# The Greek Position

## A NOVEL BY
## Robert Roderick

Wyndham Books
New York

Copyright © 1981 by Robert Roderick
All rights reserved
including the right of reproduction
in whole or in part in any form
Published by Wyndham Books
A Simon & Schuster Division of Gulf & Western Corporation
Simon & Schuster Building
Rockefeller Center
1230 Avenue of the Americas
New York, New York 10020

WYNDHAM and colophon are trademarks of Simon & Schuster
Designed by Jeanne Joudry
Manufactured in the United States of America

10   9   8   7   6   5   4   3   2   1

Library of Congress Cataloging in Publication Data

Roderick, Robert, date.
   The Greek position.

   I.   Title
PZ4.R6875Gr          [PS3568.03455]          813'.54  80-17850
ISBN  0-671-61015-5

1\91

*Beware! . . . For at least another hundred years we must pretend . . . that fair is foul and foul is fair; for foul is useful and fair is not. Avarice and usury and precaution must be our gods for a little longer still.*
—JOHN MAYNARD KEYNES,
"Economic Possibilities for
Our Grandchildren," 1930

# Contents

# I.
# Lions

*December 24, 1965*
*Zurich, Switzerland*

SHORTLY AFTER dawn, an SAS Boeing 707, the first aircraft into Kloten Airport that day, came to rest at the immigration entrance.

Usually, such early arrivals interest only relatives of those aboard. The Swiss, however, have their own royalty.

So the reason for the turnout of SAS and airport brass seemed clear enough to the baggage handlers and ground-crew men also there: The plane's passenger list, teletyped from Rome, included a Prince of Zurich.

A nobleman did grace the manifest: "E. Schotten."

His behavior, however, contradicted his status. He left the plane last.

Moreover, despite falling snow, he came down the boarding steps in a faultlessly cut gray silk summer suit. Tall and tanned, with sun-bleached blond hair, and boyishly handsome at forty, he moved with a pronounced limp, favoring his right leg.

But neither flight nor early hour nor his infirmity lessened the enthusiasm of the handshake with which he greeted each member of the welcoming committee.

If, however, a subtle wariness seemed to lie behind his engaging and youthful smile, that had to be expected.

*Zürchers*, such as those who met him, and members of the world's financial community, knew that look. They called it "cautious sensitivity." It marked men who risked fortunes in far-off places among strangers.

Herr Schotten indeed belonged to that elite. He owned a premier private Swiss bank.

So, treated accordingly, he limped to the terminal.

There history, not wealth, colored his welcome.

For to the gruff *Zürchers* inside, ex-army men now in civil service, Herr Schotten and Christmas Eve were inextricably intertwined.

11

Anton Raus, a mean-faced, bespectacled immigration official with the elongated skull and sloping forehead of a weasel, saw him first. Smile baring rapierlike incisors, he darted from his grilled cage, inkpad and stamp in hand, to personally admit Herr Schotten to Switzerland. A bow, with flourish, completed formalities.

That rankled in one of the most crustily democratic places on earth. Raus, however, ignored local sensibilities.

Brusquely ordering passengers at his booth to shut up and stay in line, he gestured along the aisle to the far end of the barnlike reception hall. His wave brought Chief Customs Inspector Max Haupt.

Haupt, a tall, intimidatingly burly former career army sergeant with a fiercely bristling military mustache, stared down onlookers in the immigration area. Next, turning to Herr Schotten, he nodded at an elegantly thin Moroccan leather attaché case. With thumb and forefinger and sense of high drama, Haupt withdrew from it a flimsy typewritten manuscript stapled inside a blue paper wrapper. Shaking and inverting the case, he passed it back and forth for the benefit of those watching, to prove it held nothing else. A solemn wink accompanied the demonstration.

Then, arm embracing a clearly embarrassed Prince of Zurich, Haupt led the way to a lobby exit.

His luggage? Herr Schotten asked at the door.

A wave of the hand dismissed the matter. A customs van would take the bags to Bank Schotten, Haupt said. Standing around while a plane unloaded was a hell of a way for a game leg to start off a morning.

Anton Raus, also in worshipful attendance, agreed.

Nodding, Herr Schotten entered the lobby.

"Merry Christmas," he said.

But his actions seemed at odds with the sentiment. Smiling affectionately and sincerely for the first time, he made an infantryman's thumbs-up sign.

For Raus and Haupt, that gesture made the day.

It did mark *their* Christmas Eve: that of 1944.

Its sense of community reached even farther back.

For *Zürchers*, that began in the thirties.

Town bankers, after all, made war on Hitler first.

In 1931–32, they looked away while he made rabble-rousing speeches about "international Jewish financiers," many of whom were colleagues and partners. Germans, they knew, had a weakness for scapegoats.

But by 1933, with Nazis in the streets burning and looting Jewish businesses and synagogues, the stolid bankers of Zurich had seen enough.

They took immediate action. They sped passage of a new Swiss banking law.

The reason for the Banking Act of 1934 has long been forgotten, but two provisions, still in force, brought Hitler his first defeat as Führer.

The first allows nameless, numbered accounts. The second makes it an imprisonable crime for a bank employee to reveal information about depositors without very specific authorization.*

In 1934, the clear-eyed already saw the destiny of the Third Reich and wished to leave Germany. The new Swiss banking act provided an escape hatch—at least for worldly goods. Numbered accounts were quickly opened.

Hitler and his chief economic adviser, Dr. Hjalmar Schacht, had elaborate plans for plundering this wealth from the Jewish middle class to arm the Wehrmacht. A few wily Swiss bankers, using pens instead of guns, had put much of that capital out of their reach.

Hitler, historians say, never forgot. Many believe that a need to avenge this defeat explained his often-voiced desire to invade Switzerland.

So, to caution him, the Swiss made a solemn vow: Should German infantry march on their borders, or paratroopers appear in the skies, every bridge and tunnel linking Switzerland to the outside world would be destroyed. Then the 500,000 troops of the Swiss Army, one of Europe's best-trained and most modern forces, would go into action—and fight to the last man. What incentive had they to survive a war from which one's country might never recover?

Switzerland, in short, promised *Götterdämmerung,* an invitation to the end of the world.

Hitler understood that, and it restrained him.

But, defeat looming, he became unpredictable, and many Swiss then saw their vow as a death sentence, the execution date a madman's secret.

Meanwhile, tension rose as German troops repeatedly overran borders, pursuing Jews and political foes fleeing to Switzerland. Those incursions mainly went unprotested, for fear of provoking reprisals.

*Zürchers,* with their worship of property rights and wealth and dislike of appeasement, had been the most vocal Swiss opposing that policy.

So faint irony shaded the voice of a Swiss border guard at Schleitheim crossing on Christmas morning, 1944, as he phoned his Wehrmacht counterpart 150 yards down the tree-lined road.

He would soon pass through an ambulance from Schaffhausen canton medical chambers, he reported. It held the bodies of six German nationals. All had been found dead Christmas Eve from mysterious causes deep in the Swiss part of Schleitheim wood.

A German colonel called on receipt of the remains.

Had he said six corpses? he asked the guard.

*Ja,* the Swiss laconically replied.

* For years, hearsay has held that no one, not even the government, had access to depositors' identities. This has never been so. The Swiss Banking Act spells out the exceptions in detail. Generally, they give authorities access if there is good reason to believe that a crime under *Swiss* law has been committed. Tax evasion in other countries is not considered such a felony. Publicly, the Swiss say they are not tax collectors. Privately, they concede it would not be bad for business if they were.

The Nazi slammed the phone down.

Of the six bodies, two had been those of patrol dogs. All, animal and human alike, had throats slashed virtually to the point of decapitation.

In the Schleitheim area, border violations ceased Christmas Day, 1944.

The Swiss troops responsible, *Zürchers* of the First Pre-Alpine Infantry Regiment, took this improved German behavior as a matter of course. They knew how to talk to Hitler, they said. Death was his mother tongue. He had only to remember that the retribution visited upon his men and dogs was but another way of saying, "Switzerland—*Götterdämmerung!*" That would make him swallow his vengeance.

So, at least, said Anton Raus and Max Haupt.

That view, they freely acknowledged, came from the nineteen-year-old lieutenant who, despite a shattered ankle, led them against the Germans.

A banker's son, they said, he understood psychology.

Smiling, Herr Schotten entered the coffee shop.

At seven-thirty, he left for a phone booth.

Less than a minute later, he crossed the airport lobby, passing display cases of Swiss watches, in the awkward, rolling gait that served as his reminder of Christmas Eve, 1944.

At the red-and-white Iberia Airways counter, he bought tickets for Christmas Day flights the following morning on the eight-o'clock plane to Madrid and the eleven-o'clock from Madrid to Tangier. He would leave Tangier at 5 P.M. on Air Maroc. From Paris he would fly BEA to London, arriving at 1:30 A.M. the twenty-sixth.

Handing over the tickets, the Spanish girl in the booth rolled her outsized brown eyes accordingly.

"*Frohe Weihnachten,*" she sympathized in German.

Merry Christmas indeed. Herr Schotten saw it otherwise.

"But it will be, *guapa!*" he argued. "It will be!"

The clerk smiled delightedly. A long time had passed since someone had called her "good-looking" in Spanish. With her eyes, she followed the tall blond man across the airport lobby. He walked as though he had a thorn in the ball of his right foot. She was glad for him when he got into the back of a black Mercedes limousine. The chauffeur had put down a jump seat so that the disabled leg could be rested on it. That made her feel better.

The Crisis Phone rang in the office of Herr Dieter von Kootze, head of von Kootze & Cie., Privatbankiers, at precisely 7:33 A.M. At most, a dozen people in the world could reach von Kootze on this phone. None had in over seven months.

Von Kootze, a former army general with a stiff Prussian brush cut, was the fifth of his line to occupy this large oak-paneled fourth-floor office overlooking

Lake Zurich. His reaction to the sudden ringing paid tribute to the selective breeding practiced by prominent Swiss banking families.

He looked at his watch. He saw it was too early for the London and Paris stock exchanges to be open, and still night in New York. So he knew there had been no dramatic price break since he had last heard the news.

Shrugging fatalistically, he reached behind the desk to the built-in combination lock on the lower right-hand drawer. He set the four numbers without a miss. Then, lifting the receiver and leaning back in his brown leather chair, he excused his secretary, Frau Annamarie Meier, to whom he had been dictating, with a nod.

"Yes?" he said softly into the mouthpiece.

"This is Christian," came the equally quiet response.

Christian Reymonde was the executive vice-president of Bank Schotten. In 1963 he had recruited von Kootze into the group of currency speculators whose actions caused a stampede against the English pound in 1964.* Von Kootze made 88 million Swiss francs† in the fall of sterling.

Eric Schotten had masterminded the attack on the pound. He put only one string on von Kootze's profit: half of it was to be available for reinvesting the next time a suitable "position" presented itself.

Von Kootze had waited ever since, knowing full well that most bankers lived and died without getting one such opportunity. Now he was suddenly sure that in his lifetime he would have at least two. As his conviction deepened, he felt the fingers holding the phone grow perceptibly cooler.

Inhaling, he kept the excitement out of his voice. "How can I help you, Christian?" he asked.

"By being ready to be picked up at four-thirty this afternoon. We've been invited to supper."

"Oh. By whom?"

"Eric. He just got off the plane at Kloten. He's anxious to see us."

"On Christmas Eve, Christian?"

"Eric thinks it's lucky for him. Besides," Christian Reymonde said dryly, "I think he's earned the right to disrupt a holiday of ours. Don't you?"

"Of course. I'll be ready."

"Good. His car will pick me up first."

"By the way," von Kootze asked, "where did he say he came in from?"

"He didn't. All he said was he's calling our pledges."

"Yes? All—or partially?"

"All, every centime. We're back in business, Dieter. But this time, big."

*"Gott sei dank,"* von Kootze murmured. "I feared I wouldn't live to see it."

"Amen. Now we'll do some real banking. See you at four-thirty."

* An action for which the indignant English dubbed them and their colleagues "the Gnomes of Zurich."
† $20 million in 1964.

An hour later, von Kootze still hadn't resumed dictating. Concerned, Frau Meier went into his office to see if he was all right. Never felt better, he said. This had just struck him as a perfect time to redraw his will.

At 10 A.M. he rang through on the intercom and asked Frau Meier to get Franz Schwarz, of the Union Banque Suisse, on the phone.

Of the 1,600 Swiss banks, Union Banque Suisse is the largest. With $8 billion in assets, it's about one-fourth the size of the Bank of America, the biggest in the United States. Unlike U.S. banks, however, it deals in gold as well as paper. To Swiss, both are legal. But the gold is more real.

Franz Schwarz, the man von Kootze called, was concerned solely with gold. As an administrative vice-president of the bank, he had as one of his responsibilities the *täglicher,* the day vault. In it, the bank kept the supply of gold bullion used in daily trading.

The difference between a private banker like von Kootze and a corporate banker like Schwarz is one of perspective. To Schwarz, money was only money. And someone else's at that.

But Schwarz sensed the undercurrent of excitement in von Kootze's voice, and it disturbed him. Von Kootze was no bedwetter. He was used to money. Why, then, was he suddenly short of breath inquiring about it?

A moment later, an answer occurred to Schwarz. It caused him to rush up to the third floor to seek out Herr Doktor Klaus von Salomon, a research economist and the resident gnome-watcher of Union Banque Suisse.

Von Salomon was a tubby man with prematurely white crewcut hair and preposterously thick eyeglasses.

"Aha, the keeper of the keys," he quipped, blinking out over a foot-thick stack of computer printout sheets.

Schwarz nodded. "I thought you'd like to know that the little people are on the move again."

"Oh? Do they come down from their Alps on Christmas Eve, too?" von Salomon inquired. Unconcerned, he resumed his study of the computer sheets before him, a yellow pencil clenched between his teeth.

"It seems so," Schwarz replied judiciously, ignoring the sarcasm. "Field Marshal von Kootze just called, inquiring about the state of the *täglicher.*"

"How much did he want?" von Salomon asked absently.

"Forty-five million francs."

Von Salomon spat out the pencil. "Good God! It's '64 all over again."

"Worse," Schwarz said quietly, savoring his moment of triumph. "That time, all he needed was ten million."

Von Salomon nodded and rose. "Excuse it, Franz, if I put you off at first. Half my time I'm chasing down dark plots—all imaginary."

Five minutes later, a senior vice-president of the bank summed up von Salomon's news with a wry grimace: ". . . and where Dieter von Kootze goes,

Christian Reymonde goes, and Eric Schotten leads. And who can anticipate Eric? In '64, he had the whole world dancing to his tune—including us. What now? What's next? Where can he have a position so big that Dieter von Kootze's share alone is forty-five million francs? Find out, Klaus. Find out, at once!"

The ferret had been given the scent.

Herr Doktor Klaus von Salomon nodded vigorously. Ironically, at that moment he had only to look out a window to spot his prey.

Eric Schotten's Mercedes crept past the drab, fortresslike Union Banque Suisse. Ahead, all the way up the Bahnhofstrasse to the railroad station itself, the wide, glittering avenue beckoned in its Christmas best. The gray sky and falling snow could not diminish its opulence. The Bahnhofstrasse spoke for its people brusquely and to the point. In tone and texture, it uttered but one word: Money. Massive brick and gray limestone banks celebrated making it. Luxurious shops and stores glorified spending it. Like any true *Zürcher*, Eric Schotten delighted in both.

At ten-fifteen, the black limousine pulled up at Number 69, Jelmoli's department store. At ten-thirty-five, Jelmoli's doorman handed several large packages over to the chauffeur for safekeeping.

Schotten, meanwhile, crossed the Bahnhofstrasse, awkwardly dodging the blue-and-white electric trams that ran down its center. At Number 62 he entered Franz Carl Weber's five-story toy store.

At eleven-thirty, he and two of Weber's clerks loaded more packages and a menagerie of Steiff stuffed animals into the Mercedes. The chauffeur would deliver them that afternoon to the children of Bank Schotten employees, as custom decreed.

At eleven-thirty-five, the limousine stopped at Number 36, a building of understated elegance. Gubelin's, Zurich's most exclusive jewelers, was located here. At eleven-forty, Schotten was back in the car. A small square jewelry box outlined itself in the right coat pocket of the gray silk suit.

Shopping done, the chauffeur continued up the Bahnhofstrasse to Amtshauser. There he turned right for the Urania Bridge. Across the Limmat River lay Niederdorf, the hilly bohemian quarter of Zurich.

At the top of Niederdorf's hill stands the University of Zurich, long one of Europe's most formidable and liberal institutions. Albert Einstein took his Ph.D. there in 1905 and stayed as a faculty member.

In the 1930s, Germany contributed several other great teaching minds to the university. One belonged to Herr Doktor Professor Yigal Heim.

For Herr Doktor Professor Heim, the Banking Act of 1934 had special meaning. Before the year ended, before he himself came to Zurich, his small inheritance made the trip. By 1964 Herr Doktor Professor Heim, who had no head for business, was a millionaire. He could only marvel at what his bankers had done for him. His gratitude was boundless.

In 1964 he also had an opportunity to express his thanks. The president of his bank had come to him with a problem that called for all of his learning and talent. Since then he had given of himself joyfully and grown quite fond of his banker in the bargain.

Shortly before noon, then, on Christmas Eve day, the professor left his comfortable home in Niederdorf. A slight nearsighted man with a reddish-brown beard, he hurried past the gray stucco house on the Spiegelgasse where Lenin had once lived, and down the hill toward the Limmat River.

Promptly at noon, he entered the Odeon Café, now unnaturally quiet with the students home for the holidays. Eric Schotten rose to greet Heim from a table in the rear, two away from the one at which James Joyce wrote much of *Ulysses,* the professor saw.

The first hour, they reviewed the typewritten manuscript in Schotten's attaché case. Every page had been peppered with question marks, statements and written questions. The professor responded to each in precise, academic German. Schotten took notes.

At 1 P.M., when they finished the manuscript, a waiter brought fresh *café filtre* and a plate of pfeffernüsse, anise-flavored Christmas cookies.

At eight minutes after one, Professor Heim unbuckled his valise and withdrew a sheaf of newspaper clippings. A slip of white paper was carefully pinned to each. These he and Schotten reviewed as carefully as they had the manuscript.

At 2 P.M. they finished. As he departed, the professor indulged himself in a bit of academic humor.

"*Salaam aleikum,* Herr Schotten," he said, in the faultless, liquid Arabic of a world-renowned authority on Semitic languages.

At precisely 4:30 P.M., Eric Schotten's black Mercedes glided to a stop before the ornate wrought-iron entrance to von Kootze & Cie., Privatbankiers. The bank's front door flew open, and Dieter von Kootze stumped down the stone steps as if parading to a distant drum roll.

He motioned curtly to the chauffeur to raise the glass partition before he entered the car. Then, leaning back against the gray upholstery, he turned to Christian Reymonde.

"So, Christian, what is it?" he demanded in an impatient whisper.

"Impossible to say. I'm as much in the dark as you."

Christian Reymonde shrugged, underscoring the difference between *Genevois* and *Zürcher.*

In Geneva, Reymonde's birthplace, bankers speak French and act like wealthy men. They come to work at 9:30 or 10 A.M., and lunch long and luxuriously, with due attention to wines and *ambiance*. They appreciate the arts. They enjoy ideas. They like to laugh. They have style.

In German-speaking Zurich, it's another story. Even corporate bankers are at their desks by eight-thirty. Three-hour lunches are unheard of. Local custom honors hard work, practical solutions, and directness. To many foreigners, *Zürchers* are so intense they lack finesse.

Christian Reymonde had mastered both approaches. A few years after his sister married Eric Schotten's father, he merged his small family bank into Bank Schotten. By 1965 he thought like a *Zürcher*, but still behaved like a *Genevois*—a devastating combination for many wealthy widows who wanted the management of their fortunes in able, sympathetic hands.

At sixty, Reymonde looked forty-five. He was tall and slim, with jet-black hair and an impeccably trimmed mustache. A widower with four grandchildren, he was rumored to have a mistress. That she was a ravishing brunette with the Theater am Heckplatz was entirely believable.

"Eric told you nothing?" von Kootze insisted.

"Nothing. He left in October, saying he'd be back for Christmas, and so he is. All I've seen are a few scraps of paper—which don't add. At least not to me."

Von Kootze eyed Reymonde through his steel-rimmed spectacles. "They have to add. Banking is a business of addition. Everything adds! That's the beauty of it. Now tell me what you saw, and I'll find the clue."

"I doubt it, but I'll tell you anyway. In November I received articles of incorporation for a company registered in Lausanne named Lion Holdings. The papers were full of all the usual gibberish, so I checked the *Vaud Canton Commercial Register*. Nothing there either but the capitalization—eight million six hundred thousand francs.* Half that came from Eric's personal account at Frisch et Compagnie in Geneva. Where the other half came from I have no idea."

"From our silent partner, no doubt."

"Of course. But who do you think he is?"

"A technician, some sort of specialist," von Kootze shrugged. "What's four million francs alongside the forty-five million from each of us? Nothing. No control there. It's only a carrot, a share to make him produce."

Reymonde nodded. "That's how I saw it. Nothing new there. So much for Lion Holdings. A week later, another document came. It was the charter for the Helvetian-Judaic Foundation, headquartered in Geneva. And don't ask me what that is, either."

"No need to—another of Eric's complications. That, or a joke. He finds humor in names."

---

* $2 million.

"I assure you, Dieter, Eric is not joking. Along with the charter came a bill from our good friends in Bern, Advokaturbureau Rigel, Ullreich und Krieger. We now owe them over four hundred thousand francs."*

"Lawyers!" von Kootze whispered. "We went all through '63 and '64 without one of those bloodsuckers. Now we need them? Why?"

"To create these legal fictions, of course. But I ask you, Dieter: are they fictitious? I ask you because a week ago the lawyers sent me another letter. It was written blind† by a very fancy English solicitor with offices on Temple Square in Hong Kong. He confirmed arranging for an escrow account of one hundred million dollars at the Fuji Bank in Japan."

"*Gross Gott!*" von Kootze hissed. "First, the three of us don't have half that. Second—"

"Another party you don't know is also pledged for forty-five million francs," Reymonde interjected.

"Was he with us in '63?" von Kootze asked sharply.

"Oh, yes. But 'he' is a she."

"God in heaven," von Kootze sighed. "Nevertheless, even with this unknown, the four of us will have a position of roughly only fifty million dollars. Where's the other fifty coming from? And Japan—what have we learned from twenty years of experience? That loans are fine, but it's lunacy for a foreigner to invest there. More difficult, even, than here in Switzerland. What can be in Eric's mind?"

After a few moments, Christian Reymonde leaned over the armrest in the Mercedes and said softly, "Let me tell you something, Dieter."

"Yes?"

"Eric is deep. Deeper, perhaps, than even we know. It's no use guessing. This may go far beyond banking."

"To what, then?"

"To power. To power beyond wealth."

Von Kootze pondered this, sitting very erect.

"Why are you so glum?" Reymonde asked.

"Because power is a sham. Can you bank it? Does it pay dividends? Will it pass itself on to grandchildren? No, and no, and no! In the end, it only erodes. But gold begets more gold. And 'more' is the point of banking."

"A narrow view, Dieter. A little power is good for you. Just ask anyone without it."

An hour later Christian Reymonde wondered.

* $100,000 plus.
† The practice of lawyers responding to or giving instructions to others on their letterheads, their clients remaining nameless.

*December 25, 1965*
*Tangier, Morocco*

THE COUNTESS was still warm from her midday bath, and soft, erotic invitations swirled off her body. Her breasts, swelling out of the white caftan, bore traces of dusting powder and the musky challenge of Ritual perfume.

She sat in the corner of the ocher-colored stone gallery. Her legs were stretched out on the blue velour divan that ran under the Moorish windows lining three sides of the porch. Her outsized brown eyes, with their arrogant cat-green glints, regarded Eric Schotten unblinkingly.

Still eying him, she leaned forward so that the long pale-blue cigarette rested in the yellow-white flame of the gold butane lighter. After a moment there was a soft, crackling sound. Then she gulped the smoke. It hit her at once. By the time she exhaled, her eyes had narrowed into hard, needle-sharp points of inquiry.

"Now tell me about the position, dear," she commanded in her crisp French-accented English, her face as compact and willful as a fist.

"Must you indulge yourself now?" Schotten asked.

She smiled indolently through the cloyingly sweet clotted smoke. "You are warped from a lifetime of Sundays in Zurich, dear. Of course I must indulge myself now. That's what money is for, and that's what life is for. Now. Do you know what Buddha said when he was asked to sum up in a single word all of his thought?"

Schotten shook his head.

" 'Now,' " she whispered with quiet satisfaction. Then she turned away to gaze at Europe through the high arched window at her right.

She was literally the last person in Africa. Cape Spartel, the rocky promontory on which her house stood, marked the extreme northwestern edge of the continent.

Hundreds of feet below, a muffled drumbeat of surf tolled the end of the Atlantic's three-thousand-mile journey under the boisterous southwest trades. Tangier sprawled off to the right—an abstract checkerboard of faded yellows, whites, and deep greens. Directly ahead, the Straits of Gibraltar streamed across the horizon like a cobalt pennant. Beyond, Europe rose pale and remote in the purplish haze.

"Get on with it, dear," she suggested, her hand resting casually on Schotten's thigh. "Or else I shall suggest another way for us to celebrate Christmas. You look that gorgeous—just like a little British schoolboy in your blazer and gray slacks."

She spoke wistfully. Nothing would happen, and she knew it. A banker raising money for a position had no interest or time for sex. Such men always found cash, and the next step in the plan, far more exciting.

Her knowledge came from experience.

To the world, she was a rich White Russian with an eccentric's flair for arbitrage.* Supposedly, her family fled the Revolution with a fortune in art, jewels and negotiable securities.

A few discreet bankers knew otherwise.

In point of fact, her family left Russia penniless. She mastered arbitrage as a child in her father's open-air currency exchange at the foot of the hill on which she now lived. Initially, she disliked it. It lacked challenge, and it didn't pay enough. In her midtwenties, however, she found her true vocation, an area of finance that did offer rewards equal to her gifts.

Gold.

In time, she knew how to buy, sell and move gold—legally or illegally—anywhere in the world. In financial parlance, she became a "submarine."

Schotten conceived the attack on sterling. She executed it.

With a surgeon's deftness and a ballet master's sense of timing and leverage, she arbitraged the English pound in its weak markets until it had to fall. Then, sufficiently alarmed, the rest of the international financial community stepped in and finished the job.

"I was in Egypt last year," Schotten began, "and all I heard was jihad—"

"But they are imbeciles, dear," she sighed. "They run up and down the streets, eyes bulging, screaming 'Holy war!' And it never comes. All they do is talk—talk, talk, talk!"

"Not this time," he assured her. "Now the Arabs have a charismatic leader whose destiny they are eager to share—Nasser. And Nasser has Russian tanks. A year ago I saw them being unloaded in Port Said. Last month I saw more. And when he gets enough he will make war on the Jews. He has no choice. Islam cries for blood. And, politics aside, he suffers from a terminal case of religion. That is our position. Everything else follows."

"And when will this war start?"

"From what I know, in about eighteen months—in June or July of 1967."

Unimpressed, the Countess puffed on the pale-blue cigarette. Still looking toward the green western side of Gibraltar, she said, "So we buy oil. But even then, what will we have? Nothing. It will be just like in 1956, when they closed the Suez.† Oil is too cheap in the first place, dear."

---

* Arbitrage involves the *simultaneous* purchase and sale of a commodity, security, or foreign currency in two markets. The difference in price between one place and the other is profit. It sounds simple, but an army of penniless ex-arbitragers would tell you otherwise. The game requires a vast knowledge of world trade and politics—plus, of course, a spy's talent for intrigue and developing information.
† In the U.S., for example, the price of crude oil rose from $2.79 a barrel to $3.09—far too modest a rise to justify tying up money for eighteen months.

"Agreed. But we won't be in oil."

"No? Where else could we be?"

"Be subtle. Who made all the money in 1956?" He smiled at her ingenuously, heightening her puzzlement.

"Why do you give me a riddle?" she demanded.

"To help you judge our chances. If you can't recognize our position, how will the rest of the world? I'll even give you a hint," he said quietly. "Yesterday I returned to Zurich from Japan."

Hashish was no match for provocation. She snubbed the cigarette and spun around, jet-black hair flying off the shoulders of the white caftan.

"I am not the rest of the world," she whispered venomously. "I am the best of the world. Don't say another word!"

Several minutes later, she nodded to herself and leaned forward. Unmindful that the tops of her breasts were riding out of the caftan, she waggled a square accusing forefinger in Schotten's face.

"As I recall, you have friends in Japan, don't you dear? What's that *zaibatsu*\* there with the beautiful name? The singing something?"

"The Singing Willow," he answered. "But that was years ago, and it was supposed to be secret. How did you know of that connection?"

"I'm an old family friend," she said cryptically. "All that you do is of interest to me."

She also knew what the relationship implied.

"You went to Japan then to buy, not to sell. No?"

He nodded.

Christian Reymonde and Dieter von Kootze had not gotten that far the previous evening. But they were provincials alongside her. They had spent their careers financing Swiss industry and its customers. She had spent hers sniffing out tiny, exploitable imbalances between nations. She needed only the single clue. With it, she homed in on the answer as surely as a seabird wings its way over the featureless deeps.

"How does one buy most advantageously in Japan?" she began. "In dollars, of course—she needs them to buy coal and iron ore in America. So my job will be to move gold east for dollars. Very well. I have a stunning idea for that—a 'first,' dear! And perfectly legal too, which is nice."

"For your added comfort," he dryly observed, "I can assure you that throughout this will be perfectly legal, as well."

"Even better," she answered. "Then our only problem is to make ourselves invisible, and I know how to do that, at least, with gold. So," she went on, returning to his riddle, "what does one buy in Japan—in dollars—cheaper than anywhere else in the world? Since we are not shopkeepers, we have no use for consumer products. It follows, then, that you went there for capital goods,

\* A banking, industrial, and manufacturing combine.

heavy industrial equipment. But what kind? What would one need to make money from an Arab–Israeli war?"

After a long pause, she shook her head in disbelief. "This position is not concerned with banking or finance at all, is it, dear?"

"Only now, in the beginning."

"I have it, then." She nodded. "It can only be that. Your Singing Willow also owns shipyards. You want us to build oil tankers! Tell me, dear, what do you estimate the payout on those ships would be?"

"With luck, ten times our investment by 1970."

"And how much do you want from me?"

"The full pledge—forty-five million Swiss francs."

"That's ten million dollars American," she said. Eyes narrowed, she did the multiplication and conversion in her head. "So my share of the payout will come to one hundred million dollars."

"Yes. With luck, it might even go to one hundred twenty million dollars."

Her response to the good news was a deep frown. "But tankers are huge," she remonstrated. "How can they be hidden so that others don't put two and two together and also build them for your impending war? If they do—poof! There goes the shortage of ships and our profit. That has a lot of risk in it, dear."

"Not if we're careful. Steps have been taken in Japan to insure secrecy."

"And what about in the Middle East?" she asked. "We will have Mukha-baraat* and Mossad† to contend with in this. The Egyptians are nothing—a bunch of nigger Charlie Chaplins. One bribes them or fucks them or sucks them. And that's that. No matter. But Mossad—they're the best, and abso-lutely incorruptible. I fear them. They are so righteous."

"Mossad may not be a problem, but a potential ally," he observed. "When I get home, I'll be seeing the Israeli ambassador about the Helvetian-Judaic Foundation, and I'll sound him out."

"A perfect pretext." She nodded sagely. "Yet another damned charity. Are you connected with it?"

"Oh yes. And so are you."

"I—how?"

A smile curled the corners of Schotten's mouth. "The purpose of the Helve-tian-Judaic Foundation is to raise funds for Israel. You, I and our associates in this position shall be its patrons. And believe me, we shall contribute mightily. One hand must wash the other."

"Of course!" she agreed warmly, not begrudging a little charity if it was good for business. "They must do the necessary when war comes—see that the Suez Canal is blocked—or we can't make the money they need."

"Exactly."

* Egyptian Foreign Intelligence.
† Israeli Secret Service.

"That is genius, dear. Truly. But can you bribe a country?"

"Israel, yes. Its national debt is approaching one billion dollars* and keeps rising. After the war—which, of course, the Jews will win—they will be even worse off. They will be alone and need money even more desperately."

"Oh yes, that I agree with. That filth, de Gaulle, will surely sell them out the first time Boumédienne looks cross-eyed at ERAP and CFP.† You'll see. *Zut!* No more Mirage jets. No more ships. No more credit. And England will do the same. British Petroleum is too important for them to upset Iran and Iraq over a few Jews. In the end, the Israelis will be left with only the Americans, and God help them then. ARAMCO‡ makes U.S. policy in the Middle East. If presidents didn't need Jewish votes, do you think there would be an Israel?"

He nodded. "You see, you're making my point. Suppose you are Israel, and I come to you with a proposition. I offer you, perhaps, a quarter of a billion dollars for doing what you probably intend to do anyway. Am I bribing you or insuring your survival?"

"Perhaps, it is possible," she conceded. "But what about Russia? Our position helps the Jews. The Russians want them weak."

"Oh, where is that written?" he asked. He mimed scanning the reddish stones in the arched ceiling, as if expecting to find an inscription there.

That was the last straw. She was accustomed to the initiative, particularly in her dealings with men. Today, quietly and adroitly, their conversation had been turned into an interrogation, with Schotten the inquisitor. Now he had the gall to mock her.

"What do you mean, 'where is that written?' " she rasped. "The whole world knows where it is written! Didn't the Russians come running to Egypt's aid in 1956?"

"But reality in 1967 may be quite different."

"And what, exactly, is that supposed to mean?"

"In peacetime," he explained in a quiet but unmistakably pedantic tone which further irritated her, "patron states seek only weak client nations as partners. Why? For one reason only—so that they can impose their will upon them. Very well. What, then, is Russia's will in regard to Egypt?"

"What it has always been—naval bases in the Mediterranean to counter the American Sixth Fleet. But I know all this!" she protested. "Why are you patronizing me? Why do you ask me these stupid questions?"

---

* In 1972 it passed $3.4 billion, tripling since the Israeli arms buildup of 1966. In 1979 it stood at $9 billion.

† Acronyms for French-owned oil companies in Algeria. De Gaulle, of course, did exactly as she predicted. The Algerians nationalized both concerns anyway on February 24, 1971, as part of Société SONATRACH.

‡ Arabian-American Oil Company, a joint venture of Jersey Standard, Texaco, Standard of California, and Mobil.

He smiled disarmingly, then shrugged. "Because when I ask them to myself, I get stupid answers."

"Oh?" she asked, eyes suddenly slit.

"Yes. Accept as a premise that Egypt destroys Israel and becomes dominant in the Middle East. Would Nasser then want the Russians as permanent house guests?"

"Of course not!" she replied heatedly. "What would he need them for?"

Schotten nodded. "Exactly. He'd boot the Russians out and, socialist or not, ally himself with Libya and Saudi Arabia—both have more oil money than they can count—and go merrily on his way, which is to dominate the entire southern shore of the Mediterranean at Algeria's expense."

"Probably so," she agreed. "There's no love lost between Nasser and Boumédienne. Each wants to be the Arab strong man."

"All right." He smiled. "If we see this, why don't the Russians? Why are they willing to risk their presence in the Mediterranean to let Nasser make war? Has that occurred to you? I find it puzzling, myself."

She sat up straight, spilling more of her full, aggressive breasts out of the caftan. Her already large brown eyes widened further. "Are you suggesting . . ." she said tentatively as his line of thought became clearer, "that the Russians want Egypt to lose?"

"Exactly. A stupid answer. But there it is. And it won't go away."

"If you are right," she continued haltingly, placing each word in front of the other like a timid footstep, "the Russians won't want a peace settlement, either—at best, only an armed truce. Is that true?"

"Absolutely. For the Russians, that would be best of all. They would have an excuse to stay in the Mediterranean forever—to stand by their defeated comrades. Russia would want a permanent stalemate."

She brightened. "And so would we!"

"That's right. And logic tells us this will happen. But to find that logic, one must hold it up to a mirror and read it backward. Nice, eh?"

"So it's all a charade," she mused. Nasser gets his jihad only because he'll lose it. Oh, I like that, dear! What irony! And then we make all this money because of the Bolsheviks—even better, and so fitting too."

Still, she had reservations.

"But the Americans don't want the Israelis too strong, either," she cautioned a moment later. "If the Jews win and get snotty, the Saudis might sit on all of ARAMCO's cheap oil. Has that occurred to you—that our position lands us right in the middle of the Americans and the Russians?"

His face set flinty-hard. "Is that a reason to run from a billion dollars? They are flags, and we are money. When flags act in their self-interest only, money has the same right. And we must exercise it. Otherwise, the high-minded statesmen of the world will try to gobble us up, too, when it suits them. There's no morality in any of this, only oil and politics—and flags against money."

There was no answer to that, so she nodded, her eyes lingering on the handsome tanned face and the sun-bleached straw-blond hair.

"You really are quite fearless, aren't you?" she asked. "Your father said you were, but I never believed him. You were always too boyish, too pretty."

"I'm a banker. I understand the price of things."

"Yes, I see that. I like what you said about partners, too. The deep thinkers sometimes overlook a basic truth like that in their quest for the grand design. I'm with you in this. Call my money when you wish. Now, what do we do next?"

"We find another man to bring fifty million dollars more to the position. Ideally, he will be sympathetic to the Jews and based in New York."

"I know such a man," she said casually.

"Can I speak with him?"

Now she had the initiative.

Shrewd little glints of green flickered in her eyes. She had lived up to her pledge, and that said nothing about finding another man. Therefore, the price of that service could be negotiated.

"Do you know what you're asking, dear?"

"Of course."

"I have but six clients. The value of their identities is incalculable."

In short, the price would be high.

"I appreciate that. But I don't use a sharp pencil with my friends, nor do I expect you to."

"I'll give you a name. And this is what you will give me—whether or not this man joins us." Her voice dropped to a husky imperative. "From the moment that war starts, you will manage my account—all of it—and you will not fail to earn eleven percent a year for me. Do you understand, I don't care what happens in the rest of the world? In my own little corner, I want to see eleven percent. Every year. Is that clear?"

"How could it not be? If I don't earn eleven percent, the difference comes from my pocket. I'll set up an escrow account for you to cover that."

"Yes, and in the Swiss Credit Bank."

"As you wish."

"And, dear, you will not charge me one goddamned penny's worth of management fee! All this, of course, my lawyer will write up in Zurich."

He nodded. "Fair enough."

At the very least, the name of her client would cost him a million dollars in management fees, plus untold millions more in liabilities if he failed to produce an eleven percent return each year.

"I call the man you want *L'Apache,*" she said. "He has not your financial resources, but he is very bold. He lives in New York, too, although he operates mainly in South America. I think you two would get along, and I would like him in this. I'll contact him."

"Christian knows where to reach me in London," he said, rising.

Satisfied, the Countess nodded. Reaching into the enameled box on the red stone windowsill, she withdrew another pale-blue cigarette. The beginnings of a smile crinkled her hard small mouth.

"And, dear," she said softly, but still in the hoarse, commanding tone she reserved for negotiation, "you look a little peaked. It must be all this travel. On your way back from New York, I want you to stop here for a few days. The sun will be good for you at this time of year."

Without speaking, he placed on the windowsill the small jewel box he had picked up the day before at Gubelin's. Then he leaned over the blue velour divan to kiss her cheek.

"*Enchanté,*" he murmured.


*December 27, 1965*
*London, England*

> E SCHOTTEN CLARIDGE'S HOTEL LONDON UK DE ZURICH
> SUISSE EX TANGIER STOP HOWSAM BATTLECO STOP ONE
> EIGHTEEN BATTERY PLACE NEWYORK ELEVEN AYEM WEDNESDAY
> 29TH REPEAT 29TH STOP RESERVED YOU CARLYLE 28TH
> REPEAT 28TH STOP WHO HOWSAM FOLLOWS STOP
>
> CHRISTIAN


*December 28, 1965*
*New York City*

> E SCHOTTEN CARLYLE HOTEL NEWYORK DE ZURICH SUISSE
> SMALL PRIVATE BANK STOP YOUR CONTACT UNKNOWN
> STOP
>
> CHRISTIAN

*December 29, 1965*
*New York City*

HOWSAM STOOD behind a bare antique cherry dining table at the far end of the room. The fingertips of his left hand rested lightly on a favorite talisman of international bankers, a small ebony carving of the Three Monkeys.

As the Countess had indicated in her oblique manner, he was an American Indian. He seemed quite young, less than forty; tall, crewcut, and very fit. Heavily muscled arms and shoulders bulged beneath the yellow short-sleeved dress shirt, and thick, cordlike veins latticed his hairless forearms.

"Your leg hurt?" he asked in a quiet, deep voice as Schotten appeared in the doorway.

Schotten stopped in midstride. "No more than usual," he admitted.

"Try the couch at the fireplace. Stretch out. The fire won't hurt, either."

"Thank you. Somehow, I thought you'd have me squinting into the sun all morning." Schotten nodded at the four windows behind Howsam that looked out on the Narrows.

"Is that the style in Europe?"

"Oh yes, without exception."

"Some bankers," Howsam shrugged. He lifted the heavy high-backed Windsor armchair behind him in one hand and started across the long red-carpeted room. At the fireplace, he turned the chair to face Schotten and sat down without offering to shake hands. Instead he leaned forward, his sharp-featured face looming over the bright-yellow shirt like an angry cinnamon-hued bird of prey.

"I want to ask you something before we get started," he said.

"Ask me anything." Schotten smiled. "Today you're the buyer."

Howsam thrust his square chin toward Schotten. "Where'd you get the suit?" he asked.

"This?" Schotten blinked. He unbuttoned his coat and peered into the inside breast pocket. "At Anderson and Sheppard's."

"They in London?"

"Yes. On Savile Row."

"What'd it cost?"

"A hundred guineas. Call it three hundred and fifty dollars."

Howsam reached over and rubbed the taupe twill lapel between thumb and forefinger. "Jesus, it feels like cast iron—perfect for riding airplanes. I'll get me one the next time I'm in London. That price isn't bad, either."

"Oh, no, it's a money's worth. This is now five years old. But write for an appointment before you go over, and mention me. It may help."

"Thanks. I'll do that, but what's your first name?"

"Eric."

Howsam nodded. "Okay, it's your nickel. "

So much for amenities, at least on his part. Typical behavior.

To most private bankers, partnership is one thing, friendship another. When the two are mixed, others notice, and that can be dangerous. For the financial world reflects nature. Big fish eat little fish. Besides, the introduction from Countess Tanya Tatarovich meant only that they were very private bankers, nothing more.

In reality, they were adversaries at that moment. Howsam wanted a "free look," a chance to identify and assess the position before committing himself to it. Schotten was there for money. He would disclose as little as possible until he had backing. Meanwhile he risked divulging the position. Obviously, he would be very careful.

"You are unknown in Zurich," he said pointedly, handing over the previous evening's cable.

"Pretty much here too," Howsam agreed with casual unconcern. "Comes from keeping a low profile."

"I'd say you did that rather well," Schotten observed, recalling the outside of the narrow three-story red brick building, which had been depressingly shabby. Even the bronze plaque proclaiming the structure a part of "New York's Heritage, built 1778 . . ." was weathered a dull brown and pocked with corrosion. "But I had no idea inconspicuousness paid such dividends," he went on, waving a hand around Howsam's sumptuously appointed office.

That was true. The inside of 118 Battery Place had been a genuine surprise. The painstakingly restored old house glowed with fine antiques, gleaming brass and silver, and extravagant arrangements of fresh flowers. And, unlike Howsam's office, the rooms on the two lower floors flaunted yet another arrogance: Aubussons. In Europe, a prosperous bank might hang one as a tapestry. At Battle & Company, they were rugs.

"Oh, I poop around South America a little," Howsam admitted. "I never get into anything real big, but with tips and overtime, I make out."

"You're modest to a fault."

"Well, you know how it is." Howsam shrugged. "If I blew my own horn, I'd disturb the neighbors, and that's not nice, either."

"But many people confuse humility with craftiness."

"I send those to 59 Wall," Howsam said flatly, "to Brown Brothers Harriman. They're real good private bankers."

Howsam obviously valued his privacy.

"Very well." Schotten nodded. "What did Tanya tell you about this?"

"Nothing. Only that we should meet. She doesn't trust the overseas phone."

"In that case, I'll come right to the point. I need a man in America. He must be sympathetic to the Jews and unafraid of playing the game at the highest international level."

True enough. But that was only the first of many points. Each would be a qualifier, requiring a positive answer. The conversation would end the moment Howsam stopped saying yes.

"Keep talking," Howsam answered. "We don't go on *The Eleven O'Clock News* to advertise it, but in Germany this was a Jewish bank—Battelzweig and Company."

"The Battelzweigs are German refugees?"

Howsam pointed to the single picture over the fireplace. It was a faded sepia print of a fiercely mustached captain in the Civil War Union Army.

"Were," he said laconically. "In 1842."

An American Indian in a Jewish private bank raised more questions. But Schotten let them pass. They could wait. A banker raising money lives in the here and now. He moved on to his second qualifier.

"And how do you feel about mixing in international politics?"

"You mean, will I bump heads with the heavy hitters?"

"Exactly."

"Sure, if the money's right. Who wouldn't?"

"My dear fellow, the world is full of bankers who are allergic to events."

"Come on," Howsam scoffed. "Those guys are afraid to get out of bed. They're not bankers. They're bookkeepers."

"All right, then, I assure you, this position is not for bookkeepers. It assumes there will be war in the Middle East within eighteen months and that the Israelis will win. We will profit from the peace."

"Am I missing something?" Howsam asked. "What does being sympathetic to the Jews have to do with that?"

"A quid pro quo is involved."

"A what?"

"If they do something for us, we will do something for them."

"Yeah? What are they supposed to do?"

"I don't want to tell you that now."

Undiscouraged, Howsam tried the other tack. "Okay, what'll this position do for them?"

"Give them what they'll need most after the war—money. Lots of it."

"What's 'lots'?"

"In round numbers, a quarter of a billion dollars."

Howsam nodded. "That *is* a position."

"Oh yes, quite enough for now." Schotten smiled. "I already have fifty million dollars committed to this. If you were to come in, could you raise another fifty within, say, three months?"

This was the third qualifier.

Something amber glinted in Howsam's eyes at the mention of $50 million.
"Maybe sooner," he answered.

"Yes? How much sooner?"

"Oh, if I got real lucky, I suppose by the day after tomorrow."

*"Fantastisch,"* Schotten whispered. "Your modesty aside, may I compliment you on your taste in clients?"

"You'd be making a big mistake. The orphan-and-widow trade goes to Morgan Guaranty and United States Trust. They all want a whiff of that old Ivy. The ball-busters come here. If they don't get ten percent a year on their money, they call up and ask if I'm running amateur night. They're all doing the poor Indian a favor . . ." Howsam trailed off bitterly.

"Be that as it may, how many of your group would you have to tell—"

"Hold on." Howsam uncrossed his legs and sat up straighter. "What's the lockup on this?"

"The money will be out of reach no less than three years and no longer than four."

"And the payout?"

"Short term, a billion dollars by 1970."

Howsam shook his head. "I'm not real good with figures. Is that ten times the investment?"

"Yes. A thousand percent return in four and a half years."

"Straight shares?"

"Yes. Everyone gets the same percentage coming out as going in."

Howsam considered that for a moment. He sat well back in his chair now, motionless, like an eagle on a rock. Behind their hooded lids, his black eyes circled lazily over Schotten's face.

"You place the contracts yet?" he asked quietly.

"I beg your pardon?"

Schotten's right leg, comfortably stretched out before him, jerked so violently that his foot flew off the deep red carpeting.

Howsam did not notice. He had closed his eyes and tilted the chair back so that his head rested against the faded red fireplace bricks.

"Sure," he continued, "only one business in the world pays like that, and you want dollars because you're buying in Japan. Right?"

"That's part of it," Schotten conceded.

"Yeah. Now I got the other part too. It's geography. If you raised this fifty million in Europe, you'd have everybody in London in your pants."

"You're very quick." Schotten sighed, glancing at his watch. "It's only eight minutes after eleven."

Howsam opened his eyes and left his chair. He pulled a large log from the bin at the left of the fireplace and put it on the fire with one hand.

"You can't sneak up on an Indian," he said over his shoulder.

So much for plans and qualifiers and bankers who did not run to type.

*   *   *

"Come on, let's tear it apart," Howsam said a few moments later, seating himself in the armchair again.

"You're serious?"

"Interested. So far it's all concept and no facts."

"As I said earlier, ask me anything," Schotten suggested mockingly.

"Okay, how do you know this war's on in the first place?"

"How do bankers like us learn anything?"

Howsam nodded, like a surgeon recognizing a familiar malignancy. "You found a man in a high place."

"Yes, a member of Nasser's cabinet. He started sending us money about eighteen months ago. I wondered why, so I went to Cairo and had a little chat with him. No need even to mention treason." Schotten smiled. "That type is always solicitous of a banker's well-being."

"Same thing happened here once. A pal of Batista's brought us money while Castro was still in Mexico. He was so scared we'd blow the whistle on him in Havana, he couldn't tell us enough. Currency, sugar, cigar leaf—you name it, everything we did with him worked. God, but we made a ton," Howsam recalled fondly. "And he didn't do too badly, either; wound up owning half of Acapulco. Anyway, you check your guy out?"

"Of course. But that was easy. The Egyptian arms buildup I saw for myself. The problem was learning Israel's intentions. Without that, there would be no gauging the risk. So I went home and put out a few lines."

"And?"

"And nothing." Schotten shrugged ruefully. "Israeli security is airtight. I should have saved my money. Then, one night at the home of a Jewish friend in London, I got it all—how that war will be fought, and how it will be won. And it cost me nothing. Not a cent! I have it here."

Schotten opened one of the two tan Moroccan-leather attaché cases and withdrew a freshly typed version of the document he and Professor Heim had reviewed in Zurich.

"These are excerpts from a book entitled *Mosoch shel Chol,*"* he explained. "It was written by a former Israeli general, Yigal Allon."†

Howsam's eyelids narrowed. "And *this* has all the answers?" he asked, waving the flimsy sheets of onionskin in their blue paper wrapper. "What'd he write them down for? Why'd the government let him?"

"I think this book takes the place of normal diplomatic relations. If the Arabs and Russians had military attachés in Tel Aviv, this is the kind of information the Jews would let them steal."

Howsam nodded slowly. "Maybe, but that's just more concept. Don't get me wrong. You could be right. But what are the facts?"

* English title, *Curtain of Sand.* Published in Israel (1960), by Kibbutz Hameuchad.
† Who rose to deputy prime minister. He died in 1980.

Schotten's blond eyebrows arched quizzically. "Facts?" he gently chided. "There aren't any facts. If there were, would we be here? Facts earn bookkeepers six percent—eight, if they're lucky. Insight makes fortunes."

Howsam winced. "Jesus, you sound like Siegmund Warburg,* and that makes me nervous. What the hell do I know about philosophy?"

"But you don't have to know anything about it." Schotten smiled reassuringly. "That's the beauty of Warburg's message: 'Progress in thinking is progress toward simplicity.' And what we must think about here is simple enough: human nature. We can take this book as Holy Writ, because Yigal Allon is a first-rate man. He would never lie."

"Come on," Howsam scoffed. "Washington is full of first-rate men, and not one of those overeducated sonsofbitches will even tell us the right time about this Vietnam thing. Do you mean to sit there and tell me you want fifty million dollars because you read a book?"

"Exactly. Because I say to you, in the long run human nature triumphs over all—even money—and Allon is a case in point. He shines with truth."

"Never heard of him. The only Israeli general I know is Moshe Dayan."

"That's because Allon did other things. He was, in fact, always ahead of Dayan in the army. In the Israeli War of Independence, in 1948–49, he was the Jews' best general. He was only twenty-eight or twenty-nine then, so with peace he left the military for college—first in Israel, then in England. After that he ran for the Knesset and was elected. He's still there.

"But to this day he's regarded as Israel's top field commander. Even now he has quite a voice in military matters, although he will never be minister of defense. He's become a dove. Nevertheless, people who know him tell me that psychologically he remains a general.

"All right. What does that mean? To me, it says honor is his first god and tactics his second. Therefore, he's unlike your men in Washington. His integrity is less accommodating. It tells him that truth is truth and must be spoken. Witness his dovishness. No power on earth—not even a government—can induce such a man to sign his name to a lie. Secondly, as one who influences the Israeli generals, he will never prove his own strategy wrong, either.† That you can be sure of. Human nature again. Read a bit," Schotten suggested, motioning toward the excerpts. "See for yourself."

"Well, whatever he is, he's sure got a way with words," Howsam said a few moments later. "You ever hear of an 'anticipatory counterattack' before?"

Schotten shrugged. "Don't forget he's a politician too. They debase language faster than money. Still, his meaning is clear: if threatened, Israel promises the Arabs a Pearl Harbor. Now, would a man of his stature say that, or

* A London merchant banker of vast charm and erudition, known for his ability to cloak the most ferocious financial moves in lofty philosophical contexts.
† Allon did not. Nor did Moshe Dayan or any of the Israeli generals. *Mosoch shel Chol* reads as though it had been written after the Six-Day War rather than before.

outline conditions which Israel would consider acts of war, if he were not speaking for his government? I doubt that very much."

About fifteen minutes later, Howsam looked up thoughtfully. "You know something?" he said. "I think you're right. If there's going to be a war, and we know there is, it has to be fought like this. Otherwise, the Israelis lose."

"So it would seem."

"Okay, then. So how do you get the Jews to do what you want?"

Schotten reached into the open attaché case again and handed over a sheaf of papers. "This is the charter for the Helvetian-Judaic Foundation. Under certain conditions, it will raise a great deal of money for Israel."

Howsam read, harsh vertical lines framing the bridge of his nose.

"You ever done business with Israelis?" he asked.

"No."

"They still think we're a Jewish bank, so they give us a job once in a while. You know what that's like? That's like being a bitch in heat. If you stand still you're gonna get screwed, and if you run you're gonna get your ass bit. Where Israel's concerned you can't win, and I'll tell you right now, bribing them'll never happen—at least, not in real life."

"Of course not," Schotten conceded. "This will have some effect on the peace. But on the war—never."

"No?"

"No. Absolutely not."

Howsam's eyes widened slightly. Otherwise his expression remained unchanged. "Play that back again," he said, leaning forward in the high-backed chair, "I can't make it add. It sounds to me like Tanya got conned."

Schotten smiled broadly but shook his head in disagreement. "That she did to herself. I just made it a little easier for her to believe what she wished. 'Suppose you are Israel, and I come to you with a proposition . . .' I said. She filled in the rest. Bribery is how she moves gold. So she thought, Why not bribe a nation? It was as simple as that. To her, venality is the great truth of life—the eternal verity." Schotten shrugged disdainfully.

"So why did you just try to palm off this foundation on me?"

"To see your reaction. If it had been the same as Tanya's, I would have been out the door by now."

"I don't get it."

"What?" Schotten smiled, feigning surprise. "You've been ahead of me all morning. Now you're not? Tell me, did you think we could hire this job done?"

The reds slowly faded from Howsam's face. He looked down, as if what Schotten had left unspoken lay at their feet. "So that's the punch line," he said in a resigned, unsurprised tone. "I knew you were building up to something. But that—guaranteeing to block the Suez Canal if the Israelis tell us when they're going to move—you call that banking?"

"Indeed, nothing but," Schotten replied curtly. "And classic banking, to be sure—a Baring or Rothschild position.* If it goes, we will be that rich. If it doesn't, we will lose more than our money."

Howsam shook his head reprovingly. "Goddammit, I should have known that," he said pensively. "When you talk heavy money, that's what it all comes down to. Nothing else."

Schotten nodded, his tanned, evenly featured face suddenly as coolly remote as a sculpted Roman head. "A high-risk business, history," he observed. "But life's too short to be lived at six percent, anyway. So, when that war comes, our friends will want certain other things to happen. And it will be our job—yours and mine—to make sure they do."

"You think it will come to that?"

"I *know* it will come to that. That's how Jews do business, you said as much yourself—with all the 'insurance' they can get. And what else will we be at that point with the deal done? I would insist on the same in their place. The odds say we'll be in no danger—that Nasser will close the canal on his own. On the other hand, though, we could find ourselves in the middle of a Hollywood war film—without an Errol Flynn or John Wayne to help us."

That became the final qualifier. But Howsam had no sense of drama. Baring and Rothschild wealth had not impressed him. Neither did risk.

He nodded. "Okay, I'm in for twenty million bucks. I'll go after the rest tomorrow."

"Done."

Schotten extended his hand, but Howsam had already turned toward the red telephone on the bottom shelf of the bookcase behind him.

"Margie," he said in the phone, "ask Dr. Fabian to come in, will you?"

Dr. Fabian appeared a few moments later, a tall, austerely handsome woman in her early thirties. She wore a dark-green skirt and cashmere cardigan and brown loafers. Her auburn hair streamed back in a careless ponytail from a high intellectual forehead.

"Do me a favor," Howsam said.

Dr. Fabian nodded, less casual than she seemed, nonchalantly leaning against the paneled mahogany door. Peering nearsightedly through her round tortoiseshell reading glasses, she immediately noted the sweat-stained armpits of Howsam's yellow shirt. By the time the pale-green luminous eyes reached Schotten, they were frankly hostile. Unintimidated, he returned her gaze with

* An apt allusion. During the Napoleonic Wars, the Barings engaged in blockade running. Their profit went into another chancy venture, the East India Company. At the same time, the Rothschilds financed Wellington's army, smuggling gold through France, through the French lines, and finally into Spain. Both firms, of course, remain premier private banks to this day. The bones of equally monumental risks repose in the vaults of most other major private banking firms.

a singularly disarming smile. Something other than philosophical detachment stirred fleetingly in her face, but Howsam's voice extinguished it.

"Call Ann Arbor," he said, "and tell whoever's there I'll be out tomorrow morning around eleven."

"What if—"

"Not interested! I'll be there, regardless. Then get hold of the little old winemaker, and tell him to have someone meet my plane in San Francisco."

"About Account 60-J?" Dr. Fabian asked in an almost British accent.

"Right. And if he gets skittish, tell him I want to move all the dough—every penny! That'll straighten him out in a hurry."

She nodded, frowning.

"Good. Then call Lake Forest, and tell them I'll be in touch as soon as I know my schedule, probably tomorrow night. I want the eight-A.M. American flight to Detroit and the five-o'clock TWA plane to San Francisco. Oh yeah, and call the Mark Hopkins. I'll need a room for tomorrow night, and maybe the next. Got it all?"

Lips set in a thin line, Dr. Fabian nodded and left the office.

A moment later, the phone behind Howsam rang.

He listened briefly. "Thanks for the advice. Just call Ann Arbor," he said in a steely tone.

"Got a mind of her own," he said to Schotten, putting down the phone. "But what the hell—if she were a man, she'd have my job."

"I'd make allowances. She's very attractive."

"You married?"

"No. Never."

"Want to meet a nice Jewish girl? No, forget that!" Howsam said almost immediately, shaking his head. "There's no joke there. Life owes her."

"Oh? She looks fine to me."

"Some other time," Howsam suggested, with a resigned wave of his hand. "It's a long story. Where were we, anyway? Oh yeah, you never said how you planned to make the shove."

"I don't follow."

"How do you get the dollars to Japan?"

"Oh, you mean the conduit. I have it here." Schotten withdrew another sheaf of legal-sized papers stapled with a blue paper wrapper.

Howsam skimmed the long sheets of onionskin incorporating a company named Société A. G. Lion Holdings, in the city of Lausanne, canton of Vaud, Federal Republic of Switzerland.

"You're doing this in the open?" he said, when he had finished.

"Yes. People don't suspect what they see, only what they sense. So we'll be perfectly legal and aboveboard. We'll register this company with all the government agencies concerned. And what will they do? They'll say, 'Ah, another new little company,' and the papers promptly will be buried in a basement somewhere, if not lost altogether. Then, after a while, what happens to most new companies?"

"About eight out of ten go down the drain."

"Yes. And here was this funny little Swiss company. It too went the way of most corporate flesh."

"That beats sneaking around," Howsam agreed. "And no one gets hurt, because it's our money. Okay, so that means you've got to float the stock in Canada.* Now, how do you get the dollars there?"

Howsam listened attentively as Schotten described a highly complicated currency manipulation. "It'll never fly," he said when Schotten had finished. "The concept's good, but it's contrived—*The Thirty-Nine Steps*. Jesus, Louie Rasminsky'd† be all over it before we even got started. No—where you want to be is in wheat."

"Wheat?" Schotten asked, puzzled. "How?"

"Easy. We're going to be a bunch of grain brokers buying Canadian wheat futures for Latin America. Only we're not going to buy any. We're just going to put money on deposit and spread it around all over the country. Then later we'll make withdrawals to buy stock in Lion Holdings. No sweat about that either. We'll do it long distance. I know someone who'll line up stockholders in Montreal for us, too."

"You sound like Warburg." Schotten smiled. "Brilliantly simple."

Howsam shrugged. "It comes with the territory. Down in South America, with my skin, I'm just one of the boys, so I hear things. Hold on a minute, and I'll get a real expert on wheat in here."

Howsam picked up the red phone again and punched the intercom button. "Jorge, can you come in? . . . Hell, bring your lunch with you. We're thinking about buying a little wheat."

The small, wiry middle-aged Cuban who sat in the office next to Howsam's appeared. He had owned a bank in Havana. And he knew about wheat. By two o'clock, Schotten had the information he needed.

"What are you doing tomorrow?" Howsam asked after his assistant had left.

Schotten shrugged. "Nothing very much. Just a courtesy call in Long Island City. Archimedes Angelakos, the naval architect designing the tankers, has an office there, and Costa Lianides, our Admiral of the Ocean Sea, who will run the ships after the war, is helping him out. But they'll wait until you get back."

"Good. I want to meet those guys. In the meantime, how'd you like to go up to Montreal tomorrow and get briefed on the stock part of the deal?"

* Canada provides virtually no control over the sale of common stocks as does the Securities and Exchange Commission in the United States.
† Then governor of the Bank of Canada. One of the most respected central bankers in the world.

"Fine."

"Margie, put Dr. Fabian on, will you?" Howsam said into the phone. ". . . Ilona, call Montreal and tell Evelyn that a friend of ours who needs some help will be up there tomorrow morning on the ten-o'clock plane. . . . Hey, don't give me 'Evelyn who?' . . . Never mind why! Just do it! And see that there's a ticket waiting for Mr. Schotten at Air Canada at Kennedy. . . . S-C-H-O-T-T-E-N.

"A tall gray-haired chauffeur named MacKenzie will meet you at the gate in Montreal," Howsam told Schotten. "Now, where are you staying?"

"At the Carlyle."

"Okay, be there tomorrow night, and I'll get in touch." Howsam rose.

At the door, Schotten finally succumbed to curiosity. "How long have you been here?" he asked.

"Eighteen years."

"A long time. Did you always want to be a banker?"

Howsam shook his head. "I overmarried."

"I think not."

Howsam smiled tentatively. "Well, if that's your position, I'll bring you around to the house when this is all over, and you can tell that to my wife."

Then they shook hands for the first time—partners.


*December 30, 1965*
*Ann Arbor, Michigan*
*Montreal, Canada*
*Ukiah, California*
*New York City*


ON JUNE 9, 1865, exactly two months after Lee's surrender at Appomattox, a deed was recorded in the Kalamazoo, Michigan, courthouse. The document transferred ownership of fifty-one acres of land to a man named Hiram Weesaw.

Family legend has it that less than fifty dollars changed hands. Nevertheless, the transaction was no small matter. The purchase represented Weesaw's mustering-out bonus and savings as a sergeant in the Third Michigan Cavalry. And more than that, it marked him as an exceptional man.

He was an Indian who had prevailed.

He had done more than survive the Civil War. He had also bested lumber barons and politicians who had tried for years to drive the Indians west, out of Michigan. With his deed, Hiram Weesaw was there to stay.

He spent the rest of his life ankle-deep in muck, bent double, growing celery, green onions and mint. He and the other Indians and Poles who lived in the marshlands about twenty miles south of Kalamazoo came to be known as "Swamp Angels." Their descendants still are.

That could have been the fate of Hiram Weesaw's grandson, Jake, as well. But an imaginative high-school chemistry teacher intervened. He did so by writing a letter to a West Coast university, then virtually unknown in Michigan. His note echoed the laconic farmers' sons he taught.

He coached football on the side, the chemistry teacher wrote. He had an outstanding halfback who was also doing sophomore-level college chemistry. If the school still wanted Indians on its teams, what could be done about transportation and tuition? The boy would work for everything else.

An enrollment form came in April, a train ticket in August. In due course, Hiram Weesaw's grandson, Jake, became one of the most legendary of Stanford University's gridiron Indians.

He returned to Michigan years later, a Ph.D. in chemistry, and took a job at a paper mill in Parchment, a small town near Kalamazoo. That was in 1927.

For eighteen football seasons after that, Jake Weesaw crisscrossed Michigan in what seemed a romantic but hopeless quest. He sought other young Indians with Stanford brains as well as football skills.

Finally, in 1945, in a hamlet just six miles from his own birthplace, he found one. The boy who met his standards was an awesomely violent fullback with the cool, analytical mind of a hunter: Prentiss Howsam.

Eventually, Howsam's fame at Stanford surpassed Weesaw's. But nothing in football impressed Howsam as much as what Jake Weesaw told him the night before he left for college.

They had said goodbye, Howsam still standing by the car, when Jake cut the motor to lean out the driver's window and nod curtly at the chickens running loose in the yard and at the ramshackle, weathered house.

"A couple of things," he said quietly. "They think you're going there to play football. But you and I know better. You're going there to get out of this, and don't you ever forget it. You'll need good grades and plenty of sixes to keep that football ride. So if a guy won't block for you, run right over him. You hear me? Right over him—cleats in the back! Nobody gives a poor Indian boy anything." Then Jake drove off.

Harsh counsel, but only Francine Battle made a liar out of Jake.

She had given Howsam everything, and it seemed almost inevitable to her that she would. He had made her feel like a girl. She was intelligent, darkly handsome, and wealthy, and she should have had her pick of Jewish boys. But she had an unusual problem. She was six feet tall.

They were lab partners in freshman chemistry. At first, his dark hawk-sharp features and hooded eyes seemed sinister to her. But after a few weeks she began to enjoy working with him. He did things well, quickly and decisively, like her father, Ike Battle.

By November, her respect had become interest. She knew then he was very bright, and she started to wonder about the person in the magnificent copper-shaded body. He seemed solemn and uncommunicative, but she saw flashes of something else. Try as she might, however, she could not divert his attention from chemistry.

But one day he confronted her on the steps of the lab building.

"Hey, want to go to a football game Saturday?" he asked.

She nodded dumbly. He thrust a single white sidelines pass into her hand and disappeared into the stream of passing students. Until then she had thought he was at Stanford on one of the scholarships for Pit River Indians from northern California. He had never mentioned football.

The game was between the University of Washington's freshmen and Stanford's. But Francine Battle hardly noticed. The day belonged to Howsam. He scored three touchdowns; the third, running right over his own quarterback. His left cheek was scraped raw, and there were four stitches under the Band-Aid on the bridge of his nose. But he was ecstatic.

The freshman season was over, and the coaches had told him he would be the varsity fullback the following year. That meant he would have at least half of his college education, for sure. His euphoria made him more talkative than she could have imagined.

Over lunch, he told her about Jake Weesaw and life as a Swamp Angel. That was done, he said. Now he knew about the world beyond Michigan. He wanted his share. Someone else could do the farming.

A regiment of manufacturers' and merchants' sons had been paraded through the stone mansion on Long Island Sound for her benefit. But none of them, her father, Ike Battle, had warned, would be an exceptional man. She had always wondered how he could be so sure. Now she knew. This boy, naive and socially inept, would run right over life just as surely as he had run over his quarterback. He would be anything he wanted to be. It was as simple as that. By the time they entered the stadium that afternoon for the varsity game, she was helplessly and hopelessly attracted to him.

They eloped to Elko, Nevada, on the first day of Christmas vacation, December 19, 1945.

Ike Battle took the news calmly. The world had not ended with the Depression, the New Deal or World War II. It would not collapse because his daughter married an Indian. Besides, Francine was a serious girl. He had confidence in her judgment.

A month or so later, it was confirmed.

His new son-in-law was noticeably short on manners and certainly no beauty. The bronzed skin, with the cold, hooded eyes and hard, beaky mouth, made him seem frighteningly feral. The angry red stitch marks across the bridge of his nose were even more sinister.

Still, Battle had noted with a banker's detachment, there was no denying the kid's intelligence or his cynical, bluntly outspoken honesty. And, surprisingly, he had in abundance what the sophisticated Eastern society boys who dated Francine lacked. At eighteen, he had a view of the world as harsh-hearted and illusionless as a seasoned Wall Streeter's.

In short, he thought like a banker. Moreover, he had strong genes. He would have sons. If he passed his brains along with his guts, Battle & Company would endure another century.

Weighed against that, the prospect of halfbreed grandchildren meant little to Ike Battle. Others, including his wife, could be impeccable. That had never been one of his failings. Banking was a game with damned few rules. There was nothing genteel about it. In the end, bloodlines, religion and social graces were meaningless. History, he believed, backed that view.

The fastidious bankers he knew had all gone for walks, out of high windows, in the thirties.

And that was that, Howsam reflected sourly, concentration broken as the plane lurched through the smog and downdrafts over Detroit. He had hoped that recalling the events that led him to Ann Arbor this morning would yield a clue to the man he would meet there. But no such luck. He had run out of time when he most needed it.

He still disliked Thorstein Rademacher, and could not understand him, even though they had never met.

By 9:25 A.M. he had the rented Ford on the expressway for Ann Arbor. He wished he were going to Parchment instead. But this was out of Jake Wee-saw's league, even though he owned the paper mill now and much of south-western Michigan besides.

Thorstein Rademacher, on the other hand, had slightly more than $20 million worth of stocks in Battle & Company's second-floor safe. After capital-gains taxes, his holdings would exceed $16 million. More to the point, in September he had casually observed to Ilona Fabian that he seemed to be losing his appetite. He attributed this to the unusually hot, dry summer. But in November, when the ponds had frozen over and he still felt too logy to go skating, he thought that something might be wrong. His doctor mentioned a bowel obstruction and suggested the surgeons "take a look."

So the surgeons put old Rademacher on the operating table in University Hospital and split him open from breastbone to groin. Forty-five minutes later, neatly stitched, he was in his room. Four days later he went home. He would be dead in another four or five, Howsam had been told.

A childless widower, he would have no interest in return on investment. If he came in, the entire $16 million could be earmarked for the Helvetian-Judaic Foundation. By 1970 that would account for $160 million of the $250 million set aside for the Israelis. Without Rademacher, the investors would have to contribute the full sum, or 25 percent of the profits. With him, the bite would be only 9 percent. That made a difference.

Howsam, who professed to be poor at figures, had worked it all out in his head while sparring with Schotten. In his case, Rademacher's participation meant an extra $32 million, and over the first four years only. But that was easier said than done. Rademacher, by all accounts, was formidable.

Adolf Hitler was responsible for his presence in America, and the Glass-Steagall Act of 1933 put his life and Howsam's on converging courses. This law required American banks to limit their activities to either commercial banking or investment banking, the underwriting of stocks and bonds. They could no longer do both.

Battle & Company, remaining a commercial bank, was a principal beneficiary of this decision. Many refugees wanted to keep their money with their own kind. At least until they got the feel of their new country.

Rademacher turned up in 1935. He had taught at the London School of Economics and had taken a post at the University of Michigan. Stocks were his conceit, he said. He knew the market so well he could chart it from one year to the next. Therefore he changed his portfolio only during the summer months, when classes were not in session.

Ike Battle need only execute his orders and keep the account current for tax purposes. No, he did not want Battle phoning him with information. Like his friend in London, Siegmund Warburg, he read only a newspaper's index. The rest was for idiots. The same applied to stock market gossip. A crank, to be sure, but private banks are full of them.

He made an uncomplimentary remark about dirty windows, deposited $8,000 and left. He bought stocks two weeks later. After that the value of his portfolio soared, regardless of depressions, recessions or World War II. In several years it doubled and trebled in worth.

After the war, Ike Battle visited Ann Arbor, but they never became close. Rademacher's arrogance put him off. That, Battle knew, also caused the squabble with Howsam, and was not entirely his son-in-law's fault.

The row stemmed from the discretionary account.

Initially, Rademacher's quarterly and semiannual dividend checks were deposited. That money would be used the next time stocks were bought. By 1950, however, large sums lay idle from one summer to the next.

Ike Battle suggested that he invest this cash, without consulting Rademacher, as it came in. Rademacher agreed, and a genteel contest evolved. Battle tried to make the discretionary account, which he managed, outperform Rademacher's portfolio. That never happened, but the game amused them anyway. They made wry jokes about it when not playing chess the two evenings a year they spent together in Ann Arbor.

In 1958, however, Battle had his first heart attack. Howsam took over with spectacular results, cashing in on positions related to the Cuban situation. At year end, as a matter of course, he wrote the following note:

> I am pleased to inform you that adjusted yield on your Discretionary Account, weighted for time, was 41.7% per annum.
>
> As of December 30, the balance stands at $433,527.71. Hopefully, you will find this performance satisfactory.

Rademacher immediately called Ike Battle with a blistering harangue. The letter's patronizing tone outraged him. Furthermore, the bankers he knew were cultured, not tradesmen. This Howsam, whoever he was, did not even know the language. How could he be trusted with money when he wallowed around in linguistic imprecisions?

The first part of the diatribe Ike Battle understood. The discretionary account had bested Rademacher's portfolio. The *Oxford English Dictionary* explained the second: "hopefully" was not a word, but a corruption.

Predictably, Howsam exploded when he was told of this. Ike Battle, taking a cue from what he knew of his son-in-law's vengeful character, made sure that the two men never met. Shortly before he died, he introduced Ilona Fabian to Rademacher, and she had serviced his account ever since. They had much in common. They were both Europeans, and she had taken her doctorate at the London School of Economics.

But neither Howsam nor Rademacher forgot the other. And judging from the questions Ilona Fabian had to parry, their mutual dislike deepened rather than abated.

The past held little hope, but Howsam turned off the expressway and drove through Ann Arbor undaunted. He had a plan, and he liked it. It covered both contingencies. If he did not get the $16 million, he would at least get that much in satisfaction.

Rademacher lived in a white frame house with a narrow curving roof over the front door and a broad fieldstone chimney. Howsam knew the design well. Hundreds of similar homes had been built throughout Michigan just prior to World War II. They sold for $9,000 then, $500 down, and, after the Depression, they seemed the height of luxury.

A nurse appeared at once, a compact blonde with wide-set blue eyes and a square face. She sized him up through the glass panel in the aluminum storm door, frankly puzzled. Local Indians did not wear cashmere chesterfields with hand-sewn velvet collars.

"Dr. Rademacher isn't seeing anyone," she said. "He's very ill. He won't even see the rabbi from the Hillel Foundation."

"He's expecting me."

She shook her head. "Only his banker."

"Goddammit, I am his banker!" he snapped, handing her his card. He stepped into the living room and threw his coat on a green horsehair couch which Rademacher must have brought over from Europe in 1935.

"He upstairs?"

"Yes," she conceded, still bewildered.

"You're Miss Ten Houten?" he demanded, matching the Michigan-Dutch face to the name on checks he had signed the last month.

"That's right."

"You from Holland or Zeeland?"

"Zeeland, but how do you know that?"

He smiled cryptically. "You just see we're not disturbed."

She nodded quickly, eyes wide. He had that effect on lots of people. No one ever expected to meet a bright Indian.

Rademacher lay on his side, burrowed down in an oversized hospital bed, like a soldier in a foxhole. Behind him, a large picture window looked out on a drab ravine. He was staring at the doorway as Howsam entered.

Howsam remembered him from photographs. He had been tall, squarely built, with aggressive cheekbones. Now he seemed diminished with a beige blanket under his chin like a napkin. His lips were drawn back over gray, septic-looking gums in either a smile or a grimace.

"Ah, the fancy New York banker," he whispered in a heavy German accent. "What brings you here?"

"Your money."

"You and the rest of the world," Rademacher sighed disgustedly, "all drowning in a sea of good causes. Now, suddenly, I'm important."

"Don't flatter yourself. I'm here for Ike. If he were alive, you'd be the first person he'd see today. As far as I'm concerned, you're still his client."

The beige blanket moved almost imperceptibly over Rademacher's shoulders. "High marks for honesty, if not for charm. But you'll be wasting your breath. I already have a little cause. Sit down, and I'll tell you about it. Then you can leave."

Howsam took a copy of the *Wall Street Journal* off the chair at the bed and sat down. Almost at once he had to fight back the breakfast he had had on the plane. The stench of rotten eggs surrounding Rademacher was stupefying. It could only have come from the cancer.

Still lying on his side, Rademacher focused his right eye on Howsam. It was pale blue, the white milky with fever.

"My neighbor, McClure, does pharmacological research," he began. "He's brilliant, into everything. He stops by to see me almost every evening, and when the pain is bad he gives me a little sugar cube, which I chew.

"Those nights, I see my little friend. At first I thought, What a stupid disease. It's only a fragile one-eyed head with a tiny V-shaped beak. It was drowsy then, gentle. The most I ever felt was a twinge, and not always unpleasant either.

"But recently it's grown, and it's become frantic. Now it has a long green furry body, and it's very quick, as if it knows it will never get its fill of me. Oh, yes, these days it plunges and soars through my guts like a demented eel—twisting and wrenching at my flesh quite mercilessly. But I don't hate it. On the contrary, I sympathize with it. It's driven. Terribly. Twice, in desperation, it even hurled itself all the way down to my scrotum. That, I can tell you, was truly . . . exquisite. I woke up both times screaming for my mother. But I was too spent to scream. Nothing came out. Only the moon knew the agonies my friend and I endured those nights.

"Now, the do-gooders come here with wondrous tales of what my money will do for their worthy causes. But you know something? Only my starving, tormented little friend interests me. And not one of those charity vultures has even mentioned him. Oh no, they're too selfless for that. Now, you tell me, Mr. Discretionary Account, what you can do for my little friend. Then, perhaps, we'll talk money and wills."

"Wise up. Nothing's going to whip that thing. I want you to beat death."

"Oh, yes. You—and you alone—know the secret of my immortality."

"Sort of."

Rademacher sneered, rolling his fever-dulled eyes toward the ceiling. "A fool, a *goyishe* Indian fool playing with words."

Howsam nodded philosophically. "Maybe I came too soon," he mused. "If I'd waited another day or two, that little green friend of yours might have bitten out some of your nastiness."

Rademacher gasped. A bony hand darted forth from under the cover, toward the nurse's call button, but Howsam slapped it away, hard. Then he leaned over the bed, inches away from the dying man's face.

"You old fool. What did you expect? I came here because Ike would have wanted your money to live on and on to help Jews. And what are you doing? You're insulting me!"

Rademacher's lips drew back triumphantly. "Old news. I don't need you to tell me how to take care of Jews. I've already done that. Every penny goes to Israel to build a hospital. Do you know what kind of a hospital you can build there with that much money?"

"Rademacher," Howsam roared, "you've got cancer, not insanity! For Christ's sake, you were smart enough to make twenty million dollars. Is that your idea of how to help Jews?"

"What do you mean?"

"I mean that country's already up to its ass in hospitals! Every Hadassah lady, every nightclub comedian, every cloak-and-suiter who strikes it rich—

they all run to Israel to build hospitals. You know why? Because they get to name them after their parents. They're all such dummies they think that's great. They don't know the difference between sentiment and sentimentality. The Jewish edifice complex, my wife calls it. But you—you're a moneyman. You're supposed to know better! Tell me, you think a hospital's going to win a war or increase gross national product?"

Whatever else he was, Thorstein Rademacher was an economist. He knew economic truth when he heard it. He was listening. With great effort, he propped himself up on one elbow, head off the pillow.

"You give me that money," Howsam went on, "and by 1970 the Jews'll have one hundred sixty million dollars—with plenty more to come. Then Israel will have what it really needs to survive, cash—cash for guns and planes and tanks and factories!"

Rademacher sighed and raised himself still higher.

"That beats hospitals, huh?" Howsam reached across the old man and pressed the button to raise the bed. "Come on, now, sit up, and I'll tell you how to help Jews."

Just then, Nurse Ten Houten, alarmed by their voices, entered the bedroom. She busied herself at once at a small medicine table.

"Do that later!" Howsam ordered.

"I can't. Everything has to be ready for Dr. Gilkey when he comes," she said, eying him suspiciously.

Like any banker after money, Howsam too lived in the here and now. He edged the chair closer to the bed, totally immersing himself in the cancer's putrid aura, and cupped his hand to Rademacher's ear.

He spoke twenty minutes, without interruption, in a quiet whisper.

Then Rademacher turned to him. "It's complicated," he said, "iffy."

"Of course. If it were easy, everyone would do it."

"And what happens if you're caught?"

"I'll let you know—sooner than you think. I'll be as dead as you."

Rademacher's pale-blue eyes brightened. His thin lips flattened against the gray gums.

"I like it," he whispered. "Either way, I win."

"Right!" Howsam agreed. "No matter how it goes, you get a money's worth. Is that some kind of a deal?"

"I'll call Hawley tomorrow about changing the will."

"No, goddammit, I'll call him now! I didn't come out here for promises. Resign yourself! You're going to die, and you're going to die soon. And if you really want to help Jews, you're going to die balls-ass-naked broke, because I'm going to take all your money. Today! Now, do I get hold of that lawyer or do we call it quits?"

Rademacher cringed, violently shaking his head through Howsam's outburst. Then he sank back upon the pillow, spent. Finally, when he stopped gasping, he nodded submissively. Sweat drenched the sides of his face. He dabbed nervously at his forehead with a red-striped pajama sleeve.

Howsam reached over and felt his cheek. "Jesus, you're on fire. I'll get you some water."

"*Nein! Nein!* With the fever, the water is so bitter it makes me vomit. Orange juice—there." Rademacher pointed to a small bar refrigerator set on the lower shelf of a bookcase.

Howsam held the paper cup. Between sips, Rademacher told him how to reach the lawyer, Hawley, who was on the law school faculty.

Hawley showed up twenty minutes later, a small man with a lot of forehead, less chin, and skeptical gray eyes. His yard man was an Indian. Like Nurse Ten Houten, he had trouble squaring his image of bankers with the one before him. Still, he listened and promised to have papers ready when Howsam's lawyer arrived from New York the next morning.

The odor, heightened by Rademacher's fever, hit Howsam as soon as he reentered the bedroom.

"Jesus, don't they ever give you a bath?" he asked.

"*Nein.* Only a wipe with the towel when they change the bed."

"But you stink!"

"Dr. Gilkey's orders. He's afraid of pneumonia."

"Come again."

Rademacher nodded, underlining the idiocy. "You heard."

"That horse's ass. Take your top off," Howsam ordered. "You're going to get a bath. I'll be right back with a washcloth and a towel."

"But what about the nurse? What if she sees?"

"Fuck her—and fuck that doctor too. I'll be goddamned if any client of mine is going to lie around like a pig in slops. That's worse than cancer."

Rademacher smiled, this time unmistakably.

A few minutes later, Howsam blotted the old man's back dry and turned him around to do his chest. "How does it feel?" he asked.

"Good, better than sleep."

"That's the idea, but hang on. I'm at the scar, and it looks raw."

Rademacher obeyed, putting both hands on Howsam's shoulders. He gazed at the bedroom door, his thoughts far beyond his body.

"Tell me," he asked, "who will know of this?"

Howsam looked up. "Oh, you, me, Ilona."

"And not the Israelis?"

"No, why should they?"

"It seems so strange. I'm going to change their country, and they'll never even know who I am."

"What's the difference? *You* know, and that's what this is all about. Don't you feel better?"

"Yes, but I'm all alone. I don't even have anyone to say Kaddish for my soul. Do you suppose someone in Israel could do that?"

"Leave that to me. I promise you, they won't see penny one until that's done. And they better find the rabbi of the world to say it for you."

Finished, Howsam unrolled his sleeves, put on his coat and walked to the side of the bed. "Get some sleep now," he told Rademacher. "Tomorrow, when you sign that will for the Helvetian-Judaic Foundation, you're going to change the world. And if that little green sonofabitch shows up again, tell him so—it'll take the bite right out of him. You'll see."

Rademacher raised himself higher on the pillow. "Will—will you come back when this is all over? I'd like you here. You and Ilona."

Howsam nodded. "Don't worry, now. The hard part's nearly over."

"I know."

Rademacher clung to Howsam's hand. *"Mazel tov,* Prentiss."

At two-thirty Howsam was in a phone booth in Metropolitan Airport, waiting for Ilona Fabian to answer at the other end. When she did, he said just three words: "Sell out Rademacher."

"You heartless bastard," she answered.

"Have it your way, but be at home tonight. I'll call you from San Francisco. I may want you to get hold of Schotten."

Then he hung up and went into the coffee shop, not at all hungry.

Evelyn ducked the question with one of his own.

"Some smoked salmon?" he asked. "It's really quite good, and, after breakfast on Air Canada, you deserve something special."

Eric Schotten considered the silver tray at the right of the deep green velvet wing chair. "Thank you, no."

"Well, then, a little Crema Danica? That's a lovely cheese, especially on the dark rye, and should be, too—at damned near four dollars a pound."

Schotten smiled. "A little later, perhaps."

Evelyn nodded resignedly. A short pudgy man with thinning blond hair, he leaned casually against the library's marble fireplace, cup and saucer in left hand. The blazer and the Breton red slacks were for New Year's in Nassau, he said. When they finished, a company plane would fly him to his winter home there.

His face seemed to have been on permanent holiday. Round and beaming, pink-cheeked and smooth, it belonged in the elegant château in Westmount, Montreal's wealthiest English-speaking area. It projected the diffident, somewhat fatuous sense of well-being that marks a middle-aged man who has always known that little in life can hurt him. But, hospitality exhausted, he finally came to the point.

"What have I to do with the Jews?" he said in a deep, jovial baritone. "Oh, that's a long story. Very long indeed. We Welshmen have a reputation for being a tricksy, two-faced lot, you know. And I must say," he observed happily, "in most cases it's richly deserved. You've read *Under Milk Wood*, by Dylan Thomas? No? Do, Eric. Do! You look a banker who enjoys more than balance sheets. At any rate, kids the world over study the poem now for what critics call its 'moving and sensitive portrayal of Welsh village life.' It's all about a place named Llareggub. Spelled backward, you know, that comes out 'Bugger All,' which is really what poor Thomas had in mind all along. Oh, that's very Welsh. And a good thing, too, for a bit of that old Celtic sly must have rubbed off on me. I took what you might call the glandular approach to history, you see. I grew up in Palestine."

"Your family were colonials?"

"Good heavens, no! We've never been smart, or even middle-class. I bumbled into the Mandate—living proof of Maugham's maxim that it's better to be born lucky than rich! I'd gone down to London in 1935 looking for work, and prospects were bleaker than the pit. Geologists were three a ha'penny, but when I went round to the Combined University Appointments Board, they told me Iraq Petroleum had a job going begging. I hadn't even the wit to ask why! Instead, I traipsed right over to Whitehall and saw a portly old gent with walrus mustaches named Pocock. He knew Cambridge, of course, but what caught his eye was my college there, Selwyn. Had I, by chance, been a parson's son on church stipend? he asked. I nodded.

" 'Anglican?'

" 'No, Fundamentalist.'

" 'Excellent!'

"I tell you, I hardly believed my ears. Welsh Chapel's never been in very good taste in England, you know—too much fire and brimstone. But old Pocock positively beamed!

"The firm wanted men with 'rigorous Christian backgrounds' in the Middle East, he said. In fact, they'd left a good job open months waiting for such a chap. They needed a production expediter in their Haifa refinery. Was I interested?

"I told him I wasn't sure. Geology was my mum's idea, you know. I'd been a weak, sickly child, and she thought the outdoors and all the fresh air'd be good for me. And right she was, God rest her merry soul! What I really wanted was fieldwork, I said.

"Pocock winked. Slyly. Expediters often spent months checking just the Palestine portion of the pipeline, he said. And with my upbringing, I'd like some places that it passed. His face lit up so mentioning them, you'd think he was Father Christmas handing out sweets."

" 'Ein Dor!' The Witch of Endor lived there, you know.

" 'Megiddo!' Armageddon, we call it.

" 'Harod!' Where Gideon and his three hundred routed the Midianites.

"Enough said. Three weeks later I landed in Haifa, and O'Hara-Forster, the plant manager, told me why the job had gone begging. Delightful chap, Michael, and not given to flights of fancy. 'Stay in bed nights,' he told me, 'or you'll wake up some morning with your peter in your mouth. Haj Amin's on the warpath.'"

"Haj Amin el-Husseini," Schotten said, "Grand Mufti of Jerusalem."

Evelyn nodded cordially, placing the oversized Quimper cup and saucer on the mantel over the fireplace.

"Himself," he smiled, "and leader of the Husseinis, Palestine's toughest Arab clan, to boot. And make no mistake, when that little nigger got testy, God and gun were on his side! Every mullah in every mosque preached his hatred; every muktar in every village paid him tribute; every politician supported his extremist National Party. Furthermore, by 1935 he'd arms to match his influence. He'd found a friend, you see, who shared his feelings for the English—Hitler.

"But England saw war coming, and it wanted Arabs on its side. So Mr. Chamberlain threw Haj Amin a bone: the Jews.

"In effect, the Balfour Declaration, which backed a Jewish national homeland in Palestine, was suspended—League of Nations police restraints in the Mandate, too. Good, practical politics, for Jews died cheaply then. They feared offending the English—"

"And you knew nothing of that?"

"Nothing," Evelyn affirmed. "At Cambridge, half my class lost dads in Flanders and Passchendaele. We couldn't have cared less about so-called 'civil disturbances' in Palestine. We'd had it with war—even as late as 1935.

"And to crown my sorrows, that filthy old swine, Pocock, had lied about the job too. There wasn't any fieldwork. I read gauges and ran specific-gravity tests on each batch of crude coming down the pipe from Iraq. Scutwork, Eric—scutwork! Why, I might as well have been a chartered accountant for all the fresh air I'd get out of that!

"But I've always sat at the foot of the cross, and six months later none of it mattered. None! Not the job, not the shooting, not even the loathing everyone had for the English. We'd hired someone to come in afternoons, you see, to get our reports in shape for London, a young Jewess— You're sure you'll not try the smoked salmon?"

"Thank you, no. Not just yet."

"But your foot's bothering you, isn't it? I can tell from the way it's twitching about."

"It needs to stretch," Schotten admitted. "Perhaps I'll try the couch."

Evelyn shook his head. "No, no! Don't get up. You're already in the best chair in the house. I'll just fetch a footstool from the lounge whilst you give me a refill on the cocoa." He bounded out of the library in short, surprisingly quick steps, to return with an oversized yellow hassock comfortably canted against the bulging blue blazer.

"There. You're comfortable? Good. Now, where was I?"

"The girl," Schotten said, adjusting his right leg.

"That'll take some doing." Evelyn smiled. "At my age and weight, you know, you don't run round singing The Song of Songs—especially mornings. Still, I'll do it now, and appearances be damned, for I'll hymn you joys and honor delights old Solomon never knew. Promise! My gal had all of his, you see, and more, Eric—more. Black jasmine-scented hair . . . tiny waist astride lush, rolling hips . . . long, gorgeous legs that seemed to go on forever? Solomon sang not a word of those, you know. And couldn't.

"How come? The old fraud'd never really seen them! His 'fair daughters of Jerusalem' hadn't worn white shirts and shorts as mine did.

"But she was half a head taller than I, and a beauty, so I never dreamt of happy endings. There wouldn't be any, and I knew it—no miracles either, not with Mandate politics and religion. Still, I was mad for her, mad out of my mind. Poor, tubby little fool—I couldn't help myself.

"Day after day, we sat facing each other, not six feet apart. And sometimes I'd look up and catch her measuring me. Her eyes'd bound away like frightened does when that happened, and I'd watch them go—achingly painful moments, those. I never knew what to think, you see. For we never spoke and were rarely alone.

"Her dad saw to that. Afternoons at four, he met her at the front gate, and he got a wide berth from everyone, especially me. A real *shtarker*, he was, and all in black, from hat to beard to knee-high leather boots—hardly the type to give a little *goy* calling privileges.

"But one day he didn't show up, and I found her waiting outside. So I offered to see her home. Not necessary, she said. She always met people she knew on the bus. All right, I'd walk her to the stop. Would she mind? 'No . . .' she said, thinking of the old man, I'm sure.

"Well, I carried her off like a hostage into the first Greek ice cream parlor we passed. And before she could even open her mouth I'd ordered two great, whacking bowls of pistachio ice cream. And there we sat.

"She'd never been alone with a man before, and I thought she'd bolt for the door. She looked that scared. But gradually I drew her out, and things got better. Mornings, she told me, she went to the Technion, the Jewish scientific institute. I made the appropriate fuss, but she shut that right off. Child's play, she said. Her big brother was a *bocher*, in Talmud school, studying to be a rabbi.

"My line of country at last, and you should have seen me go. I dazzled her with science, flabbergasted her with my knowledge of the Book, and before you knew it she was laughing. I've not words for what I felt watching those heart-stopping black eyes shine on me . . . Kid stuff? Sure. But that's what life's all about, isn't it—at least the parts that count?

"No matter. By the time we left, she'd enjoyed herself, too, and it showed.

Even Arabs, who despised seeing women in shorts, nodded approvingly. She was that lovely, that sweet, walking down Allenby Street all in white—smiling. I've not the language that moment rates, either.

"And just as well. It died three blocks down.

"Usually, at five, Arab workmen and little old Jewish ladies going home from vegetable market queued up at the bus stop. There was never any fuss. They were all too tuckered out from the heat. But that day, by crikey, they were all milling about, the Arabs laughing and carrying on and the women screaming bloody murder.

"I didn't get it—I never had any brains—but the girl did, from a block away. She'd seen the English constable in the intersection laughing—"

"A Jew-baiting," Schotten interrupted.

"Exactly. How'd you know?"

"My father told me about them in the thirties, when I was a little boy. He saw them in Germany."

Evelyn nodded. "Oh, yes, quite the thing then. When we got closer, she squeezed my elbow and said, 'Stop it—before someone gets hurt.' Dear God in heaven, I should have run for my life! I was a preacher's boy. I knew nothing of fighting. But she'd touched me. So I pushed through the crowd. A regular donnybrook it was, too, five teenagers battling along the curb—three Arabs against two Jews. The brawl was about who had got on line first. I put my arms out, like a sleepwalker, and got in between them.

" 'Fair's fair! It's three against two,' I shouted, trying to sound like my public-school headmaster.

"What a laugh that was! Got me a smack right in the mouth from one of the Arabs. He hadn't heard about fairness—nor had the Jews either. They tripped me up from behind, and I went down like a shot, clutching at arms, legs, belts, anything. But all I got was shredded knees. The damned cobblestones ate them alive below my khaki shorts. I never made it back to my feet. The five of them just clambered over me, throwing punches as they came and went. Oh, it was awful.

"I promise you, I'd be there still, but for a bent old *alter kocker* of a Jew with a dirty yellow beard. Believe me, he didn't know from fairness either! He came rushing in—long black coat flapping—screaming like a dervish, and swinging a monstrous knobby cane in both hands. Thought it was a cricket bat. One Arab got it right across the face—smashed his nose absolutely flat. Another caught it on the ear, and what a shot that was! Caved the drum right in. Blood spurted out clean over the kid's shoulder. And that put paid to that. All three Arabs were legging it down Allenby Street. Oh, you should have heard that little fiend cackle then!

"But his biggest laugh was on me. He thought the blood gushing from my lips and knees even funnier. And so did the others—Arab and Jew alike. I got the same message when I looked at the girl too. She'd the good grace not to show her contempt, but that was all. I tell you, I wanted to cry. My eyes smarted with shame.

" 'For God's sake,' I alibied, as if I'd only done her bidding, 'he wanted to kill somebody with that club.'

"A waste of breath. Jews have their own notion of reality, you know. For them, honor is to survive. Glory is to prevail. I'd done neither.

" 'Yes,' she said, eyes dimming behind that cool, solemn reserve Orthodox maidens wear like veils. 'You were . . . reasonable.' Then she got on her bus.

"If it weren't for Haj Amin, I'd have died of heartbreak. But the very next day we heard he meant to broaden the general strike he'd called the year before, in 1935. That meant round-the-clock tanker loadings, so between the heat, the stench and sixteen-hour workdays, I stopped thinking altogether.

"The Arabs, of course, ran fevers overnight. But nothing happened. They're easily stirred but quick to lose interest, and Haj Amin knew this. So he let them stew. In fact, it wasn't till an afternoon three weeks later that Yassir, a plant messenger boy, came running down the loading dock for me. He was a bit of a prankster, but not then. No ten-year-old could feign joy like that. I mean, he was ecstatic.

" 'Ing-lase! Ing-lase! Come see the funny Jew!'

"Sure enough, behind him the tarmac road leading to the main gate was jammed with Arabs, all of them sprinting flat out and most yipping like desert dogs. Oh, that's a sound. It goes right through you: a high-pitched and hungry *whoop!* . . . *whoop!* . . . *whoop!* It carried all the way down to me, on Haifa Bay, a good three quarters of a mile off.

"Sunny afternoon and all, the bloody racket scared me shitless. But I dropped what I was doing and took off after them anyway. I'd no idea what was happening, but I knew it had to be bad when Jamal, the plant foreman, scuttled by, a knowing smirk on his crafty ferret's face. Oh, he looked happier than a dog with two cocks, and he'd not stir his lazy, spiteful backside for the Second Coming, that one.

"It was Jamal, you know, who first called me 'English' rather than 'effendi.' He'd told O'Hara-Forster I was too young to respect. As Haj Amin's agent in place, he'd got away with it, too. After that, my life'd really been hell. I'd no 'face,' you see—I'd lost it all just like that.

"I could hardly walk, let alone run, because of the scabs on my knees. So when I got to the gate, three or four hundred Arabs were ahead of me, all squatting on their haunches in a semicircle. Happy as larks they were, too, giggling and nattering and holding each other's hands like schoolgirls. They'd shut up a bit when one of the deeper thinkers'd mutter *'sharaf,'* their word for honor. But the next moment they'd start right in laughing and yipping all over again—as if that bothered the Jew."

"Yes, what was he doing all this time?"

"Nothing. Poor devil couldn't have cared less, either. He was stretched out, straddling the yellow line in the blacktop road, arms and legs flung every which way. He looked as though he'd fallen through space and landed on his back right between the guardposts at the main gate. Fact was, he'd no such luck at all.

"They'd yanked his white shirt out and pulled it down round his knees, and from tails to second button, it was drenched in blood. Thick, red streams of it ran out the corners of his mouth, too, and trickled down his face, like clown's makeup. That's what he looked like, you know: a clown. His lips were skinned right back from his gums, ear to ear, as if he were afraid we'd miss the peter jammed between his teeth.

"I'd been warned, of course. O'Hara-Forster'd told me that was standard Arab operating procedure—and no pun intended. Still is, in fact. In December 1947 it happened again in that very refinery, but to forty-one Jews. In 1948, at a place called Kfar Etzion, another thirty-five got more of the same.

"Still, words don't prepare you for that. All I wanted to do was to be sick—and I would've, too, but for Jamal. The filthy cadaverous swine saw my face and broke out laughing. I'd be damned if I'd give him more satisfaction, so I swallowed hard, instead, and shook with dry heaves.

"I knew the Jew right off, you see, by his black knee-high leather boots.

"I couldn't take my eyes off him, so I never saw the girl. She just slipped up behind me, soundlessly in sandals, hands pressed flat against her white shorts in dread, through all the giggling and yipping. The Arabs went dead quiet then, as if someone'd thrown a switch. And when she got closer, they all sucked breath. I heard it—a great, collective gasp. Oh, the little buggers were coming, I'll tell you, smiling like naughty boys and licking their lips in anticipation. That's why they go in for mutilation in the first place, you know: to intimidate the survivors. They wanted to hear her wail.

"But she didn't—not ever. Dry-eyed and silent, she walked straight to the body, steady as you please. No doubt about her being a dutiful daughter. She knew what to do, and she did it. She set them a proper example.

"She knelt down in her dad's blood and leaned over to close his eyelids. But they weren't there, Eric. His eyes, either. His balls were. Poor dear thing—that's what she found. She'd no way of knowing, not in that mess, what she'd be touching. It straightened her right up, I'll tell you.

"But then she went into a sort of slow motion, tilting her head until the long black hair hung 'cross the right shoulder of her white shirt. She stayed that way, baffled and questioning, trying to reconcile the childlike, dreamy smiles all round her with the blood dripping off her hands.

"My stomach gave up the ghost right then and there, and I was still head down when the screaming and cursing started—"

"The police?" Schotten asked.

"Police, my bum! They only turned out when English property was in danger. Haifa belonged to Haj Amin in those days. It was the girl, Eric—the girl!

When I looked up, I got the shock of my life. She was walking away, right through the Arabs, and those closest to her were scuttling off backward—literally cringing, I mean—and not taking their eyes off her. They were shaking their fists and spitting at her for ruining their afternoon, but they weren't yipping. And, by God, they were bloody well keeping their distance. Know why?''

Schotten looked up from the silver tray alongside the green velvet wing chair and absently shook his head.

"Jamal!" Evelyn said exultantly. "He was on his knees, shrieking and tossing his head about like a fevered horse. Two of his pals were trying to lead him away, but he wouldn't budge. He had both hands at his eyes, rubbing them, as if they were on fire. And maybe they were. She'd thrown a perfect strike, you see, right into his bony, leering face, with what'd been in her dad's mouth. I saw it, lying on the blacktop, right at Jamal's feet, its head pointing right at him, so he'd not miss its accusing eye—"

"No disrespect," Schotten interrupted, "but you're right."

"Yes? About what?"

"The salmon. It's the best I've ever tasted."

"Oh, really? As advertised?"

"Absolutely! I pay a fortune to those robbers Fortnum and Mason to fly me Scottish salmon from London, for our English clients' tea, and it's not within light-years of this."

"All in the smoking, and the Indians up north, where I found all the iron ore, really have that wired," Evelyn explained, once more the chatelain of Westmount. "But do try some with pepper—to bring out the flavor. Black's in the rosewood mill. Cayenne's in the pewter. That's it. . . . Good? If you think that's something, just wait till spring. I'll send you fresh-smoked Arctic char. You'll think you're in heaven, old chap—in heaven!"

"*Fantastisch!*" Schotten agreed. "But please—let me fix you something. I feel guilty eating so well alone."

Evelyn's eyes brightened. "Can't have that, can we? And since Mummy and the girls aren't here to hound me 'bout my diet, we'll do it up right! Spread a little Crema Danica on that light rye, will you? Then two slices of salmon and a heavy spoonful of diced onions."

"Pepper?"

"Indeed! A turn's worth of black."

"Done—and I'll refill the cocoa too."

"First rate!" Evelyn declared a moment later, smacking his lips. "My compliments to the chef, and tell him an encore's in order. Just like the first, Eric, but a little heavier on the Crema Danica, please."

His enthusiasm continued unabated through a second heaping open-faced sandwich. When it appeared that a third might be required, Schotten immediately brought the conversation back on its original course.

"That must have been some day," he said.

Evelyn nodded, wistfully licking his thumb after dispatching the last bit of cheese-covered crust.

"Oh, that wasn't the worst of it by half—not by half. The old man had been killed on company property, and if the family held us responsible, it meant a lawsuit. So O'Hara-Forster, the plant manager, wanted to pay them off at once if they freed us from liability. I forget what he decided on, but it wasn't much, twenty or thirty pounds at most—laughable, really. But not to me," he said, pointing a forefinger at his blue blazer. "As the junior Englishman on staff, I got elected to deliver the check.

"The family lived in a Jewish quarter about halfway up Mount Carmel. So, at seven that night, I was in an old yellow-and-blue Leyland bus, wheezing up the side of the hill. We'd barely turned off Allenby Street when I heard the wailing. At first I thought I knew whose it was. But as we crept higher I learned better. It came from every block and ricocheted off the old yellow houses and filled the sky like heat lightning. Haj Amin had all the Jews in Haifa screaming that night, I'll tell you.

"And my timing couldn't have been worse. I guessed the old man'd been in the ground about an hour. By the time I arrived, the mourners'd be back from the grave, and the *shiva*'d be going full blast. That gave me a chill, all right. You've seen Jews sit *shiva?*"

"Once," Schotten nodded. "In Zurich. A friend of my father's died."

Evelyn shook his head patronizingly over the yellow cup and saucer, a connoisseur dismissing the ordinary.

"Not the same. Not the same at all. I'm talking hard-liners now, the kind who covet grief—greedy as they come with suffering. They want it to hurt. And the more it hurts, the better. Because when they can't stand it anymore, they stop mourning. There's no pain left. That's why they sit *shiva* in the first place: for the misery. Good therapy, actually. It gets it over with fast. It's not for nothing Jews say, 'Life is for the living.'

"They know what they're doing, so they help it along. They darken the rooms, so it hurts to see. Then they lift the rugs and take off their shoes, so it hurts to walk. The furniture goes, too. Crates or rough pine stools are better. They make it hurt to sit. Add some bawling, and you've got yourself a nice little orthodox *shiva*.

"None of which laid a patch on what I found: thirty or forty wild Moroccan Jews all jammed into a dinky two-room basement flat. Feisty and delirious with death they were, too—just as I expected. They'd hardly started, and they were already sending out regular shock waves of sweaty heat, stink and ear-splitting sound. Just getting through the dark, filthy brick passageway leading back to the place was like swimming upstream. They'd not missed a trick inside either, I'll tell you.

"The temperature stood at eighty-five, but they'd nailed and shrouded the

two cellar windows opening on the alley. The only light in either room came
from a single *yortzheit* candle—a big brass cup filled with rank rendered lamb
fat. I never did find the bloody thing, but it must have been low down somewhere. All it did was throw grotesque shadows. The furniture'd been cleared
out and the straw mats rolled back, too. Then—and this was inspired—someone'd put the nick on a bushel of granite chips from a paving job and spilt
them over the beaten earth floor. If that burning lamb fat didn't bring tears to
your eyes, those pointy little chips would—not that the women needed help.

"They had the front room all to themselves. And in its center, four of them,
robed and scarved in black, swayed and danced barefoot round the widow.
They were clapping hands and keening her in a long, wracking wail. She kept
time, screeching like a banshee and raking her nails down her face with each
handclap. I never saw the poor woman, just her shadow on the whitewashed
wall behind her. But that was enough. Later, I heard, she took great pride in
the scars from that little bit of business. She had four on each cheek, and they
were as deep and wide as a Zulu warrior's, she boasted. Such had been the
measure of her grief. A fierce, weird people, Moroccans. Primitives, as Jews
go."

"A far cry from what I saw," Schotten agreed. "I'm surprised you got that
close to the doorway."

"Oh, the dancers were quiet. The runners made the real din."

"Runners?"

Evelyn nodded. "Five or six others scattered about in the murk were running in place. Sprinting would be more like it. They ran as if they'd be air-
borne and levitated with the very next step—all the while groaning and giving themselves great thumping shots to the chest, Catholic *mea culpa* style.
Lean as hounds they were, too, and tireless. Exertion'd soaked their robes
through, but their grunts roared through that little cellar like cannon fire. The
men, in the back room, hadn't a chance. All their chanting, and God only
knew what else, came out as background music.

"The fact is, I didn't even hear the zealot, and she was lying right at my feet
in the doorway. The poor dear thing'd already worn ruts in the dirt floor
kicking and clawing at each handclap, but the chips'd made her pay dearly.
Her hands and feet dripped blood—her chin too. She whimpered with every
spasm—I saw her mouth work—but I never heard a sound.

"I found the girl's older brother right off—a tall blond kid in a blue-and-
white prayer shawl, with long earlocks and a ferocious case of acne. He stood
by a beaded curtain covering the cooking alcove. His forehead had a big
round circle of blood on it, and so did the whitewash opposite him.

"I never got through the doorway. Suddenly, the girl stepped in front of me,
her blood-spotted legs showing through the gap in her mourning robe. I
should have known something more was wrong right off. A tidal wave of grief
surrounded us, but none of it seemed to touch her. Fact was, she looked serene,

staring at me over the poor zealot's convulsing body. She'd not wept a tear, either. Her black eyes were dry and knowing, and she had the drill down pat, too.

" 'So, English,' she said mockingly, 'they sent you with the blood money. Good! We need it. Tell me, is it . . . reasonable?'

"What could I say to that? Absolutely nothing. So I shook my head and handed her the envelope. Then I fled back down the passageway, too rattled even to remember that I needed her signature on the waiver.

"I'd never been so unstrung in all my life. I had to do something to get my wits about me, so I went back to the office. I thought I'd do the reports I should've that afternoon. And, of course, I couldn't. I couldn't do a bloody thing. But I kept trying until eleven, anyway. Then I packed it in. I got my flashlight, turned out the lights, and started downstairs.

"The last shift had gone home at ten-thirty, leaving the place dead quiet. So I heard the noise as soon as I stepped out on the covered front porch. It came from the right and sounded like animals pawing the ground.

"Well, in those days, before the refinery sprawled all round Haifa Bay, laborers had a choice of three whizzers, all on the main tarmac road. The first was on the dock; the second, halfway up, where the cracking took place; and the third, right next to our building. It was a corrugated iron shed like the other two, but for some reason the side facing the road had a shoulder-high gap between wall and roof. Arabs being what they are, the place became a sort of social club. Chaps making wee-wee said hello and transacted all manner of business with chums passing by on the main road.

"That's what I thought was going on then—a few Arabs in no rush to get home, telling jokes after hours about the funny Jew.

"Well, I'd already had a full plate for that day, so the last thing I needed was any more Arab repartee. They'd hoot and holler me up to the main gate, besides. So I did the first smart thing I'd ever done in Haifa. I peeked round the corner of the porch. If I saw Arabs in front of the latrine, I'd decided to tiptoe back through the office and leave by the rear door.

"A dim little sixty-watt bulb hung over the crapper's entrance. But it showed enough to stop my heart, I'll tell you. The girl and her brother were backed up against the side of the shed, facing three Arabs. All five of them were feinting and swaying, watching the knives in each other's hands like cobras following a snake charmer's flute.

"The big brother had got them in that spot, I thought. He'd put his head in the Book, and he'd not stopped looking until he'd come to good old bloody Deuteronomy. Chapter Thirty-two, Verse Forty-one would do: '. . . I will render vengeance to mine enemies, and reward them that hate me.'

"That's what the Book said, so that's what he'd do. Then he collared the little sister and asked if she was a dutiful daughter. What could she say? They'd probably planned it all at the cemetery. That's why she was so cool later. Her mind was on other things. He must have been psyching himself up for it, too. Chances were, everyone at the *shiva* had simply passed out or gotten so delirious they never even noticed them sneak away.

"Whatever—bloody Deuteronomy'd put more Jews in early graves than all the Romans, Crusaders, and Nazis combined. Just as it would those two—whilst I cowered on the porch, wondering what in God's name to do. Then the Arab closest to me, the one opposite the brother, turned his head.

"Jamal. Well . . .

"I'd not so much as bloodied a nose before. But he'd laughed at me. And she'd called me reasonable. So what had I to lose? That's how one's mind works at twenty, isn't it? Stupidly. And full of pride. But I had a bit of the old Celtic sly going for me, too.

"If I could sneak up behind the Arabs, and hit them hard enough, I'd drive them right into the side of the shed. That's why the filthy little bleeders hadn't already charged. It was dicey for them too. If they did and missed, or the girl or her brother sidestepped, they'd run smack into the corrugated siding. Someone'd get a knife in the back then, for sure.

"Well, I took a firm grip on my trusty six-cell Eveready and tiptoed down the porch steps. Then I sprinted up the sidewalk, building a head of steam, all two hundred pounds of me. I had a tremendous advantage.

"I've always had bad feet—something to do with metatarsals—so I was wearing crepe-soled shoes just like now. See? Soundless.

"They were maybe thirty feet away, the other two Arabs in shadow, so I didn't recognize them until I got halfway there. When I saw the red fez and green pantaloons, I knew the one in the center had to be Kareem, the store-keeper—a bully and a thief. The small one on the left in the black boiler suit could only be Abu, the loading-dock foreman. He was a chum of mine, a good soul. He'd eleven kids at home, too—bred them faster than lice. Dear God, I wondered, what's he doing here? *Sharaf,* I guess, honor. Jamal and Kareem'd probably thrown it in his face, so he'd had to go along, like the girl, when the big brother laid Deuteronomy on her.

"I was moving like a train. About six feet out, I aimed right for the center of Jamal's back and raised the flashlight. Make no mistake, I meant to pound his head down like a tent peg. But at the last second, he sensed something. He turned round, dark bony face one big O of surprise.

"All I got was a glancing shot off his shoulder. Maybe it broke his collar-bone. Maybe not. More important, he'd flinched. So instead of making contact, I flew right by him and into the corrugated siding. I was going so fast, I thought I'd knock the shed down. Lord, but I hit it! From the sound, you'd have thought Big Ben struck one.

"I went down like a shot, but after Allenby Street I knew better than to stay there. I was on my feet instantly, despite groping round for the flashlight. I beat Jamal, anyway, and that's what counted.

"He was halfway up when I hit him again, and he still looked baffled. That's all he was: surprised; not angry or even fearful. He just couldn't fathom how Allah could visit such an untranquil day on clan Husseini. I'd aimed for his head again, but missed, hitting him squarely in the chest instead. I had all I owned in that shot—felt it all the way up my shoulder and into my neck. The next day, my elbow was puffed up like a grapefruit from it. Anyway— bones cracked, and they were Jamal's and he dropped.

"The big brother immediately flew right by him, going backward. He fetched up against the shed white-faced and sweating, pop-eyed. Even his acne looked scared. He'd caught himself a swipe from someone's knife, and his white shirt had the beginnings of a diplomat's red sash on it from shoulder to hip. Kareem came crashing out of the darkness after him, bellowing and looking like a deranged bear in green harem pyjamas. I swung at his head, too, but got him in the neck. Christ, I missed everything that night. A moment later, though, I had his blood gushing 'cross my face.

"And then it was over. Silent, save for our gasping. Off to the left, I saw the girl on her knees, apparently unhurt, toss her hair back over her shoulders. Thank God, I thought. She'd managed to kill Abu. I'd been too scared even to think of her. No doubt 'bout him being dead, either. He lay flat on his back, black felt slippers pointed outward, like an upturned penguin. I'd seen her dad the very same way that afternoon.

"Well, I'll not be coy." Evelyn smiled apologetically, leaning against the oak-paneled wall, crepe-soled shoes casually crossed over each other. "Prentiss called me yesterday afternoon and told me what was on. So I talked to a chap in Ottawa who has friends in Tel Aviv who know people in Zurich, and word's come back you've swung a little steel, too. So you'll know what I mean. I looked down at my hand and saw that I'd not picked up the Eveready at all, but Jamal's knife, and it felt . . . right?

"I'd been turned, just like that.

"All that in a blink. The big brother was really bleeding by then, so I threw him my key to the bicycle shed and told him to leave it open—showed him the way to a hole in the fence, too. He bounded off like a scared rabbit, clutching his shirt to his chest.

"Then I heard the girl. She was sobbing her eyes out—still on her knees— with yet more blood on the white shirt and shorts. God, how she cried, her face right alongside poor, dead Abu's, as if they'd been lovers.

"I rushed over, praying she'd not been hurt after all. Kneeling down, I saw she'd not been. She was bawling for another reason. She still wanted to be a dutiful daughter. She'd had her head in Deuteronomy, too. But she'd stopped at Chapter Nineteen, Verse Twenty-one: 'And thine eye shall not pity; but life shall go for life, eye for eye, tooth for tooth, hand for hand, foot for foot.'

"She meant to do for Abu what they'd done for her dad, you see. She'd the knife right at his eyes. But she couldn't do it. After all her courage and control, she'd failed, and that would stain her conscience forever.

"I put my hands under her arms, lifted her up, and took her over to the porch in front of the production building. Her breath came in great, gasping sobs, jerking and twisting her body about unmercifully. So I sat her down on the floor in a corner and patted her hair and rubbed her shoulders—anything I thought'd help. But nothing did. She just kept saying 'Shame' over and over again, her mouth quivering like a great open wound.

"So I went back and did it for her . . . to the three of them . . . till they looked just like her dad.

"It only took a moment. You know how it is when steel starts to fly. All at once it gets a life of its own. It begins to wheel and soar like a bird, right there in your hand, and drags your arm along with it.

"And by the time I was finished, I was proud of them. They looked so well, in fact, I didn't want them wasted on some solitary sweeper who'd discover them at five-thirty in the morning and call the police to cart them off. I wanted all the gigglers and yippers to have a little peep at their chums, too, and to remember.

"So I dragged them into the whizzer one by one and sat them down on the two long boards that served as the communal toilet seat. And they seemed just fine there, proud as punch and as close as they'd been in life, three little niggers all lined up on their potties for their morning squeeze.

"Then I went back to the porch and nodded. The girl stopped crying and got up immediately. Reaction'd set in by then, and we raced to the bicycle shed, took two messengers' bikes, and got out the way I'd told her brother. She led. My knees hurt so, I could barely pedal. The scabs'd split on both. But we tore out of town, past the Old City, and 'cross the Plain of Acco. Then she headed out Acre way, up the coast road, with the Mediterranean on our left, bigger than the moon, and just as orange.

"Then, suddenly, she couldn't go fast enough, as if she were fleeing something. And, of course, she was. But God only knew what. So much had happened that day. Anyway, she leaned over the handlebars, her long black hair snapped out in the slipstream, and in seconds she was just a silent white speck up ahead. I didn't even try to catch up. I knew I couldn't and my knees were killing me, besides.

"Finally, though, I saw her standing by the road in the distance. She'd stopped under the old Crusader fortress at Acre—a nice irony. The place had become a prison, full of Jews who'd fought Arabs and English unsportingly. Altogether, we'd gone ten miles—far enough. We took the bikes off the road, hid them in some brush, and walked down to the water.

"I found myself a high, smooth rock and flopped back against it like a beached whale. What I'd felt at the refinery, I realized, was just the urge to flee. Now shock had come. The girl, standing at my side, breathing in quick, shallow gulps, might have been on another planet. I know I was.

"By the time I finally did look over at her, she'd started undressing. She'd turned her left side to me, but I saw that her shirt and bra were already off and that she had her shorts down round her knees.

"That didn't register at all. Nothing did. I'd seeped into that rock like water. Physically, I knew, I was there, but somehow I seemed outside myself. In fact, I remember wondering how I remained standing. I'd no answer for that either. So I gave up thinking and turned back to the stars.

"When I saw her next, she stood directly before me, gorgeous and fawn-like—just heartbreakingly beautiful in that orange moonlight—with her hands on my shoulders.

" 'Come, Evelyn,' she said. 'We've got to bathe. We've got to get this blood off us.'

"I couldn't move. Nor could I speak. My tongue seemed to fill my mouth, wedging the jaws open. Classic reaction to fear, that. I just stood there, terribly cold and trembling—helpless.

"So she undressed me, as if I were a child, and led me down to the water. And since she was the taller, when we got out shoulder-high she put her arms round me and gathered me in. I laid my cheek on her breast then and clung to her, eyes shut, past all pride or shame, praying only for my teeth to stop chattering. But they didn't. So she pulled me even closer, and we stood there till the warm sea'd washed the blood from our bodies.

"No need to speak. We both knew it'd been fated. We'd just taken a little longer to work it all out. God loves man, Eric. He never sends us more than we can bear. Never!

"And so it was. When my shivering stopped, we went back. She'd just turned eighteen the week before, and we were both virgins. So what we did with each other on that beach at Acre was very tender and touching—beautiful, in its way, I suppose. And if God looked down from behind that great luminous orange moon, I daresay He approved, too.

"So thirty years and five children later, I have her to do with the Jews. And more . . . much more."

"More?" Schotten wondered.

"Oh, indeed. Indeed!" Evelyn beamed delightedly, bounding across the library like a messenger bearing good news.

"My wife'd been read out of her family as soon as they'd heard she'd married a *goy*," he went on, seating himself on the yellow hassock alongside Schotten's foot. "We'd not heard from any of them. Word was, in fact, they'd sat a *shiva* for her too—same as for the old man.

"So you can imagine my surprise when I opened the door in our flat in the English quarter a few months later for my new brother-in-law. Oh, he looked the perfect little *bocher*—had the whole kit, black felt hat over blue-and-white skullcap and tieless white shirt. At first I thought he'd come to lay some ancient curse on me. But he hadn't. He wasn't all that holy.

"The little bleeder was in Haganah, the underground Jewish army, up to his earlocks. Fact is—" Evelyn rolled his eyes expressively—"he's so high in Mossad now, Ben-Gurion made him change his name twice.

"Anyway, he wanted me to help out on a little job. . . .

"Well, what would you have said, especially with your new wife sitting right there on the couch beside you? Truth was, the idea rather appealed to me, too. If I'd not found my calling that night at the refinery, I'd at least discovered . . . a what? A propensity? Yes. That'll do.

"So I joined the family business.

"It wasn't much, just the usual bits and pieces, but I learned steel. And a year later, a tall, red-haired Englishman turned up in our doorway, just like the *bocher*. You know how you can always spot the cops or spies in a cheap film, no matter what they're wearing? Well, this chap sent the same type of signal, white linen suit notwithstanding. But the message was: army."

Schotten leaned forward in the green velvet chair with a knowing smile. "Orde Wingate!" he exclaimed.

Evelyn nodded happily, an alumnus of an exclusive school meeting a fellow classmate in a godforsaken corner of the world.

"I can see you've done your homework."

"One must. There's always more than money to a deal."

"Indeed. Indeed." Evelyn chuckled. "Except this time. My company, Iraq Petroleum, got Orde out there, you know. They didn't give a damn 'bout Jews being killed, but when Arabs started diddling with the refinery, that was different. That struck at England's reason for the Palestine Mandate: Haifa; a Mediterranean port from which to ship Iraqi oil.

"So after the pipeline got cut a few times, Pocock and gang went to Number 10 Downing Street and tore a strip off Neville Chamberlain. Forget Haj Amin and foreign policy! Profits were in jeopardy!

"Well, politicians being what they are, that monkey promptly landed on the War Office's back. They were told to defend the pipeline without chasing Haj Amin all the way into Hitler's bed.

"That ruled out direct military action, so the army decided to do the job with a commando officer. They'd give him a few Englishmen and let him fill out the force with Jews—the first time, incidentally, they'd legally bear arms in the Mandate. They picked Wingate to lead, a perfect choice but for an oversight. As Pocock'd say, he came from a very 'rigorous Christian background' indeed. He believed literally that Jews were the Chosen People and Palestine their Promised Land.

"As an English officer, he'd defend the pipeline. But as an Old Testament Christian, his first duty was to God. So he dedicated himself to building a

Jewish army to speed the Tribe of Israel's day of deliverance. His group—it didn't even have a name then—would train the officer cadre.

"What a schemer! Orde didn't run ads for broken-down policemen or ask the brass for names of 'good' Jews. Instead, he got in with Haganah. And there he was, standing in my doorway.

" 'Mr. Waddell,' he says in his droll Sandhurst way, 'you've made a bit of a name for yourself with some friends of mine. May I come in and tell you why I'm here?'

"So he told me, but very generally. I didn't catch all his nuances by half, but I had only one question anyway. Quick as a wink, I asked, 'It's outdoor work?'

" 'Oh, yes, guarding the pipeline—and discouraging the Arabs.'

"Well, my wife took to that last part right off. To him too. Those fevered blue eyes were right out of Deuteronomy, I'll tell you. So she gave me the nod, and that was that. Two nights later, I put on the dark-blue shirt of what came to be known as the Special Night Squads.

"We tried our wings for a month or so in the hills round Haifa, learning signals and tactics and Orde's theory of 'active defense.' We wrote the book for commando forces in World War Two, you know. It all boiled down to a single word: Attack! Attack! Attack! Attack!

"Then we went on ops, and what a laugh that must've given the Jew-haters in the Mandate political department. They thought they'd the best of two worlds, you see. They told London they'd fielded Wingate's force, and Haj Amin what it was: six very irregular Englishmen and a dozen sheenies. What harm could they do? Or so experts reckoned.

"They didn't know 'bout our other chums. They were boys then mostly—fifteen, sixteen, seventeen—but every evening 'bout sundown they'd sneak out of kibbutzes and towns to join us. Haganah sent them, and they were eager to learn. So they'd fight the night's action and then slip off in the dark, back to their beds, for a few hours' shut-eye before school or work.

"Good times then, Eric! And good chaps too! Allon—"

"You knew Yigal Allon?"

"Soldiered all through Galilee with him, and Shimon Avidan, and Yitzhak Sadeh, the Haganah commander—we were all in it, all comrades. And we were devastating. I mean, we swung a lot of steel! Attack! Attack! Attack!

"To this day, you know, the officer's standard command for moving men forward in the Israeli Army is unique. It's what Orde taught us in Special Night Squads: not 'Charge,' but 'Follow me!'

"Creaky metatarsals and all, I loved it. Yes—I loved every moment. And I kept getting better too. So after a few months Orde got Moshe Dayan out of Haganah to be his aide-de-camp and gave me my own squad.

"I sent for the *bocher* first thing," Evelyn recounted, reaching across Schotten's leg and taking a slice of rye bread off the silver tray. "He'd been hiding most of a year on a fishing boat in Ashdod, and he turned up tanned and fit and thirty pounds heavier. He'd shed the acne and earlocks too, and become quite decent-looking, blond and Nordic. Later, in fact, he led several British paratroop raids into Germany posing as a Nazi officer. Never got another scratch either, after I taught him 'active defense.' Fought through the Israeli do's in '48 and '56 the same way.

"So all through '37 and '38, Orde's squad and mine roamed Palestine. I saw the country then, I'll tell you—all the places old Pocock mentioned—but as a commander, and at night.

"Ein Dor first—a classic job, that," Evelyn said, critically eying the Crema Danica and adding more. "Sixteen Arabs lying in a wadi in ambush. They'd other squads along the road, too, so guns were out. We bellied down the hill and loved them instead, just like the Book says, as brothers. Oh, it was gorgeous . . ." He trailed off in a soft, almost wistful tone.

"We'd not hurt our brothers—not for anything. So first we clapped our hands over their mouths so they'd not scream in fear. Then we embraced them, so they'd not hurt themselves falling. And, finally, we proved we'd not come there to pain them. There's so little from ear to ear 'cross the neck, I doubt they even felt the steel. We were that quick and merciful. And we laid them down to rest the same way. They'd such a gentle passage, you'd have thought they were smiling twice. Their windpipes gleamed white as snow in the moonlight.

"Great fun!" Evelyn pronounced, waving the rosewood pepper mill for emphasis.

"Megiddo too," he went on, "and I bollixed that from start to end. I stabbed a lamb there, you know. True, Eric. True!" he remonstrated. "In the fog—I thought he was an Arab in a white robe. How the poor creature got there I'll never know. But no harm done. We ate him that night.

"Took me till Harod, though, to live that down—had to shoot the woman in the brown robe to do it, too."

"You shot a woman?"

"Indeed. Indeed!" Evelyn joyfully admitted, biting down on his sandwich. "Stitched her right open with a Thompson submachine gun. We were all hunkered down across the street from the village muktar's house that night, watching a raiding party form up, when this old baggage comes sashaying down the street.

"My Lord, you should have heard the *bocher* and the rest of the gang natter away when I put the gun on her—regular Victorians, they were. But they should've gone told that one on the mountain, not to me. The old sly said there was something funny 'bout her robe. It didn't sway right. So I just waited till they opened the door for her, and she stood in the light."

"And then?"

Evelyn rolled his eyes expressively.

"Strong stuff under that brown robe—blew the roof clean off the muktar's house and set off the rest of his goodies too. We heard later the oldest male Arab left in town was exactly two weeks shy of his thirteenth birthday.

"Well, you can just imagine my enthusiasm when Prentiss called yesterday and told me what was on. I hopped right over to the Israeli Embassy in Ottawa and got through to the *bocher* in Tel Aviv straightaway—spent the whole bloody night on the howler sorting things out, in fact. But before we get into that, tell me something, Eric—"

Evelyn leaned forward confidentially, blue eyes sparkling guilelessly.

"With all this heavy money flying round," he said, round face curling into a diffident, wheedling grin, "it's sure to attract some rowdies. Do you think we'll have to swing a little steel?"

The history of Battle & Company Account 60-J was equally bizarre. It had begun with a phone call on December 22, 1959.

"Mr. Howsam? My name's Courtney Montgomery," a cool, assured voice announced that afternoon. "I'm a senior partner in Cox and O'Shea—we're lawyers out in San Francisco. I'd like to stop by and talk a little banking. There might be some business in it for you."

Howsam heard three or four such overtures a month and answered them all the same way.

"Thanks for your interest," he said. "But I doubt if we could help. We're so small, we only take new accounts on referrals. It's a house rule."

"Nice try." Montgomery chuckled. "But I've got a reference—Perry Black. He's *our* client, too."

That placated Howsam. Black, a former Stanford classmate, managed family holdings in Central America. When he needed irregular banking, which was often, he came to Battle & Company.

"Well, then, come on over," Howsam said. "Where are you now?"

"Just around the corner. Be there in minutes."

"Great the sooner, the better."

At thirty-one, Howsam knew enough about private banking not to take anything at face value. Leaning forward in the high-backed Windsor armchair, he punched another button on the red telephone to dial one of Wall Street's most prestigious law firms. A moment later, Archibald Rothwell, his lawyer and Ike Battle's Princeton classmate, came on the line.

"Archie, you know a law firm named Cox and O'Shea?"

"They on the West Coast?"

"Right. In San Francisco."

"Jesus—"

"What's the matter?"

"That gang's in politics, not law," Rothwell declared in his gruff Establishment voice. "They're killers on anything to do with federal regulation—airlines, broadcasting, defense contracts, the works. They've got a whole damned floorful of partners with pull. House Democrats, house Republicans, and, yes, if the Russians ever get here, you can bet your ass they'll have house Commies crawling out of the woodwork, too. What in hell do they want with a crooked little Indian?"

"How do I know? That's what *I'm* asking *you*. I just got a call from one of their partners. A mutual client gave him my name, and he's coming over."

"Well, watch yourself. You get greedy with those guys, and they'll get you so tangled up in Uncle Sam's beard you'll never climb out."

Montgomery had arrived a few minutes later: tall, spare, fiftyish, strikingly handsome in charcoal-gray flannels. He reeked of money. The December tan suggested a weekend place and horses in Big Sur, or a little winery up north with a lovingly restored Spanish mission house.

He shook hands briskly and sat down across the antique cherry dining table, smiling broadly at the statue of the Three Monkeys. His teeth were perfect and all his, which still impressed Howsam. In rural Michigan, almost everyone had plates at thirty-five.

"Perry Black says you're very creative," he began.

"You have that kind of problem?" Howsam countered.

"A beaut," Montgomery admitted, casually hooking his right leg over the chair arm. "The California Community Property Law."

"Isn't that a little out of your line?"

"You know that law—here, in the East?"

"Know it? Hell, I live off of it! You think Hollywood shysters'd ever get divorced if they had to split down the middle with the old lady?"

Montgomery nodded. "In this case, it's our managing partner's biggest client. The guy's had wife trouble forever. So a few years ago he did a little selling—didn't even tell us. Now things are boiling over, and he wants his money where it won't be extraditable or have his name on it."

Howsam wondered.

The very rich he knew lavished foresight on divorce that others did on retirement. They set the alimony stash before proposing. Unless human nature had been repealed, this client would have done that, too.

But the story went unchallenged. If false, it revealed the true purpose of Montgomery's visit. If true, it said nothing about whether the business was worth taking. Either way, a banker's next question remained the same.

"How much is involved?" Howsam asked.

"A substantial amount."

"What's that—five figures, six, seven?"

"Oh, let's just call it 'substantial' for now."

"And the client?"

"For your purposes, a Mr. John Doe."

"Then you've got a real problem. Nothing personal, but this country's crawling with dirty money—"

"Hey! That's insulting . . ."

"Yeah? So's jail. I don't need that grief."

"But *we* do?"

Howsam nodded, as if the point had been well taken, and cast another line, again in the direction of quantity.

"Tell me," he asked, "have you tried this out on any West Coast banks, where you've got some leverage?"

"Wouldn't dream of it." Montgomery smiled. "The going rate out West for this kind of fun and games is a million-dollar deposit or a pension fund for the bank's trust department to administer."

Howsam nodded again. But he knew better.

That might be the price to some law firms. But to a Cox & O'Shea, with their potential? Never. Many bankers would help them, and for free. Big banks swallowed money in $500,000 gulps and spat it out just as fast through "Overs, Shorts, and Damages," the ledger entry for teller errors, bad arithmetic, and misplaced money. When billions in cash changed hands, things happened. Auditors accepted them. But there was just one catch.

When big banks buried money, they wanted names. But Cox & O'Shea had none. So they made up a divorce story and went looking for a shady banker instead. Montgomery then came East to make a plain, old-fashioned cash dump—an unrecorded deposit—that would unload a ton of illegal funds under false pretenses.

For a variety of reasons, such deals always had takers. Since the transactions broke the law, they were kept off the books. The same applied to the fee, which went straight into the banker's pocket. Next loomed the money hidden on deposit. Sufficiently crooked or hungry men saw that as "principal" from which they could conveniently "borrow" to finance the investment and/or real-estate killings of their dreams.

So, on balance, Howsam liked the overture.

He had no gangland clients, nor did he knowingly launder dirty cash, but he knew exactly what to do. He did it regularly for blue-chip American firms wanting "hot money"—legitimate funds—buried abroad for future illegal currency speculation.

Montgomery's business would be worthwhile, too. He had at least $500,000 to dump—the amount a bank could safely hide, plus more, which auditors might question.

That was Howsam's first scenario.

The second he liked even better. This concerned fees.

Lawyers made money marking up time. But what could they charge for two lunches, say, at the Rainier Club, up in Seattle? Nothing, certainly, alongside their bill for finding an obscure private bank all the way across the country. That could be big business—and for the banker as well. And that raised the key question: How much money justified two tremendous fees? The brown stitch marks bridging Howsam's nose suddenly reddened.

That answer he knew from experience: millions.

"You want me to hold this dough?" he asked, crossing his legs and leaning back in the Windsor armchair.

"If the price is right."

"Where is it now?"

"On me."

Leg still dangling over the chair arm, Montgomery reached inside his dark-gray flannel jacket. A casual toss placed a tired kraft envelope before Howsam.

Howsam removed a rubber band and withdrew the checks, riffling their right edges, like a dealer flexing a fresh deck.

"That's some divorce you've got there," he said, dropping the envelope on the polished cherry table.

Montgomery shrugged. "What's so special about two million six hundred thousand dollars?"

"Nothing. Just its weight. That could get noisy."

"But you could move it—quietly?"

"Oh, yeah. Sure. No problem. I buried twice that, in one lump, a few months ago."

"For how much?"

"Same as I'd charge you. Three percent now, plus three percent of the balance every January first the dough's on deposit, plus one hundred twenty days' interest and notice when you want it to walk—"

Montgomery could multiply, too. "Hey, wait a minute—one hundred fifty-six thousand dollars for the next nine days? That's more than we'll get for the whole job."

"Maybe you guys work too cheap."

Montgomery smiled at the solicitude. "Be sure to bill us for your time," he said, rising. "I've got to check some flights to Geneva."

"You're serious?" Howsam asked.

Montgomery retrieved the kraft envelope. "What do you think?"

Thick dusky forearms crossed over his blue short-sleeved shirt, Howsam thought of Ike Battle's pricing strategy: first you make the client sick; then you make him well. He judged that time had come.

"I think you've been reading too many thrillers," he said. "That night flight to Switzerland only works for gangsters and secret agents. For the rest of us, it's disaster. First of all, Swiss bankers don't want dollar deposits. What the hell for? They run their banks like mutual funds, and take a percentage of each account for managing investments. That's how they get paid. So you go to one of those guys and ask him to sit on some cash for you. Sure, he'll say, and charge you minus three to four percent a year, maybe even five. Then, when you bring that dough home, he'll hit you for another year's interest as a withdrawal charge. After that, you're on your own. You'll have to find a conduit—usually, a foreign firm with business in the United States—that can move money here. If the banker puts you onto one, he'll want another percent or two—a finder's fee. Then the conduit'll take another five to seven percent—I know one gets nine—"

"That much?"

"Sure, that much," Howsam laughed. "Why not? You think the Swiss raise dummies? Your only other choice is the Mob. They'll move dough for one or two percent, sure. But sometimes they don't think that's enough. So the courier never shows. What do you do then? Go to the cops? Call Interpol? Punt?"

Montgomery sat down abruptly. He was sick.

Howsam now proceeded to make him well. "After all that, I don't sound so bad, do I? I'm here, not there. I'm no hood. And my price is right. I move the cash home for free. And I'll bring you back more than you gave me. I'll make you money."

"How?"

"That's my business."

"Where?"

"That's my business, too."

"And mine! You think I'd tell a client that—nothing?"

"Right, and just like that! He'll love every word, too. Know why? Because you're also going to tell him that next year he'll make ten percent on that dough—$260,000. And after that, never less than fifteen percent. You hit him with those numbers, and he'll keep right on smiling—even when he hears it cost more than you thought to find a banker, and you need a bigger fee to cover expenses."

"You know something," Montgomery said, a boyish smile creasing his tanned features, "I like your style. Just give me a receipt, and I'll be on my way," he said, tossing the kraft envelope on the table.

"Sure thing." Howsam scribbled one on the top sheet of his memo pad.

"I'll be in touch," Montgomery had said, pocketing the receipt and shaking hands warmly.

Richer by $156,000, Howsam had wasted no time gloating. Montgomery had acted like a beginner, and he chided himself for not expecting the request for a receipt. That meant the checks had to move at once.

Picking up the red telephone, he had placed a call to Eusebio Pérez, president of Banco Pérez de Panamá. For once, the Miami radiotelephone circuits were free of atmospherics, and Señor Pérez came on the line immediately. The call meant $10,000 to him, so he listened carefully.

Yes, he would write the letter.

Yes, he would see the minister who ran the postal system.

Yes, he would join the midnight Avianca Cartagena–New York flight.

Yes, he would take the checks to Gerhard Stumpf.

Yes, he had correct certification numbers and amounts for each check.

Yes, he would buy two pounds of Sierra Negra coffee for *café solo*.

Done, said Howsam.

Not quite. One small matter remained.

What was that?

The Minister.

He was still doing business?

Oh, yes. But not for $600. Now he wanted $1,000.

Howsam screamed he was being screwed.

Senor Pérez agreed.

Seven hundred?

Impossible. The Minister was *muy macho*. That would offend him.

Eight hundred?

That would have to do, Eusebio Pérez declared. He had no desire to spoil the natives, either.

Done?

Done!

Howsam had smiled. The receipt would "vanish" immediately. Within thirty-six hours, the checks would also.

Next, seeking the client's name, Howsam had called the most Byzantine banking mind he knew, Norbert Nygaard, of La Jolla, California.

A huge, ill-tempered man, Nygaard had first visited Battle & Company in 1942. He arrived as an auditor in the Treasury Department's Alien Property division. He left with a connoisseur's appreciation of chicaneries sensed but not found. A year later, he became a claims investigator for bank insurers. His savings arrived at 118 Battery Place shortly thereafter.

Since then he had moonlighted for Ike Battle and Howsam. In return, his money joined theirs in special situations.

The phone rang forever, as Howsam expected. He had seen Nygaard labor up the stairs from his basement model railroad, long-ashed Pall Mall dangling from his lips. In time, panting replaced ringing.

"Norbie? Prentiss."

"Yeah?"

"I just got a bunch of postcards from California."

"So?"

"They're dirty—"

"Hey, Prentiss! Don't start that again! You already gave me that line twice this year. And twice I shagged ass all up and down the coast—for what? For nothing! For your goddamned Indian second sight."

"Well, this time I got dumped for sure."

"And pigs'll fly! All I know is, I chased Gert out shopping so's I could lay a little track—"

"Norbie, somebody shipped me two point six million postcards."

"How many?"

"You heard."

"You get a lot of views?"

"Forty-one."

"What'd you get the most of?"

"Los Angeles—785,257 copies."

"The least?"

"Walnut groves in Fullerton—51,750."

"Where are the others from?"

Howsam read off the city and amount on each check.

Nygaard snorted. "Jesus! Don't you know anything? That's a real-estate deal. Those are all county-seat towns."

"C'mon. Who uses Cox and O'Shea—"

"They the guys in San Francisco?"

"Right. Who sends them to dump clean goods?"

"Don't ask me! I crunch numbers. But every figure there is a multiple of the going price index for one-acre industrial sites in those counties."

"How do you know that?"

"How do you suppose? I talk to realty boards and keep all that shit in my head. Sometimes it shows where money went. What do you think I get five hundred dollars a day for—adding and subtracting? Now, you just got a forty-one number hit. You call that coincidence?"

"And the lawyer wanted a receipt!" Howsam shot back. "You call that real estate?"

"That don't make it dirty."

"It does in my book. Check it out."

"Now—right before Christmas?"

"Right! Right now!"

"Jesus, you're paranoid!"

"I'm telling you, I was dumped!"

Events proved them both right.

At eleven the next morning, a yellow cab had stopped at 118 Battery Place. Its passenger was a tall crewcut cocoa-colored man of sixty in a *café-au-lait* shantung suit. Haughtily erect, unmindful of the cold, he bounded up Battle & Company's eight stone steps with feral grace. Passersby eyed him curiously, as if witnessing the return of the Noble Savage.

International moneymen had no such illusions. Eusebio Pérez was the most sophisticated of men: a Class 1 Panamanian banker, licensed to do business worldwide. He did much, mainly with Howsam, in Latin America, where both, naturally, were called *los Indios* (the Indians).

Howsam had greeted him formally, with handclasp and deferential bow, then motioned to the armchair before the cherry dining table. Señor Pérez nodded and removed his coat. The pocket of his yellow short-sleeved shirt bore the "S" of Sulka's Paris custom-tailoring department. After a final adjustment to his heavy pink-and-yellow gold Peruvian tie clasp, he sat.

Was he comfortable? Would he like *café* after the long taxi ride?

Señor Pérez said yes to both questions. Howsam punched the intercom button on the red telephone and asked his secretary to bring in a pot of *café solo*. He stood until she did. Then he filled two demitasse cups, handed one to Señor Pérez and toasted him with the other.

*"Salud y pesetas."* Health and wealth.

Señor Pérez nodded appreciatively.

Amenities observed, *los Indios* began laundering $2.6 million.

Howsam had started with a rapid-fire account, in Spanish, of Montgomery's visit. Next, from the manila folder before him he produced the kraft envelope. Then came a mimeographed goldenrod form. Typed in triplicate, it recorded bank name, certification number, and dollar amount for each check, required by the Trading with the Enemy Act of 1917.

Resurrected in the 1930s, the old chestnut helped Franklin Roosevelt pierce bank secrecy to identify rich men profiting from the Depression. The act also mandated reporting "any foreign deposit or withdrawal deemed unusual." Bankers found nothing unusual. Ever.

In 1951, during the Korean War, Harry Truman invoked the act again to curtail *sub rosa* U.S. trade with Iron Curtain countries and Red China. Knowing bankers, Truman stipulated that "any deposit or withdrawal of $2,500 or more" be reported. The Senate Banking Committee liked the reporting feature so well they let it stand.

The form had been proofread by two typists, Howsam's secretary, and his Cuban assistant, Jorge. Howsam read it again, aloud, in Spanish, while Señor Pérez confirmed each item.

That done, *los Indios* enjoyed another *café solo*. Next came Internal Revenue Service Form 1087, which U.S. banks or lawyers must file for aliens. Howsam removed the brass paper clip and slid triplicate copies across the cherry table. Then he read from an accountant's pale-green spread sheet.

Ninety-one items later, Señor Pérez had looked up, twisting his mother's diamond wedding ring, which he wore in mourning on the little finger of his left hand.

*"Qué es eso?"* he asked, nodding toward Form 1087.

Howsam told him: A report of dividends and interest on $2.6 million of stocks and bonds sold December 14, 1959.

Could that be substantiated?

Yes. A stockbroker in Beverly Hills, California, was preparing buy/sell tapes now. One would be sent to Señor Pérez. Inspectors would feel lucky to find that much. Brokerage firms were *indocumentado*. They lacked documentation for most of their deals.

*"Cuánto cuesta?"*

"Eighteen thousand five hundred dollars."

*"No comprendo,"* Señor Pérez had sighed. As a banker on a great oceanic trade route, he did many things with money. But nothing like this. He wanted to learn.

Howsam refilled the demitasse cups and asked for the letter written the day before, on December 22. Señor Pérez opened his alligator briefcase. First came two one-pound coffee bags, then a sheet of flimsy copy paper.

The carbon was dated December 19, 1959. The original, now on a New York–bound plane, bore that registry date and postmark as well. This anticipated Montgomery's visit by three days and followed the "sale" of the securities by five—thanks to the Panamanian minister.

The text notified Battle & Company that it would shortly receive forty-one checks from Cox & O'Shea. These remittances were itemized below. They were to be held until further word from Banco Pérez de Panamá, which awaited instructions from an unnamed South American client.

Pointing to the paragraph describing the checks, Howsam wondered why a lawyer wanted a receipt for an illegal transaction.

*"Por qué?"* Señor Pérez asked.

For only one reason, Howsam answered. Montgomery feared the dump would be discovered. With a receipt, he could claim he had only been an agent. He thought he had performed a perfectly legal, proper errand. He had been told to take the checks to Battle & Company. How could he know the checks' blind trusts represented corpses, or that the client who brought him the job, never seen again, had false credentials? In short, he had been duped. Fishy? Sure. But it would get by.

Then, Howsam had explained, the burden would fall on him. Who was the client? Where was the money? Who told him to send it there? Señor Pérez' letter, on the other hand, made him an agent, too. He knew only his part of the deal. And, clearly, it made Montgomery's receipt "vanish," as well. Now that marked a stop, not a destination.

*"Y las otras formas?"*

The other forms tidied up the story. They gave the checks a legitimate history. If the dump surfaced, Señor Pérez would take the brokerage tape to the U.S. consul in Panama City and make a deposition. The matter would end there, Howsam declared. No banking or tax treaties existed between Panama and the United States.

Eusebio Pérez had tapped his temple with a forefinger and allowed himself a solemn, thin-lipped smile. What he said required no translation:

*"Tú eres muy inteligente—por un Indio."*

Howsam mentioned that a respected associate had called him paranoid for taking such precautions.

Was this man a banker?

No.

Señor Pérez had nodded knowingly. For a banker, he said, twisting his mother's diamond wedding band, a little paranoia was no bad thing.

Then they went downstairs to be driven to Long Island, where Ike Battle was slowly dying of heart disease.

At 3:30 P.M. Eusebio Pérez had kissed his old friend goodbye.

An hour later, he boarded a DC-7 at Idlewild.

At 9:30 P.M., he stepped into a cool, humid Mexico City night to launder $2.6 million.

At 10:20 P.M., he sat in the laundry—a two-story white stone, mahogany-beamed living room on fashionable Paseo de Palma. Snacking on Guaymas shrimp, he recounted his New York visit.

Gerhard Stumpf had listened, nearsighted brown eyes opaque and bored behind thick steel-framed round glasses. A balding, moon-faced man in white hand-embroidered Costa Rican planter's shirt, he knew all the punch lines. He had laundered Ike Battle's money since 1938.

His education in Mexican finance began even earlier. An admirer of precision, he fixed the exact moment as 7:02 P.M., February 27, 1934.

At that instant, the introductory "Deutschland über Alles" had faded from German overseas radio, and news of the Reichstag fire, in Berlin, followed. Goebbels' announcer said Communists were responsible.

Stumpf had heard the broadcast in Tampico, Mexico, as purser on a Hamburg-American Line freighter. Shipboard reaction that night mirrored Germany's. Armed with axes and chipping hammers, the Nazis went berserk. Within moments, the cries and footsteps of "political unreliables" rang out through the steel companionways.

A child of the proletariat, whose father's Hamburg saloon catered to Communist dock workers, Stumpf had no use for miracles. Taking thirty dollars American from his purser's safe, he lumbered across the boat deck as quickly as ample girth and stubby legs allowed. Grabbing a stanchion, he heaved himself up on the railing. Then, with the foresight and caution that would distinguish his entire financial career, he clapped one hand over his nose and the other around his glasses. Thus poised, he stepped off, feet first, into the oily waters of Tampico Bay sixty feet below.

Three days later, he had arrived in Mexico City.

Off the bus, he immediately sought out a music store. Finding one, he bought a secondhand concertina. He then presented himself to the owner of the Berghof, *"Bierstube Alemana, Muy Típica,"* as a singing waiter. He was hired for two meals a day and a rent-free room above the café. More important, the boss knew people. A week later, Gerhard Stumpf turned in his seaman's passport and applied for Mexican citizenship.

Nights occupied, he next searched for a day job. He found that one morning on the Reforma, Mexico City's equivalent of Park Avenue.

Scattered over a black velvet cloth in a bank window were a hundred matchbook-sized bits of orange metal. Wafer-thin, they weighed three ounces each and would easily fit inside a tourist's vest pocket or glove. Later, Stumpf would know them as "smugglers' bars."

Now he was struck by their beauty. Growing up in the post–World War I German inflation, he heard much of class struggle and revolution. The quiet, warm glow before him seemed infinitely more comforting, real and attainable. He opted for gold on the spot.

Naturally good with figures, he had advanced from clerk to accountant in the steamship-line office before going to sea. Pulling down his ill-fitting coat, he walked in and applied for a job.

The following Monday, he reported for work as a clerk-translator. His bank pay went for clothes and a book a week. All were about his adopted country's banking system. To his surprise, he found it unique. Its safety record was absolutely perfect. The Depression broke three of the "Big Eight" Swiss banks and thousands of others in the United States and around the world. But not one depositor in Mexico lost a centavo.*

Stumpf's introduction to Mexican banking took place in a *financiera.* These investment banks, similar to U.S. savings and loan associations, existed to lure foreign capital, mainly dollars, needed for industrial growth. They paid high interest, offered Swiss-style confidentiality, and guaranteed income tax relief (international tax treaties were eschewed).† Inheritance taxes were not imposed, either.‡

These attractions, however, went unheeded. Apart from the Depression, Americans remembered Pancho Villa, Emilio Zapata and the Revolution of 1910. Mexican banks needed money so badly they paid commissions to middlemen for delivering dollar deposits.

---

* That record stands.
† All true today.
‡ They still are not.

Finder's fees quickly obsessed Stumpf. If he landed a few, he thought, he would have capital and be on his way. The question confronting him and all of Mexico, of course, was how to attract dollars from the States.

Such achievements are seldom recorded. Nor are they likely to be advertised. But several informed sources believe that Gerhard Stumpf, the portly singing waiter, was the only man in Mexico to find an answer.

It came to him three years later, in 1937, while watching a newsreel of an air raid on Shanghai. At the time, it seemed so simple he doubted it. Yet the more he examined his solution, the more unassailable its truth seemed: politicians were the same the world over. They seldom led. They only appeared to. More often than not, to stay in power they pandered to the mob. What happened in Germany, Stumpf reasoned with remorseless logic, could happen in some form or other in the United States.

He knew three bank customers who could say if his idea made sense. So, cautiously, over the summer, he sounded them out. Impassive men all, they merely nodded. But that fall, armed with their letters of recommendation, Stumpf took a bus north.

He spoke to every local Japan Society and *shosha* (businessmen's association) from San Diego to Seattle. Describing his bank and the tension between Tokyo and Washington, he said prudent Japanese might want some money in Mexico. If he was wrong, no harm done. Deposits would earn twice the interest they could in the States. Was that so bad?

Nisei, American-born, had dismissed him. The immigrant Isei listened.* With a banker's reserve, and a singing waiter's feel for the audience, Stumpf asked for no money. Instead, he thanked all for their patience.

He was rewarded in January of 1938. The mail that month brought him over $2 million American. The government-authorized commission for the deposits he initiated was one half of 1 percent, or $10,000. His superiors paid him that again, under the table, for bringing them the money.

February had brought $750,000; March, an office behind the Reforma.

April produced a tall mustached American whose closely cropped iron-gray hair clung to his scalp like a helmet. His card identified him as Ike Battle, a New York private banker. He said he knew Shintaro Awasa, a client of Stumpf's.

Sensing an investigation of some sort, Stumpf immediately invoked Mexican law. Any bank, broker, or investment adviser divulging facts about a client committed a crime, he told Battle.

Battle had said not to worry. Awasa, a client's gardener, had suggested that he look him up. Since he had business in Mexico City, he had done a little personal checking and decided to stop by.

---

* With good reason, it developed. Japanese Americans, relocated during World War II, suffered estimated property losses of $40 million. They got back $4 million.

Why? Stumpf asked with Teutonic directness. To make a deposit?

Battle had smiled. No, he was interested in what Stumpf would think of next, when he ran out of Japanese. He hoped to hear from him then.

To what end?

To back him if the idea was big enough.

Stumpf said he did not understand.

Battle had nodded, hands in pockets, slouching in the wooden chair. He was a dinosaur, he said. The Depression had all but made private bankers extinct. The coming war and postwar period posed equally grave threats. Big American banks would finance both, squeezing smaller ones out of business. While the giants rebuilt Europe and the Far East, he would entrench himself in Mexico and Central and South America.

How? Stumpf asked.

Battle would trade that answer for a big Mexican idea. Fair enough?

Thoroughly perplexed, Stumpf had watched him leave. He did not grasp the visit's classic simplicity until August. Then he saw why a banker followed a Japanese gardener's financial lead. For just one reason: to learn. But what could Shintaro Awasa teach Ike Battle?

Simple: a new way to bury money.

Unencumbered by education or economic theories, Stumpf had something many classically trained economists hungered for. He had the knack of instinctively relating events to money. Having labored four months to discover the obvious, he disposed of the subtleties in moments.

What kind of money, he had wondered, would Battle want to bury in Mexico? Dollars? Never. Dollars were stronger than pesos. But with war, Mexican pesos were safer than any European currency, even Sweden's or Switzerland's. Who could say Hitler would not attack either?

So, Stumpf had theorized, Battle had European funds.

Undoubtedly, he was the New World end of a conduit originating in Europe. But as recently as April, the money had been homeless. After listening to Awasa, he came running to Mexico.

Why? For two reasons.

The first was obvious: greater profit. The second had real subtlety. For long-range purposes, Mexico suited Battle better than the United States. It gave him, in 1938, a Latin-American foothold on other people's money. His, regardless of events, could stay at home earning more profit. Then, with peace, those fat war dollars would move south, into a financial vacuum. Their impact would be six or seven times the same amount prewar. Time and that strategy, Stumpf thought, could indeed give Ike Battle and his associates a formidable foothold in Central and South America.

But "something for nothing" did not exist in banking. Battle did not need help to make *financiera* deposits. He could handle those himself and keep the one half of 1 percent commission if he were greedy.

Why, then, had he approached Stumpf? Stumpf knew and smiled.

Battle wanted an idea that yielded more profit than Mexican banks.

In September, research done, he had dictated a one-sentence letter. He said simply that he had an idea which Señor Battle might find interesting.

Two weeks later, in a corner suite of the Hotel Reforma, Stumpf met with Battle and Eusebio Pérez, whose bank's excellent reputation he knew. Pérez's presence said that Battle's plans were already operational. The future alluded to in April, Stumpf saw, was now. The time for theory had passed. So he hit them with the most direct statement he could make.

He could take all the money they could send him from the bank in Portugal, he said, and guarantee a yearly return twice the bank rate.

That had the desired effect.

Ike Battle, mouth open, half rose from the green-and-yellow striped couch. Eusebio Pérez, alongside him, seemed unable to lift the demitasse cup the rest of the way to his mouth.

What bank in Portugal? Battle had asked.

Having recently taken inscrutability lessons from several hundred Japanese, Stumpf fielded the question with absolute aplomb. His round face remained impassive, his balding forehead uncreased.

The bank they either owned or had close ties to, he told Battle calmly.

A faint light of recognition passed over Ike Battle's face. Then he pulled quizzically at the corner of his steel-gray mustache.

What had Portugal to do with anything? he asked.

Everything, Stumpf had replied. They wanted to move European currency, not dollars, and Portugal would be neutral in the war. More important, it had historic ties to the richest country in South America, Brazil. If he had to guess, he would say they owned a Portuguese private bank.

Battle turned to Pérez with an I-told-you-so smile.

Pérez nodded solemnly. In 1936, he told Stumpf, they had bought a Lisbon bank with branches in Bahía and Rio.

Had he deduced anything else they owned? Battle asked.

No. He had quite enough difficulty finding the problem, Stumpf told Battle. Besides, he took him at his word. If they liked the idea, he expected a full explanation of their holdings and plans.

Very open and aboveboard, Pérez commented.

Stumpf had smiled. He could afford to be, he said. His idea required a Mexican citizen. If they knew any who impressed them, Battle would not have climbed three flights of stairs to a dingy office behind the Reforma.

Pérez returned his smile. Overlooking the Spanish, he said, he had just met an impressive Mexican. Now what was the idea?

Stumpf laid it out with Germanic precision.

Four types of banks were authorized to operate in Mexico, he said.

The first was the government bank, obviously no concern of theirs.

The second was the commercial bank, like those in *los Estados Unidos,* too big and visible for their tastes.

The third was the *financiera,* the type in which he deposited money for Japanese. They loaned funds to business and industry, paying depositors 6 or 7 percent interest and charging borrowers 8 or 9 percent.

The fourth type of bank, he continued, was the *hipotecaria,* or mortgage bank. They charged much higher rates than even *financieras.* They had to. The turnaround on their money was much slower.

He wanted to start an *hipotecaria.*

Were their rates twice as high as *financieras*? Pérez had asked.

No. But they offered other advantages, Stumpf replied. Mexico was poor. There were many foreclosures.

Was either gentleman familiar with the Mexican Constitution of 1917?

Battle and Pérez shook their heads.

Mexican law prohibited foreign ownership of the most desirable land, Stumpf had said. Aliens could not own property within a hundred kilometers of a border (sixty-two miles) or fifty kilometers (thirty-one miles) of an ocean.

He, a Mexican citizen, could buy land anywhere. Moreover, with an *hipotecaria* he could earn high interest on one hand and foreclose on properties in default on the other. He had spent a month talking with realtors. They told him entire parts of the "forbidden zone" would triple or quadruple in value after the war. Take a look, he said, handing over letters and appraisal forms. Battle and Pérez read them avidly.

Then Stumpf had spread a map on the coffee table in front of the couch. His finger traced the red line defining the area prohibited to foreign owners. It stopped at the states of Guerrero and Jalisco. These were the best places, he said, where values would rise fastest.

And the yearly rate of return? Ike Battle asked.

Infinite, Stumpf said.

Battle and Pérez leaned forward questioningly.

They would use none of their money, Stumpf said. When European funds came, he would put them in a *financiera,* as he did for the Japanese. His one half of 1 percent commission would start the *hipotecaria.* Then, each year, instead of leaving interest on deposits in the bank, he would withdraw it. That would fund the next year's operation.

After the war, they would sell land and pay depositors interest earned in the *financiera.* The balance would be profit. Assuming that values doubled in five years, they would make 35 percent a year on the money handled. But with no investment, return would be infinite.

Eusebio Pérez clapped his hands. He had just seen every banker's dream: something for nothing. He toasted Stumpf with a fresh *café solo.*

Fingers pulling at the corners of his mustache, Ike Battle had continued his thoughtful study of the map. That, indeed, was a big Mexican idea, he told

Stumpf. But he could make it even bigger. He knew how he could buy land for nothing. Not even interest. And they would cheat no one.

Pérez' grin widened. Suddenly he had that answer, too, a premature proof of Branch Rickey's famous aphorism: luck is the residue of design.

Two Swiss companies, fearing Hitler, had each sent $1 million in gold to the Lisbon bank, Battle said. They wanted it safe in Rio. Instead, Lisbon would sell the gold for pesos and send them to Stumpf. After the war, they would buy gold for the Swiss. Meanwhile, they had $2 million free. Gold earned no interest. It just sat.

Now for terms. He and Pérez each wanted 30 percent of Hipotecaria Stumpf, Jalisco y Guerrero, for the use of their conduit's funds. That left Stumpf with 40 percent for the idea. Fair enough?

Stumpf was flabbergasted.

Battle noted his surprise. He had never thought good ideas were a dime a dozen, he said. That was the cliché of businessmen who never had any.

Then they shook hands and left for supper. "Jalisco and Guerrero ..." Pérez mused in the elevator. Did they have any nice towns?

Stumpf shook his head. Just fishing villages. But after the war they would be the Pacific's Miami Beaches. His favorite was Zihuatanejo.* Two others, not so good, but with potential, were Puerto Vallarta and Acapulco.

That had happened in 1938. Twenty-one years later, as the saga of Courtney Montgomery's cash dump unwound, Eusebio Pérez handed over the kraft envelope. He asked what Stumpf would do with the money.

"Lo mismo," Stumpf shrugged. The same.

He would deposit the checks in several *financieras,* earn 13 percent interest, and "age" the money. When thoroughly Mexican, it would go to Hipotecaria Stumpf to earn 20 percent or more a year.

Pérez nodded approvingly.

Basically cautious and conservative, they were exemplary bankers: scrupulous with clients and honest with each other. They just did things differently.

A century earlier, Thomas Jefferson wrote of such men, "Merchants have no country." Stumpf and Pérez discounted that. Jefferson was a politician, they pointed out with equal disdain. He distrusted all who used power for their ends rather than his. Still, they were not cynics. They knew what money could buy and what it could not.

So, business done, they went into the large patio strung with red-and-green Santa Claus paper lanterns. Modest Gerhard Stumpf wanted his old friend to see the piñata hung from a hook high in the whitewashed wall.

In Mexico, a piñata is a clay pot shaped like a pig and stuffed with coins, favors and sweets. On Christmas Eve, Stumpf's five young sons, armed with bamboo poles, would smash it to bits. The resulting scramble would signal the start of La Navidad.

---

* Interestingly, Zihuatanejo is now touted as the Acapulco of forty years ago.

Smiling, Pérez dropped five U.S. dimes into the piñata.

Then Stumpf had asked about Ike, and they sat down at the wrought-iron-and-glass patio table. They stayed there, under the stars, speaking quietly and sorrowfully in the chill night air, until Stumpf's chauffeur came to return Pérez to the airport.

Two days later, Howsam had excused himself from Ike Battle's Christmas table and gone upstairs to the master bedroom. Seating himself on Ike's bed, he called Norbert Nygaard.

After the usual wait, Nygaard's slow, heavy breathing came on the line.

"Norbie? Prentiss. Any luck?"

"Yeah, I was just thinking about calling you, but I got plaster setting downstairs. I'm putting in the mountains for the Feather River Canyon—"

"What'd you find, Norbie?"

"It was real estate, just like I said. I didn't have time to trace 'em all, but eleven checks tie back to land sales."

"And the owners?"

"Mrs. Fior Consentino, of Shaker Heights, Ohio, and Mrs. Naomi Neuberger, of Miami Beach, Florida."

"Women?"

"Yeah."

"Who the hell are they?"

"Oh, they're daughters," Nygaard said vaguely.

"But whose?" Howsam insisted.

"Itch Cohen's and Speed Immediato's."

Who were they? Howsam wondered.

Isaac Cohen and Spedante Immediato were developers, Nygaard had told him.

What did they develop?

"Big stuff—commercial property, mostly."

"What kind of commercial property?"

"Hotels."

"Where, Norbie?"

Nygaard took a deep breath, shoring up professional pride against an inevitable onslaught.

"Vegas," he admitted.

"Gorillas! Goddammit! What'd I tell you?"

"But the stuff they sold was clean as a spanked baby's ass!" Nygaard protested. "What I found they owned six, seven years."

"You mean they're straight now?"

"I didn't say that. I said this was. But to tell the truth, I thought they were, too. They don't even go near Vegas anymore. Immediato lives upstate in the wine country, and Cohen and his wife gypsy around to wherever it's warm, she's got arthritis so bad."

"Then what's this all about? What'd they dump clean money for?"

"The word I got was war," Nygaard had wheezed. "The Vegas gangs are all making muscles over how they want to split the town up next. I knew it had to be something like that as soon as I saw the checks were clean. So I called a pal in a bank out there, and he told me."

"But who told him?"

"Local real-estate deals—they're going on all up and down the Strip. Bulletproof guys like Cohen and Immediato always try to get into cash before the shooting starts, he said. Then they're ready to pick up the pieces when a hotel or something big all of a sudden goes on the market at a fire-sale price—"

"Goddammit!" Howsam bellowed. "I already bought a brokerage tape and created a client. Are you telling me I put twenty-nine three down the chute?"

"Oh, boy, are you quick."

"You're out of your mind, Norbie! If that's so, why'd Montgomery come to me in the first place? He could have gone anywhere with that dough."

"You don't get it?" Nygaard had asked incredulously. "For God's sake, you had it all figured out when you told me he asked for a receipt. You just had his reason for wanting it ass backwards."

"I did?" Howsam had asked, increasingly confused.

"Sure. You said it made him an errand boy, which it did. Then, you told me, if some West Coast anticrime squad traced the checks to him or a bank examiner found footprints at your end, he'd just flash the receipt and say the Lone Ranger gave him the money—a guy sent by a client who either died since then or left the country."

"That'd work, wouldn't it?"

"Of course it'd work, but, like you said, it'd leave a little smell. The checks tie Cox and O'Shea to the Mob, and that'd kill their legitimate business. So Montgomery has to keep those hoods hidden. But meanwhile their retainer'd choke a horse, so he takes orders. They told him to make a quiet deposit, and he did. He just let you think it needed laundering and acted so dumb he faked you out of a receipt. Why? Because if the law finds that money, the auditors' first thought'll be that it's dirty. Then your lawyer pal flashes his piece of paper and bucks the cops to you. He's clean. They'll swallow anything he tells them, too, because they'll *know* he got suckered. After all, who's stupid enough to want a receipt for what he thinks might be a cash dump?"

"Isn't that what I just said, Norbie? That's my story, too—why I put everything on record and had the letter from Panama backdated."

"Watch it now, Tonto," Nygaard warned him with joyous malice, "because here's where it gets tricky! This is what you didn't say—the real reason for the receipt, what you forgot to ask yourself when I kept telling you this was clean money: what happens when those guys with badges discover you generated a brokerage tape for checks that didn't need any and that the real-estate deals behind them lead to gangsters? What'll they think then?"

That possibility had not occurred to Howsam.

"Jesus," he sighed, totally bewildered, "what would the cops think, Norbie?"

"Why, they'd think what any law enforcement officers would: that you and the hoods figured all this out to take advantage of Cox and O'Shea—that you set them up to be the fall guys in this."

"But why?"

"Because everybody wants to know how Mob money moves in and out of legitimate businesses. So, who'd ever think a partner in a distinguished law firm like that had been conned into acting as a courier for organized crime?"

Howsam finally grasped Nygaard's lesson.

"That sonofabitch! As the Chinese'd say, he's so subtle as to be profound. He not only cost me twenty-nine three I didn't have to spend, but he set me up so cops'd be looking over my shoulder the rest of my life, and he put all that money at risk, which I'd have to make good. If a court ruled this was a conspiracy to falsify a government report, they could confiscate that dough, and I'd be stuck! The clients didn't ask for that brokerage tape. I gave it to them because I thought the dough was dirty. You think for a moment Cohen and Immediato'll sit still for that receipt?"

"Those two," Nygaard had laughed in his high, reedy voice. "They don't have the brains they were born with. I'll lay you a hundred to one that receipt's in the lawyer's safe, and nobody even knows he has it, let alone what it could do. Hoods are the easiest lays in town for lawyers with clout. They think all that prestige is cheap insurance."

"Christ, nobody's that dumb."

"You were," Nygaard snickered. "Check around."

Howsam did. He went downstairs.

Archibald Rothwell, who with his wife had come for Christmas dinner, had waited with Ike in the oak-paneled library overlooking Long Island Sound for the rest of the story.

The two older men enjoyed it, and Rothwell assured him that Nygaard's assumptions probably were right. Firms like Cox & O'Shea, he said, knew people, not law or ethics. In the main, they were opportunists. Howsam had learned a cheap lesson at $29,300, he laughed.

"Look," he went on, "there's little enough risk in any cash dump being discovered, so what are the chances that this one will be?"

"None!" Howsam retorted. "I blew twenty-nine three I didn't have to on brokerage tapes making sure those checks'd be 'legal' when they already were."

"Then forget it," Rothwell advised. "That receipt's just needless 'insurance'—a lawyer's dirty trick."

Ike, lying on the couch, wrapped in an afghan, agreed.

Howsam did not see it that way.

The next day he told Nygaard to get Immediato's address. Then he phoned Eusebio Pérez and asked for a receipt for $2.6 million.

He received both on January 2, 1960. Then he wreaked several times $29,300 worth of vengeance on Courtney Montgomery. He wrote Immediato, at his vineyard in Ukiah, California:

> Since your lawyer requested a receipt for your recent remittance, I thought you should have one for your records as well. It is enclosed.
> Banco Pérez de Panamá will send quarterly statements of your account to Cox & O'Shea and a copy of their yearly summary to me, which I shall forward to you.
> Please do not hesitate to call whenever you have a question or need service.

Perfect. That said Cox & O'Shea had run a game on Immediato—and would, if things got sticky, walk away from his $2.6 million—to protect the firm name. Since the client should have remained anonymous, the note also said the lawyers were unaware that their little move had been discovered. Six days later, a picture postcard of the Cape Mendocino, California, lighthouse arrived. Its text, printed in block letters with a Magic Marker, read: "THANKS BANKER."

Eight months later, in August of 1960, Speed Immediato had expressed his gratitude more tangibly. A lawyer from a distinguished Park Avenue law firm arrived unannounced one afternoon. Like Archibald Rothwell, he was austere, craggy, and in his late sixties. He too had a kraft envelope. It had contained a check for $1.4 million and a clipping from the *Atlanta Constitution*. The story announced the sale of a building on a prime downtown corner of Peachtree Street.

In all, Cohen and Immediato gave Howsam $4 million. Moreover, they were ideal clients. After that he never heard from either of them.

And that was the background of Battle & Company Account 60-J.

Howsam put the point outline he had prepared for Speed Immediato back in his breast pocket and watched the 707 let down through the rain squalls blanketing San Francisco Bay.

In thirty hours it would be January 1, 1966. As of that moment, with interest applied, Account 60-J would exceed $10 million. That much Immediato would understand. But, recalling the block-lettered postcard, Howsam wondered if he could grasp anything else.

The trip to Ukiah raised more doubts. It began a step beyond the plane gate when a tall young Indian blocked his way. He wore ranch clothes—rain-curled Stetson, Levi's, sheepskin jacket—and a pained expression.

"Howsam?" he asked.

"That's right."

"Speed sent me. You got any other bags?"

"Just this." Howsam raised the blue canvas Crouch & Fitzgerald one-suiter that fits beneath plane seats.

"Okay, then. Let's go. It's rainin'."

A hundred miles and ninety silent, hair-raising minutes later in an enclosed jeep, they turned off Route 101 at Ukiah to a blacktop road. Then came a narrow gravel trail winding through a wooded canyon. Then they passed between two high gateposts of round creek-bottom stones. Manzanita and oak trees, swaying in the rain, stretched beyond.

Howsam peered through the windshield-wiper arc. Vineyards marched up and down the hills on either side of the road as far as he could see.

"Jesus, how big is this place?" he asked.

"Fourteen hundred acres."

Howsam shook his head, recalling the agonies sixty had inflicted on his family in Michigan.

Finally the road skirted a hill and circled back on itself, past a series of board-and-batten homes and buildings with creek-stone foundations.

"They're in the back of the aging cellar," the driver said, cutting the jeep's motor. "That's the one half in the ground."

"Who's 'they'?"

"Itch's here, too—got in from Palm Springs about noon. Just walk straight down the aisle. They're at the back, in the tasting room."

Howsam left the jeep, sprinted across the rainswept cement apron, and down an inclined ramp. The cellar was dark, damp, soundless, and filled with the heady aroma of grapes. A small patch of light spilled out of the tasting room, perhaps a hundred and fifty feet away. Five-foot-high oak casks, on their sides, faced each other across the narrow aisle.

He walked the full length of the darkened building before he found a sign of life. A yellow rain slicker dangled from the bung in the very last barrel on his right. He draped his chesterfield similarly over the cask opposite. Then he glanced into the tasting room.

Prints of castles and vineyards covered the whitewashed walls. Among them were framed wine lists from well-known hotels and restaurants. Howsam supposed they served Immediato's wines. To his surprise, only one came from Las Vegas. The right side of the room, however, was empty.

So he stepped through the doorway and turned left.

He saw Courtney Montgomery first.

Still tanned and casual in gray flannel slacks and natural linen sport coat, he sat on the left side of a round rosewood pedestal table. His hair had whitened in the past six years, and he looked more distinguished than ever.

His lips tightened, and a flush crept under his widow's peak, when he saw Howsam. He hunched his shoulders as if to rise, but thought better of it. He suddenly realized his position. Since Howsam had found the clients, he knew the checks were clean. Also, the purpose of the receipt. But the big question was, did Cohen and Immediato know? Neither gave any sign.

Speed Immediato sat next to him, fleece-lined aviator's boot casually propped against the table's edge. The faded denims and blue-and-yellow plaid shirt said country. But his face was vintage Vegas: pit-boss sharp and drenched in expensive cologne.

His partner, Itch Cohen, sat on the right side of the table. At first sight, he resembled a stolid middle-aged businessman. At second, a piece of sheet steel: cold, hard, and all gray—suit, straight-back hair, eyes. A silver dollar walked across the knuckles of his right hand as he measured Howsam. His glance matched the glints on the chrome-plated frames around his glasses.

Immediato rose, discarding the paper matchbook cover with which he had been picking his teeth. They were caps, unnaturally white under his dyed jet-black hair. He looked more like an aging nightclub crooner, Howsam decided.

"I'm Speed Immediato," he said, extending his hand. "This is Itch Cohen. The counselor, you know."

Howsam shook hands and turned to Cohen.

"Pleased to meet you, Banker," Cohen said. "You're our front-runner. That twenty percent a year still holding up?"

Howsam nodded. "You've got it. I found something better, though, but I want to hear it from you before I move anything."

Montgomery's flush deepened. The implication that his clients had other bankers handling buried money suggested that other lawyers might be in the wings as well. He glanced furtively at Howsam for some kind of hint. Howsam let him stew.

Immediato seemingly took no notice. Instead, he turned to the sideboard behind him for a long-stemmed tulip glass and a wine bottle.

"For that we'll listen," he laughed. "But first, a little cabernet?"

"No, thanks," Howsam said. "I'm not much of a wine man."

"This'll make you one," Immediato promised. "It's so good, we don't even ship it—only to Itch's kids and mine—and a few cases to Ernie's, down in Frisco, so we always get a table. Here—try a little," he insisted, filling the bottom quarter of the glass and thrusting it across the rosewood table.

Howsam did. "Sensational!" he said, meaning it.

Immediato nodded knowingly.

"A classic red—from flinty soil and cool Zone Two climate, same as in Bordeaux, France. We'll send you some. You still live in Oyster Bay?"

Howsam's surprise brought forth a thin smile from Itch Cohen. Unlike Immediato's impeccable show-business caps, the teeth in his upper plate were slightly oversized. The effect was awesome.

Immediato filled Howsam's glass and leaned back, aviator's boot still against the table. "So, okay. We're all comfortable. Deal," he said.

Howsam now faced the problem of presenting the position. He had two choices. He could talk it, in which case Montgomery would undoubtedly interrupt and do everything possible to confuse the issue. Or he could stick with the point outlines already prepared. The drawback there was that Cohen and Immediato looked like lip readers. Still, on balance, that seemed the lesser evil. Reaching into his breast pocket, he withdrew the two-page memoranda. One he gave to Cohen, to share with Immediato. He handed the carbon to Montgomery with a truly wicked smile, noting with satisfaction the sweat beads forming over the lawyer's upper lip.

As expected, Montgomery finished first. He immediately went on the offensive, talking to protect his retainer and, perhaps, his skin, or both.

"All right, Banker," he said. "When this is over—when this war nobody sees has been fought and won, when this crazy gnome's scheme works out—what's on the bottom line? What's in it for my clients? That is, if they haven't been killed off, too, with the rest of you maniacs."

Howsam had been waiting for that.

"I want your ten now," he told Cohen and Immediato, "and in 1970 I'll bring you back ten times that—one hundred million dollars. Guaranteed. Otherwise, the Swiss and I and God knows who else'll be dead."

What Cohen and Immediato lacked in style they had in nerve. Their reaction was worthy of a Wall Street boardroom. Neither so much as blinked. First-rate executives, their business just happened to be crime.

"That's a real heavy face—that dwarf," Cohen finally commented.

" 'Gnome,' " Montgomery corrected.

"Gnome, dwarf—c'mon," Immediato told Montgomery out of a lifetime's experience with high-priced lawyers, "you're fly-fucking. You're talking words, and the Banker's talking takedown. You're gonna need an iron umbrella to keep that dough from knocking your brains out," he warned Howsam. "It's gonna rain on you!" Then, turning to Cohen, he asked, "What do you think?"

"I think we're two punks shaking pennies out of gumball machines, that's what I think," Cohen answered. "Look at him," he ordered, bathing Howsam in chrome-plated highlights from the frames of his glasses. "He's not even forty yet, and he's gonna own the world."

Immediato pointed to the outline. "I meant about this—the deal."

"I don't know. I never bet a war before." Cohen shrugged. "So that makes it an automatic six to five against—like anything else in life. But Israelis or not, the dwarf's making the play," he reasoned, "and that gives him the edge. The rest of the world's counterpunching, and counterpunchers went out with Tony Zale. Downside, I see it more like a push. Even. But it's maybe eleven to ten to go. No more, though."

Montgomery relaxed, sure of the proposal's rejection. Since no betting line existed, his clients would soon find themselves in over their heads.

Howsam disagreed. He liked what he heard. The first rule for making money was to be sure of not losing any.

Cohen was doing that now, flip-flopping the silver dollar. Significantly, he ignored the payout. That came later. Not losing took priority.

"That eleven to ten—that's not a heart bet?" Immediato asked.

"I gave at the office!" Cohen snapped. "This is business."

Immediato nodded, acknowledging receipt of information, not necessarily agreement. Tipping his chair farther back, he turned to Howsam.

"How big is this altogether?"

"A hundred million."

"And what's in already?"

"Eighty-six."

"How much of that is yours?"

"Twenty—the same as the Swiss—but I laid off ten to the guys who've been handling your dough for me. We're in a lot of things, and I don't want to get too far ahead. Otherwise I'd have to go find new partners."

"Smart," Immediato agreed. "It's easier to find new dough. But we get a hundred million for our ten?"

"Right."

"So?" Immediato wondered aloud.

Itch Cohen, reversing the silver dollar's direction from right to left with a lightning-fast sleight, answered him.

"We'll take what's open—the whole fourteen million," he told Howsam.

"For now you only get ten. I'll let you know about the other four later."

"Why's that?" Immediato asked.

"Somebody in Chicago gets first refusal."

"Who?"

"The daughter of an old client who was tight with my father-in-law."

"What's she like?"

"An armchair liberal." Howsam shrugged. "She's sitting on thirty million bucks of her old man's money, so she and her husband drive Mercedeses to show Germany and the world they don't believe in collective guilt."

"Oh, brother, are you on a lemon there," Immediato laughed. "That kind never hurts anybody or does anything."

"For sure!" Cohen chimed in. "They're nothing—*nebbish*es."

"I know," Howsam agreed. "But that's how it is."

"Promises . . ." Cohen nodded resignedly. "What are you gonna do? Respect the dead, may they rest in peace. Call us after she tells you no, Banker. Then we'll all be clean."

"Just hold it right there! Christmas was last week," Montgomery pointed out. "Do either of you hear what he's saying? He's not talking about dumping a fight or rigging a horserace. He wants to fix a war—change history!"

Cohen shrugged. "What history? We're making a move. So we're gonna do a number on Egypt. Well, what's Egypt done for us lately?"

Montgomery's eyes widened in disbelief. "Are you nuts? You know who plays around in the Middle East? Guys like David Rockefeller and André Meyer.* They go down to Washington to talk foreign policy with LBJ, and he listens. He may not always do what they want, but, by God, he listens!" he roared, thumping his fist down on the rosewood table. "You know why? Because they can hurt him. They're that strong!"

Having invoked names, he next related the general to the specific, adding a dash of irony. "And if any of that big oil crowd finds two little *shleppers* from Vegas in their scene, I promise you, they'll start such a boot and shoe factory up your ass, you won't know what hit you!"

"What's that supposed to mean?" Immediato asked. "This is a free country, isn't it? Don't we still have free enterprise here?"

"No, we do not!" Montgomery assured him with all the conviction a senior partner of a politically oriented law firm could muster. "We have a foreign policy that serves our national interest. And I can tell you, in the Middle East it's to keep those oil companies big and profitable. Billions are involved, thousands of jobs, Wall Street—even the economy here."

Immediato shook his head. "The government protects those guys?"

"Exactly. They're in the national interest."

"I don't get it. Hell—all they're doing is making money. Anybody could do that," Immediato insisted. "How do you know I wouldn't be more in the national interest? Or the Banker? Or Itch? Maybe we wouldn't be so smart about the taxes. What makes those guys so special?"

"They got there first," Howsam said.

Immediato suddenly made the connection. National interest and power politics were like putting a race wire in a Bronx cigar store. People just spoke better English.

"Sure," he said. "First you buy the precinct. Then you buy the squad."

"Talk about a lock," Cohen mused "You can't get in the race if you're not on the track, and they won't let you on. But if you're big enough, you're already there. You're in the national interest."

"That's what they think," Immediato told him. "We're getting in, too. That national interest's got it all over free enterprise. Anytime everybody runs for himself in partners with the government, it's a license to steal."

* The chairman of Chase Manhattan Corporation and the then senior partner of Lazard Frères & Co., investment bankers, who in 1958 set up the Iranian Development Bank. Iran then was the world's leading oil exporter, with Abadan the world's largest refinery. Nevertheless, the country's most spectacular energy-related project remains the 700-mile-long pipeline delivering natural gas to Russia. The role of the Iranian Development Bank in this venture remains shadowy and undiscussed. The Rockefeller family, of course, through its holding company, Jersey Standard, controls Standard Oil of New Jersey, a partner in ARAMCO.

"Well, then, mister, you'd better have your sprinting shoes on, because that's going to be the fastest track you've ever seen!" Montgomery shouted.

A third demon now pursued him, more terrifying than losing his retainer or even incurring the wrath of Cohen and Immediato: his partners.

He could already anticipate their reaction. They would view the night's events as potentially ruinous on two counts. First, firms like Cox & O'Shea could not afford public disclosure of gangland connections. Second, being identified with Israel in a war would be even more costly. Multinational companies, in Arab markets, would shun them. After ten years of fees, however, the only way out of the situation seemed to be through persuasion.

Desperate, Montgomery marshaled his strongest case: competition.

"Look," he said reasonably. "Forget the oil companies. Forget the Egyptians and Russians. Maybe their spies are just newspaper talk after all. If you go ahead with this, you'll go foreign. And that means the CIA."

Cohen's silver dollar continued its deliberate stroll across the knuckles of his right hand. Immediato, similarly unimpressed, sucked his teeth and eyed the matchbook cover on the table.

"You think they're a bunch of dumb Irish Fordham Law School boys worrying about pensions, like the FBI?" Montgomery challenged.

"No?" Immediato asked.

"No! Not on your life! They're the cream—better than anything you've ever been up against, including hoods."

Immediato found that meaningful. Nodding, he turned to Howsam.

"Tell me, Banker," he asked, leaning forward in his chair, "where'll this play—here in this country?"

"New York," Howsam answered.

"Got it. Okay, then, Counselor," Immediato went on, "when you were U.S. attorney, in Frisco, how much better was the CIA than the FBI?"

"What do you mean, better?"

"Just that. Was the CIA better?"

"Of course. I told you. They're the cream."

"Okay. So they were fifty percent better?"

"Sure. At least."

"Seventy-five?"

"How would I know?"

"Take a stab: sixty percent better—eighty?"

"Hey! What're you doing—trying to make odds on this?"

Immediato shrugged. "That's what I do. Right? I figure odds. Itch keeps 'em that way."

"Jesus," Montgomery sighed, flopping back in his chair. He shook his head helplessly, but what he had heard would not go away. "All right. Call them sixty-five percent better."

"And it plays in New York," Immediato repeated for Cohen's benefit.

Itch Cohen nodded briskly, weighed it all up, and supplied the answer.

"On my mother's grave, may she rest in peace," he vowed through his hard, chrome-plated stare, "if this plays in New York, at sixty-five percent, that CIA'll never get on the track."

Face shining with sweat, Courtney Montgomery stared at him incredulously, his once high, distinguished widow's peak plastered across his forehead in damp, flat streamers.

"How . . . can you say that?" he asked.

Speed Immediato, not looking at all like an aging crooner, explained.

"Itch'll disappear 'em," he said.

Ninety minutes later, Dr. Fabian stood before her living-room window.

Glasses off and ponytail undone, she looked like a slightly older version of the models in *New Yorker* ads. The classic, even features were unflawed, the long center-parted auburn hair thick and lustrous. And at thirty or so, she clearly knew that in life, as well as in art, less is more. Black silk slacks and gold lamé blouse understated an equally elegant figure.

Drawing back the turquoise silk drape behind her, she smiled sardonically and pointed her brandy glass down the snow-covered block on East Eightieth Street. Then she turned to Schotten, to justify the price she had paid for the handsome town house in which they now stood.

"You're clever," she said. "Howsam told me so. What do you see out there?"

"Fifth Avenue," he answered.

"Yes—seventy-four feet away, to be precise—and that's why I paid sixteen times the yearly rent for this building. When you're that close to Fifth, the 'greater fool' theory applies—"

"In real estate?"

"Of course in real estate. Especially in real estate. It's just like growth stocks in a bull market. No matter what you pay for a Xerox or IBM, a greater fool will always come along and pay you more. This little house is like that   the key to the corner. See?" she asked patronizingly, pointing the empty brandy glass toward the Metropolitan Museum. "Sooner or later, some builder will have a dream about that corner. And when he does, he'll see a big apartment building there with a fancy Fifth Avenue address and vulgar little steel balconies. He's my greater fool."

"And what will you get then?"

She cocked her head judiciously, flame-dark hair spilling over the right shoulder of the metallic gold blouse.

"Three or four times my investment—maybe five. With the lower three apartments rented, mine is free. So, tell me," she asked with elaborate irony, "do you think I did so badly tying up my little nest egg this way?"

He shook his head.

*"Kauf billig, verkauf teuer,"* he murmured, citing his grandfather's maxim. Buy cheap, sell dear.

"Exactly."

Then she left him at the window.

He pondered her attitude, watching the snow fall on Fifth Avenue. Then, turning away a moment later, he found her seated on the large pumpkin-colored couch alongside the fireplace. Bolder after the exchange at the window, she raised her freshly filled glass in a mocking toast. That he took in stride. Women with brains and money and not much else were constants in a private banker's life. The hard, steely edges around her smile, however, were another matter. Their hostility concerned him.

Hoping to find the reason for her attitude, he met her challenge head on, but with a disarming smile.

"Dr. Fabian," he asked, starting across the room in his awkward, rolling gait, "do I offend you?"

Placing her glass on the tile-and-chrome cocktail table before the couch, she considered the question.

"Yes," she said as he approached. "You come here from that old brothel in Tangier with the guileless face of an IBM typewriter salesman and a copy of *Mosoch shel Chol* under your arm. You say you're an international banker." She smiled. "Others might call you a . . . thug?"

"There's a difference?"

"And you smile too much!" she whispered.

"I'll tell you about that," he said, seating himself beside her. "But first, may I have a brandy?"

"Of course. It's Fundador, though. You may find it a bit strong."

"Thank you. I'll be careful."

Then, leaning back against the couch, he told her about smiling.

"I was graduated from the École Supérieure de Commerce at eighteen—"

"In Neuchâtel?" she asked in frank surprise.

He nodded casually. "During the war. Perhaps it was easier then. We still had Germans, but no English. At any rate, my father was a widower, and he couldn't get away for the graduation. So my grandfather came instead—an absolutely first-rate banker. After the ceremony, as we left the school, he turned to me in the back seat of his big Mercedes and slapped me on the knee. 'Eric,' he said, 'let me tell you something they don't teach in there. You've the great good fortune to be indecently handsome, and this is a jealous world. So smile a lot. People never believe good-looking men have brains in the first place. And if you seem happy in the bargain, you'll be home free. No one will ever think you've brains enough to blow your nose. After all, who in this life ever met a happy, good-looking man who knew what was going on?' So I smile a lot," he concluded somberly.

"That's the most cynical story I ever heard. Why did you tell me that?"

"So that you will always know that whatever passes between us is completely candid and aboveboard."

She raised her glass, not in the least disarmed.

"Just a simple little Swiss country banker, aren't you?" she asked. "It's all candid and aboveboard, but Howsam's out, going his own remorseless way tourist class, raising thirty million dollars from gangsters and dead men, and you spent the day with that cutthroat in Montreal—"

"What do you know of him?"

"Everything." She smiled. "I was raised in Jerusalem."

That explained the not-quite-English accent, as well as her attitude. She resented his using Israel.

"Don't prejudge," he cautioned.

"Prejudge?" She laughed quietly. "What's there to prejudge? You went to Evelyn Waddell. So you plan to start a war. For money."

A shrewd guess, but it indicated that Howsam had not divulged the position to her.

"There are wars enough for all," he said evasively. "A banker needn't start one, only learn its time and place. Profit, after all, is a function of information. In the end, truth is money's greatest ally. And besides that, what we propose to do is perfectly legal. Even the people in Tel Aviv agree."

"Yes, men like you would call it 'high finance.' "

"No, just the way of the world. As Clausewitz—"

"Stuff Clausewitz!" she retorted, recalling her years at the London School of Economics. " 'War is an extension of politics.' Is that your idea of a deep thought? What has that to do with banking?"

"Everything, because it raises the real question: of what is politics an extension? And, like it or not, there's only one answer: money. *'Gott regiert in Himmel und Gold auf Erde.'* God reigns in heaven and gold on earth. 'Ever thus . . . ever so,' as my grandfather used to say. And that's what this is all about. Who rules, Doctor, flags or money? So where can a banker go to get enough gold to make his weight felt politically? To only one place." He smiled. "To war."

His casual, relaxed answer turned her green eyes agate black. But the phone preempted her reply. Springing from the couch, she strode to a small table at the far end of the book-lined fireplace wall.

"Howsam," she snapped. "For you."

A moment later, Schotten was at her side. She stood her ground, glaring at him. Turning to shield the phone, he found himself facing a hand-signed Chagall print of the fiddler on the roof. The subject seemed apt.

"Yes," he said carefully.

Howsam's deep, quiet voice came over the line, drowning out the San Francisco Airport flight announcements.

"You get to Ilona's all right?"

"No problem. I even got a cab in the snow."

"Good. Then I don't feel guilty about disturbing you. I don't like talking through switchboards. I'm on my way to Chicago now, but that's only a duty call. The fifty's in regardless. So I'll catch an early-bird flight and pick you up for breakfast eight-thirty, nine. You see Evelyn?"

"Oh, yes. A charming fellow. I'm glad he's on our side."

"He mention the *bocher?*"

"Who?"

"His brother-in-law."

"Of course—the one who was going to be a rabbi! Yes. He said he spent the night talking to him in Tel Aviv."

"Figures. What'd he say?"

"I'll fill you in tomorrow. It's somewhat confused."

"Fair enough. And Ilona?"

"Equally charming."

"Yeah?" Howsam sounded genuinely surprised.

"Absolutely."

"Well, great, then. After I get through telling her what this is all about, I want you to tell her how the entire corporate setup'll work—"

"Is that wise?"

"It is if we go down the drain. She and my lawyer are my executors. I want them changing my will on the way out to Michigan tomorrow."

"You don't trust my associates?"

"Let's not get maudlin," Howsam laughed. "Would you—with fifty million dollars of a stranger's dough?"

The question went unanswered.

"Okay," Howsam said. "I'll see you for breakfast at the Carlyle."

Schotten handed over the phone and returned to his brandy. Howsam, his usual succinct self, took less than a minute to brief Dr. Fabian. Her only response was a single drawn-out "I see." Then she stood before the couch, her knuckles whitening around the brandy glass.

"Voltaire was right," she said. " 'If you see a Zurich banker jump out a window, follow him. There is money to be made on the way down.' He just had no idea 'down' could be so low."

"Your friend Evelyn put it even better," Schotten answered. "An Arab proverb. 'Take what you want, saith the Lord. And pay for it.' "

She downed the brandy in a gulp and poured another.

"So why not buy blood?" she wondered, as if that followed logically. "Tell me, who gave you that right?"

"My mirror. I looked into it on my fortieth birthday, weighing this position, and it told me a great truth. It said that, left alone, the politicians will steer east and west to the same place. They'll just give it different names. And why not? Their business, after all, is power—not money, or ideology, or perhaps even politics. So I went ahead. If we win, we'll brighten the twilight of capitalism. Who knows? We may even prolong it. We'll have enough to buy a few heads of state of our own."

Hardly gospel as taught by Keynes, Laski and other left-leaning English economists who had influenced her. But not wholly without truth. Smile steelier, she seated herself on the couch. Her right arm dangled over the corner. The left stretched along the back, brandy glass in hand.

"You Germans," she said in the European slur on the Swiss. *"Sturm und Drang! Götterdämmerung!* We all face the Apocalypse! Any moment," she whispered, "I expect to hear *'Ein Volk! Ein Reich! Ein Führer!'* "

That went too far.

Conceding whims of personal chemistry, he gave her the right to dislike him. Her bad manners he excused, too, as much as they puzzled him. Why had she, after all, to be so forthcoming in showing her enmity? What end did that serve?

His tolerance, however, stopped there. One concession he would not make: that anything in his actions, his past, or this situation merited insult.

So, a warm smile echoing his grandfather's advice, he returned the compliment. At the same time, in a tone of mild reproof, the very least he thought she deserved, he reminded her that they were still allies.

"It's the same old heaven, Doctor," he said, "a place where how many?—six million of your recently murdered people now reside. I'd think of that, if I were you, before I mentioned führers to anyone who stands on the side of Jews—for whatever reason. Unless, of course, you think they died nobly, gorged on martyrdom."

"You pig!" she shouted. Then, turning to face him, she brought up her right hand in a swinging, roundhouse slap.

Until then, he had seen her hostility as petulance. Childishness afflicted many beautiful women. Now, however, he thought otherwise. Something else could have caused her behavior.

With great care, he sought a name for that impulse. Charity aside, his selection made him uneasy. The word he chose seemed improbable, ominous: irrationality.

So, reaching up, he caught her wrist. Then he shook his head, almost apologetically.

A retort had done what civility had failed to. Nostrils flared, lips parted, her face no longer recalled a remote, stylized mask. Either sexually or vengefully, she had been aroused. He also.

For good or ill, in a banker's world, the desirable is seldom simple. So he found her, lusting to hurt him, wildly attractive. Part of her appeal, valid or not, he knew, came from her loss of control.

Of the many beautiful, worldly women he knew, none, in his view, had ever distinguished herself for candor or the force of her beliefs. An analytical, cautious banker, mindful of his wealth and conscious of his limp, he thus questioned the motives of all.

Dr. Fabian's rage, on the other hand, whatever its origin, rang with authenticity. Moreover, it made her seem equally flawed, vulnerable. At the least, he reasoned, he owed her sympathy, perhaps understanding.

Leaving in a climax of insult, then, demeaned both compassion and good manners. Those were the minimum, he believed, that civilized adults brought to every transaction; at any rate, after banking hours.

And, of course, he wanted her. That made it easy to excuse her instability. Logic vanished just as quickly. Now he hoped only to ingratiate himself with her. "Enough," he said. "Talk won't work for us."

Unstable or not, she still perceived reality. Green eyes dark in rage, she sneered at the obvious.

Few words had passed between them, fewer ideas. So far, they had dealt only in abuse, and she knew it. Her expression said as much.

Lips compressed, she tried to free herself. He prudently maintained his grip on her wrist.

Still, he thought, he might not have been wrong. Talk might not ever work for them. And, conceivably, that might not matter, either. Attraction could be perverse. They already knew how to hurt each other, he mused. Sometimes, such insights led to intimacy.

He felt that desire himself acutely now. His need had more to do with self-knowledge than with sexual pleasure, and it had no relationship at all to affection. If he could hold her nude, be enveloped by her, he sensed he might better label the feelings she aroused in him. Looking at her, he thought he saw that same yearning flicker through her anger.

Regardless, he knew, they had broken a rule. Still strangers, they had overreacted. They had gone too far too fast to part that night as friends or acquaintances. Already exposing much of themselves by word or act, they now had but one choice, it seemed to him. They could either reveal the rest or be done with each other.

Always a banker, ever assessing likelihood, he put his chances of bedding her at better than fifty-fifty. She did not seem one to do things by halves.

Reinforcing that belief, she took a deep breath and lunged at him again. Unable to free her wrist, she then sank back resignedly in the deep cushions of the pumpkin-colored couch. Looking ahead, eyes quizzically roaming the far end of the room, she seemed finally to him to be pondering the choice he recognized the moment before. He let her think. With her, he knew, thought could dissipate anger.

Soon it had seemed to, so he turned away to pour her another Fundador.

Knocking it back in a gulp, she gestured for more.

Nodding, he filled the bottom of her snifter.

Then, that brandy drunk, too, he confronted her with the business outstanding between them.

"So, Jerusalem?" he asked softly.

Without answering, she rose and led him the length of the floorthrough apartment to an all-white bedroom as chaste and small as a convent cell.

He congratulated himself then on his insight. He had been right again, he thought. She needed him, too, to better grasp her feelings.

He would soon learn otherwise. What she sought went far afield of understanding.

Later he found a name for that as well: retribution.

It began as she left the bathroom, nude, in black satin high-heeled mules. Until then, Evelyn's "fair daughters of Jerusalem" had waxed and waned beneath his consciousness like voluptuous, cloud-shrouded moons.

Now those images were disconcertingly clear.

Dr. Fabian projected them all: the long, gorgeous legs that seemed to go on forever . . . the tiny V-waist . . . the lush, rolling hips.

*"And more, old chap, more . . ."* he imagined the sonorous baritone hymn, with its warm Welsh lilts, continuing. *". . . shapely, high-slung breasts, improbably full for her slender frame, with silky-smooth, pink aureola . . . and a dark incitement—a firestorm of flame-glinted hair—sweeping 'cross her belly."*

At forty, he thought himself immune to looks. She proved he was not.

Guardsman-straight, she stood over him at an arrogant parade rest, hands behind back, shielding nothing, giving him his fill of her. Then, lips pursed judiciously, she ran the red-lacquered nail on her right forefinger just once over the full length of his erection. It quivered greedily.

Her knowing smile acknowledged the reaction.

"How frail you look," she said absently, glancing at the heavy support bandage wrapped around his right instep, "just like an injured little bird."

Sympathy ended there.

Joining him on the narrow brass-framed bed, she pulled him over her. Then, without embrace or foreplay, rushed him in between her legs. They met like swallows in flight, in a brief, frenzied flutter which he could not control, and parted almost immediately.

Now she lay on her side, the long nail again lazily skimming his body, down the creases of his thighs, around his genitals, along the bridge behind them. Green eyes wide and unblinking, she seemed totally detached from the minute contractions and swellings, sudden races and skips, pulsing just beneath his skin.

"Schotten," she asked mockingly, "is that your idea of romance? Bip, bip, bip—and you're all through? Done?"

He shook his head, flushing in the pale-blue light of the bed lamp.

"Finance and Fundador . . . " he mused. "You could be right. Maybe they don't mix."

"They might." She smiled encouragingly. "It's a long night. We'll see."

Her words had the desired effect. Gratefully, eyes shut, he sank deeper on the turquoise pillow as she snapped off the light. Nervous tension diminishing, he began to enjoy the tiny erotic impulses trailing after her touch. No longer taunts, but invitations, they crept inexorably higher. A little more, and he would be ready, and do well. Later, still immersed in sensation, he vaguely felt her shift position. A breast lingered momentarily on his rib cage. Her body brushed his in warm but too-brief intimacy, as if they were not strangers. Then her mouth closed over him.

Lulled by her bogus sympathy, he overreacted. His stomach bucked against her forehead. He reached into the deep thicket of hair tumbling over his groin to push her off.

"No! I'll be all right. You needn't—"

She looked up, eyes glittering in the darkness.

"You fool," she said. "This isn't for you. It's for me. Do you hear? For me."

Then her face vanished once more behind the shroud of auburn hair. Quite drunk, she seemed to understand her motives far better than he.

She acted as though she were winning, as she had at the living-room window, besting him. Since he obviously found her attractive, his judgment as a sophisticated man was being violated as well.

His climactic, shuddering sigh quickly followed.

Lying back in the darkness, she savored her victory. Without question, he had been physically humiliated.

But his little homily about smiles had gone right by her.

So she underestimated him. By half. He lived by his judgments.

And still desiring her, he saw no need to alter his view of her now, only to learn why she craved such vengeance. That, he knew, cost dearly. And the more intelligent the woman, the higher the price.

Her account came due about twenty minutes later.

"Aren't you ever going to leave?" she suddenly asked, in the dark.

"Not for now," he casually replied.

Propping himself up on an elbow, he leaned over the perfect, sculpted face, his gray eyes opaque and metallic. His teeth flashed in the darkness. But the Zurich banker, and not the good-looking man who smiled a lot, presented the bill, in full, interest applied and compounded.

"Doctor," he asked, wincing at what would be said, "where else at one-thirty in the morning can one find so accomplished a cocksucker?"

What she did was one thing; naming it, another.

Her body flinched its full length and shot off the pillow, then fell back as quickly as he blocked the way. Realizing she had won nothing, she threw her hands up to her mouth and flung herself over on her side. Breath wrenched past her knuckles in explosive gusts.

He never knew whether she cried from guilt, hurt or shame. Nor did he care. He was touched that she wept at all. The European women in his past would not have. They knew better than to mind what anyone called them. If they could not do business where they wished, they did it where they could. Life was long, looks were fleeting. Men were economic concerns.

He reached over in the darkness for her shoulder, saluting emotion, however misdirected. She wanted no comfort from him.

But she had never been touched that way, for that purpose, either. Shaking his hand away, she began to sob aloud, a single high-pitched open-mouthed note. Barely audible, it carried her to a peak and then died, the mattress and bed frame pitching and yawing in its wake.

Finally, still lying on her side, her back to him, she spoke. Her voice, flat and routine, tied off a loose conversational thread.

"I used you," she said, into the darkness.

"Oh? That's what people do with people, isn't it?"

"Not like this. I wanted to see if you could kill a ghost."

"A ghost . . . ? Well, did I?"

Her back to him, she nodded on the pillow. "For now, at least."

"Was I the first?"

"Oh, God, you're all the same, aren't you?" she whispered, still facing the wall. "Greedy little boys. 'Was I first?' 'Was I best?' 'Was I biggest?' Why is it none of you ever asks what counts: 'Will I be the last?' "

"That's unfair, and you know it. I meant about the ghost."

"If it makes you feel better—yes, you were the first. But only to succeed. Before, it was always the same. Nothing. So here I gave up trying. It made life simpler."

"Simpler? How simpler? We're in this world, Jerusalem, not the next." He tapped her hip lightly with his fist for emphasis. She did not draw away, so he left it there. "Ghosts have no business here," he went on, "only we. Life is for the living."

She nodded again, sorrowfully, shoulders bobbing with silent weeping.

Her tears mourned the loss of mystery, he thought. Bed left women a single privacy: the past. That disclosed, they were utterly revealed. She felt that way now, he guessed. She had no more secrets.

Or so she thought. Soon, she would have even fewer.

A born negotiator, he had an exquisite sensitivity to people and situations. It told him now to take charge. Cradling her head with one hand, he slid the other, on her hip, between her body and the mattress. Then, tenderly, he pulled her over to face him.

Calculating, even with his own emotions, he had no regrets about the pain he would shortly inflict. He dealt in futures. Her past permitting, she might fit into his. But unexplained history led nowhere. Still, for a banker, he trusted her. She seemed sufficiently off balance to be truthful. When he spoke, his voice was warm and sympathetic.

"Tell me about your ghost," he said.

So she did.

Israel had an elite, she began. The air force. Fliers got the best of everything. That may have determined her job the summer before graduate school. She was assigned to a kibbutz near an airfield. Whether by chance or by policy, all the college girls there were attractive.

At any rate, she met a flier. She did not go back to college. He moved in with her instead. A year later, during the 1956 Sinai campaign, his plane exploded over Port Said. His loss brought another. She miscarried. She had been unaware of the pregnancy. Psychologically devastated, she did things.

She paused, stretched her legs, digging the heels of the black satin mules into the turquoise bedspread as she sought the right word.

"Haywire?" she tried.

He nodded in understanding.

"That's it," she agreed.

She went that way with men, she said.

By her reckoning, fate owed her two lives: one lost in Egypt; the other within her. She knew she could not raise the dead. But after she recovered, she sought substitutes.

Her lover's squadron mates selflessly sought to make amends for events. She was quite desirable then, she observed, and the fliers had a very good time with her indeed. In retrospect, they were merciless.

Both losses, however, remained outstanding.

"But what about your family? Why didn't you go home?"

She had no family. Her father had been a doctor in Budapest. By 1935 he sensed the inevitable. Although Jewish physicians were denied emigration, he took steps to get his two small daughters out of Hungary.

One March morning he took a Danube ferry, as he did every week, to see patients in Pest, nuns in a teaching convent. Examinations done, he had his usual cup of tea with his old friend the mother superior.

On Maundy Thursday, 1935, the black wrought-iron convent gates in Pest closed behind Ilona Fabian. She never saw her father again.

"Do you remember him?"

She shook her head in curt dismissal. "Only a smell. Wool. It rained torrents that night, and his coat must have been drenched."

"And your mother?"

"Nothing . . . nothing at all. I was three."

The next day, Good Friday, the nuns took the convent chorus to sing at Easter services. Magda and Ilona Fabian went with them.

She recalled nothing of Vienna or the journey across Europe, to Copenhagen, with an official of the Zionist Immigration Department.

But six weeks later a rusty old freighter hove to off a beach on a dark moonless night. She remembered that. She recalled a Danish seaman too, a blond boy of fourteen or fifteen. Magda said his name was Nils. Ilona sat at his feet as he helped row the lifeboat ashore. He kissed her on the cheek and handed her over to a man standing in the water.

She awoke the next day in a Jerusalem foundling home.

Her destination was fortuitous, the one time in her life that chance favored her. Two eccentric London dry-goods heiresses, who once visited Palestine and found it too Jewish, financed the orphanage. They insisted that English and English manners be taught inside its walls. She grew up there.

"So where was your sister when the flier died?"

Magda had been blown up, too. She vanished in the *Palestine Post* bombing of 1948. Her luck was like that, Dr. Fabian said. The orphanage saved her life, but took Magda's. It helped her get a job on the *Post,* Israel's English-language newspaper.

Six months after the flier's death, she continued, Ike Battle appeared. He said his wife was her mother's second cousin.

"What took him so long? The war was over ten years."

The Battles had no idea of her mother's married name. They had to trace her through Hungarian records.

"How did they get those?"

Through the State Department. Ike helped out in South America.

Typically soft-spoken, Ike came right to the point with her. He had checked around. He knew about her life. But she was his wife's only living relative, and he wanted to help. He had some ideas if she was not irrevocably committed to life in Israel. Was she?

No!

Her intensity misled Ike. It sounded like rapture. So he called it gratitude. She knew it for what it was: relief.

Actually, she cared little about a new life. Moving on meant continuing the old. That remained unfinished.

Why not come to America and start graduate studies in mathematics? Ike suggested. He owned a bank. He needed people who understood figures.

She needed privacy first. So she lied. She said she was not ready for America. She might never be. She felt European.

Ike—poor Ike—understood. Very well, he said. She had an option. With her English, she could go to England. It had fine schools, and she would not be alone. He had many friends there. She could fly over and get acquainted with his family and the United States on holidays.

So she went to London. She spent three years there, but lived six. In reality, she said, she led two lives. She passed back and forth, as she put it, through Alice's looking glass every day.

On one side: the ordered, serene world of mathematics and higher economic theory, pure and fulfilling.

On the other side: men.

Her ego shrieked at their banalities. Her body ached from their weight. Still, she submitted to them. One, she thought, might free her from her past. For by then she saw the nature of her grief: she mourned her lover.

His image, in fact, became a constant in her life, so she called that presence her ghost. Its disappearance, however brief, would be a signal. She would know then that the past had ended.

So she kept trying.

But no man, however ardent or skilled, made her forget.

Another possibility occurred to Schotten. "Could the ghost have been the child?" he asked.

No! she said hotly, denying a slight on her research. She proved that her second year in London. She helped in the children's ward of St. Mary's, in Paddington, held scores of infants—and felt nothing.

Desperate then, she built an elaborate theory that the ghost was the Danish boy, Nils. A Christmas in Copenhagen ended that notion. Seamen were brutes, she wryly observed.

But she avenged herself on those sailors, the only way a woman could, as she had with Schotten. She never had before. Once past inhibition, she enjoyed that power. Why should she always be the one who got hurt?

She took similar vengeance on the snide, supercilious Englishmen who thought her easy. They never asked what she really wanted, what she could give. They just took. Used her. Such men, of course, were children. How she embarrassed them, shocked them into impotency!

But finally that no longer amused her, either. Then she was done.

The ghost, she knew, would be with her always.

Finished with men, she passed through the looking glass to the tranquil world of intellect and reason. She liked life better there and hoped never to leave. It had art, music, money, and, for sleepless nights, Fundador—also, less feeling and absolutely no ghosts.

Occasionally, an attractive man threatened to pull her back. Others seemed capable of rekindling unwanted feelings. No matter. She made her hostility patently clear. If they persisted, she punished them too. She already had had enough emotion for a lifetime.

"Not so," he quietly disagreed, looking squarely into her wide-set almond-shaped eyes. "Your ghost just died."

Disengaging herself from him, she reached over to the nightstand at her side of the bed for a cigarette. Lighting it, she coolly said the ghost no longer mattered. It did once. Not now. Currently, tranquility took priority. Then, lying on her back, she inhaled in deep, lung-punishing drags.

He recognized the rank, acrid odor of the smoke at once.

"Those Gauloises will kill you," he warned, with the stern disapproval of a confirmed nonsmoker.

"One must die of something," came the soft, matter-of-fact reply.

Finally, after a last lingering puff, she snubbed out the cigarette and turned her head to the right on the turquoise pillow.

"So, Schotten," she asked out of the darkness, with gentle, detached irony, "where are you now?"

"In the casino at Estoril, outside Lisbon," he answered, still gazing at the ceiling, hands folded over his chest. "It's spring, and you're wearing a lime-green chiffon gown, and my foot has miraculously healed so that we can dance under the stars. Amalia Rodrigues, the *fado* star, is singing 'April in Portugal.' "

Slowly, she propped herself up on her right elbow and looked down at him. Her eyes seemed stricken.

He smiled self-consciously. "The banker as romantic—banal, eh?"

"Schotten," she whispered, "you're making love to me—now?"

"Oh, yes."

"But I told you . . . no. I don't want that."

"Then why are you crying?"

His hands went up to her face, cradling it, before she could turn away. She tossed her head, mouthing a silent no as he drew her closer.

"Surely, at our age," he continued, turning her words back on her, "it's time for a little romance."

Her tears came faster then, glistening in the dark, coursing down his fingers. Finally, still helplessly shaking her head, she collapsed across his chest, confused and fearful. So he took her.

Then she took him, twice, by simply locking him within her thighs until he responded.

Ever the realist, he suspected her body acted on its own. Her mind, he thought, still yearned for the safe side of the looking glass. He saw that in her face as guilt and pleasure animated her features.

An hour later, he knew it.

Standing in the doorway of her apartment, in a white terrycloth robe, she said goodbye. To avoid misunderstanding, she spoke in German, a language of several farewells. The one she chose is absolutely final. It marks the end of a certain kind of relationship. With Germanic thoroughness, it looks both ways. It notes shared success and gain beyond cost in the past. It promises lifelong respect in the future. Translated, the expression says, "Live well."

She said that to him. *"Leb wohl,* Schotten."

Not entirely surprised at her decision, he paused at the door of the self-service elevator and smiled, shaking his head in disagreement.

"If I forget thee, Jerusalem—"

"Don't joke, please."

"I'm not," he said, opening the door. "We're not yet done with each other—not by years. Know that."

She shook her head. "Please, no. I don't want that. Leave it as it is. It wouldn't be good for either of us. I'm not ready. I may never be."

"Resign yourself, Jerusalem," he warned her from the small elevator cage. "This is an imperfect world. Who in this life gets what he wants?"

"Oh? Tell me, what was it you wanted, Schotten?"

He shrugged, blocked the elevator door with his shoulder. The tanned handsome face rose out of the gray topcoat like a solemn statue, without irony, as impassive and resigned to the emptiness of time as marble.

"To be a priest," he said.

# II.
# Cowboys

*December 31, 1965*
*Chicago*
*New York City*

AT 3:45 A.M. Howsam squeezed into a phone booth at O'Hare Airport in Chicago.

He put through a collect call to Ukiah, California, identifying himself as "Mr. Banks."

Itch Cohen answered, sounding wide awake. "Speed ain't here," he said without elaboration. "What I say, consider it comes from him too."

"You were right," Howsam told him. "I struck out, just like you said."

"So what are you light?" Cohen asked.

"Four."

"Okay, Banker. You got action for fourteen. When the time comes, send somebody out and we'll tell him how to get the other four. It moved out of the country, too."

"Well, thanks—"

"Done. And, Banker—Speed and I think you're some finished piece of goods. You need help, holler. You hear?"

"If it goes right, we won't."

"You can never tell. We carry lots of juice, 'specially in New York. Plenty people owe us, so don't hesitate. You and that dwarf are in the jungle. Not us. Got it?"

"Got it," Howsam said.

At 8:45 A.M. Howsam looked up from his poached eggs on buttered rye toast. His hair rose in a straight, precise brush. The whites of his eyes were clear and unclouded. The past day and night of flying showed only in his skin. A flat brown, it had no red in it.

Schotten, in the much-admired taupe twill suit, seemed equally fresh. Like

109

big-game hunters who finally bring a trophy-sized animal within range, they could have gone on forever. They were high on money.

"Okay," Howsam asked, "what did Evelyn say?"

"He said he talked to the *bocher,* and the *bocher* said no," Schotten answered, spreading orange marmalade on an English muffin.

"No? Just like that?"

Schotten shook his head. "There's all kinds of hedging going on there I don't understand."

"Like what?"

"Evelyn's very words: 'They'll not make war for money. They'll not be bribed.' In fact, he assured me," Schotten continued, pausing to lift the coffee cup to his mouth for emphasis, "they'd do everything they could to avoid that war—even though they know they'll win it."

"Weird," Howsam commented. "That war's inevitable. They can't stop it. Evelyn told me so himself, not three weeks ago."

"Agreed. But he also told me Israel's a country, not a fortress. They might not even be able to afford a victory."

"But what if it's still on, whether they want it or not?"

"In that case, they'll be delighted to help—but only if they see war's inevitable. I quote," Schotten smiled derisively, unsuccessfully attempting a Welsh accent, " 'Till then, we'll just cruise round on station submerged, old chap, like one of the Americans' Polaris submarines.' "

Howsam shook his head. "But where does that leave the deal?"

"There is no deal," Schotten said flatly. "Our friend the *bocher* promised we won't hear from Tel Aviv unless and until . . . Then, if they give us a time and a place, the Helvetian-Judaic Foundation becomes a twenty-five percent shareholder in 'Lion Holdings.' Evelyn, however, will hold the—again his words—'watching brief' in the meantime to see that we don't step out of line. Frankly, I've never heard anything so high-handed in my life. We're doing for them what they should do for themselves, but there you are. Those are the terms. I don't understand all that hedging. Do you?"

Hooded black eyes narrowed, Howsam reached across the table with his coffee cup for a refill. Then, silently, he carefully stacked the last bit of bacon on the remainder of the eggs and toast.

"I'm beginning to," he said a moment later, lifting his fork. "Sure," he nodded, speaking as he chewed. "We're all thinking like *goys*—Evelyn included. We look at this thing and all we see is the money. The Israelis look at it and all they see is Fagin and Shylock."

"I don't follow."

"Public opinion. The Jews' first reaction to anything is: How will this look to the rest of the world? Well, this time we don't even have to ask, do we? The answer is: Not so hot. Why, can you just imagine the stink if anybody ever stumbled across this? And you know what it'd be, too: 'Just what you'd expect from kikes, isn't it? They're fighting a war with one hand and making a little *Gescheft* with the other.' "

"That's Talmudic logic, war by opinion poll?"

"Who said it was? I'm only saying how things are, not how they should be. Don't worry, though. If they're talking a time and place and twenty-five percent, the deal's on. The Prince of Death, up there in Montreal, doesn't work on cheapies, either. He's one of their big guns. That's how Ike met him—financing the '48 War of Independence. If he's looking after us, they mean business. They just don't want any embarrassments. Follow?"

Schotten nodded.

"No sweat, then." Howsam smiled. "At least on this end. It's those Greeks of yours I worry about."

"Angelakos, the designer, is a child. Our problem is to convince him that this is a profit-making venture. He wants to put every penny into ships. Nothing is good enough. Lianides, the Admiral of the Ocean Sea, on the other hand, is a thief of virtuoso ability. He began in Greece as a boy in the war, first robbing Germans and then the British, from whom, in fact, he stole a ship. In either case—" Schotten smiled as he signed the breakfast check—"I suggest you watch your wallet. They're waiting for us now."

Forty-five minutes later, the position surfaced publicly. It was discovered in an office in the Time-Life Building by Shirley Carmichael, a twenty-two-year-old secretary from Englewood Cliffs, New Jersey.

Miss Carmichael, an attractive brunette who advanced to the executive suite without benefit of college or Katharine Gibbs, regularly skimmed a dozen or so trade papers and journals. Doing her morning's reading, she immediately noted the headline over a short item on the back page of that week's issue of *International Commerce.*\* Using a steel rule, she neatly tore the story out and put it in the "To Read" folder she kept for her boss.

She never saw the clipping again or understood its significance.

Her diligence, however, resulted in the violent deaths of three people.

Her interest in obscure periodicals stemmed from an oilfield poker game played on a flatbed truck near Ponca City, Oklahoma, in 1928. The winner that freezing December night, oil historians say, was a wiry blond rigger with the suspicious squint and tight-lipped smile of a small-town cardsharp, A. C. (initials only) Stiles.

The story goes that he won $180, an old Chevrolet pickup truck, and oil leases on 2,875 acres in south-central Texas. Years before, the rig foreman had picked them up for a song, and he hoped to drill there himself someday.

Stiles, aptly nicknamed "Acey," did instead, although he never intended to.

\* Published weekly by the U.S. Department of Commerce.

A roughneck, scuffler, and penny-ante promoter for fifteen of his thirty years, he originally planned to sell a major* an interest in his holdings in return for putting down a well: a time-honored swap. But after the stock market crash, the majors had no taste for wildcatting. So that left him a single alternative: to "poor-boy" the well. He would trade future oil, if any, for drilling help. As might be expected, he had few takers.

But about eighteen months later, shortly after midnight on July 3, 1930, the ground shook and the "poor boy" came in with a deafening hiss.

It stood in the middle of nearly four square miles of charted traprock. Estimates of the oil beneath it ran to 750 million barrels, for which Acey Stiles expected $3.2 million.

Three days later, an oil company lawyer told him he should have read his leases first. He absolutely owned 2,875 acres in the northwest corner of the Burroughs ranch—there wasn't a soul on God's green earth arguing that. But the road off the highway, back to the well—that didn't belong to Burroughs at all. That belonged to his brother-in-law, Kincaid. Now, Kincaid wasn't going to be hard-nosed about a little traffic coming through if it meant a well on his sister's place. But tanker trucks were out, a pipeline too. The man didn't want his cows scared.

His company owned mineral rights to the Kincaid spread, the lawyer said, and it wasn't ready to drill there yet. So a pipeline would have to wait until they put down a well and found oil. In short, there was no access.

"When'd you think all that up?" Acey Stiles asked.

"Last year, after our geologists had a look-see, while you was out poor-boying round," the lawyer said.

"That ain't legal, boxin' in oil like that," Stiles answered.

That wasn't the point, the lawyer said, smiling. The point was, it was arguable in court. Now, did he want to hang around eight, nine years while the thing got settled, or take $1.2 million and get his white trash the hell out of the neighborhood?

Acey Stiles took the money.

Eight months later, he popped up in the Middle East. Thinking the Persian Gulf far enough from the majors to safely find oil, he bought at cut rate a concession that had floated around Houston for years. His card said he was president of PANARTEX, Inc., a modest acronym for Pan-Arabian Texas Explorations.

With him, as general manager, was W. Huber Garrison. A brawny black-haired Texan, Garrison was as much a roughneck and a gambler as Stiles, and more. He had degrees in petroleum engineering and geology from Rice Institute. He had learned international operations with Mene Grande, the Gulf

* In those days, Standard Oil, Mobil, Texaco, Gulf, and California Standard. Since joined by Royal Dutch Shell and British Petroleum, they are now called the "Seven Sisters."

Oil subsidiary that pioneered the Lake Maracaibo basin fields in Venezuela. As events developed, he needed everything he knew.

Exactly one hundred days later, PANARTEX discovery well number one, put down alongside the sea to save pipeline money, came in at fifteen thousand barrels a day. Then, to show they meant business, they immediately sank another. That, they told the sheikhs, would prove out the field. It did, to a fault, as befitted a two-billion-barrel pool which is still pumping. It blew the top fifteen feet off their dilapidated drilling tower.

They now urgently needed to do some selling. But all either man really knew about oil was how to find it. The Depression added another complication. European industry, their natural market, was all but closed down. So while Garrison kept drilling, Acey Stiles left in an ill-fitting white linen suit and his good black boots to peddle crude. Shunning the majors and their subsidiaries, he scouted the Far East.

Three months later, he had contracts with independent refineries in Australia and New Zealand. With the first royalty checks, the sheikhs called him *effendi* and vied for his presence at feasts. Suddenly he had a business, an oil company. In 1932, Hubie Garrison went to the States for executives and technicians to run it.

New men in place, Stiles went to the Orient, selling crude in China and Indochina. Next he looked west. South Africa, he felt, despite being Anglo-Iranian* territory, would be a market, too. It was.

Sales doubled and organizational problems solved, he then declared Saturday night. Like any roughneck, he headed for "town." In the Middle East, that was Paris. Legend has it that he took $30,000 cash and a letter of credit from Barclays Bank, in case anything expensive caught his eye.

He returned four months later, addicted to Pol Roger champagne, Beluga caviar and statuesque women. The supply of all, happily, seemed limitless—as easy as finding oil—and, good Christ, he had five more continents to search! Meanwhile, he would explore the vast desert interior of his concession, which looked even more promising than his producing area.

His euphoria vanished shaking hands with Hubie Garrison. PANARTEX, he learned, was losing $20,000 a week, with bigger losses in sight.

The turnaround, he correctly surmised, was a major's work. It started, though, in 1929. That fall, directors of California Standard met in their walnut-paneled boardroom in San Francisco to assess the effects of the stock market crash.

SOCAL, as it is called from its days as Standard Oil of California, was in an enviable position: cash-rich, but somewhat oil-poor. The coming Depression, then, top executives reasoned, could be a blessing. Drilling costs would plum-

* Today, British Petroleum.

met, making it an ideal time for exploration. Where? Since all the easy domestic oil had been found, SOCAL would go overseas.

In 1930, company geologists landed on Bahrain Island in the Persian Gulf. In 1932, they had producing fields. But with few foreign outlets, SOCAL was in the same fix as PANARTEX.

Its chairman, however, did not knock on doors or haggle with shipowners to move oil. Texaco, he knew, had good foreign marketing, but little crude. So managements met to form a joint subsidiary: Caltex.* Its purpose: to produce, refine, and sell in Africa, Asia and Europe.

By late 1933, Caltex crude leaving the Persian Gulf helped tanker owners revive the law of supply and demand. Whoever paid more—Caltex or PAN-ARTEX—got the ship. The Depression laid up so many, a shortage existed. Oil that PANARTEX moved to New Zealand at $1.00 a ton suddenly cost $2.50 or $3.00 to deliver.

Tanker rates meant little to Caltex. They passed costs on to consumers. Acey Stiles sold at contract rates. Shipping time came out of his pocket.

That was some of the loss. The rest occurred when PANARTEX crude reached port. Harbormasters kept ships from docks, delaying off-loading. New local taxes were imposed. Twice, obscure favored-nations trading clauses were invoked. As a result, PANARTEX paid heavy penalties to buyers and shipowners, who charged by the day for late deliveries.

Hubie Garrison hiked up a khaki trouser leg and removed a shaggy brown boot. Pouring out sand, he leaned back behind his desk and smiled.

The majors were just saying howdy, he said.

Shitfire! Acey Stiles exploded.

A Chinese in Shanghai had predicted all that eight months earlier and told him what to do about it. He even gave him the name of a man to see in London. But the whole damned thing sounded like such a slick way to make a fast buck off a white man, he ignored it.

What was the story? Hubie Garrison asked.

It came from a goddamned Chinaman.

Don't fire up so, Garrison said. What did the Chinaman say?

So Acey Stiles told him what he had heard in Shanghai.

Then Garrison made a surprising suggestion, based on his experience in South America. He told Acey Stiles to look up the Panamanian ambassador when he got to England.

Stiles snorted derisively, but heard him out.

Ten days later, he was in London.

The first day there he spent in Barclays Bank.

The second day, the Panamanian ambassador took him to lunch.

* In 1962, Standard of California's subsidiary, Chevron European, bought the Caltex outlets in Western Europe and Britain.

The morning of the third day, he vanished into an ancient narrow building in Seething Lane, a tiny alley behind Lloyds of London.

The man mentioned in Shanghai was blond, urbane and tweedy, a former Royal Navy destroyer captain. Drawing on his pipe, he bore a striking resemblance to the actor Leslie Howard, lanky slouch and all.

His name: Pericles Travassaros.

The day before, when Acey Stiles phoned, he took it as a perfect matter of course that a Chinese knew of him. He was in that sort of business, he said. Now, waving his guest to an exquisite old red leather armchair opposite his desk, he observed that he had just what was wanted.

That afternoon, he and Stiles left for Glasgow.

The objects of their interest were nine mistakes committed by the Burmah Oil Company* in 1921. The errors were due to a post–World War I industrial boom that never arrived. Now, like children born not quite right, they were hidden away in a quiet backwater of the Clyde in neglect.

Rimed in half-inch-thick ice and rusted a scabrous reddish brown, they were anything but impressive. But Acey Stiles, who never loved anything in his life, loved those decrepit old tankers at first sight. Each could move six thousand tons of PANARTEX crude at seven or eight knots at a cost of one tenth of a cent per ton per mile.

Desert-thinned blood rattling in his veins, breath clenched in gasps in the freezing wind, he told Pericles Travassaros to buy all nine.

Two days later, Travassaros did. He paid slightly less than $17,000 a ship, or $2.75 a ton. Scrap iron currently sold for $3.00.

How had he gotten such a price? Acey Stiles asked.

Well, the broker chuckled, he rang up this chap Terence at Burmah and said he thought he had a buyer. But the party he represented had no intention of paying wreckers' bills. There was too much scrap iron around for that. Terence saw through this story, of course, but he wanted those dogs off his hands.

Since brokers work on commission, the price cut came as a surprise. For one of the few times in his life, Acey Stiles said thank you.

Not necessary, Travassaros insisted. That was just to demonstrate his worth. He had an ulterior motive. He hoped to become general shipping agent for PANARTEX. Did Mr. Stiles think he knew enough about ships to commission, outfit and man those tankers?

"How much?" Acey Stiles asked, thinking of the old poker maxim "If you can't play, you gotta pay."

"Two thousand pounds a year," Travassaros answered.

* A firm with interests far beyond Burma, where it began exploration in 1886. Moving west in 1904, it helped form Anglo-Persian Oil in the Middle East, now British Petroleum, of which it still owns 22 percent. BP, in turn, has a controlling interest in Standard Oil of Ohio. Burmah recently bought Signal Oil, one of the largest U.S. independent exploration and production firms.

Having saved £6,000 on the purchase price, Stiles immediately said yes. Then it was his turn to surprise Travassaros. Call the Panamanian ambassador, he told him, and have him register the ships.

Was Mr. Stiles Panamanian? Travassaros asked tentatively.

Of course not.

Was PANARTEX a Panamanian company?

Hell, no. It was a Texas company.

Well, then, why—

Because Panama was the best place for ships to come from, that was why! Panamanians didn't give a damn about an owner's nationality. For a nickel a ton, he could register ships and fly their flag. That had advantages. First, Panamanian safety standards were insurance company minimums. Second, there were no taxes on shipping profits. Then—

There was more?

Hell, yes! The Arias family and bankers ran that country. They wouldn't stand for currency or exchange regulations, or anything else that would cramp their style. So shipowners got the same privileges, too.

How long had all that been going on?

About three years, Acey Stiles laughed. Ever since the government got itself dead-ass broke and dreamed the thing up to get fresh money.

Thus, from the New World, and not the Old, came the cornerstone of many future international shipping fortunes: the flag of convenience.*

A short while later, an upstart Greek operating out of Buenos Aires, Aristotle Onassis, sailed his ships under the red-and-white Panamanian flag. He came to be regarded as its discoverer.

That never bothered Hubie Garrison or Acey Stiles. They cared little for credit. Only cash. And by then they were into other things. For them, World War II began in 1934.

Like so many fortunate PANARTEX decisions, that too was a reaction to the majors. For the tankers solved one problem and aggravated another.

Ships could indeed move crude cheaply, and at predictable cost. But they could not get it unloaded any faster in British ports. Nor could they lobby against suspicious, hastily imposed embargoes on foreign oil in Saigon. They were no help, either, in unblocking funds frozen in Australia or easing New Zealand's exchange rates.

Nor were they likely to be, according to Pericles Travassaros. He brought that news himself on the last tanker out of mothballs, eight months after meeting Acey Stiles. Now on retainer as general agent for PANARTEX ships, he had a vested interest in the company.

The word in the City of London, he said, was that Compagnie Française

* Costa Rica, Honduras, and Liberia also went into the flag business. More recently, Cyprus and Formosa.

des Pétroles was the culprit. It was frantic for Persian Gulf oil.* It meant to bankrupt PANARTEX and then buy the concession. Since CFP was 35 percent government owned, that was taken as French policy, English Foreign Office concurring. The British majors were glad to help. One good turn deserved another, and they owed Whitehall a few after Versailles.

What the hell did Versailles have to do with that? Acey Stiles demanded. Naive and unread, he still regarded oil as a big poker game.

Travassaros did not disabuse him of that notion. Still, he did him a great service. He taught him how to read the deck.

Acey, old chap, he chided, waving his black-shell pipe, that's what this is all about—history. The Allies created the League of Nations almost as soon as they went to war, so as not to put too bad a face on divvying up the spoils. Versailles was the payoff.

Now, World War I, at least in the Middle East, was fought for control of the Turkish Petroleum Company, of which Germans owned 25 percent. France, especially, wanted oil in this part of the world. So, at Versailles, the Allies gave her the League of Nations mandate in Iraq.

But that gave her too much. So, to balance that, England got a similar mandate in Palestine, with Haifa, from which the oil would be shipped.

Then, to even things out further, the Allies formed the Iraq Petroleum Company. That gave them all a share in Iraqi oil. CFP, Anglo-Persian,† Royal Dutch Shell, and the Middle East Development Company each got a 23.75 percent interest. A shadowy Armenian operator, Calouste Gulbenkian, took the remaining 5 percent for services never fully explained.

All clear? Travassaros asked.

Acey Stiles bit the end off of a thick black Havana cigar and applied match to boot heel. It took a while to sink in. But when it did, he clamped down on his cigar and swallowed redneck pride and paranoia.

Those sonsofbitches, he said.

Battling the majors was one thing, fighting nations another. He would go to Bahrain Island and talk to SOCAL. They had just gotten a big Saudi-Arabian concession.‡ As the two American companies in the area, they could mount a joint defense. One thing was sure: If the English and the French wanted PANARTEX out, they would go after SOCAL and Caltex next.

Pericles Travassaros laughed out loud.

"You've not been paying attention," he said, wagging his pipe.

Acey Stiles eyed him questioningly around his cigar.

Travassaros repeated the key words: "The Middle East Development Company."

* A wish eventually fulfilled when CFP, as a partner in Iraq Petroleum, moved into Qatar and Abu Dhabi.
† Precursor of Anglo-Iranian and finally British Petroleum.
‡ The beginnings of ARAMCO.

Still drawing a blank, he explained: "Esso and Mobil."

"How in hell did they get to Versailles?" Acey Stiles demanded.

"The same way Calouste Gulbenkian did—by means mysterious and diverse. No one knew exactly, but they got the American share of the spoils," Travassaros answered with his Leslie Howard smile.

That got through. So did its implications. Both firms, and SOCAL, were in the Rockefeller Standard Oil trust. They probably still did things together.* So Esso and Mobil would protect SOCAL. They had influence in Washington. And since the State Department put them in the Middle East, it doubtless knew the current situation, as well.

But no American diplomat or oilman had a word of warning for PANARTEX. Where that left Acey Stiles and Hubie Garrison was obvious. Silently, they exchanged nervous glances, like small boys suddenly ambushed by bullies on the way home from school.

The first objective of his trip achieved, Pericles Travassaros reloaded his pipe. His clients were now contemplating the future. He wanted them to, for he brought more than bad news. The mails, after all, could do that. A letter, however, could not do justice to his plan for avoiding the dilemma. That had to be done face to face, with the timing just right. A patient man, Travassaros lit up, tamped down the tobacco, and lit up again.

Finally he spoke, carefully choosing his words and measuring his phrases. He wanted no mistakes about this. If his plan was accepted, he would sell dozens of ships and everyone would make gobs of money.

Politicians could change their minds a dozen times before anything happened, he began obliquely. So while chaps in Whitehall might not approve, patriotism began for him when the first gun sounded in anger. Until then, he left that virtue to civil servants. They could afford it. They were on salary and had pensions awaiting them.

Already at war with England, France, and the American majors, Acey Stiles leaned forward expectantly.

A few months later, tankers with distinctive house flags painted on their stacks—a buff outline of the state of Texas beneath a ruby-red Arabian scimitar—became familiar sights in Kobe and Yokohama.†

At the time Travassaros broached the idea, Acey Stiles called it a stay of execution. It would make him rich, all right, but he worried about the company. His real concern, making the majors treat him as a "white man," he left unsaid. He needed a weapon for that. What happened, he asked instead, when Japan "pacified" China and finally made war on the European powers in the Far East?

---

* And still do. Texaco was SOCAL's first partner in ARAMCO. Esso and Mobil joined them in the 1940s.

† In 1938 sometimes lying alongside Onassis ships on charter to independent producer J. Paul Getty.

Hubie Garrison answered that.

Silent, dark as old leather in sun-faded khakis, he straddled a chair, chin resting on forearms draped across its back. Seemingly unresponsive to the discussion, he had not stirred since it began.

Leave that to me, he said languidly. When they were set in Japan, he would go out and stay out until he found safe oil. That meant in North or South America, because Hitler would go to war, too.

Earlier, Travassaros wrote off Garrison as being too physical to be much of a thinker. But having saved German rearmament as his *pièce de résistance,* the final reason for buying more ships, he quickly revised his opinion.

Others, including heads of state, would not have that opportunity.

All paid dearly.

As befits a *Fortune 500* company (asterisked, and with a footnote explaining name and business), PANARTEX in its benefits booklet given to new employees devotes a page to corporate history. Understandably, the Ponca City poker game is treated in detail and the years 1934–41 are passed over. More specific with World War II, however, the story proves W. Hubei Garrison as good as his word. On December 7, 1941, PANARTEX also had producing fields in Canada, Louisiana, and Argentina.

"Mr. Stiles," the report also states, "invested all available capital in what would become one of the Free World's most important wartime assets—the comany's fleet of twenty-seven oceangoing tankers."

The law requiring all vessels of U.S. and Panamanian registry to be leased to the U.S. Maritime Commission for the war's duration is unmentioned. Neither are financial arrangements. But the smallest PANARTEX ships, the six survivors of the original nine Burmah Oil tankers, each earned slightly less than $40,000 a month on charter.

Profits ran as high as 50 percent. They were kept, too. No PANARTEX vessel ever shipped a sea under the Stars and Stripes. Legally, they belonged to a Panamanian holding company. Personal income taxes did not apply.

In recognition of its expertise in oil transport, PANARTEX also ran government-owned T–2 tankers for the War Shipping Administration. For these, it received the standard wartime payment of 10 percent of operating expenses. When hostilities ceased, it had contracts for eighty-one such ships.

Acey Stiles and Hubie Garrison had a great war. No one had been at it longer, either.

Had she thought to ask, Miss Carmichael could have had firsthand observations of much that was glossed over in the corporate history. Her boss would have given them to her.

He had first sailed into Yokohama in 1935 as a sixteen-year-old ordinary seaman. At eighteen, he brought oil to Bremerhaven and Hamburg as well.

He saw the rest of the world during the war as an officer, courtesy of the Coast Guard's New London, Connecticut, upgrade school.

Since her superior was flying back from Amsterdam that afternoon, Miss Carmichael gave the "To Read" folders to Mr. Garrison's secretary. The chairman of PANARTEX, never one to stand on ceremony, would have his chauffeur drop them off in Greenwich on the way home to Ridgefield.

*January 1, 1966*
*Greenwich, Connecticut*

HAVING FLOWN in from Amsterdam and gone straight to a New Year's Eve party, Loren Wade finally arrived at his rambling fieldstone home in Greenwich at 3:25 A.M.

Any thought of sleep, however, vanished the moment he opened the front door. A large buff PANARTEX interoffice envelope lay across the top of the umbrella stand, to the right of the doorway. That, he knew, was the work of Balvina, the Mexican maid.

His wife, alongside him, nodded knowingly, handed him her mink, and, unfastening the back of her dress as she went, mounted the broad circular staircase. Still fresh from catnaps on the plane, Wade hung the coats in the hall closet and headed for the large brick-and-beamed kitchen.

Balvina anticipated him. The tea kettle was on the range. The Chemex, coffee in filter, stood on a tray beside it. So did his cup. Smiling, he punched a button in the copper stove hood and went upstairs to change.

He returned in crisp faded khakis and a dark-blue wool shirt, a five-foot-six-inch grab bag of Texas clichés. His paunch said six-packs and Mexican food; his face and water-wet sandy hair, Future Farmers of America; the darting narrow-set eyes, Regular Army noncom.

Pausing only to pour boiling water into the Chemex, he loped across the kitchen to switch on the sun porch lights. A few moments later, he placed the coffee tray on a glass-and-wrought-iron end table and sprawled on the chintz-covered chaise beside it. Pulling the shirttails down over his belly, he sighed contentedly, and raised the two-cup captain's mug bearing the PANARTEX house flag, red sword lying across buff outline of Texas.

Then, blue eyes as bright and frigid as a Wilson's petrel sighting its Antarctic nesting ground, he unwound the string on the oversized buff envelope. Removing the manila file, he proceeded to do what he did best and loved most. He took command of one of the world's largest tanker fleets.

Miss Carmichael, who made up three or four "To Read" folders a day, knew tanker operations and how to keep him interested. So, atop the stack of radiograms, Telexes, memos, correspondence, and clippings lay the item she had found most amusing.

It came in a long, thin airmail envelope bearing a Hong Kong postmark and held an invoice signed P. Barker-Benson, administrator, St. Elizabeth Hospital, Kowloon.

Wade, like all tankermen, constantly cultivated useful people around the world. Peter Barker-Benson was one of his more creative finds. He bought medical supplies for PANARTEX in the Far East. He did so, unknown to his board of governors, on the hospital's letterhead, at institutional discounts. He kept 20 percent of the savings. The arrangement brought him about $2,500 yearly, useful money in Hong Kong, so he had an interest in the company.

He now asked, across the bottom of the invoice: "A bit much, Loren?"

Just possibly, Wade conceded.

The bill covered air freight charges, delivery from Kai Tak Airport, and goods ordered by Sixtos Bolanos, master, *PANARTEX New Territories*. A week earlier, according to the invoice, he had left Hong Kong with 1.4 billion units of CIBA-Geigy penicillin in handy one-shot syringes. Only gold was more saleable in the Far East.

A dour agate-eyed six-foot-four-inch Filipino, Bolanos sold ships' stores. Or so said former employers when he joined PANARTEX a year earlier. Wade ignored the reference. No one was perfect. Besides, smart captains made more with performance bonuses. Not ruling out theft, however, he recognized another possibility. From Hong Kong, *New Territories* went to Bangkok to have a new propeller fitted.

That gave the crew a night ashore with the lovely doll-like massage girls in Bangkok's bathhouses. An avid student of sailors' pleasures, Wade predicted the exact degree to which the evening would be memorable. A minimum of seventeen of thirty-two men aboard *New Territories* would get gonorrhea; five, syphilis; two, both.

High marks for Bolanos if he tracked such things. Wade liked skippers who did. How to be sure? Easy. Asian clap came faster. So the captain already knew how much was aboard. Wade would radio him and ask.

If Bolanos reported fewer than ten cases, he would be lying and out of a job. If he had more than fifteen aboard, he needed additional penicillin. In that case, Barker-Benson would have fresh stocks waiting when *New Territories* next made Hong Kong. By then, the first syphilis chancres would also be itching up a real storm under those naughty brown foreskins.

A half-dozen items later, giving him time to focus his concentration, Miss Carmichael had clipped a series of communications, a sure sign of trouble. Eyes narrowed, he read a terse radiogram printed on pulpy yellow Teletype paper. Then, brows knit, he leaned forward in the chaise and read it again:

PANARTEX NEW YORK
DEPARTED DHAHRAN 0740 DEC 27 STOP FIRST
ASSISTANT ENGINEER B SWINBURNE UNABOARD STOP
MASTER PATRIOT

Hubie Garrison saw ship-to-shore messages in Wade's absence. He had immediately answered via marine radio station WAG, in Thomaston, Maine:

MASTER PANARTEX PATRIOT
EXPLAIN YOURS 27TH INSTANTLY STOP
CHAIRMAN

Unawed by titles, *Patriot*'s skipper refused:

PANARTEX NEW YORK
LETTER LOREN FOLLOWS STOP
MASTER PATRIOT

Garrison's and Wade's concern, and the captain's reticence, stemmed from a distinction *Patriot* shared with two other PANARTEX ships. She sailed under the Stars and Stripes. Her Defense Department contract for hauling jet fuel to Saigon required U.S. registry.

Sailing an officer short in Honduran, Panamanian, or Liberian ships meant little to those countries, or to Wade. To the U.S. government and Coast Guard, however, it could be a criminal offense.

Beneath *Patriot*'s second message, Miss Carmichael clipped the letter, postmarked Dhahran, Saudi Arabia. The envelope remained unopened. Hubie had a sixth sense about what not to know. So, apparently, Wade saw, did Miss Carmichael. Smart girl.

After a deep draft of coffee, he removed two pages of tall angular script reflecting the person and style of Captain Milo Kuykendall.

Shortly after 1730, on December 21, First Assistant Engineer Buster Swinburne, on thirty-minute supper break, went to cabin for quick shower. Entering stall, he stepped in cat shit. Did Wade remember Buster?

Indeed, and with trepidation. Buster was blond and piggy-looking, with forearms on him like Popeye. His family ran tugs in the Gulf of Mexico, which helped him get hired six years before. Since then he had made a name for himself on his own. He liked to fight.

Buster berserk, Kuykendall continued, running around stern looking for Chief Engineer G. Weller's cat. Found him under galley bake oven, put full turn in neck, threw overboard. Witnesses: Cook Wofford Haines; Second Cook and Baker Drummond Sattersthwaite.

Still nude, Buster next appeared in the officers' saloon. He told Weller what had happened. Weller said nothing. Wade believed it.

Altogether, Gus Weller weighed maybe 120 pounds. Most of that, however, was experience. So at 0410 the next morning he climbed to the top deck, where wide, waist-high buff funnels flanked either side of the smokestack. The port ventilator lay directly over the engineroom desk, bolted to a bulkhead eighty feet below.

Buster would be there, Weller knew from two years' observation, writing up the log, coffee mug in hand. Wanting a straight, soundless fall, he reached into the airshaft until his hand was in the center of the twenty-four-inch-diameter duct. Then he dropped a two-foot-long, six-pound Stillson wrench. He scored a direct hit.

Buster never had brain fucking one anyway, Kuykendall wrote. It didn't hurt him at all. He put twenty-one stitches in his head, gave him enough Demerol and Jack Daniels to kill San Francisco, and got him back into his bunk. He should have stayed there a day. Instead, he had lunch and stood his next watch at 4 P.M.

Two days later, though, Buster started humming Looney Tunes and seeing things upside down. Kuykendall immediately had him sign a Workmen's Compensation form and initial the ship's log, as required by law. Both documents showed cause of injury as an engineroom fall. The oiler and the wiper on watch with Buster at the time had no use for him, either. They were glad to sign their names as witnesses to the accident.

At Dhahran, Buster was unable to stand. So the captain took him to the ARAMCO hospital on a stretcher. Then he called the American Embassy in Jidda for a waiver to sail shorthanded. His Saigon cargo got him one without questions. In the meantime Gus would ship as first, and maybe Buster would learn manners. No real harm done, Kuykendall concluded.

Wade agreed. He even saw some good in the incident. That down-the-ventilator dodge was so old it had hair on it, but it might just chase that troublemaker Buster out of the company.

Having provided vicarious sea time, Miss Carmichael now inflicted the remainder of his job on him. PANARTEX chartered twenty of its fifty-one ships, so monitoring the world tanker market was vitally important.

Wade's approach to this Byzantine activity was simplicity itself. He checked everything: the hundred or so men and corporations who owned the world's tankers; their three to four thousand oceangoing ships; the seventy-five yards that built them. Demanding work, but profitable.

In 1965, PANARTEX ships earned $208 million on charter. Twelve percent of that was profit.

Swallowing more coffee, he began reading Miss Carmichael's clippings. The articles came from *Petroleum News Service, International Commerce, Shipping*

*Statistics & Economics,* and *The Oil and Gas Journal.* They were heavy reading, filled with data, graphs, and algebraic symbols.

Forty minutes later, vaguely dissatisfied, he got up to reheat the coffee. Sensing a discrepancy, he reread items from *Shipping Statistics & Economics* and *The Oil and Gas Journal.* Still not finding what he wanted, he put the articles on the wrought-iron-and-glass table beside the chaise and tackled the remaining correspondence.

After tedium, Miss Carmichael lightened the mood with an airmail envelope sure to bring him a laugh.

Andrés Bejirano-Sáenz, counsel for the six PANARTEX companies incorporated in Panama, wrote to announce his daughter's upcoming marriage September 9. Naturally, he hoped to see Wade at the wedding, if not before.

Naturally.

Señor Bejirano-Sáenz wondered about *PANARTEX Panama.* Could she make Balboa on that date? His daughter dreamed of a wedding reception on her. Would that be too much trouble for *estimado* Loren to arrange?

Of course not.

And the girl had excellent taste. *Panama* was built in the midfifties as a playpen for Acey and his chorus girls. Aft she had an owner's deck in the best Onassis style with wood-paneled lounge, dining room, and three three-room suites opening off the lounge. The veranda held a Portuguese-tile swimming pool and a fantail-shaped dance floor.

Wade's only problem was that the old hooker cost $27,000 a day to run. Currently, he had her going coastwise between the Gulf and New York. A year's scheduling had to be juggled to send her south with a paying load.

The father of the bride worried about other matters.

There would be two hundred guests. It might be best to engage white stewards, with passenger ship experience, for the trip. Did Wade agree?

Absolutely.

A final thought. Could *Panama* weigh anchor and make a little voyage to nowhere, returning at 10 P.M. to enable the newlyweds to make the midnight plane to Madrid?

Without doubt. And forget the $1,600 in tug and pilot fees involved.

The night's easiest read. Who said no to the brother-in-law of the Vice-President of Panama?

Finally came the inevitable, frustrating letter from Barlow, Corchia, Chambers, Donchian, and Rabinowitz, admiralty lawyers.

This concerned the *Ponca City.*

The ship, a 20,000-ton "clean" tanker, belonged to Nippon Transport, Ltd., a PANARTEX subsidiary. Nippon leased her to the parent company. Wade then chartered her out as a "relet" at less than he theoretically paid Nippon. The "loss" reduced PANARTEX taxable profit accordingly.

During the early-morning hours of December 27, *Ponca City* had begun discharging naphtha in Lagos, Nigeria. An old Liberian tanker, *Leicester Square*, pumped out gas at the same time on the other side of the dock.

*Leicester* finished first. At 2:30 P.M. two gray-and-yellow tugs began horsing her out of her berth. Backing, she turned to starboard, past the end of the dock. Engine stopped, she carried sternway as her bow swung for the harbor mouth. Lining it up, the pilot rang SLOW AHEAD.

Then he left the wheelhouse for the bridgewing, to be sure *Leicester* did not turn the full 180 degrees. If she did, she would throw propwash directly on *Ponca City*. To the pilot's dismay, exactly that happened. *Leicester* had not responded to SLOW AHEAD.

Nor would she answer HALF AHEAD or FULL AHEAD. An oil nozzle, shaken loose by vibration, had fallen between *Leicester*'s gears, jamming them. An unusual occurrence, but no more so than many that befell ships that went five years without survey.

One hundred feet later, dragging the tugs with her, *Leicester* came down on *Ponca City* in a three-knot, slow-motion collision guaranteed to go unreported in the press. The impact drove *Ponca City*'s bow through six feet of reinforced concrete at the head of the slip and another two feet of the highway beyond. Her stem folded back on itself like an accordion, squeezing the foredeck forward of number-one tank eight feet above the bulwarks. Thirty feet of her stern would never be the same, either.

About sixteen hours later, Wade had seen the damage for himself, on his way to Holland. New ends would have to be built and put on her. But first she had to be towed where the work could be done—Capetown.

But not for a while, D. Donchian, of Barlow, Corchia, Chambers, Donchian, and Rabinowitz, now wrote. The problem was fixing liability. Tokyo Fire and Marine, which insured *Ponca City*, would not pay repair money (about $3 million) until the claim was subrogated to *Leicester*'s insurers. She had several, Donchian said. But none admitted responsibility. Such situations were common involving ships flying flags of convenience, he pointed out gratuitously.

*Leicester* was owned by a Liechtenstein corporation (two Greek Cypriots) and insured at Lloyds. But she was chartered to an Athens Greek who relet her to a Panamanian subsidiary of BP. BP then manned her with a contract Chinese crew whose recruitment agent also carried liability coverage. So who paid? From whom did PANARTEX collect? Donchian confessed he did not know. All parties, he thought, had at least arguable cases for avoiding payment. In the meantime, he explained with barely concealed ecstasy at the prospect of $200-an-hour consulting fees, the firm's insurance specialist was digging into the matter.

Anticipating that response on the dock in Lagos, Nigeria, Wade had taxied downtown to a brand-new building still sour with the smell of uncured cement. Basil Ndhotu, Q.C., a lawyer PANARTEX occasionally employed on the Gold and Ivory coasts, had offices there.

Barrister Ndhotu, a portly, dignified man so black as to seem gray, ignored $200-an-hour legal niceties. Shaking his head at a balky window air conditioner, he developed a sound line of attack within an hour.

Ndhotu wanted $50,000; $20,000 would go to a Nigerian high-court justice for permission to sue the government in behalf of PANARTEX; another $20,000 would find its way to the Minister of Trade, responsible for marine safety and codefendant in the suit.

The legal action would make the Minister, already stuck $1 million for dock and road repairs, Ndhotu's ally in collecting $3 million more for PANARTEX. Since *Leicester*, empty and damaged, was worth less than half that, he would have to look elsewhere. The $20,000 would help focus his attention in the desired direction.

On January 2, *Berkeley Square*, also belonging to *Leicester*'s owners, would make Lagos. She was a newer 40,000-tonner; her net worth, loaded, exceeded $4 million. Ndhotu predicted the Minister would seize her. That had as little to do with law as Levantine Liechtensteiners or flags of convenience, he conceded. But it might get the job done.

Unable to think of anything better, Wade had gone to the local branch of Barclays Bank and drawn the money on his London account. So, while Donchian still tried to pass "Go" and collect $200 an hour, he had $50,000 riding on Ndhotu. All in all, a good bet.

Now he finished his coffee, pulled down the tails of his dark-blue wool chief's shirt, and dozed off thinking it had been an easy mail.

Balvina, the maid, woke him shortly after 7 A.M., and he followed her into the kitchen chatting in Spanish, which gave him a lift. Wife and daughters asleep, he conned her into making his favorite breakfast.

At 8:05 A.M., fortified by two cans of Gebhardt's chili and four fried eggs, with Oysterettes and diced onion over all, he suddenly remembered Miss Carmichael's clippings. Captain's mug freshly refilled, he returned to the sun porch chaise and reviewed the troublesome articles.

This time, he found the discrepancy. It lay in two small charts, one in *Shipping Statistics & Economics*, the other in *International Commerce*. Ninety-nine out of a hundred times, differences were errors in typesetting. Still, he would call Ursall Majors on Monday. Urs would know.

Pleased that nothing in the "To Read" folders eluded him, he told Balvina to wake him in time for the Cotton Bowl game. He would phone in some radiograms and then nap on the den couch in the meantime.

*January 3, 1966*
*New York City–Washington, D.C.*

AT 8:55 A.M. Wade bounded into his corner office on the forty-first floor of the Time-Life Building. Seven blocks to the west, a dazzling panorama presented itself. A blustery nor'wester swept down the Hudson, scouring the sky, giving the sun a clear path to the ships below. Gleaming in the clear, warm light, *France, United States,* and *Queen Elizabeth,* back from holiday cruises, looked as though they were still celebrating.

He barely gave them a glance.

Striding across the beige carpeting, he threw his suit coat over the teak compass binnacle Acey had taken off one of the original Burmah Oil tankers. Then, blue eyes again gleaming with anticipation, he folded back his white shirt cuffs, opened his collar, and readjusted his Masonic tie clasp.

Eagerly leaning forward in the oversized red Do-More chair, he attacked the fresh "To Read" folder in the center of the bare rosewood desk. That, he knew, held the weekend's Telexes. Miss Carmichael, downstairs in the Savarin with his half-gallon coffee thermos, picked them up rather than waiting for the interoffice mail.

The first long yellow sheet contradicted Captain Milo Kuykendall. J. M. Stahlberg, M.D., director, ARAMCO Hospital Services, Dhahran, Saudi Arabia, said Buster Swinburne had a brain. A bone splinter from a radial skull fracture pierced it, causing death at 1438 G.M.T., January 2. Remains reposed in a mortuary awaiting further instructions.

That got Buster out of the company, Wade thought. It also meant getting him home and buried, but that would be time well spent. Fair enough.

Sixtos Bolanos, master, *PANARTEX New Territories,* he noted, on the other hand, had been right, but optimistic. He reported twenty-two cases of gonorrhea aboard. He wanted Wade to have Barker-Benson standing by with more penicillin when the ship next made Hong Kong.

The captain further mentioned an unauthorized cash disbursement. He gave cooks and messmen four days' pay for not going ashore in Bangkok. With cooking no problem, he wanted *kuhol* waiting in Hong Kong, too.

No sweat, Wade thought, Bolanos rising in his estimation. He would airfreight six bucketsful. *Kuhol* were river snails, a Filipino delicacy. He would also send fifty cases of Manila San Miguel beer.

*New Territories'* deck and engine gangs signed off ship's articles in six weeks. He wanted those men swaggering away from the chartered DC-3 in Manila International Airport fat and sassy and in good health.

Flush with a payoff, they would brag about their sunshine cruise with the Red Sword in sailors' bars all up and down the Philippines. Their audience would listen and remember. No ship of Loren Wade's, by God, ever waited for crew as Greeks and Chinamen did.

The next Teletype, from Athens, took Wade back to December 1956 and Acey's death. That, according to doctors, resulted from cirrhosis of the liver.

Wade knew better. Gamal Abdel Nasser killed Acey.

In June 1956 he nationalized the Suez Canal. That October, a British-French-Israeli force moved to take it back. Only Eisenhower's order to stop aborted the action. Meanwhile, Nasser, out of spite, blocked the waterway. Since the voyage around Africa took twice as long as the Canal route, Europe and the United States suffered an acute tanker shortage.

With most of their vessels on time charters for as long as ten years, independent shipowners, led by Stavros Niarchos, promptly cried *force majeure* ("acts of princes, war, and God") and broke their contracts. Freight rates immediately zoomed as the shortage intensified and ships were offered only through spot charters, a voyage at a time. On the Persian Gulf–United States run, for example, the cost of moving a ton of oil rose from $3.94 to $60.

But by 1953 Acey Stiles thought he knew tankering. Finding chartering cheaper than ownership, he sold most of his fleet. Royal Navy Captain Pericles Travassaros, killed in Denmark Strait during World War II, was not there to tell him contracts mean different things to different men.

So in 1956 Acey learned for himself, and the lesson put him in New York Hospital. By November, one month after the Canal closing, his projected first-half 1957 chartering losses topped $205 million.*

Waiting to die in a private room overlooking the East River, he replayed that deal endlessly until he found its key. His revelation came as a final order at the brief meeting at which he handed over tanker operations to his most bucko skipper. Tight-lipped to the end, he said but four words.

"Find yourself a Greek," he told Wade.

Left with an abiding fear of being caught in a move on the spot-charter market as Acey had been, Wade quickly found himself a Greek.

A Manhattan shipbroker, Dimitrios (Taki) Keriosotis, gave him a direct line to the world's tanker capital, London; its main province, Athens; and a quiet but influential backwater, New York's Greek tanker community. Taki had family in the business in all three.

Besides being a listening post, he was also one hell of a broker, Wade thought. His Athens message proved it:

PROSPECTS WANT SEE YOU LA WANDA STOP
RADIO TIME PLACE STOP

---

* A big loss, but not exceptional, then or now. In 1974, Burmah Oil borrowed $650 million from the Bank of England. Reason given for the loan: losses on tanker operations.

Smiling, Wade jotted "Mon., Feb. 14—Kobe" on the radiogram and put it to one side. Dumping the twenty-seven-year-old *La Wanda Stiles*, named after Acey's mother, would make his year. With her cranky engines and loose hull, only a supersalesman persuaded anyone to even look.

The next yellow sheet brought even better news:

BERKELEY SQUARE SEIZED LAGOS JAN 2 STOP
LLOYDS LONDON ENROUTE SETTLE STOP

Justice, Wade thought, was the same the world over. You paid the two dollars and got the locals on your side. At that, he got off lightly for $50,000, which explained some of the high cost of saying "Fill her up" at a gas station.

By 4:30 P.M. he had attended three meetings, lunched with Hubie Garrison at "21," bought a coffin, booked Buster Swinburne home on TWA Air Freight, notified the family, and finished two more "To Read" folders. Now, with the last mug of his half gallon of coffee, feet on the gray metal windowsill behind his desk, he recalled the *International Commerce* clipping which he read New Year's morning.

Reaching for the phone, he punched the intercom button.

"Shirley, honey," he said, "get hold of Ursall, will you?"

A moment later, Ursall Majors came onto the line. Normally the company's lobbyist but now an assistant secretary of commerce, Majors had Harvard and Sorbonne degrees. Neither, however, to the dismay of his correct Washington secretary, made the slightest dent on twenty years around oilfields and tankers, or a Zapata County, Texas, boyhood.

"Wade? Wade, who?" he shouted into the phone. "The only Wades I ever knew were a raggedy-ass bunch of south Texas cotton choppers."

"This ain't one of 'em!" Wade squawked back in his high-pitched Galveston drawl. "This here's Captain Wade, an' if you don't stop bein' so hateful, I'm gonna get hold of Hubie, an' that blind trust that's makin' you so rich an' keepin' uo up nights is gonna be full of A T and T! How you, buddy? Got a minute?"

"A minute? Shit! You name it, Loren. I got till 1968 for any old thing you want. This here's the world's biggest circle jerk. I ran into His Eminence, Lyndon, at a Christmas party an' asked him, did the ship of state ever sail. Shut up, he told me, you don't understand government. It moves by fallin' forward—"

"You're pullin' my coat."

"I ain't, either! Who do you think helped flush out all those Harvard clothes dummies running around Washington these days? Old Urs, that's who. Now, what do you need, Loren?"

"I want you to check somethin' out for me, an article in last week's *International Commerce*."

"The one about Japanese shipbuildin'?"

"Right."

"I read it, too. Their order books are up again."

"Have been for years. Nothin' new about that. I'm wonderin' about somethin' else. You know that English service I get—I used to give you the year-end issues—*Shipping Statistics and Economics*?"

"Sure. That's the best of the bunch."

"Well, *International Commerce* says the Japs are buildin' half a million more tanker tons than they do."

"It does?"

"Yessir."

"What do you suppose that means, Loren?"

"Damned if I know. The two've always been the same. I hope it means somebody hit the wrong typewriter key. You can check that, Urs?"

"Red Sword forever!" Ursall Majors answered.

Smiling, Wade hung up. Harvard and all, old Urs was a tiger.


*January 5, 1966*
*New York City–Montreal*


AT EXACTLY 4 P.M. the intercom buzzer interrupted Howsam's packing.

Turning from the saddle-stitched dark cowhide attaché case on the antique cherry dining table he used as a desk, he picked up the red telephone.

"Mr. Waddell," his secretary said, "from Montreal."

Glancing at his watch, Howsam punched the lighted extension button.

"It's teatime," he told Evelyn accusingly.

"I know. But I flew up to Ottawa from Nassau last night, and I've been trying to reach you or Ilona ever since."

"We were at a funeral, in Ann Arbor, Michigan."

"Oh, my," Evelyn sighed. "I trust the estate's all in order?"

"Absolutely. There's nothing tied up in the will but the house and furniture. Everything else Ilona sold over the phone and put into Treasury notes last Friday. Archie did some kind of job out there—"

"Archie Rothwell's the best. If he were Canadian, he'd handle all my affairs. Oh, that's excellent!" Evelyn said, smacking his lips. "So all that's left is to get everything here, and—"

"You eating?" Howsam asked.

"As a matter of fact, yes. A touch of salmon and Crema Danica. I'll be back to yogurt and Ryvita damned soon enough, when Mummy comes home. But, as I said—"

"I'm way ahead of you. The fact is, I only came back here for some papers—didn't even look at my messages. At six I'm flying back to the Coast again, but this time to see La Jolla Fats."

"Your model railways chum?"

"Right—the *maven*. He says he'll walk everything right up to Montreal without leaving a footprint or even bending the grass."

"He's in this?"

"Oh, yeah. Only he doesn't know what it is, or even care. He and his old lady just bought a mountain on Maui, out in Hawaii, to retire to, so I asked him if he'd like twenty-five K of this for a quarter-of-a-mil payout. He liked."

"Were you twenty-five thousand short?"

"No. Schotten and I each gave him a piece of ours."

"Well, that's very generous of you."

"Generous, my ass. That's the cost of doing business. I've got a hunch anybody who gets greedy in this thing will be very, very sorry."

"A sound assumption."

Then, after pausing, Evelyn got to the real point of the call. "Tell me, Prentiss. Do you think our Greek friends understand that?"

Howsam had spent the previous five days considering that very question. Finally, after a lengthy glance at the darkening Narrows through the windows behind his desk, he answered. "I'd say Arkie does—"

"He's Angelakos, the naval architect?"

"Right, Archimedes Angelakos. He's not in this for the money, anyway."

"He's not?"

"No."

"Well, then . . ."

Eyes narrowed, Howsam leaned forward in the Windsor armchair, as if Evelyn were sitting across from him at the cherry table.

"Listen," he said, trying to logically explain an illogical answer, "we don't meet many guys like Angelakos. It's like you say. Money makes everybody on Wall Street three feet tall. So I could be all wrong. But it's my guess he's doing this because he wants to be . . . creative?"

"Creative?"

"Right—creative. We've got a hundred mil tied up and a tricky piece of business to fix. But the whole morning we were in Long Island City, he talked about what came next—the two-hundred-fifty-thousand-tonners. What's that sound like to you? All he was thinking about was form and function, and structural integrity, and what did we think of his sketches."

Nonplussed, Evelyn cleared his throat. "Well, how were they?" he asked.

"Don't ask about the engineering. But I'll tell you one thing: he's an artist. I know from Francine and Ilona dragging me to all those auctions. He's bigger than the great white whale—with enough hair to sod a football field—but he's got the eye. Can he draw. He may even be a genius. But Schotten says he's about six mentally. He lacks *polymetis*."

"That last, Prentiss?"

"Greek for a head for business. Between us, I think he'd do his end of the thing—including what comes later—for zip. Ships get him off."

"Then why did he get one percent?"

"Because the Greek's his uncle, that's why!"

"And he touched a nerve end, did he?"

"You want a twinge? Try three hundred seventy-five thousand dollars' worth! That's what he figured he'd need to get the owner's quarters of his flagship in shape."

"But whatever for?" Evelyn asked reasonably. "Busy men take jets these days. Why does he need owner's quarters in the first place?"

"Because Ari has them."

"Onassis?"

"Right. And all the other Greek sluggers. It's traditional. So, according to the scenario, he figured he had to have them, too."

"Understood. But how does one spend that on a couple of rooms?"

"If you're asking, you don't know your Greeks!" Howsam snorted. "You priced square sunken Carrara marble tubs lately, or sapele—"

"What's sapele?"

"An African wood for paneling that not even you can afford. Or Scala-mandré drapes, or bidets with gold fixtures—"

"Bidets?"

"Oh, that's nothing! I'll show you Greek *chutzpah*. After we killed that owner's-quarters shit, he turns right around and says we owe him the difference between tourist and first-class air fare back from Japan. His plane was sold out tourist. That'll be $381.75, please. How's that for balls? I'll bet you he's never even taken a subway first class."

"Well, at least he's not cheap."

"Cheap? That's the worst of it! He doesn't give a damn about money, either. Couldn't care less."

"He couldn't?" Evelyn asked sharply.

"Hell, no."

"Then what's he in this for?"

"To live Californialy," Howsam explained sourly.

"Californialy?"

"Like a movie star, with a villa on the Riviera."

Evelyn sighed. "He was the best Eric could find?"

"The best!" Howsam sneered into the phone. "He's so crooked, Lloyds of London won't even touch him. He's beat them out of a fortune."

"Then suffer him, Prentiss! Suffer him!" Evelyn, a great admirer of the bottom line in all things, immediately counseled in his deep, soothing baritone. "Don't be petty. Go look at Ike's Book: Ecclesiastes, Chapter Ten, Verse Nineteen," he chuckled, hanging up.

Rushed as he was, Howsam strode across his red-carpeted office to the bookshelves alongside the fireplace. He hated not knowing anything someone else did. Taking down the old Bible Ike's grandfather had carried in the Civil War, he turned to Ecclesiastes.

Evelyn, he saw, was right as usual. Chapter 10, Verse 19, read: "A feast is made for laughter, and wine maketh merry: but money answereth all things."

*January 11, 1966*
*New York City*
*Washington, D.C.*
*Tangier*

WADE WAITED seven days.

On the morning of the eighth, a meeting canceled, he called Washington. Anticipating a humorous response, he inserted the needle ever so gently.

"This the late Ursall Majors?" he asked.

The assistant secretary of commerce ignored the opening. "I was just fixin' to call you," he answered. "That was no misprint, Loren."

"You sure?"

"That's what took so long. I had to Telex those dead-asses in Tokyo three times before I got it pinned down."

Frowning, Wade peered down on a gray, rain-swept Hudson. "You find out out who ordered that half-million tons?"

"No way. It was tough enough just learnin' who was buildin' it. At first they said the Singing Willow—"

"That's wrong, Urs! Wronger than tits on a nun. They were booked solid last year. They don't have open buildin' capacity—not yet at least."

"They don't," Majors agreed. "And I didn't think so, either, so I got the commercial attaché in the Tokyo embassy to piece off somebody for a look at their order book. He found that tonnage, all right, Loren—five one-hundred-thousand-tonners—but it turned out they're not buildin' those ships at all—"

"They're not?"

"No. Hasegawa Shipyards, Limited, is. They've already started, in fact."

Slowly, Wade spun the red chair and leaned over the rosewood desk as if facing a cryptic message in one of his "To Read" folders.

"Urs," he asked quietly, "who in hell's Hasegawa?"

"You don't know?"

"Never heard of 'em."

"Jesus, I hadn't, either, but I thought you would, for sure. Hold on a minute, an' I'll read the Telex. That's what my third call was all about. I figured I'd at least try to keep even. . . . Yeah, here it is: 'HASEGAWA INLAND SEA PILOT YARD SINGING WILLOW.' "

"They say where it's at?"

"No, That's all."

Wade reached for the ever present skipper's mug, sandy-brown widow's peak corrugated in forehead wrinkles. The silence lengthened.

"What's wrong?" Ursall Majors finally asked.

"That's stronger'n fifty acres of horseradish," Wade told him. "You know that Singing Willow group?"

" 'Course I do. Who doesn't? That's a *zaibatsu*-and-a-half. It may not be Mitsubishi or Hitachi, but it sure as hell's right up there with 'em—"

"An' with a big difference," Wade explained. "That chairman of theirs, he's got a dream—he's had it for three, maybe four years now. He sees a shipyard where you put iron ore into a steel mill at one end an' tankers come out the other, like popcorn. In between, he's got all this Detroit assembly-line bullshit, but beefed up for ships—computerized loftin', laser-cut steel, jigs for automated weldin', modular assembly, the works."

"You mean he wants to change the game?"

"You got it."

Ursall Majors had a $60,000 mortgage on a home in Greenwich, a handsome wife with expensive tastes, and two small boys. He also had two daughters by a first marriage at Wellesley. He took seriously any news affecting the value of the PANARTEX tanker fleet or the company profit-sharing plan. A Singing Willow threatened both.

"Loren?" he asked at length. "Question."

"Yeah."

"If this is such a great leap foward, how come they're so shy?"

Wade chuckled. "You remember when Ishikawajima-Harima an' those other guys tried the great leap forward?"

"Oh, Christ!" Majors chided himself for forgetting. "That was when—in '60? Didn't they even have ships split on the building blocks?"

"You better believe it!" Wade assured him. "They were poppin' all over Japan like Rice Krispies. After seven or eight, I even lost count. But every one of those yards got the book thrown at 'em—from customers, the Shipbuilders' Council, even the government. After all that shit the Japs turned out in the thirties, they don't need no bum tankers. They're churchfolk now, hellbent on the pursuit of excellence—whatever the fuck that is."

"That's in the eye of the beholder." Majors laughed. "The whole world got that religion from Jack Kennedy, as if he ever knew. What he meant was, 'Do it my way.' "

"Regardless," Wade answered, "you can just bet your ass anybody still dreamin' about the great leap forward is gonna keep it to himself. Them willows ain't gonna advertise or send any salesmen around this time until everythin's just so. There's too much face at stake. Here, if the chairman of the board fucks up, he gets a fat-ass consultin' fee and retires to Sea Island or Palm Springs with all the other lucky losers. Over there, they got more sense. They call him a horse's ass an' tell him to go home an' try for a nice twelve-inch hara-kiri slash to prove he at least has balls. So quiet ain't the question," the high-school dropout told the Harvard man. "What I want to know is who's buyin' them five pigs in a poke—an' why."

Ursall Majors liked that even less than the briefing on the Singing Willow. Wade's question said that others saw the future differently. They had sufficient faith in it, in fact, to order five large innovative vessels at the bottom of a shipping slump. Such optimism suggested a knowledge that events might drastically affect tanker spot-charter rates. The last time that had happened, when Nasser closed the Suez, PANARTEX had very nearly gone into bankruptcy. Majors, who had seen that firsthand, viewed grimly the possibility of a similar situation recurring.

"Christ," he said, "I want my mommy. That's scary. You think someone's out there in the high weeds?"

"Maybe," Wade conceded. "Could be a lot of things."

"How long'd we last this time before we went down the tube if there is a move on to rig charter rates?"

"Eighteen months—maybe two years."

"That's all?"

"Sure. Even with ships I got chartered out, I don't have enough to haul our own oil if anything happened at Suez—an' world oil consumption's way up, so a tanker shortage'd goose prices higher an' faster'n last time."

"Well, what're you goin' to do, Loren?"

"I'm gonna go have me a look—"

"To Japan?"

"I'll be there anyway. In Kobe. Taki found a live one for *La Wanda*—"

"He did! How in hell'd he do that?"

"Don't ask me." Wade laughed. "All I know is, he did. Listen, Urs," he continued, leaning over the rosewood desk and whispering into the phone, "you didn't say nothin' about this to anybody down there, did you?"

"No. Of course not."

"Okay. Great. Just don't—not even to Hubie. That'll wait till we see what we got. But if this is a move of some kind, an' we read it first, we may just hit the bigs a few licks of our own."

"Oh, I read that loud and clear," Majors replied. "Everybody's gettin' rich out of Vietnam but us. We got hind tit. Exxon guys are runnin' in an' out of the State Department like they were plannin' grand strategy—"

"Includin' who ships how much!" Wade interrupted bitterly. "They got both feet in the trough, for sure. An' those mothers'll figure some way to leverage all that dough against us by the time they're done. The same goes for Gulf. You can't tell who's company an' who's CIA over there anymore. Acey was right. They're all after our ass—just for breathin'."

"Well, let's hope we can even out. When do you go to Japan, Loren?"

Wade's bird-bright eyes darted to the open appointment calendar on the desk before him.

"February fourteenth."

"Good. Let me know what I can do from this end when you get back."

Countess Tanya Tatarovich, in Tangier, planned a trip relating to the Singing Willow that same day. Her journey, however, took her to London. There she would make $50 million of gold vanish, render U.S. dollars invisible, and effect anonymous delivery in Japan.

*February 13, 1966*
*London*

THE COUNTESS smiled.

Robbie Sturrock licked his lips.

The hydraulic lift, soundlessly inching down the narrow, dimly lighted brick-lined shaft, normally held a thirty-inch-square loading pallet. So they stood chest to chest. She enjoyed the proximity. Sturrock, tall, balding, fiftyish, found it unsettling. Most men would have.

She saw to that. Worshiping simplicity, she applied the principle to herself. Her appearance resulted from ruthless subtraction. What remained, seemingly uncontrived, incited desire. A silvery-gray sable made the jet-black hair tumbling over the shoulders look darker, more sensual. A chaste high-collared white silk cheongsam, by contrast, did the same for the voluptuous body and the frank, knowing face. Authentic save for hemline, it also bared a modest but tantalizing four inches of left thigh.

Her presence, enigmatic as always, raised questions in Sturrock's mind. Some related to business. He had been on the periphery of the 1964 attack on sterling, which she had executed. Just standing there, he had made £40,000. Shaking his head as if in a quandary, which he indeed was, he went fishing for an answer—any answer.

"Silly season," he asked, "or is more fiscal mischief in the wings?"

"No mischief, dear," she said. "Just a little swap, and legal too."

"That's not like you."

She shrugged modestly. "It's a changing world, dear. One must adapt."

"On Sunday?"

"Of course on Sunday! You don't expect me to waste a perfectly good shopping day on business, do you?"

He would have believed that from any other woman. But not from her. Still wondering why she wanted to see him, he tried another tack.

"Just get into town?"

"Yes, dear. Yesterday."

Actually, she had arrived four days earlier.

Thursday, she had gone to Cambridge for tea with an elderly don, a meteorologist. She sent him £1,000 every year, whether or not she consulted him, and thought it a marvelous investment.

That night she had read Commodity Research Bureau reports, which Howsam airmailed. Prizing anonymity, she had another client order *Oil World.* This, possibly the world's dullest publication, covers commodity oils. Those copies, also waiting at Claridge's, she saved for the next evening.

Friday she had lunched with a sugar broker, reviewing beet-sugar production in Iron Curtain countries. After supper, she tackled *Oil World.*

Saturday she had flown to Paris, to a friend's Chinese seamstress, for a final fitting on the white cheongsam. That, she saw, had been time well spent. Robbie was in a state. The odor of sweat overrode his cologne.

As the lift crept past a red 15 painted on the side of the brown brick shaft, he tried yet another tack.

"Jamia's still on holiday in Antigua," he said.

"That's nice," she answered cryptically.

An aging ingenue, she thought. In five years, when his face, chest, and stomach sagged, he would resemble a basset hound trapped on its hind legs in a large barrel.

At the twenty-foot level they came to a stop. Above them, a lemon-yellow steel plate slammed shut with a hiss of compressed air.

Reaching into his green-and-brown hound's-tooth jacket, Robbie withdrew a small bronze cruciform key. Twice he failed to cap its hollow end on a square switch pin within a stainless-steel cylinder inset into the bricks.

His failures softened her firm, determined mouth.

"You're not thinking about business at all, dear," she chided. "You're having trouble with your prick."

He was. The cheongsam, revealing nothing, forced him to rely on highly colored memory. Under the white silk, he knew, lay a magnificent bush, as dark and lush as Africa. But the last time he had seen her, as now, she was maddeningly aloof.

"We'll do something later?" he asked. "Special?"

"We'll see, dear," she said, smiling, as if the matter were under consideration.

They rode the rest of the way in silence.

The building above them, erected after the Great Fire of 1666, was thought by guidebooks originally to have been a convent. Actually, a wine merchant built it. Robbie let the error ride. The Portland limestone cellars, forty feet below street level, held his stock in trade: gold.

At the bottom of the shaft, he cupped her elbow in his hand and helped her off the lift into the packing room. A small whitewashed cellar crammed with workbenches and bandsaws, it resembled a woodworking shop.

Almost immediately she pointed to the freshly sawed oak planking beneath her stylish gray kid pumps.

"You burned the floor, dear?" Frugal men, bullion brokers did that periodically. The flames enabled them to retrieve gold ground into the wood.

Sturrock shrugged. "It was down fifty years last May. Time enough."

"How much was in it, dear?"

"Thirty ounces."

"Did it pay?"

"Just barely."

"Perhaps you'll do better this morning."

Puzzled, but still clutching her elbow, he steered her to the right, to another lemon-yellow door. Inserting the bronze key in another stainless-steel cylinder, he turned on the lights as the door raced across its tracks.

"The family jewels," he said.

From the doorway she surveyed the cellar. Her eyes moved rapidly, ignoring the pinks and yellows glowing through the cold blue-white fluorescent lighting. The bullion lay in $1-million piles on about twenty small wooden pallets casually scattered over the oak floor.

The tiny 3.75-ounce, 10-tola bars which so entranced Gerhard Stumpf comprised the bulk of Robbie's inventory. Destined for Dubai, they would ultimately reach India by smuggler's dhow.

Two pallets held 10-ounce bars that Malaysians took in trade for opium.

Eight pallets held kilo bars for Europe. The French buried them; Belgians and Germans plastered them into walls; Italians sent them to Lugano.

Robbie watched from the doorway, his fixed smile making his lean, long-jawed face seem even toothier.

He really was a fool, she told herself. He thought gold excited her.

It never had, only time.

Buddha said: Now. Confucius spoke of ten thousand Golden Days, no more. Why were both men so imperative? Why did they ignore faith, love, or truth? Because they knew what mattered was terribly finite: self. And what fulfilled self? Sensation. At forty, she saw two thousand Golden Days left.

After this, she would devote herself to them, in Switzerland, in a villa near Dr. Niehans' clinic. His hormones from young goats worked for de Gaulle, Chevalier, and Noel Coward. Why not for her? With luck, they could add three or four thousand more Golden Days. Then, done with lust, she would try food and drugs, and surely die fat and ugly, but sated.

"See what you want, luv?"

All business again, she shook her head. "The heavy bars, dear."

"Ready and waiting."

The vertical creases framing the bridge of his nose deepened. Heavy bars meant big money. Serious business. Regaining her elbow, he led her down the narrow center aisle to another steel door. As it slammed open, a faint flush crept into his face.

The cause of his embarrassment and faintly sweaty aroma immediately became clear to her. He meant for her to see the bar vault last.

Someone, unquestionably Robbie and the wizened old guard upstairs, had humped all the bars into a single pile. Hip-high, three feet wide, and perhaps five feet long, it held about six and a half tons of gold.

An impressive display.

It would also serve as a couch.

A droll prospect, she thought.

If things came to that, it would be another first.

Her smile deepened the reds in his face as she walked to the gold. Then, standing behind the pile, she made a show of inspecting the top row of bricks nearest her, running a black-kid-gloved forefinger from left to right.

"Germiston *dreck!*" she said of a dull yellowish-brown 400-ounce bar from the Rand refinery near Johannesburg.

"Johnson, Matthey," she said of the next three bars.

The firm produced ingots for the Bank of England and owned six of forty-nine sources worldwide recognized by the London market as acceptble melters and refiners. Its mark guaranteed a normal "good delivery" bar no less than 995 parts in 1,000 pure gold.

She tapped each brick with her forefinger. *"Dreck! Dreck! Dreck!"*

Next were two squat, square-sided highly polished ingots. They came from the Denver, Colorado, mint, noted for the jewellike quality of its bars.

"Pretty. But *dreck* . . . and more *dreck!*"

To their right lay a wan, sick-looking brown brick.

A product of the Refinery of China, in Peking, it recalled a $3-million 1961 Canadian-wheat purchase. It did not rate an expletive. A roll of the huge brown eyes, alight with green, said worse.

"Dear," she said reproachfully, "you have nothing but *dreck.*"

Baffled, Robbie leaned against a yellow mini-forklift electric truck alongside the doorway.

"It gets us by," he answered tentatively.

Bored with the game, she got down to business.

"Would you like some truly good bars?" she asked.

To a bullion broker, that had only one meaning.

"Russian?" he inquired back.

She nodded.

"Moscow State Refinery?"

A languid, patronizing shimmer of shoulder-length black hair told him no. "All Union Gold Factory," she said.

He licked his lips. That was *crème de la crème.* "How much are we talking about, luv?"

She shrugged. "Oh, call it forty-five tons."

He reacted as any gold bug would. He grew wary. "Isn't that a bit much for you to tote around?"

She leaned across the stack, smiling ingenuously. "I saved it from my allowance, dear. Mother sent it to me. At finishing school. Are you interested or not?" she finally demanded.

He was.

Russian gold is the best in the world. Moscow State Refinery bars almost always assay 999.9 parts in 1,000 pure and fetch five or six cents an ounce over maket price for added quality. All Union Gold Factory bricks meet that standard without fail and bring one fourth of a cent an ounce more.

Forty-five tons meant roughly 1.5 million ounces. At five cents an ounce, the premium alone was worth $75,000. He had no illusions of keeping it all, but, whatever she took, this looked like good business. He knew another trick or two to make it even better.

"What do you have in mind?" he asked.

"I want to swap forty-five tons of All Union Gold Factory, ounce for ounce, for London market *dreck,*" she said. Those choice bars had been quietly husbanded by Schotten and his uncle, Christian Reymonde, since 1961. They, in turn, induced Dieter von Kootze to do the same.

"We deliver to Schiphol. You also," she concluded.

That way, both trails ended in Holland.

Robbie's freight forwarder would move the Russian gold out of the airport with papers to which the Swiss had no access, Dutch Shipper's export declarations. Her customs broker would similarly put London shipments on the first appropriate plane, and that was that. Simplicity itself.

"First rate," he said admiringly.

Now all that had to be settled was price.

And so much for simplicity.

"I want four and three-quarter cents over market," she began.

He swallowed.

That left about $15,000 as his share of the $75,000 premium price.

"At an average of each week's Monday and Tuesday prices, dear," she continued, her voice assuming its harsh, imperative negotiating tone.

That made him wince. "Luv—" he entreated.

"Why not?" she asked, stepping out from behind the waist-high bullion stack. "We'll have two tons on each Friday's ten A.M. KLM flight from Kloten. It will be in Schiphol by noon. My client wants Friday delivery."

She had no client. She expected one later. The lie fed his greed. If it rushed a commitment, she had a big edge in the haggling.

It hurried him.

"Five minutes?" he asked.

"Of course, dear," she smiled.

Wryly amused, she lit up a Balkan Sobranie as he walked back toward the lift. He would give her Monday and Tuesday prices every week of the year, and then some, she thought, for Friday delivery.

He would have his buyer pay him in London Friday afternoon, when the gold left Schiphol. He would loan those dollars over the weekend on the Eurodollar market. They would earn interest Saturday, Sunday, and Monday. That could mean $75,000 over the twenty-two-week shipping period.

Or so he undoubtedly thought.

He did, at least, seven minutes later, when he returned.

Upstairs, he had phoned a Madrid banker who had open buy orders on Russian gold from Argentina. The Spaniard was now calling Buenos Aires to arrange dollar accounts in London. He and Robbie had closed the deal without papers. Bullion was a small world. It operated on trust.

"When do we start?" he asked. "It's all settled."

"Very nice," she said.

He stepped forward for his reward, palms smoothing the wavy gray fringes of hair flanking his baldness.

"Time to celebrate?" he asked.

For answer, she leaned over the bullion and snubbed her half-smoked cigarette on the Refinery of China bar she found so offensive. The gusto with which she ground in the dark tobacco precluded using the gold as a couch. Then, eyes green with feral glints, she turned back for the kill.

"Now, dear," she asked, "what about the interest?"

"What interest, luv?"

"The weekend interest."

"That's between me and my buyer," he said.

"Where did you get that idea?"

"It's always been." He shrugged.

"Dear," she said with a faint tone of warning, all the more ominous for the mouth framing it, "don't assume. Don't ever assume that anyone with forty-five tons of gold doesn't know what it's worth. What did you think—that I was the Tooth Fairy and that after leaving you all this I'd just steal away? Are you that naive, dear or do you think I am?"

His face dropped in shock.

Revising her estimate, she saw him as a basset in three years, not five.

"My buyer's on the phone," he pleaded. "He's transferring dollars."

"That's a pity, dear, but you had no right to be so optimistic—"

"Bitch!" he shouted into her face. "I'm committed!"

Leaning against the bullion, she held up a gloved hand placatingly.

"It won't do to be emotional, dear," she said coolly. "You're in enough trouble as it is. But I'll bend. We'll work something out. A compromise. It's only money. Do you think I'd ever leave you in a position where you'd have to make a fifty-million-dollar renege?"

He did.

Drenched in grateful sweat, he happily accepted 10 percent of the interest his client's Friday payments would earn in the Eurodollar market.

Twenty minutes later, she crossed the Sunday-morning emptiness of Piccadilly Circus. Disappearing into the Regent Street entrance to the underground, she emerged from the Haymarket side, to hail a cab. Once around the Circus, she ordered, then northwest on Regent Street.

Where northwest? She would say later.

The privacy her next meeting demanded made this rigmarole necessary. She had once interested Inland Revenue. Now, perhaps, someone else. Customs men used strange chalk on her luggage. At any rate, satisfied that no one followed, she gave the driver an address in St. John's Wood.

The first phase had gone well. She had moved the Zurich gold, without leaving tracks, at $150,000 over market. The day's real profit, however, hinged on the next hour. Then, if things worked out, forty-five tons of London *dreck* would vanish, to surface in Tokyo as untraceable U.S. dollars.

The man awaiting her, whom she did not know, had a reputation as a top-flight economist. According to her reading in Tangier, he was also quite ruthless. History held him accountable for 35,000 deaths.

Thinking of him, she lit a Balkan Sobranie and inhaled deeply. It failed to calm her. Instead, her stomach rumbled, and the metal clips on her garter belt bit into her twitching thighs.

Fear, her father said, was the thief of dreams. She had never been afraid. She seethed now, instead, with anticipation.

Halfway through the second cigarette, they turned into St. John's Wood Road. An impressive gray stone apartment building stood at the address given her. She guided the cabby to its rear. As promised, a strip of electrician's tape held the catch back on the loading dock's black steel door. Removing the tape, she closed the door and entered the freight elevator.

At the twelfth floor she took a last deep puff on the cigarette and ground the stub beneath her sole on the highly polished marble. The door she wanted was battleship gray, with a one-way glass peephole, an empty nameplate, and a brass bell push. She rang once.

The man for whom she wore the cheongsam appeared immediately. He was small and slight, with a receding chin and long black hair. His face glowed with warm, apricot-tinted highlights above a somber black suit.

"Good morning, Mr. Chen," she said.

Wey Yu Chen, London economist for the Bank of China (Mainland) and former governor of Soochow Province, bowed.

"*Chère madame,* do come in. Please."

Mr. Chen, she thought, mocked history. The 35,000 souls in his past weighed as heavily on his gentle unlined face as a falling feather. Moreover, he mocked nature as well. The brown eyes, boyishly bright and inquisitive behind the round steel-rimmed glasses, were seventy-two years old. A dangerous man, she decided. He needed watching. Still, she wanted her price for the gold, not his. That meant taking the initiative.

She did so at once. While he hung her sable in the foyer closet, she walked through the apartment. It was lavish, hardly the place for a Mr. Chen, unless of course, he was less revolutionary than his past indicated.

That seemed worth knowing.

She smiled as he turned from the closet. The sweep of her hands and head told him what she meant.

"Chairman Mao must be a believer," she said. Then she quoted Sun Tzu, a Chinese philosopher of war: " 'Regard your soldiers as your children and they will follow you into the deepest valleys; look on them as your own beloved sons, and they will stand by you unto death.' "

Mr. Chen giggled. He did not bother denying her implication.

"Jeremy has a side to his life better left unremarked," he said of the apartment's tenant, a Chartered Bank* officer, who had arranged the meeting.

"But, *chère madame,*" he asked, "how do you know Sun Tzu?"

"I know everything, Mr. Chen," she said, turning from the front window's faded, rain-wet view of Hampstead Heath. Smiling, arms crossed over the white cheongsam, she got right to the point of her visit. "I also know that Eastern Bloc countries aren't buying beet sugar . . ."

Mr. Chen stopped poking an absurdly low white love seat, as if registering an interesting but nonusable fact.

Actually, that had just been a tease. The sugar-beet crop in Eastern Europe is sometimes an indicator of the year's Russian wheat harvest, which, in turn, determines Soviet gold sales. Sophisticates use other data. This she casually tacked onto the end of her sentence.

". . . and I know the Siberian polar air mass has not moved west this year, either. So there is no winter kill in the Ukraine. They will have spring wheat. And, unless the world tips over, a big fall harvest too."

That said Russia would sell no gold in 1966 to buy wheat from Argentina and Canada; bullion would be scarce and more expensive.

Mr. Chen appreciated that. In 1965, he and fellow economists had become alarmed about England's economy. To the West's surprise, they sold most of

* Regimes come and go. The bank has been in China since 1858.

China's silver to buy gold: one hundred tons. By the time the Countess reached London in 1966, they had sent another eighteen to twenty tons to Peking.

"But, *chère madame*," he said to discourage her, "we already have all the gold we will need for some time."

"No, Mr. Chen dear." She smiled. "What you have is only all the gold you wish the world to know about. Correct?"

That put the conversation in an entirely different light. Mr. Chen patted the white love seat.

"Here. Please. Do sit beside me, and we'll chat."

He smiled delightedly as she sank down next to him.

"Now, *chère madame,* you have some gold?"

"Yes, A lot."

"How much is that, please?"

"Forty-five tons."

Eyelids retracted in shock, Mr. Chen no longer looked boyish. Nor did the 35,000 murders in his past seem so unlikely. More than anything, he resembled an angry, fierce little bird of prey. She would eat him alive on price, she thought, watching him rearrange his avuncular smile.

"And where is the gold now?" he asked.

"For your purposes, at Schiphol Airport."

"And what kind of gold is it, please?"

"London market *dreck*." She shrugged. "Untraceable."

He understood and fiddled with the copper health bracelet on his tiny left wrist as he pondered a price. She denied him that luxury, insistently tapping him on his thigh as her voice deepened to negotiating pitch.

"Now, dear," she said, "let's talk privacy and what it's worth."

Mr. Chen's eyelids retracted farther. He had not heard that tone from a woman before.

In due course, he paid a premium of $4.21 an ounce for privacy. Was that possible? he asked, to his own surprise, when the price was finally set.

She assured him it was—in Chinese. *"Chin shih wang neng-te."* With gold, anything is possible.

Mr. Chen would send to Japan, through a route of her devising, $56,062,-400 in American paper money. Most of it would be earned by Saigon whores and heroin sellers. After Hanoi delivery, Uncle Ho would send it to Chairman Mao for arms.

And the balance? she asked.

Mr. Chen's apricot-tinted highlights deepened. The Cultural Revolution was not without its own hypocrisies.

Yum-yum girls on Hong Kong's Lockhart Road would earn it, he said.

So ended her career in gold.

Forty minutes later, she returned to Claridge's.

Sitting on the edge of her bed, still wearing the sable, she completed the day's most gratifying transaction. She made two brief calls.

The first, to BEA, reserved a seat on the 4 P.M. Zurich flight. The second, to the Swiss hamlet of Feusisberg, arranged for her to be met at Kloten. Hanging up, she grabbed a huge armful of clothes from the closet and joyously tossed them on the bed.

She would sleep that night in a stone mansion high on a wooded hill. Its master bedroom, overlooking Zürichsee, held a canopied bed with a three-piece, board-hard German mattress. She would smoke blue-papered cigarettes at leisure there and fuck Schotten unmercifully, she thought.

Now was just beginning.

*February 15, 1966*
*Hasegawa Shipyards, Japan*

LOREN WADE took his pleasure differently.

Moreover, neither heavy rain nor a skittish blue Toyota lessened his enthusiasm.

The *La Wanda Stiles* sold, he gloated all the way down the narrow winding road skirting the Inland Sea.

His high spirits continued through Hasegawa's main gate and to its yellow stone pagodalike administration building. Buttoning the naval officer's black raincoat and jamming down his white Stetson, he sprinted from the car feeling friskier than a yearling in a field of bluebells.

His mood lasted one step into his host's office.

The red flannel shirt and the denims said that the small, wiry man at the gray metal desk actually got down into the docks and built ships. The blue-and-yellow University of Michigan football pennant on the oak-paneled wall said he could do a whole lot more.

His career, Wade guessed, had begun at a secret supper. After defeating Japan, Douglas MacArthur had held several. His guests were *zaibatsu* chiefs. Heads of banking and industrial groups, they sat down expecting reprisals.

Instead, MacArthur sounded a new call to arms. Its name: Economic Recovery. Its goal: to limit Russian influence in Asia. For that, America needed a strong partner. So the United States would aid Japan's industrial resurgence. Summation: business as before, but better.

Savoring the sweet taste of defeat, most *zaibatsu* chiefs booked freighter orders into shipyards. A few pondered "Economic Recovery."

Doing so, they earned about $500 billion.

They, of course, anticipated ever larger tankers. More important, they

found neither men nor skills to build those ships. Developing talent to overcome those handicaps immediately went into their forward planning.

Takeo Kono, superintendent of Hasegawa Shipyards, became part of that
strategy at fifteen. One day in 1946 his father, foreman in a Singing Willow
factory, mentioned his son's math grades at work. The *zaibatsu* soon had the
boy in Tokyo's First National High School, the country's most prestigious secondary school. After that, it sent him to the University of Michigan. In 1958,
destined for top management, he went to MIT for a master's degree.*

Now, standing at his desk, smiling confidently, Kono found his career in
jeopardy. At thirty-five, he had no illusions about that.

He knew this gang of Texans. They did business with whites. Europeans
built their ships. No good would come of this visit, Kono thought. But refusing it would only have heightened suspicion. Hence his dilemma.

His welcome, however, conveyed no misgiving.

*"Dai Kon Gei, Akai-Katana!"* Great Welcome, Red Sword!

Smart little monkey, Wade thought. He even had great color for a Jap:
light Tex-Mex skin and reddish-brown wavy hair. A real *zaibatsu* prince. If he
were American, he would have made Webb Institute, the world's best school
of naval architecture, instead of the world's second best. But old Mother
Wade's little boy, Loren, he told himself, had been around some and seen a
few sights, too, so chances were he would learn something.

Full ahead!

*"Dom arrigato go zai mas,"* he shot back faultlessly. "An' that's all she wrote
for my Japanese, 'cept for gettin' laid or gettin' fed!"

Hubie called that down-home flannelmouth. It worked.

Kono laughed delightedly. "A sufficiency, Captain," he said, stepping
around the desk to shake hands. An inch or so shorter than Wade, he pointed
to a gray metal armchair.

"Have a seat, Captain. But first—it's only a quarter of eight—some tea?"

"Great! The greener an' stronger, the better."

Smiling, Kono perched on the edge of his desk and jabbed a button on the
white phone behind him. Almost immediately, a young secretary in a blue
smock appeared and placed a tray beside him.

"Not exactly '21,' " he apologized, lifting a red-checked towel recalling the
restaurant's tablecloths, "but this is country down here."

Just plain folks, Wade thought. The little bastard looked about nineteen
with his snub nose and freckles, but he bet Kono knew Wheeler's, Haerlin,
and the Jockey Club,† too, all the fancy places where tankermen buy and sell
over fine food. The black Dunhill's De-Nicotea cigarette holder cocked between his teeth said so. Hubie had had one before his ulcers got so bad.

---

* A not uncommon grooming for a potential star who has given the *zaibatsu* the customary
lifetime commitment in return for its pledge of lifetime employment.
† In London, Hamburg, and Rio de Janeiro, respectively.

Kono lifted an oversized white mug. *"Kampai,* Captain."

"Cheers."

Lifting the warm cup, Wade answered his host's expectant smile.

"I had me a day to kill, so I thought I'd better get a look at all this. We got ships Greeks won't even buy—bottoms near to fallin' out—an' my pals say you're makin' the great leap forward."

In truth, he had never mentioned Hasegawa. He feared gossip. If he found something here, he wanted it for himself. Then he could hurt everyone, especially the majors. They were all his enemies.

Recognizing the lie, Kono lied right back.

"No leap forward," he said. "Only the first step. We just want to see what happens with modular components. You know, build the bow separately, the stern, even the superstructure—then fit it all together."

"Is it workin'?"

"We think so. But it's too early . . ."

"Can I look?"

Kono gestured to the wide green-tinted window behind his desk. "Be my guest."

Consciously slowing his pace, Wade crossed the gray floor tiles, steely blue eyes locked on the foreground. Directly below Kono's office lay the largest graving dock he had ever seen. Its grimy concrete floor, eight stories deep and 150 feet wide, extended to the muddy brown waters of the Inland Sea a quarter of a mile away.

A short keel section, dwarfed by the pit's soaring sides, stood at the far end. Workers, yellow dots in slickers and hardhats, crawled through its forest of reddish-brown steel frames and floors.

Four sister graves lay to the right. Their size enabled builders to float out hulls too large for launching from ways. Long yellow arms of Mitsubishi traveling cranes swung over each, signaling activity. Puzzled, Wade glanced back, ignoring the keel section, to the dock below them. It troubled him.

Standing at his side, Kono knew why. The pits were four hundred feet too long for 100,000-tonners. They were lengthened for five 250,000-tonners which the buyer also optioned. Those ships were larger than any currently known to be on drawing boards or even considered. They were Hasegawa's real secret, never to be mentioned.

So ordered the *zaibatsu* chief when he assigned Kono to Hasegawa. Kono then raised the subject that had been artfully avoided throughout that meeting.

Who was the buyer? he asked. An old and trusted friend, he was told.

The chief cited another compelling need for secrecy as well. National pride demanded it, he said. Early tries at new production methods shamed Japan. Yards involved suffered recalls, penalty payments, and official censure. All hurt sales. So at the 1965 meeting at which foreign tanker orders were approved, the Shipbuilders' Council and government conspired. They decided to ignore Hasegawa's 100,000-tonners. Those ships would not be publicized, they said. Therefore, they did not exist. In that climate, the chief concluded, 250,000-tonners, set for 1967 construction, surely would have been disallowed. So he had not mentioned them. That could wait until Kono had successful progress to report on the approved vessels. Delaying the announcement also caught foreign competitors unaware, an important advantage.

But neither *zaibatsu* nor Council anticipated a zealous clerk who released correct tonnage figures to *International Commerce,* or Loren Wade, who spotted them.

That put Kono in a no-win situation.

Pondering the dock, Wade would soon see the reason for its size. Diverting him seemed equally risky. That meant playing show-and-tell with drawings of the 100,000-tonners, which could hold clues to the owner's identity. Kono found none. But that gave him scant comfort. Wade should not have been at Hasegawa in the first place.

So the problem, like many bridge hands, had no safe answer, only a best play. The gamble had to be taken to shield the 250,000-tonners.

A little *aisatsu*—elaborate, self-effacing, helpful courtesy—would make the move less obvious. Lightly tapping Wade's blue flannel coat sleeve, Kono pointed to the keel section rather than the dock.

"They're hundred-thousand-tonners," he said, as if Wade did not know, "907 feet overall with 105-foot beams. If it weren't raining so, I'd take you down for a look. But I've got the next best thing—the presentation paintings. They're sexed up to sell, but they'll give you the idea."

"I never miss a chance to spend another guy's dough!"

Kono pointed to an easel in the corner of his office. "Bring your chair, Captain," he suggested.

Wade did, figuratively licking his chops. Ships, like handwriting, he thought, reflected men. And he knew more about tankers than anybody else. He could spot the nationality of an owner from a single detail.

Standing at the easel, Kono fished a pack of Kents out of a red flannel shirt pocket and reloaded his cigarette holder. Then he turned a twenty-by-thirty-inch art board. It revealed a paining with a black background, similar to those Howsam rhapsodized over to Evelyn Waddell. The subject, however, was a 100,000-ton tanker.

Wade shot forward in his chair. "Great God Almighty . . . damn!" he flannelmouthed. "You guys buildin' yachts or ships? That's gorgeous!"

In truth, he regarded tankers as ranchers did cows. At best they were nasty, hateful creatures. This one even had a black hull and a sky-high stern superstructure. He despised both features. Still, he meant every word. No shipyard design department drew that, he thought.

Then, hoping to catch Kono off guard, he immediately put on a move of his own, flouting tankering's unwritten law of compulsive secrecy.

"Who they for?" he asked excitedly.

Kono, expecting no less from the Red Sword, pointed to the red, white, and blue stern ensign. "Panamanians," he said blandly.

"So's the whole world." Wade laughed. "I am, too. They got names?"

Kono shook his head, secure in truth. "These are escrow Panamanians."

Unusual, but not unheard of. Varsity tax dodgers, mostly American and Greek, often went that route.

At the same time, the flag eliminated Norwegians. Norway's law prohibited owning foreign flaggers.

The design on the gracefully swept-back funnel told Wade even less. Navy-blue bands, top and bottom, bordered a red field. In its center stood a white rampant lion. He had never seen that house flag before.

Squinting, he tried unsuccessfully to read the tiny white draft numbers painted on the bow.

Kono helped him out, further distracting him from the graving docks.

"They'll draw fifty-two feet, Captain," he said.

Another negative clue; three, in fact.

New York Harbor allowed forty-four feet of draft. the Suez Canal permitted thirty-eight feet. By the same token, Africa and South America had no need or facility for 100,000-tonners.

Three more boards deepened the mystery. The crew's quarters, with red carpeting and drapes, double bed, desk, chair, and recliner, were unmistakably American. The galley, however, had a stainless-steel cafeteria steam table opening on the crew mess. Scandinavians, stuck with high wages, used those because they eliminated stewards.

The bridge, on the other hand, looked Greek. It held more electronic equipment for high-speed steaming than Wade had ever seen in one place before. Onassis and a few other spot charterers ran property that fast.

The engine room, in contrast, seemed British. It held two main boilers, the most expensive items in a ship after turbines. Greeks put in an auxiliary, and in bad weather and breakdowns those puny standbys led to many groundings and distress calls.

Then came the fifth board, which would haunt Wade for the next fifteen months. The only vertical, it seemed prosaic at first glance. Its white lines traced the structure of a ship's bow. Perspective placed the viewer on the bottom plates looking up and forward.

The area defined roughly equaled an eight-story building a half-block wide by a half-block long. Apart from sheer size, Wade had never seen so much heavy steel in one place before. When Kono finished explaining modular construction, he realized that only main members were shown.

"Where do the tanks go?" he asked.

"This is the bow tank," Kono said quietly.*

"Good Christ Almighty, what'll it hold?"

"About nineteen thousand tons, a little more than a T-2."

"Sweet Jesus . . ."

Wade had never seen anything like it. In fact, no one had. Kono had shown him the forerunner of a new breed of ship, the high-speed supertanker especially designed to take oil from the Persian Gulf around the Cape of Good Hope. The many features that seemed unusual or unnecessarily expensive have all since proved their worth in that rigorous service. But then, after another cup of tea, Wade left, thoroughly confused.

Profoundly relieved, Kono saw him out. Only then did he note his anxiety. A warm, fearful rush of sweat bathed his arms and chest. Absently reaching into his denims, he withdrew a blue-and-white bandana and wiped his palms dry. His forehead needed mopping, as well. Adrenalin receding, his freckled face no longer looked nineteen.

He had won their little duel, he thought, mentally framing his report of the meeting. Show-and-tell had been the best play. The 250,000-tonners were safe. Yet he felt no triumph; at best, only a sense of reprieve.

No one in Tokyo mentioned this yard. No foreigners knew of the lengthened graving docks here. *Zaibatsu* men checked that daily. For years, Hasegawa had done repairs. It continued to, the rest of the world believed.

That made Wade, with his farmer's face and seaman's crude manner, smarter than he looked, smarter than anyone else, in fact. He alone suspected what was happening here.

Such a man, it seemed to Kono's cool, analytical mind, was not likely to lose interest in Hasegawa Shipyards, Ltd. Picking up the white telephone, he told that to the *zaibatsu* chief in Tokyo.

Nursing the blue Toyota up the coastal road in the rain, Loren Wade agreed. That little *zaibatsu* prince had whipped his ass, he thought. But, regardless, he would find the owners of those 100,000-tonners. There was no dog in any of the Wades, and he would gumshoe this thing to death. Besides, he had learned a hell of a lot.

The designer was the best he had ever seen, and an artist besides. Moreover, he had gone to sea. That showed in the details: the placement of navigational instruments; the simplicity of engineroom controls; the choice of gear. So few naval architects had sea time; that alone would make this one easy to track down, he thought.

Being in the same business, he knew that the operating man was something

---

* At that time, usual building practice called for 35 to 40 tanks in a 100,000-tonner. After the Six-Day War, to make more room for cargo, ships up to 250,000 tons were built with five and six tanks. Now, to lessen oil spills from collisions and groundings, owners have returned to the earlier system.

else, too. Anyone who sent ships out with those electronics aboard had only one thought in mind: Full ahead. This guy, he thought, had to be as bucko as the South Americans, a real gaucho.

What that said about the owner was too confusing to sort out. But one point required no further thought. Those ships were meant for the spot-charter market and to extract every last penny from it. In short, to make a killing. Ursall Majors had been right. He had found someone in the high weeds. No one needed five speedballs like those to earn the normal 10 to 12 percent return on investment from time chartering.

Then there were those bows. He knew in his bones they were meant for waters no tankers now sailed.* But where those seas were he had no idea.

That put him farther behind Square One.

But he had a clue, a "maybe."

Peering through the rain-streaked windshield, he stepped on the gas pedal. *Full ahead!*


*March 31, 1966*
*New York City–Curaçao, N.W.I.*

TWO DAYS later, Wade started back for New York.

He made the same trip, via London, three or four times a year, dimly aware of circling the world. As PANARTEX cheerleader, taskmaster, goodwill ambassador, and salesman, it was all the same to him.

He had business everywhere, and it was all local. To move oil, in Hubie's words, you "got out among 'em." You showed your face. You pressed flesh. You ate, drank, and womanized with the men who counted, on every tanker run, until they treated you like a hometown boy.

This trip, however, had another aim: to identify the owners of the ships in Hasegawa's graving docks. On the plane from Japan, though, the "maybe" recalled alongside the Inland Sea had given way to what he considered an "obvious": charters. No one, he reasoned, would build five speedballs like those he had just seen without some business on the books. His grapevine, he believed, would know who, in that depressed tanker market, had managed to be that fortunate.

Skip Hong Kong, he heard at his first stop from two bankers. Local shipowners, save for Y. K. Pao, were not building. Stuck with low cargo rates, they barely eked out mortgage payments on present ships.

---

* Actually, there were a few. After the 1956 closing of the Suez, Onassis vowed never to be dependent on the Egyptians. He then built ships too large for the Canal and ran them around the Cape of Good Hope. That decision was regarded as another example of his eccentricity/flamboyance. Few took it seriously.

He heard the same in the Philippines. Smart money there went into real estate, not ships, his Manila agent, Ceferino Reyes, told him.

A bureaucrat in Jakarta from whom he rented dock space echoed Reyes. No tanker owners he knew calling at Indonesia were building new ships, he said.

He drew a blank in Singapore as well. Neither his banker nor his lawyer could report local Chinese money moving north to Taiwan tanker owners or to Japan.

Equally unsuccessful at stops in Iran and Saudi Arabia, he flew to Suez to make the Canal transit aboard *PANARTEX Levanter,* whose steering gear he wanted to check before putting her into drydock at $35,000 a day in lost time plus repair costs. Most of the trip he spent on the bridge, pumping the pilot, who knew of no independent tanker owner building new ships.

At Port Said he hitched a ride to Cairo in a Mercedes limousine with a Suez Canal Company director who knew world shipping even better than he. An investment of a fifth of Wild Turkey, however, brought no results.

In London the next day at a Safety at Sea seminar in Trinity House, London Greeks and Scandinavian owners were all crying so loudly about business he did not bother to ask. His London banker, Henley, confirmed their sentiments.

At 7 P.M. he loped aboard a New York–bound Pan Am 707. Tossing his suitcoat into the blanket bin, he loosened collar and tie, unzipped his trousers, and sank back in his seat. Considering the Atlantic home waters, he fell asleep before the plane left the ramp.

He awoke with four and a half hours to go. That left time for his monthly, a multigraphed letter he sent to ships' officers. Tankerman's house organ, profit-sharing report, and travel guide, its hotel, restaurant, and brothel reviews were also widely read at the home office.

Turning on the overhead light, he opened the airline pilot's flight bag he preferred to a briefcase. Then, fishing out notes and traveling two-cup skipper's mug, he hit the stewardess call button.

A tall blond girl immediately went on shuttle service.

"You put four sugars an' three of them toy creams in, honey," he said, handing her the mug. "Then fill 'er up with coffee, stronger the better."

Three cups later, he finished writing. Fly unzipped another notch, legs comfortably crossed in front of his pot, he busied himself with the manicurist's white pencil which he carried à la John Kennedy. Reprising the trip, he decided it had been great, all except for Kono's 100,000-tonners. His efforts there were a total bust. Zilch.

Still, he felt optimistic. Another "obvious" had occurred to him: money.

That was in New York. Most cash for tanker construction came from there. It reposed, in fact, within minutes of his office. Big insurance companies had it.

They were in the business because of that intrepid "discoverer" of the flag of convenience, Aristotle Onassis. He had found insurers in 1946, while canvassing New York for loans to build ships. Banks, he quickly learned, had little interest in shipping and even less in Greeks. Undaunted, he looked elsewhere and came across the Metropolitan Life Insurance Company. The Met had no such prejudices. Moreover, it welcomed Onassis. He helped solve a pressing problem.

The firm had cash but, owing to investment regulations governing insurance companies, few places to put it. With only a fraction of its funds in stocks, vast amounts of money languished in low-yield bonds and mortgages. Discovering a more profitable place for that capital, the Met quickly gave Onassis his loan. He paid a full point above the going interest rate for it, too, which thrilled the lending officers and bothered him not at all.

Having found the money, he soon became the biggest independent tanker owner in the world. The insurance companies prospered equally. Supposedly, they have never made a bad tanker loan. They prefer, however, not to publicize that success. Jet-set Greeks and foreign wheeler-dealers fight the homey images they foster on TV commercials.

Wade, of course, knew everyone to see.

Turning off the reading light, he gazed out at the night sky, planning his next move. Faces, restaurants, and dialogue passed through his mind in free association. In the midst of those images came a mild surprise.

The "maybe" that had occurred to him leaving Hasegawa Shipyards suddenly surfaced. It was still a "maybe." But now it commanded more respect.

What the hell, he thought, what had he to lose? Nothing.

He always asked questions. No one saw any significance in them. He had a reputation for being nosy. Reaching into the flight bag for a ballpoint, he hastily scribbled a line across the bottom of the monthly's last page: *"P.S. Who white lion on hind legs in red field?"*

The next day, in New York, he began earnestly to track down the millions of dollars taking shape in the graving docks of Hasegawa Shipyards. By March 8, he had lunched all the U.S. insurance men and the few bankers who, in 1966, regularly put up money for tanker construction.

Still on Square One, he grew increasingly uneasy.

The paintings in Kono's office said that the men behind the 100,000-tonners, if not tanker operators, were at least on the fringes of the business. They knew ships. Now, unable to trace their activities anywhere in world tankerdom, he realized they knew more as well: money. Anyone who hid that much, in fact, had it down cold.

That worried him. Tankermen gambled. Moneymen did not. When they moved, something was on for sure.

What? He had no idea.

Two weeks later, conceding defeat, he no longer actively pursued the matter. Instead, it chased him. New approaches kept coming to mind. Unfortunately, they made even less sense than tracking down the money. So he thought harder and grew increasingly frustrated.

On March 31, however, he found the morning's "To Read" folder especially engrossing. As of ten-fifteen, the image of Hasegawa's graving docks had yet to make its first daily appearance. It sank even deeper in his subconscious when Miss Carmichael buzzed him on the intercom.

"Captain McCall," she said curtly. "From Curaçao."

"Ben? *Carib* ain't due there till tomorrow!"

"When did schedules ever matter, with women waiting?"

"You got it!" Wade agreed in high good humor. "Say, honey," he asked, "how'd you like a little trip to Abadan next month? There's no tellin' what Ben'd do with you waitin' on the dock."

Miss Carmichael cradled her phone, hard.

Laughing, Wade leaned forward in the red Do-More chair and punched the lighted phone button. He had every reason to grin and overlook the captain's cavalier disregard for schedules and estimated times of arrival. Esteban McCall was making him look very good indeed.

In 1965, through miscalculation, PANARTEX had come up 300,000 tons short of Persian Gulf crude for U.S. customers. So Hubie Garrison borrowed it from BP, who owed him a favor and had surplus oil in Curaçao.

All well and good, but PANARTEX owed BP reciprocal deliveries, and Wade hated such deals. They only lost money. If ships lagged two or three days behind schedule, out-of-pocket costs neared $100,000. Those were charged to him on year-end balance sheets.

Determined not to subsidize Hubie's mistake, he rejuggled voyages to free Esteban McCall, master, *PANARTEX Carib,* to repay the loan. A darkly handsome twenty-eight-year-old Tex-Mex, McCall was Wade's youngest skipper and most unrelenting shipdriver. A self-described victim of opportunity, he was also a womanizer of notable achievement. Normally, he shuttled crude from Venezuela and Curaçao to Bahía, Rio de Janeiro, and other ports, on charter to Petrobras, the Brazilian state oil monopoly.

Invoking a hefty performance bonus, and telling McCall to run flat out without regard for fuel-oil cost, Wade persuaded him to make five round voyages to the Persian Gulf. *Carib* was soon two days ahead of schedule. Now it looked as though she had tacked on another twenty-four to thirty-six hours. With one more run to make, that began to look like found time, about $100,-000 worth.

Wade greeted him in a delighted high-pitched Galveston drawl. "Hiya, Ben! How they hangin'?"

"Lower'n whale shit!" McCall whooped. "Man, I just come a cup!"

A woman's laugh sounded over the atmospherics in the radiotelephone circuit. While not verifying the brag, it suggested its possibility.

Wade had spent many similar mornings in Curaçao. An image of McCall and the lady, lying nude beneath a sheet, immediately came to mind. He saw them in a second-floor bedroom of a red-tile-roofed white house. To judge by McCall's style, it was in Scharloo, he thought, Willemstad's parklike residential district. Outside, the southwesterly trade was setting up shop for the day. Purple bougainvillea began to move. Their fragrance floated in on the warm breeze.

"Is that what you're callin' for?" he asked with mock gruffness. "You want to put a nine-dollar-a-minute brag on a dry-balled old man?"

"Not me, *Jefe*—never! I'm all business."

"Oh, lordy, yes!" Wade agreed with a squeaky giggle. "You're just a regular little comp'ny stiff—wouldn't say shit with a mouthful."

"Now you got it," McCall laughed back. "Who else you know reads your monthlies in bed—motherlickin' P.S. an' all? You still lookin' for a white lion?"

A moment later, Wade's "maybe" had a name: Costa Lianides.

*April 4, 1966*
*Greenwich–New York City*

THE BLACK Cadillac glided to a silent stop before the sprawling fieldstone house at precisely 7 A.M.

Loren Wade, moving even faster than usual, scampered out his front door and across the circular driveway to meet it. Shoulders hunched, he clambered in, slammed the right rear door shut, and dropped his white ten-gallon Stetson alongside the chauffeur.

"Okay, Red, let 'er rip!" he ordered. Then, leaning back, he executed an eager half-turn.

Hubie Garrison sat quietly in the limousine's left corner, watching the arrival over the gold frames of his half-moon reading glasses. Jet-black hair, still thick and widow's-peaked, brushed the gray ceiling upholstery as he nodded in greeting. Sliding the *Wall Street Journal* between his body and the car's side, he extended his right hand.

"Hiya, buddy," he drawled softly. "Long time no see."

It had been, in fact, six weeks and four days.

"By God, Hubie, you're a sight for sore eyes!" Wade crowed, taking the hand in both of his. "I mean, you look tougher'n whorehouse pussy!"

He meant it, but appearances were deceiving.

Big oil abounded with rangy, flat-bellied men. But few seemed more than merely physically formidable. Hubie did. He looked presidential. His tanned even features held all the contradictions the industry demanded. At sixty, his firm chin and straight, level mouth still suggested the high-stakes gambler. The high, thoughtful forehead and pale-gray eyes had the cool, detached intelligence of a Karsh boardroom portrait.

The rest of him, to the delight of secretaries and stockholders, looked as if it had just ridden in from Marlboro Country. The back and shoulders beneath the three-hundred-dollar Dunhill gray glen plaid suit recalled roughnecks and drill pipe. Crow's feet, deeply etched, bespoke wild places and punishing climates.

He had suffered twenty years of both, Wade thought. But not abroad. Manhattan had ravaged him.

After the war, instead of finding more oil, he had sat at a desk and tried to control Acey. No one could. So, with the '56 Suez closing, that stubbornness cost $205 million in tanker charter fees, which left PANARTEX near bankruptcy. Wade took over tankering, and Ursall Majors ran foreign business. But the real burden of recovery fell on Hubie.

With the majors for competition, the rescue took a lot out of him; medically speaking, about a third of his stomach. He left his gall bladder at Harkness Pavilion, a kidney at Columbia Presbyterian, and, over the years, about five inches of ulcerous small intestine at New York Hospital. His last operation took place the day the *La Wanda Stiles* was sold. Since then he had recuperated at home in Ridgefield, on his ranch in Texas, and deep-sea fishing off Panama.

Ursall had shed a wife and a drinking habit, but acquired a nervous tic and gray hair since '56. Old Mother Wade's little boy, Loren, in contrast, had gained thirty pounds. Thriving on what literally nearly killed his two closest friends and associates, he felt fiercely protective of both. He pondered Hubie's latest surgery now as the Cadillac moved down the driveway. Still clasping his hand, he spotted the chalky dust of an Amphojel tablet filming the tanned lower lip.

"How you feelin'?" he asked anxiously.

"Piss-poor," Hubie admitted.

Lifting his jacket, he pointed his forefinger at the dusty-pink shirt just below his right rib cage.

"I got me a little burn right there," he said.

"You think the croakers missed somethin'?"

"No way. They really cut on that sonofabitch. Saw the X rays myself—"

"Then what's all that heat from? What's wrong? Goddammit, Hubie, you weren't eatin' paprika again, were you?"

"Forget it—not after that last time!" Hubie protested. "Nope—Jolene give me this heat," he explained, shaking his head at mention of his oldest daughter, twenty-four. "She checked in Friday, too, just before I got back from Panama. With the kids."

"Oh, Jesus . . ." Wade sympathized softly. That bad news preempted his own. He decided to save his account of Hasegawa's 100,000-tonners until breakfast at the Dorset Hotel, in New York, or even for the ride home.

"In spades," Hubie agreed. "I got me a no-hitter goin'. Three up, three down—not a damned one of those gorgeous girls can stay married."

"What happened this time?"

"She felt neglected."

"Judas priest! Don't everybody?"

"Don't ask me," Hubie sighed wearily.

Fists clenched on knees, he leaned back heavily in the limousine's corner.

"That's her mama's version, at least," he went on, "an' you know Cora. Once she gets that mouth of hers limber, there's no stoppin' her. She'll do three hundred words a minute in cruise, an' she hit me full bore—had me hammered before I even got in the house. What Jolene needs, she says, is a trip to Europe, with maybe a little flat in Paris or Rome, so's she'll have time to find herself. You know, what women dream up, sufferin' around the pool at the Fairfield County Hunt Club."

"That all?"

"Oh, yeah."

"That's some medicine."

"About twenty, thirty thousand bucks' worth." Hubie shrugged. "But Cora's gonna even out, no matter what. All those retired cheerleaders will. Don't worry." He smiled wickedly. "Your turn'll come with Willa Mae in about five years, too. Know what I mean?"

Wade nodded in reluctant understanding.

At first small-town women loved charge cards, expense account entertaining, and travel. But after ten years or so the view cleared, even in Greenwich, Lattingtown, and Short Hills. Wives saw they were mistresses.

Husbands camped in their beds. They were truly at home wherever they could find, ship, or sell oil more profitably than competition. As Cora Garrison put it, oilmen really lived to screw each other.

By the time women saw that, they were too comfortable to leave, but too hurt to be forgiving. So they got hard-mouthed, spoiled the kids, and started spending big. They had to even out somehow, Wade thought. Honey, the wife of Taki Keriosotis, his shipbroker, seemed the exception that proved the rule. But he saw much in that marriage he would never understand. Besides, Honey, he reflected, had more brains than most men he knew.

"So how'd you leave things?" he asked.

"Oh, I went right along." Hubie smiled. "No blowups. I took their dump. Now you give me yours, an' I'll know I'm home for sure."

"Mine?"

Hubie's cool gray eyes rose lazily over the tops of his reading glasses.

"Sure, for God's sake, you think I'm Blind Tom? You haven't even unbuttoned your coat, let alone pants. We lose a charter?"

Caught out, Wade scowled at the button on his blue suit coat and once again told himself never to underestimate W. Huber Garrison.

"A ship?" Hubie persisted.

"Get a hold on yourself, Hube."

What Cora and Jolene Garrison failed to do in a weekend, Loren Wade accomplished in eight words. "Somebody's fixin' to rig the spot-charter market," he said.

After 1956, the reaction was natural. A thunderous belch tore Hubie's mouth open. Then the heat beneath his rib cage reached him. Wincing, left eye shut, he leaned over the armrest.

"You're sure?" he demanded, bathing Wade in warm, sour breath.

"Dead sure."

"Who's doin' it?"

"I got a name, but it ain't worth squat— Oh, Jesus, Hube . . . there's blood. You're bleedin'. You want some water? You want the air on?"

"Who?" Hubie insisted, shaking his head.

Gently pushing him back into the limousine's corner, Wade reached into the walnut bar cabinet behind the front seat for another Amphojel tablet.

"Here, give yourself a fresh hit," he ordered.

Then he patted the chauffeur's shoulder. "Red, hike up the window, will you, buddy?"

Slumped against the seat, Hubie dabbed at his mouth with a Kleenex. "Must've popped a bubble," he said, eying the blood.

After a lifetime of fighting the majors, fear had ceased being a condition. It served instead as a signal, shunting him to heightened awareness. As the partition rose, he gained absolute control of himself. Only the thick forehead vein pulsing from left eye to widow's peak betrayed stress.

"How do you know that name's no good?" he asked.

"Because I never heard of the guy."

"You know everybody?"

"Yeah, everybody who'd build five 100,000-tonners."

"You're sure?"

"Believe it! Now, just cool yourself out an' listen. Otherwise, we'll be goin' around the barn all mornin'."

Nodding as they swooped down the ramp to the New England Thruway, Hubie bit into the Amphojel tablet and listened. At the Greenwich toll booths he gingerly lifted his glasses from the throbbing forehead vein and turned to Wade as the car passed through the gate.

"You're right," he said. "Nobody in shippin's that smart about money. So where'd your name come from?"

"Ben McCall—"

"Ben McCall's shuttlin' the Persian Gulf."

"He knew the guy before, in Rio. He's a Greek—Costa Lianides. He run for Petrobras, same as us."

"Never heard of him."

"He owned three T-2s," Wade admitted sheepishly.

"T-2s? Petrobras quit T-2s ten, twelve years ago."

"Not his."

"Oh, c'mon. Loren! How in hell could anyone use those old spitkits?"

"On nickel-and-dime coastwise hauls. The story is, neither of the two he run were in Rio a week a year. They were always back in the weeds. The third he stripped for spares."

"I never heard of any crazy deal like that!"

"Neither did I." Wade smiled. "But we never boffed a provincial governor's daughter to get a charter, neither."

"He's a womanizer?"

"Lianides? Ben says he'd fuck a snake, you hold the poor thing's mouth open! Had himself a penthouse higher'n Christ of the Andes—overlookin' the Jockey Club an' Rodrigo de Freitas Lagoon—an' the whole shebang was always decks awash in politicians and jism."

"He's not there anymore?"

Wade shook his head. "He turned U-boat commander."

"Had a little accident, did he?"

"Ever know a Greek with insurance who didn't? Last May he run his two workin' ships into each other in the River Plate. You know how tough that is? First, you gotta be some kind of genius to even find anythin' in those mornin' fogs down there. Then, to collide without hurtin' anybody, you gotta be a double genius. Well, Lianides did it—without radar, loran, or anythin' else. That's what we're up against—"

"What'd the insurance pay?"

"Ben thinks about a million."

"Shit!" Hubie complained. "He ain't the money."

" 'Course not," Wade agreed. "He ain't a pimple on the money's ass. What I saw at Hasegawa looked like eighty, ninety million bucks' worth. That's part of what boogered me all weekend—"

A man who noted buttoned suit coats used all of his senses. "Part?"

"Take a brace," Wade warned softly. "That sonofabitch may be right here in New York."

Hubie belched again. His mind, however, raced ahead with customary Red Sword bucko. "New York!" he panted, not questioning how or why Wade had reached that conclusion. "What'd you do?"

"What the fuck *could* I do?" Wade shot back, voice squeaking as he vented the anxiety he had lived with since New Year's Day. "I didn't hear from Ben till Thursday, an' I ain't no detective. So I looked in the phone book. An' you know what? There ain't a goddamned Lianides in it!"

Eyes shut, head resting again on the seat back, Hubie reached over the arm-rest and tapped Wade's thigh consolingly.

"You got all that from McCall?"

"Right. Ben run into him in Rio last July—just after he got his insurance check—absolutely dipped in shit. He's even sold his third wreck to some Athens Greek. Said he was leavin' to deliver it the next week. After that he was comin' to New York, to get sharp, he said. He had relatives here—"

"You believe that?"

"Not for a minute! Not after what I seen in Japan. No, sir! He don't have time for no relations."

"So why would he come here?"

"To see the money?" Wade asked.

"I wonder. You didn't go to Taki with this, did you?"

"Oh, Christ, no! Our general agent or not, Taki's the last guy I'd talk to. If him or any of the Keriosotises ever found another Greek in a deal like this, you'd never know what they'd cook up. Deep down, they're all brothers. You get two of 'em together, an' right away it's 'us' against 'them.' "

"No question. So what's next?"

"I got a trip to B.A. to do in May, so I thought I'd move it up a few weeks an' stop off in Panama. You know, give things a short obsquintical."

"Do that, you'll disappear up your own asshole," Hubie warned. "Anybody smart enough to buy Panamanian flags already knows the whole bit. All you'd find is dummy companies an' untraceable bearer shares. Besides that, Panama's a small place. You'd raise dust."

"Okay, then. You tell me what to do."

Shaking his head, Hubie looked out of the Cadillac at Scarsdale's center-hall Colonials. Unable to reconcile them with 500,000 tons of rogue tankers or an invisible Greek U-boat commander, he turned away. The possible promptly claimed his attention. Reaching into the bar cabinet, he withdrew a large brown Maalox bottle. Uncapping it, he took a long pull.

"Jesus," he sighed, glancing down at his pink shirt, "what am I doin' here? I'm all sweated through."

That, for him, was an orgy of self-pity. After a moment's indulgence he reached into Wade's lapel pocket for the manicurist's white pencil. Then, silently, eyes narrowed, he set to work on his fingernails.

Never having tracked a man before, he pondered the next step all the way into Manhattan. The problem, he quickly saw, had two parts. Both were difficult. But only the first dealt directly with Costa Lianides. He had told Ben

McCall nine months before that he would come to New York. He could have. But where was he now? More important, could he be found without alarming him?

After frequent recourse to Maalox, Hubie had the answer. Finally, over his soft-boiled egg in the Dorset Hotel's dining room, he let Wade in on it.

"Call Urs," he said.

"Urs!" Wade yelped across the white tablecloth. "Urs don't know shit about money, neither! He's down brown-nosin' in Washington."

"That's the point."

"I don't get it."

Hubie drew him a picture.

A few minutes later, as the elevator rose in the Time-Life Building, he did even better. He remembered why he was still in the oil business, sweating through thirty-five-dollar Custom Shop shirts.

"You, me, Urs—that's all who know about this, right?" he asked.

"Right."

"Let's see it stays that way," Hubie said through his level, unblinking gunfighter's stare. "If this is what we think it is, I want it all—every bit of it—so's I can share it with my pals. You know—spread around a few belly burns of my own. Get what I mean?"

He lit fires sooner than he knew.

*April 25, 1966*
*New York City–Montreal*

HOWSAM FELT the heat first.

Downing his *café solo* in a gulp, he cradled the red telephone and immediately refilled the cup. Speaking to Courtney Montgomery anytime, he thought, automatically called for seconds. Now, if he had not drained the small aluminum espresso pot, he would have gone for thirds.

Drumming his fingers on the antique cherry table, he picked up the phone again and told his secretary to get Montreal. Then, leaning forward as if to pounce, he finished the coffee and waited for the call to go through. When it did, he wasted no time on salutations.

"Are you ready for this?" he asked.

"Ready?" Evelyn Waddell chuckled.

" 'I will render vengeance to mine enemies and reward them that hate me,' " he intoned with mock solemnity. " 'I will make mine arrows drunk with blood, and my sword shall devour flesh—'

"That's Deuteronomy, Chapter Thirty-two, Verses Forty-one and Forty-two, and it's not funny, Evelyn! The Greek's been blown."

"But I gathered that happens daily—"

"Not by *los Federales,* it doesn't!"

"Oh, dear. It's not just another bout of Hellenic *joie de vivre* that ran afoul of the law?"

"Not on your life. Tuesday he showed up here—and that's *verboten*—with two of the goddamnedest forms I ever saw in my life. IRS sent one, Immigration the other."

"But those could have been routine, Prentiss."

"No way. All the years Jorge, my assistant, was a resident alien, he never got either."

"That does sound ominous," Evelyn agreed. "I'll ring up Home Office," he went on, alluding to the Israelis, "and try to find out what happened."

"Don't bother. We already know. What happened is, we've drawn a crowd. On April fifth, a guy down in Washington named Ursall Majors initiated inquiries with the Justice Department and IRS."

"Oh? Where'd you learn all that?"

"I called the winemaker's lawyer."

"You did? Him? Whatever for?"

"Because every one of his firm's juniors goes to Washington—to learn the ropes from the inside and to buddy up with the civil-service stiffs who'll be there forever. They're wired into every department."

"First rate, Prentiss! That'll keep Home Office out of it entirely. But what did our Greek chum think of all that sudden interest?"

"Think!" Howsam exploded in the high-decibel roar he reserved for mention of Costa Lianides. "When did he ever think? He came in, took one look at Ilona's tits, and his tongue swelled up so he could hardly talk! Security aside, that's why I won't have him here. It's tough enough getting sense out of him anytime, but when a skirt's around—"

"Oh, I know, I know," Evelyn sympathized.

Never having met Lianides, he did not know. He had, however, heard Howsam on the subject. The Washington intelligence confirmed, he pressed for details in his clubby conversational manner.

"But tell me, Prentiss," he asked, "who's this man Majors?"

"An assistant secretary of commerce. In real life he's vice-president of foreign operations for PANARTEX—"

"By crikey, that's familiar—but I can't place it."

"You're not supposed to. The lawyer says the guys running it specialize in keeping their heads down. They come on like poor Texas cowboys always trying to stay a step ahead of the sheriff. The fact is, though, they're small to medium in oil but big in tankers. They own more than Onassis."

"Poor cowboys indeed. Have they Middle Eastern oil, Prentiss?"

"Plenty. They were one of the first American outfits there in the thirties, but ARAMCO and the war got in the way."

"And Majors is an assistant secretary. Isn't that just a notch below cabinet level?"

"Right, but that title only proves they're the turds in the punch bowl. If they had real clout in oil, Majors'd be in the Department of the Interior with all the rest of the hondlers, angling around for mineral rights and defense contracts. The lawyer says that appointment was probably the cheapest way LBJ could pay off a campaign gift."

"They sound able, nonetheless."

"For sure! And they'd better be. How'd you like big oil on one side of you and every sleazy tanker owner in the world on the other? And chances are," Howsam went on, "those yahoos are smarter than all of them. It could be they found us in February."

"How did you find out?"

"From the dwarf. His pals out East told him a guy named Wade—the cowboys' tanker honcho—came calling. They swore up and down, though, he didn't get anything."

"Well," Evelyn mused, snickering, as always, at the code name that Itch Cohen had unwittingly provided for Schotten, "so much for invisibility. But that's nothing to panic over, either. All they've found, apparently, is a name. And none of us ever dreamt we'd keep all our secrets forever, anyway. It can't be done—the nasty things are just too bloody big. The important thing is that you and the dwarf—and what happens next—be kept in the shade, and that looks safe. But, Prentiss, I do wish you would have told me about that visit as soon as you heard of it," he gently chided.

Howsam testily defended his and Schotten's reaction to Wade's Hasegawa visit. Practical bankers made a fine art of calculating probability.

"Hey, c'mon!" he objected. "Don't give me that twenty-twenty hindsight cloak-and-dagger crap. He had a perfectly natural right to be there. Those guys are always shopping around for new equipment. Besides, how do you tell a something from a nothing?"

Evelyn, who dealt only in certainty, told him. "My point exactly," he said. "One can't. So one always assumes the worst. Overkill's the first order of business in this game. Understood, Prentiss?"

Howsam grunted reluctantly.

"Now, where was it you said the cowboys had their Middle Eastern oil?" Evelyn asked out of the lengthening silence.

"I didn't!" Howsam snapped, still smarting at the earlier rebuff. "But it's in the Persian Gulf."

"I see. Prentiss . . ."

"Yeah?"

"I wonder if you'd be a good chap and do me a small favor."

"What?"

"Put me in touch with the winemaker's partner. I'd love a little chat, and I'll go wherever he—"

The soft, wheedling tone seethed with longing. The image of Itch Cohen, with his piercing, chrome-plated glare and oversized shark's dentures, seemed equally ominous. Howsam, who had committed himself to a risky, offbeat position, but not to murder, reacted violently.

"Whoa, there! Hold on!" he shouted. "Nothing's happened yet—remember? All they've got is a name."

Evelyn sighed, an understanding minister instructing a strayed member of the flock. The sin, in this case, was a refusal to face up to the obvious.

"Those are resourceful chaps, Prentiss," he patiently pointed out, "with powerful allies."

"Who?" Howsam demanded. "The lawyer says they've been at war with big oil for thirty years and they're just hanging on by their fingernails."

"Believe me, they've friends. But that'll wait till we get together. You know nothing of the politics involved. Just be a good chap and arrange a meeting, will you? Being prepared is never wrong, Prentiss."

"Well, I don't like it. Not that way."

"Nor I," Evelyn agreed heartily.

But motives, rather than murder, worried him.

"Remember," he said, "we've not a clue to the cowboys' intentions, and till we do we can't afford to guess. That little graveyard behind the Church of the Unwarranted Assumption is already full up with cockeyed optimists, thank you. Trust me, Prentiss. Trust me, and mark my words. We've not heard the last of Messrs. Majors and Wade."

"You think they're coming after us?"

"Oh, absolutely! I know it in my bones. They've not survived thirty years in that game being casual." A nicely turned phrase underlined the argument with wit and grace: " 'Swift instinct leaps; slow reason feebly climbs.' "

Unable to dispute the thought, Howsam impugned the source. "You bastard, you!" he shouted. "You made that up yourself."

"Oh, no. Not at all. That's from a chap named Edward Young."

"But who's he?"

"I dunno, but I read it somewhere," Evelyn chuckled sheepishly, putting down the phone.

Loren Wade, whose reading was solely determined by Shirley Carmichael, did not know, either. Nor would he have agreed. As he wrestled with more facts than Evelyn or Howsam realized, neither instinct nor reason so much as twitched for him. Pensively raising the two-cup skipper's mug behind the rosewood desk in his office, he saw the upcoming weekend as the only factor in his favor. It gave him two more days to make some kind of sense out of Ursall Majors' findings. Fortunately, he thought, Hubie had vanished for parts unknown earlier in the week after receiving a mysterious phone call. For once, Wade had absolutely no difficulty containing his curiosity.

*April 28, 1966*
*Greenwich–New York City*

MOUTH SET in the tense, watchful lines of a five-card stud player calling a four flush, Hubie Garrison observed Wade's entry into the Cadillac.

Blue Dunhill suit aside, Hubie projected little of the boardroom and less of Marlboro Country. He looked, in fact, like an affluent drunk in the throes of terminal hangover. The purplish forehead vein bulged ominously. Sweat darkened the yellow shirt collar. The uncapped Maalox bottle in his right hand completed the picture.

But Hubie did not drink. Ever. So his condition, Wade guessed, stemmed from his mysterious trip of the previous week.

"Good Christ Almighty, Hube," Wade squawked, anxiety pinching his voice to its highest pitch, "I seen better heads on pus! What happened to you? I mean, where'd you have to go to get yourself into that kind of shape?"

"To hell an' back," Hubie sighed as the car started down the driveway, "an' runnin' harder'n a turkey through the corn."

"But where, exactly, was that?"

"Vancouver."

That meant nothing to Wade. Still, he used it.

"They got the best roast beef an' Yorkshire puddin' in the world there," he said, shooting a line, "in a place called the Georgia—"

"Are you nuts?" Hubie snapped, recalling his diet of baby food. "I'm not even up to the Beech-Nut chicken and rice dinner yet! All I had was oatmeal, with a little nutmeg to spice it up. Caskie ate the beef—"

Sympathy promptly gave way to self-interest. "That little pissant!" Wade complained at mention of Caskie Horne, the PANARTEX vice-president in charge of exploration. "Every time he shows up, you get drillin' fever, an' I lose me some ships. What'd he do now, bring in more dusters—or just find a fresh spot where he'd like to? And what's he so proud of, you had to haul ass to Vancouver?"

"That was so's we wouldn't be seen."

" 'So's we wouldn't be seen.' Christ on a bicycle, all he had to do was fly home! He's got an office right here in New York, just like the rest of us peons."

"The bigs were onto him," Hubie said, lowering his voice despite the glass partition behind the chauffeur. "A whole damned gang of their Ivy League rock knockers is chasin' him, wonderin' what he found. Fact is, he's into more crude than the Shah of I-ran. He didn't want it to look like he was comin' home to report."

"In Canada? There's nothin' in Canada everyone don't already know about—includin' Eskimos and Renfrew of the Royal Fuckin' Mounties!"

"Caskie wasn't in Canada," Hubie said.

"No?"

"No."

Squinting, Hubie pushed the gold-rimmed reading glasses up into his black hair. Then, measuring Wade, he reached into his coat pocket and handed over a sheaf of the buff-colored onionskin sheets that oil companies use for geological reports and surveys.

"Caskie wants to do a little leasin'," he said.

Skipping the charts, Wade concentrated on the text. The report made curious reading. It omitted place names. Regardless, Horne wanted to lease several hundred square miles, millions of acres. He had located three distinct fields, he said. He strongly suspected there might be a fourth, but much deeper than he had probed.

Wade knew just enough about drilling and recovery to see that this could well be the world's most costly crude. He also knew Hubie. Like all geologists, he just plain loved to find oil. It thrilled him. Many times, that craving for discovery had gotten in the way of profit. This situation, with its secret meeting, report without names, and chance to screw the majors, had all the makings of just such a case.

Still, things could be worse. Acey would bet the whole company on a parlay like that, Wade thought. With that small consolation, he handed back the buff sheets.

"So what's all this hope gonna cost us?" he asked.

Grimacing, Hubie muffled a belch. "Caskie says forty-five million dollars for leasin', sonar shoots, an' core samplin'. Then megabucks—maybe two billion dollars before we pump pee-drop one of crude—"

"Oh, Christ . . ." They were back to Acey's round of showdown, Wade thought. The only difference was, Hubie would play the hand. Even the bet, despite nine zeros, remained the same: all or nothing.

Neither winning nor losing fazed Wade. He feared only losing his "motion."

A true tankerman, he roamed the world with godlike disdain for time and space. He craved constant movement, the excitement of arrivals and departures, rapid changes of plan. Eating, drinking, and scheming were bonuses. All reinforced a favorite cliché. Rich men held the tickets, but he was seeing the show. Facing that loss, he glanced at Hubie.

Hubie, he decided, was something else. Doctors might have taken most of his stomach, but they never touched his guts. His face had enough *High Noon* in it to make Jack Palance sing soprano. His manner, too.

"You don't like it, gimme an out," he told Wade. "If the bigs beat us to that crude, they'll drown us in it. They'll leverage us on price—not only here, but all over. So, if we don't have both feet in the trough when pumpin' starts, it's all she wrote, buddy."

"Sweet Jesus . . . what are we gonna do?"

Hubie shrugged. "What else can we do? It's like stud. If you got a call, you got a raise. I told Caskie to start leasin'. If we don't, I see us goin' down the tube in maybe ten, twelve years—somewheres in there."

"But, Hube, where's the two billion dollars comin' from?"

The purple forehead vein, puffed finger-thick now beneath Hubie's faded Panamanian tan, pulsed clearly. "That's my mornin' problem," he said.

Wade could only sympathize. "Lordy," he said, "I got in thinkin' all you had on your mind was Jolene, but I was scared to ask."

Hubie's macho smile vanished abruptly. "No, that's all settled. She an' Cora left yesterday for Rome. Before I got back."

"I thought they was goin' to Paris."

"They decided Rome had a better ambience."

Two years of Texas high-school English gave Wade a vocabulary he found ample anywhere in the world but in Greenwich. There, the brokers, executives, and lawyers who were his neighbors thought him quaint. Hearing one of their words, he promptly threw in the sponge.

"Ambience?" he repeated.

Hubie, after forty years around oilfields and tankers, knew how to put the Fairfield County lexicon into old, simple words. "What that means is Jolene wants to try herself a few Guinea muff-divers, too," he said.

Wade declined comment. Hubie nodded understandingly, as if wishing he could do the same. "That's Darlene's word," he added, naming his middle daughter, who, after a brief stay in Paris following her divorce, had left for Rome. "Darlene's real sophisticated now," he observed. "Urs says she's even gettin' known down there in Washington—an' not only in our office. Just don't ask me at what."

This time Wade took refuge in a question. "What's Cora say to that?"

" 'Real neat,' " Hubie answered. "She thinks girls should kick up their heels. You know, have experiences. Yes, sir . . . 'real neat,' " he mused, slowly shaking his head as if biting into something excruciatingly sour. "Can you feature that comin' out of the mouth of a fifty-two-year-old woman?"

Stretched out, feet on the jump seat before him, he spoke in a tired monotone, looking straight ahead, like a patient on an analyst's couch.

"The girls can get away with anythin', she says. So why not? They can't get hurt. We're upper-class now—heavy money. That's the East for you, with its 'background' an' 'breedin'' bullshit—bucks. Christ, who in Port Arthur ever talked about class? There wasn't any in the whole goddamned town, an' none of us ever went lookin' for it, either! But a mother of girls, she talked that way, she'd damned well get her butt shipped, an' that's what got me spooked. I don't know if Cora means it or she just wants to get me pissed. Same with Darlene, always agitatin'. But I'm here to tell you, there's just no way in this world or the next you'll ever catch her at it. No way! You know that yourself. Lookin' at her, you'd swear an' be goddamned butter wouldn't melt in her mouth—Jolene an' Charmaine too. They're all like that, from Cora down—sneaky-smart."

Family portrait drawn, Hubie pulled himself up in the gray felt seat and made an appropriate transition. "Which gets us back to your Greek."

His tone implied that between daughters and finding $2 billion, Costa Lianides was just another distraction. He had a point.

But Wade saw things differently.

Raising money mattered, of course. But not finding it would hurt ten to twelve years down the road. The Hasegawa 100,000-tonners, though, would be at sea within a year. If the move for which they were built hiked spot-charter rates just half as much as Niarchos did in '56, it would sink PANARTEX. Wade saw a first-year loss of $350 million.

Selling that theory, however, took more than logic. It also required Hubie's attention. Costa Lianides, luckily, came with his own red flag.

"He's a Hydra boy," Wade said.

"Hydra?" Hubie responded as expected. "I been to Hydra," he told Wade. "Cora dragged me there in '61, after they took out my gall bladder. That's tourist country—not a seaman in sight except the ones you see on ferries, an' the whole place is poorer'n Job's turkeys, to boot! The damned fools went an' chopped down all the trees centuries ago, an' not a one grew back, so there's no wood for boats, an' fishin' stinks besides. Hotels polluted up all the water—same's in Acapulco. Between hills an' rocks, I mean, goats don't even scratch out what to eat.

"All they're doin' on Hydra," he concluded, a board chairman killing an aide's idea, "is knittin' heavy sweaters an' raisin' new-style Greeks—just bartenders an' bellhops. Name one tanker owner who comes from—"

No sale.

"Oh, man, you're pathetic," Wade said quietly. "You're gonna wrap yourself around an axle tryin' to wish that Greek away, an' I'm tellin' you, he ain't about to go. I been there, too, so forget about *taverna*s an' *bouzouki* music an' guys in fisherman shirts dancin' *syrtaki* an' playin' grab-ass with all that Swedish cunt down there for the sun. Good Lord, if you think that's real, the next time we're on the Coast I'll take you to Disneyland so's you can see Mickey and Pluto—alive!"

Hubie stared out of his corner of the Cadillac.

Old Mother Wade's twice-torpedoed little boy, Loren, kept right on talking. "I mean," he concluded in a hand-wringing, impotent tone, "this boy hit the Lutine bell* two God Almighty awful licks before he even quit pullin' his pud—"

To shipowners, beating Lloyds of London out of anything is virtually impossible. Beset by that kind of guile, Hubie promptly reconsidered Costa Lianides. But his reluctance to do so surfaced as skepticism.

"Urs got that off some government form, did he?"

"No, sirree! Urs most certainly didn't get that off no government form. I got that right off the horse—my pal at Scarborough and McKinney.† They got the biggest book of Greek tanker business of any syndicate at Lloyds, so I figured I better give London a call."

"An' your guy knew Lianides?"

"Did he ever! Got cramps just hearin' the name. Turned out he had a piece of him both of those earlier times. But you know the lockjaw they got at Lloyds. All he'd say was, 'A most irregular gentleman.' "

Hubie indeed knew that sort of reticence. "He was sendin' you a message there," he told Wade. "That was a joke, an irony—"

"You mean, like ambience?"

"Right. That's what an English newspaper called Jack the Ripper."

"Well, then, there you go. What'd I tell you?"

Nodding, Hubie gave up. But, beguiled by insurance, he got his questions out of order. "Where'd he get ships in the first place?" he asked.

"Where do any of them Greeks get ships? He had a 'Been America' uncle, Spyridon Angelakos—"

"You mean some diner Greek who went home to live it up on his American Social Security?"

"Right. Only this was a produce Greek—wholesaled Peconic Bay scallops out on Long Island, in Riverhead. Sold the business off to a brother, though, so he had a few bucks, too. But he's hell an' gone down the road—"

"I thought you said he bankrolled those ships."

"He did. But those weren't Lianides' first ships."

"They weren't?"

"Oh, hell, no. Not by a damned sight. For God's sake, he had his first ship before he was nineteen."

"Loren, that makes him six years smarter than Onassis."

"Ballsier, for sure. Smarter, maybe. All I know is he oughtta be dead, but ain't. Instead of goin' along with the crowd, he's got his house flag on a half-million tons of Rolls-Royces. Which ain't so bad, considerin' all them hungry goats on Hydra. In fact, I rate that ten ... "

"You better start at the beginnin'," Hubie said.

* Tolled at Lloyds of London if a ship insured by Lloyds underwriters has gone missing or sunk.
† Members of the Lloyds syndicate "Minas & Others" will recognize these men.

Watching him hoist the brown Maalox bottle, Wade nodded approvingly. "Take yourself a real belt," he suggested. "It's a thrill a minute on the good ship Annie No-Bottoms."

Caveat sounded, Loren Wade began his morning's work.

In 1941, he said, Nazi commanders in Greece got an order confirming the rumored invasion of Russia. They were told to replace Wehrmacht troops with Greeks for housekeeping jobs. Complying, the mess sergeant of an Athens military hospital hired some locals as kitchen help. Their names, of course, went to Gestapo and police headquarters for checking. This review brought Costa Lianides to official notice.

Athens cops, seeing his name, guessed he had not quit fishing merely to eat better. Petty larceny, like hemophilia, flawed the family history. The father, a Lykiardopoulos* man out of London, was a well-known bit of Piraeus Harbor trash with a criminal past.

But the Gestapo heard nothing of that. Detectives, Greeks first, hoped Lianides would rob the Nazis blind.

"Where in hell'd you get that?" Hubie asked.

Wade smiled ingenuously. From egg money, he said. Like a farmer's wife, he had windfalls. His restored budget cuts. One, a Greek shipping-paper editor, ran down gossip. Mostly, though, he double-checked information from Taki Keriosotis, the shipbroker, and his Athens relatives.

Hubie shook his head in wonderment.

Within ninety days, Wade continued, Lianides organized a ring to steal meat from the hospital. Most of it went to the black market, of course. But he got some to the resistance. So the cops left him alone.

Soon, however, they felt otherwise. Lianides found a fancy Plaka district whore, and she wanted more money. So what began as a small-time, somewhat comical profiteering scheme turned into something else. Drugs and medicines became available. Most were cut with water or talcum powder—

Maalox in hand, Hubie took that personally. "Goddammit, that was murder!" he protested.

Absolutely, Wade agreed. Three, four folks were dead in no time, and all the wrong ones—partisans.

The whore died soon enough in an alley. Lianides vanished.

For police, the matter ended there. They had no idea of what happened next. Moreover, the case stayed closed. By 1945, key witnesses were dead.

"But you know?" Hubie asked.

"Oh, yeah." Wade shrugged. "A fisherman'd sail to Turkey. The Turks were neutral. So I got to thinkin' I better have a little Bombay gin with Tubby Crampton an' hear a few of his Royal Navy war stories."

"And Tubby knew Lianides?"

* An old and rich London Greek shipping family.

"For sure an' in spades!"

"You mention any names?"

"Me? I'm churchfolk. Tubs did, though, an' our boy's third on his list of all-time great wild men."

Hubie winced. Jovial Cunard executive Tubby Crampton, C.B., D.S.O., O.B.E., D.S.C., had been deputy director of British Naval Intelligence, Mediterranean Theatre, during World War II.

Three weeks after the Athens deaths, Wade went on, Turkish fishermen from a mousehole port near Chesme met a barepoled smack in heavy seas. Bounty hunters pure and simple, they took off a lone Greek, sank the boat, and went home. Town police, automatic partners in all such ventures in that part of the world, jailed the hostage.

The chief of police sold him over the phone. The next morning, a man named Cyril took delivery. Slight and fair, he wore the inevitable blue blazer and gray flannels of a Royal Navy officer in mufti. His face, flinty beyond its years with command and experience, suggested a Death Row priest about to walk the last mile.

He had shanghaied many Greeks, and, age aside, he thought, traitors and petty criminals all ran to form. So he had no qualms about handling a fifteen-year-old. Once in the hostage's cell, he sat down on the straw mattress and held out a box of Players cigarettes. Striking a match, he shook his head and spoke softly in Greek.

A shame, he said. Capture meant internment camp.

The prisoner, a chunky boy with strawberry-blond hair, rare for a Greek, looked up. Then, despite split lips and tremendous shiner, he smiled. Sharp-featured face alight with cunning, he challenged Cyril.

What was so bad about camp? he asked. Lots of RAF and Royal Navy men were already there. All would live to see the end of the war.

Cyril smiled back, wanly. Inwardly he rejoiced. Every guttersnipe sang that chorus, but none seemed to know the verse. He guessed he would have his man within sixty seconds.

British prisoners would live, all right, he said. Greeks had rather different prospects. Turks killed them right off.

But the Geneva Convention—

That? Cyril scoffed. Turks got right round that! Camp guards just saved the last lentils in the stewpot for Greeks. Their bits of mutton fat, also from the bottom, were sure to be a trifle gamy, too, rather greenish, in fact. So, if one missed hepatitis, a trying enough death, one got amoebic dysentery and died even harder. At most, Cyril gave Greeks ninety rather nasty days.

Even so, he said, that showed progress. In the old days, Turks were less merciful. They never bothered with prisoners at all. They simply drove iron spikes through hostages' boots, into their heels, and then told the poor buggers to walk home.

"That was true—what Tubby's guy said?" Hubie asked.

"Oh, yeah. Every word. Turks are some kind of haters."

"Then what was he sellin'?"

"A berth in his kamikazes, a bunch of old fishin' boats they had—caiques, they call 'em—fitted with humongous Thorneycroft diesels. The damned things'd outrun striped-assed apes."

"For runnin' spies?"

So Wade had thought, too. Crampton, however, kiboshed that theory. Agents? Good heavens, no! he laughed. Planes did for spies. Cyril looked after practical politics. His job, Crampton said, was to see that friends came to power in Greece after Hitler.

"So he ran guns," Hubie said, unsurprised. An oilman, he understood practical politics. A few nuances of friendship, however, eluded him.

"Right," Wade replied, "but to both sides."

Which meant caiques were often ambushed by all three interested parties—Communists, Nazis, and partisans. Initial losses were so high, Cyril soon began buying Greeks. After that, Royal Navy men did the sailing, but rubbish like Lianides took arms ashore in rubber life rafts.

It wouldn't do to have white men killed off in that game when there were all those wily Levantines about who would never be missed.

But the Nazis got Type E torpedo boats, and British losses kept rising. Lianides became a deckhand then; a year later, a mate. Finally, with his original Royal Navy petty officers dead, Cyril made him a skipper.

No one else had sufficient local knowledge.

Nor did anyone else put it to quite such exquisite use.

One dark, moonless night, a submarine from Malta surfaced off Crete. By dawn, its crew had transferred three hundred Sten guns, eighty thousand rounds of ammunition, and sixty-one cases of hand grenades to one of Cyril's caiques. Bloody Costa Lianides snaffled the lot, and no Nazi, Communist, or partisan ever touched him, Crampton said flatly. He was never heard from again by the Royal Navy, but Cyril called him a born haven-finder, the highest praise one seaman can give another.

His choice of cargoes had been pluperfect, his timing even better. He vanished three weeks before V-E Day.

Lloyds had found him in 1950, Wade's London chum said. The *Sultana of Izmir,* an old tramp, supposedly hit a mine in the Gulf of Enez, off Turkey. Others had there, too, so a claim was paid.

Lloyds paid him another in '53. He beached an empty Liberty ship on Palawan, in the Philippines, that time. "A Frog corvette put him there," Wade told Hubie. "They did that to Uncle Ho's gunrunners."

At the time, however, the French were telling Ike they needed just a few GIs to quell hamlet uprisings in Indochina. An 8,000-ton arms cargo bound for

Hanoi queered that pitch. So, fearful of gossip getting back to Washington, Saigon officials denied all responsibility when asked by Lloyds.

Which left the insured's version of the incident. His steering gear failed, he said. It was, after all, typhoon season, with a full storm in progress.

Disarming or not, the story played. Moreover, it brought $500,000.

Lianides dropped out of sight again. Wade guessed to the French Riviera. Ben McCall mentioned a stone cottage on the Haute Corniche high above Menton. At any rate, the daughter of a Brazilian provincial governor, a young widow, he heard, summered there in '59.

The visit resulted in three T–2s, with rampant white lion stack marks, coasting Brazil for Petrobras—

"All right! Okay! Enough!"

Shaking his head, Hubie leaned back, watching cars in the right lanes turn off the Thruway for Port Chester and the Tappan Zee Bridge. His glance clearly conveyed a longing to go that way, too.

His mind, however, stayed put. But, having enough of insurance, he shrugged resignedly and put the question to Wade about Lianides that should have come first. "Where's he now?" he asked.

"Accordin' to Urs, in a subleased penthouse at Seventy-eighth and Park, payin' eleven hundred seventy-five dollars a month, an' doin' not too badly at all for a poor boy from Hydra."

"He's not just visitin'? He's a resident alien?"

"Oh, yeah. He's been roughin' it there since January."

"Well, who sponsored his work permit?"

"Christanthanou an' Archimedes Angelakos."

Hubie winced at the names, then gave up trying to keep them straight. "What's-his-name had two brothers?"

"No. Just Christanthanou. Archimedes is his kid."

"An' Archimedes took over the scallop store?"

"No, he went into tankers. That's what I was tryin' to tell you when you got that bug up your ass about Caskie's two bill—"

"Tankers! Tankers—how?"

"Grab ahold," Wade cautioned. "He's worse yet—"

"For God's sake, you know him?"

"No, just *of* him. But that's enough to give you Old Yellow Stain all by itself. Archimedes is one of them Webb Institute geniuses, only he went to the Merchant Marine Academy first, so, besides the diplomas, he's a chief engineer to boot. Now he owns Marine Cargo Systems—a shop over in Long Island City that modifies tankers—an' there ain't a doubt in my mind, either, but what he designed Hasegawa's hundred-thousand-tonners too. I know for sure that little Jap showed me his sketches."

"You do? How?"

"Because the gyro case in the bridge drawin' had a tiny little 'AA' in its corner—which I never remembered till Saturday night on the sun porch."

Hubie dismissed blame with a curt nod. Only the result mattered. That, and where the name fit in the equation.

"We ever do business with Angelakos?" he asked.

"Are you kiddin'? That guy's one of them antique-car shops where they hand-rub thirty coats of paint, an' he's got the majors standin' in line. Whenever they get an idea they don't know what to do with, he's the man. If he can't improve it, or get it done, he'll invent a framus that will. Any flies on that boy, bet your ass those little suckers pay rent, too."

"But is he the money, Loren?"

"Oh, hell, no. How can he be? He's just startin'."

"In other words, we found us a Greek position, only the Greeks don't count. The real Lions in that house flag of theirs aren't Angelakos an' Lianides, but the guys behind them who're buyin' those ships."

"Seems like," Wade conceded.

"Well, then, it's simple. The problem's still the same. How do we get to the money before it moves to find out what in hell's goin' on? That's your job, and I don't want you fussin' with shipyards, or schedules, or any of your old clapped-up buddies out on the briny deep till you're back to me with names, dates, and places!"

"Done!" Wade squeaked in his highest register. "But if I rate Lianides an' Angelakos as tens, what must the guys runnin' 'em be? So just tell me how."

Hubie had an answer for that too. "Be creative," he said. "All I know is I got me two billion dollars of my own to find."

Marching orders given, he slid his reading glasses into place and reached down alongside the jump seat for his briefcase. Unzipping it with an expectant smile, he withdrew a much folded buff-colored photostat. Spread out, it draped across the armrest and onto Wade's thigh.

Wade identified it unopened. It had to be Caskie Horn's survey map.

Hubie's lips were moving in and out as if he were a poker player debating whether to draw or stand pat.

Furtively glancing sideways, Wade wanted to fold.

He knew the name at the bottom of the map: Valdez Narrows. Weyerhaeuser skippers had told him about that place. They called it the brickyard, to honor its rocks.

Scrawled across the top of the map in thick grease-pencil outline were three red circles denoting "certain" oilfields and a blue for a "probable." Beneath them lay another name. Wade knew that too. Young geologists said old geologists went there to die: North Slope.

Alaska would be their Little Big Horn.

Even worse, Wade thought bitterly, looking across the seat, the massacre was inevitable. Neither talk nor logic nor experience mattered. General Custer's eyes had already seen the glory. It was as if his life had never happened.

For thirty years, Hubie had drawn his own red circles. Eleven out of twelve had marked dusters. Nevertheless, the map had him smiling all the way to the Triborough Bridge. Then, as the Cadillac made the long, sweeping left onto the East River Drive, he refolded the buff-colored sheet and finally spoke.

"You know what?" he said, his eyes following a black Moran tug going downriver in the morning sun. "Let's do breakfast at the Barclay today."

Wade grimaced. That used to be a once-a-year yen. Lately it had become a staple, and he hated it. Breakfast there meant a four-block crosstown trek, uphill, across the spine of Manhattan. A man suffering the afflictions of decades of watch-standing did not go hiking casually.

"Christ Almighty," he grumbled, "that's hell an' gone from the office, an' oatmeal's the same all over."

"I know," Hubie agreed, turning away to better view the tug, "but the walk'll be good—the garbage hasn't heated up yet, the way it does summers."

Perfectly true, but contrived. Oilmen found refineries sweeter than baby's breath.

So something was being sold. Obviously, the Barclay. But why?

Wade promptly floated a trial balloon. "You want legwork so's you can go huntin' again?"

"Oh, Christ, no. I can't hold a gun, I'm so weak."

"An' you ain't all of a sudden sick of the Dorset?"

"Didn't I just sign a new lease on the suite there?"

The suspicion grew that the four crosstown blocks were punishment for being less than eager about Alaska.

"Well, then, what is it? Why in hell are you so hotted up about the Barclay? You lose somethin' there, or what? Goddammit, you know between my piles an' my feet, all that hoofin' around just about kills me dead!"

"To tell the truth, I thought it'd be nice to hear the birds while we ate."

Wade bolted upright. "You mean them parrots in the lobby?"

Hubie turned back from the window, his face suddenly making the thick jet-black hair above it seem like some kind of joke toupee. "Lovebirds too, Loren," he answered entreatingly. "Some days they sing real good, almost as sweet as the bobwhite down at the ranch . . ."

That made it Wade's turn to look away. He had seen enough anyway. He had it right the first time. In oil, only the players changed. The macho smile had been phony all along. Its corners, finally twitching in panic, summoned up the true image. Acey. Sober, his mouth always shook like that. Now, he saw, Hubie had that honor.

Which left an awkward corner to round.

"Well, shit," he said softly, glancing down at his opened trousers as he smoothed shirttails over paunch. "Since I'm doin' the Bermuda Race again this year, I guess today's as good a day as any to do a little walkin'. I left my rubber tire at home for sittin' on in the office, too, but screw it. . . ."

So Hubie got that wish. The other, however, eluded him.

The money had already begun to move.

The Swiss, usually so zealous of privacy, have no use for it in some matters. So a small room atop Zurich Central Post Office is filled ceiling-high with files of unusual cables to banks.

This library, on microfiche, covers twenty years. It exists to enforce laws of escheat. These require the passage of two decades without contact before a bank may presume an account holder dead and claim his money. After eighteen or nineteen years, bankers tend to forget messages that make no apparent sense or are signed by aliases.

The 1966 Bank Schotten drawer holds such a cable. In English, French, and Yiddish, it originated in New York City on April 25, 1966, and reads:

> MAVEN MOVING NORTH STOP RESERVED DWARF
> QUEEN LIZ MONTREAL MAY 19 REPEAT 19 STOP
> LAPACHE

Translation: Norbert Nygaard, the querulous model railroader of La Jolla, California, had smoothed the way into Canada for $50 million through the Rio de Janeiro branch of the Bank of Halifax.

*May 19, 1966*
*Montreal*

A FAINT metallic click sounded behind Schotten.

He barely noticed.

Someone in the next suite had tried the lock in the connecting door, he thought. Dimly, he wondered if that person had flown with him from Paris. Curiosity ended there.

The effects of the trip concerned him more. His foot had cramped that morning boarding the plane. Aloft, his sinuses ached ceaselessly in sympathy. Now, head in hands, right shoe off, he sat on the edge of the bed, hoping to revive before the phone rang.

Jorge, Battle & Company's Cuban aide, would call at any moment. Over supper, he would further explain wheat buying and how money from Howsam's group could be placed in Canadian banks under that pretense. Time permitting, the papers created by Norbert Nygaard to move funds from Brazil and the United States would be covered, too. Howsam said they were "pretty slick."

Translated, that meant stupefyingly intricate.

The evening, Schotten knew, would never end.

Then, as his sinuses throbbed anew, he heard. Dr. Fabian's voice. It came from over his shoulder.

"So, Schotten," she asked softly in her not-quite-English accent, "you had a difficult trip?"

Turning, he saw her in the doorway to the adjoining suite. She stood behind the gilt-and-white armoire that stood along the wall to his right.

Surprised, he half rose. Then caution, as always, overrode impulse. He pondered her presence. He knew of no reason for her to be in Montreal. Beyond that, he judged she had watched him for a while. And not alone. Her old chum Fundador had been there, too.

Her right hand, resting atop the chest, held a chunky half-full hotel water glass. The whereabouts of the missing top two inches of brandy posed no problem. Looking past the shoulder-high wardrobe, he saw a tan silk blouse, collar askew and unbuttoned, and a jumble of auburn hair.

Thoroughly baffled by her attitude and presence, he sank back onto the bed. "I expected Jorge," he said by way of greeting.

Smiling, she leaned back, away from the armoire, shaking her head.

Watching her, he knew why he had not risen. He recalled her expression.

She had smiled like that at her living-room window the previous December, treating a polite question as if it were a challenge. She had humiliated him then, with her Greater Fool Theory of real estate. The corners of her mouth curled now in equally hard little parentheses.

Seeing them, he grew increasingly uneasy. Those arcs had served as storm warnings before.

Now, however, they seemed curled only in wryness. "Jorge?" she said with a flippant shrug. "Jorge's down with flu. So Evelyn got a Brazilian passport at the last moment—a woman's—that only needed my picture. He thought the whole wheat story would be more disarming if I came with you, instead. Puns intended, I'm sure."

She paused while he digested that. His confusion amused her.

"So I reserved us these," she told him, glancing at her suite beyond the connecting door, "and in the eight other cities as well."

Her words were simple enough. But not her past. So he pondered what he had just heard. Was it a threat or a promise? While solicitous, she offered no help.

"You're confused, Schotten? Unhappy?" Toasting him mockingly, as she had in New York, she took a long pull of brandy and put the glass down. "I'll make you happy," she assured him.

Then she stepped away from the armoire, nude but for open blouse and black satin high-heeled mules. Since their night together, memories of her began with those slippers. From them, his mind's eye rose, lingering on each carefully hoarded image, like a miser fondling coins.

Enjoying those reveries then, however, he conveniently forgot the reason he had been able to see her so. Reality, in contrast, brought instant recall. Confronting her nudity again, he recognized what in Zurich yearning glossed over: the cause of her behavior; the state of her mind.

His first impression, he knew, remained valid. Her actions could only be described as irrational. Motion, meanwhile, opened her blouse. Logic and discretion promptly diminished. Albeit guiltily, he still gazed at her covetously.

Chin down, green eyes slit, she noted her cleavage with a negligent, satisfied nod. Then, looking up, she met his glance, inviting inspection.

Bleary-eyed with fatigue, he knew she had changed, but not how.

Casually leaning on the armoire, knee up, right foot braced against the chest behind her, she let him ponder the problem. Seeing he needed help, she swung right leg over left and pivoted to stand in profile. Then, pawing the tail of the gauzy blouse behind her, she led the red lacquered nail on her forefinger across the subtle line ringing her thigh.

"You like my color?" she asked.

Still disoriented, he nearly shouted a warning. As her nail vanished in the fold between thigh and stomach, the vague, menacing image that often intruded into his erotic memories of her suddenly materialized.

Harsh, coppery flames rose in a cloudless vaulted sky, searing it white.

The next moment further unsettled him.

"I've been in the garden . . ." she said.

He knew that place too. It existed in her mind, in London. It lay behind the looking glass in Alice's house. She went there to use men.

The thought bit deeper into his face than pain. His anguish, however, went unnoticed. The garden had frustrated her as well.

". . . but it doesn't work just in one's head," she lamented. "I got this lovely tan sailing with Howsam's boy, Jake. But Jake's only fourteen . . ." Still leaning on the armoire, she smiled wryly, as if relating a perfectly obvious, rather dull fact.

In New York, of course, she said just the opposite. Then, she told him, the garden no longer interested her. She had only gone there anyway, she claimed, to kill the ghost. She wanted him at rest. He would be, she knew, if she could somehow reduce him from presence to memory. Remote, beyond her consciousness, he would be unable to continue to hold her hostage.

She thus needed a man to effect her escape. But none of the men she found on the other side of Alice's looking glass could help. She failed to respond to any of them. So, in time, demeaned and discouraged, she sought an alternative. The answer she found worked for a while. She suppressed all emotion. Life, indeed, seemed simpler that way. In the long run, though, the upshot of so extreme a course could easily be predicted: she feared ever feeling again.

So Schotten's killing the ghost had made no difference. She still insisted on ending their relationship. A classic case, he had thought at the time. The cure had done more damage than the disease.

Crazy or not, that outcome had a logic. He accepted it. Now, always analytical, he wondered. Her actions were inconsistent with the story. Finding no satisfaction in the garden, why had she so suddenly, so ardently, wished to return? With the ghost dead, what compelled her to? Moreover, supposedly outlawed, one of her emotions had ordained this episode. Which?

He had several candidates, all equally distasteful. Analytical to a fault, ignoring his anguish, he reviewed the full list. He began with what he considered to be the least likely possibility:

*Lust.*

For all her protests, he mused, she had spent much time in the garden. Perhaps in New York, he rekindled some of her pleasure in its delights.

Plausible, but dubious, he thought. Controlled and detached, he had never excited women.

Still, the idea sired another. Sometimes, behavior contradicted motivation. If it did now, he reflected, she might be seeking the opposite of enjoyment: pain. In his view, that reflected a quite different cause:

*Guilt.*

He had never doubted her sincerity when she spoke bitterly of how men had used her. Could it be that with the ghost slain by the methods she so abhorred, she had conscience problems? She might well, he concluded. With her intelligence, she would see that hypocrisy. If so, what she proposed now and in the eight other cities would be suitable punishment.

Those covered the obvious answers, he thought.

He gave them virtually no chance of being right. The forces moving her, he believed, had to be fully as convoluted as her mind. Education and sophistication were paid for in complexity. Noting that principle, he had two more candidates that might explain her presence, nude, in a Montreal bedroom. The first he considered a bit straightforward. But it had to be included.

*Vengeance.*

What if she really loved the ghost? She might, he thought. But, knowing that others would call her sick if she admitted it, she wisely pretended otherwise.

Or, the wraith might serve a different end. Suppose she had lost the capacity to love. What could be handier than having a spirit in the wings to scare off men and to discourage involvement?

Either way, he thought, her subconscious would make her believe the party line best suited to its purposes. So, if one or the other of those suppositions were correct, she would want vengeance now, he reflected. Slaying the ghost, he had made her respond. In effect, he had shattered her cover story. If that had happened, she would crave retribution. How better than humbling him as she had done in New York?

But did the ghost matter at all? He had to wonder.

He had never taken the Flying Dutchman seriously, either. The dead were dead. A mind such as hers would be among the first to acknowledge that immutable fact. From there, he saw the outlines of what seemed to him to be the fourth and most likely cause of her behavior:

*Self-preservation.*

Her actions were real enough to her, he thought, as were the garden and the ghost, but all existed to masquerade as authentic effects of her past. She needed them to convince herself as well as others.

Beneath that veneer, so painfully hidden from her, he sensed, lay the essence of her torment. It would be something about her, or something that happened to her, that she feared she lacked the strength to face.

He had no idea what the secret might be. But, confused or ignorant, he remained a banker. Infatuated or in love, he remained a banker. He still prized return on investment. He had thought of her constantly since they met. And his ego had paid dearly for that past of hers. So he wanted the secret the ghost concealed in exchange.

He sensed that a trade could be made. She had changed since New York. Then, she ambushed him. Now, she declared her intentions. Her candor, he hoped, might be saying, Help me.

Rushing her at truth, however, failed before. So, now, he led her the first step toward it. He answered her as if he believed her charade.

"Tell me, Jerusalem," he asked, "after Vancouver—what happens to me? Burial in the garden?"

She shrugged.

So much for hope, he thought. Given an opportunity to step out from behind her myths, she clung as ardently as ever to garden and ghost. Revising his first judgment, he decided she had not changed.

He would soon be as wrong about himself. She had indeed changed.

Now, seeing his face, she felt a need to apologize. "I—I don't want these feelings," she sighed.

"Which feelings, Jerusalem?"

Frowning, she shook her head, trying to sift words out of an overload of conflicting ideas and images. In the end, she could only summarize. "I'm not at peace," she sighed. Then anger displaced contrition. "You're smiling, damn you!" she said. "You think that's funny, don't you?"

"Funny? No," he assured her.

Promising, yes. She had left an opening, after all. He moved into it as casually as possible. Neither garden nor ghost concerned him now, but the path that led beyond them to what they shielded. "Actually," he said, "I wasn't thinking of you just then, anyway. Lemmings suddenly popped into my mind."

She tensed warily at that.

Seeing her surprise, he lightened his tone even more, as if they were indeed discussing lemmings. "I wondered," he told her, "if they're really happy, or only painfully misguided, when they heed their inner voices and head for sea. They don't swim, you—"

"Signifying?" she cut in, increasingly impatient.

"Just that we're so like them," he said. "In our case, though, we scurry along, looking neither here nor there, telling ourselves, because we have intelligence, that we're doing the right thing."

"And we're not?"

"No. I don't think so."

"What is it, then, Schotten, that fatal impulse, that siren's song, that lures us in over our heads?"

Her directness surprised him.

Chin still on shoulder, he shrugged as if he now had to find the precise phrase. He took his time, pondering her reasons for rushing him. His strategy had overlooked that possibility. In the end, unable to read her motives, he opted for cautious generality.

"For most of us, what we hear, I think, is bogus guilt," he hedged.

"An interesting theory," she conceded. She cocked her head as if considering it.

But a moment later she passed judgment. Garden and ghost, of course, prevailed.

She gave him no chance to trick the truth from her. Smiling serenely, green eyes glittering with dark glints, she pushed off from the armoire with her right leg. Like a model showing the dress beneath a coat, she spread the blouse with her palms. Then, fists on hips, spiky black mules digging into the beige carpeting, she started toward him.

Nothing would keep her from the garden, he saw. The inevitable recognized, the focus shifted. His concern suddenly turned to his emotions.

Mainly, he seemed to feel fear. He knew the sensation. He linked it with the memories of her he enjoyed in Zurich. But then he called the feeling anticipation. Now, seeing her firm stride and ruthlessly set lips, he realized he had had the same apprehension almost every moment he was with her or thought of her.

He knew when it had begun: when he held her wrist as she tried to slap him. But she had not been the object of his fear then. She had been its cause. Now he saw he had been frightened for himself.

With reason, he thought. For, responding to her, he had, in effect, renounced his faith. Short of that, he surely had violated its prime tenet: he had entered knowingly into a losing transaction. Other men did, of course, with women, but not Princes of Zurich. They were taught to honor profit in all matters. So involvement with Dr. Fabian raised doubts.

The most serious concerned emotional stability. Bankers considered detachment a tool of the trade. Could he afford to question his?

Some of that uncertainty showed in his face. Seeing it, she smiled. Then, sauntering by the foot of the bed, she drew up before him in a last arrogant, hip-swinging stride.

That gesture, however, went unnoticed. Dusk provided the flourish, instead. A first sigh of night breeze, rising from the St. Lawrence, gently lifted the Venetian blind on the window behind her. For a brief moment, through its open slats, he saw a layered twilight. Then soft golds, and silvers, and muted neons fell over her like a transparent diagonally striped sari.

The illusion vanished instantaneously. Moreover, he knew its cause. Rising, the blind let in short dashes of light from an IBM sign on a building across the street. They hung in the dusk behind her like airy light-blue veils being gathered to her body. The beam reaching her right hip, however, suddenly diffused instead of becoming a stripe.

And where he had seen fire, he now saw smoke.

It curled out from beneath the bulge of her abdomen like fog caught in wine-dark trees. A few ragged mares' tails and streamers, seemingly spun free, hovered above. Swirling upward in a long, straggling elephant walk of blues and grays, they blackened the V between her thighs and dulled to rust the down climbing to her navel.

The next stripe, starting at her ribs, crossed her body, growing progressively darker. It ended, gunmetal gray, on her left breast, like a faded bruise. Its neon blue spillover bathed the underside of her chin.

That made her face even more disconcerting.

He wondered, in fact, if she had been masturbating. Driven, highly strung women did such things. He saw the signs occasionally in the Countess. The underlighting accentuated that look now: wide, slightly protuberant eyes; hard, thin-lipped mouth over slackened jaw. The sweat filming her cheekbones further supported that suspicion.

Or, he thought, he might just be seeing Fundador.

Watching him, she saw only his face. "What's wrong?" she asked. "Sorry I'm here?" Clearly in command, she put the question tauntingly.

Ever the dealmaker, he ducked the ultimatum. Most, he had learned, including his, were only melodrama. He had by then, as well, invoked the patron saint of lost causes: hope.

So, shaking his head, he lied.

"Good, then," she said curtly. "That's settled." Leaning over, she cupped her palm around the curve of his left cheek and continued. "And since they eat late in Montreal, I've made us a reservation at Chez Bardet for nine-thirty. Yes—" she nodded, looking down as she cradled his other cheek with her right hand—"nine-thirty's about right. We'll need all of two hours. You've developed a funny little tic, you know, that wants looking into. Your tongue's always on the go now—in and out, in and out."

Then came the point of her presence in Montreal. Expressed as action, it translated as punishment. Who should suffer it, however, remained unclear.

"Tell me, is this what you so want to taste?" she asked, suddenly pulling him into her thighs.

His hands rose to push her off. But surprise gave her leverage. His body bent to hers. At the same time, she moved closer, her knees virtually straddling his.

"Or," she mused, continuing her quest for atonement or vengeance through the same implacable, steely-edged smile she used for matters relating to garden and ghost, "are you thinking of someone more . . . accomplished?"

He could not answer.

The sari reflected his rational view of her. It showed a soiled, used woman.

But, moving closer, she obscured that rational view. She stepped into the golden light of the nightstand lamp. Then, finally, she looked as he remembered. More to the point, she felt as he remembered. And, ultimately, he confronted truth.

It appeared as his senses registered touch. His answer flowed back as quickly: he had no need to trade with her. Neither ghost nor the lie it might shield mattered. What lay under the sari did not count, either. Disturbed or deranged, sick or dangerously drunk . . . he wanted her, regardless of cost.

In concert, his body committed similar treacheries. His cheek, seemingly held by force, stealthily slid down her abdomen, seeking the touch of more hair. His hands, supposedly on her hips to push her off, rested on the swell of her buttocks instead. Fingers splayed and outstretched, he yearned to caress her. Only pride, and fear of the comment to follow, restrained him.

Meanwhile, he felt his face warm with shame.

Was this love? he wondered.

He rejected the proposition out of hand. Most of the young fell in and out of love at will. Adults sought or rejected it just as handily. Save for extreme cases, love could be controlled.

So, in all likelihood, this was not love. But, if not—what?

Lust? Even less likely, he decided. He felt pity for her today, perhaps revulsion.

So, then, which state ruled him now?

While not quite right, a word suggested itself: thrall. That caught his helplessness, suggested his shame. In addition, it brought a new insight.

It explained husbands and lovers who gave lifetimes and riches to faithless women; wives and mistresses who similarly squandered themselves on the wrong men. Such bonds might puzzle the rest of the world. He now understood them. Shrouded in silence, they only seemed mysterious.

The loyalties in those relationships, he knew, were fixed by unspeakable secrets that ensnared and addicted as surely as drugs. But who, so burdened, he reflected, ever spoke of those cravings or hymned the joys of their fulfillment? Indeed, who without at least a remnant of banker's detachment would even admit having such urges?

His own case made the point, he thought. The dirty little unmentionables twitching his cheek and stiffening his fingers were alarmingly clear:

The heat within a woman's mouth.

The rasp of spiky heels across his back.

Musk that scented love with almond blossoms.

How did one justify bondage to those? And where, he mused, did they leave background, or culture, or education, or values?

Thinking, a better word than "thrall" came for what he now felt: betrayal.

Her actions mirrored similar conflict.

At some point, she slid her right hand around his cheek and turned his head. Now she cradled him almost maternally, as if reminding herself, regardless of her personal demons, that she had only to use this suddenly fearful man, not to hurt him.

Meanwhile, seeking truth, he found weakness: his.

So he put the question to her he refused to face.

"Jerusalem," he asked, "don't you know what you're doing to yourself?"

Beset herself, her reply could have been his.

"Who does, Schotten?" she answered. "Who does?"

So began their trip across Canada.

Eleven days later, they parted in Vancouver, no nearer understanding themselves or each other. Loren Wade, that day, was on Long Island Sound, taking the ocean racer he would skipper home to Newport for the start of the Bermuda Race.

*June 24, 1966*
*Hamilton, Bermuda*

LOREN WADE lifted his paunch, crossed his legs, and settled back against the Royal Bermuda Yacht Club's fine old mahogany bar. A member in good standing, he felt at home there. He visited the island often. Bermuda gave tanker owners tax breaks, and he ran a PANARTEX holding company out of a lawyer's desk drawer in Hamilton.

Reports put the boat he would sail home sixty miles away, which left him another day of rest. So, happily lifting his pink gin, he looked across the snooker table to the start of his third Bermuda Race Week.

He had much to see.

The first boat had arrived the night before. Now, the next afternoon, past the open French doors at his right, twenty more lay anchored, courtesy Union Jacks under starboard spreaders snapping in the southwest trade.

They were mostly fifty- and sixty-footers; their masts rose higher. Dressed with code pennants, they blotted out the green hills and white-roofed pink stone cottages across the harbor. Rolling gently in the swell, they splashed the sky with costly glints of chrome, paint, and varnish.

Captains in tan chinos roamed decks, checking for race damage. Paid hands put red and blue nightcaps on compasses and winches; coiled lines for port; set white Dacron wind sails pouring dry air down hatches.

Meanwhile, Wade knew, the real show took place just past the French doors. Lowering his gaze to bring the crowd into view, he quickly saw that Race Week's most serious business had indeed started with a vengeance.

White-jacketed stewards, trays aloft, offered gin and tonics or rum swizzles. Blond English waitresses, on loan from resort hotels, passed hors d'oeuvres. At the head of the lawn, club chefs prepared charcoal in long stainless-steel troughs for steak and chicken. In the distance, at water's edge, the Talbot brothers, oil drums and washtubs in fine tune, welcomed launches to the dock with the island's anthem, "Bermuda." Watching over all as hosts, in traditional blue blazers and white ducks, were officers of the Cruising Club of America, sponsor of the race.

The next week would see a party a night. To Wade, they were PR, put on to make the race look democratic. This evening's do, he felt, had another aim: to define current lines of financial force.

Keeneland yearling sales aside, no event drew more wealth more privately than these receptions that took place in midocean every two years.

Honored guests, of course, were the owners of the anchored yachts. Since speed depended on size, they had the largest boats and were the richest men in the fleet. They stood now in a small circle on the veranda, drinks in hand, swapping notes on a race of calms and squalls.

Noting their obvious good fellowship, Wade saw that power had not moved since the last race. The New York Yacht Club WASPs were still playing *We Happy Few.* They did so by casually leaning against the club's whitewashed siding, automatically assuming the role of hosts.

Their taste for old money and older ways showed in aged blazers, brass buttons salted green. Establishment elders, tanned and sharp-eyed in their sixties and seventies, had an even better putdown, Wade thought. Besides the tired jackets and limp cotton whites, they wore sneakers but no socks. Their bony, veined ankles said their money had so much time in grade they learned to sail Bermuda races that way, before deck shoes were invented.

The New York Athletic Club Catholics and other new boys were not impressed. Loyalty on Wall Street, an old saw went, was worth a quarter of a point—twenty-five cents a share. That priced religion and style too. The Old Guard was on the run and knew it. Vietnam and LBJ's go-go market promised more fortunes than any in-group could corner.

Moreover, Wade saw, the upstarts got a maximum bang per buck from their new money. They served notice with it. Most had Gieves blazers, bought in London after the '64 transatlantic race. Others wore French fishermen's shirts or caps from last summer's Mediterranean cruises.

And, meanwhile, they smiled patiently.

In another race or two, wealth would replace ploys. Then, on this veranda, a man now leaning oh-so-casually against the wall would mention cocktails and supper at a rented cottage in Smith's or Pembroke Parish. Mergers could follow that evening of sailing small talk; in time, perhaps, marriages; at the least, to show friendship and mutual interest, sons would be asked into banks and brokerage or law firms now closed to them.

So, while heels were dug in against the inevitable, cordial, correct company manners prevailed.

Crews mimicked owners.

Big boats raced with eight to ten hands, so nearly two hundred men milled over the lawn, led by watch captains. Old-timers in their forties and fifties, they had been to many Race Weeks. Most Wade recognized. He knew them from the Yale Bowl parking lot. Their faces went with custom Mercedes station wagons, martini mixers, blanketed tailgates, pots of foie gras, and $100 wicker baskets from Maison Glass.

Many had financial ties to owners—as partners or employees, or as their bankers, brokers, or lawyers. So they took care with the pleasantries. A pat on the back, an arm around shoulder, a toast, went to counterparts in faster boats. Those who came in later got praise for making a race of it. Sure laughs were fixed in each routine—holes worn in rawhide deck shorts, unlikely bruises and rope burns, fluorescent sunburns.

No meeting of ins and outs took five minutes. None was sincere. No lunch dates at the Anglers' Club or the Lawyers' Club were set. Nor would parties in wealthy enclaves like Lattingtown or Comfort Island see any new faces. Still, Wade knew, the chats had merit. Men nodded to each other on Wall Street. Occasionally, they shared a seat into town on a Gold Coast commuter train. Beyond that, the encounters educated the young.

Most were owners' sons or grandsons. College kids or just out, they wore the football jerseys with class year on back that Ivy League schools sold as sweatshirts. As usual, Princeton black and gold and Yale blue stood out. "Comers," twenty-five to thirty-five, in bold tartan shorts and slacks and rabbity smiles, made the Grand Walkaround, too.

All had much to learn from Race Week.

The watch captains were now teaching poise. Some also held later classes in hideaway bungalows in Somerset or Southampton parishes. New York call girls ran those. These folks, Wade knew, bought their kids professional instruction and supervised entertainment whenever possible.

But now decorum ruled, and, framed by French doors, the men outside seemed very remote. They were indeed. Watching them, Wade rejoiced for his daughters. Better to marry those sharks than to fight them, he thought.

Christ, he wondered, downing his gin in a gulp, did just watching money do that to Texas populists?

Two drinks later, the women arrived. Usually, old debutantes named Binky, Dee-Dee, Fluff, and Muffy made him laugh. Not this time. They too flew in on Monday, and he found them fully as imposing as their owner and watch-captain husbands.

He saw them in the airport lobby, moving an Everest of luggage, golf bags, tennis racquets, and scuba gear with a nod here, a flick of white gloves there, to maids, daughters, and juvenile sons. Hardly breaking stride, a few sent porters to smoking Madison Avenue meat-market cartons full of dry ice and prime beef as they picked up small square "21" boxes.

Scottish woodcock, flown in at the start of hunting season, he guessed. He had had them last week. Regulars got some to do at home. At eight dollars a copy, the tiny birds were a steal—the perfect "something extra" that turned social sell into a memorable supper party 670 miles from home.

Good business and a nice touch.

Tuesday, he saw more of each. Shopping Hamilton two days early, the women got the best Ballantyne and Pringle sweaters and Daks and Jaeger slacks in Race Week stocks. Wise to duty-free-shopping ways of wealth, Archie Browne's and Trimmingham's clerks had Christmas wrappings ready and waiting.

Wednesday, the ladies tended hair. In the Elbow Beach Hotel for a business breakfast, he saw the dawn patrol waiting for the beauty shop to open. At noon, late risers in yellow oilskins stood in the rain before a Front Street hairdresser's. Cabbing to the Mid-Ocean Club for supper, he delivered a Babs and a Mugs to the Castle Harbour for the same treatment.

Thursday morning, he spotted Babs in a St. George's liquor store. Ash blond, tanned, and girlish in slacks and sweater, she ordered the movements of a clerk behind the counter from a small red leather address book. That logged guests' favorite drinks, he knew. He saw similar guides in fish stalls, flower shops, and even at a tobacconist's. Details mattered.

Such women, he thought, seeing them pass through the club, also noted dusk. They wanted outdoor spots to come on and wind to die. Then, poised and smiling, and looking ten years younger, they appeared on the lawn. No last ray of glare crinkled crow's feet in that soft, silvery light. No final cat's paw of dying breeze raised a single lustrously brushed or coiffed hair.

As with the men, he knew them from their clothes.

Old Guard wives wore black skirts and white blouses. Brown wicker purses with scrimshaw whales recalled Nantucket and New York Yacht Club cruises. Made by an island artist, they were sold only at his shop.

New Boys' wives countered with looks, youth, and designer dresses. Some carried straw cigarette cases or purses. Those said Nassau and the Southern Ocean Racing Circuit. With paid hands, air fare for amateur crew, food, and fun ashore, six or seven winter races cost $20,000 to $25,000.

Babs, as Wade guessed, had married a real slugger. A strapless white wool gown with blue edging, which his wife had shown him in an Athens shop, implied Aegean sailing the summer before. The straw bracelet on her left wrist disposed of cold weather as lavishly.

Arriving alone, she made her regal way through the crowd of admiring men standing inside the French doors. Wade, equally taken by the play of ash-blond hair over elegantly tanned shoulders, leaned forward on his stool to watch her passage across the veranda.

Doing so, he got his first shock of the evening.

At the steps going down to the lawn, Babs suddenly froze and jerked her arms upward. Wade saw the move as the start of a hug. His daughters did that, running to him, when he returned from trips. But now the gesture died as quickly as it began. Elbows scarcely rose.

Memory, he guessed. She had something to hide and realized who and where she was and how this bunch loved gossip. Nosy as ever, he eagerly bent farther forward to see the object of her covert affection.

And then turned away. His stare had led to Demosthenes Elias Keriosotis.

How or when Keriosotis had arrived remained a mystery. But, leaning against the pinrail at the base of the flagpole, he had finessed the center of activity on the lawn.

Casually pointing, he unerringly spotted owners and watch captains in the darkness behind him and greeted each woman. Those in black gowns and white blouses got a sedate buss on the cheek. Those flaunting Bahamian straw got the kiss plus a pat on the fanny. Whichever, all savored the welcome. Some, in fact, lingered, in no rush for firsthand race news.

At first glance, he recalled an estate country host urging guests to the striped party tent in the backyard, Wade thought. Then he decided that that view slighted looks and style. No millionaire commuter he knew had straight black hair, a classic profile, and a thirty-two-inch waist.

Damned few could match three or four hundred faces and names, either.

Fewer still would grasp his secret for putting every Race Week guest instantly at ease:

For Old Guard, brass buttons greener than theirs.

For Establishment Elders, sneakers and white ducks.

For New Boys, a spectacular sixty-five-dollar Sulka ascot.

For Babs, a discreet, playfully arched eyebrow.

He had something for everybody, Wade mused. In Wade's case, an account overdrawn by $41,000.

At that, it may have been fair value. Since 1957, when Acey Stiles ordered Wade to "find yourself a Greek," Dimitrios (Taki) Keriosotis had served as shipbroker and general agent for PANARTEX. With Taki and the Keriosotis family offices in Athens and London, Wade had a big edge on American tankerman and most Europeans as well.

But the deal had always rankled. Taki, childless, had a surrogate son, his nephew, Demosthenes. He included the boy's security in his price for becoming the PANARTEX Greek.

Xantippe, the boy's father, he told Wade, made that necessary. The brightest of the Athens Keriosotises, he had come to New York in 1935 to establish a family presence. He did, but, listening to his wife, he put profits into Brooklyn real estate instead of ships. So, in 1950, almost broke, he died of shame.

It took until 1954, Taki said, to turn the business around. Then, fixing his first tanker charters, he saw money in New York. So, finding a Brooklyn congressman who had an opening to fill for Kings Point, the Merchant Marine Academy, he began selling Demosthenes on the family trade.

The boy preferred to go to college. He got that from his mother. A retired manicurist with airs, she called shipping a dirty game. Luckily, she married that summer and moved to L.A. Ducking parenthood and tuition, she promptly signed the kid into Kings Point.

That made him responsible for the boy, Taki said. Setting his price, he told Wade that apart from family business the rest of his time would go to PANARTEX. But, besides the usual fees, he counted on the company to do something, when and if needed, for Demosthenes.

Desperate to rebuild their tanker fleet after the 1956 Niarchos move on the charter market, Hubie and Wade had no choice but to go along.

Their first "something" came due in 1960. A couple taking the *United States* to Europe that summer hit the U.S. Lines with a $2-million damage suit. Their daughter, they said, had been taken to an officer's cabin and seduced while intoxicated. The girl, fifteen, named Third Mate Keriosotis as the father of the unborn child.

A nothing, according to Taki. Kids. But no American line would hire the boy. So, could he ship third in PANARTEX until things blew over? He could.

Captains lauded his navigational and watch-standing skills. They ignored his manner. That implied that tankers were just a step to better things.

They were indeed.

In 1963, Wade diversified. As furtive as ever, and with an eye on taxes, he formed a company to bid on a ten-year charter for hauling aviation fuel from the Staten Island refinery to New York–area airports. That trade, with its time and traffic pressures, called for young skippers.

Taki, naturally, had just the man to head Flight Fuel Delivery, Inc. Besides, he said, the deal needed three "clean"* mosquito tankers. The year before, the city had bought some of Xantippe's junk Brooklyn land, so Demosthenes had cash. With his own money in ships on a cost-plus basis, the kid would be serious.

Ever gracious, Wade agreed.

A month later, having flown from the Persian Gulf and lunched royally at the Hemisphere Club with Taki and Wade, Demosthenes agreed to run the new company. Handshake sealing the job, Wade then mentioned money.

Deal closed, Demosthenes coolly shook his head. PANARTEX had to finance everything, he said. He had no money.

But what about the check from the city? Taki asked.

The answer left him speechless. That had bought a town house on East Forty-ninth Street, he heard.

A town house—what in hell for? Wade demanded.

For when he came ashore, Demosthenes said. Because prep school had taught him a truth: if one wanted to be rich, charm and image came first. A home in Turtle Bay provided a perfect backdrop.

Hearing that, Hubie roared with laughter. He seldom saw Wade, a careful man and a very hard loser, holding the short end of the stick. Look at the figures and pay the two dollars, he said. He was right. Clan Keriosotis had been a money machine.

So the deal stood. Tenants out, Demosthenes began redoing his town house, with occasional nods, of course, at his mini-tankers. He ate up cash faster than a shoat in bran, by Wade's lights, and Hubie loved it. He told Ursall Majors, who told Wade, he got $40,000 a year in laughs alone seeing Loren try to keep the kid from screwing him worse. He would also enjoy hearing about an unannounced week off, or maybe two, to sail in the Bermuda Race. He would probably call that "cute."

Like the nickname, Wade mused. It should have been Demo. But, seeing his tiny son at birth, Xantippe had begun calling him Demi. And it stuck, through all six-two of him. At five-six, that bothered Wade. It always had.

So, turning to loathe anew all that charm and image, he got his second surprise of the evening.

* A ship that has never carried crude oil or any other substance likely to clog aircraft or other fuel lines.

Demi had lost his smile.

Face anxious and earnest, he looked, in fact, to be pitching for his life. The attitude of the woman before him, however, said she had no intention of catching. Left knee bent, body thrust over it, she seemed not to have stopped, but only to have put off finishing her stride. Heightening that impression, she nodded and waved to people on the lawn behind Demi.

A tall, long-haired brunette, she had the best back Wade had ever seen. It rose from a narrow waist in so steep a V that the swell of her breasts curled out from under her shoulders. In the silvery glow of the outdoor spots, each rib depicted a perfect, flowing arc. The valley in which they joined her spine ran relentlessly straight, deep and high-sided, a shadowless cleft, with voluptuous hummocks of muscle and tendon rippling its surface.

Babs, Wade decided, had only been a cull after all. She had elegance, but lacked strength, sensuality. This woman had it everywhere. He saw it. Then, for the first time, he realized why. She dressed differently.

She wore white sneakers, white slacks folded to midcalf, and a white T-shirt of light cotton. Moreover, her shoes looked gray; wet, as if she had just arrived from surf casting or dinghy sailing. Knowing people there, she undoubtedly also knew the dress code of the evening. Yet, while she showed it less respect than a New Boy's wife, the faces to whom he saw her wave all belonged to the Old Guard.

He found Demi's actions more interesting. His gaze hungered after her as she walked away. That never happened.

So, nosy as ever, Loren Wade slid off his barstool. As usual, he felt foolish indulging his curiosity. But what could he lose? he asked himself. The answer, as always, remained the same: nothing.

Besides, he thought, her name might damned well come in handy someday to use against Demi. How or why he had no idea. But facts were like money. Workingmen never got enough of either.

Crossing the veranda, he took a shadowed side path past the flagpole, unseen by Demi. Then, finding cover in a food line, he spotted the brunette.

She looked even better head on, he thought.

She had what he resentfully called the Privileged Look. Her smile bespoke an expensive orthodontist; her complexion and body tone, a childhood diet of a quart of milk a day and two green vegetables with each meal.

As he expected, she had married very well, too. A pear-shaped diamond marked her engagement. More diamonds celebrated her wedding.

Then she had set up house on Long Island. The red burgee with white chevrons of the Manhasset Bay Yacht Club stenciled on her T-shirt under her left shoulder placed her near wealthy Sands Point. It implied Old Guard ties as well.

She stood with three women. All in their late twenties, they explained her clothes. The name printed on their windbreakers excused them from dressing, too. That tub, Wade knew, a smaller yacht undoubtedly sailed by their husbands, lay far behind his on the course to Bermuda. So, as junior in-group members, they came to show the flag, careful not to let looks or attire outshine older wives working that night. An hors d'oeuvres plate in one hand and a glass in the other, they howdied everyone who could do them or their old men any good.

The brunette, however, had another object in mind. Nodding and smiling brightly, she gradually let the flow of the crowd inch her around until she stood almost at a right angle to her companions. Wondering why, Wade turned slightly to align himself with the white T-shirted back ten or fifteen feet away.

What he saw moved him right out of the food line.

Extended over her right shoulder, her profile hung in the dark as starkly as a deeply etched cameo. While flawless, it disturbed him. He knew that look. Only naive or incurably optimistic men, he thought, saw desire in a hardened cheekbone or narrowed eye. For him, those always marked something else: not available women, but accessible women; negotiators.

Her sight line went straight to the flagpole.

With Demi, that could be trouble someday, Wade told himself. She would only have to set a price that could be stolen. He set off at once to find someone who might know her name.

Fortunately, he saw Les Commons, a watch captain on Jakob Isbrandtsen's *Good News,* leaning on the ramp rail leading to the launch dock. A short, balding, muscular Long Island dentist in *Lederhosen* shorts and Dartmouth-green football jersey, Commons waved him over.

After asking about wind and Gulf Stream conditions, Wade pointed his gin glass at the circle of young wives.

"Who's the looker?" he said. "She new this year?"

Commons, a veteran of seven or eight Bermuda races, glanced toward the brunette and leaned closer, speaking over the steel band playing on the dock behind him. "You mean Fiona?" he asked, trying to be specific.

"The one in the T-shirt," Wade affirmed.

A moment later, he blessed his stupidity. Race Week unfolded all around him: lawyers stroked clients; bankers pushed loans; brokers pumped Big Board company chairmen for stock tips. Small groups of their marine counterparts—owners, builders, agents, and oil company brass—did the same. But he had overlooked the obvious: that Demi and the woman knew each other through business. Naturally, he had guessed they had met yachting. So, seeing that she came from Long Island, he had asked a neighbor to identify her, rather than a shipping man who might remember his interest later.

A Sands Point girl, Les Commons said in answer.

Her name was Fiona Angelakos.

Her husband, Arkie, did something in tankers.
Did Wade know him?

*July 6, 1966*
*New York City*

HUBIE SAT erect at his $8,000 Irish bogwood desk.

His eyes held darker glints than the four heads on the knotty-pine wall behind him. A hunter's grand slam of North American sheep, they inspired Wade to call the office Frank Campbell's, after the fashionable Manhattan funeral chapels.

Today, however, ignoring mood, Wade rushed past the thirty-foot window row framing the Hudson on the right side of the office.

He had primed himself for this talk since June 26.

He had no recollection, in fact, of the sail home. The first two days he spent determining how to use what he had seen. Then, getting an idea, he retired to the front of the cockpit, under the white nylon dodger. There, fussing with his manicurist's pencil, he made up a lie for Hubie. It had to be right, he thought, or he lost the sale. Embellishing, refining, and testing that story took the rest of the trip. Finally, on July 2, when he left Newport, all the pieces fit.

So he radiotelephoned Hubie—only to hear a maid say he would be in Texas until the sixth. Calling home, he had Willa Mae invite Ursall Majors and his wife for the weekend, instead. He and Majors spent that time further polishing the tale.

Now, reaching the gorgeous petrified-wood pedestal desk with its stunning reds, whites, browns, and blacks, he told himself not to rush things. Easing into the black leather and chrome conference chair opposite Hubie, he pushed back his shirt cuffs.

"Watch me now," he said, "my fingers'll never leave my hands! I found the way to the Lions."

"The who?" Hubie asked.

That confirmed Wade's guess about the Garrisons' July 4 weekend. Cora had told Willa Mae they were flying home to go to some barbecues. Hubie's amnesia said they had—and come up short on takers for North Slope action. Judging from Hubie's face, Wade figured they were light about $2 billion, which still left them at Square One. That suited him.

He had never thought Hubie could raise that much money. He wanted him to fail quickly and turn to other matters, like the Lions' move to rig tanker spot-charter rates. Most of that he got into his reprise.

"The money behind Lianides, buildin' them five speedballs at Hasegawa's for God knows what," he said.

Uneasy with good news, Hubie immediately reached for his gold half-moon glasses and squinted across the desk. "You did? How?" he asked.

Wade did not intend saying. He needed involvement first. He got that, typically, through indirection. "Oh, I got to puttin' things together." He shrugged casually. "An' I kept comin' back to *Anzac.* Remember?"

Hubie did, of course.

In 1962, *PANARTEX Anzac,* steaming from the Persian Gulf to Wellington, New Zealand, had come down with engine ills. Rather than order her to Japan for repairs, Wade sent her to Seattle. On the second day of her run back under reduced power, he got a call from a New York shipbroker. Listening, he learned a cardinal rule of shipping: anything is cargo.

The night before, the broker told him, a catcher in an Antarctic whaling expedition had rammed its factory ship, springing her holding tanks. Could *Anzac,* the closest vessel to all that whale oil, head south and take it on?

She could, and in due course her eight-knot detour earned $650,000.

That windfall started Wade thinking. Why not build a convertible: a ship to take one kind of cargo outward bound and then return with another? Two loads a round trip beat one.

Hubie, however, killed that proposal. PANARTEX, he said, was in the oil business; others could pioneer shipping advances.

So Niarchos did. In the process, he proved Wade right. His oil–bulk-ore carriers were big moneymakers.

Wade still liked the idea, and whenever Hubie went off on a drilling binge he mentioned convertibles, hoping for conscience money.

Now, however, Hubie found himself $2 billion short. So the reference to *Anzac* baffled him.

"What's she got to do with Lianides?" he asked.

"Why, Judas priest an' Jesus Christ Almighty, she's what it's all about!" Wade exclaimed, as if underscoring the obvious. "Them boards in Japan had stuff on 'em a good five, maybe ten years ahead of the rest of us peons. So, shippin' bein' what it is, that's about all she wrote for tankers till everybody catches up an' some guy needs a design edge. Right?"

"Could be," Hubie conceded.

Wade sailed on, as if agreement had been total. "Then you got container ships, but they're already figured out, too, an' planes've got the passenger trade all locked up. Right?"

"Probably so."

"Okay, then. What's left?"

The question answered itself, since only one other type of deep-sea cargo carrier remained.

"Convertibles?"

Wade nodded. "Exactly. There's nothin' else goin' for front-runnin' designers—an' what's Archimedes Angelakos?" Then, unclipping his trouser waistband, he divulged the first part of the plan conceived on the sail back from Bermuda. "So I got to thinkin'," he went on, "that Archimedes might be real receptive if he all of a sudden got a design job for a convertible."

Hubie belched, slamming into his chair back as if he had been struck across the chest. Then he spun around to the sideboard behind him and turned back to face Wade, frowning, Amphojel in hand, savagely popping a tablet out of its cellophane jacket.

"You want to chase those Lions like *that?*" he asked. "For God's sake, as soon as they hear you found Angelakos—and they will, because he's still working on their ships—they'll know you're onto something."

Wade shrugged. "If they're as smart as we think, they've probably got that far already, or, at least, suspicioned it. For sure, that little Jap, Kono, passed word on to somebody I was at Hasegawa."

"Then it's simple. Archimedes'll just say he's too busy for any design work, and where'll you be then?"

"Right up the creek," Wade conceded. "Only it ain't that easy for him to tell me that. Remember—if them Lions've rigged the spot-charter market, they ain't hidin' just from us, but from the whole world. So they don't want anybody askin' how come a poor Greek like Archimedes nixes a $250,000 job for a $10-million convertible that'd bring him more work. No, sir! That's the last thing they'd want. That'd make anybody wonder. So their safest move is to tell Archimedes to act interested—to play business as usual." Having blunted Hubie's objection, Wade now moved on to the next step in his plan. "Besides that," he asked slyly, "who says I got to go anywheres near Long Island City to send a design inquiry there?"

Disarmed and surprised, Hubie followed right along. "Then who would?" he demanded. "Whenever we've let somebody else boss shipbuilding, it's been a goddamned disaster until you've jumped in. Contracts or not, the yards are too smart about charging costs for our guys."

"I'll give you that," Wade nodded agreeably, pleased with his progress so far. "But you know," he continued, "goin' through the books, I found a funny thing. With all the expense-account screwin' around that went on, the best job we ever did of puttin' new construction into service still was on those mosquitoes of—"

"Demi!" Hubie roared.

Half rising, he slammed the palms of his fists down on the desktop with such force that the stainless-steel pedestal column rang. "That little cunt!" he went on. "He's your idea of who should ride shotgun on this? He's already into you a hundred grand in three years just foolin' around, an' now you want to let him near real dough? Why, that's the goddamnedest thing I ever heard! You need a keeper! You're nuttier'n a sunstroked lizard at high noon!"

Wade knew better. Carefully lowering and clasping the zipper on his fly, he looked up, bright-blue eyes nearly white, to deliver the clincher. "Angelakos has got a wife," he said. "I seen her down in Bermuda."

Hubie dropped into his chair. Then, sensing what came next, he leaned forward, across the desk. "An' she's stuff," he said softly.

"Even better. On a scale of ten, she's an eleven. Got a face on her like the *Mona Lisa* an' enough shade under her tits to grow mushrooms."

Hubie squinted, like a poker player squeezing cards to see his draw. Suspicious that this scenario might be just another way for Wade to get a convertible built against his wishes, he dug in his heels.

"That don't excite me a bit in the world," he said. "I got a wife an' three girls at home that good."

"You're not gettin' the drift," Wade sighed. "Demi already knows her."

Hubie had an answer for that too. "Hell, Demi knows all that yachtin' snatch! That's a small world. They all know each other, an' when they ain't too drunk to leave the bar or to get off the boats, they're all out diddlin' an' divorcin' each other every which way. So, if she's in that gang, it'd be contrary to natural law if Demi didn't know her. But what's that to us?—talk about one of your 'maybes.' "

"That ain't no maybe! I seen 'em on the lawn down there in Bermuda, an' they got a little thing for each other. Only she ain't buyin'—not for now at least. She's a negotiator, that one, an' so far the price ain't right. But she sized him up when he couldn't see her, like a hunter squintin' through a scope, just waitin' for a prize buck to step into the clear. So if we send Demi to Angelakos with a design inquiry that could turn into big bucks, you can bet your ass Mrs. A'll be happy to use hers too, if she gets the idea it'll help close the deal. An' a thrill seeker like Demi ain't above lettin' her think that, either."

"Then, with Demi in the bedroom, an' her in fits of animal passion, she's gonna tell him what her husband is up to in Japan, because she can't hold anything back," Hubie said, jumping to the story's climax. "There's only one problem with that," he went on. "You're dreamin'. I never laid eyes on that woman in my life. But if she's like the rest of that society bunch she runs with, I'm tellin' you, she's not about to spill the family secrets for that old delightful tingle once or twice. An' you know Demi—he's not about to stand at stud, either, an' turn himself into a spy for two crudeos like us. He's the Prince of Forty-ninth Street—loves himself better'n anybody—an' that'd get in the way of his dignity. Slick as you are, you'd never sell him that kind of action."

"An' I'm tellin' you I don't need to!" Wade shot back. "I seen 'em, an' they're on! If a judge'd been there, they'd both've got thirty days for mopery with intent to gore! Good Christ Almighty, you know how I am. I'm so old it only gets hard on one side. An' most times, Old Pink an' Pearly won't even do that without I first sneak in a little whiff of mucket, either! But I mean, those two had me goin', just watchin' 'em eyeball each other with all their damned clothes on—"

"No sale!"

"What do you mean, 'no sale'? It's the only way I know to get in back of Liani—"

"Loren, for the love of Christ, grow up! Where you been, anyway? That's straight out of Secret Agent X-Nine."

"Well, goddammit, you think of somethin' better!"

"That's your job. Mine's gettin' to the North Slope. I'm just here listenin' for ten million bucks' worth of idea, an' so far I don't hear it."

"Who said anythin' about ten million bucks?"

"You said you were goin' to Angelakos for a ten-million-dollar ship."

"But I never asked for the ten million, did I?"

Forehead vein suddenly pulsing, Hubie pushed the gold-rimmed glasses back into his hair and spun around again to the sideboard. Returning with a Maalox bottle, he leaned across the desk, waiting, clearly at a loss as to where the question led.

Wade smiled guilelessly. "How you fixed for fifty grand instead?" he asked.

"Fifty grand?"

"You heard."

"You can't build a ship for fifty grand!"

Wade country-boyed his smile without speaking.

Hubie heard him, anyway. "That's the stupidest goddamned thing you ever came up with!" he bellowed. "You want to make believe you're buildin' a convertible. First, you've got to con Taki—"

"Forget about Taki. He'll wind up thinkin' this is all his idea. I got that part all figured."

"An' Demi?"

"What do you think I need the fifty grand for? It's like fuckin' ham an' eggs—the hen's involved, but that pig, man, he's committed! That's how I want Demi. I want him in so deep he tastes it. An' don't bet he won't stand at stud, or spy, or do whatever we say if he thinks he's lookin' at a cost-plus operatin' contract for a hundred-thousand-ton convertible—maybe even three of 'em!"

"An' Mrs. Angelakos—she's just waitin' for all this to happen?"

"Bet your house, lot, Cora, an' the three girls on it! How she eyed Demi, she's tough enough to bite nails an' spit razor blades, an' she's a merchant besides, or she's gonna trade! An' how much out are we if—"

" 'If'? If she don't trade, you mean? Now you got an 'if' on top of two 'maybes.' You call those odds?"

"Hubie, whether she flops or not, it puts us right where we want—next to the money behind Lianides."

"No, goddammit! I don't want us showin' in this. That money thinks two or three moves deep an' four or five crosswise. If they ever see us, they'll fake us so far back into the tall weeds we'll never get out, an' I got enough on my mind already. Alaska don't sell to the boys down home. All they want to talk is off-shore Gulf leases. To hear them tell it, the South'll rise again, soon's they put the boots to natural-gas rates. An' that's real! That's now! No ifs! No may—"

"Sweet Jesus, don't get hotted up so!" Wade protested. "There's no way this'll start for three, four weeks anyway. Taki's leavin' for Athens tonight to take in the baptism of the century. That niece of his that married into the Hadjidimitrious last year just threw a son, an' soon's the holy water dries, all the men in both families are goin' off to somebody's island to whack up what's left of world shippin'. Then, him an' Honey are runnin' off sightseein' some-wheres. In the meantime, call Urs. He liked—"

Hubie put down the Maalox bottle. "You talked to Urs about this?"

Wade nodded nonchalantly. "Saw him, in fact. Him an' Bonnie Sue come up to spend the Fourth with us, an' he says the odds—"

"Odds! What the fuck's Urs know about odds?"

"For God's sake, what do you?" Wade demanded back. "Eleven out of every twelve wells you ever put down come in dusters, an' you're tellin' me about odds? Besides, I never called this a lock, but it sure as hell beats twelve to one, an' it don't take ten years or two billion dollars either. On top of that, it may just keep us in business till you get Alaska out of your—"

On his feet, Hubie leaned across the desk, forehead vein finger-thick and purple to his widow's peak. "Hey, Loren! Who's *el Jefe* around here, any-way—you or me? I told you no, an' no, by God, it is! Now get outa here with your goddamned 'ifs' an' 'maybes.' You're sourin' my Maalox before it ever hits bottom!"

Wade had an answer for that too. If he did nothing, he saw himself jobless in about twenty-four months. The Lions' move would bankrupt PANARTEX that soon, he believed. So he gambled that sure time.

"Well, then, *Jefe*," he said, rising and clipping his trouser waistband, "I'll just do it myself."

Hubie smirked. "With what?"

"With my egg money, that's what ! An' if push comes to shove, I got enough hid to build me that convertible too. You go tell that to all them fancy Har-vards an' Yales you got downstairs keepin' books on me."

Hubie, who took anything from Wade, took that too. Surrounded by M.B.A.s, he still saw Little Loren as the company's best mind and something more: the rusty nail that hung in no matter what. And, besides, the fable of the fake convertibles might just work. In fact, freed from defending the Alas-kan move, Hubie saw merit in the tale. It happened now. It offered a way to get past Lianides. Its price was right.

But first he had to deal with insubordination.

"Okay, you got the fifty," he muttered grudgingly. "Just you see the hog don't eat the butcher." That offered a graceful chance for apology.

Wade, however, rising, ignored it.

The rebuff moved Hubie to threaten punishment. "By God," he continued, as Wade strode past the windows overlooking the Hudson, "if it works it might even be creative. You know—presidential."

That put Wade ashore, without his "motion."

Ignoring the threat, Wade started for the door.

Hubie watched him go. Then, sagging against the edge of his $8,000 desk, he suddenly knew how Acey felt during similar *mano a manos*. If wrong, he preferred going bust on the North Slope to a merger and respectable retirement. He knew plenty of men better than he who had died goats. Beyond that, miracle or not, he also knew he would find $2 billion.

But, unable to explain pride or hope, and needing allies, he surrendered. Mouth curling into disarming smile, he wondered if he too, like Acey, resembled a Bowery bum panhandling two bits for a pint of muscatel.

"Loren . . ."

"Fuck you!"

The grin widened. A nervous belch was swallowed. ". . . no need to call me sir, buddy!"

Thirty feet away, Wade paused and looked back, his glance filled with contempt. For answer, he slammed the eight-foot-high rosewood door with thunderous force.

So began what Hubie called the "spy caper."

It ended no less explosively.


*July 31, 1966*
*New York City*


TAKI'S GRIN shone in the best tradition of European dockside dentistry. Pleased at Wade's call on his first day back, he flashed his full set of gold-jacketed teeth. "I got just the thing for you, Loren," he said.

Reaching into the top drawer of a rusty green filing cabinet, he removed an unopened quart bottle, which he dangled enticingly by the neck.

Wade leaned forward in the rickety plastic-covered armchair. Unable to read the label under the cellophane wrapping, he shook his head.

"Ouzo?" he guessed.

Taki smiled sorrowfully. "I look like that—some kind tourist?"

Not to Wade. Neither did Pearl Street, a narrow lane meandering across lower Manhattan, suggest tourism. Dating from Colonial times, when shipowners lived there, it now housed maritime sweats: ships'-stores dealers, freight forwarders, electronic-repairs services, and the like. Taki's block, paved with cobblestones brought back as ship ballast, rivaled the least inviting in the mile of dingy, unwashed storefronts. His second-floor office in a 250-year-old building, over a venerable firm of chart agents and compass adjusters, seemed of a piece.

Xantippe, Demi's father, had bought the chairs and the filing cabinets when he arrived in America in the thirties. The oak desk, pocked with wet rot and gummy varnish, came from a Canal Street liquidation sale when Taki took over. Only the Telex at the head of the stairs looked new.

Nor did Taki conjure up the image of a shipbroker. In a group known for tailoring and grooming, he alone contrived to look like a supermarket manager. He lacked only a tan jacket, breast pocket full of colored pens, Wade thought. Everything else he had: the white shirt, frayed collar already limp with sweat; the heavy, flat-footed stance and gray-tipped thinning brown hair; the tired, ashen rings under his eyes, with matching lids and even grayer polyps in their corners; the forehead deeply set in the pleading arcs of a man forever trying to please.

Seamen, however, saw more. A small dull-green anchor tattooed between left thumb and forefinger marked a rounding of Cape Horn under sail. With the death of windjammers, men Taki's age, in their midfifties, had done that trip at thirteen or fourteen.

But now, tempting Wade, he seemed far more the store manager, behind the liquor counter to make a quick sale, than the deep-sea man.

"Raki Arak Razzouk!" he exlaimed in a surprisingly light, boyish voice, fondly slapping the bottle. "Honey never seen Beirut, so I took her down to Saint George's, an' we found this—best in house an' bought full price right from bartender!"

"Jesus," Wade sighed, "ouzo's a kid in short pants next to that stuff."

"You don't like raki, Loren?"

"At eight-fifteen in the mornin'?"

Shrugging, Taki acknowledged the point and dismissed the oversight. In common with many New York shipbrokers, he got to his office between 6:30 and 7 A.M. That gave him time to answer the day's first Telexes before it was lunchtime in Athens or London. So, closing the file drawer, he knelt before the Astral refrigerator tucked in the corner behind his desk.

"You like Yoo-Hoo?" he called over his shoulder.

"Yoo-Hoo?"

"Tsoc'late, Loren. Real good!"

"On top o' eggs Benedict?" Wade asked. "I just come from breakfast with Hubie at the Dorset."

"I got it then, another cup coffee! I'll send to Tsock Full o' Nuts an' get coupla wholewheat doughnuts too—with sugar on top!"

"Lordy," Wade groaned, opening his trouser clasp, "it's already in the eighties. Nothin' hot—please."

"But, Loren," Taki protested, slapping the sides of his thighs in frustration, "you're my guest!"

So, twenty minutes later, unable to wash the crumbs off the roof of his mouth, Wade began chasing the money behind Costa Lianides.

"I got somethin' real sneaky to play with," he said.

Taki looked around uneasily, with good reason. His stupendous lack of business sense, he once told Wade, had persuaded his Athens uncles to keep him at sea thirty-three years. There, at least, he said, he kept a master's wages in the family. So, with little at risk, at age forty-six he had been plucked off the bridge of a Keriosotis tanker and sent to New York. His assignment: to close the office established by his dead brother, Xantippe.

Instead, business boomed almost at once. The few prospects who came to him left certain he had an uncanny sense of estimating the safe life of a ship. They told friends, and within a year he had a reputation. He had also made big money: 1.5 percent of the sale price of the vessels he recommended buying.

Then he made his brokerage clients even more money. After decades in his family's fleet, he knew every trick for coaxing antique engines and rusty steel through more trips than builders ever intended. Those skills brought him his first lucrative tanker charters and, a little later, Loren Wade.

Meanwhile, his uncles, who had suffered him as the family *malaca,* the jerk of the Keriosotises, for thirty years, called him lucky and told him to be grateful for his big break. In spite of having acquired a million dollars or so and a beautiful young wife, Honey, he remained what he always had been: a docile old-school Greek seaman.

The convertible fable had been created accordingly. If served the story whole, Wade believed, Taki would gag in confusion. The tale, therefore, had been broken into three digestible bites. First, a reason for PANARTEX to build such ships had been found. Next, a possible change of attitude on Hubie's part had been structured into the scenario. And, finally, a subplot had been developed to bring Demi onto the scene.

Once Demi arrived, Wade reflected, he knew exactly how to steer him to Archimedes Angelakos and how to sweat him for the information about the Lions he needed. In the meantime, though, everything hinged on Taki understanding and believing what he had been told.

"Remember, that big spic weddin' me an' Hubie are flyin' down to Colón for next month?" Wade began.

"The one with party on *Panama?*"

"Right. Well, last week I sent her down to Newport News Shipbuildin' an' Drydock to get cleaned up. Then Hubie gets this bug up his ass that since he's throwin' the reception I should honcho the refit in person. So, down I go, but I never did shucks' worth of work. I got to thinkin' instead, lookin' at them Norfolk an' Western docks right next door."

"Loadin' coal?"

"You got it." Wade winked. "For Japan. That's what makes it so beautiful. Guys down there say the railroad might just as well have one solid train an' run it round an' round, from the mines in West Virginia to the docks. They're loadin' coal twenty-four hours a day to go through the Canal an' then up to Japan. The coal never stops comin'!"

Shaking his head, Taki loosened his tie. "*Skata* cargo, Loren," he warned. "My cousin Minas, figures man in Athens, he say coal pays four percent on investment, tops. Is all low rates an' spot tsarters a trip at a time."

"No question," Wade agreed expansively, watching the bait go down. "But what happens to all them ships after they discharge in Japan?"

That Taki knew from bitter experience. "If their owners ain't found no better cargo, they come back U.S. for more coal."

"Exactly, an' haulin' oil, that's our bind, only eastbound."

Taki nodded. "Sure, you gotta sail empty to Middle East for another load."

"Right, an' that's what's killin' us! We bring in a ship a week to Curaçao or Staten Island with Persian Gulf crude, an' then what happens? We turn that sucker right around and send her back light. Ain't a way in the world we can make a penny off that return trip. Odds are, in fact, we'd do a damned sight better lookin' for soft-lipped chickens! So what in hell can we do? How do we beat the motherlickin' geography?"

Brows fiercely beetled, Taki leaned forward.

"Watch me, now," Wade warned softly, right forefinger at lower eyelid in the Middle Eastern sign for caution. "Suppose our westbound ship from the Persian Gulf unloads crude here an' cleans tanks at sea. But then, instead of goin' right back to the PG, say she goes into Newport News to load coal. Then, imagine her goin' to Panama, through the Canal, an' up to Japan to discharge the coal before she heads for the Gulf. What do you suppose the books'd look like on that kind of voyage?"

Taki struggled through the geography. ". . . from Japan to PG for oil an' then back here to States to discharge oil—that's worldaroun', Loren!"

"It works that way, you go west far enough."

"Lotsa miles worldaroun'," Taki said glumly. "Why send s'ip on three-month voyage for bum tsarter?"

Wade shook his head. "You ain't gettin' the drift," he said. "We better do all the numbers. Find yourself a pencil."

The center drawer of the oak desk yielded a pencil. An old Telex, taken from a twenty-five-gallon cardboard chemical drum which served as a wastebasket, provided the paper.

"Okay," Wade began, "how many miles from the PG to Staten Island?"

Taki smiled in recognition. Like Wade, he regarded every sea route in the world as "home waters."

"Eighty-three hundred twenty-five!"

"Right! You loaded or unloaded?"

"Loaded. Wit' crude."

"Make an *L* by the miles."

Pausing, Taki considered whether to put the *L* to the left or the right of the mileage. At length, he decided it belonged to the right.

Wade waited patiently. Then, nodding in relief, he continued. "Now, how many miles from Newport News to Panama?"

"Sixteen hundred!"

"Exactly. Loaded or unloaded?"

"Loaded . . . wit' coal."

"You got it! An' from Panama to Japan?"

"Seventy-six hundred!"

"Loaded or unloaded?"

"Still loaded wit' coal."

"Right. But, goddammit, make an *L* there too, same's the others! Now, what's the run from Japan to the PG?"

"Forty-seven hundred fifty-two."

"Loaded or unloaded?"

"That leg, we're light. No?"

Wade nodded. "Right. We discharged coal in Japan. Put a *U* there. Now what do you see?"

Taki added the distances. "Ninety-day trip, twenty-two thousand miles, four percent profit. *Skata*, Loren," he concluded, shaking his head.

"Good God Almighty, man—look! Even Hubie saw it! How many miles'll that ship run light before she makes Staten Island again with another load of crude?"

Taki ran his turquoise pencil stub down the strip of Telex paper again. "Forty-seven hundred fifty-two—from Japan to PG."

Then, lips pursed, oak chair creaking, he leaned back to regard the faded green paint on the twelve-foot-high ceiling and what he had just said. After a lengthy silence, the significance of the 4,752 miles from Japan to the Persian Gulf became clear to him. Having found the answer, however, he had difficulty believing it.

"Reg'lar voyage PG to Staten Island . . ." he began, retracing his thought, "s'ip runs light one way—eighty-three hundred twenty-five miles. World-aroun', you save over half cost return passage to PG. Right?"

"An' I got paid for goin' to Japan on top of it—even if it was only four percent!"

Smiling as if he had the prize steer at the country fair, Wade unstuck his shirt from the plastic chair back. Taki, he saw, had swallowed the reason for PANARTEX to build convertibles. His next bite would soon follow.

A long moment later, it did.

"But, Loren," Taki sighed, sagging back into the loose-jointed chair, "we don't run no convertibles."

"Who said we did?"

"But you said you talked this with Hubie."

"Don't I talk everythin' with Hubie?"

"An' he liked it?"

"This time he listened."

Taki took his cue from the coy, teasing smile. "Oh, boy! We're gonna do convertible after all!" he exclaimed, slamming his palms down on the desktop for emphasis. "You deserve it, Loren! You had idea first. You got the credit comin'—"

"Now, now," Wade chided, hands out as if warding off an affectionate Great Dane. "Good Christ Almighty, credit's the last thing we need. As a matter of fact, we don't want the Red Sword anywheres near this."

"No?"

"No way!"

Wade shook his head and leaned forward for dramatic effect. Then, reviewing dialogue for a last time, he set Taki up for the third and crucial bite—the one that would bring Demi into the fable.

"What we want," he told Taki in his best conspiratorial whisper, "is to find us an operatin' man who'll find us a designer who'll draw an eighteen-knot hundred-thousand-tonner . . . real quietly. Then, if his speed curves test out, we'll get us bids on two or three for openers, an' me an' you'll go to Nippon to find us a *zaibatsu* who'll fix us a time charter on coal—"

Taki shook his head, as if to a stubborn child. "Loren, I tol' you. Japs only spot-tsarter coal—"

"An' I'm tellin' you right back," Wade retorted, "there ain't a *zaibatsu* chief in the world who won't buy our deal before the tea's even cool! Remember, all we need goin' to Japan is enough profit to cover the leg we're empty from there to the PG. That's less'n half the run back to the U.S. You don't think them little monkeys over there won't buy all that bargain shippin' we're willin' to sell?"

What he lacked in quickness Taki made up for in enthusiasm. Finally understanding the price play to the Japanese, he slapped the top of the desk again. "If I'm *zaibatsu* chief, I'd buy myself!"

Wade shook his head. The story went down because its economics and geography were true. Taki's Athens uncles, however, would wonder. They would ask who in his right mind put big bucks into new ships to save half the cost home from the PG. So, widening his smile, he gave Taki another reason for sending a ship around the world. This too had the benefit of an underlying truth.

"An' while we're sellin' coal—" he winked, resting both forearms on the edge of Taki's desk—"ol' W. Huber G.'ll have both hands an' a downhill drag on the majors' gonads! He's gonna cop some gravy the Pentagon gives bigs for haulin' PG crude to the East Coast stockpile. Ain't a way in the world, with public bids, Uncle Sam can miss layin' five years of that cush on us. We just lay back in the weeds so's the majors bid on sixteen-thousand-mile round trips. With convertibles, we got half the delivery distance—which gives us eight thousand miles of their cost to build into our price as profit."

Taki sat back questioningly. "You gonna tsarge it all, Loren?"

Wade shrugged, as if conceding a meaningless point. "Hell, we'll sneak in six to seven thousand miles' worth anyways, even after we're done Jewin' down the price. As we say in Jamaica, 'Do that sweet you?'"

A moment later, he saw that it did not. Given a six-figure yearly fee, Taki blinked, rubbing the gray polyps in the corners of his eyelids.

Once a *malaca*, always a *malaca*, Wade thought.

There were, he knew, two kinds of Greeks. "Been America" Greeks took their savings back to the Old Country so they could die in their villages as rich men. "Die America" Greeks, on the other hand, said their lives began when they reached the United States. Taki, with great pride, counted himself a member of the latter group. He took exception to screwing his government.

Regardless, he had pledged Wade his full resources. Leaning forward with an accommodating smile, he honored that promise, a disapproving accomplice. Turning both palms up, he looked like a grocer offering a favored housewife of the neighborhood a choice of eggplants.

"So, Loren, what's first for me to do?"

"First, you get us off Square One. You find us an operatin' man, only you don't approach him, an' you don't mention the Red Sword. Got it?"

The operating man would, of course, be Demi. But never having taken a course in speedthinking, Taki would need at least a week to dope that out, Wade thought.

Then blood, or just being Greek, would beat hell out of patriotism.

*August 21, 1966*
*New York City*

WADE SURVEYED the sunroom of Restaurant Lutèce.

Eyes brighter than usual, his gaze panned over the trellised walls and climbing plants, wicker furniture, and translucent-plastic ceiling. Occasionally, he held his glance appreciatively on an attractive woman.

His smile begged indulgence. Appetite thus excused, he moved to the attack.

Leaning across the yellow plaid tablecloth, he broke the crusty roll on Demi's butter plate in half. Then, sighing, he split the roll again and began dabbing at the red lobster sauce before him in tiny, though precise swipes.

"Goddamn," he gloated between bites, "this is what I call eats! Old Mother Wade ever cooked up gravy like that, little Loren'd never run off to join the maritime, I'll tell you. Judas priest," he exulted, using a last bit of crust to lick the plate cat-clean, "I mean it's like what Elizabeth told Philip on their weddin' night: 'This is too good for common people!' "

Enthusiasm or put-on? Demi wondered. With Wade, he never knew.

Meanwhile, he winced discreetly for the benefit of the waiter and two expensive-looking women at the next table watching the cleanup. He hoped they understood the gesture. He meant it to say lunch had not been his idea.

Lutèce, however, had been. He calculated it would give him a better chance.

Parted from his status symbols—the skipper's mug and tanker models in the office or his favorite table at "21," Pietro's, or the Palm—Wade might be managed, he hoped. That, at least, had been his strategy when he got the call a week before, summoning him to a meeting.

He should have known better, he thought bitterly. Wade thrived anywhere. Drawl aside, he ordered *quenelles de brochet, nantua* in such perfect French that André Surmain, Lutèce's autocratic owner, cocked an eyebrow in surprise. He took the order out of curiosity, Demi believed, after spying Wade's white cotton tanker-slop-chest socks.

Monsieur had an interest in gastronomy? he asked.

In eatin'? Oh, hell, yes! That was the most fun you could have with your clothes on, he was told.

In that case, Surmain prompted, testing the fitness of an acolyte for his temple of *haute cuisine*, Monsieur might like morels, not on the menu.

There followed an informed and lively chat, much of it news to Demi, about the fleshy, spongelike mushrooms. *Cèpes,* an even rarer variety, were also mentioned. Surmain had flown some in from Paris for a private dinner. The upshot: Lutèce looked like a real nice spot, but a little tearoomy, so, to be safe, Wade ordered an entrée of each.

Surmain left enchanted. A salon painter, he had discovered his own Grandma Moses.

A member of the Kennedy family, passing their table, recalled Lot's wife on her way home from a gang bang. The prominent diplomat with her needed only a big white purse to make a fortune peddling his ass on Eighth Avenue.

More commentary followed. To Demi's growing unease, it reflected a pet Wade theory: the best way to hide a secret was to put out lots of blab. Today he touched on everything but a reason for the meeting. Before, that had been a given; they met to fight about expenses. Now he acted as if he were at a social lunch. He called Lutèce a great idea. They would do it again, and soon, he said. Promise made, he then gave the women at the next table his best village idiot's smile as they watched his double entrée arrive.

Baffled by this attitude, Demi waited until the final pastry flake and last bit of cream sauce had left Wade's plate. Then he sought answers.

"Uncle," he said, in the mocking tone he affected when referring to Taki, "told me you might be the bearer of glad tidings, Loren."

"Maybe, maybe not," Wade allowed, licking the tip of his forefinger. Then, leaning forward, he began to lift the covey of crumbs surrounding his plate. "It could be a terrific pain in the ass too, with nothin' to show for it," he went on, not looking up.

Demi brightened at the opening, however nebulous. "Well, then, Loren," he said as the waiter arrived with spectacularly purple currant ice and poured *café filtre* from a gleaming brassbound glass pot, "since we're here, hadn't you better tell me about it?"

"Oh, yeah," Wade sighed.

Repeating what he had told Taki, he made sure his tone carried an unmistakable undercurrent of reluctance. He needed that later for credibility. At the same time, he held back many details. Used wisely, they could be like the sloping sides of a minnow trap, he thought. As they became increasingly specific, they would close in on Demi until he had but one way to go—through the narrow open end of the entry cone.

The journey, in fact, had already begun.

Brown eyes glinting, Demi considered the merits of sending convertibles "worldaround." Pondering hearsay, he took his time, tamping a pencil-thin Schimmelpenninck cigar on its slim oblong metal case. At length, he lit an equally exotic inch-long French waxed match.

A role in new construction could be very good news, indeed. But, knowing Wade's dislike for him, he put off asking about his place in the plan. He wondered, instead, if a plan existed at all. Little Loren had more curves than a corkscrew. So, to gain time to see where the talk led, he turned to banter.

"And Uncle understood all that, Loren?" he asked.

"The second or third time through," Wade conceded.

"Without calling Auntie Honey or Athens? That's very good for him. He's flowering, Loren, flowering—entering his quick-study period. He'll be doing short division next. And my compliments to the chef on the idea. But doesn't Niarchos just charter convertibles out and back?"

Probe launched in his East Side tone of bemusement, Demi sat back.

Minnow trap in mind, Wade responded as casually.

"Bein' a Greek, that's his only choice," he said. "The Pentagon can't ship in foreign bottoms. So, what he does, he hauls grain from Canada, here, or Argentina—dependin' on who's got the crop—to Europe. Then he goes on to the PG for crude bound for this side of the Atlantic. He ain't above carryin' coal either, if business is slow. He don't have the luxury of Uncle Whiskers payin' for that leg back from the PG."

That sounded like a plan to Demi. He also saw its profit potential. Less suspicious, he now grew bolder.

"That's so good it's vulgar," he said. "You charge round trips, but you only pay for half a one-way passage—maybe not even that if you get lucky with the Japs. And that makes you vulgar, too," he told Wade, hoping a left-handed compliment might draw out more of the story. "You're sitting on more money than God, and you look like you want to go to the ladies' room and see if they have Midol, your tummy hurts so. What's wrong? Is this just a gleam in Daddy's eye, and you need my testimonial to go along with Taki's? Is Hubie still hanging you up on convertibles, and you can't sell him by yourself?"

"No, no! Nothin' like that! Hubie's sold," Wade protested. "He already give me fifty grand to get started. He's in for the first step, anyways."

"The first step, Loren?"

"Development."

"Then what's biting you? Why the face?"

"Goddammit, I'm hot to trot, but I ain't got horses!"

"Horses?"

"An operatin' man an' a design—"

"Loren, for God's sake, the only operating men you couldn't get are maybe the Onassis and Niarchos cousins. Anybody else'd work free until those ships are launched, for a piece of the pie they're going to earn! You know that. All you have to do is put out the word."

"Right," Wade agreed slyly. "An' what do you think the bigs'll do, once we put out the word?"

The question answered itself. The majors would start designing convertibles, too, and PANARTEX would lose its competitive advantage.

With a connoisseur's eye, Demi regarded his Schimmelpenninck. Tapping off a minute section of pearl-white ash, he shrugged matter-of-factly. "So, what's wrong with one of your boys?" he asked. "How many are in your operations department now—forty or forty-five?"

"An' ain't a one of 'em ever rode herd on more'n a big coffee order from the Savarin," Wade answered. "To say nothin' of twenty or thirty million bucks, or a designer, or all of them shipyard sharpies who figure out how to do everythin' on overtime. But we think we found us a guy, anyways."

"Oh, who?"

"You," Wade replied.

Demi reached up to brush back his forelock. He had Keriosotis black hair. But his grew out of a widow's peak instead of straight back, so the right side tended to fall over his forehead. He confided once to Wade that nothing disarmed a sophisticated woman more rapidly than that tousled look. Since then, Wade saw he swept forefinger past eyebrow whenever stalling, the way pipe smokers fiddle with ashes.

He did so now. But this time, openmouthed, he found no hair to sweep back into place.

The waiter, however, chose that moment to bring the check, proving Wade's law: that snobbishness in New York restaurants varies inversely with prominence given to prices.

In many Wall Street clubs, only members got menus showing costs. At Barbetta's, a tony theater-district spot, charges appeared, but the bill came in a parchment envelope. Lutèce, not to be outdone, sent its bad news in a hollowed-out book; the "Bible," to regulars.

Worldly Europeans handle that snootiness simply and surely. They find the owner and pay him. That achieves two objectives: first, it reminds the boss of the buyer of all that expensive food; second, it puts money into his hand, emphasizing that he is only bourgeois after all, to be paid for goods or services by the gentry like any other shopkeeper or tradesman.

Demosthenes Elias Keriosotis, who coveted such ploys, used it now to compose himself. "I'll be right back," he told Wade. "Get some more coffee and dessert if you want. If you pay the bill first, seconds are usually on the house in these joints. The old image muddies up, don't you know"—he winked at Wade as he took the check—"if they start charging nickels and dimes after they've already whacked you for a forty-buck lunch."

Wade watched him go. The rust-checked hacking jacket with red leather piping, maize gabardine slacks, and brown suede shoes were the best London offered. The New York Yacht Club tie was even better. Slim and erect, he strode by the lush plants and handsomely groomed diners in Lutèce's sunroom as if he, and not Surmain, owned the place.

But not even the most assured minnow, Wade reminded himself, swam into the trap without looking both ways. Nor, apparently, without an eye on overhead.

"They tab those?" Demi asked, returning to the table and seeing a fresh pot of coffee and two lemon tarts.

Wade shook his head.

"Timing is all," he heard. "The bastards kill you on wine, but you come up a winner on this nine times out of ten. Once a week, it's worth two to three hundred bucks a year."

A shrug mocked the money. Wade knew better. Every penny mattered to Demi. His $50,000-a-year salary fed a $100,000-a-year lifestyle. The left arm draped over the back of the wicker chair similarly suggested casualness; the finger sweep across the forehead, something else.

The voice, however, remained as playful as always. "Now tell me how I become a millionaire tanker Greek, Loren?"

Wade shook his head. "Don't spend a penny yet! That's years off, if at all. What we're talkin' about now is fifty thousand dollars to get us a set of drawin's, so's we can start."

Given secrecy, the convertible plan could not fail. So, as intended, nothing in the qualifier deflected Demi from his central suspicion. The doubt lured him forward as surely as breadcrusts do a minnow.

"But why me, Loren?" he asked.

"Who else we got?" Wade demanded. "Judas priest, with the market goin' soft, I'm runnin' hard's I can just to keep us even. Where'm I gonna find time to poke my honker into new construction?"

"But *I* surely wasn't your idea, was I?"

Suspicion aside, Demi relished inserting the needle. For him, three tanker bosses, Colocotronis, Karageorgis, and Niarchos, had style. The rest violated his view of the universe. He enjoyed particularly making Wade squirm whenever possible.

Wade, who knew his audience, reacted accordingly.

"Jesus, buddy," he sighed placatingly, "you know how we operate. I got to talkin' to Taki—"

"And when did you ever listen to Taki about—"

"I ride both ways with Hubie every day I'm here, too."

"I was Hubie's idea?"

"C'mon! Who in hell knows whose idea anythin' is, how we chew it around? An' what's the difference, anyways? It had to be you. You're in the family, an' you already built ships."

That disclaimer, as unconvincing as the first, had, however, the same effect. It drew Demi further down the funnel being constructed for him.

"So it was Hubie," he smirked.

In point of fact, it had been. Wade had planned on that from the beginning. His opportunity to use Hubie, however, had come sooner than anticipated. Taki had called the evening after their meeting. "Hey, Loren, what in hell we thinkin' about, anyways?" he had begun in the urgent whisper. "We already got guy for Prodzect X!"

His candidate, of course, had been Demi.

His reasoning: the kid ate off PANARTEX, too, so he could be counted on to keep quiet. Besides, Taki added, where would he or Wade find time to gumshoe around until they found exactly the right guy?

Wade had fielded the suggestion perfectly. He agreed, but with a reservation. Time troubled him, too, he said, so he thought Taki should try the idea on Hubie. *He* would, but he had a flight to Curaçao the next morning. If Hubie okayed Demi, so would he—provided, of course, Demi could be policed. Loose change in building a convertible could run into hundreds of thousands of dollars.

A quick call then reprised that chat for Hubie. The next morning, he had responded to Taki on cue.

Now, doubt at rest for the moment, Demi leaned over the yellow plaid tablecloth. For all his posturing, he never suffered from hypocrisy. "Well, thanks anyway, Loren, for not turning Hubie around on this. If you wanted to fight hard enough, I know you could have," he told Wade.

Then he assessed the situation, taking advantage of the opportunity.

"The way I see it, this is like a Texas gunfight," he said, the merest trace of a smile curling the corners of his mouth. "Right now, we're sneaking down the alley, past the hotel and saloon, to get to the stable, where we can turn left and blast those gringo sonsofbitches in the back the moment those bids are opened in Washington. So, if we need a designer, we can't go to a shipyard for plans. Business is so slow, the story'd be out as soon as anybody who looked like a live one asked, 'What's new?'"

Sipping his coffee, he dismissed foreigners as well. "Europe'd be even more dangerous. They've got the designers, but they're all tied to owners one way or another. It's like the old guilds. Each artist has his patron. There's a social thing too. The wives almost always come from shipping families on top of it, and you never know where they're reporting, either. Which, it seems to me, makes a case for our finding an independent here, where we can keep an eye on him."

Pure Demi, Wade thought. He ran on like a teacher and never missed a chance to point out the "social thing." Still, he was right.

"That's where I come out, too," Wade agreed. "What about Gibbs and Cox?" he asked, naming the designers of the *America* and the *United States*.

"No good on two counts. First, they get more work than they can handle. Second, most of it comes from the Navy, and those guys look at everything. Tell me," Demi asked, raising his coffee cup again, "what would you think of Sparkman and Stephens?"

"I thought they might get mentioned," Wade snickered. Sparkman and

Stephens were premier designers of ocean racing yachts.

"Oh, they do more than yachts! In Liberia two years ago I saw one of their powered lighters come into Monrovia with latex from the rubber plantations up the Pickaninny River, and it looked like a jewel."

"An' what would we ever do with a jewel except run its engine right through the floorplates? You know us. We ain't in that elegance game."

"Then maybe we should talk to De Fever or Garden. They made their names doing working ships."

"I know, but how big's a tuna clipper? Or one of them crab seiners Wakefield uses up in Alaska—three or four hundred feet? We're talkin' a thousand, now, maybe more. An' those guys are on the West Coast."

"Okay, we'll stick to New York. What would you say to the Rosenblatts?"

"They'd be more like it," Wade agreed, deciding the time had come to add a fresh crust to the minnow trap. "We used them before on some repairs, an' they did good, but unless we're luckier'n we've ever been, Uncle Sam'll throw our ass the hell out of his feed trough soon's he can an' get right back in bed with the majors. So, what I want now is technology that'll still be ahead of the rest of the gang's in five, ten years, when we have to get them convertibles chartered out again. I don't think you're gonna get any breakthroughs that big from guys who ain't workin' tankers seven days a week."

"Loren, is that you? 'Breakthroughs'? You want to be the pace setter, instead of letting Ari and Stavros pay for all the research?"

"Why the hell not for once? I ain't against progress if it's the only way a deal makes sense. You want any more of that lemon tart?"

Demi withdrew a fresh Schimmelpenninck from its metal case. After a prolonged bout of tamping, he confirmed his hearing. "You're serious? You want innovative ships?"

He got a nod back as his tart crossed the table.

Lighting up, he dropped the tiny stub of the French waxed match into the ashtray, and leaned forward.

"I've got a guy for you," he said. "He's here in New York, works seven days a week on tankers, and maybe knows more about them than you."

"Who's that?"

"Archimedes Angelakos."

And so the minnow negotiated the entry cone.

The genius of the trap, however, lay in its design. Past the funnellike entrances at each end, it widened into a free-swimming environment for tiny fish. Rather than trying to escape, they finned contentedly in the center of the snare, unaware of being captured.

No man honored that principle more than Loren Wade.

He looked up now from the dessert plate before him. "How's that again? That's *mucho* Greek on a full stomach—first time through, anyways."

"Arkie Angelakos. He owns Marine Cargo Systems, a shop over in Long Island City that modifies tankers for the majors. I was at Kings Point with him. Then he went on to the Webb Institute."

"Never heard of him."

"You wouldn't. He gets all the work he wants from the bigs, and at top dollar, so he doesn't solicit."

"An' he designs?"

"All the time." Demi grinned. "Why do you think he gets so much business? He won't notice, though, until somebody asks for an entire ship. He's an even bigger *malaca* than Uncle. As a matter of fact, he got the money for his company designing. He figured out how to stretch T-2s."

"Oh, shit," Wade scoffed. "Half a dozen guys tried that, an' they all should've gone to jail."

The modification, explored in the fifties, promised to enlarge old tubs at minimal cost. The procedure entailed vertically cutting through the forebody of a T-2, inserting a 70- to 90-foot-long hull section, and then welding back the bow. In practice, only the first Japanese attempt at modular ship construction produced a greater debacle.

Demi, however, knew of a successful try. "The ones Arkie stretched are still going," he told Wade. "And he built them for half a million bucks less than anybody else, too."

For that much money, Wade gladly played straight man. "How'd he do it?" he asked.

"By going to the best Dutch yards and—"

"He never saved that kind of dough in Holland."

"He never meant to. But he did want Dutch quality."

"Then where'd he make the savin's?"

"Loren, think breakthroughs! Where do you go for big savings?"

By then, thoroughly adrift, Wade lost patience. "Now, goddammit, you're talkin' Japan, not Holland!"

"Why not both?"

"Both? How can that be?"

"If you're a *malaca* like Arkie, it's simple. He was the only man in the world stupid enough to think it out. Quick, Loren! What else can a ninety-foot hull section be?" Amusing himself, Demi provided another clue. "Suppose you closed off both ends," he said.

Wade continued to shake his head.

"Well, Arkie imagined those sections were floating drydocks," Demi went on. "So, after he got that Dutch Old World Craftsmanship, he just towed them to Japan, where all that cheap labor spliced them into the hulls. Is that the kind of innovative mind you're looking for?"

And then some, Wade thought. That kind of brain, he told himself, remembering the sketches he had seen at Hasegawa, could innovate a ship's bow into a 19,000-ton tank.

"Jesus," he said, "you think we could get him?"

"He'll come running," Demi promised. "He did those T-2s when he was sailing with Gulf as a first assistant. He can't stop designing. It's all he ever wanted to do. His business now, he says, is turning into a factory—nothing but production and cost accounting. I'll get him in for lunch next week."

Wade shook his head. "You're forgettin' somethin'," he said, licking his lips over the last taste of Demi's lemon tart.

"I am? What?"

"PANARTEX can't be anywheres near this. Guys from the majors'll be runnin' all over his place. If one ever seen our name on a convertible plan, school'd be out. So, as far as this Angelakos is concerned, you're the buyer. Who knows, anyways, but some four-eyed clerk at the Port Authority, who owns Flight Fuel Delivery, Inc.? I ain't gonna show until final plans, an' you're ready to shop yards. Get it?"

Oh, did he love that! Wade thought.

The brown eyes opposite him shined brighter than a champion retriever's in field trials. They seemed to be tracking a statuesque brunette as she crossed the sunroom. What they really saw, he knew, were expense checks.

Being the buyer meant trips.

London would be first. Niarchos convertibles unloaded wheat there. Lloyds also had claims histories with multicargo ships. Gaining that data cost lunches and suppers. Most, the story would go, were paid for in cash. Bootmakers, shirtmakers, and tailors on Jermyn Street, meanwhile, would enjoy a little flutter.

After London, a mandatory stop at Saint-Nazaire. The yards there were considered masters of high-arc welding. Where else to bone up? Not by accident, most of the town house furnishings came from there, as well.

Seaway ports were also musts. Montreal, especially, held the best of all possible worlds: a parade of grain and ore carriers of every type; Holt Renfrew for clothing that could not be hidden in London expenses; Paris wine merchants; and French cooking in the bargain.

"Understood," Demi agreed, ostensibly still eying the statuesque brunette.

He would shortly enjoy a more intriguing prospect.

"Good. Only one thing troubles me," Wade went on. "Is that guy gonna be able to deliver? If he's as busy as you say he is, where's he gonna get the time? This ain't repipin' a tank, you know, or installin' bigger pumps. This is Big Gazoo—the whole works—an' on a convertible, where there's two of everythin' an' four times the engineerin'."

"Loren, I promise you, as soon as I tell him we're looking for a breakthrough convertible, he'll be like a kid in his playpen! He'll be on that mornings, nights, weekends, and maybe days too. I wouldn't be surprised if he even cut back on his workload. He's done that when the job's interested him. Did it last year, in fact, to do some consulting in Europe."

Oh yeah, Wade thought. He saw five of those consultations—in Japan.

"He married?" he suddenly asked.

Demi promptly abandoned the brunette in the white linen suit. "What's that got to do with designing ships?"

"Plenty! We got a schedule, an' he's moonlightin'. That's six or eight months of twenty-hour days, so I don't want him frettin', too, why his boy's Little League team don't make the double play, or how come his daughter ain't in the front row at ballet class recital. If he's that way—"

"Forget it. He doesn't have kids."

"An' his old lady? She'll sit still for . . ." Wade trailed off.

The vigorous nod and eyebrow sweep, Schimmelpenninck forgotten between index and middle fingers, told him what he had to know. Overshadowed by travel and expense account opportunities, a prime fringe benefit had gone unnoticed. He redirected the conversation accordingly.

"You know her too?" he asked.

That brought another nod as more coffee was poured.

Wade pressed his advantage. "What's she like?"

Shrugging, Demi finally regained his composure. "Fiona . . ." he mused. "She's a little girl from Greenwich. But Daddy didn't go to Yale and become a big-company type, so she didn't get to Smith, either. The money wasn't there. She missed out on the Grand Tour with Mummy, too. Pan American gave it to her, instead, as a stewardess. Always on the outside looking in, that's Fiona. Remember *A Christmas Carol*, Loren?"

"That been on TV?"

"Right, with Tiny Tim and the rest of the lovable, deserving poor drooling on the windows of the rich man's house at the Christmas goose. Well, in Greenwich those waifs are all women, and it's not food they crave, but a style. They're taught to ride and sail, play golf, like football, know theater, and be 'good sports'—"

Wade halted the lecture. He had already named that phenomenon. To the vast displeasure of his wife and Hubie's, he accused both women of believing in it. At the risk of seeming brighter than he looked, he told Demi what the WASP upper middle class did in Greenwich.

"They're raisin' geishas," he said.

"Geishas?"

"For the *Fortune 500*."

The line was promptly auditioned for future use. " '*Fortune 500* geishas' . . . that's very good, Loren! Exactly," Demi agreed, stirring his coffee. "So, after college, girls've got life taped. It's Hobe Sound winters, Maine or Martha's Vineyard summers, and lots of fun dinner parties and shopping in between. Those are God-given rights. Besides, what the hell else are they good at? Damned few, though, have names or bank accounts to marry that well, so most settle for Arkies. But they never forget the dream. They know how 'nice'

people live. They owe that to themselves. That's why they took all those lessons, and developed those great smiles, and were so careful about whom they
let into the Dark Tower, as if it held some kind of precious secret. So, don't
you worry about Fiona. She'll good-sport it with *The Late Show, Gourmet,* and
her travel brochures, and keep that poor *malaca* awake and working on sandwiches, coffee, Benzedrine—even needles, if it comes to that!—and tell herself
she's doing it for him."

It took one to know one, Wade thought. No couple he knew deserved each
other more.

"Music to my ears," he said, sliding out from behind the table, "a lovin',
frugal woman! You call this Arkie an' see if he'll take the job. If he says yes,
you want three hundred-thousand-tonners, fifty-thousand-dollar plans fee
paid soon's you see an eighteen-knot model tank test from Stevens Institute.
Standard design fee, expenses, an' the usual blah-blah-blah paid as customary. You want delivery December '67."

"I think the time's too tight, but I'll call you in the morning to confirm."

"Don't bother. I'll be long gone. I'm on my way to Kennedy. Me an' Hube
are off for Rio an' the yearly Banana Belt goodwill tour, so's we end up in
Panama the eighth to meet Willa Mae an' Cora for a big spic weddin'. I'll see
Flight Fuel Delivery gets a little check from there, too. But you call Shirley,"
Wade added, tapping his fist on Demi's shoulder for emphasis, "an' set up a
lunch here for the eleventh. Snackin' aside—" he winked—"I'll be expectin'
great things from you, Babes."

Outside, in the heat and glare of a windless August afternoon, Demi turned
down Second Avenue, wishing they had lunched at La Grenouille. From
there, Tripler's and the silk summer suits he had long coveted lay just a short
stroll south on Madison Avenue.

The purchase would be a snap. Arkie, he calculated, would work for $35,-
000. The $15,000 balance, meanwhile, would buy lots of suits and clean up
embarrassing bills.

But petty graft, he decided, could wait. He had more important business to
consider.

At the same time, he reminded himself, he had heard Wade's version of
events. That needed checking. Still, he believed he had handled the situation
well. He had just spent two and a half hours in a mined channel and brought
his ship, if not to safety, at least to more open water.

Such skill, he believed, deserved a bonus. A florist's shop across Second Avenue suggested a suitable indulgence. Stepping inside, he bought a yellow carnation. That, he thought, put him one up on Niarchos.

He had always chosen white flowers for his rust-and-white-checked hacking
jacket. All wrong. The petals got lost in the background. At first glance, they
suggested a blob of shaving cream.

The carnation had a half hour to the wastebasket; he would change clothes then to run jet fuel from Staten Island to La Guardia. But as he crossed Second Avenue, glancing down at his lapel, his little lark took on new meaning. A reward for coping with Wade, it also said that when and if convertibles became reality, he would be ready. He had the style.

Still dubious, but feeling more like a big-ship man with every stride, he turned into Forty-ninth Street, choosing not the uptown side on which he lived, but the downtown. At midblock he slowed his pace to consider the serious business the luncheon had raised: a pink stone row house.

Totally undistinguished and dating from the 1860s, the black iron fence in front of the three-story house had sprouted a FOR SALE in April. The home still remained on the market. For him, it had an irresistible appeal: its side of the street.

That put it *in* Turtle Bay Gardens.

In 1919 a developer bought twenty houses on Forty-eighth and Forty-ninth streets, turned floor plans front to rear, and joined the backyards in a common garden. The result is a charm and tranquility unique in New York. His house, opposite, might well have been on the other side of the moon.

Jacket open, hands in pockets of the maize slacks, he affected an aimless stroll past the pink stone house. He had wanted to pace it off since the FOR SALE sign appeared. He had, however, restrained himself. The economics then seemed impossible. No longer.

Three 100,000-ton ships might cost $25 million. He needed only a little bit of that.

The building, as estimated, ran seventeen feet wide. That posed a problem. With a southern exposure, a built-in seat under the living-room windows seemed mandatory. He knew where to get such units, already assembled, but they would be at least four feet short. Maybe, he thought, crossing the tree-lined street, he would get lucky in Saint-Nazaire.

Letting himself into his house through the service entrance, he passed through the kitchen to the hallway. Another three steps and a right turn brought him to his "office." A nook perhaps five feet wide and six feet deep, it had been furnished to resemble a T-2 chartroom. A gray metal six-drawered chart table ran the wall left of the doorway. The right wall held a standard War Shipping Administration four-foot gray leather chartroom settee.

Swinging back the glass panel covering the felt-lined chronometer case inset into the tabletop, he took out a phone with one hand. With the other he pulled over a gray metal navigator's stool. Perching himself on its oak seat, he threw the rust-checked hacking jacket on the settee, loosened his tie, and swept back the shock of black hair.

Then he called Taki.

Events were as Wade had reported, Taki said. Moreover, like all brokers, influencing clients gave him great pleasure. So he recounted in detail how he had made the sale to Hubie.

That convinced Demi. Taki, he knew, lacked imagination to tell anything but absolute, unvarnished truth. So, shaking his head, he reached into the gray metal book rack over the chart table and took down a catalog.

He found Arkie's number in his ad. Ten minutes later, he had lunch set at the New York Yacht Club the Tuesday after Labor Day. Hanging up, he immediately began another call.

Two numbers into it, however, he stopped dialing.

Arkie's reactions puzzled him. In retrospect, they seemed all wrong.

Coiling the cord, he put the phone away. The pink stone house, he decided, could wait.

Closing the glass top of the chronometer case, he moved to the settee. Then, brown suede shoes braced on the rungs of the stool, he reviewed the day. Seemingly perfect, it had begun to make him increasingly uneasy.

Arkie, he told himself, should have jumped at a design inquiry. He had whined, instead, about his workload. The backlog, he said, made him brown-bag lunch.

His indifference had forced disclosure of the project. But convertibles had not moved him that much, either. Interesting, he conceded. Naturally, he thought about them. He doubted he could do the job, but he would pass on his ideas for free anyway.

*Jesus!*

Was that just backing away from a job, or . . . *what?*

Even more baffling: suppose, Demi thought, Arkie had been sincere. Given, he was a *malaca*. How could he ignore a $250,000 to $300,000 job? That needed looking into. But how?

For guidance, he turned to Aristotle Onassis, who often looked as though he slept in his suits and salted his collars with dandruff: "In shipping, the advantage is always to the one with the most patience."

Neither witty nor profound, he thought. Only universal.

That applied to another enigma as well: W. Huber Garrison.

Wade would have preferred anyone else to him, Demi knew. Hubie, undoubtedly, knew that, too. Yet, this time, he listened to Taki.

For that matter, Wade had gone along, as well. His reason for doing so seemed simple: he knew it would please Hubie.

But why?

Turning the question this way and that, speculating on possibilities, he drifted into a reverie. The nature of the problem encouraged it. For Hubie left damned few words. So, instead of clues from their relationship, he found himself considering attitudes. Most had no name.

Gradually, however, gaze fixed on the record player on the yellow wall next to the ship's clock, Demi became aware of the movement in his lap.

Looking down, he saw the yellow carnation. It spun idly between his left thumb and forefinger.

His hand had come to rest on his jacket when he shifted to the settee, he thought. Then, as he reran scenes and talk, hoping memory would explain Hubie's motive, his fingers absently coursed the coat's lapel to the flower. At that, he found, it claimed his attention sporadically. Rotated forward, its wiry stem nudged his inner thigh through the maize slacks. Otherwise, it seemed weightless.

Fanciful or not, it gave him his answer. The yellow carnation, he told himself, said it all.

Ships were built in a year. After that, deals over lunch in fine restaurants, or with brandy in living rooms at places like Turtle Bay Gardens, determined earnings. By now, Hubie appreciated that, too. In '56 he may not have. Then he obliged Acey and let him name their most aggressive skipper, Loren Wade, marine superintendent.

So, this time, he had more sophistication. Choosing his next operating man, he ignored bucko. Now Hubie sought another quality, one he valued, too: style.

As adept as the next man at telling himself what he wanted to hear, Demi took the thought further. So far, he guessed, he had clipped PANARTEX for $100,000. Wade had fought him for every penny. But Hubie?

Hubie had just smiled and called him "Babes."

Had he been "auditioning" him? Demi wondered.

He might well have been. He could have spotted the polish and ingenuity that went into a good operating man from the beginning and let him grow up, learn the moves. In that case, the money hardly mattered.

Men who managed big-league oil and shipping bosses, on one hand, and Foreign Legion rejects who sailed ships, on the other, were worth any price. All of which, Demi noted, confirmed his mother's favorite teaching: with style, you could get away with anything.

That also applied, he knew, to the pink stone house across the street. At first, he had wanted to be met and shown through. All wrong, he thought. He saw now just how that should go. The realtor had to come to him.

In that neighborhood, the broker would be a faded deb, fortyish, married to a loser, who lived on Beckman Place up to her ass in debt. Why else would she hustle real estate? That woman he intended to impress mightily.

She would have coffee in the floorthrough room upstairs. He wanted her to tell him about the pink stone house seated on a twelve-foot-long couch, in more space than any apartment she could ever afford. That way, she could also see the other things beyond her reach: the walnut paneling, better than in any New York club, he had been told; the chandeliers; and the custom-designed black iron spiral staircase featured the year before in the *New York Times*.

Then, going out, he planned taking the scenic route through the kitchen: around the massive maple butcher's block; past the stainless-steel gas range with its six burners, twin ovens and three-foot-wide griddle; over the glowing caulked and holystoned teak flooring.

For aging debs, the décor established his *bona fides*. That could be worth as much as $20,000 to him.

For, across Forty-ninth Street, he would immediately start knocking down the price. Every shopper did, and always for the same reason: renovation and remodeling expenses. Brokers, naturally, ignored that routine. His, however, would know better. She had seen his home.

Suddenly, talk of gutting a floor, moving walls, or other changes equal to the cost of the house would ring with truth. Chances were, those plans would go back unedited to the realtor, who, in turn, would pass them on to the owner. He had found a serious prospect, but . . .

The price then might come down. The odds, he estimated, were seventy-thirty in his favor.

The people living in Manhattan's pink stone houses were realists. They never expected to buy at the bottom or sell at the top. So, offered a respectable prospect, the property owner across the street might take less.

But shaving price for a pushy orthodontist from Queens, or the president of that year's hot ad agency, could be demeaning. Undoubtedly, several such offers had already been rejected. Accepting one, however, from an exotic Greek shipping tycoon might well be worth the money.

It could provide years of conversation.

That would satisfy many rich.

For stylish wealth always sought more style.

Tastes were forever being cultivated and refined.

Exotics like him were coveted.

The insecure needed them to brighten dull backdrops.

The pink stone house might belong to such a fool.

Which brought Demi to his principal fringe benefit: Fiona. She had that kind of insecurity, too. He had seen it in Bermuda.

With $250,000 of design fees to spend, his image no longer posed a problem. But Greenwich did, he realized. Little girls from there learned not to give themselves impetuously or cheaply. So, she would need time to consider the value of his goodwill.

She could have months, he decided.

He would ask her to lunch at Lutèce in November. Afterward, he would show her the pink stone house. By then, of course, the dickering over price would be in its final stage. His ex-deb broker would be frantic for her commission, too. So, from the instant she met them, she would do his selling for him. Fearful that Fiona could queer the deal, she would do all she could to make him and the property look good. He had only to be casual and modest, as befitted a man who could order $30 million worth of convertibles.

He would defer to Fiona, weigh her comments.

What could be more natural then, or more flattering, than to invite her across the street to his place, where they could talk out a few ideas over coffee or a brandy?

It could work, he told himself.

The floorthrough living room would put her into shock.

He might not even have to suggest that Arkie seemed a little slow, or preoccupied, or whatever.

By then, she might well just love him for himself.

Smiling, he rose from the chartroom settee, thinking of his mother. She had said it all: With style, you could get away with anything.

The idea amused him all the way upstairs.

In less than 290 days, it would also kill him.


*October 17, 1966*
*Moose Factory, Ontario*

THE GEESE were about a half mile off.

Silhouetted against dawn's weak light, they skimmed the flats of James Bay, the southern tip of Hudson Bay, like elegant, stylized arrowheads.

They sought a last snack before continuing south.

They had already left their summer nesting grounds, above the Northwest Territories, 1,200 miles behind them. With luck, they would ride the rising northerly nonstop to similar marshes in Texas and Louisiana.

Evelyn Waddell sighed rapturously. Then, kneeling in the icy water, he leaned out from behind the small hummock topped by stunted arctic willow, silently half cupping his mouth with his right hand.

Fifty feet away, Gregory Mousecall, surname honoring a grandfather whose cry of a wounded rat had put owls into Cree stewpots, took the signal in the driving rain. The bill of his Montreal Internationals baseball cap bobbing beneath the hood of his polar-bear parka, he nodded slowly.

For Howsam, that made a bad week worse. The geese, he thought, were as good as dead.

The Cree, whose land is barren, harvest only living things. Famed hunters, they are deadly wing shots. But, shells being expensive, they seldom fire at birds beyond point-blank range. So their celebrity rests far less on marksmanship than on calling.

Learning that art begins in a boy's second summer. At twelve, he will mimic the call of every creature in the marshes and skies above the permafrost line with seemingly supernatural accuracy. After that, he will get better.

At seventy, Gregory made a case in point. Shoulders raised in a deep breath, he leaned back, hands cupping mouth. Then, still kneeling, rain pelting his face beneath the baseball cap, he flung the high, one-note flight call of the Canada goose into the north wind after the morning's first birds.

Crouched beside Evelyn, Howsam hoped they were out of range. He had not shot a goose in four years. Nor, since his wife had shown him a soaring bronze sculpture, *Bird in Space,* by Constantine Brancusi, at the Museum of Modern Art, had he cared to.

That, of course, amused Evelyn. He called it hopelessly sentimental. So, watching the lead bird, he needled Howsam. "Oh, I think he likes Greg, Prentiss," he simpered, eyes gleaming Meissen blue beneath the round brim of the black rubber Canadian miner's hat he wore hunting.

"Oh, yes! Look—he's turning his head!"

Howsam noticed something even more ominous. The flock's wingbeat had slowed.

He saw six birds, flying in line, parents leading and trailing. Ma and Pa Kettle, he mused, and four kids hatched on the ice that summer.

Head cocked critically, Gregory studied their passage. Encouraged, he tolled twice more, slowly. *"Awww . . . nk! Awww . . . nk!"*

Halfway through the second note, Pa Kettle extended his right wing like an oar and went into a diving turn. The rest of the string followed.

Gregory began calling faster, inviting them closer.

Evelyn sighed rapturously. "God and Greg always provide," he said. The what remained unuttered.

Howsam knew: *confit d'oie,* the preserved goose that with salt pork, beans, and sausage goes into *cassoulet,* Quebec's cold-weather stew.

"And far be it from me to offend Brancusi's shade," the soft clubman's baritone went on even more unctuously, "but I'm sure it'll forgive your helping preserve these birds—in light of the number you'll eat this winter . . . and, of course, since I'm the client."

"You dirty little bugger!"

That meant sleepless nights. A dozen heavyweights were needed, and the drill never varied. Afternoons, birds were plucked, dressed, quartered, and brined. At 2:30 A.M., time dictated for dawn return to the blind, parts were fried in lard, stewed two hours, stacked in earthenware crocks, and sealed in more lard. The meat kept for months and gave a gamy, hearty flavor to stews far superior to that provided by domestic geese.

An Alpine bivouac tent, seven feet long, five wide, served as kitchen. Bent over Coleman camp stoves, men acquired a cloying stench on hair and arms that lasted well into winter, according to Francine Howsam.

All of which Evelyn had heard firsthand.

So, chuckling, he straightened up and began calling from his knees as the geese neared Gregory's hummock, to the right. His note, more nasal, faster, and softer, imitated the feeding chatter of young birds.

He had learned that call thirty years before.

Expelled from the Palestine Mandate as a terrorist by Colonel Montgomery,* the police commissioner, he had gone to Canada seeking oil. He liked to say he found Gregory and the Cree instead. Two years later, though, just in time for World War II, he had made his first ore strike. Wealth freed him to hunt and fish with the Indians. As a result, few whites knew more than he about northern Ontario and Quebec.

Geese were his specialty. The feeding note he now tolled, for example, he called easy. A few years earlier he had taught it to Howsam. "One simply humps up one's tongue, lays it against the roof of one's mouth, and says 'hand,' but without the *d,* and whilst exhaling," he said.

Howsam never got it. Still, the sound seemed childishly simple.

*"Haa . . . nh! Haa . . . nh!"*

Hurtling toward Gregory, Pa Kettle turned his head.

The decoys off Evelyn's rise, mounds of blue clay topped by white feathers, fooled him. He veered before the first note died. He climbed before the second ended. Wings flapping louder than untended window shades in a summer storm, he beat against the gusting northerly.

Thirty feet below him, Howsam saw the fixed amber eyeglint in the greenish cheek. The poor sucker, he thought. He wanted to guide strays, too. Canadas were like that. Only Italians loved kids more. The family followed him, all now past Gregory's hummock.

Evelyn, meanwhile, kept calling. *"Haa . . . nh! Haa . . . nh!"*

Answering, Pa swung his feet down and fanned his tail feathers open, hovering in the rain over the decoys.

Smiling gently, Evelyn pulled his right trigger.

A thin iridescent spray streamed out on the wind.

Head shot, Howsam knew, seeing the green. Pa Kettle fell like a stone.

A moment later, a son joined him. He seemed to explode in a puff of white smoke. Breast shot, Howsam thought, white feathers.

Tolling frantically, Ma Kettle wheeled and dived. Dropping faster than Gregory could lead her, she leveled off, skimming the water, and got by him. Her youngsters turned after her but failed to dive, flying back line astern and naively bunching up in panic.

Gregory settled for "new" goose. Slowly raising the rusty Simpson-Sears

---

* Later, Lord Montgomery of El Alamein, World War II British European commander. His notable enmity for Jews developed during this period, probably because they beat him at his own game. Unable to control their reprisals against Arabs and police, he frequently conceded defeat by imposing daytime curfews, bringing business to a halt and jeopardizing his career. Among his chief tormentors: Menachem Begin.

shotgun acquired years before at the Fort George trading post farther up James Bay, he fired just once. He doubled on the leading birds.

The third, a "blue," so young his feathers had not yet bleached white, quickly aged. Folding back his wings, he swooped down to water level.

He rose a hundred yards past Gregory's hummock.

Ma Kettle awaited him, circling upwind in a huge arc.

Gun reloaded, Evelyn watched her, nodding sadly. "Poor darling, she's looking for survivors," he said. Then he resumed his feeding chatter. This time, he added some deeper notes.

Hearing them, Ma Kettle altered course. Monogamous, she no doubt had her mate in mind. She and the "blue" struggled crosswind, like swimmers in surf lines.

"Stupid, stupid dears," Evelyn sighed between calls.

He caught Ma Kettle twenty feet upwind of the rise.

She took a full shot pattern in her chest. Wings spread gliding downwind, she somersaulted as if she were in a back swan dive. Then, folding up, she plummeted out of the sky like falling mountain ice. A fourteen-pounder, she entered the water with a plunging gurgle.

The "blue," boring in after her, spun once, end for end sideways, from Evelyn's second shot, passing so close they ducked. He thumped off the base of the rise and gently splashed into the water.

So ended the Kettle family's flight south.

The occasion allowed Evelyn a moment's brag. "Small wonder, was it, Prentiss," he asked drolly, "that the tribal elders named me Fierce Fat when they made me Cree? You saw that shot on the 'blue'? Hit his bill—period! Greg won't find a ruddy pellet to pick out!"

Reaching into his sewage and slime poncho, he withdrew "survival steel," the top of the seven-and-a-half-inch blade sporting sawteeth. Guided by casual flicks of the wrist, its cutting edge effortlessly sliced the half-inch willow saplings atop the hummock in single strokes. Armed with sharpened sticks, he left to "upgrade" decoys.

Hearing him slosh around in the ankle-deep water, Howsam swore no man had greater solicitude for the dead or loved them more. He had sympathy for all.

"Poor chap, you stuck to Mum just as she said, and look what you got," he told the "blue" downed behind them. "A fella like you should be seen, but your mouth's gone. So, you'll go on this lump, neck tucked under, as if you've a full tum and need a little zizz to sleep it off."

To Pa Kettle: "Arrogant man. See what happens, flying on *Shabbath?* Not even being a Good Samaritan helps. Our God's a vengeful God, and rightly so. Still, he fed you fat as a whale, because He knew you'd look so well in front. This stick won't hurt a bit. See . . . it's already through the top of your head."

To Ma Kettle: "Poor dear, I'm sure your family knew you deserved better. But since you were his wife, you'll want to face him. How's this, with a willow in your throat, as if your head's down for a bite?"

To the son who fell with Pa Kettle: "Oh, my, you're a bonus—ten pounds! From last year's hatch, and a real *macher* too—had to be with Dad, right? If you loved Mum more and hung back, you might be alive yet. But good boys lead, so next to Dad you'll go. Nice?"

To the second youngster in Gregory's double: "Greg shot your *pupik* off. I knew he'd get something. He always does. But your head's so sweet you rate the highest mound and a stick to make you look—"

Gregory's tolling interrupted the condolences.

The last "new" goose under his arm, Evelyn sprinted for the blind. Rushing back, bilious poncho fluttering after him, he reminded Howsam of a fastidious crab fleeing an avalanching sewer stoppage. Rounding the corner of the rise on his knees, he shouted and pointed behind him.

"They're on the move, Prentiss—on the move!"

Howsam nodded. He had seen them before Gregory.

A greenish black carpet, a half mile wide, darkened the splintered eastern sky. Riding the gusting northerly, it came within a quarter mile of the blind before revealing itself as a near-solid mass of geese in coils, strings, and vees. The formation swept south over James Bay to the horizon.

To Howsam's ear, Evelyn no longer sighed. He seemed, rather, to whimper in ecstasy.

"You're sure you'll not help us with the spare gun, Prentiss?" he asked. "Remember—Greg needs at least a hundred birds salted down for winter, and I've not seen flights like these since the thirties. Oh, they're prime—absolutely, unbelievably prime!"

The geese skimmed the bay in waves. Then, at the shore, the leaders rose to avoid tricky ground currents. After that, they died.

Gregory's flight call slowed them. The Kettles turned them right.

Evelyn's feeding talk brought them closer. At fifty feet or less, he fired.

Survivors, wheeling, flew back to Gregory.

The Adamses came first.

The Browns followed.

The Campbells were next.

The Davises arrived after them.

So it went through Howsam's imagined phone book.

He had never seen so many geese die in so many ways. Watching them, he had the sensation of wandering into a lunatic version of *12 O'Clock High*, where the Germans win the movie by shooting down all the B-17s.

Other differences were more disturbing.

Movie planes fell miles away. Here, bodies veered, tumbled, and knifed wing-first through a killing ground a hundred feet square and fifty high.

Images telescoped accordingly. Black, white, gray, and green blurs whistled down accelerating, irreversible arcs crisscrossing the hummock. Smaller birds fell silently. All splashed or thumped into death so quickly that impact joined shot in one sound. Beaks, feet, feathers, heads marked their wakes.

Shattered cries and calls, shrieks and squawks, and flappings and flutterings similarly rent the narrow cube of airspace between Evelyn and Gregory.

Then, after an hour, they ceased. Rising winds put down the flight.

Frequently glancing north, lips pursed in frustration, Evelyn hacked more willows. Then, brim of miner's hat blown flat against cheek, he left to pay last respects and to arrange comfortable and suitable repose for his newfound friends as he had for the Kettles.

Howsam fled to the lee of the hummock, where he had found Evelyn, under a bearskin, eating a softball-sized onion as if it were an apple.

He could not remember being in so foul a mood.

The day before, he had realized he had to go north. Rushing home, he had changed into hunting gear, got a Toronto plane at Kennedy, then a DC-3 with freight for Timmins. There six hundred dollars lured a bush pilot from a rusting mobile home used as a brothel. Defying Canadian law and common sense, they left in darkness and landed at Moose Factory in the even more treacherous glow of false dawn. Then he trudged two miles through the muck and rain.

At the blind, things had gone further downhill.

"Hul-lo—what's this," Evelyn had asked, peering out from beneath the bearskin, "an old member rejoining? Couldn't keep away from the *mishpokeh,* after all, could you, Prentiss? You saw all your cousins and aunts and uncles on the way out of town, I trust?"

"You know why I'm here?" Prentiss had asked.

Judiciously thrusting the onion into the rain, Evelyn glanced upward. "Well," he observed, "since a good bit of sky's falling, I'm sure it's for something major. I wonder, could it be the cowboys're on the move?"

Chaos then followed anticlimax. Gregory chose that moment to send Evelyn dashing. He flung his first flight call after the Kettles.

Now, again in the lee of the hip-high rise, Howsam raised the bearskin over his head, sat down, and lay back against the side of the hill. He would be there awhile, he knew. Scores of birds had fallen. A few minutes later, he heard that judgment confirmed.

". . . seventy-one, Greg," Evelyn called out. "About half you, me, need for eat."

In time, decoys set, he lifted the hide, backed in, and plopped down. His "on-holiday" smile ignored chill, rain, and any urgency Howsam's presence suggested. He looked, in fact, as if he were poolside at his winter home in the Bahamas taking wicked delight in being so comfortable. His tone further reflected that Caribbean state of well-being.

"Well, Prentiss," he said, as warmly reassuring as ever, fingertips in brown fur propping up his side of the bearskin, "from what we know of Messrs. Garrison and Wade, we never expected those two to lie doggo, did we? So, which of their wicked pranks brings you up here 'gainst will and wish?"

Still rankled at his welcome, Howsam took revenge, delighted to share some of his past week's anxieties. "They found Angelakos," he said curtly.

The rim of his miner's hat raising with his eyebrows, Evelyn clearly considered that redundant. "Oh, but hadn't they done that in April, Prentiss," he asked, smile still courteously intact, "poking round Lianides' Immigration file? Didn't Angelakos have his name on everything as sponsor of the work permit?"

Still seeking vengeance, Howsam tried another tack. "Right," he agreed, "only nobody gave him ten days to reply under penalty of law. He got lunched at the New York Yacht Club instead."

"By the Immigration, Prentiss?"

This time, Howsam resorted to understatement. "No," he said after a headshake, "by a bird dog from the cowboys, a Demosthenes Keriosotis, and he brought along a proposition."

That put them about even for Evelyn's flippancy, Howsam thought.

Until Monday, he had thought he had a solid-gold position. Now $50 million could go belly-up at any moment.

The Israeli "watching brief," which Evelyn called his little giggle, serious because of the money involved but absolutely safe, had also undergone a change. Now all that stood between discovery of the men and the country behind Hasegawa's five 100,000-tonners were two highly unpredictable Greeks and Evelyn's judgment.

To Howsam's mounting dismay, however, Evelyn showed no sign of appreciating the increased precariousness of the situation. Instead, idly poking around in the water and marsh grass at the feet of his black waders, he retrieved the outsized onion, dropped at Gregory's first call.

"Here, take a bite," he said, "best breakfast there is—purifies the blood."

"That? It's full of mud!"

"What—this little blue between the petals? Not enough to hurt, Prentiss, not enough to hurt—just so long as it doesn't enter our souls! It's full of borium besides, a very valuable trace element. C'mon! Your belly's grumbling so, we can't hear to talk, anyways."

Grimacing, Howsam took the onion.

Nodding approvingly, the host returned to business. "An offer, Prentiss? Well, that *is* different," he mused. "Tell me about it."

As breakfast passed back and forth, Howsam did.

There were, of course, no clues or insights. The ambiguities, however, sufficed for Evelyn.

"Oh, that's bright—bright, bright, bright!" he said admiringly. "How's a chap to say no to that without due and proper explanation?"

"Exactly."

A sigh, as if the Kettles had just appeared in the dawn, betrayed the casual tone of the next question. "You wouldn't happen to know whose little gem that was, would you, Prentiss—Garrison's or Wade's?"

Howsam, ever pragmatic, had given that no thought. Tracking down the threat had kept him fully occupied.

"It's there," he said. "What's the difference?"

"Well," came the reply, tone as diffident as always, "if we knew who put this probe forward, I think we'd have a peek at their intentions. That, in turn, might suggest a strategy to us. Garrison, for example, has fought so hard to keep that company afloat he might be bought off if the price was right. But Wade—clever little tyke—found us in the first place. Suppose he's in charge of this. Where are we then? He and Garrison might have very different aims in this, as I'm sure you know."

That idea had not occurred to Howsam, either.

Correct then, it did not hold true throughout.

Hardly pausing, Evelyn hurried past what seemed so obvious to him. "At first blush, I'd say this is worthy of the mind of Wilmer Garrison—tuned to concert pitch, of course, where, incidentally, it operates most of the time. He's a reader, you know," he told Howsam, citing his own research, "a student. His degrees are far better than mine, and he speaks a very good Arabic too, which 'Home Office' says is only surpassed by his grasp of Islam's politics. So, I'm sure he's onto his Greeks as well. I'll wager, in fact, he's even consulted the sage Churchill on the subject: *'They have survived in spite of all that the world could do against them and all they could do against themselves . . . quarrelling among themselves with insatiable vivacity.'* Oh, yes, Wilmer Garrison'd think it jolly bright to send Greek after Greek. It's only hypothesis, but that has a roundness, a symmetry.

"Of course—" Evelyn chuckled mischievously—"the only trouble with giving Garrison credit for the idea is that it fits Wade better. It's him to a 'T'; flank speed, collision course, and damn all! He sank a U-boat in the war like that, you know. Cut right 'cross a convoy lane to ram a surfaced sub cleaning up with deck gun and torpedoes. Getting there—" he winked, taking back the onion from Howsam—"he nipped the stern off a British frigate taking a somewhat more temperate view of the action. Be assured," the tale went on in mock solemnity, "the Royal Navy had very hard lines for him. But yours gave him rather an exclusive medal . . . and, sweeter still, his scrofulous old ship had to be towed to Murmansk and sunk by the Russkis after they got the oil out—a two-million-dollar trifle in insurance for PANARTEX—which the Admiralty believes may have crossed our chum's—"

"You get all that for his retirement dinner?"

"Oh, that'll be a do, and, unless I'm off the mark, notable for its pregnant silences! Believe me, he'll not want to swank round that past of his! Most of it, flat out, isn't up to repeating. He's an original, that one! Did I mention he took me to lunch not long ago?"

Howsam looked up sharply, unamused.

Evelyn's enthusiasm for the subject continued unabated. "I picked him up one noon at the Time-Life Building my last time in New York just to see how he was keeping, and he led me to the best Italian restaurant in Manhattan— Amalfi. He met a child there of the most gorgeous blond persuasion I've ever seen, and I tell you, the little brute—he's even shorter than I, which I like— was magnificent! The poor dear hung on his every word, and he hardly gave her a squint for the food. As they say in the mines round Timmins, he's a 'volume forker,' your basic, straight-ahead, ingestive type. And, if sending an offer to Angelakos isn't straight . . ."

Trailing off, Evelyn's eyes scanned the bearskin. Then, slowly, his smile changed. Concern displaced appreciation.

Howsam now understood his flippancy. Some of it he even forgave. Still gun-deaf when he sat down, Evelyn thought he had heard something else.

"But you said that meeting with Angelakos took place six weeks ago Tuesday, Prentiss . . ."

"Actually, closer to seven, the day after Labor day."

"Oh, dear. Oh, dear, dear, dear . . ."

"Welcome to the party," Howsam added.

"But where was Angelakos all that time, Prentiss? He wasn't really considering taking the job, was he?"

"No, of course not."

"Well, then, why didn't he come to you sooner?"

"Angelakos hasn't come to me yet. I got all this from Lianides. He called me Monday."

"He told Lianides but not you, Prentiss?"

Howsam pushed back the hood of the olive-drab Orvis rain poncho and ruffed his crewcut with his palm. Then, sighing, he shook his head. "Lianides didn't know till then, either. He went over to Long Island City last Monday—for what else, to get an advance on his paycheck for the fifteenth—and there's Angelakos up to his ass in balsa wood and X-Acto blades carving a new set of tank washer nozzles. Well, I don't have to tell you how our Admiral of the Ocean Sea took to those new nozzles. You know the way he gets when anything cuts into his share of the take. He was all over that poor fish Angelakos before he could breathe. Then he got the story."

"Oh?"

"Sure. Those weren't for us, Angelakos said. They were for a Merchant Marine Academy pal of his, Demosthenes Keriosotis, who got lucky and found backing to build three convertibles—they haul oil, bulk cargo, and ore—and washing systems are key because of the different flashpoints of what all they carry. 'A really cute problem,' he told Lianides. He even said he'd been offered the whole design job, and his wife wanted him to take it, but he didn't think he had—"

"And Angelakos never thought to mention it to anyone?"

"Oh, hell, no! What for?" Howsam scoffed, sourly requoting Lianides. "He got four, five design pitches a year, but they were all shit *skata* jobs until we let him do it right and blow a hundred seventy grand—"

"And what did Lianides say to all that, Prentiss?"

"Not a peep. He put his head down and looked those models over real good. Then, when he got all he could, he hit the bookkeeper for his cash and ran to the nearest diner. That's when I heard we had Demosthenes Keriosotis, of Flight Fuel Delivery, Inc., in our pants since Labor Day."

"And good on you, Costa Lianides," Evelyn intoned softly. "You know not to wake baby."

"Amen."

"Then came the paper chase, I suppose, to see who Keriosotis was?"

Howsam nodded.

The company name had told him where to look. Archibald Rothwell, his lawyer, had a clerk search Port Authority records. An Albany associate would also visit the secretary of state's office. The corporate charter, filed there, had names and addresses.

Dr. Fabian, meanwhile, had uncovered another lead. The phone book listed a Dimitrios Keriosotis, shipbroker, with offices on Pearl Street and in Athens and London. Before that, the matter had seemed simple: Garrison and Wade had dreamed up the offer to Angelakos. Now a new possibility had to be weighed: Could Demosthenes have been sent by his family?

Howsam had rejected the idea. Coincidence had no part in big money plays. Tuesday, though, he began to wonder. Monday's research had proved nothing to the contrary.

"Nothing, Prentiss?"

"Zip-po!"

Archie Rothwell's clerk had found Flight Fuel Delivery, Inc., and its president, Demosthenes Keriosotis, certified to effect aircraft fuel shipments to commercial airports under Port Authority jurisdiction. The Albany report had more of the same. The corporate charter listed six other Keriosotises. Stockholders, all lived in the New York area. Three were company officers as well. A Pearl Street address, care of Dimitrios Keriosotis, provided a place of business.

"He heads the family's New York branch?" Evelyn asked.

"Right, a terrific shipbroker, everybody says, and he must be. Ilona calls his building a Sutton Place gas guzzler full of duplexes and triplexes overlooking the East River—on the river side of the street. He lives like he owns a shipping company. The one to check, she said, was Demosthenes. She called him a fraud and a cheap swordsman in the bargain."

"She knew him, Prentiss?"

Howsam shook his head.

"*Of* him?"

"Oh, no, nothing like that. This is straight out of the intuition department. She found his address in the phone book, too, and you know how she is about real estate, so she took a walk down Forty-ninth Street to comparison-shop town houses, and she saw black corduroy drapes on his third-floor bedroom windows. Every budget Romeo goes for them, she says. They all want caves—lightproof and soundproof. The fact is, they're the cheapest things you can buy."

"Trust the feminine eye for the unerring, insightful non sequitur," Evelyn observed sarcastically.

"I'll let her non-sequit. She knew what to do next."

Distrusting corduroy drapes in the town house of a shipping company's president, Dr. Fabian had refused to believe the corporate charter or the Port Authority records. She insisted they learn where Demosthenes got his money. "Call Norbie," she had told Howsam.

"Your bank *maven*, Prentiss?"

"The same."

"But wasn't he in Calif—"

"There's an Old Boy network for everything, and tax guys have something else going for them: reciprocity."

Evelyn reset elbows on thighs. Then, crimping the bearskin to pour the rain off in a manageable stream, he shook his head.

" 'Reciprocity?' " he asked.

"The buddy system. Every April fifteenth, billions of dollars in the U.S. that should be paid in taxes aren't. The feds and state tax departments compete for those bucks—finders keepers."

"They do, Prentiss? Compete, I mean."

"Ever see a tax case brought jointly by a state *and* the government? You won't, because a federal claim takes precedence. So, with IRS agents and offices everywhere, in most cases the only way states can reach uncollected dough first is to swap what they know. A tip from the East brings a Western guy a big score. If he wants more, he'll do the same for whoever helped him. They're all lodge brothers, Norbie says—Civil Service stiffs bucking for promotion—and somebody in those gold-domed capitol buildings keeps score, so it's the old story: you scratch my back, and I'll scratch yours."

"And your *maven* has that kind of influence."

"Once removed. He's the best snoop going, so he sells downtime to state tax departments out West for a hundred twenty-five dollars a day instead of five hundred, and they snap it up. Then, if he needs a favor, he calls whoever has reciprocity with the state he wants to reach, and that guy makes the contact to pay off his IOU."

"Of course," Evelyn assumed. "In reality, states owe the *maven* three hundred seventy-five dollars for every day he works for them."

"No," Howsam said in correction, "they paid for his time. What they really owe Norbie is the convictions, fines, and recoveries that he got but they took credit for. Wiring Demosthenes Keriosotis cost him a hundred forty-one years' jail time, $1,750,000 worth of fines, and $3,275,000 in late remittances of unpaid taxes."

"That much, Prentiss, just to peek at a few tax returns?"

"Stick around. I'll show you a few tax returns."

Recognizing Howsam's tone, Evelyn said nothing.

So began the tale of Norbert Nygaard's paper chase. It started, Howsam reported, taking out a small note pad, with the tax return Demosthenes Keriosotis filed in 1962. That year he showed a taxable income of $4,670 and listed Straits Transits, Ltd., as his employer.

"Is that a something, Prentiss?"

"Norbie called Straits Transits a 'Claude.' "

" 'Claude'?"

"For Claude Rains, the Invisible Man in the movie. This Claude officed in Singapore and had three tankers so wrapped up in the Liberian flag that you couldn't find him. We learned, though, on the next year's return that he spoke Spanish and banked in the U.S."

"You did—how?"

"Simple. In 1963, Demosthenes reported $6,872 from a Sociedad Internacional Financial de Vapores. That $6,872 made the society a son of Singapore Claude."

Evelyn rolled his eyes helplessly under the black miner's hat.

"That's fifteen percent of two years' pay and overtime for an American mate in the Far East," Howsam explained, "plus eight percent compound interest, what pension funds earn these days, so it had to be a profit-sharing plan. The check came from Banco Internacional de Panamá, but in its lower left, where we print magnetic code numbers, an American account number appeared in the exact place for it to be read by one of our electronic scanners. See?"

Leaning, Howsam held the note pad before Evelyn: "11203 8."

"Surely, Prentiss, that wasn't on the tax form?"

"No. Demosthenes had already drawn flies because Flight Fuel Delivery shows a profit of about thirty percent of industry average. My guess is that came from some snoop in the U.S. Maritime Administration or the Admiralty and Shipping Section of the Department of Justice."

"You don't know?"

"And won't. When the society surfaced, Norbie's man called a pal in Ohio, where they build Great Lakes ships. So the Columbus guy cashed one of his Washington IOUs and got everyting we wanted—plus a lesson on making ships invisible, which, it developed, we needed, because that same year, '63, Demosthenes also showed $35,000 from a Short Line Marine, Inc."

"And who are they?"

"They're P.O. Box Twenty-three, in Wilmington, Delaware, a bank. They built Flight Fuel Delivery One, Two, and Three. Legally, they're a corporation run by trust officers—"

"And, no doubt," Evelyn cut in, telescoping the story, "Short Line Marine left a trail of collapsed corporate shells behind it—with names of no living men attached."

"Right. It's a 'street name' hiding somebody."

"Yes. 'Asset, asset, who owns the asset?' "

"Exactly. Short Line Marine was our second Claude. Then, on his '64 return, Demosthenes showed us another. That year he got $35,000 from Flight Fuel Delivery and $15,000 from Gibbs Hill Associates. Flight Fuel operated part of that year. So Gibbs Hill, experts say, paid him for the rest to supervise construction of the ships."

"Isn't Gibbs Hill a lighthouse on Bermuda?"

Howsam nodded. "Here, though, Norbie says it's more likely a shoebox in some lawyer's office in Hamilton."

"And surely there to duck taxes, which would seem to make Short Line Marine redundant."

"No way. Short Line serves another purpose. If it proves American ownership, it can get a shipbuilding loan for up to forty percent of cost. We could get rich with a ferry on the Central Park lagoon in that kind of deal."

"But if it's a blind trust, how can Short Line prove it has American ownership?"

"Simple. The president of the bank'll swear it has. Then a Mississippi senator and a congressman from Pascagoula, where the ships were built, go around to the Maritime Administration crying how that part of the state needs an order, jobs. Votes being what they are, Short Line gets the loan, and everyone's happy. It should happen to us."

"Yes! Because once the ships are built, Short Line charters them to Gibbs Hill, who, in turn, charters them to Flight Fuel Delivery—"

"And Flight Fuel pays through the nose, so Demosthenes makes thirty percent of industry average, and what should be taxes goes to Gibbs Hill as charter fees instead."

"But all the while, that still didn't tell you who owned Flight Fuel Delivery, did it?"

Howsam shook his head. "Both the Keriosotises and the cowboys own Liberian ships. The answer came from income Demosthenes reported in '65. Something called the Deepseaman's League sent him exactly fifteen percent of a master's wages for a vessel of fifteen hundred tons or less. The check came from Banco Internacional de Panamá and had the same account number as the one he got from Singapore Claude in '62. It even carried the full U.S. magnetic code, which put it in the Time-Life Building branch of Manufacturers Hanover Trust—"

"Where the cowboys have offices, Prentiss!"

"And where Dimitrios Keriosotis also banks. We found out later that he does a lot of work for PANARTEX. And that's as far as the feds got. They still don't know who owns Flight Fuel Delivery."

"With all that on the check, Prentiss? Why?"

"Because the Deepseamen's League is hidden in Panama. Banks there won't let gringos in, so you're out of luck unless you know a local with clout, which I do: my partner, Eusebio Pérez. So he took somebody to lunch, showed him that magnetic code, and nailed it all down. It turns out to be the Deepseamen's League fronts for another Claude: Amigos de Zapata. You know who Zapata was?"

"Zapata was a Mexican, Prentiss."

"You know what else he was?"

"Besides being a revolutionary? No."

"Archie found it in the Rand McNally Road Atlas in his office yesterday. Zapata was the man they named the county for where two of our pals were born—A. C. Stiles and that guy in Washington, Ursall Majors."

"Of course." Evelyn nodded. "It's always that way with these tricksy little games if you look far enough. Dimitrios, that awful Greek of Eric Ambler's, summed it up for all time: 'In the end one is always defeated by stupidity. If it is not one's own it is the stupidity of others.' "

"You're missing the point," Howsam said. "Nobody got defeated, and nobody was stupid. These guys are smarter than we thought. There's a real good chance, in fact, Archie says, Short Line Marine may be legal."

"I'd not be surprised at that either. Style aside, and that only matters to snobs, that's a fine old firm. If they can beat Nygaard et Frères, I shudder to think what could happen to us if we lost sight of them."

"That's why I'm here. I think Angelakos ought to take that job."

"By all means, Prentiss. We've got to know their intentions."

"Agreed. But what do we do in the meantime?"

"On-holiday" smile as benign as when he sat down, Evelyn raised the bearskin and regarded the unceasing rain. Risks weighed and decision made, he clearly saw a possibility that had eluded Howsam.

"In the meantime," he proposed, "I think we should go back to the tent, and whilst you and Greg do the geese I'll just nip over to Ships Sand Island and kill us six or seven mallards for supper."

A few weeks later, Hubie Garrison would question the future as Howsam had done, and get a far more specific answer.

*November 24, 1966*
*New York City–Greenwich*

THE CLOCK in the International Arrivals Building at Kennedy Airport said two-thirty.

Aging blue canvas Val-Pak and black leather airline pilot's flight case at his feet, Wade debated whether to go home or to New York City.

Then he saw that the decision had already been made. Red, Hubie's chauffeur, waved at him from the exit.

Wade lifted his bags and followed him to the black Cadillac. Getting in, he thought of Shirley Carmichael. He wished she had put him on a later plane.

Seated in his usual corner in a gray Dunhill summer suit and velvet-collared chesterfield, Hubie looked like an expensive corpse at a $350 funeral. His face, under a fading tan from the September jaunt through South and Central America, had a yellowish, waxy sheen. His cheekbones, similarly, seemed splotched with too much rouge.

Wade had his mouth in gear before he sat down. "Good Lord Almighty, all the time Mama was alive, I sent money home. All the time I been married, I sent my paycheck straight to Connecticut Bank an' Trust, an' I'm a sonofabitch if anyone but you's ever welcomed me back from foreign shores!"

"I just got in myself on Aeronaves de México, so I figured I'd pick you up," Hubie told him.

Wade unclasped his trousers. Scratch Mexico, he thought. Ten days before, when he had left, that promised money. A New Orleans oil broker said he had a "sure" lead to $250 million, maybe more. The face across from him, however, said otherwise.

Still, for form's sake, he had to ask. "You do any good?"

A forlorn wave reinforced his first impression. "I never lit anywheres long enough to find out," Hubie answered. "Some runaround. From Mexico City to Acapulco to Puerto Vallarta to Cozumel—and nothin'. What'd you get?"

To Hubie, Wade knew, that now meant in Japan.

Sighing, Wade watched as Red turned the Cadillac off the airport's inner traffic circle for the Van Wyck Expressway and Manhattan.

"We got six months for sure, maybe seven," he said.

"You saw those ships again?"

Nodding, Wade winked. "Real good," he told Hubie. "But from maybe sixteen thousand feet high an' three miles off through my little Bausch and Lombs," he added, pointing to the flight case alongside Red in which he packed his marine binoculars. "I took a charter flight down to Sasebo, so's I could get me a short obsquintical, an' you know the only things I never seen?"

Hubie shook his head.

"I never seen any bows or sterns. So, my first day south, I chased dump trucks—"

"Oh, Jesus!" Hubie moaned as Red turned right onto the Belt Parkway rather than going straight ahead. "I bet you we're in for another tour of scenic Long Island! That goddamned Van Wyck must be still screwed up—was the day I left— Sonofabitch! You said dump trucks?"

"Right—lookin' for ones loaded with green sand."

"For castin's?"

"You got it! Chase enough trucks, an' sooner or later you find a foundry where all that green sand is laid up in patterns for castin' bow an' stern members an' thirty-five-foot propellers—that's when you see what the launchin' date is an' who's buildin'—"

"I told you!" Hubie groused as Red turned right, off the Belt and onto the Cross Island Parkway. "We're gonna lose us twenty minutes, a half hour, this way. So, what'd you get from your foundry tour?"

"What I got was *aisetsu*ed, *kampai*ed, an' *sushi*ed to death," Wade sighed. "But I never seen castin' one. What that means is Hasegawa's so hipped on not flashin' anythin', they're gonna do their own—an', as far as I know, that may be a first."

Hubie shrugged. "They could've gone somewheres else."

Wade shook his head. "Life don't work that way. All the time you bought machinery, you ever see a factory that wasn't right down the railroad track, or river, from its foundries?"

Looking back in memory, Hubie nodded. "Why is that, Loren?"

"Because United Parcel can't deliver. Prop shafts in those Hasegawa monsters'll run a hundred fifty feet long by three feet in diameter. The rudder post'll be one chunk of steel four stories high by ten feet across an' maybe fifteen, eighteen feet long that could weigh a hundred sixty tons. How's that gonna get in from outa the neighborhood?"

"An' that leaves six months from when the ends go on to launch?"

"Like I said, maybe even seven. There's a hell of a lot has to be hooked up, an' then there's trials an' final fittin' out."

"All well an' good, but how do you know they haven't started castin' yet?"

"Because Angelakos is supposed to deliver finished design drawin's December sixteenth. Then, he told Demi, he's gotta take off for Nippon the eighteenth for a consultation. Since the ends are the only important stuff left to do, I predict that trip is gonna consist of him standin' by the molds eyin' that hot metal for bubbles an' measurin' it for shrinkage soon's it cools."

Frowning, Hubie watched the exit for the Northern State Parkway, which would take them into Manhattan, go by in a light powdery snow flurry.

"So, when's the ship sail with Demi?" he asked.

"I further predict," Wade chuckled, "Demi'll be on the horn to Mrs. A the moment the wheels go up in her old man's plane. He's doin' New Year's Eve again for the clan, an' he had to go up to Montreal twice to check out Brazilian wheat ships before the St. Lawrence froze over—" he winked at Hubie— "so you know he brought back enough cut-rate bubbly to service a few worthy society gals—"

"Red! New York's that way!" Hubie shouted, pointing to his left as the exit for the Long Island Expressway receded. "Where we goin'?"

"To Greenwich," Red said.

"Greenwich?"

"Today's Thanksgiving, Hube."

"Is it?" Wade muttered.

Red nodded in the mirror to him.

"Then we're having Christmas," Hubie told Wade as he settled back for the trip north to the Throgs Neck Bridge and the New England Thruway.

"I got Urs an' his wife an' kids this mornin' at La Guardia," Red further volunteered, confirming his news.

"They stayin' with us?" Wade asked.

Red nodded again.

"Good! We'll get him in on this, too," Hubie said. "But if Angelakos is through with us December sixteenth, how are you goin' to get what we want?" he asked Wade.

"Oh, he's gonna have a lot of revisin', I promise you." Wade laughed. "Same's Demi an' Mrs. A—they'll all just have to keep practicin' till they get everythin' just right."

# III.
# Greeks

*December 19, 1966*
*New York City*

IN 1936, the venerable Peninsular and Oriental Steam Navigation Company set the events in motion responsible for the birth of Fiona Angelakos.

That year, sensing a Far East war, the firm sent Jack Davies, a young, personable skipper, to New York as freight solicitor.

Management saw Japan ruling the Pacific. America and England would win it back, but British industry east of India, source of P&O cargo, would be in ruins by then. Rebuilding, given Britain's depression, might take years. China as well could go Communist, be lost. U.S. Asian firms, however, had capital that would generate cargoes, so courting Americans with business in the area was crucial.

Jack Davies proved perfect for the job. Tall and dark, with black hair and green eyes, he had the warm smile of a passenger-ship officer and the easy, low-key manner of an even rarer type of master—a man unawed by either his authority or his responsibility.

He soon got cargoes and made friends. One shipper, in fact, with a marriageable daughter, asked him out to the Indian Harbor Yacht Club in Greenwich for a sailing weekend. Chance, however, scuttled that match before it began, a circumstance for which the host blamed himself.

At the launch dock, he greeted a group of lightning sailors and introduced his guest. Jack Davies thus met a coltish young girl in faded khaki shorts and navy-blue sweatshirt whose dark Celtic good looks equaled his.

But for someone's sick sister, Caitlin Lewis would not have been there. To be sure, the skipper who invited her did so only after much thought. Her father managed the club.

Jack Davies had no such qualms. He married Caitlin in January 1937.

Greenwich then seemed remote from New York, so they paid $11,000, $800 down, for a center-hall Colonial a short walk from the train. Fiona was born the following November.

In 1939 Davies began going to Washington on lend-lease matters. Except for trips to P&O ships sent to the States, that remained his wartime beat.

Separations aside, Caitlin loved those years. Her folks, like many Greenwich workers, lived in Port Chester, New York. With a house in town, she finally felt free of the "servant" class.

The future promised a further rise. She knew that much Fairfield County wealth came from shipping. She had a husband in the business. Moreover, they were being asked to owners' back-country Greenwich estates and mansions. Fiona, a great beauty, would marry into one of those homes, Caitlin hoped, and she groomed her daughter accordingly.

She had never been a snob, she told friends in 1942. But Jack got some French coloring books in Canada, and, undeniably, Fiona had an ear for the language. Private Greenwich Country Day taught it better, and sooner, than public schools, so the child would go there.

In 1946 the Davieses joined Riverside Yacht Club. For its junior program, Caitlin said. Kids had to sail. Ballet and riding began that fall, too.

Greenwich, meanwhile, was changing. By 1952, it had been discovered. It had become an increasingly popular bedroom for Manhattan-based middle and upper management. A house like Caitlin's and Jack's brought $48,000. Other prices rose apace.

So, as Loren Wade suspected of his neighbors, the Davieses began playing "catch up": hoping a year-end tax refund would break them even.

In 1953, Caitlin finally admitted defeat.

That year, Fiona's sixteenth, she knew that even in Greenwich, with its uncompromising standards, she had an uncommonly pretty and presentable girl. A good student, Fiona excelled at other skills valued in town, too. She could ride, sail, ski, swim, and play tennis, and she got lots of calls—but none from the estates and mansions Caitlin and Jack still visited.

Her child snubbed, she recalled Jack's comment as he turned down what seemed a good offer from another line: "In shipping, there are only two kinds of people: owners and others." A raise meant nothing, he argued. She would spend it without noticing. So he would go into debt and stay with P&O. To her, that seemed a vow of perpetual poverty at $27,000 a year. Now she saw he had grasped what had eluded her all her adult years: despite house, Greenwich Country Day, and yacht club, she still had not escaped the "servant" class.

Only ownership, she knew, assured that departure.

Fiona, the next year, entered the University of Bridgeport, while Jack worried about retirement. But two years later, generous to a fault, he returned from London with a P&O fortieth-anniversary check. It fell short of two years at Smith or Wellesley, he said. But an old pal, Paul Bondurant, who got one, too, said it would see his youngest, Liese, through a quite ritzy Swiss finishing school, thank you.

What did the ladies think of that?

Caitlin saw it as a triumph. Education abroad had real *cachet*.

Fiona kept her thoughts to herself. But she had her hopes.

Bright and competitive, she had looked around. Aside from money, she thought she had more of everything that men wanted than most women her age. European sophistication could help overcome the financial drawback.

She also knew that in life, not just in shipping, there were only two kinds of people: owners and others. Her mother put it even better: "Never marry for money, but don't just give yourself away either, dear."

She came home with a mastery of French, German, and Italian, a wish to travel, and a taste for worldly, successful men. A month later, she entered Pan American stewardess school.

She provided Pan Am with a rare asset: an American girl who knew how to live abroad. The line wanted to base her in Paris. She immediately accepted. The next year she went to Rome. Then Frankfurt.

U.S. executives then flying abroad on business all made $35,000 a year or more. Foreign firms sent stars, too. So she met a few men who interested her.

Their attraction held for a night or two. Then, in a *grande luxe* hotel or country inn, she found another "servant" posing as an eager achiever.

She heard a lot about stock options, profit sharing, retirement plans, and "riding it out," all employees' synonyms for hope: nothing of buying and selling, capital gains, and wealth—the more fulfilling concerns of owners.

Then, in 1961, after four Christmases in Europe, a scrubbed flight put her in New York for the Propeller Club holiday dance, an event well attended by New York's maritime community. Her folks, naturally, insisted that she join them.

At twenty-four, she had become an even greater beauty. So most young shipping men felt obliged that night to stop by at Jack's table to greet him. Many, with rueful smiles, had been Fiona's classmates at Greenwich Country Day. Most, needless to say, lived in back-country estates and mansions.

Their interest gave Caitlin no sense of triumph. She worried, instead, about Fiona. She looked beyond her beauty and youth.

In repose, she saw, the right corner of her daughter's broad, sensual mouth now arched upward in a calculating curl. Smiling, her eyes crinkled in amusement or delight, but never stopped moving. Typically, she had no idea of the origins of those mannerisms. But she wondered, as a mother would, if bright men, and Fiona had met many, had seen those telltales, too, and gracefully retreated to other, less demanding women.

So, when Archimedes Angelakos came to the table at eleven-thirty, she watched. Big and very Greek, with a swarthy, heavily featured face and unfashionable crewcut besides, he bore the mark of a marine engineer. A furrow of scar tissue, bone-deep and an inch wide, ran from the corner of his right eye-brow into his brown hair. It traced a live steam leak, she knew. Earnestly talking shop with Jack, he gazed worshipfully at Fiona.

Unlike the other men, he did not ask her to dance. And when Jack mentioned that she was Frankfurt-based, he just smiled sheepishly and said he often got to Germany. Then, bowing, which struck Caitlin as a bit much, he left. She put him down as not too bright.

On the way home, though, Jack called him the ablest man they had met. A few months before, he said, he had earned a $15,000 fee from P&O. A liner, 1,100 passengers aboard, had broken down in Singapore. Ship's officers and London engineering staff voted to wait for a Clyde shipyard to manufacture and fly out a new part. Arkie, coming home from Japan, made a replacement better than the original, in a local machine shop in forty hours. He got him that job, Jack said, and not even the iron-fisted Scotsman at headquarters said a word about price. Since then, he had done more work for P&O.

The next afternoon, Arkie called Fiona.

He was at Herb Hild's, on City Island, having sails recut, he told her. Greenwich being a twenty-minute drive, he hoped he could come up and take her to supper. He knew a nice place, he added gratuitously, and if her folks felt cheated, since she got home so rarely, why not have them along, too? He owed Jack a lot, he said.

So they all went, and to a very nice place indeed: Emily Shaw's Inn, in Pound Ridge, New York. Soft-spoken and diffident in contrast to his size and ability, Arkie mostly asked Jack's advice about business.

Nevertheless, he interested Fiona. She knew many executives, but few owners; none still in their twenties. He had the quiet maturity of the sixty-year-old corporation heads with whom she frequently chatted.

He had, at the same time, a sense of play. At twenty-eight, he had a boat and belonged to Manhasset Bay, as tony a club as Indian Harbor. Liking cars, he had three. Toys, he called them. Set up in business, he would pursue his dream. He wanted to design a $250,000 house. His tone implied that money had no meaning other than what it would enable him to do creatively.

Fiona remembered that. She wanted a showplace house, too. The status that went with it she could handle.

In late January he called from Hamburg. He had a job there. Could they meet that weekend?

Of course! But would he please come to Frankfurt? She had had flying for that week.

So they drove to Heidelberg and tramped *schloss* and town, holding hands and shielding each other from the sudden blinding snow squalls that roared down the Rhine Valley. Then, in the Red Ox, over venison ragout, she proposed a toast.

To a glorious day! she said.

Glass raised, he shook his head and smiled sappily.

He wouldn't drink to that? she asked. He disagreed?

No!

Then why did he shake his head? What didn't he believe?

Just—being there . . .

Yes?

. . . in that out-of-the-way place . . . with her.

She hoped he would get used to that, she said.

Her smile made his hand tremble. Moselle lapped at the sides of his glass.

Later, at the Frankfurt airport, to encourage him, she kissed him goodbye, a cheek brush, and he blushed.

She had heard from two other men after the Propeller Club dance. The first had been a classmate at Greenwich Country Day. Calling from Paris, he reported that, meetings over, he had a Ritz suite for the weekend. The second, another back-country squire, had attended her birthday parties without inviting her back. He wanted her for Lisbon, he said.

Neither man had seen her in six years.

And she had never been easy. Certainly not cheap or vulgar. What right had they to treat her so?

Those two sapped her spirit. They underlined what she had been thinking herself the past year or so, that her life had begun to feel like a four-for-a-dollar record club offer:

YOUR CHOICE: POP-ROCK-COUNTRY-CLASSICAL!

God knew, she had tried to be all things to all men.

FREE TRIAL!

She had given a few of those as well. Perhaps, too many. Sex had never moved her, besides. It seemed messy at the time, stupid the morning after. She had mastered it, as she had cooking, another foolish pastime to her, because the life she wanted meant doing everything well.

GUARANTEED SATISFACTION!

She had given that to some men; received it from none. Yet she always felt she was "on approval," not they, merchandise to be returned if not found satisfactory. That had to stop. No one deserved that kind of insecurity.

So, back in her apartment, thinking of Arkie, she sounded a retreat from ambition. She could withdraw with honor, she reflected. No one had ever looked at her so adoringly or treated her so deferentially. She had no fears about his ultimate financial success either. What he lacked in shrewdness and social finesse she would supply. Two doubts she never had: that he would be infinitely gentle . . . and dull.

Ten months later, on her twenty-fifth birthday, they married. Her father died three weeks before the wedding, so her surrogate uncle, Paul Bondurant, who had looked after her while she was at finishing school, flew over from London to give her away.

Caitlin, having married off her daughter in Christ Episcopal, the Greenwich society church, sold the house, paid the debts, took what little was left, and went to Florida. There she joined the sisterhood of attractive, charming, and worldly middle-aged women who knowledgeably advise others on good times by day in exclusive boutiques and ponder bittersweet memories by night in small apartments far from the ocean.

Most of which that great student of things social, Demosthenes Elias Keriosotis, knew or could guess when he called the Monday after Arkie left for Japan, as Wade suspected, to start casting bow and stern members.

Like Wade, Demi also sensed Fiona's restiveness.

He too had seen her discreetly regard other men: in Bermuda; at parties; on New York Yacht Club cruises.

They were both, he thought, in the same game: hunting. They both wanted . . . more.

Moreover, she seemed as serious about it as he. To a "hunter," that only heightened her appeal. Bedding her would be taking a trophy.

So he misread her when the maid got her on the phone.

"Hi, Demi!" she said.

He knew that tone. It came over as pure enthusiasm, unclouded by doubt or surprise. That delight sounded suspiciously akin to what he had earlier come to call her "breathless Pan Am rush." Developed for repeat passengers, it had been honed, he thought, for shipowners.

When Arkie left, she always felt a letdown. Her despondency, however, had nothing to do with his absence. The feeling stemmed from where they lived.

Shortly before their wedding, they had looked at an old coach house on Sands Point. Converted from a stable into a garage in the twenties, it had been abandoned in the forties. Apart from its price, Arkie liked its lines and stone exterior and thought it would be fun to redo. Finished right, he said, with its view of the Sound, it would bring over six figures.

So she went along with the idea.

He failed to say he and his two brothers, Pete and Steve, the Riverhead scallopers, would do all the work. With, of course, help from the wives. Later, he blamed the oversight on taking family tradition for granted.

Poor Greeks did for themselves, he said. Tirelessly, she would have added.

Work began the first Saturday morning in December. By noon, the north and east walls had all but vanished under sledges and a rented jackhammer.

The next weekend, massive Thermopane windows raised on boatyard jacks were cemented into place. Christmas Eve, back locked in pain, she helped tap the last red brick into the last course of the new floor.

She saw the new year in before a huge fireplace made of stone taken from the walls. Seven nieces and nephews, unlike any Greenwich kids she ever knew, lay in sleeping bags on the hearth.

Twelve months later, they were all in the same room again New Year's Eve. She knew by then, for what it was worth, and to her the price had been too high in effort, that she had a showplace home.

Their view through the clear night stretched to Stamford, fifteen miles away. Execution Rocks Lighthouse, beneath them, flashed white. Stepping Stones, to their left, blinked green.

The brick floor, waxed and polished and dotted with Scandinavian area rugs, cast warm glints on whitewashed walls and oiled ceiling beams. Italian lamps, in poster-bright oranges, reds, and yellows, spiced the room with bold primary colors. Danish and modern furniture, much of it bare wood with cushions covered in striking fabrics, echoed the browns, blues, and greens surrounding them by day.

She had wanted Bloomingdale's to do the decorating. But Arkie, who read architectural journals and visited designer showrooms, called the store "trendy." He had her fly to Amsterdam instead. Then, his job done in Rotterdam, they shopped Copenhagen and Helsinki.

He did have exquisite taste, she thought. Most of what they bought he chose, after soliciting her approval, of course, in his maddeningly shy, self-effacing way. She just wished he took design less seriously. She had had enough of "function," "integrity," and "purity."

She found the house beautiful. She conceded its comfort. But for her it just missed. Its simplicity somehow made her seem vulnerable. It failed to project the affluence she needed to feel secure.

Within a year, though, word about it had got around.

The previous week, upstairs still undone, she had gotten a note from Manhasset's Congregational Church. The writer hoped she would show her home on the church's spring house walk, a prestigious North Shore fund raiser.

Arkie had thought the invitation pleased her. She saw it as added work. But, at his urging, she had agreed to open the house. So, more grateful than usual for a respite from do-it-yourself, she had seen him off for Japan the day before.

She would rest the first week. Books and TV would alleviate some of the boredom. Apathy would then follow.

The fault lay in the nature of suburbs. Women her age who rode and played tennis with her all had small children and tight budgets. Few had traveled. Fewer still had her sophistication. Moreover, they all thought they had "arrived."

Those in their forties, with means, had other interests. Sexual appeal fading, they seemed to be in a tacit conspiracy. They plotted to keep what they already had, she guessed. They did this, it seemed, by helping each other provide "safe" climates for their husbands. Dinner parties. New York shows. Cruises.

Thus chaperoned and insulated, men enjoyed harmless illusions of variety. They saw lots of faces. Most had bright, winning smiles. Some were interesting. One or two might even be animated by a drink too many. But all were the same age as their wives.

Attractive younger women threatened those parties, she thought. They mirrored the world. They suggested dangerous possibilities better left forgotten: youthful secretaries; divorcées; out-of-town temptresses. So she and Arkie seldom saw middle-aged couples either.

Motherhood, of course, would have made her much safer socially. But that meant giving up too much. It put her future at risk.

She had an option there, never verbalized. But her actions acknowledged an awareness of it: a second marriage.

So she welcomed Demi's call.

She had no plan to marry him. She hardly knew him. Nor did she crave a man. Sexually, she never did. But she found his looks and polish attractive. She enjoyed his sense of humor too.

He offered more than amusement, as well. Besides being Arkie's client, he belonged to a vast shipowning family. If she stayed married, where he sent relatives for new ships could mean a lot. Part of the convertible design fee, for example, had already bought a Caribbean vacation she and Caitlin would enjoy in April. Arkie called that her bonus for being alone so much that fall and winter while he sat at the drawing board. There could be many more. The Keriosotises were quiet, but everyone knew they owned a lot of tonnage.

On a deeper level, she had another reason for pleasing Demi. Like remarriage, it too remained unspoken: he recalled the world she had fled in desperation—to suburban boredom.

Surprisingly, he had told Arkie he might call her. Probably, she thought, for a lunch in town. She had half expected him to do that months before, surreptitiously.

So, intrigued at what his motives might now be, she followed up her initial gush of recognition with enough innuendo to give him an opening. "I don't know if I should even be talking to you," she began, the laughter in her tone suggesting she felt otherwise, "not after what you've done to my man! Poor Arkie came home in a daze Saturday after seeing you, and I put him on a plane for Japan yesterday the same way. He never even saw me the whole weekend," she protested. "Is that any way for a client to treat a distinguished naval architect who's gone without sleep for two months to produce the most beautiful set of plans ever—"

Demi slouched lower on the gray leather settee in the tiny "office" in his house. Then, smiling, feet braced on the bronze handles of the chart table facing him, he prepared to enjoy himself—and her.

She would be great fun, he thought. He rarely encountered such world-class glib. Just saying hello, she boxed the compass. Her tone excused him for killing Arkie, implied she had been a loving, dutiful wife, and even insinuated she might have become a little horny in the process as well.

A wary women, he decided. Suggesting everything, she revealed nothing. That implied an interest in his intentions. Which meant he had better learn hers.

So he cut her off in a melodramatic, pleading tone. "Fiona, don't! Stop—please! You're desolating me," he whimpered. "You're judge and jury, and you're convicting me without due process of a crime I'd be the last man in the world to commit."

He sank back lower on the settee, awaiting results.

The strategy had worked before. He simply played against a woman's typecasting. Clearly, she had expected a cool, sophisticated reply. He had given her low comedy instead. With luck, an unguarded response might just follow.

"Crime?" she mused.

"Fu-fu-fu-fu-ucking up your sex life," he stammered.

Great, he thought a moment later. So far, it had worked. He heard her swallow, probably in confusion. Then she tumbled to the game. And that suited him even better.

"Sex life?" she asked icily. "Is there a life of any kind for a woman who has a 108,000-ton convertible for competition, especially when—"

He sighed, as if trying to calm her. "Fiona—"

"—especially when an unreasonable client," she went on in a bogus, quiet, well-bred tone of outrage, "browbeats her husband into committing to a full set of hull lines within sixty days, and—"

"But that was two months ago, Fiona."

"Oh, I know. I know that, all right, Mr. Client."

"And nothing since then?" he asked.

The question trailed off in silence.

His voice grew more conciliatory. "Surely, once or twice?" he ventured.

She let that go by unremarked, as well.

"Not even a little quickie?" he asked tremulously.

Finally the ridiculous triumphed. He got an unguarded response. She giggled.

Even then, he thought, she boxed the compass. Her voice still conveyed all things: anguish, embarrassment, reserve. And, beneath those, another tone: a note of complicity. It joined him in mocking Arkie. Derision shaded her voice like a whispered secret. However subtle, it represented an invitation.

It also explained her interest in him.

The obvious reason, helping Arkie, he discarded at once. Her laugh put her in business for herself. Realistic about women, if little else, he abandoned as quickly any idea that sex figured in her overture. If it had, she could have been far more direct.

So, he reasoned, she had a purely selfish motive. She saw him as possible prey. At thirty-one, with a likely $25-million order, he certainly looked it.

Considering that, he widened his smile. Someday, he thought, he would thank Loren.

Meanwhile, he admired her wiliness. She had covered herself all ways. He might suspect, but would never be able to prove, or care to repeat, that she had once stalked him. No basis in fact existed for that assumption. He had, after all, heard only a tone. To his ear, it implied she might be reached.

If he let that signal pass?

The call would go on, of course. But her invitation would not be repeated. Doing so would give away the game. Dull men had uncertain futures, besides.

In the meantime, though, he had her overture. How he handled it determined the next step. She might or might not then decide to go hunting. Either way, who would know? Only he, and only if she pursued him further.

He wondered then, as he always did about women like her, if such a move came from brains, experience, or instinct. Regardless, he knew how to proceed. He understood the urge to hunt in both sexes. Men so moved saw life as a series of games. He did himself. So, why not try for a trophy? With luck and timing, it could be won.

Women, in contrast, had a deeper need. Consciously or not, they were searching, he thought. At some point, he mused, they had begun seeing themselves as commodities, marriage as a transaction. Moreover, if purchased, what they had to sell—background and birth, looks, social graces, and taste—assured them further anonymity. As wives, they became adjuncts to successful men's business and leisure needs.

Psychologically, huntresses made that tradeoff as girls, Demi believed. Then the thought ruled their acts like a self-fulfilling prophecy. But, with age and sophistication, the nature of the exchange became clearer. That, in turn, made them cagier, more demanding, and increasingly selective about how and with whom they entered into negotiations.

Others regarded them as grasping, greedy women. He saw them as insecure children with a need for external approval. Men defined their identities. Things—clothes, furs, homes, jewels, travel—measured their acceptance. So, the more they got, the more they wanted, because the more they had, the higher they valued what they had traded away: images of self-worth.

That followed from Wade's observation, he thought. Married or rented, some geishas always aspired to top market fee—regardless of personal cost. Still, he knew, their egos demanded more. For, however grandly indulged or treated such women might be, in their own eyes they remained bought. Employment as bed toys, hostesses, or showpieces forever denied them equality. That made them vulnerable. They all craved recognition.

So, abandoning low comedy, he accorded her in voice and manner the headiest compliment she had ever received. "Others," by her father's definition, had flattered her similarly, of course. But no shipowner ever offered her, future unseen, expectations unspoken, what his words now implied: partnership.

"I need your help on something," he said.

That put her further off balance, as he intended.

It also brought the response he expected: silence.

He took that as a sign she had gone on the hunt. If she were just massaging a client of Arkie's, she would have been as bubbly as when she came to the phone. A prompt "Sure, what can I do?" would have followed without waiting to hear his request. Now, instead, stepping out of character, she paused.

She needed that moment, he knew, to regroup. What began for her as sexual had become serious. Facing this unexpected turn, she had much to ponder before proceeding.

First, she had to determine whether he had received her invitation and, if so, responded to it. At the same time, he speculated, she might well be asking herself if that really mattered. The initiative could have been all his. In either case, she would think she had an edge if she remained glib and elusive and kept him coming to her. But glibness would be all wrong if he sincerely saw her as an equal.

Amused at the maze he had led her into, he welcomed her pause. He needed time, too. He had many images to move her past interest, but they had to be presented just so, he thought. To him, in fact, the order in which he put them far outweighed their content. If their flow seemed contrived, or if he began to sound like a salesman, he knew she would shy away.

Women like Fiona, he held, were resolutely middle class. They had to explain their subconscious mischief to themselves in socially approved terms. Vocabularies might differ, but in all other respects they resembled corporate hired guns weaseling out of contracts. Hellbent for money, power, and better fringe benefits, men piously invoked challenge, the need to be creative, and security for their families as causes for corporate divorces. Their female counterparts, successfully consummating hunts, similarly referred to incompatibility or mental cruelty.

Leading her, then, as he saw it, became a matter of suggesting acceptable motives to her for impulses which she preferred not to admit. That made order important. Appropriate thoughts later would be scoffed at now.

Initially, she would tell herself her interest came from being a dutiful wife, he reasoned. So, naturally, he helped her reinforce that idea first.

"Arkie mentioned I'd call?" he asked.

"That you might," she allowed.

He smiled at her choice of words. He had told Arkie he *would* call. "Might" made that conditional. It implied that she had thought casually, if at all, about hearing from him. Or, just as subtly, it suggested that her mind had wandered when Arkie had given her the message.

He let that pass, however. Partnership, after all, had stopped her cold. So he knew what had to come next. His manner, accordingly, became more businesslike as he framed an image calculated to start moving her.

"I've got this house on Forty-ninth Street . . ." he began, letting the statement trail off so that she had time to visualize herself in the midst of what for her would be a glamorous setting, ". . . and I need a hostess for my big holiday do—the annual Keriosotis family reunion. I wonder, Fiona," he went on, "would you help me preside?"

Put just right, he told himself. She could make a whole lot more out of that than just an evening on the fashionable East Side.

By then, he thought, she knew Greeks. She had seen beneath the quick smile and the open manner. She understood the lust for privacy and the sense of kin. In a world where only blood could be trusted, few outsiders were asked to family affairs. Even fewer acted as hosts. His request, then, could be taken as a compliment of high order. As a member of a shipowning clan, he belonged to the most exclusive group in an already closed-in society.

She responded as predicted. "Of course, I'd love to," she said.

Glamour and flattery introduced, he next reinforced the partnership image. He did that with truth. Instead of selling the pleasures of the evening, he outlined her responsibility. His other aims aside, she had a role to play. If she bungled, it could be costly to both of them.

"Marvelous!" he shot back at her acceptance. "Last year I tried to do it by myself, and it was a shambles. I warn you," he confided, further heightening her sense of collaboration, "you'll wish you were part lion tamer. At this point, the family does most of its business with itself, and the women don't get along."

"They don't? Why not?"

"Why not?" he laughed. "Do Greeks need a reason? Marina's mink is blacker than Melpomene's, but Melpomene lives in Short Hills, which is classier than Greenwich. Aphrodite, on the other hand, dresses like a slob, but owns ten acres in Lattingtown that make Short Hills look like a slum. Marina, though, summers in Greece next to my Great-Uncle Zavvas, the family head, which she doesn't let the others forget. But Honey, my Uncle Taki's wife—"

"Taki's the broker?"

"Right, and Honey wee-wees on everybody—partly because they all live so well off of their piece of Taki and partly because she's from Lumberton, North Carolina, and never liked Greeks in the first place."

"And, naturally, you want me to keep the girls happy so the men can attend to business instead of each other's throats."

"Exactly, only the men don't count. The women own everything. They're Keriosotises—Taki's cousins—so what he says in New York goes. But what none of them realize—because they think only Greeks can make a shipping buck—is that Honey's the chairman of that board. Then, for added piquancy, Taki's sisters, Phaedra and Artemis, who hate the others, and who should never be confused with Doris Day or Patti Page, will be there, too. Auntie Phaedra tried to rip off Melpomene's dress last year. She's had four divorces and still craves men. Auntie Artemis, who's smarter than hell, and who always manages to hire longhaired brunette maids just about your size, tags along to smoke my pot."

"In other words," she chirped, the cheerful Pan Am stewardess, "a normal working night."

"And then some. How are you at handling paranoia?"

"Is it knee-high or hip-high?"

"Head-high."

"I swim!"

"You'd better," he cautioned. "At this point, the girls are ready to tear the family apart."

"Oh? Over what?" she asked, abandoning flippancy.

"Over what else?" he taunted. "Money and power."

He had liked her confidence. Nothing she had heard of the Keriosotis women had lessened her belief that she could handle them. Now her wariness impressed him even more. That showed a real zest for intrigue, calculation.

So, sensing more help from her than he had expected, he explained the conflict smoldering behind the evening. The argument, common in Greek shipping clans, offered him another benefit. It could make her more compliant.

"In the next five years," he told her, "1,250,000 tons of ships in the family fleet have to be replaced. Some of us think we need 1,750,000. So, after that's settled, comes the hard part: who pays how much and what that means to dividends. And then, of course, there's all the nitty-gritty to work through."

"Like what, Demi? I'll need to know to help."

Trust her, he thought. She got that message. However the family resolved the argument, as much as $1 million in naval architect's fees would be thrown up for grabs. That made the party vitally important to her, whether or not she later decided to go into business for herself. The situation also enhanced Demi's stature, so he gave her the facts she wanted.

Beyond scope, there were many other important specifics to be decided, he said. How much of that new tonnage should be in tankers? How much in freighters? Should they be built for time or spot charters? Or both? And before those came the key question: philosophy.

"Philosophy, Demi?"

"Sure. The real fight's over 'smaller' versus 'bigger.' "

Greek owners liked small ships because they needed less crew, he said. They ran family-owned companies and hated to pay strangers. They thought like seamen, too, instead of executives. They wanted to spread their bets. The old men in Athens, Zavvas and Lycourgos, brothers of his dead grandfather, Demosthenes, felt that way. They would always embrace "smaller." He, Taki, and Artemis, on the other hand, argued the case for "bigger." They had great respect for Onassis, who pioneered the trend.

Meanwhile, the debate raged. A decision would be reached at the family meeting in Athens in May. Marina would support her father, Zavvas, on the "smaller" side. Her sister, Melpomene, however remained uncommitted. She disliked Marina sufficiently for being the favorite child that she might well back "bigger." Aphrodite, who resented the way her father, Lycourgos, treated her husband, could vote "bigger" as well just to spite the old man. Phaedra, as she would see, had no mind to make up. But her support was there to be bought off by the highest bidder.

"If that's what's going on, why do they even bother getting together?" she asked.

"Good God, Fiona," he retorted in a bantering tone, "aren't you a Greek yet? They're family! Family'll only stab you in the chest. Bad as they are, strangers are even worse!"

"The customer is always right!" she laughed without conviction. "And it is your house. When's the date? I want to get it in my appointment book."

"New Year's Eve," he said, anticipating her reply.

"Oh, Demi, I'm so sorry," she apologized. "I'm on to go to the New Year's party at the club with the crew Arkie races with. They promised to look after me."

Clever girl, he thought. So shrewd. She had let him ramble on, without asking the date, so that she could be busy that night. She wanted him to beg her to change her plans. Then her presence would become a favor from her rather than from him.

He knew how to handle that. He had offered the carrot: partnership. And she had tried to use it to get an edge. So now he gave the stick: an owner's ultimatum. She could say no, of course. But he never doubted how she would respond.

"Fiona," he told her, "that's insulting. You sound like girls I knew in prep school who always washed their hair nights I wanted dates. Here I am, stuck with two million very cranky tons of Greek shipping, and you're saying you have to do the businessman's bounce and wear a funny hat with suburban lawyers, or whatever, and their Betty Crocker wives."

"I'll see what I can do," she said a moment later.

"Fair enough."

Then, smiling to himself, he stretched lower on the gray chartroom settee.

Order, he thought, meant as much to success as timing. She had answered the key question. She would be at the party. After that, when she arrived became a detail. He had now only to present the request.

"I'll call, of course, to firm things up the thirtieth," he went on, "but could you plan on being ready at about twelve-thirty?"

"When?" she asked sharply.

"I thought we'd have a little lunch first," he said casually, turning the conversation to the final image he wanted her to have. "I'm meeting a real-estate broker then to go through a house I'm dickering on. I've heard so much about what you've done to yours I'd like you to have a look before I go ahead—just to see what you think of some of my ideas."

He understood her hesitancy. That expanded an evening into virtually a day together. Still, they had a chaperone, so she had the problem of gracefully refusing the invitation. A little flattery never hurt, either, he thought.

In the end, though, curiosity won out. "You're buying in town?" she asked.

"Yes, on Forty-ninth Street."

"But isn't that where you live now?"

"This place is in Turtle Bay Gardens," he explained.

She paused, impressed, but still dubious. "I'd love to see it, but I think I'd better pass, Demi. There's just too much to do, and I'd have an entire evening outfit to bring—"

He had an answer for that too. "Fiona, you're my guest," he reminded her in a tone of good-natured admonishment. "Don't make so much work for yourself! I'll be food-shopping then, so I'll send my car, and Sal, the driver, will do the rest."

A special conceit, the money-green Cadillac gave him nearly as much pleasure as the house. It made his success image even more precocious. Few men his age had places in town. How many owned limousines too? Moreover, how he afforded such a trifle baffled his *malaca* family, which greatly increased his enjoyment.

A fellow hunter made it possible. He had turned up one night saying he had discovered the imaginary limousine. Inspiration struck, he said, in another citadel of make-believe, Washington, D.C. Riding in a rental vehicle, he noticed that the upholstery carried monograms. After some prodding, the driver explained why. The car, he said, had been "borrowed." It belonged to a customer who rented garage space. He got free rent and a wash each day the livery operator used the vehicle to supplement his rental fleet.

If they could shop that deal, and find a buyer, Demi's friend told him, they could buy a Cadillac jointly and both ride in style. Demi liked the idea so well, he offered to sell it. Doing so, he saw that his pal had not invented the imaginary limousine at all. He had, in fact, *reinvented* it.

New York livery operators offered him free rent and washes—and an added fillip. They would give him the same driver, so that he had virtually a personal servant, at half price when he used the car. At five dollars an hour, plus gas and oil, he would cut taxi and car rental costs by half.

The ploy, he later learned, amounted to a secret of the rich, or those who wished to appear so. Thereafter he always watched the movers and shakers enter or leave limousines on TV news, musing if their washes were thrown in—and who owned the other half of the car. Neither question, he knew, occurred to middle-class viewers. They thought money put people in big cars beyond sharpshooting. So he felt sure he had Fiona sold.

"You just be ready," he told her. "Sal'll run you into town, drop your evening things off at my house, and you at Lafayette or La Grenouille, since Lutèce won't do lunch on Saturday, and I'll take you over from there. It's that easy. Now, what do you say?"

Indeed, what could she say, gracefully, to that?

A moment later, rising from the gray leather settee, he placed the phone in the chart table chronometer case. Then, smiling, he picked up Arkie's roll of initial design drawings and left to meet Wade.

The plans, he knew, were exceptional.

Things were looking up all over, he thought.

A few hours later, homeward bound in the right rear corner of Hubie Garrison's Cadillac, Loren Wade agreed.

He had been asked if he had seen Demi that day.

"Take a look at these," he said.

The limousine had then gone perhaps a hundred feet. Looking away from the folded, sepia-toned sheets of paper Wade offered, Hubie shook his head. The prospect of more reading, in addition to the jaywalking Christmas shoppers who stopped them dead in the middle of Sixth Avenue, deepened his scowl.

"Just tell it to me," he ordered wearily. "Christ knows, I don't need any more written reports, not today, tomorrow, or any day, for that matter."

"This ain't no memo," Wade objected. "I went all over hell's half acre an' back till I found a blueprint place that'd make reductions on the spot."

"Those're the plans?"

"First design drawin's, lines an' profile."

"Enjoy 'em. What in hell do I know about ships?"

"You wanna see if we got somethin', don't you?"

Reluctantly, Hubie reached across the armrest.

Sighing, he wedged himself into his corner as they crept by the Radio City Music Hall and the four-abreast Christmas-show line that wound into Rockefeller Center. Holding the drawings in gray neon marquee glow, he thus became acquainted with the work of Archimedes Angelakos.

The top sheet he shuffled under the other at once. "Goddamned lines," he muttered. Then, squinting, he turned and flopped against the seat, flicking on the reading light at his left shoulder.

Reaction immediately followed.

"Loren," he whispered, "that sonofabitch is movin'! Look at it!" he ordered holding the paper horizontally at its edges between thumbs and forefingers and passing it in the air from left to right. "Just as sure as I'm sittin' here, on Fiftieth Street, that mother's headin' south. It's got motion!"

Wade grinned. With luck, he thought, he could get a convertible yet.

The second impression seemed equally encouraging.

"How'd he do that? This don't even have color. All it is, is an outline. Where'd he get the movement?"

"Look at the bow," Wade instructed.

A moment later, holding the photostat as if he were reading a book, Hubie nodded in recognition. "Got it," he said. "That's the angle of rake you drew to show what the sketches in Japan looked like."

"Yeah, so we know we found us the man. Only here he had a different problem. Keep lookin' at the bow, but take in them uprights back at the stern supportin' the boat deck over the main deck at the same time."

"They're raked forward, too—same's the bow. Is that all he did, Loren, just repeat the bow angle?"

"Right, an' that's art, instead of the weldin' we get from those shipyard yo-yos we go to when we build. He hit it another pretty good lick too."

"He did? Where?"

"The damned thing's so slick you're lookin' at it an' you can't even see it."

"Show me."

"Look again at the stern."

Hubie raised the sepia-toned sheets closer. Then, after a moment, he shook his head. "Shee-it," he murmured. "He tilted the stack mark."

Nodding, Wade eliminated coincidence as a factor.

"Right," he agreed. "He tipped Demi's K an' the anchor nineteen degrees forward, exactly one-third the angle of the bow rake. Makes a difference, don't it?" he asked, smiling across the armrest. "Your eye gets sucked in at the funnel, sorta leans forward with the house flag, an' picks up speed when it drops down to them stern uprights. That bigger angle gets you lookin' quicker. By the time you're at the bow an' see it again, you're goin' so fast you'll swear the whole shebang's on the move."

Shaking his head, Hubie turned to his left to gaze at the brilliantly lit five-story-high Christmas tree dominating Rockefeller Center.

"Some stuff," he muttered. "You suppose we could do that with our house flags—tilt Texas an' the swords, I mean?"

"Sure," he was informed sardonically, "all I need's the budget. Just don't expect me to pay for a bunch of dead-ass painters with one-inch brushes to redo a hundred an' some funnel sides."

The challenge was met at Fiftieth and Fifth Avenue. "Let's do it!" Hubie said.

Wade, after ten years of hearing nothing other than that ships cost too much, promptly took it from there. "Turn the light back on, an' I'll show you somethin' else," he said. "Get the line drawin's out."

"You can't read surveys. I can't see those curves" Hubie protested. "They always stay flat for me."

"Dammit, do like I say! Hold that sheet straight out, just under your eyes, with the stern almost at your nose. Now squint, same's if you were sightin' a rifle, an' rock that paper up an' down round the centerline. Whatta you see?"

After another slow block, Hubie saw the curves. At Fiftieth Street and Madison Avenue he flicked off the reading light and turned to Wade.

"Underwater, it's like a sailboat at the stern," he told him. "Do we have any ships like that?"

"No."

"Then what's he want to do that for?"

"To whip cavitation—"

"Whip what?"

"What happens when the propeller bores a hole in the water, an' it don't have anythin' to bite on. You can't get speed unless the prop turns, but by the time you get it goin' fast enough to do you some good, it sets up a corkscrew-shaped suction ahead of it. Between hull form an' that twist, the damned sea ain't ever where it oughta be! Mostly, it just rolls by. So I told Demi to get us eighteen knots, 'cause that's about the state of the art these days. My bet, though, is that the model of what you're lookin' at's goin' to tank-test a hell of a lot closer to nineteen an' a quarter."

"It's that good?"

"Maybe better. It could hit nineteen an' a half."

"What've you got, then, to string along Angelakos?" Hubie asked as they turned left on Park Avenue.

"Leave that to me," Wade answered sorrowfully as a traffic light halted them between Fifty-second and Fifty-third streets. "I'll fuck that gorgeous thing up somehow," he sighed, gazing at the thousands of tiny white lights on the small trees set into the reflecting pools in front of the Seagram Building.

"An' the other part?"

"In motion, too. The Duke of Forty-ninth Street informed me today he invited Mrs. A to the family New Year's Eve party. What with all the revisions an' deadlines we'll lay on the old man when he gets back from Japan, he told me, he figured he'd better get the old lady on his side."

"Under him, you mean."

"Oh yeah. He's too cute for words, that boy."

Hubie chuckled. "Christ, I bet you got everybody in this thinkin' three or four deep, at least."

* * *

Fiona, for one, had given the matter much thought.

The first order of business, then, would be to find a suitable dress. It would have to showcase her as well as the other women presented themselves, she knew. If not, they would patronize her for lacking style. At the same time, what she chose had to be sufficiently quiet to avoid competing with them, yet still set her apart.

After lunch, telling herself she could not embarrass Arkie, she drove to the artsy bookstore in Locust Valley for the European fashion magazines.

That evening, watching *The Tonight Show* in robe and pajamas, she found the Continental designers disappointing. With the mini still popular, they were content outdoing each other in kookiness.

What she wanted came from the American *Vogue*. Rose Kennedy wore it, but they were the same body type, so she knew it would work.

With a few tricks, tightening it, deepening the décolletage, and slitting a side seam, the dress, a Pauline Trigère, would be perfect.

But in fuchsia.

And Demi would send his car, she thought. Interesting. . . .

*December 31, 1966*
*New York City–Zurich*

FIONA BESIDE him, Demi opened the gate in the black iron fence fronting the pink stone house.

Then, glancing around, he smiled.

The sky seemed unusually dark, even at four-thirty, when dusk begins to fall in New York during early winter. Looking up, over the housetops on the other side of the block, he saw pillars of pewter-gray cloud and ragged wisps of scud sailing south.

Normally, mushroom-shaped cumulus formations meant rain. Tonight, chilled by a harsh northwesterly, they promised snow. Perfect, he thought. Facing long drives home, his guests would leave sooner.

Turning, he leaned into the wind, putting his hand around her waist to steer her into the lee of his body. Coat whipping about her knees, she quickly took shelter. Moreover, in heels she stood nearly as tall as he, so, laughing, she matched him stride for stride in the dash he suddenly led across Forty-ninth Street.

Her height disconcerted him. She fit, he thought. From shoulder to knee, her body flowed into his.

He thought about kissing her, to see her reaction, and guessed he could carry it off. After all the tone and sophistication that had gone before that afternoon, their impromptu dash certainly excused an equally high-spirited act of impulse, he reasoned.

But patience overruled curiosity. Pointing to his black steel street-level kitchen door, he led her across the sidewalk. A last wave sent the real-estate agent down the block to Second Avenue.

Then he played his role.

"Enough *House and Garden*." He smiled, holding the door open for her. "Now to work."

She smiled back radiantly. As well she might, he thought. The joke so far had been on him. The day had been planned to dazzle her. Instead, it had turned out the other way.

He had chosen La Grenouille for lunch, because Seventh Avenue designers and fashion writers had made the place a "local." They would impress Fiona, he thought, and then there would be the other women.

Weekdays, they warmed La Grenouille—always awash in anemones, daisies, tea roses, and tulips—with a glow of their own. Against their presence, fashion magazine photographs of them became a kind of visual hearsay.

Saturdays were even better. Garment District lords arrived then, as trade gossip had it, with their mattresses, floor and runway models who sold high fashion in showrooms. To Demi, they were the most alluring females in New York. Older, livelier, and sexier than cover girls, they dressed better, knew how to walk, and handled themselves with assurance and humor.

But gorgeous women rarely impressed Charles Masson. As La Grenouille's owner, he fed them twice a day. If disposed, he might nod at one of them. But bow? Or leave his post by the front door? Abandon the phone and the reservations book? Never!

He did for Fiona. Moreover, his approval went beyond looks. Her sense of style and place had been unerring.

With the image of Jacqueline Kennedy's trim little pillbox hat still vivid, she arrived bareheaded, center-parted blue-black hair lushly swirling over her shoulders. December and a dab of lipstick did for cosmetics.

Her dress, similarly, got right to the point. Pastel-green wool with pleated skirt for walking and deep slash pockets for warmth, it said country: little girl from Greenwich, Demi thought. Her belt put her in the yachting order of the species; a gold pelican hook, used to close lifelines, cinched its brown leather ends. Her attire implied that she saw lunch with so many formidable beauties, in such a citadel of style, as a challenge she could cope with quite casually.

And she had. The conquest of the real-estate agent followed. Within minutes, she knew that Joey, a lank-haired blonde in a tired B. H. Wragge black suit, had gone to Sweet Briar. Raising her martini, she convened a finishing-school girls' reunion. Sisters, she said, had to stand up to arrogant Smithies and all-American Wellesley girls, and, faded-blue eyes shining with shared hurts and prejudices, Joey laughed with her.

He almost went for it himself. If Fiona had just kept her eyes still, instead of measuring the other women and sizing up the men like the hunter she was, the effect would have been perfect, he thought. Still, he had to concede, she made it work.

She did even better at the pink stone house.

He meant that to awe her, to give her a picture of great shipping wealth, no matter how vicariously. Instead of being cowed, she told him what to do. And Joey thought her ideas were marvelous. One he liked himself.

She told him to cover a dining-room wall with a pink-tinted mirror. They were dirt cheap at bar supply houses, which bought them when nightclubs and taverns went broke. They took years off women's faces.

Leaving, she said the house had fantastic potential. She offered to get him into the Center for Design some Saturday, when showrooms were less busy. She had a friend's decorator's pass and used it to get discounts.

What, he wondered, did that mean: hunting? Interest in the house? Stroking a client? He had no idea. So he told her to call when she had a Saturday free.

Then came the dash across Forty-ninth.

Comfort and security quickly replaced menacing sky. Heat, light, almost pink with glints and rays from hanging copper pots and pans, and the aroma of food met them behind the kitchen door.

Nando and Euralia were also inside. A Filipino couple, they did the cooking and serving at Turtle Bay's most stylish cocktail and supper parties. Since those were one-night jobs, Demi had first call on their services. Euralia straightened up the house three mornings a week and did his laundry and marketing.

Her black dress and cap hung on a hook in the pantry door along with Nando's red jacket and cummerbund. Now, red-tipped Marcovitch cigarette dangling from her lips, she stood at the diner sized grill in turquoise slacks and purple rayon blouse printed in a wild floral design.

Using tongs, she turned bacon with her right hand. Her left shook a huge copper pan filled with chicken livers on the six-burner stainless-steel stove. Tossing the thick fall of black hair, generously streaked with gray, from her left eye, she looked up.

"Hi, luv-uh," she greeted Demi, heavily lipsticked mouth curled into a kiss. Her wink included Fiona.

Patting Euralia's behind, Demi stole a chicken liver.

Nando nodded approvingly. White shirt collar open, cuffs up, he perched on a high kitchen stool at a three-foot-long maple butcher's block. Before him ranged unopened Bombay, Beefeater's, and Tanqueray gin bottles. To their right, possibly in deference to European taste, stood the distinctive green decanter Gordon's reserved for its United Kingdom trade. In his hands he held a quart of Stolichnaya vodka.

Fiona's eyes went from him to the butcher's block. At first her gaze creased his dark, acornlike face into a shy smile. Then, as her expression grew sterner, he covered both eyes, doing "See No Evil."

"Is all of that for us?" she demanded.

Her naiveté rocked Nando with mischievous laughter. "Only for Gibson! Tak-kee look 'frigera-to-ah," he exulted, pointing to the double-doored look-in stainless-steel restaurant unit to her left. "Demi know plen'y damn good how keep aunties happy!"

As ordered, she turned to look into the waist-high glass panels. The top shelf held two large copper roasting pans draped in cheesecloth.

"The *pièce de résistance,*" Demi said idly, leaving Euralia, his eyebrows arched as if he were letting her in on a secret.

Fiona let that pass to count the bottles instead.

Who knew how many of Nando's Gibsons the twelve people at the party would drink: a magnum and two quarts of Moët et Chandon, a quite good, but not great, champagne; a quart of Pol Roger, regarded as the very best; and six quarts of Spanish Rioja red wine.

"I thought he was joking," she told Demi, shaking her head.

"Oh, no," he assured her, reaching into the case to turn the Pol Roger label down. "We're simple seafarers. Nothing succeeds like excess with anybody from Chios. Just look at the *mezedes.*"

The hors d'oeuvres filled an eight-foot-long steel table at the far wall.

*Taramasalata* came first. It looked parsley-green through the inch-thick sides of a huge flat-bottomed semispherical Italian bowl. From the top, though, its beaten carp roe glowed a familiar rosy pink.

A similar bowl held *tzantziki,* another traditional cold appetizer. Lifting a thin-sliced cucumber round and onion ring out of the velvety sour-cream sauce with the tips of her fingernails, Fiona tasted. Then, smacking her lips for the last bit of flavor, she looked over her shoulder.

"There's more than sour cream here," she called out.

Euralia grinned, showing a gold front tooth to rival Taki's best. Wiping her hands on a bar towel tucked in the waist of her slacks, she came over.

"You got good mout'," she said. "You cook?"

Fiona nodded.

"Whe-uh you learn?"

"In Paris."

"Cord'n Bleu or private?"

"Cordon Bleu. That's why I took a job there, I had four days a week to go to classes."

Deftly pincering the red-tipped Marcovitch with left little and ring fingers,

Euralia dabbed at the sauce with her right forefinger and tasted. "You try again," she said, licking her lips.

A moment later, Fiona shook her head. "I can't get the taste. It comes and goes, but it makes all the difference. What is it, please?"

"Tablespoon yogurt beat in sour cream."

"Yogurt. That's not even Greek. That's Armenian!"

Head bobbing, Euralia fell back against Demi's chest. "Anythin' good Greeks cook, Armenian! Right, Demi?"

"And the dill?" Fiona went on.

"Armenian too. They got from Russians. This gang"—identified by a disdainful wave over the table—"don't know diff'rence. On'y eat."

Demi smiled. "As I said, we're from Chios."

"And this?" Fiona asked, tapping a copper mold of a steamship, funnels and all, about three feet long.

"Honey say she no come if I don't make for her—*ratatouille.*"

"That's French!"

"Ker'sotises no care. Jus' eat. You try. I got big *ratatouille* secret too."

Fiona took a pinch of the vegetable stew from the mold between thumb and forefinger. Eying it, she smiled appreciatively. "You've julienned the eggplant and zucchini," she said, "so they'll pick up more of the onion, garlic, and tomato flavors. Very nice. I'll give you a secret back for that. The next time, add a little mint when you take the vegetables out of the pan to cool."

"Mint?"

"It'll make the flavor fresher and cut the garlic."

Brown eyes narrowed, Euralia nodded. "I try! Now you taste."

Fiona chewed thoughtfully. "Where's the zucchini?" she asked.

That brought a delighted handclap. "That's my secret! I learn from chef La Toque Blanche. Ce'ry root. No zucchini—nevah!"

"Marvelous!"

"Zucchini shit," Euralia confided, one cook to another, Marcovitch again dangling in left corner of mouth. "No taste, no crisp neither, like you wan'"

Feeling more at ease, she took Fiona's arm. "Hot *mezedes* here," she said, pointing to a battery of double-handled restaurant-sized silver serving trays. "First we got *soutsoukaki.*" She shrugged, tapping the platter of miniature meatballs. "Then *spetsofai,*" she went on, passing sausages and peppers floating in tomato sauce redolent of garlic. "An' then *spanokipites,* bes' in worl', from Lambros—"

"The Greek caterer?"

"I go Lon' Islan' City this mo'nin' fo-ah fi' dozen. Sal take me. Upstair', hot, they taste better, but you try one now."

"Simple country fare," Demi slyly observed, seeing the pleasure the sample bought. "An inch square of phyllo pastry with a spinach pie inside."

"I won't say another word," Fiona promised.

"This fo-ah chick' liv-ah, bac'n," Euralia went on, pointing to a fourth tray, empty, "an *kalamari* go here," she said, tapping a fifth, also empty. "But I no do that till las' minute."

"Don't do any for me," Fiona laughed.

"You wait! You see!" Euralia ordered, grabbing her arm for emphasis. "You like my fried squid plen'y, too. I no do like old bouboulina Greek lady wit' olive oil an' garlic. I learn mine Indonesian chef Manila who teach me how wit' saté pow'duh."

Which left a visiting Cordon Bleu one question. "No fish?" she asked.

The Marcovitch, scissored again between little and ring fingers, promptly pointed to the door at right. "He-uh we do fiss course 'lone. I got nice red snapper, *à la spetsiota,* in pantry 'friger-to-ah to bake durin' drinks." The cigarette then swung to the look-in refrigerator behind them. "Same time, meat go in o-van—mo-ah lam', bet-tuh, this gang, blaah!"

Fiona shook her head. "They're going to eat all this?" she asked Demi.

"Every bite," he promised.

"I'm full already. Get me out of here," she sighed.

Looking at his watch, he nodded. "You've got to see the house, so you'll feel at home, and I've got a stop to make over at the Poseidon Bakery."

"On Ninth Avenue? Whatever for?"

"Why, to pick up the *vasilopita,* of course."

Then, seeing her expression, he smiled. "The New Year's Eve cake."

"Oh, Lord," she moaned.

"You need son'thin' upstair', jus' buzz," Euralia called after her.

"You made a friend," he said, leaving the kitchen. " 'You got good mout.' "

Hanging her coat in a small closet under the stairs, he pointed down the gray-carpeted hallway. "The ladies' deck," he said.

Three steps later, he nodded left at an oak door. A brass plate on it read: FIRST-CLASS PASSENGERS ONLY.

"The head," he told her. Doing an about-face, he opened the door opposite. "My office," he said.

She nodded. "T-2 chartroom. Cute."

"I'll put on records when I get back," he told her, pointing to the unit on the yellow wall next to the brass ship's clock. Then, closing the door, he ushered her down the hallway to the first-floor dining room. "And here's your office," he said. "This is where you'll be captain."

Flicking on lights, he crossed to open white drapes at the glass doors. The contrast, while muted, had its share of drama.

Outside, he saw, the northwesterly had strengthened. The towering pewter-gray cumulus, more ragged now, moved by faster. Depending on lull or gust, creeping heavens behind the houses on Fiftieth Street either tore at the sky or flogged the barked-pine fence separating backyards.

Inside, the red filaments in the six-bulb cut-glass chandelier showered the room with warmth. More came from the red-and-brown-brick walls. Ceiling-high limed-oak bookcases, gaudily splashed with dust jackets, offered a different ease. Below them, chocolate velour couches and floor pillows promised another.

Leaning in the doorway, Fiona surveyed her "office." Her face, he saw, showed no more than polite interest. But her eyes skittered feverishly.

Still at the drapes, he let her savor the details. Arms crossed over pale-green dress, she looked as though she owned the room, he thought.

Nodding coolly, she stepped inside.

The square French dining table, with its elaborate yellow-and-white fruit-wood marquetry, usually centered under the chandelier, had been broken apart into four small tables and set across the width of the room. The outside two held scoring pads and cards. A backgammon board lay on the inner right table; brandies and liqueurs on the inner left.

"Melpomene and Marina do gin—Hollywood—at two bits a point," he said, nodding to his left. "Serious. They also like to drink, so they get their own champagne bucket. Artemis and Aphrodite play canasta, but no one knows for what, since they're always too stoned to pay up," he added, turning right. "And that," he ended, eying the backgammon board, "is where you'll graciously lose to Phaedra, so she'll love you. I saw you playing in Bermuda, and that's her game, so you're nominated."

"Accepted," she answered, head thrown back, hands in dress pockets, as she strode around the tables as if to mark out her territory against Phaedra's arrival. "But I won't lose, and she'll love me anyway."

"I'm telling you, Fiona," he cautioned. "you'll do well just to lose. You know what we call Phaedra, don't you? The *skilapsaro*—the shark."

"If she proves too much for me," she asked, running her finger around a brandy snifter on the drinks table, "can I assume that Dr. Courvoisier or Hennessey'll know how to keep Auntie Phaedra happy?"

"Oh, yes! Yes, indeed, you may!" he laughed.

Then, ingenuously fluttering her eyelashes, she took a cigarette from a silver tulip cup on the drinks table and passed it under her nose. "May I also assume," she added, "that if I'm really strapped, she and I can share a house-brand cigarette, which smells suspiciously like those I enjoyed during my wicked, wicked stew days in Paris?"

"Oh, God!" he moaned, taking the cigarette. "Sharks are everywhere, and you stay the hell away from the grass! You're here to keep law and order—remember? Besides, if you're a good girl I'll give you something really nice after, if you want a naughty smoke. Now let's get out of here." Flicking off the lights, he pointed down the hall to the stairway.

Then, upstairs, she abandoned teasing.

"Oh, Demi!" she said. "I've never seen a room like this."

She probably had not. Few rooms like it existed in New York, especially in homes. Twenty feet wide, two stories high, and capped by a vaulted ceiling, it ran the length of the house: fifty-one feet. With a ten-foot-wide arched window nearly as tall at each end, it recalled a Venetian *galeria*.

"Did *you* do this?" she asked.

"Undid it," he explained. "At first this building was a loan society office. This used to be its banking room, with the clerks upstairs and down. Then, in 1910, it was bought for a house. That owner put in a kitchen, left this room as is, and had bedrooms on the top floor. By the 1920s, though, Turtle Bay Gardens had caught on, so a new buyer bricked in the windows, stuccoed the front, and where we are now became two floorthrough apartments. The ground and third floors were the same. That made it easy. I just peeled it all off until I got back to 1871. And, do you know something, Fiona?"

"No? What?"

"It looks even better with lights on." Turning away, he reached over to a light switch.

A soft glow crept through two chandeliers twice the size of those downstairs. Fifteen feet above the floor, they rode remote and serene through a vaulted dusk like pink-tipped icebergs. Then, yellowing as bulbs warmed, their light bent and split through faceted Murano glass beads, splashing over the center of the room.

Expert at showing the room, he waited for her sigh. Then he turned the dimmer switch to the next click.

"Now what do you think?" he asked.

The chandelier light then reached the walls.

She turned to him at once, face lit in the sensual, winey glow she had told him to get from a pink mirror. He had used wood instead.

Walnut paneling twelve feet high lined the room. Grained in browns and reds, it soared and swirled over the walls like distant fire. Intricately carved, and relieved by horizontal moldings, it reflected light as readily as glass, but in warmer colors.

"Where are Rhett and Scarlett?" she asked.

He shrugged modestly. "It's a nighttime room, so I used nighttime colors—beige, black, brown, camel, and charcoal. But you're right. It's that *vin rosé* blush of pink or red from the wood that gives it life. Come," he said, pointing to the window at the far end and cupping her elbow, "I'll show it to you. We're going that way, anyhow."

Keeping left, they passed two serving tables draped in damask cloths. Laden with heavy, pistol-gripped silver, they also bore stacks of purple-bordered plates with the golden anchor and intertwined "K" of the Keriosotis house flag in the center.

Halfway down the room, they came to the couches.

Twelve feet long, they flanked a small white marble fireplace, nubby charcoal-gray peninsulas rising from a beige-carpeted sea. Behind each stood a black table the same height and length. They, in turn, each held a tall polished-brass lamp with pink silk shade at either end. Demi had a compulsion common to many seamen: reading. American magazines, neatly fanned by issue across its width, covered the near table. The one beyond the fireplace held European titles.

Pausing to neaten the row of *Salmon and Trout,* an English fishing journal, he stopped and looked up. He judged the time right for another little trick. Magicians made things vanish. He made them appear.

The stunt had worked so well on Joey, the real-estate agent, he believed it had lowered the asking price on the pink stone house by at least $10,000. Fiona, with her wary eye, would be even more susceptible, he thought.

So, turning, he pointed back toward the stairs. "The loan society had supplicants climb the stairs and follow a railing to here," he said, "where they were allowed to warm themselves. Then, after they'd probably fretted to death, they got the big heat—the officers' fire," he added, swinging his arm to the left.

A larger fireplace stood in the wall opposite them.

"Never saw it," she laughed.

"And the piano?"

"Piano?" Brow creased, she scanned the far wall.

He expected that reaction. She wondered how anyone could overlook a piano. He knew: easily. He had planned it that way. A black grand stood before the Forty-ninth Street window. Everyone saw it, but few perceived it. The arch around it swept the eye upward instead.

"A Steinway, no less," he said, following her gaze.

He left it at that, not wanting to oversell. Then, guiding her elbow and turning her to the Fiftieth Street end of the room, he resumed their passage.

A few steps later they came abreast of the drinks table. Draped in a heavy cloth and set with glasses, it shot as many glints upward as it received. The silver champagne bucket beside it bore the austere "C" and laurel wreath of the Cunard Line.

Nodding in recognition, she took another look. Observation confirmed, she pointed. "You're not serving that too are you?" she asked. Her glance went to the stand holding the champagne bucket. Nestled within its feet, discreetly hidden, stood a half-gallon jug of white wine.

"You'll see what the Gallo's for," he promised.

"What?" she insisted.

"You don't know?"

She shook her head.

"You can dress 'em up, but you can't take 'em out," he sighed.

He got an elbow to the ribs, sharply, in reply.

"Truth is truth."

Veering farther left, past the built-in bookcases, he sounded his final grace note in the floorthrough room.

"Just look at that soffit," he told her, tapping the eight-inch rounded cornice sealing the joint between the side and end paneling. "I had a party one night, and this funny little guy in a white suit—in January yet—kept poking at the wood and tracing the grain with his fingernail. Some of my galas," he said, rolling his eyes, "end up with friends of friends of people I invite here, too, so we never met. But the next morning he called and wanted to buy the soffits. Said he was from Griffin and Howe."

"Who?"

"Fiona," he asked, "doesn't Arkie ever let you come into town, just to walk around? Griffin and Howe are gunsmiths. By the time they're done with gold and silver inlays, and wood carvings, one of their creations'll cost more than a Cadillac—and I don't mean a Coupe de Ville either! Anyway, he said he'd pay forty-five hundred dollars a soffit—told me they never got enough Italian walnut for custom rifle and shotgun stocks."

After the brag, he needed modesty. Humility gave him his next line. "If this were in the East Sixties or Seventies, or the Eighties, near the Met—who knows?" He shrugged. "I might not even have to worry about convertibles. But here it's just cute. Now upstairs."

She took a step back toward the entrance to the room.

He smiled. "Unh-unh. There's no stairway there."

Placing both hands on her shoulders, he turned her to her right 180 degrees from the left wall. "That," he said, pointing to the green velour sofa in the center of the room, "is where I have my afternoon nap with the Sunday *Times.*"

Then he turned her ninety degrees more, until she faced the Fiftieth Street end of the room. "And that's how I get to the third floor," he said, pointing to the spiral staircase, with its cantilevered steps, rising at the left of the arched window.

"On that?" she asked. "There's not even a railing! It's just plates welded to a pipe—how high?"

"Twenty-two feet."

But he knew his Greenwich girls. "Are you game?" he asked.

Mouth firmed up, she accepted the challenge. "Lead on!"

"I intended to," he said, foot on the first step.

"So you at least had that much decency," she chaffed.

"Of course. Just keep your left hand on the pipe and grab a handful of my coat—but not too hard. It's Abercrombie's best cashmere."

That brought him a punch in the back. He was moving her, at that, he decided.

"I thought this was black," she said, halfway up.

"It was when it ran in the *Times,* but when I finished the upstairs I decided it wasn't an exclamation mark at all, just a comma between floors. So I mixed red and brown and resprayed it to match the wood."

"You mean there's more of this?"

"You'll see."

Shoulders through the circular third-floor hatch, he felt her hand pull his coat back. He expected that reaction too. She wanted a last look. He gave her plenty of time. He knew the effect of the view. The smaller the piano looked, the better he did. Then, he thought, she would have another surprise.

Stepping off the spiral staircase, she did. Eyes wide in disbelief, she pointed. "Where did you find that?" she asked.

"What do you mean, 'that'?" he retorted. "It's like a Lionel train: every boy should have one."

Shoulders heaving with laughter, she ran her fingers over the silky smooth tawny teak, as if to convince herself it was there.

"On Forty-ninth Street, Demi—a Japanese hot tub?"

"Of course. What's the big deal?" he asked. "Huey Long," he told her, mentioning a prominent shipbroker, "lives a few blocks away—he's got a sauna. Niarchos, over at 25 Sutton Place, has a steamroom. Taki even had one put in for Honey."

She shook her head, patently unconvinced. "Steamrooms are one thing. That—that's bizarre."

"Bizarre? I spent two years shuttling the PG to Japan in Liberian flaggers, and the only time I ever felt alive was neck-high in hot water in a tub just like this in Yokohama. I vowed then I'd never be without one—instant heaven! So, when I got the house, I wrote and had this built. Seats four comfortably," he said, putting his arm around her waist and guiding her so that she could see the holystoned teak seats, "and more, intimately."

"It actually works?"

"I've got the two-hundred-fifty-gallon hot-water tank and high-speed submersible water pump in the basement, and this heater," he said, tapping a gray plastic box under the seat facing the windows, "to prove it—all thirty-five hundred dollars' worth. And a year ago tomorrow," he went on, "it paid for itself. The four of us—Honey, Taki, Phaedra, and I—spent the best afternoon of our lives here, getting rid of hangovers, washing down caviar with Pol Roger, and watching the Rose Bowl Game on the SONY over the hatch there."

She glanced at him.

Very good, he thought. That really outsophisticated her. He had only to keep the suggestion without letting it become a dirty joke. Humor did that nicely. "It was all family." He shrugged. "So who looked? Besides, other than a prude, what healthy woman wouldn't want to give her bubbies a nice warm little New Year's Day float in Arpège bath oil?"

Smiling, she ignored the bait. Instead she pointed to the white porcelain bidet. "And every boy should have one of those too?"

"Fiona," he said placatingly, helping her off the six-inch-high platform on which the tub rested, "I want this house to be like the Democratic Party—to have something for everyone. What kind of a host would I be if I thought only of my own comfort?" he asked, walking her across the black and white diamond-tiled floor, past the bidet and the door to the center hallway. "That's why I have this makeup table and lighted mirror," he went on, "and this reading room." He smiled, opening a door in the far wall to show a pink bathroom hung with a magazine rack. "And this," he concluded, sliding back a frosted-glass door to the left of the "reading room" to reveal a square sit-in tub/shower. "And, of course, that," he tacked on, pointing to a white stool alongside one of the windows looking toward Fiftieth Street, on which Euralia had neatly stacked a white terrycloth towel, robe and pair of slippers, and, over all, a shower cap in an unopened box. "Now, surely," he appealed, opening his arms in a call to reason, "after that care for your comfort, you don't begrudge me the pleasures of my bath, do you—for which I paid thirty-five cents a visit in Japan?"

She could play that game as well as he. Brow wrinkled, she studied the shower-cap box. "Do you buy these in quantity?" she asked.

Reaching over, he took the box from her. "That such a small mind dwells behind so lovely a façade . . ." he mused. "If it pleases the court, I read from the label, which you may enter into the record as evidence: 'Beekman Place Chemists—$1.79.' Does that sound like a volume buy? As a matter of fact, I'll see why Euralia paid so much."

Ever mindful of good exit lines, he saw one now, and used it. "Since you obviously wouldn't even stand in a model bedroom with a furniture salesman not your husband," he said, lightly tapping her behind with the box before dropping it on the terrycloth slippers, "I'll just say your things are in the first room on your left."

He looked back from the staircase hatch. She stood where he had left her, in silence, hands on hips of the pale-green dress, a small smile playing over the corners of her mouth.

She was ravishing, he thought.

Glad to be alone, Fiona rushed down the hallway.

The dress concerned her now. It might need steaming in the shower. Nothing but perfection would do. She had fought that hard for the gown.

The battle had begun the day after Demi called. She went then to see the designer, Pauline Trigère. But Trigère had gone to Washington that day. To fit Lady Bird, the receptionist said.

And the principal *vendeuse?* she had asked.

Busy. With regular customers.

In time, a woman of forty or so had appeared. Tall and slim, she had the flowing walk of a model and startling chestnut hair. Drawn back, it revealed an equally dramatic triangular face, marred only by deep crow's feet. From elbow to wrist, the left sleeve of her natural-silk smock bristled with pins. She had introduced herself as Marcelline.

Could she help? Her smile seemed patronizing and perfunctory. It implied that children had no business with Trigère.

Undaunted, Fiona used the *Vogue* photo of Rose Kennedy to show what had to be done to the dress.

Marcelline heard her out, then shook her head. The ideas were sound. But with the holidays so near, and so many customers needing dresses for Florida and Palm Springs right after—

Fiona had cut her off then and there. She handed over Arkie's card. On call round the clock, he gave his clients and prospects his home address and phone number as well. Firm name plus Sands Point had its effect. Young or not, anyone in shipping with a Greek name was taken very seriously by high-fashion houses.

Marcelline suggested a visit to a fitting booth.

Waist? she asked, closing the curtain. Fiona told her.

"*C'est vrai?*" Truly. Marcelline sighed enviously. They had no eights for that bust or those shoulders. But they would see what could be done. Madame would please wait in her slip.

A moment later, a young blond girl appeared. She handed Fiona the dress, in yellow, to try on.

Marcelline returned with a basket of clothespins and a huge woman in a purple-and-gray sleeveless housedress. Barelegged, the woman padded into the booth in shaggy red wool slippers. Black hair pulled back as severely as Marcelline's, she reminded Fiona of women who tend bar afternoons in Marseilles. Two gold thimbles glittered on her right hand.

"Luciana, Madame Angelakos," Marcelline said. Then, moving behind Fiona, she gathered the back of the dress and clipped it snug with clothespins. "Fashion photographer's trick," she said, "just to get the front right. Then we'll look."

Overflowing a small stool, Luciana watched intently.

Quickly done, Marcelline joined her. "What do you think?" she asked.

Motioning Fiona closer, Luciana reset a few pins.

"*C'est possible?*" Fiona asked.

"Depending . . ." Marcelline hedged, probably preferring not to make another dress during the holiday rush, but wanting Fiona to come back. "With the changes you want, the body must be just—"

"With the right body, anything's possible!" Fiona said.

Luciana met the issue head on. "Madame Angelakos, please to disrobe," she rumbled. Having seen her share of desirable, expensive, and pampered bodies, she spent the next few moments fishing a blue Gitanes box out of her apron. Then, exhaling pungent white smoke, she looked up. Pointing impatiently, she shook her head.

"All off, please," she ordered. "Everything!"

Bra, hosiery, and panties were obediently removed.

"Now stand in your pumps, and please to turn . . ."

A whisper followed. It mixed awe and rapture in equal parts. *"Marcelline, regardez les fossettes!"* That Fiona understood. "Marcelline, look at the dimples!"

She had two, one at either side of the base of her spine, just above the coccyx. They were the mark, she had been told by European dressmakers, of a perfect back mated to equally faultless hips and buttocks.

Turning, she addressed Luciana. *"Alors?"* she asked.

A wanton, Mediterranean sweep of eyes answered her. The gesture made the words redundant. "Myself, I would go everywhere just like that."

Smiling, Fiona held up the *Vogue* photo once more. *"C'est possible?"*

*"Très possible!"*

Four fittings and $1,600 later, Fiona had what she wanted.

So now, finally alone, she rushed down the hall to see if her investment might need steaming in the shower.

The first door on her left, fittingly, she thought, bore a brass plate inscribed FIRST OFFICER. Heavy oak, its lower half had the louvered kickout panel prescribed by International Safety at Sea Regulations. Seeing that, she knew what the room held: gray metal bunk, lee boards head and foot; matching desk and chair; settee like the one downstairs in Demi's "office"; and a gray steel clothes closet.

Stepping inside, she had but one surprise. Someone, she saw, had anticipated her. The fuchsia dress already rested on the berth. It lay on tissue paper, isolated from lint from the white chenille bedspread under it. Seams and hem aligned, it had been smoothed by hand.

God bless Euralia! she thought.

Dress cared for, she sat on the settee, shower things beside her, and kicked off her dark-green suede pumps, growing increasingly optimistic.

Demi would have understood her attitude perfectly. He had, in fact, predicted it when he called her. He knew how the day would affect her. As a seaman, he had enjoyed the same satisfaction: journey's end.

For her, however, the voyage took place in her mind. There she marked another passage: arrival in the world of owners.

An hour later, Honey encouraged her further.

Opening a door hidden in the mantel over the large fireplace, she produced a bottle and two sherry glasses. "Real Bristol Cream," she laughed, pouring, "an' my little nit niphew, bless his pointy head, don't dare mess with it! I bring it from home."

She stood six feet tall in organdy silk pumps, with the kind of slim but extravagantly contoured body Las Vegas hotels featured on billboards. Her face, in contrast, outwholesomed the euphoric young mothers illustrated on disposable-diaper cartons. A luminous smile brightened a wide, generous mouth. Enormous brown eyes seemingly absorbed further warmth from her hair. Long and wavy and tied in a white ribbon, it spilled down her neck like butterscotch.

Fiona had no idea what to make of her. No beauty in her midthirties hid the past, she thought. Men saw to that. They left marks. So did ambition, disappointment, shame. But Honey's face denied any rough usage. So did her mannerisms. Her gaze should have been quick and wary. Instead, it remained calm and unsearching. Listening, hurt women often thinned their lips defensively. Hers stayed full. The softly drawled and slurred Southern voice, with its built-in laugh, complemented everything seen.

Her warmth, in short, seemed guileless. Underlining that, it came naturally. She had used no cosmetics. At the same time, she had a sense of theater. From ankle to shoulder, white lace slacks and tunic offered intriguing glimpses and grounds for speculation. Her left nipple, caught in the wide mesh and darkened by a brown body stocking, stood proud in arrogant, perfect definition. Equally sharp outlines of thighs, hips, and buttocks implied that she wore little else underneath.

The outfit suggested a type: the sex bomb untouched by the past. So, at least, ran shipping-community gossip. Fiona took that as envy. Demi supported that assessment. He called Honey a Greek turned inside out. In the four years she had been married to Taki, he said, she had learned as much shipping as the men in the family and had more brains in the bargain.

Fiona had already glimpsed that intelligence. She had seen it from the spiral staircase. Dressed, she had wanted to explore the floorthrough room. But, clear of the hatch, she saw Honey. So she watched her.

Honey had stood at the piano, arranging bouquets. She took pains, made combinations, eyed variations. Then, flowers set out, she paced the room to view them. The vases on bar and middle serving tables thus replaced each other. Red roses went into the bowls at either end of the cold appetizer spread to play off the paleness of *taramasalata* and *tzantziki*. Fresh deep-green sprigs of rosemary and thyme were banked over the base of the tray reserved for the lamb, then arranged anew.

Seeing her, Fiona recalled Arkie. He too saw endless combinations of color and line. Beyond knack, that took a keen intelligence.

Which made Honey all the more difficult to assess.

Obviously, no mystery lurked in her smile now. Sherry poured, she sat down on the charcoal-gray couch opposite. Scanning the champagne satin pumps and the fuchsia dress, she raised her glass.

"To charmin' wild shippin' Greeks back into their trees," she drawled, "an' the most gorgeous woman that's ever been under this roof."

Fiona, ever facile, toasted her right back. "Excepting blondes."

"At thirty-five, goin' on old? Never! Everybody knows blondes have more fun besides, so the rest don't really matter all that much."

"Then, certainly, to the most stylish."

"An' don't count me in yet on that either!" Honey laughed. "Lord knows, I might jus' be passin' through. Fact is, I hope I am. I got other plans," she said with a negligent wave around the room. "If this is anybody's style, it's yours. You got the couth for it, as a pal of mine says. But you oughtta be nappin'!" she scolded with mock severity. "Won't anybody be here for maybe an hour, even Demi. He just called not two minutes ago from the Poseidon to bitch about traffic an' to remind me to wake you at six, so you'd have time to get ready. That's why I thought for sure you'd still be upstairs in that bunk, 'specially after trampin' through that damned ol' white elephant 'cross the street."

Fiona had found the pink stone house disappointing, too. Still, she did not admit that. Her mother had taught, instead, always to be positive. "To tell you the truth, I couldn't wait to get down here," she laughed. "I want to try everything, see how it works. I've never been in a room like this before."

"It's somethin', all right. What I call real Saint-Nazaire modern."

Met by a baffled glance, Honey explained further. "Saint-Nazaire's where the shipbreakers are. I call Demi founder of the grave-robbin' school of interior design. Your daddy went to sea, didn't he?"

"Yes. In the P and O."

"He take you on trips?"

"Whenever he could, especially cruises."

"Okay, then. Don't this remind you of a passenger ship?"

Another question gave a further hint. "What'd you do rainy days at sea?"

Fiona raised her sherry in an I-don't-know gesture.

"Your mama never took you down to the library for a book?" Honey asked laughingly. "Sure she did! Only you never saw a ship's reading room like this before, 'cause it took Demi to put it together. The chandeliers an' all this gorgeous wood," she went on, with another airy wave, "came out of the *Conto di Pastafazoole,* or some other wop liner Mussolini sent troopin' in the thirties an' France took after the war as reparations. The breakers cut her up for steel, then took the panelin' out piece by piece. Leave it to them, they knew what was comin'—veneers an' then wood-grained Formica! Same's these couches—only eight were ever built. These two are out of the first-class lounge of an ol' Cunarder, the *Aquitania.*"

"But the tables fit perfectly," Fiona observed.

"Naturally." Honey smiled. "They're from another Cunarder, the *Caronia.* The lamps too. Take a look. They're bolted through the tables. Kitchen's like that, too—come out of a U.S. troopship, the *Gen'ral Disturbance* or some such. You see anythin' else here looks familiar?"

Helping, she nodded over her right shoulder.

Fiona saw only the Fiftieth Street end of the room.

Honey turned that way on the couch, too. "You ever on a Liberty ship?" she asked.

"As a matter of fact, last summer. Every so often, my husband'll cannibalize one for spare parts."

"Then I bet you been on the fantail too."

"Where they keep the auxiliary steering engine?"

"That's it! Well, you know that funny little ladder inside the hatch? Our spiral staircase there is two of 'em welded together. Demi got it for thirty-five bucks down in Mississippi!"

"Well, at least I got the upstairs doors," Fiona laughed. "I knew they had to come from a Liberty."

"For sure, but out of a yard on the Chesapeake, an' only after very heavy negotiatin'," Honey laughed back. "To the Greek eye," she said, pouring more sherry in an ironic toast, "an' if you think this is somethin', jus' remember Demi's the kid in this family."

Fiona distrusted such openness. She wondered what Honey hoped to gain by it. Did she need a friend? Had she tried to dissuade a new girl from worming her way into the family's graces? Or, sensing an ally, were her confidences an invitation to become further involved?

Regardless, the gesture had to be acknowledged. If not, Fiona knew, she would seem rude. Or, even worse: dull.

"I'll drink to that," she answered, "but standing. Because another Greek eye found you."

Smiling, Honey reached out to touch glasses. "Now let's go see how Euralia's doin'," she urged.

Fiona shook her head adamantly. "No. Now show me how all this works. I want to try the chandelier lighting, see where you've put the ashtrays and silent butlers, and hide some towels in case we get food spills."

That brought a warmer response than her toast. "Sweet Lord on high," Honey sighed. "I think I jus' died an' went to heaven! Me an' Euralia have always been the maids around here before."

An hour later, they were fast friends.

When the bell rang, Demi, a victim of traffic and forced to wait at the bakery, was still upstairs changing.

"Remember," Honey whispered, smiling mischievously, as they walked to the door, "anybody of either sex with a mustache but Demi and Taki owns tonnage. You got to be nice to them—but not too nice. Otherwise they'll eat you alive. The men are just along for the ride."

Marina, Demi's Greenwich cousin, who stood on the "smaller" side of the family debate, and her husband, Zenon Linakis, were the first guests to arrive.

He, fiftyish, tall, dark, dour, needed only red stocking cap and white skirt to pass as an officer of evzones, the Greek Army honor guard.

She, about forty, short, dark, and equally serious, needed nothing to resemble a Cartier's counter. With rings, earrings, and brooch pinning a midnight-blue chiffon shoulder train, she displayed about thirty carats of diamonds, Fiona guessed. In big stones only. The estimate, probably light, ignored the popcorn-sized pearls strung around her lacquered beehive hairdo as if it were a Christmas tree.

Like Zenon, she had a mustache. But only hers counted, Honey said. Zenon owned a quarter interest in three tugs that never ventured beyond Piraeus Harbor. Marina, on the other hand, had real tonnage.

Eldest daughter of Zavvas, the clan's head, she had married to meet her father's need for cheap T-2 tankers. The Linakises, though poor, could then buy eight at low rates from the U.S. Maritime Administration. Bright for sixteen, she resisted marriage—until Zavvas agreed to put one of the falsely registered ships in her name.

She now owned four modern tankers and a piece of Taki, and would inherit half of her father's fleet. Meanwhile, Honey reported, she scrimped along on $300,000 a year, said Taki robbed her, and agitated for Zenon, who worked for Taki, to take over the New York office.

She gave Honey the darkest mink coat Fiona had ever seen to hang in the closet on the landing. Then, black eyes glinting warily behind dark-purple eyeliner, she turned, extending a chunky, bejeweled hand.

"You're no Greek?" she asked Fiona.

"No. Just my husband."

"And Angelakos—what kind of name is that?"

"An island name," Fiona answered. "From Hydra."

"S'ipowners live there, on Hydra?"

"None that I know of," Fiona laughed.

"We're from Chios," Marina told her.

That gave the Keriosotises awesome credentials in the hierarchy of Greek shipping. Origins there implied a family seafaring tradition centuries old and possible blood or marriage ties to the legendary Livanoses.

"Even Zenon comes from Andros," she laughed, naming another traditional spawning ground of shipowners.

Nothing subtle there, Fiona thought. She had just been downgraded in the pecking order. She had expected no less. So she had a suitably bland reply ready.

"Beautiful places—I've been to both," she said.

Marina, intimidatingly, pressed on. "Your husban'—he's in s'ippin'?"

"Oh, yes. A naval architect. He's doing Demi's convertibles."

"He's good?"

"The best." Fiona smiled. "From Webb Institute."

That made it Marina's turn to raise her eyebrows. Arkie belonged to an elite as exclusive as hers.

But staying even had never interested Fiona. She had paid for Hydra. Heeding Honey's advice, she returned the putdown. Moreover, she did so with consummate irony and subtlety, for maximum sting. "My husband's family's one of the biggest scallop wholesalers on Long Island," she said proudly.

Smile glazed, Marina decided she needed a Gibson.

Her younger sister, Melpomene, who might back "bigger" in the family debate to spite her, arrived next. Nostrils flared, lips tight, she flicked her black kid gloves at Honey and swept by.

"What was that all about?" Fiona asked, watching her march into the floorthrough room.

"The coat," Honey whispered back. "She called Taki yesterday and asked if she could wear it so Marina'd eat her heart out."

"Over a sable? She could buy one anytime."

" 'Course she could. But for eighty-five hundred dollars? No way! As good as Greeks hate, they do one thing better—envy. She'll make believe she's got big fam'ly news that can't wait, an' Marina'll see the coat, an' ask a question or two, an' before you know it her belly'll be on fire!"

A minute or two later, when Melpomene returned, her smile provided confirmation. Watching her hand her coat over to Honey, Fiona saw she had never been a beauty. Thin, yes, which, to Greeks, was the next-best thing. Her face and body bore the marks of too strict a diet. Her skin lay taut from the corners of her mouth to the underside of her chin. But hollows were forming around her eyes and in the front of her neck. Her collarbones and the ribs across her chest were prominent, as well. No bra yet had been designed, either, to camouflage slack, fleshy folds arced over the tops of breasts, sure signs of painful weight loss.

Bathed in pink light from the paneled room, she had a waxy, translucent sheen. Shadowed, that chandelier glow turned a wan, less appealing violet, as if all her bones were bruised.

No doubt anticipating Marina, she too wore an off-the-shoulder gown, but in black silk. An even chunkier brooch secured the train. Between that and her earrings, Fiona credited her with about forty carats of emeralds.

Right hand ablaze with cabochon rubies, left with square-cut diamonds, she put both on Fiona's shoulders. "I tol' myself," she said, her voice a deep baritone, as if her reedy body were a sounding board, "all the way to Marina an' back, 'That girl got purple hair like Maria Callas.' Is yours, or some kind tint?"

"Mine!" Fiona laughed, taking her hand. "I got it from my father."

"No fertile chicken egg in V-8 like Maria do?"

"No—nothing. All I take is vitamin C for colds."

Melpomene removed her hands from Fiona's shoulders. With the disdain for personal rights of the very rich, she traced Fiona's right eyebrow with a skeletal forefinger. Expecting it to be smudged with eyebrow pencil, which would prove that the hair had indeed been tinted, she found nothing.

Nodding ruefully, she too walked off for a Gibson. "So you're young," she said despairingly over her shoulder, confronting her enemy in yet another guise.

Cursing chauffeurs, her husband, Ferenc di Nagy, smiled his way through the front door and into Honey's arms a moment later. The handsomest thing alive, she called him, until he whipped out his cigarette lighter, or went for fresh drinks, or made over you on the walk down the aisle at a Broadway show. Then he looked like just what he was: a man who lived off women. Meanwhile, she said, he gave lessons in suave to the rest of the men in the family, who, God knew, could use them.

A stockbroker serving wealthy refugees from pre–World War II Hungary and Poland, he had the knack of reading a balance sheet. So he backed Taki against Marina and Aphrodite. He also did well with family investments. But, Honey predicted, Melpomene would punch his ticket, and his ride in the upper reaches of wealth would end, with the bull market. He not only lived off women, but he liked them. In quantity.

Tall and slim, with a leading man's wavy blond hair, he regarded Fiona with a connoisseur's appreciative eye. Finding no encouragement other than social in her smile, he nonetheless bowed with a dash and duelist's sense of punctilio that suggested the "Saber Dance" being played in the background. Then he moved off, right hand deep in his tuxedo jacket pocket. Groping, no doubt, for his lighter, she thought.

Aphrodite next appeared timorously at the door.

The "Iron Mouse," Honey called her. Her father, Lycourgos, like Marina, had wed for the family good. In his case, the quest for more tonnage led to Norway. There he married a shipowner's only child. Aphrodite resulted.

She made a case for breeding to type, Fiona thought. Clearly, her genes had fought each other and lost. Tall and heron-thin, she had a deep, pelican-shaped Scandinavian chin and coarse swarthy Levantine features. Her hair and eyes, similarly, were battlefields on which neither side claimed victory. The English had a word for their color: "peaty." The shade of bog water.

Her personality matched, Honey said. The buoyant Greek spirit had spent itself trying to ignite a spark of levity in that Nordic dourness.

Her looks and way, family legend ran, had convinced her parents that she should remain an only child. That gave her an edge. She got twice as much from Taki as Marina or Melpomene did and had more say in the business, most of which came from her husband, Holcombe Wainwright II. "Yeah, Hokey the deuce," Honey said. "Piping Rock Club, Westbury Horse Show—real Long Island society."

Marriage, she went on, had addled Aphrodite. She knew what young ship-owners' sons looked for in a woman: tonnage, and, preferably, less than ten years old. So, like Melpomene, she ignored Greek men and did not marry until she came to America to work in Taki's office. Wedlock followed within a year. In Athens, feelings were mixed. To Greeks, ships were real, so Zavvas and Lycourgos rued her marrying a stockbroker. But they also saw pluses. Wainwright & Company, an old WASP Wall Street firm, had ties to in-vestment capital they did not. But Honey, who got the tale from Taki, said the overriding sentiment seemed to be wonder that Aphrodite got a man at all.

That explained itself two years later. Wainwright & Company went broke.

So Aphrodite had a choice. She could be laughed at to her face by her fe-male cousins, or behind her back by Hokey's family. She opted for her more genteel in-laws. Since then, Honey said, she had gone steadily downhill. In her shame, she had disassociated herself from the Keriosotises physically and emotionally. Diffidently and quietly, she had remorselessly attempted to be-come a WASP.

In Lattingtown, on Long Island's North Shore, horses and tennis kept her busy. Skiing and trout necessitated a home in Manchester, Vermont, an old town restored by the rich to a condition in which it had never existed. Both places favored full-length wool skirts and black velvet jackets. With those, Aphrodite, hell-bent on distancing herself from vulgar, jet-set relatives, wore a heavy silver cross. Of course, Honey conceded, it might have been sincere. Religion came easier with that kind of face.

Still, humility aside, Aphrodite remained a Keriosotis. When Wainwright & Company failed, she had got Taki to make Hokey his marine insurance agent. In return, she fought Marina's efforts to make Zenon Taki's successor. But, Honey laughed, she told her father and uncle in Athens that with the New York office "mature"—whatever that meant—they needed a lawyer to run it. Guess who in the family had gone to Yale Law School and passed the bar?

Glance skittering nervously, lips trembling in and out of a shy smile behind the outthrust underslung chin, Aphrodite extended her hand. "So nize . . ." she said with a little head bow.

Nodding, Fiona ignored the diffidence. She saw only appraisal. The weak tea eyes were suddenly a hard agate red.

Hokey, equally self-effacing, followed. Fiftyish, portly, in wrinkled tuxedo, he dabbed a buttonhole mouth with an equally tiny pointed tongue. Salt-

and-pepper hair center-parted and pomaded, eyes wide behind gold-rimmed glasses, he had the fearful smile of the unsuccessful rich.

Fiona ignored his smile, too. She probed the weak, watery blue gaze instead. Its edges held enough ice to walk on, she thought.

Honey, however, dissuaded her from being impressed. "Small change," she whispered behind Hokey's back, from the closet at the head of the landing. "Wait till Athens gets here."

No sooner had she spoken than the bell rang again.

A short dark man with gold teeth came in first. Taki, Fiona thought.

Honey kissed his forehead, rubbed lather off an earlobe, and with a red lacquered fingernail reset the few brown hairs lying across his scalp. Then, taking his coat, she pointed him down the landing.

"Mrs. Angelakos," he said, taking the offered hand, gold teeth winking in the light, "Dimitrios Keriosotis. Your husban's dzenius!"

"Why, thank you," she laughed back. "I've always thought so, too. But wives are supposed to. I just wish my father were still alive to meet you. Besides a good opinion of Arkie, the two of you would've had something else in common."

"Oh, yes! What?"

"That," she said. Teasingly, she gently tapped the faded green anchor tattooed in the web alongside his left thumb.

"Your fodder went to sea?"

"Oh, yes!"

"In sail?" he asked, with mounting interest.

"Of course, and around Cape Horn too, at fifteen."

Smiling up at her, he waggled a forefinger, warning that two could play the game. "But later in passenzer s'ips," he said.

"Yes—in the P and O."

"An' then they made him skipper."

"Yes. But you knew that!"

"That don't matter." He winked slyly, as if making a pass. "Anybody with looks to make daughters like you," he explained, "he don't go freightin' long. Comp'ny puts him on bridze of great white liner."

"And anybody that smart about shipping owns the liner," she retorted.

Blushing, he denied the compliment. "How smart I am is after t'irty-five year at sea my bes' s'ip I got secon'han' from Esso wit' my two sisters. But I got secret you s'ould know, anyway."

"Oh?"

"Yes . . ." he whispered. Clearly smitten, he took her arm and turned to the serving tables, the top of his head just below her ear. "Euralia cook our place once, maybe twice week, an' we got a little thing—us two—Honey an' Nando don' see," he told her, with a wink that creased his earnest, solemn face into a caricature of guile. "So, later on," he suggested in his conspiratorial whisper, drawing even closer and rising on his toes, "after you got everybody fed, you come eat your lamb wit' me. Euralia save you bes.' I promise! Yes?"

Another branch of the family, for sure, she thought. But she knew precisely how to respond. Accent and manner aside, what remained? A man exactly like her father. So she quickly took a step back and, just as suddenly, grasped his lapels.

"Are you propositioning me?" she asked.

Fearful he might have offended her, he nodded uncertainly.

"Good," she whispered back, "because you're on!"

Then, to that, she added another surprise. Pulling him in, she kissed him full on the mouth. A trifle arch for her taste, to be sure. She would never do that in Greenwich, or with Demi.

But she knew Taki loved it. He walked off shaking his head in delight. Old-school seamen were all alike, she thought. They wanted all women to act like dockside whores.

His sisters, she guessed, would be more worldly. The first, she saw, stood at the closet now. Phaedra, she knew, without being told.

Her coat, Fiona saw, would have sent Melpomene home in shame. It was full-length Russian lynx, its hood alone holding $8,500 worth of fur to her eye. Short and compact, she shrugged out of it with the calm assurance of a leading lady coming back for yet another curtain call.

Taking the coat, Honey regarded her dress. "You crazy?" she asked.

"Whatta you mean, 'crazy'? I seen this on that cow Leine Renaud at the Café de Paris las' year, an'—"

"But Leine Renaud's nearly six feet tall."

"Fuck tall! Who's got better body? Who's sexier?"

Honey silenced, Phaedra sought corroboration. "Hey, Fi-o-na!" she shouted across the ten feet or so from the closet, without waiting to be introduced. "How 'bout it? Sexy?"

"Sexy," Fiona thought, missed the mark. "Stunning" came closer.

From where she stood, Phaedra had been in profile, so she had seen only the right side of the dress. Then it had seemed a rather conventional but somewhat garish turquoise gown, almost fluorescently bright, with a mesh top across shoulder and chest, and long sleeves. Viewed head on, however, it became another kind of garment. Visually, it had no left side. There a mesh panel ran from hem to armpit.

It clung to Phaedra like a cinnamon-tinted shadow. The fabric, cunningly scalloped to reveal a maximum of leg, thigh, and breast, joined the transparent panel in front and back under a blue-and-white rhinestone strip. Swirling over the thigh crease as low as possible, the jeweled band then snaked right, across the abdomen, and left, skirting a thick, aggressively raised nipple. In outline, the glittering gems recalled a musical clef.

A ridiculous, vulgar dress, Fiona thought. Except . . . Except that one woman in a million could wear it. It just took the right figure and look. She herself had the body, she knew, but not the face. Phaedra, on the other hand, had both.

At forty-seven, Phaedra had the rounded, muscular form of a high-school cheerleader. She kept that way skiing and hunting, Demi had said. She liked sports that gave men strong thighs. The tan she would arrive with, he had told Fiona, she got in North Africa, chasing Barbary sheep in the coastal plains and Austrian ski instructors in the Atlas Mountains.

Her face, round and small, looked thirty-five. It seemed to go from strength to strength. Chin, lips, and cheekbones all thrust forward, as if willing the body to follow. Enthusiasm, unjaded and unsated, lay over all, framed by short lustrous jet-black curls. Willful jaw aside, only a too-thick Greek nose kept her from being a beauty. But flaws counted for little in the net effect. Energy and spirit made looks irrelevant.

Smiling broadly, she drew up before Fiona. "What you think?" she asked, hands on hips. "Is sexy?"

As with Taki, Fiona read her immediately, too. The family tomboy: a sailor in a woman's body.

"You're the night's big winner!" she told her.

Laughing, Phaedra pulled her in, arm around waist. Like Demi, she had a notable lack of hypocrisy. "What winner?" she whispered. "Who's competit-sun? Marina peddled her ass. Melpomene couldn't. Aphrodite wouldn't. An' you," she chided, slapping Fiona on the behind with her purse, and then pointing it toward the floorthrough room, "you're worse than them. You're prettier'n Honey even, an' you wear ol' lady's dress. Where's fun in that? Who's gonna give boys tickle?"

Reproachfully waggling a finger, she left. "I s'ow you how to dress later," she laughed over her shoulder,. "when we play backgammon."

All present, Euralia turned off the front light and triple-locked the door, typical security for a Manhattan party at which jewels were worn.

Honey, similarly, dimmed the chandelier over the closet landing, mouthed "wee-wee" and descended the stairs to the first floor.

Which, of Taki's sisters, left Artemis. The most complex of the lot, Fiona thought.

An hour before, she had seen her as "Demi's lesbian aunt." No longer. What Honey had told her went against any stereotype. The smartest one in the family, she had called her. Moreover, Artemis had made Taki's fortune. When he came to the United States, she helped him.

How?

You had to understand Greeks, Honey said, smiling. Briefly put, Artemis bit her uncles' balls off.

The youngest child of Demosthenes, the grandfather for whom Demi had been named, she had been the favorite and brightest of his four as well. She had, in fact, been the only girl in the family to go to college, and in France, at that. So her father named her executor of his estate. With Demi's dad, Xantippe, cut out of the will for failing in America, she controlled Phaedra's and Taki's legacies.

In the fifties, that meant nothing. Phaedra married,.Taki remained at sea in family ships, and dividends were sent to the appropriate banks.

Later, with Taki's success with the New York office, that changed. Artemis, who had title to Phaedra's house according to terms of the will, sold it after a bitter fight and put all three inheritances into cash.

To buy ships, Fiona concluded.

No, to hire lawyers, Honey answered. Artemis sued to dissolve the family partnership. With Demosthenes dead, Zavvas and Lycourgos had started skimming his children's dividends. To make up for losses incurred from his son, Xantippe, they said. The partnership agreement had no such provision. The uncles could not, however, stand a lawsuit, so they paid up.

That money bought Taki his first tankers. Artemis then came to New York to oversee his office, which led to another typical bit of Greek nonsense. She and Taki ran ships as partners of Zavvas, Lycourgos, and the London branch of the family. Meanwhile, they operated others for themselves and Phaedra. As trusting as they were trustworthy, their Athens uncles immediately sent Aphrodite and Melpomene to New York to see that the books were kept straight.

Thus began the rift within the Keriosotises. The children of Demosthenes no longer needed Athens. They had their own ships. Meanwhile, they owned part of the family fleet too. So they were of the clan . . . and not. Moreover, Zavvas and Lycourgos, ignoring advice, took the shipowners' traditonal 10 percent return on investment, while Artemis and Taki did twice as well.

They made a wonderful combination, Honey observed. Taki knew ships and runs. Artemis knew how to make them pay. They had, in fact, on a smaller scale, outperformed Onassis and Niarchos during the past decade. That, in turn, had increased family factionalism, for those on the "bigger" side of the argument had results behind them.

That made the evening difficult, Honey went on. Marina, tied to Zavvas, would back the old men. Tonight she would give them further aid. She would also police Aphrodite and Melpomene, who were uncommitted. Demi would get even more heat.

Oh? Fiona asked.

Hadn't she noticed? The Keriosotises, Honey said, had a Greek problem. Zavvas and Lycourgos were in their seventies. Their principal heirs were women in their forties. Even worse, the girls were all slow learners, and had picked the wrong husbands. So, who would next head the family fleet?

Artemis, who had the brains, would not. Her enmity for cousins and uncles ran over the skimmed dividends too deeply. Taki? He had the experience, but would not lead, either. She, Honey, would see to that. He and Artemis would play with their own ships. The rest of the time, he would enjoy his passions. Fortunately, Honey said, grinning, they were hers too. They had a vegetable garden and loved to fish.

So, whom did that leave to lead? Demi.

And that compounded his difficulties, she said. At the moment, he owned only what was left of his father's share in the New York office. But if he sold out to the old men, he would quickly get credit to build ships of his own and a bigger piece of family profits. But that chained him to relatives and a fleet which, twenty or thirty years down the road, would be worthless. Who, contemplating middle age, even with a fortune as bait, cherished being publicly labeled the goat responsible for the death of a family dynasty? Certainly not Demi.

Fiona questioned that. She knew plenty of "goat" millionaires. Greenwich and Hobe Sound were full of them. And they all seemed quite happy. No one ever called them losers, either. Their money still talked.

Regardless, Honey elaborated on that theme. Demi had the trickiest game of all to play, she said. On the one hand, he had to sell "bigger" to get ships he wanted. On the other, he had to do so without offending Zavvas or Lycourgos. If he did, one of the lah-di-dah London Keriosotises would become family head. Could Fiona imagine Greeks named Colin or Derek?

Listening, Fiona named Demi's convertible backers: Artemis and Taki.

It had to be they, she thought. Those ships gave them a play all ways. As independent owners, they were building "bigger." As family members, they were shaping the future of the Keriosotis fleet, of which they were part owners. How? By buying Demi's vote.

That had to be, too, she believed. If not, why would he back "bigger"? That jeopardized his chances with Zavvas and Lycourgos as heir apparent.

So, clearly, Artemis and Taki had given him an interest in the convertibles in return for his support. With that premise, everything fit. If Demi sold "bigger," he, Artemis, and Taki won everything. They got ships they wanted and control of the family. As a bonus, he had a share of the convertible earnings. If he failed, he would undoubtedly manage those new ships. What with pay, profit, and Flight Fuel Delivery, he would soon be rich. That worked from the personal viewpoint as well. Honey had already said that she wanted Taki to cut back on work, and that he loved Demi as a son.

That logic ruled Fiona throughout. It brought the Lions, rational to a fault, much trouble; in the end, her too. But at the moment she congratulated herself on her reasoning. It left but one person whose motives she had not fathomed: Phaedra.

Phaedra, Honey said, had a foot in both camps. Her reasons were commercial as well as personal. A tremendous spender, she needed big money. The family fleet paid more than the ships she owned with Artemis and Taki.

Zavvas cut her in on bribes too while he held power. Added to that, her father's will gave Artemis some control over her income; she and Taki made decisions on ships they owned. Phaedra could only listen, and that rankled. She had not yet forgiven Artemis for selling her house, or Taki for backing that decision.

She also had a guilt problem.

Guilt? Fiona asked.

Oh, yes. Phaedra, the gutsy daughter, got herself pregnant at sixteen. Her father, as she knew he would, made the boy marry her. The honeymoon, sophisticated even by Continental standards, began in a Swiss clinic with an abortion. She shed the husband that year, too. She then went on a tear with other wild daughters of European shipowners. They had their own fun and games—quieter, but wilder than anything gossip columns could print.

And Demosthenes had financed that?

Of course, Honey said, smiling. As a Greek, he had "face" to lose. His little girl had to keep up with the others. Otherwise his pals would rank him and spread stories about how bad business had become for the Keriosotises.

So, Artemis, the "baby," had paid for Phaedra's freedom. Sent to a French convent school at fifteen, she went to an equally Catholic women's college at seventeen, and came home at twenty-one. To stay.

Demosthenes, a widower, saw to that. The family had a bad World War II, and they were up against it in the forties, so he needed a cheap cook, maid, and laundress. Shy, nunlike Artemis became all three. By the time the Korean War came, and profits from it got back to Athens, she had pretty much become a recluse. Bright and sensitive, she had spent seven years as a scullion in a dark, somber house with an unloving and unlovable old man.

Her idea of prosperity, then, well . . .

Honey shrugged.

She had hired a tall young maid with long black hair. Others since shared the same characteristics. Whether she had tilted that way in convent school or in college, no one knew. Demosthenes, playing stern Greek patriarch for the sake of a few drachmas, could have turned her by himself. Whichever—who had sentenced Artemis to the house? Phaedra, by her actions. So she had a part, too, in what Artemis became.

That much seemed simple, Honey said, but what do we feel for people we've hurt? Enmity. They keep reminding us of our darker sides.

So, on the one hand, Phaedra disliked Artemis. On the other, shamed by conscience, she could be fiercely protective of her little sister. When others attacked Artemis, she defended her more than she should have. She made many enemies protecting Artemis.

At the same time, she ran little deals with Zavvas behind her sister's back. Still, she felt guilty about her. So no one knew, really, where she stood—Phaedra included.

Artemis represented the opposite pole. She had the calm certitude of an avenging angel. Whether in Athens or in one of the spectacular apartments of Paris, she fended off the rest of the family on behalf of the children of Demosthenes. Xantippe having been her favorite brother, she counted Demi as her ward.

Very *luxe,* she had at the same time a touch of the *religieuse.* She came to New York summers to visit Taki and Honey at their place on Long Island. She scrubbed floors then, baked bread, cooked fish, and made salads.

Timid and self-effacing, she depended on Phaedra's vocal, and sometimes violent, protection during family confrontations. Still, distrusting her, she came to New York for these New Year's Eve parties.

Artemis summed them all up, Honey said: tricky and dangerous.

Seated on the gray couch, Honey raised her glass. To the future, she said. Normally, she confided, she kept family matters to herself. But Taki liked the convertible plans, so a full briefing seemed in order. However the "bigger–smaller" debate was resolved, they might see a lot of each other in years to come.

Honey's openness now became understandable. Knowing Greeks, Fiona translated that perfectly: "might" meant "if . . ." If what? If she and Arkie were seen as desirable friends. First Greeks did business with family. Then friends. Never strangers.

Honey, she saw, watched her appraisingly. She wondered, no doubt, if the message had been received.

And then the bell rang.

Walking to the door, Honey dismissed her thanks. Forget it, she laughed, arm around Fiona's waist. With her there, it would be a great night for the white race. That would be thanks enough.

So she had Honey on her side, Fiona thought. A good start.

Then Marina stood before her, asking if she was Greek.

Now, twenty-five minutes later, she faced Artemis.

Honey, slighting her own looks, ignored others' altogether. So Artemis caught Fiona totally by surprise. She had a surpassing beauty. Moreover, it denied place and circumstance.

The face rising from the bowed white satin blouse and black moiré jacket collar had been painted by Sir Joshua Reynolds. It belonged to a member of the English aristocracy. In the portrait, fresh from riding, the woman glowed with the bite of morning mist, like Devon cream under nutmeg. Her hair said there had been wind that day, too. Short and brown, its ends turned to show chestnut glints. Now, two centuries later, she appeared in Artemis.

And so did someone else. Head down, body shyly bent back at waist, she looked up, far more the convent-school girl than the implacable avenging angel. Her lips, backlit by the dimmed landing lights, quivered tremulously in and out of shadow until they set in a timorous smile. Then, fingers trembling, she extended a hand.

Fiona responded accordingly. She had Honey, she thought. She had Taki. She decided to go for broke. She took the proffered hand in both of hers.

*"Bonne année, Tante Artemis!"* she said.

Artemis leaned farther back. But this time her smile held genuine delight. "You speak French?" she asked in perfect English.

Fiona nodded.

"And you did your homework, too, for being hostess."

"Honey filled me in, but I didn't know about your English. I thought you might find French more pleasant."

Freeing her hand, Artemis threw both arms out in an expansive hug. "Pleasant?" she laughed. "Oh, that's sweet, so very, very sweet! Happy New Year indeed, Fiona! If you spoke to Honey, you know how often anyone ever thinks of being pleasant at these things."

Hands at sides, Fiona remained calm. Warm breath curled over the inside of her left ear. Occasionally, lips brushed its tip. That could be happening as much by chance as design, she thought. How else did people whisper? The pressure of thighs and abdomen could also be coincidence. Greeks were nothing if not enthusiasts. But the subtle spreading of legs for more contact? That seemed open to question.

Artemis promptly resolved her doubts. "Tell me," she cooed, arms affectionately settled around her shoulders, "could you love me?"

The message now clear, Fiona responded. She hugged Artemis back. Her hands found her hips, pulled her in for a brief, guileless moment in which their bodies folded into each other from knee to breast.

"Oh, yes!" she answered. "I do already, the way I love Honey—but we've decided she should be my big sister. So will you be the aunt I never had?"

Stepping back, she then kissed Artemis. With Taki she had been playful, smacking his lips, a teenager thanking Daddy for the stereo on Christmas morning. Now she let her mouth soften and linger, as if she were an affectionate child getting as much as she could of a favorite friend or relative.

Smiling, Artemis cocked her head appraisingly. Sensitive to nuance, she read the signal: turndown.

Still, she patted Fiona's cheek. She could have been embarrassed or rebuffed. Instead, she had only been disappointed. Such delicacy deserved reward. "You'll be my niece," she said sincerely. Then she left.

So she had Artemis too, Fiona thought. Relieved, she craved a cigarette. Her legs began to tremble, as well. Suddenly, she had to sit down.

Almost as quickly, she decided to join Aphrodite. Shy and without say in choosing the designer of the new ships for the Keriosotis family fleet, she posed no threat. Moreover, ignored by her husband and cousins, she sat alone on one of the gray couches. She would welcome a few minutes of innocuous Locust Valley shopping gossip.

That, and one of Nando's Gibsons, would be what she needed to regain her composure, Fiona calculated. For all her thought, she never asked why she had submitted to this situation or why it unsettled her so. She knew. She had learned that from her mother. Women like her had to do these things. Wives with looks and social skills took the lead, made opportunities for husbands like Arkie.

And, she thought, for themselves.

For her, that avoided suburban matronhood and, while not being like the women here, having what they had: the freedom of wealth. Even more, she envied their arrogance. How sick she was of always having to be the one who ingratiated herself!

So she passed no moral judgments on the Keriosotises. She knew they were crude, offensive, and uneducated. But she needed them.

As she went to Aphrodite, her gaze swept the magnificently paneled room, the elegantly coiffed and jeweled women, the men who looked so at ease in black tie. She forgot the origins of Saint-Nazaire modern, the fishwife manners, the conflicts, jealousies, and lies among these people.

Seeing them, she wanted *her* place in their midst.

She remembered the party later for four incidents. Five, in fact, concerned her. But her shading of memory could well be excused.

She called the first such happening "The Look." It occurred twenty minutes later.

Having put Marina, the Connecticut cousin, further in her place with tales of Greenwich Country Day School and a wedding in Christ Episcopal, she left to join Demi and Aphrodite at the cold-appetizer table.

The green velour couch behind her, she commanded a full view of the room. At the far end, idly leaning on the piano, Zenon and Ferenc, Melpomene's husband, seemed to be chatting quietly. Light from the far chandelier, however, disclosed a fixed glint in Ferenc's eyes. It went directly to the spiral staircase.

Phaedra stood on the fourth step.

Casually observed, she could have been scanning the books on the right wall. Watched closer, another image emerged. Her arched back, rolling hips, and swaying body suggested a miniaturized Dance of the Seven Veils to a far-off flute that only she could hear. Then, mesh panel of her dress facing the far end of the room, she cupped her breasts, tilted her head so that it could be seen, and silently mouthed a question: "You like?"

Ferenc, blond leading man, replied as discreetly. Eyes now on Zenon, he smiled broadly and nodded.

Laughing to herself, Fiona thought no more of it. Phaedra was giving the boys "a little tickle." Rough humor at its roughest—a gang from Chios.

The second such incident occurred two Gibsons later.

Hokey, who had had three, precipitated it. Artemis, Phaedra, and Zenon were similarly involved. And Nando starred.

As predicted, the hot and cold appetizers and red snapper had been totally devoured. Then, with suitable ado, Demi produced the *pièce de résistance,* the favorite party dish of Aristotle Onassis: unborn lamb, split and roasted with rosemary and garlic.

Virtually impossible to find, save for a Loren Wade, who bought forty tons of lamb a year, the treasure brought rare agreement between Marina and Melpomene. They gave it a standing ovation. Zenon, grim and taciturn, showed even more appreciation. Handlebar mustache bristling, he sprang to the serving table with what Fiona took to be a wild Greek battle cry. Smiling covetously, he tore off the right rear leg without benefit of knife.

Ten frenzied minutes of carving later, only bones and the head lay on the platter. They too were destined for speedy removal. Zenon, who meanwhile had been downstairs, returned. Walking directly to Euralia at the second serving table, he carried with him a green plastic kitchen garbage bag. Nodding curtly, he put everything but the head into it.

A gesture from Demi stopped him there. Smiling, Demi put his arm around Zenon's shoulder and eyed the table questioningly. "What's the matter?" he asked. "The food's no good?"

Zenon, obligingly, played straight man. "What you mean?"

"I mean there's four loaves of pita here and twenty more downstairs and half a tray of pilaf. I'm wondering why you're not eating."

Zenon looked at him uncomprehendingly. He had, after all, eaten a quarter of the lamb.

Turning away, Demi looked across the serving table. "Euralia," he asked, "you made the pilaf the same?"

"Same's always, Demi! I sweah!"

"But why so much?"

Face buried in hands, she shook with giggles. Laughing harder, she bent lower, behind the table.

"What'd you say? I can't hear you," Demi complained.

"I say, 'cause I do 'nodder lam'!" she answered.

Rising, she produced it from under the white damasked table. The platter was set into the heating tray, the alcohol burners spluttering blue beneath it.

Inspired corn, Fiona thought. But it worked. The women applauded, and the men cheered.

Zenon promptly tore off another right rear leg. He had poorer luck, however, with the pilaf: the serving spoon missed his plate entirely. Phaedra, rushing for the tongue, spilled her wine. Fortunately, no one noticed either mishap. Both wound up in the empty *kalamari* tray.

Watching from the small beige love seat to one side of the large fireplace, which she and Taki shared, Fiona decided to go back to work. The party would soon be food-drunk or wine-drunk. Whichever, it needed a few steady hands.

"I think I'd better help Euralia serve the pilaf," she said, rising.

Having seen both spills, too, Taki nodded approvingly.    "You'll be back?" he asked. "We got baklava for dessert!"

"I'll leave my purse," she promised.

"Good girl!" Demi whispered, tapping her thigh as she rounded the end of the serving table and stationed herself behind the pilaf tray. "As you can see," he went on, nodding toward Euralia, carving the lamb, "nothing succeeds with the Keriosotises like a little excess."

Plate filled, he then joined Marina at the piano.

Looking over Nando's shoulder at the drinks table ten or fifteen feet away, Fiona thus had a perfect view of what she called "The Wingshot."

It came during the second helpings on the second lamb, which also marked the fourth Rioja stop. All involved had drunk by then at least two Gibsons and nearly half a bottle of wine.

Idly glancing up, Fiona saw it all.

Artemis, standing in profile to her, had put her hand out for Nando to fill her glass. Hokey faced her. He, Demi had told her, owned an arsenal of Griffin & Howe custom shotguns. Moreover, he had also had three Gibsons to Fiona's knowledge. Now, finding Zenon sufficiently interested, he demonstrated the correct way to lead a bird from right to left.

Hokey's back being to Artemis, the result was inevitable. His arm glanced into hers. Wine followed, spattering her white satin blouse.

Fiona first saw her eyes widen in shock.

Hokey's reactions were equally visible. His brow creased, his gold-rimmed glasses shooting up. Then, turning, he saw the Rioja spill over his hand.

Seeing his face, Artemis literally cringed. "Sis . . . sy!" she cried, like a terrified child.

"Goddamned dyke!" he shouted back. His voice did not ring true to Fiona. She heard as much fright as rage in it.

Phaedra, meanwhile, gave as good as Artemis had gotten. Leaving Demi and Marina, she ran to the drinks table. Arms menacingly raised, she echoed family sentiment. "Goddamned society asshole!" she called Hokey.

Nando, in red jacket and black tie, reacted faster than Phaedra. Reaching behind him, he gathered up two bar towels and darted toward the silver champagne bucket at the right side of his table.

Fiona moved from behind the pilaf tray to help him. But Ferenc, just served by Euralia, stopped her. Hand around arm, he quickly pulled her to his side.

"It's nothing," he whispered. "Lots of bad blood. And, besides, there's no way you can use it." He smiled knowingly, one outsider helping another.

She wondered what he meant.

By then Nando had rounded the drinks table, picking up the Gallo wine jug, and wormed his way past Zenon to Hokey's back. Turning, he met Phaedra with his cocoa-brown smile.

"No pro'lem, Missy Phae'ra," he assured her, blocking her charge, though he stood at least four inches shorter than she. "Fix right up—you see!"

Glowering, Phaedra stood aside.

Euralia, leaving the table she shared with Fiona, joined them. Taking a bar towel, she held it out while Nando soused it in white wine. Then, smiling, she moved to Artemis, motioning for her to untie the bow of her white satin blouse. Patting her arm reassuringly, she opened the top two buttons as well and folded the wine-soaked towel inside and outside the spotted area. Nando, his towel similarly drenched, did the same to Hokey's left coat and shirt sleeves.

Grasp still firm, Ferenc turned Fiona to her left. "Don't tell anybody," he chuckled softly in her ear, "but I gave Demi that trick. White wine's the only thing in the world that'll take out red. Learned it in France last summer when a waiter tripped and spilled a glass on my jacket. The captain came over and got it right out, just like Nando's doing. Never cleaned the coat till we got home, either. White'll work on grape juice too, but not as well. But then, nothing does."

Nando and Euralia defused the incident as quickly as it had flared. Moreover, no one else there seemed to act as if anything unusual had happened. Moments later, in fact, they urged Zenon on as he opened the green plastic garbage bag to collect the second lamb's bones.

"What's he doing?" Fiona asked.

"You'll see," Honey, who had joined her and Taki on the beige loveseat, laughed. "Jus' you remember, Greeks are primitive people."

Demi seemingly underscored that remark, Fiona saw. Arm around Marina, with whom he shared the piano bench, he pointed to Zenon and rose. Then, moving to the right wall, he turned the dimmer switch back.

The chandelier light then just touched the paneled walls. The effect, Fiona thought, moved them all back through time beyond history. They could have been a clan, a family, a tribe in a massive, vaulted cave, warmed and illuminated by the fire locked in the wood ringing them. The theme of *Never on Sunday*, meanwhile, piped in from the chartroom record player, filled the room.

Zenon, face as solemn as ever, spun the bag shut. Then, turning it lengthwise, he held it over his head in both hands and began to dance as the others applauded on the beat.

"He got Easter lamb before it go on the spit," Taki whispered. "Wats what he do nex'."

Fiona wondered what could top a dour tuxedoed man in handlebar mustaches dancing with a plastic kitchen garbage bag. She soon learned.

Moving faster as the tempo quickened, Zenon danced into the aisle between the charcoal-gray couches. Then, with a last spin, he faced the small fireplace. Dropping the bag on the hearth, he went to one knee to crack the bones with his fist. Then, by popular request, he rose and, jumping, finished the job with his heels.

Nando, in the meantime, grinning demoniacally, circled the room with the last of the Rioja. A bottle in each hand, he topped off all glasses.

Zenon followed, bestowing bones from the plastic bag as if he were the sower in Millet's painting.

"Now we get to suck the marrow," Honey snickered.

"A gran' lady." Taki winked. "She grow up in sout' on catfiss that ain't got no scales even, an' live in mud an' eat it. So don' listen to her," he advised. "Marrow bes' part."

Struggling to keep a shinbone from dripping on her dress, Fiona nodded gamely, now knowing what topped dancing with a garbage bag.

The third incident marking the evening Fiona labeled "Ice Cubes."

Its scenario began unfolding at ten-forty-five in the dining room.

Shortly before, Phaedra had excused herself, so Fiona had crossed the room to watch the gin game between Marina and Melpomene. As Demi predicted, they seldom spoke. Cards sailed back and forth across the table with deadly, rapid-fire precision. The tempo slackened only as one or the other reached for the Moët et Chandon at the side of the table.

Champagne, however, proved unequal to the occasion.

Melpomene, bony face gleaming under sweat, mustache glistening full width, seemed even more translucent than before. Marina, beehive hairdo listing over left ear, either from its weight or from that of the pearls in it, had similar problems. Her tension showed in a constant, compulsive harrumph. So, pouring a fresh glass of champagne, she sipped and grimaced. Melpomene watched her, a tight, mean smile crossing her face.

They wanted something stronger, Marina said. They liked brandy on ice spiked with champagne. With Phaedra gone, would Fiona get the cubes?

Of course, Fiona replied, rising.

A moment later, in the hall, she rued her eagerness to please.

Light suddenly flowed over the far end of the hall. Backing out of the kitchen, Ferenc came into view.

Glancing right, at the stairs leading down from the floorthrough room, he cocked his head, as if anticipating shadows or sounds. Satisfied there were none, he looked left as quickly, straightening up.

A step past the chartroom by then, she had nowhere to hide.

Smiling boyishly, Ferenc acknowledged her presence. Mouthing "Shh," he made the sign of the cross.

"A little tickle," he whispered.

"It's our secret—now we're even," she answered.

She did owe him, she thought. He had kept her from the drinks table. She had had no business in that fight.

Nodding thanks, he turned for the front stairs. She went back to the dining room as quickly. She had no business in the kitchen, either, she knew. Phaedra had mentioned "a little tickle."

The icemaker was still working, she told Marina. It would take a few minutes for more cubes.

Then, instead of watching more of the gin game, she went to the backgammon table to calm herself—again. Turning the board, she sat down with her back to the Thermopane doors. A thoughtful hostess, she had wanted that seat; then she would be sitting in the draft, rather than a guest. But Phaedra had insisted on it. Looking down the hall, she had a full view of the traffic from the floorthrough room.

Seething, she thought of what she would tell Demi on the way home. She had gone along with this, thinking his family would be just another bunch of snotty rich. But nothing could be further from the truth. They were just a bunch of animals with too much money.

She realized just as quickly that she would say nothing. The splinter group—the children of Demosthenes—was already on her side. They could be worth a half-million dollars by themselves. Like it or not, she realized, the more you got, the more you paid.

The idea no sooner registered than Phaedra appeared. Unnaturally erect, she lurched down the hall. Her appearance reminded Fiona of confession magazine covers.

Rising, Fiona rushed into the hall, pointing to the chartroom. "Quick!" she whispered, moving to the right wall to block the way with her body. "Get inside."

Phaedra's head snapped around, black eyes focusing, blunt, aggressive features becoming more pronounced as her lips peeled back in rage.

"Goddamn you!" she shouted, bringing up her hands. "Who do you think you are, some kind—"

She never finished. Making a tactical error, she grabbed at the collar of the fuchsia dress to pull Fiona to one side. No one would damage that dress. Lowering her shoulder, Fiona bulled her into the chartroom, slamming the door behind them.

"Look at you!" she ordered, ending her charge with Phaedra pinned against the chart table. "The cheapest Piraeus whore wouldn't walk around that way! And you're going back in there to sit down with that man's wife?"

Phaedra looked down and laughed. "What we gonna do?" she asked.

That needed no answer. First they had to unjam a zipper. The problem lay in repairing its ravages. Phaedra had drunkenly run the zipper over the body stocking below her hips. The nylon promptly laddered. Unstressed, it fell away. A provocatively bulging lambchop-shaped island of bared flesh thus rose from a cinnamon-colored sea over a good bit of abdomen and down the thigh to the knee. To make matters worse, the gown, caught in the undergarment, no longer hung correctly. Distorted, the strip of blue and white rhinestones hiding the seam between mesh panel and fabric now exposed a thick clump of black pubic hair.

What to do seemed simple enough to Fiona. First she had to cut the gown free. Then she had to repair the stocking.

How? With what? she wondered.

The chart table's top drawer held answers to both.

Taking the scissors, she went to her knees. Then, reaching up inside Phaedra's dress, she cut the stocking as close to the zipper as she could to minimize damage. The fastener opened, she went to work on the nylon. For that she first used Demi's stapler, Phaedra squealing whenever the cold chrome metal brushed her skin. With the top of the stocking stapled through its elastic waistband, a base existed against which the material could be pulled. Scotch Tape, applied around the inside of Phaedra's thigh whenever possible, then welded the edges together. Dress adjusted, Phaedra again looked presentable.

The others, having heard her curse in the hallway, looked up as they returned. Ignoring them, she poured a brimful snifter of Courvoisier and took the seat facing the Thermopane doors as Fiona indicated.

Artemis, regal and serene, smiled at their arrival. Then, noting the rigid back and stiffly held shoulders beneath the fuchsia dress, she turned to Fiona. Living on the edge of desire herself much of the time, she saw that posture as a reflection of the struggle for composure it masked.

"Listen to Auntie," she said, enticingly waving a freshly lighted cigarette. "Take a few puffs."

Fiona regarded the marijuana. She had ignored it until then. She had gone easy on food and drink as well. She wanted her nerves and mind "up," alert. That judgment had been correct. She wondered now, though, what else could happen in the hour or so before Demi came to take them upstairs. Perhaps she might get through the rest of the evening better if she came "down" a little.

So she reached for the cigarette. Artemis nodded approvingly.

"Now watch your luck change, too," she said.

It did, dramatically.

In the next hour, she won four hundred dollars from Phaedra, who, shocking everyone, lost without a whimper. Moreover, when Demi came for them, she paid and went upstairs with her arm around Fiona.

In Greece, the end of the year brings families to the dining table. A fresh cloth has been laid, and wineglasses and the best bottles the budget allows are set out. In some homes, "company" demitasses, with gold or silver spoons and a newly made, aromatic coffee, will appear.

In either case, the centerpiece of the celebration will be *vasilopita,* the New

Year's Eve cake. Round and full of eggs, nuts, and raisins, it will give off scents of yeast and cinnamon, and its top will be decorated by a cross of white sugar frosting flecked with colorful bits of citron.

Its appeal, however, goes beyond the senses. Greek custom has the baker hide a gold coin in its dough. Whoever gets the slice with the prize, legend holds, will have a lucky year.

So it was on East Forty-ninth Street, but with modifications. Appreciating the jealousies that animated his aunts and cousins, Demi had the Poseidon bake twelve *vasilopita*, each about twice the size of a large sweet roll. Then every guest could be a winner. Anticipating prosperity from operating Wade's convertibles, he had flat gold Dunhill cigar clippers for the men and Tiffany gold ship Monopoly tokens for the women. They pleased everyone.

So, just before twelve, chandeliers set for dimmest light, they all gathered happily as Demi poured from the second magnum of Moët et Chandon.

Taki, ringed by the group, self-consciously rubbed the gray polyp in the corner of his right eyelid. The tuxedo and $1,000 gold Rolex notwithstanding, he looked out of place with his naive, uncertain smile and thick, muscular deck ape's body. Still, as the oldest family member present, he had the responsibility for ushering in the New Year. Brow fiercely beetled, he consulted his watch, silently counting down the seconds. Finally he raised his glass at the precise moment.

*"Hronia anno!"* he said, with obvious pride.

Turning and rising on his toes, he kissed Honey three times in the Greek fashion. All the men kissed all the women the same way.

For the first time, Fiona heard warmth in the women's deep, husky voices. It sounded like friendship. More likely, she mused, it would be relief. Clan Keriosotis had survived a rough shipping year. Those present, as well, had just negotiated an evening potentially as ruinous.

Taki, however, ended the party twenty minutes later. Chatting with Ferenc at the Fiftieth Street end of the room, he idly pulled back the tobacco-brown velvet drape to glance at the backyard.

"Hey, we got snow!" he called out. "An' from wes' by nor'wes'—plenty more to come."

Hearing that, the others rushed to the phones, as Demi knew they would, to call chauffeurs. They recalled the twenty-inch snowfall on New Year's Eve of 1964 that had ushered in John Lindsay's mayoralty. It had taken hours then to get out of the city to expressways and turnpikes.

So, coats on, waiting for their cars, they gathered on the front hall landing, glasses in hand, finishing the last of the champagne.

Those heady moments, so full of satisfaction, came so quickly they blurred into a single incident, which Fiona called "The Goodbye."

It began with Marina, who had slighted her for not being Greek. Holding both of her hands, she promised to call in early February, when she returned from Florida. She needed Fiona's help redoing a bedroom. So she said. She really wanted a note to Greenwich Country Day for her daughter. No matter, Fiona thought. Marina acted for the old men in Athens. Her voice gave Arkie a champion on the "smaller" side of the family argument.

Waxy, skeletal Melpomene, who searched her eyebrow in vain, left next. Kissing Fiona on the mouth, she said she hoped to see her again soon. Anyone who could shut up that slut, Phaedra, and beat her out of four hundred dollars, she whispered, was a friend of hers.

Anyone who could just shut up, Ferenc added, with a rakish wink, patting her cheek, was a friend of his.

Shy Aphrodite, a genuine eccentric, departed next. Underslung jaw warmed by a six-foot-long Dartmouth green-and-white scarf and the collar of a soiled down-filled parka, she told Fiona to call the next week. She would be at home, and she had wild onions pickled in Vermont that her in-laws would love.

Phaedra, stiff-legged from Scotch Tape binding her left thigh, promised to call if she had a lunch free in New York. She would not, of course.

Artemis, who would, asked her to meet her at the Plaza the following Wednesday. She also handed over her card so that Fiona would have no excuse for not getting in touch with "Auntie" in Paris that summer.

Honey, equally sincere, made a supper date for the sixteenth, when Arkie would be back from Japan. Taki, rising to kiss her, said maybe they could get a little thing going, like he and Euralia had.

By one o'clock she had changed her mind. The Keriosotises were not so bad, after all. They could be handled, she thought.

She felt her thighs and spine relax as stress began to ebb. Relief stabbed at her nervous system. Soon, she knew, it would show as shakes. Demi, at the door, glanced at her quizzically. Turning before he could speak, she went to the floorthrough room for a tray and started collecting champagne glasses. Playing hostess, she told him she wanted to get them into the sink and police the dining room a last time.

So began the prelude to the incident with no name.

Later, sitting on the green velour couch facing the Fiftieth Street window, Demi watched her return and smiled.

She had stoned herself out of her mind, he saw.

He had sensed smoke behind her fixed, stopped-down stare when she came upstairs. He guessed she might want more, watching her smile tremble, from the front door. She had found it, he knew, in the dining room.

Now she looked as though she were wading a stream. Each prolonged stride saw a champagne satin slipper firmly toed into the beige carpeting. Then, following a brief pause to square her shoulders for better balance, she swung her rear leg forward.

Watching her, he began to feel quite confident.

His timing had been perfect, he told himself.

Physically, she had nothing left. She had spent it all. He knew she would. She had been "on" since lunch, playing to every cue and move. Now she had come down. She had to. It had only been a question of when.

He knew her attitude had changed, as well. Hunting, he had experienced similar states of mind. Stoned or not, she reveled in triumph. Placed in a high-risk situation with much to lose, she had performed magnificently. And her victory, judging by the leavetaking, had been total. It even showed in her face, he thought. Winning had heightened her beauty. The fuller mouth and relaxed, wider eyes gave her warmth. She looked giving.

Those changes, however subtle, encouraged him. Their promises were assured by experience. It had taught him what transformed women like her: acceptance.

He had seen others arrive at the same realization. Its force had transcended marriage vows and pride.

The idea flew to what meant most to Fiona too: identity. That, paradoxically, made her more vulnerable. For, finally won, she now had that to lose.

So he took her staying over as a matter of course.

Arriving at the brown velvet drape over the arched window, she turned to face him. Arms over chest, right hand holding brandy snifter, she drenched him in a smile so dazzling he deferred talk. Head back, laughing, she had an arrogance that suggested she was the mistress of Tara and Scarlett was only the maid, he thought.

He gave her the moment. She had earned it. As with a hunter after a trophy, which, indeed, was how he saw her, his respect had grown with observation. She could play the game, he mused. In time, she would match any of the great ladies of the Big Money with whom he wanted to deal. If he had the means, in fact, he knew he could be serious about her.

He saw ships of his own, though, and wealth to keep her from hunting again, at least four or five years off. By then, her spectacular good looks would have begun to fade, and he would need someone younger to help build an image of tonnage, style, looks, and charm tailored for big oil company brass. Brokers fixed those charters, to be sure, but the deals were made with the ladies in attendance, in pink stone houses, on yachts in Edgartown, or in salmon clubs on the Miramichi or Tobique. So, he told himself, he had best enjoy her now. They had no future. Still, the sense of regret and waste he felt came as a surprise.

She had had no time to play "What if?"

What she had won that evening she could have lost as easily, and she knew it. She had just to let stress get the better of her once. One misstep would have ended it. The Keriosotises, who indulged themselves in every whim and excess, clearly welcomed to the family circle only outsiders who had competence and sophistication they lacked. Honey had said as much. As a result, she had been an unqualified success.

But, in the end, her nerves had given out. How could they have not?

So, downstairs, in the kitchen, she had had as much brandy and marijuana as she could. And both had worked. She knew the smoke had calmed her body. She no longer shook, and she felt in control of her legs and shoulders again. The brandy, she believed, had done the same for her mind. It had made her a little drowsy, true, but it had taken the edge off her excitement. That let her put things into better perspective. Sleepiness aside, she felt fresh and clearheaded, able to handle anything. Her optimism stemmed from the relief of finding a problem solved, as it had when she saw that Euralia had properly set out the fuchsia dress. Further bolstered by her earlier triumph, she thus confidently turned to the last bit of her evening's business: saying good night.

That had to be done just so, too, she thought. She could lose everything in a priggish, suspicious dash for the door. He would laugh at her, and, after what she had seen that night, she knew the rest of the family would, too. So the key to leaving without awkwardness, she had decided, lay in her behaving exactly as she had: casual, open, and, above all, with great assurance. That would discourage any fantasy he might be harboring.

Moreover, she added, they were equals. He had been host, all right, but she had run the tough part of the job. She wondered what the evening would have been like had she not been there. She got that from Honey as she left, who had heard the same from Marina and Artemis.

So she decided to wind things down the way she did at home with Arkie. After guests left, and she got the ashtrays and glasses out of the living room, she would come back for a last drink. Then, on the Finnish couch before the picture window, they would look out over the Sound, quietly trading impressions of the party and what had been said and done. She savored those moments. They had a sense of partnership about them.

She wanted to create the beginning of one of those endings now, lingering and relaxed, low-key, friendly, shared reminiscence. Then, when the opportunity arose, she would suggest leaving, and it would seem right. So, leaning against the edge of the drape, she began.

"We charm the wild shippin' Greeks back into their trees?" she asked, borrowing Honey's accent and line.

"Fiona, you were tremendous."

"Drink to that?"

"Anytime!"

Rising, he lifted his brandy glass from the table alongside the green velour couch and toasted her across the ten feet or so of beige carpeting.

"To the top of the tree," he said, with a bow.

Laughing, she tipped her head back. It stayed there for a quarter inch of brandy. Way too much, he thought, watching her. She quickly confirmed his estimate.

Bringing down her glass, she let her breath out in a long, trailing sigh. Then, rubbing her mouth across the back of her left hand, she looked up.

"My turn?" she asked.

"You want to make a toast?"

She nodded. "Nice party, nice people—to *kefi!*"

"To high spirits," he answered back.

"If I live to be a hundred," she said, incandescent smile still intact, "I know I'll never see another man dancing with a garbage bag."

"Zenon?" he laughed, following her lead. "He had *kefi,* all right! He—"

Leaning alongside the arched window, listening, she idly lifted the edge of the tobacco-brown drape to look down on the backyard. There she found the opening she wanted.

"Oh, Demi!" she cut in, trying to convey anxiety, regret, and surprise. "It's still snowing. Shouldn't we start thinking about getting me home?"

"I checked just before you came back up here," he told her easily. "It's already slowing down—nothing to worry about."

"Except the Expressway. You know how that gets."

Looking away from the window, she assumed a rueful smile. A yearning pout, it acknowledged possible inconvenience that her demand might cause. At the same time, the expression implied that she expected him to humor her.

He shrugged casually, hoping to mollify her.

"Look again," he suggested. "There's twenty-five, thirty miles an hour of wind outside. The Expressway'll be blown dry to Holbrook. No problem."

Looking down, she shook her head again, objecting. "Demi, the yard's absolutely white," she patiently insisted, counterfeiting a hopeless sigh. "The bowl's already full in the little Buddha fountain, for that matter, and snow's all the way up to his belly button."

"That's a half inch, an inch, tops."

"Here in town, maybe," she wistfully conceded, "but out on Sands Point that means two or three, with drifts because of the hills. And we're the richies who always get plowed out last. Please . . ."

That ruined it for her. She thought she had said "please" with three dots. But brandy or marijuana punctuated it sincerely. He heard an exclamation mark. A virtuoso of exit lines, he knew what that meant. Bitch! She had been playing him.

Up to that moment, he had believed her. He had even felt sorry for her. Meanwhile, sober, drunk, or high, she had seen this as a night's work. He had sold her to the family, done all he could to be charming and to put her at ease to insure her success—and had never moved her. How she must be laughing at him, he thought.

A moment later, though, he began to think she might not be. A smart hunter, he realized, would already have been on her way home. She would have hitched a ride to Long Island with Aphrodite and Honey, leaving him there dick in hand. While not quite East Side form, in view of the snow she would have been entitled to that finesse. What could he have said? Nothing. She had done a superlative job, as requested. Whom could he complain to? No one. The family would have laughed at him. He would have been disappointed, certainly, had she left, but unable to fault her. She, after all, had just played the game better than he. Why, then, he wondered, had she chosen to stay?

Pondering that, he saw her in sharper focus. She needed a lot more seasoning, he decided. A lesson in humility would help her, too. She obviously thought she could handle him. Experienced hunters would have understood bed rights, and the place of morality in $25-million deals. Her behavior, in contrast, suggested that her know-how had only been instinct. Realizing that, he guessed he had a beginner on his hands. In all probability she had never come this far before, he believed.

If so, he knew what to attack: her sense of sophistication.

So he glanced at his watch, even though she still had her back to him, looking down on the backyard.

"It's, what," he said, answering her "please" in a tone of good-natured compromise, "only one-twenty-three? Early yet. Come here, and we'll fuck a little, and then we'll decide what to do about the snow."

The shock hit just above her ankles. It stiffened her legs. Locking her thigh muscles, she kept it from her back. But she had been unable to do anything about her face. She felt her features contort in alarm. So her gaze stayed fixed on the backyard.

In her first involuntary start, though, her arm had pushed the velvet drape slightly to one side. That gave her his reflection in the arched window to look at, too. The lamp on the table alongside the green velour couch, the room's only light, illuminated him perfectly. With his right hand, she saw, he had just completed combing back his widow's peak. He sat quietly, relaxed, smile assured and inviting at the same time, jacket open.

He had also exposed himself.

Her eyes went quickly to the Buddha fountain in the corner of the yard. The wet, heavy snow had already crested the figure's navel. Fighting panic, she told herself she had to stay calm. She could still get out of this, and without offending him, if she kept her poise. That meant putting him on the defensive, but nicely, so that they could laugh about this later. Somehow, she had to reverse their roles. She now had to be the good-natured adult and he the whining, demanding kid. So, still looking out the window, she mustered up her most forgiving Pan Am stewardess voice.

"Demi," she coaxed, "don't be childish—please."

He meant to break her, to pay her back for laughing at him, and he expected a struggle, so he led mildly.

"Don't you be," he laughed back softly. "You're randy, Fiona, a very naughty girl who came here to get fucked and wore no pants—"

That spun her around as if lashed. "How did you—"

He silenced her with an airy, amused wave. "Phaedra," he said, smiling. "She said you were seething."

Of course! She recalled a nudge with her purse on the landing. Trust that slut to broadcast a thing like that. Fortunately, she had the perfect retort. If delivered coolly enough, it would cheapen him.

"Trigère's *vendeuse* said not to wear any because—"

"Yes, and we always listen to our dressmaker, don't we? She knows best—just like the Tripler's salesman who assured me last June ascots were out. You see a few down there in Bermuda on the Old Guard?" he asked, not at all impressed with Trigère's *vendeuse*. "And the fact is," he added, with a slyly arched eyebrow, "You've wet yourself rather badly, too—"

"I what?"

Had she? Tensing buttocks and thighs, she induced a minute movement between her legs. It seemed to her he might be right. Oh, Lord, she wondered, beginning to despair for the first time, how had that ever happened?

Eight or nine feet away, he wrinkled his nose.

"I can smell it from here." He nodded, sniffing mockingly. "It happens—even to nice girls. So don't be coy. I want to help."

She felt her back sway across the drape and come to rest with her shoulder blades pressed against a raised molding in the paneling. The high, sharply beaded edges of the wood roused her. A kind of weightless lassitude had begun to creep up the backs of her legs. More alert, she reminded herself again to stay calm, to remain light and sophisticated. Righteous indignation would be wrong. Morality too. They had to laugh about this later, and he had to be made to feel childish.

So she shook her head, tolerantly. Her voice lost its stridency. "We're not high-school kids in the back of a car, Demi," she reminded him with a soft, melancholy smile, as if she almost regretted they were not. "And I'm not some abandoned suburban wife either, with her husband wintered in, in a cabin in Maine, dedicating his life to literature and the Great American Novel."

He marveled at her. She had stoned her mouth into slow motion. Words came singly, without flow. Yet none of the booze or dope had touched her glibness. That facile, pseudosophisticated patter marking the upward-climbing little girls from Greenwich could survive anything, he thought. It had to be a gene. But he could be patient. He knew where she would lead him. Then he would start teaching her the facts of life.

"Arkie's only in Japan," she concluded, with the kind of casualness that impressed the women she played tennis and rode with, "and he'll be home in ten days. How could I hurt him like that?"

That, indeed, put him where he wanted to be. The lesson could begin. Smile in place, he spread his palms.

"But who's hurting Arkie?" he asked softly. "He's eight thousand miles away, and this is just a little secret between us, between consenting adults who know how to take their pleasure without hurting."

She, of course, had heard that before, he thought. Every married letch in New York who gave his secretary his paycheck to cash, so that she would be impressed with how much he made, used it. So must have pilots and men she met flying. But familiarity had value. When what seemed familiar turned out not to be, composure often vanished. Seeing her head rise as if she had a reply for that old chestnut, too, he thus robbed her of all her glibness.

"After all, Fiona," he pointed out, smiling, as he ran his fingers through his hair again, exercising leverage he did not possess, "I've got quite a stake in Arkie, too. The last time he and I looked, in fact, I found I had twenty-five million reasons for not wanting to hurt him in any way."

She felt weightless now to her waist. A byproduct of another surrender to stress, the sensation came from shock without reaction. Normally, fear would have set off a fresh adrenalin charge. But her body held no more.

Then instinct replaced thought: She knew Demi had to be pleased.

Mind fogged by brandy and smoke, she sought to put words on that idea. Then she could talk it away. But language took time. It had to be chosen. Images came faster. Fantasizing or hallucinating, she saw them at once. They had a compelling and unique vivaciousness.

She immediately recognized them as truth.

She recalled Ferenc, whose ticket Melpomene would punch; Hokey, who cringed before Artemis, because she, undoubtedly, ruled him through Aphrodite. She could see Phaedra's face, rigid with hate, because she had touched her in the hallway outside the chartroom.

She had words for what she sensed then: the Keriosotises were hard users. They expected more than their money's worth. People who gave less were disposable. Demi, she now knew, saw her that way, too. He had said as much. Now, sitting on the green velour couch, hard and throbbing, smiling like a celebrity who took being ushered to the best table as a matter of course, he gave her abundant proof that in his mind, at least, the design fee paid for her as well. He, after all, as he had so pointedly suggested, had twenty-five million reasons for her not wanting to hurt him. If she did, he could steer his and family business elsewhere.

So, refusing, she would lose the convertibles for Arkie. She saw him then for the first time that night. His design order gone, his arm still circled her consolingly. She had just described running outside to flee Demi. Unlike the others, Arkie's image came with sound track. "Gee, Fiona," he said in the dumb, diffident way that made the inexorable logic that invariably followed so unsettling, "how'd you get in that bind, anyway? You knew Demi was a little wild. Why didn't you just go home with those people from the Island?"

She had no words to explain that away, either. The answer belonged to her, and to her alone. And, guarding it, she knew she had to submit.

She sensed that her mother might not even understand. Caitlin had told her to ignore snubs from the Big Rich; she said she was as good as any of them. Those slights, however, were never forgotten.

Nor had she ever felt "as good as"; "better than," yes. She still did. And that, of course, included Arkie. She simply had too much to offer.

The Keriosotises were a case in point. She had won them all, she thought, but Demi. So she had stayed behind for something special: a sweep. She wanted him captivated, as the others were, too.

Then, his pass gently rebuffed, she would have gone home happy. She would have proved "better than." That also would have demonstrated that she belonged; that, in fact, she deserved more. Instead, he pulled his thing out and reminded her of twenty-five million reasons for not crossing him.

So she had no words for Arkie, whatever she did.

For Demi, she had only one.

"Please . . ." she begged.

"Come, Fiona," he said, waggling the fingers on his right hand toward himself, "you know what maidenly reserve counts for in this house."

Summoning up a last bit of pride, she pointed. "There?" she asked contemptuously.

Having no qualms about embarrassment, he had shown himself to her to shake her poise. Then he intended to take her upstairs. But, seeing her distress, he changed his mind. The couch would be better. Junior League matrons or whatever seldom made love there, on their knees in hosiery and pumps, with dresses pulled over their backs. That did away with foreplay and preliminary insincerities too. Altogether, he decided, that would be an instructive beginning to his little lesson. It would teach her to be very careful indeed when the prey could hunt back.

He knew how to make what she learned chastening as well. He had seen her flinch when he used the word before.

"Of course, on the couch," he laughed. "Just like in the back of a car. Isn't that where America learns to fuck—at the drive-in? Even you, Goody Two-Shoes, when you were a little girl, didn't you drive up to Norwalk or Bridgeport to see the movies and to fuck a little in the back seat if you liked the boy?"

She shook her head, slowly, silently, pleadingly.

Satisfied that he could be as glib as she, he reached over to a green jade box on the table alongside the couch. Raising the lid, he gave her his warmest smile. After all, he told himself, he wanted her humble, not terrified. Holding up his hand, he displayed a long cigarette wrapped in silky translucent red paper.

"Remember?" he asked.

She shook her head.

"I said before that if you did a good job I'd give you something really naughty to smoke afterward. Well, you did a tremendous job. So come here and I'll give you some," he told her, rolling the cigarette enticingly between thumb and forefinger.

Dimly grateful for any change of topic that got him off drive-ins and what she would shortly do, she leaned forward.

"What is it?" she asked.

"A little something nice a friend of mine brings me once or twice a year from the PG. Really good—half hash, half kif. The kif's special, from the Pakistani hill country. They sneak it into Iran, and it's harder to get out than Pahlevi. We'll share," he suggested, waggling the red cigarette invitingly in her direction.

"Kif . . . ?" she mused. "I've never had that."

"The Arabs have a word," he observed, "for pleasure and well-being: *kaif;* from which comes our little friend here," he ended, pointing the cigarette at her invitingly.

So she left the window. Eyes lowered, watching the placement of each champagne satin pump, she saw him. An ugly, crooked blue vein pulsing in his foreskin, he looked huge. She had no idea men could be so big. After that, she kept her gaze fixed on the red cigarette.

Reaching him, she stopped, looked down wonderingly.

He nodded, pulling his chin back.

He meant it, she saw. They were going to do it there, like that.

Oh, Lord, she thought, he really was crazy. No one did things like that. Merely submitting, she also began to sense, would not be enough, either. She would have to please him, as well.

Leaning over, she put both hands on his shoulders. Then, moving her feet around his, she braced her shins against the couch. Looking down, she saw his eyebrow rise. Her face warmed in a blush. Her movements had shown more than passing familiarity with back seats.

"Be careful," she whimpered.

He nodded in understanding.

Her first concern that night beyond herself, he guessed. Maybe the dress *had* come from Trigère. At first, when she had invoked the *vendeuse,* he had suppressed a laugh. Glancing at the workmanship in the collar, he began to think he might have been too cynical. Regardless, he saw, she had taken her best shot. Her pumps, a $100 item to his knowing eye, were brand-new, too.

An idea he had had before about her came to mind again. He questioned whether she realized she had gone over to the hunt. Lots of Greenwich girls never did, he thought. They were raised that way, to be upwardly mobile.

Then, reaching down with both hands, he lifted the fuchsia dress over her knees, past the burgundy satin garter belt, and finally up over her hips. Gathering the material, he held it loosely, so as not to crush it, in both hands, over the small of her back.

"Ready?" he asked.

She nodded.

Bending her right knee, she slid the lower leg past his left thigh onto the green velour cushion. Then she repeated the procedure with her left leg and slowly let her body settle down on his thighs.

A moment later, he dropped her dress and, cradling her face in his hands, patiently gave her further instructions.

"Fiona," he told her, "nice girls put it in."

So she did. Effortlessly.

He quickly regathered her dress. He wanted to feel the small of her back under his hands again. He sensed mysterious, surprising contours there worthy of further exploration. Then, estimate vindicated, he leaned back.

"You see, Fiona," he told her, chuckling softly, "you do need a friend. And, judging from the state of things, rather badly."

He had no illusions about what had wet her so: acceptance.

And he had no qualms about taking credit for it.

That had just reached her first.

His turn, he would move her more.

Her chin bore down on his left shoulder. Glancing up, his gaze fixed on her right eye. It glittered black now and seemed as wide and vacant as a skull's. Staring through the darkness toward Forty-ninth Street, she sighed.

"Demi . . ."

"Yes?"

"Take me home, please . . ."

"Home?" he asked, as if giving the matter serious consideration. "I don't think we'd better. Not yet."

She nodded in insistent slow motion. "I've got to get home, Demi . . ."

"We'd never make it," he answered soberly, drawing on experience with other women in similar states. "Look at you. You're bouncing up and down like a jackhammer. If we left now, I'd have to fuck you on the Expressway, and that wouldn't look—"

"But my maid's waiting up . . ."

"Oh." He nodded.

Nothing serious there, he thought. An easy fix.

"Stop," he said, putting his hands on her thighs to hold her down. "Just let it soak while we come up with something."

Trembling, she pressed her chest to his. He looked down on the tops of her breasts, heaving with exertion. Gorgeous, he thought, full and round. He would have to do something with those later, too.

Her chin still on his shoulder, she turned to him dependently. Even slack with drugs, her face still had a breathtaking, arrogant beauty. That would change, he told himself. Somehow, she had managed to keep her ego intact so far. She had probably already explained this away in her mind to her satisfaction. But upstairs, as she climbed the walls and tried to walk on the ceilings, those flawless features would rearrange themselves very respectfully. Besides being a marvelous technician in his view, he also had something for her to smoke. Overreachers had to be taught, he reflected.

But first, he would keep her a night or two.

"Who's your best friend, Fiona?" he asked.

"Liese . . ." she answered.

"Liese who, darling?"

"Liese Bondurant. But Liese's in Hong Kong now," she sighed. "She married Taffy, the P and O manager there."

"Perfect!" he laughed. "Now, here's what we'll do. First I'll call your house. Then you'll tell the maid you ran into Liese by surprise at the party, and you're going with her to the apartment she's staying at until the snow stops and the roads are cleared. You think you can do that?"

Frowning, she nodded solemnly.

Reaching out, he brought a notepad and a felt-tipped pen back from the side table. Then he scrawled a long, inch-high number on it.

"That's the phone at the apartment where you'll be staying with Liese," he told her, holding up the pad so she could see. "I'll hold this, and all you'll have to do is read it off. Okay?"

"And someone'll be there, Demi . . ."

"Bet on it. They'll be Liese Bondurant, too, with an English accent. It's a personal number I keep at my answering service."

Putting the pen back on the side table, he turned the touch-tone phone and began tapping out her number on Long Island.

He felt her thigh rise against his left hand.

"What's the matter?" he asked.

"Demi . . ."

"What?"

"I'll be talking on the phone . . ." she protested.

"Yes."

"I can't. Not like this . . ."

"Sure you can. Now I'll finish getting your number and hand you the phone," he told her, a chief mate outlining the drill for a slow deck gang, "and you're going to sit here very quietly. Then I'll put my right hand under your dress and help you relax. I'll hold my number up in my left hand, right in front of you, so you can read it off. Understood?"

"You're sure?"

Nodding, he completed tapping out the number.

The call took less than a minute. She even managed a sympathetic laugh for the maid at being snowed in.

Hanging up, she trailed off in a luxuriant sigh.

He felt her body growing warmer under his hand.

"What are you doing?" she asked.

"I'm rubbing something."

"With one finger?"

"Actually, two."

"Where did you learn that?"

"If I told you, you wouldn't like it."

"Where, Demi?"

"In Constanţa, Rumania, from a gypsy woman."

"A whore, I bet."

"You see," he laughed, "I told you, you wouldn't like it! Now give me the phone and I'll tell the answering service about Liese Bondurant."

That done, he picked up and lit the red cigarette. He took a deep drag, knowing now he could enjoy himself. The more, the better, he thought. No matter how much he had, she would still be ahead of him. Slowing down, he would also have more control.

He wanted her to have a few hits, too. They would edge her back from hysteria or shock. So, shaking his head in pleasure, he took another deep drag, holding in the smoke before handing her the cigarette.

"Here." He smiled. "Take some. It's your bonus."

Nostrils flared, she sniffed speculatively.

Amused, he watched her shake her head.

"I don't even let Artemis near that," he told her. "It's for the grownups— real pleasure seekers."

Hearing the challenge in his tone, she remembered that she had to please him. So, putting on a smile, she brought the cigarette to her mouth.

A long, rapturous "Ooh . . ." followed. And another.

Unlike marijuana, which seemed sweet and cloying, kif had a cool, bitter taste. Freshening her mouth, it reminded her of gin. It had another quality, which she sensed but could not describe. It distanced her from herself. It was as if she were standing at the green velour couch watching Fiona.

That had advantage, it seemed to her. Disembodied, she still shared the sensation she knew, for example, that Fiona had never been as full as Demi made her and that it felt good. She marveled at the number and new sights of pleasure that his size induced. It went all around, inside her. Able now to watch, she also wished he would do again what he learned from the gypsy. In retrospect, that had been very special, traveling all the way up her spine and around the back of her head. If she could see how it had been done, she would know something valuable.

At the same time, detached, she forgot about pride or modesty. Those were Fiona's problems. Unencumbered by either, she would concentrate on enjoyment. Who said there could be no gratification without commitment?

Oh, yes. Arkie.

So, eyes widened apologetically, she took another deep puff on the red cigarette, thinking how nice Demi had been to share it. Had it been hers, she would have smoked it all. Exhaling, she handed it over.

"Here, Demi," she said. "It's your turn."

Very nice, he thought. The kif had muscled its way past the marijuana. She sounded like a child. She must have had decent impulses then.

She, meanwhile, watched him intently. Then, cigarette finally snubbed, she began to move.

Quickly getting his hands back beneath the fuchsia dress, and aided by kif, he thought of crepes. He often made them for overnight guests, and the procedure never varied. After beating the eggs and the milk, he took the flour down from over the stove, where Euralia placed it to keep dry. Sifting it into the center of the bowl, he would form a high white peak rather than spreading it evenly over the surface. Passing his forefinger through that warm, featherylight, satiny mass to disperse it gave him a tactile pleasure he enjoyed nowhere else.

Fiona's body, he thought, felt like that flour.

So, celebrating his trophy, he began taking his pleasure. He saw that as mastery. Her earlier rebuff had denied him enjoying the sense of partnership that enriches and informs one of the most collaborative of human acts. He knew full well what motivated her eagerness to please.

Applying lessons from others fully as knowledgeable as the Constanţa gypsy, he quickly found the muscles and nerves in her back and thighs he wanted to reach. Then, gently kneading, prodding, and stroking with the tips of his fingers, he helped her along.

What began for her, he thought, as a slow dance of rigid, exact movement rapidly changed. Responding to his touch, she started off on a wild, careening ride in search of undiscovered pleasures. Quickening her tempo almost at once, she bumped into his chest, scraped over his thighs—and, past inhibition by then, gathered him in closer. Her hands, seeking better leverage, reached behind him to pull against the loose folds of his tuxedo jacket. Head braced under his jaw, she clamped her body to his. Her knees dug and twisted in the cushion alongside his thighs for more support.

Moving faster, she began to pant. Sweat misted her belly and the recesses along her spine hiding the nerves he wanted. Her wet matted the hair through the opening in his shorts. Sucking noises trailed after her passage over him. A runaway, he thought, as her efforts became more frantic. With no destination that he would sense as imminent, he crooked his thumbs in her thigh creases to stop her. He wanted her fresh for later.

She looked up at him, questioningly, fearfully.

"Enough for now," he said, cradling her buttocks.

"But, Demi, you haven't finished . . ."

Bitch! he thought.

He knew then that she had in fact been a user, too.

She sat there, giving him her little girl's voice, slack-mouthed and greedily rocking her bottom, as if she craved more. At the same time, breathless and quivering, she expertly flexed and tensed her abdominal muscles and underside, trying to make him come first. Drunk out or drugged out, he reflected, she had to win. She had to rank him out somehow.

The hunter's will.

Yet the dampness on him seemed real, too.

Realizing that duality, he saw that nothing had changed. It had only been made clearer. He still had to best her sexually before he could attack her arrogance. Then he could chasten and intimidate her as she deserved to be. So he sought to further disarm her.

"I've got a surprise for you upstairs," he said. "We'll do better there, too."

"Upstairs, Demi. . . ?" She glanced down uncertainly. He knew what that meant. She questioned her legs.

More important, feeling her wet, she feared staining her dress.

"No problem," he told her, gently lifting her from him. "It only takes a little bit of genius."

Then, still holding the fuchsia dress over her hips, he rose after her. Turning her back to him, he gathered the material in both hands over her belly and pulled her closer before whispering in her ear.

"Now," he said, "we're going to march in lockstep to the staircase when I give the order. You can do that?"

Facing away from him, she nodded.

"Good," he said, drawing her shoulders to his chest.

She drew away immediately. He pushed her stomach back as quickly. That gave her arrogance a little nudge, he thought. Closer, he had slithered in between her buttocks.

"An old Greek custom," he said, holding her. "Now get ready. . . . Left! Right! Left! Right! Left! Halt!"

They came to a stop before the spiral staircase.

She swayed a little. He took the opportunity to move closer.

"Now," he continued his commands, "right foot on first step. Left hand on stair column. . . . Left! Right! Left! Right! Left!"

Halfway up the staircase, stretched taut, dilated so that she wanted to spread her legs, she agreed with what he had said earlier. Indeed he had a little bit of genius. It resided in using that bludgeon of his as if it were a feather, and of always being able to find her clit. He even had it now beneath his index finger as they climbed and lurched around the center post. In truth, it seemed lighter than a feather, more like a warm breeze that had found its way inside for her private pleasure.

Detached again, as she had been alongside the green velour couch, he told Fiona to cant right slightly to better accommodate herself to his touch.

Below her, she heard him chuckle.

He knew everything, she told herself.

Still, it felt nice, like hearing a great promise.

How he stayed there, with her walking, baffled her.

Occupied between pleasure and speculation, she thus passed through the top-floor hatch, into the brilliant fluorescent lighting, immediately noting the difference in temperature. Stepping off the staircase, facing right, she saw why and ran out of his hands.

"Tub's full!" she cried joyously.

Unsteady, dress gathered around waist in left hand, she barged into the teak siding. Ignoring the step, she tried to swing her right leg over the top. Kicking too high, her calf cleared the lip, bounced down on it, and then away. A tearing sound followed.

Spinning away, eyes bright for the first time since the party ended, she gratefully took support from him.

"Demi, the dress! My dress! It's all right?"

Laughing, he tapped her inner thigh. "Only the ribbing on your hose tore. It's heavy stuff, so it twanged."

Sighing hoydenishly, she fell back against the tub. Then, almost as quickly, as she felt the heat, her slack, relieved smile, after all that had happened to her that night, thinned into a hard, questioning line.

She glanced at the water, then at him.

More arrogance, he thought.

She suspected him of taking her for granted.

"I filled it at seven, on my way down," he told her to salve her pride. "I do every night I'm home. Taper off in that hundred-and-five-degree water, and you'll go to bed with a better rush than you will from one of my cigarettes."

"You will?"

"Oh, yes, but not as good as you'll get from both." He laughed, removing two cylinders in the familiar red paper from his handkerchief pocket and placing them in the tray on the side of the tub. "Now stand up and put your arms over your head, and I'll show you."

Giggling, swaying unsteadily, she did as told.

The dress passed swiftly over her head.

He stood back, his face twisted in alarm.

"Fiona, honey," he asked, "what happened to you?"

Looking down, she casually brushed her forefingers over the flesh-toned Curad adhesive bandages lying across the tip of each breast.

"You mean these, Demi . . ."

He nodded.

"Model's trick," she said, "to hide the nips . . ."

That made it his turn to sigh. "May I?" he asked, nodding toward them.

She fluttered her black eyelashes coquettishly. "Gently, Demi . . . ?"

"Hand to God, Fiona."

Delicately, as if peeling tape off tissue paper, he lifted both bandages. Her nipples were sized and shaped like the short, thick filters on Euralia's cigarettes. Now, gorged with blood, they seemed as red and rock hard. Behind them rode full, perfectly elliptical breasts.

Nudity heightened that sensuousness. What puffiness or lack of tone hid in other women she flaunted. He saw every bone. His eyes lingered on unexpected deeps and rises, new contours. He traced the flow and symmetry of muscles so voluptuously bulging her buttocks and thighs and rippling her abdomen and pelvis.

Engrossed in himself, he had little curiosity about women. He took them as his due. In bed, expecting them to be alike, he had no surprises. Seeing Fiona, he felt otherwise. He speculated on her astonishing topography. He wondered how it would change if led past her familiar sexual horizon. If adequately aroused, he thought, she promised what all men dreamed of, few achieved, and even fewer had the guts to seek—pleasure akin to pain.

Stealing an upward glance, he finished removing the last bandage. Her gaze went vacantly across the room to the shower stall. A small smile lifted the corners of her mouth. Relief brought it, he thought, reaching for a hanger from the clothes hook on the wall to his left. The fuchsia dress, now over his arm, would soon be safe.

The next moment proved his thoughts wrong.

The dress hung, he turned to her expectantly.

Her mind had been elsewhere, he saw.

"Can we finish now, Demi . . . ?" she asked.

She lounged casually against the tub, forearms on its dark varnished lip, her body facing his. Right leg bent, she braced the champagne satin pump on the teak side behind her to take her weight. Leaning back, she beckoned him closer, lips curled invitingly in a little girl's pout of longing.

Bitch! he thought. She would never quit. Her smile had nothing to do with the dress. She had sensed her impact on him, instead.

Now, in her burgundy satin garter belt and little else, she challenged him. Her knee slowly opened out from her body until it spread the dense, opaque black thicket of hair curling over her lower abdomen. What she showed to prove her desire gleamed under the bright fluorescent lighting. A shiny magenta, its edges, rigid with swelling, throbbed with erratic pulses. She wanted him to see her that way, he knew, because she understood what had happened when she had removed her dress. He had gone ahead of her. Drunk or drugged, she still realized that if she could entice him to her, she could win. She could have him finished, humiliated and unsatisfied, in seconds. Then she could dictate terms. Even leaving.

He marveled at her instincts. Whore's trick, he thought. Wham, bam, thank you, ma'am. He knew that from a youth of dockside carousing. So he answered in kind.

Grabbing her hips, he growled like a playful puppy. Then he thrust his face straight up her thigh.

Squealing in fear, she turned away, back to him. Lips trembling, she sagged against the tub. Her last try, he thought. He had her now.

She knew it, too. Sighing, hands at sides, she turned to face him.

Quickly unclasping the garter belt, he got her out of her shoes and stockings and lifted her into the tub. He sat her down, thinking of Wade, who said never to be a hard winner. So, reaching the shelf over her head on the left wall, he took down the bath oil, poured it in, and patted her cheek without looking at her or speaking. Then, to amuse her, he added bubble powder and threw in the thirty-year-old Japanese celluloid models of the *Rex* and the *Normandie* that Honey had gotten at a garage sale on the Island. Smiling, swirling the water, he said every boy should have his own ships, too. She seemed unconvinced. Patting her cheek, he turned to undress. In her condition, he thought, the heat rush would reach her at once. Then she would feel less sorry for herself.

"Demi. . . ?" she called a moment later.

"Umh . . ."

"I need something for my hair, Demi . . ."

Reaching up, trousers below hips, he fished out the lace from the décolletage of the fuchsia dress and waggled it behind him until she took it.

Finally nude, he turned off the fluorescents, leaving on the ceiling spots at the left and right of the tub. They would sit then in a sort of protracted twilight, which made for a nice effect, he thought. Then, swinging his right leg over the side, he entered the water with her.

She sat facing him on the left seat, arms outspread and floating just below the surface. Her head rested on the scrubbed teak ledge behind her. Her eyes were shut, her lips parted, as if in a blissful, silent sigh. Banks of gossamer, iridescent bubbles crowded under her chin and around her ears, framing her face. She seemed lovelier than before, hair pulled back to reveal her features, and tied in a topknot with the fuchsia lace. She looked sixteen to him, gorgeous and unused.

The rush, he saw, had arrived, too.

". . . 'swon-ner-ful, mar-vel-ous . . ." she sighed in tuneless pleasure, syllable by halting syllable.

Quickly lighting a red cigarette, he took a deep hit.

Head back, she sniffed languidly, eyes still shut.

"Bonus time, Demi . . . ?"

"Come and get it."

So she sat with him, and they smoked, feet braced against the seat she had left. Between puffs, they flicked the ships back and forth, he smiling, she giggling, when they disappeared in the bubbles.

Sitting there, seeing his face, she knew he would never hurt her. His smile was as dopey as Arkie's. She could even get out of the tub if she wished, although she knew she would not. Her detached self had already said that once hardly mattered, and that he had been very good and still needed finishing. She had only to keep things light.

So, when the *Normandie* arrived, she tried a small experiment. Instead of flicking the model back, she put it on top of the bubbles.

"Look, Demi," she cried, "it floats!"

"Everything floats," he told her solemnly.

"Everything, Demi . . . ?"

"Everything," he affirmed.

Right arm around her shoulders, he dropped his hand to wedge the bubbles away from her side. "See?" he said, pointing his chin down.

Her right nipple gently bobbed on the water like a fleshy, bloated carmine pupa. It hardened, grew a more fiery red, and immediately took on a cylindrical shape with a minimum of manipulation. Reaching over his body, he found her left breast and fondled it with his fingertips, too.

She inhaled, breath catching in her throat. The sound came out bass, as if she were a man. As she hardened further, he lightened his touch. That deepened the tone, made her pant. Then, guiding her nipples, he turned her to him.

"You know, Fiona, you could float, too," he said.

Her eyes, as usual, he saw, gave her away. They scanned him, the tub, the water. She knew perfectly well what he had in mind. Still, aroused, lips trembling, she did her charade.

"I could, Demi . . . ?"

"Oh, yes," he said with authority. "Just like on the couch, and it'll be very good for you with all the warmth and weightless—"

Reaching past his left shoulder to the ledge behind him, she brought her legs and body over his thighs in a vast upheaval of bubbles.

So, coupled under that twinkling, iridescent cloak, one hand and mouth ministering to breasts, five knowing fingers creating more pleasure in back and thighs, he showed her how to float. Joined, they shared another red cigarette and floated again. Then, lifting her from the tub, he toweled her off, carried her to his bedroom, and took her a third time.

Nice, she said, and promptly fell asleep.

Bitch! he thought. She had won, after all. He had never moved her.

Opening his nightstand, he removed a small glass jar.

Then, lying beside her, he pondered his next move.

Fiona looked up from her pillow.

The darkness to her left held a small pink glow. Before it, radium green hands said five-fifteen.

Turning away, she found the bed empty.

Farther right, a narrow seam of soft orange light outlined the edge of the hallway door, which stood ajar.

Good, she thought. She could find the john.

Woozily sitting up, she threw back the covers and groped her way out. Demi, foreseeing the state in which many guests would find themselves, had thoughtfully put passenger-ship handrails in the halls. Grasping one in both hands, she gingerly followed it to the bathroom.

A few minutes later, feeling better, face splashed in cold water, she returned to the bedroom. Leaving the door slightly ajar as she had found it, she stumbled in the darkness past the bed to the black corduroy drapes.

Looking out, she saw snow in the glow of the street light beneath her. Hoods and tops of cars parked on Forty-ninth Street were white, as well.

She guessed that only four or five inches had fallen. Nice, she thought. The roads would be plowed soon. She would be home soon.

But not too soon, she thought, spreading her thighs as she had done on the spiral staircase. She felt that full again, and the ache seemed stronger. After more sleep, she decided, she would give Demi a little bonus.

That would be nice for her, and it would help make him like her more. She hoped he would. She wanted all the Keriosotises to like her. They were friends. Demi deserved something extra too. He, after all, had asked her to the party to meet his family.

Then she would go home.

One little bonus, once, would make him call again. Then, over the phone, he would have to ask nicely. And she could accept or refuse, as she wished. That would be nice, too.

Meanwhile, looking down, she felt grateful for the moist steam heat. Soothing, it clung to her as warmly as the water in the tub. Feeling taut and stretched all over, she wanted nothing else on her. Even silk sheets had seemed cold and scratchy, getting out of bed.

Letting go of the drape, she heard him behind her.

"Aha!" he called. "You're up. I brought food."

He stood in the doorway in a white terrycloth robe bearing a U.S. Lines crest. Probably from the steamroom of the *United States,* she thought.

His left hand cradled the Cunard champagne bucket. From it, she saw, protruded the neck of a green bottle. His right hand balanced a large serving tray supporting glasses and several small bowls.

"Breakfast already?" she asked.

Eyes narrowed, he regarded her nudity. "You've something better in mind?" he asked.

"It's not too early to eat, Demi?"

"Wait till you see what I've got," he said. "Then ask if it's too early."

Placing the bucket and the tray on the chest of drawers to his right, he turned to the bed's rosewood headboard. Reaching to its far left, he tapped a switch on a small black tube lamp. Its light, falling in a diagonal swath over apricot silk pillows and sheets, made the room seem warmer. Folding back the black spread, blanket, and top sheet, he began to smile.

Finally, he thought, he saw what had happened.

He could only think of Aristotle Onassis. His respect for his teachings deepened: "In shipping, the advantage is always to the one with the most patience."

A universal truth.

Breakfast? He had had his at noon. Early? He had already seen the Cotton Bowl game and the first quarter of the Rose Bowl.

She had thrashed around and snored so loudly he had gone downstairs to spend the afternoon watching football. He had only brought these goodies up now to get her the hell out with a decent taste in her mouth. He had a La Guardia delivery to make on an early tide the next morning and wanted a good night's sleep.

And what had happened? His patience and forbearance had been rewarded: Fiona had misplaced twelve hours. She read the clock as A.M. rather than P.M. She had given him another night.

So, he told himself, breakfast it would be. He would call his backup man later.

In the meantime, he thought, the windfall deserved his best effort. Opening the headboard bolster, he took out two pillows. Then, considerate host, he patted them full, set them up side by side, and bowed over the bed.

"Your breakfast, madam," he said, with an elegant, sweeping flourish.

Glancing down, he nodded approvingly. She had brushed her hair out, letting it spill over her shoulders again. Framing her face, it made her seem more knowing; by implication, more exciting. Apart from swallowing, in fact, as she tried for more saliva after all the booze and drugs, she looked as gorgeous as ever.

"You deserve better," he said as he took the champagne bottle from the bucket and held it up for her inspection, "but men don't make it."

Recognizing the Pol Roger bottle, she smiled.

Twisting out the cork with a thunderous report, he turned to the food tray, filling two tulip glasses. Handing her one, he sat down beside her.

"To secrets," he proposed.

Squinting, she guided her glass to his. Then, tipping her head back on the apricot pillows, she drained the wine, hoping to slake her thirst. That much, that fast, immediately put her back into the night before, he saw. Her left hand, closer to him, unashamedly crept into his robe and up his thigh.

Her eyes sought his. "Demi . . ."

Patting her cheek, he slid off the bed.

"Demi . . . !" She impatiently waggled her empty glass at him.

If not one thing, the other, he thought. She would soon be in a fine, quiet frenzy.

Smiling, he steadied her hand. Taking the Pol Roger off the headboard, he poured a refill and began gathering the purple-banded white bowls on the food tray. He had three, nested on each other. The first, cherry tomatoes rising above its sides, he put on the apricot sheet next to her hip. The second, still exuding oven heat, held pita bread, split crosswise into wide round tops and bottoms. The third, extending the line away from the headboard, reached the top of her knee. It held unsalted white soda crackers.

Gulping the champagne, she eyed the food, then him.

Pleased at her interest, he compounded the mystery. He handed her a small wooden ice cream cup spoon. Then he held up a wide, flat tin, anodized bronze. Its white label had blue Arabic script.

"Breakfast, Forty-ninth Street style," he said, slipping onto the bed with her. "What's good enough for Pahlevi may be good enough for us. We'll see."

"The Shah, Demi?"

"No less, and here's his special conceit," he said, handing her the tin, still cool from the refrigerator.

"Caviar, Demi?"

He nodded.

"Thought so . . ." she mused. "Mustn't ever use a metal spoon, 'cause you'll taste it if it tarnishes."

"Very good, Fiona. Very good indeed."

She held out her empty glass as if for a reward.

"Take a tomato intead," he told her. "It'll do a lot more for your thirst."

So, facing him for approval, she bit into a cherry tomato. Its juice spurted onto the apricot sheet and dribbled down from the left corner of her mouth.

Shaking his head not to bother, he gently ran his thumb down her chin. Then, smiling, he turned to face her, holding the tin between them.

"Now," he went on, as if telling a child a parable, "the world's full of caviar, and if you were the Shah, a kid who's supposed to have everything, you'd want a very special kind—and all of it—wouldn't you, to lord over everybody else?"

They were all alike, he thought. Hunters never learned enough.

Brows furrowed, she recited her Cordon Bleu litany: "Beluga ... osetra ... sevruga ..." she said, going from largest- to smallest-sized eggs.

"There's a fourth, too—sterlet."

"That shouldn't count, Demi," she said reprovingly. "It's too small."

Nodding, he allowed her exception.

"And a fifth—Pahlevi," he continued, "named for you know who."

"There is, Demi?"

"Yes, but except for a few cases that go to gourmet snobs who'll buy anything if the price is high enough, he keeps it all for himself and a few key embassies and, of course, shipowner and oil company pals who got him back on the throne and the smart journalists who forget to mention he tells a lot of jokes with 'suck' in them. Now, what do you suppose," he went on teasingly, "makes this little half-pounder here so special?"

Wide-eyed, she shook her head. A harder drug overrode the effects of liquor, kif, and marijuana: a view, as near and as real as his hand, of the sphere in which she had always imagined herself—the heady, glamorous confluence of shipowners, royalty, and vast international business interests.

Carefully using the tip of his spoon, he pried off the top. Then, with the lid on the headboard, he moved the tin into the light of the small tube lamp.

"There," he said. "You ever see caviar anywhere like that before?"

"It's golden, Demi!"

Another romantic, he thought. Everyone called it that. In point of fact, it always seemed to him to be a shade or two lighter gray than good beluga.

Suddenly animated, she grabbed the tin from him, sniffed it, passed it in and out of the light, prodded the eggs with a fingertip. "It's like osetra, but gorgeous," she said.

"Exactly," he agreed. "These are osetra eggs, but taken from fish right before spawning, when the color's lightest." Knifing the edge of his spoon into the top, he wedged out a good, restaurant-sized portion, each egg perfectly round and glistening in the light. "Here," he said, "try some."

"That much, Demi?"

"Fiona, this is a half-pound can."

"Did it cost a fortune, Demi?"

"It's cheaper to eat money, but I've got another downstairs. Uncle Zavvas did a deal for the Shah, so we get a break on the price. Now, take it."

"Oh, God bless Uncle Zavvas," she sighed.

"Try it with a tomato," he suggested.

"I like it this way, Demi."

"Try it."

"But how, Demi?"

"First, bite off the top of the tomato, like so," he said, demonstrating. "Then swish it around in the caviar until you've got all it can hold, like so, then eat," he finished, holding the finished product before her.

"Marvelous," she announced. "But look at the sheets, Demi . . ."

"Fiona, darling, these sheets are already bound for glory from last night," he said, watching her face color. "Why deny them Pahlevi?" Then, taking the half-bitten tomato and loading it with more caviar, he handed it back. "What do you say?" he asked. "Do we need the pita and crackers?"

She shook her head. "Just more stain . . . and champagne . . ." She giggled.

He put the unneeded bowls on the chest and poured more champagne before getting back on the bed. She seemed to be growing stronger. More animated, but making no more sense, she had now gone "up." The Pahlevi had done it, but he discounted it as an aphrodisiac. It had never moved him. Why women loved caviar, he believed, had nothing to do with sex or taste. The images behind it, its cost, and the other people who ate it, usually more "social" than they, excited them.

Not having eaten in thirteen or fourteen hours, she had a ravenous appetite and thirst. So, a few minuters later, he went downstairs for more of everything: another bowl of tomatoes, the other can of Pahlevi, the reserve bottle of Pol Roger he kept with his "emergency" wines.

Returned, he found her stretched out, à la Goya's *Naked Maja,* green eyes fever bright. She gave the food a brilliant smile, which he took as promising. Wade had observed offhandedly, as the little pig usually did when dispensing pearls, that, drunk or sober, eating gauged a woman's sexual capacity. Did she have an appetite? Lick her fingers? Forget to wipe her mouth? Gobble her food? The more of those indicators, the merrier.

So, lying across from Fiona, watching her eat, he waited patiently. She met all of Wade's criteria. She had her fill halfway through the second tin of caviar. Sighing languorously, she rolled onto her back, wiping her fingers on her hips.

"Done?" he asked.

She nodded. "All done, Demi."

A long moment later, sighs deeper, absently eying the Pahlevi, she picked up the tin and placed it behind her, on the headboard. Then, bracing her hands against his left shoulder, she pushed herself off the bed.

"Piddle, Demi."

He watched her go, thinking of Wade's law. He had found it infallible.

Rising, he leaned over to take away the tomato bowl and to sweep the sheet with his palm. Turning away from the chest of drawers, he refilled the champagne glasses. Then, taking off his robe, he opened the jar he had put on his nightstand the night before. Shaking out a cigarette, he lit it, turned off the black tube lamp, and got on the bed.

She appeared at the doorway, uncertain at the darkness.

"Just shut the door halfway, and follow the light to the bed. The room's nicer that way," he told her.

"This much, Demi?" she asked at the door.

"A little more. There—that's it."

Soft orange hall light then fell across the foot of the bed. Later, he would seem to be passing back and forth between darkness and dawn.

Feeling her settle beside him, he reached up for her champagne glass and handed it to her. Then he smiled and toasted what would follow.

"*Hronia anno,* Fiona."

Touching his glass, she drank.

Then she sniffed. "What's sweet, Demi?"

He reached into the ashtray on his nightstand.

"This," he said, holding his cigarette in the light.

Licking her lips, she blinked. With reason, he thought. It looked rained on. Mottled brown, its shriveled paper held deposits of a chalky white substance both dry and gummy. Still, he knew, it had an appeal for upper class women that made caviar seem dull. Many who shared his bed knew the joys of Pahlevi. Not one had ever smoked anything remotely like what he now held in his hand.

After more champagne, she sniffed again. "What is it, Demi?"

"A Pall Mall," he said. "I made it myself."

"How?"

Experience told him this had to be presented with a dramatic revelation, just like the floorthrough room.

"I can't say," he teased.

"Why not?"

"Because it's a secret."

"Demi!"

Relenting, he turned the cigarette toward her. "Want a puff?"

Head cocked skeptically, she weighed the offer.

"Take one, and I'll tell," he promised.

"It's . . . all right, Demi?"

"Fiona, darling, I'm smoking it myself."

"Nice . . . lemony," she said a moment later. "And now I feel it," she went on. "It's behind my belly button, on the way down." Grabbing his hand, she took another drag. "You said, Demi . . ."

"What I do," he told her, "is open a pack of Pall Malls and put them on a shirt board. Then I take a bottle of paregoric and pour as much over them as they'll soak up. After that, the whole shmear goes on the stove shelf, where Euralia keeps flour and the rest of the things that have to be dry. Then, in a day or so," he went on, smiling at her vexed expression, "I turn the cigarettes and souse them again. That goes on till they won't absorb any more paregoric.

Then, Fiona, after a little pour of lemon extract, for flavor only, what do you think's left on those Pall Malls?"

"What, Demi?"

"A nice dusting of opium, not ever enough to hurt, but just right to give you a little tickle all the way down to there," he said, lightly tracing his fingertip over her abdomen beneath her navel.

So long, Pahlevi, he thought. What chance could it have against that, especially with hunters who sought to be "good sports" always and whose stock in trade was an encyclopedic knowledge of earthly delights?

"Opium, Demi!"

"Umh-umh. That's what makes paregoric such a good stomach relaxant."

"It won't hurt, Demi?"

"No, no, no! Fiona, I do these for Artemis."

And Artemis, like the Shah, wanted something no one else had. In this case, however, desirability resided in her mind. Nothing in the world, he thought, could beat gin and the rush from a hot tub as aphrodisiacs. Both were so relaxing they imparted staying power as well, which, with many of the women he knew, tremendous technicians, was a definite prerequisite.

Reassured, she took the cigarette out of his hand.

"It's better than the red cigarettes. It goes to different places—nicer ones for here . . ."

And soon it would be in her head, he thought. She would see pictures then. He often did, too. Now, amused, he watched her legs work in search of whatever sensation silk sheets could offer."

"Where did you learn that, Demi?"

"At sea."

"Arkie never learned that at sea."

"Arkie's very serious. That's why I respect him."

She took the cigarette from him again. "It's nice," she told him. Then, leaning over, she held up her empty glass. "And so's Pol Roger," she added.

He put the champagne bucket on the bed between them.

"That's cold and wet, Demi!" she objected.

"I promise we'll never notice," he laughed, filling her glass. Then, looking at her, he put his arm around her shoulder and pulled her closer. "Here," he told her solicitously, "you'll be out of the light."

There, silently, they drank and smoked.

After two cigarettes, he snaked his left arm along the headboard to the tin of Pahlevi she wanted near her. Then, heaping the wooden ice cream spoon, he brought it back and spread the caviar.

"Demi . . ." she sighed out of her reverie.

"Umh . . ."

"My shoulder's icky. What are you doing?"

"Dining on Pahlevi better than even the Shah has it."

"Your mouth's warm, Demi . . ."

She leaned back, partly to say she liked a joke, partly to show she wanted him to enjoy her. Giggling, she drew on the third cigarette. Then, when he had finished, she handed it to him.

A few puffs later, he reached out again.

Her body stiffened at his touch. Ducking his head under her arm, he found the nipple erect and full under the caviar. The curve of her breast swelled under his tongue. She sat rigid throughout, head thrown back against the pillows. Her right hand cradled and caressed the back of his neck, stroking it so that she brought him more fully around her.

"Demi . . ."

"Umh . . ." he murmured again.

Tonguing the underside of her breast, he felt her ribs brush his cheek. Eyes shut, he saw spilling flour.

"Would you like to kiss me, Demi?" she asked.

"Oh, yes, Fiona. Very much," he told her.

Moving from under her arm, he drained his glass and put it on the headboard. Emptying hers, he set it there, too; the bucket as well. Then, urging her forward, he threw the extra pillows on the floor and slowly let her settle back on the mattress.

Poor rabbit, he thought. She feared where he would put the caviar next. She sounded like a kid playing spin the bottle.

Well, she would grow up very soon.

So, patting her cheeks and smoothing her hair as if she were a child, he lay beside her, head and shoulder across her chest. Her face gently cradled in his hands, he kissed her eyes and temples, brushed her lips, slowed his mouth over the hollows between breasts and arms.

Then, lowering his head, he followed the pulse in her neck down to her collarbone, took it lower, tonguing both sides of her cleavage. Guided first by one contour and then another, he circled her nipples, first dabbing at them, next sucking them in short, hard little pulls that made her gasp, finally scratching them and inciting them further with the delicate bite of the sharp edges of his teeth. Whimpering, shoulders rising as if to embrace more of that momentary, suggested pain, she slipped her hands under his arms to draw him closer, threw her right leg over his thighs.

Mouth open, moist with saliva, he enveloped hers. He flicked at the corners of her lips and traced their shape, pecked and nipped at the seam between them.

Sighing, she responded, parted.

Nails raking his back, she sent her tongue out in a long questing, yet tentative probe. Encircling it, he pulled it in until his cheeks hollowed. He felt its tip writhe in the void under his palate, restlessly search for more contact. Unappeased, she loosened her hold.

He followed her back. Trembling, she let him wedge himself between her teeth and upper lip. Then, hands still cupping her face, he moved his thumbs lower, gently tracing them across the gumline over her mouth. Her knees rose, pushing her head deeper into the apricot pillow, seeking to better embrace his surrogate penetration. Bridging as if she were a wrestler, she slid under him. His thigh felt cold and damp where she had been.

Reaching behind him, he gently tapped the inside of her right knee and crawled between her legs. Kneeling, he left her mouth, tenderly kissed it closed, circled it above and below as if putting in a safety stitch. The masculine bass note marking her arousal the night before appeared again. The tone deepened as his teeth snicked their way across her skin from her left collarbone to the nipple beneath. It grew raspier still as his right hand slid around her hips and his fingertips gently began stroking her ovaries. Mouth distended, head thrashing the apricot pillow, she pulled him off by his hair when she had enough. Then, eyes closed, moaning like a man clearing his throat, she unerringly guided his mouth to her right breast.

A moment later, pushing him away again, she skidded across the pillow, the top of her skull slamming against the headboard. He sighed in sympathy, bent lower. Soon his mouth roamed the voluptuous bands of muscle spanning her abdomen. His left hand, meanwhile, journeyed softly along the thigh crease under it. Its quest ended at her femoral artery. He could slow her heartbeat from there, he knew, numb her right side from the hip down. Instead, gently massaging the pulse beneath his index finger, he got her to drop her leg. Seemingly unmindful of action and reaction, she murmured luxuriantly as she spread the limb across the apricot sheet.

Changing hands under her hips, he smiled to himself and thought of a Chinese acupuncturist and chiropractor off Collyer Quay, in Singapore. He had gone to him with an officer who had a bad shoulder and, for twenty dollars U.S., had learned how and where to start immediate, involuntary orgasm. A cute little parlor trick with the right crowd, it also had other uses. Once, the imperious daughter of a German shipowner had ordered him to do certain things. He brought her such bliss instead that she went home to a clinic and vanished from social view for five months.

Now, just brushing that place evoked a rapturous sigh. Tonight, however, the site served no purpose. He wanted to punish Fiona in other ways.

Meanwhile, his tongue traced its way down the right side of her abdomen and around her thigh crease.

She reacted at once, as she had the night before.

Stiffening, she thumped into the headboard again, breaking the bed, she thought. It squeaked in protest, like an animal in a trap.

She tried to sit, got her shoulders off the pillow, then fell back. Closing her legs and squirming out from under him failed, too. Finally, in desperation, she put her hands on the top of his head, placatingly.

"No, Demi! I've never had that. Please . . ."

His tongue moved faster. A finger touched something between her legs that had never been touched before.

Her feet rose, fell, legs spread wider than before.

She heard him laugh.

His touch left a pleasant tingling sensation. In spite of herself, she began to feel a soft, insinuating band of warmth start to creep up from his mouth.

She pushed harder on the top of his head. "No!"

"Shhh . . ."

Stymied, fearful of what she began to feel, she raked her nails down the sides of his cheeks and neck.

"No, Demi! I don't do that. That's not nice!"

He had been waiting for something like that.

Toes curled, he pushed himself off from the foot of the mattress, sliding over her until his knees jammed between her legs. Keeping her spread so that she had no chance to roll away, he dropped to his forearms, his face directly over hers.

Her head shook wildly, soft rustling sounds marking its passage over the bolster behind her. Grabbing her hair, he trapped her face between his hands.

" 'Nice'?" he asked. "Fiona, darling," he went on, gracing her with his softest, most patronizing laugh, "you've rollicked in the hot tub, gorged yourself on Pahlevi, washed it down with Pol Roger—and now, after all that, you still want to fuck middle class?"

Smiling, he watched her, as if expecting an answer.

Instead, a hurt beyond pain shrouded her face.

Welcome to humility, he thought.

In a few minutes, she would seek salvation from it. She would beg.

Unable to move, she escaped symbolically. She flung out her right arm.

Its force tore her head out of his hands and drove her cheek to the apricot pillow under her. Sobbing, she instinctively nipped at the silk case with her lips. A last stab at pride, he knew. She wanted to eat the pillow. That would deny him the satisfaction of hearing the anguish she now felt rising in her throat.

Chuckling, he shifted his weight.

Cry stifled, she sank deeper into herself.

The journey hardly began, however, before she felt his tongue again. This time, more alarmingly, it seemed to be chasing something. Judging by heat and quickness, she sensed the new presence bounding around within her, just out of his reach, as a sly, sneaky little animal.

Despising his touch, terrified of the intruder, she threw her hands down, pushing at the top of his head.

"No, Demi! No! Please! No, no, no!"

"That's reaching you, Fiona?"

"No, goddamn you! No!"

Unsuccessful in moving him, she lashed out again at his face and neck with her nails. Closing her legs, she tensed her thighs until they locked, swollen with effort. She took in breath, in short, bass sniffs and gulps.

And, looking up, he laughed.

Their eyes met across her body.

Together, glancing down, they saw her stomach rise, as if against her will, from the apricot sheet.

No sooner had he raised his head, in fact, than the little animal had reversed course and darted back down between her legs. She felt it there now, its hot, greedy mouth nipping and sucking after his.

Smiling, he gently patted her cheek.

Then he lowered his head.

She fell back on the pillow, biting her knuckle.

She had bought in bed and sold in bed.

She had traded in bed, too.

But not once had she ever been had in bed.

Now, she knew, she would be.

So, closing her eyes, she mourned her loss.

Never secure, always trying to please others, she had long seen innocence as an obstacle to the status and life she wanted. Her grief, instead, celebrated another virtue, one, he could have told her, most women like her, whether actively hunting or not, valued just as highly: control.

Something brushed her side, a pillow. She felt it slide under her hips.

Oh, Lord, she wanted to laugh aloud, he planned to eat her on that, as if they were the lead two-page photo in a Swedish porn magazine under a catch headline like "Dining at Fiona's."

Well, let him, she thought. Let him do anything. So long, pride. So long, shame. And good riddance to other petty little middle-class niceties.

After that, time stopped. . . .

He followed her moan with a tremendous shiver.

She sank back, trying vainly to roll free of a gummy substance under her left hip. Unable to, she turned her head away, making no effort to cover herself. Why bother? she thought. She had gone beyond shame. Forever. At least with Demi. She had let him use everything.

Her life had always been like this, she thought.

Just as she seemed to have what she wanted, someone thought up a new game. So it never ended. It just got more humiliating. Like now.

She had tried so hard to please them, to make them like her. And she had, she knew. She had been one of them. Never once, in fact, had she shown them how much better than they she could be. She won playing their rules. And what happened? This. What made the rich so greedy? Why, always, had they the right to expect more than fair value? And where did that leave her?

So musing, she felt him stir on her.

His cheek lay in the crook of her neck. "Fiona?" he whispered.

She nodded, not wanting to talk to him.

"You need anything?" he asked.

In spite of herself, she turned to his voice. It sounded different.

She saw that he looked different, as well.

His face seemed pinched, compacted, nearer to pain than pleasure. His eyebrows and mouth had an earnest, solemn set she had not seen before, either. Smoothing her hair, he raised himself, softly stroked her cheeks.

"Can I get you something? You want anything?"

She shook her head.

Then, gently withdrawing, backing away from her on his knees as if he were an Oriental servant, instead of climbing off American style, he gave her a greater victory than she had achieved in the floorthrough room:

"Was it . . . was I . . . all right?"

Disoriented, full of self-pity, she did not answer. She doubted his sincerity. She had, after all, been used, abused, and outraged. She knew that much.

Suddenly, it no longer mattered. Reaching down, she found the nature of the gummy substance under her left hip: caviar. Rather than breaking the bed, they had turned the tin on its side and it had rolled up and back on the mattress. That became her ultimate triumph.

Poor little Fiona Davies, she thought, the pathetic little girl who had so much to offer—who always tried so hard to be better and brighter and more attractive and to have better conversation—had finally arrived. Those back-country cows from the estates across the Merritt Parkway got the men, respect, and lives they wanted because their fathers had money. But none would achieve the position or nearness to power that she could.

She had been wallowing in caviar: Pahlevi, no less.

Moreover, she had him begging. She saw that in his face.

Drugged far more deeply than by anything she had drunk or smoked, she had her first insight in thirty-six hours free of greed, lust, or suspicion: she wished her mother could see her.

It came and went so quickly she forgot it. But then it recalled an exchange she and her mother had enjoyed in the first seven years of her life. "What's better than one penny?" her mother would ask, and she would answer, "Two pennies!" That principle guided her now.

"Demi," she called urgently and quite sincerely, "come back. Hurry back. I'm not through!"

And she meant it. Such was the power of Pahlevi.

*Oh, Jesus,* he thought. *Where's this going?*

At that moment, Costa Lianides could have told him.
Prentiss Howsam knew as of then, as well.
Evelyn Waddell would know the following morning.
Loren Wade would learn at lunch that day.
And Hubie Garrison would know that afternoon.

Eric Schotten, meanwhile, slumped lower in his easy chair in the small pic-ture-lined parlor of the *pied-à-terre* he kept in Niederdorf, the student quarter of Zurich.

It had been a melancholy holiday for him. It fell too close to the first anni-versary of the night he had spent with Dr. Fabian.

Beyond that, the page from the December Boat Show issue of *Yachting* which he held in his hand had heightened his sense of mortality. He had felt it the night before, at midnight services in Grossmünster Cathedral with his uncle, Christian Reymonde, and his mistress. As he regarded pictures, words, and Howsam's blue ink script, apprehension swept him again.

The advertisement extolled the virtues of a small flat-bottomed outboard-powered boat named the Boston Whaler. The main photograph, under a headline reading "Impossible to Sink!," showed a hull sawed in half afloat in Boston Harbor with a man sitting in the stern. Under that Howsam had writ-ten assuringly: "Anything up to three-inch shell'll go right through."

The motors, circled in blue ink, led to a similar note in the margin: "Arkie says he'll get us 40–45 m.p.h. Not bad for 16 feet."

A final ring in the lower right enclosed a feature of paramount interest to all bankers: the price, $995. That, Howsam accorded his highest compliment. "A money's worth," he wrote. His postscript in the bottom margin invited Schot-ten to see a Whaler at the Boat Show and then to join him in Florida for three or four days to put one through its paces.

Nodding ruefully after a last glance, Schotten rose and walked toward his bedroom. He would get an airplane ticket the next morning, he thought. At least he would have a final weekend with Dr. Fabian.

*January 2, 1967*
*New York City–Lyford Cay, Bahamas*
*New York City–Greenwich*

HOWSAM SNATCHED at the phone.

The Waddells, he had heard the day before, were away for the weekend.

Now, between nerves and *café solo,* he returned his cup and saucer to the antique cherry dining table with a clatter. Then, leaning forward in the Windsor armchair, he vented his frustration.

"Is that your idea of 'holding the watching brief?'" he shouted. "For God's sake, it's eleven-thirty! Where the hell've you been?"

"In Jamaica, and Happy New Year to you, Prentiss," Evelyn answered in his cordial clubman's baritone. "I can only say things are coming to a boil, and your little frolic looks more likely every moment. But, good heavens, you sound shirty! The sky's not fallen in at your end again, has it?"

"You tell me!" Howsam demanded. "Demosthenes just surfaced again."

"Did he? Well, that *is* news! I always thought he might blossom into more than the red herring—too many connections there just for that. Too much credibility. Tell me, Prentiss, what else is he up to?"

"Just what he should be—screwing the ass off of our designer's wife."

"I beg your pardon."

Ever vengeful, Howsam smiled grimly into the phone.

Evelyn's aplomb rode a tremor of anxiety. "You're sure, Prentiss?"

"Got it straight from our Admiral of the Ocean Sea, Costa himself."

"From him? But how could he know?"

"Easy as pie," Howsam laughed. "He called his niece by marriage yesterday to wish her Happy New Year and got the telephone-answering device instead. The maid said that in an emergency the lady of the house could be reached at the apartment of a Liese Bondurant in New York City. Otherwise, to please call again after one, when she got back from church, and she'd take the message."

"Liese Bondurant, Prentiss?"

"A figment of somebody's newton. There's nobody in the Manhattan phone book with that name."

"Then what makes the Admiral so sure—"

"Simple! No pun intended," Howsam said, taking his last bit of pleasure from the situation. "The Liese Bondurant number rang a bell with the Admiral. It ended in eight instead of seven, but other than that it'd reach the phone on Pearl Street where Demosthenes offices with his uncle."

"Talk about luck . . ."

"Luck, my ass! The Admiral's call was inevitable."

Evelyn let that pass. "Well . . ." he trailed off a moment later in a deep sigh of satisfaction. "Well, well, well—that tells us a bit of what we want to know, doesn't it? 'For all that is in the world, the lust of the flesh, and the lust of the eyes, and the pride of life, is not of the Father, but is of the world.' "

"That's John, First Epistle, Second Chapter, Verse Sixteen."

"Yes, and more to the point, Prentiss, who'd be the more likely to use sexual bait: the chairman of the board or the tyke? For that matter, which of them would be in a spot to know of a connection or an acquaintanceship between the red herring and the lady?"

"Ask me another," Howsam scoffed.

"Fierce little tyke," Evelyn laughed, "I love him. He's just like a terrier, never gives up—sniffed us out a year ago and hung on for dear bloody life, and look where he is now, and we with our hands tied! There's nothing we can do without confirming his suspicions. We've just to sit here and let nature take its course until we see what his intentions are. Oh, I tell you, he's brilliant, Prentiss, absolutely—"

"Hey! Wait a minute! Don't get carried away."

"Oh, I shan't. I shan't. But still and all, a job like that deserves to be recognized, even by us, and doesn't it sit better with you, knowing his priorities, that this was his idea rather than the chairman's?"

"No question of that," Howsam grudgingly conceded. "That's a real edge. We know how the little bastard's mind runs, and he's got the shorts, so he'll be playing defense all the way."

"Exactly, and the chairman of the board, rumor has it, is looking for something on the order of two billion dollars. If he were running things, he'd be inclined to rush—to get a little desperate."

"I'm with *you,*" Howsam agreed. "If they ever see the light, they'll have all they can do just to protect themselves against what's coming."

"And in the meantime," Evelyn gloated, "that little brute's right where we want him, too. He daren't make a move, either, unless and until . . ."

"Right—'unless and until' our designer tells his mommy, and that's as likely as my ever telling Francine what we're doing or what we did."

"Yes, it would've been better, of course, if we'd kept everything in the dark, but, all things considered, I'd as soon have the two who're sniffing about now in the picture as anyone. They'll not do anything rash—not those boys! When did they put Demosthenes to work? In August! And look how long they've waited before taking the next step. Mark me, Prentiss—they'll leave us and themselves plenty of options. They're bright enough for that, all right. Who'd've ever guessed that anything as intricate as this could be found in the first place?"

"Amen."

"One thing, though, still puzzles me, Prentiss."

"Yeah?"

"You called this inevitable."

"Exactly. Didn't you mention once having a wrangle with the Admiral about his expenses?"

"Once?"

"Yes, but that time you chatted up the designer for confirmation—only to learn that he never saw the Admiral anywhere but in Long Island City, because his wife had declared him *persona non grata.*"

Howsam laughed in reminiscence. "Oh, Christ, yes! She hates his guts. The week he got here, he brought some belly dancer from a Greek café in Astoria out for Sunday dinner and never took his hand out from under her dress. You can just imagine how that went over—especially at a very chi-chi buffet for ten young Republican yachting pals."

"And how long ago was that, Prentiss?"

"Nearly a year."

"Yes. Well, that's what puzzles me. After being snubbed all that time, why ever would the Admiral call to wish her a Happy New Year?"

" 'Why ever?' " Howsam scoffed. "Everybody's always underestimating that wild man, and he's always right. Why, to take a run at her himself! He said last summer the designer was in over his head, that any sailor with half a brain'd know what he married—and never mind the looks and finishing-school manners—and I thought he was just telling me another sea story. How could I know? He's always talking wild. Like this latest kick he's on: that the dwarf and I just forget our end of the deal and go tarpon fishing in Costa Rica instead."

"That'd never do with Home Office, Prentiss!"

"Of course not. Besides, a deal's a deal. Anyway, he says Greeks even have a name for her kind."

"They do?"

"Oh, yeah. *Proshtighi*. It'll suggest something to you if you roll it around awhile on your tongue."

"Delicious!" Evelyn said a moment later. "Utterly, indescribably delicious. It means everyone's in place. She and the herring'll swim round the aquarium to their hearts' content, and all the little chap'll be able to do is watch."

"You think?"

"Absolutely! It's human nature, Prentiss, and you know what our friend the dwarf says: in the long run, it overrides everything."

"You're that positive?"

"Indeed, indeed! Everyone's in sight. We've just to lie doggo now and go 'bout our business. Delicious!"

For others, the situation had a bittersweet taste.

Hubie Garrison frowned as Wade entered the Cadillac.

"So?" he demanded.

"It's on! It's on!" Wade reported, flopping back against the seat to open his belt and pants for the trip home. "I had lunch with Honey over to Lutèce's, an' she thinks the kids even got in a little tick—"

Frown deepening, Hubie shook his head. "I mean in Athens, with Zavvas. We got how much, two hundred forty thousand tons, comin' off charter the end of April with Tokyo Tankers? What's he done to find us a new taker for all that iron?"

Wade grabbed the armrest as Red, the driver, gunned the limousine across Sixth Avenue. He took the interest in Zavvas as a sign of trouble. It meant that a meeting earlier that day with investment bankers had also failed to produce all or some of the $2 billion required to put PANARTEX on the North Slope. The news from Athens, he thought, would do little to improve Hubie's mood. So he stayed silent until they came to a stop alongside the Rockefeller Center skating rink.

"Taki called this mornin'," he answered. "He said he just got off the Telex with Zavvas—that they had us a nibble."

"They did? From who?"

"BP."

"British Pete—that can't be much! They use that slope out there in Hong Kong to haul what they can't— What's his name? Not Pao . . ."

"Tung. Ol' C.Y."

"Yeah. So what do they want with us? They know we can't go as low in price as him."

"They need more bottoms, an' his bankers don't like the looks of charters these days, so he can't get up the dough to build."

"So what's BP talkin'?"

" 'Bout world scale," Wade reluctantly admitted.

"Plus or minus?"

"Minus."

"Minus how much?"

"Minus twenty."

"What? Those four ships we got out with Tokyo now are runnin' for world scale plus sixty!"

"Yeah, but times change."

"Well, one thing don't change. You know what that is? Red ink! You're goin' from a four-million-dollar-a-year profit to—to what?"

"To break even."

"You mean four million right off the top."

"You rather be Reksten an' have five hundred thousand tons anchored in some Norwegian fjord, with more comin', or Onassis with three hundred thousand in Eleusis Bay?"

"Je-sus . . . the market's that bad?"

"Hell, now's the big delivery season here for home heatin' oil." Wade laughed. "Wait till April or May, an' I'll show you somethin'—"

Hubie, hearing the tonnage Onassis and Reksten had laid up, had a new respect for break even. "So what'd you tell Taki?" he asked Wade.

"Just what I learned off my old Norski pal Hagbart Waage: 'Never fix a time charter in a bad market.' "

"But you just said it was goin' to get worse."

"Till May or June anyways, so I told Taki to keep puckered."

"You did? But why? Where's your reason?"

Smiling, Wade turned away from his window as they crossed Fifth Avenue. " 'Cause Mrs. A told Honey—"

"Hey, if I want *All My Children* I'll get it at one o'clock on Channel Seven!" Hubie shouted. "What in the name of Christ does what Mrs. A said to Honey have to do with you lettin' four sixty-thousand-ton ships go unemployed? What's that goin' to cost us out of pocket each month if somebody else comes along and takes that business?"

" 'Bout a quarter of a million a month."

"How much? Are you totally nuts? You're riskin' three million bucks a year 'cause Mrs. A told Honey?"

"Jesus, will you just take a hit an' get a hold on yourself?" Wade asked, reaching into the walnut drink cabinet on the back of the front seat and withdrawing an Amphojel. "Honest to God, you're gettin' more like Acey every day. If it ain't your idea, it's no good."

Belching ferociously, Hubie pried the white tablet out of its cellophane packaging and leaned back heavily against the gray plush seat.

"Like I said," Wade went on quietly, murmuring into Hubie's ear, "Mrs. A told Honey they weren't even gonna put their boat in the water this year till July, 'cause Archimedes had to go back to Nippon in April an' maybe wouldn't be home before July Fourth. That says he'll sea-trial those Hasegawa speedballs for a week, ten days, an' then hit the road. So whatever's gonna happen'll happen between then an' sometime in June. Demi'll know sooner, though—" Wade winked— "from Mrs. A."

After ten months of failure raising money, Hubie, understandably, had become skeptical of any plan that appeared to be working. "You got it all programmed, huh?"

"Hey, Hube, he already topped her."

"Honey told you?"

Wade nodded smugly. "She called Mrs. A yester—"

"To check that out?"

"She says no, but I don't believe it. You know how her mind works. Anyways, she got the maid on a recordin' sayin' Mrs. A stayed over at a girl friend's place here in town—only the girl friend's number turned out to be Demi's private line down at Flight Fuel Delivery."

"Jesus . . . an' she never tumbled to why you were so interested in Mrs. A?"

"C'mon!" Wade protested. "Soon's I heard Mrs. A slept over, Honey had all she could do to keep me from firin' that little pissant Demi off them convertibles right then an' there! Here I am trying to stay hid an' get them plans against this impossible deadline you give me, an' he's boffin' the designer's wife—maybe the one sure way to queer the guy off the job!"

"Oh, man!" Hubie laughed, spilling the chalky white Amphojel powder out of the corner of his mouth. "You are somethin'! Tell me, Loren, you got enough revisions in your head to keep Angelakos busy till April?"

" 'Till April?' " Wade mimicked. "Till April of 2001! All we gotta do is sit back an' see what them 'Lions' do next."

Had he attended the Boat Show the following Sunday, he would have known, and he would have felt considerably less relaxed about the future.

The Lions, with understatement typical of financial men, referred to the matter as "insurance."

*January 8, 1967*
*New York City*

SUMMERS, Dr. Fabian told Schotten in the cab crossing Central Park, kids in New York's affluent Long Island Sound suburbs think less of cars. What they want then is boats. And none so fascinate well-to-do children as the hot rod: the Boston Whaler.

This appeal explains why Whalers are usually shown just past the entrance on the Coliseum's first floor at the New York Boat Show. There they immediately divert the young, so Chris-Craft, Hatteras, and other big boat builders can sell interested parents without undue distraction.

Predictably, then, the lobby rang with youthful squeals and shouts.

"I told you, Schotten," Dr. Fabian said, waving a mink-clad arm at the Whaler display, "this would be *The Children's Hour.* From here to Maine, anywhere there's water, you see even eight-year-olds in them, running flat out day and night. I can't believe you'd go in those—they look like Tupperware."

"What?"

"A plastic soap dish!"

She got no argument.

Thirteen feet overall, with scarcely eight inches of freeboard, the boat in front of them did look remarkably like a soap dish. Flat-bottomed, with stainless-steel bow and stern rails, it had a pale-blue nonskid floor and three varnished mahogany seats. A white vinyl-clad steering wheel protruded through a fourth slat in front of the helmsman's position amidships. Everything else, of white fiberglass, bent and flexed alarmingly under the weight of the youngsters swarming over the hull.

"Fortunately," he said, in a tone fully as ironic as hers, "this is only the tender. What we want," he went on, consulting Howsam's ad, "is the sixteen-foot Center Console Sport Fisherman. Yes—" he nodded, turning her to the right of the blue-curtained backdrop—"that's it on the end."

The manufacturers of the Whaler, knowing boat shows, discouraged kids by placing the Sport Fisherman on a dolly. Three blue-painted wooden steps led to a raised ramp, putting the gunwale shoulder-high.

Rapping the stern quarter with his knuckles, Schotten nodded more confidently as he helped Dr. Fabian onto the walkway. "More like it," he said, smiling.

"More Tupperware, you mean," she answered, leaning over the hard white plastic half-round fender riveted to the gunwale. "Only this one looks like a sled with sides, or maybe a coffin with the lid off. I thought the idea was crazy when Howsam first told it to me, and now I think it's even crazier. These are for children—rich little boys and girls on Nantucket or the Vineyard, or the East End of the Island."

"Not so, Jerusalem," he said, tapping a forefinger against a plasticized reprint of an ad hanging on the stern guardrails. "Listen to this: 'U.S. Coast Guard buys 100 Whalers to protect safety of life at sea,' " he read.

" 'To protect safety of life at sea' from bullets, Schotten?" she asked.

"Look there," he ordered, pointing under the seats at what appeared to be white plastic partitions. "Each of those, from hull to the underside of the wood, is one solid block of polyurethane foam for flotation. If we had water right up to the sides, the hull still couldn't sink. Then there's this," he said, reaching into the boat for a foot-square piece of material used to explain its construction. "See how this works: an inner and outer skin of epoxy, which can't shatter because it has fiberglass cloth running through it for strengh— and, sandwiched in between, this layer of balsa wood."

"Howsam's boys use that for model airplanes!"

"Yes, marvelous stuff—too soft to shatter and much lighter than water, so it will always float, no matter how many holes are shot into it."

"And you, Schotten?" she asked, brow creased under the mink hat.

His face hardened beneath the gray homburg. "I, presumably, would float, sink, and rise again—days later. But first I would have to be hit. At forty-five or fifty miles an hour, that is an acceptable business risk."

"That fast?"

"Maybe faster."

"My God," she murmured.

Pushing her hand against the hull side, she saw the gleaming white fiberglass bend under her brown kid glove.

"Don't be misled," he told her. "That bends for the same reason an airplane wing bends. If it were rigid, it would crack under the stress. Besides," he laughed, cupping her elbow, "I won't be there, anyway."

"You won't?"

"No, Howsam will. He's stronger, so he'll pull in the others. I'll be here," he said, pointing up to the steering console.

"You're going to do the driving?"

He nodded.

"You must be mad! What do you know about boats? Have you ever run anything like this?"

"That's what Howsam and I will do down in Florida this coming week. He'll teach—"

"Fool!" she whispered with such vehemence that she drew a stare from another couple on the walkway near the bow. "He's never been in a Whaler, either. A friend of his has one at his house on Marathon Key, and he'll be away. That's why you're going there—to save on hotel bills and boat rentals. A fishing guide will show both of you how to—"

"Then so much the better. The expenses are way ahead of plan, anyway, and we'll have professional instruction. If an eight-year-old can run one of these, so will I, by a week from today, when I fly over to Nassau."

"You're going to Lyford Cay?" she asked sharply.

Knowing her hostility toward Evelyn, he refrained from mentioning names. He nodded instead. "Yes. He called me last Monday after speaking with Howsam—said he'd been rethinking strategy and wanted my approval, that he'd found some interesting political possibilities that I would appreciate."

"All of them," she sneered, "I'm sure, involve 'swinging a little steel.' "

"I think not. He can be fiendishly clever, too."

"What did Howsam say to that?"

"I was told not to mention this to him. I'm going over to the Bahamas for a quiet Sunday, and I'll fly to London a week from tomorrow."

Pondering that, she grew silent, pensively running her gaze over the varnished mahogany steering console in the center of the boat.

"So that's where you'll be when it happens . . ." she said at length.

He nodded. "Only we'll remove the seat and windshield and put in a special deep-sea compass."

"But you'll be standing then, Schotten—exposed!"

"Yes."

Smiling faintly, he looked down the length of the right arm of his gray chesterfield. She held his hand in both of hers with what seemed all her strength. Her face, which he had always seen as a perfectly sculpted but impassive mask, mirrored the intensity of her grip. Her expression showed neither love nor affection, but he saw something else in it which heartened him nearly as much: concern. He took that to mean she no longer saw him as merely playing a role—exorcist of the ghost—but as a person.

Coloring under his gaze, she tacitly admitted her new attitude. To herself, she dated that change from the last time they had been together.

That had been in November.

She had gone to Zurich one Friday with $1.5 million, which another of Itch Cohen's and Speed Immediato's lawyers had put into a Geneva bank.

Calling Christian Reymonde at home, as instructed, she had been told to take the checks to Eric's apartment. He would be back from Bern that evening. They thought it best for her not to be seen at Bank Schotten.

Were such precautions necessary? she wondered.

Reymonde thought visitors to the bank were being monitored.

By whom? she asked. Agents of the cowboys? Their Arab clients? The Egyptians? The American CIA?

No, by a far more effective force, Reymonde said: agents of the Swiss Bankers' Association. The group disapproved of members who engaged in "irregular practices," even if legal and for their own accounts.

So, late that afternoon, in a light snow, she went to Niederdorf. She had not seen Schotten since May. As "wheat traders," they had crossed Canada to deposit the money Norbert Nygaard had moved north from Mexico. They had parted after twelve nights of loveless lovemaking with the relationship as ambiguous as before. He called her behavior "self-destructive," begged her to forsake the ghost and other private demons to live in the present. Smiling, she replied with a phrase she knew he would find especially distasteful. Worldly European women applied it to lovers taken in convenience. Their bones did not clash, she said. Besides, she added with a cruelty he did not deserve, the ghost provided certain comforts—mainly intellectual—that no banker could.

She had thought then she knew Schotten. She had found another side of him in Niederdorf.

She guessed he lived on a tree-lined avenue with a view of the Limmat River or near Grossmünster Cathedral. Leaving the Mercedes diesel cab, she found, instead, that he resided in what charitably could only be called an alley one car wide and two blocks long. Volkswagens, Fiats, and bicycles parked over curb and sidewalk made it seem narrower. So did the odors, a brisk November afternoon notwithstanding. Like most European quarters, it had its own bakery, bistro, and butcher shop.

His apartment had more surprises. On the top floor of a narrow buff-stuccoed four-story building, it held as much first-rate modern art as she had seen outside of museums. She had always thought of him as serious, very bright, to be sure, but without much humor. His walls challenged that view with Arp, Chagall, Ernst, and Klee, among others. And beneath the eaves and around the dormers, where no paintings would fit, were books—hundreds and they too were at odds with her stereotype of a Swiss banker.

So was his appearance. He wore a red velour shirt with a long rounded collar turned up at his neck and baggy yellow doeskin slacks. Red socks rose out of his black Moroccan slippers. She had never imagined he *had* old clothes, let alone wore them.

He stood silently, arms crossed, enjoying her surprise as she toured the parlor. Then, pouring sherries, he sat down on a blue velvet couch facing a small coal-burning fireplace, waiting for her to finish.

"Schotten," she said, "you're a closet intellectual."

He shook his head vigorously. The paintings were his joys, he said. At the bank and at home in Feusisberg, he had art for clients. Here he pleased only himself. As for the books, a few years before he had tired of whodunits.

Nothing more?

He shook his head again. To him, intellectuals were entertainers. A pleasant hour or so of reading in the evening. No more.

Surely he didn't mean that?

This time he nodded.

"Look at them!" he said, flinging an accusing red-veloured arm at the bookshelves flanking the fireplace. All the intelligentsia were there: Brecht, Camus, Sartre, plus Marx, Malraux, Kocstlcr, Kierkegaard, Freud, Teilhard de Chardin, Barth, Buber, and on and on. And what had they changed? Child labor laws . . . perhaps. European children no longer went to work at eight but at fourteen. Was that power? Or change? Intellectuals had done no more, he contended. Europe had been to the precipice twice that century. Both times deep thinkers were out in the streets inciting the unwary with dreams of impossible tomorrows. In the meantime, a Neanderthal like Hitler nearly wrecked the Continent, and another, Churchill, saved it. Now a true intellectual, the mad attendant of the madhouse, de Gaulle, shuttled back and forth from the nineteenth century, serving up the contents of history's bedpans as if they were new ideas: honor, glory. And what had he, with all his infinite wisdom, done to make Indochina and Algeria more livable for the natives to whom they belonged? Nothing. Ever thus . . . ever so, he said, quoting his grandfather. Intellectuals and liberals were too caught up in good deeds to consider money and trade and three meals a day as a decent place from which to start improving the world.

He threw up his hands apologetically, to atone for the tirade. He had, of course, disparaged many of her gods and virtually all of her beliefs.

Too surprised to argue, she smiled instead. His voice held something she had never expected to hear in a Swiss banker: the cry of a frustrated idealist. Her view of him altered at that moment.

So, Schotten, she asked, what was to be done?

He knew then, too, that her feelings had changed. So, glancing at his watch, he rose.

What was to be done, he announced, was to eat.

So they ate in the bistro next door, a dark, noisy, overheated cave full of students, thick ragouts and kegs of Hürlimann's dark beer.

And that night she did not see the ghost. Nor did she see him the next night in Feusisberg. He chose not to appear the past weekend as well.

Now, considering the steering console of the Whaler, she could only speculate as to what all that meant. Love?

She knew otherwise. She had once fallen in love. This felt nothing like that. For now, she let her statement in Canada stand: their bones did not clash.

Still, she acknowledged a concern for him that she had not had before.

"And you'll be there how long?" she asked, bobbing her head in the direction of the white steering wheel.

"In the gauntlet or outside?"

"Does it matter?"

"Oh, yes."

"Inside, then."

"Two miles."

"That long, Schotten?"

He shrugged.

"Insurance costs more every day." Then, seeing her frown, he turned her to the stern and motioned for her to walk. "Enough?" he asked.

She nodded vigorously.

Fifteen minutes later, only their unusual good looks distinguished them from other Manhattanites entering the Plaza Hotel for Sunday brunch.

In their case, however, it could very well be their last meal together.

*January 14, 1967*
*Freeport–Roslyn, New York*

THE STUDY of Boston Whalers continued.

It resumed the following Saturday, at a showroom in Freeport, on Long Island's South Shore. A tall swarthy man, pockmarked and crewcut, with the beginnings of a paunch, conducted the inquiry. Unlike Schotten or Dr. Fabian, he ignored aesthetics.

Boarding a Whaler, he took a red pencil stub and a wrinkled pink receipt from his shirt pocket and quickly drew the top of the varnished mahogany control console. Using a machinist's stainless-steel tape, he then painstakingly measured and recorded each dimension. He repeated the procedure, with even more care, at the transom, where one or two outboard motors could be mounted.

Once more on the showroom floor, he eyed the boat critically and tugged the stern liferails, testing for rigidity. Understandably, both salesmen present ignored him. The bulk of their suburban buyers typically wore fleece-lined Antartex coats or Abercrombie & Fitch parkas. Black leather jackets, high-topped shoes, and gray work pants invariably meant boatyard carpenters or mechanics sizing up repair jobs.

The researcher, however, left in a most patrician vehicle, a beautifully maintained 1951 navy-blue Mercedes 300 SL, the model with gull-wing doors. Drawing envious glances, he sped north through the early-morning mist the length of the Meadowbrook Parkway before turning west on the Long Island Expressway.

Getting off at Exit 37, he went north again, to Long Island Sound, before reaching Roslyn Harbor, a town of white clapboard houses, church spires, and boatyards. Lying in green hills on a bay twenty miles east of New York, the village is familiar to many Americans; it often passes for New England in TV commercials. There the blue Mercedes drew up before a marine supply store. Inside, new research began.

An elderly clerk in khaki chinos was asked if he had a Danforth-White Constellation. Yes indeed, he answered. After a last tuck in a halyard splice, he set aside the coiled Dacron-and-stainless-steel cable and crossed the store.

From a display case on the far side he withdrew a square gray cardboard box. He placed it on the countertop almost reverentially. Then, reaching inside with both hands, he removed a six-inch-diameter compass. Metal parts sprayed with a black crackle finish, two circular red-lensed bulb housings rode on the front of its high spherical dome. Its size, and the provisions for night lighting, indicated that the instrument had been designed for large power yachts or ocean-racing sailboats. Boston Whalers, in contrast, normally took slightly larger versions of the familiar AirGuide car compass, if one was fitted at all.

What about that black compass card? the clerk asked. Was it all right? If not, he could get a white one.

He liked the black card, the customer replied. It was better at night.

And the ten-degree notation?

Fine. Compass headings in numbers every ten degrees were quite enough for amateurs. None of them could steer closer than that, anyway.

Considering the sale made, the clerk relaxed. The customer, meanwhile, casually hefted the twelve-pound compass on the fingertips of his left hand. Squinting, he turned it to the light coming in the front window. Then he searched the top of the dome for tiny incipient bubbles in the fluid with which it was filled. At the same time, he withdrew a Phillips-head screwdriver from the right pocket of his black leather windbreaker.

His right hand, matted with black hair, engulfed the tool, amber handle and all. Then, with thumb and forefinger on the driver shaft, he deftly began loosening screws in the black metal housing beneath the bowl.

Somewhat surprised, the clerk asked why.

To check the gasket on the expansion chamber. See? the customer said. Instead of being black, the rubber looked gray, dry. In a few months it would decompose. When that happened, the fluid would run out and the card would swing too fast.

Alarmed now, the clerk began to sell. But what harm could that do in Long Island Sound? he asked. The compass could be filled in a day and ready for the next weekend. On top of that, why write off the gasket? It might still last years. All true.

He liked things right, the customer said. Besides, he didn't want the compass for Long Island Sound.

For twenty-five dollars he would have Tony Spino, at New York Nautical Instruments, refill the bowl and put on a new gasket. Now, how much was it?

One hundred seventy-two dollars and seventy-five cents.

Bills were promptly produced and counted out.

After watching the blue Mercedes pull away, the clerk resumed his splice, wondering where the customer did his yachting. In all his years around boats, he had never seen anyone so fussy about a compass.

*January 21, 1967*
*New York City*
*Riverhead, Long Island*

FIONA CONSIDERED the note sandwiched between the chrome frame and glass of the bathroom mirror: "See you at Ma's 6–6:30."

That meant, she guessed, Arkie's brother Steve had called at 5.30 A.M. and picked him up on the way to New York delivering scallops. Arkie would unload the truck, so the third brother, Pete, got a morning off. Then, in Riverhead that afternoon, the three of them would tear up Steve's basement floor, put in new drains and a sump pump, and re-lay concrete in time for supper at their parents'. Altogether, a typical Saturday.

Still, she thought, crumpling the note and putting her toothbrush back into its holder, it had its merits: she had the day to herself.

Back in her bedroom, she consulted the clock radio. Eight-fifty-five.

Late enough, she thought, reviewing the recent past.

She and Artemis had had a marvelous lunch at the Plaza and an even better afternoon in Greenwich Village. It began as an introduction to boutiques and shops that visitors to New York rarely saw. Almost at once it turned into a wild shopping spree, a day when all the right colors and sizes were in stock. By suppertime, they had spent $2,600. At the table in the Coach House, where they met Phaedra, Artemis called it the best time she had ever had in Manhattan. They would do the Village again, she said.

The next week she spent a day at Aphrodite's, in Lattingtown, tramping through horse barns and six inches of snow on the vegetable gardens until her ankles were blue. Still, she did something right. She and Arkie were invited to Vermont for a weekend in February.

The previous Saturday, Arkie's first day back from Japan, they had had supper at Sutton Place. That had been a success, too. Taki made over her, and Honey wanted her help on clothes. Euralia even kissed her and told Arkie she had a cook's mout'. Then, touring the triplex, Taki mentioned their summer home and fishing on Peconic Bay.

Arkie had grown up there doing just that, so charts were produced to take advantage of "local knowledge." After an hour, rods and tackle appeared. The seminar lasted until 1 A.M. Then Honey asked could they get together again, and would he help them choose gear?

The date made, Fiona felt that the family had accepted them.

That made Demi's silence all the more baffling.

They had not spoken to each other since New Year's.

So, sitting on the edge of the bed, she called him.

As time passed, she had seen why she had to make the first move. She was married, so that initiative had to be hers. Demi had reasons, too—twenty-five million of them, she thought—for not wanting Arkie hurt. He had to trust her to pick the time and place. She thus rationalized her way around any possibility of rejection, as she usually did.

It could never hurt to have the others as friends, she told herself. But Demi had to be. He was the client.

She felt sure, too, she could manage him. By then, the Keriosotises no longer awed her. She had spent more time with them, seen how they lived. They were rich—God, they were rich!—but nothing else. She had more taste in her little finger. If she were in the family, and she told herself she had no desire to be, her influence could be greater than Honey's. It would be in a year or so, she thought, even if she just stayed a friend. She had what not even their money could buy.

The house on Forty-ninth Street seemed less imposing, too. Demi had been an inspired scrounger. Nothing more. He could become very dependent on her, she believed, if she guided him properly. And being invited back by the client, Arkie said, was the secret of success.

Moreover, she felt she had nothing to prove. She knew already she could handle the Keriosotises. So she got right to the point.

"Hi, Demi!" she said.

She had the decorator's pass, she told him. For that day only.

Pass?

To see furniture. For the pink stone house.

Oh. He said he'd be ready at ten-thirty.

By one-thirty, he had had enough. The cheapest thing she found anywhere that she liked, a silk print, ran $3,200 made up as living-room drapes.

Promising to take the matter under advisement, he led her up Third Avenue, to Serendipity, where they had great soups. He needed that pause.

He had kept away believing she had no more to give. He had had the pleasure he wanted from her, he thought, and its bottom line had been discomfort, not ecstasy. One such lesson should be enough for any man.

Now he began to wonder what harm another might do.

Part of that, he knew, came from her looks. Other times at Serendipity, he had seen Catherine Deneuve and Sophia Loren. Neither got as many admiring nods as she had. And, he wryly told himself, her clothes were even more casual than they were at La Grenouille.

She wore a high-collared chocolate-and-black Irish tweed dress. Nothing could have been simpler. With a silk scarf her eye color, blazing lime emerald fire in her bodice, nothing could have been more dramatic either.

Even so, he thought, looking at her over the table, he had no choice but to stall. If he dawdled long enough, she might say or do something to make him lose interest. A long shot, true, but still a possibility. Beyond that, he needed time to determine why she had called.

She no longer needed him. Her acceptance by the family's women already showed. More open and relaxed, she acted as if nothing had happened.

So, over Serendipity's red spice soup, he pondered her interest in the pink stone house. It could be real. Who, so programmed, would not be fascinated furnishing a Manhattan town house at a prestige address?

Or she could be fantasizing. He had seen her doing that more than once, too, arms haughtily folded over her chest, New Year's. Shopping could give her that same vicarious sense of well-being. His theorizing ended there.

Over coffee, she asked to see the new house. She wanted to take some measurements, she said.

With the owner of the house wintering in Tucson and in no rush to close, Joey, the real-estate agent, had given him a key. So, still baffled, he returned to the kitchen after setting the circuit breakers, to find it empty. No mystery there, he thought. He knew where to find Fiona in this house. He had only to swing open the door and look through the dining room.

She stood at the living-room bay window.

Leaning against its molding, eyes shut, head back, arms over her chest, she made the best case he had ever seen for sun worship. Her face mirrored an absolutely radiant, thankful smile.

Her pleasure, however, defied the facts. The weather had not changed. Looking past her, over the manicured boxwood hedges that gave Turtle Bay Gardens its character, he saw only a dark, windy January day.

She was playing lady of the house again, he thought.

That, he knew, implied other behavior as well.

He took her upstairs, resolved to be very careful.

Some of his suspicions were confirmed on the third floor. Strong and athletic, she needed help on and off the miniature two-step stepladder for hanging drapes the previous owner had left. More often than not, when she reached for his shoulder, her fingers brushed his neck. Going for his arm, she invariably got a hand or a wrist. She never missed, he told himself. She always touched skin to skin.

He began to wonder then what she knew about him.

On the second floor, her voice began to deepen. She had a fixed stare as well. Usually, that look marked a woman expecting or wanting a sexual advance. Having insight into her mind, he presumed nothing.

Still unable to determine the reason for her call, he resolved not to commit himself. There had to be an advantage of some kind in it for her, he thought. Until he saw it, and how it applied to him, he would keep his hands to himself. Meanwhile, the symptoms—the stare, the touching, the deeper voice—subtly grew more acute. So did his remembrance of pleasure, rather than of pain.

In the kitchen, leaving the ladder, after measuring some shelves, she looked at him questioningly. Her lips, he saw, were pursed in hard, drawn lines, expectant, tense. Whatever else she had in mind, he thought, some of her needs were clear. But those could wait. Smiling blandly, he helped her down without comment.

That left the living room. There she grew more obvious.

"Some reach!" she said, indicating the distance from the rickety windowsill-high bookshelf circling the bay to the curtain rod. Pointing to where she wanted him to put the ladder, she nodded for him to stand close by.

Smiling tremulously, like a kid about to go off the high board, she placed her palm alongside his neck, then pushed her weight off against it as she got both feet on the first ladder step. Arms outstretched, leaning over the bookshelf, she reached for the curtain rod above the center window in the bay. Just missing, she was carried forward by the weight of her body. She grabbed the casement moldings to stop herself. The ladder, meanwhile, rocked under the sudden load shift.

"Demi!" she cried in mock terror.

He pulled her back, holding her by her hips.

"Now stay there!" she laughed, mounting the top step.

Then, her behind braced against his chest with more pressure than necessary, he thought, she began to strip the steel tape out of its case.

Looking past her, through the diamond-paned leaded glass, he sensed that her interest in the house might be real. The reason for that enthusiasm lay beyond the bay window. The garden, crisscrossed by walks and ringed by handsome stone homes, some ivy-covered, had a safe, serene beauty even now, under a somber winter sky and bare shrubs and trees.

The scene recalled London's elegant mews and squares. The elite lived in them secure from crime and decline of empire, and when they left those enclaves they got the respect to which their addresses entitled them. That adulation could be considerable.

Fiona would love that, he thought, particularly the part about the elite. People behaved impeccably in that world. They understood "nice." He realized he had only to attack the image she saw through the bay window to attack her. That fell short of entirely explaining her interest in the house, but it did give him the intitiative.

So, watching her, he waited a moment longer.

Then, as she leaned forward to measure the window, he slid his hands under the brown-and-black dress and pulled the elastic band around the top of her panties down over her buttocks and thighs.

Stiffening, she inhaled with a loud hiss. *"No!"*

*"Shhh. . . .* Don't move, and don't worry," he told her before she could say more. He just wanted to say hello. Besides, he went on, with a bow to her sense of propriety, no one could see him. His body was right behind hers.

The moment lengthened. Gradually, he felt more of her weight settle against his chest. With more time, he heard the sibilant snick of the measuring tape as it ran back into its steel case. It fell with a soft thud to the white shag rug the previous owner had left in the bay. Reaching down, her hands stroked his face, entreatingly.

"Demi-i-i . . ."

He smiled in recognition. He had heard that soft sigh of remonstrance before. She had used it New Year's. Then she had moaned, "Please . . ." The word framed an entire sentence, he thought: "Please don't make me walk to the couch and do that awful thing." And, all the while, she had been ready.

Now, her stomach writhing in his hands, he ignored that plea. He had the initiative. The problem lay in keeping it. As he weighed the next move, the stainless-steel tape measure, lying in the white shag, caught his eye.

Why not? he thought.

A sense of stealth had accompanied them through the empty house. Now, with rain coming, the gloom recalled the Saturday afternoon B movie mysteries he saw as a kid. If she felt it, too, he could preserve his advantage. So, speaking to her back, he gave it a try.

He had an idea, he told her. Why didn't she get off the ladder, so they could do something nice?

What?

Yes, he went on urgently. He got a laugh into his voice, so that it sounded as though he were choosing a picnic site. Here, on this nice shag rug, he explained.

She came down with all the athletic agility with which he credited her. She even managed to turn, so that when she landed she faced him.

He saw then the extent to which her friendships with the women in the family had bolstered her confidence. She knew how to say "No!" now.

Was he crazy? she demanded. Did he think she was some kind of animal he could take on the floor—that she'd sit down that night at her mother-in-law's table without having showered, with him all over her . . . in her?

He shrugged, trying to save the situation. The sweat filming her face gave him hope.

Where could they go? he asked. Nando and Euralia were across the street cooking for when he returned from the Knicks game with his pals.

"Then, damn you, forget it!" she told him.

Reaching under her dress to rearrange herself with a contemptuous lack of self-consciousness, she strode from the room.

He followed. He had to. Her touch still enveloped his hands.

He caught up with her in the kitchen, where she had left her coat, and sweet-talked her to the other side of the street. Then, sneaking her in the front door of his present house, he led her across the floorthrough room, up the spiral staircase, and down the hall to his bed.

So she had her way after all. She chose the time and place. She had made a stud out of him, he thought. That gave her control.

Determined to regain it, he brought her along with his tongue to a climactic shriek which had to be stifled with his hand. Any advantage he won he lost as quickly. Sober and undrugged, she had great strength. More often than not, her body rode under his completely off the bed. That contact now overloaded him with sensation. Gasping, whimpering in equal parts of ecstasy, guilt, and pain, he withdrew to see a disconcerting glitter lighting the cool emerald eyes watching him. Those shrewd, speculative glints mocked the tender, compassionate smile below them.

The hunter's instinct, he thought. She had had enough men to know or guess she had an unnatural effect on him. Fearful of how she might use her advantage, he sought to erase it. Rolling her over, he got her on her hands and knees, taking her through the legs. She readily complied, as if to say that nothing he did could wrest control from her. But by then he had gone too far to stop.

Later, he sat in the tub/shower. The finest spray at full pressure and highest temperature had pelted him for twenty minutes. After that, he knew, her imprint would still be as strong. It would be for days.

Before, somehow, only his hands had been involved. Now, from midthigh to chest, despite the rush of water, he felt warm, satiny flour spill over him.

And now, crazily, he thought, he wanted more.

Rising, he let the spray hit him full in the groin.

Fiona slowed down.

The rain coming harder now, she dawdled along the Expressway thinking about the pink stone house.

It would be just another example of what Honey had called "Saint-Nazaire modern" if Demi had his way, she thought. And judging from his actions that morning, he seemed to have that in mind.

Still, some of her ideas must have gotten through.

He had asked her to get the decorator's pass again for next Tuesday or Thursday. Or had he done that because of the other thing? she wondered.

No. He had said he wanted to see some other places, at Serendipity—before they had gone to the new house—when she mentioned walling one side of the dining room with sawed limestone. Arkie had a pal who got it cheap.

That would be more like it, she thought. A little quiet elegance. No one had to know where it came from. It would be worthwhile, too, to look in at Hanson Lamps, she reflected. A few, custom made with longer extension arms, would be perfect upstairs. As her mother had taught her, it never paid to skimp on anything that could be seen.

All the electrical fixtures, in fact, seemed to her to need replacing. But that, she knew, would take some doing with Demi's tight-fisted approach. She wanted to do something about the plumbing too. The tub off the master bedroom, for heaven's sake, had feet!

She would not call Demi until the following Thursday, she thought. Then they might get together the week after.

Let him wait for once.

Why give Arkie any cause for concern?

Arkie too would be discreet about that Saturday.

"We got a minute?" he asked as his older brother Steve turned the truck onto 25 and the road into Riverhead.

"What for?" Steve asked.

A stop at Peconic Bay Marine, Arkie said.

Was he buying another boat?

No, a friend of his wanted to race his Whaler down in Florida, Arkie lied, and he wanted him to put a little juice in the engines.

Okay. Steve, bigger than Arkie, straightened up behind the wheel in enthusiasm until his blue wool watch cap brushed the cab of the truck. No one knew more about engines than his little brother, the genius.

They wanted to see 100-horsepower Evinrudes, Arkie told the manager of Peconic Bay Marine.

The manager knew the Angelakos boys. To see or to buy? he asked.

Arkie smiled sheepishly. First to see, he said. Then to buy. He wanted to build in some pizzazz.

In the shop, the manager said. They had a couple there torn down.

The engines were clamped to rusty oil drums, their shafts and props submerged in the water inside. Their streamlined blue-and-white casings had been removed, as were the tops of the engine blocks.

Reaching into the red-and-black-checked wool jacket he wore winters ashore, Arkie took out a stainless-steel vernier caliper. Thumbing the button at the top of the rule, he spread the points.

"What are you doing?" Steve asked.

Measuring the cylinders, Arkie told him. Did he see the tops of the tubular sections set within each other in the engine block?

Yeah.

The inner one, about an eighth of an inch thick, was steel, the cylinder, Arkie said. The one around it, silvery, aluminum, absorbed heat. He wanted to shave the cylinder wall and use a bigger piston for more power.

How much could he shave off? Steve asked.

Maybe seventeen thousandths of an inch, Arkie said.

But then what would he do for pistons?

Buy spares for Ford truck engines, Arkie said. He would turn them down to size in his shop.

And how much power would that give him?

Arkie didn't know, but he said it had to help. Real power came from re-working the manifold. Designers ran the exhaust into the water to deaden sound. He would reroute it through the top of the engine block. With no back pressure to reduce revolutions, horsepower could increase by twenty percent. Then he intended to install a turbo-blower.

Did he mean a supercharger, like in cars?

Yeah. A guy in Long Island City would cast new tops for the engine blocks, allowing for manifold changes and the turbo-blower.

Reaching over to a workbench, Arkie lifted the top of an engine block per-haps eighteen inches long and showed Steve the alterations to be made.

And how much more power would that give him?

Another fifteen, twenty percent.

Jesus! Steve shook his head. He was talking thirty-five, forty percent more power. How fast would a sixteen-foot Whaler go with two bombs like that?

Arkie smiled sheepishly. He never said, for fear of scaring the guys who'd be running the boat. But it'd do about eighty, he guessed. In flat water, maybe eighty-five miles an hour.

Satisfied that the Evinrudes would do, Arkie led the way back to the show-room. There he bought two. Producing a roll of hundred-dollar bills, he counted out thirteen. The overage should be applied to the family account, he told the manager. He and Steve would settle later.

Two ninety-pound engines, packed in stout wooden shipping cases, were carried to the truck under the arms of the brothers Angelakos the way florists' delivery boys tote a dozen roses in their long, weightless cartons.

Would Steve drop them off at Long Island City the next time he came into New York? Arkie asked.

Steve nodded.

In the cab, though, he turned to Arkie. A bright man who could have gone to an Ivy League school to play football, he had a last question. If the cylinder walls were shaved, he asked, his broad swarthy forehead wrinkling the blue wool watch cap, wouldn't that shorten engine life?

Without doubt, he heard. The thinner the cylinder wall, the sooner it would wear through, especially at extremely high speeds.

Then those Evinrudes in the back of the truck—how long would they last? Going flat out?

Yeah. At full power.

About an hour.

Steve got the picture. A joke. In their blue-and-white engine cases, the motors would be "ringers." They would pass for 100-horsepower Evinrudes. But inside, each would have forty more horses. Still, something else seemed crazy enough to need an answer.

But who paid twelve hundred dollars for an hour's speed? he asked.

Anybody who had a big bet to win, Arkie said. "Only, for God's sake," he added, "don't tell Fiona."

Chuckling, Steve backed the truck out of the lot.

*January 27, 1967*
*London*
*Greenwich–New York City*

SOME STORES throughout the world achieve the status of shrines, and London has its share of these remarkable establishments. Foyle's, in Charing Cross Road, to name one, has the pull of Mecca to booklovers. The showrooms of Holland and Holland, with matched pairs of shotguns at $25,000 a set displayed, have similar appeal to hunters. Anglers pay homage at Hardy's, in Pall Mall, where they revel in rooms filled with exquisite bamboo fly rods.

Foreign yachtsmen, with equal ardor, find their way to Piccadilly Circus and then a hundred yards or so up Albemarle Street to the shop of Captain O. M. Watts, Ltd.

The Whaler for Arkie's Evinrudes was bought there.

The buyer, a dapper little fellow with gold-rimmed spectacles, pencil-line mustache, and heavy Middle European accent, represented himself as Maxime Masiloff, a French national with Nice and Paris addresses.

To the delight of management, M. Masiloff in fact bought two Whalers, sister ships. A raffish tilt supplied to black homburg by an ivory-headed cane, he explained his purchase with a lascivious roll of watery-blue middle-aged eyes. He occasionally financed films, he said. With a place on the Riviera, in that business, he needed two boats to keep the girls from tearing each other to pieces over him.

The manager and the clerk waiting on M. Masiloff nodded agreeably. Catering to European yachtsmen, they understood excess. Moreover, the old lecher had so much money his personal check came from London's Rothschild's bank. With that bit of authenticity, man and story went the way of most things typical. They were forgotten.

Leaving instructions for the boats to be delivered to Nice in April, M. Masiloff, the morning's first customer, wished everyone well. Sauntering out, homburg at rakish angle, he strode up Albemarle Street with the air of a man whose day had started gloriously.

Three thousand miles to the west, the morning began less auspiciously.

Hubie Garrison, home for a day in the office after two weeks of looking for money, opened the right rear door as the Cadillac came to a stop.

"So?" he demanded.

Smile abruptly fading, Loren Wade scrambled in from the darkness, threw the white Stetson over the partition, and settled back, unclasping his trousers. That did it for the Pacific Northwest, he thought.

Lumbermen, supposedly choking on a half-billion dollars in cash from a recent boom in housing starts, apparently invested only in trees.

Confirmation of that theory came at once.

"Well?" Hubie insisted, as if getting even.

"Oh, man," Wade sighed, "talk about a mean squeeze. Here I ain't even had a chance to say hello, let alone get my tunky down on the seat, an' you're hammerin'—"

"Fuck hello and your tunky too, Loren! You tell me about Angelakos! Demi get anythin' off him so far?"

"He ain't even seen him yet—won't till two weeks from next Monday—"

"Goddammit, that's the middle of February!"

"I know."

"Jesus Christ!" Hubie muttered, flinging away his copy of the *Wall Street Journal* in frustration. "Won't anythin' around here go right? You're not even started yet, an' you're already runnin' short on time. When did Mrs. A tell Honey that Archimedes had to be in Japan again—in April?"

"Judas priest, Hube! Give him a chance to breathe, will you? He never made it back here from Nippon till the thirteenth, an' the day after he was at Taki's an' Honey's with his ol' lady, cryin' his eyes out over all the work come into his shop from Gulf while he was gone. Now, you want us to lean on him, so he starts wonderin' why he can't have ten workin' days to do the job right—'specially on a first revise, where there ain't even buildin' bids out yet? Besides, you never know what'll happen in the meantime. Tomorrow the four of 'em are goin' out to Altenkirch's on the Island to buy some boat rods an' have supper. It's comin' along better'n we coulda hoped—they're all gettin' tight with each other."

"An' Demi?"

"Spoke to him yesterday. Tol' him he better keep Fiona sweet, 'cause we're really gonna put the boots to her ol' man on the revisions."

"Fiona?"

Wade tipped his head and smiled insinuatingly. " 'We' call Mrs. A Fiona," he said. "Anyways, he told me he seen her last week an' was havin' lunch with her next—she's got the hots to help decorate his new house. Oh, yeah."

"An' while they're all gettin' chummy, the clock's still tickin'!" Hubie protested. "You got ten, twelve weeks at most, only you don't dare show yourself or say anythin'. So what in hell do we do in the meantime?"

"Keep puckered," Wade advised.

"You call that a strategy?"

Crossing his legs, Wade reached up to turn on the reading light. Then, taking out his manicurist's white pencil, he went to work on his nails.

" 'Course," he said in a faintly mocking tone as he regarded his right hand under the lamp, "it's still your comp'ny. If you got a better idea—or can't stand the suspense—just play your ace."

"What ace?"

"The one you got in the hole—up on Seventy-fourth Street."

"Not yet—maybe not ever."

Hubie glanced across the back seat with increased respect. Trust little Loren, he thought. Nothing went by him. He knew where to get the money, too. It had always been there—two billion dollars, or four, whatever he needed. He would as soon go broke first, though, as ask for it.

"You know your Koran," he told Wade. "Remember the part that goes: 'Take what you want and pay for it, so saith the Lord'? What do you think our little ace in the hole'd cost if we went there for it empty-handed?"

Nodding, Wade buffed his nails on his lapel.

"Then keep puckered," he said.

*February 16, 1967*
*New York City–Lyford Cay*

EVELYN'S VOICE rose poolside in Nassau.

"Ah, yes!" he said into the phone. The Admiral of the Ocean Sea had just called? To him that meant Costa Lianides, a man for whom he had developed considerable respect in recent months.

"And what had that worthy to say, Prentiss?"

Knee propped against the edge of the antique cherry dining table, Howsam summed up the week's events.

The first revise on the convertible plans, he said, had gone to Demosthenes Monday, the thirteenth, on schedule. He liked the ideas fine, but wanted his uncle, in San Juan on a ship survey, to see them when he got back.

That killed Tuesday.

Wednesday, Demosthenes had booked a private dining room in the New York Yacht Club, and the three of them had had a working lunch. Its net effect boiled down to at least another month's design work.

The designer took changes in stride. The alterations, however, puzzled him, he told the Admiral of the Ocean Sea, who just happened to be in Long Island City that afternoon. The work involved pumps and piping and took a grasp of hydrodynamics. He knew that the uncle and Demosthenes had good working knowledge of modern ships. But somehow he never thought they had theory as well.

That poor, poor clod, Evelyn sighed. The theory, he said, came from the little tyke. It had to. He knew more about the subject than anyone else.

Of course, Howsam agreed. The design changes bought the cowboys another month for Demosthenes to romance the lady in question.

Oh, yes. Yes indeed. And that proceeded swimmingly, the droll baritone voice in the Bahamas continued. The lady could be seen in the neighborhood of Forty-ninth Street and Second Avenue two or three times a week.

How did he know that? Howsam asked.

The same way he knew she also drove a green Pontiac station wagon, Evelyn said. He had a pal, he went on, savoring a new turn of phrase, who "carried lotsa juice" in the Seventeenth Precinct.

That brought a smile of recognition. Itch Cohen talked that way. "You clever bastard," Howsam said into the phone.

One used what was available, came the modest reply. Flattery, however, did not diminish vigilance. "But, Prentiss . . . ?" Evelyn continued uneasily.

Yeah?

Was the designer really that thick?

Thick?

Not at least to have sensed something.

Why should he? Howsam asked. If he was dumb enough to think the convertible order just flew in by accident, without a connection to something else, how much would he need before he started suspecting his wife?

And he hadn't told her?

Oh, Christ, no! Howsam said. He had asked Costa that again not ten minutes before and got the very same answer: absolutely not! The designer was a *malaca*. He did what he was told.

Poor sot, Evelyn sympathized, so thick.

Not thick, trusting, Howsam answered.

Even worse, came the reply from the Bahamas.

*February 28, 1967*
*New York City*

WADE WOULD fly to Curaçao later that morning.

From there he would go to Maracaibo, in Venezuela, and then to Trinidad. So the ride in had been devoted to reviewing events likely to take place in the marine division during the next eight days.

The discussion had continued in the Dorset. Now, the usual bowl of Scottish oatmeal eaten, and woefully shaking his head at his second cup of Postum, Hubie raised the question which most concerned him.

"An' when's the good ship Angelakos sail?" he asked.

The subject had last come up Friday, four days earlier, a record so far, Wade noted, for restraint. The answer had not changed. Still, he knew, it had to be restated, and without any smart-assed comments.

Hubie, Wade saw, had wound himself about as tightly as a man could. In '56, what with Nasser, Acey's death, and the Niarchos' move on charter rates, he had become ashen. Then the operations had begun. Now, despite light-gray pinstriped flannels and a yellow shirt, the first signs of that coloring could be seen again. His face had charcoal shadows. So Wade answered fully, knowing it made Hubie feel in control. This time, too, he added a detail Taki had given him the night before.

"The ship sails March fifth," he said. "Mrs. A's goin' down Thursday or Friday for a week or so at Marina's on Hobe Sound to play ten—"

"I thought you said she was goin' to see her ma."

"I did, but when I heard Florida, I assumed."

"She's movin' right into the family, ain't she?"

"Why not, with a husband in that game? For all I know, she maybe sees herself in the new house too. Her kind makes lots of nice first marriages. Anyways, with her gone, Demi's gonna spend Sunday with Archimedes over to his joint in Long Island City an' take the plans to Taki. Then, Wednesday, when I come back from Trinidad, I'll get my licks in at lunch."

And how much time did that leave?

Six, eight weeks.

Was that enough?

Plenty, Wade said. He knew what to revise next. Moreover, the nature of the change would fly right by Demi and Taki. But the Lions would find a message there. And, bet on it, they would answer. The first part of their secret, the when, the date Arkie left for Japan and when he expected to return, came to them from Honey, who got it from Mrs. A. That had been an accident, he said. The what would not be.

Why?

Wade used the Lions' word: insurance.

Admittedly, in deference to Hubie's condition, that put the best face on the situation. Still, he believed he had a fifty-fifty chance, which beat hell out of the odds you bucked trying to raise $2 billion.

Insurance? Hubie asked.

You been chasing money too long, Wade said. Reaching out with the silver coffeepot, he half filled Hubie's cup and topped off his own.

"Cheat a little." He smiled, winking at the coffee. "You may need it." Then, leaning forward, elbows on tablecloth, cup in hands masking mouth, he explained insurance.

Halfway through, Hubie extended his cup for a refill. "You mean we're bein' watched?" he asked.

" 'Course we are. Have been, probably, since Labor Day. That's why they let Archimedes do the convertibles in the first place—so's they'd have Demi under lock an' key, where they could watch him an' keep him quiet. How do they know who he's gonna talk to in the meantime? Now, if you were them, an' he come by wavin' twenty-five million bucks in his hot little hands, wouldn't you be just the least bit nosy 'bout where he got that dough? I sure as hell'd be. That's why I'm gonna send 'em a message. Anyways, that's their problem. I got one of my own. What I need now's an out."

"An out?"

"Sure, 'cause this time, unless I'm wronger'n hell, we'll get the what—if we get it at all—from Mrs. A. With her out fuckin' up a storm for the comp'ny good, I got this sneaky little hunch Archimedes don't have no more idea what's goin' on here'n Demi or Taki."

Cup out for more coffee, Hubie leaned forward. "You mean they're lettin' her bang—"

" 'Course they are! It's another way of keepin' Demi busy an' out of trouble. If you think they maybe know by now where he got his money, you gotta believe they been watchin' her too—Archimedes is too big a part of the package for 'em not to—an' they don't mind young love, neither. Why in hell should they? Who's hurt? So it's obvious, as of now, she don't know no more 'bout what's playin' down at the Bijou'n we do. If she did, an' it scared 'em, how tough would it be to slip her daddy word she was maybe spreadin' her ass round a little? Hell, that wouldn't even have to come from a stranger! His cousin Lianides'd do that. What the hell else is he here for but to look things over?"

"But you're sayin' we need the out for Demi?"

"Exactly. So's we can play our ace."

Sipping his coffee, Hubie still looked baffled. "I don't get it," he said.

"It's somethin' I overlooked," Wade admitted. "The way the line of communication works on this, he's gonna get the news before we do. You think he's gonna settle for runnin' three convertibles if this thing turns out to be as big as we think it is?"

"Christ," Hubie confessed in return, "I never saw a chance for this to work, so that never occurred to me, either. He'll want the moon!"

"An' then some. We'll wind up workin' for him."

"An' what about Taki?"

"You kiddin'? Demi share? Hell, by the time he gets done with us, we'll be all hung out to dry. He don't need Taki to know what he's got."

"Jesus, Loren, what're you gonna do?" Hubie asked.

For answer, he got the Levantine sign of shrewdness, tip of forefinger pulling at the bottom of the right eye. Somehow, on Loren Wade, despite his being fat, sandy-haired, and unmistakably Anglo-Saxon, the gesture fit.

It did nothing, however, to solve his problem.

He thought then in terms of aces and outs.

The violent combination of the two would not occur to him until June 5.

*March 6, 1967*
*New York City–Lyford Cay*

BACK RIGID, Howsam turned in the Windsor armchair.

"Yeah," he said into the phone.

"Good morning, Prentiss," Evelyn replied. "Good—"

"What's up?"

"Why, nothing's up. I just wondered if you hadn't heard a small note of reassurance over the weekend."

"You mean from the meeting yesterday in Long Island City? No, and I won't. The Admiral of the Ocean Sea's afraid of looking too nosy, so he's giving that beat a rest until Thursday. The designer and Demosthenes are having lunch again then, anyway, so that's when I guess the job'll be okayed or sent back to the drawing board."

"Bright," Evelyn said approvingly. "Our Admiral's a chap with a sense of nuance, but, actually, Prentiss, I had rather another sort of note of reassurance in mind. With you and the dwarf so dubious about the event going forward, I'd wondered if you'd read your Sunday *Times*. It reported an incident you'd find of interest and, in a melancholy way, encouraging as well. It's hardly the usual smash-and-grab type of thing Mother's neighbors go in for, where a few children are killed. This suggests future activity of a more organized sort. It puts me in mind of going to the theater and hearing a musician or two warming up in the pit. You know then the overture can't be far behind—just a matter of time."

"Where's the story?"

"You'll find it on page three of the first section. And, Prentiss, when was it you said Demosthenes and the designer were lunching?"

"Thursday, the ninth."

"And the Admiral'll be in Long Island City later that afternoon?"

"That's the plot. Then we're having supper."

"I see. I wonder, Prentiss, are you free to fly to Montreal Friday morning? I've some business you should look at, too, so it'd be a worthwhile day."

He sensed something, Howsam thought. He had no idea what it might be, but he felt better. For Evelyn to come north, the deal had to be on.

"Sure," he answered. "My pleasure."

"Leave your flight number at my office, and they'll have MacKenzie at the gate to drive you in."

Switching phone buttons, Howsam called downstairs, to a girl named Carol who clipped magazine and newspaper articles for reference. She had the Sunday *Times*.

He read the story, feeling fear, greed, and sorrow. On March 5 an Israeli farmer, plowing a field near Kibbutz Shamir, on the Syrian border, had been injured when his tractor struck a land mine.

Nothing smash-and-grab about that. That suggested practice, or seeding an infantry escape route. Otherwise, why waste a mine?

*March 8, 1967*
*New York City*

OLD ARCHIMEDES had outdone himself, Wade thought.

The plans were perfect. If the project were real, he would skip tank tests. He knew enough about hull lines to see when plans offered eighteen and three quarters knots. Moreover, his fifty-odd tankers, with every type of loading and off-loading system, had given him a college education in tanks and piping. Archimedes, he guessed, had a Ph.D. in each subject.

Which left only one way to go, he knew, to get a message to the Lions. He had to set up a strawman.

In the meantime, he saw, the Prince of Forty-ninth Street lounged against the steps of the spiral staircase. With his hands in the pockets of the brown-and-white-checked sports coat and sun streaming in on him, he outsmugged whiskey-ad men of distinction. He had the right, Wade thought. He had done the job. No one in the PANARTEX office could have guided Archimedes better. Demi knew a hell of a lot of shipping.

That knowledge dictated the strategy. First, the work needed praising. After that, Wade believed, the talk would steer itself. So, lifting the ashtrays off the right side of the cocktail table in front of the green velour couch, he let the plans roll themselves up. Then he threw out his arms.

"You done it, Babes! I'll swear an' be goddamned if you didn't! There's more here'n I asked for!"

Demi's smile grew into a smirk. "It has its points," he said modestly.

"Good Lord Almighty, yes! On a scale of ten, that little sucker weighs in eleven! Has Archimedes got a modelmaker goin' an' tank time lined up so's we can show Hubie hull speeds an' not give him no place to hide?"

Demi shook his head. "Not yet. I thought you'd better sign off first."

"Oh, man," Wade sighed, moving the strawman into position. "That shoots another week."

"I'll call him right away. The modelmaker's the cheapest part. We could pay him overtime."

Nodding, Wade slid the left side of the plans from beneath the ashtrays, holding them on the cocktail table. Demi had put them there that morning, before they met for lunch. The kid had been in a hurry, he thought, watching the sheets coil into the roll. He had covered a matchbook. Its front bore the red-and-white burgee of the Manhasset Bay Yacht Club, Mrs. A's. She had gone down to Marina's last Friday for a week or ten days of tennis, and here she was, back in town early. Had to be here. He knew how that went. He had that problem, too. She could have come in yesterday, he knew, but that would have cut the visit too short. So, he guessed, she had landed that morning, and Demi's phony limo had taken her here to matinee. That explained his being late for lunch. With the strawman in place, however, he looked away from the matchbook and got on with sending a message.

"An' the specs?" he asked.

"Next Monday. He needs the weekend to get numbers together. That piping system you like'll take a fortune in custom foundry work."

"I'm smit," Wade acknowledged. "Give him all the time he needs, but remember numbers never built zilch. We gotta get that model started."

"He'll be on it this afternoon, Loren."

"Okay, just so's we don't lose no more time. But what's your guess we're talkin'—ballpark costs?"

Demi shrugged. "At the low end, nine million five a ship; at the top, nine million eight-fifty," he said, still leaning casually against the spiral staircase.

That raised the strawman to his knees, Wade mused. He had, in fact, first considered price as his decoy in sending a message to the Lions, but rejected it because of its obviousness. It would never get past Demi and Taki. They expected him to know what convertibles cost. Then, searching for another idea, he got the answer. Money played a role, but time bore the burden. More important, the new ploy gave him the white hat, let him be the good guy. So, hearing that estimate, he commiserated, mainly with himself, for Demi's benefit.

"Oh, Babes," he moaned, flopping back on the green velour couch, "what're you doin' to me?"

"What do you mean, Loren?"

"I mean where do I find that kind of dough? Didn't I say goin' in we had twenty-five million dollars to build three hundred thousand tons?"

"Sure you did, but you never said it was firm. You know convertibles run fifteen to twenty percent more than regular tankers."

" 'Course I do! Christ, Demi, where do you think I got the twenty-five million dollars in the first place? Hubie gave me seventy dollars a ton—the goin' price for new ships—an' tol' me if I was so keen on convertibles, I could eat that fifteen to twenty percent plaster outa my operatin' budget."

That came over, Wade knew, as pure Hubie. He liked to say oil companies made money finding oil. Ships were there to save a few bucks.

Accepting that, Demi still had no cause for alarm. Having sailed in Straits Transits, Ltd., and been the nominal head of another hidden subsidiary, he knew a bit about normal PANARTEX operating procedures.

"What about your egg money?" he asked, smiling.

"That's how come there's twenty-five million dollars in the kitty to begin with," Wade retorted. "As a matter of fact, I give you guys more'n a twenty percent cushion, so's for once we'd do something right."

Nodding, Demi tried another rational approach. "Well, I don't say being twenty percent over budget is any way to run a business, but it's even dumber, isn't it, not to bite the bullet for another four million dollars when there's a hundred waiting to be made?"

"It sure as hell would be in Esso, Gulf, or Texaco," Wade agreed. "But we're talkin' Hubie now, an' he don't care squat 'bout a hundred million dollars. That's for accountants. He's thinkin' riches of the earth! Billions—who in hell knows, maybe trillions! So he's got his eyes on that twenty-one million dollars I euchred outa him, an', so far's he's concerned, that's twenty-one million dollars he can't put in the ground for that great come-together day he taps the underside of the China oil dome an' we all sit on a golden throne forever after, eatin' lamb with the Lord, as the A-rabs say."

That too presented an authentic picture.

"I think we'd better scrap the new pumping system, then, and go back to what we had," Demi said.

"Won't do, Babes."

"I don't say it's not great for safety, Loren," Demi conceded, fixing blame for the overage, "but before it and the new tanks came into the picture, we were right on budget."

"I know." Wade nodded sorrowfully. "But we'd only be kiddin' ourselves. You seen any figures lately on world oil consumption?"

"Sure. It's rising. The Japs and West Germany are finally getting their manufacturing in stride."

"Exactly. An' in five years or so, when we get the boot from the Pentagon, tanker demand'll pass tonnage. Then, with all them ships, an' more comin' off the waves ev'ry month, we'll see accidents you won't believe! An' not just collisions at sea, but dumb stuff like oil spills or blowin' up in downtown Newark or Philadelphia, 'cause then it'll be like baseball. Sure, you got all them expansion teams in the bigs, but how many can play? An' while all that's goin' on, we'll see Thor Heyerdahl on TV tellin' us our naughty tankers're makin' a garbage dump outa the oceans, or that frog Cousteau sayin' we already killed 'em—not to mention the Sierra Club an' God knows who else'll finger us for—"

"I hear that already from East Side liberals," Demi said, waving his hand as if they were present.

"Sure, 'cause lots of it's true."

Having gone around the barn to justify the convertibles' pumping systems, Wade now applied the clincher. "An' what'll happen then," he asked, "to insurance on five-year-old ships without safety systems put in by Father an' blessed by Holy Ghost? I predict, that'll go through the roof, that's what! An' us stuck with three with fifteen years of operatin' life in 'em? No, thanks."

That conclusion caught Demi totally by surprise. Moreover, the economics brooked no argument.

But, glib as ever, he tried another idea. "Well, then, let's scale them down! They only came out to a hundred eight thousand tons because the hull seemed to work best that way. I bet if we shaved two feet of beam off—"

"You'd be back to maybe a hundred thousand tons, with maybe a million-and-a-half-buck saving, an' that'd be it. If you went any smaller, you'd need a fourth ship." Wade sighed. "You read the terms in that bid same's me."

Nodding, Demi absently reached up to comb the cowlick from his forehead.

"But if we got them down to a hundred thousand tons," he said, "we'd only be two and a half, three million over budget. Do you mean to say, Loren, that Hubie'd walk away from a hundred million dollars then?"

"You wanna go sell him that?"

"I'd sure as hell try."

"I'll only tell you," Wade said ruefully, reporting truthfully, "he just leased another eight hundred square miles in western Canada, an' he's even skippin' cinnamon on his oatmeal so's his belly's in shape to be there six, eight months from now when the riches of the earth come gusherin' in. The only reason it might be eight months instead of six is he's out scratchin' round for twelve million dollars he don't even have in his exploration budget to get those holes down. Your timing'd kill you."

"But that's nuts, Loren! That's not business."

"Maybe not, but it's Hubie," Wade said, again in truth. "You're forgettin' somethin'. We may call him chairman of the board, but deep down, when he's sittin' on the crapper all alone, with the door locked, thinkin' his thoughts, he's still Acey's partner—a wildcatter. An' you know what makes those guys different? They want it *now!* Don't go talkin' to him 'bout a hundred-million-dollar payout over five years, 'cause he'll laugh you right out of the Time-Life Building. He's lookin' for that in six, eight months—an' the hell of it is, he's hit like that before an' will again—so convertibles don't move him!"

Shaking his head, Demi went for his cowlick again. He looked panicked, Wade thought. Sure, he saw everything going.

*Now!*

Rising, he cut off further protest.

"I think you better get Archimedes on the horn, an' call a halt," he said, stuffing his shirttails into the trousers of the blue serge suit he wore for lunches at Lutèce, "at least till we rethink—"

"When? There's no time! You just told me I blew a week not getting the model started. Well, he has to go back to Japan in five—"

Trousers still open, Wade abruptly sat down.

Seeing his look of shock, Demi had interrupted himself. "What's wrong?" he demanded. "I told you that! Why in God's name do you think I kept pleading with you to make things simp—"

"Oh, Jesus! Jesus, Jesus, Jesus . . ." Wade moaned. "I know, I know, Babes. I'm blamin' *me,* not you. I've had this thing in my head on Archimedes for three weeks, 'cause I guessed he'd maybe go over budget an' put us in even worser shape on time doin' more revisions. Your sayin' Japan now, the handle just come to me."

Demi, who had moved closer to more forcefully blame him for the time bind, turned to him questioningly.

"Archimedes put them stretched T-2s of his together in Nippon, didn't he?" Wade asked.

"Right. He built ninety-foot midships sections in a Dutch yard and then towed them to Japan, where they were spliced into the hulls."

"That's what I thought!" Wade snapped. "But I lost it. Must have. Anyways, that's how we can maybe get well on the time an' dough."

"What is?"

"Remember—you give me a real slow jerk on what else those midships sections could be?"

"Sure. To Arkie, they were floating drydocks."

"Well, now I'm askin', what else could they be?"

Demi shook his head.

"Modules," Wade snickered. He would pay dearly for that later, he thought. For now, however, it got the strawman on his feet. One thing at a time.

Demi, meanwhile, tapped a Schimmelpenninck cigar on its long, thin metal case. He had been alarmed, of course, that Wade might pull the plug. But instinct said there had to be a saver. No one walked on $100 million that fast. Still, he knew, Hubie might. This made the possibility, however unlikely, scary.

Beyond that, his confidence had eroded. Proud of his shipping knowledge, he had taken two hard ego shots. The first came on budget. Questioning Wade for wanting costly safety systems, he had missed what might happen to insurance. The second blow hurt more. That had just come.

A master ad-libber, he had been beaten to a saver. Moreover, the idea gave them the edge mentioned in August. If Arkie could do it, they had a breakthrough. But, caught between chagrin, resentment, and relief, he tended to distrust his deliverance. It could be too good to be true.

"You're talking about modular construction?" he asked.

Wade nodded. "How else can we do it? Time is money, an' that's the fastest way known to man to get a ship built. So, it solves the time bind: when we need 'em—an' the dough bind: which is to save twenty percent."

"Which is all great in theory except for one fact: so far, no one's been able to do it."

"I know. But who's tried? A bunch of little Japs who stand round the shipyard gates mornin's to sing the comp'ny song an' do exercises! Anybody like Archimedes? Hell, no! Christ, Babes, if everybody thought like you, where'd the zipper be? You 'fraid to be first?"

Still skeptical, Demi raised another objection. "In a leaky boat, yes."

Nodding, Wade met the safety issue head on. "As between leaky convertibles an' no convertibles, which'd you rather have? Besides, who says Archimedes can't keep 'em from fallin' apart?"

Lighting a French match, Demi's hand shook. He had all he could do now to contain his relief. Still, one factor kept him from being optimistic.

Reaching past Wade's knee, he picked up the plans. "He leaves in five weeks," he said, brandishing the roll, "and he says there's a thousand hours here. So he's almost two hundred short if he works twenty-four hours a day going in on the modular version. You think he'll have time?"

"That's *his* problem. If he'd quit bein' so Greek, he'd hire a few draftsmen an' have it whipped."

"Christ, Loren, I was just there Sunday, and he had three of them in. He says that thousand hours is just his thinking time."

"Well, now it's easier. We just done his thinkin' for him. We told him to go modular. He wants a check for two hundred fifty thousand dollars, he'll figure out the rest."

Afraid of disappointment, Demi remained dubious. "And after we've got the plans—what then? There isn't a yard in the world who can build modular."

"Christ, Demi, I never said any yard's gonna go put up a steel mill, but the way business is, I think lots of guys'll take another look at how much modular they can do short of that—an' that's all we need, ain't it? That way, we got a shot. Otherwise, it's all she wrote."

Like leaky convertibles, it beat no shot.

Still, Demi had to sell it. "But, Jesus, Loren—he's got to sleep."

"Sure, but on his time—not ours! How much is he into us for, anyways, as of now?"

"Forty-one five."

That made it message time for Wade. "Okay. You call him, an' lay it all out. An' if he starts to whine 'bout his sleep, or his other work, or his old lady, or whatever, you tell him either he guarantees a full set of modularized construction plans before he goes to Nippon or you'll pay him off in full an' go talk to somebody else."

Typical Wade. Full ahead! with or without Arkie. That made it real to Demi.

He nodded. "Don't worry. I'll tell him, and we'll start the model. I'll call Fiona too. She'll help."

Message delivered, Wade started on his shirttails. Rising, he shook his head at the plans offered him. "You keep 'em," he said, putting more pressure on Demi. "I don't show Hubie maybes. Jus' let me hear from you this afternoon."

Then, walking the length of the floorthrough room, he paused before the Forty-ninth Street window to don black raincoat and white Stetson.

"Remember," he shouted, "if he don't guarantee delivery, you'll go talk to somebody else. Say it just like that: you'll go talk to somebody else."

That had to do it, he thought, letting himself out. The Lions had to get that message.


*March 10, 1967*
*Montreal*
*Hydra, Greece*
*New York City*


HOWSAM BROUGHT the message to Montreal.

Evelyn considered it.

Lips pursued ruminatively, he sat at a gold-embossed leather-topped desk, surrounded by a fortune in Regency antiques. Outside, a Calgary Express, his name for a blizzard coming from the western provinces, swirled by his twenty-second-floor office window in Place Ville-Marie. He treated weather with the contempt it deserved, he told Howsam. So, wishing to be in Nassau, he wore a pale-tan summer suit as if he were.

Nor did he seem the least intimidated by the news. On the contrary, his face, burned a deep iodine, wore its usual on-holiday smile.

"Demosthenes said it just like that?" he asked.

"I made Lianides repeat it: '. . . or else he'd go talk to somebody else.' "

"Well, that's certainly pointed enough. But whom, exactly, do you suppose they have in mind, Prentiss?"

"You got a phone book? I made a list coming here. Try the CIA, or the U.S. State Department, or their landlord in the Persian Gulf, the Emirate of Armpits, or Egypt, or even their bankers, or—"

"Or none of the above."

"Absolutely. Is puzzlement."

"But they've not run to head either," Evelyn said, harking back to English boarding-school talk to describe the situation. "So, if one wishes," he went on, peering across a dazzlingly yellow Quimper teacup, "one can take that in it self, too, as a sort of signal—"

"You mean about intent?"

"Umh-hmm."

"You've ruled out a bluff?"

"One daren't rule out anything. Still, where's the gain? From what we know of our chums, they're nothing if not goal-oriented."

"I got that far myself," Howsam acknowledged. "So what do we do?"

"First, I'm to be kept in the shade. Just so long as there's no face to connect you and my client, there's no harm done. Wars breed all sorts of wild tales and stirring dramas, many true, but they're not to be believed, because once the story's told, authors can never find flesh-and-blood characters to step forward. Clear?"

"I told that to Schotten a year ago."

"Yes. I'm sure Ike taught you that early on. Then we have to respond, and no later than— When do Angelakos and Lianides leave?"

"Monday, April seventeenth."

"So be it! We'll take that, then, as our deadline for silencing the hounds— and the later, the better. In point of fact, if we could engineer things round to happen on the sixteenth, we'd eliminate the problem of reaction time altogether, and that'd be best by far."

"Sure. But how do you . . . shut them up?"

The deep, rich baritone voice, warming in color as if it were making an inconsequential request, also echoed the smile in its boyish mischievousness. "I wonder, Prentiss," it purred as a forefinger traced tentative circles in the maroon leather desktop, "if you'd send me Lianides."

That meant only one thing to Howsam. He had, of course, pondered Evelyn's intentions as soon as word came back that Wade had seen the ships in Japan. Knowing the man and the situation, two answers had come to him. Both were distasteful. One strategy meant murder; the other risk. This course, unimagined, combined both.

The stitch marks in the bridge of his nose whitened. "What!" he shouted.

Evelyn, sipping tea, raised a hand in demurrer. "Eric agreed it might be the thing to do if this happened," he said, lowering the cup.

"He did? When?"

"In January. After his week with you in Marathon."

"Why wasn't I told?"

"Because I thought it best to insulate Lianides."

"Him? From what?"

"From what he might think of as a negative. I'd no idea then, you see, he'd be such a stalwart."

"Jesus, he's bulletproof."

"So I've learned. Well, now I want to chat him up a bit, so he can have a word with Angelakos."

"Here?"

Evelyn shook his head.

"You can't use Nassau either. You'd be traced."

"I know. But with this tan and all, I think I look sufficiently local to pass myself off as the master of Halfway Tree. Of course, I'm not tall and wiry, and I don't have a black mustache either, but think of the fun that'd cause after, if someone told a naughty tale out of school. Anyway, the laird of that particular fief'll be away on another little errand for Home Office and he said to give it a try. What do you think?"

Halfway Tree lay outside Kingston, Jamaica. It belonged to another client of Howsam's, Rupert Stone-Martin, who, like Evelyn, had a Sabra wife and a Special Night Squads past. After selling off a fortune in bauxite to ALCOA, he had become a Caribbean trading Tai-Pan. His hotel, oil, and sugar holdings ran from Bermuda to Trinidad and across to Venezuela.

Howsam could only shake his crewcut head. "Boy, have you got balls," he said.

"I?" Evelyn modestly protested. "You should have seen our friend the dwarf. There's *chutzpah* for you! That chap'll take a back seat to no one in the gumption department. I assure you, I trod very lightly putting this to him. The whole brilliant idea, after all, came from him, and he'd put twenty million dollars of his own in it, so he'd the right to be shirty as you please. Instead, he had the words beatified and sanctified before I'd even got them out. Said we had a classic move there."

"He did? Eric?"

"Indeed. Even supplied chapter and verse as well; 'The art of power is not how to use your friends, but how to use your enemies.' "

"Not a bad line."

"I should say not, and it's from Napoleon, who—"

Rising, Evelyn pursued a more pressing subject. "Good Lord, Prentiss," he exclaimed, consulting his watch, "it's five after twelve! And in this season," he said drolly, pointing to a sky white with snow, "that's the time *cassoulet* ships dock all over Montreal. We'd best get cracking!"

On Hydra that year, seasonal patterns did not hold.

Usually, with little or no tourist business until May, the island's winter population consisted mainly of women, children, and family patriarchs. Able-bodied men who, summers, tended bar, bellhopped, waited tables, and ran boats were on the mainland working in factories, or at sea.

All, that is, but the Angelakoses. They, instead, were coming home, causing much local speculation.

The gossip, in fact, had begun ten days earlier.

Yorka, a lame ship's cook and baker, even slower in the head, landed then on the Piraeus ferry. That night, roaring drunk in Taverna Poseidon, dockside to Hydra's watch-charm harbor, he told Archangelo, the owner, he wanted to buy the place.

With what? Archangelo asked.

With this! Yorka said. His coin purse hung from a chain around his neck. Opening it, he counted out sixteen U.S. hundred-dollar bills.

It would take many times that, Archangelo told him.

By summer he would have many times that, Yorka said.

The next day, an even stranger incident occurred.

Fotis, a clan elder, waited at the dock to take the ferry back to Piraeus. A brawny graybeard who repaired yacht engines summers, he wore a shiny black suit seen only at Christmas, Easter, christenings, and funerals. That indicated serious business on the mainland. A retired chief engineer, he answered the questions of his dockside buddies with the modesty of a long-faded Hollywood starlet who had been suddenly recalled to play a plum character part. He had a delivery job, he said, that a former owner felt could be entrusted only to him.

Everyone wished him well. Poor Fotis, all recalled, had not been to sea since the fifties, when he had been shipwrecked in the Philippines. Before that, a ship of his had gone down off Turkey.

Two days later, Zavitsanos returned. A captain, he had spent the last four years coasting Brazil in a T-2. Locals wondered. Unlike other Hydra men who had been in that trade, he came home untanned. He sported, instead, an eau de cologne, identified as Parisian, and wore a fine English tweed suit and the best shoes seen on the island in decades.

The ferry after his disgorged his younger cousins George and Alexander. Bright, good-looking fellows who had gone to the national maritime college, they served as deck officers in Karageorgis passenger ships. Sure to be captains, they surprised neighbors by saying they had left their berths for a better opportunity.

The next ferry brought their younger brother, Nico. He had left the maritime college, he told the curious, to assess his future. He wondered if he wanted a career at sea. In the meantime, since they would all be away most of the summer, he said, he and the other boys would whitewash their widowed mother's house.

The last to arrive were the sons of Fotis: Ioannis, Orestes, and Theodosius. Engineering officers like their father, they spent the time at home as all marine engineers did. Making the rounds of family houses, they repaired electrical and plumbing systems and did odd bits of carpentry.

So, by March 10, Archangelo began to wonder.

Looking across his bar in the Poseidon to the right-hand corner of the room, where Zavitsanos presided over the nightly meeting, only Angelakoses were visible. Physically, the family produced the biggest men on the island. But Archangelo's speculations went beyond awe that the windows overlooking the harbor were blocked out, or that three tables for four were required to seat nine men. His thoughts concerned lost wages.

They had enough officers there, he noted, to man a ship.

He wondered why.

By March 10 Demi too had a riddle to ponder. He believed Wade had saved the convertibles. Still, a doubt kept nagging at him. But, try as he might, he kept missing its handle.

*March 11, 1967*
*New York City*
*Long Island City*

FIONA STAMPED her foot.

The phone booth seemed to be getting smaller. Shifting the receiver, she stretched her back. Where was he? she wondered. He had said he'd be there. Sighing, she looked at her watch. Four-thirty-five. Almost too late. Still . . .

The ringing stopped abruptly. "Fiona!" Arkie answered without asking.

"You said you'd be working on the plans," she began.

He was, but in the back, he apologized. He needed the big drawing board there. He guessed someone had pulled the phone jack out of the plug without noticing. Anyway, he had barely heard—

She laughed to mask her impatience. She wanted to report a change of plans, she said. Honey had called that morning to say the fishing tackle had arrived. With Taki coming in that afternoon from three days in Houston, she thought it would be fun to give him a surprise party and to rig rods and reels after supper. If they could make it, she'd food-shop and have the garage men save a parking space for them in her building.

So she had said yes and taken the train into town, Fiona told Arkie. Then she could drive him home. Was that all right? she asked, knowing his answer.

Oh, great! Great! he said. But . . .

But what?

Wouldn't all that fishing talk bore her?

Little boys needed toys, she laughed. Just be there by six-thirty, she ordered. She had come straight to Bloomie's to get him his shirts and had another stop to make, so she would be there then, too.

Where was she going?

To Hanson's, she said, reviving an idea shot down by Demi because of cost. She thought a couple of swingaway wall lamps might be a nice, easy way to finish their upstairs bedroom in time for the house walk. Everyone used them in living rooms, but if they had different shades—

Hey, great idea! he agreed. She should go to it.

Hanging up, she rushed to the escalator. Outside, on Lexington Avenue, she got a cab at once. She told the driver to take her to Forty-ninth Street.

Then, finally on the way to Demi's, she leaned back. Eyes shut, she enjoyed her anticipation.

For his part, Arkie had been no more truthful.

He had not been near the convertible plans that day. He had not looked at them, in fact, since Wednesday. He had, instead, indulged himself.

Savoring the joys of precision, the suggestion of seeing metal take form, he had spent the best part of the week at lathe, milling machine, and drill press. It had been great, he thought, hanging up the phone.

He liked designing, but its rewards were aesthetic, abstractions on sheets of paper. The Hydra Greek in him cried out for reality, textures and shapes. When he got back, he decided, he would do something really big with his hands that took a lot of sweat, like build a swimming pool with Pete and Steve. That would be good therapy.

Closing the office door, he went downstairs. There, on the abandoned machine shop floor, he put the final loving touches on the machinist's project that had so gratified him.

With saw and Yankee screwdriver, he set in the last heavy wooden members on the export crating that would house what he guessed was the greatest pair of 100-horsepower Evinrude outboards ever put together.

*April 8, 1967*
*Greenwich–New York City*

SIGHING, WADE looked around his sun porch.

Jesus, he thought, why couldn't it be fall? TV had football on then. That, at least, made rainy Saturdays tolerable. Now, instead, with Willa Mae and the girls in New York at the dentist, he had nothing to do but think.

He had done that already for three weeks. The results, predictably, were doubts. The Lions, he knew, had to reply. They had too much at stake not to.

His message should have reassured them, as well. They had to know he had nothing to gain by being the snitch. So what had gone wrong?

He wondered again if he had left anything undone.

This time, however, he believed he had.

Half rising from the chaise, he flopped back on the chintz-covered pillows shaking his head. Jesus, he told himself, he had become a worse old lady than Hubie. A moment later, though, he no longer cared.

He knew he had to make the call. Besides, what had he to lose?

The answer, as always, came back the same: Nothing.

So he left the sun porch for the kitchen to refill his two-cup skipper's mug from the Chemex. Then he went to the phone in the den.

Demi answered on the second ring.

"That you, Babes?" Wade asked, using the nickname he and Hubie reserved for Demi. "What's doing?" . . . Archimedes was on schedule? Good. An' when did he plan to deliver? . . . A week from today! Aw, Babes, wasn't that cuttin' it too close?

What did he mean?

He meant Archimedes'd be in Nippon a day later! What happened if they had to make a change? Or found a mistake, or somethin' they couldn't correct? How in hell did they get hold of Archimedes?

He'd see? What did that mean? he asked Demi.

Archimedes didn't want to talk about where he'd be in Nippon? Well, by God, he'd better!

There was a matter of what? Of *confidentiality?* Confidentiality, his ass! Good Christ, he had dreamed up the deal! Of course he understood it. The question was, did Archimedes? He got fifty thousand dollars when the model tank tested eighteen knots. He got the other two hundred thousand dollars for December 1967 delivery. Well, that was out, an' it was on him, wantin' the whole thing done up modular, so he'd give him two months' grace—call delivery February 1968—but they had to know where to reach him in the meantime so's things could move if they got boogered. Wasn't that only fair? Sweet Jesus, he was doin' that boy a favor!

He didn't know Arkie? No, he didn't, he agreed. But he knew Hubie! he told Demi. Would Hubie sit still for *approximate* delivery? Did Babes know what it'd cost to charter in three hundred thousand tons a month waitin' on those convertibles? Who had guts to sell Hubie that kind of a— Hey, wait a minute . . . wait a minute! Had Demi seen Mrs. A lately?

No? "Then screw Archimedes! What he don't know won't hurt him. You get hold of Mrs. A right away quick, an' lay all this on her at lunch Monday or Tuesday. Women are more practical. They run the fam'ly checkbook. You let her decide if confidentiality's worth two hundred Gs."

There, by God, he thought, that pointed the finger. He could do no more.

No, he answered, he didn't know Mrs A neither.

*Betrayal?* Who was she betraying? "You're not plannin' on anythin' bein' wrong, an' neither'm I. The odds say there won't be. So whatever Archimedes is so proud of'll be your secret, too, but you gotta know how to find him, don't you, if there's an emergency? Otherwise, what can you do? You gotta stop! As far as Mrs A knows, you're in the same boat I'm in with Hubie. How in the name of Christ do you tell your money that delivery's *approximate?*"

That put a catch in Demi's breath.

Was that really the case with him and Hubie? Demi asked.

Jesus, he hadn't thought about it but maybe it was, Wade answered. They might have played out the string. Goin' modular had just barely kept them alive.

*Approximate* delivery, though, could be the end.

". . .you'll see what you can do, Babes?"

Oh, if they hit, would that cost him, Wade thought, putting down the phone. Would he pay for that one.

And still no out in sight. Even so, he had had to do it.

They had just come in through the kitchen when the chartroom phone rang. Using the opportunity, Fiona went upstairs to get her stockings, badly splashed by a taxi, washed and dried in time for supper, leaving him alone.

So, cradling the receiver in the chronometer case in the top of the chart table, Demi sat down on the gray leather settee opposite to ponder the call. It had come at the worst time possible, he thought.

He had chosen this weekend to start disengaging. With Arkie on twenty-hour days and motel naps to meet the deadline, they had been together almost constantly. He thought the affair would peak then, too.

Others had after that much heat. This should have, as well. Besides, he constantly told himself, it served no purpose. She had been a right woman at a wrong time. Nothing more. Losses, therefore, should be cut.

But emotion had ignored logic. Increased contact, instead of satisfying appetites, had only whetted them. The more he had of her, the more he wanted. To further aggravate matters, her hungers seemed as intense.

Today, he reflected, had been the worst of all.

Artemis had asked her and Honey to spend a week in Paris after the May family meeting. So, with Arkie in Norfolk for the weekend consulting an engineer classmate at Newport News Shipbuilding, Fiona and Demi had decided to devote this Saturday to fashion. First, lunch at La Grenouille, to see what Seventh Avenue wore that spring, then, with *Women's Wear Daily* passes, showroom visits to watch department store buyers choose.

But with the entrée, her green eyes had begun to stare and her voice had deepened. "I'm not hungry," she said, putting down her fork.

Nodding, he rose and pulled out the table.

She looked baffled, fearful. He felt that way.

They had been overtaken, of course, by the obvious: love. But they were too sophisticated to realize that. So they got doused chasing cabs to get them to bed.

And now this, he thought, sitting in the chartroom.

Just as he wanted distance, Wade pushed him closer.

So far, he reasoned, he and Fiona could be excused. They had been selfish, perhaps weak. What Wade wanted them to do now, though, went past forgiving and changed the nature of the relationship. The little bastard could weasel it as he wanted. It still came out the same: betrayal.

Not that he blamed him. In his place, with money on the line, he too would insist on access to Arkie. The problem would be making her see that. Then he could steel himself to shed her again.

Still, he told himself, he had used her for pleasure. Why not for business? The prospect made him wince.

But, weighing how best to persuade her, he left for the kitchen. Pol Roger made a start, he thought. The pantry refrigerator "emergency stores" held a bottle. Behind it stood a mayonnaise jar, lid punctured to admit moisture. Nodding resignedly, he unscrewed the top and withdrew four red-papered cigarettes. She had liked those since New Year's, he remembered.

Pocketing them, he got a sudden insight.

The idea that had nagged at him for weeks, formless and without handle, as Wade said modular had eluded him, concerned Arkie. How or why he could not guess, but he knew Arkie stood at its center.

Then, passing the butcher's block, he spotted the *Times,* still folded and unread. Like all tankermen, he had an abiding interest in the Middle East, so an item he had missed scanning the front page over coffee stopped him now.

The day before, Syrians had shelled three kibbutzes at the foot of the Golan Heights. Israeli Mirages took off to silence the guns. Six MIGs rising to defend them were destroyed. Two were shot down in flames over the suburbs of Damascus, presumably as a caution to the populace.

Same old story, he murmured.

Dismissing the item, he got out a tray and glasses. Pahlevi would have been nice, too, he thought. But Brie would have to do. He had blown the last tin of golden caviar on yet another daughter of shipping royalty. He should have known better, he told himself. After Fiona, tonnage and wealth notwithstanding, the heiress had all the excitement of milk.

His melancholy deepened in the floorthrough room. Finally, on the spiral staircase, he stopped and, leaning against the center pillar, asked himself why.

Sophistication denied him an answer. He did not acknowledge love.

But something else surfaced, instead: the elusive handle.

Arkie had leaped at redoing the plans.

He had been positively eager, in fact, to get into modular construction. He had wanted to mention it, he said, but had thought it might seem too radical. Still, he knew its time had come. Moreover, the technique fascinated him, and he had done a lot with it on conversion and repairs. He knew exactly what to do. That summer, he would refuse design work so that he could help in the shipyard.

Strange, Demi now thought. Everyone else discredited modular. But he had the one man in the world who liked it. Suddenly, the fit seemed more than mere coincidence. Had Wade known that? If so, how? Did Arkie's job in Japan explain that interest?

He stopped, weighing conflicting ideas. He, after all, he reminded himself, had brought up Arkie's name in the first place. Beyond that, Wade had now sunk over $50,000 into design fees, and he had hit him for another $8,500 in expenses. In view of the way Wade and Hubie nursed a buck, that bespoke a sincere interest in the convertibles.

Still, moving around the spiral staircase, Demi sensed that Arkie's forwarding address might be more than it seemed. Having no idea, however, of what that might be, he got gloomier. He blamed that on Fiona.

Suddenly, he felt guilty. Not about what had happened, but about what would. He hated the idea of giving her the red cigarettes. He despised using her that way. He loathed himself even more for being willing to do it.

Why? he wondered.

What had he done to deserve conscience?

*April 15, 1967*
*Eleusis Bay, Greece*
*Sands Point, New York*

THE BAY lay nine miles north of Piraeus.

From sea level, it resembled a steep-sided cup.

Hills, 1,500 feet high, crowded the shores ringing its bight, which pointed northeast. Salamis, a rugged 1,200-foot-high island, provided visually unbroken walls to the west and south.

Sheltered, near offices and a shipyard at the head of the bay, the few square miles of water thus enclosed have significance beyond size in the world of shipping. Greek owners send old elephants here to die, or to be sold, or, in more hopeful moods, to await new work.

Days, the place recalls an abandoned graveyard. But under a full moon, hills rising in starry sky, the bay seems the beginning rather than the end. Soft light mutes corrosion and rust. Darkness straightens twisted railings and bent booms. The ships, riding to their chains, look pristine and perfect, new and ready to voyage the world.

One, in fact, seemed to prove the point.

An aged T-2, it crept down the closely packed lanes from beneath the cliffs of Salamis, distinctly the low-rent end of the bay. Dark save for running lights, it had no tug or pilot, an act of nerve and parsimony rarely seen even there.

Turning at Eleusis, it shaped course for the narrow channel to Piraeus and the sea, sliding broadside to the moonlight. Its name, newly painted, could then be read: *Dynamic Papachristou.*

Then, bow behind Salamis, the stern swung, briefly passing through the light to illuminate the house flag on its stack, a faded rampant white lion.

A few hours later, 4,500 miles to the west, the departure of *Dynamic Papachristou* would be discussed in a bedroom. The ship seemingly had a life expectancy then of six weeks, eight at the outside.

Arkie lay back, forearm across his eyes.

Fiona, brushing her teeth in the bathroom, had left the door ajar. He seemed to see that light against his eyelids. It made his headache worse.

The letdown, he thought. He had hoped momentum would keep him going until he boarded the plane for Japan.

Working through the previous night, he had met Demi for breakfast, spent the morning talking specifications, and gone to lunch at the New York Yacht

Club with Taki. Then, driving home, he had picked up Fiona for the trip to Riverhead, where, never mind dates, the family would celebrate Easter because of his presence. His dad had gone all the way to New Jersey for the live baby lamb which he butchered for the occasion.

Between work, food, wine, children, and this, the goodbye night, events should have swept him along. Instead, he felt spent. He blamed that on Costa Lianides.

Breezing in Friday night for some gear, Costa had remembered the deadline and brought supper. He also had the start of a tan. The high cheekbones framing his compact, square face had suddenly sported freckles, and coppery glints had begun to appear in his strawberry-blond hair.

Where had all that come from?

Jamaica, he said. Wanting a change, he had gone there to meet someone English and blond. Not half bad either, he laughed.

So, leaving the draftsmen to finish cleaning up the plans, they had eaten Chinese food at the office desk and discussed what had to be done in Japan.

Then Costa mentioned their trip after Japan. A cable from Zavitsanos had come that morning, he said. He would sail from Eleusis Bay the next night.

And when would he reach Ancona?

In five or six days.

What! That long? Italy was next door to Greece.

Yes, but old tramps like *Dynamic* had been around. They didn't like to be rushed.

And the explosives?

The Israelis had told Howsam they already had the stuff in Ancona. So they would be all set when they got there. And Fiona? Costa suddenly asked.

Fiona—what about her?

She still didn't know?

No! Of course not! That was the deal, wasn't it?

Sure, but he just thought . . .

Thought what?

That maybe Arkie had mentioned a date or a place to— Costa, interrupting himself, modified that. He casually held up a hand. The meaning of this remark changed as rapidly. From accusation it suddenly verged on suggestion.

What he meant, he said, was that from the first, in 1965, when he had brought Schotten to him, what had been stressed? Security. To build the ships without anyone getting nosy. All right. That had been done. Kono, at Hasegawa, had told them in January, when they went to Japan to do the final castings, that no one had been around.

A shrug said the obvious: They had been unseen in Japan.

And here, in Long Island City? Costa went on. Had any strangers turned up? Had there been any mysterious inquiries or—

None! Arkie knew everyone who had come to the shop.

So there he was. With both of them dropping out of sight when they left Japan, security, perhaps, no longer posed the problem it once—

How long had he been thinking that?

Costa's brush mustache glinted copper as he smiled. Since hearing from Howsam that the explosives had arrived, he said. He doubted they'd blow up anything. Still, gelignite was real. If they had an accident—*pfft!* Who would know what became of them? He and the cousins had no worries. The old ladies on Hydra had lost so many men to the sea they took that as part of life. But he had suddenly remembered Fiona. Did Arkie owe her a hint, maybe, so she'd know what to do if he didn't come back? Could he leave a note?

No. If he gave it to her, she'd know something was funny and open it. The same with anybody in the family.

What about a lawyer?

When? He had to work straight through that night, deliver the plans, and then go out to Riverhead.

Nodding, Costa rose from his chair.

Then maybe it was better not telling her, he said. The risk seemed too small to worry about. He discounted the physical danger altogether. He had, in fact, told Howsam and Schotten to stay home, to forget the Whaler, and to leave the last voyage to them. So far, security had been perfect, and, while Fiona had only her mother to talk to—which she probably wouldn't do anyway— why tempt fate? He was sorry he had even mentioned it.

Shaking his head to dismiss the matter, he moved on to other things. From his jacket pocket he took the tiny gold ring for which his left ear had been pierced, indicating he had sailed each of the seven seas, and inserted it. Then, turning to the table behind him, he put on the British officer's raincoat, ra- kishly knotting the belt. Last came the chocolate-brown fedora, brim down all around, European movie director style. A knowing tap inclining hat to pre- cisely the right angle, he spun back, presenting himself in his favorite role: ex- otic Greek shipping millionaire.

He had a long, tearful goodbye to make with a French model, mad to go villa shopping on the Riviera with him that summer, he said, winking. Then he had left, saying goodbye over his shoulder. "See you Sunday . . . and forget the other thing."

But Arkie had not forgotten the "other" thing.

How could he? He had dragged it around as if it were an anchor.

At first, he had thought indecision made it so heavy. *Should he tell her? Shouldn't he?* Now, in bed, limp with fatigue, forearm across the steamline scar throbbing with pain over his right eye, he understood what had begun to weigh on him: guilt.

He had been selfish, he thought. She had a right to know. But he had had showboat fever.

He had gone into this for a chance to overwhelm her with a sailor's Halloween, the payoff for a long trip. He had pictured it when Costa brought him Schotten. He had seen Fiona's face as he casually handed her a six-figure check and told her that more was on the way.

He should have known better, he told himself. Flamboyance had never been his style. He had already staged a sailor's Halloween, after his first trip, when he had been paid off with seventy-one hundred-dollar bills; he had wanted to see his parents' expressions when he tossed up the full deck and those paper snowflakes wafted down over the kitchen table. But all the way home he had feared that some tough guy from the docks was following him and would go after his money belt. From then on, the company had sent a monthly check to his bank.

Now not telling her seemed worse than cheating. Lots of guys fooled around, went home, and lived happily ever after. What he had committed himself to, on the other hand, could turn her life around overnight. She should have had a say in that, he thought. Part of his decision had belonged to her. That transcended $2 million.

Who wanted to be that rich, anyway? He already made more than they could spend.

Besides guilt, he had a full cargo of irony.

Conning himself, he had dismissed the idea of a sailor's Halloween, as any adult would. He had told himself, instead, that the job had been irresistible, that he had wanted to pioneer and this had been the chance. The ships, however, had disappointed him, and he blamed the clients. Costa had wanted them only to be fast; Howsam and Schotten, cheap.

Enter irony.

He had signed on for a possibly fatal voyage with Sindbad the Sailor—and been frustrated. Then, doing nothing to find design work, he got Demi's convertibles. They were so perfect, such advances on the state of the art, they would put him into the naval architecture texts.

So, feeling guilty, he now felt foolish as well. That made telling Fiona all the more difficult. For his motives were better left unspoken. Promising to make her happy, to protect her, he had been childish, selfish, and stupid. Insecure, naive, he felt disgust sweep over him.

He had left her but one conclusion: that his actions reflected his regard. He could never humiliate her like that. She had done nothing, ever, but bring him joy.

Wallowing in conscience, afraid to confess, he sensed the darkness behind his eyelids begin to brighten. That meant the bathroom door had swung open. She had about finished. She would be with him soon.

His guilt deepened.

So began the event proposed by Loren Wade, approved by Evelyn Waddell, and triggered by Costa Lianides. As befitted the best thinking of three extremely bright, cautious men, the incident proceeded exactly as planned.

A moment later, Arkie felt her hand on his cheek.

Looking up, he saw her standing alongside the bed.

In the darkness, the light from the bathroom seemed gray. Filtered through the diaphanous white nightgown, it fell as shadow, making her body seem more voluptuous and mysterious. Seeking her face, he caught a glimpse of the black triangular cloud that hovered between the curves of her thighs. It had become blue. The points of her breasts, which he thought of as pink, now looked magenta, deeper in color, more demanding.

"You looked so sad coming home, I decided to put this on," she said.

He saw her teeth flash above him. Next came the glitter of three white satin bows as she undid the top of her gown. His sense of remorse intensified.

She had worn that gown on their wedding night.

After that, honeymoon or not, she wore pajama tops. She had never seen such a hairy man, she said. He could scratch her to death. He had felt a sense of incompleteness ever since.

Now, showered, powdered, and cologned, she stepped out of the gown and slid into the bed, kissing him on the shoulder. Nestled against his side, she traced her fingertips over his pectorals.

"The sendoff committee got a little somethin' nice in there for a neighbor girl?" she asked mischievously. Her tone recalled Honey, whom he adored.

Then, doing things Demi had taught her, she gave him the night of his nights.

Afterward, lying in darkness, arm around her bare shoulder, he could only marvel at his good fortune.

Married, he thought, he had found the other Fiona.

Her great beauty, poise, and knack with people were just veneers, qualities others saw. Beneath them lay childlike, incredible generosity. So forgiving of his weaknesses, she already pardoned his dullness, shyness, and what she called his peasant's addiction to work and family.

He dreaded asking for more of that charity.

But, like the calm he now felt, it seemed endless.

Surely, he thought, it would cover a sailor's Halloween.

She could understand and forgive that, he believed.

She would even comfort him in his confession.

Then, cloaked in Perfect Contrition, he could go.

He would have restated his love: pure and total.

So, awash in guilt and gratitude, he told her.

Lying beside him, she did not sleep. She knew her life had reached a turning point. A decision had to be made, she thought. Before that, though, she had to curb her emotions.

First she had felt shock. She had thought she had known Arkie. Obviously, she had not.

So diffident, so inept at everything but engines and ships, he had kept a secret for two years. That took guts she had never seen. He had a toughness, an integrity, she now knew, beyond her. By then he should have been her man. Quiet and shy, he would forever be his own man. That frightened her.

Then, after the surprise, came the hurt. She knew then, as well, what Demi had done to her.

She could have understood that he wanted her in bed. Many men had. But most men had been decent about it. She had never resented their interest, either. Some of it had been flattering.

Now, though, she only felt used.

She should have known better, she told herself. The rich never changed the game. They just kept making the rules more humiliating. Like this, she thought.

She had wanted to help Demi. Bed aside, he was her friend. All the Keriosotises were. Besides, he had warned that Arkie could lose the rest of the convertible design fee if he vanished after reaching Japan. Laborers, he said, hired out, delivered, and got paid. Others had to be flexible. He respected confidentiality, of course, but he wondered if it could be worth $200,000. She might well think so, too, but he left the matter to her to decide. . . .

She had found nothing improper in Demi's request. If anything, she had believed, it had complimented her business sense. Arkie, she knew, had none; only a knack for earning big fees. But whatever he made as a pieceworker fell far short of how she wanted to live or the wealth that the patronage of one of tankerdom's first families could bring.

His asking her help, in fact, had seemed like a confidence shared, rather than a favor. Now she knew. Nothing had been real, she thought. Beyond hurt, she felt a sense of loss. She lamented her shattered illusions.

For Demi had been more than a lover.

Isolated in suburbia, surrounded by Arkie's family, she had been lonely. She had missed someone to talk to who saw life as she did. Demi had fulfilled that need. He had the sophistication she missed, the equally keen eye for the detail that mattered in a dress, a meal, or a room. He laughed at the same things. They had been, she thought, their own best company.

The French had a word for men and women who enjoyed each other in that way. But, being French, they assumed that friends could never be lovers as well. They called such couples *copains:* pals.

She had that sort of rapport with Liese Bondurant. She treasured it. She had been that close to Demi. But to no one else.

Her goals made confidences dangerous.

Still, she needed someone with whom to be intimate. Everyone did.

But who would be her *copain* now?

Demi had only wanted what she had just heard, she knew. He had known all along, she now believed, about the ships nearing completion in Japan. He had only to learn why they had been built and when they would go into ser-vice to have facts he could sell to make his fortune, with or without convert-ibles, and regardless of how his family settled the "bigger–smaller" debate. All that had passed between them, she now believed, had been false on his part, aimed at getting what she had just been told.

While not as conversant with tanker mathematics as Honey, she had a good idea of what her information might be worth. Later she could make Demi pay that price—to the last penny—if she wished, she thought. But first she had to calm herself.

At dawn, however, she found herself more upset. Her sense of loss and de-pression had deepened. So she crept out of bed and showered. Then, having given the maid the weekend off so that she and Arkie could be alone, she went downstairs to fix a going-away breakfast.

In the kitchen, she recalled Demi's cousin Marina, of the beehive hairdo, whom she had visited at Hobe Sound in March. Unlovely, coarse, and a bully with servants, she had one evening exposed a surprising sensitivity. It revealed itself over a third martini in some small talk about marriage. Now, from the depths of her own sense of abandonment, Fiona saw she had been reaching out, as well. Tough-minded Marina too, she thought, had been seeking some-one with whom she could be intimate.

The most painful burden women could bear, Marina had observed, was either too much money or too much beauty. The wrong men lusted after both, so love could never be assumed. Prudence required, then, that such perishable commodities as looks and wealth be protected. But what defense existed against predatory males? Only one: independence.

She had learned that, she told Fiona, seeing what had happened to other shipowners' daughters. So, when her father had urged her to marry at sixteen for business reasons, she had insisted on a dowry. In her name. A ship. Now she owned four. Like it or not, her husband behaved accordingly. If that seemed distrustful, she apologized. Life, however, went on with or without love. But in either case it went on better with money.

Love belonged to the poor, she said. God obviously invented it for them. Only they could afford its risks.

Raising her glass, she downed her third martini and poured in the bonus from the bottom of the pitcher. In retrospect, her smile seemed to Fiona as empty and plaintive as she now felt.

The airport cab came for Arkie at seven-thirty. They said goodbye in the kitchen. Then, standing at a window, she watched him leave.

As the cab turned into the street from the driveway, he leaned forward in the back seat. Hand raised timidly and tentatively, he looked like a little boy on the bus leaving for his first day of school.

Still pondering what to do, she waved back.

She never saw him again.

# IV.

# All Together

THE CHARTROOM phone rang at 5:45 A.M.

Leaving the kitchen, Demi went to answer it.

Fiona did most of the talking. She would be there in an hour, she said. She had something for him to sign. After that she would tell him about Arkie's traveling plans.

Her tone told him not to gloat. Beyond that, her rage seemed directed at him. She had stumbled onto something big, he thought. Its magnitude made her feel he had betrayed her. His eagerness would only confirm that suspicion. So he tried being casual.

Fine, he answered, but he had a run to Kennedy that morning. Wouldn't it be better if they had supper—

No! she told him. From his place she would drive back to LaGuardia to get a nine-thirty plane for Florida.

Hearing "Florida," he grew alarmed. She had planned on a Friday flight. That Sunday, she and her mother were leaving for ten days in the West Indies.

What about the tickets for *Cabaret* he had already bought? he asked. They were for Wednesday, and he had paid scalpers' prices.

Her answer heightened his unease. She had such a bad taste in her mouth she wanted a few extra days south to get rid of it. Antigua—did he remember? she asked with pointed irony—had been Arkie's gift to her for his spending so much time on the convertibles.

Then she left him with a suddenly buzzing phone.

He held it in his hand almost fearfully. That last bit, he thought, went beyond anger. It had sounded like conscience. But if it troubled her so, why would she tell him? And what was that business about signing something?

One thing he knew beyond a doubt: Wade had jobbed him.

But how?

Shaking his head, he called his relief skipper. Then he went back to the kitchen for more coffee.

By 7:05 A.M., alone again, he knew everything.

He sat then, as before, at the butcher's block.

The steel door had just slammed behind her. She had left without a good-bye.

Arriving, she had not acknowledged him, either. That had been at 7 A.M.

He knew she would see the open kitchen door as she walked up Forty-ninth Street from where she parked, so they met there. She entered silently.

He saw at once that she looked different. Usually, he thought, pastel greens worked for her. Today, an elegantly cut silk traveling suit did nothing. The creamy Celtic complexion seemed faded, worn. Violet fatigue shadows shrouded her eyes as well.

Closing the door behind her with her heel, she took a step to her left. Then, leaning casually on the edge of the stainless-steel range, she opened a zipper on her black leather shoulder bag and withdrew a beige envelope. A casual flip placed it before him on the butcher's block.

"Sign that," she said. "Then we'll talk."

Her mouth had changed, too, he thought. It seemed drawn, less humorous, more demanding. In a few years, he knew, when she grew more used to having her own way, as she obviously expected to now, she would still be a beauty, but those lips of hers would strike a distinctly cautionary note. They did now.

Nodding, he reached for the envelope. Unsealed, it lay face down. So, lifting the flap, he took out a letter. It consisted of two brief typewritten paragraphs.

Reading them, he felt his face flush. That bitch Marina, he thought. Unwittingly, she had told Fiona exactly how to write a marriage contract.

Shaking his head, he looked up questioningly.

Had she been too bold? she asked with mock concern. He so loved to eat and fuck her she had hoped he might have eventual wedlock in mind. Or did he do as much for all the ladies of his acquaintance?

A savage smile preempted an answer. She had never used those words, he thought. She delighted in punishing him with them now.

Folding her arms over her chest as she did when she had command of a situation, she tipped her head sympathetically, as if soliciting a reply.

Hearing none, she left the first paragraph of the letter. In that, he had only proposed marriage. The second dealt with a far more delicate matter. Or, she asked, did he balk at community property?

She could have anything she wanted! She could have anything he had, but—

She held up a black-kid-gloved hand for silence.

Her dowry, she said, tapping her temple, would make him very rich. It seemed only fair that she share in the wealth she brought to—

Smiling, he regained his composure. She really ought to sit down and have some coffee, he said. She had plenty of time to get to the airport, and he knew she had been under a strain. She needed to relax, to rethink things. Surely she didn't expect him to sign a blank check for half of his lifetime's earnings?

Her answer indicated she had done her homework. Surely he didn't think, did he, that half of what she had in mind would leave him poor? If it did, where would she be? On the contrary, she purred as glibly as ever, this was like that best of all Irish toasts. She wished him only what she wished herself.

He changed course abruptly, and sincerely. He knew beyond doubt now she had something big. Her feelings, however, concerned him more.

Yes, but did she have to spell it out so? he asked. And what was all that crap about her option to liquidate all assets, if she wished, for a share-and-share-alike settlement, regardless of which party initiated divorce proceedings? For Christ's sake, where was love? That sounded like the penalty clauses for late delivery that smart lawyers wrote into shipyard contracts—business!

Business? she asked. Of course it was business! Hadn't it been that for him? He needed money to be done with his family. Well, how else could she become independent and make a third marriage for love?

Fiona—

Sign! she said, pointing to the letter.

It wasn't necessary, he insisted. He loved—

Sign! she said again, more imperatively.

Smiling, he patted his blue wool chief's shirt. He had no pen.

Finding one in the black shoulder bag, she threw it at him. A yellow ballpoint, it bounced off the butcher's block, up to his chest, and then down, coming to rest on the envelope. Then, arms crossed once more, she leaned farther back on the range, waiting.

A moment later, pen capped, he looked up.

She shook her head. She wanted the letter back before she talked.

Shrugging, he picked up the envelope.

Already stamped, it had been addressed to her, care of her mother in Florida. Smart, he thought. She had only to walk up Third Avenue to the FDR postal station and get it registered. Received, it would then go, unopened, into a safe-deposit box to await her pleasure.

Refolding and inserting the marriage contract, he pushed the envelope to the edge of the butcher's block.

Nodding, she took a step forward. Her eyes suddenly looked smoky, venomous.

He had been had in this, too, he began.

She told him not to worry and to skip how and why. Soon, she said, dabbing the envelope flap with her tongue, he would be rich enough for both of them. He wanted that, didn't he, to be a real shipping Greek like Ari and Stavros and the others, with apartments, houses, and servants waiting wherever he went? No matter. She wanted that.

Gently patting the flap shut with gloved fingers, she returned the envelope to the shoulder bag, closing the top zipper with a flourish.

Then, arms crossed, casually leaning on the range again, she told him.

What she said went beyond his wildest imaginings.

The war closing in on the Israelis would create the greatest shipping opportunity in history, he believed. Whoever won, tanker owners would make billions the first year. If fighting ended stalemated, with the Suez Canal closed, profits could reach hundreds of billions.

If the standoff persisted, earnings would nudge the trillion-dollar level. That, in fact, seemed to him the likeliest outcome. The United Nations had only to sell out again to the Third World countries that wanted Israel destroyed. A peace proposal without guarantees would do that. There had been plenty before. A state of war, he reminded himself, had existed in the Middle East since the UN created a Jewish nation in the first place.

Meanwhile, he knew he had been had royally, but how?

He kept returning to the first lunch at Lutèce.

He had suggested Arkie. But unable to reconstruct that conversation, and blinded by ego, he rejected the obvious answer: that he had been set up from the start. He decided, instead, that Wade had lucked into the situation.

It would be just like that little bastard to snoop around without letting on, checking Arkie's credentials. Then, when he found those ships in Japan, he got Fiona into the picture. That had been in November. With her old man in Nippon for the holidays, he had asked, did he think she might enjoy New Year's at his place with the rest of the family?

Sure, he had wanted a little slap and tickle. Why not?

But, Christ, look what had happened.

She had his signed marriage contract in her purse. And looking at her, he knew that vengeance had motivated that document as much as greed. Moreover, he had to concede that her enmity might be lasting. What reason had she ever to believe his side of the story?

From there, he feared, the scenario never varied. Hurt women turned to booze, drugs, or lovers.

Where did that leave *him?*

He vowed Wade would pay for the pain he had caused.

With all that, he had her facts to keep straight, as well. After he decided what to do, he had to report what she had said, and that had to be right. Just the bare bones, without nuances of detail and timing, and their relationship to one another were mind-boggling.

A shadowy Japanese shipyard that had five 100,000-tonners about to go and five 250,000-tonners well under way; an equally obscure repair yard in

Ancona, Italy; an old T-2 called *Dynamic Papachristou* that would go there to refit and leave with a half ton of gelignite aboard; a Boston Whaler capable of eighty miles per hour; a thirty-five-year-old submarine that might or might not play a part.

A captain's daughter, she knew distance, speed, and time. She sounded like a second mate recounting possible course changes. The image quickly vanished, though, as she got more specific. Then, under the weight of her brisk, precise, cheerily impersonal recital of bearings, headings, and positions, he began to form a quite different idea.

She had just put a dozen lives at risk, he thought. The guys in the Whaler were goners for sure. Those on *Dynamic Papachristou* could die, as well.

He felt himself wince as the realization deepened.

She abruptly stopped talking.

Piety seemed a bit much coming from him, she said.

He shook his head as if to deny having made a value judgment of any kind. He had to mollify her somehow, he thought. Her rage seemed murderous. She looked ready to spring away from the range and pounce on him.

Names? he asked in a detached, businesslike tone.

She told him he already had two: Archimedes Angelakos and Costa Lianides. Her smile said she wanted them on his conscience.

Was it so bad not to want to be bored? she asked. They would be very, very rich.

Then, marriage vow given, she left.

Wade had to pay for what he had done to them, he thought, still sitting at the butcher's block. He knew he could never make him pay enough, and pride demanded that he make him pay until it hurt.

Otherwise, he would be as big a *malaca* as Arkie.

His chief barrier to revenge, he knew, lay in Form 10-K. The document, required yearly of publicly traded companies by the Securities and Exchange Commission, named names and detailed important transactions. Moreover, it had to be updated quarterly.

With war in the Middle East, he knew that second-quarter 1967 reports of all companies in oil or tankering would be closely scrutinized. Everyone would want to know who stood to gain or lose. Besides securities analysts and competitors, readership would also extend to the State Department, the CIA, the FBI, and other federal agencies. That much opportunity made for weird politics.

So that ruled out obvious moves, he thought.

Stock options, bonuses, and consulting deals with deferred income were for employees. Going to him, they could conceivably look like payoffs.

Whatever he did would have to be more subtle. Ideally, it would not appear on Form 10-K at all.

Moreover, he knew, the sooner he acted the better. The more time he put between whatever had to be signed and that war, the less likely outsiders would suspect that he had known about it. At worst, they would call him a lucky Greek. He could live with that.

Deciding not to call Wade until he determined what to do, and still reacting to Fiona's rage and distrust, he thus found himself thinking again about the marriage contract. After he got past his shock and humiliation, he began to see that it had a principle he could use.

He had to be careful, of course, and he also needed another document. But as far as he knew, what he wanted could be kept out of Form 10-K. If it had to go in, it could, in fact, be dated today, and its roots could be shown in a check sent to Arkie the previous fall.

That, he decided, looked promising.

So, leaving the stool behind the butcher's block, he refilled the coffee mug and walked down the hall to the dining room. Then, seated on one of the overstuffed chocolate-brown velour couches beneath the bookshelves, he thought things through.

At nine-thirty, he went into the chartroom.

He had the outline of what he wanted then, but he needed a yellow pad to get the key phrases in writing. Dealing with Loren Wade, he knew, they would have to be airtight and watertight.

At ten-twenty, everything looked perfect.

He called Shirley Carmichael, Wade's secretary, then.

Finished, he returned the phone to the chronometer case in the chart table, slowly lowering the glass top hinged over the compartment.

As he did, he idly glanced at the ship's clock. It said ten-thirty-seven.

Fiona would be about in Jacksonville, he thought.

He considered having her paged at the airport. She might feel better talking to him, he mused.

He had, after all, just made them about $41 million. The first year.

Shirley Carmichael, meanwhile, typed the dictation.

At ten after eleven, proofing done, she buzzed Wade.

Sure, she could come in.

Why the hell not? he thought. What could she do to make the morning worse? Taking a last disconsolate glance at the Hudson, he spun the red Do-More chair to face her over the desk. He had never felt lower. He should have heard from Demi by now, he thought.

He had half expected to yesterday at home. He had, in fact, had a hell of a row with his wife over her tying up the phone so long. That evening, only pride had kept him from calling New York.

Had Hubie been in Ridgefield, he would have. Hubie hated waiting on anything. To avoid that, he had flown again to Vancouver for the weekend to dream more dreams of North Slope riches. The reprieve would end, however, Wade knew, at two o'clock, when Hubie arrived at the office from Kennedy.

But court, he saw, had been called to order early. It showed in Shirley Carmichael's face. She stood timorously in his office doorway. She had just got a funny call from Demi Keriosotis—

She broke off as he shot up from the red chair.

He sat down as quickly to let her finish.

—and he had told her to type up what he dictated and to give it to him to sign and get notarized in the legal department before he went over to Forty-ninth Street for lunch. Demi had something to tell him.

So the ship had come in after all, he told himself. Jesus, talk about a thrill. It had war beat to hell. His throat suddenly seemed full of Adam's apple. If he tried to talk, he knew, his voice would come out sounding just like Daffy Duck.

Quiet seemed in order on another count as well. He still had not thought of an out.

First, he had to see how smart Demi had been. He took the papers silently over the rosewood desk.

Miss Carmichael knew better, but she stayed to watch his reaction anyway. She had seen vast sums exchanged as his secretary, but those had been on checks to shipyards and governments. Nothing of this magnitude had ever involved an individual.

She also knew something of Wade's feelings for Demi. They had remained unchanged, she saw, noting the thinned lips and the color rising above the white shirt collar. His slow, careful reading, though, implied that he might be giving the proposals serious consideration.

At length, finished, he took a large gray envelope out of a drawer, put the papers in flat, and stood up. Miss Carmichael, reaching over to the teak compass binnacle from the first of Acey's old Burmah Oil tankers, got his coat and held it open for him.

The blue in his eyes, she noted, seemed frosty gray.

Demi had some nerve, she thought. Could he have anything worth a $22.5 million loan guarantee and a letter of agreement making him a partner in a company that would build and operate ships? Yielding to curiosity, she asked obliquely.

Would he be in Legal if there were any calls?

Nodding curtly, he left.

Fifteen minutes later, though, going down in the elevator from the legal department, he began to smile. He had found an out, he thought.

Judas priest, he thought, the thing had become so real he had gone for that letter of agreement himself.

\* \* \*

He returned at two o'clock.

Scampering past Hubie's receptionist and secretary before they could react, he entered the office without knocking, kicking the door shut.

Phone in hand, Hubie looked up sharply.

Gray and travel-worn, he had obviously just arrived. His attaché case stood unopened on the bogwood desk. He had probably just called Ridgefield to check in with Cora, Wade thought.

"We got it, Hube!" Wade shouted. "We got it!"

Speeding up, he lumbered past the thirty-foot-long window row overlooking the Hudson, judging his stride to snag the black conference chair alongside the desk on the fly. Then, seating himself, he reached out.

One hand around Hubie's neck guiding his right ear to his mouth, and the other pulling on his lapel, he thus whispered what Demi had told him.

The news brought an immediate and violent reaction.

A thunderous belch, the loudest Wade had ever heard, racked Hubie's body and left him gasping. Bent double, chest nearly to knees, he pointed to the water carafe on the sideboard behind him. Then, yanking the top drawer open, he blindly rummaged through it with both hands and produced a small brown bottle. Turning away as he unscrewed its cap, he tapped the bottle with his forefinger and watched three reddish drops descend through the water held before him, coloring it as they went. Throwing his head back, he drank it down in a gulp.

"What's that?" Wade asked.

"Belladonna. It paralyzes your guts."

"Jesus. . . . That something new?"

Hubie nodded. "A real elephant killer."

Then, ashen, but as if to prove that his body and mind were separate entities, he sat up briskly and wiped his mouth on the back of his hand.

"Go on from the Whaler," he said.

Two more sentences completed the story.

Jeopardy had long been Hubie's natural element. He felt at home in it. So, once over his initial shock, he took Wade's report in stride, regarding it this way and that as other, more cultivated men held up wineglasses.

He spent at most ten seconds deciding what to do.

"Get all the voyage abstracts an' charter bills out of the '56 files," he told Wade, "an' have Shirley call Willa Mae so she can let Cora know we won't be home for a while—at least not tonight."

Nodding, Wade had already started out.

"An', Loren—" Hubie called after him, "get a cab on the Fiftieth Street side, will you, buddy? I don't think I can hoof it over to the Dorset."

Wade nodded sadly. The Dorset was three blocks away.

The suite's two-story living room faced Fifty-fourth Street. Pine-paneled, its high walls held more of Hubie's hunting trophies and models of Wade's favorite ships. A kitchen fronted by a serving bar occupied its rear wall. Three bedrooms and baths were upstairs, making it an ideal but offbeat place for cocktails, lunches, and suppers, and for executives and friends of the company stranded in town overnight.

Wade sat at one end of the dining table in front of the bar, his blue canvas-bound abstracts and ledgers at his feet and before him. Hubie, at the other end, asked the questions, working his slide rule and jotting down the answers on a yellow pad.

They worked until seven without a break. It took that long to digest the '56 tanker move. Then supper came. Pushing their papers away, they ate silently.

Afterward, they turned to the future.

At nine-forty-five, they were done.

The North Slope lay within their reach.

Wade knew how to get them there.

Seeing Hubie's approving nod, he pushed his chair back and rose to tuck in his shirttails.

"Well, then," he said, "I guess I better saddle an' get on with it."

"You know what you've got to do first?"

" 'Course I do! What in hell do you think I brought my bags for? I gotta send them guys a message before some wild sheenie comes lookin' for us."

"You can do that so there's no mistake?"

"Leave that to me. In two, three days—"

"How long?"

"I'm goin' to Panama first."

"Panama?"

Buckling his belt, Wade farmboyed his grin. "I got me some egg money down there I wanna free up, too."

As he passed by, Hubie reached out to touch his cheek. Anything he felt then would have embarrassed him to say.

So he sat at the table as Wade left, and when the door closed he got out the belladonna. Then he called the town house on Seventy-fourth Street. The time had come to play the ace.

Going up Fifth Avenue, Hubie opened the cab's window for some fresh air alongside Central Park. Stomach calm, eyes shut, he let the breeze lave his face. The relaxation it brought seemed as good as sleep.

This ended his career, he thought. After tonight, the rest would be nest-sitting. PANARTEX would be there to stay. Not that it mattered or that he really cared. The North Slope had been only a measure, a definition of his ability and worth.

He owed the outcome to Loren, of course. But that in no way diminished his pleasure. Others, particularly the moneymen on his board of directors, called Loren an embarrassment, lacking executive style, and wanted him fired. He had fought them, believing that character and brains came before all. They would like a member of their own elite as marine superintendent, he suspected, a mannerly Annapolis graduate from a family they knew. The majors, with their corporate mentalities, leaned to that type.

He had never bought that argument. Loren had outperformed them all. That made him feel especially good about himself.

The situation pleased him, as well.

Beyond doubt, he had a buyer for what he knew.

The Arab world, he reflected, had always been a myth. For him, it broke down into two political camps.

The countries along the shores of the Mediterranean were socialist. They wanted a redistribution of wealth. There Nasser led the way. By 1962 he had nationalized 90 percent of Egypt's assets. Moreover, he had emerged as the spokesman for Pan-Arab causes.

The Persian Gulf states, on the other hand, where he operated, were feudal, owned by the emirs, kings, and sheikhs who ruled them. And, while Nasser made noise and took Soviet aid, they were anti-Communist and rich. But no one listened to them in the Arab world.

They wanted Nasser cut down to size, he thought. They would pay any price for that.

The diplomatist would leap at what he brought. More important, he would know how to use it. He would help the Jews too, if necessary. Both the fact and the irony pleased Hubie. For he wished the Israelis well.

Hubie had had business at the Haifa refinery and spent time in Israel. He liked the country, and he liked the people. He felt at home there. Sitting at a sidewalk café on Dizengoff Street in Tel Aviv, sipping an orange juice, he always thought of Texas.

The scene recalled Houston to him, before it got so sophisticated, and tried to act New Yorky. In Tel Aviv, millionaires wore sport shirts, the way they used to at home. They laughed a lot, too, and looked at girls.

A student of history, he appreciated their regard for the past as well. They had learned from Napoleon. He planted the cypresses lining the main roads of France so that his troops would always march in the shade. In Israel, main routes east and west, to the Syrian and Egyptian borders, had double rows of trees to hide men and armor from the air.

So he liked the Israelis, as did Wade. They knew how to fight and how to live. Oilfields and tankers held the same kind of men. They beat boardrooms any day.

Rashid met him at the curb.

"Garrison, effendi, good evening," he said, opening an umbrella against a barely visible evening spring mist. "Our pleasure."

Short, with tightly curled brown hair that clung to his scalp, he had a square, features-thrust-forward face common to many Arabs. When he smiled, as he did now, he always reminded Hubie of a mustached, iodine-stained turtle. But then, Hubie had his prejudices and fears.

First, he wondered what, exactly, Rashid did. There were many possibilities, all sinister.

He could be a spy. Custom forbade the diplomatist's succeeding his father. The throne instead would pass to another surviving son of his grandfather, a member of a different branch of the family. Rashid might be that group's agent in place for the day power changed hands.

Or he could as easily be overseer of his country's United Nations delegation. Attached to the diplomatist, who had no official standing, he had access, a base, and a low profile in the local international community. All suited an Arab decision maker who preferred to remain in the background—as most did.

Or he might be an intelligence agent, one of a few from Persian Gulf states, apart from Iran, sent to the United States to handle joint area needs.

Second, Hubie distrusted his religion.

An army officer in his midthirties, Rashid, like Faisal and the diplomatist, came from a line of desert warriors. Brigands, really, who gained control of vast reaches of land, they followed the tenets of Wahabism. By far the most puritanical of Islam's sects, it permitted only the pleasures of the marriage bed. Austere, fervent, those who were committed to its principles were capable of the most extreme excess, for to them the word of the Koran came literally from God, not Mohammed.

Fortunately, the diplomatist no longer believed.

But Rashid did, Hubie knew.

That accounted, he supposed, for his endless hours in the gym at the Young Men's Hebrew Association at Ninety-second and Lexington. He had to dissipate that pent-up sexual energy. All that weightlifting made him ominous. The massive chest, arms, and shoulders dwarfed his head.

Smiling, wide-set white teeth flashing under the umbrella, he cupped Hubie's elbow in his hand, mounting the steps of the house. His head came only to Hubie's shoulder, but Hubie could imagine him lifting him just like that, by the elbow, with one hand if he wished.

He wondered again what Rashid did.

The diplomatist met him at the second-floor landing.

The gesture showed great respect. His outspread arms indicated affection as well.

"Welcome, Wilmer, our brother," he said in Arabic.

The only son of his father's favorite wife, a light-skinned Egyptian Bedouin princess, he had inherited from her the legacy of an ancestor and an act of violence two thousand years in the past. His face bore a flawless Roman profile.

In his midfifties, he remained the most handsome Arab Hubie had ever seen. As tall as he, and with hair as black, he had known much the same life as well. He too had been sacrificed to oil. For him, however, the decision had been involuntary.

In the thirties, before Acey Stiles and Hubie started to drill, his father had thought oil rights to his lands issued after World War I would expire. So he had talked to the French, and money had changed hands. As a sort of escrow and hedge against dealing with his future partners, he sent his son to France to be educated. He should have known better.

So should Ibn-Saud, in Saudi Arabia.* His sons were being corrupted at the same time. With oil company "uncles" supplying allowances and suggesting entertainment, what chance had Wahabism with teenage boys in London, New York, Paris, or Las Vegas?

The diplomatist's life changed on a Sunday morning in the Bois de Boulogne. Drunk, showing off to a fancy prostitute with whom he had been provided, he fell off his horse, fracturing his right hip and pelvis.

The hospital emergency-ward doctor, seeing his name and skin color, mistook him for an uppity Algerian *pied noir,* a black foot, whose family had made money at the expense of Frenchmen. He had had a busy Saturday night besides. So he set the fractures with a bit less than his usual precision.

Six weeks later, casts off, the diplomatist found he could walk only when he thrust the right side of his body forward at a forty-five-degree angle.

With winter came a more disconcerting discovery. The ball joint in his hip had become arthritic. The excruciating pain led to morphine. And the morphine led to a new circle of friends. They, in turn, led to syphilis.

The cure in the thirties involved arsenic and prolonged induced fevers. In many cases, it produced side effects fully as severe as the disease. So, between malady and medication the diplomatist returned home with a painful sensitivity to light and a considerable hearing loss.

Miraculously, his misfortunes were purely physical. His mind and personality escaped damage. Disciplined by a rigorous curriculum at the Sorbonne, his thought had a precision and breadth unusual in an Arab of any age. He left for France a friendly boy. He returned a friendly man. Most people in the West had been good to him.

Beyond that, he once told Hubie, Europe had given him a chance to con-

---

* Ibn-Saud died in 1953, the second-richest man in the world according to some estimates. His son Saud succeeded him as king. He and his brother princes, no doubt recalling the good old days of wine, women, and gambling that marked their "coming out" in the West, had the monarchy teetering on the edge of bankruptcy by 1958. The royal family then pressured Saud to put his half brother Faisal in office as prime minister to bail out the country's finances.

sider Middle Eastern aspirations and wishes. He had met the full range of Zionist students at the Sorbonne. Some, now high in Israel's government, came to visit him still. Many were wild-eyed in those days about Communism, he said, but they grew out of that. Meanwhile, their hopes for a nation built on agriculture and industry made sense. It fit with the times.

His father and his fellow sheikhs, similarly, had an equally valid right to their dream—to live the desert warrior's pure, uncomplicated life—but he wondered if they could afford the old ways at the expense of the new. Oil, he believed, would change everything. Managing it meant more than wealth. A culture stood at risk. Quietly, in the thirties, he set out to clarify the Arab vision. He and Hubie, the only educated men for a thousand miles in any direction, had often discussed his activities and aims.

Educated beyond the princes of other nearby states, and painfully sophisticated in the ways of the West, he became a key man in the Persian Gulf despite his youth. Always in the background, never mentioned, he had a say, Hubie knew, in every oil contract signed in the region. That remained true in 1967.

He presented himself as an eccentric expatriate, a recluse somehow in love with Manhattan. Those who knew better let that stand. They respected his wish to keep his history to himself. A few understood, as well, the reality behind the fey impression. In truth, he chose to live in New York because of the pain research being done in the city's hospitals.

Meanwhile, international oilmen equally interested in anonymity came to the house on Seventy-fourth Street to launch deals or to have the final terms blessed. In effect, he acted as a negotiator for all the countries neighboring his own. How long that role would endure, however, when an uncle, possibly jealous, became king remained moot.

But now the diplomatist had influence everywhere on the Arabian Peninsula. Hubie had long suspected, in fact, that its nations shared the upkeep of the lavish establishment in which he now stood.

Once it had been a row of three identical houses. Gutted, they were united by structural steel and redone as an austere version of a sheikh's palace. Ibn-Saud's sons put Las Vegas neon lighting in their castles. Here, the art and furniture reflected the diplomatist's long stay in France; the stone floors and priceless rugs, the land of his birth.

The front room on the second floor, Hubie supposed, supported his eccentric's image. He assumed, at least, that it had been conceived for that purpose. Stretching full length across the width of the house, it ran twenty feet deep. Lined with couches, its center held a king's ransom of chess tables and sets purchased at the world's premier auction houses. In thirty-five years, Hubie had never heard the diplomatist mention the game.

He dressed for effect, too. He often said clothes helped him will away the weather. He must have had some real rubes in for supper that night, Hubie thought, and told them that clouds made him want a day in the south of France. Barefoot, he wore the white ducks and blue-striped jersey traditional along the Riviera.

But there would be no tricks now. Despite opposing interests, they were friends. Each, in a way, too, had become the product of the other. The diplomatist had taught Hubie much Arabic and much about the Arab way. Hubie, in turn, had provided him with his introduction to international oil.

So, regarding his caller, his eyes softened.

He had been expecting this visit, of course. Still, he had hoped it would not take place. It signified defeat. The majors wanted to destroy PANARTEX. Who but he then had $2 billion to lend? He wanted asking for it to be as easy as possible. His terms, he knew, would be ferocious enough.

Arm still around Hubie, right hip pointing toward the front room, he nodded reassuringly. Then, scuttling ahead like a crab, he led them through the entrance and left to a two-piece sofa in the far rear corner. Like the drapes and the damasked walls, its color, a soft celadon green, had been chosen as a concession to his eyes.

Rashid entered then bearing a huge gold tray. On it were two bowls of mint ice. The diplomatist handed one to Hubie.

"You've had a long ride," he said, alluding to the search for $2 billion.

In common with Faisal, he shared a favorite proverb: "God gave man two ears and one tongue so we could listen twice as much as we talk."

He heeded that wisdom now. Sunk in the corner of the deep sofa, immobile, valanced ceiling lights on low, he barely seemed present. His face shadowed, the white duck pants and the stripes in his fisherman's jersey looked muted and far off as well. He wanted that effect. It made asking easier.

But, in due course, instead, he heard about a war. He had known it would come for at least a year. Hubie, he now saw, wanted to sell that.

"Brother . . ." he said, trying to avoid embarrassment. "A *naksa* for Nasser, nothing more." That put the matter in perspective, he thought.

"A setback?" Hubie asked. He believed it might be more.

The diplomatist then heard about the Lions.

*"Mesh momken, brother . . . ,"* he whispered. *"Mesh momken."*

"Impossible?" Hubie asked. "Possible." Loren had found it and checked it out. Today he had learned why those ships were being built.

But what outsider could learn of such a war?

A banker, from a member of Nasser's cabinet, Hubie said. He then went to the Israelis with a deal. In return for the time and place of their attack, he would make the Jews a lot of money.

*"Mesh maaul . . ."*

"Inconceivable?" Hubie asked. Not at all. The Lions were moneymen. They saw only money. To them, nothing seemed inconceivable. They had an old T-2, *Dynamic Papachristou . . . .*

Cupping his ear, the diplomatist leaned forward.

At story's end, he sighed in awe. *"Al nakba!"* he whispered.

The catastrophe indeed, Hubie said, nodding. Could Nasser suffer a harsher fate? he wondered. He would finally be brought to heel, made to respect his Arab brothers. Could Persian Gulf states ask for more?

Shaking his head, the diplomatist looked upward. *"Allah maana!"* he said softly and gratefully. "Allah is with us!" Then, softer still, he sent forth a prayer. He asked Allah to watch over the Jews in their war. After that, he turned to earthly matters. Dates? he asked.*

Hubie could only shrug. He had an approximate idea at best.

Then how would they know?

Simply by watching *Dynamic Papachristou.*

Yes, that could be done. Where would she be?

In Ancona, Italy.

Thoroughly shamed, the diplomatist sank back in the corner of the celadon sofa. He had feared this meeting. He had expected his old friend to beg. Instead, his friend had been the giver. He had brought the most precious gift one person could offer another: unconditional trust. The gift had value as well. Its price went beyond measuring.

What he had just heard, the diplomatist knew, made him secure in this house, near doctors who brought him peaceful, undrugged nights, for the rest of his life. Regardless of who became king after his father, the other sheikhs would insist that he stay in New York. He had only to tell them he wanted to, when the time came. Their debt to him, after this night, would be eternal, and they would see that their wishes prevailed.

He, in turn, had a similar obligation. He sought now to honor it.

"Wilmer, brother . . ." Emotion choked his words.

Sinking farther back into darkness, he tried again. Many doors, he knew, had been shut in his brother's face in the past year. They would always be. The lone rider seemed easy prey. His sheikhs, in fact, thought that in time he would fall to them. Happily, all that had just ceased to apply.

This no longer involved business. It concerned . . . *sharaf.* Honor. Only that repaid trust. The gift he had taken could not go unacknowledged. What did his friend need?

Hubie told him. He wanted $221 million—very quietly.

* A question of more than military significance. A few observers have surmised that Faisal of Saudi Arabia, knowing the date when fighting would start, found it wise to be in Europe. He sent Nasser a message of support. Radio Mecca also said Saudi troops had entered Jordan to fight on the Arab side. The Israelis, supposedly, never saw one of those fellows. Further credence to the theory that the Persian Gulf states had a fix on timing comes from the immediate financial aid Kuwait gave Egypt, Iraq, Jordan, and Syria at war's end. It amounted to nearly £60 million, estimates say. Such sums are not withdrawn on the spur of the moment. As it was, the size of the withdrawal had a noticeably weakening effect on the pound sterling. The Saudis sent money also, but from dollar reserves, which were not as visible in money markets.

That was all?

With the ships they had coming off charter and new ones they would build, they would earn $2 billion for the North Slope in two years.

The diplomatist leaned forward. Only now did he appreciate the nature of what he had been given. He had saved thousands of men, billions of dollars in military equipment, and the national honor of several states. And it had been a gift. For $221 million could be easily raised. The interest would be murderous, to be sure, but in a tanker move, when rates zoomed, no one would notice.

His sheikhs had had no such gift in mind for Hubie. Why he came to them baffled the diplomatist.

He shrugged, indicating himself. "Why, brother?" he asked. "Why here?"

Hubie wiped his lower lip with thumb and forefinger. He felt frustrated. He had already talked himself dry, and nothing had come out right. He had been unable to tell Loren how he felt. He had that problem now. Still, he had to try. He owed it to this man who, never whimpering, had given him an example of how to live with adversity.

They had played their hand in the game of oil over thirty years, he said. Soon history would deal a fresh round, power would shift, and new players would sit down at the table. Then they would go separate—

He shook his head, as if erasing that. Too pompous, he thought. Too dramatic, too macho. Poker hands belonged in cowboy movies, not here. They had done something quite different. They had shared life—and with damned few laughs. So he tried to say that. As usual, he spoke with great economy.

What would they remember of each other, dying? he asked. Learning. Pain. Time.

The diplomatist, he observed, understood. His head nodded in the darkness.

Those things went to *sharaf,* Hubie went on. When shared, they too involved honor. So whom should he have helped if not his brother?

Brown eyes glistening, the diplomatist came forward in the light again. This war would drive oil prices up, he said, and his country had no investment strategy for that additional income. Until someone came up with a plan, why not hold those surplus royalty dollars on the PANARTEX books as promissory notes?

In effect, that made the loan interest-free.

Hubie thought of the Koran: "God giveth manifold to whom he will."

They were on the North Slope.

Another mint ice? the diplomatist asked.

Good. He wanted to call Washington.

Then they could see a little of Johnny Carson, and Rashid would drive him back to the Dorset.

## April 20, 1967
## Hasegawa Shipyards, Japan
## Genoa, Italy

TAKEO KONO cradled the white telephone.

Then, head back, he regarded the graving docks just outside his office window. His pride of lions, painted now and almost ready for sea, blocked out the sky. The white heraldic cats on their red stacks towered sixteen stories above ground level.

The week before, he had thought they provided him with a clear path to the *zaibatsu*'s executive suite in Tokyo. A delegation from the Standards Committee of the Shipbuilders' Council had come to the yard to review the ships. They had been enthusiastically approved.

Then, in his office, when he described what he had learned of modular construction and how quickly 100,000-tonners could be built in the future, the members of the party had become downright ecstatic.

They had even laughed at the midships sections of the five 250,000-tonners in the docks with those about to be launched. They had no idea Hasegawa had anything that large on its order books. Nor had they authorized construction. But seeing how well the new technique had been mastered in the five smaller ships, the gentlemen of the Standards Committee took the monsters to follow as a little joke on themselves.

Nervously patting his shirt pockets for his Kents and cigarette holder, Kono wondered if the project would be his undoing instead. Absently gazing at the gleaming white superstructure of *Lianides Triumphant*, he saw in his mind's eye at the same moment the battery factory in Sapporo where his father worked. He could very well be there, toiling alongside him, in a week, he thought.

His anxiety stemmed from Oriental inscrutability. His *zaibatsu* chief, a traditionalist, hissed a lot. He did so to show impatience, pleasure, or rage. Kono had always known which had been which. No longer. What he had just heard defied translation. Beyond that, he had only been following orders. Moreover, a check from Bank Nippon lay on his desk. The chief should have taken that as good news. He hissed it, instead, like a burning green log. Kono found that mystifying.

Finishing his recital, he grew even more bewildered. And what about the check? he asked.

The question brought forth the single longest hiss Kono had ever heard. It could only indicate profound embarrassment, he thought.

He would have to see, the chief said.

*See?* See what? Kono wondered. From whom?

Who in this world, or the next, for that matter, did the chief of an eight-centuries-old *zaibatsu* feel required to consult? And what would the chief say of him?

Kono wiped his face with a blue-and-white bandana.

Strange, he thought. Very strange.

Halfway around the world, Kono had company.

Some stevedores in Genoa shared his puzzlement.

They had spent the morning on the cargo-passenger liner *American Excalibur,* one of the famed "Four Aces" belonging to American Export Lines. By far the most interesting freight they had taken from the ship had been a heavily constructed crate plastered on each side with red arrows and stencils:

> THIS SIDE UP!
> CONTENTS:
> Marine Compass
> 2 Outboard Engines
> NO FORKLIFT!

Living near the water and fishing on their days off, the stevedores would have liked to steal that crate.

That afternoon, finished on *Excalibur,* they moved one ship forward on the dock. There a French tramp set to cross the Med and coast North Africa to Port Said and then up to Turkey took on its last cargo. Shortly after 3 P.M. the coveted crate reappeared with a garish red tag stapled to it, indicating that customs had passed it in and out of Genoa.

Such a transit required new papers and the services of a freight forwarder. Why anyone would do that when he could ship direct from New York baffled the stevedores.

An expensive whim, they assumed.

Crazy Americans.

*April 22, 1967*
*Oyster Bay, New York–Ottawa, Canada*

EVELYN ANSWERED the moment the phone rang.

"Prentiss?" he asked. Howsam recognized that tone. It oozed satisfaction. That surprised him. Moreover, coming from Ottawa, it made him suspicious.

Howsam had had an anxious enough week already.

Lianides had called from San Francisco, before boarding the plane for Japan, to report that Arkie had told Fiona what would be happening.

After that, Howsam had heard nothing.

Had Fiona passed the message on to Demosthenes? If so, had he let Garrison and Wade in on the secret? And, finally, if they knew, what had they decided to do? He and Evelyn thought they would acknowledge receipt of the information and then use it for their own purposes. Why, then, were they still silent?

So, seeing the maid's message to call the Château Laurier Hotel, he had assumed that something else had gone wrong. Evelyn went to Ottawa to visit the Israeli Embassy. Usually, that meant trouble.

Puzzled, he shut the door on the great front-hall debate as Francine and the boys, still chilled from the Mets' first Saturday night game of the season, decided what to eat hot with *The Late Show*. Then he grunted warily in acknowledgment.

Evelyn continued, voice full of sly secrets. "Home Office rang yesterday to say someone in Bern wanted me here on the scrambler phone to—"

Schotten? Howsam thought. Jesus, what could have gone wrong in Europe?

"What happened?" he demanded, sure his suspicions had been justified.

"The dwarf's just heard from the cowboys, and—"

"He's what?"

"—and the signal's affirmative!"

"You're sure?"

"Yes, yes. God may be subtle, but he's never mean, Prentiss. Good news happens—even in this life!"

Sighing, Howsam sank back in his red leather den chair. Of all the communications channels open to Garrison and Wade, Schotten had seemed the least likely. Why go abroad when they had men in Washington who could pass a seemingly innocuous message to New York without understanding its contents? Garrison, a member of the Council on Foreign Relations, could have reached people in the Israeli UN delegation who could see that word got to them. For that matter, a phone call or a telegram to Battle & Company would have suited Howsam equally well.

Wade and Garrison, however, he learned, unfettered by orthodoxy, had made those options seem as pedestrian as they were. They had, he thought, found the best of all ways to speak to them.

"What'd they tell Eric?" he asked.

"I blush to say," Evelyn, the man who had correctly sensed their intentions from the start, admitted. "Hang on, Prentiss," he ruefully warned, having been as wrong as Howsam about how the message would arrive. "It's not so much *what* they said, but *how* they said it. First off, they never got within eleven thousand miles of Eric."

"They didn't?"

"No. Of course not. The tyke turned up, instead, in the Land of the Rising Sun the day before yester—"

At Hasegawa? Howsam wondered. What reason would Wade have to go there?

One occurred to him almost at once. "Jesus! He didn't go looking for Arkie or Lianides, did he?" he asked.

Evelyn chuckled wryly at the suggestion. "Oh, no! Not that boy. He must've been drooling for a look, but he never boarded one of the ships—did his business in ten minutes instead, and went his way, which Eric and I assume'll be a merry one indeed the next few weeks. At any rate, he told the superintendent the hundred-thousand-tonners looked better than the sketches, and since they'd be out of the graving docks soon, he wanted five like them for himself—subject, of course, to the present clients' okay, who might have options to build more, or a say about who cashed in on what the yard had learned about modular construction at their expense. If they did, he said, he wanted them to know he'd wait his turn in line and build elsewhere in the meantime. But, regardless, his order stood. Does that suit, Prentiss?"

"Almost . . ." Howsam answered.

Evelyn continued in admiration and amusement. "The *zaibatsu* chief passed word to Eric within the hour, and no one who hadn't known what was going on had been exposed—and so much for all our clever ideas of how they'd get in touch!" he laughed.

"Except for one thing," Howsam added. "You think he was for real? He could have been fishing, too."

"Not likely. My apologies, but I forgot to mention it. He left a check."

"He did?"

"Yes, for three million dollars. Earnest money, he said."

That made it real for Howsam.

"And he's no *schnorer*, either, Prentiss." Evelyn laughed, recalling more of the call from Schotten. "He even passed on a stock tip to return the compliment—said they'd have some good news of their own to report soon, and between oil and ships their shares'd be selling for fifteen times earnings in the seventies, higher than any of their competitors."

"So they hit up north after all," Howsam concluded.

"Without doubt. And that's another proof of their sincerity. For now, that bit of news is as valuable to them as ours is to us. It hasn't gone out yet over the Arctic grapevine, and the majors think they've got them stymied for financing, which gives our cowboy friends a tremendous advantage."

"But they found money for ships . . ." Howsam mused.

"Indeed. Remember my rather dreary lecture on the politics of the Middle East last fall in James Bay and where I said they'd go as a last resort? Well, two of our chaps, who just happen to have an apartment on Seventy-fourth

Street, saw the chairman of the board pay a visit to a certain distinguished party Monday night—"

"And you didn't tell me?"

"Prentiss, they see each other every ten days or so. They're old chums, so that meant nothing by itself. But somehow I've a hunch now that one hand washed the other at that little tête-à-tête and the chairman came away with the money to get the tyke his ships."

"Which in turn'll pay their way up north."

"Exactly, and the silence of the tomb'll descend on what they've taken from us!" Evelyn crowed. "That whole gang represented on Seventy-fourth Street'll jolly well wear their beads out praying for you!"

Slumped in the red chair, Howsam ignored the irony.

Thinking hard, he considered something else.

"You know something?" he said at length. "With the ships they'll charter, plus what they'll build, I think he may have pegged the price–earnings ratio on their stocks too low. There's no reason, the way they do business, why their shares couldn't sell for twenty, twenty-five times earnings while the majors poop along at six, maybe eight, times if they're lucky. That's a man who can send a message, *bubeleh!*"

"Oh, yes! God bless him," Evelyn answered, "look how careful he was. Look what he gave away just to be sure we'd read him. One could turn that little bull loose in any china shop in the world, and he'd not so much as chip a tea-cup, Prentiss. That's the beauty of dealing with professionals—it almost doesn't matter whether things develop according to plan. Old, established firms see there's no waste, no misunderstandings, no accidents."

"So, that's it, then. At least on the front," Howsam concluded.

His sigh of satisfaction trailed off in silence. "It isn't?" he asked.

"Only for the cowboys," Evelyn conceded. "They've got what they came for, and they're bright, so they'll go on about their business and leave us to ours. But there's an old Welsh proverb that applies here, I think: 'Fate does not work in trivialities.' What that means, my father used to say, is that there's a natural order to things. We'll not be done in New York, I believe, until we know everyone else is satisfied, as well."

"You mean Demosthenes?"

"Indeed. And the lady in question, certainly. It seems to me she's burnt a bridge. If she doesn't like what she's found on the other side, we could be hearing from her, besides Demosthenes. It depends on what their information bought, don't you think?"

"You see that kind of payoff there?"

"I'd be shocked if there weren't. You don't chalk up what they've done to young love's first sweet blush, do you?"

"Jesus, am I dumb!"

"Not dumb, just blessed. You married your college sweetheart and lived happily ever after. Your mind has no experience in that line of thought. Mine either, for that matter. The suggestion came from the dwarf. With his looks and money, he's a sophisticate in problems of that nature."

"Christ, it could be. How'll we find out?"

"We won't until it happens."

"But that could put the weight on Ilona!"

"That's why I plan to be in New York for the first two weeks of June. With company."

"You're bringing guys down?"

"No, but I'll have a friend there and access to others if I need them."

The friend, Howsam knew, would be Itch Cohen. He had been in frequent, cordial contact with Evelyn. They had, in fact, scouted the homes and offices of all their likely targets should violence be required.

As distasteful as he found that possibility, Howsam had begun to live with it, accepting Evelyn's view that such an outcome would be an act of war. On one level, he knew it would be. For him, however, it would still be murder. Money had gotten him into this, nothing else, and he never kidded himself about that. If the price was right, he could go along with a lot of things, he had discovered. He had not enjoyed learning that.

So now, suddenly, besides conscience, he faced the likelihood of assuming responsibility for Dr. Fabian as well. She had hated this from the start. He worried about how she would react to suddenly finding herself cast in the role of fingerman. More important, he feared the effect on her already precarious state of mind of delivering someone to Evelyn and Cohen.

She had, he thought, gone steadily downhill since the January weekend with Schotten. She drank and smoked more, seemed edgier, sank into deep silences that often ended in convulsive shudders. He sensed she had decided on a showdown with her private demon, regardless of cost. Watching her, he preferred not to predict the outcome of that confrontation. He hoped, as well, she would reach that crisis on her own, without any help from him.

Evelyn, ever prescient, offered assurance. "Eric thinks there'll be no problem," he said. "He says she's ready for that sort of responsibility."

"Yeah, but he's in love with her."

"I know."

"He say that just now?"

"Oh, as early as January. We mentioned it when he came over to the Bahamas, after your week in Florida."

"You guys saw all this developing then?"

"Saw the possibility would be more like it," came the reply. "Some men, like the tyke, are irresistible. You can't stop them short of death. It remains to be seen if the other two—Demosthenes and the lady—are cut from the same cloth. They might not be, you know. Who's to say?"

That increased Howsam's concern for Dr. Fabian. Everyone involved seemed equally irresistible.

"But the other two—we can't see if they're happy?" he asked.

"Short of waiting, I think not."

"So what do we do in the meantime?"

"Well, I, for one," Evelyn replied in the simpering tone he reserved for his most outrageous pronouncements, "have been sitting here thinking that a seven hundred or eight hundred percent return over the next ten years, whilst nothing alongside what you stand to make, would do me rather nicely. I think we ought to start building a position in that stock we mentioned earlier—say, five thousand shares a month over the next few years—well hidden, of course. It might do you to come in with me, too, and we'll bury the shares up here with some pals of mine. Would you look into that Monday, Prentiss?"

Howsam had to laugh. "You little *gonif.* You never get enough, do you?"

"Well," Evelyn chuckled back, "there's nothing down anywhere that says I can't make a quid out of this, either, is there? Your late father-in-law, you know, would already have buy orders out. Home Office wouldn't mind, either. It wants its friends to prosper. Even Aeschylus'd approve."

"Aeschylus?" Howsam protested. "That Greek's been dead forever! What the hell could he ever have to say about misusing insider information?"

"Everything, Prentiss! Everything!" Evelyn gibed.

Then, asking him to call Monday, he let his voice drop to an appropriate tone, fitting both the subject of the evening and the quotation: " 'God is not opposed to deceit in a righteous cause.' "

Who was he to argue that? Howsam thought. Still, he worried about Ilona.


*April 26, 1967*
*Dhahran, Saudi Arabia–Nice, France*


THE PLANE dipped on final approach to Dhahran.

Loren Wade zipped up his trousers.

A great trip, he thought, buckling his seat belt. So far, it had been a thrill a minute. He had never wanted more than that.

Monday he had gotten the last Miami flight from Kennedy. Tuesday, at 7:30 A.M., he left Miami on Air Panama. What with a nice nap on the couch in Pan Am's executive club, two breakfasts on the plane, and a longer snooze aloft, he hit Paitilla Airport in full stride. Andrés Bejirano-Sáenz, counsel for the six Panamanian PANARTEX subsidiaries, alerted by Hubie, took him at once to the Gallo de Oro. Fortified by shrimp and chicken, beans, and rice, they then plundered pension and profit-sharing plans set up there to give Wade that option.

Shortly after lunch, the local branch of Bank Nippon delivered a certified check for $3.5 million.

At 4 P.M., Ursall Majors called from Washington. He had a way east that day without a trip to Bogotá or Mexico City for a connecting plane. The Navy ran a weekly freight flight to Pearl Harbor and Manila. Using his influence and invoking a fictional captain's reserve commission, he got Wade on it.

Wednesday morning, fresh from a good night's sleep amidst a jumble of submarine spare parts, Wade presented himself at the Pan Am counter at the Honolulu airport. What did they have for Japan? he asked the clerk.

A 7 P.M. flight to Tokyo, came the answer.

What about that Japan Air Lines 707 parked outside? he asked.

A charter, the clerk said.

Did they have a seat on that 707? he asked.

Yes, but that was a charter flight, he was told.

Who chartered it? he asked.

The SONY Japanese Honor Workers' Brigade.

Fishing in his own pocket, Wade smiled ingenuously. He was a Japanese Honor Worker, he said, handing over a card identifying him as president of Nippon Transport, his Japanese tanker company, and a fifty-dollar bill.

The plane left at 10 A.M.

*Sushi*ed and noodled aloft, he returned the smile of the Honor Worker across the aisle. Slant-eyed, the man still recalled Acey with his cardsharp's squint. Other Honor Workers grinned and hissed, too. One brought forth a bottle of Johnny Walker Red, in fact.

Teacup out, Wade said, *"Dom arrigato go zai mas."* At least, he mused, Japs liked good whiskey. Ferocious gamblers, they were fond of round-eyed marks as well. In high good humor, he left the plane two hundred dollars ahead.

Thursday, at 5:30 A.M., at Sasebo, he and the pilot of the chartered Cessna twin breakfasted in the airport employees' cafeteria. He got a shave, rented a Toyota, and sat down in Takeo Kono's office at 7:35.

Check and message delivered, he next visited SSK, a yard as famous as Hasegawa was obscure. The first two of four 60,000-tonners coming off charter the next week would refit there. Knowing the approximate start date of the war, he wanted to rush in the third and fourth.

Succeeding, he returned to Sasebo at 11 A.M.

He spent the afternoon in Tokyo at Nippon Transport, had a big supper with the manager, and caught a red-eye flight to Hong Kong.

Friday, at 6:30 A.M., he went aboard *PANARTEX New Territories* at Hong Kong. From there she was going up to Sasebo and SSK. He wantd to see the work her officers had ordered. He had ideas, too. She would be spot-chartered, and those trips could take her to Europe. New routes might call for structural modifications.

He had also watched her master, the dour six-foot-four-inch Filipino, Sixtos Bolanos. Magnificently color blind when measuring performance, he had decided to give one of the Hasegawa 100,000-tonners to Bolanos, so they had much to discuss, as well.

Saturday, at 5:30 A.M., another red-eye deposited him in Jakarta, where he went through the drill again with *PANARTEX Kowloon.* Now skippered by old pal Ocie Culpepper, she would go next to Sasebo for refit.

He wanted Ocie on one of the 100,000-tonners, too. The party following the announcement led to Serang and one of the great restaurants in that part of the world. After an all-night falldown built around a whole pit-roasted pig, he got back to Jakarta just in time to get a flight to Singapore.

*PANARTEX Luzon* there would go to Borneo next, then to Manila and up to Japan. Engineroom heat stood at 124 degrees. Munching salt tablets as if they were popcorn, he okayed $600,000 worth of engine work in ninety minutes. Topside, he went for another $875,000.

Never known for generosity, he smiled at the bemused expressions around him. He had just spent, he and Hubie estimated at the Dorset six days before, the profits of *Luzon*'s first two weeks on charter when that war began.

Done, he taxied to the Raffles Hotel. Its Sikh doormen and bellmen and barefoot little Malay waiters had never impressed him. He liked the Raffles for its bathrooms. Their huge tubs took a week's wash at one shot.

He had bathed and done the laundry by the time the lawyers arrived. Alerted by him Thursday in Tokyo that he would be coming, they brought the necessary ledgers and documents. Chinese, they were known in his office as Charlie Chan and Number One Son. As counsel went, they were among the best he retained around the world. They had to be. He kept a lot of "egg money" in Straits Transits, Ltd., based there. Singapore, unlike Panama, had strict laws and currency regulations.

Finding the cracks in those prohibitions kept them busy until 1:30 A.M. Monday. Then, with time out for sleep, they worked until bank closing Tuesday.

Chan and Son had done it again, he thought, boarding the TWA red-eye that night for Riyadh, Saudi Arbia. He had expected to leave Singapore with about $1.5 million. Instead, he had a letter of credit in his pocket to a London bank for $2.7 million.

Wade felt even better now as the plane from Riyadh lowered over the ugly brown waters of the Persian Gulf and passed across the green strip behind the shore that marked the ARAMCO company town. With its neat white bungalows and deserted Little League fields, it looked like a suburb of Los Angeles with the kids in school.

His fourth 60,000-tonner, *PANARTEX Nippon*, lay here. She would leave that night for Yokohama. Then, after discharging, she would make her way south to Sasebo. He wanted her master, Joaquin Wainwright, one of his young stars, to be responsible for *Luzon* too in the yard.

As usual in the desert, with thermals everywhere, the plane came down like a kite. Lurching this way and that, bouncing three times, it eventually grabbed the runway in a rubber-burning skid and stayed landed.

Glancing out of his window, through the heat waves rising across the field, he thought the buildings were underwater, they shimmered so. Shaking his head at the prospect of another day here, he looked away.

He turned back almost at once. Sensing something unusual, he glanced at the terminal again. Sure, he thought, seeing what had caught his eye.

Why would a Japan Air Lines 707 freighter be there?

Who, he wondered, besides himself, could be so dumb as to need a $40,000 charter flight to put aboard a ship what should have been there in the first place? At that, he had required such expensive medicine only once, when he had just started running his fleet.

Ever curious, he bounded down the boarding steps to have a quick look at that precious cargo before getting on the ARAMCO bus that met every flight. Wooden crates, he saw, steaming with dry ice, were being forklifted out of the plane's side doors into a waiting red van.

The Japanese words stenciled in black on the tops of the boxes seemed familiar. But they went beyond his reading. Stretching his neck, though, for a better look, he saw a red symbol below the writing. At first he took it for a flower. Tiny and blurred, it hid in shame, he thought, reluctantly identifying the shipping company responsible for so costly an error. Then, squinting, he brought the image into focus and what it depicted: a set of Olympic rings.

Seeing them, he laughed aloud. Even the mighty Onassis screwed up provisioning! He could hardly wait to tell Hubie. It had taken him years to live down the incident.

Still grinning, he boarded the bus. Then, gradually, his expression grew more thoughtful.

By the time they reached the refinery and tank farm, his brow engulfed his sandy widow's peak. He remembered why the Japanese writing he saw on those crates at the airport seemed so familiar. The Friday before, he and Sixtos Bolanos, celebrating the captain's promotion, had gone to Hong Kong's Japanese steak house. Then, afterward, standing on the curb waiting for a cab to take him to Kai Tak and the red-eye to Jakarta, they both had to pee. So, ducking into the alley behind the restaurant, they did, surrounded by shoulder-high stacks of boxes like those he had just seen.

Kobe beef, Bolanos casually remarked, reading the thickly stenciled characters, the best in the world and the most costly. Japanese cows fed on rice. There were a few like that in the Philippines, but nowhere else.

Onassis fed a crew Kobe beef?

The question bothered him all through lunch and his inspection of *PAN-ARTEX Nippon* that followed. Then, when he had finished, he stopped at the port captain's office to say hello to the staff, all of whom he knew.

Opening his airline pilot's flight case, he removed a bottle of Wild Turkey bourbon with a suitable flourish and passed it around. Out of deference to its Wahibite hosts, ARAMCO allowed no Jews or booze, so glasses were quickly produced. Metal chair tipped against the cinderblock wall, he joined the shop talk, patiently awaiting an opening. One quickly came in the friendly kidding.

He wasn't so dumb, he protested. Not as dumb as whoever was responsible for the Kobe beef he had seen coming into town that morning.

Oh, that! Cal Jenks, a harbor pilot, scoffed. That wasn't dumb. That was crazy. Onassis had his OTR* bug again. His captain said they were set to provision in Taranto, Italy, but then they were ordered not to use the Suez Canal getting there. That meant they would be about twelve days short of beef. So, for once in his life, that sonofabitch Ari did the right thing. He bought a planeload of the best and arranged for it to be kept in Dhahran so that ships calling there could draw on it.

Hearing that, Wade wanted to run.

But again, awaiting better timing, he took another two fingers of whiskey. Then, leaving the half-empty bottle, he said goodbye and stumped out into the afternoon heat to clamber back aboard *PANARTEX Nippon.*

Sure that ARAMCO and/or the Arabs taped phone and cable lines,† he wanted to get a message to Hubie quickly and privately. Composing a long radiogram, he ordered it to be sent as soon as tug lines were cast off. His European itinerary, for which he required hotel rooms, would take him to the principal shipbuilding cities. He wanted Shirley Carmichael to update PAN-ARTEX ship movements in and out of those places and to photostat thirty sets of Angelakos' convertible plans. They were to be in London the next day, even if she had to buy a seat for them on Pan Am.

Then, cursing himself for having dawdled on his way around the world thus far, he rushed to the airport to get the first plane back to Riyadh and the first red-eye going wherever the hell west it went.

ARAMCO yo-yos might buy Optimum Track Routing. But old Mother Wade's little boy Loren? Never!

OTR in this case meant the best way to Europe around the Cape of Good Hope. Hell, that had been known in 1488, when Bartholomeu Dias rounded Africa and called its tip "Cabo Tormentoso." In 1498 it gave Vasco da Gama,

---

* Optimum Track Routing. The art of determining the quickest, most economical course between two points, using seasonal winds and currents to best advantage.
† A shrewd guess, but possibly too conservative. It developed after the Yom Kippur War in 1973 that Mossad, Israeli intelligence, had been tapping both parties' cable lines, as well. No one would admit, however, how long the taps had been in place.

going east instead of west, the key to one of history's most fabled sailing routes: La Carreira da India, the Passage to India. A few years shy of five centuries later, nothing had changed.

Moreover, Onassis had been running ships around the Cape since 1956, when he vowed never again to be hostage to Nasser and the Suez Canal.

And now, suddenly, he bought his crews Kobe beef. Then he sent them to Italy the long way around. Jesus, he really had to move, Wade thought.

Onassis knew about the war, too.*

The Lions too took a step forward that day.

They took delivery of the Boston Whalers ordered in January from Captain O. M. Watts, Ltd., in London.

M. Maxime Masiloff, the purchaser, stood on the Quai Papacino, in Nice's Port Lympia, to receive them. With documents freshly stamped in a consulate on the Rue d'Alger, he ordered the boss stevedore to have one boat taken to the bonded warehouse to await the arrival of a Turkish tramp bound for the eastern Mediterranean.

A cordial, sunny type, M. Masiloff then reached into the pocket of his gray flannels and produced a roll of franc notes. Holding them before the boss, he asked if two or three of his boys could help him put the other Whaler into his truck for the run west down the coast.

Eying the roll, the boss said of course.

A few minutes later, a tarpaulin over the boat, and lines holding it down, M. Masiloff drove off in a Chevy truck with Spanish license plates. Red flags fluttered from the lowered tailgate and a blonde gorgeous enough to be in films squealed with delight as he left the dock, gas pedal floored and tires screeching.

The stevedores took the incident in stride. The clerks at Captain O. M. Watts would not have. Their Maxime Masiloff had been a little sparrow of a man, with glasses, mustache, and graying black hair. The Maxime Masiloff on the Quai Papacino, on the other hand, stood well over six feet tall and had a lifeguard's physique and blond hair. He seemed about twenty-five.

Ten days hence, a Maxime Masiloff would receive the other Whaler on Cyprus and send it along to its ultimate destination. He, courtesy of Israeli intelligence, would be a Russian defector with a patriarchal graying beard, well known on the island.

* Steadfastly denied by that most modest and unassuming of men. Some shipping observers maintain, however, that the date he started sending all of his ships around the Cape of Good Hope, regardless of European destination, occurred, in fact, a week earlier. That aside, no Onassis ship lost a moment shaping a new course when war broke out.

*April 28, 1967*
*Dublin, Ireland*
*Hasegawa Shipyards, Japan*

THE ROOM-SERVICE waiter wheeled in breakfast.

Wade stepped into the parlor to sign the check.

Then, congratulating himself on having wrought yet another triumph of timing, he sat down by the fireplace. On the silver platter before him, usually reserved for whole Dover soles, reposed four impeccably basted eggs, yolks recalling tennis balls. They were surrounded by an equally impeccably broiled mixed grill. The platter behind them held a high mound of cottage-fried potatoes and onions, done just as he wished, flanked by toast soused in melted butter.

Such were the joys of Dublin's Gresham Hotel.

He deserved no less, he thought, hefting the quart silver coffeepot that would be replaced hourly. Events had really moved since Riyadh.

The first red-eye from there for Europe Wednesday night had been a Lufthansa 707 Frankfurt-bound, with an Athens stop. Piling on, he had quickly fallen asleep, only to be awakened in Istanbul, courtesy of a balky engine.

Rather than wait for repairs, he got an SAS flight to Copenhagen, which would have put him fifty minutes from London. At Zurich, though, owing to Channel and North Sea gales, they were grounded indefinitely.

Having grown up in Western Europe's storm systems, he immediately handed his baggage stub for the Val-Pak to a clerk. Taking a receipt, he said he would get the bag Sunday in Copenhagen. That done, he bought a ticket for London on the first BEA flight scheduled to leave.

Then, after glancing at a clock, he followed the signs to a telephone exchange, counted out $19.60, and called Takeo Kono, at Hasagewa Shipyards.

Out of the booth within ten minutes, smiling, he forked over $11.80 more and got Hubie on his way to bed.

Zurich! What in hell was he doin' there? Hubie asked.

Buyin' ships, he laughed.

Ships? He was supposed to be sendin' a message!

The *ships* were the message, he said. He had just gotten word from that Jap, Kono.

And Kono had heard from the Lions?

Believe it!

And what did they say?

That they would be honored to share their gravin' docks an' good fortune with trusted, discreet friends!

Jesus, what a bunch! Hubie laughed. Thank God they weren't in oil. If they were, they'd own it all. Then his tone deepened. What had Loren bought, anyway? he asked.

A half-million tons. Five 100,000-tonners.

How? What had he used for dough?

He had optioned them with egg money.

Egg money? He had that much hidden? Millions?

Oh, yeah. In Panama. He had refueled in Singapore too.

Jesus . . .

His egg money had been an office joke for years.

"Loren . . . ?"

"Yeah."

"Don't buy anythin' more till you see Henley."

*Trouble,* Wade thought. He had a supper date with Henley that night. He handled their London banking.

What had happened? he asked.

Henley would tell—

"Loren!" Cora Garrison came on, taking the phone from Hubie, her voice ringing with the transparently false notes of delight that marked a woman who wanted something.

"Hiya, sweets!"

Hubie had said Loren was going to Dublin, she said. Was that so?

'Course it was. Hubie was the boss, wasn't he?

Would he have a little free time there?

Sure. Saturday afternoon.

Well, then, Cora wondered, could he just run up to Arnott's, on Grafton Street, and get her two of those Aran sweaters like—

"Cora . . ." Hubie protested.

"Shut up!" she told him. Didn't his family count? What made him think business always had to come first? Besides, those sonsofbitches at Saks Fifth Avenue were getting forty dollars apiece for what Loren could buy for twelve.

"Loren?" she called.

"Yeah."

"Get two, large. One with a white background—"

"Cora, we're dealin' a big—" Hubie came back.

"—the other with a gray," Cora continued, "like the one Willa Mae got for herself there two years ago—"

"Cora!" Hubie shouted.

"Bye-bye, sugar," she told Wade. Then, her business concluded, she hung up.

Shaking his head, Wade left the phone booth. That would be some scene, he thought. The women had to even out somehow.

As he knew they would, the April gales came in from the Atlantic, swept England, and then tracked up-Channel to the North Sea. So, while Copenhagen remained closed, he boarded the BEA flight to London.

He had never seen the Connaught Hotel doorman. But the doorman, spying the Stetson, knew him. Opening the cab door, he helped him out and put the airline pilot's case on the sidewalk for a bellman.

Ah, that would be Mr. Wade, he said, smiling. Good trip?

Real class.

It supported Hubie's assessment. The Connaught, he said, poshed with the Savoy and trailed only Claridge's, due to Queen Victoria's visit, in prestige. Its staff, however, treated Americans, especially Texans, better. Catering to British gentry, most of whom were big oil investors, they saw plenty of boots, string ties, and ten-gallon hats. Blue-suit Arabs, many educated in England, favored the hotel for the unselfconscious hospitality they got there, too.

The desk clerk, knowing him, saw nothing unusual about his arrival without luggage. "On the run again, Mr. Wade?" Should he ring and tell the barbers to stand by? Or would he prefer the hall porter to take the toilet kit Mr. Garrison kept in his garment bag at the hotel so that he could shave in his room?

"Do that." Wade had calls to make.

Yes. He would also find a packet in his room.

The parcel held the photostats of the convertible plans, the list of PANAR-TEX ship movements he had requested, and a telephone message. Mrs. Wade had called. She wanted him to stop at Harrods, in London, and get a dozen bars of the good Spanish soap that Bonwit's no longer carried. On the way back, he thought, making a note.

Then, taking his phone book out of the pilot's case, he started calling English shipyards—none on the Clyde, who were too gossipy for his taste.

Always furtive, he became more so buying ships. He made a habit of never negotiating in the country in which the yard was located. Everything he had to say to the British, for example, would be said in the Gresham, in Dublin. If deals were made, he would sign the papers here, on the way home, in a Connaught suite.

At seven, shaved and showered, he entered the bar.

Henley rose to greet him.

Tall, rapier-thin, and extremely handsome, Henley had little in common with other powerful City of London bankers. A member of the fifth generation of a British family of Malay tea planters, his complexion and cast of eye suggested that, somewhere in the distant past, one of his grandfathers had married a local princess, for either land or protection, or both.

An urbane Oxford man with a native's sense of touch for things east of Suez, he had been sent to Indonesia by his bank in the fifties to handle PANARTEX business there. The next year Hubie insisted that he go back to London to handle the company's English banking worldwide.

So, at twenty-six, he met Arabs. They liked him, too. Touch of tarbrush aside, that seemed natural to Wade. Many sheikhs' sons who would shortly control oil were the same age and had been similarly educated. They liked having a banker of their background and generation involved. It lessened their differences. It also meant that when they got power they would deal with a man they knew well and could trust.

Now, ten years later, Henley served both camps. Moreover, his integrity dominated the situation. He had never been accused of favoring either side.

So, shaking hands, Wade got right to the point. He had talked to Hubie, he said. What had gone wrong?

Henley shook his head. Nothing had gone wrong, he answered. But the plan had changed. Only 25 percent of the funds pledged had been forthcoming.

A renege?

Oh, no. Whatever had happened on Seventy-fourth Street involved *sharaf*. That had to be acknowledged and would be. The diplomatist had told him that himself. So had his clients in the Middle East. On the other hand, they feared that if the loan were made all at once it would call attention to itself. There would be a burble.

Burble?

A sudden, unexplained drop in the pound sterling.*

Could that happen?

It couldn't be ruled out.

And when would the rest of the loan come through?

Soon.

What did that mean?

Henley shrugged.

Summoning a waiter, he ordered two more stouts and a refill of the Connaught's homemade potato chips.

Regardless, he promised Wade, they could cope. He had called Charlie Chan, friend and mentor of his Indonesian days, that morning, and Chan had had many ideas. Orientals very bright! Henley said. Smiling, he tapped a disconcertingly blue eye.

They went to the bank, where two secretaries were typing necessary documents, and worked until ten-thirty on some finer points of ship financing. Then Henley took Wade to a theatrical club in Haymarket that began

* As indeed occurred shortly after the Six-Day War when Kuwait, Libya, and Saudi Arabia withdrew an estimated £60 million in sterling to give to a defeated Egypt. The amount pledged to PANARTEX ran over £70 million.

serving only when final curtains fell. At midnight they returned to the Connaught.

Then came the key question.

Leaving the cab, Wade looked across the rear seat. What did Henley think? he asked. Did they have a deal?

Henley touched his knee warningly. Then, as if fearing eavesdroppers, he spoke Malay.

He knew nothing of what had transpired between Hubie and the diplomatist. Nor did he need to. He had spoken to his other clients east of Suez, the sheikhs.

"*Baik-baik, Tuan,*" he whispered. The phrase had two meanings. Tourists thought cute little bellboys used it: "I'll say bye-bye now, Master." For Wade, it had a more direct meaning: "Watch out, Boss, or it's bye-bye!"

Nodding, he went into the hotel. He had suspected as much in Zurich. Someone had shaded the diplomatist. Full ahead! But eyes sharp now.

Rising at five-thirty, he checked out, reserved a suite for late in May, and got to Heathrow in time for the eight-o'clock Aer Lingus flight to Dublin.

Now, thanks to British lassitude, he enjoyed a proper Irish breakfast. His first caller, sales director of an English yard, had told him he would be along at one-thirty or two. Roads, he had said, were a rum lookout from the London suburb in which he lived to Heathrow. No guarantees, mind, but he would go flatout to catch the ten-o'clock flight. Making the eight-o'clock plane, or going to Dublin the night before, had never occurred to him. That, Wade supposed, might strike the guy as unseemly haste. They were, after all, only talking a $30-million order.

In due course, the gentleman arrived. Opening his attaché case, he shielded a small paper bag that did not go unnoticed. He had done some duty-free shopping at Roche's department store first. He approved the terrace suite, Gainsborough over mantel, peat fire in marble fireplace. Rather nice, actually, he allowed, for Irish.

What he could not cope with, however, were the wash-and-dry shirt and pair of tankerman's white cotton slop-chest socks hanging in the bathroom. He arrived talking $100 a ton. He left forty minutes later quoting $88.

The chairman of a Southampton yard appeared next. He took the laundry and the T-shirted client in stride. Arkie's plans, however, threw him off balance. He had never seen such an elegant profile. Pricing construction accordingly, he asked $106 a ton to build. Departing, he agreed to construct three 100,000-tonners at $86.91 a ton.

After him came a hard piece of work from Liverpool, a former captain in the British-India Line, who, hearing Wade's drawl, assumed he must have been a farmer. Quickly learning otherwise, he left with one of Henley's patented letters of credit committing him to build at $82.50 a ton.

And so it would go, Wade thought. The next morning he would play host to three guys from Belfast. They would rank him and laugh at the way he talked. Strangers always did. But he would buy all the tonnage they could deliver, anyway.

Then he would buy Cora's sweaters and fly to London and get a plane to Southampton. He had a ship in Hamble Saturday. He would take the skipper and the chief engineer to supper and spend the night aboard.

At that, he knew, Dublin would give him two of the most profitable days in his life. He would leave with 1,250,000 to 1,500,000 tons of ships bought at an average of $85 a ton. He had no intention of building an ounce of that tonnage.

When the war started, he would sell those shipyard contracts to other owners who wanted in on the gravy. They would stand in line to pay $125 to $150 a ton for building commitments. So, if he got lucky, he could make as much as $97.5 million here. At the least, he could clear $50 million.

In the meantime, he thought, putting on his shirt, he would meet Dickie Dugan, one of Dublin Bay's wildest port captains. Then, suitably fortified by supper at the Royal Hibernian Hotel, they would start a pub crawl that would bring the city to its knees. Not a bad life at all, he had to admit.

Takeo Kono, that evening, also would have agreed.

He stood on the floor of Hasegawa Shipyards' No. 1 graving dock surveying the party. *Lianides Triumphant,* the cause of the celebration, lay across the harbor at a fitting-out berth, taking on final stores.

Just back from sea trials, she had logged a shade under twenty knots and proven as responsive for a big ship as a twin-engined power boat. Arkie, Kono mused, called the design conventional. He saw it as the next step in the state of the art, the "best of breed" that set standards.

More important, while Costa Lianides and *zaibatsu* brass marveled at its speed, he and Arkie had measured stress and vibration. The infamous Southern Ocean, as seamen called the waters south of the Cape of Good Hope, would be the final judge. But the instruments said their engineering approach to modular construction had been a breakthrough, too.

None of these hulls would crumple. No welds would pop. And with assembly bugs mastered, they would build ships faster than anyone imagined. The 250,000-tonners to follow would be afloat in seven months.

The PANARTEX 100,000-tonners, the bottom plates for which would go into this dock Monday, would be ready then, too—and that from a standing start! Engineroom sections of the 250,000-tonners had already been built.

Especially gratifying to Kono, the *zaibatsu* chief had told him to tell Wade that the present client had only one stipulation: that PANARTEX build to a design Kono developed and not to one Wade already had. Kono did not understand that, but he appreciated it.

Wade, hearing he could have ships in seven months, readily went along. He said he might even buy 250,000-tonners with the right design.

Perhaps, Kono thought, they would be friends yet.

Regardless, leaving that evening for Tokyo, where he would take Arkie and Costa Lianides so that they could get a plane to Europe, the *zaibatsu* chief hissed effusively. He had brought much respect to the Singing Willow and to Japan, he told Kono, the order of his sentence leaving no doubt as to where the respect did the most good.

Meanwhile, No. 1 graving dock, Kono thought, looked like Carnival in Rio. A survivor of one, he knew. When he told the *zaibatsu* chief that, the chief replied that they must go to one sometime, before he got too old, but with his wife staying in Nippon.

The five Brazilian tanker crews Lianides had recruited prepared the pit. Crisscrossing colored paper lanterns across its top, the electricians had also arranged for them to light sequentially and in varying patterns. The high concrete walls around them thus not only constantly changed appearance, but looked different in different places. Firelight illuminated the floor.

Two truckloads of charcoal grilled the truckload of Kobe beef, steaks, and short ribs that supplied the base for a *churrasco*. Then a quarter ton of sweet and hot sausages, found on a freighter from Santos, and several hundred chickens had been bought. His poor office girls, Kono saw, already looked high on garlic, which Japanese cuisine shuns.

While everything cooked, a record player, spliced into the yard's public-address system, sent a conga through the pit. At the moment, 250 carioca seamen, what seemed to be his entire yard force of 1,200, and his adminsitrative and engineering staffs of 150 swayed past Kono in a solid line. The only place he had ever seen anything like it was Ann Arbor. At pep rallies for Michigan–Ohio State football games, the snake dance around the bonfire could stretch for three blocks.

Seeing the beautiful receptionist at the main-gate waiting room whom Kono had been hoping to meet for months, he broke into the line, put his palms on her hips and picked up the step.

The desire to meet may have been mutual, Kono, a bachelor, thought. Her body began doing things in his hands independently of music. Later, he would show her how to eat *churrasco* and see if he could take her home.

Altogether, not a bad life at all, he reflected.

*Banzai,* Singing Willow!

*Banzai,* Lions!

*Banzai,* Red Sword!

*April 30, 1967*
*Copenhagen, Denmark*

WADE LANDED at Kastrup Airport at 2:30 P.M.

Burdened only by his airline pilot's chart case, he scampered through the lobby to the SAS information desk. Being a traveler to whom the possession of luggage made absolutely no difference, he immediately saw the bag he had left on the plane from Istanbul to Zurich.

Producing his receipt with the nonchalant manner of a man who saw nothing miraculous in things going right, he thanked the clerk, ambled over to a newsstand filled with the latest Danish and Swedish skin magazines, and for four dollars bought that Sunday's *New York Times*.

At 2:55 P.M. he entered the Kong Frederik Hotel, where more things went right. It was a favorite, its paneled first floor resembling a home more than a lobby. Greeted and signed in, he went up to a third-floor corner suite overlooking Vester Voldgade, which the staff knew he liked.

By the time he arrived, a silver tray, laden with rich Indonesian coffee and accompanied by freshly baked almond macaroons, awaited him.

Seeing it, he smacked his lips, tipped the bellboy, and opened the closet to hang up his coat.

As he did, the phone rang. The Kong Frederik, with seventy rooms and a hundred employees, knew how to welcome a guest. Jens, of the Queen's Grill downstairs, greeted him. Many believed that had his restaurant been in France it would have been among the dozen or so with three stars.

Hello, and good afternoon, Mr. Wade! Would he be having supper with them?

Oh, Christ, yes! An' shrimp toast an' crab puffs for openers—an order of each, same's always. Conscience demanded both, he thought. Danes, like Hollanders, had traded for centuries in the Orient. No serious eater could afford to let either go by in Copenhagen. The Kong Frederik did them so that kids had fun-finger foods. Meanwhile, he knew Chinese who were ready to kill for their secret—which had been given him for Christmas a few years back, when weather kept him at the hotel for the holiday. A bit of cognac thoroughly mixed into each cup of meat before frying made the difference. Trying that at home, his wife, a practical sort, said he should get stranded there some New Year's Eve if he saw a chance of coming home with their orange duck glaze.

His order, then, was seen as business as usual.

Of course. And what time would he be down?

Eight, eight-thirty?

That late?

He had a lot of calls to make.

In that case, Jens thought, he might need something at, say, five o'clock to help him through his last calls. He had in mind a small plate of smoked salmon and eels, with a little akvavit, of course. Did he agree?

He agreed.

Tie loosened, he opened belt and trousers and sank into a brocaded 250-year-old wing chair. Ahead through the doorway he saw the high double bed and its spotless white down pillows and comforter. Full of gentle swells and sharp little peaks, they reminded him of a meringue. Then, coffee poured, he reached into the pilot's case for his phone book and, smiling, feet on footstool, placed a call to Hamburg, Germany.

About then, at Kastrup Airport, Costa Lianides and Archimedes Angelakos received a message.

Just in from the Tokyo polar flight, they too had gone directly to the SAS information desk. Anything for Mr. Lyons, of New York? Lianides asked.

The blond clerk manning the desk nodded. A moment later she produced a brown clasp envelope. Their introduction to Mossad, Israeli intelligence, came in the form of a Copenhagen street guide.

Moving away from the desk, Lianides opened it up to find a route drawn with an orange felt-tipped pen. The line ran from the airport, down the highway to the city, and then west on Amager Boulevard to a circled "X."

A message appeared alongside the destination: "Belle Terrasse. Have passports ready, and ask for wine. Check luggage Kastrup."

Arkie, who knew Copenhagen, nodded. A classy restaurant in Tivoli Gardens, he said. He had been there a year ago.

Sunny days, he thought, Fiona liked lunching at La Terrasse. Then, jalousies on side windows and two story glass roof drawn back, the elaborate scrollwork interior came to life, she said, offering the best of both worlds. On the one hand, red carpeting, gleaming tablecloths, and armchairs in bright floral prints suggested a formal European dining room; on the other, white painted wooden arches and trusses recalled garden bowers used for summer lunch and supper in Greenwich.

Now, Arkie thought, despite a gale-torn sky and the emptiness of an off-season Sunday, the place still glowed. Copper- and glass-beaded chandeliers, which he had failed to notice before, were spaced the length of the room. More copper hung on the walls as pots and pans. Yard-high sprays of flowers stood on the sills before the beams.

Lianides smiled. Very Mediterranean, he said, like Nice.

They would like to see the wine list first, he told the maître d' as they took their seats at a corner table. Then, after deciding what to drink, they would order the meal. He understood that La Terrasse was noted for its fish.

Nodding appreciatively, the captain withdrew.

Lianides watched him leave. Was he in on it? he wondered. He had new shoes. Guys like him, on their feet all the time, liked old shoes.

Arkie shrugged. He had seen no sign of any kind.

The sommelier appeared next, a swaybacked, barrel-chested fellow, as tall and fair as the captain had been short and dark. He looked about fifty-five, with blond hair darkening into brown as it made its way to gray. He had two two-foot-long wine lists tucked under a black tuxedo sleeve.

Reaching the table, he cocked his head in front of his left shoulder, pale-blue eyes sparkling inquisitively.

"Good afternoon, gentlemen. Mr. Lyons?"

What difference did that make? Lianides asked.

A valued patron, the sommelier said, had told him that a friend of his, a Mr. Lyons, would dine there today and he had given him something to pass on.

Nodding, Lianides peeled back the edge of the beige linen napkin, folded to suggest a scallop shell, on the serving plate before him. The raised cloth revealed the dark-blue corner of the Brazilian passport he had just placed there. He was Mr. Lyons, he said.

In that case, the wine steward said, smiling, he would be the one staying in Rome for a bit.

Staying in Rome? Arkie asked.

Business, Lianides said, stroking his gold earring.

Ignoring the explanation, Arkie regarded the move. The earring had appeared in Tokyo at sight of a blond goddess of an SAS stewardess. Real cute, he thought. He could just imagine the business in Rome.

Folders shuffled, the wine steward handed them off. Casually looking around, he then lowered his head and said it would be wise to choose now. Their end of the room seemed empty.

Opening the soft red leather covers, they found a long white envelope in the crease of each wine list. A second or two, no longer, accomplished the switch. Then, new passports in breast pockets, they told the sommelier they would let him decide.

Delighted, he said. The night shift of customs and immigration went on at Kastrup at four o'clock, he told them, so he thought they should have a nice leisurely meal. Then no one would be around at the airport to see new names on old faces.

Why not start with crab puffs? Then sole Castiglione, a nice change from Véronique. It had mirepoix vegetables under the fillets and a truffled dry white wine and Madeira sauce. They had also received a basket of marvelous endive from Belgium that day. Very cold, and served with oil and vinegar, it made a perfect contrast to the fish.

He would tell the captain, and, trust him, the wines would be somewhat out of the ordinary, as well.

Meanwhile, as they ate, he said, their passports would be on the way to Home Office, where they would be kept until the venture had been completed. Then, folding his wine lists, he left.

Arkie shook his head. As simple as that? he wondered.

Why not? came the answer. They were in the hands of the world's best secret service.

But that guy was no more Jew than they were.

That was his strength, Lianides told Arkie. Who would suspect him? And did it matter what he was?

The same question had been put to Lianides in Jamaica by an Englishman. Smiling modestly, the man had confessed to running the operation for Home Office, all the while fondling the most vicious-looking knife Lianides had ever seen. He intended using it in New York should the need arise, his host assured him. A very naughty piece of steel, it had been made to order in Arizona.

Mossad must have other strange pals, Lianides told Arkie.

A moment later, casually reaching inside his jacket, he made the point another way. Peeking inside at his new passport, he grinned broadly.

"Guess who we are!" he said.

"Who?"

"Nicaraguans."

Despite apprehension and guilt, Arkie had to smile.

Nicaraguans! Who could ever trace Nicaraguans?

"You watch," Lianides told him. It would be like that at the other end. They would be there and gone, and no one would know.

*May 1, 1967*
*Copenhagen, Denmark*
*Ancona, Italy*

THE KNOCK sounded precisely at 7 A.M.

Wade abruptly dropped the "Week in Review" section of the Sunday *Times,* which he had read in vain for anything suggesting the war he knew would come soon. Smiling, he scampered across the sitting room in his stockinged feet to fling open the door.

Joop Hendrikse, as expected, stood before him.

He built ships. Eleven of the fifty-one that PANARTEX sailed were his.

Hendrikse not only knew the client but liked him. So at 4 A.M. he had left his three-hundred-year-old farmhouse near Rotterdam and driven to Zestienhoven Airport to leave in a chartered plane at first light for Copenhagen.

Seemingly oblivious to the rain still dripping off his austere black fedora and raincoat, he too grinned broadly. Tall and portly, with neatly trimmed salt-and-pepper goatee and gold-rimmed glasses, he had the benign smile and lavishly broken nose of a priest who had spent his youth running a Catholic seamen's mission.

He had in fact followed a riskier calling. He had skippered a deep-sea salvage tug. Nothing made a man more bucko. Like Wade, he also had intelligence.

Called home following World War II to help restore the shipyard in which generations of Hendrikses had built canal barges, he had seen what had eluded the rest of his family.

Amsterdam, the boast goes, rests on herring bones, a tribute to diet and Dutch ingenuity in wresting a city from the sea. Rotterdam, as all who have been there at dead low tide know, perches on a far less exotic base: bucket after stinking bucket of muck and sand. So, at least, all of the waterfront seemed to him in 1945, save for the small acreage owned by his family. That point, flattened by the Germans, stood about twelve feet above sea level and actually consisted of land.

Idiots! he told his relatives. They were sitting on a fortune. They should build drydocks and then real ships, like the ones he rescued—no more spitkit barges!

Offended, his stiff-backed family promptly named the bigmouth president and told him to go ahead. So he did.

Long a millionaire, he still preferred wardrooms to boardrooms, seamen to company men. He thus limited his clientele to hardheaded Dutch and Danish owners and the few "in-through-the-hawsepipe" marine superintendents who understood his ways. He did nothing for English and American majors, whose Royal Navy and Annapolis types were put off by bluff manners, profanity, and tattoos.

He and Wade were thus uniquely suited to each other.

"Zo, little vart," he said in greeting, "vot brings you down to Kong Frederik, zo var over your station in live?"

"Sun and sea breezes!" came the prompt reply as an especially vicious fusillade of rain rattled the windows fronting on Vester Volgade.

"Vere's breakvast?"

"No work, no eat, vatzo! What kinda Kraut are you, anyways, you gotta eat before you work?"

Sighing, Hendrikse turned from the closet, rolling up the sleeves of a purple silk shirt. Then, lumbering across the sitting room, he sat down on the couch next to the brocaded chair. Opening a much-traveled airline pilot's chart case, a twin to Wade's, with basketweave embossing, which Hubie had had a San Antonio saddlemaker do up for him, he withdrew a deep-sea salvageman's typical breakfast: a quart of Genever gin and a large glass jar of pickled herring awash in bay leaves and red onion rings.

"Lifeboat stores," he said with mock dolefulness.

Nodding approvingly, Wade handed him a plans sheet, telling him to take a short obsquintical at how far he could rise above his station in life as a barge builder, and scuttled off to the bathroom for drinking glasses.

Fearing that Hendrikse might know the designer from the profile, since Arkie had done much work in Rotterdam, he then handed over the convertible piping plan. He said he and Hubie had originally been thinking in terms of oil–bulk-ore carriers, but now had decided on five-tank oilships.

What did Hendrikse think?

The answer would take time coming. Pumps and piping were the most complicated parts of tankers. Moreover, to Wade's knowledge, no one had ever solved the problem as Arkie had in the convertibles.

Three inches into the gin and halfway through the herring, breakfast supplanted by something of far more interest, Joop Hendrikse eventually looked up from the low table on which the plans had been spread. His brown eyes shone with discovery behind the gold-rimmed glasses.

"How many, vart?" he asked, stroking his goatee.

"Four."

"Ven?"

"Eight months."

"Impozzible! Fourteen."

"Ten, then."

"Twelve, und—"

"The clock's tickin' now!"

"—und you pay overtime on top contrac' price."

Shrugging, Wade turned to the table alongside the brocaded chair to hand over a pink-and-white English bank check, heavy with brown and black certification stamps. Payable to Hendrikse for $2.5 million, it represented some of the Singapore "egg money" liberated by Chan and Son.

Carelessly stuffing the down payment into his purple shirt pocket, Hendrikse topped off the gin glasses.

"To vair vinds, vollowing zees, und delivery a year from today."

"Done!"

Deal made, the price per ton would follow.

Reaching into his pilot's case, Wade next produced Kono's plans, which had been sent to Copenhagen awaiting his arrival. The new design looked even faster than the Lions' ships. But compromises had been made for speed. Kono's vessels took an hour longer to load and unload.

Speed, of course, redeemed all faults. But turnaround time counted, too. At ten trips a year, each of those 100,000-tonners ate a day in port. In ten years, as long as Wade knew he could keep them until upkeep got too high, that lost time neared $250,000 a ship. Multiplied by ten or twelve, the number he wanted, those wasted days could keep up to $3 million profit dollars from the bottom line.

Nodding, Hendrikse saw the problem at once. The answer, he knew, would take a bit longer. It meant adapting Arkie's pumping and piping plan for the convertibles to Kono's design. Those ships, however, had eight tanks instead of five, greater depth, and different construction details.

Sighing at the ordeal they faced, they began work.

The herring lasted until 11 A.M.

The gin ran out at noon.

At 1 P.M., akvavit, Tuborg beer, and a trayful of smørrebrod, Denmark's famed open-faced sandwiches, came.

At 6 P.M., akvavit and beer had gone the way of gin.

At 7 P.M., hungry, thirsty, bleary-eyed in the fug of Hendrikse's yellowish-brown Sumatran Velásquez cigars, they broke for supper. Needing some real food, and not the delicate *haute cuisine* served in the Queen's Grill downstairs, they went to Krogs, despite the rain.

Undoubtedly one of Europe's best fish restaurants, Krogs delights in serving hearty appetites, as its décor suggests. It is a vast, cavernous place, its walls lined with murals of fishing ports and markets and muscular men opening oysters and gutting fish.

A specialty there, the fried-fish platter, recalls the planked-steak extravaganza once so popular in the United States. A wide, eighteen-inch-long oval steel tray is heaped with sole and flounder fillets at either end. The flat part holds fried oysters, scallops, mushrooms, peas, rice, and tomato and lemon slices, with smoked salmon and boiled shrimp as starters. Ringing all, on the raised rim, is a band of fluted and oven-browned mashed potatoes. The whole is served on a gilded pedestal, with sea creatures curled over each end, meant as a table decoration.

Ignoring plates, they ate from the trays, washing everything down with Tuborg. Still hungry, they sent for a third tray, to be filled with oysters and scallops and heavied up with two three-and-a-half-pound lobsters.

They closed the place. The cabs had left it before them, so, leaving Gammel Strand on foot, they made their way down the canals alongside Christiansborg Palace toward Town Hall Square. Arriving, however, they found that the rain and the chill had renewed their appetites. Diverting themselves accordingly, they reeled down Vesterbrogade across from Central Station. Favourite, one of the best smørrebrod take-out delicatessens, stayed open all night. It boiled pork, then broiled it in herbed breadcrumbs, to make a sandwich Wade especially liked.

Arriving at the Kong Frederik with food and a dozen bottles of Tuborg, plus gin and akvavit, they gave their suits to a hall porter for pressing. Then, in underwear, they again attacked the pumping and piping problems.

At 2 A.M. they surrendered, Hendrikse stretching out on the couch.

At 4 A.M., Hendrikse suddenly sat up. "Hey, vart," he shouted into the bedroom, "I got it! I got it!"

Yanking the white down comforter off Wade, he shook him awake and turned on a light. "Like zo, und zo, und zo!" he said.

Wade watched his hands depict piping. They looked good to him.

Glancing at his watch, he scuttled into the sitting room and placed a call to Japan. Within ten minutes he had Takeo Kono on the line.

He knew how to make fast ships offload faster, he told Kono.

Oh?

Five minutes later, Kono knew, too.

The answer involved relocating bulkheads, but since the ships were still on paper an eraser could do that.

The plans would be changed that night, Kono said.

Hanging up, Wade saw Joop Hendrikse behind him, brow furrowing bald head. The yellow, red, green, and blue butterflies tattooed on his muscular shoulders flapped their wings as he strained to open a pound jar of that spring's first herring, purchased at the Favourite. Finally, with a triumphant grunt, he succeeded in twisting off the lid. Pointing it at the tumblerful of gin on the coffee table, he sat down on the couch and raised his own glass, passing Wade the herring jar.

"Now ve party, vart! *Ja?*"

"*Ja!*"


Archimedes Angelakos had a far less enjoyable day.

His problems, in fact, had begun Sunday night.

Delayed in Rome, he reached the shipyard in Ancona just in time for the last launch run to the roadstead. Sweaty, out of breath, he handed down his heavy canvas bag and negotiated the slimy ladder hanging from the dock, to the amusement of the other passenger.

An English officer, he decided, taking in the brown homburg, the waxed reddish-brown mustache, and the superbly cut camel's-hair topcoat with chocolate velvet collar. He had spent time coasting Africa, Arkie guessed, probably in the Union Castle Line. The ostrich-hide overnight bag, its zipper threaded with a blue-and-white Al Italia baggage tag from Venice, said so. The alligator shoes confirmed the signal. Highly prized by clothes-conscious seamen, they were custom made in Zanzibar, where the Portuguese were less fastidious about what they shot.

Enveloped in the heady aroma of an exotic after-shave lotion, his fellow passenger extended his hand.

"Archimedes?"

"Yes?"

"Your cousin, Zavitsanos."

Arkie shook his head in disbelief.

A shipmaster and rogue to equal Costa, Zavitsanos had commanded one of the T-2s in the artful River Plate collision in which both vessels sank without loss of life. Insurance money from that accident bought the family's share of Lianides Bulk Transport, a company Schotten had formed to build and operate the ships now under construction in Japan.

The face behind the faultlessly groomed mustache, however, with its deep-set eyes and fine, firm features, contradicted derring-do. It seemed ascetic. Pale and unlined, it belied a life in which twenty of its thirty-five years had been spent at sea. If anything, Arkie thought, Zavitsanos looked like Sands Point lawyers his age, destined for senior partnerships. Only his hand seemed to belong on a shipyard launch in Ancona, Italy. Rock-hard, it had enough size, Arkie believed, to envelope the head of a twelve-pound sledge.

Costa had stayed in Rome, on business, Arkie told him.

That could happen, Zavitsanos observed. *"Then berazzy."* Usually that phrase meant "It doesn't matter." His cousins, Arkie would find, also used it to say, "What's the difference?," "Why bother?," and "What do you want from me?"

He had had an affair of that sort to look after in Venice, too, Zavitsanos went on, nodding tolerantly. He had found the town a bit touristy, however, not like Rio or London, which were sophisticated places where people did more than walk around looking at old buildings.

And the trip from Eleusis Bay?

Leisurely.

The ship ran well?

Zavitsanos waggled an index finger meaningfully.

*Dynamic Papachristou,* he sighed in his world-weary, City of London manner, like all hookers, young or old, needed a lot of tweaking.

Then they were alongside the scaling, pitted black hull. Zavitsanos boarded the accommodation ladder first. Arkie, following, put a foot on the bottom platform and reached for the outboard stanchion to hoist himself and his bag up. He nearly fell into the water, instead, as the pipe came out of its socket. Perilously swinging out between launch and ship's side, he managed to hang on with one hand, a tribute to his strength.

Jeez! Why didn't somebody fix that? he demanded of Zavitsanos when he reached the main deck. All it would take would be five minutes with the welding torch.

*That?* That had been that way since the old days in Rio, when *Dynamic* had been the third ship Zavitsanos and Costa ran for Petrobras. Had they thought she could get to the River Plate, Zavitsanos said drolly, they would have sunk her instead of one of the other two.

"*Then berazzy,* Archimedes," he said, unconcerned.

Tapping Arkie lightly on the shoulder and lifting his ostrich overnight bag, he said he would see him at seven for breakfast. They would want steam at eight sharp, he added, for going into the shipyard.

Shaking his head at the sad condition of the ship, Arkie trudged back to the sterncastle, to the engineers' quarters and the engineroom.

Entering, he felt worse. The passageway sides, gray in all T-2s, had a rosy glow in *Dynamic Papachristou.* Here and there, they were blistered. Soon, he thought, the triumph of rust would be total. Similarly, the narrow floors, painted red at building, revealed only cracked and chipped cement. To make it even less inviting, about one light in three had the weakest sort of glow.

What slobs, he mused. His family, too.

Then his contempt became alarm. He had what seamen called "a nose for steam." A dark gift from an unknown god, it enabled him to detect the slightest trace of bronze, copper, or steel—supposedly odorless materials—lurking in the ever present aroma of steam, machine oil, and asbestos pipe wrapping permeating all enginerooms. He now smelled bronze and copper, sure signs to him of corrosion in pipes and valves and of imminent breakdown. The ship even felt and sounded wrong. More sensed than experienced, the whirring of generators, the chuffing of pumps and fans, and their vibration said a lot to engineers about a vessel's health. Here everything seemed to be missing a beat.

*Dynamic,* he thought, would be fragile at best.

The voices, though, in her officers' saloon, down the narrow passageway, sounded cheerful enough. Still keyed up from the Tokyo flight, the passport switch in Copenhagen, and the dash to Ancona, he knew he could not sleep anyway, so he decided to say hello.

His cousins Ioannis and Orestes rose in greeting. Brawny engineers, they both wore undershirts over greasy khaki chinos and had more underarm hair than most men had on their heads, he thought.

Ioannis, who wore a red bandana instead of the usual black cap, had a fierce black mustache and an awesome build. Orestes, less intimidating, had a mustache to match and a tattoo on his right biceps to even things out. The phrase "Try me!" appeared in descending lines in English, Greek, Italian, and Spanish as a warning to all who worked in his engineroom.

Having been home when he and Fiona visited Hydra, they knew him and embraced him warmly. They wanted to know all about the ships being built in Japan. Ioannis, hospitably, went to the sideboard to draw him a mug of coffee from the urn.

Shrugging out of his topcoat and sport jacket, Arkie sat down at the long gray linoleum-topped table, brown with the rings of countless cups of coffee. Then, carefully finding a safe place for his elbows, he told them of the first sea trials in Japan.

As they oohed and aahed, he sipped the coffee.

What was wrong? Ioannis immediately asked.

The coffee was sour.

Sour? Orestes asked.

Jesus, didn't Yorka ever change the filter?

*"Then berazzy,* Archimedes. Be glad it's coffee," Orestes said.

And hot too! Ioannis added. Some Greek owners were too cheap even to buy coffee urns. With Costa, you went first class.

Arkie said nothing. There could be no answer. With country boys like these two, there would always be plenty of accidents at sea. They would sail in anything. They were that hungry.

A few minutes later, leaving them in what Orestes called the lap of luxury, he climbed the ladder to the boat deck and the chief engineer's cabin.

Fotis, the family's resident engineer on Hydra and father of Ioannis and Orestes, had bunked there for the trip from Greece. The bed, freshly made, still smelled like the lion cage at the Bronx Zoo.

Tearing off linens and blankets, Arkie horsed the mattress out of the bedroom, through the dayroom, and down to the main deck. Dragging it after him, he searched empty cabins until he could make a satisfactory swap. Then, on his way back, he passed the door to the engineroom casing and stopped for a glimpse of the domain he would rule.

Two steps out on the flyover, the twelve-inch-wide railed catwalk that led to the central ladder of steps, he called it quits. Forty-five feet below him, he knew, lay the engineroom floorplates. He, however, could see only the top of a fogbank. A cloud of gray steam filled the rest of the space. Under it he heard the measured clank of metal on metal. That would be Theodosius, he thought, another son of Fotis, trying to hammer open a stuck relief valve. Turning, he left, shaking his head.

Later, bed made, he unpacked, undressed, entered his shower, and opened the valves. The domestic hot-water system of *Dynamic Papachristou* promptly greeted him with a flatulent hiss and a trickle of rusty water.

So ended his Sunday.

Monday brought more of the same.

At breakfast he told Zavitsanos he could not have steam at eight. First he and the others were going to mark all the engineroom pipes and valves that needed fixing. Then they would make steam.

British understatement underlined the response. He found the engineroom a bit humid?

He did indeed.

*"Then berazzy,"* Zavitsanos replied. His shrug said he had a spoiled American to humor.

That afternoon they met again. They stood in the drydock, at the foot of *Dynamic*'s bow, black paint flakes and henna-colored rust wafting down over their shoulders as the ship settled deeper on the wooden chocks upon which it rested.

Their tour of underwater hull fittings done, they watched the shipyard workers hanging a thick electrical cable from bow to stern along the plating at deck level, abetting the fallout. With a second strand girdling the waterline, degaussing could begin.

The treatment wrapped a ship in a strong electrical current. Its charge neutralized the residual magnetism in the steel, especially the welds. Vintage T-2s such as *Dynamic,* fitted with conventional magnetic compasses rather than gyrocompasses, needed the fix periodically.

Meanwhile, the rain of paint and rust kept falling.

The only problem, Arkie said, was that by the time they got the second cable on, all that banging around would shake a ton of steel off the hull.

As if to underscore his observation, a four-inch-square piece of black paint fell between them. Striking the cement floor, it promptly exploded in a cloud of red dust—steel, literally held together by paint.

He pointed to it meaningfully.

*"Then berazzy,* Archimedes," Zavitsanos laughed. What did it matter, anyway? he asked. Old girls like *Dynamic* wanted degaussing, and they needed only a little steel to get them where they were going, so it would all work out.

Then, stepping back, clearly amused at the ravaged condition of the hull, he shook out the wide-brimmed hat with its leopard band that he favored over an officer's cap. That, and his khaki bush coat, brown suede recoil pad over right shoulder, and shell loops filled with .378 magnum rifle cartridges, paid homage to years coasting South and East Africa.

Picaresque or not, he had left that trade with the best attributes of the British white hunters, the men he so admired: a talent for friendship and a sense of humor.

So, when Arkie asked why not rename the old hooker *Then Berazzy?,* he looked at his chronometer and pronounced the workday ended. As master of the vessel, he had that right, he said. Then, putting his arm on Arkie's shoulder, he declared he could also order a chief engineer to muster at the gangway with the junior deck officers in a half hour for supper ashore.

Ancona, he pointedly observed, was no town for new boys from America and children to explore unsupervised. It had a second-century Roman arch, which would be the objective of their Sunday outing, one cinema that reeked of urine, two very bad whorehouses, in which Ioannis and Orestes, visiting nightly, had already fallen in love, and no restaurants of note. It did have, however, a glorious beach, on which there were several *trattoria* that did fish and pasta rather well.

Besides, he added with a malicious grin, the mother of the boys remembered the beautiful wife of Archimedes and knew he would not go whoring around. She hoped he would be an example for her sons.

Arkie had to smile. Zavitsanos was a hard man to stay mad at.

Impatiently twitching his waxed mustache, Zavitsanos nodded at a de-gaussing cable hanging waist-high above the cement floor. Now, he said, if Arkie would just clear away that snake, they would leave this shithouse.

Were the compasses really bad? Arkie asked.

No, Zavitsanos answered, bending under the cable Arkie held up for him.

Leaving the dock, neither mentioned the other reason for degaussing a ship, discovered during World War II. Once its latent electrical charge is neutral-ized, the vessel becomes invisible to magnetic mines.


*May 3, 1967*
*Hamburg, Germany*
*Ancona*


THE PLANE turned southeast on intermediate approach.

Wade sighed in satisfaction at the Elbe below him. High with spring rain, it looked as muddy as ever.

Hamburg, in the mist, seemed no lovelier, either.

Just as it should be, he thought. It was one of his favorite cities; he had been coming here for thirty years. He had liked it even better before World War II and its reconstruction, when it had been uglier. His love of the place, then as now, came from his always having felt at home there.

It remained one of the few towns on earth centered almost solely around ships. Its bankers financed them. Its old Hanseatic families owned them. Its merchants and traders found them cargoes. Its women had a marked and in-satiable liking for men who sailed them.

Hamburg police, Wade told Greenwich neighbors, were also unique. The tough guys with the Kaiser Wilhelm helmets on duty in Saint Pauli, the wa-terfront area, were so good they never arrested seamen for fighting. They just automatically whipped their tuncases and delivered the bodies to the ships. They knew what delayed sailings cost.

The hotels were that way, too. Keyed to seafaring, with its round-the-clock arrivals and departures, they reminded him of Las Vegas, where you could get breakfast at 2 A.M., or supper as well, with no questions asked.

Tonight, since Hubie had made the reservations, he would stay at the Vier Jahreszeiten, one of Europe's most elegant hotels. The Atlantic, where Onassis and other Greeks hung out, suited him better, and he liked the spartan little seamen's places in Altona, near the docks. But with two Swedish shipbuilders coming to see him the next day, he supposed Hubie had been right. He, and they, unnoticed at the Vier Jahreszeiten by the local shipping fraternity, would occasion no gossip.

Meanwhile, he had other business in Hamburg.

Over the Elbe, in fact, he thought he saw it. Looking down, he saw two tugs nudging a gray-hulled, buff-stacked tanker to a berth. The ship, he knew from his schedule, had to be *PANARTEX Payloader,* commanded by Alonzo Irish, the best captain in his fleet.

He meant to shanghai Irish to skipper a Hasegawa 100,000-tonner.

But Irish, a balding, denture-chewing grandfather, and fearless afloat, had a monumental timidity ashore. Seven years in *Payloader,* running on fixed company delivery routes from the Bay of Biscay to Helsinki, had given him a sense of security. He knew his ship, and he knew his operating area. Weaning him from those to the gypsy life of spot-chartering would take some doing.

Still, Wade thought, it had to be done.

On final approach, he began to see how.

He would hit *Payloader* at four o'clock, after the tiger of the North Sea and the Baltic had napped and logged his afternoon Bible time. Then, pleading loneliness, he would cajole Irish into a rare visit ashore for supper.

Ehmke's, the patrician mausoleum in the Gansmarket, would be perfect. As far as Wade could recall, he had never seen a waiter there younger than seventy, or a female guest on the near side of fifty. Moreover, they all seemed to need size 48 bras. Mrs. Irish being built along similar lines, Alonzo would feel right at home, he thought. With luck, they might even get a famed Hamburg specialty too: venison from the rolling green hills of Schleswig-Holstein surrounding the town.

He would mention the 100,000-tonners there and get Irish back to the hotel to see the plans. Then, after offering him the job and being refused, he would say why not call Newport News, and that would do it.

He could flannelmouth the lady of the house.

Emmalou? This here's Loren, honey! Listen, how'd you like to get the old man home day after Labor Day an' then take off with him after Christmas for Nippon, so's he can give some new ships we're buildin' there a short obsquintical an' take one out himself to show the kids how? An', on the way, if it ain't gonna be too much for you, honey, what with packin' and unpackin', I'd mightily appreciate it if you could stop in at Singapore, Jakarta, Bangkok, an' Hong Kong before you get to—

Along about Bangkok, just as he was getting Hong Kong out of his mouth, Wade guessed, she'd tell him to put her Poppy back on the phone.

So that gave him the morning free.

Fair enough, he thought as the plane slowed.

He knew an oil wholesaler in town who kept tabs on local shipyards for him. He would take him to lunch at Haerlin. What he learned would help him in Oslo, when he saw his Germans. Besides, Haerlin did plaice, the Rolls-Royce of flounder, better than even Wheeler's in London.

That recalled another great Hamburg favorite of his; *currywurst,* spiced *Thüringer* sausage, hotter than four-alarm chili. The *schnellimbiss,* or quick-snack bar, in Fuhlsbüttel Airport had the best in town. Leaving, he would get one. No, he told himself, he better get two.

Fuhlsbüttel lay hell and gone from town, and he still had an hour and a half to kill before lunch. His work that day began after supper, anyway.

In Ancona, the Lions too had a late workday.

That morning, a shipyard crew appeared on "Devil's Island," the exposed flying bridge over the top of the midships house. Then, with Zavitsanos watching, they welded a flat butt plate with a circular socket and four heavy steel padeyes to the deck.

They were back after lunch as one of the drydock's black traveling cranes hoisted aboard a steel mast forty feet long and four inches in diameter. Stepping it into the round socket, they fixed the shrouds dangling from it to the padeyes as Zavitsanos directed.

Then the four men looked at him questioningly. They had just erected a radar mast. The radar unit, however, was not on the mast.

Shrugging, Zavitsanos touched forefinger to eye. They were delivering the ship east, he said. They had strange ways out there. Perhaps the new owner might not fit radar at all. Maybe he just wanted something to scare demons.

Muttering, the foreman led his crew below.

*"Se Christo vedesse . . ."* he sighed, shaking his head. "If only Christ could see what's going on."

He had reason to wonder. Scraped and primed, *Dynamic* had shed what seemed half the thickness of her hull. A foot of paint, scale, and wafered steel plating lay on the cement drydock floor under her. Ships in far better shape went to wreckers' yards. And now this—a radar mast, but no radar.

Later his confusion would have been compounded.

Shortly after seven, in the soft light of May dusk, Zavitsanos reappeared on the flying bridge. He brought Arkie with him, an electric drill in hand. Its black cable snaked over the gray deck behind him and down the ladder to an electrical socket on the bridge.

Quickly scaling the wedges welded to either side of the mast as steps, Zavitsanos stopped at the tangs, to which the upper ends of the shrouds were secured. Then, reaching out in space, about thirty-five feet above deck, he scrambled onto the foot-round platform provided for servicing the radar unit. Casually leaning against the mast, he next unbuttoned his shirt and removed an aircraft pilot's headset with tubular microphone. Placing it over his reddish-brown hair, he again leaned out, letting the lead-in wire, attached beneath the right earphone, uncoil from his hand.

Catching the loose end, Arkie, on his knees, led it this way and that, looking up. When Zavitsanos nodded, he drilled a hole in the deck, inserting a female phone jack with a black anodized watertight screw-off cap.

The rest of the lead-in wire followed. Six feet of slack were taken from the deck fitting, and the remainder was snipped off with wirecutters. Zavitsanos, tearing a rag in half, came down able-bodied-seaman style, a piece of cloth in each hand wrapped around a shroud.

Very nice, he said. Actually, too good for a clod like Costa, who undoubtedly sat at this moment on the Via Veneto with an Italian starlet.

Meanwhile—on to *Trattoria Ptomaine*. They could save the wire for when they got back. It would make an exciting finish to the evening.

*May 5, 1967*
*Ancona*
*New York City*

*Dynamic* FLOATED out of the drydock at 5 P.M.

Boilers flashed and steam up, she took a brief turn around the roadstead, celebrating the new respectability of fresh black hull paint and white topsides. Her stack mark had been freshened up, as well. Where once rode a white lion, there now appeared a bright-orange winged "P" in a canary-yellow background.

It honored, Zavitsanos told the yard manager, the Papachristou family, of Belo Horizonte, Brazil. Having received a check for work done to date from a Swiss bank in Lugano, the manager had no desire to ask why the Papachristous felt obliged to repaint the funnel for a delivery run to new owners. prompt-paying, crazy Greeks could do what they liked.

And they *were* crazy, he thought. After paying $15,000 for paint, they balked at the $350 charge for tying up overnight at the fitting-out dock. Instead, cargo boom and net rigged, they would take stores aboard at anchor, they said. That would be an all-night job, the manager knew, with two ships in the harbor leaving the next morning taking priority.

So at 6 P.M. *Dynamic* lay at anchor.

At 7 P.M., the oil barge came alongside.

At 8 P.M., the ship chandler's delivery came via a workboat. Its afterdeck held the usual naval stores and drums of machine oil and baled rags used for wiping down in the engineroom. Those swiftly hoisted away, the delivery crew then motioned for the boom to be swung to the bow of their boat. There, straining, three of them manhandled two large wooden cable reels into the net and signaled for them to be taken topside.

They came from an electronics plant in Milan. Each three-foot-diameter spool held a mile and a half of twelve-volt plastic-sheathed copper wire.

They were not usual. *"Che cosa è questo?"* one of the deliverymen asked, pointing, as the cargo net bore the drums aloft.

Cranking his right hand and holding his left to his ear, Zavitsanos answered, *"Per las telèfonos."*

"Aah," the deliveryman answered. *"Buono viaggio!"*

At 9 P.M., the Israelis arrived.

Two-mile light combing the deck, they found the cargo boom and, throwing out rubber tires for fenders as they came, brought an old pilot launch alongside. Motor backed, gunned forward, and killed, their vintage crate responded as precisely as a Lippizaner in dressage drill.

How they had arranged to deliver the food, no one knew.

Their leader posed a far more intriguing question.

Standing on the gunwale of his old tub, two vertical planks from the wheelhouse missing, he signaled to lower the cargo net. Throwing it on the deck, he put his right foot into the empty hook and motioned to be hoisted away. Then, one hand around the guy, the other holding two yellow tins against his chest, he rose forty feet to the deck as immobile as a statue.

Balance like that belonged exclusively to seafarers. Where had that boyish little fellow acquired his?

Wiry, he had blond hair and fair skin typical of a northern Italian. He dressed the part, too. His greasy dungarees and sleeveless chambray shirt would have shamed Orestes, surely the dirtiest man aboard. His hands, however, were white, without a blister, callus, or broken nail. Smiling as he stepped onto the deck, he looked as bucko as a concert violinist.

"Señor Caruello?" he asked, using the name in which Arkie's Nicaraguan passport had been issued.

Nodding, Arkie stepped forward to shake hands.

Smiling, the Israeli lifted a tin in either hand. Then, placing the smaller one at his feet, he turned the larger one over, removed a key soldered to its back, and stripped off its top as if it were a sardine can.

Inside, in a clear plastic bag, lay eight pounds of a yellowish-white substance that looked like putty. Red and black self-stripping electrical lugs protruded like ears from each end of the polyurethane.

The gelignite, Arkie was told. A toe tap on the smaller tin can indicated the detonator caps. He had the wire aboard?

It had come that evening.

Excellent, then. *"Mazel tov!"* went with another handshake.

Foot in the hook he had ridden aboard, the visitor nodded to Alexander, on the cargo winch, to haul away, with a casualness that rivaled Zavitsanos'. Rising, he waved to all hands.

Zavitsanos enjoyed the call more than anyone else. What humor, he told

Arkie, pointing to the tins. They had packaged the explosive as Polish hams. The detonators had been smuggled in as Danish bacon.

Food, however, came aboard first. Then, forming a bucket brigade, they passed the tins packed with explosives into the officers' salon. Within forty minutes they had enough gelignite to sever the stern section from the rest of the hull. Arkie and his three engineer cousins would spend that weekend installing and wiring it to a detonator on the bridge.

Finished, the blond Israeli who did not look like a seaman, but who handled his launch and rode a boom guy like one, leaned out of the wheelhouse side window. "All set?" he asked, smiling up at the deck.

All set.

"Next year in Jerusalem!"

Then, with wheel hard to starboard, motor gunned, and a final wave, the launch sped off into the darkness with as much dash as when it had arrived.

At that moment, Demi too heard a good exit line.

He, however, had doubts about its sincerity.

Mrs. Angelakos, Fiona's maid said, had told her to tell him, if he called, that she had gone to New York City to see a friend—Liese Bondurant.

He shook his head at the irony.

Liese Bondurant had the fictitious apartment where Fiona could have been reached New Year's Day. Her presence in Manhattan seemed highly unlikely. Her husband managed the P&O office in Hong Kong.

The message said Fiona still had no wish to speak to him. Three weeks had passed since she had, when he signed the marriage contract.

He hung up, stepping out of the phone booth in the TWA terminal at Kennedy. His plane for Athens and the yearly family meeting left in ten minutes, so he crossed the reception area to the tobacco stand for Schimmelpennincks and paperbacks. Let her pout, he thought.

She would be off to Paris herself soon for ten days with Honey and Artemis. By the time she got back, it would be the first week in June, and she would be horny enough. In a way, he took her silence as a compliment. It implied that she had implicit faith in his ability to get top dollar for what she had told him.

He had done that and acquired insurance as well.

The operating contract, he knew, meant nothing. It ceded half ownership to him of a company sending convertibles around the world, delivering coal to Japan, and picking up oil on the leg back to the United States for the Defense Department. But why would Wade and Hubie do that now? In his view, they would not. They had no reason to. They could make much more, without partners, by chartering out conventional tankers.

The guaranteed-loan agreement, however, had been just that. Drawing it up had taken all the time that Monday morning when he last saw Fiona. There were no references to convertibles in that document.

He wondered, in fact, if that had occurred yet to Wade and Hubie. He doubted if it had. They were too busy, he thought, making their own killing. Besides, since they had sucked him into the scheme, they probably assumed he would be too dumb to know what to do with it.

The loan guarantee was his joke on them. It covered him all ways.

If Wade and Hubie built convertibles, he had half of those profits. If, on the other hand, they let that business pass, as he thought they would, he had what amounted to a $25-million letter of credit.

The moment the first gun went off in that war, he would fly to Europe and do exactly what Wade had been doing: buy shipyard time to sell at a profit. Then he would have some ships of his own built.

He might not beat Onassis or Niarchos or a few of the others, but plenty of owners would need a week or two to come up with cash before talking to yards. That was all the lead time he needed.

Meanwhile, he would go to Athens and play nephew. Entering the tobacco shop, he broadened his smile.

He would have it all, he knew.

Fiona would love him, too.

With convertibles, they would make $41 million in a year.

With the guaranteed loan, they would do even better.

He had finally outsmarted little Loren, he thought.

He had, indeed. But not others.

That oversight left him with thirty-one days of life.


*May 8, 1967*
*Haikko Manor, Finland*
*Ancona*


IN HAMBURG, Wade bought four ships from the Swedes.

He would build two. They would be free. He would sell building contracts on the other two. Sale profits would cover his costs. So it had been a profitable stop.

But his Swedish shipbuilders were slow studies and suspicious besides, so it took until Friday for them to arrive at a price.

Then Joop Hendrikse called from Rotterdam saying he had found a way to shave four dollars a ton off building costs. Could he come and check it out? For four dollars a ton on over a million tons of ships, he could.

So, instead of being in Finland Friday, as he had hoped, he arrived Monday morning. A girl friend of Cora Garrison's had found Haikko Manor. Hubie liked to go there after his operations.

A fourteenth-century castle thirty miles from Helsinki, set in a forest, it had indoor and outdoor swimming pools, great for firming up incisions, Hubie said, gentle walks, and a tranquility especially soothing to ulcer patients. Even the sunlight seemed a soft, calming green, coming through the tall pines and birches surrounding the forty-room inn. Psychologically, the bland Finnish food served to the other guests helped, too. Against it, convalescent fare seemed no great hardship.

Wade liked the place for its lakeside sauna. After a couple of trips down there, he always found himself five to ten pounds lighter, refreshed, and eager to eat his way further around Europe. In point of fact, he also enjoyed dining at Haikko Manor. For his money, the forest on the grounds held the start of the world's best soup: a small black mushroom found in Finland, not at all in Sweden, and here and there in Norway.

The lake had monstrous northern pike that went crazy for Rapala plugs, as well. So, after his sauna, he took a small fish for his supper that night and a large one for lunch with his Norwegian builders the next day.

Napped and showered, he now felt fresher than he had the first day out, on the way to Panama, and eagerly awaited the silver tureen of mushroom soup with which he began lunch and supper at Haikko Manor.

The waiter, however, tapped him on the shoulder. Cook would keep the soup on the stove, he said. He had a call waiting in the lounge.

The Athens operator put Taki on the phone.

"Loren?" he asked as stupidly as ever, Wade noted.

At the same time, Wade grew very alert. Taki might have heard something, he thought. Demi could have blabbed. Maybe he saw a better deal cutting in the family.

A moment later, he knew otherwise.

What did he think, Taki asked, sounding as puzzled as usual, about ten-year charters on the four 60,000-tonners going to the shipyard in the Far East? He had a few nibbles that could lead to something.

Absolutely not, he answered. Hubie and some of his Harvards had been looking at world inflation, and in ten years, at 2.5 percent a year, that would be like running at World Scale minus ten or twenty. Athens Greeks who figured to put ships to work that way so that they would have ten years of the full season at Saint-Moritz were living in a dream world.*

Taki sighed, a prophet without honor. He no doubt had already told Zavvas and Lycourgos that. Hearing it, they probably had called him a *malaca*. So he had called for confirmation.

Satisfied now, he asked if anything else was new.

Wade took advantage of the opportunity. No, he said. He was just playing

---

* As indeed they were. Those who chartered out after the 1973 Arab oil embargo, when tanker rates fell so sharply, are worse off. Some new owners, in all likelihood, will be forced out of shipping.

mother superior, making the rounds of ships and yards. But prices were so low he had a real itch to build. He would scratch it, of course, by the time he got back to New York. By then the war would be on, or almost, and the Keriosotises, wheeling and dealing and making millions chartering PANARTEX ships, would call his itch luck. He helped that impression along with another question.

What did Taki think they could get per ton on their ships over ten years old? he asked. With the right price, maybe building made sense.

He would check around and call him in Oslo, Taki said. In the meantime, he had to get back to the meeting and a friend wanted to say hello.

He heard Taki call and a door close. Then Honey came on.

She had no use for the Athens Keriosotises, so she and Taki stayed at the Grande Bretagne. "How you?" she asked.

Bored an' poorly, he sighed, playing for sympathy. With Taki on his way to Glyfadda, an' her all alone, he wished he was in Athens. He'd sneak right over to the Grande Bretagne an'—ugly, shorter'n her, an' fat—he'd have himself some kind of run at that sweet little thing of hers.

They run out of food up there? she laughed.

Fact was, he told her, Finland worked best in late summer. The Laplanders moved south then, an' you could get reindeer hearts an' livers, which, sliced an' fried in wild mushrooms an' onions cooked up good enough to eat at least three times a day with—

As expected, that put her in her place.

She came right to the point, affecting the down-home neighbor-girl tone she used to imply that white folks surrounded by Greeks could trust only each other. If, as Demi had described her to Fiona, she served as chairman of Taki's board, Wade also sat at her directors' table. Between them, they had made a lot of money for each other. Neither Hubie nor the Keriosotises realized the extent to which they relied on each other.

She didn't understand somethin', she began.

Demi had suddenly begun to make noises as though he backed small rather than big in the family debate over what kind of ships to build. Did he have any idea what that was all about?

Leave it to her, he thought. She knew what to listen to. He wondered whether the question came from Taki or from her. From her, he decided. Demi was the son Taki had never had. And, like most Greek fathers, as far as Taki was concerned his boy could do no wrong.

Fortunately, the Keriosotises had such a snake pit of entangled and intertwined alliances, he had no trouble in suggesting another.

Maybe, he said, Demi had made a deal with Zavvas too, even though he hated him. Phaedra had.

Lord God! that had never occurred to her.

Artemis had always been Demi's favorite. Maybe she should talk to her.

She would. The next mornin'. They were goin' to a dressmaker together. When was Loren comin' home? she asked.

Early June.

That long?

Eggs to lay an' work to do . . . he sighed.

Shoot! Somethin' didn't feel right. She didn't know what it was, but somethin' didn't fit. He'd call when he got back to New York?

For sure! They'd have lunch and a half, he promised.

"See you then," she said, still musing.

"See you."

Hanging up, he expelled a long breath. Goddamn! That woman had antennae. Talk about close.

He knew exactly why Demi was backing smaller. When that war came, and what would shortly happen at the Suez Canal took place, smaller ships would be all but worthless for years to come.

Smaller gave Demi his chance to even out with all of those dear relatives of his who had killed his father, badgered his mother, and tried every which way to screw him out of what little he had inherited.

Charlie Chan, in Singapore, had a Chinese saying that applied to such doings: "Every good deed should be avenged." Of course, that made it tough on Taki. But Wade saw now he never should have doubted Demi.

Ego always made greed and vengeance equal partners.

The Lions, that evening, were less philosophical.

They had a tangible problem to ponder. Moreover, it had come as a surprise.

Lianides had arrived the afternoon before from Rome. Then, donning German Afrika Korps shorts liberated in World War II, a matching tank commander's jacket, and Mexican huaraches, an outfit he would wear until he left the ship, he had toured the topside with Zavitsanos and the brothers George, Alexander, and Nico.

Shaking his head in wonderment at the effort that had been expended, he led the group aft to see what cousin Archimedes had done.

However much work had been done on deck, the pace below must have been frantic in comparison. Somewhat to their surprise, opening the door in the engineroom casing, they saw the floorplates. The cloud of steam, after the replacing of nine valves and the repacking of thirty-one more, had gone. Barring the chatter of a tired pump bearing, which Arkie vowed to fix, all of the machinery sang on one note as well

Cosmetics aside, the engineers had also checked and renewed many of the weak links in any power plant: pipes, circuit breakers, boiler tubes, and tips and nozzles. At Arkie's instigation one night they had even taken topside a steamline they had aboard and scoured the galley while Yorka was ashore, and had swept out a bucketful of roaches in the process. For good measure, they had done the dining table in the salon as well.

So Happy Hour and supper that night were jovial and optimistic. They had more ship under them than they had expected. All but Arkie and the young-sters had sunk at least one ship with Costa. Knowing the risks in such ven-tures, they were grateful for small favors.

The next morning, after an equally hopeful breakfast, they weighed anchor to rehearse the operation. Zavitsanos called it The Game.

It had nothing to do with sinking the ship.

The exercise consisted of steaming a mile forward, stopping the engine, and then coasting while George and Alexander took pelorus bearings on buildings ashore to measure the distance covered. After that, lining up a church spire and the tower of a shipyard crane, they were to back down three miles, keep-ing the ship centered within the imaginary half-mile-wide channel depicted by the landmarks.

Dead slow, engine astern, without tugs, it was like a flea steering an ele-phant, Zavitsanos said.

Their first attempt supported that contention.

"I say, old chap," he drawled into the wheelhouse from his post on the port bridgewing, looking over Alexander's shoulder, "I do believe we just put her aground." They had backed down barely a quarter of a mile.

Costa, standing at the engine revolution indicator mounted on the over-head at the center wheelhouse window, quickly looked away. Bouncing on toes and heels, he had been trying to gauge the feel of propeller speed through his huaraches. By the time they left Ancona, that sense would be regained. Then, in common with the select few superlative shipmasters of every genera-tion, he would know at every moment, through the soles of his feet, to within three revolutions per minute, what *Dynamic* turned, and, consequently, her speed.

Now, however, one glance astern sufficed.

*"Then berazzy!"* he laughed, slapping the thighs of his dark-green Afrika Korps shorts. Lucky they had a week or two to practice.

What did he think? he asked Zavitsanos. How much ballast did they need to stiffen her?

Two thousand tons? Zavitsanos ventured.

Why not?

Walking behind young Nico at the wheel, Costa rang the engineroom and asked Arkie for two thousand tons. "Let there be salt water!" he laughed, winking at the kid, who looked awed by his infamous cousin.

Finally trimmed fore and aft to everyone's liking, they made another wide sweep at half ahead, centering the ship between church spire and shipyard crane.

Clicking his chronometer, Zavitsanos said, Stop. He would command the ship through this part of the exercise. Then Costa would back her out. For now, he had to know, to within a hundred feet, no more, precisely how much way *Dynamic* would carry with a given amount of ballast.

Nico, leaving the wheel midships, rang STOP.

Alexander, brown hair almost blond in the sun, bent over the pelorus like a rifleman using a raised sight and called out his bearings on the buildings ashore.

Costa and Zavitsanos, behind him, looked about with the casual interest of men seeing a movie a second time. The chart, handily folded, sacrilege on most ships, lay on top of the steel box enclosing the port running light.

They were stopped, Zavitsanos said at length.

Only then was the chart consulted.

*"Malaca!"* Costa laughed. Jerk!

"What? On the second try? And with new ballast—" Seeing Costa laugh, Zavitsanos broke off. Then he laughed, too. He had overstood his mark by about a hundred yards. A piece of cake, he said.

"Nico, astern, please," he called inside.

A moment later they felt the vibration.

The wheelhouse phone rang immediately. Arkie said they were shaking to bits back aft.

From what? Costa asked.

None of them had any idea. "Let's anchor and look," Arkie suggested.

So that night, over supper, the Lions had a problem.

With the engine torn down, the answer still eluded them.


*May 10, 1967*
*Zurich*
*Montreal*


THE MESSENGER arrived at Schotten's at 7:30 P.M.

A tall, gangling blond youth, he stood at the door of the hideaway in Niederdorf shaking his head. He had no time to step inside, he explained. He had prevailed upon his professors at the University of Zurich to give him his doctorals early. That way he could be home in time if he were needed. He commanded a tank battalion.

Meanwhile, he said, handing over a white envelope, Schotten would find a plane ticket and confirmation of hotel reservations inside. He would be met at his destination, and his Swiss passport would be replaced by one he had used earlier, in Canada, the year before.

Then, Schotten recalled, he had been Janos Kupchek, Brazilian national of

Czech origin, and wheat trader. The Iberian Airlines ticket, he saw, would take him to Barcelona, Spain, Friday morning, May 12.

And where would Senhor Kupchek be staying? he asked.

Shrugging, the youth shook his head.

Schotten nodded.

*Mazel tov!* the messenger said, extending his hand. He wished he could step in, because he thought it would be years before he saw such paintings again, but his oral examinations had him terrified. He had to study.

Leaning back behind his Regency desk, Evelyn acted as messenger for Howsam.

He had read a thriller, he said, in which the hero had the assignment—and don't ask him why—of smuggling an elephant into an unfriendly country. No problem. The elephant passed over the border unnoticed as a member of a traveling circus.

The novel stank, but he revered its lesson, Evelyn said. He told Howsam this, he went on, opening the center drawer of his desk and withdrawing a Canadian passport, to assure him humor had no part in his new identity.

Howsam took the passport. He knew nothing of espionage or forgeries. Nonetheless, the document seemed authentic to him.

Opening it, he knew beyond doubt it was. Alongside a recent photo of himself, he found that he had become an old friend and hunting companion of his and Evelyn's: Gregory Mousecall, of Fort George, Quebec.

Pretty slick, he had to agree.

Of course, why bumble around faking things?

An airline ticket and hotel reservation followed. Next came a Goren pocket bridge guide. Evelyn waggled it before handing it over.

"Your hotel," he said, "has a lounge with antiques I'd kill for, so, after supper the first night, you'll go there for coffee and a brandy and read a little Goren. Eric'll come in and chat you up a bit, and then our people'll stop by and ask if you two'd care for a rubber or two before going to bed. As simple as that. You'll be in the Whaler next day."

"Now, as to the war—"

"You know an Egyptian named Sadat, Prentiss?"

Howsam shook his head.

Evelyn smiled. "They call him Nasser's poodle—bit of a bootlicker, I gather, but quite bright and Gamal's chum and chief of army relations. Home Office says he's due to see Kosygin or Podgorny* tomorrow or the day after. We'll know what they tell him, and so will you. The lads on *Dynamic What'sitsname*'ll get word over radio and the details of the final arrangements. If, as expected, the Russians led the Egyptians into a charade that could only bring war, Is-

* Premier and President of the USSR.

raeli naval forces would be at their disposal. And his boys'd fix the war to suit!" Evelyn laughed.

His client assured, he looked at his watch. Twenty after four, he mused. They could be in Val David in fifty minutes. What would Howsam say to a bon voyage supper at La Sapinière? It had the best French food in North America.

What more could he do for a son going into battle?

*May 12, 1967*
*Oslo, Norway*
*Ancona*
*S'Agaró, Spain*

WADE SAVORED the view.

He seldom did anywhere. Like almost all seamen, his visual memory bank of places consisted of buoys, leading marks, and channels to which stubborn ships had to be bulldogged.

Oslo, however, proved to be an exception. He never pictured it from the sea. He saw it, instead, from here. Moreover, his view, as now, always came at dusk.

Above him, atop the Nordmarka hills, pines floored a graying sky with jagged symmetry. Closed terrace doors notwithstanding, their scent entered the dining room. Below the restaurant, granite outcrops in the sides of Oslofjord winked blue and pink in the lowering sun.

The city's lights twinkled below and straight ahead. At their far edge, the docks glowed yellow. Beyond them the water matched the sky.

Tonight he had a bonus. Fog, a pale blue new to him, crept up the fjord.

With crayfish coming, to be followed by sole caught that morning in Stavanger, the trip just kept getting better, he thought.

In Hamburg, he had succeeded in shanghaiing Alonzo Irish.

In Rotterdam, Joop Hendrikse had saved him four dollars a ton.

Yesterday, at Haikko Manor, had been the best yet. He had ordered two more 100,000-tonners from Ervin, his Norwegian builder, without arousing his suspicions. He did that by asking for one. Ervin, his yard on repair work in the slump, suggested three for volume savings.

Hell, he answered, he needed four, but the budget got in his way.

Then how about two at the per-ton price of three?

Feeling guilty, he thus made the best buy on the trip: sixty-eight dollars a ton.

Such ploys were necessary with Norwegians. Their laws allowed shipowners to build abroad, but in practice they seldom did. In a small country, Ervin said, people helped each other. Usual buyer–seller adversary relationships did not exist.

That made dealing with Norwegian builders tricky. If an Ervin heard a secret, he would take it to countrymen first and build for less rather than stay silent and build ships later for more.

Wade approved. He appreciated loyalty.

Tomorrow, however, he would be less forgiving. He would see his Nazi, Klaus-Heinrich, then.

Klaus-Heinrich's Hamburg yard had built four ships in the early sixties for him, and they had done little else but break down. Repairs? Make-goods? Modifications? Never! The Germans said crews were at fault.

Wade had sat still for that, vowing to even out. He would, and good old Klaus-Heinrich would never tumble to it, which made revenge sweeter. He would go home thinking he had sold little Loren the moon. Then, in a month, he would find his yard tied up for a year and a half with low-cost contracts during the greatest shipbuilding boom in history. Meanwhile, Wade, selling construction orders, would make the money.

And that damned Nazi would call it luck, he knew. The thought warmed him more than cognac.

Then, back at the Hotel Bristol, it lost its glow.

Taki called first. A nervous laugh masked his anxiety.

"Hey, Loren, what in hell's goin' on?" he asked. Did Loren know that damn-fool kid Demi? Guess what he was doing! He was startin' to talk "smaller," just like Zavvas an' Lycourgos, over what kind of ships to build next! Where had that come from? Did he know somethin'?

Wade told Taki what he had told Honey two days before. Could Demi have made a deal with Zavvas?

"What! Come on, Loren. Demi go against *me?*" Taki asked. Who had raised that kid since he was seventeen? Taki knew Demi got a little nuts aroun' women an' money, but he had a good heart with no room for treachery in it. Had he ever lied about anythin' big?

Wade let him ramble.

What about his older ships? he finally asked.

Dzesus! He had forgotten all about them, Taki admitted. He'd call tomorrow or the day after. This "smaller" thing really had him going.

Honey, obviously, had said nothing. She would wait for Taki to mention the matter. Then she would give him advice. What an operator she was, Wade thought. She never let him think she ran the show.

Henley called ten minutes later.

Without being told, Henley saw what was coming next. An Arab loan to Americans to build tankers for which no demand existed meant only one thing to him: that the market would soon change. That, in turn, implied a Middle Eastern war, affecting the Suez Canal.

A banker, he also understood unsecured loans. Generally they were gifts. Otherwise, they paid for services. In this case he had no illusions. He also knew the only intangible worth $200 million to several nations: the time and place of that future war.

That knowledge put all who had it in jeopardy.

So, readying the next step of Wade's buying binge, he had been especially careful. When building contracts and mortgages were reviewed by the European governments subsidizing most shipyards, he wanted nothing on paper that might smack of rush or suggest he and Wade had read the future with help denied others.

Always, however, he implied nothing over the phone. Instead, he made a little joke of being at the bank at nine o'clock in the evening.

He hadn't seen anythin' yet! Wade laughed. Wait till he, Wade, got done with the Nazzy, Klaus-Heinrich. He had him comin' in the next mornin'.

He could wait, Henley answered. As a matter of fact, he wondered if he could put off for a day or two their date in Stockholm to go through the mortgage rigmarole, so that he could move more paper through the mill. Then they could backtrack through Hamburg, Copenhagen, and Dublin without interruption and finish off in London at the end of the month.

No sweat, Wade said. He had some sneaking around in Scandinavia of his own to do. Meanwhile, had the diplomatist sent more dough?

Umh-hum.

How much more?

Ten percent.

Wasn't that kind of slow?

Sheikhs said a lot of beads, Henley laughed. By the way, he went on, Hubie had sent him a copy of a guaranteed-loan agreement. That didn't apply just to the convertibles they were thinking of building?

No. He had let it go open-ended. He had run out of leverage at that point. Was that causing any trouble?

No, no, Henley assured him. He just wanted to be sure he had read that correctly. It paid to keep all the details in mind. Would Wednesday, the seventeenth, do to get under way in Stockholm?

Sure. Wade would see him then. He'd call with the name of the hotel.

*Details?* Wade thought, hanging up. What details?

They were guaranteeing a loan, not making one. It applied to them only if Demi failed to pay it off. And how could that happen with that war coming? He looked at his watch and decided to call Hubie. It would be three-thirty in the afternoon in New York.

He was just talkin' to Henley, he began, an' the guaranteed-loan agreement came up. What was goin' on? What business was that of Henley's?

That wasn't any of Henley's business, Hubie agreed. Someone had told him to ask for that.

The diplomatist?

No.

Who, then?

Hubie didn't know.

Wade pondered that a moment. If not the diplomatist, who else would know about the loan agreement? Only someone in the Persian Gulf. That explained the slowness of the money, he thought. The sheikhs wanted to see how airtight that was, too.

Maybe he'd find out Monday, Hubie went on. He and the diplomatist were having lunch then. He'd goose the money along then, too.

Not likely, Wade believed. He knew his Arabs, too. If Henley had just got that loan agreement, they'd be jawing it over for days. That lunch would be to put more heat on Hubie. How was Hubie feelin'? he suddenly asked.

Apart from the suspense?

Yeah.

Better'n ever.

He had an idea, Wade told Hubie. What was this—the second week of May? Just right. Tarpon were beginnin' to roll down in Costa Rica. Why didn't he jus' follow 'em all the way north to Marathon or Islamorada, in the Keys. They didn't have no phones in most of them places, an' he had a hunch the diplomatist wouldn't mind, either.

He maybe had somethin' there, Hubie allowed. By God, he'd take Cora, too. But when would they meet?

Saturday, June 3, at the Dorset, unless—

Got it! Hubie said, stopping him in midsentence.

Unless, of course, the war started earlier.

Hanging up, Wade called home.

Away three weeks, he had another three to go. He thought he had better see his wife in London. Otherwise, he had no idea when he would. When war came, he saw two or three weeks of Dorset nights making charter deals and selling the building contracts he had been so busy acquiring. After that, he would go back to Japan, Holland, Norway, and Sweden to start his own 100,-000-tonners. So, barring emergencies, he would be on the run at least until August 15 and probably Labor Day.

Jesus, he wondered, what more could happen?

Looking out the window at the blue fog rolling up the Stortingsgata as he waited for the call to go through, he thought of several possibilities.

All made him grimace.

\* \* \*

Those on *Dynamic Papachristou* knew how he felt.

Anchored after the mysterious vibration, they put a lifeboat over to inspect the stern. Diagnosing the difficulty required no expertise.

A fist-sized chunk of bronze had departed the top propeller blade.

Young Nico, who had done a lot of diving off Hydra, slipped over the side of the boat and beneath the water. He surfaced with no surprises. The other blades were dented, and the shaft looked as if it had been wiped clean.

Arkie, Costa, and Zavitsanos nodded knowingly. Experience told them they had backed through some dunnage, planks for stacking freighter cargo in holds. Inevitably a few slipped into the water. They were a menace in every port in the world.

*"Endoxi!"* Costa said. Okay!

*"Then berazzy!" Zavitsanos predictably said.*

*They weren't going to the yard? Arkie asked.*

*With forefinger, Costa tugged at his right eye.*

*After lunch they would see what they would see, he said. Another day in drydock and a new screw would cost a fortune, and were they not tankermen? They would try to make do with what they had first. Besides, it would be just like those two banker pals of theirs to refuse to pay that bill. Since it had not been* budgeted, they would say he had dreamed it up.

By Friday afternoon they had begun to make do, and without vibration. But the price had been high.

Their speed forward had been reduced to ten knots, from the T-2's theoretical top of eighteen and the real thirteen that *Dynamic*'s tired plant produced. Backing, they had thirty-one turns a minute before shaking began. In terms of engineroom telegraph speeds, their maximum reverse power lay somewhere between half astern and slow astern.

*Endoxi!* Costa described the situation. Stately grace, Zavitsanos called it.

Arkie and the engineers thought otherwise.

Now, as Wade stood at a window in Oslo, they sat at the saloon table trying to sell the wisdom of a day in drydock. But, like deck officers, Costa and Zavitsanos had little sympathy for the inherent fragility of engines. Costa, eyes wide in exaggeration, palms up, made the deckmen's case. They could run forever at those speeds without fear of shaking the screw off, he said. So why was everybody so worried? He and Zavitsanos had to drive the bus, not they. All right. They would go a little slower. The difference in speed meant nothing to their safety. Good God, at five hundred yards' range, and with a white light above two reds, they would have the whole town to themselves, war or no war!

He didn't understand, Ioannis objected. There was an imbalance. Whether they felt it or not, it was there, and every time the screw turned, the ship would feel it.

Where? Zavitsanos asked.

Arkie shook his head in answer. How the hell could they know? Had he any idea of how much down below could be affected by a shake or wiggle they couldn't feel?

He never inspected the undersides of women either, Zavitsanos admitted. He assumed, however, that if he felt nothing amiss, nothing was. So far he had never been wrong, with ships or ladies.

"Let's vote!" Costa said, smiling ingratiatingly.

There being five deckmen and four engineers present, the visit to drydock was rejected. Shrugging, Costa looked the length of the table.

Arkie shrugged back, accepting the risk.

How big? Neither knew.

Unrolling the charts before him, Costa slid the top one down to Arkie, withdrew red and blue pencils from the breast pocket of his Afrika Korps jacket, and announced that the evening's business would now begin.

From tomorrow on, he said, they would play The Game off Ancona by chart. Every man had to know where he would be every moment and how many seconds would elapse between engineroom commands from the bridge.

Clear?

The engineers nodded.

Starting, his finger traced the western breakwater shown in the top left chart inset opposite the heading "U.S. NAVAL OCEANOGRAPHIC OFFICE" and the legend:

UNITED ARAB REPUBLIC
SUEZ CANAL

Only at the Hostal de la Gavina, in S'Agaró, Spain, did events march forward that evening without doubts.

The hotel, a rambling stuccoed 100-room structure set high above a beach, is considered to be the best on the Mediterranean. But an hour's drive from Barcelona, in the heart of the German tourist's budget Costa Brava, it represents an out-of-the-way place in all but summer months and holiday weekends.

So, with few people there on a Friday in early May, a Brazilian grain trader, Senhor Janos Kupchek, had no difficulty noticing three fellow guests enjoying a postprandial brandy in the lounge while they discussed the latest edition of *Goren's Bridge Tips*.

Walking over, Senhor Kupchek, an unusually handsome blond man with a limp, stood diffidently before the group. Excuse me, he said, but were they bridge players? And more to the point, did they need a fourth?

No longer! said a tall, powerfully built man with a coppery complexion, a crewcut, and a flawless Spanish accent, who introduced himself as a Canadian, Gregory Mousecall. Why not join them for a drink? he suggested. And then they could enjoy a rubber or two.

But first he would like to introduce Señor Maxime Masiloff and his wife, Hélène. Señor Masiloff, Mousecall said, came here so frequently he kept a boat in the hotel anchorage, a Boston Whaler.

Did he like boats? Señor Masiloff asked; he was a small wiry man in his early sixties, and rose to shake hands.

Oh, yes! Senhor Kupchek said. Whalers especially.

Then he would get a Ph.D. on his by the time they left! Masiloff laughed.

Senhor Kupchek agreed, noting the small green anchor tattooed between Masiloff's left thumb and forefinger.

Masiloff proved as capable at bridge as well.

# V.
# Prelude to War

# May 12–June 4, 1967:

*As of May 12, Lions, Cowboys, and Greeks sank from view as the affair in which they had so consuming an interest came to world notice.*

*Sometime that night, a Russian Embassy official in Cairo awakened President Nasser. He had a message from their Damascus embassy, the Soviet said, claiming massive Israeli troop movements along the Syrian border.*

*The report, an outright lie, began the march for war.*

*United Nations forces there had never seen more than a company of Israeli infantry (about 120 men) sent to thwart Syrian commando raids.*

*The UN Security Council was informed of the mythical troop movement on May 19. Momentum, however, made that immaterial.*

*A daily log of publicly recorded incidents during that crisis, or historical charade, depending on point of view, suggests why.*

*The following journal, then, is a compilation drawn from* From War to War *by Nadav Safran,\* The Six Day War *by Randolph S. and Winston S. Churchill,† the* New York Times, Time, Newsweek, *and so on. Movements of the principals focused upon here are also included.*

*Conventional wisdom says events outstripped Nasser and swept him into an unwanted war. That is the view of Safran, a professor of government at Harvard.*

*The Churchills, on the other hand, having a more intimate view of power, suggest that Eric Schotten's analysis of the situation may have been closer to the truth. They go so far as to say, in fact, that while the U.S. ambassador to Israel, Walworth Barbour, told Jews not to fight, they may have seen a "wink" passed through unofficial channels by President Lyndon Johnson. They also speculate that through intelligence or surmise the Israelis assumed the Russians would not—repeat, not—intervene, a matter on which the life of Israel depended. This suggests, certainly, that the Russians might accept the defeat of their allies, possibly welcome it.*

*In light of what we are learning of truth vis-à-vis reality as regards Vietnam, the Bay of Pigs, and Cambodia, a review of events leading up to the Six-Day War similarly raises more questions than it answers.*

\* Indianapolis and New York: Pegasus, 1969.
† London: Heinemann, 1967.

## MAY 13, 1967

Soviet President Nikolai Podgorny repeats claim of Israeli troop movements on the Syrian border, saying that Israel's aim is to invade Syria, that the USSR will help Syria and Egypt in a war with Israel, and that Egypt should be ready for such action.

"You must not be taken by surprise," Podgorny says. "The coming days will be fateful." Later, Foreign Minister Gromyko tells Sadat the same.

## MAY 14, 1967

Egypt's armed forces are suddenly put on maximum alert. The press says the measures are taken in view of reliable information that Israel plans to attack Syria and that Egypt will enter the fight if Israel attacks.

## MAY 15, 1967

While Israel holds its Independence Day parade, Egyptian troops move through Cairo toward Suez. Israel alerts its armed forces.

## MAY 16, 1967

Egypt, declaring a state of emergency, pronounces all military forces "in a complete state of preparedness for war." As the Sinai buildup continues, the Egyptian chief of staff, General Fawzi, sends a letter to the commander of the United Nations Expeditionary Forces, General Rikhye, asking him to withdraw UN forces from "the observation points on our frontier."

## MAY 17, 1967

Egypt and Syria say they are in "combat readiness." Hussein announces from Amman that Jordanian troops are being mobilized.

## MAY 18, 1967

Iraq and Kuwait announce mobilization.

Egyptian Foreign Minister Riad writes to UN Secretary General U Thant informing him of the United Arab Republic's decision "to terminate the existence of UNEF on the soil of the UAR and in the Gaza Strip."

In Tel Aviv, Israel says "appropriate measures" had been taken.

## MAY 19, 1967

UNEF is officially withdrawn.

*Al Ahram,* semiofficial Cairo daily newspaper, says Riad's letter was sent in response to an inquiry from U Thant about the "scope, limits, and meaning" of the previous decision of the UAR.

U Thant's immediate compliance, never satisfactorily explained, allows Egyptian troops to swarm over the Sinai past the demilitarized zone. Suddenly the war looks infinitely more winnable to Nasser.

U Thant's action, never forgiven by Israel, trying to avoid a war, moved Golda Meir, at his death, to send him on his way with one of the bitterest, most ironic epitaphs recorded in the English language. "His passing was as the falling of a leaf," she said.

In response, Israel calls in more reserves.

Oilmen and others familiar with practical politics in the Middle East believe that if President Johnson winked to the Israelis, he did so then. Knowing Nasser, Johnson probably saw war as inevitable.

## MAY 20, 1967

Israel completes partial mobilization and begins to put naval forces in a state of readiness. Only one of the Israelis' three destroyers is operational. Of their three submarines, all pre–World War II vintage, one is in mothballs, and another, the *Rahof,* is too old to submerge. A base is established at Ashdod, from which motor torpedo boats and other light naval craft can operate. New radar and guns are fitted, and the *Rahof* gets sonar and depth-charge racks for anti-submarine work.

## MAY 21, 1967

Egyptian forces end the takeover of UNEF positions and reach Sharm el-Sheik, at the tip of the Sinai Peninsula, controlling the entrance to the Gulf of Aqaba.

## MAY 22, 1967

Israeli Premier Eshkol says Egypt has increased its Sinai force from 35,000 to 80,000; proposes withdrawal of Egyptian and Israeli troops to earlier positions; disclaims any aggressive intentions on the part of Israel.

Nasser, talking later that day at an Egyptian Sinai air base, announces closing of the Gulf of Aqaba to Israeli ships and others carrying "strategic material" to Israel. "They, the Jews, threaten war; we tell them: welcome. We are ready for war."

## MAY 23, 1967

The most bombastic day yet.

King Faisal, in London, announces he has ordered Saudi-Arabian forces to be ready to join in a battle against Israeli aggression.

The Soviet Union also weighs in: "Should anyone try to unleash aggression in the Near East, he would be met not only with the united strength of the Arab countries but also with strong opposition from the Soviet Union and all peace-loving countries."

Premier Eshkol tells the Knesset, "Any interference with freedom of shipping in the Gulf and the Strait [of Tiran] constitutes a gross violation of international law, and an act of aggression against Israel."

President Johnson declares on TV, "The United States considers the Gulf to be an international waterway and feels that a blockade of Israeli shipping is illegal and potentially dangerous to the cause of peace. The right of free, innocent passage of the international waterway is a vital interest of the international community."

In New York, the UN Security Council meets in an emergency session at the request of Denmark and Canada. The debate trails off in following days without reaching a conclusion. Efforts of the United States to obtain a resolution that would essentially require Egypt to desist from blockading Israel while the Council discusses the issue are blocked by the Soviets.

## MAY 24, 1967

Israeli Foreign Minister Abba Eban leaves for Paris.

De Gaulle tells him not to do anything, that it should be done by the four great powers. Naturally.

A man whose fondest wish, it was said, was to die in his own arms, he considers *himself* one of the four.

## MAY 26, 1967

Rhetoric soars to new heights this day.

Lyndon Johnson to Abba Eban: "I want to see that little blue-and-white Israeli flag sailin' down those Straits."

But Johnson makes no commitment. He tells Eban, an old friend from the latter's days as Israeli ambassador to the United States, that an enabling resolution would have to go through Congress before the United States could help Israel openly. Eban, having been in Washington, knows what that means—weeks. Israel has to go it alone.

Nasser, reacting to Eban's Washington visit, tells a meeting of the Pan-Arab Federation of Trade Unions that if war comes "it will be total and the objective will be to destroy Israel. We feel confident that we can win and are ready for war with Israel. . . . This time it will not be like 1956 because we were not fighting Israel at that time, but Britain and France."

Earlier, his Ministry of Religious Affairs tells all muktars to make jihad, holy war, Saturday's Sabbath sermon topic the next day. The preachers will stress the honor of dying a martyr in holy battle.

Pope Kyrillos VI, head of the Coptic Orthodox Church in Egypt, similarly rouses Christians. He backs all steps to "regain Palestine from those who crucified Christ."

Egyptian Defense Minister Badran, meanwhile, arrives in Moscow to confer with Soviet leaders.

## MAY 27, 1967

Senhor Kupchek and Gregory Mousecall, tanned, fit, and absolute masters of the Boston Whaler, leave Hostal de la Gavina. They share a car to Barcelona Airport. Kupchek leaves on an Olympic Airways plane to Athens. Mousecall takes a TWA flight terminating in Istanbul.

## MAY 28, 1967

Sabbath out of the way, politics resume.

Sudan proclaims general mobilization.

Eban reports to the Israeli Knesset on his Washington trip; Eshkol speaks to the nation, saying that the cabinet has decided on "the continuation of political action in the world arena" to find ways to reopen the Straits of Tiran to Israeli shipping, drawing up policy lines designed "to obviate the necessity of Israel having to use its armed forces."

In Cairo, Nasser holds a press conference to spell out his position to foreign correspondents: "The Tiran Straits are Egyptian territorial waters over which we exercise our sovereign rights. No power, however strong it may be, can touch Egypt's sovereign rights or skirt them. Any such attempt will be aggression on the Egyptian people and all Arabs and will bring unimaginable harm to the aggressors. . . . If war breaks out with Israel, conditions in the Suez Canal will remain unchanged, but in the event of intervention by other countries there will be no Suez Canal."

Many historians call this Nasser's Rubicon. He has regained all that he lost in the '56 war with Britain, France, and Israel. He stands as leader of Pan-Arabism. All other Moslem rulers look to him. Even Persian Gulf Arabs have pledged him men and supplies.

With everyone dressed, how can he cancel the ball?

The Russians seemingly believed he reached that point sooner. They may have been right. At 3:30 A.M. the previous Friday, their ambassador got Nasser out of bed to tell him not to start the fighting. The advice could be likened to that of a pusher who, after leading an addict all over town before finding a fix, then warns him it might be habit forming.

The response, of course, was equally predictable. Muktars were told to talk about the glories of holy war.

The world believes Nasser. No one rushes out to build tankers. No one stockpiles oil.

The only skeptics, apparently, are two political analysts from Hydra, Costa Lianides and Zavitsanos Angelakos. Hearing the report of the news conference over the BBC overseas service, they spread their palms in a we-told-you-so gesture and ask their engineer cousins to please get up a little steam. They would like to start.

An hour later, in violation of all international maritime law, *Dynamic Papachristou* leaves Ancona twenty-eight men short and with a half ton of gelignite aboard. The voyage will either decimate the Angelakos family or forever remove it from the ranks of poor Greeks.


MAY 29, 1967

Meanwhile, the Israeli Knesset, alarmed at the Arab noise level, presses Eshkol for more action. Restrained, always moderate, hopeful of a means of avoiding war, Eshkol says he expects the United States, Britain, and others to move shortly to end the blockade in the Straits of Tiran as they have assured him they will. "It is our duty to put the pledges to the test. Very shortly, it will be clear if the prospect materializes," he says.

Nasser, that evening, before the Egyptian National Assembly, enhances his stature as Arab spokesman. He preempts another cause. "The issue today is not the question of Aqaba, or the Strait of Tiran, or UNEF. The issue is the rights of the people of Palestine, the aggression against Palestine that took place in 1948, with the help of Britain and the United States. . . . They want to confine it to the Strait of Tiran, UNEF, and the rights of passage. We say: we want the rights of the people of Palestine—complete."

He adds that Minister of Defense Badran brought him a message from Soviet Premier Kosygin "in which he says that the Soviet Union stands with us in this battle and will never allow any state to intervene until things go back to what they were before 1956. If the Western countries slight us and deny us our rights we shall teach them how to respect us. . . . We are not facing Israel but those behind it. We are facing those who created Israel."

Then comes the threat, to be explained the next day: "Preparations by the UAR and her allies for the liberation of Palestine are complete."


MAY 30, 1967

Nasser delivers on his warning.

King Hussein of Jordan, who of all Arabs shares the longest border with Israel, 325 miles, flies to Cairo at the controls of his Caravelle jet.

After a two-and-a-half-hour conference with Nasser, he signs a five-year defense pact putting Jordan's forces under Egyptian command during a war. He also allows Iraqi troops into his country during this emergency.

For good measure, Hussein permits a sworn enemy, Ahmed Shukairy, head of the Palestine Liberation Organization, to return to Jordan.

Why all the concessions?

Hussein has been a pariah among Arabs since 1948. Nasser refers to him as "the Hashemite harlot." Radio Damascus calls him the "Tom Thumb Tyrant." He fears the vengeance of Palestinian refugees.

His grandfather, Abdullah, schemed to annex Arab Jerusalem during the '48 Israeli War of Independence. A Palestinian assassin murdered him for that in '51. Now Shukairy, the man who probably ordered the killing, will fly back to Amman, Jordan, with Hussein.

Nasser, pleased at the concessions he has wrung from Hussein, kisses him goodbye that afternoon before thousands at Cairo Airport.


MAY 31, 1967

Iraqi troops and armored units move into Jordan.

In New York, the United States tries to bring Western sea powers into a plan of action to contest the Egyptian blockade of the Gulf of Aqaba.

The Soviet Union is reported to be sending more ships to the Mediterranean.


JUNE 1, 1967

Iraqi aircraft leave Habbaniya air base, near Bagdad, for H3, Iraq's westernmost airfield, closest to the Israeli border.

The Nasser-Hussein kiss confirmed, the Israeli Knesset pressures Premier Eshkol into reshuffling the cabinet. Moshe Dayan, chief of staff during the '56 war, takes over the defense portfolio from Eshkol.

Dayan, an ally of David Ben-Gurion and a political foe of Eshkol, quips, "It took eighty thousand Egyptian troops to get me into the cabinet."

No matter. He is there. More to the point, he doesn't see any Israeli ships passing through the Gulf of Aqaba.


JUNE 2, 1967

England's Prime Minister Wilson meets with President Johnson in Washington. They discuss issuing a *declaration* on freedom of passage in the Gulf of Aqaba to which Western maritime powers would subscribe.

A declaration at this late date?

The American Jewish community, as well as many pro-Israel members of

Congress, considers that tantamount to shouting "Fire!" after the barn has burned down. Lyndon Johnson smiles blandly.

## JUNE 3, 1967

The Egyptian commander in chief, General Mortagi, issues a Sabbath order of the day to his soldiers in the Sinai: "The results of this unique moment are of historic importance for our Arab nation and for the Holy War through which you will restore the rights of the Arabs which have been stolen in Palestine and reconquer the plundered soil of Palestine."

That afternoon, many units of Israel's forces are sent on leave and are seen by the foreign press and on world television at—where else?—the beaches.

So perhaps Dayan has found a way to avoid war.

The same afternoon a radiant Fiona Angelakos lands at Kennedy Airport after ten days in Paris. She senses that she can be the dominant woman in the Keriosotis family if she wishes. A better politician than Honey, she has become something more than a make-believe niece to Artemis, perhaps a surrogate daughter, and Phaedra's arbiter of taste.

Kissing Honey goodbye and Taki hello, she rushes for a Long Island limousine. Events confirming what Arkie told her, she decides to call Demi that evening. Honey has mentioned enough of the convertible deal for her to realize that he too may have been used.

No matter. After ten days of the shipowner's life in Paris, she knows that the Keriosotises must be her next stop. They will be her launching pad to the upper reaches of wealth, position, and power.

Sabbath ended, Radio Damascus comes back on the air to call on all Arabs "to undertake the liberation battle that will tear the hearts from the bodies of the hateful Jews and trample them in the dust."

Radio Cairo is philosophical: "O Arabs, prepare to die as martyrs so that we may be assured of victory. Martyrdom is the hope of every fighter."

Nasser broadcasts again to say that any war with Israel "will be total, and the objective will be to destroy Israel. We feel confident that we can win a war with Israel with God's help."

Eshkol, known as "the Great Compromiser" in Israeli politics, answers in an address to the Knesset: "I would like to say to the Arab countries, particularly to Egypt and Syria, that we harbor no aggressive designs. We have no possible interest in violating either their security, their territory or other legitimate rights. We, on our part, expect the same principle to be applied to us." The talk does not go down too well in the Knesset.

Elsewhere, spurred by the Nasser-Hussein kiss, and knowing that war is inevitable, Dayan and Ezer Weizmann, the army's director of operations, are at work. Weizmann, a six-footer, perhaps one of the tallest men to fly Spitfires in the Battle of Britain, is known as the architect of Israel's air force. Regarded as an intellectual among military men, he recently told Pentagon visitors, "We have got a plan for everything—even for capturing the North Pole."

He has a plan for the following Monday as well.

Shortly before eleven, Alexander Angelakos, aboard *Dynamic Papachristou,* goes to the radio room. Tall and blond, and handsome enough for passenger ships, he is a licensed radio operator as well as mate. Leaving the lights off, he flips a switch on the black metal Collins high-frequency receiver built into the bottom module of the RCA 250-watt transmitter.

Guided by the dial bulb, he tunes to 8280 kilocycles, an international calling frequency, and leans back in the metal-and-green-leather swivel chair. Every night since leaving Ancona he has done this without anything happening, so, legs on the transmitting table, he relaxes.

Tonight, however, promptly at eleven, Alexander hears the call sign the Israelis have given *Dynamic* for this trip. Turning on the transmitter motor-generator in the bottom of the gray cabinet, he rises to check the copper antenna-selector knife switch, slips it into the high-frequency position, and watches the black needle in the voltage dial creep up to the red line at 1,400 volts. Turning the antenna-inductance regulating knob in the front of the gray panel, he loads the rig for maximum signal strength.

Normal marine radio calling procedure is for the sending station to repeat the call sign of the station it wishes to reach, followed by its own call letters, three times. The Israelis break off Alexander's signal after they hear theirs once. Their operator, on a "bug," an automatic sending device, does this by holding his key against the dot post.

What comes over 8280 kilocycles is . . . *dit, dit, dit.* . . .

Stopping, Alexander next hears the Israeli operator send 7270, a working frequency where messages are sent. *Dit-ditt*ing acknowledgment, he shifts his transmitter frequency, tunes the receiver, and taps *dit-dit* again.

Then from the pocket of his khaki shorts, he takes out the slip of paper Costa has given him to use if contact is made. He taps out M23, an area of the Mediterranean on a chart the Israelis put aboard with the gelignite. The area lies about four hundred miles northwest of Port Said.

Acknowledging, the Israeli operator taps back CU5.

*Dit-ditt*ing, Alexander turns off his transmitter.

The Israelis are on the air in three minutes. "Orange and pink," they send back.

Pink Alexander knows. That means half a knot.

Costa, hearing the motor-generator run, knows that contact has been made and waits in the chartroom. He and Alexander look at the green-lined yellow sheet of tablet paper stuck on the bulkhead over the chart table with electrician's tape.

Orange, they see, stands for six.

Stepping off the distance to Port Said on the chart and doing the division by six and a half in his head, Costa nods as he works out the answer.

He knows Ezer Weizmann's plan.

"War, Monday morning," he says. "Our turn comes that night. By Tuesday, we'll all be trillionaires!"

Alexander looks unconvinced.

Costa slaps him on the back. "You'll see," he says. "Piece of cake!"

Then he cranks the chartroom telephone to tell the engineers to reduce speed.


JUNE 4, 1967

Nasser, it seems, has faced down the Jews and the world.

Prime Minister Wilson, out peddling the joint Anglo-American declaration to keep the Strait of Tiran open, finds no takers.

Washington announces that Egyptian Vice President Zakariyya Muheiddin will shortly visit the capital and that U.S. Vice President Hubert Humphrey will soon go to Cairo for more talks on the crisis.

Cairo sees that as a sign of U.S. appeasement. It may be.

Lyndon Johnson seems unusually subdued. Tel Aviv mirrors his mood.

The unimaginable has happened. The Arabs have at last united. Iraq, adhering to the Jordanian-Egyptian defense pact, places its forces on Jordanian soil under Egyptian command. Israel is thus ringed by the armies of Egypt, Jordan, Iraq, and Syria acting in concert.

Something subtle, however, has taken place.

Israel now has surprise on its side. Who would attack when surrounded so?

So that afternoon Major General Mordechai Hod, Israeli Air Force chief, briefs his wing commanders.

At 8 P.M., wing commanders brief squadron leaders, who, it can be presumed, do little more than nod. They have heard variations on the theme for sixteen years. As Hod will say later, explaining one of the most remarkable victories in the history of war, "We lived with the plan, we slept on the plan, we ate the plan. Constantly we perfected it."

At 11 P.M., Alexander transmits again from *Dynamic*.

Mossad, Israeli intelligence, had a plan, as well. It orders speed increased to seven and a half knots.

"They've moved up the attack," Costa says.

"Obviously," Zavitsanos agrees, stepping off the distance to Port Said with disreputably tarnished brass dividers on the chart before him. "They want it over and done in time for them to have a decent lunch."

Later, his assessment will seem eerily correct.

Shortly before midnight, in New York, Loren Wade walks through the International Arrivals Building at Kennedy Airport and takes a cab to the Dorset. His wife took a plane from Heathrow, in London, the night before. He slept in the lounge there, then waited all day. He and his wife had seats on a Pan Am flight coming from Cairo, but all equipment moving west from the Middle East has been diverted or detained because of the crisis.

So, smiling, he leans back in the cab.

The Jews'll pull the cork any minute now, he thinks.

At the Dorset the first floor of the suite is dark. Where's Hubie?

Hubie is asleep upstairs in his bedroom.

Wade grins, seeing Hubie's face and arm in the light coming over his shoulder. Hubie looks as good as new, he tells himself, with all that tan. Tomorrow, or the next day, when the Jews start to kick ass, he'll be as good as new.

Smile widening, he goes to his own bedroom.

# VI.

# June 5, 1967

*June 5–6, 1967*
Dynamic Papachristou
*Tel Aviv, Israel*
*Washington, D.C.*
*New York City*
*Port Said, Egypt*

## 0000 LOCAL TIME,* JUNE 5

A T-2 requires three men in the engineroom at all times. With only four engineers aboard *Dynamic,* each man works eighteen hours and sleeps six. Yorka brings them food. Between fatigue and 110-degree heat, they are keeping the plant going out of habit.

That, at any rate, is what compels Arkie, nominally chief engineer, to make a last tour before going topside for some cool seventy-degree night air.

His domain is a cross section of the hull, perhaps fifty feet high, forty feet wide, and fifty feet long. Its sides and ends, from diamond-patterned floorplates to forced-air fan grates on the boat deck, are painted a garish sulfur yellow. Harshly lighted, it is a four-story factory, its levels defined by black iron gratings and polished steel railings.

The machinery exists to change salt water into distilled water, which boilers heat into steam to turn a motor-generator. The 2,300 volts of electricity drive the propeller and meet the ship's other power needs.

Every step of this energy cycle has its own "feel."

So, after making room for Ioannis at the log desk, Arkie probes the floorplates with the toes of his oil-soaked, steaming shoes, as Costa tests bridge and wheelhouse decks through the soles of his huaraches.

"She feel heavy to you?" he asks Ioannis.

* A note about time. For clarity, entries concerning *Dynamic Papachristou* are noted in local time. *Dynamic*'s position puts her time five hours ahead of Eastern Daylight Saving Time. Tel Aviv, to the east, is another hour later than Washington or New York.

Ioannis, in dungaree shorts, looks up from adjusting the red bandana over his bald head. With his high-topped shoe he toes the plates around the main engine, hung from the boiler flat above him.

He shakes his head.

Over here, Arkie says. He stands beneath the condenser.

Smiling, Ioannis makes the sign of the cross.

The condenser is as vital to the ship as the motor. Its role is to cool unused steam into distilled water so that it can return to the boiler. Sea water, coming in through a hull inlet, circulates within ten-foot-long yellow-painted steel condenser jacket. Suspended within it is a serpentine of piping carrying steam from the boiler. If the condenser breaks down, one of two things happens: the ship's evaporators fail to make distilled water fast enough to satisfy the boiler's needs, or salt water from the condenser contaminates the distilled water. In either case the result is the same. The ship must stop. Salt water will disable boilers almost immediately.

Ioannis toes the plating under the condenser. Reaching up, he slaps the jacket. Then he shakes his head.

Arkie, reading the temperature/vacuum gauge mounted on the opposite side of the steel casing, shrugs back. Everything is as it should be. He must be getting old, he muses.

This will do it to you, Ioannis agrees.


0100 LOCAL TIME

Ioannis too has suddenly begun to age. Sprinting up to the third engineroom level, to the mattress put down on the flyover above the boilers for the spill from the forced-air fans, he shakes Arkie awake.

What's the matter? What's wrong?

There's water over the floorplate, Ioannis says.

How much?

Two inches.

Alarm overrides shoes and trousers. Arkie follows him down in jockey shorts.

Another few inches of water will end the voyage.

T-2s were built with the main propulsion motor hung vertically from the second level, or boiler flat. The bottom of the motor passes through the floor-plates into a watertight well inset in the bilges. The condenser and other pumps and motors ride in similar recesses.

Each of these boxes has a lip, or cofferdam, welded around it for added protection should the floorplates flood. World War II chief engineers, protesting that they might have saved ships had they more time, got these barriers raised. On most T-2s they range from eight inches to a foot. On *Dynamic,* one of the first hulls to the design, they are four inches.

So they are two inches from disaster.

Salt water will short out the main motor. No repair is likely at sea. Or, if this is a hull leak, the ship can sink.

Ioannis, for all three inches of his waxed mustache tips, red-and-white pirate's bandana, and wrestler's build, is an old-school Greek seaman. He has done nothing but run to his chief.

So Arkie starts the bilge pump. Notifying the bridge can wait. They have a firm Port Said arrival time, and this could be many things. Some might not affect speed, so why alarm anyone? Then, ankle deep in warm water, he and Ioannis try to diagnose the problem.

At 0115, however, the water is higher.

Orestes, the strongest of the engineers, breaks a bilge pump coupling and connects a general-service pump, used in passing salt water through a lubricating-oil cooler. The increased output stems the rise.

At 0130 the water begins to recede. Zavitsanos, however, on the bridge on watch, has seen the heavier discharge aft and calls the engineroom.

What's all that dishwater going over the side for? he asks. Don't they know they're disturbing the ship's trim? That's why he and Costa topped off fuel oil tanks before they left Ancona. They wanted to make Port Said with the same amount they had aboard the last day they played The Game so they could gauge the way she'd carry.

First they have to make Port Said, Arkie answers.

They have a problem down there?

Yes. Water's over the floorplates.

Any idea why?

Not yet.

Zavitsanos clucks in sympathy.

In that case, he'll just ring off, he says, and take the night air. There wouldn't be any percentage in waking Costa yet, would there?

No.

"Call me if in doubt," Zavitsanos replies, hanging up.

Even Arkie has to smile. That line is standard in every master's and chief engineer's standing night orders in every merchant ship in the world.

Leaving the phone, he walks over to the condenser and consults the temperature/vacuum gauge. The heat within the jacket, he sees, has risen thirty degrees. That means less sea water is passing around the pipes inside that circulate the leftover steam back to the boiler as distilled water.

The nature of the malady is now clear to Arkie.

"Orestes, bring the horse screwdriver," he calls.

"Will you please take up that plate?" he asks. He points to a floorplate in direct line with the condenser butted against the ship's side.

Orestes shakes his head disbelievingly.

Ioannis, the fierce, crosses himself. This time he means it.

The standard fix for what he fears they will find beneath the floorplate is a mattress against the ship's side, wedged there by timbers, a general alarm, and a dash to the lifeboats.

Orestes, "Try Me" tattoos on right biceps bulging with strain, lifts the three-by-four-foot, quarter-inch-thick steel plate.

Then he sighs fearfully. His brothers join him.

Arkie, nodding, rubs the steamline scar that runs from his right eyebrow into the front of his crewcut.

They see what they all have expected. Sea water, just under the floorplates, roils with miniature geysers. Some spout up past their shoes.

The vibration no one felt has fractured the condenser inlet pipe. No peacetime mishap can put a ship more at risk. The water rushing in now is about the same as if *Dynamic* had taken a torpedo hit.

The three brothers exchange glances. Theodosius, twenty-three, six feet two, and two hundred and twenty pounds, is the youngest and smallest. He glances up to the third level, at the mattress.

Arkie orders him elsewhere instead. "Theo," he says, "take a wrench and hose clamps, and put one of the heat exchanger pumps on the bilge line, too, and on your way back please bring my shoes."

Ioannis, standing across the opening in the floor from him, wrinkles his brow beneath the red bandana. "You can fix?" he asks.

Arkie nods.

But first they have to dry her out and stop the main motor. Meanwhile, he and Orestes can take up the next floorplate so that they have a three-foot-wide trench the run of the condenser inlet pipe in which to work. While they do that, he will call the bridge and tell Zavitsanos.

Costa Lianides, character notwithstanding, is a consummate shipmaster. Bounding across the flyover, he grasps the polished steel railings of the top ladder, leans back, feet in air, and slides down on his forearms. Three graceful swoops deliver him to the floorplates. In Afrika Korps shorts and huaraches, he reaches Arkie's side, seemingly as he hangs up the phone.

He looks at the opened floor, then at Arkie. "You stopping her?" he asks.

Arkie nods. "Then get a couple of lifeboat covers," he tells Costa.

He didn't notice, but they don't have any.

No?

No. They cost a hundred and fifty bucks apiece.

What about hatch covers? Arkie asks. He's seen two aboard—one over the steering-engine hatch aft and the other on the forecastle.

They've got those. They were stolen off the two ships that collided in the River Plate, for the trip to Greece, Costa says with a nod, understanding the repair to be made. He'll go wake Nico then, to do the diving.

Arkie shakes his head. Let him sleep, he says of Nico.

It will be a while before she's dead in the water. The strategy then is simple.

First, before repairs can be made, the sea must be kept out. The hatch covers will do this. When pulled over the condenser inlets, two twenty-four-inch screened openings in the ship's side, they will slow the rush of salt water to a manageable rate. Nico will put the hatch covers in place.

Has Costa ever seen a T-2 stopped? Arkie asks.

Costa shakes his head. Stick around, Arkie tells him. Nothing will happen anyway for another ten, fifteen minutes.

Leaving the log desk, he walks to the main motor, about sixteen feet in diameter, painted yellow like all else in this engineroom and hanging from the boiler flat above. Before it, three bronze throw levers, handles painted silver, rise from the floorplates. They look exactly like streetcar motormen's brakes, which is what they are. Later, T-2s are fitted with geared cranks. On *Dynamic*, "Swedish Steam," muscle, stops her.

Leaning on the waist-high lever at the left, Arkie shouts above the din to Costa that first you have to slow down the turbogenerator. As it puts out less voltage, the motor is slowed accordingly with the middle lever. Then, when the motor has slowed, the lever on the right is pushed forward to disengage the propeller. Jacking gear, a three-horsepower motor at the bottom of the main motor, is then switched on to keep the motor turning so that the rotor may cool gradually, without distortion.

He has no sooner pushed the right-hand lever and tapped the red button for the jacking gear than Costa looks at him wide-eyed.

It is nothing like in the movies. No bells ring. No klaxons sound.

Instead, the engineroom suddenly becomes silent. Lights start to dim.

Theodosius, already on the boiler flat, drops Arkie's shoes. Ioannis and Orestes, lifting the second floorplate out, fling it to one side and dash for the ladder. Arkie dashes after them. Costa follows.

The generator has tripped.

It will put out juice for about two minutes, as the turbine coasts. Then everything will stop—feedwater and bilge pumps, fuel oil pumps, forced-air fans providing draft for boiler fire, lights. And then, having no emergency generator, *Dynamic* will be as dead as if she sank.

Theodosius, closest to the generator, immediately punches the generator circuit breaker. It pops back.

Ioannis, on the boiler flat, sprints to the main switchboard. Unmindful of the 2,300 volts normally passing through it, he pulls fuses and resistors, looks to see that no knife switch has closed of its own accord.

Orestes, at the other end of the generator from Theodosius, starts yanking at wires, hoping to find one loose. At the same time, he opens caps on oil filter tubes and grease cups.

"*Ochi!*" Ioannis shouts as Arkie reaches the flat. No!

Orestes, with a last savage tug, shakes his head. "*Ochi!*"

Theodosius, still at the restart, does the same. "*Ochi, Archimedes!*"

Arkie regards the generator. The electrics are in order. There is no smell of burning wire. Therefore, the problem has to be mechanical. Probably, he believes, the men who designed the generator built fail-safes into it that would stop it before serious damage if a part got too far out of line.

So he does what any housewife irritated by a jumpy picture on the TV set would do, albeit somewhat more forcefully. Reaching down, he picks up a sixteen-pound maul, used for hammering boiler and condenser tubes into place, and pounds the generator casing. After the fourth whack, the machine kicks in, lights brighten, and pumps and fans pick up speed.

Standing back, he smiles sheepishly. Sometimes with vibration, he tells Costa, all you can do is hurt the thing until it runs in self-defense.

Costa joins Ioannis in crossing himself. Come on deck when she's stopped, he tells Arkie, so Nico'll know where to dive.

First, Arkie says, he'll find his shoes and start the boys on repairs.

What can they do now? Costa asks.

They can get the stuff they'll need. The engineers' order of battle follows.

Theo, with the heaviest bolt cutters aboard, is to cut two hundred feet of steel cable out of the rigging used for hoisting cargo discharge pipes aboard. That, in turn, is to be snipped into eight-foot lengths. Orestes will go to the forepeak and bring back two one-hundred-pound bags of cement. A sack of soda ash, on the boiler flat, should also be moved to the floorplates. Ioannis will tear up the wooden grating in front of the switchboard and saw the longer pieces into eight-foot lengths. Then—

They don't have a wood saw, Ioannis protests.

A hacksaw? Arkie patiently suggests. Then, he continues telling Ioannis, he is to get an old broom from Yorka and a hammer and nails.

Ioannis shakes his head. This is a steel ship, he says. It don't have nails.

Then he should get screws.

Ioannis looks increasingly confused. He rubs his scalp through the red-and-white bandana. "Archimedes," he replies, "you know Costa. He don't buy spares. Where's screws?"

In the wooden backs of the chairs in the officers' saloon. They'll need seizing wire too.

By then, it is 0137.


## 0151 LOCAL TIME

*Dynamic* is dead in the water.

Coast and Zavitsanos stand with the boy Nico at the ship's rail. The hatch covers, long lines tied into their brass grommets, lie at their feet.

Arkie, in jockey shorts and steaming shoes, strides out of the sterncastle. He rubs his arms and shoulders in what for him is a cool seventy-degree night.

With one hour of sleep in the last nineteen, he is tired and headachy. Squinting, he massages the steamline scar over his right eye as Orestes lumbers by, a hundred-pound cement bag riding on each shoulder.

Shrugging, Arkie looks over the side. About a foot forward, he tells the deckmen, who are positioning the hatch covers.

Then, joining them, he nods in confirmation.

Costa and Zavitsanos lift the steering-engine tarpaulin to the port rail, stand it on its edge. Nico steps out of his dungarees, clad in a woman's red bikini bottom, a reminder of a Swedish visitor to Hydra. At eighteen, on this ship, he is entitled to his badge of worldliness, surrounded as he is by tattoos, earrings, and broken noses.

Blond and slight like his brothers, George and Alexander, he steps from Arkie's knee to the bulwark. There he begins to hyperventilate. He will need all the breath he can store.

He must drop thirty feet to the water, then follow the ship's side beneath another thirty feet, locate the inlet, and lay the hatch cover over it. Zavitsanos and Arkie will pay out the lines as he goes and cleat them. Then, dropping beneath the keel, Nico will swim to the other side with lines attached to the opposite ends of the tarpaulin, girdling the hull.

After that, he will repeat the process.

A moment later, Costa asks him if he is ready.

He nods, passing looped lines into elbow crooks.

Then he turns in the moonless night, hands at sides.

A perfect dead-man's dive follows.

An amber plume in the Mediterranean marks his entry.

Costa, at the right moment, drops the hatch cover end first. It enters the sea with maximum penetration. Arkie and Zavitsanos each palm a line tied to a corner grommet. After fifteen seconds, they sense Nico swimming aft, toward Arkie. Zavitsanos, nodding, plays out slack. Then they feel nothing. Nico is on his way to the other side.

Costa scrambles over the pipework under the catwalk. Thirty seconds later he is ready when Nico surfaces. Down goes a heaving line with a weighted Turk's-head.

Nico passes it through his two looped lines.

Then, tying a bowline, he treads water.

Costa tells him to go back to the other side.

Arkie and Zavitsanos, having made fast their lines to cleats on the port side, do the same here. They take as much strain as they can, pulling the hatch cover as close as possible to the hull.

The second cover is more difficult to position. It is larger, and Nico is already in the water. But after a moment they have a plan. This time, Arkie will hold both lines for the starboard side which governs Nico's diving slack. When they go taut, Costa and Zavitsanos will drop the tarpaulin so that it will come part of the way through the water on its own momentum, without Nico having to drag it down.

Treading water, Nico asks for the lines.

Costa and Zavitsanos get the hatch cover on the rail.

Hips out of sea, Nico takes a tremendous breath. Then he porpoises.

Watching the lines in his hands, Arkie shouts, Now! Grunting, Costa and Zavitsanos drop the tarpaulin. Arrival perfectly timed, it splashes into the sea.

Ninety seconds later, the general alarm sounds. Those on deck smile. The bells are a signal from the engineers, The inrush of water has slowed to a trickle.

Now how long before they'll move? Costa asks.

Noon, Arkie answers.

That long!

Two and a half to three hours to make the fix, then six to eight hours for the cement to dry, Arkie explains.

Nodding, Costa walks away. Meanwhile, Zavitsanos helps Nico off the Jacob's ladder. The hero of the moment is kissed on the cheek.

Really that late? Zavitsanos asks.

They'll be lucky if they're ready then, Arkie says.

Then get set to do eighteen knots, he is warned.

What? That's top speed on a *new* T-2.

Zavitsanos shakes his head. He knows Israelis, he says. When they make a deal, it sticks. If it comes unstuck, someone dies. In the forties, when he first went to sea, he ran immigrants past British blockades. He nods to underline his sincerity.


0200 LOCAL TIME

Alexander, returning to the radio room, calls Mossad.

"Stopped M16," he sends.

"Switch," the Israeli operator taps back.

This sends them to a prearranged working frequency in the 16-kilocycle band. There they can talk more privately.

Mossad comes right to the point. "Why?" the Israeli operator asks.

"Condenser breakdown," Alexander answers.

"CU5 . . ." the Israeli signs off.

He returns, by the radio room clock, in forty seconds.

"When finished repairs?" he asks.

"Twelve hundred."

"Proceed. Friends meeting you," the reply comes back in Morse. "Advise soonest when under way again."

Alexander acknowledges and goes off the air.

Costa Lianides, standing behind his shoulder, reads the penciled message on his note pad and shakes his head. He recalls an afternoon in Jamaica.

Yes, Schotten and Howsam would be waiting for them in Port Said, the blond Englishman had said, and so would other friends. They would be there whether or not the Suez Canal was closed. So it wouldn't do to be unseemly and second-guess the deal, because the Israelis had fifty-knot motor torpedo boats with first-class radar, and they would find *Dynamic* and sink her. A destroyer might even be in attendance. No one needed another ten men running around the world with knowledge of what had gone on. Understand?

Besides, fair's fair, the Englishman had said. A deal's a deal. Otherwise, if people ad-libbed and improved upon commitments, who would know whom to trust?

None of which had impressed Costa. He had heard that little homily before.

All the while he spoke, however, on the sun-dappled balcony of the spacious white stone house in Jamaica, his host had fondled the meanest-looking knife Costa had ever seen. He called it his "swinging steel," if need for that arose in New York. Holding it in his right hand, he idly sliced hairs off the back of his left hand one at a time, with a smile of benign appreciation. Each success brought a delighted rise of eyebrow.

That had impressed Costa.

Now, reading the message, he strokes his left earlobe. Not finding his gold earring, he reaches into his pocket and inserts it. He needs its reassurance. Talisman in place, he strides to the chartroom to call Arkie.

When will they start the repair? he asks.

In about an hour, when the water's out of the bilge.

What can they do on deck?

Sleep, Arkie says. And send a man down. They'll need one more hand.

## 0300 LOCAL TIME

Arkie, still in jockey shorts, eases himself into the gap within the floorplates nearest the ship's side. His steaming shoes rest on the inside of the turn of the bilge four feet below floor level.

Orestes, five feet away, enters the trench nude, but for shoes. Between them lies the main circulating pump. On Arkie's side, the 24-inch, 3/16-inch-thick copper inlet pipe runs from the inlet to the pump. The section before Orestes joins the condenser to the pump.

A glance confirms that vibration caused the damage. The surface of the pipe is rent with longitudinal splits. They show the invisible joins in the metal as it was pressed into a sheet and then formed into seamless tubing. If corrosion were the culprit, it would reveal itself as jagged holes, where pitting had started, expanded, and eventually eaten its way through.

Orestes looks confused. Ioannis tugs at his bandana. Theodosius leans forward expectantly. None of them has ever seen the repair Arkie will do.

The first order of business, he says, resuming the engineering seminar he began in Ancona, is to bind the pipe with seizing wire.

He means spiral around? Orestes asks.

No, he means to wrap five or six turns on the pipe every four inches. That does two things: first, it clamps the splits; second, it makes a base for the steel cable Theodosius cut from the cargo discharge rigging.

The cable, similarly, serves two purposes: first, lying over the pipe fractures, it will act as a caulk; second, it will reinforce the cement which they will pour around the condenser pipe.

Ioannis is now ordered to snip the two hundred feet of steel cable into lengths matching the pipe run on either side of the circulating pump.

Theodosius will make wooden boxes from the gratings Ioannis removed earlier at the main switchboard. He must make two. One must butt-fit between the ship's side and the main circulating pump; the other, between the pump and the steel jacket of the condenser.

And, Arkie warns, Theo must not forget to get a brace and bit and bore holes in the bottom every six inches to fit Yorka's broomstick. Then he must cut it in six-inch lengths and put a piece in each opening.

What are they for? Ioannis asks.

Drains, Arkie answers. The patch will not be waterproof. If leaks had no place to go, their pressure would eventually burst the cement.

Arkie learned all this in college? Orestes asks.

No, from a chief who learned it from a Scotsman who saved a ship during World War II this way. He and that chief and two other guys, in turn, saved a tanker in the South China Sea doing this in 1961. What a night that was, Arkie recalls. They all got seasick rolling around in a typhoon. What they would have given for a flat calm like they have now.

Calm sea aside, the job has difficulties. Dead in the water, *Dynamic*'s ventilators pass no cool air below. The heat soon passes 120 degrees. Extractor fans slowed, fumes from fuel and lubricating oil also grow stronger.

Arkie and Orestes, standing in the bilge, have other problems. Balanced on the curving hull plates, they have all they can do to keep their footing. The bilge, after all, is where all the loose oil on a ship settles: oil from the cargo tanks; oil from every loose gasket in the engineroom; oil from the bunkers. Swishing around in rough seas, it films everything, and even when bilges are pumped that slippery coating remains.

So, wrapping wire, twisting, snipping, and crimping the jagged ends underneath each band, a slip or sudden shift to maintain balance generally means a nasty cut. By 0315, their hands are bathed in blood.

## 0345 JERUSALEM LOCAL TIME

The average age of Israeli combat pilots is twenty-three, and planners noted this. Wanting their boys to get at least *some* sleep the night before the war, they have set the first strike over Egypt for 0745.

So, at 0345, orderlies at Israel's air bases awaken the fliers. As they make their way across the fields in the cool night air, ground crews are finishing prepping their planes. Fuel and oxygen are aboard. Bombs, ten for each aircraft, lie below the wings, waiting to be armed and mounted.

A squadron leader, mug of tea in hand, stands before maps and photos at the head of each briefing room. The tactics are simple enough. They would make the most grizzled veterans blanch, but to the young boys who will fly the missions they are, as they were to their commanders the day before, strictly routine.

They will fly their 1,400-mph Mirage fighter-bombers at thirty feet of altitude to selected Egyptian airfields, where they will attempt to destroy an air force on the ground.

The extremely low-level approach, it is hoped, will slip them by Russian and American naval radar patrolling the Mediterranean. Takeoffs are timed to put them over Egyptian air bases between 0845 and 0900 Cairo time.

Mossad spooks, squadron leaders say, helped pick H-Hour. This is the time, they have learned, when senior Egyptian air force officers are on the way to their headquarters. On the fields, pilots and ground crews will be going from mess halls to training classes or duty assignments.

Dawn attacks are for movies, commanders say. With daylight, defenses slacken. They will do much better at breakfast. They have Mossad's word that the air force is the only thing in Egypt open for business promptly at nine o'clock in the morning. Getting the laugh, the briefings become serious.

## 0400 LOCAL TIME

Zavitsanos wrinkles his nose. What a filthy place, he observes.

He was the volunteer? Arkie asks.

Yes, but his mother never said it'd be like this, Zavitsanos complains. Then, looking around, he fixes on Orestes.

He tells him to get out of there and to go topside at once so Costa can sew up his finger. Good Christ, he can see the bone.

Glancing down, Orestes inspects his finger. It's not bleeding, he protests.

He said *now,* Zavitsanos reminds him. "And leave me your shoes," he adds.

Rib-deep in the bilge, Orestes shakes his head. "The sweat's running over their tops," he says.

"I know that, you oaf! You think I want to do that to mine?" Zavitsanos asks, extending a helping hand. "And when you die," he adds, "leave me your chest. I may want it for a scouring pad with all that hair on it, animal!"

Smiling, Orestes steps out of his shoes and trots up the ladder for some rough-and-ready stitching.

Is this clean? Zavitsanos asks Arkie, pointing to one of the silver-handled engine speed levers.

Arkie nods.

Shirt and shorts safely hung, Zavitsanos steps into the sweat-soaked shoes Orestes has left behind. Nude, he surveys the condenser pipe beneath the floorplates. At that point, the first set of seizing wire bands has been completed. Now the cables are to be laid over the splits and similarly wrapped.

With a last tight twist of mustache tips to firm them up against the heat, he drops down into the bilge and takes up pliers and seizing wire.

Is this all engineers do for a living? he asks Arkie.

Every family has a Sun God, a boy with grace. For the Angelakoses, he is Zavitsanos. He is half again faster than Orestes and clearly quicker than Arkie. Moreover, he completes binding the cables on his side of the pump and helps with the other side without getting a scratch.

At 0530, they are ready for the next step.

The three-sided troughs Theodosius has fashioned from the switchboard grating are fitted to either side of the main circulating pump and hammered into place against hull and steel condenser jacket. Copper tubing is hacksawed to length and shimmed beneath the bottom to support the forms.

Arkie emerges from the bilge to mix the cement.

Cement, of course, goes aboard every ship as a hull repair material of last resort. When welds crack, plates spring, or collision holes a side, the procedure is to cover the hull as Nico did the condenser inlets and to lay cement over the damage from the inside. More often than not, it will get a ship safely to a repair yard.

Arkie splits the first blue-and-white bag on the floorplates next to the eight-foot-long trench with a fire ax. Turning its head, he breaks the chunks into powder as Ioannis and Theodosius hump buckets of fresh water from the evaporators on the opposite side of the engineroom. Then, motioning to Zavitsanos to do the same, he starts sifting the cement and rubbing it between his palms as if he were a child in a sandpile. Satisfied at last that all the big lumps have been reduced, he forms the powder into a flat-topped pyramid with a depression in its center.

Then, reaching, he takes a bucket in one hand and pours its water into the hollow, folding the sides of the mound into it. Another bucket of water is added, and part of a third. Too dry, he tells Zavitsanos. The rest of the third bucket and a fourth go into the mixture. It becomes properly soupy.

Looking up, Arkie asks Theodosius to please put the bag of soda ash within reach. Calcium carbonate, it is used to maintain the purity of boiler water. Several handfuls are scattered and then mixed into the gruel.

Was he worried about the water? Ioannis asks.

No, the soda ash made the cement dry faster.

It did? How?

A chemical reaction.

*Chemical?*

Arkie explains.

Ah, *synergia,* Ioannis says, tapping his temple.

Orestes, still nude but for eight stitches and a bandage on his left index finger, regards the cement. He will go for two more bags, he says.

No, he will stay, Zavitsanos tells him with an eye for limits that ships' workhorses never have. His oaf of a brother, Ioannis, will get cement while he vacations on the bucket brigade with Theodosius.

And first take some salt tablets, Arkie adds.

Ioannis, a bit of a soldier, looks chagrined. And while going forward he should shout up to the bridge that he wants fifteen feet of antenna lead-in wire, Arkie orders.

"Very well, dear," Arkie goes on to Zavitsanos, scooping a bucket into the cement mix, "I'll serve and you pour."

Nodding, Zavitsanos lowers himself into the bilge between the condenser and the circulating pump. Pouring the first bucket, he splashes his groin.

It's all so depressing down here, he mutters as Arkie laughs at his grimace. Everything's so real . . .

## 0700 JERUSALEM LOCAL TIME

Forty Israeli Mirages are on their way to Egypt.

Forty more stand poised on runways. They are to form the second wave of the attack. A third and a fourth will follow. All will strike at ten-minute intervals.

Then the first wave, rearmed, will return to Egypt.

Now, in the Israeli Air Force command post near Tel Aviv, all is silent as Moshe Dayan and Mordechai Hod, the dark, mustached commander of the air force, wait. Only the sandy hiss in the communications equipment suggests that the channel to the planes is open.

Nervewracking, the quiet is also heartening. It implies that the aircraft have not been detected.

At 0705, tension noticeably mounts.

At 0710, there are audible sighs.

Dayan and Hod exchange glances. If the attack fails, they will be the goats. The coalition government has seen to that. Dayan will be blamed for starting a war. Hod will be damned for go-for-broke tactics. Twelve planes currently defend Israeli airspace.

Then, at 0714, a word comes over the radio: "Commencing."

A flight of four Mirages, in two pairs, a leader and a wingman in each, has reached its destination. Dayan and Hod lean forward in their chairs. Their aides glance imploringly at the wall speakers, as if willing them to talk. The plan, however, calls for seven and a half minutes more of silence. The fliers are allowed that much time for a bombing run and three strafing sweeps over the target.

The Israeli Air Force is remarkably close-knit. With 250 Mirages, there are perhaps a thousand pilots on duty. Men in the command post enlisted them, trained them, in many cases served with and grew up with them. Some are related by blood or marriage. So tension mounts as the minute hand creeps around the electric wall clock.

The first-wave pilots, however, maintain silence.

At 0724, though, the second wave arrives at targets. Its leaders have no need to observe silence. The Egyptians send up antiaircraft fire. Still, this attack is easier for the Israelis. They have no need to navigate at destinations. Smoke pillars provide unerring guidance.

The pilots report devastation.

Hod allows himself a brief relieved smile.

Dayan picks up a phone. He calls army headquarters. Almost immediately, an army operator taps out a message to field commanders in dry, metallic Morse. Decoded, it has the ring of a call to arms: "*Nahshonim,* action. Good luck."

Nahshon, leader of the tribe of Judah during the Exodus, is generally named as the first person to enter the parted waters of the Red Sea.

Israeli Brigadier Generals Sharon, Tal, and Yoffe, of Southern Command, in the Sinai, respond accordingly. Within moments, the soft morning desert air is rent with the staccato bark and cough of starting diesels. Leaves on trees hiding the armored columns—inspired by another leader in history—suddenly turn skyward in the exhaust.

The dash to the Suez Canal has begun.

## 0730 LOCAL TIME

Zavitsanos takes a last curving sweep of his palm over the top of the cement girdling the condenser pipe from the pump to the ship's side.

"Was this what you wanted?" he asks Arkie.

"Was it perfect?" Arkie asks back. The cement had to be of uniform thickness the run of the pipe. Otherwise, that antenna lead-in wire, wound into it as reinforcing, would quite likely crack it.

It was as good as he could get it, Zavitsanos says.

Nodding, Arkie extends an arm to help him up. The other engineers applaud Zavitsanos' appearance. He is now as filthy as they.

When will they be able to move? he asks.

Looking at the clock over the log desk, Arkie shrugs. With luck, one, one-thirty.

They would have domestic hot water by then?

Yeah, sure. But why?

Why, to shower, of course, and to make port like a proper licensed shipmaster, Zavitsanos the impeccable replies, gamely trying to coax the wilted tips of his mustache back into a horizontal plane.

## 0800 JERUSALEM LOCAL TIME

Kol Israel, the state radio service, has served up martial music, mostly from *The Bridge over the River Kwai*, since going on the air. Now Dayan announces that stiff fighting has begun in the Sinai. He concludes:

"Soldiers of the Israel Defense Forces, on this day our hopes and security are with you."

The call-up of reserves follows. As of this late date, only three quarters of Israel's 260,000-man army, four out of five of whose members are civilians, have been mobilized. Sergeants and lieutenants are already out knocking on doors and piling their men into jeeps to take them to marshaling points as the outfits' names are announced: Alternating Current; Close Shave; Love of Zion; Men at Work; Open Windows; and three presumably feminine units called Woman of Charm, Good Friends, and Fleshpots.

## 0934 JERUSALEM LOCAL TIME

What the Israelis call the second phase of the air attack begins. In fact it has been continuous, with pilots flying one-hour round trips.

The number of enemy aloft convinces Egyptians that Americans are flying missions, too. They assume that Israeli ground crews, like their own, require two hours to ready a plane. Mirages, however, are rearmed, fueled, and back in the war in seven and a half minutes. Turnaround time too was part of Hod and Weizmann's plan.

Another aspect of the strategy is more demoralizing. Weizmann has always seen his air force's role as that of preventing enemy planes from bombing Israeli cities, as the Arabs have repeatedly promised. With no desire to kill civilians, he has limited his planes to fighter-bombers, best for aerial combat and destroying military airfields, particularly runways.

Ordinary bombs, though, dropped in a long, shallow, supersonic dive, skip and do only superficial damage. Israeli scientists, however, come up with an answer. So the "smart" bomb is part of the plan, too.

This, designed to destroy runways and to discourage their repair, fires a retrorocket to slow its forward impetus as soon as it leaves the plane. Contact with the runway fires a booster rocket to drive it into the concrete. A time fuse then detonates it.

Imagine engineering crews watching Mirages streak back into the eastern sky and then having bombs that were dropped ten minutes before suddenly explode. Some go off as much as eighteen hours later.

So, with turnaround time, "smart" bombs, and some of the most accurate gunnery in the history of aerial combat, the Israeli Air Force has itself a morning. The Egyptians suffer *Al Nakba:* The Catastrophe.

By 11 A.M. they lose 304 of their 419 aircraft; ten to twelve of their fourteen military air bases are rendered inoperable; at least sixteen of their radar stations are destroyed.

Israeli losses are six pilots killed, two taken as prisoners, and three wounded. Nine planes are downed.

## 0250 EASTERN DAYLIGHT SAVING TIME

Walt Rostow, Lyndon Johnson's special assistant for national-security affairs, is awakened by a White House duty officer with word that a war is going on. He leaves his Georgetown home for the White House at once.

## 1150 JERUSALEM LOCAL TIME

Syria has received word of the attack from Egypt. Its MIG–17s leave Damascus to bomb Israeli resorts and settlements on the Sea of Galilee.

## 1200 JERUSALEM LOCAL TIME

The Jordanians, responding to Egypt's call for aid, bomb an Israeli satellite air base at Kefir Sirkin. They destroy a transport plane on the ground.

## 1215 JERUSALEM LOCAL TIME

Dayan, who has spent as much of the morning as he could in the air force command post, reports that Hod deals with the Syrian and Jordanian air strikes with a melancholy shake of the head and four words:

"Plan Syria! Plan Jordan!"

His duty officers, leaning forward in their chairs, speak crisply into their microphones. They divert eight flight formations on the way to Egypt.

By evening Syria loses almost 50 percent of its air force, 53 of 112 planes. Its bases at Damascus, Damir, Marjarial, Seikol, and T-4 fare as badly.

Hussein, placating the Arab left, pays more. Jordan's entire air force of 28 planes is destroyed, as are its airfields at Amman and Mafraq.

## 1230 LOCAL TIME

Costa rubs his earring and regards the condenser pipe.

It ain't ready yet? he asks.

Arkie shakes his head.

How does Arkie know?

By its color. Cement should be bluish white, like a new sidewalk.

It is now, and, besides, it's hard as a rock, Costa argues.

No, that's an ivory. There's yellow in it, and the outside would be hard. Concrete cures outside-in.

Well, then, when will it be ready?

A shrug. Another hour, maybe two.

Costa rubs his left earlobe harder. Can Arkie divide? he asks.

Arkie nods.

The numbers involved are formidable. Port Said is 244 miles to the southeast, and dawn there will come at 0458. If they leave now, they will have to steam at fifteen knots to arrive with the sun. If they leave in an hour, they will have to make good closer to sixteen knots.

The engineroom log indicates that *Dynamic* last made that speed for twenty hours on a leg from Manila to Seattle. Named the *Glorieta* then and with five years of abuse behind her, she dashed to what her master thought would be a boneyard or a wrecker's torch. A company now no longer in business ran her for the War Shipping Administration. The year was 1945.

## 0435 EASTERN DAYLIGHT SAVING TIME

Confirmation of the attack, probably from the U.S. Navy, since Israeli pilots no longer needed to observe radio silence, comes to Walt Rostow in the White House Situation Room. He has Lyndon Johnson awakened. At the moment, they know only that a war is in progress.

## 0555 EASTERN DAYLIGHT SAVING TIME

George Christian, White House press secretary, puts the first communiqué out to the press. He too knows only that there is "stiff fighting in the Sinai between Egyptian and Israeli infantry and armored forces."

## 0603 EASTERN DAYLIGHT SAVING TIME

Dawn came an hour before. It brings a slowly rising sun that seems to be lying on its side. Soft, voluptuous light, as gentle and warm as morning love, spills over eastern Long Island. Trees green in it. Moisture drawn from freshly tilled fields rises out of the soil like pink ostrich plumes.

Even the rust spots on the right front fender of the solitary faded-silver Ford Falcon lumbering west on Sound Avenue between Southold and Mattituck acquire a golden glow. The car's occupants ride in silence, listening to the scores of yesterday's major-league doubleheaders. On the move as early as local potato farmers, they do not look or dress like East Enders.

The driver wears a long-collared white-on-white short-sleeved shirt open at the neck with a Countess Mara silk tie and a diamond clasp. Tall and power-fully built, he has a high-domed skull fringed with black hair. His face has the boyish expression and unlined complexion seemingly reserved for jolly men who go bald young.

His passenger has all his hair. Once black, it is now gunmetal, and combed straight back, without part, accentuating a broad, flat face far too deeply tanned in early June to be local. Sun winks and glitters on the passenger's chrome-plated glasses as he listens to the scores, popping his upper plate back and forth like a retriever mouthing a bird.

Suddenly both men lean forward. The disc jockey has interrupted the sportscaster. The war is announced in a sentence. Details will follow, the disc jockey promises.

Grinning toothily, the passenger regards his watch.

Slow down, he says. It may be a long day.

## 1330 LOCAL TIME

It's white, just like Arkie said, Costa tells him.

Arkie nods.

Standing in the bilge, Theodosius swings the sledge. Four blows knock the form off the condenser pipe.

She's ready, Arkie says.

By then, Costa is on the boiler flat. Does Arkie think it'll last sixteen hours? he asks.

Arkie shrugs. At sixteen knots? Who knows?

It better, he hears. Zavitsanos says Jews don't count effort, only results.

## 0712 EASTERN DAYLIGHT SAVING TIME

The bedroom phone rings in the Sutton Place duplex. Stretching, Honey reaches for it. It's Taki, she thinks, to wish her a happy birthday.

Instead, he tells her about the war.

Always solicitous, he asks if she can please call "21" later and move their supper reservation back. He will be at the office all hours—at least until the guys in Europe collapse from lack of sleep or hear that—

The Suez Canal is closed? she asks.

Right. "But dis ain't nothin'," he tells her, laughing.

Now, he explains, everyone is going crazy diverting European- and North American–bound cargo south, around the Cape of Good Hope, so "s'ips ain't caught in dits," as he calls the Suez. Tomorrow or the next day, when they see what really happened, there'll be a scramble for tonnage like no one's ever dreamed of. He's already chartered in 290,000 tons for six months for him and Artemis, and he's looking for more.

Shaking her head, she sits up, pushing herself off the pillow with her elbow. Both feet on the carpeting, she drops her mouth closer to the phone. She has avidly followed the crisis since it surfaced. She and Fiona were in Paris then, visiting Artemis. She hopes he will take her lowered tone as a suggestion to slow down.

But Nasser said he wouldn't close the Canal unless the Jews got outside help, she reminds him.

He knows.

"Well, are we helping the Jews?"

Nobody said.

And what about the Canal now?

So far, still open, he answers. Zavvas, in Athens, heard of ships in the Mediterranean that left Port Said after going through in Sunday's night convoy. He got a Telex from Derek, in London, that morning transits in both directions look normal, too.

Then how can he be so sure the Canal will be closed?

"Honey, you don't believe Nasser, do you?" he asks.

She knows that scared, stupid tone. He uses it whenever he suspects he might be doing something without her full approval. But he goes on.

Nasser's crazy man, he says, citing what she considers hunch for fact. He's like Hitler. If world don't love him, he's gonna make it suffer—

He's gotta go. The Telex bell's ringing. But he wanted to wish her happy birthday and let her know he'd take her to supper, no matter what. Does she know what else he's been thinking since he got in and heard the news? he asks.

No.

"Demi's finally gettin' his break! He's gonna make fortsun wit' dem convertibles."

Poor little sucker, she thinks, shaking her head as she puts down the phone. Just like him, in all this, to think of Demi. And he would be just as wrong about him as he would be about Nasser, she knew.

She quickly concluded in Paris that if war came and closed the Canal, Demi could forget those convertibles. Who in his right mind would build those when straight tankers cost so much less? For sure, not little Loren.

Arkie would lose the rest of his fee then, too. She knew about that arrangement from the start from Taki. So, seeing Fiona spend dollar for dollar with Artemis, which took real doing, she kept her thoughts to herself.

Demi, she knew, discounted a closing of the Canal. It would never happen again, he said. When Nasser tried it in '56, he bankrupted Egypt. That history, in fact, became an argument for backing "smaller" in the family debate over the type of ship to build for the Keriosotis fleet. The Canal favored small vessels and cheap labor, Demi said. Greek seamen were cheap.

He said that, she recalls now—her memory jogged by Taki's news—despite facts showing that interest rates would go up faster than labor costs. In the long run, those numbers make "bigger" the obvious way to go.

Demi himself liked "bigger" in New York. Puzzled now, as she was in Athens, by his changed thinking, she feels still happy for him. As long as the Canal stays open, he'll just have to struggle along running Loren's convertibles and jockeying jet fuel at $150,000 to $200,000 a year. That will make him the poor relation, true, but she can think of a lot worse ways to go.

Still, as she rises, she feels increasingly confused. Demi's about-face seems even more curious to her.

## 0718 EASTERN DAYLIGHT SAVING TIME

The silver Falcon, meanwhile, proceeding west on the Long Island Expressway, turns off on the southbound ramp at Exit 34. Following New Hyde Park Road to the Jericho Turnpike, it then makes its way west to a small suburb just over the New York City line, Floral Park.

The town has two peculiarities.

Its houses are perhaps the smallest single-family dwellings in the United States. Some are twelve feet wide. Set on neatly clipped and trimmed postage-stamp lawns, the tiny bungalows also may well hold the highest ratio of handguns per capita in the country.

Floral Park is the bedroom for the patrolmen and detectives of the New York Police Department's Manhattan South and Midtown divisions.

Pulling up in a no-parking area at an intersection on the Jericho Turnpike, the Falcon is brought to a stop, and the tall balding driver with the jolly face steps around the front and opens the right-hand door. Waving to an orange-and-blue Nassau County police patrol car on the far side of the six-lane thoroughfare, he follows his passenger into the establishment on the corner: GI Giulio's Diner.

Inside, Giulio Infusini leaves his grill to greet the newcomers. Leaning over the counter, the Falcon's passenger silently shakes hands. Going to a rear booth, he acknowledges the welcome of patrons of the diner, all large, sturdily built men, as mutely. A nod or a tap on the shoulder visibly straightens the few so graced.

Giulio pours two coffees for the Falcon's driver. "Same?" he asks.

Smiling, the driver nods. "But for four."

A typical New York breakfast starts on the grill: eggs and onions with hashed browns and bacon; toasted onion rolls on the side.

That begun, Giulio leaves for the cash register.

Two other men have arrived.

The first, tall, sandy-haired, and lantern-jawed, wears a cheap, much rumpled gray plaid summer suit. His calves are silhouetted through the polyester by the light coming in the storefront window. He surveys the other men in the diner somewhat patronizingly.

Pointing to the cigarettes behind the cigar case, he asks for two packs of Kools and reaches inside his jacket for a small black leather case. Its right panel holds a plasticized ID card. He takes out a bill from behind it. The left side of his wallet, meanwhile, sprays the front of the diner with orange-and-yellow rays. On it is screwed the gold shield of a New York City Police Department detective officer.

His companion, in khaki chinos and red, white, and black sport shirt out at the waist, is dark with the wide shoulders, narrow waist, and thick thighs of a middleweight boxer. A snub-nosed .38 caliber Police Special bulges on the right side of his belt. In his left hand, a blue short-sleeved shirt with sergeant's stripes is just as obviously going home for washing.

The shirt's silver collar numerals put him in Manhattan's elite Seventeenth Police Precinct, whose area extends from Fifth Avenue and Forty-second Street to Fifth and Fifty-seventh and to the East River. This, the "Silk Stocking" stationhouse, guards the United Nations, the Waldorf-Astoria, Beekman and Sutton places, the diplomatic residences, and the touchy people in them.

Its headquarters are two blocks from Demi's house.

Making change, Giulio curtly nods to the rear. The officers suddenly abandon their police swagger.

"You brought it?" the gray-haired man asks, looking up, as they reach the last booth.

Nodding, the detective reaches inside his coat and produces the NYPD Patrolman's Handbook.

"What's it got on B and E?" the bald man asks.

"Breaking and entering?"

"Yeah. When does it say you can shoot?"

The detective reads a paragraph.

Nodding, the gray-haired man listens, gumming his upper plate and regarding the ceiling as the fluorescent lighting flashes off his chrome-plated eyeglass frames. Then he leans forward over the shiny black tabletop.

"Okay," he says, "here's what we gotta do. . . ."

Council is now in session. Presiding: Isaac (Itch) Rabinovitch Cohen.

## 1430 LOCAL TIME

*Dynamic* has now been under way an hour.

Grinning, Zavitsanos enters the wheelhouse. He has just worked out a sun sight. "What do you think?" he asks. "We're making seventeen!"

Costa smiles and shrugs. It's all in finding the right harmonic, he says knowingly. She did thirteen and a half with the prop making fifty-four turns a minute. So he increased speed nine turns at a time, and—

Balls, Zavitsanos says, smiling.

What happened was cousin Archimedes came aboard and did what Fotis and those three cretin sons of his should have done going to Ancona. He replaced and repacked all the valves. This may be the first time in twenty years *Dynamic*'s had the steam she was meant to have. A proper English ship would die of shame, too, with that neglect.

Still, Costa replies, looking for some credit, it's the harmonic that holds down the vibration. Flexing on the toes of his huaraches, he says it feels like they've got a full load going into small head seas. Nothing.

Zavitsanos grants him that. "It's much better than I thought," he says.

Those in the engineroom have their doubts.

The tremor, while slight, has not eluded the laws of physics. Moreover, the vibration shows itself in a way none of them has ever seen. About fifteen minutes after they got under way, it begins shaking paint loose.

The 65- to 70-foot-high airspace up to the forced-air fans is filled with sulfur-yellow dust. Microscopic particles float beneath the ladders.

At first, Arkie leads a frantic dash to shroud exposed machinery with dropcloths. Grit will eat through moving parts faster than acid. Then, following the lead of Ioannis, bandanas come out of hip pockets and go over heads. For breathing, cotton waste, rags for wiping and other cleanup chores, substitutes for Japanese cold masks.

Recognizing the fire hazard, Orestes and Theodosius begin sweeping full time. So Arkie and Ioannis must tend the plant with no relief.

At 1430 no one looks up. All see yellow powder rising on floorplates.

Heat, despite forward motion, rises to 126 degrees Fahrenheit.


## 0735 EASTERN DAYLIGHT SAVING TIME

The bedroom phone rings again.

Honey knows who that is, too. Putting down the hairbrush, she leaves the bathroom.

She has done a lot of thinking standing before the mirror. She leaves it sensing that this war may be more than it appears to be. She knows only that Arabs are as mad at one another as they are at Jews. Without knowing how or why, she has also begun to question Demi's change of heart.

She picks up the phone, masking her doubts.

"Hi, lover! What're we gonna do with all this money?"

He can't talk. There's someone in the next room. Would she see him later? Of course, it's her birthday, isn't it?

Same time and place?

Right.

Then she hears a click and the hum of an open line.

Cradling the phone, she sits on the edge of her bed. She looks into the top of her white summer nightgown. God, she thinks, does she have a case. Guilt aside, she knows she's being dumb, as well. Nothing can come of this.

Still, her nipples are so swollen they hurt. She knows from experience they'll be like that all morning. Just from his voice, she muses.

It's always been that way.

It proves there's a first for everything, even for her.

Bitch in heat, she thinks.

## 0757 EASTERN DAYLIGHT SAVING TIME

The phone rings in Lyndon Johnson's bedroom.

The message he hears is a first in American history.

The Moscow hot line is up.

Premier Kosygin, Johnson hears, has a message and will wait for him in the Kremlin. Johnson goes downstairs to the Situation Room.

By then, both men know that Israel has all but destroyed the Egyptian Air Force. Both also know what happens to armies unprotected against air power. So, however one reads history, a curious exchange follows.

The message, clicking over a Teletypeprinter a few minutes later, Johnson says, "expressed Soviet concern over the fighting. Kosygin said the Russians intended to work for a cease-fire and that they hoped we would exert influence on Israel."*

That from the man who armed Egypt, Iraq, and Syria, presumably allowed the lie about the Israeli invasion to be circulated, and said as recently as May 23, "Should anyone try to unleash aggression in the Near East, he would be met not only with the united strength of the Arab countries but also with strong opposition from the Soviet Union . . ."

Academics hold that Kosygin has two goals in mind with this somewhat premature surrender, less than seven hours after the fighting began.

His first goal, the world is told, is to cut losses. Skeptics ask: What losses? Equipment sent to Arabs was denied to Soviet forces the moment it went aboard ship.

Kosygin's second aim, history says, is to avert U.S. intervention. That over-

* Lyndon B. Johnson, *The Vantage Point: Perspectives of the Presidency, 1963–69* (New York: Holt, Rinehart and Winston, 1971).

looks America's role in Vietnam. With one unpopular war already upsetting the public, how likely would it be for the Administration or Congress to plunge the country into another military action? This argument also ignores Lyndon Johnson's behavior throughout the crisis. Not once has he publicly offered Israel aid in opening the Strait of Tiran, beyond jawbone or document.

Others who follow Middle Eastern affairs explain Kosygin's hasty surrender more simpy: that, as of 0800 Eastern Daylight Saving Time, he had what he wanted.

By then, the Israeli Air Force had guaranteed a Soviet presence in Egypt for years to come. His quick contact with Johnson, these observers say, is to let him know this and to assure him that Russia is now interested in stopping the shooting before a mistake can happen. He is even willing to be called the loser. Altogether, cheap insurance.

But naughty Kosygin receives no reprimand. Texan Lyndon Johnson knows better than to be a hard winner. He replies, instead, "that we would use all our influence to bring hostilities to an end and that we were pleased the Soviets planned to do the same."*

In the days that follow, Johnson is seemingly as deliberate and ineffectual as he was throughout the crisis. But five days later, at war's end, he has what he wants, too: a stable Middle East for years to come and, some say, with the Israelis occupying Sinai to the Suez Canal, the beginning of his "unsinkable" aircraft carrier in that part of the world.


## 1500 LOCAL TIME

Costa Lianides ponders a simpler question: Is the Suez still open?

He concludes, from the port bridgewing, that it is. The evidence lies just above the horizon. Through the binoculars, he sees a coil of smoke. A pelorus sighting shows it's moving northwest.

Zavitsanos, standing behind him, appeared on the bridge five minutes earlier to take another sun sight. Normally, lines of position are run up every hour, but he is concerned about the suddenly overcast sky. The *khamseen* wind starts blowing over the desert in March and continues for fifty days, into May. Then, after a few weeks of perfect weather, summer heat haze begins. Fearful that the *khamseen* has run its course, he takes a sight every half hour to confirm their speed while there's still sun.

Now, with his observation worked out, he squints beneath his gray felt hunter's hat with the leopard fur band and scans the horizon. More familiar with these waters than Costa, he interprets the smoke for him.

Too fast for a freighter or a tanker, he says, and too small for a passenger

---

* *Ibid.*

ship. A reefer bound for Italy or France with New Zealand lamb and mutton. They have that kind of speed. That's about the course, too, from Port Said—probably went through the Canal in last night's convoy.

Nodding, Costa considers *Dynamic.*

What'd she make in the last half hour? he asks.

Zavitsanos consults his sheet of scratch paper. Eight point six miles and change, he answers. Well over seventeen. They'll be there before dawn.

Costa, like Taki, is a hard man to convince about Nasser. "We'll be on our way to Eleusis Bay by then," he says.

Alexander, joining them, shakes his head. Looking worried, he hands Costa a message. At 1330 he radioed Mossad they were moving. "Compliments engineers," they sent back. At 1400 they said, "Proceed course fastest." Now they say, "Friends will meet you/look you dawn."

Which means, since an outbound ship from the Canal has just been spotted, there could be a naval battle in progress when they reach Port Said.

Costa shakes his head. Waste of fuel, he proclaims, and out of his pocket!

Zavitsanos, twisting his mustache tips, regards his cement-spotted legs and nods aft. His mind is on the engineers. Will they have hot shower water by then? he asks. He won't make port looking like rope ends.

And so much for the night's work from those two.

## 0801 EASTERN DAYLIGHT SAVING TIME

For Demi and Fiona, the day has just begun.

At the moment, they sit at the maple chopping block.

Smiling, he nods his head in satisfaction.

The reconciliation went more easily than he expected. He called Friday, knowing she would arrive Saturday, and left word. She returned the call Sunday, cool and aloof and after a suitable time lapse, but still early enough to have supper in town, he noted.

They had nothing to discuss now, she told him. Why had he called?

He wanted her with him when the war began, he said.

He thought war would break out Sunday night?

Oh, yes.

Why?

Because all those Israeli soldiers and their little Uzi automatic rifles that they'd seen at the beaches on TV would be back then with their units.

He really believed that?

He had to. He knew history and had looked at maps. The Israelis' only chance was to catch Nasser off guard. When could they do that better than Sunday night? He would send Sal with the car.

No, no! she answered testily, as if recalling what happened New Year's Eve when she found herself without transportation. She would drive in.

So he took her to White's, on Fifty-seventh Street, which had one of the city's loveliest outdoor dining patios and exceptional seafood, and made her listen to what a man named Wade had done to them.

Then he told her what he had done to Wade.

That made things better than they had ever been. Her smile lit up the shadows beneath the umbrella. She liked owning half of three convertibles or $25 million worth of new ships. Either, she said, made a nice start for what she had in mind for them.

She shouldn't expect too much, he told her. He was getting on. He would be thirty-two in a couple of months.

Later, sitting on a chocolate-brown velour couch in the dining room, watching TV, she said that one thing had surprised her about Artemis.

What was that? he asked.

The poor quality of her pot.

Smiling, he left for the pantry refrigerator. A shipment of red cigarettes had just arrived, he told her.

After two of the cigarettes, with brandy, *The Eleven O'Clock News,* saying there was no movement toward war in the Middle East, failed to impress them. They knew where *Dynamic Papachristou* was. They knew where the bankers, Howsam and Schotten, were.

By then, too, from their teasing each other on the couch, her hose and panties were off and her skirt was around her hips. He was exposed, as well.

Pouting, she told him to do something "nice."

There? he asked.

The blinds were down.

But who knew who might walk through the passageway?

Did that matter? she laughed. If anyone was there, they wouldn't see his face.

So he obliged.

That came from Artemis and Paris, he thought. A taste of the owner's life had done that to her. She no longer valued inhibitions. She felt safe now. Underneath, he reminded himself, all hunters are just scared little girls fleeing to the safety of money or status. No longer needing restraint, she would become wilder, he believed. In a little while he would be able to start teaching her new things. She would be eager to learn them, too, he knew.

But he had no illusions. Her willingness to expand her sexual vocabulary would have nothing to do with love or even sensuality. Something else would motivate her. Every "forbidden" act she enjoyed with him that she dared not do before would serve as a milepost. Each would show her how far she had come from her past.

He felt a surge of anticipation. In his mind, he felt her satinlike skin over his. But he cautioned himself again to slow down. It was only a matter of time, he knew. A marriage contract and community property insured it.

He would be the beneficiary of all her compensation.

Her response that night proved him correct.

Now, the next morning, listening to the portable radio Euralia keeps on top of the stainless-steel range, he is even surer of the future.

Egyptian air bases have suffered severe damage.

Israeli armor is moving west across the Sinai.

He knows that the Jews always feel safer with the desert mountain passes behind them. Egypt runs as clear and flat then as a billiard table to the Suez. They will occupy that too. Dayan did in '56, in less than a hundred hours, taking Sharm el-Sheik, the town on the Strait of Tiran, and the land lying just east of the Canal.

So one way or the other, Demi knows, the Canal will soon be closed.

The Israelis will do it.

Nasser will do it, out of frustration, as in '56.

Or *Dynamic Papachristou* will do it.

Whichever, he stands to make millions of dollars.

Rising as the newscast continues with on-the-spot reactions from world capitals, he goes into the kitchen pantry for the Pol Roger in the "emergency stores" and for glasses. He deserves no less, he believes. His estimate of the war has been far more correct than the rest of the world's. Her look tells him she appreciates that.

So, uncorking the champagne with a thunderous pop as the newscast runs down the baseball scores, he pours as she holds the glasses. Then they toast each other at the maple chopping block as her hand creeps inside his white terrycloth U.S. Lines steamroom robe.

Soon hers is open, too. Then, silently, she mounts him on the high stool. Guiding her buttocks around him, he understands.

For them, the news is the headiest promise of all. Which aphrodisiac can match its rewards? This is a moment to share, to revel in without the movement that would bring an orgasm and foreclose on the pleasure of fulfillment. Now there is a future they can safely savor, instead of yearn for, as well.

Thus arranged, and accompanied by Pol Roger, they plan their day.

He will call Wade to see whether he will be a half owner of convertibles or a full owner of ships. But he knows that Wade will be too busy to piddle around with a $25-million deal, so he will leave word to call back at the house that afternoon. Then he will go down to Taki's to mooch the overseas phone and to see what's coming in on the Telex. He'll also make reservations on Pam Am to London for tomorrow night and the two following so that he'll be in Europe as soon as Wade tells him which way to go.

She opens the top of his robe, moves closer. Lunch? she asks.

He shakes his head. Can't, he says. Too much to do. But what about her? he asks, shifting her slightly. What has she decided about her little idea?

Her thought came to her on Antigua. Her mother, there with her, no doubt unwittingly inspired it. She, after all, used to ask, "What's better than one penny?" The idea was as simple as that.

If Wade and Garrison went to such lengths to learn what had been going on, the secret obviously had great value before or after the fact. World opinion aside, how much would it be worth to keep Arkie from knowing what partners and relatives let go on behind his back?

Conscience money, Demi called it the night before. She agreed.

But Lianides Bulk Transport, as the company would be called, would earn $1 billion to $2 billion in profit, she pointed out. What was 1 percent or 2 percent of that? Hardly worth mentioning.

She could be a silent partner, he observed, with her share going to a blind trust somewhere.

Exactly, the way shipowners hid assets. And she wouldn't be at all threatening. Big oil had a history of violent, unexplained death. It went back to the twenties, when the British got their foothold in the Middle East. More recently, it included Premier Mossadegh in Iran in '53. Did he really commit suicide? Many people believed the CIA killed him. Then there was Enrico Mattei, the head of the Italian government-owned energy company. In 1962 he died in an unexplained plane crash. Prior to that he had been negotiating to import Soviet oil, which would have broken the majors' price control in key European markets.

No, she told Demi, she wouldn't even mention reprisal. The past spoke for itself. She would talk in terms of embarrassment. Bankers knew what happened to people who got in the way of big oil. What would she do? She would sleep on it.

Now, gathering more of him in, she answers. She's getting on, too, she says. She'll be thirty soon. So she thinks she'll make a call. Arkie has mentioned a Dr. Fabian.

## 0957 EASTERN DAYLIGHT SAVING TIME

Dr. Fabian does not rise as Fiona leaves.

Instead, she ponders her sudden insight.

Surprisingly, it is not at all cerebral. It seems, in fact, less a thought than a sensation. Nevertheless, she acts on it.

Speaking into the intercom, she tells her secretary to place a call. That done, she settles back in her maroon armchair, absently puffing on yet another Gauloise.

Then, unaccountably, she begins feeling heady. The transition puzzles her. But, ever the analyst, she thinks of several possible reasons for it. The most likely, however, she dismisses at once: She does not feel afraid.

How, then, does she find a subtle cause?

A trick of theoretical mathematics occurs to her.

She reverses her reasoning. She substitutes exultation for fear.

Doing so, she promptly writes off semantics. Feeling neither thrilled nor gratified, she knows subtlety has nothing to do with her headiness.

That puts her deeper in the hole. What she wants to name, she sees, probably has no handy label to help cue behavior. Yet it changes her mood. In a high-stress situation, that takes doing.

It also raises another question: Can such a force be nameless?

She has no idea. In about sixty seconds she will have a terrifying answer. But then, as the headiness gains definition, she quits thinking and gives her attention to what she feels.

A mild electrical charge seems to be passing over her eyes and forehead. The sensation, she guesses, comes from blood rushing to her brain or nerve ends. She does not know to which. Nor, for once, does she care. She likes the feeling. It tingles. No plateaus or valleys diminish its effect.

Pleasure ceases abruptly as a plastic phone button lights. With a last, mechanical puff on the Gauloise, she picks up the receiver, intent on masking her loathing.

"Evelyn?"

"Yes, darling. Yes . . ."

Cordial as always, he seems unsurprised. Hearing him, in fact, she thinks of freshly fallen snow. His deep, rich baritone wafts into her ear that coolly. But she hears a tremor pulse beneath its hearty surface.

Nerves? Not that one, she thinks. He's fearless. His voice holds something else, not quite under control. Dread? Hardly.

Reflexively, she again reverses her reasoning.

The opposite of dread: anticipation.

That puts him in focus, all right. She knows then he stands rigidly at a sixteenth-floor window in his suite at the Plaza. Phone at ear, he will be gazing at Central Park, Cupid's-bow lips curled entreatingly, like a gluttonous baby begging for another spoonful. He smiles that way whenever he thinks of Wingate and the Special Night Squads.

Sinking lower in the armchair, she tucks her chin against her breastbone, as if hiding, ashamed. But now she feels nothing. Her hollow, dry-mouthed whisper seems to come from someone else. "There are two people you have to meet."

"Oh?"

"Yes!" she hisses.

His voice steadies at once. But the reply comes slowly, as if rushing somehow diminishes the prospect. "I'd adore to, Ilona—adore to. I'm at your pleasure, darling. Just tell me when."

"Tonight."

"Poor lovers."

His sigh, so patently false, suggests a greedy undertaker showing his $6,000 top-of-the-line bronze casket.

Still, she thinks, he really is diabolically bright. How he knows which two eludes her. She could have meant the cowboys, Wade and Garrison.

Had she been in Nassau in January, she would know. He saw blackmail then and asked Schotten how he thought she would react if the burden of exposing the threat fell on her, as had now happened. Both were correct in judging she would do what she had just done.

Evelyn, meanwhile, answers her unspoken question. "In point of fact," he goes on sorrowfully, "the winemaker's partner and I guessed they'd be naughty from the start. They're both really only spoilt, wicked children, you know. So we did a little recce of our own, without mentioning—"

"And in Greenwich and Ridgefield too?" she asks venomously, offended at his obviously bogus regret.

"Oh, yes. Yes, indeed. Those places too."

Placating her, he adopts the cheerful, simplistic tone of a nuclear physicist visting a ninth-grade general-science class. "Remember, Ilona," he cautions, "we deal in eternal verities. One can't be slack about those. Oh, no! As you mathematicians say—" he chuckles ingratiatingly, a virtuoso explaining the arcane foibles of his art—"we've a 'zero error model.' So everything's already laid on—right down to our hidey-hole. My chum's on the scene, too, standing by. I've just to ring him up—and I'll do that straightaway—to get things moving. Now, what time was it, darling, you had in mind for me to stroll down Forty-ninth Street?"

"They're expecting you at eight-thirty."

"Good girl—ver-ry good indeed!" he tells her. "The sun's lowering then. Eight-thirty it is. And just right, too! After we tidy up, we'll nip on over to '21' for supper. It's still early June—may not be too late for shad roe at all. But if it is, we'll just make do with soft-shelled crabs . . . "

He plans the rest of the menu alone. She hangs up.

There, she thinks. She's done it. She's killed them. He will swing his steel, but only as an officer of the court. *She* pronounced the sentence.

So, fixing responsibility for the summary executions of Fiona Angelakos and Demosthenes Keriosotis, she notes another change. It comes as she sits with her hand on the phone, her part in two cold-blooded murders irreversible and unredeemable. She expects to feel regret or remorse; at the least, shame.

Instead, her headiness returns.

## 0958 EASTERN DAYLIGHT SAVING TIME

Wade reaches Hubie's office on the run.

Talk about sailor's Halloween, he thinks.

He got to his desk at seven-thirty-five to find a roll of Telex messages 141 feet long awaiting him. The stack of radiograms measured two inches. Added to those, the night switchboard operator reported ninety-four calls.

Shipping is distinguished for its sharp-eyed men, so many of the Telexes are from brokers, oil companies, and owners. They all ask about his four 60,000-tonners, which came off charter the month before. Two now lie in the Persian Gulf load-ready. The other two, still in the repair yard, await food and linens being put aboard.

Yesterday the going price for delivering crude to a Western European port from the PG in one of those ships was $7.75 a ton. So far today, his best offer is $11.78. And that's just "insurance," he believes. That's somebody thinking the unthinkable: What happens if the Canal closes?

He will ignore those bids.

He knows that the "unthinkable," one way or the other, will happen. In a day or two, he tells himself, the boys'll wake up and find that the distance from the PG to Western Europe has increased from 6,270 miles to 10,710 miles. Events, of course, will prove him correct. He will charter his four 60,-000-tonners on June 8. The three-day wait will earn him $2 million. By then, the rate will jump to $20.46 a ton.

The radiograms are from his masters, who, according to his policy in any emergency, report their position, amount of fuel and food aboard, and anything else he needs to know to intelligently divert ships.

Most of the telephone calls are also charter inquiries. They will be ignored, too. The others are from wives of men on ships bound to or from Suez. He will answer those in person, if it takes all night, and give each concerned woman her nickel's worth. They're entitled, he feels, and, besides, he knows from his own days as a seaman that he got fried eggs every Sunday whether or not Acey could afford them for himself. Loyalty cuts both ways.

Shirley Carmichael is a case in point. Hearing the war news on her clock-radio, she skips makeup and breakfast, arriving at the office at seven-forty. By the time the call from Hubie comes, they have answered all the radiograms, replied to the Telexes that need answering, and sorted the phone messages.

Now, opening the high rosewood door, Wade sees the "elephant killer," the belladonna, in Hubie's hand.

Christ, he thinks, Hubie's head belongs up on the wall behind the desk with the other sheep. It looks as dead. Nature has given the desert bighorn a drab, gray-brown coat to match the sand and hills of the U.S. Southwest and Mexico. Hubie's face is that color. Wade wonders what's wrong.

At the Dorset, hearing news of the war, instead of expressing joy or relief he seemed preoccupied. He had none of the questions a boss would ask a subordinate who had just committed $350 million of the company's money without supervision. He seemed to Wade, in fact, to be sad. Yet, physically, he said, he had never felt better.

Striding past the long row of windows overlooking the Hudson, Wade sees that that no longer holds. Hubie's face is shiny with sweat. The Custom Shop white shirt is gray with it. The blue forehead vein is pulsing under forced draft, and is a bright magenta in the bargain.

Tapping the belladonna into the water glass before him, Hubie raises his left hand to Wade for silence. Then, as the water assumes the shade of strong iced tea, he sighs and drinks it down.

He just got off the phone with the diplomatist—

A convulsive belch, sounding like a bark, sends him sprawling forward over the oval Irish bogwood desk. His saliva, bitter with belladonna, sprays Wade. Wincing, Hubie grabs his stomach and, doubled over, crabs sideways to the small bathroom behind the right side of his desk.

A moment later he calls, "Loren!"

Wade comes on the run, thoroughly alarmed. That was a shriek.

Hubie looks up at him from the toilet seat. Both of his palms press in against his abdomen. All of his tan has yellowed. Sweat beads the size of kitchen matchheads have popped out along his upper lip. He seems walleyed as well. Only the undersides of his irises show.

Jesus, Wade wonders, what's happened?

He reaches down to take Hubie's head in his hands.

Hubie nuzzles his cheek against his belly.

"Loren . . . " he begins.

Wade shakes his head, trying to figure out what the fix would be for this if it happened at sea. Christ, he thinks, it's worse than he imagined. Hubie sounds and feels like a little boy whimpering "Mama . . . ?" while the doctor stands by to start the stitching.

"Somethin' bust, Loren. It's all red down there." In modesty, or fear, Hubie presses his hands harder against his abdomen, as if to hide his shame.

But Loren Wade is hardly the man to be put off by a foul toilet bowl. He has slid his pals, boys he grew up with, over lifeboat gunwales into the sea. He has torn the dead, cooked flesh from others with his fingers to put sulfanilamide powder where it works best. He has seen his share of dangling ears and eyeballs and white, splintered bone ends rising through skin in compound fractures and not cringed, either.

So, reaching down, he pulls up Hubie's shirttails and looks down between his legs. Jesus, is it red! It's flaming.

Like all who go to sea with fifty or so frail bodies in their care and no doctor aboard, Loren Wade had seen a lot of blood as well. He has, in fact, become a pretty fair diagnostician of it. Ulcers bleed pink; abscesses, brown; cysts, black. What he's looking at now, he knows, is arterial blood. The cure, of course, is to sew Hubie up and start the transfusions.

So time is the key factor.

Hubie, meanwhile, knowing he is dying, returns to his conversation with the diplomatist. Gasping in pain, he explains why the Arabs' money has been slow in coming.

"He said the long swords back home, includin' his father, insisted on knowin' where you got all this, an' that I had to tell him. Otherwise, there was no deal. Well, goddammit, I can't do that! You know what they mean. Killin's a mortal sin!"

"Then fuck 'em! We may not need 'em, anyway. The charter rate's already up damned near fifty percent in the first fifty hours, an' accordin' to the news them Jews are on the way to Suez like shit through a tin horn. I figure we'll do near a billion in profit alone off ships in the next twelve months, an' after that it'll all be downhill to the North Slope. This ain't like in '56, when Nasser closed the canal. Now that sonofabatch'll have to deal his way back into openin' it—"

Scanning the gray bathroom tiles for something to work with, frantically trying to think of how to get him to a hospital, Wade feels Hubie shake his head. "We can't do it alone, Loren."

"We can't?"

"No."

"Why not?"

Hubie shudders. "Because the long swords say they'll expropriate our oil unless I go along—"

"Leave me worry 'bout that," Wade answers calmly. He pats Hubie's head consolingly. But he shouts within himself, *Allah maana!* Allah is with us!

He has found his out for Demi's loan guarantee.

It may not be worth murder to Hubie, but it is to him. He'll gladly carry Demi and that slut, Mrs. A, on his back to the grave. He's seen better than those two take the Big Swing every day of the week.

That solved, he also sees what do do next. With luck, there's a chance.

Hubie now, briefing over, ponders the same question. "You think I'm gonna make this?" he asks.

" 'Course you are, lover!" Wade laughs "All you got is some kind of lesion on your colon," he lies. "What we're gonna do is take a shower towel an' twist it into a nice little Kotex an' then take another one an' diaper you with it an' hold it up with your belt. Then you an' me are goin' to a hospital where they can make a fix on that an' get some blood back in you. Nothin' to it. I'm only worried 'bout spottin' your suit."

*Lover?*

That's what he just called Hubie, he thinks.

Jesus, is he queer?

No, he decides. He knows his preferences.

But, while he goes home to Willa Mae every night, she and the kids and the house are only incidents on the way to *his* life. That existence he shares with

Hubie. It is Hubie, and maybe Urs, he loves, he realizes. What would he have without them and the ships?

Then, leaning over, he reaches into the gray-tiled niche at Hubie's right side and dials his number on the intercom. He tells Shirley Carmichael to take his coat and to meet them at the Fiftieth Street entrance with a cab. He feels Hubie nod against his belly.

"Roosevelt Hospital's right up the road," Hubie says.

They're goin' to New York Hospital, Wade tells him. All of his records are there. His croaker may even be around doin' an operation or waitin' to do one. Either way, the hospital'll be able to reach him quicker so that he can tell the other guys what tracks to follow.

Twisting the towel and getting Hubie to pull his shirttails out of the way, he wonders about the Lions. Do the long swords want them too?

Hubie shakes his head.

Then, pulling himself up against Wade's shoulders, he explains that the Lions are as safe as they. They, like the Arabs, have too much face to lose ever to brag. Besides, the diplomatist thinks they're being run from Montreal by a man who is called *Al Nakba* in the Middle East.

The Catastrophe?

Oh, yes. Far better to keep that one docile than ruffle a single hair on a Lion, the diplomatist says.


## 0958 EASTERN DAYLIGHT SAVING TIME

Seconds have passed since she spoke with Evelyn.

Dr. Fabian feels increasingly uneasy.

Alarmed, all the crafty defenses of a brilliant, neurotic mind spring into action. They tell her what she wants to hear. Headiness, they theorize, can stem from purely physical causes. In this case, nerves.

A pat answer, that should suffice.

But self-deception is a nonunion vice. It never quits. It works, scheming, all three shifts to stay ahead of fact. So now it decrees proving the theory.

That she knows nothing of physiology hardly matters. Neither will her tests. They need only be sufficiently convincing to fool the rational part of her mind. She will then still be Ilona the Objective Analyst. She needs that role. It helps her believe that the books are closed on the past.

Her subconscious, appreciating that need even better than she, creates a perfect ruse. Promptly loading the dice, it tells her to look for signs of shock or relief. She does and finds none.

She inhales easily, without shortness of breath. Her palms are warm, dry. She presses her fingertips to her temples: her pulse seems slower, but perfectly regular.

Certain that her face will convey reaction, she studies her image in the glass desktop. A serene mask gazes back. She finds no lines in the high, arching forehead. Her mouth too, she sees, relaxes in a somewhat bemused smile.

Those contradictions, however, fail to register. For her, reality lies in the scenario being devised by her subconscious. Reacting to its demands, she sinks back in the maroon leather armchair as if exhausted.

Then she reaches for a Gauloise.

That too has been programmed. The cigarette lends credence to the nervous-reaction theory. It also fixes her memory. All her days, she will remember how desperately she needed that smoke to calm herself.

Taking more stage direction, she tips her head and strikes a match. Another second has passed since she put down the phone. But now her intellect ponders the headiness, too. With murder, not even defense mechanisms can suspend thought.

Thus poised, flame alight, Gauloise dangling from lips, Ilona Fabian, Jewess, thirty-two, unwillingly aborts her flight into fiction. The fact prompting her change of destination can be neither argued nor denied.

Her headiness grows increasingly pleasurable.

Contrary to all expectations, the longer she thinks about killing Demi and Fiona, the better she feels. Admitting that, she rouses a tiger.

An impulse, actually, it has lurked hidden, unseen and unsuspected, in self-deceits all her life. Anonymous to her, it nonetheless has a familiar name: truth.

Put another way: the urge to know one's self.

A wary hunter, it now pads along softly behind her subconscious. It knows that trying to outrun so fleet a quarry will be futile. Strategy here, instead, calls for stealth, then cornering the victim. So the chase begins as if she is still playing safe academic games:

Why now, she wonders, now that she has eliminated fear and exultation, relief and shock, understandable and perhaps justifiable reactions, does murder still please her so?

Her subconscious, still on the job, tries again to cloud the issue. The subtle delight flicking at her like a lover's tongue, it suggests, is a new thrill: the sense of evil.

Murder being the ultimate sin, she nearly believes that. God knows, she wants to. It would stop thought. But the tiger now stands between her and counterfeit emotion. She feels no guilt and knows it.

That means dropping bogus contrition and penance as well. Thus depriving her of cosmetics to make self more presentable to conscience, the hunter moves closer: What, then, does she really feel? it asks.

She balks at answering. She senses how easily reality can erase her image of Ilona the Objective Analyst. Who will she be then? Will she like that person? Will she respect her?

Truth, she finds, doesn't care. It wants answers. Spurning her identity problem, it asks the key question: Would she order the killings again?

*Yes!*

The answer explodes through her consciousness.

Its ardor appalls her.

Dread arrives at the same time. It comes realizing that the tiger is on the run. With her intellect in charge, she knows there will be more questions.

Finally, with typical academic detachment, she sees her reply as instructive. Until then, she thought she loathed violence. Her life has been ravaged by it. Now she finds that for her, at least, murder has its place.

Shocked and frightened at her feeling, she becomes consciously aware of being threatened. Still, she manages to keep her head. Intent on salvaging what she can of her self-image, she has to keep up appearances. So she resumes as pedantically as before.

If guilt has no place in the inquiry, what does? Innocence? Certainly not. The two are as unlike as apples and oranges. She cut her teeth in semantics learning that difference.

Then she considers happiness and unhappiness. The opposite of happiness is not unhappiness. It is merely not being happy. Unhappiness is another state.

That idea, so basic, intrigues her mightily. It gives her an out. It implies why it's so difficult to name the cause of her headiness. All along, she has assumed that an emotion has triggered it. But suppose it wasn't? What if her reaction came from an absence of guilt?

Truth, canny old tiger, has set a perfect ambush. It doesn't even have to run. It needs only a lazy swipe of paw. The idea dies as quickly as words form it.

Then the tiger, teeth around neck, drags its prey into the thicket to finish it off. It will be an easy matter. Only one defense mechanism remains. A question or two will dispose of that.

Sensing what's coming, she sinks lower in her chair.

But truth is an efficient killer. It needs no bellow, no ferocious gesture. Instead, it speaks conversationally. It sounds, in fact, amazingly like her own voice.

How can one feel an absence? it asks.

Since she would kill them again, she obviously has no guilt, no sense of wrong. So, if something isn't there, how can it be felt?

Moreover, how can what does not exist induce a very real sensation—for her a tingling over her scalp, less intense, to be sure, but as pleasurable as an orgasm? That has to spring from something.

So, if not from guilt or innocence, from what, then?

She shrinks deeper into the maroon leather armchair.

The words have yet to form. But the gist of the idea is already clear. She cringes from it, as well she might. Her self lies on the other side of it. Then the confrontation she fears most will occur. She will face the home truth of her life.

Meanwhile, she sees, there is devastation enough.

As the realization of where this is heading grows, she can feel her value system slip away. Her attitudes, which Howsam calls "knee-jerk liberal," no longer seem so correct, or so righteous.

Reexamined, in fact, they do not hold up.

She took years to form her beliefs. The trauma of murder demolishes them instantly. Only painful admissions are left.

Howsam is right: life is pitching, not catching.

Schotten is right: one looks in one's mirror.

That little monster at the Plaza is right: killing is good for lots of chaps.

By then, she knows what accounts for the pleasurable tingling coursing across her scalp: the sense that justice will be done.

That realization puts her further off balance. Can it be? What has so noble an idea to do with all this? This position concerns money. Just as quickly, she changes that opinion. She again considers the men involved.

Then she sees that this too is about justice.

Howsam, his wife, Francine, tells her, is so greedy that on Saturdays he likes to go to supermarkets to see all the food he can buy. His stinginess and temper are also legendary in the family. He has gone through life, Francine says, believing that the rest of the world thinks he married for money. The truth is, Ike told her before he died, Howsam made coming to America pay for the Battelzweigs. Prentiss was twice the banker he had ever been, bolder and far less intimidated by an Establishment and government wanting him out of business. Her father, Francine says, had been happy to survive. Prentiss has other ideas. Wealth has never fascinated him. His youth prevents him from enjoying it. For him, money is a weapon. When he gets enough, he will confront his enemies, and those battles will not be fought to survive, or to prolong the agony, but for him to win. Such men are to be coveted, Francine tells her. Who risks these days? Who fights?

And tonight he may die, Dr. Fabian thinks. For what? For *his* justice.

And Schotten will be with him.

His reasons for being there are far more abstract, but to him they are as real as Howsam's. He wants to "prolong the twilight of capitalism."

That, he says, gives the West a chance to survive. With enough time, a new leader is sure to emerge from the pygmies. An Israel, meanwhile, is a necessary part of that equation, moral considerations aside.

Why? Because Arabs are stupid.

They talk of crippling the West with oil embargoes. They threaten using oil as a weapon to destroy Jews and to regain a homeland for Palestinians. In the meantime, they speak grandiosely and let their brothers in Islam starve in UN refugee camps.

Like children, they want instant gratification and something for nothing. Only a few see they are fated to crawl back to the West long before their wells run dry.

When? When Arab masses rise against their rulers.

Democracy aside, Schotten points out, Israel has the only lawfully constituted and functioning government in the area. All the others are either warriors' fiefs or hand-me-down puppet regimes installed by the British.

But another event, he says, may rule out civil wars. It could come before then. When will that be? When the Russians judge conditions right. In the eighties, they too will thirst for oil.

Where will Arab leaders turn then? They will scream for aid to the West, of course.

In a conventional war, because, after all, no one wants nuclear-contaminated oil, who will provide Arabs with their first line of defense?

Israel, Schotten believes. Israelis can fight.

Unlike Mediterranean Arabs, they have also made no pretense of their distrust of Russia. David Ben-Gurion sent them packing in the fifties when Israel most needed aid. Jews know all about isms, Schotten says.

But Arabs have no monopoly on stupidity, he goes on. There would be no war if the West had leaders. They would bring the Arabs to heel now.

Money would. It acts. It rectifies situations before they worsen. So money needs more money. Then it can slow the panic until men of political vision arrive. Now the leaders of the West govern with an eye on how history views them, on winning reelection, on being loved. Ego rules those, not ethics or rationality.

You watch, he warns, what happens if America elects a weak President and the Arabs put pressure on him with oil. He'll suddenly shift policy about that "Proud and Noble People," the Palestinian Arabs, at Israel's expense. The fact is, he goes on, the Jews have a better claim to that country. They, at least, won it once.

No one, on the other hand, has ever bothered to kick out the Palestinian Arabs. Palestine has never been a nation. The Turks held it for nearly five hundred years before World War I. The Mamelukes, from Egypt, ruled it for nine hundred before that.

So, for Schotten, this war is a murderous charade. "There's no morality in any of this, only oil and politics and flags against money," he assures her. When the ineptitude of flags threatens to destroy the world, those who own it must act in self-defense. The issue is central to the age: who rules, flags or money?

For him, there is no question involved.

So tonight he too may die. For what? For *his* justice.

Which brings her to Evelyn.

Surprisingly, she begins to understand him. For her, he is the saddest of the three. Old Testament Christians like him, along with Jews, live for the Millennium, that great come-together day when all men will love each other as brothers.

He cheerily admits he will never see it. Who, with self rampant, loves even his brother?

Still, he tells her, the Day will come. And when it does, "the tribe," the children of Israel, will lead the way. So they're worth putting oneself out a bit for, aren't they?

Poor tubby little fool, she thinks, using his own words, how desolate he must have been in the Mandate—naive, terrified, and stripped of self-respect by Arab, Jew, and Englishman alike, scorned for his view of what the world might be. Who could trace the devious lines of thought that led him to identify as he did and to exercise what he euphemistically calls his "propensity"? For swinging steel, that is.

How desolate he must be now, she thinks, forever fighting someone else's battles to win a triumph he will neither see nor enjoy. Careful, she warns herself even then. Don't get melodramatic. He loves what he does.

Still, tonight he too may die. For what? For *his* justice.

In that context, she thinks of the cowboys.

At some point, she knows, Wade and Garrison learned they were in danger. Did that stop them? Not at all.

The world, as viewed from oil company boardrooms, Whitehall, the State Department, and Versailles, was too fine and clubby a place for Texas wildcatters. So there was no room for a Wilmer Garrison or a Loren Wade. Now it looks as though there is.

They too put their lives at risk.

For what? For the right to exist. For *their* justice.

That brings, for her, a stunning insight. She sees there are no villains in any of this. Perhaps, she thinks, they may all be heroes.

Still, the rest of the world is right to fear them.

These are men who understand the nature and price of justice. They know her for what she is: an energetic and tireless whore who takes on all comers and charges what the traffic will bear. She is not a right, as the politicians say, but the greatest of all privileges.

So those who understand her, and she is routinely all things to all men, depending on their needs, have no qualms about upsetting the natural order of things, or trade balances, or estate and retirement plans.

With nothing at risk, how can "little people" expect anything but to be buffeted about, forever at the mercy of others? They have only the law to protect them, and, as Goldsmith says, "Laws grind the poor, and rich men rule the law."

Laws, like foreign policies, also change at the whim and convenience of those in power. So what right, she wonders, do the meek have to expect anything but crumbs? If they think life is a benign experience, they do so at their own peril. They exist at the sufferance of others. They think their taxes buy *their* justice. In fact taxes only rent it—subject to new statutes.

Does that make the world seem like a jungle?

Surprisingly, the ray of hope comes from the one she considers the most disillusioned: Schotten. To console her, he quotes Keynes, the English economist: " 'Beware! . . . For at least another hundred years we must pretend . . . that fair is foul and foul is fair; for foul is useful and fair is not.' " Then, perhaps, he adds, man will have more sense.

A bleak prospect? Keynes is more optimistic than Sophocles, who says, "The highest form of development is withdrawal."

In effect, Sophocles shuns society. He too must believe that crowds get only scraps of justice.

Hunt it, as the tiger does a meal, alone and stealthily, he advises. Ignore your fellow creatures and their needs. Stalk your prey instead. Be sure of its strength. Then pounce on it and kill it, and your quarry's power will then be yours, and you will have that much more justice.

David Ben-Gurion, who understands justice, uses coarser words. But, two thousand years later, the thought comes straight from Sophocles: "What counts is not what *goyim* say, but what Jews do."

That works for everyone, she suddenly thinks. Substitute "others" for *goyim;* "you" for Jews.

She sees then what her life has been. The Fundador, the men, the degradation, the tears, have paid for her survivor's guilt, she has told herself. Now she knows that is a lie. Her parents are dead. Her sister, Magda, is dead. The Israeli flier, Seth, is dead. And she feels sorrow. But nothing more. If anything, as miserable as her life has been, as full of grief, she celebrates being alive.

Tonight at nine o'clock, she knows, she will sit in her lovely living room, with its Chagall and Shahn prints, and worry about Howsam, Schotten, and the Greeks. But at the same time she will rejoice.

Oh, yes, she will be ecstatic. Cringing, she will luxuriate in an orgy of greedy delight with every breath while she knows that the beautiful Mrs. Angelakos is dying in a town house on Forty-ninth Street.

Better she than I, she will think. And she will have no sense of pity. Only relief.

So, finally, she sees what has ruled her life: shame.

The rest comes in a rush.

Shame of what? Of being a victim? No, of not fighting back; of cowardice.

She has always known what kind of place the world is for those who entrust their justice to others. How could she not? That insight came with her first remembered kiss. A Danish boy named Nils, fourteen or fifteen, gave it to her when she was three before handing her from a lifeboat to a man from the Zionist Immigration Department.

How that must have terrified her, she thinks.

Grown, she never fought for herself or her people. She settled for any justice. Safety lay in martyrdom, self-pity, resignation. Those attitudes brought some sympathy as well.

So, in time, she even felt superior about compromise. She turned the other cheek. She believed in being civilized. She saw the other side's point of view.

Education put those ideas into her head, Evelyn said. Schoolteachers knew who signed their checks. The managers of society liked reasonable citizens. They went along. If the bosses didn't know more than they, the crowd reasoned, they wouldn't be the bosses.

And that gave the ignorant and the enlightened a license to murder? she retorted.

Of course not! he answered harshly. Killing could never be justified.

*That from him?* No? she asked in surprise.

No. Killing was never right. It had to be balanced against its alternative.

An alternative to murder? she laughed.

Oh, yes. Then, piling shock upon surprise, at least to her, he quoted a general confession, to be said by the whole congregation after the minister, from the Episcopal Book of Common Prayer: " 'We have left undone those things which we ought to have done; And we have done those things which we ought not to have done, and there is no health in us.' "

So to be alive is to be troubled, Evelyn said. Man, after all, did have a moral sense. "Health," he said, meant good conscience. We could never have that if we think and feel. The best we could aspire to is less anguish. The prayer suggested how to avoid some despair. Do look, Ilona, at what comes first: "We have left undone those things which we ought to have done . . ."

Now she sees. Sins of omission come first. That explains the tingling in her scalp. She knows why she has never experienced it before.

Today she has finally fought for *her* justice.

Discovery ends with pain. The flame on the match she lit for her Gauloise has begun to burn her fingers. The tingling stops at the same moment. Match blown out, she discards the cigarette too.

Then, leaning back, closing her eyes, she prays to a God she reasoned out of existence years before. She asks forgiveness for herself and mercy for the souls of Fiona Angelakos and Demosthenes Keriosotis.

## 1040 EASTERN DAYLIGHT SAVING TIME

Days, the diplomatist is the most cosmopolitan of men.

Nights, he is a desert Arab. He sleeps in a *thawb*, the long white cotton shift which is usually worn during the day under a robe.

Awakened at 3 A.M. with news of the war, he has not had time to change. He serves as the communications link between home, his nation's Washington embassy, and the head of its UN delegation, whose phones are thought to be tapped by Algerians or Egyptians.

He sits on one of the couches by the telephone in the second-floor room with all the chess sets. A radio, between newscasts, softly plays "Top 40" tunes beside him. As he rises, his shattered hip points through the flimsy *thawb* like the bow of an icebreaker, Wade thinks.

His wife says he's cuter than Omar Sharif, but not today.

Today he looks sallow, wan, and even his arms and legs where they protrude from the *thawb* seem gray. The whiskers on his chin and cheeks, always well shaven, are white. Appropriately so. Only a flashing smile and a quietly buoyant manner disguise the fact that he is a man well into middle age. As he sees Wade's face his grows older. The lines deepen.

Wilmer? he asks.

Wilmer had a little accident, Wade tells him. His secretary called ahead, and she had a stretcher waiting for them when they got to New York Hospital, so he's in the operating room now.

He'll be all right?

Wade shrugs. He wouldn't bet on it. This was the closest call yet. A croaker started a transfusion right there in the courtyard before they even wheeled the stretcher inside.

Stepping back from their embrace, the diplomatist tells the serving girl to bring them coffee and a large cup for Wade effendi. Then, shaking his head, he sits down, palms despairingly on thighs, as if he were very old.

How could this happen? he asks.

Wade reached over to touch his knee consolingly. Wilmer doesn't blame him, he says.

That makes no difference. He did this to him, the diplomatist answers. He will dress and go to the hospital as soon as they are done. They've already won their war, he adds with obvious irony, and he's had enough of it. Is there anything more to say? he asks Wade.

Wade nods.

The diplomatist taps the buzzer on his phone as the girl brings coffee.

Rashid arrives a moment later. Listening, he jots down names and addresses. Where would Keriosotis be now? he asks.

Home, countin' his money, waitin' on me, Wade says.

Rashid considers the arrangements he must make. Tell him you'll see him early tonight, he suggests.

Nodding, Wade dials Demi's number. No answer.

He holds up his hand for silence. He has another idea. He dials his office.

"Shirley, honey? . . . Hubie's with the croakers. . . . Yeah, under the knife. . . . Nobody knows." He'll go back to the hospital soon's he can. What's come in for him in the meantime? A call from Demi?

He listens impassively.

Nothin' there to keep him away from Hubie. He'll see her later. In the meantime, why doesn't she call the Dorset an' get a room so's she can bunk in there the rest of the week, too? Any clothes an' whatnot she needs the company'll pay for. He just called a halt to the eight-hour day.

Hanging up, he nods in satisfaction. Demi'll be home from three o'clock on, he says. He tells Rashid where he himself can be reached at three-thirty.

Then Rashid excuses himself. He needs a picture, he tells the diplomatist.

Nodding, the diplomatist watches him leave.

Shaking his head, he looks appealingly to Wade. Wade, rising, takes his hand, tells him not to worry. Those two are on his head. God owes them to him, and many more who died in World War II.

## 1900 PORT SAID LOCAL TIME

A hotel manager in the Rue Sultan Osman similarly owes police two souls in his charge. Foreigners, in theory, have been confined to their lodgings since the first air raid alert. They are now being logged into protective custody. Tomorrow they will be moved to Cairo under guard.

The manager is nonchalant about his missing guests. *Baksheesh* usually redresses such oversights. Besides, he has another defense.

"How far can they go without these?" he asks in what may well be the understatement of the day, holding up the two passports.

As of that moment, however, he has an argument.

The men he refers to, Mousecall, a Canadian, and Kupchek, a Brazilian, are only blocks away. They are under a rotting pier near the Rue Sultan Hussein, where no light reaches them. Yusef al-Amer, a ship's agent, keeps the Boston Whaler there that he uses to run back and forth from shore to the vessels he services.

Overnight the boat has been painted black. A new top, holding a Danforth deep-sea compass, has also been installed on the steering console, and all rails and handholds have been wound with black friction tape.

At the moment, shaking their heads in admiration at the workmanship they see, Messrs. Kupchek and Mousecall are mounting two customized 100-horsepower Evinrude outboard motors on the transom.

## 1105 EASTERN DAYLIGHT SAVING TIME

The messenger hands Rashid the manila envelope. Its back bears the brown wax seal of his country's mission to the United Nations.

Nodding, he signs for it and goes to his office in the rear of the first floor of the diplomatist's mansion. Then, door locked, he breaks the seal and withdraws the contents of the envelope.

The top sheet, a mimeographed job application, has been completed by a security man at the mission. It has everything Rashid needs to know.

The assassin's name is Mimouin al-Salaan. He has experience.

He has held similar positions twice before. Once in Paris, and once in Houston, Texas. He must be quite good, Rashid thinks. Neither of those killings, to his knowledge, surfaced.

He wants part-time work.

He gives his occupation as "Student—Columbia Univ."

His parents and two sisters live in the emirate's capital city, where his father is an engineer.

Rashid lifts the sheet to look at the photo beneath. He feels his cheeks warm. The boy is beautiful. And the resemblance is uncanny. He could be the diplomatist as manchild. Mimouin has the same softly rounded cheekbones and long-lashed, gentle Italian eyes. The top sheet puts his age at twenty, which Rashid knows is the truth. Tall and slim, he looks sixteen.

Stroking his mustache, unconsciously grooming it, Rashid fixes the image of the boy in his mind.

Turning the picture over before burning it in the wastepaper basket, he reads the confidential notes, in blue indelible pencil, which could be incriminating. Family origin: Algeria. That explains his name. "Mimouin" is popular in North Africa. Reasons for emigrating: political. Previous residencies: Palestine/Jordan.

Rashid knows that story. The father, no doubt an Algerian nationalist, got into trouble with socialists or the French and had to flee. Then, after the United Nations bent to Truman, allowing Jews to fight their war of aggression, the family fled again to Jordan. Agents of the emirate, prizing engineers, plucked them out of a refugee camp. With parents and two sisters at home, and citizenship conditional, Mimouin has to perform well.

Personality: shy, needs support.

Putting a lighter flame to the photo, Rashid smiles.

With Keriosotis away until afternoon, he will take a stroll down Forty-ninth Street. Then, after seeing the kinds of locks on the house, he will go uptown to Mimouin and bring him some support for his evening's work.


## 1823 LOCAL TIME

Atomized sulfur-yellow paint dust keeps falling.

Gaps between the raised diamonds in *Dynamic*'s nonskid floorplates fill up every twenty minutes.

Sweeping furiously, Orestes Angelakos, index finger pointed away from the broom, its bandage as yellow as everything else in the engineroom, can barely keep up. Still, he is grateful at not seeing any red dust.

When he does, Arkie tells him, it's time to swim.

That will be the red lead under the yellow surface paint. When that goes, the steel it primes, presumably, will shortly follow.

Looking down, however, as he nears the condenser inlet pipe, Orestes suddenly forgets fallout. "Archimedes! Archimedes!" he shouts.

Arkie, on the engine flat above him, cannot hear him.

Turning the broom end for end, Orestes pokes the handle through the black iron fire-escape gratings into the soles of Arkie's shoes.

"The pipe jacket—it's going!" he shouts up.

A moment later, Arkie drops into the bilge.

The cement from condenser casing to the enclosed round circulating pump is intact. The jacket top from pump to ship's side, however, has a crack in it over its full length. Ducking the riser to which the floorplates were attached, Arkie puts his thumbnail into the rent.

Only the edge of his nail will fit.

As he moves his hand toward the hull, however, the split gets deeper nearing the source of the vibration.

At the flange at the ship's side, he shakes his head.

"You remember that copper antenna wire we put in to reinforce the top layer of cement?" he asks Orestes. "I can see it in there."

"How long's it gonna last?"

Looking up, Arkie can only shrug. He's never sailed with this kind of vibration before.

## 1200 EASTERN DAYLIGHT SAVING TIME

Dr. Fabian sits back in the cab.

Two hours of busywork behind her while she pondered her discovery, she feels, at last, at thirty-two, fully and finally revealed. She finds that a not entirely pleasing prospect. But only delusions have died, not hope.

So she knows how to cope with this situation. First, she will buy a dress. She is, in fact, going to Hattie Carnegie's now.

She wants something very tailored, she thinks. But sleeveless, and with a matching bolero jacket. Linen or silk would be perfect, and the color must be lime green. That will be her wedding gift to a man who already has everything. Her saleswoman has told her that three dresses in the summer collection meet those requirements.

Dr. Fabian sees that as an omen, so the ride up Madison Avenue is a happy one. For the first time in years, rather than miring herself in the past, she reflects, she has looked to the future, and what she wants is there.

Then, dress packed, she will go to Zurich.

When Schotten arrives, she will marry him or buy him.

She remembers what Francine said of Howsam. She now thinks that of Schotten. Such men are indeed to be coveted. To live in truth is to deny one's ego, and that is their ultimate strength. They see things as they are.

At Thirty-fourth Street they stop for a red light. She idly watches the cross-town traffic. A yellow cab leads the race across the intersection. The Israeli pilot, Seth, sits in its back seat.

She watches him go east, out of sight.

So long, ghost! she thinks.


## 1320 EASTERN DAYLIGHT SAVING TIME

Honey lies back on the crisp, cool hotel sheet.

She raises her knees.

As always, he enters in a single smooth motion.

The light show behind her eyelids starts at once. Her head seems filled with colors. White, yellow, pink, and blue forms, all pleasingly shaded, dip and soar across the area she imagines behind her forehead. They arc through their trajectories like the bouncing white ball she remembers from the Saturday-afternoon movie sing-alongs of her childhood. Gone from view past her temples, they explode, but never painfully. Shock waves of those concussions pass down through her body, growing ever stronger, as the colors do, until, as they finally engulf her, there are no more.

It's been like that from the first, almost from the day she came to New York after the wedding and started to meet the "family." Some family!

It's that way for him too, she knows. Otherwise, he wouldn't be here now.

His, she now realizes, like that of the men now fighting, is the day's ultimate risk. It far surpasses the money involved. The next few days will determine how he lives the rest of his life. If events go against him, he will be killed in action as surely as all the others.

Still, for all his faults, he has guts.

The only time he stops scheming, stops trying for an edge, is when her legs are around him. She would never know now, she thinks, that he is under any kind of stress. She tightens her hold around his neck, pulls his head closer. Her breasts, still wet from his mouth, stick to his chest, ride with it. Their bellies meet and lock in the synchronized ebb and flow of practiced, satisfying love-making.

Good, she tells herself, feeling the tension drain from his neck and shoulders. She knows what he has done to her, Taki, and the rest of the family, but she wants him to have that release. That will be her last present to him, and it may help him through the afternoon.

Meanwhile, she will enjoy her generosity.

After Taki with all his hair, she savors the cool, smooth feeling of this body on hers. She loves the quick little shocks of heat, too, that he leaves behind as he gently slaps her across her bottom. He knows how and what to touch down there as well, she thinks, and that gives her a great sense of security. She never has to worry about how it will be for her.

His hand is there now.

The colors are brightening. . . .

They lie back spent but not sated.

A moment later, casting off the towel, he starts bringing her along again. She wonders then if he too knows this is to be the last time. There's a reluctance in his touch she has never sensed before. Fingers, lips, and tongue linger longingly, hoardingly, as if trying to fix or store a lasting impression.

Finally, on their sides, they face each other, their heads on a single pillow. She, as loath to accept the loss as he, hooks her right thigh over his, lets her leg trail down full length against his calves. Her left hand slides under his head; her right, over his cheek.

A sharp scarlet thumbnail lying at the corner of each eyeball, he looks at her questioningly.

She has lived a life calling for some very hard decisions, and she has always made them. She knows he senses she will now, if necessary. She hopes it will not come to that. Then there would be nothing left, and they owe each other more, she feels. She has never bargained her way to this bed, or put conditions on what she would do in it. She couldn't. It means too much to her.

For his part, he has never exploited their secret. Like herself, he has had to invent his own standards of conduct, and, like hers, they can be amoral, ruthless, and selfish. Still, he has honored this relationship.

That implies trust.

Certainly affection.

Perhaps love.

Whatever, she ends what she cannot define.

She doesn't believe all that much in coincidence or foresight, she tells him. She doesn't believe in using others' weaknesses and ignorance either. That's like taking advantage of the handicapped. There are things you do and things you don't, especially with friends. Those convertibles—what's behind them, and what happens next? she asks.

So Wade tells her.

## 1400 EASTERN DAYLIGHT SAVING TIME

Rashid snips at his British brush mustache.

Standing at the mirror, he feels very optimistic.

He has the whole thing figured out, he believes. He had only to walk by the house on Forty-ninth Street to get the basics. The kitchen, he saw, would be the way in. He knew the lock on the door, as well.

The neighborhood, however, posed the problem. Even in New York, with its polyglot population, an Arab boy would call attention to himself on that block.

Mimouin, he saw, needed some kind of camouflage. But what?

Pondering that, he continued his stroll, turning south on Third Avenue and then east to United Nations Plaza. There a security man at his nation's mission gave him the appropriate lock pick.

Then, outside, as he watched two young boys pass while he waited for a cab going uptown, the problem of Mimouin's camouflage solved itself.

Changing his plans, he walked back to First Avenue, where he remembered passing a hardware store. Inside, he bought a long-hasped padlock and the heaviest pair of compound wire cutters in stock.

Now, shaved and showered, he trims the corners of his mustache before putting the scissors down to shake a little bay rum into his palms. He adds a few drops of henna to each bottle for the coppery complexion he likes and would have were he at home in the sun every day.

Leaning over the sink, he looks to see if the color is right. It is. His teeth are dazzlingly white against it. They suggest his cleanliness, his purity.

His body must also display his strength. It has to reflect his office. Face rubbed, he puts on a white short-sleeved shirt which will show off his forearms and biceps, two of his best features, he feels. He already wears the trousers of an electric-blue raw-silk suit, the jacket of which, his friend and weightlifting partner, Mahmoud, tells him, does so well at suggesting his pectorals and shoulders.

British silk rep tie knotted, he enters the bedroom of the apartment next door to the diplomatist's mansion. So much for appearance, he thinks.

He looks representative of the Mujahideen, or Holy Warrior Department, as the Saudis call his bureau.

For substance, he opens the bedroom closet door. From the top shelf he takes down a small gray plastic attaché case. Freeing its latches, he swings back the top. Three niches are carved into the black Styrofoam interior. They enclose a very fine Italian .25-caliber automatic pistol, a four-inch silencer, and a seven-shot ammunition clip.

He takes out each component, holds it to the light, blows off an imagined or real piece of lint. Satisfied, he returns the parts to their niches.

Now for "shy" Mimouin's support, he tells himself.

Smiling, he goes to his small Pullman kitchen. He brings the attaché case, open, with him.

From the built-in refrigerator he removes a small round jar that originally held artichoke hearts. Half full, it now contains a paste or jam, depending upon definition, light brown to amber in color. His friend Mahmoud gives it to him from time to time, and with it they have passed many joyous nights. A Moroccan specialty, it is called *majoun*.

Twisting off the airtight lid, he sniffs traces of caraway, anise, and nutmeg. Their aromas are fresh and pungent, unspoiled. Dabbing at the surface with the tip of his index finger, he carries the pale-brown film to his tongue. He tastes the honey, feels the grit of the ground walnuts, recognizes particles of dates and figs. All are sweet. What he cannot taste is the kif.

That, boiled in water, sends its essence to butter bubbling in the pot with it. Cooled, the butter forms the base into which all else is mixed.

A teaspoon or two on sweet biscuits, Rashid thinks, will enfold a man in heaven for a day. That will be too much for Mimouin, he knows. It will affect his vision. So, screwing on the top, he reaches into his breadbox for a partial roll of Ritz crackers. They will give him a taste, he reflects. Afterward, he can have biscuits. Squeezing in jar and crackers, he closes the attaché case and steps into the living room for his coat.

He pats his pockets at the door. Has he forgotten anything? Yes.

Returning to his bedroom, he opens the top drawer of the dresser. From the corner behind his socks he brings out a thin red braided cotton rope. Folding it carefully, he places it in an inside jacket pocket.

It saddens him that Mimouin will wear it.

Still, he muses, the night may have its compensations.

Smiling, he picks up the attaché case as he leaves.

How fawnlike the boy is, he thinks.

## 1530 EASTERN DAYLIGHT SAVING TIME

Hanging up, Wade feels shitty.

Jesus, does he ever, he thinks.

He never saw anything like it. Honey didn't say a word. She just got dressed and left. She wanted out so fast, in fact, she wouldn't even slow down for her pants and hose, threw them into her purse instead.

Meanwhile, he lay in bed expecting her to talk.

But her departure spoke for her. She paused, briefly glanced back over her shoulder, and then, with one hand on the knob and the other on the edge, silently pulled the door closed behind her. She had no tears to blink back, no angry words to swallow, no tremors of grief to control or disguise.

He knows that glance. He has seen it in funeral homes once or twice a year. Men like him look that way at caskets of parents of the women with whom their wives play golf or tennis. How the hell else could anyone react? Is anything more remote than a stranger's death? Facing it, then, what's the best expression to have? None, obviously.

And that's how Honey sees him now, he thinks.

As he sits there on the couch downstairs in the Dorset suite, his sense of loss deepens. To his surprise, it ignores her looks and body and bed skills, which are considerable, and the kick he gets out of any kind of petty larceny. His feeling of abandonment goes deeper than that. He begins to see what Honey has meant to him.

Jesus, who will he talk to now? he wonders.

Until then, he thought he led a simple life. An illusion, he suddenly realizes. Only here, with Honey, has his life been simple. Otherwise, it's been anything but.

Now, looking back, he sees that his existence has been more like one of those building contracts he and Henley got headaches over in London: a complicated, ongoing transaction full of bonuses and penalty clauses. Moreover, everybody he lives with has some kind of deal going down, and those closest—Hubie, Urs, Taki, the kids, and Willa Mae—all want to get over him one way or the other.

It's like they were incomplete or unsure and needed a piece of him either to feel they were finally finished or had proved something.

All, that is, except Honey. She has always been whole, and she had nothing to prove. Nor did she need him, not even at first, when she thought she did, unable to decipher clan Keriosotis. So they were equals in bed and out.

And with nothing to gain and no impression to make, they were never reluctant to show each other what they liked. That led to the usual jokes, of course, and then to questions, and finally to confidences exchanged.

It should have ended there, he thinks. That's where most extracurricular diddling stops. The past suggests more than it tells, but it's safe. History, after all, is fact and dead in the bargain.

Soon, however, they were deeper than that. He can't remember when; nor, he feels, could she. But suddenly they were talking feelings.

That came easily, he muses, snuck right up on them. He sees now it should have. After what went on in that bed upstairs, they had nothing more to hide. By then, having already brought each other so much pleasure, they were secure too; safe from criticism or embarrassment. And the humping got better, as well. He thought all along that went with practice. Today he knows it came from something else: closeness.

That idea further unsettles him. He used to talk to get a woman. Now, he sees, he's been doing just the reverse. He's been diddling her for the excuse to talk. It's backward, he thinks. Still, he's never known anything like it.

So what else could he do but tell her about Demi? He owed it. They had that kind of a fit.

And now it's over.

It's crazy. They should have met when they both were single, he muses.

The whole world's nuts, he decides. A few minutes ago, when he informed Rashid that Demi had told him to stop by at seven-thirty—because guests were coming in at eight-thirty—that crazy A-rab was squeaking like a mouse all the while they were on the phone. He wonders what the hell was going on, and where, and who was with Rashid.

Rising, he shrugs into his suit coat. Five minutes ago, Hubie was still under the knife; things don't look good. It's time for him to go stand what maybe will be the death watch with Cora and the diplomatist.

At the door, he glances upstairs.

A last thought flashes through his mind. Jesus, what they could have been together, married.

## 2235 LOCAL TIME

At 1800, Mossad ordered a continuous radio watch.

At 2157, the Israeli operator returned to the air on the 16-kilocycle working frequency. Since each man knew the other by now by the rhythm of his sending and the tone of his transmitter, the question came without benefit of call sign or signature:

"That U northwest corner M7?"

Turning the transmitter, Alexander consulted his chart.

"Yes," he replied. How could they know that? he wondered.

Israel must have a destroyer or a sub in the area, he decided. Since they had seen no planes during that day, they could only have been spotted by a periscope or radar.

"Look southeast soonest," the Israeli advised.

*Dit-ditt*ing in response, Alexander called the bridge.

Now, an hour later, a new message in, he goes to see for himself.

*Dynamic* is about sixty miles from Port Said.

Stepping onto the port bridgewing, he finds Costa and Zavitsanos draped over the weather rail. At their eyes are special night-vision binoculars developed by the U.S. Army and put aboard as an Israeli gift in Ancona. They will also be tested in tank combat that night and following nights. From them will come sniper scopes that will save many American lives in Vietnam.

But what they see a few minutes later, just above where they assume the southeast horizon will be on this overcast, moonless night, requires no optics of any kind. The sky faintly begins to brighten.

Lightning? Alexander asks.

Zavitsanos chuckles softly. Rain is unheard of at this time of year.

Costa, who has been shot at by everything thus far invented by man, nods knowingly. "Look a little higher," he counsels. "Watch how the color of the clouds changes. You'll see it all better."

The orange-yellow twinklings are from cordite, he says, the primer charge in naval shells. So there's certainly a destroyer out there firing, maybe two. When the overcast grays, that's from tracers.

And the reddish-blue streaks?

Rockets, Costa answers. The Frenchman who chased him and Zavitsanos from Indochina to the Philippines shot over four dozen at them and never hit shit.

Nothing to worry about, Zavitsanos affirms. But what's he doing here, anyway? he asks.

Alexander produces the latest message. It repeats the last, but, with the condition of the sky as it is, far more forcefully: "CU A.M."

Nodding, Costa crosses the wheelhouse to the phone. He tells Arkie to slow down to fifty-five turns.

Then, shaking his head and muttering that the fuel they are burning is coming out of his pocket, he rejoins Alexander and Zavitsanos to watch the battle of Port Said. They will be there at dawn.

## 1600 EASTERN DAYLIGHT SAVING TIME

The short, portly man turns off Third Avenue.

A faintly English air envelops his clothes. Still, he seems to belong in the neighborhood.

He wears a dark-brown coconut-straw fedora with a white band with maroon polka dots, burgundy suit, shirt, and tie, and crepe-soled matching canvas shoes. Latest edition of the *New York Post* tucked under his arm, he could be an advertising agency art director coming home a little early or an editor in a publishing house. Third Avenue's office buildings house such enterprises. Many in those firms choose to live nearby.

Looking neither right nor left, he strolls down the south side of Forty-ninth Street with an utter lack of curiosity that implies he probably belongs there.

To draw that inference, however, would be incorrect.

What he has, instead, is a total familiarity.

He has walked this block many times since November. He has done so mostly out of curiosity. Now Evelyn Waddell knows he has only been prudent. He has stepped onto his killing ground.

The burgundy suit, in fact, commemorates another: Acre Prison, outside Haifa. The English gave condemned men there outfits very nearly the same color in the days of the Palestine Mandate. If he can find a closer match to that shade than he now wears, he will buy it. It will make his departed comrades seem nearer.

He halts for a car leaving the U.S. Plywood Building garage, passes Le Marmiton, a fair restaurant by Montreal's standards, and meanders by a half-dozen or so houses fronting on Turtle Bay Gardens.

Just as casually, he steps off the sidewalk, opens a waist-high black wrought-iron gate, closes it behind him, and enters the kitchen entrance of a four-story olive-drab stucco home.

Painter's dropcloths cover the floor. Two suits of coveralls lie crumpled in a corner. Nodding with approval, he enters a narrow passageway leading straight ahead to the dining room or right to the stairway. He turns right.

Itch Cohen is waiting at the second-floor landing. "You said four o'clock," he deadpans.

"What time is it?"

Cohen looks at his watch and smiles. "On the dot," he answers, teeth gleaming voraciously.

Then he leads the way up to the fourth floor.

Turning left, they pass a small bathroom and enter the back bedroom overlooking Forty-ninth Street. It has two high, narrow windows.

The driver of the Falcon sits to the left and about three feet back of the left window. A small pair of black Zeiss seven-by-thirty field glasses lies alongside his chair. Looking down and diagonally to his right, he is watching the opposite side of the street without squinting.

Hands on shoulders, Cohen places Evelyn behind him. "What do you think?" he asks in a whisper.

Evelyn nods. "Perfect! Spot-on-perfect," he whispers back. Indeed it is.

Manhattan rises from the East and Hudson rivers to its Fifth Avenue spine, so crosstown streets are rarely level. One of the steepest slopes lies between Second and Third avenues in the forties. On Forty-ninth Street, Third Avenue is about twelve feet higher than Second Avenue.

Their house is about two feet higher than Demi's.

Their angle of view is further improved by being a floor above his bedroom. They can, in fact, see through the Venetian-blind slats on his windows. Looking right, their line of sight almost reaches Second Avenue, a big edge. They can see what's coming. Traffic goes west on Forty-ninth Street, from right to left beneath them.

Arms crossed over the chest of the short-sleeved white-on-white shirt, the driver of the Falcon tips back in his chair, eyes still on Demi's house.

"He come in five to three," he updates Evelyn. "She's still out loose."

Itch Cohen, hand on his shoulder, turns him around. Then, addressing Evelyn, he makes the introductions. "Controller, meet Stan the Man, our vice-president in charge of Eastern operations. Only this one's the real hitter—bats a thousand! Right, Stashke?"

"I hit a few," Stan the Man modestly acknowledges.

His smile is infectious. Looking up, his blue eyes dance over Evelyn's face. Hand extended, widely gapped brilliantly white teeth exposed with his grin, he seems even more boyish, baldness notwithstanding.

"You like a sandwich?" he asks, rising. He and Itch have only had breakfast, he says.

They've food there? Evelyn asks, always interested.

Stan'll get some, Itch Cohen answers.

And be seen?

No one'll see him, Stan the Man answers. It'll be just like this morning, when he and Itch got there. His brother-in-law drove up in his painter's truck, they got out in coveralls, and Itch held the dropcloths while he picked the lock. Twenty people must have passed by on the sidewalk, and nobody saw them. Service guys are always around wealthy neighborhoods, especially vacation time. Who wants to be home for the painters when they can be in Europe, like the family that owns this house? So, downstairs, he'll just get back into his coveralls, go out, and again nobody'll see him.

"Besides," he adds, "there's been a shift change at the Seventeenth Precinct, and our guys are on the street."

Finally placated, Evelyn nods.

He folds his coat, places it on the white tufted bedspread behind him, and takes Stan's chair. Finding it too low, he reaches to the unfinished pine bookcase on the wall to his left for a volume of *Encyclopaedia Britannica*. That suits him. He smiles in anticipation, as if seeing geese on the horizon.

Itch Cohen takes a place to the rear and right of the right-hand window. The back of his chair brushes the head of the child's bed behind him.

He looks down and diagonally to his left, west. Shadowed, his eyeglass frames gleam a dull pewter. At first, so does the silver dollar. Then, as it walks across the fingers of his right hand, it flashes in the sunlight, which is beginning to move west.

Nice day, he observes, and the war's going good. Does Evelyn think he'll go in early or late?

Depends, Evelyn answers. If they see them both in the bedroom, he'll nip right over and do it then and there, regardless of time. It's so much easier to be neat if they're together. There's less chance of one slipping away. Otherwise, he'll just ring the bell at eight-thirty and chat them along a half hour or so, until it's dark. He'd like shadows when he walks away.

Cohen nods in agreement.

They say no more.

Their seemingly blank gazes never leave the street.

In attitude and posture, they are perfect previews of Second Avenue tenement dwellers a half block away who, after supper, will kill the rest of the night mindlessly watching traffic beneath them.


## 1821 EASTERN DAYLIGHT SAVING TIME

Taki stands in the doorway.

High blood pressure tinges his swarthiness pink.

She's never seen that before, Honey thinks. This had to be the wildest day of his life.

But he never brings home business worries. To do so would be to diminish two of his great joys: her and the elegant home she has made for him.

So, shaking his head in dismay, he smiles gamely as he plucks a pinch of shirt through the gap in his coat for her to see.

"Sweated through," he says. "Gotta tsange." Then they can go.

She leans over to kiss him, then looks at her watch.

No rush, she says, leading him through the mirrored foyer into the living room. The reservation's for seven-thirty. He can have a drink first and cool off.

He shakes his head. "We can't be late, Honey," he cautions her. "After tsupper, we gotta stop by an' see Demi. I got some ideas to go over wit' him."

Does she realize, he asks, that if the Suez Canal closes down, Loren won't build those convertibles, that he'll make much more with straight tankers? He's thought of some things Demi can do to get in on those.

In the midst of this day, she thinks.

She makes a face as if that's a fresh thought, but still looks at her watch, then points to his favorite beige wing chair facing the window wall overlooking the East River. "Sit," she says insistently.

Then she walks to her right, to the butler's pantry.

Did he have any luck that afternoon? she asks.

Yeah, he answers, sitting. He did just like she said when she called. He chartered in everything he could—490,000 tons for a year.

She knows tankering math as well as Hubie and Loren. They've told her so. Her call will make about $65 million, she thinks. She feels nothing.

In the butler's panty, she uses the wall phone to cancel the "21" reservation. Then, turning, she opens the bar refrigerator under the counter and doles out ice chunks until a tall glass is a quarter full. Pouring colorless ouzo over the ice, she reaches to the sink, taps the cold-water faucet, lets it run a moment, and fills the glass. Stirring it with an iced-tea spoon, she eyes it critically as it turns milky.

She sniffs the anise. Just right. Satisfied, she puts the glass on the sink.

Then, without pausing, she hikes up the navy-blue skirt of the Lanvin suit she bought in Paris two weeks before and pulls down her pants. Kicking them off with her blue-and-white spectator pumps, she throws them on the counter. She will have the skirt off in thirty seconds, as well, but for now it must stay on. It will heighten the sense of nudity when it goes.

The $65 million is meaningless, she reflects. She and Taki have never lived that big. They've never wanted to.

But now, she thinks, she will do him a real service. Taking the drink, she returns to the living room. She puts the glass on the table alongside his chair. Patting his cheek, she sees him squint. Too much sun, she thinks.

It's coming in from the south.

She tells people her living room has five windows. She fails to say that each is a six-foot Thermopane sliding door. The room is nearly that deep as well. So it takes her a while to reach the drapes. Loosening a brown velvet cord, she lets them fall, sees the beige carpeting darken.

"That better, sugah?" she asks.

He looks at her questioningly, concerned about time.

Smiling, she takes a couple of turns around a clip with the brown velvet cord to secure the drape and walks left to the center of the window wall.

As he watches her, his head comes up. She knows why. The backlighting silhouettes her limbs.

The light will also shine through the butterscotch hair tumbling over the shoulders of her white blouse. Some of those ends will gleam as yellow as gold. Others will throw off reddish flashes, like tiny flames. Still more will have caramel-brown glints.

It's like that between her legs as well.

Her best feature, she notes sardonically.

But he's thinking that, too, she sees. So, grin broadening, she takes two steps closer.

She canceled "21," she tells him. Then, hands on her left hip, she opens the clasp and the zipper and steps out of the dark-blue skirt.

Seeing him in the doorway, she explains, she all of a sudden got a tickle that needs attention. So, it's her birthday, but he gets the party, too.

Leaving the skirt where it falls, she steps forward again, automatically striking a showgirl's pose, hands on hips, head thrown back. Body twisted just so, she lets him see a little cloud of that luscious hair he loves so much behind her left thigh, but not the promised land it hides.

Dear God, she thinks, this can't be me.

The real Honey's in Mattituck, at the summer place, in raggedy jeans shorts and one of his undershirts, without a bra. If she's not weeding the garden, she's in the Whaler, cutting up squid for weakfish bait.

She's never used sex this way. She's always given it away.

She's shared it, in fact, with almost every man who wanted it. She started in junior high. She fucked all the little boys then, she thinks. She loved it, and how proud they were after. How they strutted off! How their chests puffed up! She had been voted, after all, a few years later, the prettiest high-school cheerleader in North Carolina, and hadn't her picture been in the paper? Wasn't she also, with her willowy legs and seductive body, the one the dramatics teacher always chose for the sexiest roles in the school musicals?

Those parts led to beauty pageants, and, ultimately, to the office of a local furniture store. Still, she muses, she hadn't gone there to win. She had already won. She wanted to see if it would be more fun with an older man.

Ten weeks later, his abortion money in hand and a story to her folks behind her, she met a smiling young British doctor in Nassau.

"Nothing to it," he assured her. He would "just let in a little air." He did it all the time for Paradise Island showgirls.

Afterward, he was just as casual. "Just a little nick," he said. It would heal in no time.

So, on the way home, she stopped at Paradise Island. Six months later, her picture graced the color postcards the resort put in its hotel rooms. Two years after that, she went to San Juan as the lead dancer in a hotel floor show there. And, on her own in those places with no fears of pregnancy, she fucked almost all the men who physically appealed to her or who made her laugh, she now remembers, seeing some of their faces.

And how proud they were! And how they strutted—grown men, smart, successful, worldly!

*Over so little.*

But she had fun, and she had never wanted more than that. In many ways, the San Juan years were the best of her life. The parties were spectacular, and the gifts, which she frequently received, fabulous.

In time, though, she found that the presents were worth more than she made dancing. She had no idea of what the other girls she partied with called that situation, but she had a name for it, and she didn't like it.

She had just had her twenty-sixth birthday.

So, with savings, an eye for style, and clothes on consignment from some New York boys she had known for years, she wheedled the hotel into giving her an empty lobby shop for a percentage of the gross. When she met Taki, at thirty, she had two more stores.

An old chum, then balling someone else, introduced them. A Miami lawyer with a lot of business in Puerto Rico, he asked if she'd join him for supper. He hoped she'd look after a Greek who was there with a client of his to help him buy some ships.

It might be fun, the lawyer laughed. The Greek was a bachelor. He could also make a $100,000 commission that day approving a sale.

The invitation intrigued her—not, however, because of the Greek's marital status or commission prospects.

She had seen ships in San Juan harbor, of course. But she had assumed that gigantic corporations, rather than individuals, owned them. Until then, she thought the showgirl's fare of cloak-and-suiters, car dealers, and owners of foam-rubber-furniture outlets represented the cream of wheeler-dealers. She wondered what a man who could make $100,000 in a day would be like.

So she met Taki. To compound her shock, he had blocked the sale.

"Fair's fair," he said, dismissing the matter. Who wanted commitsun if client wasn't happy? There'd be more s'ips. In the meantime, he was always comin' in or out San Juan. Would she have lunts wit' him sometime, maybe tsupper, dependin' on plane connectsuns?

She'd haunt his conscience if he didn't! she laughed.

"Fair's fair" had reached her. That's what she had always felt. So she married him a year later. She learned what he owned, and the extent of his family's holdings, when he brought her to New York.

His wealth hardly mattered.

She still thought she had the best of the bargain. She gave Taki youth, a beautiful woman, which he could have bought anywhere. He, in contrast, gave her what she had never had: credibility—at least, to herself.

There had been too many men in her life. Now she wanted just one.

There were plenty of volunteers for a night at a time, but none, in view of her past, who saw her as a reasonable risk for the long term. And she craved the long term. She had to prove to herself that she hadn't spent all those years dancing just to party and to get gifts. She sensed feelings she needed to express. She knew they would be years forming.

Love, or something near it, came on a brisk sunny afternoon the fall after they were married. They drove out to Long Island that day on what he called "Mission Mysterious." She had no idea what he had in mind.

But at Mattituck he turned off the main road and headed for Peconic Bay. There, at the bottom of a hill, on a tiny point of land on the water, he stopped the car and helped her out into the waist-high grass.

His right hand swept the horizon. Like Chios, he said. On good days no one knew where the sea ended and sky began. This was that beautiful.

What did she think? he asked, earnestly looking up into her face. He wanted to buy it.

He did?

He nodded solemnly.

He knew from her brothers, he said, that she had always been a tomboy, so he thought she might like this after town—a little house, nothin' fancy, old clothes, an' no company unless they agreed on the people. But she'd have a garden for corn an' tomatoes an' a boat for fis'in'. This would be the kind of place where they could be alone an' have . . .

Shaking his head, he looked at her imploringly, inarticulate.

And have what? she thought.

. . . an' have a few laughs together, he ended, blushing.

A few laughs together. The multitudes who had wanted a few laughs with her! And got them, she reflected.

But none had ever suggested she might be fun to be with in a garden, sweaty, with dirty fingernails. None had ever imagined, either, that he might find a sweet, quiet joy sitting with her, sun-drugged and sleepy, in a small boat on a summer afternoon.

Nodding, she looked at the red buoy off the point. She had to blink back tears. She had never cried for any man. After that, she felt differently about Taki.

Meanwhile, Loren had begun showing her the colors.

So she knows who's posing, hands on hips, letting the bottom of the white silk blouse sway over the rise of her belly. It's Honey, all right, she thinks, with her moist, parted-lipped smile and voluptuous, welcoming showgirl's thighs. At least, it's a new side of Honey.

This part remembers what Taki said in San Juan: "Fair's fair."

She's ready to live that way now, too.

She doesn't want to see Loren's colors anymore.

She doesn't want to be clever anymore.

She finally understands this life, she thinks: it's serious.

There are things you do and things you don't.

Mostly, there are things you don't do.

You don't betray family. You don't betray friends. You don't lie. You don't shade trust. You don't send men out to die—at least, not for money.

And there's a last "don't."

She's pondered it since leaving the Dorset.

The answer came as she looked at Taki in the foyer.

Unlike Dr. Fabian, she has no handy quotes or historical figures to help her resolve the matter. But she has just as keen a mind and an infinitely more acute understanding of the human condition. In the end, she comes to exactly the same place: *You don't tolerate those actions in others.*

So, seeking retribution, she opens the view for him a bit and starts across the beige carpeting, putting into her stride every little incitement to lust, which, even when clothed, she had made sufficiently provocative to be worth $650 a week to the hotel management in San Juan.

Watching, he hastily puts down his drink. He rubs the polyps in the corners of his eyelids. Then his jaw slackens.

Her smile widens encouragingly. Her tongue darts out to moisten her lips. He's confused, she thinks. He accepts the idea of a sexual encounter in the living room, but he's never seen her like this. He's wondering, too, she knows, because, after all, he is a man, how bold he can be and what he can do, without scaring her off.

He reaches out as she nears the beige wing chair.

She bends at the waist, draws her buttocks away.

She knows what he wants. She can see where he wants to put his face.

Maybe later, she thinks.

Yes, certainly, she tells herself. Why deny him anything?

From now on, she won't. He'll get it all, whatever she's held back. She owes it.

His eyes are practically in the top of his head as she slides behind the side of the chair and reaches over the arm to unzip him.

"First," she coos, in what she calls her slurriest, most sex-crazed drawl, while stroking him, "I'm goin' to suck you dry . . ."

"Honey . . ." he whimpers uncomprehendingly, looking at his watch.

She goes on as if he made no demurral. She's more interested in what his body's telling her. That's begun to inch down almost imperceptibly in the chair to make things easier for her. At the same time, he's arching his back so that her hand can envelop more of him.

"—then I'm goin' to fuck you dry," she continues, "an' after that, I'm goin' get you up again—"

"We gotta go over to—"

"Later," she says. "But first I'm goin' to make us a mess of raw fried potatoes an' onions with fried eggs, an' then, when we're both full, comfy, an' relaxed, I want you to give me one of those nice, long, slow drags—maybe with me up on the arms of this chair, leanin' over its back . . ."

That's one of his little fantasies. He whispered it to her when they bought the chair.

Seamen are full of those ideas, she knows. Loren's like that. Demi too. The Athens members of the family who went to sea are the same way. And no wonder. It must have to do with enforced celibacy and then learning how to do it on the docks, she thinks.

Taki was twenty-three before he made love with his shoes off, he told her. He went to a very fancy brothel in Montevideo. His captain, a cousin, logged him three days' pay for misconduct. The place, he found out, had been set aside for officers.

So they won't go out tonight, she knows. She will give him sailor's Halloween instead.

He slumps lower, reaches for her face."Honey . . ." he sighs.

He wants to thank her. But no thanks are necessary.

She knows now what he is, what the others are.

She will honor him thus for the rest of his life.

She will only regret she didn't start sooner.

Face cradled in his hands, she nods imperceptibly, lets the upper part of her body be drawn across the arms of the chair.

He looks at her reverentially.

Then, leaning over, knowing they will not leave the apartment that night, she does what she can to kill Demi and Fiona, too.


## 1827 EASTERN DAYLIGHT SAVING TIME

Mrs. Angelakos arrived shortly after four-thirty.

She had been shopping. She left the cab with two purple Bonwit Teller bags.

Across the street, they wondered what she had bought. Stan the Man hoped Bonwit's took returns.

That got a big laugh all around.

After that, they saw nothing.

No light went on in the third-floor bedroom.

A little after five, when offices closed, the sidewalk opposite them grew more animated. Now they are watching pedestrian traffic just after its peak. A few jobholders are still straggling home, some with an attaché case in each hand. The dogwalkers are out. The late shoppers are returning from the carriage-trade fish, food, and meat markets that stay open for them until seven on Second and First avenues.

Suddenly, Evelyn leans forward in his chair. "Oooh, ooh," he says softly. "Here's a something."

Itch Cohen bolts from his chair. Stan the Man comes forward from the child's dresser in the back of the room where he has been listening to race results since bringing back sandwiches.

Both stand behind Evelyn at the pine bookcase.

"A what?" Itch Cohen asks.

"Right there," Evelyn answers.

He points to the near side of the intersection at Forty-ninth and Second.

"Where?" Itch Cohen asks again.

Rashid has indeed seen how to put an Arab boy on that block without calling attention to him. Judging from the actions of others near him, no one is aware of such an exotic in their presence.

But for Evelyn, he would go entirely unnoticed.

"The delivery boy," he tells Itch Cohen.

"On the bike?" Stan the Man asks.

"Oh, yes," comes the reply. "That lad's here on serious business, I assure you. He's wearing *agal*s."

Then, as the boy, Mimouin, slowly resumes pedaling after a car pulls out of a parking place in front of him, Evelyn realizes what he has just said.

"Itch, old chap," he says, leaning back in his chair, "what would you say if I told you that our chums the cowboys got their shipbuilding money from the Arabs and that those boys are just as shy 'bout announcing their good works as Home Office?"

Itch Cohen leans farther over his shoulder, the left side of his face no longer shadowed. Sun winks off his chrome-plated eyeglass frames. "That kid's no Arab," he says.

"Oh, but he is," Evelyn insists. "Someone in the family just got thick with a Crusader, or perhaps even a Russian, thousands of years ago."

Itch Cohen seldom operates on faith. He also has the curiosity marking all good minds.

"How'd you get that?" he asks.

Evelyn points a pudgy forefinger, hand on chest.

"See under his chin?" he says. "That red cotton cord's standing in for an *agal*. Desert Arabs use them to tie their headdresses. But worn round the neck that way, they're the traditional Bedouin call for blood vengeance."

"But what's he advertisin' for?"

"Yes, indeed—why?" Evelyn replies. "I can only chalk that up to the Arab psyche. They're bright enough to get their man in there unseen, but they can't bear to let it go at that. Their egos won't let them. They've got to mark him to satisfy themselves. Nasser's like that, too, isn't he? Full of ego. That's what makes them so dangerous. They're unstable."

Mimouin, meanwhile, alternately pedals and pushes the bike west on Forty-ninth Street with his left foot as if the bike were a scooter. He wears a tan waiter's jacket taken from his dormitory's dining room, and looks like a delivery boy reading house numbers just to make sure he is on the right block.

Passersby ignore him.

At Demi's he pauses, glances at the house over his right shoulder, reaches into the cardboard box in the basket over the low front wheel of the bike as if to rearrange its contents. Then, turning to his left, he seemingly gazes at the fourth-floor window from which he is being watched.

None of the three looking out moves.

They are all experienced.

They know where Mimouin is looking.

Evelyn nods. "Checking the sun," he observes approvingly. "He wants shadow, the same as I would. A bright little chap, and I'll wager he's made similar social calls before."

Below them now, Mimouin glances back at traffic and placidly pedals off west in evening's first soft light. His hair flashes with chestnut glints in it, and they see he is quite young.

His youth, however, fails to impress Stan the Man. "I was sixteen when I started," he says. With that he returns to the dresser. Ear bent to his pocket portable radio, he twists the dial, vainly trying for more news of the war. It's still a minute or two early for the six-thirty newscasts.

Itch Cohen tells him to be patient, then takes his chair by the right window. He knows there's no rush. The procedure is always the same.

"How long you think he'll be gone?" he asks Evelyn.

Sighing in anticipation, Evelyn leans back.

"Fifteen minutes at least. Probably a half hour. His escape route depends on whether the stop lights are red or green, and he'll have to ad-lib lots of choices. What happens, for example, if the light's red at Forty-ninth and Third when he gets up there? He'll have to get out of the street, walk the cycle over the sidewalk, and then go uptown on Third to keep moving. If the light's green, on the other hand, he can either go right, onto Third, or straight crosstown to Lexington. Then where will he leave his trusty steed, ditch the jacket, and melt into the crowd without arousing notice? Is someone waiting for him somewhere with a car? If so, how long will he wait? Can the bicycle get him there in time? No, Master Itch, I don't expect to see him back for some time. Not only that—the sun's still high."

Considering all that, Evelyn consults his watch. He revises his estimate accordingly. "Call it seven at the earli—"

Stan the Man hisses for silence. He puts the radio on the white bedspread. The commercial fades, and the news begins. The Israelis claim two hundred Egyptian planes destroyed. Their tanks are rapidly moving across the Sinai, they say.

Evelyn smiles benignly. If they claim two hundred, they got four hundred, he says.

Nodding, Itch Cohen waves away Stan the Man.

"So then what's the play," he asks Evelyn, "when the kid comes back?"

"I think we should just sit here and let George—or, in his case, no doubt, Mohammed or Mahmoud—do it," Evelyn answers with a nonchalant shrug and a what-can-you-do? gesture of upturned palms.

Itch Cohen looks at him questioningly.

So, with an amused shrug, Evelyn continues.

"When he goes in, and we know he'll go in through the kitchen door, because he's a delivery boy, I'll just nip 'cross the street and wait for him in the kitchen on his way out. Since he'll be worried 'bout leaving, odds are he'll even have the door open for me."

"He's right, Itch," Stan the Man calls from the dresser. "I saw a couple of strips of black tape on his handlebars when he rode by."

"Yes," Evelyn goes on with the whimpering, goose-hunting sigh Dr. Fabian and Howsam find so disturbing, "and when he comes back downstairs, I'll be waiting for him behind the inside kitchen door. It won't take long, and since he's such a nice-looking boy, I'll hold up his head by his hair, just as if he had a proper topknot for the purpose, so he can say his prayers and Allah can snatch him right up to heaven, as He will all who die in battle. We'll see to him appropriately, too, as we will to Mrs. Angelakos. Remains deserve respect."

Itch Cohen has a less elevated view of the matter. For him, dispatch takes priority over disposal. "You got a piece?" he asks.

"I beg your pardon."

"A gun."

"Good heavens, no! Whatever for? This isn't the sort of thing you want in the *Daily News* as a warning to others. Here you want quickness, silence, and, when it's done, the look of a burglary that went sour with a drug-crazed intruder turning to his knife—all the things you're most likely not to get with a gun. Everyone has the notion they can outrun a bullet—" Evelyn smiles—"or that it'll miss. Distance gives them that illusion—makes them talky too. But put them belly to belly with a man holding steel in his hand, and, I assure you, they've absolutely no legs and nothing at all to say. They just want it over, so it won't hurt. They hold still."

"You use a shiv?" Stan the Man asks from the dresser.

"Nothing but," Evelyn answers, turning.

"What's it like?" Itch Cohen asks.

Smiling, Evelyn pulls up his right trouser leg.

He senses a chance to win two converts. "I'll show you my 'survival' steel," he says.

A saddle leather sheath, held by Velcro ties, rides above his ankle. From it he takes an item which, even in the Far North, men prize over whiskey and women: a Model 18 "Attack-Survival," made from Swedish stainless steel by Randall Knives, of Orlando, Florida. Guided by casual flicks of the wrist, the cutting edge of this knife effortlessly sliced through half-inch arctic willow saplings in James Bay the previous fall.

Itch Cohen, however, finds more of interest along the top of the seven-and-a-half-inch blade. "These work?" he asks, fingering a row of sawteeth.

"Oh, yes. Your helicopter boys in Vietnam cut escape hatches in one side of downed choppers with those teeth while Viet Cong shoot at them from the other," Evelyn says. "I also have it on good authority from Home Office"—he winks—"that one of those sawed a lock out of a steel fire door in the Castellana Hilton in Madrid not six weeks ago, and saved a chap's life."

With time before Mimouin returns, but still watching Forty-ninth Street, he leans over to particularize. A few blades are as good, he says, but what makes this weapon unique is its tubular stainless-steel handle which doesn't show now. Beneath the black Neoprene butt cap is a watertight brass screw-in plug. With what it protects, he believes, he can walk away from any plane crash in the Canadian North that doesn't kill him.

Survival has similar needs everywhere, he remarks. So the contents of the haft of this knife vary in but one detail from those that American boys rely on to get them out of the jungles of Southeast Asia. Instead of bare fishhooks, he packs six Tri-Color bucktails in various sizes. His three dozen pills are the same: a dozen for purifying water; a dozen codeine for killing pain; a dozen Dexedrine for quick energy; and then waterproof matches, of course. Monofilament and piano wire wrapped on the handle provide line for fishing and animal snares, he goes on. The black and brown rawhide bootlaces wrapped over them, in turn, can serve as tourniquets when unraveled.

Itch Cohen hefts the knife respectfully. He takes a few passes with it, shakes his head. "Stashke," he calls, "you wanna feel somethin'? It's like it's part of your hand."

Holding the knife as if it were a snake, he lofts it handle first over the bed, where it can't be hurt, and watches Stan the Man make the catch.

"And that's just for survivin'?" he asks Evelyn.

Evelyn nods, amused at Cohen's expression. Would he like to see "swinging" steel? he asks.

Cohen nods back.

Reaching over to the bed, Evelyn takes a six-inch-long brown object out of his left inside pocket. At first glance it resembles a harmonica with wooden rather than chrome-plated top and bottom panels. No blade shows. A rawhide thong dangles from one end.

He places it in Itch Cohen's hand. Then his face becomes more animated. "Loop the thong over your wrist," he tells Cohen.

Cohen does. Then he slides his fingers into the grips carved along the bottom of the brown wood sides.

"Comfy?" Evelyn asks. Getting a nod, he continues giving instruction.

"Now slide your thumb over the stainless-steel spine until you feel a little bump. That's a button set at six pounds' trigger pressure, so be careful. Keep the front of it pointed away from you. You're on it? Good. Now just let your thumb assume its normal grip."

A five-and-a-half-inch stainless-steel blade, about two inches wide and sharpened its full length along both edges, flicks out. It seats itself with a satisfying *ker-chunk,* like the sound of a door closing in a good car.

Arms crossed over his chest, Evelyn beams. "And what do you say to that, Master Itch?" he asks.

Cohen shakes his head. Testing the edge, he shaves skin off of his thumb. " ' . . . no legs, an' nothing at all to say,' " he muses, repeating Evelyn's earlier words.

Evelyn's smile widens. Craning farther to his left, he checks Forty-ninth Street again to the corner and then turns to Cohen with the covetous, greedy expression of a stamp collector showing off something rare.

"It's what aficionados call a 'funny folder,' " he explains, "although technically it's a spring-loaded drop blade, illegal, I believe, everywhere in the world. A chap in Arizona makes the blades and works for me, and a gunsmith I use in California uses the checkering—the little bumps you feel in your palm. They're there to keep the handle from slipping if your hand starts to sweat, the same reason they're on shotgun stocks. You make them by cutting crisscross lines in the wood—in this case, coco bolo, twenty-four lines to the inch in each direction."

"And this?" Cohen asks, eying the thong.

"Oh, every real assault knife needs that," Evelyn assures him. "What's a chap to do if he comes in a bit high or low and gets hung up in bone? Without it, the steel'd fly right out of your hand, and then you've got someone with a broken collarbone or rib yelling blue, bloody murder. That wouldn't do, would it? In point of fact, it wouldn't do at all. As our good friend Howsam says, it'd wake the neighbors."

"You do that often?" Itch Cohen asks.

"What—like tonight? No, not often enough."

"No, get hung up in bone."

"I did at first, but not anymore. All beginners do. But, with thirty years in the business, one gets a touch."

"You would. How do you close it?"

The blade retracts with another *ker-chunk.* "Opposed springs," Evelyn says, smiling.

Itch Cohen glances at Stan the Man, then at Evelyn.

Nodding, Evelyn smiles indulgently.

"Stashke, look at something wicked," Cohen says.

Knife caught, Stan the Man puts it on the dresser. He wrinkles his brow in exaggerated discomfort.

"Gotta pee," he says. "Be right back. Honest to God," he asks, "you'd think rich people'd have a toilet on every floor, wouldn't you? No wonder their kids are all hung up, holdin' it in the middle of the night all their lives tryin' to get down the stairs in time."

A moment later, Evelyn suddenly looks behind him.

"Is he making a call?" he asks suspiciously. Eyebrows arched over chrome-plated frames like an indulgent, long-suffering husband, Itch Cohen looks at his watch, then nods.

"Probably," he says. "He got some information this mornin' in a diner where we eat breakfast on a trottin' race goin' off at Yonkers tonight. You watch when he gets back here. I told him no calls."

Cohen nods when they hear Stan the Man on the stairs.

"You just make a call?" he asks, still looking west out of the right-hand window.

"Yeah."

"You get down all right?"

"Yeah."

"That horse was Fast Eddie, after the guy in *The Hustler,* right?"

"Right."

"It comes in, you buy supper. I'm finin' you just like you was on the Yan-kees an' missed bed check."

"Okay."

"At '21'."

"'21'?"

"Yeah—about two C notes' worth by the time me an' the Controller get done roughin' you up."

And they all laugh.

0300 LOCAL TIME, JUNE 6, 1967

The Israeli motor torpedo boat cuts its power.

It coasts up under the starboard bridgewing.

Its skipper leaves his wheelhouse with a loud-hailer.

They will follow them in, he says, and stand off five miles from shore. They will find three Egyptian OSSA missile ships and three sub chasers inside. The OSSAs, Russia's most advanced marine rocket launchers, are believed to be in the outer basin.

Zavitsanos knows that place well. It lies just inside the eastern breakwater, on the port side going in.

*Dynamic* will make a perfect target passing it.

No one's found the sub chasers, the torpedo boat skipper says. But frogmen are in the harbor now. If he hears anything, the Israeli captain promises, he will flash Costa on the blinker, and to hell with security.

They also believe, he goes on, that loaded tankers are docked in the inner harbor. The Egyptians know the Israeli Air Force will not bomb the town for fear of hitting a ship and killing everyone in the city.

Costa strokes his earring. That's the most unsettling news of all.

Hitting one of those ships would be the same as bombing it, but with an important difference: *Dynamic* would be the bomb.

They don't know about the Canal yet, either, the skipper reports. But whether the Suez is open or closed, the Whaler will rendezvous as scheduled and take them to his ship. The submarine is busy elsewhere that night. Does he need anything?

No, Costa shouts down.

"*Mazel tov,*" the Israeli calls as his boat surges ahead, beginning the wide turn that will put it directly astern of *Dynamic.*

They lie twenty-four miles from Port Said.

Dawn will come at 0428

Entering the wheelhouse, Costa rings down to the engineroom to reduce speed. The engineers know that means they will be going in. Still, they regard the order as a reprieve. The cement jacket on the condenser pipe shows copper antenna wire all the way from ship's side to circulating pump by now, and the yellow paint dust is beginning to waft down with an orange tinge.

The vibration has reached the red lead.

Next it will start on the steel.

So they welcome any slowdown.

Back on the bridge, Costa strokes his earring.

He knows why the torpedo boat is there: to check on him.

Five miles out, it'll line up the harbor entrance and turn on its radar. Then, lying dead in the water, its skipper'll see if he lives up to the deal.

No more business with the Jews, he vows, at least Israelis. They're as bad as Zavitsanos said. They mean exactly what they say.

## 1902 EASTERN DAYLIGHT SAVING TIME, JUNE 5, 1967

Evelyn sighs. "He's back," he whispers. "He's at the corner."

"But does he mean it?" Itch Cohen asks.

"He'd have to do another circuit around the block if he didn't."

"Why not? Who saw him the first time?"

Tipping his head, Evelyn concedes the point. "Maybe so," he says. "I'd not go with this sun."

Mimouin, however, resolves the question for them. He means it.

Slowly pedaling sixty or seventy feet west on Forty-ninth Street from the corner, he stops at the curb a couple of houses short of Demi's. Lifting the bicycle, he pushes down the kickstand and reaches into the cardboard box in the basket over the small front wheel.

He removes a plastic-coated chain. Leaning over, he wraps the chain around the frame of the bike and one of the thick iron wickets set in cement at the base of a tree. From the right-hand pocket of his tan waiter's jacket he takes the new bicycle lock that Rashid bought earlier that afternoon. Tapping his right front pants pocket, he feels the key. Nodding, he slips the shiny new hasp through the chain links and closes the lock.

Then he pauses and looks across the street again.

His hands rest briefly on the brown cardboard box.

Evelyn nods. "Clever little fellow," he says. "He's regrouping, planning the next step. He's telling himself he'll have to walk past the kitchen first and try to get a peek at the dining room and into the office before he goes for the door. Wouldn't do to disturb supper, would it? An honor student, that chap, and you can just take it as a given that carton's bound for his left shoulder."

"He's a right-hander," Itch Cohen says. "You see which pocket the lock came from, how he pushed it shut?"

"Oh, yes, but see how he's studying the sun. He'll not settle for less than all the shade he can get on his face. Wise beyond his years, that boy. It's beginners who're always in a rush. They lack confidence, so they can't stand the suspense, but not this one."

Leaning over, Mimouin lifts the cardboard box. Putting it on his left shoulder, he starts off.

Opposite Demi's service entrance, he turns right.

Then he is behind the house, hidden from view.

"What'd you say?" Itch Cohen asks.

Half rising, Evelyn starts over. His comment on the situation is Revelation 13:10, a judgment every bit as harsh as anything found in Deuteronomy: " 'He that leadeth into captivity shall go into captivity: he that killeth with the sword must be killed with the sword. Here is the patience and the faith of the saints.' "

"Sit down," Itch Cohen says. "You're playin' way outa your league."

Behind them they hear Stan the Man open a drawer. By the time Evelyn turns, the knives, left on the dresser while they joked about who would buy supper, are flung into the hall past the bedroom door.

Knives gone, Stan the Man blocks the aisle at the foot of the bed past the dresser. He stands a good six to eight inches taller than Evelyn and probably weighs forty to fifty pounds more. The silenced .25-caliber automatic pistol in his right hand, almost a match for Mimouin's, seems more a black-and-silver extension of his forefinger than a gun. Beaming around his brilliant, gap-toothed smile, he shakes his head bashfully, like a boy caught in a prank.

"I'm Polack," he says as a basis for establishing Evelyn's odds on leaving the room, "an' even I'd be smart enough not to move. Do like Itch says. Sit down an' watch the play. You know us, but we don't know you or your guys. We know ours. Besides, I'm already on the hook for supper. Right? When we're done with this part, you'll take care of the woman same as before, so why get excited?"

Lending weight to his words, the gun never wavers from its target. Having no desire to hurt anyone but the people across the street, Stan the Man, for all his casualness, aims at Evelyn's feet. No one has ever died, to be sure, from being hit there, but a well-placed bullet there, while far less dramatic than shattering a kneecap, will stop a man just as quickly.

The implied ability of a marksman who deliberately tries for so difficult a shot, however, is the best argument for listening to whatever he has to say.

Shaking his head, Evelyn sits down. His face approaches his burgundy shirt in color.

Stan the Man nods appreciatively.

Itch Cohen, meanwhile, showing the executive ability Howsam noted when he took the deal to Ukiah, California, has not looked away from the street during the exchange. He has delegated the entire matter to his vice-president in charge of Eastern operations.

Still not looking away, he asks a question. "Where's Snuffy?"

"Mac said he'd be in the basement entrance next to the restaurant near the corner."

"Then he oughtta be along any second."

"Should be," Stan the Man concurs.

"Christ, here he is."

Still flushed, Evelyn looks down on the street. But his expression changes. Wonder replaces rage.

"Police?" he asks.

By then, the sun has inched far enough west to reach Itch Cohen's face. Light streams off his chrome-plated eyeglass frames and the outsized teeth in his upper plate. Smiling, he recalls a shark in not very good humor whose dentures are fitted with diamond-tipped cutting edges.

His words have a slashing bite to match. "Here," he tells Evelyn, "I'm Home Office."

Then he shakes his head, baffled.

"I don't get you," he says. "What are you, a kook, a crazy, a kickster, or what? Forget Montgomery, that *pisher!* Here we got the best lawyers money'll buy, an' you know what they say? That they never expected a deal like this from me an' Speed: that it's absolutely clean! Everythin' we've done's legal! Everythin' Howsam's done's legal! Everythin' the dwarf's done's legal! Even those Greeks, the shyster says, have a legal right to carry as much explosives as they want through the Suez Canal. So where's the crime? Where's the conspiracy? Where's the paper that ties it all together? Who knows from bearer shares in a Panamanian corporation? An' they're legal, too! What we do about taxes is our business. So what's provable? *Eppes,* that's what. Nothin! An' you— you want to run us right across the street into murder one, when we got cops who'll get a citation for doin' our job for us! That's brains? That's business?"

Itch Cohen's face assumes its diamond-bright smile. He moves his chair left to better view the finale.

He taps Evelyn on the thigh. "Nothin' personal," he says.

He smiles again as Evelyn pulls his leg away.

By then, the black-haired police sergeant who had breakfast in the rear booth of GI Giulio's has crossed Forty-ninth Street. At the far curb he nods a greeting to a couple leaving a house a few doors east of Demi's. A few words, probably about the lovely evening, pass.

The couple turn right, toward Second Avenue.

The sergeant, smiling, goes left.

His gun is holstered. There is no reason for it not to be. He is, as the log will show, checking a relatively minor call: the possibility of suspicious entry.

At Demi's, he casually turns off the sidewalk.

"Snuffy's goin' in," Itch Cohen reports.

Stan the Man clucks sympathetically. "Post time," he says.

Mimouin, meanwhile, marvels at his good fortune.

Using the compound wire cutters Rashid had given him, he snipped the bike lock at Sixty-seventh and First Avenue with one try. Then, a few blocks from the liquor store, he found the carton in front of a Gristede's supermarket.

Here, things also went as easily.

Seeing no one through the first-floor windows, he picked the lock, taped the catch, and set the carton on the maple chopping block. Creeping up the stairs, he now finds the floorthrough room empty.

Marvelous! he thinks. Then they will be on the third floor. Bedrooms are small, so they will be near each other.

*Phfft! Phfft!* Like a small boy playing cops and robbers, he snaps his right wrist forward twice as if firing the gun. That's all he will need, he thinks. Then he will go back to his room. Rashid and the *majoun* will be waiting there. He likes both.

Stepping out of the entrance hall, he looks right, scanning the Forty-ninth Street end of the room for the stairs. Finding none, he shrugs and turns, starting for the far end. He seems to be doing a lot of walking without reaching anything.

Finally he reaches the first of the long reading tables flanking the small fireplace. Bracing himself against its edge for a moment, he regards the covers of the magazines which Demi neatly arranges by title and month. He sees a couple he'll take with him.

Then he leaves for the green love seat before the arched window at the Fiftieth Street end of the room.

Reaching it, he again pauses, leaning against it, wondering if Rashid will indeed buy him the Chinese supper he has promised him at the Shanghai Gardens. Weighing his chances, he sees the spiral staircase.

*Wallahi!* By God! That'll be something to climb. He's always been afraid of heights.

Stepping back, canting his head, he looks up to see how to climb the staircase. It seems to reach to infinity, but ascending will be easy, he believes. He will need only to keep his left hand on the center pillar. The trick, he knows, will be to keep from looking down.

He sees he will be vulnerable when his head clears the hatch at the top. So, clicking the safety off the gun, he puts his right foot on the first step. Head erect, gaze fixed straight ahead, he starts the climb.

It seems endless. He stops parallel to the top molding of the paneling. How high is that? He tries to remember. Halfway? Perhaps. The arched ceiling makes height hard to judge.

Added to that, his left hand begins to sweat.

Eyes locked on the paneling along the right wall, he tries to take in a deep breath. But it comes in gasps and spurts, making his left hand tremble. Fearful now for the first time, he yearns to have this done.

He climbs faster.

Soon his eyes seem level with the ceiling.

He stealthily wipes his left hand on the hatch rim.

Two more steps, and he sees a wall of gorgeous wood.

Ducking his head back through the hatch, trying not to look down, he rechecks to see if the safety is off. It is, but sweat has made the grip slippery, too. He almost squeezes the smooth Italian walnut handle out of his palm. Holding the gun by its silencer, he wipes it thoroughly on the bottom of the waiter's tan jacket. Then, weapon in hand, he climbs the last steps.

*Wallahi!*

The woman is facing him not three feet away. But she has her eyes closed. Her arms are around the man's neck. His back is to Mimouin.

Are they doing it? In a tub?

He takes one small, cautious step toward them. Its purpose is more to lean forward than to get closer. With his arms extended, the gun lies no more than eighteen inches from the man's back.

He remembers his instructor's rule: "Back to front, same side."

In this case, then, the man's heart would lie on the same side as his own, under the left shoulder. The woman, however, facing him, would have her heart opposite her right shoulder.

Rising on his toes, he then points the gun down under Demi's left shoulder blade.

The woman, arms still around the man's neck, senses his presence.

She opens her eyes. Her jaw drops as if to speak.

He sees she is very beautiful.

Smiling, he shakes his head for her not to talk.

*Phfft!*

A .25-caliber slug is fatal in a vital organ, but it lacks knockdown power. That's its advantage in a situation like this. As the entry hole, about as big as a cigarette, appears under the shoulder blade, the man's body hardly shudders.

But the bullet, Mimouin sees, has done its job.

On impact, its copper jacket peeled back from the lead slug in four ragged but equal curls, allowing the soft hollow point to mushroom as it passed through the man. By then, the nose had expanded to about twice its size and, taking along the copper petals sprouting from its base, had increased its cutting area about six times.

All that Mimouin knows. It shows in the woman's face. By then she is dying, too. She has grown pale, signifying a traumatic loss of blood.

He probably shot her spleen away, he thinks.

As she watches, he moves the gun right.

*Phfft!*

Entry occurs under the man's right shoulder blade.

The woman seems to rise as the bullet reaches her heart.

Then four Ritz crackers thinly filmed with *majoun*, besides the excitement and fear of the situation, bring Mimouin the most moving visual experience of his life.

With her heart stopped, the woman's arms leave the neck of the man in a wide, graceful, backward arc. Her body arches with them. It's as if she were a swimmer doing a back surface dive. But this is slow, almost languid, with no exertion or rush. The only thing he has ever seen like this is a film from Japan which he saw in a course the semester before. It had slow-motion and freeze-frame sequences just like the one he watches now. But the actresses were not as beautiful as this woman.

Nor did they seem, even with special effects, to ride in the air a fraction of the time this one did. Finally, her arc across the tub completed, she enters the water as if wrapping herself in silk. There are no waves, no splashes. Her head, he sees, comes to rest on a seat on the opposite side of the tub. Her chin is in the water, her eyes and mouth are open, as if she is amused at the appearance of the man. She shows no pain.

Her companion, relieved of her weight, is face down across from her. His arms float in the water, in a wide broken circle, as if he still held her. A billowing pink cloud trails off under his chest. The entry points under his shoulder blades do not bleed. The skin around the voids has been burned and singed a bluish black from muzzle blast and bullet heat.

Briefly, Mimouin considers pulling his face out of the tub by his hair. He wonders what a man who could have that woman would look like. But he starts shaking from the reaction. So, instead of satisfying curiosity, he wipes his face and hands dry on a huge Turkish towel.

Then, steeling himself and vowing not to look down, he mounts the top step of the spiral staircase, places his left hand on the pillar, and starts descending, gun in right hand. He will keep it there, he thinks, until he reaches the kitchen. He has spent perhaps thirty seconds at the hot tub.

The black-haired police sergeant, meanwhile, has been in the house that long, as well. He too had to see if the first floor was occupied before entering. That done, he then stepped into the kitchen.

Finding the brown cardboard carton on the chopping block, he unholstered his police .38 and crept up the stairs to the floorthrough room exactly as Mimouin did. Now, finding no one there, he smiles.

His quarry is on the top floor, he knows.

That means he can ambush him. Where? Obviously, wherever he has to come down. Looking around, he spots the spiral staircase. Gun in hand, he sprints to it.

Then Mimouin's feet appear.

Jesus, what a boat race! the sergeant gloats.

Three steps and a full revolution around the center pillar later, the gun is visible in Mimouin's right hand.

Holding his .38 before him in both hands as if it were a chalice, the sergeant waits for Mimouin to do the next three steps. Just starting down the staircase, his head and shoulders are still above the hatch.

Below, to his left, the sergeant watches. When he sees the bottom of the waiter's jacket, he knows it's the kid he just saw ride by on Forty-ninth Street.

The boy's still too high, though. He wants to get him in the chest, the heart, if possible.

He lets him take another step.

Below, he moves to his right to keep his body in line.

Mimouin pauses, taking a last look at the bathroom.

Then he reaches down with his right foot.

The sergeant sees the top buttom on his jacket. He sights slightly to the right and below it, then fires.

For Mimouin, feeling the *majoun* more as his fear ebbs, it's a sequel to the experience he so enjoyed with the beautiful woman upstairs. This, however, is even richer, more fulfilling, because it's happening to him.

He feels a warm desert sun enter his chest. It's as if he contains it, rather than being enveloped by it. With that there's a marvelous floating sensation, but in air. He knows his head has brushed something, but he's confident his passage is as serene and smooth as the one he saw upstairs.

In reality, it's anything but. Dying, he strikes the edge of a step, unnaturally turning his head. Then he tumbles seventeen feet to land on his right shoulder. His neck breaks on arrival, with a pistollike report.

The sergeant goes upstairs to run the body count. He's been in the house now about ninety seconds. Passing through the bathroom, he goes to Demi's bedroom. There he pulls the cords to open the blinds and then turns on the lights three times.

Across the street, Itch Cohen leans back in his chair and nods in satisfaction. "All gone," he says. "Three."

"And what happens now?" Evelyn asks.

"Now we wait till dark. In the meantime, you call your guys an' tell 'em to bring her car around any time after nine. Their first time around the block, they stop in front of the house an' blow the horn once. The second time, they pull right up—" Itch Cohen smiles—"into that spot by the apartment buildin' where the Con Ed horses are in the street. Our guys put 'em out. They'll take 'em in. There," he says, "now, ain't this better? You wanna fight, get yourself a ten-rounder at the Garden. They'll pay you for it."

## 0428 LOCAL TIME, JUNE 6, 1967

False dawn silhouettes the Port Said breakwater.

*Dynamic* lies dead in the water.

Costa and Zavitsanos stand on the flying bridge.

"You set?" Costa asks.

"Of course I'm set," Zavitsanos answers. "It's not like we haven't practiced this bloody drill for two weeks."

Nodding, Costa puts on the aircraft pilot's headset and microphone and starts uncoiling the wire leading from the deck plate Arkie installed in Ancona. The Israeli night glasses already dangle over his chest.

"Okay," he says. "We'll start when you get up to the bow and make sure we can talk to each other."

With that, he starts climbing the radar mast.

"I'm having Alexander and George lay out fire hoses on the foredeck," Zavitsanos shouts after him.

"What for?"

"For those two tankers in the harbor, that's what for."

"Pessimist!"

At 0434, phones checked, they start.

Zavitsanos, at the bow lookout's telephone, rings the engineroom. He asks for thirty-five turns. Arkie is pleased to oblige, as the lower speed will lessen strain on the condenser jacket. They will do six and a half knots. Maximum allowable speed through Port Said and the Suez is seven and a half.

But in a mile or two, at some point behind the west breakwater which Zavitsanos is best able to judge, he will put the engine on STOP and coast the remaining three and a half to four miles. His aim is to have *Dynamic* at a dead stop at the red and green lights marking the Canal entrance.

Costa, on the radar mast, will then be able to see to the horizon. If he finds no ships scuttled to block the waterway, they will proceed seven kilometers south, halfway to the Ra's al-'Ushsh signal station, and have Arkie set off the gelignite. Schotten and Howsam will pick everyone up in the Whalers while the timer runs down, and sprint back through Port Said to the Israeli torpedo boat.

The Egyptians have gear capable of lifting 45-ton vessels only in Alexandria. *Dynamic,* at 16,000 tons, would be where she sank a long time. More months would then be needed for dredging and repair work on the banks.

That, at least, is the plan.

No one on *Dynamic,* however, believes it will happen.

So they have rehearsed an even wilder caper.

When they find the Canal blocked, they intend to back *Dynamic* all the way out of Port Said and then sail her to Eleusis Bay. Negotiating a dogleg and then three miles of a quarter-mile-wide harbor in reverse without tugs is more difficult and more likely to result in scratched paint than parking a forty-foot trailer truck in a crowded loading dock without brakes or mirrors. Also, the Egyptians may be shooting at them. Still, the opportunity is seen as worth the risk.

Now, however, with morning mist on the water and an overcast sky above, a darker band of color looms before Zavitsanos about two miles forward on the starboard bow. Western breakwater coming up, he thinks.

Leaning over the bow bulwark, he peers down at the tea-colored ribbon of water lazily streaming off the starboard plates. She seems a little fast.

He rings the engineroom. He and Arkie spent most of their time in Ancona rewiring phones so that bow, engineroom, wheelhouse, and radar mast can talk to one another. Those were hours well spent, he reflects.

Could he have twenty-five turns? he asks Arkie.

Sure. Where are they?

Lining up, Zavitsanos says. They'll be inside in minutes.

Speaking of lining up, he looks astern, then dials the wheelhouse.

"Y-yes?" young Nico, at the wheel, answers.

Was he thinking of girls again? Zavitsanos asks.

What?

The bow has a very funny wiggle in it, Zavitsanos tells the boy. If he could find a woman who moved that way, he'd marry her.

No answer comes from the wheelhouse.

Nerves, Zavitsanos thinks.

*Chrysomu,* he laughs, calling Nico his golden one, just steer 217 and relax. Didn't he know what this was? Insurance! Nothing more. They were a "just in case," an idea of crazy bankers. So they weren't going to blow up *Dynamic,* because Nasser had already done what he was supposed to. They just had to see it. No one would shoot at them, either, not with a white light above two reds saying they carried explosives.

But how would they get out? Nico asks.

Just the way they're going in, Zavitsanos laughs. With all due deliberation! Isn't that the way he'll go in with all those Swedish girls who'll be back in Hydra next month when they get home?

Nico laughs.

Nothing like a little man-to-man, Zavitsanos thinks.

The bow steadies immediately.

At 0441, Costa calls. It's dead! he complains. Nothing's moving ashore. Those crazy Jews and bankers are wasting a fortune in fuel.

At 0444, the bow slides past the western breakwater.

Zavitsanos calls for half a spoke of left rudder.

That puts them about a hundred yards off the riprap.

Awakening gulls cry on the stone breakwater.

Buoy 3, a high black metal cage, looms on the port bow. Its green light is out. In the damp mist it smells of ammonia from bird droppings.

Zavitsanos leans over the starboard bow again.

The bow wave is smaller. Good. They're going slower.

The sky's lighter in the east, too.

At 0454, they pass Buoy 2, another darkened green flasher.

At 0456, dawn comes.

The sun's top few degrees of arc lie just above the eastern horizon, a weak, wan gray. The darkness ahead becomes that color, too.

Then a tall red metal tower materializes to port. Zavitsanos knows it. It's the light on the tip of the eastern breakwater. Very good, he thinks. They're right on time.

Costa calls again. He sounds furious.

Nothing! he protests. Nothing ashore and nothing on the water. Then he asks the big question: When will Zavitsanos stop her?

Past the lighthouse, Zavitsanos answers.

Then, hanging up, he takes an old piece of canvas lying at the foot of the bulwark to wipe the mist off the freshly painted white capstrip.

Looking over the side, he nods. He has the bow wave he wants, he sees: six knots.

At 0501, they enter the harbor proper.

Immediately past the flashing red light on the jetty protruding from the eastern breakwater on their port side, they pass the outer basin.

The OSSA missile frigates lie there. All look hit. The bridge is missing from one. Another has all its rocket-launching tubes pointing up at unlikely angles. The third has a crumpled foredeck. All look deserted.

On the starboard hand, they pass the service basin, where tugs, pilot boats and the workhorses of the port are berthed. Zavitsanos smiles at the lack of activity. That tells him all he needs to know. The rest, as he has said all along, will be a piece of cake.

The Canal is closed. Nasser did it during the night.

The lighthouse lies a half mile up to starboard. There's no one home there either, Zavitsanos sees. He senses having seen all this before. He did, he remembers, in the movie *On the Beach*. This is the same as when the American submarine visits San Francisco after a nuclear attack to find everything standing but all the people dead.

The signal station at the base of the 184-foot lighthouse is deserted, too.

Port Said, like all North African cities, now begins to look ivory, white, yellow, and tan in the morning light. Abreast the lighthouse, after enjoying the view for a moment, Zavitsanos returns to work.

He leans over the bow again.

Just a little more under power, he thinks.

There seems to be a contrary current. They may be doing six knots through the water, but they're not passing anything ashore at that speed.

A quarter of a mile later, as they approach the quilted yellow stone customhouse with its high date palms, Zavitsanos calls Arkie and asks for "Stop."

Then he calls Costa to tell him.

Costa, ten stories above the water on the base for the fictitious radar unit, belongs to the Itch Cohen school of management. "Okay," he says.

Then, hanging up, he puts the night-vision glasses back to his eyes and looks southwest in the direction of the Canal entrance.

Almost at once, however, he calls Zavitsanos back.

He always thought passenger ships, other than those transiting the Canal, called at Alexandria, he says. Are there liners that berth here?

Searching memory, Zavitsanos glances right. The mosque-like yellow dome and offices that the Suez Canal Company has built to worship itself slip by.

Then he suddenly remembers. Yes, he says. They keep pilgrim ships here.

Pilgrims?

Mecca.

How old are they?

Very old. Why?

Costa says he thinks he sees stacks.

How many?

Two.

Those old brothels'd have three or four apiece.

He'll look some more, Costa says, hanging up.

Past the Canal Company dome, the channel narrows. The Egyptians have built two islands off the port shore at the coaling basin to berth ships. The tankers the Israeli torpedo boat skipper mentioned lie here, further constricting the way to the Canal entrance. The passage is about a quarter of a mile wide, certainly, no wider than two average city blocks.

The ship at the northern island is Rumanian. A pigsty, Zavitsanos thinks, as a cook in an apron as dingy as the rusty gray hull paint throws a basin of equally dirty-looking water over its side.

Before it, at the southern island, a black-hulled Russian tanker. Its plates need shotblasting, and a man could disappear in its cracked welds. Zavitsanos also knows it will have a foul odor. Nevertheless, he orders three more spokes of left rudder, which will take them to within a hundred feet of the Russian when they get that far south.

He needs all the room he can get on that side of the channel. Past the Russian, the starboard shore jogs abruptly to the left. Then, just as acutely, it becomes straight again and leads to the channel entrance. So, with no power, he must make consecutive 90-degree turns. Then, three eighths of a mile later, if he is the shiphandler he believes himself to be, *Dynamic* will come to a graceful stop at the Canal entrance.

How Costa will back out of that is another matter. But he owns the biggest piece of the ship, so he gets the problem.

The bow passes the Russian's stern. They are then doing about two and a half knots, so it takes forever to put him astern.

They aim directly at the light south of the island.

Zavitsanos rings Nico in the wheelhouse.

He tells him to steer with one hand and to hold the phone in the other. When they come abreast of the light, Zavitsanos will want an immediate hard left on the wheel. And he means *immediate* and *hard*. After that, Zavitsanos goes on, Nico should pick up the phone again, because the next command will be for an equally immediate and hard turn to the right.

Holding the phone, Zavitsanos then looks astern. The light on the island is halfway to the midships house. Ten seconds later, it's three quarters of the way. Then Zavitsanos counts to five.

Now! he shouts into the phone. *Dynamic* swings hard left.

Another concrete island, built to serve as a partial breakwater to a basin for transient ships, lies about two hundred yards ahead.

He looks over his right shoulder at the tower for the flashing green light on the point of the starboard shore, where it juts out so abruptly.

Not far enough, he thinks. The island now lies about seventy-five yards away. Looking right again, he sees the Canal entrance. He needs still more room.

Fifty yards from the island, he nods.

About right, he thinks. Now! he shouts into the phone.

*Dynamic* swings hard right.

The bow phone rings. He sees four smokestacks in there now, Costa says. All are in water. Two pilgrim ships scuttled about halfway down to Ra's al-'Ushsh—call it six miles off. He's coming down to get *Dynamic* out of there.

When we stop, you've got her, Zavitsanos answers.

The elephant ballet continues, meanwhile, at a speed rapidly diminishing from one and a half knots. Towers of the red and green occulting lights marking the entrance to the Canal are clearly visible. The day beacon to the right of the green light is also well defined. It marks a sandbar. Egyptians have been dredging since the year Zavitsanos started to shave.

Speed slows further.

Even on the bow, the sound of the water streaming off the hull is reduced to a soft whisper. That diminishes further. Eventually, it dies altogether.

Alexander and George join him on the forecastle.

Tremendous! Alexander shouts when they stop dead.

They are exactly centered in the Canal entrance. The lights lie about fifty feet in front of them.

Not too shabby, Zavitsanos concedes. "Now get back to the fire hoses, you oafs!" he orders.

Costa has a more difficult problem. But, *Dynamic* now being worth $2 million, he is ready to meet any challenge. Torque, the twisting force, and cavitation, the tendency of the propeller to create a hole in the water around itself, are both more pronounced going astern.

Still, he knows what to do.

Ringing Arkie, he says he wants forty-five turns when he signals ASTERN on the telegraph. They will give him seven knots, more than Zavitsanos needed coming in, but speed gives the rudder bite. That dampens the ship's desire to go the way its propeller turns.

Bouncing on the balls of his feet to feel the deck through his huaraches, he winks at Nico, pats him on the cheek, and moves the engineroom telegraph to

ASTERN. Then, asking for one-quarter standard right rudder, Costa steps out on the port bridgewing.

His aim is to back out as straight as Zavitsanos came in, but he knows he will never do that with the rudder amidships. Torque will take over, and since the prop is turning left, the stern will go that way, too. So right rudder compensates for that.

*Dynamic* still swings a little left. But that's okay on this leg. He will leave differently. Rather than making two right-angle turns, he will make one of forty-five degrees. With it he intends to split the distance between the point on the western side of the harbor and the light off the southern island in front of the coaling basin. He will hold that course until he lines up the harbor mouth. Then another forty-five-degree turn should put him right in the main channel.

So, going left here lets him pass a little farther off the point on the west shore, no bad thing. After two minutes, though, *Dynamic* is farther left than he thought she would be. She also seems to be going faster, probably from pumping bilges. Bouncing on the balls of his feet, he confirms that Arkie is indeed giving forty-five turns. Entering the wheelhouse, he rings down STOP on the telegraph, then calls Arkie and asks for twenty-five turns the next time.

Back on the bridge, he hears a tremendous whining sound. Assuming it's an aircraft, he ducks and then scans as much of the sky as he can. He sees nothing. Then, realizing what the noise might be, he leans over the side, looking forward at the Canal entrance.

He smiles.

The Whaler, with Schotten and Howsam, is coming out of the Canal entrance faster than he thought any boat could go. Hitting them in that, he thinks, would be as likely as shooting bees with a rifle. He'll have to let Arkie know he saw it.

Making a wide sweeping turn off the port side of *Dynamic,* Schotten throttles back. Howsam, hanging on to the stern liferail, points vigorously out to sea and opens and closes his right fist twice.

Costa nods down to them, then waves. They'll meet ten miles offshore.

Returning his wave, they head upchannel.

Closing the distance on the concrete island off the transient basin to fifty yards, he tells Nico to give him full standard right rudder. Then, stepping inside, he rings down ASTERN on the telegraph.

Twenty seconds later, looking astern, he's pointed exactly as he wishes.

The concrete island slips by on the port side. The light on the point is off the starboard quarter. Taking a crude back bearing with his thumb, he sees he's about midway between them. Beautiful!

This was to be the hard part.

Stepping inside, he rings down STOP again. Then, watching the western shore come up, he looks right. The entire main channel out to sea is open to him. Only two miles to go. Ten minutes will do it.

A little past midchannel, he steps inside for his last commands. Ringing down ASTERN, he tells Nico to please give him half standard left rudder.

He knows he's in trouble immediately.

When *Dynamic* is going astern with left rudder, her bow should swing right. It does, but far past what is expected with half rudder.

The shiphandling he and Zavitsanos have done this morning needs, above all else, the ability to keep the vessel moving throughout a series of connected actions. While the engine is on STOP, the ship is still making way forward or astern when the next move begins. This motion lets the rudder work the moment the wheel turns. Few shipmasters have this touch, which is why there are so many low-speed harbor accidents. Stopped, there is no way to steer a ship. In effect, this has just happened to *Dynamic*.

She met a current stronger than the way she carried. So now the bow swings farther right. Broadside to the channel, she is crabbing.

Hard left! Costa shouts to Nico.

Maybe more rudder will give her bite.

Nothing. *Dynamic*'s like a log.

He gets Arkie on the phone.

He tells him he wants Full Ahead, and he means *full*, regardless of what it shakes loose in the engineroom.

Hold her hard over! he tells Nico.

The deck bounces beneath his huaraches.

Anything happening? he wonders. Maybe. They'll have to wait. But not too long. The Russian lies a block and a half away.

## 2236 EASTERN DAYLIGHT SAVING TIME

Mac, the blond detective who had breakfasted at GI Giulio's that morning, arrived on the block within five minutes after Demi's bedroom lights flashed on and off. He carried a large brown grocery bag.

The bag had their supper, sandwiches, he said a few minutes later. After talking to Snuffy on the phone, he knew they'd be in for a long night.

What was wrong? Stan the Man asked.

This, Mac said, taking Mimouin's gun from the bag. They all nodded. Burglars rarely used silencers. That was FBI, CIA stuff, Mac commented.

But he knew a guy on Avenue B who had .25-caliber pieces. He'd swap or buy one—either way, that'd kill an hour. Then, on the way uptown, he'd see a guy in the coroner's office who owed him a favor. Fixing the time of death would square him. After that, he had to cover for Snuffy. So he thought ten-thirty'd be a good time to get the woman out.

You takin' her? he asked Evelyn.

His associates would.

She would have an automobile accident.

Yes, at Exit 36 on the Long Island Expressway?

Should work with the right kind of fire, Mac said. There'd be no trace. Both slugs went right through her.

Both? Evelyn asks.

Oh, yeah. That kid had been to school. And his guys should come a half hour early, Mac added. They'd have to dress her.

By then, the street and the sidewalk were all but deserted. Hard workers live in fashionable neighborhoods.

So now Fiona leaves Demi's for the last time.

A tall blond man carries her in his arms.

She looks like a child who has dozed off while her parents were visiting friends. Her face glows briefly under a street light. It seems, finally, content. Her mouth is soft and loving, as if she has now decided to give her essential goodness a chance. Or is that only her reaction to death?

*Poor, lovely child,* muses Evelyn, who saw her several times alive, and never lovelier than she is now. *She could have been such a great joy. One'd only to know how scared she was.*

Hard-bitten men, they glance after her protectively.

They sigh not for what might have been, but for what will be.

Then she passes from the light.

## 0538 LOCAL TIME, JUNE 6, 1967

Costa has straightened out *Dynamic.*

They are backing parallel to the Russian tanker. But they were set down perilously close to her. Their worry now is the bow. Will it clear?

On the port bridgewing, Costa strokes his earring.

Zavitsanos looks down from the flying bridge.

Suddenly, he stomps his foot on the wheelhouse roof. From there he can see light between the ships' bows.

"We're out!" Nico shouts from behind the wheel.

Coming inside, Costa kisses his cheek.

Then he calls Arkie. First, he wants his thirty-five back. Then, in fifteen minutes he wants to see him on the main deck.

They are past the eastern breakwater in twelve.

In fifteen, Alexander is running the ship.

Costa is on the main deck awaiting Arkie. He greets him with a bow and a wave of grand disdain in the direction of Port Said, as if it were nothing.

Arkie shakes his head.

He's had only one hour's sleep in two days. Dried blood browns his hands.

Yellow paint makes it impossible to see where jockey shorts and steaming shoes end and he begins. But in twenty minutes he'll be in the Whaler. In thirty, he'll be aboard an Israeli torpedo boat on the first leg of the trip home. Looking forward as they back out, he sees the domes and minarets of Port Said peacefully sprawled behind its yellow-gold beach.

Where's the war? he asks.

# A Financial Postscript

Shipping is an extremely well-documented industry, so it's relatively easy to develop an accurate estimate of the Lions' profits.

A company known as Lianides Bulk Transport appears in several shippng registers as having operated tankers during the years 1967–73.

The English ship officers' guide, *Flags & Funnels,* similarly shows a white lion rampant in a field of red in copies printed during the years 1968–73.

This implies that, through either luck or shrewdness, the Lions sold their ships in 1973, when tanker prices were at an all-time high.

Moreover, nothing can be found to suggest that they bought or built more ships during this period. Indeed, this would seem to argue against their personalities. More tonnage and success would have called attention to themselves and started people asking questions.

So, we assume they ran 1,750,000 tons of ships (five 100,000-tonners and five 250,000-tonners) in the spot-charter market from June 1967 to mid-1973. Factoring charter prices over that period and assuming normal operating costs, they made close to $4 billion net. The money went to Panama, so it seems unlikely that taxes were ever paid.

Beyond that, a severe shortage of tankers, far exceeding shipyard building capacity, drove the price of secondhand vessels up to $1,000 a ton by 1973. So, selling their fleet then, they would have received $1,750,000,000.

In all, their $100 million investment brought them nearly $6 billion in profit.

Loren Wade being such a master of subterfuge, there is no way of calculating what PANARTEX made from its tanker operations during this period. It is known, however, that he sold the building contracts he bought for that purpose within ten days after the end of the Six-Day War for $490 million.

Experts guess that gross tanker profits for PANARTEX during the period from June 1967 to the 1973 Arab oil embargo may have nudged $13 billion.

# Afterword

ARCHIMEDES ANGELAKOS, remarried, lives in Oyster Bay, New York, in the modern house he has always wanted, designed by himself and mainly built by him and his two brothers. The land he lives on belonged to his neighbor, the man who is also his best friend and banker. As Loren Wade speculated in 1966, he does indeed now worry about his son's Little League team and his daughter's progress in ballet class. His firm, Marine Cargo Systems, now occupies a block-square building in Long Island City and is acknowledged to be the leader insofar as the innovation of tanker safety devices is concerned. His design practice flourishes apace.

ZAVITSANOS ANGELAKOS, from an office in Mayfair, operates a family-owned fleet of 1.2 million tons. He married into an old London Greek shipping family as well, so, in time, he will undoubtedly be one of the most influential men in that city's marine affairs. He is regarded as a bit of a dandy. While no one questions his intelligence, his obsession with maintaining highest engineering standards aboard his ships, regardless of expense, is also regarded as somewhat of a quirk.

ISAAC (ITCH) COHEN, widowed in 1971, spends spring and fall with his daughter in Miami, summer in Ukiah, California, with his partner, Spedante (Speed) Immediato, and winter in New York alone. He can be seen in Madison Square Garden at almost every Knicks and Rangers home game, often accompanied by Stan the Man. Neither seems to have aged. Twice a year they go to Zurich, where Cohen meets with an American and a local banker, to whom he and Immediato now entrust all their financial affairs.

THE DIPLOMATIST, still active behind the scenes of international oil, can occasionally be seen on Seventy-fourth Street. He is thought to be a moderating influence on his fellow Arabs, and Israeli officials in New York on other business are known to visit his residence at odd hours, perhaps for a friendly chat over a cup of mint tea and to watch a little of Johnny Carson.

W. HUBER GARRISON has not had a sick day since recovering from his near-fatal intestinal disorder on June 5, 1967. Now in his seventies, he remains chairman of the board of PANARTEX. Healthy and vigorous, he is hunting and fishing again and spends a lot of time visiting grandchildren with his wife after relinquishing his chief executive officer's duties. He rarely alludes to the Six-Day War.

PRENTISS HOWSAM still operates a very private bank at 118 Battery Place, worships his wife, Francine, and vents his short-fused temper on his two sons, who, he says in private, will be better bankers than either he or his father-in-law, Ike Battle. The funds he and the other members of his informal *sindicado*, Eusebio Pérez and Gerhard Stumpf, control is the largest pool of capital in Central or South America—larger than any individual's, larger than any big New York bank could commit to the area, larger than several governments'. And, as with Ike Battle, the rangy, soft-spoken man who conceived it, that cash remains largely unknown. Howsam, however, told Stumpf, who mentioned it to a friend, that they paid too high a price for this money. He regretted ever having gone into the position that earned it.

DIMITRIOS (TAKI) KERIOSOTIS lives very quietly most of the year with his wife and his Filipino live-in couple, Nando and Euralia, on the eastern end of Long Island. His diffident manner notwithstanding, he is the undisputed head of Clan Keriosotis, with 3.8 million tons of ships under his control. Archimedes Angelakos and his wife frequently anchor their sailboat off his house, and their children spend at least two weeks of every summer with their Aunt Honey and Uncle Taki.

TAKEO KONO, after building a half-billion tons of ships, was transferred to Tokyo, where he became second-in-command of the Singing Willow *zaibatsu*. He also plays on Japan's national contract-bridge team. Married to the beautiful former receptionist at Hasegawa Shipyards, he has three young sons; as might be expected, they are precociously bright.

COSTA LIANIDES died June 6, 1977, ten years to the day after he triumphantly backed *Dynamic Papachristou* around Port Said's western breakwater. He marked the anniversary of that occasion, as he did every year, with supper and wine at a three-star French restaurant. Driving home, he went off the Haute Corniche above Nice at 120 mph in his Mercedes. With him was his French movie starlet of that summer. He probably would have shed no tears for himself. He had managed to live very "Californialy" in the preceding ten years.

RASHID SULAMEIN AMAL, ordered home on June 9, 1967, died there two days later under circumstances never explained.

ERIC SCHOTTEN lives in his family mansion in Feusisberg with his twins, Christan and Magda, and his younger son, Eric. His wife, an auburn-haired Israeli, is considered the handsomest woman ever to grace Zurich's financial community and certainly the brightest. She left Schotten in 1972. She was last seen in Zurich in 1976, when she came home to have Christmas with her children. Her nurse—Schotten's wife now lives in a London home specializing in the treatment of melancholia—accompanied her. Her conscience, in the end, could not defend her decision of June 5, 1967. She is the price the Lions paid for their position.

COUNTESS TANYA TATAROVICH retired as planned and now lives in Switzerland near the live-cell-therapy clinic of the late Dr. Niehaus. She will enjoy many more than ten thousand Golden Days. At fifty-five, she looks and acts thirty-five and is often pictured at exclusive resorts in the pages of international fashion magazines.

EVELYN WADDELL, thirty pounds heavier and as many millions richer, is still the man to see in Montreal for making certain kinds of contracts.

LOREN WADE, president of PANARTEX, refused to concede in a recent *New York Times* interview that the international oil industry is now controlled by "Eight Sisters." His company, at best, as he put it, might be a "kissin' cousin," but from the poor side of the family, at that. While a little too colorful to represent them in Washington hearings, he increasingly influences other companies, answering phone calls from their presidents, who find him at least as bright as Hubie Garrison and much tougher in all respects.

\* \* \* \* \*

*Dynamic Papachristou,* after limping back to Ancona, got a new propeller and an extensive overhaul. As the charter rate for shipping oil continued to rise, she was stretched with a ninety-foot hull section, designed by Archimedes Angelakos, inserted into her forebody. Now, in the best condition of her career, when almost all others of her type have disappeared under the wrecker's torch, she is on five-year charter shuttling from Tripoli, Libya, to Piraeus, Greece, a run of mainly sunny skies and calm seas—a fulfilling and rewarding old age for a lady of dubious past. One of about fifty still active T-2s, she is also, fittingly, now named *Angelakos Indomitable,* for Hydra's only shipowning family.

# PRICE ECONOMICS

By

ROBERT B. PETTENGILL
DIRECTOR, TEACHING INSTITUTE OF ECONOMICS
UNIVERSITY OF SOUTHERN CALIFORNIA

THE RONAL D PRESS COMPANY · NEW YORK

# PREFACE

In this college textbook in economics, attention is centered upon individual prices and quantities of goods and of services. Prices and quantities are considered both as causes and as effects of economic behavior. Because of this approach, the treatment of prices is broader and more thorough than that of books where price theory is only a subordinate theme.

The book deals with the fundamental mechanism of a free-enterprise system. It explains how prices affect demand and supply as well as how demand and supply affect prices. The author has tried to help the reader to understand that in economics there are always many causes and many effects, even though they must be studied one at a time. Each cause is the effect of some other cause, and each effect becomes a cause at the next step. Some economists would pursue the chain of causation further in certain directions than the author has done. Others would not go so far. The choice is a matter of personal preference, and instructors may add or subtract as they desire.

The author of a text in a well-worked field can make little claim to anything more than some originality of treatment. However, the present writer has tried to contribute something by his merger of the institutional and theoretical approaches to economics. Theories are developed from real life situations selected as typical, rather than from models which often give the impression of being unrealistic. Illustrations usually precede the statements of general principles rather than follow them. Most of the recent developments in price theory are used in one chapter or another, but with no pretense of omniscience. The only portions in which the author's approach may seem particularly novel are Chapters 11 and 12 with their functional approach to competition and monopoly, Chapter 22 on factor surpluses, and some sections of the chapters on interest and profits.

The treatment is nonmathematical except in a few geometrical notes which are not indispensable to the argument. Diagrams are included because of their convenience as a form of economic shorthand. In most cases they are used to illustrate, not to expound the argument, and they may be omitted if desired. The chapter on indifference curves may also be skipped by those who feel that its geometry is not essential to price theory.

This text will probably be found most useful in the second or intermediate course in economic theory. However, it is designed to be adaptable for use at different levels, depending upon the preference of the instructor. Some will want to employ the book in advanced courses for a review of price theory. Others who believe that a study of individual prices should precede a study of the economy as a whole may choose to use this volume in the principles course. The author has tried to define clearly every necessary concept. Students need not previously have acquired a vocabulary in the field. Wherever possible, words are used in their most popular connotations.

The author wishes to acknowledge the great help he has received from his students who have read different mimeographed versions of this book during its preparation. Their criticisms have prompted much rewriting to increase clarity and to improve exposition. The author is very much indebted to Dr. Anatol Murad of Rutgers University, who read and criticized the entire manuscript. The chapters on interest were particularly influenced by his arguments, although they remain the author's view, to which Dr. Murad would still take exception at several major points. Dr. W. H. Steiner of Brooklyn College and Dr. Kenneth Trefftzs of the University of Southern California also read these chapters and offered helpful comments. The chapters on wage theory have been improved by the criticisms of Dr. Spencer Pollard and Dr. Paul Prasow of the University of Southern California and Dr. Morrison Handsaker of Lafayette College. Helpful suggestions have been received also from Dr. Emmanuel Hacker of Brooklyn College, Dr. Armen Alchian of the University of California at Los Angeles, and Dr. Val Lehnberg of the University of Southern California.

Most of all the author is indebted to his wife, Margaret Miller Pettengill. Without her unfailing encouragement the author would still be trying to learn enough to write a definitive book. She insisted that he write what he knew and let others point its defects for subsequent revision. That is what he has done. He deeply regrets that she did not live to see in print the book which she did so much to bring into being.

ROBERT B. PETTENGILL

Los Angeles, Calif.
    September, 1948

# CONTENTS

## PART I

### *The Prices of Commodities*

# PART II

## *The Prices of Services*

# CONTENTS

# PART I

## THE PRICES OF COMMODITIES

# Chapter 1

## VIEWPOINTS IN ECONOMICS

**1. Questions and Answers.**—Any expository book in the field of a science must be a book of answers. It must tell the how and why, the when, where, and how much of various problems. But before answers can be given, questions must be asked. And since no single volume can answer all the questions that might be asked about a subject, the questions that are chosen should be selected with care. They should, if possible, spring from a *central theme* or follow logically from an announced viewpoint. If this is done properly, the reader will realize that there is more than one possible approach to the field. He will not fall into the delusion that the particular exposition at hand is the only one he needs to study. Every choice involves rejection as well as selection. The viewpoints which are slighted or omitted by one writer may be very important to another who starts with a different premise.

The following outline indicates the questions to which brief answers are given in the numbered sections of this first chapter:

I. What is the field of economics as treated in this book? (2)
II. What are the prices which economists study? (3)
III. How should one approach the problem of explaining prices? (4)
IV. What terms should economists use? The problem of definitions. (5)
V. Why study economics? (6)
VI. How use economic principles? (7)

**2. The Field of Economics.**—Surely one of the first questions to be asked and answered is that about *the scope* of economics. What does it include and what does it omit? The viewpoint of this book is that economics may be considered one of the social sciences since it deals with certain actions of individuals in their relations with one another. It is particularly concerned with those actions which relate to the production, distribution, exchange, and consumption of goods and services, but not with all such activity. It excludes the physical problems of production, transportation, and marketing in order to concentrate upon two things: prices and quantities of goods and services in the market on the one hand, and maximizing net satisfactions on the other.

These two central themes are closely related. If, for instance, we suggest that economics studies the manner in which scarce resources are divided among alternative uses by people seeking to satisfy most adequately their manifold desires, we must recognize that prices and quantities are major guides. In modern capitalistic society individuals compare prices in their efforts to maximize personal incomes. Business men compare costs and selling prices in order to discover the best profit opportunities. Consumers are influenced by relative prices in deciding which things to buy to make their spending yield as much satisfaction as possible. Workers, landlords, and investors have services to sell and often choose one selling opportunity rather than another because the price offer is better.

For all these individuals the problem is not merely one of maximizing *gross* satisfactions. It is also, and more significantly, one of maximizing *net* satisfactions. This adds the problem of minimizing cost. Where the cost is a problem of buying cheaply, market prices are again the central consideration, but when we consider what must be given to get purchasing power, we often encounter the quantity problem, too. Workers, for instance, often must decide what quantity of their leisure and energy to give up to get the income which will buy what they want. The problem of maximizing *net* satisfactions includes, therefore, the problem of minimizing outgo.

The two themes might perhaps be combined in a single definition of the scope of economics if its implications are made clear. For instance, economics *as defined in this book* deals largely with market prices and market quantities, their magnitudes, changes, causes, and effects.[1] This should be understood to include among the causes, the maximum-net-satisfaction motive described above. The prices and quantities studied include those of both commodities and services. The actions of individuals relative to the market may be considered both separately and collectively. In the latter approach there are many problems of group choice. Some economists give their chief attention to questions of how to maximize the welfare of the group as a whole. Only a few welfare topics will be treated in the present volume. Its chief emphasis is upon the way in which prices and related quantities are determined in modern capitalistic society, together with the effects of such prices and quantities.

---

[1] This is the "correct" definition for this volume. Other authors prefer other definitions. The present author might use a different concept in another volume. See Section 5.

**3. Prices and Quantities from Various Viewpoints.**—The prices which economists study are chiefly transaction prices, the actual prices paid by buyers and realized by sellers in market transactions. To explain these prices and their fluctuations, economists usually introduce also the subjective prices which express the maximum amounts that individual buyers would pay or the minimum amounts that individual sellers would accept at any given time. These subjective prices exist in the minds of the buyers and sellers. They often differ from the actual market prices (transaction prices) at which goods are bought and sold. Subjective prices may be combined into demand and supply schedules, as will be explained in later chapters.

Demand and supply quantities also may be conceived in various ways. They may be the amounts actually exchanged, or the subjectively determined maximum quantities that buyers would purchase or sellers would sell at given prices. Another distinction is that between quantities as stocks and quantities as flows. Thus, there may be a certain quantity of wheat in storage at any given time (a stock). There are also certain quantities sold each day, week, or month (a flow). Quantities as stocks are absolute amounts. Quantities as flows are amounts per unit of time. They are often called "rates" of sale, of purchase, of production, etc.

Any rate of purchase is also a rate of spending. There is a total amount of purchasing power that changes hands during the given interval. This introduces the concept of the velocity of circulation of currency and brings together price theory and monetary theory. The income level is as important as the desire pattern of individuals in determining purchases of many goods. Changes in this level must be explained before price theory is complete.

The transactions which give rise to prices and quantities are transactions between individuals as buyers and other individuals as sellers. This is true whether individuals act independently as buyers or as sellers, or whether they are the agents of others. Even when a group takes action or delegates some one to act for the group, the individual members of that group make decisions before they vote or otherwise agree upon the desired course of action. Economic forces are therefore merely the market expressions of individual decisions to buy or not to buy, to sell or not to sell, to pay or ask a certain price, or to yield or seek a certain quantity. These decisions will be influenced by changes in prices or quantities that occur within the market itself and also by changes that occur elsewhere. The latter include technical inventions, natural calamities, the destruction of war, birth and death rates, education, and a host of other changes which influence human judgments.

In many cases the decisions of individuals cancel out. At other times, like periods of panic, they reinforce one another. In either situation the cumulative effect of individual decisions is generally more important in economic problems than the separate judgments of single persons. There are occasional unique sales and purchases where an individual buyer meets an individual seller and they agree on the price of a discrete good. But more often there are many individuals on either the buying side or the selling side, or on both, and their collective impact on the market is the important thing in price-quantity determination, not the viewpoint of any one of them. Economics studies individual motives chiefly to understand group activity and therefore should include elements of social psychology in its field as well as individual psychology. For prediction it must, of course, rely upon the law of large numbers just like insurance companies which pool risks no one of which is predictable but whose total outcome may be very closely determined in advance.

**4. Problems in the Field of Causation.**—When economists set out to examine the price-determining forces in a given institutional setting, there is always the question of how far to go in the explanation. It is easy to begin by saying that prices are determined by supply and demand, but what causes supply and demand to be what they are? And what are the causes of these causes? How far back should one go in examining links of the chain? Here again, as in the scope of economics and its goals, economists differ. Some want to go back through market demand to an explanation of incomes; others seek chiefly to explain human choices.

To explain incomes we must explain the prices paid for the services sold by individuals in their capacities as workers, landlords, or capitalists.[2] A circularity in causation quickly appears. The business firm usually pays its wages, rent, and interest out of the revenue derived from selling its products and therefore the amount paid out is partly dependent upon the prices of the goods sold. In similar fashion it can be shown that wages, rent, and interest represent costs which are considered by managers when they calculate the selling prices they must ask. Therefore, if one follows this line of causation far enough back, he must perceive the basic interdependence of all prices and all quantities which are in any way variable.

---

[2] Part II of this book treats the prices of these services.

Some economists insist that this fundamental truth must be firmly established before simple cause-effect problems are considered. They formulate an extensive series of equations which express the relationships which are most common in modern economic society and then demonstrate by simultaneous solution that all variable prices and quantities are so interdependent that none can be singled out as the cause of another. This approach, however, involves much simplification of the complexities of real life. Its generalizations are rarely useful in prediction or control unless greatly qualified. The exposition typically moves from the general to the particular, from the abstract to the concrete.

The alternative approach adopted in this volume begins with specific situations and moves toward the general. This requires choosing from the multitude of different market problems those which are most common, or which are most significant because of their widespread effects. Classifications must be established which are easily described and readily understood. Small sections of the causation chain may thus be chopped off for examination. This is not completely realistic but it is helpful. Eventually these sections may be linked together and the whole dynamic picture revealed.

Returning to the second branch of market demand study, that of choices as opposed to incomes, we may note that some economists follow this lead on out into the fields of psychology, history, and social institutions. Here too there is some circularity, but chiefly one encounters topics which do not impinge directly upon market prices and quantities. There are problems of the motives of men, how they choose, whence they derive their scales of preference, and the influence of impulsive, nonrational decisions. Institutional economists point out how our statutory laws and our court decisions erect a framework within which we develop both our ideas and our market practices. The present volume will consider the elementary foundations of desire and choice, but must leave to others the questions of institutional development and psychological drives.

A similar line of argument might trace through the supply side the influence of cost as a primary determinant of the prices of the factors, such as labor and land. The reasons for supply quantities being what they are would also be considered, and the origin and influence of the state of technology which determines the efficiency with which they are applied. Obviously there are here a whole host of sidelines which one might explore if time permitted, but which must be left to those who write monographs for advanced students.

**5. The Vocabulary of Economics.**—Every science has its own vocabulary of words which are the time-saving shorthand of its writers. These technical terms are abstract summaries of principles and concepts developed in the analytic process. They are used both to expedite thinking and to convey ideas. Many of the physical sciences use terms freshly coined to describe their new ideas, but social scientists find word coining much more difficult. Economics, for instance, deals with problems which are part of man's everyday experience. Both the amateur and the expert talk about rent, interest, profits, value, debt, inflation, etc. For use in careful analysis, these terms need to be shorn of their fuzzy edges and narrowed down to explicit definitions. Sometimes, however, in his efforts to sharpen these concepts into useful tools the economist has reshaped them so much that he cannot communicate his ideas to the people whom he would instruct. The inner circle can understand one another, but their language is often unintelligible to the outsider or the novice.

Therefore, a volume like this one, directed at those who have had only elementary instruction in economic theory, must be guided by two considerations in matters of terminology. It must define terms in such a manner that they can be understood by beginners and it must also bow in the direction of the esoteric so that students will be prepared for the jargon of the initiates when they reach higher levels.

Despite the dogmatic attitude of many writers, there is no single right meaning for terms used in economics nor for "economics" itself. There are only meanings which are more or less useful in analysis and communication. Some persons prefer one meaning, some another. A choice can be made by a third party on the grounds that to him a given meaning helps him in his objectives more than a different meaning. Take the term *capital* for instance. Some define it as goods used in producing other goods; others limit it to man-made production goods; while another group defines it as liquid purchasing power. Which of these concepts is "right"? None. Which then, should an author use? The one which serves his purpose best, regardless of whether this aligns him with the majority or the minority, or leaves him a maverick off by himself. If he does depart from customary meanings, however, it is incumbent upon him to make very clear both why he does it and exactly what the term means in his own vocabulary.

The present volume makes extensive use of adjectives and phrases in an effort to descend the abstraction ladder far enough to distinguish between the various viewpoints. Often all of them are useful and should be incorporated into the body of economic thought.

This is generally preferable to isolating one viewpoint or meaning and proclaiming loudly that this is *the* one which all persons should adopt. One of the important contributions of economics is its explanation and clarification of the relationships between the various aspects, viewpoints, or meanings of general terms which are often misused by people just because they are too abstract.

On the other hand, some concepts or definitions are clearly harmful. They either obstruct thought, preventing it from being as fruitful as it should be, or they mislead the thinker toward false and dangerous conclusions. Consider, for instance, the idea that the term *inflation* should always be associated with the printing of government notes in large quantities. This concept may obscure other possible causes of rising prices, such as an increase in the volume of bank credit, a rise in the velocity of circulation of currency, or even a decrease in the volume of production. It may also lead to the conclusion that governments should under no circumstances resort to the printing press to meet their needs for purchasing power, but should always tax or sell bonds. Although this latter argument is probably valid in most cases, exceptions are conceivable and must not be overlooked because one has accepted as final a given definition of the term.

**6. Purposes of Economists.**—This leads to the fundamental question of the goal of economists. Why study the science? "The proper study of mankind is man." Agreed, but for what reason or objective? Several goals have been suggested such as to understand the past including how we reached our present state, or to predict the future and how to adapt ourselves to it or to control it.

First, we may seek to understand what happened in the past or what is happening now. This involves learning facts about past events, arranging them into what seem to be logical cause-and-effect sequences, developing hypotheses, and thus proceeding by the scientific method to tested generalizations, principles, or laws. Such are the methods of the analyst who tries to answer the great group of "Why?" questions. The pure scientist seeks truth for its own sake. If past explanations seem inadequate, he tries to make them more complete; if they are contradictory, he tries to reconcile or choose between them; if entirely lacking, he poses new questions and seeks answers.

A second objective of economists is to learn enough about the workings of our economic system so as to be able to predict future developments. This problem may be approached with the detachment of the pure scientist who may, for instance, predict the date and extent of the next eclipse of the moon. But more often the individual who is concerned about the future wants to know what is going to happen so that he can adjust his actions accordingly. He may want to do that which will prevent a future event, like a depression, from doing him harm. Or he may anticipate a future change by action which makes it bring him more benefit than would otherwise accrue. Such individuals are concerned with the usefulness of knowledge. They tend to narrow the scope of their questioning to "practical" topics, often to the extent of ignoring fundamental problems of very great, but unperceived, relevance. They are often impatient with attempts to discover elementary principles when applications are not immediately apparent. This book is not for the shortsighted.

A third possible objective of those who study economics is the control of future events. This is based upon the second objective and through it upon the first. One must analyze before he can predict, and he must predict before he can plan how to control. Control differs from prediction and adaptation in that it assumes the course of events may be changed. Implicit in this objective is the desire, of course, to make those events turn out "better" than they would otherwise do. The focus of this desire need not be limited to the individual, but may be extended to the group. This is the field of the economic planner. He is concerned with the welfare of his group and seeks to promote it by applying pressures from outside the economic system to make it yield those price and quantity changes which he believes beneficial to his group. At times this means advancing one group at the expense of others, as through raids on the public treasury, striking for higher wages, or even international war. But it may also involve such goals as the welfare of the nation as a whole or even the entire world, unsemantic though these objectives may be.

In short the purposes of economists differ according to their scales of values, their vocational problems, their interests of the moment, or their endocrine balances. The present volume will concentrate upon the first of the three objectives described above, not because the author is uninterested in group welfare, but because analysis must precede attempts at synthesis. The person who attempts to say what laws should be passed, what ideas transmitted through education, or what emotions aroused should be thoroughly grounded in the principles of economic, political, and social analysis if he is to be more than a mere demagogue. Analysis therefore is given more emphasis in this volume than synthesis, although it seems neither possible nor desirable to exclude entirely the fascinating problems of applied economics.

**7. The Nature of Economic Principles.**—The principles of economics derived from the analytical methods of pure science are generalizations which purport to explain the effects which follow from given causes under certain conditions. Since it is often impracticable to describe all of the essential conditions when stating a principle, a generalization is usually intended to express a tendency that will work out if nothing interposes to prevent it. For instance, the first law of price is often stated as follows: "The price of a good varies directly with the demand for that good." This does not mean that in every case when the demand for a good rises the price of that good will also rise, but that the price will *tend* to rise if an increase in supply or some other change does not offset the effect of the increased demand. The principle merely expresses a cause-effect relationship, or in mathematical terminology, a function. If the relationship is very common, and particularly if obstacles to the indicated result rarely appear at the same time as the determining cause, then the principle is often called a theory or a law.

When individuals seek to apply economic principles to explain, to predict, or to control, they should at the outset recognize that the principles are definitely generalizations, not absolutes. That is, principles state what may be expected to follow a given cause most of the time, not all the time. The most useful principles are those which are true more often than, say, 90 per cent of the time. However, a 60 to 70 per cent generalization may sometimes be raised to the 90 to 95 per cent level by stating carefully the conditions under which it operates. These include particularly an enumeration of the other causes or variables which might influence the effect of the given cause and stipulating that they must not change. This is the familiar *ceteris paribus,* or "other things equal," qualification which hedges the application of many scientific laws. But one should remember that the law is valid even if other things do change to resist its effect. Thus the force of gravity operates upon an object even though impeded by a plane which prevents the object from falling, by friction which slows its rate of drop, or by an air blast or magnetic field which makes the object move in an upward direction.

In addition to a stated or implied *ceteris paribus* qualification, the statement of conditions should include several other things which will guide the person trying to apply an economic principle. In the first place, the institutional framework should be described. The first law of price described above, for instance, will hold only when sales are made under conditions where the supply quantity varies directly with the price. If there were individual, collusive, or governmental price-fixing, the results would not be as indicated. An increase in schedule demand would bring a change in the volume sold, but no change in the price.

In the second place, the result may depend upon the length of time allowed for a given cause to have its possible effects. Thus, an increased demand may raise the price in the short run, but reduce it in the long run when sellers realize lower costs through economies of large-scale production. Therefore, the time condition should be made explicit in most cases.

In the third place, the direction and the rate of change of the independent variable (the cause) will often be important in determining the change in the dependent variable (the effect). A sudden and sharp rise in demand will ordinarily raise the price further than the same increase occurring over a period of months. Or a 2 per cent per month rise in demand may change the price more than a 2 per cent per month drop.

This leads to a final comment about the applicability of economic principles. In their simplest form they usually express merely the fact of a cause-effect relationship and whether the changes in each occur in the same direction or in opposite directions. For instance, if demand goes up prices tend to go up; if supply rises, prices fall. In general terms, prices are a direct function of demand and an inverse function of supply. These principles become even more useful if the amplitude of the change is indicated in addition to its direction. This involves much more careful study of past records than that required to develop simple principles. Statistical materials are often inadequate, and many subjects are not adapted to statistical treatment. Often the most that economists can say is that in certain described cases the results are more pronounced than in others. For instance, the demand for bananas usually declines more after a 10 per cent price rise than does the demand for salt under similar circumstances. This is one of the elasticity problems which will be examined for both demand and supply in later chapters.

**8. Summary.**—The viewpoint of this volume is basically that of one living in a modified capitalistic economy like that of the United States after the second world war. In such an institutional setting, the writer seeks answers to questions about the causes and effects of price relationships and price changes. This involves also a consideration of related quantities. Proximate causes and near-by effects are given more attention than more distant ones, although the problems of interdependence are not overlooked. Individuals are seen making the choices which determine the trends and magnitudes of economic quantities. They also determine whether economic principles shall be valued merely for their own sake or whether they shall be used in prediction and control. Analysis is the main theme, but synthesis and applications are not overlooked.

Part I deals chiefly with the prices of tangible goods. Part II concentrates on the price problems connected with the services rendered by the factors of production.

# Chapter 2

## DEMAND AS A CAUSE OF PRICE

**1. Fundamental Questions About Demand.**—Since Part I of this book endeavors to explain chiefly the prices of goods and related quantities, it is appropriate to begin with a study of the basic market forces. These are popularly described as "demand and supply," but they take many forms and their analysis from various viewpoints will occupy most of the present volume. Demand will be treated first, somewhat by arbitrary choice, but also because most production takes place to satisfy known or expected demand.

There are two fundamental questions about demand from which others spring. The first is, "How does price affect demand?" This will be the topic of the next chapter. The second is, "How does demand affect price?" This leads to questions about what causes the changes in demand which in turn cause the changes in price. It is axiomatic that an increase in demand tends to cause an increase in price, but the causes of changes in demand are not so easily understood. The remainder of this chapter will be devoted to classifying and explaining these causes.

When demand changes are considered to be causes, price changes are the effects. There are several other ways of expressing the same idea which are used from time to time as they seem more appropriate. For instance, one may say that price is a function of demand. Or demand may be called the independent variable and price the dependent variable. One might say that price is determined by demand if this did not seem to make demand the sole determinant. Supply is always a second determinant and there are others such as government price-fixing and custom.

The alternative approach to demand is to consider it as an effect of price. Here price is the independent variable and demand the dependent variable. The other phrases may be reversed in similar fashion. The problem is sometimes said to be one of the elasticity of demand, as explained in detail in the next chapter.

The specific questions to be answered in this chapter may be outlined as follows:

   I. How may demand as a cause of price be distinguished from demand as an effect of price?
  II. What are the causes of change in schedule demand?
      A. Changes in buyer preference among goods; advertising, technology, and cross-elasticity of demand
      B. Changes in buyer preference for goods instead of currency; liquidity preference and propensity to consume
      C. Changes in income; income-elasticity of demand
      D. Changes in the number of buyers and in the degree of collusion among them
 III. What part do habit, impulse, and choice play in determining schedule demand?

**2. Two Ways of Looking at Demand: Market and Schedule.—** When we say that a change in demand changes price, we are speaking of a change in "schedule demand." On the other hand, when we speak of a price change causing a demand change, we refer to "market demand." The difference between these two concepts is fundamental. In the first, "demand" is a cause. In the second, "demand" is an effect. Many problems of price analysis are simplified by remembering the differences between these two ways of looking at demand.

The term *demand* itself, when used without any qualifying adjective, usually refers to a quantity, but may refer to a price. The viewpoint is that of the buyer. When adjectives are used, demand quantities become either "market demand" or "schedule demand." Demand prices in similar fashion are called either "market prices" or "schedule prices." The following outline shows the various viewpoints:

  1. Demand as a quantity
     A. The quantity *taken* by buyer(s) in *a given transaction* .............................. "market demand"
     B. The quantity that *would be taken* by buyer(s) at *any one price* ............. "demand quantity"
     C. The quantities that *would be taken* by buyer(s) at *a series of prices* .......... "schedule demand"
  2. Demand as a price
     A. The *price paid* by buyer(s) in *a given transaction* ............................ "market price"
     B. The price that *would be paid* by buyer(s) for *any given quantity* .................. "demand price"
     C. The prices that *would be paid* by buyer(s) for *a series of quantities* ............... "schedule prices"
  3. Demand as a schedule
     A. A series of price-quantity pairs showing both schedule demand and schedule prices "demand schedule"

The different ways of looking at demand may be illustrated further by the use of numbers and diagrams. For instance, robust John Smith's demand schedule for hamburgers to eat for his noon lunch on a given day may be as follows:

| If the price is | The quantity purchased will be |
|---|---|
| 10¢ | 3 hamburgers |
| 15¢ | 2 hamburgers |
| 20¢ | 1 hamburger |

Smith's actual market demand cannot be stated until we know the price he has to pay for his hamburgers. At 10 cents, Smith will buy 3, at 15 cents, he will buy 2, etc. In other words, *changes* in the market demand quantity may be considered an *effect* of price change. They will be discussed in the next chapter.

On the other hand, *changes* in the quantity demanded *at any one price* cannot be due to price change since the price is assumed to be held constant. Instead they are due to changed desires, changed incomes, etc., as explained more fully below. And when there does occur a change in the quantity demanded at any one price, it is likely to occur at other prices too. The whole schedule may change as illustrated by the following demand schedule which may reveal the effects of an increase in Smith's wages:

JOHN SMITH'S DEMAND FOR HAMBURGERS AFTER HIS WAGES ARE RAISED

| Price | Quantity | |
|---|---|---|
| 10¢ | 4 hamburgers | (Each quantity is |
| 15¢ | 3 hamburgers | larger than before |
| 20¢ | 2 hamburgers | at that price.) |

These two ideas of a change in demand in the market sense and a change in demand in the schedule sense may be illustrated by a diagram. In Figure 1 the changes in market demand are shown by moving up and down either curve. An increase in demand in the schedule sense may be seen in the fact that the second demand curve, $D_2$, is further to the right than the first, $D_1$. Each quantity that $D_2$ represents is greater than the quantity at the same price in $D_1$. (The paired figures in parentheses give the quantity-price amounts which appear in each schedule and when plotted on quantity-price axes give the points of the two demand curves.[1]

---

[1] The phrase "price-quantity" is more common than "quantity-price" but mathematical usage requires that quantity precede price in graphs.

The contrast between the two ways of looking at demand may be summarized once more. Changes in market demand are caused by price changes. Changes in schedule demand are a cause of price changes. When referring to demand changes in the market sense, price change is a cause; when using the schedule sense, price change

FIGURE 1

SCHEDULE DEMAND AND MARKET DEMAND

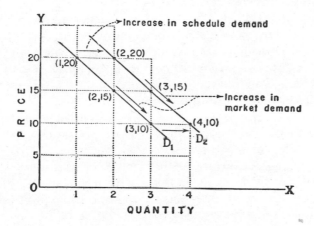

is an effect. The former topic will be examined in the next chapter dealing with the problems of the price-elasticity of demand. The present chapter will explore some of the reasons for the changes in schedule demand which tend to cause changes in price. At the same time it will cast light upon the absolute size of the quantities that exist in any given demand schedule. This is a different question from that of the changes in the quantities that occur from time to time.

3. **Causes of Change in Schedule Demand.**—It is an axiom of elementary price theory that an increase in the intensity of demand for a good tends to bring an increase in its price. More formally, the First Law of Price states that price (or quantity exchanged) varies directly with the demand. The amount of the variation, and whether it is price that changes, or quantity, or both, depends also upon the conditions surrounding the supply of the commodity, a topic the discussion of which must be deferred to a later chapter. At the present juncture, the question to be answered is, "What causes lie behind demand as a cause?" We cannot explore the causation chain very many links backward from the market situation, but some at least should be examined.

There are three main causes of changes in demand intensity: changes (1) in preference among goods, (2) in preference for goods versus currency, and (3) in income. Each of these causes may be approached from the viewpoint of a single individual, but they are most significant when they hold for a group, since changing attitudes of individuals often cancel out against opposite changes in other individuals.

**4. Changes in Preferences Among Goods.**—The intensity of demand for a given good, X, will depend in the first place upon how people value it for personal consumption or use in business as compared to other goods, Y, Z, etc. The general appraisal patterns of the members of a group are derived from the culture of that group. If they live in a highly industrialized civilization, they may prefer factory products to those that are hand-made, and speedy methods of transportation to slow ones. If it is a capitalistic economy with stress upon individual competition and the acquisition of wealth and income, people will have a scale of values in which high rank is given to consumption goods which help one to "keep up with the Joneses," or go them one better, such as fine clothing, new automobiles, large homes, etc. Income-yielding securities will rank high in the preference scale of things to buy. Or, to consider more specific desires, if smoking and drinking are prevalent culture traits, people in general will demand tobacco, liquor, and all the paraphernalia that go with these habits.

Changes in the demand for particular products within a given culture depend upon changes in the relative desires of people. Consumer demand, for instance, may be changed by advertising which makes people believe that they will be better satisfied, happier, more envied, or more successful in love, if they buy more of X than they have in the past. The slogans are varied, but they all seek to raise a given good or type of product in popular estimation so that the intensity of demand for it will increase. Ideas of desirability will also change because of education, the effect of motion pictures, the impact of religion, or the fervor of war. Certain seasonal changes in relative preferences are obviously due to external changes in the weather. Other illustrations might be found in legislation which forbids a given industry, like the Prohibition Amendment, or subsidizes it, like aids to cotton growers or shipbuilders.

In the demand for products that comes from business managers who want the goods not for personal consumption but for use in the production process, there are certain additional factors. If consumer fancy happens to turn toward a particular fabric, garment, hat, or form of entertainment, the demand for goods needed to supply these whims will rise under the impulse of the profit motive. More important in scope and in human history, however, has been technological change. The effects are both direct and indirect. When a new process is invented or a new product devised to meet a long-felt need, businessmen increase their demand for the things needed to produce the product or install the new process. At the same time they may decrease their demand for other things no longer so profitable to use as before. Thus the demand for capital goods may rise at the expense of labor in cases where labor-saving machinery is being introduced, internal combustion engines may replace steam engines, structural steel may take the place of stone, and in a host of other ways technological change may modify producer demand schedules.

The indirect effects of changing technology upon total demand are no less important than the direct, though they may take longer to become apparent. The industrial revolution accelerated the development of a capitalist class on the one hand and a laboring class on the other. This brought increasing demand for luxury goods for leisure-class living. As the ownership of tools shifted from the artisans to the business unit and as the scale of operations increased, the type of tools and machines demanded changed also. The growth of factory and commercial cities brought new ways of living and new desires. Laws were changed to aid the enterprise at first and later to protect the proletariat. In short, the entire culture pattern of modern industrialized countries has been largely shaped by a series of innovations in various fields of production, including agriculture, mining, transportation, etc., in addition to manufacturing. And this culture pattern is the basic cause of the scale of values which most people adopt relative to things to be purchased on the market. It influences prevailing demand intensities, and as it changes, they change. Through these links in the causation chain, technological changes influence the prices and quantities that prevail in the marketplace.

**5. Cross-Elasticity of Demand.**—The final point to be discussed under the general heading of things causing changes in relative preferences among goods is the prices of other goods. This is sometimes called the *cross-elasticity* of demand and will receive further elaboration in the next chapter on price-elasticity of demand. But at this point it is desirable to point out that a rise in the price of one good may cause a decrease in the demand for it and drive buyers to purchase instead some substitute good. Thus if the price of oranges goes up, some consumers may turn to grapefruit for their vitamins. But this increase in the demand for a substitute good will tend to increase its price, too. On the other hand, if two goods are complements instead of substitutes, the influence on schedule demand will be reversed. Thus if the price of gasoline is driven upward by the imposition of a large tax, people will tend to buy less of it and therefore will demand fewer automobile tires. The appropriate generalization is as follows: changes in the price of A tend to have a *direct* effect upon the schedule demand for B (and thus upon B's price) if B is a substitute for A. If B is a complement, the effect is *inverse.*

The two types of cross-elasticity are illustrated by the following hypothetical case:

CROSS-ELASTICITY OF DEMAND FOR SUBSTITUTES AND COMPLEMENTS

| Price of A (the independent variable) | Demand for B, a SUBSTITUTE for A (price of B unchanged) | Demand for C, a COMPLEMENT of A (price of C unchanged) | *For reference only:* Demand for A as Its Price Rises |
|---|---|---|---|
| 6¢ ↓ 7¢ ↓ 8¢ | 1 unit 2 " 3 " | 8 units 6 " 4 " | 4 units 3 " 2 " |

**6. Changes in Preference for Goods Instead of Currency.**—The demand for consumption goods will diminish if people choose to save more out of current income. People who saved only $10 out of a monthly income of $300, for instance, when business conditions were improving, may later become apprehensive about the future. They decide to save more seriously for a possible "rainy day" ahead. If monthly savings are then increased to $30 or $50, spending is reduced accordingly. These people are said to reveal a decreased *propensity to consume.* Their scales of preference have changed so that cash in hand or in bank accounts seems preferable to certain goods. Demand slackens first for luxury-type products and for durable goods whose useful life may be prolonged by repair. On the other hand, if people get the idea that prices are going to rise, they may spend a higher percentage of their incomes and save less. They have an increased propensity to consume. This change in consumer preferences is most clearly revealed during those periods of rapidly rising prices popularly called inflation.

The demand for income-producing goods, including securities, may also change because of a change in the relative desirability of goods as compared with currency. This is usually called a change in *liquidity preference*. The effect is more upon the disposition of past savings than upon the amount of saving out of current income. Thus, if a man has saved $10,000 and invested it in stock, he may get the idea that the stock market is going to fall and that he should protect himself against that loss. He sells his stock and puts the proceeds in the bank, while he waits for the day when he can reverse the process and buy again with profit to himself. At that time his attitude changes a second time. His liquidity preference decreases, and he chooses to hold his savings in the form of stock instead of a bank deposit.[2]

Occasionally there are people who invest regularly the amount saved each month out of income. For these persons, a decision to spend less and save more may influence two markets at the same time. The decreased propensity to consume may diminish the demand for consumer goods. The increased savings will raise the current demand for income-producing goods. But if at the same time that these people decide to save more they also get more cautious in their investing, they may reveal an increased liquidity preference by holding current savings for a longer time before investing. This will diminish the current demand for income-producing goods at the same time that the demand for consumption goods is falling. If the demand for both types of goods changes in the *same* direction, that means liquidity preference and propensity to consume have changed in *opposite* directions. This is a frequent but not inevitable relationship. During most of the downswing of the business cycle, both demands are decreasing, and during most of the upswing both demands are increasing, but at the turning points one change precedes the other.

**7. Changes in Income.**—One of the most important causes of shifts in the demand curve is changes in income. This was illustrated above in the effect of a wage increase upon John Smith's demand for hamburgers. Rising incomes, however, do not affect all rates of purchase to the same degree. Smith may buy more hamburgers for lunch, but no more coffee for breakfast. Because he eats a bigger lunch, he may not want as much for supper or may want a different type of food. If, when his wages were low, his family had to eat chiefly the cheaper foods such as beans, his wage increase may cause the family to decrease their buying of beans as they turn to meat

---

[2] Currency hoards could be substituted for bank deposits in this illustration, and real estate or bonds could be substituted for stock.

for nourishment. The following table illustrates some of the different reactions which may occur when incomes increase:

SMITH'S DEMAND AT TWO INCOME LEVELS
WHEN PRICES REMAIN UNCHANGED

| Weekly Income | Luncheon Hamburgers at 15¢ Each | Breakfast Coffee at 10¢ Cup | Weekly Beans at 18¢ Pound | Weekly Roast at 50¢ Pound |
|---|---|---|---|---|
| $30 | 2 | 1 | 2 | 0 |
| 40 | 3 | 1 | 1 | 3 |

The typical reactions are sometimes classified. Goods, the demand for which usually rises as incomes rise, are called *superior goods*. Goods the demand for which usually falls under these circumstances are called *inferior goods*. If all buyers responded like Smith, hamburgers and roasts would be superior goods and beans would be an inferior good. But buyers differ. Andy McTavish, for instance, might not increase his buying of hamburgers and roasts at all and might purchase the same quantity of beans as before. When his income increased, he might choose to increase his savings instead of pampering his appetite. And when incomes in general rise, some people's incomes rise more than others. Nevertheless, experience shows that most goods are "superior." There are certain exceptions which are generally admitted to be "inferior." Poor people have to buy them to satisfy their vital physical needs. For instance, they generally buy margarine instead of butter, flour instead of bakery bread, beans instead of meat, street-car transportation instead of automobiles and gasoline, and tickets to third-run movie houses instead of first. When their incomes increase, they begin to satisfy taste as well as hunger, desire for comfort as well as shelter. Conspicuous consumption begins to take precedence over sustenance.

For certain individuals and perhaps for the market as a whole, some goods are "superior" for a rise in income up to a certain level and then become "inferior" as the individual becomes still more affluent. A poor woman may use a washboard for the family laundry. If her financial status improves, she may enter the market for a washing machine. But if she becomes very well to do, she may send her laundry out and have no use for a machine in the house. The same story might be told for a given grade of shoes or meat or housing.

**8. Income-Elasticity of Demand.**—The whole concept of the response of demand to income changes may be summarized by the phrase *income-elasticity of demand*. This may be defined as the degree to which the demand for a good changes with a given small change in income. Income-elasticity of demand will vary with the person, the good, the income level at which the income change occurs, the direction of that change in income, etc. Using this terminology one may say that superior goods have positive, and inferior goods have negative, income-elasticity of demand. Luxury goods will generally have high positive income-elasticity, while staple foodstuffs will have low, or negative.

Certain applications of the concept may now be considered. Economists point out that the income-elasticity of demand for savings rises as incomes rise. This has an important bearing upon the end of boom periods and the arrival of the crisis which precedes a recession. It also affects the distribution of incomes among people by increasing the property incomes of those already in the high income brackets. Businessmen are often interested in what a rise or fall in the general income level of their customers will do to the demand for their particular products. If managers find that consumers' incomes are falling, they may strive to prevent demand from declining by using more advertising, or by adopting more liberal credit terms. If they cannot maintain schedule demand by such devices, they may seek a larger market demand by cutting prices.

This leads to a final comment on the importance of understanding the two ways in which a change in income may affect market transactions. To this point the implication has been that there will be a change in the quantity purchased. The other possibility is a change in the price. Or both may change. For instance, a rise in income may not lead a person to buy two automobiles, but merely to buy a better one. He may also rent a better home, pay more for his clothes, or go to more expensive places of entertainment. Or the increased income may make him willing to pay more for such items as oranges and steaks. When these rise in price at the same time that his income rises, he continues to buy, instead of dropping out of the market. In short, an increase in schedule demand, however caused, may be described as a rise in the demand quantities, with prices constant; a rise in demand prices, with quantities constant; or a rise in both. The first possibility was portrayed diagrammatically in Figure 1. It is repeated below in the more complete presentation of Figure 2, which shows also the second and third possibilities.

An increase in demand quantity means a shift of the demand curve to the right as in Figure 2A. An increase in demand price shifts the demand curve upward as in Figure 2B. When both price and quantity change, the movement is both horizontal and vertical, but is most easily conceived as moving diagonally to the "northeast," as from $E$ to $F$ in Figure 2C.

FIGURE 2

THREE WAYS OF SHOWING AN INCREASE IN SCHEDULE DEMAND

A. Increase in        B. Increase in        C. Increase in
   Quantity              Price                Both Price
                                             and Quantity

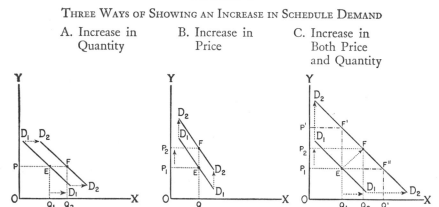

## 9. Number of Buyers and Degree of Collusion Among Them.—

The arguments of the three preceding sections have been based upon individual reactions, although the importance of the group aggregate has also been stressed. We turn now to note the importance of the number of people in the buying group. Whenever the number of buyers changes, the demand curve shifts in one direction or the other with resultant changes in prices or quantities. Changes in the population through migration or a balance of births versus deaths have been of some historical importance. The composition of the population is also significant, as when a declining birth rate decreases the percentage of children to be provided for at any given time and increases the percentage of oldsters. Immigration may change the number of people wanting particular types of goods much more than it changes the total number of buyers.

In the short run there is also the possibility that in some markets buyers may get together and agree not to engage in price bidding against one another. When this happens, as in agricultural buying cooperatives, or joint army-navy purchase commissions, there will be a decrease in schedule demand below what it was before the collusion occurred or what it might have become in the absence of such inter-buyer agreements. In a later chapter this problem will be discussed under the heading of monopsony.[3]

**10. Habit, Impulse, and Choice.**—Most of our buying is routine. We have formed habits of buying things which have satisfied us sufficiently in the past and therefore we continue to do the same in the present. This holds for most of our purchases of food and shelter, and for some of our clothing and other needs. Nearly all goods or services which we consume regularly and have to purchase frequently are bought without much conscious choice. However, the goods which are bought only once or twice a year, or even less frequently, like certain articles of clothing or other durable consumption goods, vacation trips, etc., often involve a weighing of the relative merits of alternatives before deciding upon market action. Other purchases are impulsive, made upon the decision of the moment without reflective thought, and are outside the orbit of routine buying habits. A certain food or dress may catch a housewife's fancy, or a youngster may be inveigled by a sidewalk barker into taking a dollar diamond to his girl friend.

The generalization to be made with regard to all buying of the habitual type, most of that where choice enters, and some of that which is described as impulsive, is that in its broad outlines it is largely determined by the culture pattern of the group in which the person has been brought up or in which he currently lives. This is true even where the buyer thinks he is exercising reason and trying to get the most for his money. His appraisal of what is good is chiefly a result of his social conditioning and his knowledge of materials. Impulsive buying is more apt to reveal individual differences, but much of it also reflects group-fostered desires and scales of value even if these are below the level of the buyer's consciousness.

On the other hand, nearly all market action to purchase goods is a choice between alternatives, even though the element of deliberation is not present. This follows because a person can rarely do more than one thing at a time; if he is buying a coat, he cannot at that moment be buying another coat, nor a hat, nor an order of fried chicken. If we rule out the narrow time element which makes this generalization hold for even habitual choices, we encounter a few cases where people's incomes are so large relative to their desires that they can buy whatever they want in the course of a year or so

---

[3] Monopsony is to the buying side of the market what monopoly is to the selling side. Briefly stated, it indicates that there is only one buyer, or that buyers act in collusion to reduce prices to the detriment of the seller.

and need not deny themselves anything purchasable. But even the wealthy tend to live in a *milieu* which limits their range of choices. Though freed from the trials of thrifty shopping, they are often bound more tightly by convention than poorer people to whom social approval is not so important.

Only a few enterprising and fearless individuals break from the cultural mold which governs their choices among categories and rates of consumption. At the consumer level such conduct is considered queer, penny-pinching, or irrational by the people who conform. At the producer level it may be considered a sign of greatness, particularly if the innovation succeeds in raising profits far above what the conformists make. If the enterpriser fails, he may be dubbed reckless, visionary, or a gambler. The words which the conformist uses to appraise the nonconformist are matched by those of the radical expressing his disapproval of the conservative. They represent value judgments, not careful analysis.

The significance of the foregoing discussion for the marketplace is twofold: buyers change the pattern of their purchases very slowly, but they do change, especially in particulars. Hence the seller who wants to increase his sales may benefit from spending money to try to make buyers believe his product offers greater value than another which it resembles. This is most likely to be successful with articles of infrequent purchase, but it also holds for other goods where the difference between rival commodities is not much greater than the trademark which distinguishes them. Consumers may be stimulated, educated, misinformed, or otherwise influenced in their buying of particular articles, but major changes in the categories of consumption are not easy to achieve and take a long time. Considerable attention to these problems as seen from the seller's viewpoint will be given in a later chapter.

**11. Summary of Principles Governing Demand as a Cause of Price.**—Prices vary directly with changes in schedule demand. These changes themselves depend chiefly upon four causes: (1) changes in the *relative desirability* of various goods; (2) changes in preference for *goods as compared with currency;* (3) changes in *current income;* and (4) changes in the *number of buyers* in the purchasing group. The first gives rise to the useful concept of cross-elasticity of demand. The third suggests the term, income-elasticity of demand. The second is the source of concepts of liquidity preference and propensity to consume. The fourth refers to problems of collusion, monopoly, migration, and birth rates. The causes of these causes may be examined through many links of the causation chain. Of major importance is a study of the influence of habit and impulse upon the choices which buyers make. All of these topics will receive further attention in later chapters as they are applied and developed. This chapter merely seeks to lay the foundation by defining certain important concepts in the field of demand. The related topic of price-elasticity of demand is so important that all of the next chapter is devoted to it.

# Chapter 3

## TYPES OF DEMAND SCHEDULES

**1. Demand in the Market Sense: the Law of Demand.**—There are two economic laws about demand which have become axiomatic to the man in the street, but he often confuses them. The first states that a rising demand tends to raise prices; the second says that rising prices tend to reduce demand. The economist sharpens and generalizes these two axioms. The first becomes *"Price varies directly with demand,"* and is called the *First Law of Price.* The second is made to read *"Demand varies inversely with price,"* and is called the *Law of Demand.* Chapter 2 dealt with the first of these economic laws and suggested the use of the phrase *schedule demand* in connection with it and *market demand* in connection with the second law. The present chapter will explore general aspects of the relation between changes in prices as causes and changes in quantities as results. This requires an analysis of the basic nature of demand schedules and their various types. It will be followed in Chapter 4 by an analysis of "demand-elasticity," the mathematical relation between successive quantity-price pairs in demand schedules.

The questions to which this chapter gives answers include the following:

A. How are demand schedules derived?
  1. What are subjective demand schedules?
  2. What are statistical demand schedules?

B. What are the major types of demand schedules?
  1. What is the difference between individual and collective schedules?
  2. How does a successive demand schedule differ from an instantaneous demand schedule?
   (a) How allow for the direction of price change? its starting point? its amplitude?
  3. How may long-run demand schedules be distinguished from short-run?

C. What exceptions may be found to the Law of Demand?

**2. The Subjective Nature of Most Demand Schedules.**—As explained in the preceding chapter, a demand schedule may be considered as a series of quantities that some one *thinks* a buyer or group of buyers would purchase at a series of prices. The difference between the several quantities is assumed to be due solely to differences in the price. Demand variations in this sense (market demand) are an effect of price, not a cause. Any person may describe a demand schedule. He may be a buyer telling what he thinks he would buy at various prices, a seller estimating what he thinks other people will buy if the selling price is at various levels, or a neutral third party, such as an economist who is appraising probable market activity in a given situation. These three persons, viewing the same set of conditions, would probably suggest similar but slightly different demand schedules.

Since demand schedules are subjective, they are also transitory. They change as rapidly as individual attitudes change. Unpredictable and trivial developments may be important in deciding how much an individual thinks he will buy, such as changes in the weather, an attack of indigestion, or the arrival of a bill collector. Sellers' forecasts of the demand for their product are apt to change with rumors of strikes, inflationary legislation, or war. Economists often seek objectivity by examining the records of the past and the probable conditions of the future, but prejudices and apprehensions influence their judgment, too.

**3. Statistical Demand Schedules.**—For certain staple commodities like wheat, sugar, potatoes, and butter it is possible to accumulate statistics showing the amounts which have been purchased in the past at different market prices. These prices did not occur successively through time in any regular sequence from low to high or vice versa, but they may be rearranged into such order by rearranging their dates. The price-quantity pairs thus obtained are then usually plotted on a graph and a trend line calculated which represents the best compromises between similar yet discrepant points. From this calculated line, price-quantity pairs may now be read at regular intervals and arranged in schedule form.

Statistical demand schedules thus derived may have some usefulness in economic prognosis, but they must be interpreted with care and applied with caution. Extending over many years as the basic records do, they show the effect of many other forces upon quantity demanded in addition to price change. Hypothetical or subjective schedules imply that nothing changes except the stated variables, but the statistical schedules cannot. However, this may be turned into an advantage for the latter type *if* deviations from the trend line are examined and explained in terms of the other independent variables. For instance, a year in which the supply of potatoes is exceptionally large may occur either during a depression or during boom times. The size of the national income will surely cause the resulting price to be higher in the latter case than in the former. For *any given price,* the quantity taken from the market will be greater. In other words, supplementary generalizations about the changes in income and other forces described in the preceding chapter will help the forecaster who knows probable changes in these other variables in addition to price.

Statistical demand schedules are retrospective or *ex post* and may be terminologically contrasted with subjective demand schedules by calling the latter prospective or *ex ante.* *Ex post* demand schedules of the price-quantity type may be computed from data as simple as the sales records of any given firm which changed its selling price during a given time period. There will be as many price-quantity pairs as there were prices established—sometimes only two. In such cases, the analyst must be careful not to fill in other figures by interpolation since alteration in the amount and direction of the price change would have changed the quantity responses of buyers. Statistical demand schedules are sometimes interpreted to show what the approximate demand for a given product will be in the future, judging from what it was in the past. This procedure is more likely to yield more useful results for agricultural price and production planning where there are many buyers and sellers than for single firms or for industries where either buyers or sellers are few. In the latter instances changes in the attitudes or tactics of competitors may quickly and sharply alter the response of buyers to the original price changes of a given firm or commodity.

**4. The Relation Between Individual and Collective Demand Schedules.**—Statistical demand schedules are almost always of the collective type. That is they describe the demand of a *group* of individuals at various different periods of time. Subjective demand schedules may also be collective, but they are often constructed for separate individuals.

Collective demand schedules may be constructed from individual demand schedules when needed for economic analysis. The method followed is to set up individual demand schedules with the same series of prices. The quantities which are paired with each price in the several schedules are then added together to obtain the total, or collective demand at that price. The following table shows hypothetical individual schedules for Adams, Brown, and Cross, together with a collective demand schedule according to the rule just given.

| ADAMS | | BROWN | | CROSS | | COLLECTIVE | |
|---|---|---|---|---|---|---|---|
| Price | Quantity | Price | Quantity | Price | Quantity | Price | Quantity |
| 8¢ | 2 units | 8¢ | 0 units | 8¢ | 0 units | 8¢ | 2 units |
| 7¢ | 3 " | 7¢ | 1 " | 7¢ | 0 " | 7¢ | 4 " |
| 6¢ | 4 " | 6¢ | 2 " | 6¢ | 0 " | 6¢ | 6 " |
| 5¢ | 5 " | 5¢ | 3 " | 5¢ | 1 " | 5¢ | 9 " |

Another type of collective demand schedule is of importance because of certain market situations. It is based upon the principle that a person who is willing to pay a given price for one unit of a good will be willing to buy that good at any lower price. Thus we might have a collective demand schedule for apartments, shall we say, made up of individuals Dean, East, and Foss as shown in the following schedule:

| DEAN | | EAST | | FOSS | | COLLECTIVE | |
|---|---|---|---|---|---|---|---|
| Price | Quantity | Price | Quantity | Price | Quantity | Price | Quantity |
| $80 | 0 units | $80 | 0 units | $80 | 1 unit | $80 | 1 unit |
| 70 | 0 " | 70 | 0 " | 70 | 1 " | 70 | 1 " |
| 60 | 0 " | 60 | 1 " | 60 | 1 " | 60 | 2 " |
| 50 | 1 " | 50 | 1 " | 50 | 1 " | 50 | 3 " |

Dean is willing to rent a four-room apartment if he can get one for $50 but he is not willing to pay more. East is willing to pay as much as $60, and Foss will go as high as $80. This means that there is only one apartment demanded at $80. The same is true if apartments rent for $70. At $60, however, East enters the market and his demand is added to that of Foss, who of course remains willing to buy at the lower price. The demand in the market sense rises to two at $60. At $50 East and Foss remain in the market and Dean enters so that there are three apartments demanded. This type of collective demand schedule is said to be cumulative downward. As the price falls, the demand present at the preceding higher price is added to the demand which enters the market at the next lower price so that a larger total accumulates for the group. A similar type of collective schedule will be described later for supply as being cumulative upward. The difference between demand and supply schedules lies in the fact that the quantity demanded usually varies inversely with the price, whereas the quantity supplied varies directly.

**5. Instantaneous Demand Schedules.**—Up to this point a demand schedule has been defined as showing the quantities that would be demanded at each of a series of prices. Such demand schedules may be described as being of the instantaneous type. They implicitly assume that each price originates suddenly from nowhere. The quantity paired with the prices is the amount that would be demanded if that price existed. Such might be the calculation of a person who was about to market a new fountain pen and had to decide what would be the best price to ask. Should it be priced to sell at $4, the quantity demanded would be a certain amount; at $5, another amount; at $6, still another amount. The manufacturer would have to decide between the various possible prices upon the basis of the quantity that he thinks can be sold at those prices, the cost of production, and other variables.

**6. Successive Demand Schedules Should Indicate the Direction of Price Change, Its Starting Point, and Its Amplitude.**—For all old products already on the market the seller's problem is one of price *change*. He wants to know what the demand would be at a price higher or lower than his present price when buyers will be influenced by memory of what the price was previously. His demand schedule will, therefore, be a *successive* demand schedule since it will indicate the quantities that he thinks people will buy if his price is changed in succession from one figure to another.

In a successive demand schedule the *direction* of price change must be shown. A price increase will affect demand in a different way from a price decrease. Therefore, if three prices such as $5, $6, and $7 occur in the demand schedule for hats, one must state whether the quantity shown at each figure represents what could be bought if price succession runs from $5 to $6 to $7, falls from $7 to $6 to $5, or starts at $6 and moves either $1 up or $1 down. Each of these three situations would be likely to show different quantities paired with the given price.

Most merchants know from experience that a 10 per cent price reduction will bring a different percentage change in demand than a 10 per cent price increase will bring. A decrease usually does not attract nearly so many buyers as an equal increase repels. Old customers find out about price boosts more quickly than noncustomers find out about price cuts. That is why advertising is generally essential in price-cutting campaigns. In most cases when a price is reduced and later returned to its original figure the demand is likely to be different at the end of the down-up change than it was at the beginning. This fact is sometimes generalized as a statement that (successive) demand schedules and curves are not reversible.

In addition to the direction of price change, it is also essential to know the *starting point*. The demand for hats this year at $5 will probably be different if the price has been reduced from $6 than if the reduction started from a previous price of $7. Similarly, a 10 per cent price increase will have a different effect on the demand for butter if it starts from 40 cents than if it starts from 80 cents.

This leads to the question of the effect of the *amplitude* of price change upon the change in the quantity demanded. Sellers sometimes find that their sales decline less if their prices are raised one cent at a time in five successive jumps than if there is a single 5-cent raise abruptly imposed. Therefore, if 50 units are being purchased at 20 cents, it is impossible to make a good guess about the amount that would be demanded at 25 cents without stating how rapidly the increase is to be made.

**7. The Time Allowed for Buyer Response Should Be Indicated in Demand Schedules of the Successive Type.**—When prices change, they affect the attitudes of buyers in different ways depending upon how long the price change remains in effect. For instance, when a price is increased, people at first may be repelled by the higher price and may refrain from buying. When they find that the price does not come down and they can do nothing about it, they may accept it as inevitable and resume purchases. When prices fall, it takes time for people to learn about the price cuts, and therefore the full market response is not revealed until sometime afterward. Therefore, in addition to showing the other things described in Section 6, a demand schedule of the successive type should tell the length of time allowed for consumer reaction to each price increase. This is shown in the schedule at top of page 34.

The difficulties involved in trying to make such a schedule realistic are obviously increased by making it longer. In actual practice, most schedules calculated by sellers rarely contain more than three or four prices: the going price, and one or two higher or lower alternative

A Successive Price-Quantity Demand Schedule
(Assume price rises one cent each week)

| Price | Quantity Purchased per Week (After one week is allowed for consumer reaction to each price increase; demand not shown for other reaction times) |
|---|---|
| Beginning:　5¢ | 100 |
| 6¢ | 90 |
| 7¢ | 80 |
| 8¢ | 60 |
| Final:　　9¢ | 30 |

prices. For instance, the following schedule might be made to read: Beginning at 5 cents, an abrupt change to *either* 6 cents or 7 cents would cause demand quantities to fall as indicated; i.e., the jump to 7 cents would not be through an intermediate 6-cent stage, but all at once. The seller would also be wise to add a second column of quantities to indicate what the demand is likely to be at either the 6- or 7-cent figure after a longer time, say five weeks, is allowed for buyer adjustment to the higher price.

A Seller's View of Potential Demand Responses to Price Change

| Price | Quantity Currently Sold per Week | Quantity He Expects to Sell in First Week after Change | Quantity He Expects to Sell in Fifth Week after Change |
|---|---|---|---|
| Present price:　　　5¢ | 100 | | |
| First alternative:　6¢ | — | 90 | 92 |
| Second alternative: 7¢ | — | 80 | 85 |

**8. A Classification of Demand Schedules into Short Run and Long Run.**—Economists often describe things as happening in either the *short run* or the *long run*. There is obviously a time difference implied between them. For analysis, however, it is more important to concentrate upon the number of independent variables which operate in the hypothetical or real situation being described. The *short run* is best defined as a period of time in which, actually or hypothetically, only one independent variable is present. The *long run* should then be defined as a period of time in which two or more independent variables, such as price change and desire change, operate to affect the dependent variable. The difficulty with the latter definition is that we often want to distinguish between the operation of two, of three, or of a larger number of independent variables. The phrase *long run* includes too much. We are forced to use qualifying adjectives such as the "moderately" long run or the "very" long run. This is cumbersome, but it is sanctioned by usage.

The various types of demand schedules suggested in the preceding paragraphs may be classified to illustrate this point.

I. Short-run schedules: one independent variable, the price of A, and one dependent variable, the market demand for A

    A. Instantaneous (included for completeness although the price of A really does not *change* in the usual sense of the word)

    B. Successive

        1. Reversible (probably the most common form in elementary analysis; though reversibility is often by implication only)

        2. Directional (with starting point and amplitude of changes also indicated)

II. Long-run schedules: the price of A changes, and one or more other changes occur to influence the schedule demand for A

    A. Successive, hypothetical

        1. *Two* independent variables: the change in the price of A and changes which it stimulates in buyer attitudes (many schedules possible depending upon the length of time allowed for attitudes to change)

        2. *Three* independent variables: *add* to the above a change in the price of other goods stimulated by the change in the price of A (many schedules possible depending upon time and the number of these other price changes)

        3. *Many* independent variables: *add* any other variables which are dependent as related to the price of A, but are independent as related to the schedule demand for A (such as the supply of a substitute commodity B)

    B. Statistical, historical

        1. *Many* independent variables; some of their changes may have been stimulated by changes in the price of A, but others are likely to have been caused by different forces. (Pairing the prices of A with quantities demanded often obscures these other variables and the time required for them to change and to influence demand. For instance, buyer incomes may change as suggested in Section 6 of the preceding chapter dealing with income-elasticity of demand.)

Much price analysis involves the simultaneous use of demand and supply curves. The analyst must be careful to keep their presuppositions in mind. For logical reasoning or accurate prediction it is often wise to specify each of the variables the force of whose change is being considered. Usually this brings to mind the *excluded* variables whose influence is not being taken into account, but should be.

**9. Four Exceptions to the Law of Demand.**—In most situations it is true that the demand varies inversely with the price, but there are at least four exceptions which deserve attention. These are the cases of discontinuous demand, speculative demand, style or prestige goods, and inferior goods. Much of the foregoing material sheds light upon these exceptions, which will now be examined.

The first case is that of a price change which causes no change whatever in the quantity demanded. The demand schedule or curve is said to be *discontinuous* for that interval. For instance, a decrease in the price of salt from 4 cents to 3 cents per pound may not increase John Smith's demand for salt at all. In fact the price might even fall to zero without increasing his demand. If the price should rise to 8 cents, a similar inelasticity of demand might be apparent. Somewhere above that figure, maybe at 50 cents, maybe at a dollar, Smith's demand for salt might decline a little as he chose to economize upon its use or to employ substitutes. Individual demand schedules for a great many commodities contain discontinuous segments, but few of them have as wide a gap between changes as salt. Collective demand schedules, on the other hand, usually reveal a continuous change in demand throughout the whole range of price change.

A second exception deals with the *speculative* type of market response. A rise in price stimulates demand to increase, and a falling price depresses demand. This reaction is the opposite of that described in the Law of Demand. The stock market offers an obvious illustration. A bull market attracts buyers whose added demand sends prices still higher. A bear market drives buyers away and prices fall still lower. Speculative reactions may be interpreted in the language of Chapter 2 as a change in investor preference for particular securities or for securities as compared with cash. A price increase, for instance, stimulates an increase in schedule demand which more than offsets the decrease in market demand that would otherwise be expected. In the language of Sections 7 and 8 of this chapter the speculative response might be described as a type of long-run demand schedule in which the buyer's attitude is changed. It is different, however, from the reactions previously portrayed.  In Section 7 the buyer was pictured as changing his attitudes in a way that offset somewhat the adverse effects of a price rise.  In neither case did the reaction partake of the "bandwagon" type of response.  Speculation falls in this latter category.  This exception to the Law of Demand is quite common in security markets and on the organized commodity exchanges.  It is much less common in business or consumer buying, but in periods of rapid price change it may appear quite often.

Style and prestige buying create the third exception.  Some wealthy buyers of style goods show increased desire for a new item because the rising price puts the item clearly in a prestige class open only to those with large incomes.  On the other hand, consumers who are in the habit of thinking that price measures quality, are likely to decrease their purchases of items whose price is cut below that of accepted substitutes.

The fourth possible exception to the Law of Demand is quite rare.  It is found in connection with certain commodities and services which were described as "inferior goods" in Chapter 2, Section 7. The distinction between inferior and superior goods is most clearly seen when incomes change.  In a very few cases it may appear when the price of a commodity itself changes.  For extremely poor people, a fall in the price of a staple food such as flour or beans may enable them to buy other things for taste as well as nourishment.  They do not feel the need for so much of the staple and therefore may reduce their purchases of it.  The argument may also be applied to price increases, but with greater difficulty.

**10. Summary.**—Most demand schedules obey the simple Law of Demand in that demand in the market sense varies inversely with the price.  This is clearly true for most instantaneous demand schedules and holds for all successive demand schedules except the speculative type and a few others.  When the price of a good changes, it has a direct influence upon the quantity demanded.

The price change may also have an indirect influence through its effect upon other things that may alter demand in the schedule sense. These include particularly changes in buyer attitudes and changes in the prices of other commodities.  Short-run demand schedules eliminate these secondary effects.  Long-run demand schedules allow one or more of these roundabout influences to intrude as additional independent variables determining the quantity demanded. Statistical demand schedules reveal the effect also of many completely independent variables, such as changes in income which are not caused by the change in price of the given good.

For maximum accuracy in interpretation and analysis, each demand schedule should state the variables assumed to be operating in addition to price change. It should indicate also the direction of price change, its starting point, and its amplitude.

# Chapter 4

## PRICE–ELASTICITY OF DEMAND
## AND ITS MEASUREMENT

**1. The Price-Elasticity of Demand.**—Despite obvious difficulties in constructing and interpreting demand schedules, the fact remains that the demand for A is a function of the price of A. In most cases it is true that a rise in market price reduces demand and a fall in price increases demand. This is the familiar Law of Demand defined in the first section of Chapter 3. But this law does not tell us enough. It merely says that the *direction* of demand change is usually the opposite of the *direction* of price change. Businessmen and economists want to know the *degree* to which the demand will change following a given change in price. This is the problem of the *price-elasticity of demand*. The phrase is commonly shortened to *elasticity of demand*, but the longer phrase is more precise and distinguishes the concept from the ideas of income-elasticity of demand and cross-elasticity of demand which were explained in Chapter 2.

The demand for some goods is much less responsive to price change than is the demand for others. Salt, for instance, is a traditional example of a good the demand for which does not change much with a change in price. The problem of demand-elasticity is of chief interest to growers, manufacturers, merchants, and other sellers of goods. They want to know what will happen to the demand for their products if the price is changed either by them or by persons or forces over which they have no control. Economists have made the problem one for much formal analysis, and the terms and logic employed must be mastered in order to facilitate the solution of more advanced problems.

The most important questions regarding price-elasticity of demand which are answered in this chapter are given below. The less important answers are printed in reduced type. They need be studied only by those who wish to become skilled in the use of diagrams which constitute the "shorthand" of the language of economics.

    I. What are four ways of presenting the data of a demand schedule?

    II. What are the meanings of these terms:

        A. Elastic demand

B. Inelastic demand

C. Demand-elasticity of unity

III. How may demand-elasticity be measured?

    A. By changes in total revenue

        1. Directly

        2. Indirectly

            (a) Through marginal revenue

            (b) Through average revenue

    B. By relative percentage changes in quantity and price

IV. What are the different concepts of marginal revenue?

    A. Average marginal revenue

    B. Marginal revenue at a point

V. In Notes:

    A. How may the marginal revenue be found at any point on a smooth total revenue curve (the tangent rule)?

    B. How are total, average, and marginal revenue curves related diagrammatically?

    C. How may point-elasticity and arc-elasticity be demonstrated by plotting demand schedules on logarithmic axes?

    D. How may point-elasticity be shown on demand curves using the customary arithmetical axes?

**2. Ways of Presenting Demand Schedules: Emphasis on Total Revenue.**—The effect of a change in prices upon the quantity purchased may be described by comparing the total amounts of money which pass from buyer to seller in completing the transactions at the different prices. The amount of money changing hands when goods are bought and sold at any given price is obviously the number of units exchanged multiplied by the price per unit, assuming that the price is quoted in unit terms. To the buyer this amount of money is his *total outlay (TO)*; to the seller it is his total receipts or *total revenue (TR)*. A neutral term which stresses neither the buyer's nor the seller's viewpoint might be *transaction money amount* or *total transaction money*. Despite the advantages of such a neutral phrase, for the present we shall use the term *total outlay* whenever we look at demand from the buyer's viewpoint and the more conventional term *total revenue* only when the seller's viewpoint is involved. The reader must remember that total outlay and total revenue are identical quantities.

The conventional demand schedule which shows a series of price-quantity pairs may be expanded into more complete form by computing a third column to show total outlay (total revenue) according to the equations: $TO = TR = P \times Q$, where $Q$ is the number of units changing hands at price $P$. From this three-column demand schedule it then becomes apparent that there are also two other ways of describing the demand situation defined by the conventional price-quantity demand schedule. We may set up a price and total outlay schedule or a quantity and total outlay schedule. From any one of these four schedules the other three may be obtained. The following table shows the relationship of the conventional demand schedule to these three others.

FOUR WAYS OF PRESENTING THE DATA OF A GIVEN DEMAND SCHEDULE

| "Conventional" (Price and Quantity) | | "Complete" (All Three) | | | "Price and Total Outlay" | | "Quantity and Total Outlay" | |
|---|---|---|---|---|---|---|---|---|
| $P$ | $Q$ | $P$ | $Q$ | $TO(TR)$ | $P$ | $TO(TR)$ | $Q$ | $TO(TR)$ |
| 11¢ | 1 | 11¢ | 1 | 11¢ | 11¢ | 11¢ | 1 | 11¢ |
| 10¢ | 2 | 10¢ | 2 | 20¢ | 10¢ | 20¢ | 2 | 20¢ |
| 9¢ | 3 | 9¢ | 3 | 27¢ | 9¢ | 27¢ | 3 | 27¢ |

**3. Demand-Elasticity, First Method: Change in Total Revenue.** —The simplest approach to the measurement of demand-elasticity makes use of the total revenue column in a "complete" demand schedule of the type described above. For instance, a businessman who is contemplating a cut in his selling price is very much interested in how much that reduction will change his total revenue. There are three possibilities: total revenue may increase, decrease, or remain the same. Economists describe the first result as revealing an "elastic demand." The second result is called "inelastic demand"; and the third is called "demand-elasticity of unity." These three possibilities are shown by the three different demand schedules of the following table:

DEMAND SCHEDULES OF THREE DIFFERENT ELASTICITIES

| Demand 1 ("Elastic") | | | Demand 2 ("Inelastic") | | | Demand 3 ("Elasticity of Unity") | | |
|---|---|---|---|---|---|---|---|---|
| $P$ | $Q$ | $TR$ | $P$ | $Q$ | $TR$ | $P$ | $Q$ | $TR$ |
| 11¢ | 1 | 11¢ | 11¢ | 22 | 242¢ | 30¢ | 10 | 300¢ |
| 10¢ | 2 | 20¢ | 10¢ | 23 | 230¢ | 25¢ | 12 | 300¢ |
| 9¢ | 3 | 27¢ | 9¢ | 24 | 216¢ | 20¢ | 15 | 300¢ |

In Schedule 1 the total amount of money passing from buyer to seller increases as the price falls; in Schedule 2 total revenue decreases.

In the third schedule the total revenue remains unchanged for each price drop. In order to lend greater precision to the terms, economists sometimes describe "elastic demand" as "demand-elasticity greater than unity." The example has been given in terms of a price decrease. It should be obvious that if we were to consider a price increase instead, the relationships would be reversed. For instance, demand-elasticity greater than unity ("elastic demand") would occur when total revenue declined as the price rose.

**4. Marginal Revenue as Change in Total Revenue.**—The change in total revenue that results from each change in the independent variable is sometimes called *marginal revenue*. In the "elastic" demand schedule given above, the price decline from 11 cents to 10 cents causes an increase of the total revenue from 11 cents to 20 cents, a difference of 9 cents. Similarly, the next price change from 10 cents to 9 cents causes a 7 cent increase in total revenue. The 9 cent and 7 cent changes in total revenue may be called marginal revenues. The formula for calculating $MR$ when the price decreases is as follows: [1]

$$MR_n = TR_n - TR_{n+1}$$

This holds when $n$ represents the price at the end of a change interval of one. That is, when the price changes from 11 cents to 10 cents, the marginal revenue is said to be 9 cents *at 10 cents,* not at 11 cents, nor for the interval between 11 cents and 10 cents. Applying the formula:

$$MR_{at\ 10\cent} = TR_{at\ 10\cent} - TR_{at\ 11\cent}$$
$$MR_{at\ 10\cent} = 20\cent - 11\cent = 9\cent$$

A rule may now be advanced for determining the elasticity of demand from marginal revenue instead of from total revenue. Demand is elastic when $MR$ is positive. In the schedule on page 44 the rule applies from a price of 10 cents to a price of 6 cents. Demand is inelastic when $MR$ is negative, as from 5 cents to 3 cents. Between a 6-cent price and a 5-cent price $MR$ passes through zero. When $MR = 0$ this means that there is no change in $TR$, and we have demand-elasticity equal to unity.

The same three rules also may be expressed diagrammatically. When $MR$ lies above the $OX$ axis, demand is elastic. Where $MR$ crosses $OX$, demand-elasticity is unity. And where $MR$ lies below $OX$, demand is inelastic.

The diagram in Figure 3 is drawn in steps to show clearly the

[1] For a price *increase* the formula is $MR_{n+1} = TR_n - TR_{n+1}$, and $n + 1$ is the end price. Cf. Note A.

relation between $TR$ and $MR$. If, now, the changes in price marked off on the $OX$ axis are made very small, the steps become narrower. If one could conceive logically of price changes as small as 1/1000 of a cent or less, the corresponding changes in total revenue and marginal revenue would become so small as to make steps invisible to the naked eye. The curves would become "smooth." This, in fact, is the way they are usually drawn.

FIGURE 3

DIAGRAMMATIC RELATION BETWEEN TOTAL REVENUE AND MARGINAL REVENUE

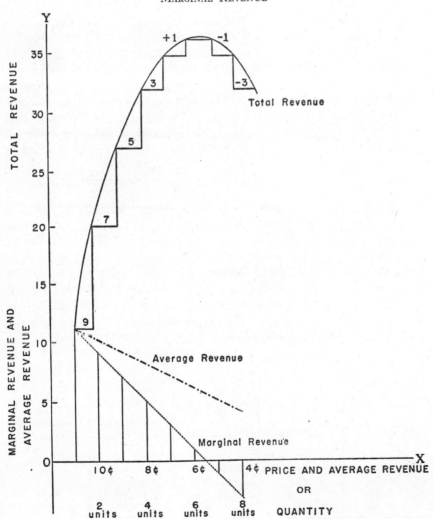

DEMAND SCHEDULE CALCULATION OF TOTAL, MARGINAL,
AND AVERAGE REVENUE

| Price | Quantity | Total Revenue | Marginal Revenue | Average Revenue |
|---|---|---|---|---|
| 12¢ | 0 | 0 | | |
| 11¢ | 1 | 11¢ | 11¢ | 11¢ |
| 10¢ | 2 | 20¢ Demand | 9¢ | 10¢ |
| 9¢ | 3 | 27¢ elastic | 7¢ | 9¢ |
| 8¢ | 4 | 32¢ | 5¢ | 8¢ |
| 7¢ | 5 | 35¢ | 3¢ | 7¢ |
| 6¢ | 6 | 36¢ | 1¢ | 6¢ |
| 5¢ | 7 | 35¢ Demand | −1¢ | 5¢ |
| 4¢ | 8 | 32¢ inelastic | −3¢ | 4¢ |

When a smooth marginal revenue curve is used, the formula given above in terms of one unit changes in price must be modified to show infinitesimal changes in price. This is done by substituting $m$ for 1 and stating that $m$ approaches zero as a limit. That is, the horizontal width of the steps is not one cent, but is assumed to be such a small fraction of one cent as to be virtually zero. The formula is written:

$$MR_n = \frac{TR_n - TR_{n+m}}{m} \text{ when } m \to 0 \text{ as a limit.}$$

The division by $m$ indicates that the change is really an *average* rate of change between the two points $n + m$ and $n$, even though it is customary to say that the change takes place *at n*. The need for an average rate may be seen clearly if $m$ is taken to be a large number, not a very small one. For instance, if a demand schedule is written in terms of 5-cent drops in price, not one cent, we would have to compute the *average* change in total revenue between each two given prices in order to find the marginal revenue per one-cent change. This is shown in the following schedule.

*Average* MARGINAL REVENUE WHEN PRICE INTERVALS ARE LARGE

| A Price | B Quantity | C Total Revenue | D Total Change in *TR* When $m = 5¢$ | E *Average* Change in *TR*: "Marginal Revenue" (D/5) |
|---|---|---|---|---|
| $1.00 | 200 | $200.00 | | |
| .95 | 230 | 218.50 | $18.50 | $3.70 |
| .90 | 250 | 225.00 | 6.50 | 1.30 |

When $m = 1$, the divisor is rarely mentioned, since anything divided by one equals itself, unchanged. The total change in $TR$ becomes equal to the average change in $TR$, and $MR$ can be read directly merely by subtraction. The concept of demand-elasticity at a point is developed further in Note A.

NOTE A.—The Tangent Rule for Finding Marginal Revenue at Any Point on a Smooth Total Revenue Curve. When smooth curves are used which have no "steps," a method must be derived for calculating $MR$ at any point. The step-type curves use the convenient fiction that $MR$ exists "at" the end of each step. Thus the step formed by reducing the price from 11 cents to 10 cents was 1 cent wide and 9 cents high. The $MR$ was therefore declared to be 9 cents "at 10 cents." Later price reductions created other steps of diminishing height until the 6-cent price was reached, after which the "curve" turned downward. Steps can be measured easily, but on smooth curves there is no visible step at all. Instead of talking about the height of steps, we speak therefore of the "rate of change" in the dependent variable at any given point. For instance, a smooth $TR$ curve corresponding to the step curve of Figure 3 might be said to rise at a diminishing rate which becomes zero just beyond the 6-cent price.

In still more general terms, we are seeking a rule for the diagrammatic measurement of the rate of change in the dependent variable at a given size of the independent variable. The technique is as follows. Choose any point $P$ on $TR$ which corresponds to a given price, and draw a straight line which just touches the $TR$ curve at that point (see Figure 4). Such a line is said to be "tangent" to $TR$ at $P$. The line itself is also called "the tangent." This tangent line makes an angle $PRQ$ with $OX$ at $R$ and forms part of a triangle $PQR$. Two sides of this triangle represent an enlarged picture of the step at $P$, which is invisible because it is so small. $RQ$ represents the width of the step and $QP$ the height (by the geometric rule of similar triangles). In our original illustration, the large step was 1 cent wide and 9 cents high "at 10 cents." This indicated a "rate of change" of 9 cents up for 1 out, or a ratio of $9:1$. We may perform the same sort of division with the sides of the larger but similar triangle $PQR$. Thus the marginal revenue, or rate of change in total revenue at 10 cents on the smooth curve is $PQ$ (the height of this similar step) divided by $RQ$ (the width).[2] The 10-cent *point* ($P$) on the smooth curve lies *between* the 9-cent and the 7-cent *steps*. Therefore, the marginal revenue *at that point* will be something less than 9 and greater than 7.

The marginal revenue rule may now be stated in the abstract terms of mathematics. It is merely one case of the general rule for determin-

---

[2] The diagrammatic distances do not precisely conform to the figures given here. $PQ:RQ$ is less than $9:1$.

## FIGURE 4
### GEOMETRIC RELATION BETWEEN THREE DEMAND CURVES

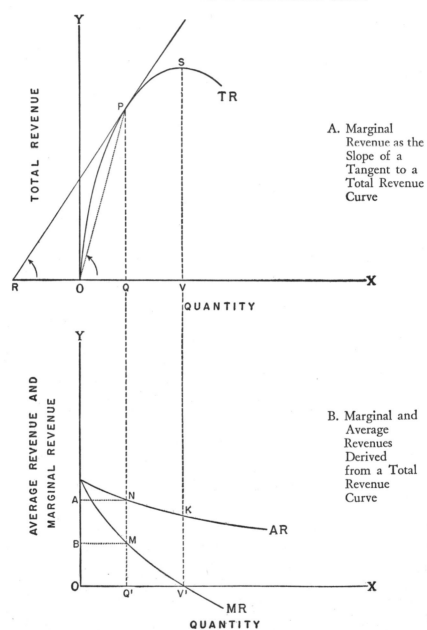

A. Marginal
   Revenue as the
   Slope of a
   Tangent to a
   Total Revenue
   Curve

B. Marginal and
   Average
   Revenues
   Derived
   from a Total
   Revenue
   Curve

ing the *rate of change*: the change in the dependent variable divided by the change in the independent variable when the latter change becomes so small that it approaches zero as a limit. In symbols it is $\Delta TR/\Delta P$ when $\Delta$ signifies an infinitesimal change in the number which follows. The $\Delta$ symbol stands for the Greek letter delta, and the ratio may be read "delta $TR$ divided by delta $P$." Diagrammatically a rate of change is the side of the triangle measuring the dependent variable divided by the side drawn on the axis which measures the independent variable. The triangle is formed by drawing a tangent to a given point on the curve which expresses the relationship between the given variables.[3]

As the point $P$ moves upward along the $TR$ curve, the tangent line drawn to it will become less steep. At the top of the $TR$ curves, a tangent would become parallel to $OX$ and the base $RQ$ of the triangle would become infinite. Marginal revenue would become zero, as may be seen by observing (1) that the angle $PRQ$ would shrink to nothingness and (2) that the ratio $QP:RQ$ would become zero.

**5. Average Revenue Is Another Way of Describing Unit Price.** —The total revenue in any demand schedule is equal to the price times the paired quantity ($TR = P \times Q$). If one takes the total revenue at each price and divides it by its demand quantity, the quotient will be the revenue per quantity unit, i.e., the average revenue ($TR/Q = AR$). From the formula, $TR/Q = P$, the quotient is clearly identifiable also as the price ($P = AR$).

Whenever comparisons are being made with marginal revenue, the most appropriate term for the quotient is "average revenue." In diagrams, $AR$ always lies above $MR$, with one exception. When the selling price is constant regardless of quantity offered, $AR$ will be horizontal and identical with $MR$. In all other cases, $MR$ declines more rapidly than $AR$, as shown in Figure 3. When only one unit is sold, $MR$, $AR$, and $TR$ are equal and meet at the same point.

**6. Comparative Areas Under an Average Revenue Curve Also Reveal Changes in Total Revenue.**—The conventional demand curve plots price on the vertical axis and quantity on the horizontal axis. Since the price is presumed to be the same for all units sold at a given time, total revenue equals price times quantity ($TR = P \times Q$). By the rules of algebra, price then becomes the total revenue divided

---

[3] In trigonometry the rule becomes: the tangent of the angle $PRQ$ (formed by the intersection of the tangent line and the axis of the independent variable) is measured by the ratio between the opposite and adjacent sides of that angle. Readers unfamiliar with mathematics may be cautioned to remember that the word *tangent* may be used in three different ways: (1) as a line, (2) as a formula for measuring the size of the angle made by the tangent line, and (3) as the quotient or result obtained by applying that formula.

by the quantity ($P = TR/Q$) which is the same thing as the average revenue per quantity unit. Therefore, it is customary to refer to the price-quantity demand curve as an average revenue curve. The diagrammatic relation between total, average, and marginal revenue curves is demonstrated in Note B.

NOTE B.—DIAGRAMMATIC COMPARISON OF TOTAL, MARGINAL, AND AVERAGE REVENUE CURVES. If a total revenue curve is drawn immediately above its corresponding average revenue and marginal revenue curves as in Figure 4, some interesting relationships may be observed. In the first place, either of these three revenue quantities may be measured directly by the height of its own curve at any given quantity. In the second place, any one of the curves may be derived from either one of the others. For instance, when marginal revenue is zero, total revenue cannot be increasing. This may be seen at quantity $OV$ in the upper diagram where $TR$ reaches its peak, $S$, and in the lower diagram where $MR$ cuts the quantity axis at $V'$.

At any intermediate quantity, $Q$, the rules for computing marginal revenue and average revenue from total revenue are as follows. First, draw a perpendicular to $OX$ to intersect the total revenue curve at $P$. From this total revenue point $P$ draw a straight line to the origin, $O$, and a tangent which intersects the quantity axis at $R$. The angle $PRQ$ shows marginal revenue by dividing $RQ$ into $QP$ according to the tangent rule. Similarly, the angle $POQ$ shows $AR$ by dividing $OQ$ into $QP$. These quotients may then be plotted below as $Q'N$ ($QP/RQ$) for marginal revenue and $Q'M$ ($QP/OQ$) for average revenue.

One should note the change in the independent variable from that given in the body of the chapter. $TR$ was there shown to vary with the price; it is shown here as varying with the quantity. Since the quantity varies also with the price, and since a complete schedule shows all three: $P$, $Q$, and $TR$, it is permissible to use whichever of the two pairs is the most useful (cf. Chapter 4, Section 2).

When comparing income with cost, marginal curves and average curves are usually used ($MR$, $MC$, $AR$, and $AC$). When considering the total amount of funds spent in the market, total outlay (same as $TR$) curves are sometimes helpful, but they do not appear very often in economic literature. All three revenue curves may be called demand curves. Some authors drop the term *demand curve* when talking about the situation faced by the individual firm planning its future sales policy and speak instead about a "sales curve." This term is not without merit, but tends to be confused with a curve showing the trend of sales quantities over a period of time.

For simplicity, most $TR$, $AR$, and $MR$ curves are assumed to be of the reversible type and no question is raised about their being instantaneous or successive (cf. Chapter 3, Sections 5 to 7).

The total revenue may be determined from an average revenue curve by selecting any point, $R_p$, on that curve and drawing lines perpendicular to $OY$ and $OX$. This gives a rectangle of which one side ($OP_1$) measures price and the other side ($OQ_1$) measures quantity. Therefore, the area of the rectangle ($P_1R_1Q_1O$) represents price times quantity, or total revenue. By moving point $R$ up and down the curve a series of such rectangles may be obtained as in Figure 5, and their areas may be compared. If the rectangle defined by $R_2$ is larger than the rectangle defined by $R_1$, this indicates that $TR$ is rising. Demand, therefore, would have an elasticity greater than unity when the price fell from $P_1$ to $P_2$. If the rectangle defined by $R_2$ were to be equal in area to the rectangle defined by $R_1$, demand would have an elasticity of unity between these two prices. If the second rectangle should be the smaller of the two, then demand-elasticity would be less than

FIGURE 5

DEMAND-ELASTICITY SHOWN BY COMPARING AREAS UNDER A DEMAND CURVE

$$P_1R_1Q_1O \gtreqless P_2R_2Q_2O \lesseqgtr P_3R_3Q_3O$$

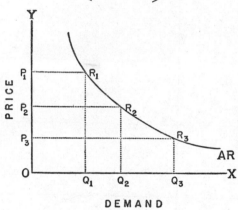

DEMAND

unity. As a general rule, the steeper the curve at point $R$, the less elastic the demand is likely to be for a price change from that point. A nearly horizontal curve would indicate a very elastic demand. This rule, however, must be applied with great caution because it does not always hold. The reasons for the exceptions and two ways of resolving the difficulties are given in Note C. In the demand and supply diagrams most commonly used in price analysis, the comparative-areas approach to demand-elasticity is generally the easiest and best.

NOTE C.—POINT-ELASTICITY AND ARC-ELASTICITY OF DEMAND SHOWN BY USE OF LOGARITHMIC AXES. (1) *Average Revenue Curve Plotted on Logarithmic Axes.* If the price-quantity pairs of the *average* revenue demand schedule are plotted on *logarithmic* ruled axes, the slope of the $AR$ curve at any point reveals the price-elasticity of demand. (The slope of the *total* revenue demand curve on *arithmetic* ruled axes reveals the marginal revenue.) Arithmetic axes start at zero and mark equal intervals for *equal additions,* such as marking points 0, 2, 4, 6, 8, 10, etc., for additions of 2 each time. Logarithmic axes start at one and mark equal intervals for *equal multiplications,* such as marking points 1, 2, 4, 8, 16, 32, etc., for multiplications by 2 each time. Thus if each interval is one centimeter long, the point five centimeters out would be marked 10 units on an arithmetic axis, but 32 on a logarithmic axis.

Figure 6 shows the way in which the elasticity of demand may be demonstrated on logarithmic axes. Since price is the independent vari-

FIGURE 6

DEMAND-ELASTICITY REVEALED BY SLOPE OF AVERAGE REV-
ENUE DEMAND CURVE ON LOGARITHMIC AXES

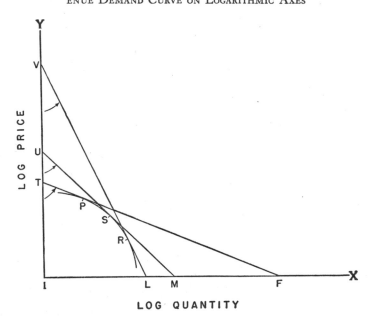

able, the angle which shows the slope of the tangent line is measured where that line intersects the *price* axis. If that angle is equal to 45 degrees (*SUI*), the demand is equal to unity. If the angle (*RVI*) is less than 45 degrees, the demand is inelastic, or less than unity. If the angle (*PTI*) is greater than 45 degrees the demand is elastic, or greater than unity. It is customary, however, to consider the "steepness" of the tangent lines and that means viewing the angles they make with the *quantity* axis. Here a small angle means great elasticity and a large angle means small elasticity.

The demand curve in Figure 6 is drawn for realism so as to bend away from the origin (the meeting point of the log *X* and log *Y* axes) instead of toward the origin. Most demand schedules are more elastic for very high prices than they are for very low prices.

(2) *Point-Elasticity Contrasted with Arc-Elasticity.* The use of logarithmic axes makes it easy to demonstrate why arc-elasticity must be considered the average elasticity between two points. On the demand curve of Figure 7 movement from point $P$ to point $R$ represents a

## FIGURE 7

### ARC-ELASTICITY IS AN AVERAGE ELASTICITY BETWEEN POINTS

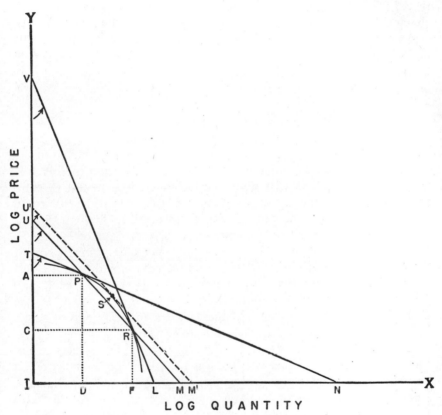

decrease in price from $IA$ to $IC$ which causes an increase in demand from $ID$ to $IF$. The *arc*-elasticity between $P$ and $R$ may be determined by drawing a straight line or chord between these two points and measuring the angle, $PUA$, which it makes with the price axis. This angle is smaller than the *point*-elasticity angle, $PTA$, for point $P$ and larger than the point-elasticity angle, $RVA$, for point $R$. If a comparison between tangents is desired, a point $S$ may be found on the arc of the curve between $P$ and $R$ such that its tangent $SU'$ is parallel to the chord $RPU$ and the angle $SU'A$ is equal to angle $PUA$.

**7. Demand-Elasticity. Second Method: Ratio Between Percentage Changes.**—A second method of measuring demand-elasticity gives numerical answers by the application of a simple formula to the changes in a conventional demand schedule. These results may then be compared with unity (1.00) to determine the degree of demand-elasticity for a given price change, the demand is said to be "elastic" if the formula quotient is greater than 1.00, and "inelastic" if less than 1.00. If price change is considered to be the cause and quantity change the effect, then demand-elasticity may be described in general as the degree to which the latter is affected by the former. The logical way to make this comparison is in terms of the percentage changes on each side of the schedule. The elasticity of demand may be expressed by the formula (in words):

$$\text{Elasticity} = \frac{\text{Percentage change in quantity}}{\text{Percentage change in price}}$$

There are two difficulties involved in the application of this formula. The first deals with the appropriate divisor to use in computing the percentages. Suppose the price falls from 11 cents to 10 cents and the quantity demanded rises from 1 unit to 2 units as in one of the schedules given above (page 41). The amount of change in price is 1 cent. This may be expressed as a percentage in any one of three ways: 1/11, 1/10, or 1/10.5. The latter possibility is the best because it recognizes that the change occurs *between* 11 cents and 10 cents and therefore the midpoint or average figure should be the divisor: $(11 + 10)/2 = 10.5$. Similarly, the quantity percentage is best expressed, not as 1/1 or 1/2, but as 1/1.5.

The second difficulty lies in the fact that one of the numerators in these percentage fractions will have a negative sign. At least this will be true in every demand schedule following the Law of Demand. In the above illustration the quantity changes from 1 to 2, and therefore subtracting the second number from the first gives a minus 1, not a plus 1. The price change is $11 - 10 = + 1$, so there is no trouble there. But if the schedule were being read in the other direction because we were interested in the effect of a price increase, the plus and minus signs would be reversed. The subtractions would be: $2 - 1 = + 1$, and $10 - 11 = - 1$. Because of the appearance of a negative sign in either the numerator or the denominator, the quotient would be negative and would, therefore, have to be compared with $- 1.00$, not with $+ 1.00$. This is illustrated by the following example based upon the figures given above:

$$E = \frac{-1}{1.5} \div \frac{1}{10.5} = \frac{-1}{1.5} \times \frac{10.5}{1} = \frac{10.5}{-1.5} = -7.00$$

The elasticity of demand is $-7.00$, which is said to be greater than $-1.00$ and therefore the demand is very "elastic." The next change in the schedule is from 10 cents to 9 cents, and from 2 units to 3 units. Applying the formula to test elasticity for this change, we find that:

$$E = \frac{-1}{2.5} \div \frac{1}{9.5} = \frac{-1}{2.5} \times \frac{9.5}{1} = \frac{9.5}{-2.5} = -3.8$$

The demand is less elastic than before, but it is still "greater than unity." Down below the middle of the given schedule, demand-elasticity becomes less than unity, as in the case where price changes from 6 cents to 5 cents and the demand rises from 6 units to 7 units.

$$E = \frac{-1}{6.5} \div \frac{1}{5.5} = \frac{5.5}{-6.5} = -.846$$

The elasticity formula may now be stated in more general terms. Instead of taking the average of the two prices and the average of the two quantities which requires adding in each case and dividing by 2, we can use simply the totals because the 2 in each fraction cancels out. Nor do we need to change the price by only one cent each time. A difference of any size is permissible, provided the corresponding quantities are used. Thus in the illustrative schedule, if the change is supposed to be from 7 cents to 5 cents, where the quantities rise from 5 units to 7 units, a difference of 2 in each case, the application of the elasticity formula gives a quotient of $-1.00$, as follows: [4]

$$E = \frac{-2}{7+5} \div \frac{2}{7+5} = \frac{-2}{12} \times \frac{12}{2} = -1.00$$

In symbols the demand-elasticity formula becomes:

$$E = \frac{Q_1 - Q_2}{Q_1 + Q_2} \div \frac{P_1 - P_2}{P_1 + P_2}$$

**8. Demand-Elasticity, Third Method: Ratio Between Segments of a Tangent to a Demand Curve.**—A third method of computing demand-elasticity is given in Note D. It is derived from this second method and is used to determine or to demonstrate the elas-

---

[4] This case may be tested, as may all the others, by applying the first method given for determining demand-elasticity. The total revenue remains unchanged at $35\cancel{c} = 5 \times 7\cancel{c} = 7 \times 5\cancel{c}$.

ticity of demand at any price-quantity point on a smooth demand curve. Although useful in the interpretation of the diagrams which constitute the shorthand of economics, it is not applicable to problems faced by economists or businessmen who want to know the probable effects of a change in price.

NOTE D.—Point-Elasticity When Demand Curves Are Plotted on Customary Arithmetical Axes. When the price change is infinitesimal, demand-elasticity at the point from which the infinitesimal movement occurs may be calculated by using a variant of the formula given in Section 7 which uses the quotient of two percentage changes. Denoting the midpoints between the two prices as $P_m$ and between the two quantities as $Q_m$, the formula becomes:

$$E_m = \frac{Q_1 - Q_2}{Q_m} \div \frac{P_1 - P_2}{P_m}$$

inverting:

$$E_m = \frac{Q_1 - Q_2}{Q_m} \times \frac{P_m}{P_1 - P_2}$$

whence:

$$E_m = \frac{P_m}{Q_m} \times \frac{Q_1 - Q_2}{P_1 - P_2}$$

or:

$$E_p = \frac{P}{Q} \times \frac{\Delta Q}{\Delta P} = \frac{\text{Price}}{\text{Quantity}} \times \frac{\text{Infinitesimal change in quantity}}{\text{Infinitesimal change in price}}$$

since, in dealing with infinitesimal changes, any "midpoint" between prices or quantities is the same as either point.

Then, by applying the rule developed in Section 4 and Note A, the second term in the final equation above may be said to equal the marginal quantity. The final equation becomes:

$$E_p = \frac{\text{Price}}{\text{Quantity}} \times \text{Marginal quantity}$$

This formula may be presented diagrammatically and then generalized into a geometric rule for finding demand-elasticity at any point on a given demand curve. Thus in Figure 8 the marginal quantity at $P$, representing price $OY$, is the slope of the tangent $APB$ with reference to the price axis. In terms of lines on the diagram this equals $OB/OA$. Then by geometry we find that $\dfrac{OB}{OA} = \dfrac{YP}{AY} = \dfrac{OX}{AY}.$ The latter term, together with the price : quantity ratio $\dfrac{OY}{OX}$ may now be substituted in the elasticity of demand formula as follows: $E_p = \dfrac{OY}{OX} \times \dfrac{OX}{AY} = \dfrac{OY}{AY}.$ By geometry, $\dfrac{OY}{AY} = \dfrac{BP}{AP}.$ Therefore, $E_p = \dfrac{BP}{AP}.$

The rule for showing point-elasticity of demand in diagrams of demand curves may therefore be formulated as follows: draw a tangent to the given demand quantity *curve* at any point *P,* and divide the lower segment (*BP*) by the upper (*AP*). This rule is very useful in in-

FIGURE 8

Point-Elasticity of Demand

(To prove $E_p - BP/AP$)

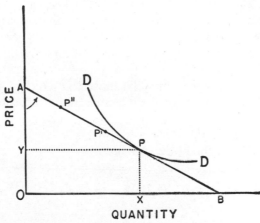

QUANTITY

terpreting conventional demand curves, which are often drawn as straight lines. At first sight one is tempted to confuse demand-elasticity with the *slope* of such lines. On the contrary, the point-elasticity changes throughout the entire length of a straight-line demand curve. The closer the chosen point (*P″*) is to *A* (i.e., the higher the price), the greater the elasticity. When it is half-way between the axes (*P′*), elasticity will be unity (*P′B/AP′* = 1). As the price approaches zero, the elasticity decreases rapidly. Incidentally, this indicates that when the conventional demand curve is drawn as a straight line, it is graphically realistic, for experience shows that the demand for most necessities tends to become more elastic at prices higher than customary and less elastic at prices below the usual ones.

It is now possible to combine some conclusions of Notes B and D regarding the interpretation of demand curves:

1. A tangent to an *AR* demand curve drawn on *arithmetical* axes makes an angle with the price axis which reveals the *marginal quantity,* or rate of change in quantity sold at that price. (In this it resembles the tangent to *TR* which was shown in Note A to reveal *marginal revenue.*)

2. A tangent to an *AR* demand curve drawn on *logarithmic* axes makes an angle with the price axis which reveals the *elasticity* of demand at that point.

9. **Summary of Economic Principles Regarding the Effect of Price on Demand.**—When other variables are held constant, the price-elasticity of demand may be measured in either of two ways: the change in total revenue or the quotient of percentage changes in price and quantity. Either method enables one to determine whether a given price change reveals demand to be "elastic" or "inelastic" by comparison with "demand-elasticity of unity." The second method gives a numerical measure of the degree of elasticity.

All finite changes in price reveal an *average* elasticity of demand between the two prices. By the use of infinitesimal changes in price, the elasticity of demand may be obtained for any given price or quantity point.

Demand and its elasticity may be shown by whichever one of four types of schedules or curves is the most useful in the problem at hand: $AR$ ($P$) and $Q$, $MR$ and $Q$, $TR$ and $P$, or $TR$ and $Q$. The most common demand curve is the $AR$ type, which plots price on the vertical axis and quantity on the horizontal axis.

# Chapter 5

## DEMAND ANALYSIS DEMONSTRATED
## BY INDIFFERENCE CURVES

**1. Outlay Indifference Curves.**—Many of the demand concepts explained in the preceding chapters may be summarized by the use of a type of economic shorthand called indifference curves. These curves also suggest a few relationships not readily apparent in either the verbal approach or in one using utility curves. The argument may be divided into two main divisions: first, the individual's position relative to two commodities; second, his behavior when one of these two commodities is defined as money. This latter approach most closely resembles the spending problems treated in the demand analysis of earlier chapters.

The first type of indifference "curve" to be studied here is a straight line which may be called an "outlay indifference curve." It is based upon certain assumptions which seem peculiar at first glance, but whose significance will become clear as the argument proceeds. These may be outlined as follows:

1. John Smith has $6 which he intends to spend on meat for his large family's Sunday dinner.
2. At the store he finds that beef roast costs 60 cents per pound and pork roast costs 50 cents per pound.
3. He does not care whether he gets a 10-pound roast of beef or a 12-pound roast of pork. Both meats are equally well liked by his family. The differences in bone, fat, etc., are such that the nourishment value of the two roasts is approximately the same in spite of their difference in weight.
4. He can, if he wishes, get some beef plus some pork instead of all of one and all of the other. It is really a matter of indifference to him what quantities of each he gets, provided only that the total purchase does not cost more than $6.

These assumptions are outlined in Figure 9. The vertical axis represents pounds of beef which Smith could buy with his $6 outlay. The horizontal axis represents pounds of pork. Point *A* on the *OY* axis shows Smith buying 10 pounds of beef. Point *B* on the *OX* axis shows him buying 12 pounds of pork. The straight line connecting $A$ and $B$ shows all the possible combinations of beef and pork which he might buy for his $6. Point $C$, for instance, reveals the purchase of 2.4 pounds of pork for $1.20 and 8 pounds of beef for $4.80. At point $D$, Smith would buy 6 pounds of pork for $3 and 5 pounds of beef with his remaining $3. So far as outlay is concerned, it is a matter of indifference to Smith whether he spends his $6 for one combination or another on the line $AB$. This line is there-

FIGURE 9

EQUAL TOTAL OUTLAY POINTS ON AN OUTLAY INDIFFERENCE CURVE

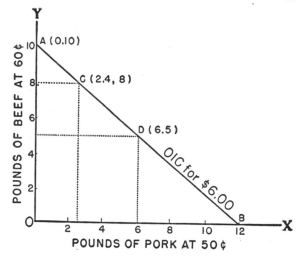

fore called an *outlay indifference curve* or a "constant total outlay curve." It is defined as a line on which all points represent the same aggregate outlay for two commodities at constant prices but for varying quantities of each.

**2. A Series of Outlay Indifference Curves.**—If we now change the amount which Mr. Smith sets aside to spend for his Sunday meat supply, we will get different outlay indifference curves. A larger amount, say $8, will give a line drawn from 13.3 pounds on the $OY$ axis to 16 pounds on the $OX$ axis as shown between $E$ and $F$ in Figure 10. If Smith has only $3 to spend, his constant outlay line will be drawn between 5 pounds on $OY$ and 6 pounds on $OX$, or $GH$ on the adjoining figure. All points on $EF$ represent a total outlay of $8, which is larger than any point on $AB$ because that line shows an outlay of only $6. Similarly, movement from $GH$ to $AB$ means spend-

FIGURE 10

A SERIES OF *OIC*'s SHOWING DIFFERENT TOTAL OUTLAYS

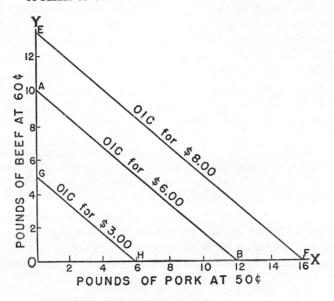

FIGURE 11

SERIES OF *OIC*'s WHEN PRICE RATIO IS 2:1

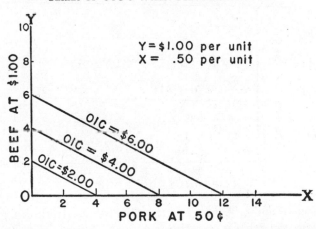

ing more money regardless of where one starts on *GH* or ends on *AB*. No point on any one line will be the same as that on any other, i.e., the lines cannot intersect. All three lines in Figure 10 and any other outlay indifference lines drawn with the same prices of beef and pork will be parallel.

If the prices of beef and pork are different from those of the original assumption, the slopes of the outlay indifference curves will be different. For instance, Figure 11 shows a series of such curves when the price of beef is $1 and that of pork is 50 cents. These lines are not so steep as those in Figure 10. The general rule is that the higher the price of the commodity plotted on $OY$ compared to the price of the commodity plotted on $OX$, the less steep will be the lines. If the ratio of the prices were 10:1, the lines would be nearly horizontal. If the ratio were, say 1:20, the outlay indifference curves would be nearly vertical.

**3. Utility Indifference Curves.**—A second type of curve based on the same principle as the constant total outlay curve just described is one in which there is assumed to be constant total utility. Money outlay disappears from the picture and in its place is put the total utility or satisfaction derived from consuming beef and pork in different ratios. Smith is presumed to experience diminishing marginal utility as he increases his consumption of either of them. This has the corollary of *increasing* marginal utility if he *decreases* his

FIGURE 12

UTILITY INDIFFERENCE CURVE SHOWING
THREE POINTS OF EQUAL TOTAL UTILITY

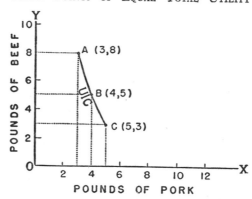

consumption of either beef or pork. Therefore, if Smith gives up some beef to get more pork, the marginal utility of beef rises and that of pork falls. But the *total* utility can remain the same, provided the amount of beef surrendered has a utility exactly equal to the amount of pork obtained.

This line of reasoning furnishes the basis for drawing constant total utility curves like that shown in Figure 12. At point *A*, Smith is consuming pork and beef in the ratio of 3 pounds of pork to 8 pounds of beef. At point $B$, Smith's meat consumption ratio has changed to 4 pounds of pork for every 5 pounds of beef. And at $C$, the ratio is 5 pork to 3 beef. By definition, Smith's total utility is the same at each point $A$, $B$, and $C$, that is, at each meat consumption ratio, $3:8$, $4:5$, and $5:3$. In terms of utility, $3P + 8B = 4P + 5B = 5P + 3B$. It is a matter of indifference to him which ratio he has. The line connecting $A$, $B$, and $C$ is called a utility indifference curve. Intermediate points on this smoothed curve also have the same total utility. The argument may appear more logical if Smith is pictured as getting his meat free in whatever ratio he desires. Or Smith may be exchanging beef for pork on a barter basis without ever changing his total satisfactions.

**4. A Series of Utility Indifference Curves.**—Following the same line of reasoning developed in Section 2, we may now construct a series of utility indifference curves as in Figure 13. Each curve

FIGURE 13

A Series of *UIC*'s Each with a
Different Total Utility

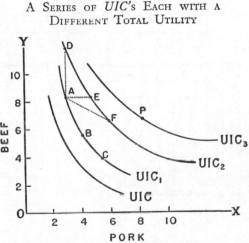

represents a different total utility comparable to the different total outlay curves of Figure 10. Movement *along any one curve* represents no change in total utility, but only a change in the ratio of consumption of the two meats. Movement *from one curve to another*, however, represents a change in total utility and also a change in the quantity of at least one of the two commodities. Thus in Figure 13, movement from $A$ to $B$ to $C$ *along UIC$_1$* does not change Smith's

total utility, nor from $D$ to $E$ to $F$ on $UIC_2$.  But a movement from $A$
to either $D, E,$ or $F$, puts Smith on a higher total utility curve.  He
would have no choice between positions $A, B,$ or $C$, but he would definitely prefer to be at $D, E,$ or $F$ rather than at any point on $UIC_1$.
Similarly, any point $P$ on $UIC_3$ represents a position preferable to
any point on $UIC_2, UIC_1$, or any other utility indifference curve to the
left of or below $UIC_3$.

Since each utility indifference curve represents a different total
utility from any other, the curves cannot cross.  In this respect they
resemble a series of outlay indifference curves.  But utility indifference curves need not be parallel, and in fact they rarely are.  They
may have many different shapes, but are usually convex toward the
origin like those in Figure 13.  This means that each of the two commodities has diminishing marginal utility, as suggested above.  In
the indifference curve analysis, however, this term is dropped and in
its place one speaks of a *diminishing marginal rate of substitution.*

FIGURE 14

DIMINISHING MARGINAL RATE OF SUBSTITUTION OF $Y$ FOR $X$

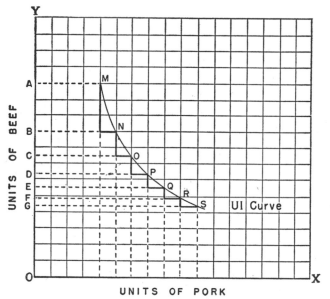

The argument is that Smith may be considered as bartering $Y$ for $X$
(beef for pork).  For each unit of pork obtained in exchange, Smith
gives up a diminishing amount of beef.  This may be seen by drawing a utility indifference curve on a grid of cross lines as in Figure

14. Moving from left to right by equal intervals represents the acquisition of equal additional units of pork. When these points are marked on the curve, as $M, N, O, P$, etc., the amount of beef that must be given up by Smith to keep his total utility constant may be seen by drawing horizontal lines from each of these points to the $OY$ axis. The distance between these lines becomes smaller as one moves from $M$ to $N$ to $O$ to $P$. This shows diminishing amounts of $Y$ substituted for equal increments of $X$ or, as stated above, a diminishing marginal rate of substitution of $Y$ for $X$. By reversing the process one may also demonstrate a diminishing marginal rate of substitution of $X$ for $Y$. Both relationships are based upon the diminishing marginal utility of the object whose rate of consumption is being increased, and the increasing marginal utility of the commodity whose rate of consumption is being decreased.

**5. Maximum Total Utility for a Given Total Outlay.**—It is now desirable to bring together the argument of the first four sections of this chapter. First we shall consider the problem of securing the maximum total utility for a given total outlay.

Assume that Smith has \$6 to spend for beef and pork as in the first illustration. Retain also the assumption that beef and pork cost respectively 60 cents and 50 cents per pound.[1] Change the assumption that he has no particular preference for more of the one rather than the other. Assume instead that he has a preference schedule that may be represented by a series of utility indifference curves as shown by the three in Figure 15. The outlay indifference curve $AB$ cuts $UIC_1$ in two places $E$ and $F$, is tangent to $UIC_2$ at $D$, and does not

### FIGURE 15

MAXIMUM TOTAL UTILITY FOR A
GIVEN TOTAL OUTLAY

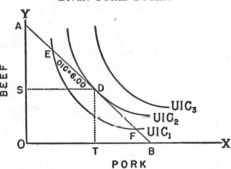

intersect $UIC_3$ at all. Smith would prefer to be on the highest possible utility indifference curve, but he is held back by his limit of \$6 to spend. Therefore, he cannot attain the total utility level of $UIC_3$ at all. On the other hand, he would not choose the beef-pork

[1] Strictly speaking, an $OIC$ is an exercise in arithmetic and need not be associated with Smith or any other particular individual. On the other hand, $UIC$'s must be associated with a specific individual.

combination represented by either point $E$ or $F$ because they are on $UIC_1$, which has a lower total utility than $UIC_2$, which is within his spending capacity at one point, $D$. That is, the *point of tangency* between the given $OIC$ and the highest possible $UIC$ solves our problem. Point $D$ reveals the maximum total utility that it is possible for Smith to obtain when he spends $6 for beef and pork at the same time, and at the prices given. This point also indicates, by perpendiculars to the axes, the quantities of beef ($OS$) and of pork ($OT$), which Smith would buy.

If it were possible to define utility in terms of definite units, a similar demonstration could be given with three $OIC$'s and one $UIC$.

### FIGURE 16
#### Minimum Total Outlay for a Given Total Utility

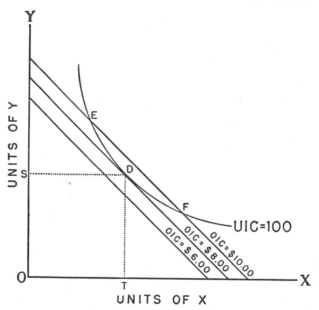

That is, if one could define for Smith a $UIC$ representing, say, 100 utils, one could then demonstrate the minimum outlay required to attain a satisfaction of that amount (cf. Figure 16). It would be the point of tangency between $UIC_{100}$ and the lowest possible $OIC$. $UIC_{100}$ would intersect higher $OIC$'s at two places, $E$ and $F$, thus indicating the possibility of moving along $UIC_{100}$ to an equally satisfying point, $D$, which would be on a lower $OIC$, i.e., which would require less total expenditure. The least outlay, $8, would be shown by the tangency solution similar to that of the maximizing problem treated in the preceding paragraph.

**6. Income Consumption Curve: A Series of Tangency Points on Parallel Outlay Indifference Curves.**—The next step is to plot on the same axes a series of $OIC$'s and $UIC$'s for a given individual and given market situation and to find their respective points of tangency. This is shown in Figure 17. Movement from $P$ to $R$, $S$, and $T$ may be interpreted as Smith's reaction to an increase in income which gives him more to spend on that Sunday meal. When his income is small, the best quantities of $Y$ and $X$ for him to buy are

FIGURE 17

INCOME-CONSUMPTION CURVE:
A SERIES OF TANGENCY POINTS

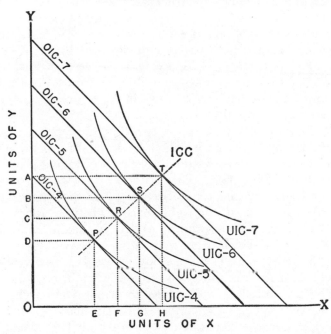

shown by $OE$ and $OD$, which are called the coordinates of point $P$. As his income increases, he should increase his purchases to $OF$ of $X$ and $OC$ of $Y$ as shown by point $R$, and so on. The line $PT$ which connects these tangency points is called an income consumption curve, $ICC$. More logical terms would seem to be "outlay consumption curve" or "optimum outlay curve," but custom dictates "income consumption curve."

One must note the assumption that the preference pattern of Mr. Smith remains unchanged as his income increases. The *UI* curves define a surface which does not alter.[2]  Only the *OIC*'s change as new ones appear further to the right.  Their shape and slope is held constant by the unchanging prices of *Y* and *X*.  The unrealism of the initial assumption does not invalidate the analysis, and it may not be very faulty if the increase in income is small and slow.  Two practical applications of income consumption curves in economic analysis are best deferred to Section 9, where the assumption of two commodities is changed to one commodity and money.

**7. The Price Consumption Curve: A Series of Tangency Points on a Fan-Shaped Series of Outlay Indifference Curves.**—Returning now to the concept of outlay indifference curves discussed in the last part of Section 2, we may construct a fan-shaped series of curves by holding one price constant and varying the other.  Beef may be held constant at 60 cents per pound while pork is assumed to sell at prices ranging from the first price of 50 cents down to 10 cents per pound. The fan of *OIC*'s shown in Figure 18 is the result.  Each of these lines has a point of tangency with a utility indifference curve.  When these points of tangency, *K, L, M,* and *N,* are connected, a price-consumption curve for pork results.

A *PC* curve of this type shows two things.  First, it reveals the effects of a falling price of pork upon the demand for pork.[3]  Second, and more important, it shows the effects of a changing price of pork upon the demand for beef.  This is the *cross-elasticity* of demand problem discussed in Chapter 2, Section 5.  If the *PC* curve slopes downward as it moves to the right, *Y* is a substitute for *X*.  Smith buys less of *Y* when he buys more of *X*.  If the *PC* curve is horizontal, *Y* is a good which is not associated with *X* in any significant way.  If, however, the *PC* curve slopes upward, *Y* is revealed to be a complement of *X*.  Smith buys more of it when he buys more of *X*. The ability to use indifference curves to demonstrate such relationships is one of their major advantages over ordinary demand curves. The principle, however, is not new and has already been stated in nongraphic terms in Chapter 2, Section 5.

**8. Price Consumption Curves Become Demand Curves When Money Is Substituted for One Commodity.**—It is now desirable to

---

[2] Of course one might define the pattern of *UI* curves as one which represented Smith's changing preferences as his income increased, but that is contrary to the customary assumptions used here.

[3] Comments on the irreversibility of demand curves and similar points apply just as much to *PC* curves as they do in the demand analysis of Chapter 3, Section 6.

enter the second half of the indifference curve analysis. This is done
by substituting money for the commodity whose quantity has been
measured on the $OY$ axis. To keep the discussion in commodity
terms, $OY$ sometimes is said to represent "all other commodities"

FIGURE 18

PRICE-CONSUMPTION CURVE FOR TWO COMMODITIES

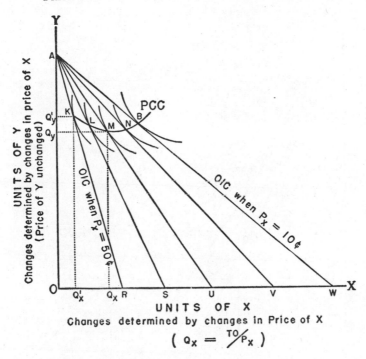

than the one measured on $OX$. This has the advantage of indicating
that money may be spent for many other things and is desired because of its ability to serve many uses.[4]

When $OY$ represents money, there will be some point on $OY$ such
as $A$ which shows the total amount of money which Smith has to
spend in the period when his purchases of $X$ might be influenced by
changes in the price of $X$. The fan-shaped series of $OIC$'s will be
much the same as in Figure 18 although the $OY$ scale will have to be
changed to money units. For most items of low price, the "ribs" of
the "fan" will be close together. To make relationships clear, Fig-

---

[4] But note that, in Fig. 19, $OY$ is the total *money* spent on *all* commodities, not
the quantity of all *other* commodities.

ure 19 therefore assumes an item whose price is high relative to disposable income. In this hypothetical illustration, a fall in the price of $X$ from $3 to $2 per unit will increase Smith's demand for $X$ from 8 units to 11 units when Smith's disposable income is $30.

FIGURE 19

Price-Elasticity of Demand Shown by a One-Commodity
Price-Consumption Curve

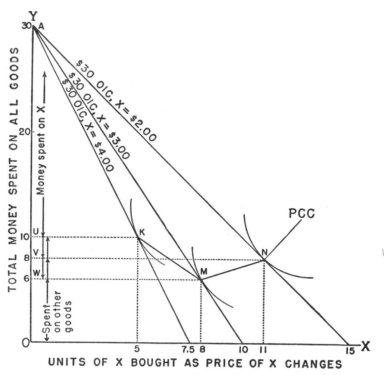

UNITS OF X BOUGHT AS PRICE OF X CHANGES

A further attribute of the one-commodity price-consumption curve is its ability to reveal the price-elasticity of demand by its slope, which the conventional demand curve can do only when plotted on logarithmic axes (cf. Chapter 4, Note C). Since $OA$ represents the total amount of money to be spent on $OX$ and other commodities, the distance from $O$ to $U$, $V$, or $W$ represents the amount spent on those other commodities. By subtraction, the distance from $A$ to $U$, $V$, or $W$ shows the amount spent on $X$. When a fall in the price of $X$ from $3 to $2 causes the $PC$ curve to rise from $M$ to $N$, it also shows the total amount spent on $X$ decreasing from $24 ($AW$) to $22

($AV$). But a decreased total expenditure on $X$ when its price is falling is an evidence of inelastic demand. Between $4 and $3, however, a falling price raised the total amount spent on $X$ from $20 ($AU$) to $24 ($AW$).[5] The generalization may be made, therefore, that when a $PC$ curve slopes downward to the right ($KM$), the price-elasticity of demand for that good is greater than unity. When the $PC$ curve is horizontal, demand has an elasticity of unity. And when the $PC$ curve slopes upward to the right ($MN$), the price elasticity of demand is less than unity.

This brings us to a theoretical advantage of indifference curve analysis. It allows for changes in the marginal utility of money at the same time that it considers changes in the marginal utility of the goods bought with that money. The conventional demand curve is based upon a diminishing marginal utility schedule for the commodity. In order to translate utils into money, each util must equal an unchanging number of cents or dollars. The marginal utility of money must be constant, an assumption which is probably near enough to the truth in most cases to be acceptable. But there are cases of small amounts of available funds or purchases of high priced items which require the use of the more general assumption of the diminishing marginal utility of money. Indifference curves fit any type of case.

**9. Superior and Inferior Goods Revealed by One-Commodity Income-Consumption Curves.**—Another advantage of indifference curves is found in their ability to demonstrate the income-elasticity of demand. This is done by drawing a one-commodity income-consumption curve in which the vertical axis represents disposable income as in Section 8. The most common type of $ICC$ is shown in Figure 20 which resembles Figure 17 except for the change on the $OY$ axis. The upward-to-the-right slope of this $ICC$ indicates that as Smith gets more money to spend he buys more of this commodity (the "$Q$" points move to the right). According to the argument and terminology of Chapter 2, Section 6, this means that the commodity is a "superior good" so far as Smith is concerned.

Under some circumstances Smith might buy *less* of a good when his income rose. Such a commodity is called an "inferior good" and may be shown diagrammatically by an $ICC$ which slopes to the left (see Figure 21). At other times a commodity may be "superior"

---

[5] $30 minus $ 6 equals $24 equals  8 times $3.
$30 minus $ 8 equals $22 equals 11 times $2.
$30 minus $10 equals $20 equals  5 times $4.

for income increases at low levels and then become "inferior" as incomes rise still higher. This possibility is diagrammed in Figure 21 where an increase in weekly income from $10 to $25 per week makes the consumption of X increase. From $25 to $30 there is no change.

FIGURE 20

INCOME-CONSUMPTION CURVE (for one commodity)

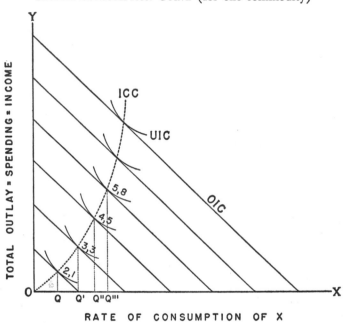

RATE OF CONSUMPTION OF X

But above $30 per week X becomes "inferior" and the *ICC* begins to slope to the left. A practical illustration might be found in the purchase of motion picture tickets to a certain theater. At higher income levels Smith might take his family to a more expensive theater, at least part of the time.

If one-commodity *IC* curves are drawn with the variables plotted on log-log axes, the income elasticity of demand may be read at a glance. An *IC* curve sloping upward to the right at 45 degrees will represent positive income-elasticity of unity because the percentage change in the quantity of X bought will equal the percentage change in other commodities bought.[6] If the slope of the *ICC* is less than

---

[6] If the percentage change in purchase of both X and Y occurs at the same rate, the change for total income will be of the same percentage since the total spent on X plus "all other commodities" (Y) must by definition exhaust the amount of income being spent.

45 degrees, the income elasticity may be said to be greater than unity because Smith will be increasing his purchases of $X$ more rapidly than he increases his purchases of other commodities. Similarly, a slope steeper than 45 degrees means income elasticity less than unity,

### FIGURE 21

SUPERIOR AND INFERIOR GOODS SHOWN BY INCOME-ELASTICITY
OF DEMAND (via *IC* curve)

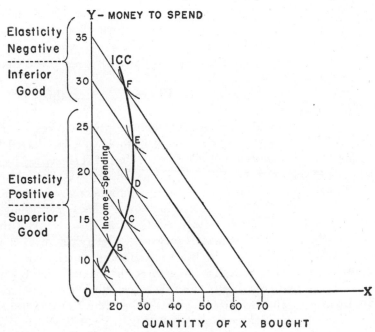

diminishing to zero when the *ICC* is perpendicular, and becoming negative when the *ICC* turns backward to the left and indicates the "inferior good" type of response.

**10. Income Effect and Substitution Effect of Price Change.—** For some purposes it is convenient to separate into two parts the effect of the rise in price of a given commodity. The first is the tendency to decrease the consumption of the good whose price has risen in the same way that a person would have to do if his income were decreased. This is called the "income effect" and may be diagrammed by a movement from the original *OIC* to a hypothetical *OIC* below it. The second part is the tendency to decrease the consumption of a good and buy more of other goods when the first becomes more expensive relative to the latter. This may be diagrammed by a movement along a utility indifference curve from one point to another. As explained in Section 3 above, such a movement does not change a person's total utility from the commodities consumed. It does represent a change in the *OIC* whose tangency would determine first the one point and then the other. The substitution effect of a price increase is always negative. The income effect is negative in most cases, but in rare cases may be positive as in the case of inferior goods. In extremely rare cases, if the income effect is positive, it may be so great as to offset all of the negative substitution effect. When that happens, the good whose price has risen may be called an inferior good on two scores—income change and price change.

The accompanying diagrams of Figure 22 show three possible cases. In each of them the income effect is indicated by the dotted line *PT* which resembles the income consumption curves of Figures 17 and 20. The substitution effect is shown by the dotted line *TR*. The price consumption curve in each case is represented by the solid line *PR,* like the *PCC*'s of Figures 18 and 19. In the first two cases, movement from *P* to *R* represents a *decrease* in the total amount of *X* purchased as its price *increases*. These represent the most common type of market response to price change. The third case shows the highly exceptional "price inferiority" case of a rise in price causing an increase in the total amount purchased. Even the second case is rare. Each of the three diagrams is intended to represent a different commodity, and therefore the *UI* curves have a different pattern. In each diagram the broken line *BD* representing the hypothetical *OIC* is drawn parallel to the line *AE,* which represents the initial price-income situation and which determines by tangency with the highest *UIC* the starting point *P*.

**11. Summary and Evaluation.**—What has been gained by the indifference curve approach to demand? In what respects is it superior to, inferior to, or no better than the conventional demand curve based on diminishing marginal utility? Both diagrammatic approaches may also be compared with (1) a strictly verbal analysis like much of that in the earlier chapters, and (2) a purely mathematical type of functional notation. Two criteria may be applied: clarity in illustrating principles, and realism of assumptions.

 I. *Clarity*—Indifference curves and their derivatives (*PCC*'s and *ICC*'s) demonstrate certain concepts better than do conventional demand curves:

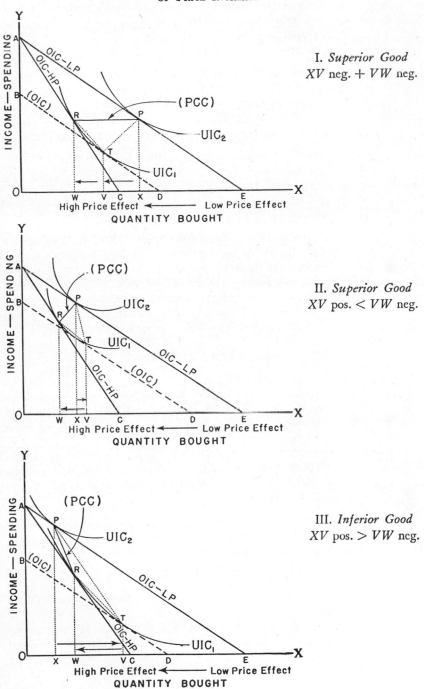

FIGURE 22

INCOME EFFECT $(XV)$ AND SUBSTITUTION EFFECT $(VW)$
OF PRICE INCREASE

I. *Superior Good*
$XV$ neg. + $VW$ neg.

II. *Superior Good*
$XV$ pos. < $VW$ neg.

III. *Inferior Good*
$XV$ pos. > $VW$ neg.

A. The income-elasticity of demand: effects of changes in income upon the quantities demanded by individuals. There are two types with varying degrees:
   1. Superior goods
   2. Inferior goods

B. The cross-elasticity of demand: effects of changes in the price of one commodity upon the demand for another. There are two types with varying degrees:
   1. Substitute goods
   2. Complementary goods

C. The twofold effect of price change upon demand:
   1. The income effect
   2. The substitution effect

II. *Realism*
   A. *UIC*'s are *more* realistic in the following respects:
      1. May make allowance for the increasing marginal utility of disposable money income as larger amounts of it are spent for a given good
      2. Do not require the use of explicit or implied specific measures of utility, such as utils, but only *relative* preferences. This is often described as using ordinal numbers (1st, 2nd, 3rd, . . .) to replace cardinal numbers (1, 2, 3, . . .). The latter must be related to utility units, but the former need not be.

   B. *UIC*'s are *less* realistic in the following respects:
      1. Imply that consumers evaluate relative *pairs* of commodities more commonly than they evaluate rival quantities of the same good or single units of rival goods
      2. Tend to obscure the unrelatedness of commodities which compete for the consumer's dollar, but are not otherwise substitutes (food and clothing, or salmon and shirts)

   C. Indifference curves and their derivatives represent *no gain* in the following respects. One should note that these defects also apply to the conventional demand curves used to illustrate points of the theory of consumer demand. The verbal method of presenting the material *may* avoid many of these shortcomings of the diagrammatic or mathematical presentations.
      1. Overstress the importance of choice and conscious planning in most consumer expenditures as opposed to the force of habit, impulse, and regimentation

2. Overstress choices between some and more of a homogeneous good rather than between this and that heterogeneous good

3. Overstress the bases of individual demand schedules, although market behavior on the supply side is more often determined by expectations about collective demand schedules

4. Imply knowledge about preference or utility schedules at prices and incomes far beyond the probable and customary ranges

5. Fail to allow for variations in demand which result from differences in the rate of change of the independent variable (price or income), its direction of change, and the magnitude of successive changes (cf. Chapter 3, especially Sections 6 and 9)

6. Fail to allow sufficiently for product differentiation, monopolistic activity, and institutional controls [7]

---

[7] An excellent appraisal of indifference curves may be found in *The Theory of Consumer Demand* by Ruby Turner Norris, New Haven: Yale University Press, 1941, especially Chapter 3.

# Chapter 6

## SUPPLY AND PRICE—GENERAL CONSIDERATIONS

**1. Statement of the Problem.**—Transactions prices are the joint result of demand and supply forces. Sometimes one of these forces seems more potent than the other. But a transaction is an exchange of money for goods, and therefore both a buyer and a seller must be involved. Both demand and supply must be present. To paraphrase Alfred Marshall, it is as idle to think of demand or supply alone determining a transaction price as to conceive of either the upper or the lower blade of a pair of shears doing the cutting by itself. The demand side of the market has received considerable attention in earlier chapters. We now turn to an examination of the supply side. It is perhaps not more difficult than demand side analysis, but it has received more attention in economic literature. The following questions must be asked and answered. The first two lay the foundation for the others, which will be studied in later chapters.

1. What are the different concepts of supply?
2. In what sense and in what situations is *supply a cause* of transaction price?
3. What are the *causes of supply* quantities and supply prices?
    (a) What are the institutional determinants of supply prices? (Ch. 7)
    (b) How may cost estimates influence supply prices? (Ch. 8)
    (c) How may production policies influence supply quantities? (Ch. 9)
    (d) How may selling policies influence supply prices? (Ch. 10)
    (e) What is the supply side significance of various types of competition? (Chs. 11 and 12)
4. What are the *effects* of supply quantity changes upon production cost and price in different time periods? (Ch. 13)
5. How can individual price fluctuations be explained in terms of demand and supply changes in typical situations? (Ch. 14)

**2. Supply as a Quantity Offered for Sale.**—Supply generally means the quantity offered for sale. Sometimes supply refers to the quantity offered at a certain stated or minimum price known as *the reservation price* or *supply price*. At other times it signifies the quantity offered for whatever it will bring, i.e., without any minimum price. Usually the reference is to the quantity offered by a group of sellers, whose size may be large or small. It may refer also to the offering of a single seller.[1] The time of supply is generally revealed by the context, but should be made explicit if confusion is likely to develop. The most common time period is the given instant of offering, or any time period shorter than that required to replenish (usually, to reproduce) the good offered. Finally, supply must be understood as referring to an amount at a certain place, although that place may be of any size, small or large, even the whole world. With agricultural products, for instance, the "supply" is often the entire amount produced by all the commercial growers in a certain region during a given crop year.

**3. Supply as a Schedule or Series of Quantities.**—Economists also use the term supply to refer to *schedule supply,* the *series* of quantities which individuals would sell at a *series* of prices. This corresponds with the concept of schedule demand explained in Chapter 2. Again the contrast should be noted between the schedule idea of supply and the market idea. The schedule is made up of a series of quantity-price pairs. Each pair represents a hypothetical market supply, i.e., a quantity offered at a price. All the comments made in Chapter 2 about demand schedules apply here. Supply schedules represent what someone *thinks* would be the amounts offered at the series of prices he chooses.[2] Only one of the quantity-price pairs can ever be known with certainty, and even that may be only an approximation. When a person himself is offering supply at a given time for a given price, he can describe *his* supply with precision, such as one used 1938 Ford coupé for $600. But the same person cannot now state definitely how many others are offering 1938 Ford coupés for $600 in a large city, or in the country as a whole. He must estimate that quantity. And if he wants to say how many *would be* offered at $700 or at $800, other estimates of still less accuracy would have to be made. The quantities would depend upon how the price is reached, whether by a rising price or a falling one, whether other prices rose at the same time, or did not, etc. Even the concept "1938 Ford coupé" is hard to define, since such cars may be in various stages of decrepitude.

---

[1] Cf. the concepts of demand outlined in Chapter 2, Section 2.
[2] They may also be historical, but these are less useful.

**4. Supply in the Schedule Sense and in the Market Sense.—**
Nevertheless, the idea of supply in the schedule sense is a very useful
one, particularly for staple commodities.  The concept is indispensable when one wishes to compare two situations in which both supply
price and supply quantity have changed or are expected to change.
Thus, if American copper miners produce and offer for sale 500,000
tons in one year when the average price is 12 cents per pound of
refined copper and 600,000 tons when the price in the next year is
15 cents, one can say only that "the market supply increased."  One
cannot say whether there was an increase in supply in the schedule
sense until he knows what the copper mines *would* have produced in
the first year at 15 cents a pound.  If that amount were 575,000 tons,
then the second year reveals an increase both in the market supply
and in the schedule supply.  Such a situation is revealed by the following figures.

HISTORICAL SUPPLY QUANTITIES MARKETED BY AMERICAN COPPER MINES

| In Year 194X | | In Year 194X plus 1 | |
|---|---|---|---|
| Supply Quantity | Supply Price | Supply Quantity | Supply Price |
| 500,000 tons | 12¢ | ?    tons | 12¢ |
| ?    tons | 15¢ | 600,000 tons | 15¢ |

HISTORICAL (AND HYPOTHETICAL) SUPPLY SCHEDULES OF
AMERICAN COPPER MINES

| In Year 194X | | In Year 194X plus 1 | |
|---|---|---|---|
| Supply Quantity | Supply Price | Supply Quantity | Supply Price |
| 500,000 tons | 12¢ | (520,000 tons) * | 12¢ |
| (575,000 tons) | 15¢ | 600,000 tons | 15¢ |

* Added for completeness, though not absolutely necessary to argument.

The foregoing argument may now be summarized by saying that
a change in supply *at any given price* represents a change in the
*schedule sense*.  This might be caused by a reduction in cost, by the
entry of new producers, by a change in selling policies, etc.  A change
in supply which is *caused* solely *by a change in price* is a change in
the *market sense*.

There is one other way of looking at supply which may now be
examined.  When the same quantity is offered at a higher or a lower

price than before, the supply may be said to have changed in the schedule sense. If the owner of the 1938 Ford coupé first offers it at $600 and then changes his mind and demands $700, the supply *at $600* has dropped to zero so far as he is concerned. Therefore, the price increase for the fixed quantity represents a decrease in schedule supply. This is a very important concept which is often misunderstood. If a gasoline station today raises the posted price of first-grade gasoline from 20 cents per gallon to 22 cents, the supply has decreased even though the station owner is willing to sell just as much as he did yesterday. Similarly, if some organized workers decide to refuse a renewal of their old contract at $1.25 per hour and demand $1.40, the supply of this type of labor has decreased regardless of the desire of individual workers to work as many hours as before. In short, a decrease in schedule supply occurs *either* when the quantity offered declines at a given price or when the requested price rises for a given quantity.[3] For increases in schedule supply the changes would be in the opposite direction.

**5. Supply as a Price Asked by Sellers.**—Just as the supply quantity is that amount which is offered at a given price, so the *supply price* is the money demanded by a seller for a given quantity offered for sale. The supply quantity concept often refers to the quantity that people are willing to sell at a given price *or higher*. Occasionally the supply price concept refers to a given quantity *or lower* which people are willing to sell at a given price. Thus, copper sellers will be willing to take more than 15 cents per pound for their 600,000 tons if anyone offers it to them. A gasoline station owner posting a price of 21 cents wants to sell all his station's daily capacity, say 5,000 gallons, but he is willing to sell any smaller amount if he cannot reach the maximum.[4]

**6. Supply Price as a Cause of Transaction Price.** The foregoing discussion has shown that the transactions price may be a cause of the supply quantity. Our attention now shifts to three general situations in which the supply price may be a cause of the transac-

---

[3] On a diagram, the movement of a supply curve to the left is the same as moving it upward:

[4] Of course, a station with that capacity cannot long continue in business if it sells only 50 gallons daily.

tions price. In the first, the supply price of an individual seller determines the transactions price at which each exchange takes place. Thus the Standard Oil Company sets the price at which its service stations sell Standard gasoline. This is the market situation most frequently encountered by individual consumers. It will be studied more fully in Chapter 7.

In other situations, the supply price of an individual seller is only one of several proximate causes of the transactions price. For instance, when bargaining occurs between buyer and seller, each names at first a more favorable price than he finally agrees to accept. During the bargaining interval there may be a secret minimum reservation price in the seller's mind, but his declared minimum changes as the higgling proceeds and he need never reveal his "actual" minimum.

A similar situation exists when there are many individual buyers and sellers whose demand and supply prices become revealed as the bidding and offering proceeds to the point where sales take place. At this point the aggregate demand quantity sought at a certain price equals the aggregate supply quantity offered at that price. The sellers are those willing to take that price or less. If the price determined by the *balancing of aggregates* is 10 cents and some seller was willing to have accepted 8 cents, the same person would have taken 9 cents, 10 cents, or any price higher than 8 cents. Therefore, he is an included seller. On the other hand, sellers who wanted 11 cents or 12 cents are excluded and do not make a sale at this time. In other words, some supply prices influence the transactions price, and some do not.

The supply price of sellers does not determine the transactions price at all in three situations. In the first, the seller has no reservation price whatever and offers his goods for auction sale to the highest bidder. In the second, the buyer sets the transactions price much like the seller in the first case described in this section. Sellers either accept that price or make no sales at all. In the third case, the government or other third party sets the price. Both buyers and individual sellers must accept it if they wish to trade. In this respect it resembles the price set by the balancing of aggregates described in the preceding paragraph.

**7. Causes of Supply Prices.**—Supply prices are determined in many ways. The first group of causes may be designated as institutional since they include such things as laws, customs, trade agreements, and attitudes. Chapter 7 explains the leading cases in this category and examines also some effects of changes in the determining institutions. The degree of price competition among sellers is particularly important since it differs from industry to industry and changes frequently. Chapters 10, 11, and 12 will shed further light on this subject.

The second group of determinants of supply price centers around the analysis of cost of production. Attitudes toward cost as a price determinant are also important. Much price theory is written in terms of the cost-price-quantity relationships which would maximize profit under various conditions. If most businessmen followed price policies based on these theories, their actions would deserve to be studied first in a book of this type. But most supply prices spring from institutional origins, including rule-of-thumb markup percentages which use cost as a base. Therefore, cost-price theory has been deferred to Chapter 8, following the institutional-price theory of Chapter 7.

**8. Causes of Supply Quantities.**—The supply quantity offered by any one seller will depend upon at least three things: (1) the price he expects to receive, (2) the quantity he can buy or produce at a cost less than his selling price, (3) the quantity he has on hand from prior production or purchase. The determinants of a seller's rate of production will be analyzed in Chapter 10.

The supply quantity for a group is a function of (1) the supply schedules of individual sellers, and (2) the number of sellers. The total supply quantity is cumulative upward through a scale of rising prices.[5] For instance, at the lowest price there may be only one seller, A, in the market. A slightly higher price may induce seller B to enter the market. The total supply at the price then becomes the amount offered by A plus that offered by B, and so on.

**9. Summary.**—The supply side of the market is very complex and will require several chapters for its elaboration. Supply generally means the quantity offered by suppliers, and is best thought of as the quantity offered at a certain price. The number of sellers, the time, and the place should be identified. Supply schedules may be constructed to show what some one thinks would be offered at a short series of prices. Supply changes in the schedule sense must be distinguished from supply changes in the market sense. Supply also may be considered as the minimum or supply price of a given quantity. This supply price may influence the transactions price in many situations. These include bargaining, the balancing of aggregates, and

[5] Cf. the explanation of collective demand in Chapter 3, Section 4.

the action of certain sellers in fixing a price and taking whatever volume of sales can be made at that price. When the buyer or the government sets the transactions price, or when auction sales occur, supply prices have no immediate effect. Supply prices have institutional and cost determinants. Supply quantities are related to output plans of producers. All of these points will be elaborated in subsequent chapters.

# Chapter 7

## INSTITUTIONAL DETERMINANTS OF SUPPLY PRICES

**1. Supply Prices When Institutional Forces Dominate.**—In Chapter 6 the term *supply price* was defined as the price at which a person declares himself willing to sell something. The supply price for certain neckties at the Honest Haberdashery is marked on their tags as $2. This is the most common situation. The marked price is the minimum price at which the seller will sell. Therefore, it becomes also the transactions price, the price at which sales take place. In a few exceptional cases, the seller's actual minimum price at that time is less than his posted or asking price. Pawnshops and other stores selling second-hand merchandise often fall in this group. In some foreign countries retail bargaining is the rule, not the exception as in the United States today. And American manufacturers sometimes shade their list prices in a form of secret price competition.

The present chapter will examine six situations in which sellers determine what supply price to ask. It will assume that the supply prices announced to potential buyers are the actual minimum prices at that time. Occasionally the synonym *reservation price* will be used. The following situations are called "institutional" because the economic environment of the seller determines his supply price decisions with very little need for conscious and independent price calculation on his part:

1. No reservation price; the auction situation
2. Supply price determined by custom
3. Supply price determined by law
    (a) Specific prices
    (b) Fixed maximum or fixed minimum prices
4. Resale supply price determined by prior seller
5. Imitation
6. Markup determined by custom, or by law

The final case to be considered in this chapter requires some calculation of unit cost before the application of the institutionally determined markup. Therefore, it serves as a very appropriate bridge to the next chapter on cost as a determinant of supply price. The cases examined in Chapter 8 deal with conscious calculations of profit-maximizing supply prices under assumed conditions of demand, cost, and competition. Institutional forces are present, of course, but are less dominant than in the situations described here.

**2. Motives Underlying the Determination of Supply Prices.—** In fixing their supply prices, sellers are influenced by a variety of motives and objectives. In capitalistic society the "profit motive" is usually assumed to be dominant. Unfortunately, this phrase has many connotations. It has been used as a synonym for material self-interest so as to include the worker's quest for higher wages. More narrowly, it applies to the desire of business managers to maximize the net income of their enterprises. But even that statement is indefinite as to scope and time. It fails to indicate whether profit maximization is sought for dealings in a particular product, for all goods produced by a certain plant, for everything sold by the enterprise, or for the managers and their friends who may have connections with other enterprises. Actions may be quite different as attention shifts from one of these profit objectives to another. So, too, with time. A profit-seeking seller may determine his supply prices according to their effect upon his current profits, his profits next month, next year, or over the next decade. The further ahead he looks, the more factors he will usually take into consideration in shaping his price policy. He is also more likely to do things which sacrifice present profits in hopes of securing larger profits in the future.

Profits, however, are usually a means to an end, not an end in themselves. The ultimate motive is the satisfaction or happiness of the business owner or manager. This basic objective not infrequently conflicts with profit maximization. Thus, when sellers are making what they consider to be a satisfactory profit, many of them are content to "let well enough alone." They do not engage in constant calculation and change in an effort to squeeze the utmost possible profit out of the situation. They accept the prices dictated by custom, law, or monopolistic pressure. This method reduces the number of variables which managers have to worry about. Some enterprising individuals prefer to depart from institutionally determined prices. They get satisfaction from the thrill of experiment, or of opposing the crowd. Even the most lethargic sometimes have to choose between retaining, raising, or lowering their prices. But even in these cases, impulse often outweighs cold, careful calculation. These are some of the reasons why this book begins with the institutional approach and defers until later a consideration of supply prices determined by cost-revenue calculations.

3. **No Reservation Price.**—The first type of institutional pricing for us to consider is the somewhat paradoxical one where the seller fixes no minimum supply price whatsoever. He may do this for two reasons. In the first case the seller may want money quickly. He does not have time to wait for the arrival of a buyer who will pay the customary asking price. Therefore, he offers his good for sale to the highest bidder or to the first buyer who appears on the scene. The auction is a familiar example of the first and a realty owner selling to a speculator illustrates the latter. In somewhat the same category is the instruction which a person owning a listed stock or traded commodity may give to his broker to "sell at the market." He will get the price that is quoted for the next transaction even though his contribution to the total sold is very small. In such sales through the exchanges the seller usually knows in advance approximately what he is likely to get, and might not tell his broker to "sell at the market" if he thought the market price was going to fall sharply for the next sale. Nevertheless, the fact remains that sellers who give such orders announce no reservation prices and therefore differ from those who do.

In the second case, we find sellers who believe it is futile to set a minimum supply price. Sellers may feel weak as compared to a buyer who has much larger financial resources. Many farmers, for instance, sell their produce or their milk to one buyer. They find it more difficult or less pleasant to deal with anyone else. So they accept the price he offers. Often the buyer argues that he is not a free agent and that his buying price is set by a selling price over which he has no control.

When buyers are few, they may organize and agree not to bid against one another in the purchase of certain goods. Unorganized sellers are impotent in the face of such agreements, and no one of them can force a higher bid by waiting and talking. It is futile for the individual seller to ask more. It is also foolish for him to accept less.

This feeling of urgency or impotence which leads sellers to name no reservation price should not be confused with the market situation described as the "balancing of aggregates" (Chapter 6, Section 6). In the latter case the naming of supply prices is very common, even though a few of those participating in a given sale on a stock or commodity exchange may be offering "at the market."

The equality of quantities bought and sold is established at a price set by some of the buyers and sellers, but not by all of them.[1]

**4. Customary Price.**—The easiest thing for sellers to do in many market situations is to offer to sell at the customary prices. This is true of old established producers and also for new firms entering the field. Some of the general motives involved were presented above in Section 3 of this chapter. Here we shall discuss the types of market situations which most frequently reveal the power of custom in price determination.

In the retail field customary prices tend to be retained for long periods on commodities of frequent purchase and low unit price, such as the 5-cent cup of coffee, cigar, candy bar, or soft drink. The fact that 5- and 10-cent prices can be paid with single coins seems to make these prices particularly stable. Twenty-five-cent commodities are purchased less frequently, and the price is less stable. Another obstacle to the change of customary prices is the frequent presence of many sellers. If one of them raises his price during a period of rising costs, some of the others are not likely to follow. This may be fatal for the first man to try it. In more technical language, the demand for the product of any one seller is very elastic when his price is raised above the customary one (cf. Chapter 4, Section 1).

An interesting variety of customary prices is to be found in the customary *percentages* involved in certain types of sales. These include the 10 per cent restaurant tip, the 2 per cent discount for prompt payment, the salesman's commission, etc. Piece-work wage rates are also a form of percentage pricing. Employers seem to resist union demands for piece rate increases more stubbornly than demands for time rate increases.

Manufacturers often maintain posted prices for a longer time than would seem warranted by changing demand or changing costs. They are much less likely than retailers to engage in "sales." Reasons for price rigidity at this level include the expense of preparing new price lists, the inconvenience and cost of re-educating salesmen, the fear of starting a "price war" among competitors, and the danger that downward adjustments when costs fall cannot be reversed readily when costs later go up again. Further explanations of these last two reasons will be given in the next chapter.

A final comment should be made to the effect that the longer a

---

[1] We ignore the exceptional case where all the sellers offer their goods "at the market." Even then potential sellers at higher prices probably exist and will sooner or later reveal their presence by offering goods at prices which will ensure sale.

price has remained in effect, the greater the difficulty in changing it. In this respect customary prices are like other customs. Ethical and moral arguments against price increases reinforce buyers' natural reluctance to pay more. Price decreases do not encounter such opposition, but neither do sellers feel price-cutting necessary to retain sales volume. Competition shifts to advertising, quality changes, and the like.

**5. Prices Fixed by Law.**—A few prices are fixed by law, either by statute or by decision of an administrative body given authority to act. Such are the government buying price for gold, certain public utility rates, and specific prices fixed by the Office of Price Administration during the second world war. In such cases the law-abiding seller has no decision to make about his supply price. He would be foolish to offer his goods for less. All he can do is to try to get the price increased. He may protest its "unfairness" or its harm to the public welfare, or he may proclaim the great good that would result for people in general if only his legitimate selling price were raised. During the depression of the 1930's the gold and silver producers talked like this. During the war nearly every seller did.

Other price-fixing takes the form of maximum or minimum prices. When the demand for goods rises more rapidly than the supply, governments may seek to hold down prices by maximum price legislation. The specific dollars-and-cents maxima described in the preceding paragraph are less common than "price freezing." This device establishes ceilings at the highest price asked by each seller for sales made during a certain base period (e.g., March, 1942). Individual adjustments are then permitted in cases of genuine hardship and public harm. Most sellers can sell their capacity output at the ceiling and see no gain from charging less. For them there is no supply price problem. Their task is to keep down costs by skillful buying, bargaining, quality debasement, etc.

During the depression which preceded the second world war, the United States tried to impose *minimum* prices. The NRA codes were soon invalidated by the Supreme Court, but for a time they reduced the amount of price-cutting. At best they did not have so great an effect upon supply prices as did wartime ceilings. Many sellers chose to offer goods at prices above the minima.

In recent years there has been a rise in the number of "guild prices." These are minimum prices imposed by quasi-governmental bodies controlled by particular trades, such as the barbers, the cosmetologists, the milk producers, etc. Other sellers are unable to get favorable legislation of this kind and arrange, instead, monopolistic agreements of various types. Violators of legal guild price minima may be fined, or their licenses may be revoked. Violators of monopolistic agreements run the risk of retaliatory price-cutting. In both cases the area of institutional price determination is being widened. Songs in praise of free competition are becoming muted.

Public utility rates have long been supervised by governmental commissions. The companies themselves must initiate most new rates and rate changes upward. This requires price policy decisions on their part. Hundreds or thousands of rates must be determined for different types of sales. Since the allocation of overhead must be somewhat arbitrary, custom and the imitation of compcting rates are perhaps more frequent supply price determinants than careful cost calculations. The companies must also meet the requirements of the law that no rates may be discriminatory and that the total net profit must not be higher than a "fair return on a fair value."

**6. Resale Price Maintenance.**—Another type of price setting which does not require independent policy decisions upon the part of sellers is called resale price maintenance. The middleman is required to sell at a price fixed by the manufacturer. This is usually a minimum price, but it may also be a maximum, as in the retailing of books. The compulsion has various institutional forms. It may be a contract which requires the seller to ask a certain price upon penalty of losing the right to buy the product in the future. The selling prices of wholesalers often are fixed by manufacturers who publish price lists showing fixed discounts for wholesale and retail buyers. Or there may be laws requiring all distributors to abide by the stipulated minimum to which some distributors are bound by contract. Other laws merely state that price-cutting may not go below a certain percentage of the list price. Nearly all states have some type of "fair trade law." Legal protection of this type has been sought by producers of drugs, toiletries, books, liquors, films, etc.

**7. Imitative Price.**—Sometimes sellers copy the supply prices of other sellers. A small seller may not want to put his price higher than that of a larger firm for fear of losing business to it. At the same time he does not dare to put the price lower for fear of starting a "price war." When the large firm changes its list price, the small firm plays "follow the leader." A new firm without cost experience may imitate predecessors upon the assumption that their prices will be high enough to cover its expenses and yield a reasonable profit. Too often the new firm fails to realize that profit also depends upon achieving a certain minimum volume of sales. If there is some product differentiation, by brands or quality, as in most packaged foods, the small seller or the new one may be slightly independent. He may advertise an alleged qualitative superiority and ask a higher price. Or he may claim equal quality and offer slight price cuts as an inducement.[2] But the fundamental approach is imitative; it is not a mathematical calculation of the maximum profit price.

In the retail merchandising of standardized or nationally branded products, as in grocery and drug stores, one firm may adopt the policy of meeting every price cut made by competitors. "We refuse to be undersold" is a claim frequently made and sometimes followed in actual prices. Such stores often hire professional shoppers to purchase goods at the counters of their competitors in order to find out just what prices are being charged. With this information, or when a customer makes a protest, the "cut-rate" store reduces prices where necessary. Occasionally they also find their own prices lower than others and proceed either to raise them or to publicize them by advertising. The knowledge that weaker Store B will follow the price cuts of stronger Store A has sometimes led the management of Store A to reduce prices below total cost on certain volume items, hoping to exhaust the resources of Store B and thus force it out of business. This accomplished, Store A may then raise prices, even to a level higher than before the reduction, thus recouping its losses.

**8. Markup Methods: (a) Markup for All Overhead and Profit Added to Direct Cost.**—A method of determining supply price which combines imitation and calculation is the markup. A middleman may figure his unit cost of obtaining a good and then add a traditional percentage markup to allow for overhead and profit. Thus, if a grocer purchases a certain brand of spaghetti at 10 cents per pound package, he may add a customary 20 per cent and ask customers to pay 12 cents. Grocers use many different markup percentages, depending roughly upon the rate of turnover of each class of goods. Bread and milk have a rapid turnover and a small markup as compared with slow-moving items like spices, bleaches, and tea. There may be several dozen such groups with inventory turnover running from once a day to once a month or longer. This explains why the markup on article A which has an average turnover of once a week should be higher than that on article B which turns over twice a week. But it does not explain why the Reliable

---

[2] Much more will be said in later chapters about problems of price-cutting in various market situations. Cf. Chapter 9, especially Section 5.

Grocery Company chooses a 15 per cent markup for A and 10 per cent for B instead of some other figures such as 16 per cent and 9 per cent.

When dozens of articles are sold by a single seller, he can never be sure that he has precisely the most profitable markup on each item. Hence he is usually guided by custom and by the price decisions of his competitors. His minimum essential task is to cover his total overhead. His total revenue must exceed his total outlays for rent, wages, taxes, etc., plus depreciation allowances, if he is to remain in business. To make a profit he must make something more than this. Unfortunately for him, however, there is no single markup rule which will guarantee a profit. Where the number of articles being sold is large, the markup combinations which may yield a profit are legion. That is clearly revealed by the random variety of items chosen for price reductions by retail sellers when they wish to attract customers by advertised "sales." It is shown also by the low markup policy pursued by most chain stores at the same time that independent neighborhood stores have high markups.

### 9. Markup Methods: (b) Markup for Administrative Overhead and Profit (after Cost Accounting).

—A second markup method of arriving at supply price is used by many manufacturers. Most of the overhead costs are allocated by accounting techniques and then a flat percentage markup is added to cover any remaining costs and to provide a profit. The chief accomplishments of cost accounting lie in distributing among their various uses the proper fractional parts of such joint costs as power, supervisory or incidental labor (foremen, clerks, janitors), and certain materials used in more than one article or process. The markup percentage becomes smaller as the cost base becomes more inclusive. But cost accounting cannot allocate expenses like research, property taxes, and administrative salaries without becoming highly arbitrary. Therefore an institutional element remains: the rule-of-thumb for the allocation of these costs or for the profit percentage added.

There is another reason for not putting too much reliance upon the cost accounting approach to supply price. Its negative value is greater than its positive. A newly introduced cost accounting system may show that a certain article has been sold at less than the estimated cost of production. But no amount of accounting can show that the volume of production used in cost estimates can be sold at a price which covers cost and the profit markup. This can only be determined by trial and error or, in a few rare instances, by market surveys which discover potential demand.  Similarly, no markup percentage is *the* correct one, guaranteed to yield the maximum profit, or any profit, for that matter.  Markup rules are as numerous and as diverse as formulas for beating the stock market or choosing the winning horse at the Derby.  Sellers in the same line of business will follow different rules, and during prosperity each will defend his rule as the best one.[3]  When a seller fails, his chief trouble may lie elsewhere than in his markup percentage.

Individual sellers themselves often use different markups at different times or for different customers.  Retail stores frequently stage "sales" and offer merchandise for less than former prices, i.e., at smaller markups.  The reductions are not often connected with the need to cover overhead costs.  More common reasons are the desire (1) to sell remainders of old stock quickly in order to make room for new merchandise of particular seasonal or style appeal; (2) to attract new customers who may buy other goods at nonsale prices; or (3) to raise cash to pay creditors.  Many retailers also depart from their "one-price" rule when selling to employees.  At the wholesale and manufacturing levels it is very common for sellers to charge different prices (use different markups) for different customers by a series of special discounts from list prices.

**10. Markup Methods: (c) When Producing to Order.**—A variant of the markup method of setting supply prices is found in those cases where the seller produces to order.  In some cases the buyer offers to pay whatever it costs.  The seller may then figure "time and materials."  The hourly rate charged for the time required includes an allowance for overhead.  In other cases the buyer says he wants something made to order and asks the seller to quote a price in advance.  The producer must then decide the size of his markup.  If he expects the order to be the only one from that buyer, he may charge more than if he is trying to build goodwill for future sales.  Other influences are the age of the firm, its competitive position, the number of orders in proportion to the total business, etc.  Production to order, one must remember, is not confined to custom tailoring.  It is quite common in the purchase of certain types of semimanufactured raw materials, specialized equipment for factories, and even some retail merchandise.  Some machinery manufacturers concentrate on producing to specification.

---

[3] They may also differ in cost accounting procedures, as in the treatment of inventories, depreciation, etc.

A variant of this situation occurs when a potential buyer states his needs to several possible suppliers and asks them to submit sealed bids. Under these conditions the potential seller arrives at his bid price in much the same way as before, i.e., a calculation of cost plus a profit markup. But other considerations may intrude. A producer who is currently running near capacity may be less anxious to get the job than one who is much in need of additional business. Profit margins may be adjusted accordingly in the bids submitted. There will also be differences in the estimated cost of production. Some firms are more advantageously equipped, stocked, or located than are other firms. The low bidder does not always set the price, for the buyer may find some method of playing favorites or may object to the bidder's materials, financial weakness, or lack of experience. Governments and some large private buyers use the sealed bid technique in purchasing both standardized commodities like fuel oil or copper pipe and nonstandardized things like factory buildings, post offices, and ships.

**11. Summary of the Institutional Determinants of Supply Price.**—Sellers determine their supply prices in a variety of ways depending upon the situation in which they find themselves. Often they exercise little conscious choice, but follow the dictates of custom, law, example, or the peculiar circumstances of the case. These institutional forces are widespread and potent. Even when some costs are calculated, the markup percentages often remain institutional or impulsive. Most of the prices we encounter in daily life spring from these institutional backgrounds and therefore we have studied them first. Now we may proceed to examine how prices may be set by using profit-maximizing formulas based upon hypothecated cost and revenue schedules.

# Chapter 8

## SUPPLY PRICE: DERIVED FROM MAXIMUM
## PROFIT CALCULATIONS

**1. Calculating the Maximum Profit Price Under Assumed Cost and Demand Conditions.**—Another group of supply prices is that in which the maximum profit price is calculated from assumed cost and demand conditions. This process differs from the methods described in the last part of the preceding chapter. It does not use any customary, legal, or imitative markups. It assumes that cost varies with output and that output varies with the rate of sales. Therefore, the price setter should estimate two functions and consider them both at the same time. The first is the cost function, or the costs of production at different rates of output (and sales). The second is the revenue or demand function. This was explained in Chapter 4 as the quantities that would be demanded of the seller at the different prices which he might set.

Many different assumptions are possible. Production cost may be viewed in various ways. Demand situations may be of one type or another. The following sections consider only a few of the possible combinations. Most of the cases show what *would be* the best price *under the given assumptions*. They do not say that sellers in real life actually do reach their supply prices in the manner shown. They say, rather, that if a seller were to seek his maximum profit price and output in this way or that way, he would obtain them by such and such a method. The major questions to be asked and answered are the following:

1. How to maximize gross revenue when cost of production is ignored?
2. What are the different types of cost schedules for the individual firm?
   - (a) Total fixed cost, total variable cost, total total cost
   - (b) Average fixed cost, average variable cost, average total cost
   - (c) Marginal cost
3. How may these cost schedules be derived from input-output data?
   - (a) In agriculture; the principle of diminishing returns

(b) In manufacturing; the possibility of constant marginal cost
4. Why are the maximum profit price and output revealed by the point of equality between marginal revenue and marginal cost?
   (a) When the selling price is beyond the seller's control
   (b) When the selling price may be set by the seller
5. What is "capacity" output and how is it related to the maximum profit output?
6. What is the effect of increases in equipment or other "fixed" expenses as output expands?
7. To what extent are the actual transactions prices of modern capitalistic society determined by these principles?

**2. Seeking to Maximize Gross Revenue When Cost of Production Is Ignored.**—The simplest type of supply price calculation in the present group is that which ignores cost of production. This occurs when goods have already been produced and the stock on hand is fixed. The seller is assumed to be able to determine the selling price by setting his supply price. His task is to determine the supply price which will bring him the maximum gross revenue within a given time. If that price is so high that some goods remain unsold, these can be destroyed, or given away. They may also be offered for sale in another time period at the same or a different price.

The solution of the problem is simple, once the demand for the good has been estimated. Set up a three-column demand schedule (cf. Chapter 4, Section 2) whose largest quantity is the maximum amount on hand for sale. Find the maximum total revenue amount in that schedule and charge the price indicated. In the following hypothetical example and diagram, the seller would make $81 by charging only 90 cents per unit. This will leave 10 units unsold. But the seller is better off than if he had tried to sell his total stock of 100 and had reduced his price to 80 cents in order to do so.

DEMAND SCHEDULE FOR 100 GADGETS
OFFERED ON ONE DAY BY SELLER
SMITH

| Price | | Quantity | Total Revenue |
|---|---|---|---|
| | $1.20 | 60 | $72.00 |
| | 1.10 | 70 | 77.00 |
| | 1.00 | 80 | 80.00 |
| (best price) | .90 | 90 | 81.00 (maximum revenue) |
| | .80 | 100 (total stock) | 80.00 |

SUPPLY SCHEDULE OF SMITH AFTER
PRICING TO MAXIMIZE GROSS
REVENUE

| Price | Quantity |
|-------|----------|
| $0.90 | 60 |
| .90 | 70 |
| .90 | 80 |
| .90 | 90 (best quantity) |
| .90 | 100 |

The diagrammatics of the situation is shown in Figure 23. Note that the supply curve is a horizontal straight line of limited length turning vertically upward at 100. Its position is unknown until the seller determines his supply price. Under the assumed conditions it

FIGURE 23

PRICING TO MAXIMIZE GROSS REVENUE WHEN STOCK IS FIXED
AND COST IS IGNORED

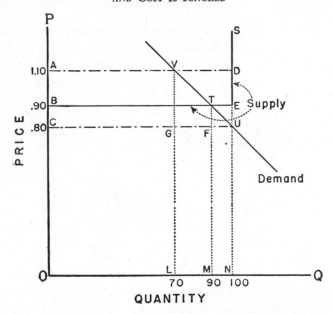

will extend to the right from 90 cents and will intersect the demand curve at T. If Smith had charged a lower price such as 80 cents per gadget, his demand and supply curves would have intersected at U. He would have sold all his 100 gadgets, but his gross revenue would have been less. At a higher price, $1.10, the quantity sold would have been less than 90 as indicated by the dotted line through $V$. This diagram also illustrates two other concepts described in earlier chapters. The higher the supply curve, the lower the supply in the schedule sense (cf. Chapter 6, Section 4). Raising the supply price reduces the supply, even though Smith insists he still has 100 units he would like to sell. And the demand schedule is obviously elastic above $T$ and inelastic below (cf. Chapter 4, Section 4). If price units were in ones instead of tens, the transition might be shown as occurring through a phase with elasticity of unity just above or below 90 cents.

**3. Cost Schedules for the Individual Firm: (a) Total Cost.—** All the remaining cases of calculated maximum profit prices require the use of cost schedules. These must now be explained. Cost schedules are constructed much like the demand and supply schedules described earlier. For each quantity there is a cost figure instead of a price. There are seven possible costs which may be used. The present section deals with three types of *total* cost: fixed, variable, and total. The next will describe three similar varieties of *average* cost. Section 5 will explain *marginal* cost.

To understand these different types of cost one must first distinguish between fixed and variable costs. These are technical terms whose definitions in economic analysis must be accepted even if they are different from those of other sciences, such as accounting. *Fixed costs* are those whose total does not change within a given range of change in output. *Total variable costs* do change with output. Administrative salaries, bond interest, real property taxes, and fire insurance usually fall in the first class of fixed costs. Raw materials and direct labor are usually good illustrations of variable costs.

Some costs fall in one category or in the other according to the degree of change in output. When the capacity of a given machine is reached, another must be added. Depreciation on the first machine was a fixed cost for a certain range of output change. Beyond that range, further expansion of output requires the addition of a second machine. This outlay may be called a variable cost. Once the second machine is acquired, however, its depreciation may be treated as a fixed amount for the range of expansion of output it makes possible. The distinction between fixed and variable costs may also depend upon the decision of the person constructing the cost schedules. If he wishes to designate as overhead a certain expense, such as that of time clerks, and treat it as a fixed cost, he may do so. But if his cost accounting system allocates this expense to units of goods produced, it may be considered a variable cost. The person who is making the profit-maximizing calculations is the one who must decide where the various expenses should be put.

The following table and figure show a hypothetical case. Total fixed costs are $1 and do not change as output rises from 1 to 4 units. Total variable costs rise from $2 to $8. This is shown as a dotted "staircase" which has been smoothed into a solid straight line for simplicity. The top line represents the sum of the total fixed and variable costs at each output. *Total total cost* sounds redundant, but the double adjective is useful to help distinguish it from total average cost, which will be explained in the next section.

HYPOTHETICAL *Total* COST SCHEDULES AND CURVES FOR A FIRM

| Total Output | Total Fixed Cost | Total Variable Cost | Total Total Cost |
|---|---|---|---|
| 1 | $1.00 | $2.00 | $3.00 |
| 2 | 1.00 | 4.00 | 5.00 |
| 3 | 1.00 | 6.00 | 7.00 |
| 4 | 1.00 | 8.00 | 9.00 |

FIGURE 24

THREE TOTAL COST CURVES

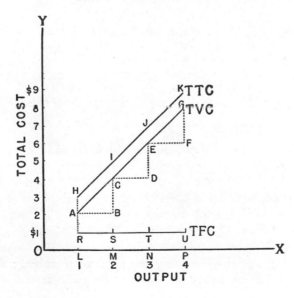

A note may be added for those who find mathematical formulation of such material interesting or useful. The equations of the curves are as follows:

$y_1 = \$1$ (total fixed cost is constant at $1)
$y_2 = x(\$2)$ (total variable cost is a multiple of $2)
$y_3 = \$1 + x(\$2)$ (total total cost is the sum of $TFC + TVC$)

Diagrammatically, $TFC$ is a horizontal straight line. $TVC$, when smoothed, is an upward sloping straight line. $TTC$ is an upward sloping straight line parallel to $TVC$ and separated from it by the distance ($1) between $TFC$ and the $OX$ axis. For instance:

$$LH = LR + LA$$

$$MI = MS + MC$$

also $LR = AH = MS = CI = \ldots$

**4. Cost Schedules for the Individual Firm: (b) Average Cost.** —The average cost figures are generally more useful than the total cost figures. They are derived from the latter by simple division, using total output as the divisor. This gives average fixed cost, average variable cost, and average total cost as shown in the following table based upon the schedules given in Section 3:

HYPOTHETICAL *Average* COST SCHEDULES AND CURVES FOR A FIRM

| Total Output | Average Fixed Cost | Average Variable Cost | Average Total Cost |
|---|---|---|---|
| 1 | $1.00 | $2.00 | $3.00 |
| 2 | .50 | 2.00 | 2.50 |
| 3 | .33 | 2.00 | 2.33 |
| 4 | .25 | 2.00 | 2.25 |

Three characteristics of the new schedule should be noted. Average fixed cost declines, sharply at first and then more gradually. Average variable cost remains constant, since the total variable cost function was constructed in the first case as a simple multiple of $2. (A later case will give an illustration of both $TVC$ and $AVC$ as curves, instead of straight lines, the $TVC$ curve bending upward and the $AVC$ curve bending downward.) Average total cost declines with increasing output, following the pattern of average fixed cost. Average total cost also may be obtained by adding $AFC$ and $AVC$.

In Figure 25 showing the three average cost curves, $RJ = RA + RE$, resembling the distances added to get totals in Figure 24. In similar fashion, $AJ = RE = BK = SF = \ldots$ . The diagrammatic

### FIGURE 25

#### THREE AVERAGE COST CURVES

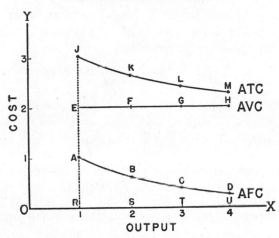

contrasts between the two figures are best seen by putting them in parallel columns as follows:

| TOTAL COST CURVES | | AVERAGE COST CURVES [1] |
|---|---|---|
| $TFC$ | —Horizontal— | $AVC$ |
| $TTC$ and $TVC$ | —Parallel— | $ATC$ and $AFC$ |
| $TTC = TFC + TVC$ | —Totals— | $ATC = AFC + AVC$ |

As a mathematical note the equations of the average cost curves may be given as:

$$y_1 = \frac{\$1}{x} \text{ (average fixed cost is \$1 divided by the output)}$$

$$y_2 = \frac{x(\$2)}{x} = \$2 \text{ (average variable cost is constant at \$2)}$$

$$y_3 = \frac{\$1 + x(\$2)}{x} = \frac{\$1}{x} + \$2 \text{ (average total cost is the sum of } AFC + AVC)$$

### 5. Cost Schedules for the Individual Firm: (c) Marginal Cost.
—The seventh cost schedule and curve for the individual firm are of the marginal variety. Marginal cost is an addition to total cost that

---

[1] In other cases $AVC$ may be curved. When this occurs, $ATC$ and $AFC$ are not parallel, nor are $TTC$ and $TVC$, though nearly so.

may be described in several ways. These should be compared with the similar definitions of marginal revenue given in Chapter 4, Section 4. In every case, marginal cost must be thought of as occurring at or just before a certain output, $x$.

When output increases one unit at a time, then marginal cost is the amount added to the total total cost at $x - 1$ units of output to make the new total total cost at $x$ units of output. In other terms, it is the difference between the total total costs at the two rates of output and may be expressed by the formula:

$$MC_x = TTC_x - TTC_{x-1}$$

In our hypothetical cost schedule one case might be that when output, $x$, is 3 units, then $MC_4 = TTC_4 - TTC_3 = \$9 - \$7 = \$2$.

When changes in the scale of production by a firm are estimated by its manager to occur in larger jumps than just one unit, marginal cost becomes *average* additional cost. When the divisor was 1, as in the first case, it could be ignored, since the average increment and the increment itself were the same. Not so when increments occur of 100 units, 1,000 units, or larger amounts. Let the increment be called $m$, then the new formula becomes:

$$MC_x = \frac{TTC_x - TTC_{x-m}}{m}$$

In a numerical illustration, a firm producing 9,000 units per month at a total cost of $90,000 might step up its output to 10,000 units and find that its new total cost was $101,000. The *average* additional cost is $\dfrac{\$101,000 - \$90,000}{1,000}$, or $11 per unit *added*. This marginal cost must be contrasted with the average *total* cost at 9,000 units of output which was $\dfrac{\$90,000}{9,000} = \$10$, and the *ATC* at 10,000 units, which was $10.10.

For diagrammatic purposes, a smoothed curve is more convenient than the more realistic staircase zigzag. Therefore, economists often use the convenient fiction of infinitesimal changes in output. Under this assumption, $m$ is made to diminish until it approaches zero as a limit. The division now gives the *rate of change* in total cost at a certain output, $x$, instead of the average *amount* of change *between* two outputs, $x + 1$ and $x$. It is this rate concept of marginal cost at a point (an output) which economists usually have in mind when they use the term. Businessmen, on the other hand, if they use the marginal cost concept at all, would be more apt to think of the average additional cost of an expanded output as described above.

**6. Marginal Cost Usually Differs from Average Variable Cost.** —Marginal cost may be the same as average variable cost, or it may differ. The simple illustration used in Sections 4 and 5 made them both the same. That is, $MC$ was always $2 and $AVC$ was likewise always $2. This resulted from the assumptions of the schedule, which can be described either as (1) a straight-line (linear) total cost function based on variable costs of the simple multiple type, (2) an unchanging average variable cost, or (3) a constant marginal cost.[2]

In most cases found in actual business practice, marginal cost and average variable cost differ at some if not at most output levels. There are two major reasons. First, there are changes in the efficiency with which the variable factors are combined with the fixed factors. Illustrations include improvements such as increasing physical returns, better coordination, reduced waste, and greater specialization. As the scale of output gets very large, decreases in efficiency may occur because of diminishing physical returns, duplication, and "red tape." A second major reason for changes in average variable cost is not related to changes in efficiency in the use of the factors but rather to their unit cost. It may result from the buying economies obtained by purchasing in larger lots. Or the increased volume of buying may raise unit costs through the need to pay freight from longer distances, pay overtime wages, etc.

There are three major types of relationship between marginal cost and average variable cost. These are shown in Figure 26. In the first, $MC = AVC$ throughout most of the output range. This was the assumption of our first hypothetical examples and might be found in many simple processing operations. Eventually, however, $MC$ rises and $AVC$ follows, but less rapidly. In the second case, $MC$ falls at first, remains constant for a large range of outputs, and then rises. $AVC$ falls slowly until it intersects $MC$ just after $MC$ starts to rise. Many factories show this pattern. The third illustration is taken from agriculture. It shows $MC$ falling and then rising in a U-shaped curve, $AVC$ falls less rapidly and again intersects $MC$ after

---

[2] Because of the arithmetic relation between five of the cost schedules of a firm, $TTC$, $TVC$, $ATC$, $AVC$, and $MC$, a schedule of any one of them with output may be used to obtain any one of the others. Only the fixed costs, $TFC$ and $AFC$, remain independent of the other five. It is interesting to note that $TTC_x - TTC_{x-1} = TVC_x - TVC_{x-1}$, since the $TFC$ component of $TTC$ does not change. Therefore, $MC$ is *either* the addition to total total cost or to total variable cost, but the former idea is usually the more useful of the two.

*MC* starts to rise. In both the second and third cases, the curves cross at the *lowest point* on *AVC*. In the first case the curves separate at that lowest point which, of course, is constant until the upturn begins.

### FIGURE 26

THREE TYPES OF MARGINAL AND AVERAGE COST CURVES

| Type I | Type II | Type III |
|---|---|---|
| (Processing) | (Manufacturing) | (Agriculture) |

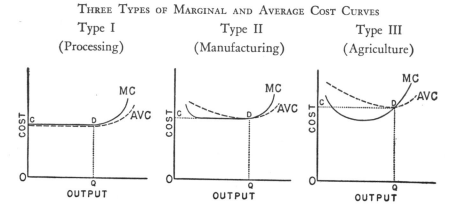

### 7. Increasing and Decreasing Returns in Agriculture.—The

traditional U-shaped cost curves of many authors were derived chiefly from studies of agricultural experiment stations which dealt with the effect upon output when different quantities of a single variable were combined with a composite fixed factor. For instance, increasing quantities of a certain kind of fertilizer have been added to a series of test plots where seed, soil, and cultivation have been held constant. On the various plots, the output per pound of fertilizer added has been observed to rise with the first few additions, reach a peak, and then decline as in the hypothetical table on page 103.

This table reveals *three* points of diminishing returns. Total product reaches a peak at 34 and begins to decline thereafter. This is the point of diminishing *total* returns. Note that at this point the additional product (column D) is zero. Second, there is a point of diminishing *additional* returns when three pounds of fertilizer are used and total product is 17. Beyond this point additional pounds of fertilizer increase the total product each time by less than 7 units of product. The 7 unit increase is the maximum. The third point of diminishing returns is that of the *average* returns column, E. This reaches its maximum at 5.75 when there are 4 units of fertilizer input and 23 units of product output.[3]

---

[3] Some synonyms should be understood: product = output = returns; and additional = marginal.

INCREASING AND DIMINISHING RETURNS IN AGRICULTURE

(Land, seed, cultivation, etc. constant; fertilizer variable)

| A<br>Composite Units<br>of the<br>Fixed Factors | B<br>Pounds of<br>Fertilizer<br>($n$)<br>(Given) | C<br>Total Product<br>in Bushels<br>(Given) | D<br>Additional<br>Product per<br>Additional<br>Pound of<br>Fertilizer<br>(Marginal<br>Product)<br>$(C_n - C_{n-1}) \div$<br>$(B_n - B_{n-1})$ | E<br>Average<br>Product per<br>Pound of<br>Fertilizer<br>($C/B$) |
|---|---|---|---|---|
| 1 unit | 1 pound | 4 bushels | 4 bushels | 4.00 bushels |
| 1 | 2 | 10 | 6 | 5.00 |
| 1 | 3 | 17 | 7 (*DMR*) | 5.67 |
| 1 | 4 | 23 | 6 | 5.75 (*DAR*) |
| 1 | 5 | 28 | 5 | 5.60 |
| 1 | 6 | 32 | 4 | 5.33 |
| 1 | 7 | 34 | 2 | 4.86 |
| 1 | 8 | 34 (*DTR*) | 0 | 4.25 |
| 1 | 9 | 31 | − 3 | 3.44 |

These points of diminishing total, marginal, and average returns may also be shown by diagrams. Figure 27 presents three typical

FIGURE 27

POINTS OF DIMINISHING PHYSICAL
RETURNS

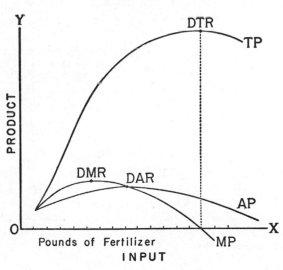

curves. They are drawn to show relationships and do not represent the figures of the preceding table. The point of $DTR$ must occur directly above the point where the $MP$ curve is zero, i.e., where it cuts the $OX$ axis. The point of $DAR$ must occur where $AP$ is cut by $MP$. Additions which raise the average must exceed that average ($MP$ points to the left of $DAR$). The point of $DMR$ is more difficult to observe visually, but the calculus may be used to prove that it occurs where $TP$ stops being convex to the $OX$ axis and begins to become concave.

8. **Transposing Diminishing Physical Returns Into Increasing Physical Cost.**—If these product curves are turned upside down, they become the familiar U-shaped cost curves. More accurately, the cost figures are the reciprocals of the product figures. For instance, column E gave the physical product per unit of fertilizer used. These average products were obtained from successive quotients of $C/B$. The average cost figures of column G are the reciprocals of column E, or the quotients of $B/C$. In briefest terms, column E shows output per unit of input while column G shows input per unit of output. Similarly, columns F and H may be considered the reciprocals of columns D and C respectively. They also may be calculated independently by the formulas given. One must remember that all of these figures represent *physical* cost. They are *fractional* pounds of fertilizer used. Not until the next section will we be dealing with *money* cost.

DECREASING AND INCREASING *Physical* COST IN AGRICULTURE

| A<br>Fixed<br>Factor | B<br>Variable<br>Factor | C<br>Product | F<br>Marginal Cost<br>$(1/D)$ or<br>$(B_n - B_{n-1}) \div$<br>$(C_n - C_{n-1})$ | G<br>Average Variable<br>Cost $(1/E)$ or<br>$(B_n \div C_n)$ | H<br>Average Fixed<br>Cost $(1/C)$ or<br>$(A_n \div C_n)$ |
|---|---|---|---|---|---|
| 1 unit | 1 pound | 4 bushels | 0.250 pounds | 0.250 pounds | 0.250 units |
| 1 | 2 | 10 | .167 | .200 | .100 |
| 1 | 3 | 17 * | .143 * | .176 | .059 |
| 1 | 4 | 23 † | .167 | .174 † | .043 |
| 1 | 5 | 28 | .200 | .178 | .036 |
| 1 | 6 | 32 | .250 | .187 | .031 |
| 1 | 7 | 34 | .500 | .206 | .029 |
| 1 | 8 | 34‡ | Infinity | .235 | .029 ‡ |
| 1 | 9 | 31 | − 0.333 | .290 | .032 |

\* Point of lowest marginal physical cost.
† Point of lowest average variable (physical) cost.
‡ Point of lowest average fixed (physical) cost.

The three physical cost functions may now be diagrammed.  Representative curves are shown in Figure 28.  They resemble the output curves of Figure 27, but are upside down.  Instead of points of diminishing returns, there are now three points of increasing physical cost.  Only one of these is very significant, the point of minimum average variable physical cost.  This occurs where the *AVPC* curve is intersected by the *MPC* curve.  The reasoning is the same as that given in the preceding section for the intersection of *AR* and *MP*.  This point of lowest average variable physical cost is sometimes called the *point of maximum efficiency* in the use of the given variable.  It represents the scale of production at which the least input is required per unit of output, so far as that variable is concerned.  But it should not be confused with the point of lowest total *money* cost, nor with the output which maximizes profit, both of which will be described later in the chapter.

One other change should be noted.  The *OX* axis in Figure 28 is changed from inputs to outputs.  This changes the shape of the

FIGURE 28

THREE PHYSICAL COST CURVES

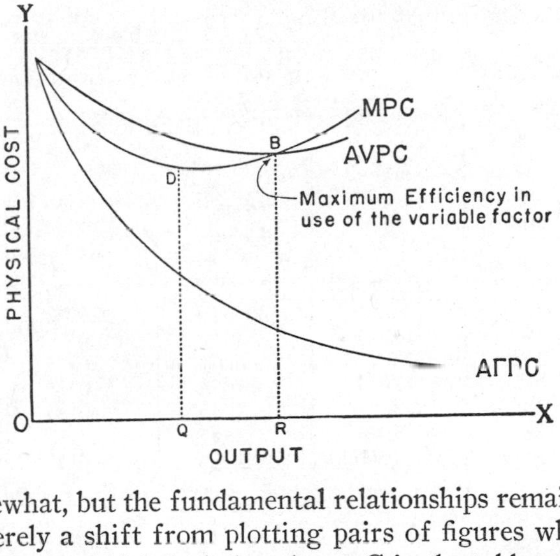

curves somewhat, but the fundamental relationships remain the same.  There is merely a shift from plotting pairs of figures which include column B to pairs which include column C in the tables given above.  The output approach is essential to the total money cost analysis soon to be given.

**9. From Physical Cost to Money Cost.**—It is a simple matter to translate physical cost into money cost by multiplying the indicated pounds of fertilizer by the cost price per pound, say 10 cents. The composite fixed factor may be treated similarly, when the appropriate prices are known. This permits adding the *money* cost of the variable factor to the money cost of the fixed factor to get a total money cost of one unit of the product at each output. (No total could have been obtained by trying to add pounds and acres.)

Another minimum point may now be shown. It is the point of minimum average total money cost, sometimes called the lowest unit cost. A few writers call the output which reveals this minimum cost the "capacity" output. The volume of production may be expanded beyond this point, but unit costs rise. This use of the word *capacity* should be contrasted with the popular connotation of the maximum amount that can be produced in a given time period regardless of cost. Furthermore, technical "capacity" exists at a different output for each factor considered as a variable. Thus, there is one capacity output for fertilizer inputs, another for seed, a third for cultivation labor, etc.

The following table shows the principle in relation to the hypothetical figures of the preceding illustration with the additional assumption of a 10 cent per pound cost of fertilizer and a 50 cent cost for the composite unit of the fixed factors.

MARGINAL MONEY COST AND AVERAGE MONEY COST IN AGRICULTURE

| B Variable Factor (Inputs) | C Product (Outputs) | I Marginal Cost in Dollars ($F \times \$0.10$) | J Average Variable Cost in Dollars ($G \times \$0.10$) | K Average Fixed Cost in Dollars ($H \times \$0.50$) | L Average Total Cost in Dollars ($J + K$) |
|---|---|---|---|---|---|
| 1 | 4 | $0.0250 | $0.0250 | $0.1250 | $0.1500 |
| 2 | 10 | .0167 | .0200 | .0500 | .0700 |
| 3 | 17 | .0143 | .0176 | .0295 | .0471 |
| 4 | 23 | .0167 | .0174 | .0215 | .0389 |
| 5 | 28 | .0200 | .0178 | .0180 | .0358 |
| 6 | 32 * | .0250 | .0187 | .0155 | .0342 * |
| 7 | 34 | .0500 | .0206 | .0145 | .0351 |

* Capacity, or point of lowest average total money cost.

Figure 29 shows representative curves for a farm product table like that above. The vertical axis is now money cost. This permits adding the $OY$ distances of the average fixed cost curve and the average variable cost curve to get a higher curve known as the average total cost ($RE + RD = RC$). This latter curve approaches the

*AVC* curve as the *AFC* curve approaches zero.  The minimum point, *C*, of *ATC* occurs at a larger output than the minimum point, *B*, of the *AVC* curve.  These two minima are shown on the *OX* axis as

FIGURE 29

FOUR MONEY COST CURVES

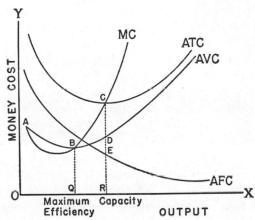

*R* and *Q* respectively.  Their designation as "capacity output" and "maximum efficiency output" must be considered technical definitions as explained above.

The marginal cost curve intersects *both* the *AVC* and the *ATC* curves at their lowest points.  This is important in the analysis to follow, which explains the use of the *MC* and *ATC* curves in calculating the maximum profit price.  The shape of these curves is determined by the conditions of physical productivity peculiar to agriculture.  In manufacturing and merchandising the curves may be much flatter, but their typical relationship is most clearly seen in this example.

**10. Use of Cost and Revenue Curves in Setting Price.**—In the preceding six sections we have completed a survey of the cost curves of the individual firm.  Now we can proceed to the solution of our basic problem.  We want to know how a business manager might determine the price which would maximize his profit if he knew his cost and revenue schedules.  The answer may be stated formally as follows.  The maximum profit price is that at which the additional cost of the last unit sold is just equal to the additional revenue derived from that sale.  More briefly, it is the price at which marginal cost equals marginal revenue.

The reasoning is simple. At any lower price the marginal revenue would be less than the marginal cost. A loss on that marginal sale would occur. Therefore, the volume of sales-output should be reduced and this means raising the price. At any higher price a profit would be made on the marginal unit. This would suggest an expansion of sales-output, but that would require a reduced price. The maximum profit price is the only one at which no change in sales-output would benefit the producer. That is why it is sometimes called the *equilibrium price* for the individual firm. Another name might be *equilibrium quantity,* but this phrase is less common. It has the advantage of pointing out the necessary identity between output and sales in this approach. Cost relates to a quantity output which is equal to the quantity sold at the price which maximizes profit.

The application of the foregoing rule for determining the maximum profit price for an individual firm may be either numerical or graphic. If a manager were to make such calculations for his own firm, he would use figures. He would begin by drawing up four schedules: (1) average revenue and quantity, (2) marginal revenue and quantity, (3) average total cost and quantity, and (4) marginal cost and quantity. For simplification, quantity might be put in the first column and then four others for $AR, MR, ATC,$ and $MC$ ranged along side. Next he would look at $MR$ and $MC$ to find the point where they are equal. This will occur at a certain quantity. If the $ATC$ is subtracted from the $AR$ for that quantity, the profit per unit will be obtained. The final step is to multiply this unit profit by the quantity to obtain the total net profit. This is the maximum profit obtainable under the assumed circumstances. The solution may be proved by adding two more columns to the table. The sixth would be profit per unit at each output level. The seventh would be total profit, obtained by multiplying unit profit times quantity. The largest figure in this seventh column would be seen to occur at the output which also reveals $MC$ to be equal to $MR$.

Curves may be used to arrive at a similar result. Businessmen would have to use figures since they want precise numerical answers. Economists merely want to demonstrate the principle involved and hence resort to their graphic shorthand. The symbols of this shorthand have been presented above in the form of typical cost and revenue curves. With the use of these symbols it is now possible to present quickly some of the many different situations which occur in real life. Although the cases can be defended as real, one must not assume that most managers of business units use these techniques in determining their actual prices or outputs.  Further comments on this qualification will be made after the typical cases have been examined.

**11. Graphic Demonstrations of Profit-Maximizing Situations When Price Is Constant.**—The first case is taken from agriculture. Farmer Smith is assumed to be one of thousands of farmers selling the same product.  The price which he expects to get for his product will not be affected by any variations in his output or sales.  He may expect the price to rise or fall between planting and harvest, but somehow he gets an idea of a probable minimum price at which he will be able to sell. Smith is also assumed to know his cost curves so that he can plot them as $MC$ and $ATC$ in Figure

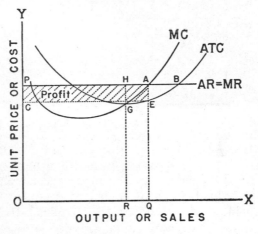

FIGURE 30

MAXIMIZING PROFIT WHEN SELLING
PRICE IS FIXED

30.  Since the price is constant regardless of sales by Smith, the marginal revenue is also constant.  The horizontal line $PAB$ represents both, $AR = MR$.

The maximum profit output is indicated by the point $A$ where $MC = MR$.  The price for this output (and all others that Smith might determine) is $OP$.  The profit per unit is $AR - ATC$, or $QA - QE$, which is $AE$.  Output $OQ$ is also equal to $CE$ or $PA$. Therefore, total profit is shown by the rectangle $PAEC$ whose area is obtained by multiplying output $CE$ by unit profit $AE$.  Under the cost-revenue conditions assumed for Smith, he benefits by producing more than $OR$, which would have given him his minimum unit cost. $AE$ is less than $HG$, but this loss in unit profit is more than offset by the gain from selling the additional product, $RQ$.  The amount of this extra profit is shown by the triangle $GHA$.  Each unit beyond $G$ ($OR$) has an additional cost shown by the height of the $MC$ line $GA$.  But each unit brings additional revenue shown by the height of the $MR$ line $HA$.  The difference in each case is positive up to output $OQ$ or point $A$.  Beyond point $A$, $MC$ is above $MR$ and additional output would be produced and sold at a loss.

FIGURE 31

ZERO PROFIT WHEN SELLING PRICE
IS CONSTANT

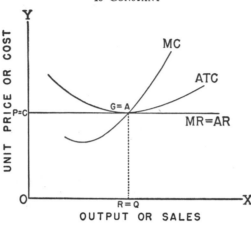

At the same time that Smith makes profit of the magnitude $PAEC$, Brown may be just breaking even, as shown in Figure 31. Here $MC$ intersects $MR$ and $ATC$ at the same point, $G = A$. This point also equates maximum profit output $OQ$ with minimum unit cost output $OR$. Brown cannot improve his position by producing more or by producing less, because moving in either direction from $G = A$ will make his unit cost exceed his unit revenue.

Jones, however, is in a still worse position. As shown in Figure 32, Jones cannot break even at any output. His task is to minimize his loss. This is done by producing at output $OQ$ indicated by point $A$ where $MC = MR$. This is better than producing $OR$ which would give minimum unit cost $RG$ but would bring greater loss.

Someone might ask why Jones produces at all. The answer could be that his $AVC$ (dotted line) curve cuts $MC$ below $PAH$ and therefore he makes something more than his out-of-pocket expenses. This operating profit may be used to pay part of his fixed costs which otherwise would be entirely unmet. Or the answer might be that Jones is just getting started and expects to have lower costs in the future.

Other reasons might be given which often ap-

FIGURE 32

PRODUCING AT MINIMUM LOSS WHEN
SELLING PRICE IS CONSTANT

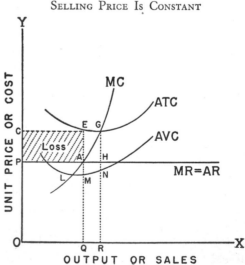

pear in agriculture, but they are contrary to the assumptions used here. The cost and revenue curves are expectation curves, not realization curves. If the latter were the case, Jones might start with the expectation of a higher $AR$ curve or a lower $ATC$ curve and find afterwards that he had made a serious mistake in his estimates. The labor of the farmer is implicitly included as a cost in $AVC$ and $ATC$ above. Most farmers do not figure costs that way and hence have much lower curves. As a matter of fact, most small farmers do not do any calculation planning of this type at all. They go rather by hunches, reactions against failures, imitation, rules of thumb, health of livestock, and the limits of human strength. A few college trained men and large scale farmers may do differently, but not many of these have any concept of $MC$ and $MR$ curves.

**12. Graphic Demonstrations of Profit-Maximizing Situations When Price Varies Inversely with Quantity Demanded.**—The next three sets of graphs deal with cases where the demand as viewed by the individual seller is a function of price. Marginal revenue differs from average revenue (cf. Chapter 4, Section 4). But the problem remains the same. The manager must decide what sales-output quantity will maximize his firm's profits. The solution is usually given, not in terms of output, but in terms of the profit-maximizing price. Since the price and the quantity are inseparably connected, the choice of the one determines the other. There is only one choice, not two, and there is no fundamental difference between this choice and that of the farmer.

The most common graph in this group is that of Figure 33. It is like Figure 30 in that Ross, the producer, is making a good profit. Again the crucial spot on the graph is point $A$ where $MC = MR$. This determines the maximum profit quantity $OQ$, from which a line may be projected vertically through $A$ to $B$ on $AR$. Moving horizontally to the left, we find point $P$ on $OY$. $OP$ and $OQ$, the price and quantity, are simultaneously determined by point $B$. When Ross finds his best quantity, he has also found his maximum profit price. The profit itself may be shown by finding the point $E$ which shows the unit cost of the output $OQ$ ($E$ is at the intersection of $QB$ and the $ATC$ curve). Unit profit then becomes $QB$ minus $QE$, or $EB$. Multiplying by the output, the total profit becomes the shaded rectangle $PBEC$.

One significant difference should be noted between the solution in this case and that of Figure 30. The most profitable output, $OQ$, is *less* than the capacity output, $OR$, whereas in Figure 30 it was greater. Some of the implications of this difference will be explored in a later chapter.

The second figure in this group shows producer Adams just breaking even (Figure 34). His $ATC$ and $AR$ curves are tangent at point $B = E$ on the quantity perpendicular $QA$. The third figure, 35,

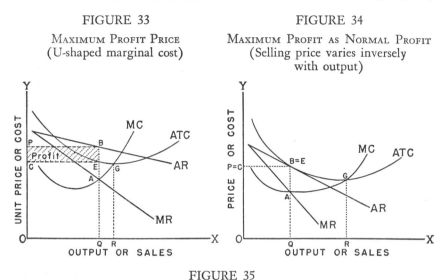

FIGURE 33

MAXIMUM PROFIT PRICE
(U-shaped marginal cost)

FIGURE 34

MAXIMUM PROFIT AS NORMAL PROFIT
(Selling price varies inversely
with output)

FIGURE 35

MINIMIZING LOSS

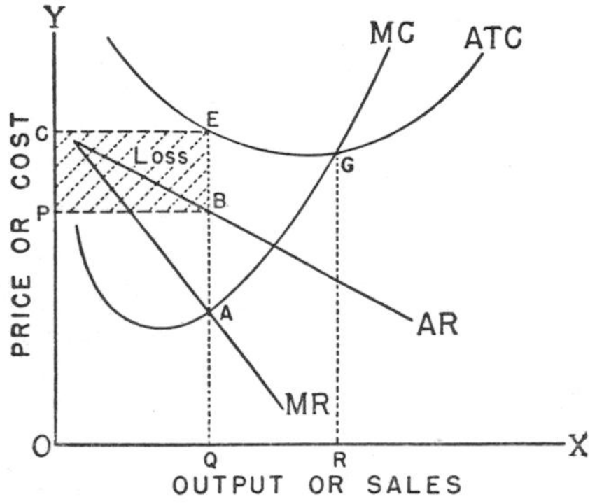

shows producer Thomas operating at a loss, $CEBP$, but minimizing that loss by choosing output $OQ$ (price $OP$) whose $MC = MR$ at $A$.

**13. Special Situations May Be Shown by the Shape of the Curves.**—Most manufacturing and distributing firms do not have deeply convex cost curves. $MC$ curves may be flat-bottomed for a considerable range, as in Figure 36. The solution is the same as

before.   The only difference is that $OQ$ and $OR$ may be further apart
when firms operate under constant marginal cost.   The same type of
$MC$ curve also may be used to
show a manufacturer just breaking even or operating at a loss.

FIGURE 36

MAXIMUM PROFIT PRICE WITH CON-
STANT MARGINAL COST

Another situation of interest is
that in which the best output is
zero.  That is shown in Figures
37 and 38 where the expected revenue is so small that out-of-pocket
costs cannot be regained.   Farmers, particularly fruit growers,
sometimes find themselves in this
predicament.    The demand falls
so low that the market price will
not cover the costs of hiring the
labor to pick and ship the crop.

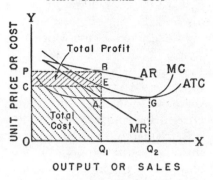

In Figure 37 the marginal cost and the average variable cost are both
higher than the potential net revenue shown by $MR = AR$.  The
manufacturer who sells in a market where his demand is a function

FIGURE 37

BEST OUTPUT IS ZERO

I. Constant Selling Price
(An orchard owner's view at harvest
time)

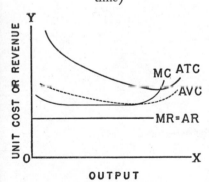

FIGURE 38

BEST OUTPUT IS ZERO

II. Price Falls as Quantity Rises
(Manufacturer's view)

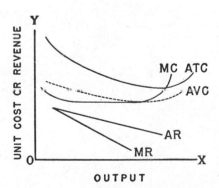

of the price faces the situation shown in Figure 38, where $AR$ and
$MR$ slant and diverge, but at no place exceed $MC$ or $AVC$.

Again the reader must remember that these are planning graphs,
not records of historical events or experiments.   They portray how

the probable cost and revenue situations look to two different individuals who are potential producers. Production occurs in hopes that the situation will be like that of Figure 30, 33, or 36. But if the producer finds he is mistaken, a different picture must be drawn, such as Figure 37 or 38.

Cost curves will have upward jogs whenever new "fixed" factors are added. The simplest group of cost curves assumes that there is only one fixed factor which remains constant throughout the entire range of output. In reality the only difference between "fixed" and "variable" factors is the greater frequency with which inputs have to be increased as outputs expand. Direct labor and materials are continuous variables. Indirect labor, like that of foremen, must be increased intermittently. Hand tools and smaller machines are added less frequently than larger machines. And so on. Graphically this introduces upward jogs in the *AFC* and *ATC* curves. *MC* rises abruptly to a point *MC'* above the upper limits of the usual graph at the moment the new "fixed" expense is treated as a variable. After this point *MC* falls below its previous level and continues its rise as shown in Figure 39A. Similarly *AVC* has a small downward jog, but not enough to offset completely the upward jog in *AFC*.

FIGURE 39

INCREASES IN "FIXED" FACTORS

A. The Cost Curves

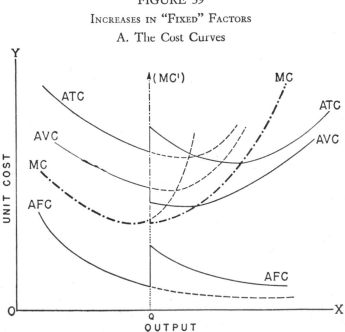

B. Maximum Profit Point

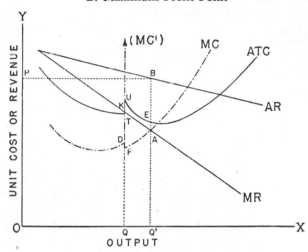

OUTPUT

Graphs of this type are clearly irreversible. They are pictures of cost changes with increasing output and would be different were output to decline. $MC$ crosses the $MR$ curve at two points, $K$ and $A$ as in Figure 39B. The former is clearly an exceptional case caused by the method of treating the additional "fixed" expense as an incremental expense at that particular point. Therefore the maximum profit position is determined by $A$ and the optimum output is $OQ'$.

Another problem of cost curves in price setting is the question of whether or not to include normal profit. In the foregoing diagrams this cost was omitted, but in a later chapter the same sort of curves will be presented with it included. The whole subject is too involved for more than mentioning at this time. (See Chapter 10, Section 13.)

**14. Some Observations on the Meaning of Cost Curves for the Firm.** In conclusion a few observations may be offered to introduce whatever realism is possible in the general subject under discussion. Few business managers use the $MC = MR$ approach in determining their most profitable selling price. The $MR$ schedule is the hardest one to estimate. It requires business forecasts which are far beyond the capacity of most firms. Even expert estimates of probable future demand are largely guesses. Demand fluctuates fairly rapidly for most products. If the $MC = MR$ formula were used rigorously, the selling price would have to change frequently. These changes would themselves affect future demand. Therefore most firms which independently set their own selling prices for new products usually follow some form of the markup rule. They hire cost accountants to tell them the base figure and then guess at the best markup. A few enterprisers estimate the price at which they can sell a certain output and then make plans to produce that much if they think costs can be kept below that price.

Once prices have become established, the pricing problem becomes one of change. Many times demand rises or falls and variations occur in cost without any change in the asking price. The inconvenience, expense, and market disturbance of changing price lists discourage application of the $MC = MR$ rule even by those who know it. Even when major changes in demand or cost do force changes in prices, many long-run considerations are influential in determining the new figure. Some of these will be examined in a later chapter.

Yet profit maximizing does remain a motive. Even crude price-setting methods strive to achieve it in either the short or the long run. Perhaps the $MC = MR$ equilibrium point is better seen as the norm about which guesses cluster than as the price-determining mechanism itself. Whether realized or not, norms are useful concepts, but they should not be confused with the actual economic behavior of real people.

**15. Summary.**—If producers could determine cost and revenue schedules for their future business they could compute the maximum profit output by use of the $MC = MR$ formula. These schedules are usually very difficult to obtain with any accuracy. Other considerations usually cause departure from the formal solution even when it can be calculated. Certain useful principles, however, may be derived from a study of this approach.

1. The *quantity* of a good which one seller will produce and offer for sale at a given place within a given period of time is a function of:
   (a) The seller's expected cost and revenue schedules
   (b) Chance factors which may upset plans

2. The *price* which one seller will ask for the goods he produces and offers for sale is a function of:
   (a) The power of the seller to set his own price independently
   (b) The seller's expected cost and revenue schedules
   (c) The formula applied to these schedules. The $MC = MR$ point indicates a probable norm, but there are many departures from it.

# Chapter 9

## DETERMINANTS OF SELLING POLICIES

**1. Statement of the Problem.**—Often the choice of the best selling price involves much more than the simple methods of the three preceding chapters. Selling cost may be added to production cost. Products may be improved or debased. Prices may be set high or low relative to current cost of production. Prices may be kept constant when costs and demands change, or they may be adjusted accordingly. One cannot understand the workings of our modern capitalistic economy without knowing the determinants of these choices.

Selling policies may be defined as those ways of action an entrepreneur chooses to maximize his profit by influencing his volume of sales. They fall into two main groups: (1) price policies and (2) demand stimulation policies. The former include markup percentages, stability, and discrimination. The latter refer to advertising, product improvement, and other ways of attempting to increase buyer desire for the product. Demand stimulation affects demand intensity, or demand in the schedule sense. Efforts in this field cost money and must be compensated by increased revenue if they are to be continued. Price policies affect schedule demand indirectly through their long-run influence on consumer desire. Their direct effect is upon demand in the market sense: the higher the price the lower the demand, etc.

The various facets of this complex problem may be seen from the following list of questions to which answers are given in this chapter:

1. What are selling costs and why do producers incur them?
2. Under what conditions does advertising pay?
3. How do selling costs influence the maximum profit price computed from cost and revenue curves?
4. How does product differentiation affect the pricing policies of sellers?
5. What long-run perspectives may influence sellers' price policies?
   (a) The attitude of buyers
   (b) Price policies of competitors
   (c) Entry or exit of competitors
   (d) Public regulation
6. What are the different types of price discrimination, their causes and their effects?

117

**2. From Production Cost to Selling Cost.**—In the preceding chapter the influence of cost upon supply price was discussed in terms of production cost. For simplicity it was assumed that the only cost decision to be made by suppliers was an estimate of the effect of changes in the volume of output upon unit cost, either marginal or average. On the other side of the market, the demand schedule was presumed to be known. It was either a fixed price for unlimited sales by an individual producer or a schedule in which the demand varied inversely with the price. It is now necessary to move from this over-simplified picture to introduce additional variables for greater realism.

The first step is to introduce the concept of selling cost. Producers do not need to accept the demand schedule as given. In the modern world they often try to increase the intensity of demand by various types of selling effort. Most firms do not sit back and merely accept orders as they are received, but reach out either by salesmen or by advertising, to influence buyers who otherwise would have bought elsewhere, or conceivably not at all. At times there even is pressure to sell some assets so as to buy others, such as the advertising which indirectly seeks to induce people to liquidate their war bonds to purchase homes, automobiles, refrigerators, etc.

Total profit is the difference between total income and total outgo, and each of these categories includes quantities as well as prices. On the revenue side this means that total income is a function of the quantity sold as much as it is a function of the price per unit sold. On the cost side there are not only the problems of the number of units purchased and the price paid per unit, but also certain other expenses associated with the general conduct of the business which are often loosely called overhead. Sometimes selling expense may be linked directly with the number of units sold, as when salesmen are paid a commission which varies with the volume of their sales. More often selling expense cannot readily be linked with each particular commodity and must be considered a part of overhead. In the latter category it represents an expense which is fixed in total amount, but declines as the volume of sales increases. Selling expense must be estimated and budgeted in advance of the selling period or calculated in retrospect as though it had been. Selling cost, however, differs from most other overhead costs in that the latter usually are planned relative to an expected volume of sales, whereas selling efforts are intended to increase that volume, to raise the price at which goods may be sold, or both.

**3. Advertising and Other Forms of Selling Expense.**—At the retail level the chief form of selling expense to try to increase schedule demand takes the form of advertising. The retailer uses newspapers and radio to tell potential customers about himself, his store, or his products, hoping thereby to induce more people to buy from him than otherwise would have bought. He may stress the high quality of his merchandise, the courtesy of his salespeople, the convenience or prestige of his location, or the generosity of his credit terms, if he wishes to appeal to those potential customers who do not buy with a thrifty eye to price. If his aim is to attract the latter, the retailer will stress the cheapness of his product, invite price and quality comparisons, tell how much the price has been reduced from former levels, "refuse to be undersold," etc.

If the advertising does increase demand, the seller will reap additional profit, provided the increase in gross revenue exceeds the additional cost. The simplest case is one in which the increased demand from *dd* to *d'd'* permits the seller to charge a higher price without loss of customers, as shown in Figure 40. Since the volume of sales remains constant at *OQ,* the only additional cost is that for advertising, *PACE.* This is less than the additional gross revenue, *PP'BE,* and, therefore, the seller makes a

FIGURE 40

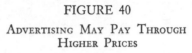

ADVERTISING MAY PAY THROUGH HIGHER PRICES

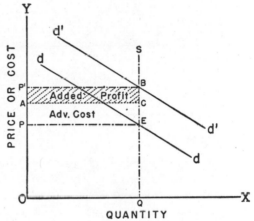

net gain from his price and advertising policy as shown by *AP'BC.*

Under other circumstances the price may remain constant either because of voluntary choice or because the maximum price is set by the government, the trade association, or a traditional policy of "follow-the-leader." In such cases individual sellers (or trade associations) may benefit from advertising and other selling efforts which increase the volume of sales.[1] The effect upon profits may be shown under either of two conditions: constant cost (of production), or decreasing

---

[1] In the case where there are many sellers of a homogeneous good such as wheat or copper, the maximum price is fixed by "the market," and an individual firm would undoubtedly find it too expensive to try to increase demand when the effect of its efforts would be felt by all sellers and could not be concentrated upon its own (undifferentiated) product.

cost. For instance, in Figure 41 the unit cost of operation remains the same, $OA = QF = Q'G$, when sales expand from $OQ$ to $OQ'$. The area $QFGQ'$ represents the additional operating expense. $FDEG$ is the advertising expense which increases demand from $dd$ to $d'd'$. This leaves $DBCE$ as additional profit.

FIGURE 41

ADVERTISING MAY PAY THROUGH LARGER VOLUME
(Constant Cost and Price)

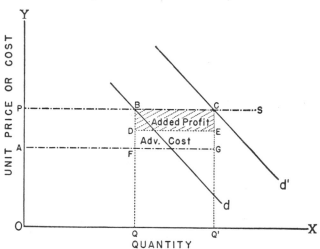

However, it is more likely that additional sales will reduce average total unit cost through the process of "spreading overhead" and even possibly through economies in operating at the larger volume. This situation is diagrammed in Figure 42 where the unit cost drops from $OG$ to $OA$ as output rises from $OQ$ to $OQ'$, price remaining constant at $OP$. Advertising cost is represented as $AEFB$ by spreading it over the entire output.[2] If $ATC'$ is the new unit cost curve, the increase in net revenue is $EGHJ$ on the former volume $OQ$, plus $JCDF$ on the added sales, $QQ'$.[3]

Both these illustrations assume that the advertising campaign is "successful," that it more than pays for itself. But that is not always the case. Sometimes the increase in gross revenue is less than the extra selling expense. This probably occurs most frequently in

---

[2] When selling expense is a variable expense like salesmen's commissions, a different diagrammatic technique must be used.

[3] $ATC'$ will not be parallel to $ATC$ because the total advertising expense will have to be distributed over fewer units if sales are $OQ$ than if they are $OQ'$, i.e., $LH$ will exceed $FB$.

cases of "defensive" advertising where competitors are taking away a
firm's trade by their own successful selling efforts or by offering a
better product, and where the injured firm tries unsuccessfully to
stem the advance of its rivals.   Instead of increasing demand by advertising, the result may be merely to prevent it from declining or

### FIGURE 42

ADVERTISING MAY PAY THROUGH LARGER VOLUME AND LOWER
COSTS
(Price Constant)

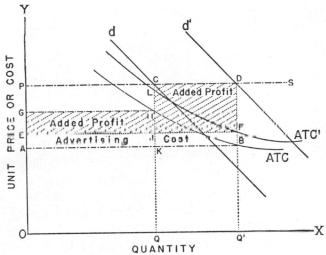

from declining as much as it otherwise would.   Some cigarette advertising would seem to fall in this category.   A similar unfortunate
result may sometimes occur in the case of an advertising campaign
designed to bring customers to a new store or to persuade people to
buy a new article.   In short, an outlay for selling expense may or
may not pay for itself, depending upon the article, buyers' willingness to purchase, the effectiveness of the particular type of advertising chosen, and the effectiveness of the advertising of competitors.

   Although the advertiser generally wants to increase schedule demand by increasing buyer information and desire, he may also wish
to change the price-elasticity of demand at the same time.   There are
two possible alternatives.   If an advertiser is contemplating a price
cut, as in a "sale" planned by a retailer, he may be content to *increase*
the elasticity of demand for the product whose price is to be reduced.
In fact, it is very difficult in such cases to distinguish between the increase in intensity and the increase in elasticity of the demand sched-

ule.  On the other hand, an advertiser may wish to *de*crease the elasticity of demand so that he may raise his price without suffering a considerable reduction in market demand.  From a different approach, there is also the possibility that the advertising may be designed chiefly to decrease the *cross*-elasticity of demand, i.e., to prevent adverse shifts in schedule demand that might result if a competitor should cut his price or improve the quality of his product.

There are, of course, other forms of selling expense besides advertising.  They include hiring and training salesmen, providing attractive and convenient places and methods of sale, furnishing customer services such as credit and delivery, etc.  Sellers at all levels may spend money to promote the sales of their goods.  Manufacturers of branded goods often advertise, and middlemen likewise. In fact, middlemen count on the advertising campaigns of manufacturers to help them sell to retailers, and the latter receive selling help from the advertising of all who previously handled the good. Such advertising does not help a retailer competitively against other retailers handling the same good, particularly if the manufacturer insists that all retailers in a certain area quote the same price.  But it will help if a retailer has the only dealer contract for a given area, like a Ford dealer in Dogpatch, and is trying to sell the product in competition with other products which are claimed to be equally good, or better.

Expenditures for advertising seem to follow a law of diminishing additional returns.  A small amount of selling expense may be relatively ineffective and the money wasted, but larger amounts may bring increasing additional revenue.  Somewhere a peak occurs and thereafter further expenditures reveal diminishing additional revenue.  Eventually a point is reached at which the selling expense no longer pays for itself in expanded demand and added revenue. Business firms seek to budget their selling expenditures so that they just reach this point, but its exact location must always remain a matter of guesswork since it varies with competitors' efforts, changes in buyers' incomes, etc.[4]  The most profitable amount to spend on selling effort also depends upon the type of sales appeal.  Some slogans are far more effective than others, some advertising media give more contacts for the money, some salesmen are better builders of repeat business than other salesmen.

---

[4] The seller must also decide how much emphasis to place upon selling expense in relation to other methods of increasing sales, such as price cuts, product improvement, etc.

Whether selling expense does increase demand in most cases cannot be proved, since much sales activity is defensive as in the case of rival brands of cigarettes. Each tries to get some slogan or sales appeal which will prove more attractive than the other and their efforts therefore largely cancel out. However, selling expense is a cost of doing business and in the long run must be compensated by income from sales. That is, unit prices asked and received by sellers must cover all costs, including selling expense, if the seller is to remain in business. Where advertising, for instance, does increase demand for a given article, unit costs of production may be sufficiently reduced by the expanded volume of production to pay the cost of that advertising and still permit the seller to quote lower prices than before. (See Figure 42 where $OA + AE$ is less than $OG$.) But the seller need not lower his price merely because his costs are reduced. It is more likely that he will retain or even increase his asking price to take advantage of the increase in schedule demand. And if the selling effort actually costs more than the decrease in per unit production expense, then a price increase is to be expected. Finally, industry abounds with trade-marked articles whose superiority over similar articles is chiefly an illusion created in the minds of nondiscriminating buyers by the clever and oft-repeated slogans of advertisements. Proof of this contention may be found in the large profits made by certain sellers in this group, such as the producers of cosmetics, as the result of being able to maintain a price far above the cost of production.

**4. Product Differentiation Aids Price Control by Sellers.—** Most selling effort is conducted by individual firms in favor of their own products. This requires that they be distinguished from similar products in some way so that the buyer can tell rival products apart. For many nondurable consumers' goods, such as food and clothing, the use of trade-marks or brands is the chief method ("None genuine without this signature" or "Look for the red label"). Minor differences in design or "quality" may be introduced to make the distinction more obvious. These become more pronounced among durable consumers' goods such as automobiles, radios, and refrigerators.

Product differentiation of the quality type often involves additional expense so that the seller is faced with the problem of deciding how much he can afford to put into such extras ("chromium grille," "dual horns," "humidor compartment"). His decision on that score is closely related to his ideas about the probable effectiveness of his contemplated selling campaign. A gadget is worth adding only if it can be magnified by advertising into a very important feature "well worth the extra money" it costs the buyer. To be profitable to the seller, it must yield enough additional revenue to cover more than both the manufacturing and the advertising expense.

Precise calculation of "the most profitable price" under such conditions is obviously impossible. The seller plans his production design and the amount and type of his selling expense according to the best guesses he can make and not according to specific schedules of estimated material costs and marginal revenues. On the expenditure side the number of variables is large, and on the revenue side the imponderables of the ever-changing market confound attempts at arithmetical formulation of maximum-profit prices. If the expected rate of sales does not materialize, the seller may increase the amount or change the type of selling expense. He may reduce the price, offer more liberal credit terms, or do nothing at all, hoping that the current selling efforts will eventually prove successful as the product catches the public's fancy or consumer spending rises. An improvement in the design or a change in the packaging or the name of the product are other possible expedients.

The presence of so many alternative ways of expanding sales makes the precise explanation of asking prices difficult. There is no standard formula or rule-of-thumb which will tell the price at which profit will be maximized in the short or long run. The seller who spends much on selling expense or in improving his product need not make large price cuts to achieve a desired sales volume. Another possibility is that he may set his price high above production costs and rely on selling efforts to evoke sufficient buying to permit him to cover both production and selling expense and make a good profit.

**5. Long-Run Perspectives in the Determination of Selling Variables.**—When a seller decides upon the magnitude of one or more of the variables involved in sales policy, he ordinarily looks farther ahead than merely the time to dispose of his current output. It is important for him to estimate demand intensity months and years ahead if he takes certain steps in the present. The importance of the effect of price changes upon the desires and buying habits of the people has already been discussed at various points (cf. Chapter 3, Section 7). The effects of variations in product are probably longer lasting, because they build up or tear down the reputation of the seller for turning out "good goods." Advertising and other elements of selling expense often do not have their full effect for months afterwards. For instance, the cumulative effect of a slogan ("They

Satisfy") repeated again and again may ultimately attract customers who were not stimulated to purchase at first. And the word-of-mouth advertising of those customers who actually are satisfied also takes time to get around.

The level at which prices are initially set or the changes which are subsequently made may have long-run effects in four fields with which sellers are frequently concerned: (1) the attitude of buyers, (2) the price policies of competitors, (3) the possible entry of new competitors into the field or exit of existing ones, and (4) the possible stimulation of public regulation. Each of these topics deserves separate discussion.

### 6. Long-Run Effect of Price Changes upon Attitude of Buyers.
—A new retail establishment often features initial prices lower than its competitors', hoping thereby to wean away their customers and get people in the habit of shopping at the new store. After a period of a few weeks or months, prices may be raised gradually to more profitable levels, but there is always the danger that the price-conscious customers originally attracted will then go off to other stores for reasons of longer familiarity or greater convenience.

Established retail stores often feature "sales" of various kinds hoping to draw customers from competitors. Some of the advertised "sale" articles may not be priced lower than before, but are merely played up in display advertising to bring them to the attention of potential buyers, who would not otherwise have thought of buying them. Where price cuts do occur, the seller must always recognize that a part of the business he attracts is made up of old customers, who take advantage of sales to stock up on the featured merchandise. In the course of a year or two they may not buy more of the cheapened goods, but merely space their purchases differently from what they otherwise would have done. The long-run effect, therefore, may be diminished buying in the months ahead by these old customers, and increased buying by new customers, who return to buy other goods after the sale is over (or even form the habit of patronizing the sales of the particular store). Price cuts also may be made defensively to meet those initiated by competitors and to make the consumer believe that he always can shop in that store with confidence in getting the lowest possible prices.

The significance of price competition in the retail field must not be exaggerated, however, since many if not most consumers are not insistent upon getting the most for their money in durability, design, and general satisfaction. Style features catch the eye more often than price tags, and consumers may not bother to inform themselves about rival products in other stores. Careful judgment is too inconvenient, takes too much time, or requires technical competence to appraise the worth of goods which only a few possess. Hence, a store may rely upon convenience of location, completeness of stocks, efficiency of sales force, generosity of terms, etc., instead of price-quality competition. The advertising of such stores may stress these points, feature a very few genuinely cheap articles, or merely publicize prices with regularity and rely upon repetition to convey the illusion of good buying opportunities.

Manufacturers have different problems to face than retailers when setting their asking prices. In the first place their buyers are more price-conscious, whether they be those who buy for resale or for use in further production. The latter also examine the quality of their purchases with greater skill and care, since business success depends as much upon efficient and economical buying as it does upon diligent selling. Sellers of industrial equipment and raw materials often stress design, technical performance, durability, and convenience more than price. Those who sell finished products to middlemen must consider the effect of their initial prices or price changes not only upon the ultimate consumer, but also upon those intervening buyers who handle the products. A manufacturer sometimes seeks to encourage wholesalers and retailers to carry his line of merchandise rather than a competitor's by conducting a vigorous advertising campaign intended to make the ultimate consumer want the products and ask for them by name at the retailers. Or he may grant "advertising allowances" to middlemen in which he cuts his list price by an amount which the buyer is supposed to use in local advertising. He may fix the final selling price so high that retail margins or commissions of middlemen are larger than usually accompany his type of product. To encourage stocking and pushing new products, special deals of various types may be employed, such as giving one case free for every dozen cases purchased. The variety of expedients is so great that no significant generalization is possible regarding the optimum price in relation to cost.

**7. Effect of Price Changes upon Price Policies of Competitors.** —The fact that price changes made by Seller A may cause Seller B to make similar or offsetting changes has already been noted in several connections and deserves further analysis. In the first place, although A's price change is obviously a causal factor so far as B is concerned, the quantitative reaction of B is unpredictable. If the product involved is one in which there is high transference of demand from one seller to another when price differentials emerge between sellers (as with many industrial raw materials and a few standardized retail products like gasoline), Seller B is likely to make precisely the same cut (or increase) that is initiated by Seller A. The firm making the first change in such cases usually is the major seller in the field and the other smaller firms merely "follow the leader." If A happens to be a relatively small seller or if most of the firms are operating near capacity, competitors may not follow price cuts initiated by A.

On the other hand, if the industry is one which has much excess capacity, or if the major sellers want to punish firm A which has become too independent to suit them, the reactions of B, C, etc., may be to make price cuts larger than A did. This may prompt A to still further cuts and a "price war" occurs in which most of the firms, if not all of them, soon sell at a loss. Illustrations may be found in the history of retail sales of gasoline, bread, milk, and other relatively standardized articles of wide consumption. At one time railroads likewise engaged in this type of "cutthroat competition" before the Interstate Commerce Commission was granted the power to impose minimum rates and to prevent rebates and other forms of secret price-cutting. A price war ends when continued losses discourage further price-cutting, or bankruptcy forces the weaker firms out of business. Some firm may then raise prices a bit and find that others are tired of the war and willing to follow. The group eventually may restore prices which approach those prevailing before, or exceed them, as in the case of some American railroads in the decade following the Civil War.

In the second place, the possibility that a price cut by A might stimulate similar or greater price cuts by B, C, etc., is something that is likely to be taken into account by the management of A if it is farsighted. Ordinarily such a prospect will be a deterrent, but not always. New firms or those with particularly aggressive management may be willing to take the risk. By secrecy or surprise they may get the selling advantages of low prices for some time before competitors follow suit. One result of such price wars or the possibility thereof is that sellers may get together in a formal or informal way to agree not to do such things. They hope that such an understanding, though unenforceable in the courts, will act as a greater deterrent than purely independent caution. The possible boomerang effect of price action makes for still greater uncertainty about demand schedules than ordinarily exists. Equilibrium theorists point out the logical impossibility of stable prices under such conditions and describe the situation by terms such as *oligopoly, duopoly, circularity,* or *the small group case.*

If products are highly differentiated in fact or in the minds of the buyer (as through effective advertising about the alleged superior quality of a given brand), sellers will be less prone to reduce prices to meet price cuts of a rival. Instead they often try to discredit the rival product as being inferior by bringing out what they call "second grade" brands to sell at the lower price while refusing to lower the list price of their "first grade" brands. Such has been the case in certain retail markets, such as that for automobile tires (chain store competition), gasoline (small refiners and casing-head gasoline), and refrigerators. Major canners have often put "off-brand" labels on their surplus pack to prevent having to make the price cuts which would be required to market their entire supply under the nationally advertised brands. Because of the lack of grade labeling or public testing laboratories, consumers cannot tell the difference. Therefore, the more prosperous among them, or the less thrifty, continue to buy the highly advertised brands instead of others which offer greater value for the money. "Fighting brands" are almost exclusively a feature of retail trade. Industrial buyers are more careful and less gullible. However, the prestige of "big names" undoubtedly does make it hard for new firms to break into the market at any level even though their products are superior in design or quality or are lower in price.

**8. Effect of Price Policies upon Entry or Exit of Competitors.** —If firm A raises the price of its product very far above the unit cost of producing it, new or existing competitors will try to take away its customers by offering similar articles or effective substitutes at lower prices. The most common case is where A is deterred from raising his price by fear that existing firms will undersell him and seriously reduce his sales volume. To prevent this he may get an agreement among his chief competitors to raise their prices at the same time—or rely on their voluntarily following his lead. Monopolistic agreements of this type to reduce price competition are generally kept secret because of fear of prosecution under antitrust statutes. Ostensible competitors may have interlocking directorates, considerable stock ownership in common, or potent trade associations which secure unity of action in regard to price. This restricts the field of competition to selling efforts and to product superiority. Even these may be limited by agreement, as in the "cartel" arrangements between firms in different countries, which frequently limit the areas within

which members are free to seek buyers, so that each member has his
own home territory free from foreign competition of any kind.

Potential sellers may be prevented from becoming actual competitors in various ways.  These include the large amounts of capital
required to get started (alloy steels) ; the situation where patents are
held tightly by one firm or made available only at high royalty
(electronics) ; exclusive franchise (radio broadcasting) ; lack of sales
outlets (automobiles) ; lack of skilled labor or management experience; and tariffs (against foreign competition).  Any firm which
contemplates asking prices which others deem "high" must consider
the effect of such prices upon its future competition if it wishes to
arrive at a wise decision.  Sometimes it will choose to set the high
price and at the same time hunt for means to secure cooperation or
retard entry.

Stated in general terms, there are probably two main reasons for
entry: prices and profits.  The prospective entrant is probably attracted most often by high prices which exceed the cost he thinks
he would have to incur in producing a similar product or service.  In
other cases, however, the new entrant is attracted by reports of high
profits in the given field.  Prices are obvious, profits may be concealed or distorted, and financial reports demonstrating their presence
do not usually appear until after high prices have been in effect for
some time.  Other reasons for entry include a desire on the part of a
hired manager to become his own boss, old firms taking on new lines
to make fuller use of existing capacity, etc.

When entry occurs, the newcomer is beset with many difficulties,
not least of which is the task of convincing buyers that he has a good
and dependable product.  Since he usually cannot point to his past
record, he must offer some special inducement to get his first sales
made.  This usually means offering goods at less than prevailing
market price, granting more favorable terms of sale, or throwing in
some "extra" for the standard price.  That is why many firms operate
at a loss during the years in which their product is being introduced
in the market.  They spend more for selling expense of various
types or they have to operate at such a low percentage of capacity
that each unit sold carries more overhead than is customary in the
industry.

If the newcomer is successful, he may take away so much of the
business of the price-raising firm or firms that they are reduced to a
smaller scale of output.  To avoid such damaging competition, an
existing firm which is tempted to raise its prices may reduce them
instead.  This will tend to discourage entrants and may even bring

greater profits through the economies of large-scale production which were impossible at the higher price.

Defenders of the capitalistic system of free enterprise acclaim self-restraint and free entry as automatic checks to monopolistic price raising. They are similar to the price competition which allegedly reduces the prices of all firms in a group when one of them introduces a process for reducing the cost of production and cuts prices to exploit its advantage. Rivalry between firms already in a field plus free entry of new competitors is supposed to keep prices so low in relation to cost that no firm or group of firms can long receive abnormally high profits. The picture is undoubtedly true in its main outlines, but these are increasingly blurred as obstacles to entry multiply and innovators seek profit through price maintenance rather than price-cutting. Established producers may also buy out the upstart rather than engage in price competition with him. Therefore, conclusions regarding desirable social policy must be reached in the light of a careful appraisal of each given situation and not by the application of sweeping generalizations either about the benefits of free competition or about the harmfulness of government regulation and public price-fixing.

**9. Effect of Price Policy upon Public Regulation.**—In deciding his proper price policy the business executive also must take into consideration the possibility that what he does may provoke public regulation harmful to him. In earlier periods of our national history, excessive prices charged by railroads, water companies, gas, light, and power companies, and street railways provoked public regulation designed to curb increases and price discrimination. In more recent years, however, the field covered by the term *public utilities* has become fairly well stabilized as an area for public control and two other trends have developed. The first dates back to 1914, when the Federal Trade Commission was set up to curb various acts known as "unfair methods of competition." Since this form of public regulation is designed to protect the seller, not the consumer, it sometimes seeks to prevent price-cutting. The argument is that a seller should not engage in temporary price-cutting in a given area in order to squeeze out an upstart competitor and then, after that has been achieved, return the price to the former level. The purpose of that kind of price competition being to eliminate future price competition, it is considered antisocial. Other forms of unfair competition are banned by orders of the FTC, but only price matters concern us here.

The second trend is for competitors to *seek* public regulation in order to avoid the profit-destroying effects of price competition. The milk distributors and producers have secured such protection in a number of states by legislation creating commissions to set minimum prices. In California the barbers have similarly organized and protected themselves, with the result that the public is paying almost twice as much per haircut as formerly. Neither of these industries has been declared a public utility, and the consumer has no representative to guarantee that prices will be held down to a "reasonable" level like that vaguely defined for public utilities as a "fair return on a fair value." Since public regulation of this type often has grown out of conditions of destructive price competition, it is like going through a war in which the survivors emerge into the promised land flowing with the milk and honey of guaranteed minimum prices.

There are some retailers, however, especially chain stores, which may read the handwriting on the wall if they press down too heavily upon their weaker competitors. Already most states have enacted "fair trade" laws to prohibit retailers and wholesalers, in certain lines, from selling at prices less than "cost" plus a minimum markup determined in various ways. Small businessmen also have secured the passage of the federal Robinson-Patman Act (1936). This amends the Clayton Act and forbids sellers to grant large buyers any more reduction from the price charged small buyers than is warranted by the economies in manufacture, sale, or delivery which result from selling in larger lots. In similar fashion the price-cutting tendencies of large retail sellers have been curbed by state and federal legislation (Miller-Tydings Act) permitting producers to set minimum resale prices for their goods and to refuse to sell to those who will not sign a contract to maintain these prices. In addition to these laws which limit freedom to cut prices, aggressive selling may also bring down upon chain stores a special tax, varying directly with the number of stores in the chain, which certain states have already inflicted.

During the depression that followed the 1929 crash, the downward trend of prices and spending became so alarming that one of the devices adopted by the New Deal administration to stop it was the National Recovery Administration. Under the NRA *minimum* prices and wages were established and industries were organized into groups to draw up codes of fair competition which limited members' rights to cut prices. The law was later declared unconstitutional, but a precedent was set and many industrial firms still feel the effect of the "price-stabilizing" codes in spite of declarations by the Department of Justice that the antitrust laws are still on the statute books.

**10. Types of Price Discrimination.**—As suggested above, certain sellers offer large lots of goods at lower prices than small lots. This price discrimination in favor of large buyers is defended on the ground that merchandising costs are less per unit of sale. But that is not the only reason, nor is it sufficient explanation of the spread between low and high asking prices for the same goods. Buyers of the same size are sometimes charged different prices which have no conceivable cost variations to justify them. This is called personal or firm discrimination and is due either to the desire to favor the low price buyer or to his more effective higgling over the price. In times of rising prices, new customers are often charged more than old customers, although they do not always know it. When business is light, the reverse may be true, and the seller may shade his price secretly to get new business. Another common practice is to grant cash customers a lower price than those who take time to pay. If we assume that prices should be proportionate to costs, then whenever they are not, discrimination is made against some one.

**11. The Basing Point System Reduces Location Advantages.**— If all buyers of steel or other commodity of a certain type and quantity paid the same F.O.B. price at the mill, the nearest buyers would have an advantage over the more distant ones. Their transportation costs would be less. Buyers who could use cheap water transportation would have an advantage over those paying more expensive rail freight rates. These buyers are discriminated against when they are deprived of this transportation cost advantage.

The most famous method of discriminating in this way is the *basing point system*. It is best known in connection with the steel industry. For many years most steel buyers in the United States were compelled to pay a Pittsburgh, Pennsylvania, F.O.B. price plus rail freight from Pittsburgh, regardless of where they bought the steel. A Chicago firm might buy steel from Gary, Indiana, but it had to pay the Pittsburgh price plus freight from Pittsburgh ten times farther away. A firm in Laramie, Wyoming, might have the same treatment when it bought steel from Pueblo, Colorado, nearby. These buyers lost the advantage of being near steel mills.

Discrimination of this type depends upon some type of monopolistic price-fixing. There may be only one producer with several factories geographically scattered. The Ford Motor Company, for instance, has many assembly plants, but all Ford dealers pay a price which includes freight from Detroit. Or there may be some type of understanding among competing producers of a standard commodity like portland cement or linseed oil.  Such firms would all quote the same prices to all buyers in a given city even though purchases were made from different sellers in different cities.  Each quoted price would be based upon an agreed F.O.B. price plus an agreed transportation cost from an agreed basing point.

Another form of location discrimination occurs when manufacturers establish the same delivered price for all buyers wherever they may be located.  The most extreme case is found in retail commodities sold at the same price throughout the nation, like Hershey bars or the latest popular novel.  This form of uniform delivered price has sometimes been called "postage stamp pricing" because of the uniformity of rates on first class mail regardless of distance.

The size of the market area in which all sellers quote identical prices depends upon the rail freight structure.  Some mail order sales have two zones, one east of the Rockies and another west of the Rockies.  If the rail freight rate on a certain type of steel pipe is the same from an eastern basing point, such as Sparrows Point, Maryland, to Los Angeles, San Diego, and San Francisco, the uniform delivered price region will be very large.  Ordinarily, however, the transportation rates to different cities as far apart as these vary considerably and therefore their buyers do not pay the same price.

The major economic significance of uniform delivered prices lies in the fact that buyers do not gain from being located close to a producer.  A San Francisco buyer might get his steel from Pittsburg, California, only thirty miles across the bay, but he could not get it any cheaper than the Los Angeles buyer, 450 miles to the south.  Both would be charged the base price at Sparrows Point plus freight to the west coast, even though the steel originated in Northern California, and this western producer would pocket the extra transportation charges, often called "phantom freight."

**12. Other Aspects of the Basing Point System.**—A uniform delivered price system of one type or another has been used in thirty or more major industries, including asphalt roofing, cast iron pipe, cement, copper, gypsum board, linseed oil, lumber, soap, steel, sugar, tiles, and zinc.[5]  Although its historic origin has differed in different industries, the chief purpose seems to have been to prevent price competition which arises when new firms commence business at points closer than old firms to important consuming centers.  Buyers

---

[5] An excellent summary and criticism of the uniform delivered price system may be found in TNEC Monograph No. 42, *The Basing Point Problem*, which contains the views of both the United States Steel Corporation and the Federal Trade Commission.

otherwise would tend to buy from their nearest supplier in order to save on transportation costs. This would cut out the older firm from markets near the new one and prevent the newcomer from invading the territory near the old one. The chief reason why new firms cooperate in such a monopolistic system probably is fear of local price cutting by the old firms, which could afford to sell at a loss for a while if they thought it necessary to prevent losing all of the business in a given area. The new enterprises must rely for their selling appeal either on speedy delivery or on buy-at-home-from-those-you-know arguments, since the article involved is ordinarily identical in form and quality regardless of who produces it.

Sometimes the new firms become so well established that they are able to force the older concerns to grant them the privilege of having their own basing point, although they usually continue to use the base prices of the industry leader. Pressure from buyers and from the government also have been responsible for introducing a multiple basing point system in place of a single basing point. The delivered price in localities near the new basing point will fall because freight charges from that point are less than from the former one, but uniformity of delivered prices will remain. Sellers in the old basing point city and elsewhere will revise their price lists to adopt the delivered prices of the sellers in the new basing point cities. This means that if they succeed in making sales in the natural market area of the latter, they will not be able to charge the full freight from their own shipping point, but will have to absorb it. For instance, if Birmingham, Alabama, is considered the new basing point, Pittsburgh, Pennsylvania, the old basing point, and New Orleans the place of sale, then the change gives New Orleans buyers a price reduction equal to the difference between freight rates from Pittsburgh and from Birmingham. Pittsburgh sellers, however, must absorb this difference, approximately equal to the freight between Pittsburgh and Birmingham.

It is obvious that the most economical procedure for the country as a whole would be for buyers to purchase from the source which can produce and ship goods the most cheaply.[6] Under the basing point system this rule is violated. Goods are shipped from west to east which could be bought in the east, and from east to west which could be bought in the west. There is much of this "cross

---

[6] It is often wise, however, not to concentrate all orders on the cheapest source of supply in case it might be closed by a fire, strike, or other difficulty. In periods of generally tight supply and rationing those with many suppliers have generally fared better than those with only one.

hauling," with attendant waste of manpower and resources in transportation and selling efforts, plus a higher average level of costs to the consumer.[7]

The basing point system has many variations, all of which involve price discrimination. If the number of basing points is large, the amount of discrimination is small, but it does not disappear unless every production center is a basing point for every item, in which case there would be no reason for having the system since it would be equivalent to F.O.B. pricing. The base prices at different basing points are often uniform, but uniformity in this respect is merely monopolistic, not discriminatory. Where base prices differ, they may reflect differences in cost of production, and to that extent the market price structure is more competitive.[8]

**13. Requisites for Price Discrimination.**—When a seller charges one buyer or group of buyers a higher price than another, he must rely upon the inability of the low-cost purchasers to resell at the higher price. This is achieved in various ways: (1) by keeping the price differential less than the transfer costs between the two buyers (includes costs of handling, transportation, and taxes, such as excises or tariffs); (2) by refusing to install the necessary equipment for the buyer who does not buy directly (telephone service); (3) by contracts prohibiting resale; (4) by the perishable nature of the article; or (5) by keeping the high-price buyer in ignorance of the discrimination against him. Efforts may also be made to convince the high-price buyer that the apparent discrimination is really to his benefit.

The latter argument is based upon the following line of reasoning: (1) The high-price buyer A is originally charged a price which, when paid by all buyers, is just sufficient to cover direct costs, indirect or overhead costs, and a normal profit. (2) If sales can be made to B only at a lower price than that charged A and others like him, A may yet gain if two conditions are fulfilled: (a) the price charged B is in excess of the direct costs of supplying B, and (b) the excess is used to reduce the total overhead costs that must be charged to A. However, if the excess is used only to swell the profits of the seller, A does not benefit. Another approach is to assume under (1) above that

---

[7] As a make-work policy during the depression of 1929–1939 some government agencies, it is reported, made a practice of ordering supplies from the most distant firm of those submitting identical bids.

[8] The basing point system of pricing was outlawed for the cement industry in a 1948 decision of the U. S. Supreme Court. The ban of this decision may be extended to other industries, but evasionary tactics are probable.

the revenue from firms charged A's high price is not sufficient to cover all costs and that the seller is faced, therefore, with the necessity of discontinuing business or raising A's price if sales cannot be made to B which will meet the deficit in overhead costs. The difficulty lies in convincing A that B really is being charged as much as he should, or that the seller is as nearly bankrupt as he contends.

Prominent illustrations of long-continued price discrimination are found in charges for railroad transportation, water, electricity, gas, and telephone service. In rail history the most famous example is the long-short haul controversy. To meet competition from water carriers or other railroads at terminal points, railroads have often charged more *per ton-mile* for hauling identical merchandise a short distance to a nonterminal point than for a long distance which includes the short one (from New York to Denver as opposed to from New York to San Francisco). Protesting inland towns were told that they benefited from the discrimination, since otherwise they would have no rail service at all. Somehow they could not envisage the rails being torn up, but the best they could do was to secure the passage of legislation prohibiting the extreme discrimination which had existed when the *total* charge for the short haul exceeded that for the long haul (larger charges per ton-mile were still allowed). Less obvious examples in the field of railway rates are the higher charges for articles of high value and small bulk (silk, tea) than for cheap articles of large bulk (cement, coal). The allegation that railroads and other public utilities "charge what the traffic will bear" attests the fact that those who must pay the high rates usually feel that the sellers are raising the price to them instead of just lowering the price to others for the benefit of those who protest. It is an axiom of monopolistic price-fixing that the monopolist sets his single or multiple rates as high as he can in the light of the prospective demand for his product by various buyers.

There are also many cases of departure from the published basing point prices discussed in the preceding section. When purchasers want the product modified in size, quality, or delivery date from what is customary, the seller is involved in additional expense. This has led to the imposition of charges known as "extras." If the leading producers operate monopolistically, they may consult with one another about these charges and set up a scale of extras which is supposed to apply to all sales, like the underlying basing point prices themselves. In such a case the extras will only approximate the additional costs involved and may be shaded upon occasion. Departures from the basing point prices themselves have also been common in some industries, notably steel. In efforts to get orders from very large consumers, price concessions are frequently offered, but the smaller firms and governmental buyers are forced to pay the full list price. These price cuts, usually secret, cannot be justified on the grounds of the economies of large-scale operation, since they bear no uniform relationship either to average or to marginal costs and since the government, though a large buyer, gets no cuts at all. The extent of price concessions varies instead with the degree of economic concentration in the consuming industries, i.e., with their bargaining power.[9]

**14. Limits of Price Discrimination.**—If we assume that a seller knows the demand and cost curves for his product throughout a wide range of quantities, which is unlikely, we can state with precision the prices which he should charge to maximize his profit. Having determined the most profitable uniform price, he should then subdivide his customers into as many groups as possible at prices higher than this one. He should also seek additional customers at prices below the most profitable uniform price until his total sales have expanded to the point where marginal cost equals market price. The problem may be diagrammed by Figure 43 which should be compared with Figure 33. If all goods must be sold at a single price, the best price is $OP = QB$, determined by the $MC = MR$ rule of Chapter 8, Section 12. If the seller can discriminate against the buyers willing to pay more than $OP$, he should seek to exploit as much as possible the demand represented by section $SB$ of the demand curve $AR$. The more finely he can subdivide these buyers and ask each group the full amount it is willing to pay, the closer he will come to the theoretical maximum profit increment, the triangle $SPB$. Having done this, the seller might seek also to exploit the demand at prices below $OP = QB$ on the segment $BU$ of the demand curve. This is often called "dumping." The maximum gain to be derived from this type of discrimination is shown by the triangle $BAU$.

In actual practice the seller does not know the full shape of his demand curve nor is it constant from day to day. Hence the best he can do is to make guesses and use trial and error methods. This

[9] John M. Blair and Arthur Reeside make the comment in TNEC Monograph No. 41, *Price Discrimination in Steel,* Washington, 1941, that "the obvious effect of these concessions to large buyers is that small purchasers are placed at a competitive disadvantage. No elaboration is needed in describing the position of a small manufacturer who in February 1939 was forced to pay for a ton of cold rolled strip a delivered value of $154.69, netting the mill $145.41, as against a large competitor, who, for this product, paid a delivered value of only $76.19, a mill net of but $70.88" (p. 26).

usually results in prices that are too high for his own good rather than too low. For instance, if the seller in Figure 43 aims at the group which would pay *OM* for *OL* units but asks them to pay *ON,* he loses entirely *KL* units of sale so that his gain (*PZCN*) from trying

FIGURE 43

Discriminatory Pricing

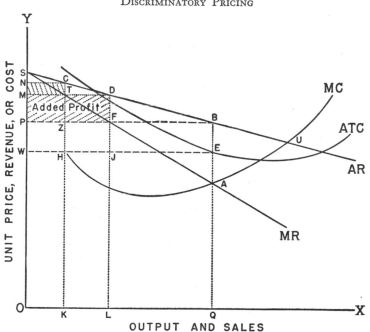

to segregate buyers is less than expected (*PFDM*), and may even prove to be a loss (if *PZCN,* the approximate gain in profit, is less than *ZFJH,* the approximate loss of profit).

**15. Summary of Economic Principles Regarding Selling Policies.**—The three groups of economic principles explained in this chapter continue the supply-side exposition of the three preceding chapters, but some of them refer back to the chapters on demand. They clearly are supplementary to the principles described earlier and in no wise constitute a sufficient explanation in themselves. The three groups are as follows:

    A. Demand intensity and elasticity are a function of:
        1. The amount and type of selling effort by the seller
        2. The amount and type of selling effort by rival sellers and those selling complementary goods

B. The asking-selling price of any given seller is a function of:
 1. Selling expense
 2. Price policies of competitors
 3. Expectations about reactions of competitors to own price policy, and the ultimate effect of those reactions upon himself (oligopoly)
 4. Expectations about reaction of public control agencies to price policy. This will be a function of:
    (a) Changes in particular prices in relation to the general price level
    (b) Profits relative to other firms and other times
    (c) Degree of price discrimination

C. The degree of price discrimination between buyers is a function of:
 1. Differences in cost of sale to different buyers (vary with quantity per purchase, credit terms, delivery and freight charges, etc.)
 2. Monopoly power to separate buyers and prevent resale among them
 3. Elasticity of demand by classes of buyers
 4. Elasticity of supply (ease of entry of new competition as price is raised for certain buyers)

# Chapter 10

## PRODUCTION POLICIES INFLUENCE PRICES

**1. Production Choices of Business Executives.**—Prior discussions of supply and price have assumed that the decisions to be made by business executives were limited to (1) price to be asked, (2) output to be offered for sale, (3) proper amount and types of selling expense, and (4) best design or quality of product. Decisions must also be made in three other fields: (5) what to produce, (6) how to produce it, and (7) when to produce it. Although these problems are among the first to be tackled by managers when an enterprise is begun, they are less familiar to the average person than the ones already examined and hence have been deferred to this point. Much of the previous discussion will prove useful background material for this further analysis of the problems of supply and price.

**2. Deciding What to Produce and How Much.**—To state that an enterpriser will choose to produce that product which will bring him the most money is to state an axiom of capitalist economics. But it ignores other possible motives and it does not tell us anything about the conditions on which such a decision depends. Some individuals choose to produce that which they enjoy producing, even though it is relatively unprofitable. Such choices, as well as pecuniary ones, usually are related to the prior experience and skill of the enterpriser. The possession of specialized equipment is also likely to influence his decision. Many decisions to begin small enterprises are made impulsively without careful appraisal of costs and revenues. In larger firms more care is exercised and exhaustive engineering and cost surveys often are made. The larger the investment needed to start producing a given product, the more likely is the new entrant to be a firm which already is producing something else. If relative market prices change so as to make product B appear more profitable than before, and A less profitable, a producer whose equipment is not too specialized will shift his output from A to B. This often occurs in farming areas where soil and climate permit producing a variety of crops. A change in relative costs of production will produce similar results.

If only one article is being produced, the problem of how much to produce can be solved in the abstract according to the rules outlined in earlier chapters.  Those who must accept or who choose to accept the selling price given by the market, market leader, monopolistic agreement, custom, or government, ordinarily will plan to produce only as much as they can sell at the given price.  At times, however, the rate of production may exceed the rate of sales or fall below it as management chooses to build up or to diminish inventories.  In order to keep valued employees, many firms produce to stock during slack periods or business recessions, hoping for future sales to expand and reduce accumulations.  The output of annual crops is planned with less care, partly because the price is not clearly predictable at the time of sowing and partly because the weather may prove to be a more important determinant of output than human decisions about planting acreage.  Finally, those who are in a position to set their own selling prices usually adjust production rates to current sales, plus or minus changes in inventory.

If two or more articles may be produced alternatively with the same material or labor, the most profitable quantity of each to produce will be a function of the technical efficiency of production and of the price of each, assuming that these are given and constant.  A high price may be offset by high cost (low efficiency) of production. Assuming that unit cost of production varies with output, the relative output of each should be adjusted until the marginal costs of each bear the same ratios to one another as do the selling prices to one another (the marginal rate of substitution equals the ratio of their prices).  This is reasonable only under the further assumption that the producer can sell as much of each as he wishes to produce without changing the market price when he varies the size of his offerings—an assumption of the theory of pure competition, but rarely encountered in the business world.  It is more frequently true that if he wishes to vary his output and sell without inventory accumulation or decumulation, he must change his asking price (or selling expense).  Under these circumstances one can repeat only the earlier generalization that profit will be maximized when marginal cost equals marginal revenue for each of the items produced.

**3. Entrepreneurial Adaptation to Shifts in Schedule Demand.** —At this point it is again necessary to emphasize the distinction between two types of entrepreneurial choice.  In the preceding section and most earlier ones we have taken demand as fixed and have assumed that the entrepreneurial problem was to choose the price and output which would be most profitable. Business managers also have to face the problem created by shifts in schedule demand caused by competitors' price and selling policies, by seasonal change, by general advances or declines in business activity, and the like. In the multiple products case examined in the last section, we may assume, for instance, that the demand for product A rises so that the former volume can be sold at a higher price, or a larger volume can be sold at the same price (or both price and volume may rise). The problem now is how to adapt production rates of each of a group of products (A, B, C, etc.) to the increase in schedule demand for A.

Under conditions of pure competition, theory states that the price will rise and that the individual firm must decide whether to shift some of its efforts from producing B, C, etc., to increase the output of A, or to expand A while keeping B, C, etc., constant. The former alternative would require an increased employment of the factors required to produce A (more labor and land used for alfalfa). The latter might involve merely a transfer of factors and a diminished output of one or more of the products B (barley), C (corn), etc., which are technically substitutable for A in the production process. If, however, one of the other products, such as B, is complementary with A in production (cf. wool and mutton), then its output will expand, not contract. The most profitable expansion of A (and its complements) will be reached when the marginal cost for A equals the new market price for A. Regarding other products, the most probable situation is one in which the firm maintains its former volume of output for them. If, however, their prices decline as a result of the increased demand for A, the firm should produce less. Finally, it is possible that the total supply of a limited factor (such as a farmer's land) may be diverted from producing other products to concentrate exclusively on A, whose price has risen. Or if the transferable factor is one which can be employed only at a rising marginal cost of production of A and is also limited in supply (such as labor in an isolated region), then output of A may expand to the $MC = MR$ point and the factor which remains after that volume is reached may be devoted to producing the less remunerative products B, C, etc.

**4. Deciding How to Produce: Choosing Proper Amounts of the Factors.**—Wherever price competition is keen, business managers are forced to give much thought to methods of reducing costs. Sometimes this is achieved by driving hard bargains with those from whom purchases of materials or services are made. But more often the economies arise from devising better combinations of the factors, that is, inventing new processes for factory, farm, mine, or office which permit producing the same amount of product with less total outlay for the factors used. These inventions may save either labor, capital, or land, or any combination of these in their various types. This is popularly known as securing "increased efficiency" and may be measured either in terms of decreased physical inputs (or total dollar cost of inputs) or in terms of increased total output if the total expenditure for inputs remains constant.

It is obvious that two things chiefly determine the most economical combination of the factors: their unit prices and the technical knowledge and skill with which they can be made to work together. Physical efficiency determines the physical cost of each unit of product, and through unit prices, the money cost. Therefore, with prices and efficiency given, the firm will make the best use of available factors when it uses them in such quantities that the price ratio between any two factors equals the marginal rate of substitution between them. The advantage of substituting one factor for another lies in the relatively greater value product per dollar spent for the former. Therefore, when the marginal value products per dollar of input for each factor purchased are equal, there is no further incentive to substitute. This concept of equilibrium may be formalized by the equation:

$$\frac{\text{Price of A}}{\text{Price of B}} = \frac{\text{Marginal value product of A}}{\text{Marginal value product of B}}$$

If we assume, for instance, that the price of one of the factors changes (wages, material costs, interest, etc.), there will be a change in the quantity used and therefore in the ratio between the quantities of the various factors employed. Specifically, let the price of factor A decline for some reason or other. A firm will tend to adapt itself to this change by increasing the use of A both absolutely and relatively to other factors. The quantity of substitute factors will decrease absolutely, while complementary factors will be employed in larger quantities than before, until a new equilibrium is reached according to the above formula.

It is very important to realize that most factors are both complementary and competitive. They are complementary in that both are needed in production, but competitive in that substitution occurs between *marginal* units. A farmer needs both land and labor, but if the price of land rises more rapidly than the price of labor, he will change the ratio between the units of each factor that he employs by using less land or by hiring more labor. In some cases the technology of production requires that certain factors be used in fixed proportions, such as one engine per auto frame, or one driver per truck, and changes in relative price are ignored. These perfectly complementary factors may be considered as single units in applying the formula for equilibrium of substitution in relation to other factors where competition at the margin occurs. In most instances of apparently fixed proportions, however, the fixity is due to the smallness of the price changes that are likely to occur. If, instead, the price of one factor goes way up as a result of a war or embargo, there is a strong incentive to economize it, and ratios that were considered fixed may be changed. Or an additional variable may intrude: a price-induced invention or change in technology which brings a substitution of another type. Instead of changing from a ratio of 5A:3B to 5A:2B, the new combination may be 5A:6C, or even 5A:1B:4C.

**5. Deciding When to Produce: The Problem of Future Output.**—In addition to the foregoing problems of deciding what to produce, how to produce, and how much to produce, the enterpriser also must consider the problem of when to produce. Sometimes the decision can be made separately from the others; for example, the cotton farmer must decide only what is the best time for planting in order to reap his autumn harvest. Mostly the decision regarding timing is linked with other decisions such as that regarding how to produce, or how much, and obviously it is related to the choice of products, which may differ in the minimum length of time required to produce them. Probably the shortest time between inputs and outputs is found in certain lines of merchandising where the turnover is very rapid, and the longest time in cases where large investment in capital equipment is necessary, as in the mining of low-grade non-ferrous metals or the development of hydroelectric projects. These latter illustrations also point to the relationship between choice of what, when, and how much, since they belong to that group of enterprises which ordinarily must be conducted on a large scale if they are to be profitable and, because of their huge capital investment, require long-range planning.

If, for purposes of analysis, the time factor be isolated and considered by itself, certain important generalizations may be made. In the first place, the decision to produce outputs for sale at some time in the future requires a corresponding decision to make inputs prior to that time. These inputs of materials, labor, and land use must be bought and paid for by the enterprise, except where contributed by its owners. This requires the expenditure of money and is commonly referred to as an investment, although this word has several other uses. If the output date is known, the investment in inputs must be made at some earlier time, determined by technical factors associated with the chosen method of production. Animal and vegetable products have a rather definite life cycle often connected with the seasons, so that there is little room for choice of input timing once the output date is decided. In certain manufacturing processes, however, and in merchandising, the enterpriser may vary the length of his production period considerably. He may speed up the manufacturing process by hiring more labor, working longer hours, or getting speedier machinery, and he will do so if he thinks it worth his while. The remarkable production records of American industry during the war indicate what can be done to shorten the production process when it seems desirable to bring the date of output closer.

In normal times, the decision regarding the timing of initial and subsequent inputs may be impulsive, rule-of-thumb, determined by availability of funds, or calculated so as to maximize profit. Established firms often have a long record of past operations to guide their judgments about the future, and the technical and trade journals offer the inexperienced manager much information of value in appraising alternatives. Many production processes become so standardized that there is only one "right" way to do them. There remain, nevertheless, a considerable number of production problems that cannot be reduced to routine. All new products present problems of timing in addition to those of factor combination, and new market situations are continually developing for old products. Small producers, as has been frequently pointed out in these pages, rarely calculate their actions as carefully as they should. Large producers are more likely to analyze cost and probable revenue with care, particularly when large investments are in prospect. In either case some element of guesswork is involved.

Interest cost often is ignored in small-scale enterprises and in firms where the funds are contributed largely by the owners. The interest cost for the time interval between input and output should be considered in rational calculations. An item of major uncertainty is the future price of the future output, or if the price is to be fixed by the seller, the future volume of sales at that price. At times the quantitative relationship between inputs and outputs is also conjectural, especially in farming, or with new enterprises, new methods, or new products. These elements of risk are sometimes allowed for by assuming that the lowest of several possible prices or volumes of sale will be realized, or the highest probable expense.

The economist attempts to generalize the essence of the calculating process by assuming that the production planner decides upon certain reasonable or probable figures for inputs and outputs and then proceeds to calculate which of several possible constellations of cost and revenue would be the most profitable. This is done by much the same method as was used above for analyzing which factors it is best to use to get desired outputs. Each input is dated and considered as a separate factor, such as one day's labor on June 23rd, or one day on June 24th. Outputs similarly are dated in order to keep them distinct. The input cost is subtracted from the output revenue on each of the planned future dates to determine the net revenue for that day, whether positive or negative. The time element is then further introduced by discounting these amounts to determine the present value of each of these net revenues on the planning date. An algebraic total is then computed of the positive and negative remainders or "surpluses." The aim of the business manager will be to select that time distribution of future inputs and future outputs which will give the largest possible total present value, thus choosing the production plan which will maximize profit in the future. Earlier analysis indicates that this maximum will be reached when (1) the marginal rate of substitution between outputs of any two dates equals the ratio of their discounted prices, (2) the same rule holds for inputs, and (3) the discounted marginal revenue of any output equals the discounted marginal cost of any factor inputs with which it may be technically associated in the production process.

It is obvious that calculations such as these would be too laborious for the average enterprise to conduct in complete detail, and also that the figures involved are too conjectural to warrant treating them with such exactitude. Near-future planning data have a lower margin of probable error, but such planning hardly requires the elaborate discounting technique suggested above. Furthermore, long-range planning is perhaps more closely connected with preparing or obtaining the capital equipment required for production than estimating the precise output of that equipment on specific dates. This is particularly true under monopolistic conditions when the possession of capacity to produce is not equivalent to production at capacity. Nevertheless, the foregoing theoretical analysis helps to point out the many details which businessmen should or could take into consideration in deciding when to make expenditures to get desired future output. The process of discounting future costs and revenues also indicates the often overlooked importance of the interest rate. Whether the funds to be invested are borrowed or owned, their use in preparing for future production involves a cost, either explicit cost or opportunity cost.

6. **Altering Plans for Future Production.**—The next problem related to plans for future production is the changes in such plans that arise from the changes in the conditions which gave them birth. Because of technical reasons and long-term contracts, changes often cannot be made quickly ; and when they are made, they may have long-lasting effects. Therefore, managers must look far ahead to estimate future obligations, future inputs, and future outputs. These estimates are all subjective : entrepreneurial ideas regarding future price or sales volume, ideas concerning physical efficiency, ideas about future cost of factor units, etc. The personal ideational basis of judgments in this field is so obvious as to render hardly necessary the oft-repeated caution that demand and supply activities in the market are the result of guesswork, impulse, and imitation more often than they are precise, mathematical computations based on objective data. There even has been developed a "theory of expectations" which tries to explain, or at least to classify, human judgments regarding future economic events. For instance, if the price of a given product has risen during the past week or month, that may be taken by some to mean that this price rise will, in the future, continue at the new level, at the same rate, or in some other way. Others may interpret recent experience as forecasting a decline, before long, to the prior level or even below.

Whatever the specific expectation, it is important to realize that people do judge the future by the present (or rather by the recent past). Present price changes, therefore, alter not only current production rates as explained in previous sections of this chapter, but also alter plans regarding future production. They raise or lower the expected net revenue of future dates and therefore may change the optimum production plan as measured by the maximum present value of expected future surpluses. Changes in expectations of physical productivity do likewise, as when reports are received of the success or failure of similar processes adopted by others or of new inventions. The oil-drilling industry with its dry holes and its gushers offers abundant illustrations in this field. Finally, there must be mentioned the prospect of future interest rate changes which might make it necessary for planners to discount the distant future at higher or lower rates than the immediate future.

The degree of uncertainty about future conditions also varies. When a manufacturer gets a contract for the sale of his product in larger quantities for the coming year than in the past, he will be more certain about his future sales than if he is producing to stock for uncertain future sales. Yet even contracts may be cancelled, as those holding wartime munitions contracts found out in 1945. On the buying side the uncertainty of rental costs may be removed by purchase of the property or, with slightly less confidence, by a long-term lease. Similarly, short-term borrowing by a series of notes, subject to interest rate changes at each maturity date, may be supplanted by refunding into long-term fixed interest obligations. Uncertainty on the buying side suggests that calculations should include the highest, or nearly the highest, conjectural cost. On the selling side, the lowest or nearly the lowest price or sales volume must generally be chosen in planning present inputs for future outputs. Allowance should be made also for possible delays or inefficiencies in the physical production process. The more conservative the production planner, the higher will he estimate possible costs and the lower will be his predictions about sales or efficiency. The ultimate decision in any particular case often depends as much upon the temperament of the person or persons making estimates and final judgments as it does upon verifiable facts.

**7. Equilibrium of the Firm, a Summary and Evaluation.**—In trying to increase profits (or prevent their being reduced) a firm may adopt any one or more of the alternatives which have been described. It may spend money on selling efforts or in improving its products. It may reduce its selling price and thus curtail its revenue until the hoped-for expansion of sales occurs. The production plan may be altered by present outlays for machinery, for managerial skill, or for a more productive group of workmen which may ultimately reduce cost by more than the proximate additional expense of getting them. Buying or renting a more favorable site might also be included in this group and represents a frequent managerial problem in retail trade. Still another alternative is spending money lobbying for favorable legislation or for laws curtailing competitors. For instance, independent stores have secured punitive taxes against chain stores in some states, and many industries have hired "legislative agents" to help them get tariff protection or subsidies. Regulatory commissions may be similarly courted or coerced.

The analytical problem for price and production economics is to represent interrelated variables by curves or simultaneous equations and show how geometry or calculus reveals the desired maximum or minimum points.  The conventional curves in two dimensions, whose intersection solves the problem, are now giving way to three-dimensional surfaces or to contour maps of substitution functions with tangency lines.  None of these refinements should obscure two very important facts about abstract analysis.  First, its schedules and curves are hypothetical and are intended to reveal principles, not quantitative answers to the businessman's problems.  Second, the variables are so numerous in nearly every management situation that they could be expressed diagrammatically only by multidimensional surfaces which we cannot draw.  Therefore, recourse must be had to the equations which link the variables, and in these equations the coefficients must be represented by letter symbols since their quantitative magnitude depends upon the unknown peculiarities of each possible situation.

The practical problem for businessmen is to choose the right combination of expenditures, but since there are so many possibilities, and results are so unpredictable, his judgment must often be based on "hunch" rather than on careful calculation.  No formal solution can be given which is more helpful to the businessman or government official than the generalizations which could be made without having recourse to mathematical presentation.  An exception might be made for certain cost functions where the relationship between variables is governed by physical laws and may be expected to repeat the experience of the past in the future.  Even in this case knowledge of average or marginal cost of production at different outputs does not give the answer to a host of questions about price policy, selling expense, and future production planning.

Most actions of businessmen supplying goods or services for sale are designed to improve their economic position according to their information, reasoning, desire, or impulse.  Economists speak of these activities in the direction of increasing profit as being supply changes promoting equilibrium of the firm.  They sometimes imply that the ideas of businessmen about demand and cost schedules reflect actual objective facts and that, since these "data" are given, the correct action to maximize profit can be accurately determined by abstract analysis.

There can be little objection to treating the "equilibrium" of the firm and the "maximum profit position" of the firm as synonymous, but one must not be led by the use of such terms to think that every action of businessmen leads in the direction of equilibrium.  Mistakes may be made because of inadequate information and poor judgment.  Nor must we think that the economic conditions of demand and cost, which are chiefly responsible for concepts of demand and cost schedules, remain constant for any appreciable length of time. They are changing continually. Even if subjective reflections of objective circumstances were completely accurate, human logic above reproach, and the profit motive supreme, any equilibrium of a given firm could last but a moment. Finally, the equilibrium formulae of the preceding pages are approximated only in part by the most careful business enterprisers and practically never with the use of academic nomenclature. For instance, most managers have no idea about their marginal costs, much less a point of equality with marginal revenue. As indicated in the earlier sections of this chapter and in frequent reference throughout the portions dealing with theoretical analysis, most business decisions on the supply side of the market (and the demand side, too) are based on a great variety and mixture of motives. Short-run or long-run profit maximization is only one motive, though usually the most important one.

Nevertheless, the concept of equilibrium of the firm looms large in recent economic theory and its basic principles should be understood by those who wish to keep abreast of developments in economic thought. It is also useful in understanding other economic concepts such as "normal price" and "normal profit," together with the issues of public policy which are related to these ideas in the framework of government regulation of competition and monopoly in a capitalistic system.

**8. Normal Profit: Equilibrium of the Industry.**—Corresponding to the expansion and contraction of output of the firm in its efforts to reach the equilibrium position of maximum profit is the entry or exit of firms engaged in the production of a given commodity. If it appears to some one that he can make a good profit in producing that commodity, he will be tempted to invest his idle capital in the materials, equipment, and labor required to do so, or he may divert his funds from other employments which he thinks less profitable. This new entrant will try to sell his output at the prevailing price, or slightly below it, or he may try to market a product of superior design and durability. If he is successful in selling his article, some or all of his customers will be people who formerly purchased from the firms originally in the field and these firms, therefore, will have to be content with a smaller volume of sales unless they are willing to reduce their asking price. In either case profit will be reduced. For instance, if a grocery store in a certain location seems to be making good profits, some one else is likely to open a store near-by, taking away some of the customers of the other store and perhaps stimulating price reductions.[1] The entry of firms into the automobile producing industry or into airplane manufacturing during recent decades furnishes another familiar example. New producers in a given field include, of course, either entirely new firms or old firms which add the new product to former lines or shift from one good to another.

On the other hand, firms may cease producing a certain good if it becomes less profitable than other goods they turn out, or if the firms themselves are driven into bankruptcy by falling demand. If a bankrupt firm is dissolved through the sale of its assets to others who do not intend to employ them in the same line of production, the supply of the product reaching the market will decline. The exit of producers in either of these two ways is generally ascribed to the presence of subnormal profits or of losses. In short, entry generally occurs when profits of industry are above "normal" and exit when profits are below "normal" (though see Section 8 in Chapter 9). An "industry" is in equilibrium with no expansion or contraction of supply either when each individual firm is making normal profit or, though profit rates of different firms vary, the average is "normal."

**9. The Opportunity Cost Theory of Normal Profit.**—The concept of normal profit has been given various definitions, none fully satisfactory. For the individual firm it may be thought of as that return to the owners of business enterprise which equals what they could get by hiring out their abilities, capital, or land to some one else instead of using these assets themselves. This is known as the "opportunity cost" theory of normal profits. The logic of the argument is that if business enterprise offers the opportunity to earn more residual profits than can be earned by contracting the sale of one's labor, capital, or land to others, people will be tempted to shift to self-employment of time and funds. Unfortunately, the argument does not hold so well when business earns less than "normal," for in many cases the capital equipment of the firm is so specialized that it cannot be sold to some one else except at a heavy loss. Hence, there is no opportunity to earn "the going rate" on the funds originally invested, but only on the shrunken value of stock shares or salvaged equipment. The best that can be done, when revenues still exceed operating expenses, is to accumulate the excess as a partial depreciation reserve and then invest it in a different line of production

---

[1] In some lines excessive entry leads to a general condition of operating at less than capacity. This keeps $ATC$ above its possible minimum, and entry may lead to higher prices, not lower.

instead of replacing equipment that wears out. The opportunity cost approach, therefore, is more useful in explaining entry than in explaining exit.

For the group of firms comprising an industry, normal profit is often taken to mean the average rate of profit being reaped by other industries at the same time. This is also a variation on the opportunity cost theme. The argument is that new entrants into the field of enterprise, or those shifting from other lines of business, will tend to go chiefly to those fields where firms on the average are making higher profits than elsewhere. Low profits appear in industries which are experiencing a declining demand for their product or where in the past there has been excessive entry. "Cutthroat competition" is an adverse factor, while monopolistic agreements or practices are favorable to profits above normal. High profits are rarely due to excessive exit, but rather to insufficient entry for one reason or another.

**10. The Bulk Line Cost Theory of the Normal Profit Price.—** Industries usually are made up of many firms earning profits individually at different rates, some high, some low. It is therefore somewhat difficult to describe a condition of "normal" profits for an industry as a whole. Even in prosperous times, when the majority of firms in an industry operate in the black, there are usually a few firms which are in the red. Several attempts have been made to define this state of an industry with precision, notably by the price-fixing agencies in the United States in 1917–1918 which advanced the concept of "bulk line cost" to divide the "bulk" of the producers who are making money from the few who are not. This line is said to be the price which is equal to or greater than the cost of production of about 85 per cent of the output of the industry. Fifteen per cent have a cost greater than this cost-price. There are many difficulties with this concept, but it is a useful one for the price-fixer. One difficulty is the accounting problem of determining what items should be included in cost. Another is trying to decide whether an 85:15 ratio should be applied to all industries at all stages of the business cycle and, if not, what alternative ratio is appropriate. A third is attempting to define the price when firms produce different yet similar products, like manufacturers of furniture or clothing.

The bulk-line-cost price approach to normal profits gives an appearance of greater precision than a simple reference to average profits, but it is far from being a good tool for analysis of conditions of entry and exit. In the first place it assumes that entry is stimulated by the observation that all, or nearly all, of the firms in an industry are making a profit as opposed to a customary 85 per cent.  A full theory of entry would have to describe many other motives and would have to admit that the 85 per cent concept is more influential among economists and price-fixers than among businessmen, most of whom have

FIGURE 44

BULK LINE COST AND NORMAL PRICE

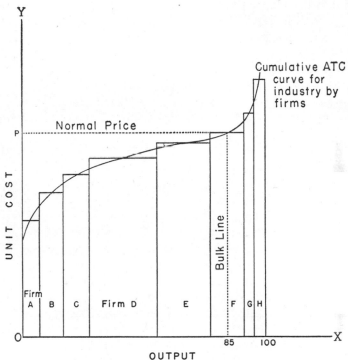

never heard of it.  In the second place, it ignores the cyclical fluctuations in the general level of profits which would make 85 per cent too low a figure for good times and too high for bad times.  Thirdly, as pointed out in Section 8 of Chapter 9, entry is probably stimulated more often by abnormally high prices than by abnormally high profits, although the two usually go hand in hand.  A careful entrepreneur is likely to compare probable selling prices in relation to his probable costs before making his decision to venture.  On the other hand, an impulsive entrepreneur is more likely to look at the large profits of a few successful firms than to compute an average for the industry and compare it with the average profit in other industries. Finally, industries differ greatly as to (1) relative average profits in good times (gold-mining versus copper), (2) relative average profits in bad times (public utilities versus steel), (3) relative ease of entry (retail merchandising versus shipbuilding), and (4) relative ease of exit without loss of capital (merchandising versus smelting).

**11. Other Uses of the Concept of Normal Profit.**—Because of these difficulties with the concept of normal profit, it would have been discarded long ago were it not for the usefulness of the idea in two connections. First, the competitive system of free enterprise is supposed to find one of its chief justifications in the alleged fact that the profit motive leads individuals to make rather quick adjustments of supply to demand, thus reducing excessive profits and transferring resources to their most urgent uses. Whenever the above-normal profits of a group of producers reveal that "demand exceeds supply" in that field, new entrants are supposed to be attracted until expanding supply forces profits back to normal by bringing prices down. This prevents a few from exploiting the many when they find themselves in a particularly fortunate situation. Competition is also supposed to force prices down when cost-reducing innovations bring large profits to those who first introduce them. However, sellers may choose to be content with a smaller fraction of the total market rather than to cut their prices when new competition appears. This is particularly common where the number of competing sellers is small (steel) or where they produce products which are slightly different though similar (harvesting machines). The argument that competition prevents the long continuance of greater than normal profits also runs afoul the facts which seem to reveal that obstacles to entry are so potent in some fields as to preserve high profits for many years running (aluminum, shoe machinery).

The second reason for keeping the concept of normal profit is that economists find it useful in equilibrium analysis and in that other abstraction, the "long run." Normal profit is considered essential to the long-run survival of each firm, to the stability of each industry and, therefore, to the stability of the economy as a whole. Abnormal profit is held to be characteristic of boom and depression stages of the business cycle and is one explanation of why these stages cannot be permanent. The concept of normal profit permits the development of many generalizations about price, the firm, the industry, and the economy which fit neatly into a coherent whole which is logically unassailable even if some of its premises are not entirely realistic. As emphasized in Chapter 1, the principles of economics are not intended to be absolute rules applicable to explain every case.

Rather they are generalizations which are true most of the time when specified conditions are present. The relation between actual pricing methods and conventional economic theory will receive further elaboration in the sections which follow.

**12. Normal Price Causes Normal Profits and Holds Supply Constant.**—The concept of "normal price" is virtually synonymous with "long-run equilibrium price," since both depend upon the ideas of "normal profit" and "equilibrium for the industry." If the entire product of an industry is being sold at a given price and if at the same time there is no tendency for the output to expand or contract by action of existing firms or because of an unbalance between the rate of entry and exit, then this price is said to be the "normal price" for that product. An alternative definition would stipulate that it is the price which would maintain a constant rate of supply if the following things were to remain constant: (1) schedule demand, (2) prices of other products, (3) factor prices, and (4) technology. Although perhaps not in existence at any given time, it is the price which would be reached in the long run if enough time were allowed for adjustment of output by individual firms and for bringing exit and entry into offsetting balance.

Certain difficulties with this concept deserve attention. First, normal price thus defined cannot exist in actual business practice except accidentally and momentarily. Conditions change too rapidly; for instance, there would be a different "normal price" with each level of demand intensity and demand could certainly be expected to change several times within the period conceptually required for the adjustment of output by firms and for the restoration of a balance between the entry and exit of firms. Second, there can be no normal price for the products of an industry selling articles which differ from one another in some aspect of design, packaging, or advertised trade-mark (automobiles, radios, pencils). Since product differentiation is very widespread in modern times, the remaining field of homogeneous products where the idea of normal price might have applicability is quite small. Moreover, some of the few cases that remain reveal monopolistic practices which establish a practical stability of supply at the given level of demand, but the profit position of firms in the industry does not resemble the bulk-line-cost price picture described above.

Finally, it is very hard to define an "industry." One hardly knows where to begin and where to stop, since so many farmers, manufacturers, and merchandisers sell more than one product. For instance, it would be hard to state just how much of the profit of General Motors should be considered in appraising the normal profit position of the automobile industry and how much should go to refrigerators, airplanes, diesel engines, batteries, and a host of other things including trucks. And should only automobile assemblers be included in the automobile industry? Or should all the parts companies be appraised, too? Many products compete for the consumer's dollar with objectively dissimilar goods. Thus it is a question of whether we should speak of "the canning industry" or one part of it such as "the vegetable canning industry," "the food preservation industry" (to include dried and frozen foods), or "the food industry as a whole." And what would be the limits of the latter? To turn to another field, is it proper to analyze "the radio industry," apart from the cinema, the legitimate stage, or all other forms of entertainment? If a broader concept is used, where would books and public lectures be included?

In the light of these and similar difficulties with the definition of a "commodity" or "industry" it seems best not to analyze the terms too closely, but instead to examine what the popular concepts can add to our knowledge of the working of the economic system. For formal analysis the terms probably should be abandoned entirely in favor of the actual maximizing or minimizing unit which is either (1) the firm, or (2) the private individual consumer, or (3) the factor source. This will get us by the logicians even though it still leaves us in trouble with the psychologists.

**13. Normal Price When Normal Profits Are Included in Cost.** —In an effort to preserve the concept of normality for price analysis under monopolistic conditions, a shift is often made to the opportunity-cost version of normal profits. Under this approach, costs as figured by the accountant are expanded to include a "normal profit" return to the owner for his otherwise uncompensated services as working manager or supplier of capital or land. The individual firm is then taken as the prototype of the industry. Its equilibrium price is equal to its $ATC$ when these imputed "costs" are included. For the firm selling under monopolistic conditions, this means that when $MC = MR$, $ATC$ must also equal $AR$ (the price). This "normal profit" situation is shown by the following diagram, (A), Figure 45. Another diagram, (B), is given to show by contrast the more common situation under monopolistic conditions where difficulties of entry permit price and sales volume to be such that a profit is made in excess of normal.

The normal profits which are said to exist under the long-run equilibrium situation shown in Figure 45A are, by definition, equal to opportunity costs as explained in Section 8 of this chapter. By a

FIGURE 45

PROFITS UNDER MONOPOLISTIC CONDITIONS

(A) Normal Profit                    (B) Profit Above Normal

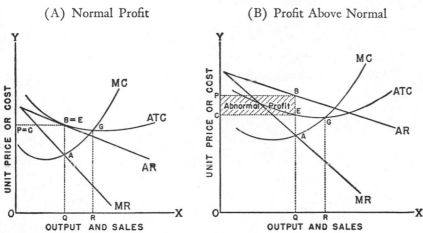

further inference these profits are considered to be the same as the average earnings of firms engaged in "competitive industry," a concept which will be analyzed in the next chapter.

Both diagrams of the monopoly revenue type shown in Figure 45 reveal that the minimum $ATC$ point $G$ would require an output $OR$ greater than $OQ$ which maximizes profit. This means that it is profitable for the monopolist to keep his selling price so high that sales and output are below that which would yield the lowest total unit cost.[2] This conclusion is confirmed by the common observation that, for a given stage of the business cycle, excess capacity is most extensive in those industries where there is the least price competition (cf. cement).

A competitive industry of the traditional type may be in equilibrium even though some firms make more profits than others. This is the bulk-line-cost-price idea of Section 10 of this chapter. In diagrams, normal profit must be included in $ATC$ as a cost ("opportunity cost"). This is done in Figure 46 where two firms with dif-

---

[2] Exception: when demand is so great that $MR$ intersects $MC$ above $ATC$ or at the place where they cross. This is very rare and if it should occur for any length of time would lead to an expansion of capacity. See Chapter 13, Section 7.

ferent costs are shown selling at the same price. The first firm is in equilibrium where $MC = MR$, even though the selling price, $AR$, equals total unit cost, $ATC$, because the latter contains normal profit. The second firm, B, makes normal profits plus the abnormal profit $PCEA$. The most profitable output $OQ$ is *greater* than $OR$, which would have given the lowest possible $ATC$. Under monopolistic conditions $OQ$ is *less* than $OR$, as shown in Figure 45.

FIGURE 46

PROFITS UNDER PURE COMPETITION

(A) Normal Profit                    (B) Profit Above Normal

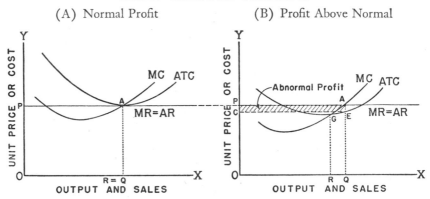

14. **Summary of Economic Principles Dealing with Production Policies Which Influence Prices.**—Since the concepts of normal profit and normal price involve the volume of production, they may be included in the summary of this chapter as determinants of the quantitative aspects of supply schedules of firms or industries. The other topics deal more with the buying policies of firms in relation to output than they do with selling and will be treated at greater length in the chapters on distribution, where the purchase of factors is under direct consideration. The following outline covers both viewpoints:

    I. Total supply offered for sale is a function of:
        A. The output of individual firms, which is a function of:
            1. Managers' ideas about profit opportunities, i.e., about probable demand schedules in relation to cost schedules
            2. Availability of the necessary factors of production, especially capital, materials, and skills
            3. Presence and strength of monopolistic agreements
        B. Willingness to expand or contract the inventories of the individual firms

C. The number of producing firms, which is a function of:
   1. Past entry and exit, which is a function of:
      (a) Profit relative to other opportunities (normal profit)
      (b) Losses relative to financial resources and determination to carry on
      (c) Monopolistic restrictions upon freedom of entry
      (d) Technological or capital restrictions upon entry
      (e) Institutional stimuli to entry (subsidies, etc.)

II. When there are joint products, changes in the relative quantities produced and sold are a function of:
   A. Changes in the relative prices of the products
   B. Changes in relative rates of sale
   C. Willingness to allow changes in inventory
   D. Changes in the prices of factors, if use-ratios differ
   E. Changes in technology

III. When there are joint factors, changes in the relative quantities bought and used are a function of:
   A. Changes in technology which alter their relative efficiencies as substitutes or complements
   B. Changes in the relative prices of the factors
   C. Changes in expected price or rate of sale of single or joint products

IV. The time at which outputs are to be expected is a function of:
   A. The time of inputs
   B. Technological processes used
   C. Expectations regarding relative future prices of products and factors
   D. Interest or discount rates, and expectations of change in them

This summary goes beyond that of Chapter 9 both by adding more independent variables and by examining certain causes of the magnitude or change in these variables. Everything that from the viewpoint of this chapter is an independent variable is itself dependent on one or more other variables, only a few of which can be mentioned in passing. The list of these determinants is not intended to be complete, either in this chapter or in any other.

# Chapter 11

## A FUNCTIONAL APPROACH TO TYPES OF COMPETITION AND MONOPOLY

**1. Difficulties with Substantive Classifications.**—Much recent analysis in the field of monopoly and competition fails to distinguish clearly between substantive and functional connotations of terms.[1] For instance, a writer may start with a substantive definition of a monopolist as the sole seller of a certain commodity and then speak of the way in which that commodity competes with substitutes. The "monopolist" may reduce his price to strengthen his market position relative to these substitutes (cf. the price reductions in aluminum in recent years). On the other hand, the "pure competitor" of classic definition may never consciously reduce his asking price to sell more goods, but always sell "at the market." And the "oligopolist" may either engage in competitive price wars with his few rivals or collude with them in a monopolistic fashion to eliminate one or more forms of rivalry. Substantive and functional definitions are too often mixed. For logical consistency and clarity of thought they should be unscrambled wherever possible.

One solution to the problem is that of expanding the list of substantive determinants until so much is said about the product, the sellers, the buyers, etc., that alternative courses of action are narrowed down to a single one. This is the process of reasoning from market structure to market behavior. It leads to very extensive classifications of market situations by a series of combinations of possible opposites. One such list has been published containing 64 substantive classes and there is no good reason except lack of space why such a list might not be extended to 128, 256, or even more.[2] In terms of behavior patterns the list of only 64 situations is obviously redundant and hence was shortened by Bain to 14 by eliminat-

---

[1] A substantive definition is one which identifies by describing states of being. A functional definition describes acts of doing. The former is supposed to be something inherent; the latter is outward manifestation in behavior. The substantive does not change; the functional does.

[2] One class, for instance, is that in which there are the following substantive conditions: few sellers of a durable producer's good whose product variation is unimportant, yet it is differentiated in important degree and there are many buyers.

See Joe S. Bain, "Market Classification in Modern Price Theory," *Quarterly Journal of Economics,* Vol. 56, August, 1942, p. 560.

ing duplicate and unimportant cases.    Each of the 14 remaining situations is apparently intended to give rise to a distinct (and complex)
pattern of market behavior.

A second solution is to begin with classes of market behavior and
work backward as needed to the market structures from which they
spring.  This would classify different types of activity by buyers and
sellers and reveal for each class one or more situations which are its
logical causes.  Or a list of combinations of forms of behavior might
be developed comparable in length to the Bain-Mason list of combinations of substantive elements.  Such a list might also be redundant
in terms of the situations which supported the complex patterns of
behavior, but this would not be sufficient reason for elimination and
condensation.  It is behavior which is our chief interest, behavior
and its results.  Hence the list of behavior patterns need be made
only as long as necessary to include the cases which interest us.  Or
if the statistical measurement of significance is preferred, only those
cases which occur with the greatest frequency need to be tabulated.

The writer has no desire to argue that the substantive-to-functional
approach should be discarded, but only that the functional-to-sub-
stantive approach seems preferable in many expository summaries,
and even perhaps as a background for empirical investigations.

Industry studies which give information regarding the relationship between price behavior and output variations on the one hand
and seller-buyer-product-institutional circumstances on the other may
be summarized with functional emphasis and functional classification just as easily as with substantive.  It is only a question of which
is preferable for the purpose in mind and which gives rise to the most
useful vocabulary.

**2. The Questions Asked in the Functional Approach.**—The
answers of economic theory will obviously differ with the questions
asked.  Hence it seems desirable to make the questions as explicit as
possible.  The ones which seem most appropriate in a functional approach to competition and monopoly are the following:

1. What are the different methods of price determination in the
   market?
2. What are the different forms of buyer behavior and seller behavior?
3. What are the causes of these forms of behavior?
4. What are the major patterns of "price behavior"?
5. What are the causes of these patterns?
6. How should these methods and forms of behavior be appraised
   in the light of social welfare?

Only the first two questions will be discussed in this chapter. The last four will be treated in Chapter 12. Many of the answers to these questions must be given in outline form to save time and space. For the same reason, many obvious inferences and explanations may also be omitted.

**3. Methods of Price Determination.**—The explanation of the actual market prices which exist at any given time is a short-run or market-time problem which must not be confused with the problem of price equilibrium in the long run. The first problem treats prices as effects of buyer and seller activities. The second deals with buyer and seller responses to price. In the traditional terminology the distinction is between schedule demand and supply as proximate causes of price on the one hand and price as one cause of market demand and supply adjustments on the other. The market behavior of individuals is our concern, not the elasticities of demand and supply. A brief outline of methods of price determination may be grouped under three headings as follows (the most common substantive equivalents are given in brackets to the left) :

I. Prices set by individuals acting independently
    A. By only one individual
        1. Classified on basis of who sets the price

[*Monopoly*]        (a) Price set by seller, accepted by buyer (because he cannot buy cheaper or on better terms)

[*Monopsony*]      (b) Price set by buyer, accepted by seller (because he cannot sell higher or on better terms)

        2. Classified on basis of motives of seller (or buyer)
            (a) Considers reactions of those on other side of market (seller considers price elasticity of demand)

[*Oligopoly* or *oligopsony*]  (b) Considers reactions of those on his side of market (seller considers cross-elasticity of demand and its effects on actions of rivals)

    B. By two individuals

[*Bilateral monopoly*]  1. By both buyer and seller. If they have unavowed overlapping range, bargaining is likely. Subsequent agreement on price and acceptance by both.

    C. By many individuals

[*Auction*]      1. By highest bidder among buyers when only one seller (or lowest bidder among sellers when one buyer)

[*Pure competition*]  2. By many sellers and by many buyers in some place where they or their representatives meet and learn of rival bids and offers. Totals on both sides at various prices are compared until one price is found at which the totals are equal.

Subsequent acceptance by those buyers willing to pay it or more and by those sellers willing to take it or less. Rejected by other buyers and sellers.

II. Prices set by individuals acting together
    A. Identity of viewpoint and interest of members of a group (borderline case, shades into the next)
    B. Price leadership of dominant member
[*Collusive monopoly*]    C. Definite agreement among members on price to be asked or offered by each.
        1. Informal agreement, usually verbal
        2. Formal agreement, usually written

III. Prices set by the government or other external authority and accepted by both buyer and seller
    A. Specific price
    B. Fixed maximum or minimum price
    C. Formula for calculating price

Since nearly everyone operates on both the buying and selling sides of the market, the methods outlined permit many possible combinations. For instance, the first two methods under I–A give rise to four possible situations:

1. Firm sets price as seller, sets it as buyer.
2. Firm sets price as seller, accepts it as buyer.
3. Firm sets price as buyer, accepts it as seller.
4. Firm accepts price as buyer, accepts it as seller.

Furthermore, since most firms buy more than one thing and sell more than one product, there may be a great variety of buying and selling methods practiced by each firm. Smith may bargain with his organized workers, set his hiring price for other workers, purchase some materials from a list-price seller, purchase others at a price fixed by the government, etc. On the selling side there is likely to be more uniformity of practice if only because most firms (and individuals) sell a smaller variety of things than they buy. The large number of different types of buying and selling activity which may characterize a single firm constitute one good reason for avoiding the blanket appellations of "monopolist," "oligopolist," etc. An individual is what he does. He becomes something different when his actions change.

**4. Ways of Competing Against Others.**—Another very useful classification from the functional viewpoint is that which includes ways in which sellers compete against other sellers and buyers against other buyers. This also includes methods of price determination, but views them from another angle, and it adds other methods of market activity not suggested in the first outline.

Firms compete when they contend against one another for sales to customers, for purchases from suppliers, or for business survival or growth. Competition as a form of action means struggle. Usually it is struggle with known rivals, such as other people buying or selling the same good. But sometimes the contest is with unidentified opponents, such as "sellers in general."[3] The "enemy" may also be governmental, the forces of nature, or one's own complacence. Minimum success in competition is a requisite to survival. Greater success permits growth in net worth or net income, or is evidenced by that growth. That which is often called monopolistic activity also influences survival or growth, but a discussion of its forms and implications must be deferred to a later section.

The major forms of competitive activity may be grouped in the following outline:

I. Direct methods of competition
   A. Marketing competition (against other sellers)
      1. Supply-price competition (usually against known rivals)
      2. Selling competition (against known or unknown rivals)
      3. Product competition (against known or unknown rivals)
   B. Purchasing competition (against other buyers)
      1. Demand-price competition (usually against known rivals)
      2. Buying competition (against known or unknown rivals)
      3. Specification competition (against known or unknown rivals)
   C. Predatory competition (against other buyers or sellers)
II. Indirect methods of competition
   A. Cost competition
   B. Production planning

It should be obvious that many of the forms of competition in this outline are forms of behavior often found in situations substantively called monopolistic or monopsonistic. This is clearly true of all the direct methods. The indirect methods are used by buyers

---

[3] Nearly all substantive "monopolists" compete in this sense even though they refrain from price competition with known rivals.

and sellers in both "monopolistic" and "competitive" situations. These arguments will be clarified by the sections which follow.

**5. Direct Methods of Competition.**—The direct methods of competition involve action in which the seller or buyer tries to help himself at the expense of others in a similar market position, or even directly to harm them. Marketing competition includes those forms of behavior which develop when the supply that a seller wants to sell is greater than the demand at the going price and terms of sale. The situation is sometimes called "a buyers' market," but it is really broader than that since a single seller may act competitively even when most of the other firms feel that there is no necessity to do so. Marketing competition is reduced in form and intensity by monopolistic activity and by the rare periods of "boom" conditions when most firms' existing capacity to produce is fully and profitably utilized.

The most widely recognized form of marketing competition is supply-price competition. Often called simply "price competition," this occurs when one firm tries to get additional sales by reducing its asking price(s). Several variations on this theme are possible. The objective may be to attract customers from known rivals or from unknown competitors.[4] Additional buying by present customers may be the goal. Or the price reductions may be defensive, not offensive. There is also the case where the price of X is reduced in hopes that customers (as in retail stores) may buy more of Y and Z whose prices remain unchanged.

Note should be taken of what supply-price competition is *not.* In the first place it is not the same as those price-raising techniques which are popularly called monopolistic, as will be explained in a later section. Price-cutting to increase sales does not lose its competitive character merely because some one expects this action to be followed later by a higher price. In the second place, price competition is very different from the market activity of persons selling under substantive conditions of "pure competition." No such seller has to reduce his asking price in order to sell more. He characteristically offers his output on the market for what it will bring. His choices involve only the amount offered and the time at which he makes his sale. Price declines are the result chiefly of reduced intensity of

---

[4] Sometimes a substantive distinction is made on this basis. Oligopolists are said to cut prices relative to *known* rivals whereas monopolists "set" their prices at the best point in their assumed demand schedules, whose elasticities are a function of the prices, qualities, and quantities of substitutes offered by *unknown* rivals. The difficulty of defending such a distinction is obvious.

demand. They may also occur because *many* sellers offer a larger amount for sale, or even because they diminish their asking prices. But prices under "pure competition" never fall merely because a *single* seller decides to reduce his asking price.

It is also desirable to recognize that any form of marketing competition may include activities which the business community or the injured firm may call "unfair." False claims may be made regarding the content of a product or the service it will render. Libelous statements may be made against rival firms or goods. Salesmen may coerce or bribe buyers in various ways incompatible with the mores of the group. In certain situations where there is an agreement or a tradition against supply-price competition, price-cutting itself may be called "unfair."

**6. Purchasing Competition.**—On the buying side the three corresponding methods of competition are less familiar because they occur only in those rare periods of capacity operation of the firms supplying a given industry. This has been characteristic of business in general only in time of war, but a similar "shortness of supply" occurs now and then in particular markets where demand becomes unexpectedly great or supply unexpectedly small. Natural calamities, strikes, shifts in fashion, and rapid changes in technology offer some illustrations.

Demand-price competition consists of raising the bid price to get scarce goods or services which would otherwise go to competitors. Occasionally the buying price will be fixed for one reason or another and the purchasing departments of firms will be able to get their desired supply of goods only by such methods of buying competition as offering prompt payment, absorbing freight, and agreeing to accept delayed shipment. Specification competition may occur parallel to product competition, as when a firm agrees to accept inferior goods in order to avoid getting nothing at all.

All of these forms of purchasing competition should be distinguished from those tactics used by buyers when supplies are not scarce. Under conditions of a "buyers' market," the purchasing department may bargain with suppliers to secure price reductions, may refuse to buy at all unless a fixed low price is met, may demand superior quality and service, etc. This type of activity is best associated with "monopsonistic" behavior and will be discussed below.

**7. Predatory Competition.**—In addition to the various forms of "unfair" competition that may occur in buying or selling, there are other things which firms may do to get the best of their rivals. These include actions intended to weaken a competitor's ability or desire to continue in business by raising his costs of production or sale. Sabotage, acid, arson, and even mayhem have been used to inflict costly losses or to raise the price a competitor has to pay to get supplies of goods or services. Laws may be sought or applied which increase the rival's cost of doing business, such as tariffs and excises on imported goods, rigorous inspections at frequent intervals, etc. A firm may hire away the best executives of its competitors thus getting a double advantage (unless too high a salary has to be offered as inducement). The losing firm will have to use inferior men and the hiring firm will have a staff better able to introduce economies or increase sales. There are also various ways of stealing from rivals the trade secrets which have given them a special advantage. These include both direct theft, the employment of labor spies, and bribing employees to tell what they know. To injure a competitor by increasing his costs, a firm may stir up labor trouble at the rival's establishment. Or it may use its influence with those who supply funds or goods to cause them to charge the competitor more than they charge the favored buyer.

These forms of competition are somewhat different from those usually called "unfair" by trade associations or the Federal Trade Commission, although there is some overlapping. That is why they are grouped at this place under the heading "predatory." With the exception of tariffs, predatory competition is usually confined to situations in which sellers or buyers are few, because only in such cases can one individual see a clear gain to himself through loss to his rival. Under the "many" case of substantive pure competition in either buying or selling, spite or malice may give rise to such action, but it can hardly be called competitive in the sense which dominates this discussion.

**8. Indirect Methods of Competition.**—The indirect methods of competition are those which are not aimed at any particular rival or group of rivals, but which may often spell the difference between success or failure. Most important in this group are efforts to reduce cost by technological improvements. Practically all firms are continually on the quest for new methods which will reduce average unit costs. These include either better combinations of existing factors or the invention of new forms, both of machines and of materials, which will give the same output with less total cost for inputs.

Cost competition is a form of behavior so widespread that it is not limited to any one substantive type. It is found where sellers are single, few, or many, where products are homogeneous or heterogeneous, durable or non-durable, etc. Successful cost competition may determine whether a firm is among the survivors when a decline occurs in schedule demand and is reflected in either falling prices, shrinking sales, or both. On the other hand, cost reductions may precede and make possible price reductions. If price cuts actually result, then cost competition may be considered one cause of price competition.

A second form of indirect competition is that of production planning. This involves timing the inputs and outputs of an enterprise so as to have them occur at those times which will bring the lowest costs and the largest revenues, i.e., the largest net profit. The best times for outputs depend on the business cycle in general and the product cycles in particular. For some products seasonal timing is important. For others the task is to secure the best adjustment of one's own efforts to those of rival producers or of potential buyers.

**9. Forms of Monopolistic Behavior.**—Monopolistic behavior is the opposite of competitive behavior in several ways. It includes action (1) to restrict certain forms of competition, (2) to restrain freedom of entry, and (3) to "exploit" buyers. When individuals compete, they make independent decisions which they expect will give them an advantage over their rivals. When they act monopolistically, they surrender some of this independence to a group or to a government agency. Competitive behavior is supposed to benefit consumers by giving them better goods at lower prices and better terms. Monopolistic behavior works in the opposite direction, particularly towards higher prices. The profits of competitive industry are proverbially low, while those of monopolies are high.

The anti-competitive and anti-buyer aspects of monopoly are interrelated. Sellers who do not "naturally" occupy a position where they can exploit buyers may seek such a vantage point. They do this by forming associations of rivals to reduce the struggle between them. They think to make greater profits by removing certain forms of competition which formerly benefited buyers. These associations may also be helpful in limiting the entry of new competitors.

The amount of freedom of action surrendered to the association usually varies with the tightness of the group. A trade association is less able to restrain competition among its members than is a holding company. Some labor unions exert more pressure on members to conform than do others. Mergers and amalgamations completely destroy the freedom of the combining units, but pools do not.

Associations may be voluntary or coerced. Firms may involuntarily agree to eliminate "cut-throat competition" among themselves. Or, paradoxically, a weak firm may be forced by such competition to sell out to a strong firm or to abide by its selling policies. Coercion may be applied in many ways, by denial of supply sources, by threats of a "price war," by cutting off bank credit, etc. Often that which appears to be "voluntary" association may contain elements of compulsion.

Governments may intervene to reduce competition as well as to enforce it. For many years the ICC has restrained rate-cutting by railroads. More recently we have had price-floors for agricultural products under the AAA. "Fair trade laws" also limit the degree of price-cutting that is legal. Sometimes industries seek to be treated like public utilities and thus be protected from the entry of competitors. In many states certain trades, like barbers, have obtained government support for guild pricing practices. They are given power to restrict entry and to set minimum prices which they then raise as rapidly as they can.

**10. Anti-Competitive Behavior.**—When firms get together in voluntary or compulsory association to reduce competition among themselves, they are seeking to reduce the number of competitors or their freedom of action. The ultimate objective in our capitalistic economy is usually, of course, to secure greater profit. However, an important intermediate objective of some business men is to reduce the number of occasions on which they must make major decisions of policy. To them decision making is painful. One major decision to cooperate may remove the need to make a whole series of other decisions which would be required if rivals were to act independently. Each cooperator surrenders part of his autonomy in order that others may be persuaded to surrender some of theirs.

There is set up a field of anti-competitive behavior which may include one or more of the following forms of cooperation among sellers. Price agreements are the most common.

FORMS OF ANTI-COMPETITIVE BEHAVIOR

I. Establishing uniform price policies
    A. Delivered price systems
    B. Open price systems
    C. Specific minimum prices, F.O.B.
II. Establishing uniform sales terms

III. Allocating markets
IV. Restricting quantity sold or produced
V. Standardizing quality

These terms are sufficiently descriptive to need no elaboration. Comments on uniform price policies were made in Chapter 9, Sections 11 and 12.

**11. Anti-Entry Behavior.**—Monopolistic behavior includes any action to increase the difficulty of entry of new competitors. Entry is opposed because new entrants will take away some of the sales of the older firms. Associations to prevent price-cutting and to reduce other forms of competition may be used to discourage entry. Their chief weapons are patent pools, control over supply sources, and other methods of making it difficult for a beginner to get started. Sometimes they do not act until a rival has begun operations. Then they engage in local price-cutting and other powerful forms of competition to squeeze out the newcomer. This is competitive behavior with monopolistic intent. Through control over government bureaus existing firms may prevent a potential entrant from getting the necessary licenses. Or they may cause certain regulations to be enforced against him which are overlooked in relation to existing firms. A newsboy may use his fists to keep another boy from muscling in on his street corner monopoly. Larger firms use more subtle pressures.

Entry may be difficult anyway. Scarce natural resources, large initial investment, rare personal skills, and limited franchises are obvious barriers. The mere fear of inability to break the hold which existing firms have on the market may deter possible entrants. Brand names with popular goodwill are hard to beat.

When obstacles to entry exist, whether natural or artificial, the protected firms often make supernormal profits. These serve as an inducement to entry. Hence monopolistic behavior may include efforts to conceal these profits, as by stock watering, excessive depreciation charges, etc. Supernormal profits depend upon the use of a selling price which is high relative to costs. At times when entry is especially feared, a temporary reduction in this price may serve as a deterrent. This problem will be discussed further in Section 13 below.

**12. Anti-Buyer Behavior in General.**—Monopolies have long been denounced for the ways in which they harm the consumer. The argument is usually that if there were more competition, the price would be lower, the product and associated services better. But such denunciation and reasoning does not furnish a norm by which prices may be judged to be either "high" (monopolistic) or "low" (competitive). Nor does it tell us how severe price competition must be for the market to become free from all taint of monopoly. The personal bias of the polemist will obviously influence judgment. Is there any place where the economist may take a convincing stand?

At the outset he should avoid the substantive definition of a monopolist as one who is able to set his selling price. This definition would include all those who from time to time reduce prices in an effort to take customers away from other sellers and who are therefore described by most people as competing with one another. There is nothing to be gained by seeking to reverse popular connotations in this regard.

The functional approach offers a better, if not perfect, solution. Anti-buyer behavior may be divided into five parts as follows:

### Forms of Anti-Buyer Behavior

I. Raising prices when demand rises, but costs do not rise, or do not rise as much

II. Sustaining prices when demand falls (maintaining "rigid prices")

III. Sustaining prices when unit cost falls (appropriating the gains of "technological progress")

IV. Charging some buyers more than others ("price discrimination")

V. Charging a "high" price; making "supernormal" profit

The first four types will be analyzed briefly in the following section. The fifth is more difficult and will be deferred to Section 14.

**13. Four Types of Anti-Buyer Behavior by Monopolies.**—The first case of anti-buyer behavior is that in which a seller raises his asking price following an increase in demand. If there were intense price competition among sellers, no seller would raise his price unless driven to do so by rising costs. Therefore, for him to ask a higher price merely because demand has risen means that he is exploiting consumers. This monopolistic analysis must be contrasted with the conventional analysis which shows an increased demand raising prices in a "competitive" market because of the upward slope of the supply curve. That positive slope results from increasing marginal cost or increasing marginal reluctance to sell. It is not the same as the present case where there is no increase in cost, but merely a changed idea of "what the traffic will bear." Or the increase in cost is insignificant in relation to the increase in price.

The second case in the above outline refers to situations in which sellers maintain prices unchanged when demand falls, costs remaining unchanged. Such sellers choose to keep prices constant rather than to adjust to the downward shift of their revenue curves. "Rigid prices" should be contrasted with what may be called "rigid quantities." In the latter case, a seller faced by declining demand tends to maintain his former rate of output and takes whatever lower price it will bring. Behavior of the first type is often called monopolistic and suggests a perfectly elastic (horizontal) supply curve. Behavior of the second type usually is associated with substantive competition and suggests a completely inelastic (vertical) supply curve. A comparison also should be made between the vertical supply curve of the extreme anti-rigid-prices school and the upward sloping supply curve of an industry in conventional analysis. Under the latter assumption some curtailment of supply is to be expected when schedule demand falls. High cost producers will be forced out and the marginally high cost production of those who remain will be eliminated as unprofitable. But this is clearly not the same as supply curtailment by those who engage in monopolistic pricing in the face of declining demand.

The third case of anti-buyer behavior is the least disputed of all. It occurs when costs decline because of technological progress or a drop in the price of one of the factors. If there is highly competitive behavior, the price of the finished product will quickly be cut and the total net revenue of the firm will tend to remain the same as before. Monopolistic behavior, on the other hand, will seek to keep prices up so as to keep for the firm most of the gain from the reduced cost. Prices will remain unchanged or will not be reduced as much as would be required if all the benefit from the cost reduction were to be passed on to the consumer. It is interesting to note at this point that the denouncers of monopoly will often admit the desirability of stimulating technological progress by temporary patent rights. This admission that monopolistic behavior is sometimes socially beneficial at the same time that it is anti-buyer in the short run opens the door to an extensive social critique of competition versus monopoly which is of great importance, but cannot be presented here.

A fourth type of monopolistic pricing which is often denounced as harmful to buyers is price discrimination. This was discussed at length in Chapter 9, Sections 10 to 14. It includes all forms of price differences quoted by a given seller which are not in proportion to differences in cost. Those who have to pay the higher prices may claim that they are being discriminated against in a way that would be impossible if competition were present. This is probably true, but competition cannot always be present, or if present might be harmful, as with certain public utilities.  High per ton mile railway rates, high utility rates for individual home-owners, etc., are often defended on the grounds that these rates are lower than they would be if the selling firms were unable to derive some revenue from business which would not be obtainable unless granted very low rates.

Not all price discrimination is anti-buyer and therefore monopolistic.  Some may be pro-buyer and competitive.  The difference may be seen by referring back to Figure 43.  All prices charged above the equilibrium (uniform) price $OP = QR$ are anti-buyer.  But sellers may also favor certain buyers by offering them goods at less than $OP = QR$.  We usually call this "dumping" and recognize it as a competitive effort to win customers from other sellers.  This case illustrates again the advantage of the functional approach to competition and monopoly.  The substantive approach would bring both types of activity together since they both depend on the presence of "monopolistic" power to set selling prices.

**14. Monopolies Charge "High" Prices and Make "Supernormal" Profits.**—The fifth type of anti-buyer behavior is perhaps best known but it is very difficult to describe with precision and is least well suited to the functional approach.  To appraise situations in which firms set prices "too high," monopolistic pricing must be defined in terms of its results in comparison with competitive pricing.  This requires the assumption that there exists a normal competitive relationship between price and cost, e.g., that which yields normal profit.  Monopolistic behavior then becomes that which sets prices which yield supernormal profit.  This may sound like a very neat disposal of the whole problem, but it is really a deceptive trap unless the terms are very carefully defined, and even then it is tricky.

In the first place, normal profits must be expressed as a rate of return on net worth.  This normal rate is not a fixed figure, but varies from industry to industry and from time to time.  It is best defined in terms of the behavior or the desire to act which characterizes firms within and without the industry or situation.  Normal profits do not attract sufficient entrants to cause an expansion of total production or productive capacity, but merely enough to offset exits.  Normal prices in an industry are those which yield normal profits at the rate of sale which results.  These are the prices presumptively set when there is "normal" competition among rival firms, although the preceding discussion clearly indicates the possibility that competition may meet with buyer approval even when it reduces profits for sellers to the vanishing point.  There is a difference between the norm of the economist talking in terms of the long run and that of the consumer appraising his short-run position as buyer.

The best that can be done along this line, therefore, is to define monopolistic behavior as that which sets prices so high that they yield supernormal profits according to somebody's criterion. If the judgment is rendered by people with money to invest who would like to earn similarly large profits, competitive behavior may sooner or later develop to force profits downward, and possibly prices too.[5] The economist is most likely to follow this approach.

On the other hand, a "substantive monopoly" may charge such low prices or experience such difficulties in getting buyers to purchase that it makes only a normal or even a subnormal profit. It should not then be denounced as a "monopoly," since from the viewpoint of results it is pricing "competitively."

Supernormal profits often depend upon hindrances to full production by restriction of output. If a single firm is involved, it will be able to maintain the "high price" which exploits buyers only if it limits its output to the amount it can sell at that price. The conventional analysis shows the maximum profit combination of price and output to be at a higher price and lower quantity than if the firm produced at minimum average total cost. If the latter point is further defined as the "competitive output," on the grounds that it will yield "normal profit," then the smaller output which yields a larger profit must be called something else, e.g., "monopolistic."[6] If several firms collude, and some or all of them have considerable excess capacity when they sell at the monopolistically established price, it is usually necessary for them to engage in further monopolistic action by agreeing to restrict output. Quotas are set so that the total amount offered on the market will not exceed that which buyers are expected to take at the fixed price. It may even be less if there are excess stocks to be moved.

A final comment about the supernormal profit approach to monopoly might be that such profits are hidden as quickly as possible. Assets are revalued upward, stock is watered, salaries are padded, and other techniques are used to prevent both buyer dissatisfaction and outsider jealousy. An economist must also be a good accountant if

[5] To simplify the discussion, comment upon obvious relations between price and quantity sold, type of product and cost of production, selling expense and total expense, etc. has been omitted in most cases.

[6] Supernormal profit for individual firms is possible, of course, without monopolistic behavior. For instance, the intra-marginal producers of a homogeneous product sold at a uniform price may make "efficiency profits" by devising ways to reduce cost. See Chapter 25, especially Section 7.

he would use this criterion of monopoly. Even then he would still face the very difficult problem of appropriate allowance for efficiency profits.

**15. Summary.**—Market prices are determined in many ways. These are most fruitfully classified as behavior types: by people acting independently, by people acting together, and by governments. When people act independently they compete against one another in marketing, product quality, purchasing, cost reduction, timing, etc. Monopolistic behavior includes collusion to set price, to control output, to allocate markets, etc. It may also involve action to discourage entry, and to exploit buyers.

The functional classification of types of competition and monopoly emphasizes what sellers and buyers do in the market. Its emphasis is institutional. Its generalizations are more varied than those of the substantive approach. It examines with semantic care the referents of words of wide usage in both popular and technical works on economics. Realism is the objective, rather than the solution of formal problems of logic. No institutional analysis can be completely realistic, because economic phenomena are infinitely varied in time and place.

# Chapter 12

## CAUSES AND EFFECTS OF COMPETITIVE AND MONOPOLISTIC BEHAVIOR

**1. Causes of Different Types of Market Behavior.**—In the preceding chapter on different types of market behavior, scattered references were made to the *causes* of action of one type or another. It is now appropriate to examine both causes and effects in more systematic fashion. In the first place, we assume that in a capitalistic society the major cause is the desire to maximize profit. As indicated in Section 3 of the preceding chapter, this goal may be sought by different methods of market pricing and behavior. Four of the most important are the following:

1. Independent price-setting and other forms of competition
2. Collusive group action to set prices and in other ways to restrict competition
3. Accepting the price (and terms) set by others; competing in other aspects of market or production behavior
4. Bargaining with buyers

In the second place, action in any of these four ways may be based upon a variety of conditions. None of them arises from a single, unique pattern. Finally, although any given condition may generally give rise to a certain pattern of behavior, the possibility of exceptions must not be overlooked. One entrepreneur may seek maximum profits in the short run, as by monopolistic pricing, whereas another may react to a similar situation by competitive pricing, believing that to be best in the long run.

Because of these varying possibilities, the classification of behavior in terms of substantive causes is difficult. It seems better to base generalizations directly upon types of behavior and take note of exceptions to causes instead of exceptions in action. Possible reasons for using each of the four methods listed above will be analyzed in the next four sections. After a couple of diagrammatic notes, the chapter will conclude with a discussion of temporal and spatial price patterns resulting from competition and monopoly.

**2. Causes of Independent Price-Setting by Sellers.**—An individual seller may choose to set his own price rather than to collude, to accept, or to bargain, if one of the following three major situations of fact and opinion is present.

I. The seller may perceive no close rival who might be influenced by the price set and therefore he feels no danger of retaliation. This assumption of low cross-elasticity of price between A and other products, B, C, D, etc., may be either a fact or an illusion. If it is true, it is due to the first two of the following causes or to the third:

    A. Product differentiation or market isolation ("a wide gap in the chain of substitutes"). This in turn is caused by:

        1. Product differentiation by a single producer, achieved by such things as:

            (a) A product design protected by patent, trade secret, time required to imitate, etc.

            (b) A trade-mark protected by copyright and bolstered by advertising, customer experience, etc.

            (c) The ownership of scarce natural resources

        2. Some type of merger or agreement among various producers of similar products

    B. A *relatively* low price for the product. (Buyer substitution is a function of relative prices as well as relative qualities. A seller may be a substantive monopolist at *any* price range, but not a functional monopolist. There is always some price above which cross-elasticity will become apparent for any good, no matter how differentiated.)

    C. The ignorance or indifference of rivals

        1. The price-cutting seller may be small in relation to other sellers.

        2. Price cuts may be secret.

II. The seller perceives rivals who will be influenced by his price, but acts independently nevertheless. (In this case there is appreciable cross-elasticity.)

    A. He may feel so much stronger than his rivals that

        1. He thinks they will tag along ("price leadership"), or

        2. He thinks he can beat them in a test of strength.

    B. He may think he can keep his price cuts secret.

    C. He may be a newcomer who must do something different to break into the field, such as price-cutting, special product differentiation, or ballyhoo.

    D. There may be general or particular overcapacity and price-cutting becomes an action of last resort.

III. The seller can postpone selling if there are no buyers at the price
he sets.
- A. He may be a single seller of a differentiated product, such
as a piece of real estate.
- B. He may be one out of many sellers of a homogeneous product who is willing to sell now if he gets his price or better,
but otherwise prefers to wait. American wheat farmers
often fall into this class.

For cross reference with the traditional approach one should
note that substantive monopoly appears above under I-A, III-A, and
possibly II-A-1, although most economists would probably put most
of II under the heading of substantive oligopoly. Substantive pure
competition should be associated with III-B, although it is rarely
presented with that type of emphasis.

To complete the discussion of independent price-setting by sellers,
a note might be added concerning the background of price discrimination. Three major causes or conditions are usually described (cf.
Chapter 9, Sections 13 and 14).

1. There is no close rival. (This is usually interpreted to mean substantive monopoly, but it need not. When sellers formerly engaged in active competition with each other find that the demand
at a fixed ceiling price exceeds what they can supply, they may
engage in various types of "black market" price and customer discrimination. There is no merging, no collusion, no change in the
number of sellers, but a different type of behavior emerges from
the combination of scarcity and price ceilings.)
2. The total demand schedule can be subdivided, with different elasticities of demand in each subgroup.
3. The cost of keeping markets separate is not large relative to the
gain from price discrimination.

**3. Causes of Collusion.**—Collusion occurs whenever a group of
sellers believes that profits can be maximized better by concerted
action in some respects than by rivalrous action. Functional monopoly is preferred to functional competition. Among the possible
methods of securing noncompetitive behavior, collusion is adopted
rather than outright combination whenever sellers do not want to
surrender their right to compete in other respects. The fear of antitrust prosecution may be an influence on either side. It may discourage collusion, may cause it to be informal, or may stimulate
complete merging of former rivals. A more detailed statement of
the causes of collusion follows:

I. The product is homogeneous or is only moderately differentiated. (There is appreciable cross-elasticity among the products of different sellers.)

II. There is excess capacity in the sense that not all firms can produce at minimum average total cost and sell the total output without forcing the price down below that figure. This, in turn, may be caused by:

    A. A decline in schedule demand

    B. The entry of new firms, usually low-cost producers

    C. The expansion of capacity by existing firms

    D. In agriculture, a short-run glut may result from unusually favorable growing conditions

III. Belief that the "industry" demand schedule is inelastic above the prices prevailing prior to collusion.

IV. Government influence.

    A. To aid sellers thought to be harmed by too much price competition. Cf. AAA, NIRA, NLRA, etc.

    B. To promote the achievement of foreign policy objectives. Cf. permissive and compulsory international cartel activity

**4. Causes of Price Acceptance.**—Sellers accept the prices set by others under quite a variety of circumstances including the following:

I. The buyer may set the price and refuse to bargain.

    A. The seller may be unable to find any other buyer who will pay more, or

    B. The seller may deem it unwise for him to wait for the buyer to relent or for other buyers to appear.

II. The seller may fear imitation or retaliation if he acts independently.

    A. Strong rival sellers may cut prices as much or more.

    B. Bankers, union labor, suppliers of materials, and others from whom the seller buys and who have an interest in uniform action by all sellers, may coerce the one who breaks ranks.

III. The seller may see no possible gain from asking less.

    A. He can sell at the going price all that he possesses or can produce. This means that either:

        1. There is a buyer who will take all that the seller offers at a fixed price, or

        2. There are so many buyers and sellers that the given seller can supply only a very small part of the total.

IV. The seller may believe he would lose by asking more.

    A. He thinks that buyers would quickly turn to rival sellers who offer similar or identical goods at unchanged prices.

    B. He fears the penalties of a law imposing price ceilings.

These four cases of price acceptance by sellers include the situations frequently defined in traditional classifications. For instance, substantive monopsony is akin to I, substantive oligopoly resembles II-A, and substantive pure competition fits III-A-2 and IV-A. The last two categories were also illustrated in Section 2 under the heading of price-setting. It should therefore be clear that the traditional categories do not give rise to any type of behavior peculiar to them. This is true whether the substantive distinction be made upon either the number of sellers or product differentiation. One cannot reason backward from the function to say that price-setting is exclusively the activity of substantive monopolists, or that price accepting is sure proof of substantive pure competition. The merits of the functional approach are also supported by Section 3 on collusion and the following section on bargaining.

**5. A Diagrammatic Note on Traditional Demand and Supply Curves for Different Types of Competition.**—The traditional substantive approach to a "monopolistic" situation defines it as one in which an individual seller, or a group acting together, chooses the selling price which is expected to yield the greatest net profit. The price-setting is said to occur against a background of a sloping demand curve with $AR$ above $MR$ like those of Figures 33–36 or 45. The $MC = MR$ point, when found, leads to the price-quantity solution of the maximum profit problem. Though there is a tendency to establish such an optimum price, the actual behavior of "monopolistic" sellers is much more complex than mere price-choosing by formula. The preceding chapter has outlined and explained many different kinds of monopolistic behavior. The argument also shows that price-setting is as much a part of competition in the functional sense as it is of monopoly.

Three other substantive classifications are worthy of consideration. The first is pure competition, described as a situation in which there are so many sellers of the same type of product that no one of them can set the selling price independently of the others (cf. Section 4, III and IV). The traditional diagram has a horizontal demand curve ($AR = MR$) like that of Figures 30, 31, 32, and 46.

The second is pure monopoly. The description and diagrammatics of pure monopoly are not as uniform as those for pure competition. The most logical picture would seem to be that of a single seller, or group, able to raise the selling price without any loss of demand. This is the exact opposite of pure competition where any rise in an individual's selling price means complete loss of demand.

Diagrammatically it is also opposite.  The demand curve is vertical instead of horizontal.  Such a situation is highly unreal, but it is the true limiting case.  If it ever did exist, the monopolist would raise his price to the point where demand began to fall off.  He would revert to the sloping demand curve of "monopolistic competition" for any further price increases.  This is shown in Figure 47.  There is

FIGURE 47

PURE MONOPOLY FOR A LIMITED PRICE RANGE

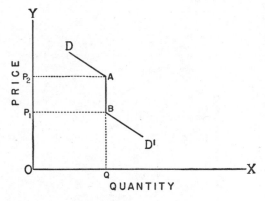

QUANTITY

"pure monopoly" for the firm selling at $P_1$, but after it raises its selling price to $P_2$, further increases encounter a sloping $AR$ curve like that of Figures 33–36 and 45.

Another substantive classification of forms of competition which appears in most discussions of the subject is oligopoly.  Here there are a few firms producing the same product, each conscious of the way in which its own actions may have a boomerang effect.  Firm F, for instance, may think that a price cut would attract customers from its competitors.  But if these competitors follow with a similar price cut, they will retain most or all of their customers.  Firm F will gain something, but less than expected.  There are at least three possibilities.  Some buyers will be attracted by F's bold move in making the first price cut and will not return to former suppliers.  Second, former customers of F may be induced to buy more than before.  Third, a few new buyers may be attracted to the product by its now low price and Firm F will get its share.  The latter two gains are shown in Figure 48 as those resulting from moving down the "industry demand curve," $dd'$, from $A$ to $C$.  If competitors had not followed suit, Firm F would have moved down its independent demand curve, $DD'$, from $A$ to $B$.  If the process is described in two steps, sales of an oligopolist may rise first from $OQ$ to $OQ_1$ and then drop to $OQ_2$.

In this traditional diagram there is no easy way to show the increment of customers taken from other firms. And if competitors

FIGURE 48

THE BOOMERANG EFFECT UNDER OLIGOPOLY

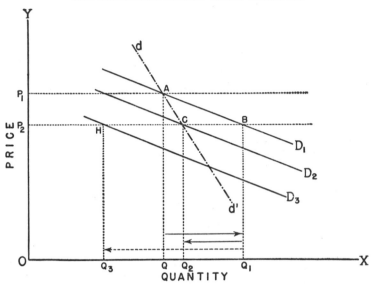

retaliate by cutting prices more than Firm F, demand may drop to $D_3$. The new sales quantity, $OQ_3$, will be less than $OQ$.[1] The boomerang effect in such cases really hurts. Even the sales increase from $OQ$ to $OQ_2$ may be harmful if costs do not decrease as much as the prices drop.

These possible adverse effects of price-cutting often lead to acceptance of the going price as indicated in the preceding section.

**6. Causes of Bargaining.**—Sellers use bargaining to determine the price when they think that the demand is inelastic over a certain price range. In such circumstances a seller sets his initial price high and shades it as little as he can. The buyer, conversely, sets his first price low and comes up as little as possible.

This is often called a "bilateral monopoly" situation, but it is a

---

[1] A line connecting $A$ and $H$ would *not* now represent an "industry demand curve" like that between $A$ and $C$. Competing firms would have different prices. This could happen if location or service differences made buyers prefer to deal with one seller rather than another. The full product homogeneity of traditional theory is rarely found in practice.

type of behavior peculiar to itself and can hardly be called anything other than bargaining or "higgling." In one sense the good involved may be considered different from other goods offered or sought. In another sense the bargaining merely occurs because either the buyer or the seller does not want to take the time and trouble to hunt acceptable substitutes. Any failure to reach a mutually acceptable compromise is evidence of belief in the availability of such substitutes.

**7. A Diagrammatic Note on Bargaining.**—A diagram like Figure 49 helps to clarify the concept of a bargaining range within which the price is determined by bargaining. Assume that $DD$ shows the demand curve of a buyer who will buy quantity $OQ$ at any price from $QF$ up to $QA$. A seller in the same market will sell $OQ$ at any price from $QB$ down to $QE$. The bargaining range is $AE$ where the two curves overlap. If the seller is the more clever bargainer of the two, the final price, $P$, will be closer to $P_1$ than to $P_2$. In formal theory the $AF$ vertical segment of the demand curve would indicate pure monopoly for the seller for that price range. It is more often called

FIGURE 49

THE BARGAINING RANGE WHEN MONOPSONIST MEETS
MONOPOLIST

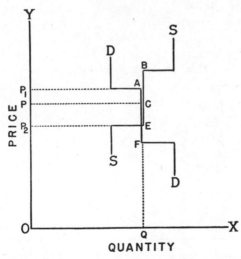

merely a discontinuous demand curve. Similarly, the buyer would experience pure monopsony as he moved from $B$ to $E$ on the seller's supply curve.[2]

---

[2] The shape of both curves above points $A$ and $B$ and below points $D$ and $E$ may be either slanting, curved, or, as here, of the staircase type.

**8. Bargaining and the Emergence of a Subjective "Surplus."—**
If the bargaining between monopsonist and monopolist results in a
price such as $P$ in Figure 49, both buyer and seller will feel that the
price is a good one.   The buyer may say to himself that he obtained
the goods for less than he was willing to pay.   He has "saved" the
amount $PP_1$.   This is often called a "buyer's surplus."   The seller
may also feel that he has gained $PP_2$, which is the amount obtained
above his minimum price.   This gain is known as a "seller's surplus."

Surpluses of this type also emerge from other market situations.
The most common is that in which the market price $P$ is set by the
seller and buyers appear who are willing to pay more than $P$ but do
not have to do so.   A housewife may go to market expecting to pay
70 cents for a pound of bacon.   When she gets there, she finds that
bacon is on sale that day for 65 cents.   She has "saved" 5 cents.
Similar illustrations on the other side of the market are not so common.   But sometimes a producer may start producing a good with
the expectation of selling it at, say, $1.00.   When the good is ready
for the market, he may find that it can be sold for $1.25, a gain of
25 cents.

There is a third possibility which has been discussed extensively
pro and con.   It is based upon continuous demand and supply curves
such as those of Figure 50.   If the demand curve represents a col-

FIGURE 50

BUYERS' AND SELLERS' SURPLUSES MAY EMERGE FROM CON-
TINUOUS DEMAND AND SUPPLY CURVES

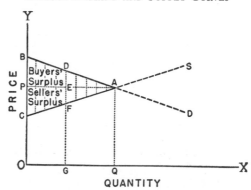

lective cumulative schedule in which each buyer wants only one unit,
such as one refrigerator, then a total buyers' surplus or consumers'
surplus ($BAP$) can be computed in terms of dollars saved.   If the
supply curve is taken as a cumulative average cost curve for a group

of suppliers, a sellers' surplus or producers' surplus ($PAC$) can be shown.

When the demand curve is the cumulative total demand of buyers who want more than one unit, a buyers' surplus is more difficult to prove. Some argue that the principle of diminishing marginal utility indicates that the buyer would have paid a high price for the first unit, a slightly lower price for the second, and so on until the $n$th unit whose potential bid price is equal to the market price. The difference between the market price actually paid and that which would have been paid for each unit *if the goods had been bought one at a time at the maximum bid price for each successive one* may then be added to obtain a total consumer's surplus ($BAP$). The unrealism of this argument lies in the fact that the *total* quantity would not be bought at any higher unit price than that actually paid for the "last" or "marginal" unit. Therefore there is no consumer's surplus at all. Even if the diminishing marginal utility approach be accepted as describing the basis of the demand curve, there remains the problem of adding utilities to get a total in "utils." When different people are involved in a collective demand schedule, the task is impossible. Nevertheless, even if a buyer's surplus cannot be measured under these conditions, the concept is a useful one in certain economic problems, such as that of achieving equal sacrifice in distributing the tax burden.

On the selling side, the difficulty arises from the usual definition of the supply curve as a *marginal* cost curve. This is desirable and logical for small changes in the vicinity of the market price, but such a curve cannot be extended all the way back to $C$ as shown in Figure 50. All the fixed costs would have to be included in computing the marginal cost of the first unit. This would cause $C$ to be very high, far above $B$. The seller's "surplus" then becomes very difficult to calculate or to demonstrate on a diagram.

## 9. Parallel Classifications Are Possible on the Buying Side.—

Almost all of the foregoing analysis has dealt with the selling side of the market. Similar classifications may be made also on the buying side. Functionally this requires description of various types of competition among buyers. Monopsonistic behavior replaces monopolistic. It includes anti-competitive efforts by collusion, anti-entry activities, and anti-seller devices. Individual buyers try to improve their buying techniques and to bargain for as low buying prices as possible. The substantive categories are also similar. Pure monopsony exists when the supply of the good being bought is inelastic for price cuts over a certain price range. Monopsonistic competition is revealed when buyers cannot get more goods except at higher prices. Under pure (buying) competition the supply curve as seen by the individual buyer is perfectly horizontal. The latter situation is very common because of the habit of sellers to quote fixed prices. It is modified by the practice of quoting quantity discounts.

Most firms operate monopsonistically in the purchase of some of their materials, equipment, or services. They operate competitively in "shopping around" to buy other things at lower prices than their rivals. They accept prices fixed by a seller only when they cannot bargain the price down or find a better price elsewhere. It is much less common for them to fix their buying prices than to fix their selling prices. Only very large buyers or well organized groups can do both.

**10. Patterns of Price Behavior.**—One of the main reasons for attempting classification in the field of competition and monopoly is the desire to explain various types of price behavior. We may also want to predict or to control price movements which we do not like. When the emphasis is upon price patterns, the classification may be either temporal or spatial.

The price changes which occur through time may be compared in terms of either their relative frequency or their relative amplitude. The prices of some commodities may change many times in a business day, like wheat on an active grain exchange. Other prices may not change for months or years at a time, like nickel candy bars, street car rides, gold at the mint, or new Fords. A price may be stable at one season of the year, but fluctuate considerably in others, like hothouse vegetables as compared with field grown. Or there may be long periods of stability interrupted by vigorous price wars, as in the case of retail gasoline in some areas.

So far as amplitude of price change is concerned, differences in range from high to low may be noted. Some prices do not depart very much from their norm of cost of production while others do. Durable goods and income-yielding property probably have the widest range of fluctuation. In other cases changes in the cost of production are significant, such as seasonal crops. Some price patterns reveal inflexibility upward, but considerable amplitude downward, while for other commodities the reverse is true.

Although the foregoing list of patterns of price behavior is far from complete, enough cases have been cited to indicate that there are many determinants of price patterns other than the degrees and types of competitive behavior. With this qualification in mind, the competition-monopoly aspect of price stability may now be explored.

**11. Causes of Price Stability.**—Prices change most frequently when the exchange price is not set by single individuals, but by bargaining or by the balancing of equal quantities at various bid and offer prices in the market. A major reason for instability in the prices of staple goods traded on the exchanges is the frequent change in expectations. Bid and offer prices fluctuate with every rumor and every prediction of change. Even without the presence of professional speculators, exchange prices would change because producer-sellers, not to mention buyers, often do amateur speculating on their own part.

Prices tend to greater stability when individual sellers are able to determine the exchange price by setting their offering price. Although custom, contract, and demand inelasticity are also important causes of stability, monopolistic behavior must be given considerable weight. The functional monopolist is one who takes steps alone or with others to insulate the market from the usual forces causing price change. For various reasons he prefers price stability. Therefore, instead of changing his offering price with every minor fluctuation in demand or cost, he keeps it constant for weeks, months, or even years. He does not act like the substantive monopolist of traditional equilibrium theory whose asking price is always set so that marginal cost equals marginal revenue. Price stability tends to become a goal in itself, a rival to that of maximum profit. This is true, even though capitalistic apologists may argue that the individual entrepreneur is always seeking maximum profits "in the long run," and that $MC$ and $MR$ curves should be interpreted in that light. As indicated above in Chapter 11, Section 12, price stability is often the most prominent tactic of collusive monopolies. It is also common among collusive monopsonies.

Periods of stability interrupted by price wars generally indicate the presence of collusion among a few big producers plus opportunities for fairly easy entry by small producers. This type of price behavior will also be likely to occur if the major firms cannot quickly adjust supply to demand, if they cannot store raw materials or finished products in time of glut, and if there are no significant economies of scale.

Firms which cannot control the prices of their major raw materials are more apt to have fluctuating selling prices than those which are integrated vertically. The same is true for those who buy in a market where prices fluctuate as compared with one which is monopolistically stabilized.

Even if all substantive monopolists sought to price their products according to the economist's formula, there would be differences in the patterns of price behavior. Demand changes and cost changes occur with different frequencies for different products. And the time-elasticity of supply varies considerably. Durable goods, for instance, reveal much greater amplitude of fluctuation on the down side than do nondurable goods. Therefore, it is wise to remember that substantive classifications of monopoly or competition in terms of frequency of amplitude of price change must be very loose, indeed. The ability to set exchange prices is only one of many variables that influence the degree of price stability.

Stable prices in the time sequence of an actual market must not be confused with stable prices in the equilibrium sense of economic analysis. Much of the traditional substantive approach is linked to the latter in logic, but has been transferred to the former by inference. For instance, the equilibrium price under "pure competition" is sometimes held to be more "stable" than the equilibrium price under "pure monopoly," whereas observation seems to show that the reverse is true. Part of the trouble undoubtedly lies in the vagueness with which the demand and supply schedules are often defined in each case, but even the sharpest substantive definitions give analytic tools inferior to those of the functional approach.

**12. A Functional View of Geographic Price Patterns.**—There are also many patterns of geographic price dispersal at any given time. Three types are quite common. One is the uniform, or postage stamp type of price. A second is the transfer differential pattern with differences closely proportional to transport costs from a central market or place of production. The third is the basing point system, where one or more cities constitute the places from which transportation costs are figured regardless of actual point of production. There is also a zone delivered system like parcel post rates where the average transportation cost, or something close to it, is considered in computing a delivered price for the entire zone. This is intermediate between the first and second types given above. Many non-systematic patterns also exist influenced by custom, differing costs of production, different degrees of competition, density of population, number of production points, etc.

Differences in geographic price patterns depend only in part upon the geographic dispersion of price-competing producers. If they agree to act together in one way or another, the pattern will depend chiefly upon the type of freight charging or freight absorption scheme adopted. If they act independently, the price pattern depends upon relative costs of production, the distances between competitors, and their fighting strength. Price competition will be more severe and the price pattern more unpredictable if dumping practices are followed than if a uniform price is charged to all sellers F.O.B.

Here again a monopolist is what a monopolist does. If a firm chooses to engage in extensive price discrimination practices, it may be acting either competitively or monopolistically. When price discrimination involves cutting prices for certain sales *below* the average total cost (including necessary transportation costs and a normal profit), then this should be called competitive action even though its intent is to extinguish price-competition in the future. On the other hand, when a seller's price discrimination pattern involves only a series of price levels *upward* above average total cost, this is monopolistic pricing. This pattern is a method of exploiting buyers for the benefit of the seller, whereas the former type of price discrimination benefits certain buyers, at least for a time. (Cf. Chapter 11, Section 13, and Chapter 9, Sections 13 and 14.)

Neither intent nor future possibilities of opposite action should lead us to call competition "monopoly." We may condemn regional dumping as likely to produce anti-social results, but uniform pricing with competitive intent might also lead to the same outcome. In retail selling all buyers may be charged a below-cost price by a given firm when it promotes a "loss-leader." This is competition and it may or may not lead to the ousting of rivals who cannot stand long-continued losses. Consistency would dictate that he who proposes to ban regional dumping should also support "Fair Trade Laws." Each proposal condemns a particular discriminatory price competition which weak firms don't like and whose results economists may disapprove.

**13. A Social Appraisal of Competitive and Monopolistic Behavior.**—Since the main purpose of this chapter has been to suggest a functional approach to the concepts of competition and monopoly, it is not necessary to elaborate upon social implications. However, certain inferences may be made explicit. We should not condemn monopoly, substantively defined, without examining its behavior. Some of that behavior is competitive and some is monopolistic. Furthermore, not all competitive behavior is good nor all monopolistic behavior bad. It depends upon the results and upon the standards of goodness which we use in evaluation. A few illustrations may be given.

Certain forms of competitive behavior seem to be anti-social according to generally accepted criteria. Most obvious is that which bankrupts newcomers or noncooperators in an effort to force them out of business and is followed by a subsequent price boost which exploits the buyers for the benefit of the firm that initiated the squeeze. But it is hard to draw the line between good competition of this type and bad. Sometimes only experience can prove that monopolistic behavior will be the ultimate result. And in the meantime consumers benefit.

When there is too much selling competition, we generally feel that resources are wasted which might have been put to more productive use. A welding of the competing advertisers into one large unit by a holding company or other technique might reduce this waste. But, of course, it might also lead to monopolistic activity of another kind which we would condemn.

The problem of excessive entry with resultant overcapacity and high unit costs is well known in some fields like retail groceries and gas stations. Behavior opposing entry has been called monopolistic, but it may succeed in preventing a waste of society's resources. Franchises and patents are governmentally sanctioned methods of restricting entry, presumably in the public interest. We restrain competitive behavior in this respect or in that and then hope that anti-social monopolistic behavior will not emerge. But it often does.

When competition becomes very keen, firms are sometimes led to exploit their workers or other suppliers, instead of their customers. The government has recognized this danger in the soft coal mines, for instance, and has introduced compulsory cartellization. But it is very hard to keep the balance. Competition between firms has been their protection in the past. Is government control sufficient for the future?

Another form of monopolistic behavior which has received the stamp of government approval is that collusion among workers known as collective bargaining. Here again arises the problem of distinguishing between the subsequent forms of activity. Some are accepted as good according to most criteria, some denounced as bad, and many are highly debatable. No appraisal will be attempted here, but the case is offered to support the argument that intelligent social control must go beyond the forms of monopoly to the types of behavior that emerge and must then distinguish among these the ones that are anti-social and should be controlled. Otherwise we may throw out the good along with the bad.  Our predilection for emotionally colored labels has often betrayed us.[3]

**14. Summary.**—The causes of market behavior patterns are found in part in the selling and buying conditions traditionally used in defining substantive monopoly, competition, and oligopoly.  Pricing methods include price setting, price acceptance, and bargaining.  These functional classes cut across the traditional categories, but seem more realistic and useful.  Parallel classifications on the buying side exist for both functional and substantive viewpoints.

Buyers' and sellers' surpluses may be distinguished under certain assumptions regarding subjective maximum buying prices, subjective minimum selling prices, and objective costs.  Temporal and spatial patterns of price behavior may be described.  Monopolistic behavior promotes price stability through time.  It also leads to geographic patterns of fixed price differentials.  Monopolistic behavior generally is socially harmful, but there are frequent exceptions.  Competitive behavior is usually beneficial, but not always.

Generalizations about methods of price determination should be made with care and applied with still more care.

---

[3] In the interest of brevity, comments upon other criteria for judging the merit of competitive versus monopolistic behavior have been omitted.  These include effect upon technical progress, saving and investing, level of employment and output, quality of goods, incentives to government control, etc.

# Chapter 13

## TIME FACTORS IN INDIVIDUAL PRICE TRENDS: COST CHANGES

**1. Introduction.**—Chapters 11 and 12 have demonstrated the importance of the degree of price competition in the determination of the market price. We now return to the cost arguments of Chapter 8. But the approach is different. We want to know why prices *change*. The explanation might be sought in changes in the degree of price competition, in laws and court decisions, in sellers' expectations, and in other things. In this chapter, however, our attention will be centered upon cost changes as causes in periods of rising demand. The next chapter will examine some of the other possible causes of price change and will consider falling demand.

Specific questions to be answered in the next few sections include:

1. What is the concept of "time-elasticity of supply" and how does it differ from simple "price-elasticity"?

2. What three time periods of supply change are commonly described as demand rises?
   - (a) What is "short-run" supply?
   - (b) What are two ways of looking at "moderately long-run" supply curves?
   - (c) What are "very long-run" supply schedules and how may they be used?

3. Is monopoly inevitable in the long run under conditions of decreasing cost?

4. What other cost changes influence price?
   - (a) How summarize cost reasons for a downward price trend?
   - (b) How summarize cost reasons for a rising price trend?

**2. Time-Elasticity of Supply.**—The definition of supply schedules and curves in terms of their setting in time involves three problems: (1) the difference in the times required for different commodities to evince the same price-elasticity of supply; (2) the different price-elasticities of supply for a given commodity in time periods of different length (usually increasing length); and (3) other cost changes, i.e., those occurring independently of the variations in the schedule demand for the commodity which produce the price changes which serve as independent variables in the first two problems.

The concept of time-elasticity of supply is useful in explaining the amplitude and duration of individual price fluctuations. The term may be defined as the length of time that is required for a given percentage change in price (or rate of sales) to provoke the same or any other given percentage change in supply (or rate of production). Time-elasticity of supply is "long" or "short" only on a relative basis as the supply of one commodity is compared with another. For instance, for a commodity such as copper, a 10 per cent increase in price may cause a 5 per cent increase in supply within a month. On the other hand the quantity of new houses offered on the market each week may rise only 1 per cent within a month under the same price stimulus and a period of six months may be required for a 5 per cent expansion.

In several earlier sections of this work the concept of normal price was discussed, but little attention was paid to its time frame of reference.[1] This deficiency may now be corrected, at least in part, by examining the different time periods allowed a given producer or an industry to adjust supply to changes in price. When price is assumed to be the independent variable, then the change in quantity supplied, the dependent variable, ordinarily will be larger if a long time is permitted for readjustment of supply conditions than if only a short time is allowed. That is, the elasticity of supply is a function of time as well as of price change and therefore a three-dimensional diagram showing a supply surface would be more realistic than any single two-dimensional curve could be. However, the cumbersomeness of three-dimensional diagrams and three-variable tables suggests the construction of a series of two-variable schedules and curves, each for a different time period. The ones most commonly used are those for the short run, the moderately long run, and the very long run, although different authors use different terminology.

Certain difficulties should be acknowledged at the outset. *First,* the time periods will have different chronological lengths for different commodities, for different firms producing the same good, and even for the same firm producing the same good under different circumstances. This greatly complicates the problem of constructing a realistic schedule for accurate prediction of future relationships. It often leads to confusion through unconscious transference of time

---

[1] See, for instance, Sections 8 and 9 of Chapter 10.

durations from one situation to another, as from agriculture to manufacturing or retailing, or from cases where price competition prevails to cases where such competition does not exist. *Second,* the quantities of a supply schedule are really time *rates* of sale (strictly, of offering for sale). That is, they are quantities per unit of time. This time unit is always shorter, much shorter, than the time period for which the schedule has been constructed. Thus, in the short run, which may cover weeks or months according to the commodity under consideration, the supply quantity in a schedule usually shows the rate of sale per hour or per day. *Third,* the causal relationship does not always run from price to rate of sale. Under the widely prevailing conditions of monopolistic competition where the seller sets his selling price, changes in the rate of sale influence changes in price (and in the rate of production) rather than vice versa. *Fourth,* it is extremely difficult to give precise definitions of different supply-time periods, but the reason for making time distinctions can be made clear without this precision. Nor is it necessary that all writers use the same terms in designating the different intervals if we realize that the concepts are slightly artificial at best. The important thing to emphasize is the need to recognize and make allowance for elapsed time.

### 3. Short-Run Supply Curves.—

The "short run" usually is defined as time long enough to permit increases or decreases in the rate of sale from a given stock of goods on hand which the seller does not have time to alter by purchase or production. It is sometimes called "market time" or simply "time period I." It is best illustrated by reference to agriculture, where seasonal changes or life cycles tend to separate the periods of selling from the periods of producing. In the temperate zone, crops usually are harvested in summer or in autumn. After the harvest period, farmers have a given fixed stock of produce on hand which they may sell at a higher or lower rate depending upon circumstances. One of the determinants is the price offered or obtainable, and its change from recent levels. A second is the urgency of sale, or the seller's need for cash to meet his obligations. A rise in price generally will induce more people to sell their stock than before. But it may cause some to think the price will continue to increase and therefore may lead to a speculative decision to hold back for still higher prices. Much farm produce is sold immediately upon harvesting for whatever it will bring. These sellers leave to speculators and those with storage facilities the problem of guessing which way the price will move in the future.

Those who set the price at which they will sell and then let the demand determine the quantity to be sold operate in a different kind of short run. Merchants, for instance, have customary order periods in which they purchase their inventories and decide upon the price which they think will be most profitable for them to ask when disposing of their goods on hand before the next order period. The price is based upon an expected rate of sale. If subsequent experience shows that sales are slower than expected, the price may be cut. If the rate of sales proves unexpectedly rapid, the price may be raised, but this is not considered good merchandising policy in most cases. Instead, the merchant seeks larger profit by increasing his rate of buying to keep pace with his rate of selling. He is content to make his gains through larger volume. Price increases might antagonize consumers and have a bad effect in the long run.

In the agricultural example which has been described in an earlier chapter as pure competition or cost competition, producers adjust their rates of sale to changes in the price. On the other hand, the merchandising example, which illustrates imperfect competition or price and service competition, shows producers adjusting their asking prices or their order rates to their rates of sale. In both cases the quantity offered at a given price is offered out of a fixed stock on hand and the cumulative totals offered by all persons selling a homogeneous good may be aggregated into a short-run supply curve or schedule. This curve may shift during the short time period whenever the attitudes of sellers change. The shift is basically the same whether it seems to be to the right or to the left as with quantity changes, or upward or downward as with price changes. A *de*crease in the price asked for a given quantity constitutes an *in*crease in schedule supply just as truly as an increase in the quantity offered at a given price.

Past cost of production or cost of purchase tends to be unimportant in setting reservation prices in these short-run cases for one or more of the following reasons: (1) the cost is not known (as often in farming), (2) speculation is a stronger motive than the quest for normal business profit, (3) the seller must accept the prices buyers offer even if they are below cost, (4) there is urgent need for prompt sale (because of need for cash or because the seller cannot store goods profitably), (5) sellers do not expect to be selling the same sort of goods in the same place in the future (random sellers, or cases where the replacement merchandise will differ from the stock on hand), (6) replacement cost is higher or lower than past cost.

Because of the many different situations involved, there is no one typical short-run supply curve. In cases where a uniform price is set by the seller, the curve is a horizontal straight line which may move up or down if the price is changed subsequently because of unexpected changes in the rate of sale. In those cases where the price is determined by the bids and offers of many sellers (pure competition), the collective supply curve usually slopes upward to the right, but any individual supply curve may be either positive in slope, perpendicular, negatively inclined throughout or concave to the price axis, i.e., partly negative and partly positive, as shown in Figure 51.[2]

### FIGURE 51

#### Types of Short-Run Supply Curves

(Most common at left, least common at right)

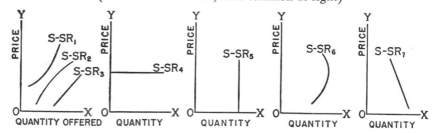

### 4. Moderately Long-Run Supply Curves.

—The moderately long-run time period usually is defined as long enough to permit expansion of production by the use of additional variable factors but not long enough to permit an increase in fixed factors. Sometimes it is called "long run," "time period II," "intermediate," or even "short run" (in cases where time period I is called "market time"). These alternative definitions are not at all precise if only because there is no hard and fast line dividing variable and fixed factors. However, this vagueness makes little difference if the main purpose is kept in mind, which is to show how an increase or decrease in production may be influenced by the relationship between price and cost.

If we make the same assumptions that were used in Section 10 of Chapter 8, that marginal and average costs can be determined, are known by the seller, and are used by him to regulate his output, then his supply curve will approximate his marginal cost curve in this time period. According to the formal analysis of selling under conditions of pure competition, he will maximize his profit by keeping $MC = MR = AR =$ Price. Since marginal cost rises with an expansion

---

[2] The negative slope which appears in the last two supply curves is decidedly unusual. However, it seems to occur in the market for some types of labor as wage rates rise. Case 5 may occur in stock markets when falling prices bring out stop-loss orders.

in quantity produced, the cost figures in the marginal cost schedule or on an $MC$ curve may be read as equivalent to price figures, so that the most profitable output can be read directly from that schedule or curve.

On the other hand, if we abandon the assumptions of pure competition, and shift our attention to the problem of a price-setter, there is no simple relationship between price and marginal cost. Maximum profit comes at that output which equates $MC$ and $MR$, but $MR$ is not equal to $AR =$ Price. Furthermore, under these conditions of monopolistic competition the increase in demand, as explained above, is not immediately reflected in an increase in price, but rather in an increase in the rate of sales, or sales orders, at the price currently quoted by the seller. (See Figure 54.)

In either case, whether price setting or price acceptance is the policy of the seller, he ordinarily will increase output with an increase in demand. The speed with which this can be done depends upon how quickly he can do two things: (1) procure the necessary additional variable factors of production and (2) combine them in the production process to create that which buyers want, whether it be services, products of a certain form, or goods at a certain time or place. For small increases in output, say 5 to 10 per cent, the factor problem usually is not difficult, although there are exceptions. Extra materials generally can be furnished upon demand from suppliers' inventories. The time required is that of securing delivery and depends chiefly on the distance the goods must move. Occasionally transportation bottlenecks may impede delivery, or problems of financing the transaction may create delay.

In wartime, the chief problem of supply expansion often is that of securing the necessary priority or allocation order from a government agency. In peacetime, sellers of production goods sometimes put their customers under quotas and refuse to sell them more than a fixed amount, so that if a certain buyer wishes to expand his output he may have to spend some time getting his quota raised, finding alternative sources of supply, or substituting other raw materials. The restrictive practices of international cartels might be cited for illustration, and collusive monopolies in this country have also restricted sales, though perhaps less openly. When Seller B does not have enough merchandise in stock to meet the increased demands of Buyer A who wishes to expand output, B must expand his own production before A can be supplied (unless the buyer can purchase elsewhere). This requires more time, but introduces no new problems in supply-elasticity, so we can return to the first firm, A, and continue with the analysis by considering the problems he may meet when trying to expand output.

Additional labor, for instance, usually can be obtained in either of two ways: (1) by hiring new workers or (2) by inducing old employees to work overtime. The latter is the quicker of the two methods though often the more expensive. If no additional workers can be recruited locally, delay may be caused by having to bring in workers from more distant localities. If they are hired away from rival firms, the cost rises sharply, since an increase in wages usually must be shared with veteran employees too. Sometimes closed shop agreements with closed unions impede expansion of output. The long apprenticeship period required by certain unions furnishes another instance where the supply of a factor cannot be increased rapidly.

Enough has been said to indicate that the responsiveness of supply to an increase in demand has different time dimensions under different circumstances even when the problem is merely one of securing additional variable factors of production. Usually the quicker an expansion is effected, the more it will cost the expanding firm and therefore the larger must be the expected profit inducement. The increase in price or rate of sale needed to bring forth a certain increase in rate

TIME-ELASTICITY OF SUPPLY WHEN PRICE INCREASES

|  | Base Price and Increase | Quantity Produced After | |
|---|---|---|---|
|  |  | One Month | Two Months |
| Original............... | 50¢ | 1,000 | 1,000 Normal rate |
| Increased to........... | 60¢ | 1,200 | 1,400 |
| Increased to........... | 70¢ | 1,500 | 1,800 |

TIME-ELASTICITY OF SUPPLY WHEN RATE OF SALES INCREASES

|  | Base Rate of Sales and Increase (Price is 50¢) | Quantity Produced After | |
|---|---|---|---|
|  |  | One Month | Two Months |
| Normal............... | 1,000 | 1,000 | 1,000 No inventory change |
| Increased to........... | 1,200 | 1,100 | 1,200 Inventory down, then constant |
| Increased to........... | 1,500 | 1,250 | 1,400 Inventory down even after two months |

of production cannot be predicted without a close scrutiny of the particular firm or industry being analyzed and of the economic environment in which that industry operates. In the "moderately long-run" time period under consideration hypothetical supply schedules should specify in some way the length of time presumed to elapse between the causative change in demand and the resultant change in supply.

These two hypothetical supply schedules show only two of many possible situations. The second schedule assumes that the price remains constant at 50 cents throughout, which would be likely to happen only if unit costs did not rise appreciably (as when 1,500 units are not more than capacity operation and unit factor prices do not increase with the firm's necessary expansion in demand for them). Neither schedule looks far enough ahead to answer questions about probable entry of competitors and possible "overproduction" which, particularly in the first case, might force the price down in some future month not shown here.

**5. Directional Supply-Elasticity.**—Finally, we should note that these are one-directional schedules; they tell what might happen to supply if the demand for the product were to rise. That is, if the price having once risen to 70 cents, should decline to 60 cents and then to 50 cents, there is little likelihood that the supply would shrink at the same time rate at which it expanded. It usually takes much less time to lay off workers than to recruit them, to decrease orders for materials than to increase them. Exceptions may be found in the case of long-term contracts which cannot be cancelled quickly. And if new firms enter an industry

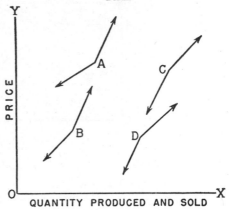

FIGURE 52

MODERATELY LONG-RUN SUPPLY CURVES MOVING FROM GIVEN PRICE IN GIVEN TIME

under the lure of large profits, they leave it much more slowly when prices and profits fall.

Therefore, the above schedules cannot be drawn into curves unless arrows are attached to indicate the direction of change in the independent variable (price or rate of sales). If such curves are to be used at all in graphic explanation of how supply fluctuates, they must all start from an assumed given price and move either up or down from it. This will give a "broken back" curve something like those in the accompanying diagram, but there will have to be a different curve for each hypothetical starting price (or rate of sale). Curves *A* and *B* of Figure 52 are probably the most common type for manufactured raw materials, i.e., less elastic above starting price than below it, while curves *C* and *D* reveal agricultural commodities (if the time period is extended to at least one year).

**6. Two Types of Moderately Long-Run Supply Curves: Industry Marginal Cost Curve or Successive Price Points.**—The moderately long-run supply curve may be of two types. The first is the collective marginal cost curve explained at the beginning of Section 4.

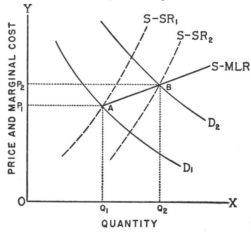

FIGURE 53

MODERATELY LONG-RUN SUPPLY CURVE

I. The Equilibrium Type Derived from the Marginal Costs of an Industry or a Representative Firm

The second is the line connecting two short-run price-quantity points. The first shows what would happen if the market price were always the "equilibrium price" under pure competition as described in Chapter 7, Section 11. The second is more realistic. It may be drawn for any type of market supply, whether hypothetical pure competition or any one of the many kinds of monopolistic competition. It should be distinguished, however, from a line connecting two price-quantity situations in the short-run time period or in the very long run. That is, the quantity increase from the first price to the second comes from new production, not from stock as in the short run, nor from increased capacity as in the very long run.

The *MLR* supply curve based on marginal cost will slope upward to the right. This is true whether it depicts the collective marginal costs of a group of firms or Marshall's "representative firm." One may say also that this type of curve will not be as steep as an *SR* curve for the same industry. The *MLR* supply curve is more elastic than the *SR* curves (Figure 53).

The second type of *MLR* supply curve may slope upward, downward, or move horizontally. The most common situation is that of a seller offering his goods at a fixed price. His *SR* supply curve is horizontal at that price as in Figure 54. His *MLR* supply curve may be identical with it for moderate increases in the rate of sales. This is the case with most manufacturers and retailers. In addition to

FIGURE 54

MODERATELY LONG-RUN SUPPLY CURVE

II. Derived from Successive Short-Run Points
When Both *SR* and *MLR* Prices Are Constant

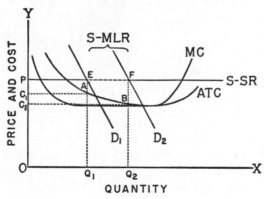

their fixed price policy which underlies this argument, most of them have constant or nearly constant marginal costs. The following diagram illustrates the situation.

Figure 54 may be interpreted as follows. Demand increases from $D_1$ to $D_2$. (Both of these demand curves are *AR* curves. No *MR* curve is shown because there is no need to find a hypothetical maximum profit price, as was the case in Figure 33.) Sales at price $P$ rise from $Q_1$ to $Q_2$, determined by points $E$ and $F$. The output is adjusted to the rate of sales. Therefore, average total cost declines from $C_1$ to $C_2$ determined by points $A$ and $B$. Marginal cost may be ignored since it does not constitute a supply curve nor here influence price.

A second possibility considers that the price does change as output expands. This is most common with goods which are relatively homogeneous, such as agricultural products and industrial raw materials. The price may rise or fall, as shown in the two parts of Figure 55. One must note carefully that Figure 55A is not the same as

FIGURE 55

MODERATELY LONG-RUN SUPPLY CURVE

III. Derived from Successive Short-Run Points
When $S$-$SR$ Rising

A. *MLR* price rising                                B. *MLR* price falling

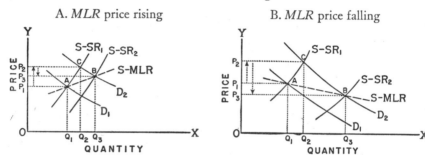

other figures which it resembles. In Figure 53, for instance, the *MLR* supply curve is drawn as a solid line to indicate that it determines both points $A$ and $B$. In Figure 55A, the *SR* supply curves are decisive and the *MLR* curve is dotted to indicate that it is derived from $A$ and $B$. Similarly, Figure 55 should not be confused with very long-run supply curves of increasing or decreasing cost. The latter could be drawn in the same way, but the line connecting $A$ and $B$ would be given in advance as equilibrium points on a curve of increasing or decreasing average total cost for a representative firm whose capacity was increased. This will be explained below in Sections 7 and 8.

A diagram like Figure 55 may also be used to explain why prices may rise in the short run under the impact of increased demand, but fall in the long run. The short-run price rise from $P_1$ to $P_2$ stimulates output expansion in the moderately long run. This causes a new short-run supply curve to appear at $S$-$SR_2$. This curve intersects $D_2$ at $B$ instead of $C$ and the price falls accordingly to $P_3$. The degree to which $P_3$ falls below $P_2$ may be slight, as in 55A, or large as in 55B. An intermediate position is also possible in which $P_3$ is below $P_2$ but is equal to $P_1$ (not shown in Figure 55).

### 7. Very Long-Run Supply Curves of Representative Firms.—

In certain situations a third period of supply time may be distinguished in relation to capacity changes of representative firms. This is called variously "very long run," "time period III," or simply "long run," and is defined as time long enough to increase the quantity of the "fixed factors" employed, i.e., the factors which are considered as fixed in the "moderately long run." All factors become variable, strictly speaking. The vagueness of this definition is apparent, and the borderline between the two long-run time periods and the two groups of variables is extremely hazy. However, it is reasonable to make a general distinction between direct labor and materials on the one hand and machines, floor space, land, or executive personnel on the other.

The usual reason for additional investment in the latter is that the intensity of demand is great enough to push output beyond "capacity," i.e., past the point of lowest average total unit cost (see Chapter 9, Section 13). Further expansion may be profitable even in the face of rising costs if the price exceeds average cost at that point, but before long the existing facilities will be overtaxed and marginal costs will rise sharply. If output is driven that far, costs can be reduced by increasing some of the "fixed factors." The farmer will buy or rent more land; the manufacturer will get more machinery or floor space; the middleman will get more storage or display room. In each case the effect will be to restore more efficient relationships between the factors of production and thus to lower the unit cost of production. This is the significant result, and the fact that such additions usually take a longer time than is required to get more labor and materials is merely incidental. When a firm is operating at less than capacity and an increase in demand causes it to expand output toward but not beyond capacity, there never will be any "very long-run" situation no matter how long one may wait for supply adjustment. Where capacity is reached and exceeded, the changes described as occurring in the "very long run" follow those associated with the "moderately long run."

The time required for making additions to fixed capital depends upon the nature of those additions and the supply conditions prevailing in the market. Orders for additional machinery may be met from supplier's stocks on hand or the machinery may have to be built, particularly if it is of special design. New floor space may be rented or purchased if available, or constructed if not, provided that construction materials and labor can be obtained. Land may also be purchased or rented. Sometimes it is logical to think of writing a contract with a new executive or research expert as resembling the addition of a "fixed factor" or making a "very long-run" investment. Such men are not always readily obtainable.

It should also be noted that the motives and occasions for securing additional fixed factors are not confined to demand increases which

FIGURE 56

VERY LONG-RUN SUPPLY CURVE OF INCREASING COST
DERIVED FROM NADIRS OF SUCCESSIVE *ATC* CURVES

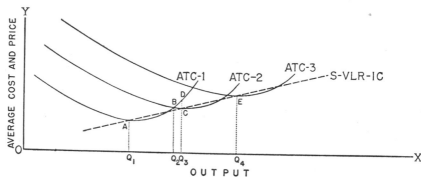

already have raised output beyond capacity. Purchases may be made in anticipation of such an eventuality either because it is thought impending in the near future or merely because there happens to occur a "good opportunity" to obtain land, or a building, or an executive. Sometimes the expansion will be initiated as a method of increasing sales, rather than as a result of such increases. This occurs when the management of a firm decides to seek lower costs through production on a larger scale, with the ultimate objective of expanding sales through the lower prices made possible by the reduced costs. Such is the traditional history of the Ford Motor Company in the days of the "Model T."

The degree to which costs may be lowered by an expansion of fixed assets will of course vary from firm to firm and industry to industry. Three possibilities are frequently discussed in economic literature: higher, lower, or constant average total costs. All *comparisons are made at successive capacity operating rates*, i.e., at the lowest possible average total cost under the larger capacity figure as compared with the smaller. These have been described by different phrases such as "increasing cost," "decreasing cost," and "constant cost," or "diminishing returns," "increasing returns," and "constant returns." In the case of "increasing cost" or "diminishing returns," the advantage of expansion lies in the fact that production with the smaller capacity has been pushed so far past the point of lowest average total cost that the unit costs prevailing before expansion are higher than those prevailing afterwards, even though the $ATC$ at capacity in the second situation is higher than in the first. This usually is shown by a diagram of successive $ATC$ curves such as in Figure 56.

When (in the moderately long-run time period) production expands beyond the capacity operation quantity $Q_1$ of the original $ATC$-1 curve, unit costs begin to rise. When they exceed the cost $(Q_2B)$ shown at output $Q_2$, it becomes profitable to expand facilities (in the very long run) so that a new unit cost curve is obtained like $ATC$-2.[3] The capacity operation point, $C$, on this curve has a higher $ATC$ than the capacity operation point, $A$, on $ATC$-1. But $Q_3C$ is much less than the cost, $Q_3D$, which would have been incurred if the expanded use of factors had been limited to those associated with the moderately long run instead of the expanded (durable) facilities usually associated with very long-run changes. Similar sequences of $ATC$ curves might be used to derive $S$-$VLR$ (Supply—Very Long Run) curves of constant cost and of decreasing cost (see Figure 57 below and also Figure 55A above).

A few cautions must be given about the nature and usefulness of very long-run supply curves. In the first place, these curves are not reversible; they must be read always from left to right and never backward. A contracting demand rarely will cause disposal of portions of the fixed plant, and even in the occasional cases where this does happen, the contraction will follow a different pattern from the expansion. In the second place, the successive $ATC$ curves must be considered either prototypes of all the firms in the field (to have them all the same size would be most logical) or composite curves for the industry as a whole. This assumption also requires that "normal profits" be included as a cost of production and, of course, that there be no restraint on competition among the firms involved. Thirdly, the $S$-$VLR$ curves differ fundamentally from other supply curves in that the independent variable is not price, but rather is the scale of capacity production which itself changes because of the postulated increase in schedule demand. Enlarging output capacity brings either

---

[3] The further assumption of free entry of competitors is necessary, because otherwise rising costs could be offset by increased prices.

rising, falling, or constant points of minimum average total cost and these nadirs in turn establish the trend of normal price. Fourthly, a rising $S$-$VLR$-$IC$ curve is not the same as a rising $S$-$MLR$ curve. The rising costs of the latter usually are due to a more intensive use of a given fixed factor. Inferior grades of the factor may be used in some firms and superior grades in others, but in each case the quantity used must be held constant. The rising costs of the very long-run supply curves, on the other hand, are due to rising minimum $ATC$ points on successive moderately long-run supply curves when the scale of production is increased by expanding a fixed factor as well as the variable factors.

Finally, if a very long time actually does elapse between the successive changes in the production capacity of typical firms, then *other changes* are likely to occur which also will affect costs. For instance, soil may become exhausted or eroded, mineral deposits may become depleted, stands of virgin timber may be cut, etc. The cost of labor or industrial materials may rise so that the chief factor causing higher $ATC$ points is a rise in the general price level, not a change in scale of production. On the other hand, improvements in technology may so reduce the cost of production as to offset all these forces and the price of goods in "increasing cost" industries may decline historically. This argument about the influence of historical change also applies in situations where decreasing costs otherwise would exist. Expanding the scale of production reduces unit costs, but this reduction is more than offset by the rise in such costs as those enumerated in the preceding paragraph. As a result the historical trend in prices is upwards, not downwards. The long-term trend of product prices in an industry is never sufficient evidence to establish with certainty whether that industry produces under increasing, decreasing, or constant costs. These classic categories belong to a static world of arbitrary assumptions, not to the dynamic world of real life where other cost changes may occur to offset them.

**8. Very Long-Run Supply Curves as Planning Curves.**—A curve comparable to the very long-run supply curve of decreasing cost has been used for other purposes than historical analysis or prediction. Some have used it for a "planning curve" to indicate how an enterpriser might reach a decision in calculating how big a plant to build. Obviously he would want to build the one which would yield him the most profit. If he contemplates producing a standardized product under conditions of pure competition, which does not happen very often in modern times, he will want the lowest possible *ATC*. This can be determined if he knows the *ATC* curves of successive plant capacities as shown for a hypothetical instance in Figure 57 where *ATC*-3 is the *MLR* curve with the lowest nadir.

The decline in the *S-VLR* curve up to output *Q* may be attributed to the economies of large-scale production, while beyond *Q* the diseconomies of bureaucratic management might increase sufficiently to

### FIGURE 57

Planning the Optimum-Sized Plant
by Using a Very Long-Run Supply Curve
Based on a Succession of *ATC* Curves

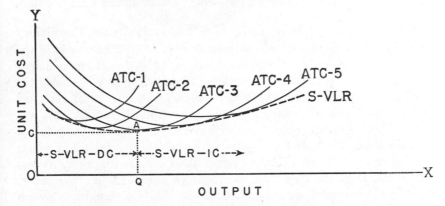

overcome additional production economies and therefore the stage of increasing costs would be reached. Each successive *ATC* curve of the moderately long-run period begins at a higher point because of the increased investment in plant capacity.

A diagram of the kind shown in Figure 57 has an extremely limited applicability at best. Most enterprisers lack sufficient knowledge of probable costs to do more than guess at a sequence of *ATC* curves like those drawn above. The actual capacity of the plant often is frozen by the size of one important fixed factor which happens to be available in a certain amount, such as a factory site or a power unit.[4]

---

[4] If fixed factors could be obtained freely in any desired magnitude, the *ATC* curves of the *MLR* all would be so close together that their nadirs would merge and become identical with the *ATC* curve of the *VLR*. The latter curve, if then considered a supply curve in the very long run, would indicate that all factors were variable and that there was no lumpiness in any of them, i.e., that there were no "fixed" factors, but all were perfectly divisible. A curve could be drawn which would be marginal to such an *ATC* curve, but it would have little practical value, since some factors always are lumpy in actual experience and the most profitable output rate is calculated upon the basis of more or less intensive use of these factors, i.e., upon the *MC* curve of the moderately long run.

Furthermore, practically all manufactured products are sold under one or another type of monopolistic competition, not pure competition as implied in the above analysis. That is, the quantity sold is limited on the one hand by the price fixed by the seller, by his trade association, or by the leader he is following, and on the other hand by the efforts of his own sales force. Hence, the most desirable capacity of the planned production unit will be determined more by the estimated sales volume than by the estimated costs. This is also true for much planning in the field of wholesaling or retailing. Finally, most planning of optimum capacity is based upon questions of changes in present facilities. It does not start from scratch, and the disposal of existing plant often will be an important factor in the final decision.

**9. The Apparent Inevitability of Monopoly Under Conditions of Decreasing Cost.**—A second use of $S$-$VLR$-$DC$ curves is in the problem of monopoly. Economists have argued that if the manager of a given firm knows that expanding plant capacity will enable the firm to reduce unit costs, he will be induced to undertake such expansion (assuming he can get the requisite capital funds). This will permit the firm to cut prices and to undersell competitors who do not expand as rapidly.[5] If the total quantity which buyers will purchase at a price equal to or slightly greater than $OC$ in Figure 57 is less than $OQ$, then the first firm can achieve a substantive monopoly. Such is the case with most public utilities. If, however, buyers want considerably more than $OQ$ at such prices, the expanding firm will experience increasing costs and firms with smaller capacity can meet its prices by equalling its costs. This explains why expanding demand in many industries has been followed by an increase in the number of firms rather than in the expansion of existing firms. The small newcomers can compete successfully with the larger old firms.

Several other obstacles to the achievement of monopoly through the economies of scale may be mentioned. One is the rise in shipping costs as additional customers are sought at greater distances and across possible tariff walls or other politico-economic barriers. There is also the ever-present possibility that the expanding firm will choose to be content with less than the whole market and will utilize its reduced costs as a method of expanding unit profit rather than cutting prices. Or the competing firms might get together at some stage in

---

[5] Note the inversion of cause and effect in this approach. Cost changes cause price changes instead of vice versa; and price-competition is antithetical to the cost-competition (pure competition) situation assumed to underlie the first $S$-$VLR$ curves.

the game and agree upon price maintenance or a division of sales territory.

**10. Summary of Possible Cost Reasons for the Downward Price Trend of a Commodity.**—It generally is argued that the historical trend downward in the prices of certain commodities (such as automobiles) can be explained best in terms of the long-run decreasing costs of representative firms, as described in Section 7. Actually, there are many possible reasons for decreasing cost. A check list such as the following may be useful.

1. In the *moderately long run,* when the major factors are held fixed and there is an expanding demand for A:
   (a) Increasing physical returns (declining $AVC$) may occur as the use of more of the variable factors makes a more efficient combination of the factors.
   (b) The total cost of the fixed factors will be spread over an increasing number of units (declining $AFC$).
   (This group of causes ordinarily would not be relevant, since the declining $ATC$ which is the joint result of these two is rarely the basis for decisions to decrease prices.)

2. In the *very long run,* when all factors are variable and there is an expanding demand for A:
   (a) Economies of large scale production may occur because of:
       (1) "Internal economies." These include all those reductions in cost which are made possible by increased division of labor, use of more and better machines, reduced waste, quantity purchase discounts, cheaper selling costs, etc.
       (2) "External economies." These include particularly those reductions in the cost of goods bought which result from their being produced in larger volume by a given industry to meet the expanding demands of the buying firm (or industry). Or satellite supply and service industries may develop.
   (These causes are the most significant ones underlying the downward sloping portion of the $S\text{-}VLR$ curves. They are usually less important for price trends over a period of several decades than No. 3 below.)

3. Efficiency rises because of inventions which reduce costs by reducing the total necessary quantity of labor, capital, equipment, or land.

(a) Improved tools or machines for the harnessing of mechanical power.

(b) New products, such as chemicals, more productive than those formerly available.

(c) New processes or ways of combining factors.

(Inventions have no necessary time pattern. They may occur at any time and be introduced at any time. If they represent inexpensive changes in the variable factors, they will be substituted in the $MLR$. If the inventions affect fixed equipment and are expensive, time must be allowed for accumulating the necessary funds (unless they can be borrowed). This may involve waiting until existing equipment is worn out and depreciation funds collected, which would indicate the appropriateness of association with the $VLR$. Again it should be stressed that $MLR$ and $VLR,$ although useful concepts, are incapable of precise definition.)

4. Decreased cost of buying factors of production, caused by:

(a) All of the above possible reasons for the decreased cost of producing any good.

(b) Other reasons for reduced factor prices than those included thus far in this cost-side approach (see Section 5, Chapter 16).

(c) Increasing supply of factors arising from causes other than increased demand for them, such as extensive immigration forcing down the wage rate.

(d) Declining demand for factors, such as that resulting from cyclical recession or a secular decrease in the price level.

5. Fortuitous improvement occurs in the quality of free goods essential to production. (Limited chiefly to agriculture where weather conditions are vitally important.)

In the above outline, points 1 and 2 assume that the initial cause of the decline in cost is an increasing demand for a certain product. The cost reductions mentioned under points 3, 4, and 5 require no such assumption, although certain demand changes are implicit in 4-d. These other possibilities complicate the problem of considering an $S$-$VLR$ curve as one existing through a period of time. Any one or more of them may exert their influence to change the price-quantity relationship of such a curve before sufficient time has elapsed for small-scale fixed factors to be replaced by large-scale factors. To avoid this possibility by having recourse to *ceteris paribus* is to run the danger of forgetting forces of extreme importance in explaining history or predicting future developments. There is also the danger of confusing the production unit with the administrative unit, as in business combinations which may bring together two or more units producing the same thing so as to increase total output without affecting the scale of production in the usual sense.

**11. Summary of Possible Cost Reasons for the Upward Price Trend of a Commodity.**—The increase in the price of certain articles over a period of years also can be explained in part by a cost-side approach. Many items in the following outline of causes of increasing cost, historically considered, parallel those for decreasing cost, but there are significant omissions and additions.

1. In the *moderately long run;* expanding demand for A:
   (a) Decreasing physical returns as output is expanded past the point of diminishing average returns.
   (Because of the inability to expand certain fixed factors, such as land sites, and the difficulties of entry, the *MLR* period may be prolonged considerably both in quantitative and temporal extent.)

2. In the *very long run;* expanding demand for A:
   (a) Internal diseconomies such as inflexibility, lack of employee interest, complex rule-books, etc.
   (b) External diseconomies resulting from the internal diseconomies forced on others by expansion of A.
   (This group of causes is not as significant as under decreasing cost, and is generally less important than point 1, above.)

3. Efficiency falls, because
   (a) Workers' morale declines.
   (b) Machines wear out.
   (c) Management becomes less capable or energetic.

4. Increasing cost of factors used in making A:
   (a) Diseconomies of suppliers when production expands under stimulus of other demand than that from makers of A.
   (b) Increased total demand for factors rigidly fixed in supply.
   (c) Decreasing supply of certain factors, such as exhaustible natural resources.
   (d) Increased bargaining strength of suppliers, such as union labor; or more competition among buyers.
   (e) Other non-cost reasons for increasing prices, particularly cyclical booms and secular uptrends in prices, tariff changes, or property taxes.

5. Fortuitous decline occurs in the quality of free goods (poor weather) or of certain raw materials forcing substitution of inferior ingredients, as in wartime.

**12. Summary of Economic Principles Governing Cost Changes Which Influence Price.**—When time is allowed for supply and cost to become adjusted to those changes in price which result from an increase in schedule demand, the basic price determinants alter. Present price becomes a long-run determinant of future price. The first change is a rise in market price. This permits an increase in marginal cost in the moderately long run. This may be followed by an expansion in the production capacity of most of the firms in the industry so that the nadirs of their average total cost curves change. Whether these nadirs rise, fall, or remain constant depends upon the balance between the economies and diseconomies, both internal and external, of increasing plant capacity. The argument is presented best through using the concept of a representative firm and presupposing pure competition. Very long-run cost and supply curves must be read from left to right; they are not reversible. The same is true, although less significantly, for moderately long-run supply curves.

During the time which must elapse for the foregoing adjustments to occur, other cost-influencing changes are almost inevitable. Therefore, the upward or downward trend of individual prices should be described as a function also of such things as changed prices of the factors used, inventions, etc. Some variables push prices upward, some downwards, and the net result may obscure the fact that opposing forces were at work. Occasionally the forces are balanced so evenly that constant cost may occur for a while and the price may remain relatively stable.

# Chapter 14

## INDIVIDUAL PRICE FLUCTUATIONS

**1. Introduction.**—The previous chapter considered chiefly long-run trends in prices, particularly as they are based upon changes in cost. This involved an explanation of the manner in which increases in schedule demand alter the average total cost curve in the very long run. Intermediate price changes also were considered, but the major emphasis was upon the trend of normal prices in the face of rising demand under conditions of pure competition. The present chapter is not so narrow in its focus. It includes a discussion of both short-run and long-run price changes in individual prices under conditions of declining demand. Institutional changes and monopolistic situations are considered. Both upward and downward deviations from normal price are analyzed and their implications examined. But the basic question remains the same, "How can individual price fluctuations be explained in the economy in which we live?" The answer again is approached chiefly from the supply side.

Specific questions follow:

1. What is the effect of falling demand upon price?
    A. When sellers can adjust output but must accept price?
    B. When sellers can adjust both output and price?
    C. When firm exit occurs?
2. Why do current prices of commodities deviate from normal prices?
    A. When prices rise?
    B. When prices fall?
    C. When supply changes suddenly?
3. What diagrams show the different supply-reaction situations?

**2. Effects of Falling Demand When Sellers Can Adjust Output but Must Accept Price.**—Most of the discussion of the time-elasticity of supply in Chapter 13 was based upon the assumption that the initiating force was an increase in schedule demand manifest in a heightened price. But what are the probable developments if demand falls, and why? The answers can be given best by considering separately the supply conditions likely to exist under price acceptance and those under price adjustment.

Assume first that the manager of the individual producing unit has to accept the going market price and that he has been operating at his most profitable output under that price. Then he will make more profit by reducing output as the price falls than by continuing to produce at the former rate. If he knows his cost schedules, he can calculate the most profitable output for any price by finding the rate at which marginal cost equals market price. This is logically true with either a moderately long-run or a very long-run $MC$ curve. But this apparently simple solution in formal analysis requires careful examination and qualification.

The marginal cost curve that prevails in a period of contraction may be based on certain variables which do not appear at the same stage in the expansion of production or change at a different rate. Instead of being concerned with additional costs, the manager has to calculate "subtractional" costs. Some costs must be incurred anyway, others may be reduced or eliminated by decreasing output. These two groups usually are called fixed costs and variable costs, but the content of each category will differ with the direction of the change in output, not to mention also the magnitude of the change and the time allowed for adjustments to occur. (Refer also to Chapter 13, Section 7.)

If output is to be reduced, obviously there will be reductions in outlays for labor and materials. There is, however, the possibility that certain labor contracts cannot be broken and wages must be paid even if the employee is not working. Such costs are not subtractional unless the demand remains shrunken until after the contracts expire. Somewhat the same situation is faced when managers are reluctant to drop skilled and experienced workers who have no contract claim, but whose replacement would be very difficult when expansion again became desirable. Materials may be purchased on contracts which still have weeks or months to run and in addition sizable inventories may have been accumulated at the plant. In the latter case the only saving from not using materials already purchased would be the salvage value of the materials when sold to some one else. A third type of subtractional cost would be the maintenance and upkeep on plant and equipment which is saved when these are not paid. Fourth, wear and tear depreciates durable capital goods even when maintenance and repair expenditures are made as they become necessary. This is physical depreciation as opposed to obsolescence. The latter will occur whether the machinery is being used or not. Fifth, in some cases a royalty payment may be avoided or reduced by curtailing operations.

When all of these subtractional costs which are appropriate in a given case are deducted from total cost at the going rate, a schedule of total costs at lesser rates may be constructed and a directional marginal cost schedule or curve may be derived therefrom for the moderately long-run period. This schedule is the one which should guide a manager who calculates his costs accurately and carefully so that he may quickly adjust his output to changes in demand as shown by variations in the price. A manager of this type probably would be hard to find, particularly in agriculture, where conditions of pure competition are approached most often. In addition to the difficulty of rapid and precise adjustment in output to the figure which the schedules or curves indicate would maximize profit, there is also the problem of price expectations discussed above in Section 6 of Chapter 10. A mere fall in price usually is not enough to provoke a changed output, but rather an expectation of a future price low enough for a time sufficiently long to warrant the trouble and inconvenience of seeking to save money by curtailing production.

Other conditions which may retard or discourage output reduction in the face of lower prices include (1) the possibility that falling profits may stimulate inventive efforts and produce successful cost reductions which were not forthcoming when prompted by the mere hope for gain. (2) Reduced prices may force out marginal firms which cannot stand losses or which prefer to shift to some other line. This eases the pressure on the remaining firms by reducing total supply and thus lessens the price decline. (3) If the owner-manager can substitute more of his own labor for that formerly hired, he can reduce out-of-pocket cost without reducing output, although this possibility is significant only in small enterprises. (4) Some small-scale producers also have tried to offset falling prices by increasing their own efforts so as to get *greater* total output, hoping that total revenue will not diminish even though prices have fallen. (5) If the owner-manager has no better alternative use of his time and resources (very often true in farming), he may continue to plant as much or make as much as before, in the hope that the future will not be as black as present prospects may indicate.

### 3. Effects of Falling Demand When Sellers Can Adjust Both Output and Price.—When a seller sets his own price and demand falls subsequently, he will experience a decline in his rate of sales. He ordinarily will curtail production as a result, rather than to continue and to accumulate inventory, but his decision again will be

affected by some of the exceptions noted in the preceding section such as long-time contracts for the purchase of labor or materials, large raw material stock piles, ignorance of precise costs, and future sales expectations.

The basic questions are, "Will he cut his price? And by what guide?" The answer must be that those who set their own prices generally do not change them as often in responses to changes in demand as price acceptors change their output. The $MC = MR$ equilibrium formula may be applied if data are known for any given demand and cost schedules, but when demand schedules shift, prices usually are not altered until demand has changed considerably. This is particularly true for reduced demand where the diminished output which results is often produced at higher unit costs than before and cost data have to be understood pretty well before prices will be cut "to reduce losses." They are more apt to be increased. As a matter of fact, there is usually great uncertainty about the exact elasticity of demand schedules, particularly new ones, and the tendency among price setters is to assume greater inelasticity than actually exists. Price setting is always something of an experiment, and the temperament of the manager may have more to do with price policy in the face of declining demand than any analysis of maximum profit positions.

In the case where the seller fixes his price in concert with other sellers, additional deterrents to price-cutting are present when sales diminish. If the decline in the sales of one firm is the result of its failure to meet sales competition by other firms, the weaker firm obviously will not succeed in getting the others to agree to a general cut in prices. It may break away from the group and try price-cutting independently, but is not likely to do so until all other avenues of relief have been exhausted. The fear of retaliatory action and ostracism also may prove an important deterrent. If, on the other hand, the entire group is suffering a decline in demand for its product, the price is more apt to break when some major firm seeks to get the jump on its competitors, but even so price agreements usually increase price rigidity and delay price-cutting.

Since one purpose of price setting is to avoid those fluctuations in price which result from changing demand when goods are offered for sale regardless of price, there is no necessary connection between demand variations and market price. Therefore, the comments about the best relation between demand, sales, and cost, which received attention in the analysis of the effects of shrinking demand under conditions of pure competition, are largely irrelevant here. However, a distinction should be made between those situations in which there is active price competition and those in which there is not. In the former case a decline in demand often is followed rather quickly by a price cut, but not in the latter case where tacit or implicit price agreements are the rule.

Another factor which influences the rapidity with which monopolistic price adjustments are made in response to a fall in demand is the margin of price above average total cost when that total includes all explicit and imputed outlays except those to the owner for his services of labor, land, or capital. If this margin is large at any given volume of sales, a considerable drop in sales may occur without causing the increased overhead costs per unit to rise sufficiently to wipe out the profit margin entirely. The immediate loss from price reductions plus the difficulties of raising prices in the future usually discourages even those price cuts which can be demonstrated to be beneficial. The history of many large firms during the 1929–1939 depression reveals numerous instances of price rigidity in the face of considerable declines in sales. Most of these firms made money throughout the depression or in all except one or two years, thus indicating the probability that prices had been set so as to yield a very large margin of profit in normal times.[1]

**4. Effects of Falling Demand on Price Through Firm Exit.—** Under pure competition the entry or exit of a single firm cannot influence the price, but if enough firms are driven out of producing commodity A by a fall in the demand for it, an appreciable reduction will occur in schedule supply via exits and the price may rise again. Or the rate of price decline may be retarded, assuming that demand continues to fall, as in the case of goods rendered technologically obsolete by a new invention (cf. natural camphor giving way to synthetic). Under monopolistic competition the exit of a single firm may or may not affect the price, depending for instance upon the degree of price competition that exists, the number of firms in the competing group, the cost curves of the survivors, and the competitive distance between the differentiated good produced by the withdrawing firm and the substitutes offered by rivals (cf. electric refrigerators displacing iceboxes).

Even though the impact of falling demand upon price via firm exit is not subject to generalization in any sweeping fashion, the relation between demand and firm exit is worthy of review. Since falling de-

---

[1] The depression also fostered economies which undoubtedly helped to maintain profits by holding down the rise in $ATC$ when sales declined, but these are not sufficient explanation.

mand implies a decline in either price or sales, it also may be linked
with those reductions which come through price competition, thus
combining the analysis of conditions under the two general types:
pure competition and monopolistic competition. Firm exit may be
either voluntary or involuntary. It may involve either temporary or
permanent cessation of production. Voluntary exit may occur for a
number of different reasons including prospective bankruptcy, dis-
couragement, physical incapacity of owner-manager, or visions of
greener pastures elsewhere. Involuntary exit is the result of inability
to meet demands of creditors, who ask the court to intervene and
appoint a receiver to protect their interests. This may lead to re-
organization of the firm with a scaling-down of fixed charges or to
a dissolution of the enterprise and sale of its assets, usually in segments. Only in the latter case does genuine exit exist in the sense
that a curtailment of supply is an almost inevitable outcome.

A firm facing a declining demand or engaging in price competition
may continue in business temporarily even though its selling price
does not cover its average total costs. It will postpone paying any
costs that it can, such as by reducing the outlay on maintenance or
stalling off demands of creditors. Individual circumstances will determine the payments which can be postponed most easily, but bondholders, landlords, and even tax-collectors are frequent victims. The
firm will, of course, do its best to introduce cost-reducing innovations wherever possible, even to the extent of bargaining more
severely with workers and with others from whom it buys goods
and services.

It is sometimes said superficially that if the price falls below the
average variable cost,[2] the firm will find it unprofitable to continue
operations, but this does not constitute a satisfactory theory of firm
exit. In addition to the numerous possible reasons for exit which
already have been given, there should now be added the absence of
financial resources sufficient to sustain operations during a period of
producing at a loss. It matters little whether the losses are measured
by a price which is lower than $ATC$ or lower than $AVC$; the latter is
merely an extreme case of the former. The important thing is the
size of the losses in relation to liquid assets or the firm's ability to
borrow. The amount of loss is also a function of the total sales made
at prices below total cost, i.e., of the length of time during which such
sales are made. It is often the prospect of a change for the better

---

[2] This would include all costs which could be avoided by closing down divided
by the total output at the expected rate of sales, both costs and sales being figured
with reference to an identical time period such as a week or a month.

which keeps a firm going, or despair about future losses which causes one to quit.

Finally, a firm may shut down on what it hopes is a temporary basis in order to reduce its losses while waiting for that upturn in demand which would make operations profitable again. Such action may be induced by a combination of operating losses, short-run pessimism combined with long-run optimism, and a minimum of selling costs. The last point refers to the ease with which sales outlets and customer acceptance could be regained after a shutdown. The selling problem also confronted many firms after the war, during which they were forced to shut down or convert from one product to another because of a shortage of essential materials for customary peacetime production.

One might add that often when a manufacturer or other primary producer shuts down, the flow of goods to the ultimate consumer is not stopped immediately. Other producers may increase their output of an identical or similar good. Even if this does not occur, the inventories of finished products which the manufacturer possesses or the stock in the hands of wholesalers or retailers may still be sold to supply consumer needs for weeks or months thereafter. The time required to drain these lower reservoirs in the stream flow of goods often delays the time considerably when the flow from the primary source becomes necessary again.

**5. Upward Deviations from Normal Price.**—Even though expansion and contraction plus entry and exit of business firms tend to adjust supply so that transactions prices generally do not deviate very much from hypothetical normal prices, minor deviations exist most of the time and major departures are frequent in some lines. Rising demand may spread overhead costs and lower $ATC$ further below the asking price than it would have been at the output contemplated when that price was established. Occasionally monopolists take advantage of buyers' needs and raise their asking prices even though production costs are falling, or at least have not risen proportionately. (Cf. Chapter 11, Section 13.) They may be able to do this successfully because at the same time demand may have become more inelastic or may have shifted upward.

In other cases of rising profit margins there is no artificial obstacle to entry and expansion, but merely the fact that technically these require time. Shifts in schedule demand occur more rapidly than supply can be readjusted. Competitive bidding may force the price up above cost, or competitive offering may push it down below cost.

There is a short "time-shift ability" of demand upward and a long "time-elasticity" of supply. As was explained in Chapter 13, different industries require different lengths of time to adjust their output to the most profitable rate following any given percentage change in prices. If this price change has been away from normal price, the supply adjustment usually will be such as to cause price to move in the opposite direction, i.e., back towards normal price. The adjusting expansion or contraction in supply may occur in either the moderately long run as explained in Sections 4 to 6 of Chapter 13 or in the very long run as described in Section 7. No absolute measure of time-elasticity of supply is possible, but the conditions which tend to make it long or short deserve comment.

In agriculture, there have been more violent swings in the price of crops, like deciduous fruits, which take a long time to mature after planting, than in the prices of grain and other annuals, although the figures are difficult to interpret because of variations in the weather and the incidence of plant diseases or harmful insects. The time-elasticity of supply expansion is also longer for certain animals like beef cattle than for others like rabbits. In mining, certain deposits may be exploited more quickly than others because of the nature of the mineral deposit, and therefore the price need not go so high nor stay up so long to bring about the supply expansion which will tend to pull it down again. In manufacturing, the more expensive goods are usually those which require the most labor to produce and therefore take the most time. Objects in this class include heavy machinery, factories, railroads, steamships, office buildings, bridges, and canals. In the field of consumer goods the best illustration is homes. The long time technically required to expand the output of some goods also tends to discourage starting to expand, because of the inevitable uncertainty about whether the price will remain high until the goods from the expansion program reach the market.[3] The result is further to increase the amplitude and duration of price upswings for goods having a long time-elasticity of supply.

**6. Downward Deviations from Normal Price: The Influence of Durability.**—Current prices also frequently fall below normal. How far they fall and how long this downward deviation occurs depends chiefly on the article's durability. Ease of repair and of transfer to other uses are additional determinants.

---

[3] The significance of expectations in production planning also has been discussed above, particularly in Chapter 10, Section 6.

Most of the goods whose expansion of supply takes a relatively long time also are durable in the sense that they take a relatively long time to wear out in use. As compared to food which is a "single-use" good, those other products are "repeated-use" goods. They have a long time-elasticity of service supply when demand is falling as well as when it is rising, but the time required for a given percentage change in supply following a given percentage change in price is likely to be different going downward from that going upward. Since the demand for a repeated-use good is for the series of services which it can render, the supply of the good is really the supply of a series of such services. If extra care and maintenance can prolong the useful life of a machine, building, or other durable good, they increase the supply of the desired services and tend to offset the contraction which may result from the curtailment or the end of new production. As a result a decline in the demand for a durable good does not bring a quick shrinkage in the total supply of services from such goods even though the output of new goods drops rapidly.

It is further true that most durable production goods are sold under monopolistic conditions with a policy of price rigidity which sustains prices even though demand falls. Therefore, one cannot turn to the machine tool industry, for instance, to find an illustration of the slowness of supply quantity to shrink in the face of falling prices. But there is one durable goods industry where price competition and flexible prices prevail and can be used as an example even though the results are somewhat oblique. The construction industry has as its products homes, apartments, office buildings, and factories, which usually are sold as a unit together with the land on which they are erected. Therefore, even though it is the land which actually does most of the fluctuating in value, the declining demand for structures sometimes depresses the price of existing buildings to the place where new construction virtually stops. But the supply of (the services of) buildings does not diminish very much since they are so durable and there is no appreciable offset on the supply side to counteract the decline in demand and send the price back up again. In the terminology of this section, there is a long time-elasticity of supply contraction.

The extreme case of durability is that of land itself, particularly building sites, which have virtually perpetual life. Urban land offers the best illustration of extreme fluctuation in price because of long time-elasticity of supply both downward and upward. But it does not have a long-run normal price because it has no cost of production by which such a price may be established. (Cf. Chapter 10, Section 13.)  A partial substitute, and source of expansion on the up-swing, is the cost of development which in some cases is considerable, as for draining, irrigating, levelling, filling, or creating means of ingress and egress via highways or railroads.  Unless it has been inherited, land in its various forms probably has had a cost of ac-quisition or development for any given owner, and fluctuations sometimes are measured from such costs rather than from the normal price used for man-made goods.

A further impetus to extreme downswings in the case of durable goods may be found in their effect upon demand.  It is in bad times that the demand for new machines, building, etc., falls off and it is also in bad times that owners try to make their existing equipment last longer.  Hence replacements tend to be bunched in the upswing or prosperous period of the business cycle and diminish rapidly during the downswing.  This irregular purchasing accentuates the fluctuations in price and/or sales which would occur anyway because the size and durability of many production goods cause long time-elasticity of supply both upward and downward, particularly the latter.

### 7. Unexpected Supply Shifts May Cause Price Fluctuation.—

If we reverse the causation picture and consider cases in which the deviation in price results from an initial shift in supply plus a sluggish adjustment of demand, we find the major illustrations in agriculture. Here the vagaries of the weather may upset the best of production plans, whereas consumption habits are slow to change.  Furthermore, farmers are notoriously given to ill-calculated expansions of planting following good price years and are only somewhat less thoughtless in contractions after poor ones.  They do not clearly foresee the total effect of the combined judgments of thousands of competing in-dividuals most of whom change in the same direction at the same time.  Even with uniformly productive weather, alternate periods of high and low prices are therefore likely and are revealed in the history of some farm products such as meat animals and orchard fruits. Some manufacturers also have been guilty of similar practices, chiefly on the expansion side, but in recent years these mistakes in produc-tion planning have been curbed both by the diminishing number of competitors in some lines and by the emergence of strong trade as-sociations able to gather needed information.  The prevalence of price-fixing by manufacturers and merchandisers obscures the results of miscalculation in those fields while government intervention in support of farm prices is rapidly becoming an impediment to supply contraction in agriculture, even though benefits are paid farmers for not planting.

**8. A Summary of Supply-Side Causes of and Restraints on Individual Price Fluctuations.**—Some deviation from normal price is more common than otherwise. The foregoing sections have sought to explain why divergencies from normal are not, in some cases, quickly overcome. Detailed explanations of fundamental shifts in demand were given in Chapter 2 and need only be summarized here by saying that they spring from changes in desire or purchasing power which either are induced by the producers of the commodity (as by advertising) or occur independently because of external forces. Analysis of cyclical fluctuations in prices and costs must be deferred to another chapter, where further comment will be made on individual price fluctuations under the question of why certain prices fluctuate in a pattern which differs from the general trend, but this is not the same as the current problem of deviations from normal price.

A few special cases deserve some brief concluding comment. First, when goods are made to order, their prices ordinarily do not depart very far from average total unit cost (including normal profit). However, if they take a long time to make (bridges and large buildings), unforeseen changes in the supply of labor or materials may develop or unforeseen production difficulties occur so that the cost may become much higher than was expected when the original contract was drawn. Second, the normal prices of secondhand goods can be only rough approximations based on cost new (or cost of reproduction) less the customary depreciation and plus cost of renovation. The possibility of self-use limits the price-depressing effect of declining market demand, but there is no ceiling except through the availability of substitutes or the presence of government price control. Third, bargaining is very important in determining the prices of articles which are heterogeneous and those whose normal price cannot be determined readily or to which the seller is indifferent. This includes land, buildings, secondhand goods, scrap, and articles, offered by speculative or necessitous sellers. In all such bargaining particular transactions prices may deviate widely from the average selling price or from a calculated norm of cost-less-depreciation. Ignorance of worth, impatience, or inability to discover better alternative bids or offers may all play a part.

**9. Diagrammatics of the Time-Elasticity of Supply.**—The general idea of variations in time-elasticity of supply among different commodities can be expressed with some simplification in a two-dimensional diagram in which the horizontal axis represents elapsed time in weeks, months, or years, while the vertical axis represents unit price of the commodity being considered. In Figure 58 there are four comparisons, two on the up side and two on the down side. Each curve is drawn in relation to its own hypothetical normal price

## FIGURE 58

### TIME-ELASTICITY OF SUPPLY IN FOUR SITUATIONS

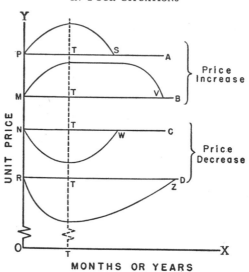

MONTHS OR YEARS

under the assumed conditions of constant cost in the very long run. (There is not intended to be any significance in the relative height of these very long-run horizontal cost curves.) In each pair of cases there is assumed to be some uniform price stimulus which is expected to continue and to which supply adjustments are therefore made. There is the further somewhat artificial assumption that all four prices reach their peak or nadir after the same interval of time. The upward time-elasticity of supply of commodity A is shorter than that of B (*TS* is less than *TV*). The flat top to B's curve is intended to suggest that there may be some delay before the new goods reach the market, but when that happens there will be a rather sharp drop to the old price. Speculative action as in farm products might hasten the decline. The decrease in price on the down side for C and D are drawn so as to be greater than the increases for A and B because supply contraction is generally slower than supply expansion. The time-elasticity of supply adjustment for D is made greater than for

C ($TZ$ is greater than $TW$) to indicate a hypothetically greater durability of D.

Curves like those of A and C or B and D might follow one another in time sequence for a single commodity E, particularly if the cause of the price drop was supply overexpansion following the first price increase. In that case an initial price change caused by a change in demand might cause a series of "ripples" or oscillations around the normal price with diminishing amplitude until stability was achieved again. This result would occur, however, only if every other force affecting demand or supply were to remain constant while producers were figuring out the best output by a process of trial and error. A state of affairs of this kind is improbable in a dynamic world, and the argument about disappearing ripples is intended merely to state a tendency, not to describe a probability. (See Figure 59.)

Under some circumstances there would be no dampening effect, or even an antidampening effect so that there would be an increase in the amplitude of the ripples. Technically, the ripples will diminish if the demand schedule is more elastic than the $MLR$ supply schedule. They will increase if the reverse is true, if producers learn nothing from experience, and if they allow the successive expansions and contractions to occur over the widening range provoked by the original $MLR$ supply curve. These latter conditions seem improbable, but the price history of potatoes, corn, and cabbage in this country seems to indicate that many American farmers learn very little from experience. Their good fortune in certain years has been the result, not of wise planting and good weather, but of war's demands and nature's adversities elsewhere.

Diagrammatically, the price-quantity oscillations give rise to a chronological curve which spirals inward or outward. Against the background of a demand curve and an $MLR$ supply curve the spiral looks like a cobweb. Hence the oscillation argument is sometimes called the cobweb theorem. It is an interesting oddity of infrequent importance except that the reasoning may help statisticians to derive static curves of demand and $MLR$ supply (see Chapter 15).

**10. Summary of Economic Principles Dealing with Individual Price Fluctuations.**—The major problems of individual price fluctuations may now be summarized from the arguments of this chapter and earlier ones. Price fluctuations may be considered as either changes from any prior price, or deviations from a "normal price." The latter has been the theme of Chapter 14. Demand aspects are slighted in the following outline.

## FIGURE 59
### THE COBWEB THEOREM

STATIC CURVES                    HISTORICAL CURVE
(cobweb)                         (smoothed ripple)

### A. Demand More Elastic than *MLR* Supply

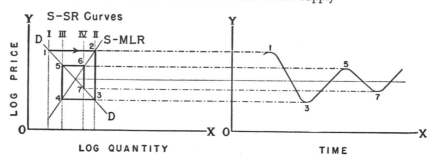

### B. Demand Less Elastic than *MLR* Supply

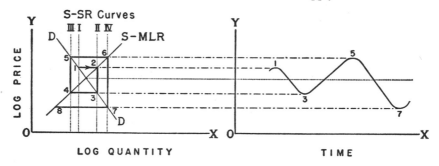

### C. Demand of the Same Elasticity as Supply

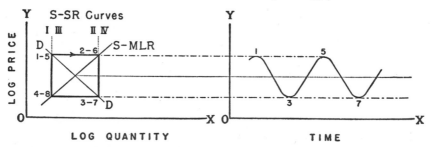

NOTE.—If price is established at point 1, the supply forthcoming in the next production period will be that shown by point 2 on $S\text{-}SR_{II}$, but this can be sold only at the price indicated by point 3, which in turn will evoke the smaller supply shown by $S\text{-}SR_{III}$ and establish the price at point 5, etc. Logarithmic axes are used so that the slopes of the straight-line curves will indicate their elasticities.

I. The concept of "normal price" involves:
   A. Two assumptions (except as noted):
      1. Entry and exit are not restricted by the government nor by collusive agreement.
      2. Expansion and contraction also are subject only to the gain-seeking decisions of the individuals involved.

   B. Two approaches:
      1. Demand: the "normal price" stimulates no change in demand intensity.
      2. Supply: the "normal price" stimulates no change in the rate of production and offering for sale. This requires the simultaneous presence of two equalities for each seller: $MC = MR$ and $ATC = AR$ (or Price).
         (a) The $AR$ and $MR$ schedules depend upon the magnitude and elasticity of demand. The latter is particularly important when competing firms produce differentiated products and set their own prices.
         (b) The $ATC$ and $MC$ schedules for individual firms depend upon
            (1) The prices of the factors, and
            (2) The efficiency of use of the factors, especially in relation to technology and the quantity of fixed factors. The latter influences the "capacity" of the representative firm, but is dependent also upon demand as explained in Chapter 13.

II. Deviations from normal price are a function of:
   A. The initiating changes in demand or supply.
      1. Their amplitude.
      2. Their duration.

   B. The time required for offsetting changes in demand or supply.
      1. For a supply change upward.
         (a) Reproducibility of product (time required to produce more of it if factors are available).
         (b) Availability of needed factors of production.
         (c) Ease of overcoming collusive or governmental restraints to expanded production.
         (d) Ease of entry of new firms.

      2. For a supply change downward.
         (a) Time required for completion of irreversible production processes already started (cf. crops).
         (b) Durability of products already sold and in use (also affects demand).

    (c)  Length of contracts for the purchase of factors.

    (d)  Ability to continue operations at a loss (liquid assets, borrowing capacity, etc.).

    (e)  Ease of exit.

        (1)  Liquidating value of fixed assets.

        (2)  Ease of shifting fixed assets or labor skills to alternative occupations.

3. For demand changes.

    (a)  Alteration of desire patterns.

    (b)  Changes in buying habits.

    (c)  Changes in the availability or in the prices of other goods.

        (1)  Substitute goods.

        (2)  Complementary goods.

The major loose ends of this summary which must await further discussion are two: (1) the prices of the factors of production, and (2) changes in the total volume of spending by business, consumers, and government. The first of these topics will be treated in Part II on the prices of services. The second will be discussed incidentally in the chapters on interest and profits. A more complete treatment must be sought in books treating changes in the general price level rather than in individual prices.

# Chapter 15

## THE QUANTITATIVE APPROACH TO PRICE CHANGE

**1. Principles of Quantitative Economics.**—The principles of economics expounded in the preceding chapters have stated that certain demand and supply forces exert an influence upon price. If allowed to act independently, they tend to force the price upwards or downwards according to whether the relationships are direct or inverse. If opposing forces are present at the same time, and that is usually the case, they tend to offset one another so that the outcome is in doubt. This uncertainty, however, does not invalidate the principles of economics because, like all scientific laws, each is based upon the premise of *ceteris paribus* (see Chapter 1). Although this is a valid defense, the pure scientist in the modern world has difficulty in retaining his detachment. The economist in particular often is asked to explain the workings of very complex problems, to predict the future course of prices or employment, or what to do about a distressing situation, such as the low incomes of farmers.

To give an adequate answer to questions of this type, the economist must develop principles which explain what happens in the intricate maze of economic life. He must first go beyond simple single-variable functions. This has been the objective of earlier chapters which have shown that economic changes usually result from the action of several variables. The second step is to shift from a qualitative to a quantitative approach. Instead of being content with principles which answer questions about the *direction* of change in an effect which follows a given cause, the economist also must seek to explain *how much* the change will be.

The specific questions answered in this chapter include the following:

1. How can economics be made a science of price prediction?
2. What are the major independent variables causing changes in the price of a staple farm product like wool? How are their "elasticities" computed and related?
3. How do quantitative economists allow for shifts in schedule demand? the "time trend" factor.

4. What are the major difficulties in obtaining quantitative formulae for explaining price change?

5. What pitfalls should be avoided in applying these formulae to predict price change?

**2. The Prediction of Economic Effects or Changes Is Desirable, but It Is Difficult When There Are Many Variables.—** Both big business and big government plan for the future. If they cannot control it, they at least want to be able to adapt themselves to it. They face practical questions such as how much the domestic sales of coffee will decline if the price is raised five cents per pound when a subsidy ends or Brazil imposes an export duty. Or if our government should negotiate a 50 per cent reduction in the tariff on flaxseed from Argentina, how much would imports increase? How much of a drop in the interest rate on realty mortgages is necessary to stimulate the building of an extra 200,000 new homes next year? What is the best rate structure for an electric power company entering a certain backward rural area? These are problems of the type which confront the practicing economist. Each one is unique and must be studied separately with careful examination of parallel situations in the past. But the more economic principles, both qualitative and quantitative, the analyst knows, the quicker and the better will be his answers.

Complete accuracy of prediction is never possible because unforeseen circumstances usually intrude during the time interval which separates the prediction and the occurrence. However, the shorter the time perspective, the narrower the market, and the fewer the variables involved, the smaller will be the margin of probable error. The forecaster is aided by the force of habit and routine in human responses. If he is dealing with large groups of people, the unusual cases tend to offset one another so that the accuracy of predictions may be increased.

Economic statistics of production, prices, income, sales, foreign trade, bank deposits, etc. reflect the reactions of large groups of individuals over a period of time. Relationships between these time series may be discovered by the use of reasoning, mathematics, and statistical methods. Experience or "common sense" may indicate which data best reveal the demand or supply forces which are most likely to influence certain other data. That is, the dependent variable is affected by one or more independent variables, and if the latter can be discovered by observation and reasoning, much time can be saved from the laborious work of statistical correlation by concentrating first on those data which seem obviously related. The others can be ignored unless the calculated curve proves to be a poor fit when compared with the curve of the original data, thus indicating that something of importance has been overlooked. This approach may indicate also the type of relationship between the variables, whether direct or inverse, simple multiples or squares, continuous or intermittent.[1]

**3. Dynamic Determinants of the Price of Wool.**—A recent study of the forces determining the price of fine wool in the United States furnishes a good illustration.[2] Elementary reasoning would suggest that the changes in the price of wool must be influenced on the demand side by changes in consumer income and on the supply side by changes in domestic production, domestic stocks, foreign production, foreign stocks, and the foreign exchange rate (since most of our wool is imported over a high tariff wall). Over a period of time, one would expect to find also some price-depressing effect from the trend toward substitution of rayon for woolen fabrics. Each supply and demand factor will have a different quantitative effect upon the price. All of these variables may be summarized by the verbalized equation:

$$Price = \left(\frac{Consumer}{Income}\right)^a \times \left(\frac{Domestic}{Production}\right)^b \times \left(\frac{Foreign}{Production}\right)^c \times$$

$$\left(\begin{array}{c}Domestic\\plus\\Foreign\\Stocks\end{array}\right)^d \times \left(\begin{array}{c}Foreign\\Exchange\\Gradient\end{array}\right)^e \times \left(\begin{array}{c}Time\\Trend\end{array}\right)$$

The small letters $a, b$, etc. represent the elasticities of price in terms of the factor in the parentheses; that is, the percentage change in price that will result from a given 1 per cent change in each factor. Time trend has no elasticity coefficient since it is the sum of all the remaining factors which operate slowly and gradually through time.

The equation may be expressed in the functional notation of mathematics by using the italicized letters to indicate the factors involved:

$$P = f(I, D, F, S, E, T)$$

---

[1] In simple mathematical terms, *a priori* reasoning may suggest not only the terms of the function, but its form, whether it is linear, curvilinear, or repeating, whether in two dimensions, a surface in three dimensions, or some undrawable figure in a multidimensional space.

[2] Charles F. Roos, "The Dynamics of Commodity Prices" in *Studies in Mathematical Economics and Econometrics in Memory of Henry Schultz*, edited by O. Lange, F. McIntyre, and T. O. Yntema, Chicago: University of Chicago Press, 1942, pp. 283–285.

By various statistical devices one may compare the time series of each of these factors and their quantitative effect upon price may be determined as an elasticity figure. This usually requires that the data be averaged or summated for successive yearly periods and that changes be expressed in terms of the difference between successive years. The probable form of the equation is decided by *a priori* reasoning and its constants are obtained by various correlation techniques. The final equation is then applied to the data to obtain calculated "should-be" prices which are compared with the actual prices in order to determine "correctness of fit" (most easily seen by plotting on the same graph the curves of both calculated and actual prices). If the fit is not good, the trouble may lie in either some factor which has been overlooked or in a time lag which has not been properly calculated.

The exact equation obtained by Dr. Roos in the wool price study is not given in his article, but he does indicate the elasticities as follows:

| | | |
|---|---|---|
| *a* (Consumer Income) | = | + 0.88 |
| *b* (Domestic Production) | = | − 0.48 |
| *c* (Foreign Production) | = | − 0.03 |
| *d* (Domestic + Foreign Stocks) | = | − 0.04 |
| *e* (Foreign Exchange Gradient) | = | + 1.38 |

This may be read to mean that a 1.00 per cent change in consumer income, for instance, will mean a change of 0.88 per cent in the price of wool in the same direction. Changes in foreign exchange rates influenced the domestic price of wool more than anything else. Changes in consumer income (that of individuals in the lower bracket) were second in importance, and changes in domestic production were third. The other two factors were not very important in the period studied, 1923–1939. The signs preceding the elasticities indicate that an increase in consumer income or foreign exchange rates increases the price, while an increase in production or stocks reduces the price. If these elasticities continue to operate in the future, they should be helpful in estimating what would be the effect on wool prices if the government were to change the tariff rate, control domestic production or sales, or manipulate foreign exchange rates. Since no time lags are indicated in the analysis, the future price cannot be predicted by examining current data. An economic or political prediction about all of the independent variables must be made first, and after that an estimate can be made of how much these expected changes will affect the price of wool.

In other analyses of time series relationships, time lags have been discovered. Where they do occur, the emergence of phenomenon X indicates that it soon will be followed by phenomenon Y, provided no unusual circumstance intervenes. Thus, a rise in the price of corn usually is followed by a rise in the price of hogs, or an increase in payrolls precedes a rise in the reported volume of retail sales. Sometimes historical data reveal characteristic fluctuations, such as the seasonal variations in the price of eggs or the volume of money in circulation. If these fluctuations tend to have a definite pattern of amplitude and a regular periodicity, fairly precise quantitative and temporal predictions are possible, but these conditions are rarely fulfilled. Thousands of men are still trying to "beat the stock market" by guessing better than the average guesser which way the prices of certain stocks will move, how soon, and for how long.

**4. Quantitative Studies of the Elasticity of Demand.**—Although our attention is now directed chiefly to the complex causes of price fluctuations, simpler studies of the same quantitative type should be noted, especially the measurement of the elasticity of demand for various products. In these, price is made the independent variable and the quantity demanded is made dependent upon it. Sometimes another independent variable is added in the form of an index of consumer income. All other variables, such as changes in consumer tastes, are assumed to change so gradually and so slowly that they may be represented as a time trend, $t$.[3]

A famous study of sugar prices was made by Henry Schultz. (See both his *Statistical Laws of Demand and Supply with Special Application to Sugar,* 1928, and Chapter VI of *The Theory and Measurement of Demand,* 1938.) In the latter work, he derives the per capita demand formula:

$$x = 70.62 - 2.259y + 0.8371t$$

to express the influence of changes in price, $y$, upon the demand for sugar, $x$, in the period from 1875 to 1895. The origin of the time trend, $t$, is taken as 1885. The elasticity of demand in this function averaged $- 0.37$. That is, on the average a 1 per cent change in the price brought an opposite 0.37 per cent change in the quantity demanded. The elasticity at high prices was greater than at low prices and for equal prices it decreased numerically each successive year of the twenty-year period in his study.[4]

Another fruitful result of Schultz's approach is its emphasis upon the shifting of demand curves as indicated by the time trend factor, $t$.

[3] Cf. the distinction between market demand and schedule demand as described in Chapter 2, Sections 1 and 2.
[4] The price data used in this study were corrected for changes in the price level.

This quantitative estimate of the trend of demand is of vital importance in public programs for the support of prices or the curtailment of production. It is not enough to know how much a rise in price will reduce demand (the elasticity coefficient), but we should know also the long-term trend of demand in order to discover probable future needs for greater or lesser curtailment of production. In some of these studies of agricultural commodities, consideration also must be given to the effects of changes in the prices of both substitute goods and complementary goods. Sugar and coffee, for instance, are complementary to each other, while beef and pork are substitutes for one another. In each class, the prices of both goods are interrelated. Statistical studies reveal the quantitative correlation between such items and help in forecasting and in controlling their price movements.

Most of the commodities studied by Schultz have a fairly stable demand but a fluctuating supply, because they are food or fiber staples of wide consumption whose output is subject to the vagaries of the weather and crop hazards. Their sellers are numerous and they cannot fix the selling price except when they get the government to do it for them. Hence the quantitative studies of price-elasticity of demand are highly valuable to agricultural policy planners. The following table summarizes some Schultz's findings: [5]

Two Measurements of per Capita Demand for Certain Agricultural Products, United States, 1915–1929 (except 1917–1921)

| Product | Price-Elasticity of Demand | Time Trend (Per Cent Shift per Year) |
|---|---|---|
| Rye | − 2.96 | − 7.66 |
| Buckwheat | − 0.90 | − 3.20 |
| Oats * (ex. 1917–1923) | − 0.60 | + 0.54 † |
| Barley | − 0.53 | + 0.69 † |
| Corn | − 0.48 | − 2.13 |
| Hay * | − 0.46 | + 2.24 |
| Sugar | − 0.34 | + 0.90 |
| Potatoes | − 0.32 | − 0.15 † |
| Cotton (1914–1929) | − 0.12 | − 0.75 |
| Wheat | − 0.08 | − 0.21 |

* Consumption per animal.
    † Not statistically significant, since the "standard error" exceeds the figure shown. This comparison is a statistical device for testing the probable precision of the averages or coefficients calculated from samples.

[5] See *The Theory and Measurement of Demand,* Chicago: University of Chicago Press, 1938, Chapters 6–15.

The above commodities have been ranked in order of diminishing price-elasticity of demand. Rye is the only one which had an elastic demand, and its experience was exceptional in these years. For all the major crops the demand was less than unity and closely approached complete inelasticity in the case of cotton and wheat. In all such cases a reduction in the size of the crop will increase the total return to the farmer-producers. This explains in part the reasoning underlying the programs for crop reduction and restriction in this country during the 1930's. The time trends are significant also. Demand was declining during the period for six out of ten crops and very rapidly for rye and buckwheat. The positive trend for oats, barley, and potatoes is not certain, since in each case the derived trend percentage is less than its standard error. Hay is the only crop showing a definite increase and that is on a per animal basis, so that it might be offset by a decline in the number of animals.

**5. Difficulties in the Quantitative Measurement of Economic Relationships.**—One should not get the impression from the above description of the use of statistics to strengthen deductive theory that all economic questions can be answered by their use. On the contrary, the usefulness and reliability of mathematical equations involving numerical coefficients, constants, and exponents in prediction and control are definitely limited. In the first place, there is much room for personal choice in the selection of the data to be analyzed— whether to use the data gathered by one agency or another, or those related to one level of transactions or another. Sometimes less reliable data are chosen in place of more trustworthy data because the former may possess advantages of continuity or completeness. Second, when certain time series are incomplete or have changed their bases of compilation or publication during the time interval, interpolation or extrapolation must be employed, with the errors inevitably attendant upon the use of these devices.

The third difficulty already has been mentioned: the problem of choosing the most appropriate equation and method of statistical analysis. For instance, Schultz gives six different answers to the elasticity of demand for sugar from 1915 to 1929 depending upon the equation and method used. They run from − 0.31 to − 0.40, which is not a seriously wide spread, but when the probable error is subtracted from the former figure and added to the latter, the range becomes − 0.08 to − 0.52, which is so wide as to cause hesitation in trying to predict the probable change in demand which would follow a given change in price. The fourth difficulty is an analytical one:

how to decide from the historical evidence whether a given regression represents a demand curve of the short-run type or a supply curve in the long-run group. If general observation of the motives and actions of producers indicates that their output may be expected to fluctuate more often than the intensity of demand, we may infer that the data should be analyzed to reveal a demand curve. If demand fluctuates more rapidly, then it would be more logical to develop a price-quantity supply curve. Certain statistical methods also have been developed to aid in making the distinction as to which curve should be sought in given historical data.

Fifth, it is important to recognize that the derived curve is essentially a picture of an average situation during the period analyzed and that this average might have been different if the period had been selected so as to begin or end at a different time. For instance, according to Schultz, the demand shift for wheat was only $- 0.21$ per cent per year during the years 1921–1929, but if 1921 to 1934 be taken for analysis instead, the time trend would be $- 0.50$ per cent, more than twice as large, and the price elasticity of demand also would jump from $- 0.08$ to $- 0.19$.

### 6. Problems in the Application of Price Prediction Formulae.
—In addition to the difficulties of obtaining a formula which correctly states the relation between independent and dependent variables, there is also the problem of knowing when, where, and how to apply these formulae. Their usefulness in prediction depends upon the future repetition of past patterns of events. These include not only the economic routine of demand and supply, but also the highly unpredictable political developments, "acts of God," inventions, court decisions, etc. Errors may arise both from failure to realize the exact situation which the basic data represent and from misapplication of the findings. But errors are not limited to the faulty application of inductively derived conclusions. If anything, they are more apt to be the mistakes of those who seek to apply deductive theorems.

One problem of application lies in the nature of the data. We are prone to think of a demand curve as applying to the purchases of ultimate consumers, but the buyers whose purchases are reflected in most of the statistical data of prices and quantities are middlemen, manufacturers, or even outright speculators. The derived demand curves picture their reactions to price change, and because of the greater speculative element in all such buying the probable error in prediction exceeds that which probably would hold for routine buying by consumers. A statistical demand curve often is pictured as having uniform elasticity throughout and also as being reversible, but we know from other evidence that the elasticity is usually different at high prices and at low ones, and that buyers react differently to a price increase and to a price drop. Similar situations exist on the supply side. Farmers in particular tend to be guided as much by the recent trend of prices as by the actual level prevailing at the time of planting. Furthermore, the weather plays such an important part in the outcome of planting decisions that if possible the supply responses of farmers probably should be measured in terms of acreage planted instead of bushels or pounds of crops harvested.

Statistical investigations of the price behavior of particular items must be limited chiefly to standardized products bought and sold by large numbers of people. They include farm products, minerals, and other industrial raw materials. If prices are subject to monopolistic control, they tend to be more stable, but any changes that do occur are less predictable by outside analysts. If the government intervenes with price-support or price-ceiling programs or introduces special devices to stimulate or curb production, predictions must be revised to take these into account. Past experience, nevertheless, will help in judging the necessary extent of these efforts to achieve the desired goals and also in overcoming the difficulties that will be encountered in striving to reach them.

7. **Summary.**—This chapter is an introduction to the problems of measurement of economic forces. Two approaches may be used. The first asks what are the forces which *cause* the price of a commodity to change over a period of years and how strong is each of them. The second asks what are the many *effects* which follow from a given price change and what are their magnitudes. Only the first has been sketched here. It must be mastered if economics is to be a science of prediction and not merely a series of generalizations regarding tendencies.

Most principles of quantitative economics cannot be developed and learned in advance. They must be formulated in terms of the statistical correlations bearing upon the problem at hand. Statistical sources, however, can be discovered and appraised. Principles of statistical analysis and advanced mathematics are fundamental tools. Therefore, the practicing economist has much to learn after becoming familiar with basic qualitative principles if he wishes to undertake the analysis of specific problems in quantitative terms.

# PART II

## THE PRICES OF SERVICES

# Chapter 16

## GENERAL PROBLEMS OF SERVICE PRICE THEORY

**1. The Prices of Services Resemble the Prices of Commodities.** —The second part of this volume deals with the prices of services. These prices have four well-known names: wages, rent, interest, and profits. The first three are paid by business firms or individuals to other individuals. Profits are received by individuals, but are paid by no one, unless by "society" for the services rendered by business units. Our basic problem is to explain the prices of these services and to examine their effects. Many of the principles of commodity price theory apply to service prices, too. But markets are different and certain behavior patterns are peculiar to buyers and sellers of services. That is why the two types of prices are usually examined separately.

Service price theory is often called distribution theory. One reason is found in the fact that wages, rent, interest, and dividends are usually paid by a business unit out of its income.[1] They seem to represent the division or "distribution" of that income. Another reason is that most individuals receive their portion of the national income in one of these four ways. Almost the entire income of the country is "distributed" to people through the prices paid for factor services which the people sell. Exceptions may be noted for charity, social insurance payments, pensions, graft, and bribes. The latter two are interesting in that when they are paid to people who do things that others want, they are akin to wages, but sometimes they are paid for *not* doing things and then are clearly in a class by themselves.

Distribution theory also may include the economic problem of the relative sizes of the aggregate shares of the national income going to each major factor group. For instance, economists study the question of why labor as a whole gets more than two-thirds of the national income in this country, and why it gets a larger share at one time than another. In a society which depends upon individual re-

---

[1] The difference between profits and dividends will be clarified in a later chapter. For the present the terms will be considered virtually synonymous.

sponse to profit prospects for the guidance of production, the size of the profit share may be very important. Expectations of percentage return per dollar invested are the prime consideration, however, not the percentage of national income going to owners of firms as a whole.

The specific questions to be considered in this introductory chapter include the following:

1. Why is service price theory also called distribution theory?
2. What are the four main classes of service payments and how may they be subdivided? Classes of services?
3. How may "use prices" be distinguished from "ownership prices"?
4. What are the general characteristics of demand and supply in factor markets?
   (a) Peculiar subjective and objective considerations?
   (b) Joint demand, derived demand, cross elasticity, etc.?

**2. There Are Many Subgroups in Each Factor Class.**—Although economists usually divide factors into four main groups and call their *payments* wages, rent, interest, and profits, there are many subgroups in each class. Price analysis that holds for one subgroup must be changed somewhat to describe another. Labor wage problems, for instance, are different for the salaried worker and the day laborer. Organized musicians sell their services in a different manner from casual farm laborers. Similarly, in talking about rents, one should distinguish many classes of rental markets. The rental problems of parking lot owners differ from those of companies owning automobiles for hire. Homes are rented differently from office buildings, and farms from factories. Dollars look much the same when borrowed, but lenders differ in their willingness to accept certain types of risk. No two business units are completely alike in revenue and cost experience. The profit price that society pays for their services is uniquely determined in each case.

Despite these differences, cases may be grouped according to the elements which they have in common. Generalizations may be made about the phenomena which are found in small groups, or in larger groups which include these small groups. Theories which describe and explain collective bargaining, for instance, have certain common denominators with theories about the wages of unorganized labor. These elements in common may then be combined by a process of abstraction into a general wage theory. The important thing is to remember the level of abstraction for which a theory is designed. No theory is a complete map of reality. It is merely an outline sketch to indicate the picture whose details may be sought or ignored according to the purpose of the moment.

3. **The Factors of Production as Services and as Sources.**—The *services* whose prices are to be analyzed in this part of the book are often called "factors of production." They are used in agriculture, manufacturing, trade, and all other productive enterprises. But they are strangely without distinct names. The services of human beings are sometimes called "labor," sometimes "work," and sometimes just "services." The word *labor* often is used also to describe a group of laborers, as when a manager speaks of "bargaining with labor." When one rents the services of land, he may seek its fertility, its minerals, its ability to support buildings, its sunshine, etc. There is no single term which describes the variety of services which the same piece of land might render. So, too, with capital goods such as buildings, railroads, and machinery. They shelter, aid the movement of goods, improve the efficiency of labor, etc. The services of capital funds are sometimes described by the alternative term *purchasing power*. But funds also are desired for the service they perform in furnishing "liquidity" and in facilitating "hoarding." A similar difficulty arises with the services of a business unit. These are usually called "production," but the profit reward which goes to the owners is not for production, a gross return, but rather for success in achieving a positive *net* return in the act of production.

Even though the services or factors have no distinct names, their prices are almost always called wages, rent, interest, and dividends (or profits). These prices are paid to the owners of the *sources* of the services. Rent is paid to the owners of tangible property, interest to the owners of funds, and dividends to the owners of incorporated business units. These three are forms of "property income." If a man's body were considered to be wealth which he owned and let others use, wages could be called "property income" too.

4. **Use-Prices and Ownership-Prices.**—Payments for services may be called "use-prices" and payments for sources called "ownership-prices." Distribution theory is largely concerned with the "use-prices" of factors of production which are obtained on a temporary basis. Wages, rent, or interest are paid on some type of time contract for services. In each case there is an express or implied promise to return the factor source substantially intact. In renting real property, an exception is made for "normal wear and tear," a vague and often litigious phrase. When borrowed dollars are returned as dollars in some form of legal tender or acceptable draft or check, the

debt is usually considered to have been fully discharged even though the purchasing power of the returned dollar may be much less than that of the borrowed dollar. Workers likewise may be worn out by their jobs, may contract occupational diseases, or may be injured in accidents. In recent years this impairment of the factor source has been made an increasing responsibility of the employer. Workmen's accident compensation laws have been followed by old age assistance to which employers must contribute. Sickness insurance, especially for occupational diseases, also is now beginning to appear on statute books in this country. It has long been common abroad.

Sometimes the source of the factor service is purchased outright. An "ownership-price" is paid which closely resembles the "transactions price" paid for commodities whose services are desired for direct consumption. It gives the buyer the right to use the services of the good without any stated time limit. For instance, the services of land, buildings, and machinery may be obtained by paying a rent-price for temporary use or an ownership-price for permanent use. A business unit also may be rented, as in the leasing of railroads, or bought, as through the purchase of stock shares. Now that slavery has become illegal, men and women cannot be bought outright like other animals or inanimate objects. Their services must be purchased on a time basis. Currency may be bought outright, as in the foreign exchange market. More often it is borrowed. The price paid for the use of funds for a period of time is called "interest." [2]

Another type of use-price is that offered by society when it employs profit prospects to entice or induce people to use factors in production. Society does not obtain permanent rights to factor sources committed to productive effort. Therefore, profits cannot be called an ownership-price. But profits also differ from most use-prices. There is no contract requiring that they be paid for services rendered. Nor is any definite time period involved like that for wage, rent, or interest payments. There is merely the implicit promise that if the income from the productive use of the enticed factors exceeds the outlays, the difference may be kept by the owner of the factor sources as his "profit" for the interval.

### 5. Subjective Considerations in the Use-Prices of Factors.—

Subjective considerations dominate the selling side in factor markets. This is the opposite of commodity price markets where the selling side is chiefly objective and where it is the consumer buyer whose

---

[2] A distinction will be made later between the services of the funds in the hands of the buyer and the services which the owner of the funds performs when he allows the buyer to use them.

motives are usually subjective.  The factor seller is usually a private
individual and the buyer a business unit.  The individual is influenced by *subjective* considerations particularly when it is his labor
which he is selling.  He considers what he must give up, his leisure,
his time which he might use for himself, the pain and fatigue of exertion, etc.  If he owns many pieces of real property which he rents,
he may consider his being a landlord a business.  He may adopt
the objective profit-and-loss attitudes of the manager of a business
unit.  But if he has only one or two pieces of property for rent,
subjective considerations of effort, of things given up, of use-
opportunities foregone, or of the condition of his property when returned, may weigh heavily in his calculations of the price he will try
to obtain for its services.  A similar line of reasoning seems applicable
to large and small lenders and to owner-managers of small business
units as compared with wealthy individuals owning many shares of
stock.

On the opposite side of the market a similar contrast may be dis-
cerned.  The buyers of factor services are usually the managers of
business units who are motivated by *objective* comparisons between
income and expenditure, between costs and revenue.  Of course there
are exceptions to the generalization.  Some services are purchased by
consumers for their direct use such as the so-called personal services
of barbers, physicians, taxicab drivers, and tailors.  The services of
property are often sought for residence purposes, either directly
through renting a house or apartment or indirectly by borrowing to
buy a home, automobile, vacation, etc.

**6. Derived Demand for Factors.**—Since the demand for factors
of production comes chiefly from business firms, it has certain peculiarities.  In the first place, the intensity of that demand depends
in part upon the demand for the product of those firms.  Therefore,
factor demand tends to rise and fall as the manager changes his ideas
about the future rise or fall in the demand for his product.  In the
second place, any single factor is only one of many which the firm
needs to conduct its business.  Factor demand is joint demand and
is therefore a function of the prices of other factors and the technical
possibility of substituting one for another.  If many good substitutes exist at fairly comparable prices, then the price-elasticity of demand for a given factor will be great.  The cross-elasticity of demand
will also be large.  A rise in the price of one will cause much substitution of others for it, as in the case of labor and machinery (or the
funds to buy it).

The factors which cost the most in a joint demand situation will have the largest influence on the selling price of the product or on the ability of the firm to continue in production. Hence their elasticity of demand will be greater both for price increases and for price decreases than will that of factors whose cost is only a small fraction of the total. The relative importance of factors will differ of course from product to product so that generalizations of wide applicability are difficult. It is at least a 95 per cent generalization, however, that wages constitute a larger part of total costs than does interest. Therefore, a 10 per cent increase in wage rates is likely to reduce the demand for labor more than a 10 per cent increase in interest rates will reduce the demand for funds. The demand for labor is more elastic than the demand for funds.

If the factor demand problem is approached from the narrower focus of the individual firm, or even the industry, the truth of another generalization becomes apparent. The more inelastic the demand for a product, the more inelastic the demand for the factors used in making that product. If unions ask higher pay, the employer is most likely to accede when the product demand is inelastic. If he has to raise the price to pay higher wages, his sales and therefore his employment will not decline very much. Bituminous coal is a good example of a derived demand that is inelastic, at least in good times. The factor demand by makers of commercial pastry products is probably much more elastic.

**7. General Aspects of Demand and Supply in Factor Markets.** —Service price theory seeks to explain the prices of the factors, their relative magnitudes, their changes, and their effects. Like all other prices, service prices are the result of the interaction of demand and supply. But factor markets are even more heterogeneous than commodity markets. Institutional variations must be examined in detail before comprehensive generalizations can be attempted. At this point only a few are possible.

There is some price-elasticity in the demand of individual buyers. This is based upon diminishing marginal productivity from use of inputs, decreasing marginal revenue from sale of outputs, or both. There is also some price-elasticity of supply by individual sellers, derived from increasing marginal costs, whether objective or subjective. Because of their cumulative character, collective demand and collective supply almost inevitably follow the usual laws. Factor heterogeneity makes for considerable bargaining. And of course there are many cases in which sellers are able to set and to obtain their offering prices. Price setting by the buyer is less common.

There is much cross-elasticity of demand for factors, although it does not appear so quickly as in consumer demand for commodities. The case of rising wage rates and their stimulus to the introduction of labor-saving machinery is well known, but the substitution takes time. There is also considerable income-elasticity of demand. Rising business incomes usually promote increased demand for factors. In both these types of demand-elasticity, technological factors influence the speed and degree of response. Subsequent chapters will examine each of these points in detail.

The elasticity of factor supply may be generalized under the same three headings. Some factors, like mineral-bearing lands, are quite limited in supply and therefore evince very little supply-elasticity of the price variety. Others can be reproduced and usually obey the law of increasing marginal cost. The longer the time allowed for supply expansion, the greater the apparent supply-elasticity in response to the rising factor price. Long-term contracts for loans and leases reduce the immediate cross-elasticity of supply. Ultimately, shifts in employment do occur at the initiative of the seller. Income-elasticity of supply is of the usual positive type in the case of loanable funds, but with labor supply a negative relationship often appears. For durable goods of fixed quantity, the income-elasticity like the price-elasticity of supply is zero, at least temporarily.

Factor markets may be classified in the traditional way as revealing either "pure competition," "monopoly," etc. A more realistic approach would stress the importance of custom in some cases, bargaining in others, legal minima and maxima, etc. The different types of collusive action by sellers should be detailed and not grouped under the artificial headings of "oligopoly," "duopoly," and monopolistic competition.

**8. Summary.**—The foregoing arguments and observations show the need for dividing price analysis into many parts. Service price theory is one main division. It has four traditional parts: wage theory, rent theory, interest theory, and profit theory. Each of these must be subdivided still further by type of factor and type of market if we are to get a more realistic picture of the causes and effects of prices in our economy. Even then, particular problem situations in any subdivided field will differ from one another.

Business firms pay use prices for the services of factors of production. Sometimes they buy outright the service source by paying an ownership price. The demand for factors is derived from the demand for their products. Joint demand situations influence both the price-elasticity and the cross-elasticity of demand for factors.

Service prices are best explained in terms of types of market behavior. Knowledge of the details of market situations involving labor, land, etc., helps to build generalizations about common aspects of service price determination. This is the inductive approach to theory. Knowledge of general principles of service pricing helps one to analyze specific problems. This is deductive reasoning. Economics has need of both. The following chapters, therefore, will consider both the institutional (inductive) and the theoretical (deductive) approaches.

# Chapter 17

## SPECIFIC WAGE RATES: AN INSTITUTIONAL APPROACH

**1. Problems in Wage Theory, a Preview.**—The problems of wage theory may be divided into at least four parts. The first would explain specific wage rates by examining the interplay of forces determining the demand for and the supply of labor in particular situations. This may be called the institutional approach and will be examined in the present chapter. The second might examine the more general problems of equilibrium situations under certain assumptions. On the demand side this includes the equilibrium of the firm in its demand for labor. On the supply side there is the analysis of equilibrium wage rates for different labor groups. This is often called "wage theory" *per se,* but it is really only an *a priori* approach to wage problems.

A third part would involve a broader approach and consider the differences in *real* wages from region to region and from one time interval to another. Finally, there is the relation between money wage rates and the aggregate demand for labor in a given economy. This is one aspect of the problem of unemployment. For convenience, each of these four parts of the theory of wages will be treated in a separate chapter, even though they are closely related.

**2. Topics to Be Studied by the Institutional Approach.**—Money wage rates are prices and may be analyzed by the approach used for commodity prices. Like the prices of goods, the prices of labor services are determined in many ways. The wages paid and received in particular situations are determined by the conditions of demand and supply that prevail. Bargaining is much more common than in the market for goods. Therefore we must examine carefully the customs, laws, and types of economic organization which influence bargaining. These are called institutional forces. They help to set the range of asking and offering prices in the minds of the bargainers. They also explain the relative bargaining power of the buyer and seller.

Because of the great variety of these institutional situations, generalizations are difficult, but they must be sought. Only thus can the study of wage rates be made useful for prediction, adaptation, or control in connection with the labor problems of everyday life. The following list of questions treated in this chapter indicates one way to classify situations. Another approach will be found in the concluding summary. Both should be studied carefully.

1. What is the nature of labor, its relation to laborers?
2. How are particular wage rates determined?
    (a) When set by employers?
    (b) When set by workers?
    (c) When bargaining occurs?
    (d) When set by law?
3. How and when are wage rates raised?
    (a) By the initiative of the employer?
       (Concepts of "labor float" and "time-elasticity of supply")
    (b) By the initiative of the worker?
       (Concepts of "time-elasticity of demand" and "elasticity of substitution")
    (c) Alternatives to increased pay?
4. How and when are wage rates reduced?
    (a) By the initiative of the employer?
    (b) By the initiative of the worker?
    (c) Alternatives to reduced rates of pay?

**3. Labor and the Worker; the Factor Service and Its Source.—** Labor is the mental or physical energy expended by a human being for something other than the pleasure of expending that energy. When a person puts forth such energy he is said to work and is usually called a worker. Highly paid workers often coin more high-sounding terms to describe themselves and their labor such as "executives" and "professional services," but the fundamental similarity remains. The economist is chiefly concerned with labor performed for others for pay in money or in goods. Occasionally he finds it useful to examine the circumstances surrounding labor performed for oneself, either to produce something for future use or to obtain immediate satisfaction. There is little to be gained by quibbling about where the line should be drawn between labor which is "work" and that which is "play."

Labor, the factor service, is inseparable from the worker, the factor source. That is why labor as a factor of production is often considered to be the worker himself rather than the effort he puts forth. More important is the fact that the factor source is inseparable from the owner of that source. For the service to be rendered, the owner of the source must be present. This is not true in the case of real estate, personal property, or funds, where all that is required is the presence of the factor source.

Because labor is a service performed by human beings, its supply is limited by things which people dislike, such as the fatigue of exertion, boredom, and the fear of injury or illness from work. Because labor may also be performed for himself or the time used in more pleasant ways, the worker is a demander as well as a supplier of labor. The owners of other factor sources may sometimes occupy a similar dual position on both sides of the market, but less frequently. The owner of rental property can rarely use it for himself, and even the owner of loanable funds usually considers those funds desirable for their income-producing potential and does not seriously consider the possibility of spending them. Both may let their property lie idle waiting a more opportune time or better terms of sale, but they do not "consume" the services of the factor source during the interim nearly as often as does the worker. The distinction can also be made in terms of the much larger number of possible uses of a person's time than of property time. Real and personal property are more highly specialized in their functions than are human beings. An unemployed machinist may not have any opportunity to use his skills at home, but he can probably think of many things he would enjoy doing with his time.

On the other hand, a man looking for work usually feels the need for pay more than the need for leisure or time to work for himself. An unemployed worker usually has no other source of income than his labor. By contrast people who own rentable or loanable property which is temporarily idle usually have other property income and often a supplementary work income. The savings of workers are usually small, but most workers now can get temporary and limited help from unemployment insurance funds. The result is that workers may be pictured as weighing alternative uses of their time when they try to decide whether to take a given job opportunity or not. They may also appraise other aspects of the job such as hours, conditions of work, etc. The point to be emphasized here is the extensive subjective element in decisions regarding the sale of labor. The decision of a worker selling labor resembles that of a consumer buying commodities when the latter weighs the satisfaction expected from the good purchased against the satisfaction of keeping his money with its possibilities of future use for a variety of other goods. The subjective valuations of both worker and consumer must be contrasted with the objective monetary valuations of the business firm on the buying side of the factor market and on the selling side of the commodity market.

There are exceptions, of course. In some cases labor is demanded for immediate personal consumption, such as the services of doctors, barbers, teachers, and entertainers. The consumer is the employer and the worker is selling labor to meet a direct and not a derived demand. On the other hand, labor is sometimes sold like a commodity as in cases where the employers hire unskilled farm laborers and sell their labor in gangs under contract to large buyers. Or a person like a professional baseball player may make a long-term contract to deliver services to some buyer who is privileged to sell that contract to some one else.

There are thousands of different services which laborers can and do render for others. Each of these different types of labor may also be performed at a multitude of different places. Hence it is possible for many different wage prices to exist at any given time and there is no single price nor any common denominator for that which we call labor. The economic analyst can study the height and movement of any particular wage price he wishes. In a general study like this he must confine himself to the quest for explanations of wage rates in the labor market situations which occur most frequently or which have the most significant effects. These include hourly, daily, weekly, or other time-period wage rates, whether called wages, salary, stipend, or other synonym. It also covers wages paid per unit of service performed, such as factory piece rates, selling commissions, and professional fees. The name is not important.

**4. Particular Money Wage Rates May Be Set: I. By an Employer.**—The specific wage rates which exist at any particular time and place are the results of agreements between employers and workers. The most common situation is probably one in which employers offer to pay and workers agree to accept the going wage for the particular type of service involved. It is customary for large employers to have a wage policy of paying certain definite rates for the various types of work. When one man quits or dies, another is hired to take his place at the same wage if he possesses at least as much skill. If not, the replacement is hired in a lower category until he acquires the skill needed to qualify him for the higher pay classification.[1] Small employers tend to follow the same procedure,

---

[1] This does not mean to imply that wages are determined by skill alone, nor that all employers follow this type of employment policy. Bargaining is very important, as will be argued below.

although more by approximate rule-of-thumb technique than by the schedules of a personnel department.

In recent years a technique of job evaluation has been developed by certain large employers. An expert analyzes each type of work to determine the demands which it makes on the worker. For instance, jobs vary in the amount of skill and experience they require and each one is rated at some number on a scale of 1 to 10. Job A may rate 9 points on the skill scale, while job B may be evaluated at only 6 points. Similar ratings are made for the amount of judgment required, the physical energy output of the worker, the risk of accident, etc. The total rating for a job might then be $9 + 6 + 3 + 4 + \ldots = 35$, or some such figure. A system of weighing the components may also be used, giving more importance to one aspect of a job than to another. A comparison of the totals reveals the relative demands of various jobs upon the worker. All those in the 35-40 group, for instance, should therefore be paid more than those in the 25-30 group. Wage scales are often set by employers in cooperation with workers, using such rating systems as a basis. Whenever any new job is created, it is evaluated by the method used for other jobs, and the appropriate wage is thus determined.

**5. Particular Money Wage Rates May Be Set: II. By Bargaining.**—Particular money wage rates may be determined also by bargaining between the worker and his employer. Unless the worker is an executive or the possessor of some very rare manual skill, he is not likely to do much bargaining as an individual. He will either accept or reject the employer's offer. But in a few cases there will be higgling, offers and counter proposals, until agreement is reached or negotiations are broken off. The principles of wage determination under such circumstances are the same as those for any bargained price. If the potential bids and offers overlap, an agreement may be reached. The precise figure will depend upon the circumstances. In general, relatively great strength and skill in bargaining lead to a wage close to the favorable end of the overlap. For the employer, this is the lower end; for the worker, it is the upper. This, however, is only an elementary statement. We must still examine many things which influence (1) the bid and offer ranges and (2) the relative strength of the contending parties and their skill in bargaining.

When bargaining fails to produce agreement, the contending parties may agree to submit the dispute to arbitration. This is most commonly done when organized labor is involved, not individual workers. The arbitrator (or board of arbitrators) listens to the arguments and then recommends a certain wage. Arbitrators use various formulae in reaching their decisions, depending on the case at hand. Sometimes they decide upon the basis of the apparent relative power of the disputants and then hunt for a formula which yields the same result but appears to be "impartial" and "scientific."

**6. Particular Money Wage Rates May Be Set: III. By the (Organized) Workers.**—In a few cases labor-unions become so strong that they can virtually dictate the money wage rate which employers must pay. They control all the available supply of a given type of labor, such as musicians. They announce the rate of pay for each service their members might perform. Employers must pay this wage or go without. No individual worker is allowed to work for less than the "union scale," under penalty of expulsion from the union. If an employer tries to hire nonunion labor, union workers may conduct a strike or boycott against him.

This is the familiar "monopoly" problem. The union behaves monopolistically in trying to get as high a price as possible for the labor involved. Wages tend to be high relative to the wages paid other workers not so tightly organized to reduce supply-price competition. Yet there is a limit to the height to which union wages can go, namely, the cost of acceptable substitutes. These substitutes may be machinery, land, or other types of labor which may be used in producing the commodity or service involved. Their prices and their efficiencies in production influence the price- (wage-)elasticity of demand for the labor concerned. These problems and that of the time required to make the substitution will be discussed at greater length below. At this point we need add only the comment that sometimes the commodity involved may be "priced out of the market" by rising labor costs. Some consumers may turn to other goods which can be produced with another type of labor, presumably cheaper than the high-wage group. Prefabricated houses are a good illustration. Or the substitute good may be produced by the same labor in a cheaper way, such as phonograph record music as compared with live orchestra music.

Employers differ in their ability to bargain with strong unions. Small employers may pay union rates without argument. Larger firms or groups of firms may engage in long and protracted negotiations at the time of contract renewals. In such cases relative bargaining strengths and skills return to the picture.

The actual wage rate demands of unions are determined in various ways. Prior rates are the starting point. Changes (usually upward) spring from changes in the cost of living, the level of employer profits, the volume of unemployment, the wages received in similar occupations, etc. Pay differentials in union scales are rarely worked out with the precision of job-evaluation analysis, although sometimes union men join in the analysis itself. Customary differences tend to be retained and justified on the basis of what has been received in the past.

7. **Particular Money Wage Rates May Be Set: IV. By the Government.**—At times the government intervenes to set particular money wage rates. This is usually done by establishing maximum or minimum rates. Occasionally there are regulations which require the payment of the "going wage." This often means the union scale in that community. Governmental units usually have civil service scales for their own employees. In times of generally rising wage rates, the government scale may be lower than that for private business. Inflexibility is one reason. Taxpayer resistance is another. Often there are also certain advantages in working for the government, such as greater certainty of employment in the future, retirement pensions, longer paid vacations, regular seniority promotions, etc. For many people these advantages offset lower pay.

Legal minimum wage rates have been established in many states, and industries affecting interstate commerce are now covered by federal legislation. Since these rates are usually higher than customary minima—otherwise the laws would be futile—they supersede custom and make bargaining very unlikely. In wartime legal maximum rates may also be established by government action as fixed dollars-and-cents amounts, as a certain percentage of the rates paid on a given base date, or whatever the rates were before ("Whatever was is right"). Again bargaining disappears because employers are so eager to keep their workers on the job that they are willing to pay all that the law allows.

In either case, legal maxima or legal minima, classification of workers is often used to evade the law. Apprentice beginners are sometimes paid less than the minimum on the grounds that they are just learning the business, and then are fired when they get experience. Evasive methods of reclassification for men at the top are easy. When it is possible to change jobs from one firm to another, workers can hunt the highest ceilings.

8. **Three Methods of Attracting Additional Labor.**—When employers need more labor, or a new firm enters the labor market, there are three distinct ways in which this labor may be obtained.

The first is to offer the going wage and make one's wants known. Unions may be asked to furnish more men.[2] Newspaper and billboard advertising may be used. Employment exchanges may be asked to send applicants from their lists of unemployed persons. Other devices include streetcorner recruiting and the establishment of special employment offices downtown or in other cities.

A second method is to offer various nonwage advantages, hoping to attract workers from other jobs which pay the same wage rate but lack these advantages. During the second world war, employers were prevented by law from raising wages to attract workers from other jobs. Hence they resorted to other methods. Some served hot lunches free, or at prices far below cost. Systems of rapid and automatic promotion were introduced. Lavatories, lockers, and showers were modernized. "Wage incentive" schemes offered higher pay rates for increased output. Vacations with pay, retirement pensions, and sickness allowances also proved attractive. At other times, workers have been attracted to certain jobs rather than others because of the greater probability of regular employment, of more work weeks per year or per decade.

A third way of getting additional workers when sales expand is through increased wages. This method will be explained in Section 10, but first a cautionary comment is in order. Firms competing in the labor market usually are quite reluctant to engage in wage-rate competition among themselves for fear of spoiling the market. Each knows that if it takes the lead in raising its wage offers, one or more adverse developments are likely to follow. First, its existing employees probably will demand higher wages to equal those of persons newly hired. Subterfuges of classification and new job descriptions often fail to carry conviction about an alleged lack of discrimination. If the wage increase is confined to a lower bracket, those in higher-paid groups whose ranks are not being increased will often demand raises so that "customary differentials" will be maintained. Second, other firms may raise their wage-rate offers quickly so that the first firm gets no special advantage in the labor market and finds itself faced with a higher wage cost without any gain. Third, the wage increase which is easy to initiate when workers are needed may be virtually impossible to abandon after the recruitment campaign is passed or in later periods when employers would rather reduce wages than to lay off workers.

---

[2] Sometimes merely signing a union contract, previously resisted, solves an employer's labor problems.

**9. Overtime Work as an Alternative to Hiring Additional Workers.**—Because of these dangers and also because of the cost of hiring and training new workers, many employers deem it preferable to persuade their existing workers to work longer than the usual time per day or week. The extra cost of overtime pay, usually time-and-a-half, is thought to be less than the cost and disadvantages of expanding the labor force. This method has the distinct advantage that it can be instituted quickly and discontinued easily when no longer needed. Nor does it disturb the basic wage structure.

On the other hand, there are several disadvantages. The last hours of a long day are not as efficient as earlier hours. Workers accustomed to a five-day week do not work as well on an extra sixth day. Therefore the labor cost per unit of product is usually more than 50 per cent higher, even though the pay rate per hour is only time-and-a-half.

Workers differ in their willingness to work overtime. Some welcome the additional pay. Employers may advertise the overtime pay opportunities as a method of attracting workers of this type. Others do not want to spend more hours away from their homes, families, rest, or recreation. When salaried workers are not paid overtime, they have another reason for not being enthusiastic about long hours. Occasional overtime work may be acceptable, but not frequent nor protracted subtractions from leisure time. Wise employers take all these possibilities into account when deciding which methods to use for recruiting new workers. Worker-management councils are very helpful in ascertaining worker attitudes in such situations.

**10. Wage Raises Are a Last Resort.**—If an employer cannot attract the additional labor supply he needs by any of the foregoing methods, he may raise his wage bids above those formerly paid. By offering more than other employers of similar labor, he hopes to attract workers from them to him. But he does not want to pay any more than he has to. This involves some guessing on his part. He estimates how much of a wage increase is needed to get the number of workers he wants at the time he wants them. The employer must take into consideration not only the probable subjective response of prospective workers, but also certain time factors. It takes time to spread the news. It takes time for workers to make up their minds and to shift from one job or one community to another. It takes time to interview applicants and to train them for their work. And during all this time, rival employers may take defensive steps by increasing either wage or nonwage inducements to workers to remain.

All these factors differ from case to case. Useful generalizations are difficult, but a few may be made.

**11. Wage Increases Vary with the Time-Elasticity of the Supply of Labor.**—The quicker an employer wants additional labor, the higher he must bid for it. This is an application of the principle of the time-elasticity of supply explained in Chapter 14, Section 2. In that chapter the concept was defined as the length of time required for a given percentage price increase to call forth a given increment in supply. In the labor market a different statement of the same principle appears more useful. The time-elasticity of the supply of labor may be measured in terms of the height of the wage increase required to attract a given amount of labor within a given time.

This necessary wage increase will differ with the type of labor, the type of employer, the phase of the business cycle, etc. It is small (the *time*-elasticity is short) when there is a large float in the labor market area of the individual firm. If the float is large enough, advertising or nonwage incentives may suffice and the necessary wage increase may be zero. But if the local float is small, many of the needed workers must be enticed away from other firms or induced to migrate from other regions where they have been unemployed. This requires a larger wage increase (shows a longer time-elasticity). When labor organizations are present, they may help get the desired labor if the employer will negotiate a new contract at higher rates of pay. This makes the time-elasticity *for that wage increase* shorter than it would otherwise have been. Put in another way, the necessary wage increase is lower than would have been required without the union's help. On the other hand, a wage increase without a union contract or without certain terms demanded by the unions may prove very ineffective. The dissatisfied unions may strike, picket, or do other things to prevent the employer from getting labor at all or to make labor recruitment very expensive.

**12. Wage Increases Are Limited by the Intensity and Elasticity of the Demand for the Labor Product.**—A second useful generalization is that wage increases are limited by the intensity and the elasticity of the demand for the product. The greater the recent demand for the product, the more labor will be wanted and the higher the wage that can be paid. If the enterpriser thinks that his profit opportunity will not last long, he must hasten his labor recruitment. Or if he has a contract with a penalty clause for delays, as on certain construction jobs, he must work fast to prevent losing money. The higher the wage that an employer must pay to get extra labor within the desired time, the more irksome is that wage increase.

The elasticity of the demand for the labor *product* is also important. If the employer believes that he can raise the selling price of his product to offset the additional labor cost, he will be more willing to raise his wage bid. This is rarely true in the situation being considered here where the employer takes the initiative. It happens much more often when the wage increase is being demanded by organized workers from a group of employers who produce a similar product. This case will be analyzed in a later section where attention shifts to wage increases initiated by workers.

**13. Wage Increases Are Limited by the Production Function.—** Sometimes employers consider their production function in deciding how much they can afford to raise wages to attract or to keep workers.[3] If the variable cost in terms of labor input remains constant, the employer is not bothered with this problem. But when additional output involves decreasing labor efficiency, employers must consider the problem of rising labor cost per unit of output. This is true whether or not wage increases are made per unit of labor. But it is even more important when additional labor is sought at higher wages. There are few institutional aspects to the problem, however, and its consideration is best deferred to the next chapter.

**14. When Should Individual Workers Demand Higher Pay?—** In most cases wage increases are not initiated by the employer, but by the worker. The problems concerned with this approach occupy the next few sections of this chapter. At first we shall consider the viewpoint of the individual worker and later that of labor-unions. Most wage increases initiated from the labor side spring from the bargaining of organized workers, but the general principles introduced in this section will prove very useful in the analysis of the group situation.

Individual workers usually think they are paid less than they are worth. They have only a very hazy idea of just how much they are worth, but it is generally something more than they are currently getting. Workman Joe Doakes is not immune to the materialistic standards of a capitalistic society. Like his boss, he wants more than he is getting. He knows that in the competitive arena one must struggle with constant self-assertiveness if he would get ahead. His ego rises to the occasion. His desires are stimulated by motion

---

[3] The production function is the relation of output to unit costs.

pictures which exalt material success as the highest good, by radio dramas, by magazine fiction, by advertising. Joe may come under the spell of Marxist oratory. He may accept the dogma of capitalist exploitation of the workers. Even without fully understanding the doctrine of "surplus value," he may look at the profit his firm is making and say that its size proves he is being underpaid. He may not attempt to use logical reasoning at all. The boss may be paying higher wages to Jim Blount than to Joe Doakes who considers himself just as good a man. So Joe asks the boss for a raise.

In many cases what employers know is not much greater. They know profits are rising or are falling and they think that they do or do not need to keep Joe in a good humor. The threat of his quitting may or may not cause concern. In general, employers are more willing to grant raises when they are prospering than when the tide is turning against them. In small firms they are also influenced by such unpredictable circumstances as whether they happen to be feeling good when the request is received, and the manner in which they are approached.

Because of the importance of these subjective forces in the decisions of both workers and employers, it is very difficult to describe with precision an equilibrium wage rate for a given situation. The worker must face the prospect that if he insists upon a certain pay scale and if the employer is unwilling to grant it, the job may be ended. Hence the worker seeking a raise must have some scale of values which leads him to prefer the risk of unemployment to continued acquiescence in the wage he is getting. It may be that he knows of alternative positions elsewhere or merely that he prefers to work for himself or to be idle. Decisions regarding such matters are often reached without careful weighing of alternatives.

In very general terms one may state, on the supply side, that when wage increases are being considered wage rates tend toward an unstable balance between the marginal desire for more income and the marginal desire for assurance of job security. The individual worker may be pictured as achieving maximum satisfaction for the moment either by accepting what he has of both wages and employment prospects or by demanding higher pay and weakening his certainty (?) of continuing at work. Perhaps the negative approach is better. He minimizes his dissatisfactions with his pay and his feeling of insecurity by accepting the status quo or by making a bid for a change. Once the demand for more pay is made, subjective and objective states will change. He may win the increase or he may be denied. He may become more contented or more discontented. Worker attitudes are in a continuous state of flux. Their extreme instability should be contrasted with the attitudes of employers, whose measurements of pro and con are stabilized somewhat by the objective figures of income and outgo on the accounting records of the firm.

**15. Organized Labor Should Also Count the Cost of Wage Demands.**—When workers are organized, the situation is more complex. Some one speaks for the workers as a group, but he also speaks for himself. A true leader influences the views of his followers at the same time that he reflects them. A union official cannot often go contrary to the expressed wishes of a majority of his followers, but there is usually much opportunity to use his own discretion. Many a democratic organization is dominated by a vocal and aggressive minority. Rivalries may exist between elected officials. Personal considerations and objectives may influence a leader's interpretation of the wishes of his group. Generalizations about union wage demands are therefore more difficult to make than those which apply to individual workers. But they should be sought wherever enough similarities can be seen to warrant the belief that a rule may hold more than 50 per cent of the time.

For instance, if workers want more pay, should they risk a strike to get it? The decision may be made by leaders under blanket authority given them, or there may be a specific strike vote by the union members. They will be influenced by their answers to many questions. Is it likely that an agreement can be reached without having to strike? Would a strike eventually win the wages demanded? Or a lesser figure? How long would the strike last and what would it cost in lost wages? Would other unions be likely to contribute strike relief funds to the workers? If the wage increase is won, is the employer likely to discharge some workers and substitute others or install machinery instead? How much would this cost the organized group of workers?

The economist can offer some general precepts to guide the decision, but he should be under no illusions about their being used in actual strike situations. Emotion then becomes stronger than logic, or rationalization makes desires seem to be logical reasoning. There is also much difference between cases. For instance, if the demand for the services of the laborers asking higher pay is elastic, then a pay increase per worker would bring an income decrease for the labor group as a whole. Union leadership should consider this possibility before taking action. On the other hand, if the labor demand is inelastic, union hiring halls or some other device may be used to spread the work among the entire membership so that individual and group alike benefit. Or restrictions upon entry into the union may gradually reduce its size as older members drop out. This procedure is limited, of course, to highly skilled craft unions and could not be applied to large industrial unions.

The real contribution of the impartial economist is to say to both sides that the cost of a strike or lockout is greater for each than they are apt to think when tempers get frayed and patience is almost gone. It is illogical to argue against strikes on the ground that the workers usually lose more during their period of unemployment than they gain by higher wages. Statistics could not be obtained to prove any such generalization. It is not sufficient to cite individual cases which seem to support the point, for the other side can tell of many cases which "prove" the opposite. In some cases the economist speaks for the rank and file of the workers against impetuous leaders. At other times the leaders have the greater vision and the followers need more caution. On the other side of the controversy, the interests and views of stockholders may be in opposition to those of the company officials. And in the middle stands the long-suffering consumer.

**16. Time-Elasticity of Demand Following a Forced Wage Increase.**—A major difficulty in reaching conclusions about the best course of action is that of deciding how long a time period to consider. When a wage increase is forced upon an employer by a strike or the threat of a strike, he may not immediately reduce his working force. He may have orders which he must fill or materials which it is economical to use up. His demand therefore may appear to be very inelastic. But after a few weeks or months he may be able to substitute machinery or other forms of labor for the type of labor whose wages have been raised under compulsion. Where unions are strongly organized and unemployment is small, the substitution of other forms of labor may be very difficult and time-consuming. In some cases the employer may find no satisfactory solution and may decide to close down entirely. In other words, the longer the period of time, the more elastic the labor demand is likely to be in the face of wage increases.

The passage of time may also influence the demand for labor by the reaction of consumers to the higher prices which employers often seek following wage increases. If purchases decline, production and employment must decline, too, and high-cost firms may be forced out of business.

Under some circumstances the elasticity of demand may decrease, not increase, with the passage of time for adjustments to the wage increase. This could occur when the immediate reaction of an employer is to reduce the number of workers hired either because he wants to vent his anger against them for forcing the wage boost, because he lacks the working capital for a larger payroll, or because he reduces his output in order to get a more profitable relationship between *MFC* (marginal factor cost) and *MFR* (marginal factor revenue). After he has cooled off, the employer's desire for profit may outweigh his impulse toward revenge, or he may see the light and seek to learn how to cooperate with labor and earn its goodwill. He may accumulate or borrow the needed working capital, or may succeed in raising the selling price of the goods made with the labor concerned. This latter outcome is likely whenever the wage increase is industry-wide (like that of the soft coal miners). The possibility that such a price increase may occur tends to diminish the initial contraction in labor demand.

There is also the possibility that the wage increase may improve the quality of the labor performed so that the employer gets more for his money than he expected, conceivably even more than he received before. This is a likely possibility when the wage increase is in the lower brackets and permits the workers to buy more food, to ride to work instead of walking, to have a happier home life, etc. It may result from a changed attitude toward the employer if he can convince the workers of his desire to work with them instead of against them, but such an outcome is improbable if the wage boost is the outgrowth of a protracted strike. Another possibility is that the prospect of loss may shock the employer into more vigorous efforts to improve efficiency and reduce costs.

Whenever any such improvement in labor efficiency does occur, the result cannot be interpreted strictly in terms of the demand-elasticity for labor, since the "labor" ultimately becomes superior to that obtained at the outset. If labor demand schedules could be constructed in terms of work performed per unit of pay received instead of wage per unit of labor time, then the picture would be one of a decrease in supply in the schedule sense, causing the initial rise in wage, followed by an increase in schedule supply as work output increased and the wage rate per unit of work dropped toward the original figure.

**17. Workers May Accept Improved Conditions of Employment in Lieu of Wage Increases.**—Increased wages are not the only demand made by organized workers. Improved working conditions are often requested at the same time. These include all the things suggested above among the nonwage inducements that employers might offer (cf. Section 8). In addition there is the question of hours of work, a topic most frequently raised by the workers. They may want a shorter working week, or a different distribution of the hours of work throughout the day or the week.

Another worker demand is the change of rules regarding the minimum output per worker. This may involve direct reductions in output quotas or may seek the same end by requiring that more men be employed for the same task. The full-crew provisions of railway labor contracts are well known. Employers denounce them as "featherbedding." When unions are strong they may force employers to agree to hire "stand-by" workers who perform no useful service whatever, as in the case of the organized musicians.

**18. When Should Employers Try to Cut Wages? And Workers Accept?**—If we turn now to the downside of the wage-fluctuation problem, we note that the prime mover is the employer, not the worker. He may cut wages in either of two ways: either reduce the pay of those already employed or offer lower wages to new recruits. Even in periods of business decline the number of voluntary quits may exceed the necessary layoffs and therefore require some recruiting of new employees. To offer these workers lower wages than the rates paid to existing employees does not arouse the same opposition that occurs when, on the upswing, new workers are given more pay than those of greater seniority. Union rules offer the only serious obstacle. Even though it may be feasible to make wage cuts in this manner, there is also a danger. The new employees may feel that they need not work as hard as the better-paid workers of longer employment. This possibility of inferior work is also the major objection to reducing wages of existing employees. They may find ways of slowing up which express their resentment without making their shirking obvious enough to be grounds for dismissal.

If an employer adopts the expedient of cutting the wages of those already employed, it may be because he wants to increase profit, or because he needs to reduce costs to keep out of the red. Occasionally an employer may use wage cuts as a relatively painless method of reducing his labor force by provoking some to quit. However, the ones who leave are apt to be more energetic and resourceful than those who remain, so there is loss as well as gain.

Whether wage cuts are a method of last resort after all other possible economies have been exhausted or are the first thing the management tries is largely dependent upon the organizational strength of the workers. *If there is a strong union, wage cuts are not likely to be proposed* until the management can see no other way out. Union leaders will probably demand proof of alleged business losses and must be shown that there are no other feasible methods of cutting expenses.

If the company argues that wage cuts will result in more jobs by reducing costs and thus prices, representatives of the workers ought to study the probable demand-elasticity for the products of their labor. It may be that a price cut would not increase sales appreciably. There is also the possibility that price cuts would not follow wage cuts or would not be as large as warranted by the reduced payroll.[4] That is why some unions seek conditional contracts which link wage rates with rates of profit. Workers on their part would seem obligated to give a pledge not to reduce working efficiency if wage cuts prove necessary.

If sales of a firm decline one-fourth, the necessary labor will decline about one-fourth. An employer might discharge 25 out of 100 workers. Or he might cut 10 out of the 40 hours each employee worked per week. If the union is dominated by older men who would benefit from the application of the seniority rule, discharges may be favored. If the younger men run the show, or if the older men are willing to sacrifice for the benefit of those more recently hired, the shortened work week may be advocated. The latter expedient is probably best for the community in the long run, particularly in times of depression, although there are many exceptions to this generalization.[5] The employer retains his work force against the day of rising demand once more. The junior employees are saved from having to go on relief. The senior workers probably contribute more through sharing the work than they would have had to pay in taxes or would have given to charity organizations for the support of the unemployed. But what they lose in dollars they can gain through satisfactions of a nonmaterial type, a greater feeling of unity with other workers, the bond of shared sacrifices, the gratitude of those helped, a better community for their children, etc.

Employers' ideas about probable future demand for their product will influence their wage and employment policies. The pessimistic employer who thinks demand will decline still further in the future

---

[4] The percentage reductions in wages and prices will obviously be unequal, for wages are only a fractional part of total cost.

[5] In 1933 the government tried to promote this policy first on a voluntary basis and later through NIRA "codes" given the force of law.

will cut his labor force more quickly than the optimistic employer who thinks the recession will be temporary. If demand for the product is thought to be fairly elastic, wage-rate cuts are more likely to be tried than a discharge policy. The employer will reason that lower wage rates mean lower unit costs, which will permit lower prices and that these, in turn, will increase sales so that he will need most or all of his working force. No amount of optimism, however, will overcome a shortage of working capital, which discourages the accumulation of inventory or prevents operating at a loss when sales decline.

**19. Elasticity of Labor Supply Following a Forced Wage Decrease.**—The reaction of labor supply to a wage cut is a function of many things including, first, the time which elapses between the wage reduction and the workers' decisions to change their status. If they continue to hold their jobs while looking for others, the decision to stay makes for zero elasticity at that time, but if some are able to find more attractive jobs after looking around, their decision to quit will make the supply curve for the longer period somewhat elastic.

The second determinant of labor supply-elasticity is the trend in business conditions and employment. If things are on the upswing, immediate elasticities will be somewhat greater and ultimate elasticities very much greater than in a period of recession. But in good times employers are not likely to cut wages anyway. Hence our chief attention should be devoted to the downswing. Here the major questions are whether the employees will quit immediately as individuals or by a concerted strike and further, whether they will change their minds and want to come back after the passage of time has depleted their financial resources and changed optimism into pessimism. When the latter happens, the elasticity of supply becomes less than it was at the outset. However it is not likely to become zero, for some workers will undoubtedly find jobs elsewhere and others will tend to shun a firm with a record of wage-cutting.

A third major factor determining supply-elasticity of labor when wages fall is the degree of union organization and financial strength. A very strong union may be able to prevent strikebreakers from crossing its picket lines and thus raise supply-elasticity to infinity, i.e., reduce labor supply to zero. Unemployment insurance and relief systems are a fourth determinant and serve to increase supply-elasticity when wages are cut. In fifth place might be mentioned forces influencing the mobility of labor such as efficient employment exchanges, vocational training programs, moving costs, etc. All of these determinants of supply-elasticity of labor may differ among

places, occupational groups, and time periods. Hence it is dangerous
to make sweeping statements about *the* elasticity of supply of labor
in the short run or long run.

There are, of course, a multitude of supply curves for labor, even
for each type of labor. When, for instance, the managers of a certain
firm use a labor supply curve in deciding upon changes in wage or
hiring policy, they use one kind; when they are planning a new
venture to take several years for completion, they use another. One
might say there are at least as many supply curves for labor as there
are individual people planning to employ labor in different places,
times, and conditions. There are also the supply schedules as seen by
the laborers themselves or their agents. Economists might add a
large number of supply curves based on observed records of the past
and on their own concepts of over-all supply in particular vocations,
regions, types of labor, or phases of the business cycle. Finally, the
discussion of this section has concentrated on only one directional
type of labor supply curve, that in which the wage is falling. However, most of the comments are broad enough so that when considered
in conjunction with Sections 4 to 7 above the reader should be able
to work out his own supply functions for cases where the wage is
rising.

**20. Summary of Forces Determining Specific Wage Rates.**—
Although much of this chapter has dealt with special situations that
arise from time to time in the labor market, certain generalizations
may be derived even from an institutional approach. For instance,
specific money wage rates may be said to depend upon three groups
of forces which may be subdivided as follows:

I. Employers' appraisal prices, which in turn depend upon:
　　A. The customary wage rates in the area, the employer's own
　　　　precedents, or wages paid by other employers.
　　B. The expected demand prices for his product in various
　　　　quantities
　　C. The expected technical efficiency of labor (the production
　　　　function)
　　D. The time urgency of profit prospects contingent upon get-
　　　　ting labor

II. Workers' asking prices, which are a function of:
　　A. The customary wage rates in the area, the wage rates
　　　　previously received, or the rates newly established for
　　　　other labor groups.
　　B. The cost of living

C. Expected efficiency as workers
D. The strength of labor organization and the guesses of its leaders about the gains they can make or hold
E. The time urgency of money income contingent upon getting a job

III. Relative bargaining strength on each side, which depends upon:
A. The number of competitors (i.e., of substitute opportunities available to the other side)
B. The willingness of competitors to engage in wage competition in buying or selling labor
C. Legal maximum or minimum wages
D. Unconfessed time urgencies (not expressed in bids or offers)
E. Expected support or opposition from other groups (e.g., the public, or class allies)

*Changes* in wage rates result from changes in the variables under each of these three headings plus the time allowed for these changes to take effect.

# Chapter 18

## EQUILIBRIUM WAGE RATES: SOME
## THEORIES APPRAISED

**1. The Theory of Equilibrium Wage Rates.**—In Chapter 17 specific wage rates were shown to result from various demand and supply forces under modern capitalistic institutions. We now turn to the opposite approach and ask how these wage rates may affect labor demand and supply. In particular, we want to know when specific wage rates may be in "equilibrium." This is the problem of normal or stable wage rates. Since our economy is dynamic, wage equilibrium can exist only in the abstract. Wage theories often summarize the general conditions of this equilibrium under static, *ceteris paribus* conditions. Some of these deductive theories are very helpful in understanding the economic world in which we live. Others have led to erroneous conclusions because their premises were not realistic or inclusive enough. Both types of wage theories will be presented and evaluated in this chapter.

The basic principle of price equilibrium is readily stated. The specific price in the market must not of itself stimulate any change in either demand or supply. When a wage rate is the price under consideration, that wage must not cause employers to change their demand for labor nor workers to change their supply of labor. Temporary equilibria are established whenever a wage contract is signed or a verbal agreement is made. If this wage causes either party to change in the future the quantity of labor sought or offered, it is not an equilibrium wage for the long run. During the time required to make the change in labor demand or supply, other economic forces in the environment must be assumed constant. For example: a wage rate of $1.86 per hour for coal miners may be accepted by the owners as the result of bargaining on a certain date. They agree to pay this amount, but they make plans for the introduction of labor-saving machinery. When it is obtained, the mine owners reduce their demand for labor. This proves that the agreed wage was above the longer term equilibrium wage. But it would not be proved if, after the contract date, the demand for coal slackened and caused workers to be laid off, if the price of coal-mining machinery fell to make its installation more attractive, or if any other change in the economic environment occurred to affect the demand for labor.

The questions of this chapter therefore may be grouped under the demand and supply headings so familiar in economic analysis:

   I. How do specific wage rates influence the demand for labor?
        A. Demand equilibrium for one type of labor hired by an individual firm?
        B. Collective demand equilibrium for one type of labor?
  II. How do specific wage rates influence the supply of labor?
        A. The supply offered by single individuals?
        B. The collective supply of one type of labor?
 III. Why do different types of labor usually receive different wages?
        A. Demand differences?
        B. Supply differences?
  IV. How true are certain wage equilibrium theories?
        A. Demand approach: the marginal productivity theory?
        B. Supply approach: the cost of subsistence theory?
        C. The bargaining theory?
   V. How does the presence of labor-unions affect equilibrium wage rates?
  VI. Why do wage differences persist among members of the same labor group?

**2. Demand Equilibrium for One Type of Labor Hired by One Firm.**—In earlier chapters we have seen that the individual firm is in equilibrium when its marginal cost equals its marginal revenue. The output which gives that combination is the most profitable one for that firm under certain assumed conditions of demand for the product and cost of production. The major part of our attention centered upon demand conditions and the *shape* of the cost curves. A change in demand was shown to alter the output which made $MC = MR$. Very little was said about a change in the *position* of the cost curves. To this subject we now turn our attention.

An increase in wage rates, for instance, would raise the variable cost per unit of output. This would raise also the $MC$ and $ATC$ curves and reduce the output rate which maximizes profit. Reduced output would lead to reduced inputs of all variable factors, including labor. In other words, an increase in the wage rate tends to decrease the equilibrium labor quantity for each firm, i.e., its demand for labor.

Another way of presenting the same kind of argument is to change back to the approach of Chapter 8, Section 7. This developed the concept of diminishing returns of grain output per unit of fertilizer input. If we substitute labor for fertilizer as the variable input, the result will be similar. After a certain point is reached in most enterprises, more labor means less output per laborer. Both the average product and the marginal product diminish.

The diminishing average product may be called "Average Factor Product" ($AFP$), meaning the average product per unit of the variable factor used, which in this case is labor. The diminishing marginal product may be called "Marginal Factor Product" ($MFP$). Since we want to compare wages with the product of the labor for which the wages are paid, both should be expressed in dollar terms. Therefore the product must be considered sold and its value computed. This revenue from sale may then be called "Average Factor Revenue" ($AFR$) and "Marginal Factor Revenue" ($MFR$).

$AFR$ and $MFR$ curves (often shown as straight lines) usually slope downward for one or both of two reasons. The first was explained above as a manifestation of diminishing returns. In wage theory it is often called the "diminishing marginal productivity of labor." But we must note that there may also be a stage of increasing returns, and a turning point of constant returns. A review of Figure 26 in Chapter 8 will help to recall the fact that in processing and manufacturing there are often "flat" cost curves. This is the same as saying that the productivity curves have a flat top. In many enterprises the addition of workers of a given type does not change the output per worker, whether computed on an average or marginal basis. The $AFR$ and $MFR$ curves are horizontal straight lines, at least for the range of production that might be influenced by changes in wage rates (see Figure 60).

The second possible reason for a downward slope of $AFR$ and $MFR$ curves is the downward slope of the demand curve for the output of the firm. This was described in Chapter 4 as occurring rather frequently outside of agriculture and certain standardized raw materials. If the Average Product Revenue ($APR$, formerly $AR$) and Marginal Product Revenue ($MPR$, formerly $MR$) decline, the $AFR$ and $MFR$ curves must decline likewise even though $AFP = MFP$. That is, $AFR = AFP \times APR$ and $MFR = MFP \times MFR$.[1]

If, now, we assume further that the individual firm buys its labor at a fixed wage rate regardless of the number of workers hired, a

---

[1] The $APR$ and $MFR$ terms in the above formulae must themselves be averages if $AFP$ and $MFP$ represent more than one unit of the product, as is likely to be the case if the input units of labor are large.

maximum profit input point may be found from the intersection of
*MFC* and *MFR*. When the firm is very large or the labor supply is
very small, efforts to obtain more labor may force upward the wage

### FIGURE 60
FACTOR INPUT PRODUCTIVITY AS VALUE OF OUTPUTS

A. Diminishing Value Returns in Agriculture and Some Manufacturing Enterprises

B. Constant Value Returns in Certain Manufacturing Enterprises

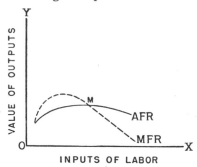
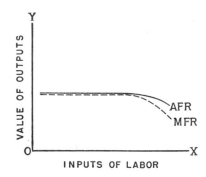

rate that must be offered. In this case *AFC* (the wage rate curve) is
not horizontal, but rises. The *MFC* curve must rise more rapidly,
according to the same principle that causes *MFR* to decline more
rapidly than *AFR*. Where *AFC=MFC*, the ideal amount of labor
to hire is shown by the point where *MFC = MFR*. Three possible

### FIGURE 61
EQUILIBRIUM OF THE FIRM UNDER THREE ASSUMPTIONS
(Constant Marginal Product of Labor (*MFP*) in Each Case)

A. Price Varies with Quantity Sold (Wages fixed)

B. Fixed Wage (Price varies) *

C. Wage Varies with Quantity Hired (Price varies) *

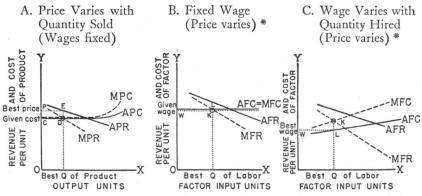

\* *AFR* and *MFR* curves would also slope downward if there were *diminishing*
marginal productivity of labor and either constant or varying price of product.

solutions to this problem of the equilibrium of the firm in regard to labor are given in Figure 61 above.

### 3. The Usefulness of Labor Demand Equilibrium Formulae Is Limited.

—The foregoing analysis is too limited in its assumptions to serve as a good guide to the actions of individual firms in the labor market. It appears to say that if organized workers were to force wages up, the marginal curves would intersect farther to the left and less labor would be hired. While true as a tendency, this influence is usually offset by other adjustments employers can make. Other costs may be reduced. Profits may be pared. Selling prices may be increased. Labor itself may become more efficient.

The marginal identity formula seems to show that wage reductions would increase the quantity of labor hired by the individual firm. This conclusion also is a low percentage generalization. There are many exceptions. Most firms hire only that amount of labor needed to produce the volume of output they expect to sell. Wage reductions would increase profit, but not sales, unless there were active price competition. Firms hesitate to engage in price competition for many reasons (cf. Chapter 12), such as possible adverse effects of retaliation by competitors. And when a whole group of competing firms cuts prices, the price-elasticity of demand for the product is much less favorable to the individual firm than if it alone makes the price reduction. Wage declines are less frequent and less permanent than wage increases. When they do occur, they often injure labor morale and reduce its efficiency, although voluntary reductions to keep a firm from closing entirely may meet with more favorable response.

Labor demand equilibrium formulae may also be used in another way. Assuming that the supply schedule of labor is given, the $MFC = MFR$ point indicates the *best quantity* of labor for the firm to hire. But here, again, the optimum labor input indicated by the formula is only a tendency. For many firms, the quantity of labor hired is determined by the production rate and that rate is a function of the orders on hand, not the firm's selling prices and wage rates. It is true that orders are a function of selling price, but other forces are also influential, such as selling efforts. In other cases the quantity of labor hired is determined by the equipment and the technology of the production process. A machine which is designed for one-man operation cannot be made to produce more by adding another operator to stand alongside the first. Technological factors of this type change very slowly.

In conclusion we must note that the equilibrium formulae for wage rates, labor quantities, or both are useful if their assumptions are kept in mind. They indicate the relation between certain variables. The omission of other variables is legitimate. But it is not legitimate to reason as though these other variables do not exist. On the other hand, one should not exalt the action of these other forces into another universal rule as limited as the $MFC = MFR$ formula. Sound reasoning and accurate prediction require that monistic explanations be discarded. The forecaster should consider the effects of many variables, including the background against which the specified variables operate.

**4. Collective Demand Equilibrium for One Type of Labor.**—The collective demand curve for a given type of labor undoubtedly slopes downward to the right. This negative slope would arise from cases of diminishing marginal productivity in the individual firms. But even where marginal productivity is constant, there are stronger and weaker demanders of labor. Maximum demand prices differ, and when they are grouped into a collective schedule the result is total demand varying inversely with the price. A change in the wage rate therefore tends to change the number of firms using that type of labor.

The equilibrium wage relative to collective demand is one which does not stimulate any change in the quantity of labor demanded by the employing group as a whole. Specifically, this means no change in the total demand which might result either from entry or exit of firms and no change from the expansion or contraction of existing firms.

**5. General Demand Equilibrium Considers Roundabout Effects.**—It is now necessary to introduce the roundabout effects of the wage rate upon the demand for the product of labor. There are two main possibilities. First is the effect of a wage rate upon the substitution of that type of labor for another factor, or vice versa. Factor substitution usually takes considerable time and therefore occurs only when there is a marked change in the unit cost or the efficiency of one of the factors. When rising wages or new inventions lead to the substitution of machinery for labor, a form of cross-elasticity is manifest. The increased demand for machinery may reduce the price of that machinery and this, in turn, may create a stimulus to further substitution in the same direction. On the other hand, if the price of the machinery rises, there will be a decreased amount of substitution for labor. Eventually, if no other disturbing changes occur, an equilibrium will develop between these two classes of factors of production.

The second roundabout effect is still more complex. In its simplest form it is the way in which increased wages, for instance, may increase consumer buying power and thus lead to increased sales. Production will then be likely to expand and more labor will be needed for the job. There are many possible complications, most of which can only be mentioned here. The workers in a shoe factory may buy some of their shoes from the store outlets of that factory, but employees of a steam-shovel factory do not buy steam-shovels. To raise the wages of the latter could have only a very roundabout effect upon sales. Increased wages may be saved, or used to pay off debts. Imports may be purchased instead of domestic goods. Further comment upon this circularity must be deferred until the payment of other factors of production has been analyzed. Even then, the supply effects must be included, too, if we are to complete the picture of general equilibrium for the economy as a whole.

**6. Specific Wage Rates Influence the Supply of Labor.**—The supply of a given type of labor depends upon forces which are both objective and subjective. The objective determinants include the number of people in a given place and their abilities. These forces are basic, but it seems best to defer their analysis until after we have examined the subjective elements. The amount of labor which a given group of people is willing to offer depends upon their rational and emotional reactions to the situation. It will be influenced by the wage rate, the conditions of work, attitude toward the employer, personal savings, economic aspirations, etc. These determinants can be seen best by considering the possible reactions of individual laborers in different situations.

**7. Labor Supply Equilibrium for the Individual Worker.**—We may begin by assuming that the wage offered by the employer is the only determinant of the number of hours worked and that all other forces are held constant. We must assume further that the individual worker is free to expand or contract his workday or workweek at will. Under these conditions the labor supply equilibrium point for each individual will be that at which the increment of satisfaction from one additional unit of labor income is just equal to the increment of satisfaction from the amount of leisure time that must be given up to gain that income.

For instance, Joe Doakes may be unwilling to give up a ninth hour every working day for $1 per hour, his wage rate for each of the first

8 hours. But at the same time he may be willing to work the ninth hour if paid $1.50 for this 1 hour of overtime. He values his sixteenth hour of leisure per day $(24 - 8 = 16)$ more than $1, but less than $1.50. Somewhere between these two figures is an equilibrium wage rate per *ninth* hour of work at which Joe would say it was a toss-up whether to work or to play. The money wage from a tenth hour of work would be less attractive than that from the ninth, while the desirability of a fifteenth hour of leisure would be greater than that of a sixteenth. Joe might still be willing to work this tenth hour for $1.50, or he might demand $2. His reaction depends upon such things as his physical energy, his desire to spend time with his family, his union affiliations, his acceptance of certain customs of wage payment, etc. A high percentage generalization may be made, however, to the effect that for hours of work beyond the customary amount, the supply curve for the labor of an individual worker slopes upward to the right.

We must now examine reductions in working hours with similar assumptions that workers are perfectly free to choose the rate of pay according to their reactions to different work loads. But we must also be realistic enough to assume that the workers in question have established certain customary levels of living (consumption of material goods) which they want to maintain.[2] The typical worker is not willing to work for a lower hourly rate when the workday is reduced. On the contrary, he usually wants a higher rate. It is more common for him to want to avoid any reduction in "take-home pay" than to desire more leisure at the sacrifice of money income. This is a valid generalization under the assumptions and is amply borne out by the history of labor wage rates in United States manufacturing firms after the second world war. In times of business recession, however, the picture is somewhat different. The worker is confronted with a third alternative, that of losing his job. In such cases he does his best to retain the going rate even though the working day is shortened. It is very uncommon for a worker to offer to work for less per hour if daily hours are cut from 8 to 7. Hours of work rarely approach zero, but if they did, a rising hourly supply price would almost certainly appear.

**8. There Are Many "Typical" Supply Curves for Individual Workers' Labor.**—The supply curve for a given type of labor by an individual laborer may now be drawn. The most significant portion

---

[2] These correspond to the customary levels of leisure implicitly assumed for wage changes upward.

of this curve is that in the vicinity of the customary workday and wage rate. The shape of the curve depends upon the direction in which wage rates are assumed to move. Figure 62 shows three possibilities. Curve $SA$ shows a rise from existing rates in terms of *marginal* increments, like the $MPC$ curve for the individual firm. Curve $SA'$ shows the same thing mathematically translated into *average* rates per hour (8 hours at $1 plus 1 hour at $1.50 brings in $9.50, or an average of $1.056 for the entire 9 hours).[3] When business conditions are not good, overtime is unlikely. If it is demanded by a particular employer, workers may waive their customary right to time and a half (see $SA''$) if not under a strict union contract. Curve $SS'$ shows what is most likely to happen to the individual labor supply if an employer attempts to reduce wages in good times. Employees refuse to work for him and strike or seek jobs elsewhere. When there is some unemployment and a recession threatens, workers may be willing to work the same number of hours at reduced pay, shown by $SB'$. If they have full freedom to choose, however, they may want to work longer hours, as indicated by $SB''$.[4] Finally, we may note that in good times when the declining variable is *work hours offered* by the employer, not wage rates, the individual supply curve of labor in terms of wage rates is likely to rise to the left, like $SC$. In bad times, reducing hours may bring no demand for increased pay, as shown by $SC'$. In short, there are many typical supply curves for a given type of labor of individuals. They differ with the direction of the wage change, the prevailing volume of unemployment, the power of unions, and a host of other things. And individual exceptions from general rules are, of course, legion.

9. **Labor Supply Equilibrium for Labor Groups.**—A wage rate may be said to be in supply equilibrium at a certain place for any given labor group when it does not stimulate net entry or net exit of labor from that group. If changes in labor supply do occur, it indicates either that the wage rate is above or below the equilibrium wage or that some nonwage force is in operation, such as military conscription, a plague, government efforts to encourage entry into a certain vocation by offers of free training or early retirement, etc. Supply equilibrium for the group need not include labor supply equilibrium for all members in that group. An increase in the

---

[3] A curve computed in this way is quite different from the sort of curve to be presented below where, to attract *more laborers,* the hourly rate itself is raised.

[4] This idea of a possible negative slope in a labor supply curve will be introduced again under the following discussion of collective labor supply.

## FIGURE 62

### LABOR SUPPLY CURVES FOR INDIVIDUAL WORKERS

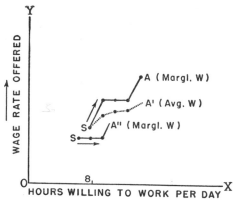

I. Wage Increases and *OVERTIME*

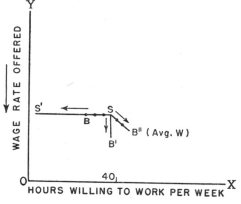

II. *WAGE* Decreases May Bring
Various Supply Reactions

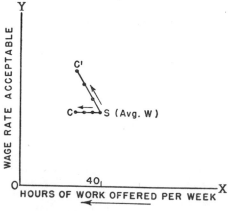

III. *HOUR* Decreases Bring Various
Wage Acceptability Reactions

average number of hours members are willing to work might be offset by exit from the group.

The aggregate labor supply for a group is a function of the number of people in that group together with the number of hours per week, month, or longer time period which each member of that group is willing to work. The supply may be considered either as a number of hours at a given wage rate, or a series of supply possibilities for a given series of wage rates. Labor supply schedules are almost always of the successive type. They involve the expected or realized *changes* in supply following changes in wage rates. One must therefore remember to watch the starting point of these wage changes, their direction, their timing, and their amplitude.

**10. The Collective Labor Supply Varies Directly with the Wage.**—The collective supply of labor of a given group rises and falls as the wage rate rises and falls. There are several reasons for this. In the first place, the individuals who comprise the group differ in their willingness to work for any given wage. They will drop out of the group at different wage rates as those rates fall. Changes in the individual labor supply may also reinforce this direct relationship between wage rates and labor hours offered.

In the second place a rise in wages stimulates those in other groups to enter the given group. This occurs in four ways. First, there is the transfer of effort from one occupation to another, i.e., to the one made relatively more attractive by its rise in pay. If radio technicians, for instance, receive a wage increase and others do not, some electricians may shift from other jobs to this type. This may happen quickly if the occupations are very much alike, but it usually takes considerable time. People are reluctant to desert a given trade for one which may be only temporarily ahead in income prospects. They may prefer to stay where they are and try to get their own wages raised. The threat of transfer may be helpful in wage bargaining. There are also union rules which prospective entrants must overcome. Mature and experienced workmen may be required to take a long apprenticeship. High initiation fees deter entrants. There are many methods that may be used to keep green pastures for those already there.

A second method of entry is to migrate from a low-wage to a high-wage region. Such migration occurs chiefly between parts of a given country. Immigration restrictions and differences in language and culture greatly limit movement between countries. This internal or external migration may add to the supply of a given type of labor immediately, as when Jewish doctors and scientists left Europe for America during the 1930's. Or the immigrants may need training and union cards like the country people who went to seaports to work in shipyards during the second world war.

The third method is the training of youth. Students in their teens are influenced in their choice of vocations by relative income possibilities. Many other factors are also involved, but in a pecuniary culture with considerable freedom of vocational choice, wage or salary possibilities are very important. Entry by this method, however, is necessarily slow.

Finally, very high wages for jobs requiring relatively little skill may attract women, children, and elderly people out of the home. This occurred very noticeably during the recent war. War fever and national propaganda also contributed to this movement, but large weekly pay envelopes were not unimportant. In general, the more highly paid occupations for a given level of ability attracted the most entrants of this type. Some of the elderly people were skilled workmen who had retired but returned temporarily to former vocations.

It should be obvious from the above discussion that the definition of an equilibrium wage rate for the collective supply of a given type of labor should state the time period involved. Even that does not help much. More useful is the concept of elasticity of supply relative to wage-rate changes. These changes may start from a hypothetical equilibrium wage or just from any prior wage. The cross-elasticity of supply is revealed by the transfer of workers from one occupational group to another.

The supply curve for labor of most types will probably have positive slope in the short run if that time period is defined in terms of individual willingness to work. This positive slope usually holds also for the moderately long run where changed attitudes influence entry or exit. One interesting exception to this generalization will be discussed in the next section. The very long-run supply of labor changes with the birth and death rates in different regions and economic groups. Economic aspects of this problem must be deferred until the next chapter.

**11. A Section with Negative Slope Appears in Some Collective Labor Supply Curves.**—For some large groups of labor, particularly the unskilled and semiskilled, higher wage rates often cause a *decrease* in the amount of labor supplied. From an individual viewpoint this refers not to overtime pay, but to wage-rate increases on an hourly or piece-rate basis.  Many workers seem to prefer a shorter work-week more than higher pay.  Or they split the difference, taking part of the gain in goods and part in leisure.  From a collective viewpoint the increased pay of the head of the family may permit his wife to quit working or his boys to go back to school.  Their exit from the labor market reduces the total labor supply in a labor group such as the "unskilled" which is large enough to include the father, too.  In terms of narrow vocational groups it is a special type of cross-elasticity of supply.  A wage increase in group A shifts workers not from B to A, but from B to C (i.e., to home or school).

This phenomenon has sometimes been diagrammed as in Figure 63.  The dotted line $S'S'$ indicates that wage *decreases* may lead to a still more pronounced negative slope.  The connection, however, is roundabout.  A general decline in wage rates is usually found only during business recessions.  At the same time unemployment grows.

### FIGURE 63

A Negative Section Likely in Supply Curve for Unskilled Labor

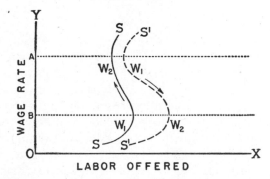

The workweek is likely to shorten, not to lengthen.  Pay envelopes become slimmer.  The wage earner may even be reduced to receiving unemployment insurance or relief.  In such cases, other members of the family often seek work to bring in supplementary income.  They increase the aggregate labor supply in the general unskilled or semi-skilled group.  Entry of this type is more pronounced than exit in the case of wage increases.  Labor supply curves of this type have only a short negative section.  At very high or very low wages, their slope is positive.

**12. Different Types of Labor Often Receive Different Wage Rates.**—We turn now to the question of why one type of labor normally receives more pay than another. We can ignore the question of the precise equilibrium wage for each group and speak in terms of norms or average wages for a group over a period of time. For centuries most judges have received more than most court clerks and most surgeons more than most nurses. Since wages are prices, the explanation of pay differentials must be found in demand and supply differences. Popularly stated, the labor demand is higher or the supply is lower. More accurately, the demand is higher at a given wage if the supply is the same in both groups at that wage; or the supply is lower at a given wage if the demand in both groups is the same. The next few sections will elaborate and illustrate this theme.

**13. Reasons for Differences in the Demand for Different Types of Labor.**—The demand for a given type of labor such as welders, machinists, salesmen, pilots, or bookkeepers depends chiefly, as has been said before, upon the ideas of businessmen about the profit that can be made by hiring them. Insofar as calculation of profit opportunities is rational, at least the following variables are considered: (1) the expected market demand for the product, expressed in terms of the quantity at a certain price, or a series of price-quantity pairs; (2) the expected technical method of production, expressed in terms of the factors to be used, some relatively fixed and others usable in varying proportions depending upon their probable prices and efficiencies; (3) the institutional restrictions upon demand such as monopsonistic agreements or practices among employers, maximum or minimum wage legislation, laws governing conditions of work, customs governing overtime pay, collective bargaining contracts, etc. Although hard to describe as rational, prejudice also enters the demand picture, as when employers dislike hiring women for certain jobs, refuse to take men over 40, or reject applicants who are colored or Oriental.

Back of the first two classes of demand determinants given above lie basic cultural conditions of the society in which the workers live. The demand for automobile mechanics in Detroit, for instance, grows out of the demand for automobiles from millions of people who have become accustomed to the possession and use of that luxury. We have developed knowledge of methods of mass production which lead to a demand for much unskilled and semiskilled labor instead of the more highly skilled labor that would be required were a smaller number of cars produced on a custom-made, hand-tooling basis. If in the future we demand airplanes in large numbers instead of automobiles, there will be some change in the types of labor demanded. The same will be true if technicians devise more efficient methods of producing automobiles than those now employed.

There is also another cultural determinant of labor demand that should not be overlooked, the opportunities for trade. The laborers producing a given article need not be the consumers buying it. Trade permits specialization which creates a demand for labor far different from that which would exist were exchange more limited. If trade were nonexistent there would be no commercial demand for labor at all! Each man would produce for himself alone. When trade exists, labor will be demanded to produce the articles for which a region is best fitted economically. Whatever affects the opportunities for trade, such as transportation costs, tariffs, foreign exchange costs, etc., therefore influences the quantities of particular types of labor that will be demanded in each given region.

The third class of causes of differences in the demand for different types of labor includes institutional developments, which often change quite rapidly. These are usually restrictive, such as anti-child labor laws, minimum wage laws, prohibitions upon the manufacture or sale of alcoholic beverages, and interunion disputes which may curtail an employer's ability to hire members of a rival union. Some institutional changes may also promote the demand for certain types of labor. Outstanding in this group are war and public works. The specific types of labor demanded under such spending programs will also be a function of technology in the art of destruction or construction, not to mention the technical aspects of making the weapons or the public improvements desired. The shift from oxidizing to atomic fission explosives is a recent change of major importance. Among institutional determinants of demand might also be listed such governmental policies as stimulate or restrain the general level of business activity in peacetime. Regardless of their cause, the different phases of the business cycle obviously influence the specific as well as the general demands for labor. Fluctuations in the demand for construction labor are a well-known case in point.

**14. Reasons for Differences in the Supply of Labor in Different Groups.**—The collective supply schedules of labor groups differ because of differences in the number of people able to do that kind of work and in their willingness to work for the wages offered. The number of people in a certain place at a given time is a result of past events. One would have to go far back into history to explain, for instance, the number of people now living in Los Angeles and still further back to explain the present population of Paris. Births, deaths, emigration, and immigration have all played a part. At any given time the labor resources of an area resemble the industrial equipment and the technology because each is a cultural heritage. In retrospect they differ only from mineral resources in that the history of their origin is more recent. Looking toward the future, they have the additional difference of being expansible.

The population of one region differs from that of another not only in numbers, but also in skills. This, too, is a cultural heritage. Although there are some changes from generation to generation, the vocation chosen by most children closely resembles that of their parents. Most sons of professional people go to college and enter the same or other professions. The present generation of coal miners is composed largely of sons of coal miners. Farm children become farmers, and so on. In a dynamic and growing country like the United States there are many exceptions to this rule, but not nearly enough to invalidate it. Even the educational opportunities for a given generation reflect the desire of the older generation that their children should be like their fathers.

There is also another viewpoint from which the skills available at any given time may be dependent upon the past distribution of similar skills, but the connection is more difficult to establish. It is the distribution of innate abilities. These abilities differ from person to person and have some tendency to be inherited. The skills which people develop are partly the result of the abilities which they possess. Therefore the skill distribution of one generation reflects in part the ability distribution of that generation, which, in turn, influences the next. This is not meant to deny the greater importance of educational opportunities as compared to heredity in determining any given distribution of skills. The argument is merely intended to indicate that heredity must not be discarded entirely.

Willingness to work for certain wage rates is also a cultural heritage. Low-income families have low aspirations. Their children do not appraise their worth to employers as high as do rich children of no greater ability or educational achievement. The wage customs of vocational groups are very strong in some countries. This is particularly true for *relative* status. Wages for a given type of labor may rise and fall considerably with the price level, but they will not change very much in relation to other wage rates.

The foregoing comments regarding differences in the supply of labor supplement, but do not contradict, the arguments of Section 8 about the elasticity of labor supply. They merely furnish the starting point relationships. When changes in demand alter wage rates, all sorts of supply changes may occur. Willingness to work may change; workers may migrate; new skills may be learned; and even the birth rates and death rates may be altered. All these comments, and many more, are needed to paint a complete picture of the labor supply differences which help to explain wage-rate differences among labor groups.

**15. The Cost of Production Theory of Differential Wage Rates.** —Cost of production differences are urged, by some, as the best explanation of differences not only in commodity prices but also in wage rates. The argument is partly true, but it accounts for only a portion of the supply-side approach and ignores the demand side entirely. The analogy with commodity prices breaks down at another point. The parents who pay most of the cost of rearing and training children have no expectation of getting all their money back. They are not in the business for profit. Nor are the childless taxpayers who contribute to the support of public schools.

The most that can be said for this theory is that it accounts for *some* of the differences in the supply of workers. Training for some vocations is obviously less costly and therefore open to more people than for other vocations. Or suppose the voters decide that more doctors are badly needed. Laws might be passed guaranteeing free tuition and living expenses for all who wanted to train for that vocation. If the cost of other educational opportunities remained unchanged, one would expect an increase in the number of doctors relative to those in other professions. The resultant decline in the typical doctor's earnings might then be ascribed to a change in the cost of production of doctors.

Some classical economists argued that the wages of manual laborers could not rise for very long above the cost of subsistence of those workers. If they did rise temporarily, the death rate would fall and the total number of workers would rise until competition forced wages down again to a bare "cost of production" level. The theory states an obvious tendency. But it overlooks the changing psychological and diet habit bases of what is called minimum subsistence. The cost of production of an American laborer is much higher now than 100 years ago and very much higher than that of an African kaffir or a Chinese coolie.

**16. The Marginal Productivity Theory of Wage Rates: a Critical Appraisal.**—Under certain conditions the differences in wage rates between different groups of workers may be explained by the so-called marginal productivity theory of wages. To be applicable, this theory requires that the demand for labor be expressed as a schedule or curve measuring the collective diminishing marginal value productivity of labor as seen by the group of employers involved.[5] The supply must be homogeneous and unorganized. The labor group must be defined as the total number which actually find employment.[6] Under these circumstances the wage rate will be determined at the point of intersection of the demand and supply curves.

This point then *reveals* the marginal productivity of the workers employed, but for various reasons the reverse interpretation has become widely accepted. The marginal productivity of the group is said to *determine* the wage. One reason for this often misleading interpretation is the fact that if the marginal value product of the workers rises because of higher prices for the product from which the demand for labor is derived, then the marginal productivity curve rises and lifts the equilibrium wage rate correspondingly. Another reason is that if the size of the group seeking employment is increased, the supply curve shifts to the right and the intersection with the demand curve comes at a lower point, i.e., the marginal productivity corresponding to the equilibrium wage rate is lower. (The converse would also be true in each of the last two illustrations.)

The marginal productivity theory of wages has very limited applicability because it is based upon assumptions which rarely apply to current wage situations. However, it may be used to explain in part why large groups of labor get lower wages than small groups, such as the unskilled as compared with the skilled. The theory here renders a service by showing that the size of the group is more important in wage determination than the skill of the workers. As the number of workers in any occupation rises, the pay will tend to fall, even though there is no decrease in the skill of each individual worker.

There are some cases in which a larger group has a greater demand for its services than a smaller group, with the result that the favorable demand differential for the larger group offsets the adverse force of its size. Automobile mechanics are more numerous and get more pay than blacksmiths; radio announcers get more than hog callers.

A second possible use of the marginal productivity theory of wages will be demonstrated in the next chapter, which endeavors to

---

[5] This has been more precisely defined above as marginal factor revenue. See Section 2.

[6] Another alternative when comparing groups would be the stipulation that an equal percentage of each group finds employment.

explain differences in real wages among various regions. In dealing with very large groups of workers, the requirement that supply must be homogeneous becomes far-fetched, but very useful conclusions may be reached.

**17. The Influence of Skill on Wages.**—The correct explanation of the influence of skill on wages may be seen by distinguishing between two different situations. In the first it is apparent that a journeyman carpenter is paid more than an apprentice, or a speedy and accurate stenographer more than a novice. Here the comparison is between *different degrees of the same type of skill.* Since pay is in proportion to work performed, the more highly skilled worker gets more pay per hour than the less highly skilled. But in the second situation, the carpenter must be compared with the stenographer, and who is to say the one is more skilled than the other? It is impossible to erect a satisfactory explanation of relative wage rates between labor groups by comparing the *degree of skill in different vocations.*

A comparison may be made between the time required to acquire the skills of each trade, but the cost of production argument is not enough. One must explain also the relative demand for each type of labor and the size of each labor group. Long years spent in training do not guarantee that the skill will be demanded once acquired (cf. wheelwrights) or that the skilled group will be so small as to command high pay for individual members (cf. public school teachers, or shipyard welders after a war). Not all people have the ability, the opportunity, or the financial resources required to get certain scarce skills, and in this sense skill influences wages by limiting the size of the group. But it is a roundabout argument that really supports the rival approach through marginal productivity.

**18. The Bargaining Theory of Wages: a Summary and Appraisal.**—Another explanation of relative wage rates among groups says that they are in direct proportion to the bargaining strength of the worker and in inverse proportion to the bargaining strength of the employer. This theory has several advantages. It brings both demand and supply forces into the picture. It says to each of the contending parties: "You can improve your position by increasing your bargaining strength." They know from experience that it is true. The theory avoids the fatalism of either the marginal productivity or the cost of production theories. It is also more realistic.

On the other hand, the bargaining theory may be misleading and is clearly only part of the explanation needed. It tends to make people think that bargaining power is something that either side can increase at will. It ignores the fact that bargaining weakness may be due to the presence of forces very difficult or undesirable to change. An employer's bargaining position with a given group of skilled workers is weakened by the presence of high profits, which are otherwise very desirable. A union's bargaining position may be weak because of the large volume of unemployment of its membership, a condition that is usually completely beyond the union's control.

The bargaining theory needs to be supplemented by explanations of the size of the labor group, the technical substitutability of one factor for another, the relation between labor demand and product demand, the interfirm competition of employers of labor, etc. All of these forces must be understood if one is to know why wage rates are what they are and why they change as they do. The bargaining theory is merely the capstone. That is why the other partial explanations were given first and it was saved for the last. With this general statement of the advantages and disadvantages of the bargaining theory we may now proceed to examine specific acts by which the one side or the other may increase its bargaining power.

Workers may improve their bargaining position in many ways. Individual workers may form unions and local unions may affiliate with others in the city, state, or nation. Alliances with unions of other types are often helpful, as through sympathy strikes and boycotts. Unions also accumulate funds which are useful in case of strikes to feed workers and their families and thus reduce the economic pressure to return to work. Union funds may be used for organizing other workers, for educational campaigns to increase group solidarity, and to work for favorable legislation. The latter method is one of the most important because laws govern not only the right to organize and to strike but also the methods that may be used in bargaining. That is why unions oppose legislative restrictions upon the right to negotiate closed-shop contracts and to engage in sympathetic strikes. They oppose the use of the injunction in labor disputes. They favor unemployment insurance for their own direct gain when out of work and also because it discourages unemployed workers from taking positions as strikebreakers.

On the other side of the picture the employers also use many methods to improve their bargaining strength and to weaken that of the workers. They seek laws to outlaw the closed shop, ban sympathetic strikes, get the right to use injunctions, etc. In case of strikes it is very important to get public sympathy. This may involve securing newspaper publicity which paints the workers' demands as unreasonable. Knowing that the general public condemns acts of violence and the destruction of property, employers occasionally employ men to pose as strikers and to urge or to perform such acts of violence. Another employer tactic is to hire people to promote dissension among the workers and weaken their solidarity.

Against this background, the bargaining theory seems to reduce to the statement that *wage changes* are best explained by acts which change relative bargaining strength. Certainly it does not *fully* explain the differences in *relative wage rates*. Locomotive engineers are as well organized as any group, but they do not get as much as airplane pilots. Organized coal miners do not get as much as organized musicians. There are also occasions where no bargaining is involved at all. Sometimes employers voluntarily offer more pay to their workers in order to keep them or to attract others. Skillfulness in bargaining at times may cover up weaknesses which the other side does not perceive. In short, enthusiasm for the many merits of the bargaining theory must not be allowed to make it *the* theory of wages. There is as much danger in its monism as in singling out any other partial theory for elevation to a place where it excludes other explanations.

**19. Unions May Strengthen the Demand for Their Services by Opposing Substitutes and by Aiding Employers.**—One of the most interesting developments of recent years in the labor field has been the increasing efforts of labor-unions to influence the *demand* for the labor of their members. They feel they have done all they can to raise wages by action on the supply side of the labor market. The next step is to reduce the elasticity of demand and to increase its intensity. There is some parallel here with the activities of monopolistic sellers of commodities who seek to raise prices by similar techniques. In the labor field, the action is of two main types: to decrease the demand for substitutes and to help employers pay higher wages.

The antisubstitute campaign has three objectives, to oppose substitute labor, substitute methods, and substitute products. It proceeds by various tactics, chiefly exclusion and cost-boosting. For instance, unionists traditionally oppose nonunionists who may want to take their jobs as strikebreakers, as rival bidders for jobs, or as candidates for union membership. This is the exclusion tactic. It has also been employed for more than a hundred years against the use of machinery or other labor-saving devices. In recent decades a supplementary tactic has been developed in the form of "featherbedding" rules by which the employer is forced to pay the partially displaced worker for as much time as it would have taken him to do the job in the old manner. For instance, faster trains do not save the railroad anything in terms of pay for the train crew because engineers, conductors, and brakemen generally get as much for 4 to 6 hours' work on the fast trains as they received on the same run formerly taking 8 hours. The gains from speedier schedules are therefore reduced, or the cost of introducing the labor-saving improvement is increased. From either viewpoint union action is calculated to discourage the employer from introducing the labor substitute.

Exclusion and cost-boosting tactics are also applied against rival goods in the production of which labor belonging to other unions (or to no union) is employed. Rivalry in the building trades, for instance, makes carpenters oppose the use of prefabricated houses produced by members of other unions and leads them to get city ordinances passed which either prohibit the erection of prefabricated dwellings or make them so expensive that they offer no economy. If that fails, the organized carpenters, and other building trades affected, may refuse to work for any contractor erecting them or may set up picket lines which other union workers refuse to cross. Another illustration of major importance is the cooperation which unions have given employers in efforts to raise tariff rates, secure interstate trade restrictions, and even city laws increasing the cost of goods "imported" from outside.

The cooperation against substitute products extends also to efforts to help employers pass on the cost of higher wages to consumers. This may take the form of pressure on Congress, the OPA, and the wage-regulating agency in time of war restrictions. In peacetime it may involve seeking industry-wide organization of both labor and employers with simultaneous or joint contract negotiation. In this way no one employer is put in a bad competitive position when he is forced to pay higher wages and all have the same incentive to raise prices at the same time.

One should also note a second group of cases in which the unions have influenced the demand for their labor by improving its efficiency. This involves conferences with employers about production methods, improving morale, job-training, etc. The Amalgamated Clothing Workers have a good record in this respect. Obviously employers can pay more if unions help workers to produce more.

A final comment on the monopolistic practices of organized labor might be that there seems to be very little that might be called oligopolistic activity. Unions rarely engage in competitive selling activities by making wage cuts corresponding to the price cuts of merchants and manufacturers. Therefore they do not have to consider what would happen to the demand for their labor if rival sellers were stimulated to cut wages, too. Employers on occasion have tried to play off individual workers against one another in such a way as to raise this problem, but the position of unions has generally been too strong.

20. **Wage Objectives of Union Labor May Vary.**—When a business firm operates monopolistically in setting the price for its product, a statement of the maximum profit price in formal terms is not difficult, but a similar statement for union wage policy is much more difficult. The business firm may logically be assumed to seek maximum net income in the total sale of its product for a given period. Unions are more often inclined to seek maximum gross return per unit of labor sold. They usually want the highest possible wage rate per hour or per week. Most unions give less attention to annual wage rates and only rarely do they plan how to maximize gross income for their entire membership considered as a group. In formal terms, they do not give much attention to the elasticity of the long-run demand curve for their labor. They are more apt to be concerned with the short-run bargaining range and to let the future take care of itself. And a bargained wage is notoriously unpredictable.

With increasing maturity, unions depart somewhat from the foregoing practices and a few show true long-range vision as indicated in the preceding section. But there is no uniformity. The most that an economist can say is that if union leaders seek short-run maximum wage rates they will probably strive for a higher figure than if they have long-run perspectives. The same is true if union policy concentrates on high hourly rates for the individual worker instead of maximum annual earnings of the group as a whole.

There is also the problem of those unions which are run (like some business firms) chiefly for the power and income of their officers. In such cases the wage policy is no more predictable than commodity price when profit maximization ceases to be the dominant motive. Racketeering obeys no formal rules. Recent demands for special retirement plans and medical aid further complicate the picture and make intergroup wage differentials greater than they appear from wage comparisons alone.

21. **Wage Differences among Members of a Given Vocational Group.**—In addition to the problem of wage differences among vocational groups which has been studied in the preceding five sections, there is also the task of explaining wage differences among members of a given group. These develop chiefly when workers are not or-

ganized, but may exist for the same type of work performed even by organized labor in different cities or firms. This is due to several peculiarities of the labor supply. First, inertia or immobility keeps workers at a given job even though the pay is higher next door. Workers like to work among old friends and acquaintances. They may even like their boss! Second, transfer to a new job may involve costs or losses which offset the gain from increased pay. Chief among these are the expense of moving and the loss of seniority. The latter may carry certain measurable retirement benefits together with the important, though intangible, assets of promotional opportunities and security against unemployment in bad times. Third, workers often lack knowledge of greener pastures elsewhere. Or if they hear about higher paying jobs, they may be suspicious about working conditions. Fourth, the other jobs may have a slightly different title or set of duties from that which a worker thinks he wants. This is one reason why even in the same firm there may exist wage discrepancies which cannot be justified upon grounds of differences in work performed or skills needed.

Intragroup wage differences may also develop because of slight differences in output per man day. Unions oppose such pay differentials, but employers often use output bonuses for their incentive value. This sometimes leads to reclassification by subdivision of a vocational group more detailed than the traditional one of apprentice, journeyman, and master craftsman. Nepotism and other forms of favoritism are all too common. Employers are also guilty of prejudice, such as that against women, married women, Negroes, Jews, Germans, Japanese, or men with gray hair. Where prejudice is community-wide, like that against races or women employees, the group discriminated against often becomes resigned to its fate and accepts as a self-valuation the relatively low figure named by the employers.

**22. Summary of Equilibrium Wage Theories.**—Following the introductory chapter which gave the institutional approach to wage determination in particular instances, this chapter has presented a more formal statement of the principles which explain wage rates in general. The problem was stated as one of explaining wages as prices and therefore the special circumstances of demand and supply were classified as follows:

I. The demand for a given type of labor is a function of:
  A. The expected intensity and elasticity of demand for *products* requiring that labor

   B. The technical methods of production (which influence
      marginal factor revenue schedules and interfactor sub-
      stitution)
   C. Existing institutional obstacles or aids
II. The supply of labor of a given type is a function of:
   A. The total population in a region (past birth and death rates
      plus migration) and their age distribution
   B. Ability to perform that type of work (includes cost of train-
      ing)
   C. Willingness to do that work (many subjective factors in-
      volved)
   D. Whether labor is organized or unorganized
      1. The type of union activity
      2. The objectives of union leaders

Both demand and supply curves shift through time as adjustments
are made to changing wage rates. Long-run curves generally have
greater elasticity than short-run curves, but the latter are the ones
which govern particular wage rates. Once a wage is determined for
the members of a group, the marginal productivity of a typical worker
may be defined, not vice versa. The marginal product is only a point
on a schedule and cannot be determined in the absence of a supply
schedule. Efforts to explain relative vocational wage rates by reference to skill fail to consider other determinants of the supply schedule and ignore the intensity of demand. An exception in favor of the
skill approach may be made for comparative wage rates of workers
performing the same type of labor.

When demand and supply curves are discontinuous in the neighborhood of their intersection, bargaining will set wage rates and the
outcome cannot be predicted. The bargaining range, however, is
set by general demand and supply conditions which are only partly
subject to control by the rival groups. The position of the wage
within that range is a function of the relative strength of the bargaining parties. Union organization aids labor in bargaining, particularly by limiting the size of the labor group. Sometimes unions
try to raise the demand curve by curbing the use of substitute products, labor, or methods. Worker efficiency may be increased. Employers also organize to improve bargaining strength. Both sides
seek public approval and government support. For these and other
reasons, wages of organized labor are indeterminate in the sense that
they cannot be described by any single principle, neither marginal
productivity, cost of production, nor relative bargaining strength.
In more advanced studies, several type situations are defined and
used in more detailed analysis than is possible in the present volume.

# Chapter 19

## COMPARATIVE REAL WAGES

**1. Statement of the Problem.**—Another problem of wage theory is the explanation of differences in *real* wages between different regions and different periods of time. We want to know whether the level of living is higher in one country than another, and why. Or we wonder how much a group of workers has benefited by its wage increases in the last ten years. This cannot be found by comparing money wage rates alone. For instance, machinists who now earn $3,500 per year may or may not be better off than when they earned only $2,000 per year. It depends chiefly upon whether the cost of living has risen less than 75 per cent or more than 75 per cent. Many other things also must be considered in making comparisons in this field. This chapter will consider the more important ones in answering the following questions:

1. What are the basic variables involved?

2. What determines the *general level* of per capita prodictivity?
   (a) The Law of Proportionality in factor ratios.

3. How explain the *changes* in real wages of a given labor group?
   (a) By changes in per capita productivity through the positive and negative effects of:
       (1) Capital accumulation?
       (2) Inventions?
   (b) By changes in bargaining strength and skill?
   (c) By changes in the labor supply?

4. What do statistics show regarding the effects of changes in the foregoing variables?

5. How explain the *differences* among average real incomes per capita in different countries *at the same time?*
   (a) What are the nonlabor factors of production which differ in quantity and quality from region to region?
   (b) How are levels of living affected also by:
       (1) War and war preparation?
       (2) The rate of capital accumulation?
       (3) The distribution of wealth?

**2. Definition of Terms and Statement of the Basic Data Needed.**
—*Real* wages may be defined as the amount of goods and services
that money wage earnings can buy when spent at the prevailing level
of prices for a given consumption budget.  To compare real wages in
different places or at different times, we need to know (1) the average
money earnings per family in each group, (2) a representative consumption budget appropriate to both groups and stated in terms of
physical quantities of goods and services, and (3) the retail prices of
the items in that budget for each place or time period.[1]  Each of these
data problems must now be examined.

The average amount of money earnings per family seems a more
logical starting point than the wage rate per worker.  It includes the
full- or part-time income of all members of the family considered
as a consuming unit.  Annual earnings are probably better than
monthly or weekly earnings.  The length of the typical workweek
may be less now than it used to be.  Or the coal miners in one region
may have only seasonal work while in other places most of them are
employed all the year round.  Statistical difficulties, however, often
force us to use data which are not as good as we should like.  Hourly
wage rates for individual workers are usually easier to get than average annual earnings per families.  Fortunately, for most purposes
their use does not seriously distort the conclusions.

Standard consumption budgets are still more difficult to obtain.
Statisticians have not been so active in this field as in that of money
wages and family earnings.  It is very hard to determine precisely the
typical consumption budget of a family of long ago.  We must rely
chiefly upon diaries and autobiographies which are far from perfect
sources of statistics.  Since 1920 scientific budget studies at different
income levels have become more frequent.  It is almost impossible to
get a single consumption budget which is fairly representative of two
groups when they represent different culture patterns.  The patterns
of life which are accepted as normal or desirable differ greatly between Orient and Occident, urban and rural communities, warm and
cold countries, or even two time periods a century apart.  The cost
of fuel for heating should be a large part of a Maine budget, but not
of a budget for Florida.  Most Americans are not interested in the
rice and fish diets of the Japanese, nor would automobiles be very
attractive to Eskimos.

The third set of data is more easily obtained than the first two.

---

[1] If the two regions are in different countries, we must also know the exchange
rate that should be used in comparing money prices and wages.

Retail prices in different regions can be surveyed fairly quickly as needed. Many countries publish cost-of-living indices which have sufficient continuity for use in comparing two time periods. Newspapers, books, and court records give major commodity prices far back into history. Many of the myriad items in a consumption budget are not very important and their price differences may be ignored.

Because of the data difficulties outlined in the preceding paragraphs, economists use various devices to simplify the problem. Sometimes they compute how many hours a certain type of worker must work to buy a single article, such as an all-wool suit or a pair of shoes. The highest level of living (real wage) is said to exist in the country, or the time period, where the fewest hours of work are required for such a purchase. At other times economists group all the people in a country together as consumer-producers regardless of their actual roles in the economy. The total national income divided by the total population will then give a per capita income figure whose spatial or temporal differences may be measured. Subtractions can also be made for the effects of war or unusual capital accumulation before reaching final conclusions as to relative real incomes. If there are marked differences in the distribution of income, the data will need further correction before they reveal the status of the working class or a certain labor group.

The ultimate form of simplification is to describe the independent variables one by one and tell how each affects the results. This is the procedure adopted in the remainder of the chapter. The first main topic is the explanation of changes in real wages which occur from one time period to another. The second is the difference in levels of living in different countries (or regions) at the same time.

**3. Per Capita Productivity Changes with the Quantities of the Factors.**—Except for war periods, the chief reason for changes in levels of living is changes in levels of output. Per capita consumption is closely related to per capita production. The money income received by workers, capitalists, landlords, etc., is spent to buy the goods produced at the time the income is paid out. There are some time lags and cyclical variations in investment, but it is true enough for our purposes to say that current consumption roughly equals current output.

Two other approximations are also useful. Changes in the national income occur much more rapidly than changes in the population and therefore may be said to reflect changes in per capita productivity.[2] Finally, since workers comprise by far the largest segment of the population, changes in per capita productivity may be presumed to indicate changes in real wages. Even though some people live without working, most of them perform some kind of labor for all or part of their incomes.

These assumptions narrow the scope of our task. We must now explain changes in per capita productivity. It is logical to make the first approach to our answer by using the principle of diminishing average returns. This principle was first used in Chapter 8 to help analyze the cost curves of the individual firm. Here it is applied to the economy as a whole. After a certain point is reached in the expansion of a region's population, additional workers will reduce the per capita output. This point of diminishing returns has been reached and passed in most if not all of the countries of the earth. At present the average output per worker is *inversely proportional* to the number of workers. The more the people, other things being equal, the less the output per person. At the same time, the average output per worker is also *directly proportional* to the quantity of other factors with which labor works to produce the total product. The more the capital with which each worker works, the greater his output will be.

**4. The Law of Proportionality and Some Applications.**—The direct and inverse relationships described above may be summarized for all factors under the so-called "Law of Proportionality." This law may be stated formally as follows: *When one factor, A, increases in proportion to other factors, B, C, etc., being combined with it, the average productivity of A falls and the average productivities of B, C, etc., rise.* The law could also be rephrased to apply to marginal products and the point of diminishing marginal returns. Both statements of the law require that there be enough of the variable factor present to push production past the relevant point of diminishing returns.

If production were to take place with fixed proportions of the factors, then each would be essential to its complement and no change in their quantity ratios could occur. Thus in certain chemical processes like the production of calcium chloride by treating calcium carbonate with hydrochloric acid neither chemical alone will make the desired product and an excess of either will also be useless. A less perfect illustration might be found in the field of labor, where to

---

[2] The changes in value terms must, of course, be adjusted for changes in the price level.

build a modern house the services of a group of specialists are needed, each one complementing the other. The carpenter cannot build the house without the aid of the plumber, electrician, painter, mason, etc. There must be at least one of each, or one person must act in a second or third capacity. There are also cases where at least two of a given kind must be present to help one another and the point of diminishing returns does not set in until the third member of the group appears.

Applied in the abstract without consideration for human values, the Law of Proportionality leads to some interesting conclusions. Densely populated portions of India or China would benefit if their capital equipment were doubled rapidly. Applying the same Law of Proportionality, they would also benefit if their population were decimated by plague. Like the Black Death of the Middle Ages, a great plague would bring anguish to many hearts, but its purely economic effects in agricultural areas should be beneficial. The average product of the survivors should be raised by the proportional decrease in the number of workers. The poorer grades of crop land could revert to pasture. The same benefits from a plague would not be so certain in an industrialized country. There it might be necessary to make expensive changes in machines and methods if the labor force were suddenly reduced one-tenth. Rapid emigration might have an effect quite similar to a plague and would cause less sorrow.

If population were to increase rapidly through immigration, per capita outputs would fall. Real wages and living levels would decline. The same would be true for a slower increase through a falling death rate or a rising birth rate. These methods take a long time. In the meanwhile there might be offsetting improvements in technology or increases in the stock of capital goods. And, of course, a reduced level of consumption is possible only if at the outset people are living above the subsistence level. If workers already are starving, one would not expect immigration to occur, nor the death rate to decline.

Factor classes should be subdivided for the best application of the Law of Proportionality. Certain types of workers or equipment may be very scarce at the same time that the class as a whole is too abundant. There are certain countries like India whose population is so fecund as to add continually to its unskilled laborers when what is most needed is people with engineering training, management ability, and manual skills. The population should not be considered as a unit and only its aggregate increase considered, for obviously the country would gain, not lose, by the immigration of persons possessing the knowledge and skills which are most scarce. And a similar comparison might be made of different types of capital equipment. An increase in farm tools might be much less stimulating to a region's per capita productivity than an increase in electrical generating capacity or transportation equipment.

The foregoing arguments may be summarized by saying that it is to the interest of any given labor group to encourage complementary factor groups to expand and particularly those factors which are most scarce in the light of prevailing or potential technology. In other words, every self-seeking group should stimulate the expansion of those other factors whose marginal productivity is highest. On the other hand, if some factors are partial substitutes for others, their increase should logically be opposed by the rival group even though in the economy as a whole the substitute has a higher marginal productivity than some other factor. That is why certain unions have opposed the introduction of labor-saving machinery and at the same time labor in general has benefited by its introduction. The Law of Proportionality may be summarized by the statement that that factor gains whose (service) quantity diminishes relative to other factors, and that the same factor loses when the reverse is true. How much it gains or loses depends upon the degree of relative change and the productiveness of the factors whose quantities change.

**5. Capital Accumulation Increases per Capita Productivity.**— When we compare average real wages in the United States today with those of a hundred years ago, we find that they have increased several fold. The Law of Proportionality offers a clue to the explanation. Population must have increased at a slower rate than the other factors. Capital goods have been accumulated very rapidly, and they have been improved by numerous inventions. In the United States the saver and the inventor have won the race against the stork by a wide margin. In certain other countries the contest between these positive and negative forces has been more even. The following paragraphs will explain some of the reasons.

Capital accumulation in the physical sense occurs when there is an addition to society's stock of machines, buildings, railroad trackage, office equipment, etc.[3] Some of the currently available land, labor, and materials are used to make these production goods more rapidly than they wear out or are discarded as obsolete. In addition to pro-

---

[3] The monetary background of savings, investment, and capital formation will be explained in a later chapter. At this point we are concerned with societal saving in terms of goods, not individual saving in terms of money.

duction of equipment in excess of replacement needs, there is continual improvement in quality. The output per worker is increased either by giving him more machines with which to work or better ones. The term *capital accumulation,* therefore, should be broad enough to include all changes in capital goods which make man's efforts more productive, whether quantitative in the accumulation sense or qualitative in the performance sense.

The accumulation of capital goods has economic, psychological, and political foundations. It tends to be most rapid in countries which are already rich in capital equipment, thus keeping them ahead of those vainly trying to catch up. "To him that hath shall be given . . ." Large individual and corporate incomes tend to promote savings and thus indirectly encourage investment and capital formation. From another viewpoint, large incomes may be said to furnish the necessary margin above survival needs which permits time and energy to be devoted to invention. The more this is done, the more rapid the rate of technological change. This in turn creates many opportunities for the profitable employment of savings by introducing the new to supplant the old. Another economic basis for our rapid growth in wealth and income has been the abundance of our natural resources at the time when our country was settled. Conditions were extremely favorable for the exercise of individual initiative in production. The free enterprise system was also favorable to the accumulation of capital and the invention of labor-saving devices. These various economic forces are and have been very interdependent.

The attitudes of individuals under capitalism might also be listed among the psychological forces, but there are others more clearly in this field. Individual capital accumulation is fostered by a desire to increase one's area of power. The owner of capital goods can give orders to those who must work with those goods in order to make a living. He can use his equipment in his struggle with other capitalists. Other individuals want to live without working and invest their savings in stocks and bonds. The sellers of these securities get control over additional funds and thus increase their power to buy and use goods and services. On the other hand, the fear of future expropriation of property or income from property may discourage saving. It may also discourage investing in the capital goods whose increase raises real wages. The fear of war might likewise cause people to put their savings into easily concealed and durable things like gold, silver, and jewels, instead of into machines and buildings. But these deterrents are often exaggerated, as will be shown in a later chapter.

The political forces influencing capital formation are both direct and indirect.  Governments may make the major decisions regarding capital accumulation and force the people to cooperate.  The Russian "Five Year Plans" offer a good illustration, also Hitler Germany's "Guns, not butter."  In this country a local school building program is ordered by the voters of a district.  Or a TVA may be proposed and financed by the representatives of those voters in Congress.  Progressive income and inheritance taxes influence capital formation in a different fashion.  Many other acts of governments have indirect and complex effects in this field, such as subsidies, agricultural price parities, tariffs, price ceilings, etc.  Further comments on capital formation must be deferred to the chapters on interest.

**6. The Effects of Inventions upon Real Wages May Be Good or Bad, Depending upon Circumstances.**—As suggested above, any invention which improves the efficiency of capital goods or the way in which they are used will increase total product and therefore the per capita real income of the group.  This generalized approach, however, says nothing about the way in which inventions may change the *distribution* of the enlarged total product.  New methods, materials, or products are introduced by capitalist businessmen presumably for their own benefit and not with a desire to benefit labor.  Just what is their effect upon the functional shares of a country's total income?  This question can best be answered by considering first the still narrower problem of the individual firm.

In a capitalistic economy inventions are usually sought and introduced because of the prospect of financial reward.  They are either cost-reducing inventions expected to widen profit margins or new products designed to attract a profitable volume of sales.  Costs may be reduced by mere rearrangement of a given group of factors or by substituting some for others.  Inventions which have the latter result are usually classified as capital-saving or labor-saving, while others are neutral, like many new products.  Land-saving inventions may be grouped separately if desired, such as building techniques which permit erecting taller structures than before.

Nearly all inventions benefit laborers as a group by improving their efficiency, by increasing the quantity of other factors with which labor works, or indirectly by providing desirable consumer goods.  Cost-reducing inventions may lead businessmen voluntarily to reduce the selling prices of their goods in order to get a larger total profit through expanded sales than would be possible with smaller output and larger profit margins per unit.  This will also tend to force downward the prices of substitute products. Consumers, including laborers, will benefit.[4]

But what about labor-saving inventions? Do they benefit or harm labor as a whole? It is obvious that in most cases their introduction means the displacement of certain individual laborers who are forced to seek work elsewhere at presumptively poorer terms. Where the demand for the product is very elastic and price competition is active, reduced prices may increase sales so much that the displaced workers may be reabsorbed in the same firm with little loss in time or job-rating, but this is the exception rather than the rule. Labor in general may benefit as consumers if, according to the argument of the preceding paragraph, the labor-saving invention leads to reduced prices of consumption goods or better quality. The degree to which prices are cut determines how much of the entrepreneur's initial gain is passed on to society as a whole. A precise balance can never be struck between the amount of gain received by worker-consumers and the loss suffered by the particular displaced employees. The gain and the loss occur to different people and are incommensurable, but society as a whole clearly gains.

Labor-saving devices are both substitutes for and complements of labor. In effect they constitute an increase in the supply of labor and thus reduce its marginal physical productivity. At the same time they increase the supply of capital (by improving its quality) and thus, according to the law of proportionality, raise the marginal productivity of labor. Which of these forces is the greater determines the net effect of inventions upon the average real income of laborers. The history of rising real wages in the past fifty years indicates that the complementary effect has outweighed the substitutionary effect. And there is no conclusive evidence that technological unemployment is cumulative.

**7. Other Effects of Inventions.**—The foregoing analysis does not treat a closely related problem, the proportionate shares of the total product going to laborers as a group, to capitalists as a group, etc. (Cf. Section 8.) The question of what governs how much individual laborers receive seems more important in terms of national policy. In fact, individual workers rarely concern themselves with anything beyond the specific and immediate effect of a certain change, such as an invention, upon themselves. They leave to economists the task or the pleasure of figuring out the larger issues. Nevertheless,

---

[4] If the new products are not consumer goods, and that is often the case, the reduced prices may not benefit consumers in the short run, but only the intervening producers or distributors. Again the degree of price competition is important.

they sometimes use his arguments about shares of national income when contending for higher wages or legislative support. Businessmen who are concerned about profits may invoke the economist and phrases like *economic progress* when they want to get workers to stop impeding the introduction of labor-saving devices. At other times these same businessmen may themselves oppose the introduction of machinery that would make their own obsolete.

There are two other interesting problems connected with inventions and real wages. The first deals with the way in which capital improves itself without having to subtract anything from current income in the form of savings. This is made possible by the joint effect of inventions and depreciation accounting. As machines, buildings, and other capital goods used by business firms wear out in use, accountants include as an expense a fractional part of their total cost in each accounting period. The depreciation "expense" is not paid out for the capital good because that good was paid for at the time of purchase. No income is paid out at all for this "expense," but it is accumulated as an increase in cash or in some other asset. By the end of the useful life of the capital good, enough wealth of some sort will have been accumulated to equal the cost of that good. It will have paid for itself and can be replaced without the need to call upon the owner for new investment.[5] If in the meantime better types of machines have been invented and offered for the same price, these may be purchased instead of making identical replacements. As the stock of capital goods in a region increases, the volume of depreciation allowances likewise mounts. New inventions in increasing number may be absorbed without forcing businessmen to enter the market for capital funds, or even to save out of their own net income.[6]

**8. The Effects of Unions upon Real Wages.**—Union leaders often claim that the improvement in labor's economic status in the

---

[5] Depreciation reserves are merely an accounting entry and do not represent cash or any property in particular. But they indicate the presence of liquid or tangible wealth equal to the original cost of the capital good at the end of its useful life, if calculations have been correct and business has gone as planned.

[6] The influence of the business cycle has been ignored in the foregoing analysis. It cannot be elaborated fully here, but two brief comments may be made. First, depreciation techniques reduce business demand for funds which other individuals save. This failure to borrow and spend saved funds may create a recession unless offset in some other way. Second, optimism and pessimism regarding the future trend of business are potent causes of the amount of capital goods purchased or constructed. On the upturn, when things look good, capital goods are demanded in large quantities. Labor is in demand. Wage payments rise. On the downturn, the opposite is true. Workers must not ignore this cyclical relationship when they examine the causes of changes in real wages.

last fifty years or more is to be attributed largely to the organization of workers into unions which increased their bargaining power. They reason from particular cases where they have been able to force employers to raise money wages to the general conclusion that workers on the average are benefited whenever any group among them improves its status. Or they argue that real wages have improved most rapidly during the recent decades of union expansion and therefore, *post hoc ergo propter hoc,* the former was caused by the latter. Despite some obvious loopholes in the logic employed, the conclusions deserve serious consideration. Maybe they contain truth for reasons other than those most commonly alleged.

In the first place, organized labor may improve its own position in particular cases if by superior bargaining strength it becomes able to win larger money wages than before. This could be done at the expense of either (1) the owners of the business, (2) those who buy the products of that firm, or (3) those who sell to the firm (other workers, land owners, lenders of capital, sellers of materials). Union labor's usual assumption is that the ones who lose when organized workers gain are the "employers" or "capitalists" who own the business and whose profits share is reduced. This may be so at the outset, but the owners usually succeed ultimately in shifting part or all of their immediate loss to other groups. They may raise the price of the articles sold if the wage cost increase applies to competitors as well as to themselves. When this is done, laborers as a whole will suffer, but not as much as the organized workers gain. The buying public includes non-labor consumers, and some of the employer's added burden is very likely to remain on his shoulders or to be shifted to non-labor factors. If the wage boost prompts employers to bargain more effectively with other groups of workers, the net gain for labor as a whole will be reduced.

According to principles previously explained, employers will probably try to substitute other factors for the laborers whose wage has been bargained upward. Substitution takes time, but eventually it brings a reduced schedule demand which may offset part of the wage rate increase. Its effect upon the total revenue of the union members depends upon what may be called the long-run elasticity of demand for that labor. In dealing with real wages, additional variables enter the picture and make generalization increasingly difficult. But the unionist is undoubtedly warranted in arguing that the average union member today receives a larger money wage and a larger real wage than he would get if he were one of an unorganized group. Some unions restrict membership and reap the monopoly gains of obstructed entry. Others contribute chiefly superior bargaining strength and skill.

The net effect of unions upon the real income of workers as a whole, including both organized and unorganized labor, involves the analyst in such a long list of possible variables working in different directions at different times that it seems best to appeal to statistics instead of to logic. Figures revealing labor's share in national income indicate that the percentage of the national income going to labor in the United States did not change much from 1899 to 1918 and from 1920 to 1939. The effects of wartime inflation and deflation brought an increase from an average of about 60 per cent in the first interval to 67 per cent in the second, the transition occurring in 1919 and 1920. If labor's share has not experienced a secular increase, then what becomes of arguments about the benefits of union organization? Few deny that the members of organized groups have benefited financially, and their gains are likely to have exceeded such increases in the cost of living as may have been the indirect effect of their gains. But the statistics seem to indicate that the *relative* position of *labor as a whole* has not improved.[7]

Other statistics show that the real income of the people as a whole, including workers, of course, has increased several fold during the past seventy years. Can this *absolute* improvement in the status of labor as a whole be credited to labor organizations? Or is it entirely the result of invention and capital accumulation as described above? The record of organized labor contains chapters in which the introduction of machines has been fought bitterly, either by outright opposition or by various forms of sabotage, including slowdown and featherbedding, which have prevented the expected labor-saving economies from being realized.

On the credit side may be put instances of unions improving the efficiency of their workers in various ways. Some unions have fine records of cooperation with management in the introduction of time-saving devices and in suggesting improvements (inventions) which reduce cost. The same unions and others have instituted training programs to improve the skill of their membership. Most of the gains in this line, however, have probably been indirect, i.e., those resulting from the improvement in labor morale and effort resulting from increased wages and a greater feeling of job security.

**9. Indirect Effects of Union Activity.**—Worker efficiency has been increased in indirect ways by union activity in various fields.

---

[7] Simon Kuznets, *National Income and Its Composition, 1919–1938,* New York: National Bureau of Economic Research, p. 22.

Collective bargaining contracts have brought improved working conditions, some participation in management, and a general sense of importance from being a member of a group possessing obvious power. Unions have led the way in movements for increased free public school opportunities, for the reduction of child labor, and for the introduction of workmen's accident compensation. Social security laws have worked in both directions. By improving health and the feeling of economic security they have helped efficiency. On the other hand, unemployment insurance may have decreased the morale of a minority. Some employers have been resentful against social security taxation and have tried to take it out of the workers indirectly.

One long-run offset may also be mentioned, the progressive reduction in the length of the work week. When the work week was very long, reductions actually raised the total weekly output in most cases. But now that a forty-hour week is fairly common, further reductions will probably reduce the total product per worker. At the same time they increase the workers' leisure. Even with reduced consumption of material goods, total satisfactions may rise. Under such circumstances one can hardly say that the worker has reduced his level of living by bargaining for a shorter work week.

Indirect gains for society may result from the way in which labor successes in bargaining force employers to search more aggressively for labor-saving devices. The increased power of unions in recent years undoubtedly has stimulated technological change in industry. It has given employers the same sort of stimulus that is traditionally provided by price competition. In other cases where business firms have used monopolistic techniques to appropriate for the small group of stockholders the gains from autonomous inventions, union demands for higher wages have been a good way to transfer these gains to a larger group of consumers.

### 10. An Increase in Labor Supply Usually Reduces Real Wages.
—The preceding six sections have dealt chiefly with factors causing increases in real wages. Now we must consider forces which cause decreases. The most obvious one is the destruction of capital goods, which is the reverse of the process of accumulation. Earthquakes, fires, insects, and other natural calamities take continuous toll. Wars cause more severe, but fortunately sporadic, destruction. Less obvious, but important, is the increase in the labor supply of a given region which results from (1) an excess of births over deaths, (2) net immigration, (3) people seeking employment who did not

work before (women, children, aged), and (4) laborers becoming willing to work longer hours.

The last two of these variables have an effect upon the level of consumption which is different from the first two. When a person works longer hours than customarily, he is likely to receive additional pay. This increases his personal income and hence presumably his level of consumption. The decline in marginal productivity per time unit of labor which generally occurs from this type of addition to the labor supply constitutes an *increase* in marginal productivity *per laborer*. Similarly when the members of a worker's family who were not previously employed add their efforts to the total number of labor hours being worked, marginal productivity tends to fall, both per hour and per laborer. But it rises *per family unit,* and hence the level of consumption increases. Another interesting paradox in this connection is the fact that these aspects of labor supply usually diminish as time goes by and their downward secular trend is interrupted only by war, depression, or other crisis. In such times they expand as offsets to the decline in civilian consumption that would otherwise occur. The plane of living may fall in wars and depressions, but it does not fall as far as it would if these additions to the labor supply did not occur.

The first two types of addition to the labor supply may be grouped under the general heading of a net increase in population or of the working force of a region. Sometimes immigration is the more important of the two, as in a large part of American history. At other times natural increase is the significant factor. Whether a net increase in population will raise or lower the marginal product of a region depends in the first instance upon the capital structure of the area. If it is primitive as in India, China, and much of Central Europe, then the principle of diminishing marginal returns will operate. If, however, the region is well equipped with capital, labor *may* be applied under conditions of increasing returns. The same may be true of the settlement of virgin territory where land is the abundant factor. It is also conceivable that a region with a relatively stationary population might experience such an increase in the non-labor factors that it shifted from a condition of diminishing returns to one of increasing returns, as illustrated in Figure 64. (Compare also Figure 27, page 103.) If the working population is at first $OQ$ with an average product curve $AP$, and then the latter curve rises to $AP'$, the point of diminishing average returns may shift from $OR$ to $OS$, so that there could still be an expansion of population beyond $OQ$ by immigration or natural increase with benefit rather than harm to the average real income of the people. A situation of this type might arise in any region where a large new factory is built or an irrigation project completed.

The form of capital and the structure of capitalistic organization tend to become adjusted to the size of the working force available, so that a war which is very destructive of human life might also push

FIGURE 64

EFFECTS OF POPULATION CHANGES UPON THE AVERAGE LEVEL
OF CONSUMPTION

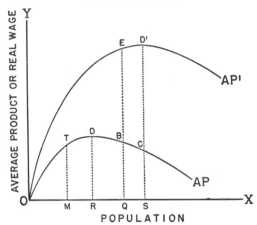

a country back from a decreasing returns position like *QB* to one of increasing returns like *MT,* although the probability is slight (see Section 9 below). Even in the primitive society of the Middle Ages, the Black Death, which took one third of the population of western Europe, may have had this sort of effect. Ordinarily, however, a regional economy operates so far past the point of diminishing returns for labor that a plague, famine, extensive emigration, or rapid industrialization would merely relieve population pressure momentarily and not nearly enough to get back past the point of optimum population. Most people who favor quantitative restrictions upon immigration into their country are probably arguing from a sound economic foundation, once the materialistic objective of maintaining or increasing consumption levels is accepted as the major goal. Exceptions would be found when the immigrants were more advanced industrially than the natives, as in the Americas in the seventeenth century and Palestine in the twentieth.

**11. The Dynamics of Real Wages—Statistical Investigations.** —Attempts have been made to investigate the statistics which are available to determine the relative influence of changes in the supplies of both capital and labor in western countries during recent decades. The most comprehensive study made in this country has been that of Paul H. Douglas, who came to the conclusion that the marginal productivity of labor in manufacturing from 1890 to 1922 declined 0.25 per cent for every 1.0 per cent increase in the labor supply. Similarly the marginal productivity of capital declined 0.75 per cent for every 1.0 increase in fixed capital.[8]

More significant, perhaps, is the cross-elasticity between the increase in capital and the increase in the marginal productivity of labor. This is determined as 3/4 of the total increase in product attributable to capital increase, or approximately 1/5 (18.9%). In other words a 1.00 per cent increase in fixed capital accumulated (in manufacturing) will *raise* the marginal productivity of *labor* approximately 0.20 per cent. On the other hand, a 1.00 per cent increase in labor will *reduce its own* marginal productivity about 0.25 per cent. Therefore, if inventions are ignored and the only two variables are capital accumulation and population expansion, the rate of capital accumulation must be more rapid than the rate of population increase if real wages are to rise, or even to remain constant.

According to the record, this condition was amply satisfied from 1899 to 1922. Capital in manufacturing increased much more rapidly than labor (1922 indexes: 431 and 161 respectively). As a result the *marginal* productivity of labor rose 49 per cent during the same interval. This figure exceeds considerably the 21 per cent increase in the real wage index for manufacturing obtained by dividing a money wage index by a cost of living index, but both results affirm the fact of an increase.[9] Perhaps part of the divergence may be explained by such factors as a time lag between increases in marginal productivity and the payment of higher money wages (the real wage index for 1923 was 128.6); the inclusion of nonmanufactured goods and services in the cost of living index; the use of retail prices in this index; an improved bargaining position upon the part of manufacturers, etc. An average value product index per employee during the same interval showed an increase of 36 per cent.

**12. Differences Between per Capita Real Incomes in Different Countries at the Same Time.**—The foregoing discussion of the dy-

---

[8] For the economy as a whole the figures were probably closer to 0.33 per cent and 0.67 per cent respectively. See Paul H. Douglas, *The Theory of Wages*, New York: The Macmillan Co., 1934, p. 493, and by implication, pp. 490–491. Also see Ch. 5.

[9] *Ibid.*, pp. 121, 125, 146, 512, and Chs. 5, 8, 20 *passim*.

namics of real wages provides tools of analysis which can expedite the answer to our next question about the reasons for differences in levels of consumption between countries at any given time. The basic reason is differences in the average productivity of the people. This is (1) inversely related to the size of the population and directly related to (2) the total hours which those people work, (3) the skill and morale of the workers, and (4) the quantity and quality of other factors which cooperate with labor. Among these other factors the more important ones are (a) the quantity of machinery and capital equipment of all kinds, (b) the amount of developed natural resources, especially fuel, power, metals, and arable land with good growing climate, and (c) the degree of managerial aggressiveness in applying new and more efficient methods of production. There are also various intangibles such as (5) the presence of an efficient system of finance and distribution and (6) a large accessible trading area permitting extensive geographical specialization and the economies of large-scale production.

Applying these principles, we may say that the high plane of living characteristic of the United States is largely the result of our having relatively large amounts of these "other factors" per worker and the fact that both management and workers have a high general average of skill and morale. In New Zealand, which had an equally high per capita real income before the war, the nonlabor resources are not so numerous, but the population is small per unit of agricultural land, workers are capable, and management is energetic. A special advantage of that country may perhaps lie in the morale-boosting effect of extensive labor organization and bargaining together with an ample social security program.

At the other extreme are the "backward countries" which lack capital accumulation, managerial enterprise, skilled workmen, and developed fuel or power resources. Technological knowledge is so cosmopolitan and so easily borrowed that the failure of a backward country to make use of it must be blamed not upon its absence, but upon the deficiencies just named. The accident of a late start down the road of industrialization is the main reason why such countries as Brazil and Russia lag behind.[10] The handicap of others such as India and China lies partly in the historical accident that brought them the benefits of modern medicine before the benefits of modern agricultural and industrial technology. They learned how to reduce

---

[10] Another effect of a late start is that the possibility of borrowing ideas and importing equipment and engineers permits the *rate* of industrial growth to be greater at the present in the adolescent countries than in the mature ones.

the death rate (especially infant mortality) before they accumulated equipment for increasing per capita productivity. In Western Europe and the United States the industrial revolution preceded the medical revolution and the plane of living rose before population growth could hold it back. Other underpopulated countries in the western hemisphere and the British Dominions have the blessing of abundant land to thank for their early start in the struggle for a higher plane of living. A detailed analysis of economic geography and economic history would be necessary to find the particular causes applicable in each case and to assign them their proper weights.

Real wages may also decline relative to other countries if a given nation decides to devote more of its resources to capital formation and accumulation than others do. This happens when, under the stimulus of a "Five-Year Plan" or other visions of greater power or productivity in the future, a nation's leaders decide to tax the people heavily to get more funds than would be made available by voluntary saving and lending. A less obviously painful method than taxation is the forced saving that occurs when deficit spending by the government raises prices more rapidly than the rise in many individual incomes.

**13. Intercountry Differences in Living Standards Affected by War.**—If a nation chooses to divert a sizeable proportion of its resources of men, materials, and machines into the accumulation of instruments of destruction, the standard of living may decline even though per capita productivity remains high. This qualification must be added to the generalization thus far made about the influence of factor quantities upon real wages. On the other hand, if rearmament begins during a depression, it may even raise the real wages of the working class as in Nazi Germany from 1932 to 1939.

Of course if war actually occurs, it affects the standard of living in various ways. First, it will probably increase the volume of production set aside for military purposes, thus tending to leave less for civilian consumption. Or it may stimulate people's willingness to work so that their services are available in far larger quantity than before the war. This is particularly true of management, which occupies a crucial position through its ability to discover and apply new methods of production which constitute in effect an increase in the intangible factor, knowledge. Women and retired people join the working forces, and regular workers labor overtime. This latter change, however, may be more than offset by the draining of manpower into the armed forces. No generalization can do more than mention the possible variables and point out the direction of their impact. Each situation will be different in over-all effect, depending upon circumstances, but most common is a decrease in civilian consumption, since both the relative and the absolute amounts taken for war usually increase.

Second, if a war results also in physical destruction at home as by gunfire, bombs, or incendiaries, there will be a decrease in the stock of capital goods such as factories, transportation facilities, office buildings, and homes. This will clearly diminish the average and marginal productivities of labor, so that a decrease in the level of consumption is inevitable. The disorganization of customary markets and sources of materials will also reduce output. The loss of life which accompanies such destruction would tend to raise the marginal product again were it not for the extra wounded to care for, the shattering of morale, and the drain on physical energy caused by insufficient shelter, clothing and food. However, even though the marginal product were to rise to its former level, the total product would be diminished. If war demands remain constant, the remainder for civilian use would have to decline.

A third way in which war affects the average level of consumption is through its effect upon international economic relations. War usually cuts off more trade connection than it establishes and therefore diminishes the quantity of factors which cooperate with the people of the warring country through division of labor and exchange. Isolation forces that country to produce substitute products at greater cost than for the exports which secured the former imports. A partial offset may be found through war-created opportunities to get imports without exporting. Foreign allies may lend or give (cf. lend-lease) more freely than in peacetime, so that domestic consumption may be maintained even though the production of civilian goods per capita declines. On the export side there may also be some saving through default on debt payments due to enemy countries, or even to allies. Other invisibles that may affect the picture one way or another include especially tourist travel, shipping services, and the international movement of bank balances or short-term capital. In connection with trade a final comment should be made about the effect of possible changes in foreign exchange rates. They usually move adversely to the warring country and therefore tend to reduce its volume of imports of civilian goods even more than would have occurred under war demands, shipping shortages, and blockades.

**14. "Economic Parasites" Reduce the Level of Living of Those Who Work.**—Countries differ in the percentage of their population which does not work. The idle have to be supported by the efforts of those who labor. *Except as they contribute indirectly* to the satisfactions of the working population, the idle may be called "economic parasites." This is clearly true of the unemployables, the sick, the aged, the crippled, and the mentally incompetent. Young children are parasites in one sense, but they give satisfaction to most parents whose labor supports them. From society's viewpoint children are people being prepared for the work of the future. If society decides that its youth should be trained better than formerly, the age for compulsory school attendance may be raised or the better students may be subsidized for higher education. Americans believe that the welfare of their country is improved by a long training period for its youth and are willing to have children remain economic parasites until they are sixteen, eighteen, or older. The high per capita income of the country helps to make this possible. If the output per family were much lower, as in many foreign countries, children would have to go to work at an early age in order to survive.

Our great wealth also makes possible an early retirement age. Many believe that it is good for the economy to force people to stop working at 65, 60, or earlier. The usual argument is compounded of a belief that there are not enough jobs for everybody and a sense of justice which says that the older people have worked enough and ought to be supported for their remaining years by the younger people whom they worked to rear.

In poor countries a higher percentage of the women have jobs outside the home than in rich countries. Here again there is a mixture of motives. The poor feel it necessary. Those with higher incomes believe that women contribute most to society by staying at home and caring for the men and the children. In times of depression, working women are criticized for "taking away the jobs that rightfully belong to men." Most men don't want their wives to work and are willing to support them in turn for their services in the home. These women are not "economic parasites" in the usual sense of the term. They contribute services and satisfactions directly instead of indirectly through working to earn money and buy goods and services for the family.

The unemployed are "parasites" through no fault of their own. They are able to work and want to work, but cannot find employment. Some of them live on their savings, others on their relatives. Some get unemployment insurance, part of which they themselves may have contributed while working. Others get a dole. Regardless of where they get the funds which they spend for food, clothing, and other items, the unemployed do not currently contribute to the production of the goods which they consume. The larger the fraction of the total population which they represent and the more they consume, the less the product that remains for those who do work.

There is also the problem of the armed forces. These men are nonproductive in the usual sense. They are "economic parasites." Yet a majority of the citizens whose level of living is reduced to support the military derive satisfaction from the thought that their country is "well defended" or is able to force its will upon weaker states. Others condemn the diversion of an increasing fraction of the national income into armed forces which are "too large" or more expensive than some other method of "defense." A few citizens get only apprehension, not satisfaction from their nation's military parasites. They fear that the armed forces may grow so large as to dominate the government and force civilians to vote ever larger appropriations. They also fear that the military influence in government may provoke war, not prevent it. The economic destructiveness of atomic war makes such apprehensions quite understandable. It is difficult for an economist to resolve such arguments. But the greater the number of military parasites in proportion to the number of workers, the lower the average level of living in terms of the goods and services which make up conventional budgets. Here again the great wealth of the United States and its small armies in the past have kept us from feeling the military burden very much. Poorer countries have suffered severely when a quarter or more of the national income has been diverted to preparedness expenditures.

**15. Large "Unearned Incomes," a Problem of the Unequal Distribution of Wealth.**—Capitalistic societies differ in the distribution of wealth among their populations. This is one cause of differences in their average levels of living. Some economies have a fairly large "middle class" like the United States. Others have chiefly the extremes of rich and poor with few between. Most of the very rich derive enough income from their wealth so that they do not have to work. They are "economic parasites." Many rich men also work. They combine earned and unearned incomes. In the middle classes, wages and salaries are supplemented to a much smaller degree by income from investments. There are others, such as widows, orphans, and retired people, whose very modest income is derived completely from property. We never think of calling these poor people "the idle rich," but only those who are fully capable of work and play around instead because of some fortunate inheritance.

All property income is "unearned" to the extent that its receipt requires no work on the part of the recipient. Whether its beneficiaries are in high or low income brackets, they are "economic parasites" when they use unearned income to obtain a share of the products of wage and salaried workers. As with similar groups examined above, some social justification is possible on various grounds. Some property owners have been thrifty savers in the past, some are philanthropic in the giving of time and money, and some cultivate the arts or promote research for the benefit of society as a whole. There is also the argument that large unearned incomes in the hands of a few are an inevitable by-product of the institution of private property which is believed to be essential to a free and progressive society. The beneficiaries of the system cultivate an acceptance of such ideas by the general public. In this they resemble other "economic parasites" such as the military who have been quite successful in getting taxpayers to believe that increasing armaments spell increasing national and personal safety. Since there seems to be an element of truth in such arguments, it is best for the workers to be happy in their support of the drones. This gives them satisfactions which lighten their load and make it tolerable, provided the "economic parasites" do not become too numerous or demanding.

The foregoing discussion is not intended to imply that the owners of private wealth should be expropriated or that state aid should be denied to youth, the aged, and the unemployed. Nor does it suggest that maximizing the average level of consumption for the masses is the proper major objective of social policy. It is merely intended to explain further variables influencing the level of consumption of those whose work is responsible for the welfare of the whole group. In some regions the bargaining power of the owning classes is probably stronger and that of the working classes weaker than in other regions. This causes differences in the distribution of income which must be taken into consideration if one is comparing and explaining the relative levels of consumption of farm labor or factory workers in different regions. If the workers at the bottom are kept so poor that they have insufficient nourishment, clothing, shelter, and education, their physical efficiency and morale may also be impaired. As a result an area where title to wealth is very unevenly distributed may have an average productivity lower than one otherwise identical, but with a much more even distribution of wealth. Considerations of this type probably help to explain why Poland or

Spain, for instance, were less prosperous before 1939 than Denmark or Norway.

**16. Roundabout Effects of Differences in Income Distribution.**—A final comment should be made about the long-run effects of various possible distributions of the national income. A complete discussion of this topic belongs properly in a chapter on economic progress, but briefly the argument may be given that in a capitalistic economy the volume of saving is probably enhanced by considerable inequality. If all of the unearned income in this country were distributed equally among the productive workers, the latter would probably save less in the aggregate than they together with the rich save now. This is so because those with low incomes generally have a much greater preference for additional present goods and services than for future security through saving and investing. Those with large incomes can buy the present goods they want with only part of their incomes and can easily create a surplus with which to satisfy their demand for expected future income or power.

The effects of the rate of saving upon real wages are roundabout and dependent upon other variables. For instance, savings which are invested in capital goods may promote economic progress. Savings which are hoarded promote unemployment of men and machines. The former result raises the level of living, the latter result lowers it. Savings by individuals are not as important as formerly in this country. Business firms accumulate most of their own savings for capital replacement and for expansion. They do not have to rely upon selling stocks or bonds to individuals as much as was necessary in an era when most profits were distributed as dividends. Bank credit and government credit are much more readily available for capital expansion than they used to be. Therefore, the deflationary effect of saving is probably more to be feared than the handicap-to-progress effect of inadequate saving. Further comments on this subject will be found in the chapters on interest.

The implications for social policy from this very brief analysis are somewhat as follows. Governments should do everything possible to promote full employment of resources in order that real wages may be as high as possible. This includes acts to reduce saving, to stimulate the investment of savings in capital goods, and to offset hoarded funds by government spending. No action should be taken in one field without considering its probable adverse results in another. If high taxes on large incomes discourage the investment of savings in new ventures, the loss to society may exceed, or be less than, the gain. If removing all taxes or profit income stimulates investment, it will also distort the distribution of incomes in favor of the rich and promote greater saving. The net balance may be good for the average citizen, or it may be bad. Unstated results also enter the picture. And there are other objectives which guide men's actions. Maximizing per capita income as a goal in our society must be supplemented with the maintenance of freedom, the securing of economic justice, and the preservation of peace. Those who contemplate legislation to bring the worker a larger share of the national income should put a whole group of the pros and cons of many alternatives on the scales, not just one or two, before deciding which course is the best.

**17. Summary of Economic Principles Explaining Differences in Real Wages.**—Real wages differ from place to place and time to time according to differences in money wages and the cost of buying a representative budget. Comparisons can best be made in terms of the marginal product on the assumption that the workers of even large groups are roughly homogeneous, or have similar differences. Using this approach the comparative real wages of any labor group are seen to be a time or place function of differences in:

1. Quantity of labor supplied by the labor group (includes number of laborers, hours worked, efficiency of work)

2. Quantity of other factors, especially capital, which usually increases through time but is destroyed by wars

3. Efficiency with which the factors are combined; especially the role of inventions of various kinds

Additional determinants which do not fit into the above approach include:

4. Number of workers in the representative family group

5. The strength of unions in:
    (a) Restricting entry (keeping down the size of their group)
    (b) Winning larger money wages at expense of employers, consumers, or other labor groups
    (c) Getting paid for work not performed (featherbedding)
    (d) Improving the cooperation or energy output of members

6. Amount of national product diverted into:
    (a) Capital formation by private initiative or government plan
    (b) Preparation for war

   (c) Support of non-working groups ("economic parasites")
      (1) Unemployables
      (2) Youth, aged
      (3) Women
      (4) Unemployed
      (5) Armed forces
      (6) Idle rich

7. Miscellaneous determinants of the size of the national product
   (a) War destruction or war stimulation
   (b) Size of the free trade area
   (c) Distribution of wealth and income
   (d) Uninvested savings

# Chapter 20

## WAGE THEORY AND UNEMPLOYMENT

**1. The Wage Theory Approach to the Problem of Unemployment.**—Unemployment exists when people who want to work cannot find work at terms satisfactory to them. The unemployed include people who have never worked before, those who have quit former jobs, and those who have been discharged or laid off. A complete study of the problem would explain the reasons for quits, discharges, layoffs, and the failure of people to find the jobs they want. It would also consider the effects of unemployment on individuals, on the economy, and on social and political developments.

In this chapter we shall discuss only those aspects of unemployment which are appropriate to the wage theory section of a book on price economics. The *effects* of unemployment upon wage rates have already been discussed in earlier chapters. Only a portion of that material need be repeated here. We now want to study how wage rates, wage offers, or wage demands *cause* unemployment. The specific questions to be answered are the following:

1. How do wage rates or their changes affect unemployment?
   (a) When product demand declines?
   (b) When other factors become relatively cheaper than labor?
       (1) Because workers demand increased pay?
       (2) Because of decreases in the prices of other factors?
       (3) Because of changed technology?
       (4) Because of reduced worker efficiency?
   (c) When employers do not pay enough to satisfy workers?

**2. Unemployment as an Individual Problem.**—Statistics of aggregate unemployment represent the total of individual unemployment situations. If a million men are listed as looking for jobs, each one of them has his own problem, but certain typical situations may be generalized. At the risk of oversimplification, we may think of unemployment as resulting when two people cannot agree about a job. The worker asks too much or the employer offers too little. They do not agree, and they do not make a deal. The disagreement may relate to wage rates or to other terms of employment. If an

319

employer wants a skilled worker and the applicant is without experience or skill, willingness of the unemployed man to work for little or nothing will not get him the job. Similarly, a union card or a college degree may be required before negotiations begin. The trouble may be merely that one or both lack information about the opportunities. The worker does not know that there is an employer offering work at acceptable terms. Or the employer does not know about Bill Smith who is willing to work at the job offered.

The individual problem may even lie in the realm of personalities. The boss does not like Jim Brown and fires him. Or employer Cross has a bad reputation. He is known as a slave driver, a man reluctant to make promotions, an enemy of unions, "unfair to organized labor," or the like. Workers may quit because an employer does things they don't like or fails to do things they want. Employers may dislike Negroes, Jews, women workers, dark-skinned people, cross-eyed individuals, etc. It is not our task to inquire into the reasons for these antipathies on one side or the other. Nor are we concerned with their merits. They are mentioned here only because if they were omitted, the hasty reader might think that the following discussion was intended to cover the entire subject instead of just one part of it.

### 3. When Product Demand Declines, Labor Demand Declines Also.

—If the demand for a manufactured good declines, output is likely to decline, too. When the production rate is reduced, fewer workers are needed. Employees are laid off, and unemployment figures rise. The sequence is obvious, but the implications should be examined with care. Each statement must be accepted as a generalization to which there are some exceptions, but not enough to invalidate the rule.

Take the case of automobiles. A decline in schedule demand means that fewer automobiles are bought per week than before. Fewer Fords will be produced, unless there is a temporary willingness to produce for inventory. Fewer employees will be needed in Ford plants. The wage rate has no direct connection with this type of unemployment. But there are some indirect connections of importance. If Ford were to reduce his price while other automobile producers kept theirs unchanged, Ford sales would probably rise, perhaps back to their former level. This would benefit Ford workers, but it might not benefit Ford. The price cut might reduce his total net profit below that which existed with the reduced volume of sales and the unchanged price. However, if Ford workers wanted so much to keep working that they offered to work for less, Ford might expect to save as much on wages as he lost on the price cut. This might be sufficient inducement for him to run the risk of price-cutting in a highly competitive industry. Such is one possible indirect connection between wage rates and employment.[1]

The foregoing illustration leads to the generalization that rigid wage rates are *one* of the things which promote unemployment in times of declining demand. But it does *not* show that in most cases of declining demand the number of workers could be held constant by wage cuts. The argument is rather that *some* unemployment might be averted in this way.

How much good wage cuts would do depends upon several other things. If the employer will not cut his price, there will be no change. If he does make a price cut, the resultant increase in sales and employment will depend upon the amount of the cut and the elasticity of demand for his product. Demand-elasticity in turn depends upon what prices are asked by competitors, the success of their advertising, quality changes in rival products, and many other possible variables. All of these things have been discussed in earlier chapters (cf. Chapter 4).

**4. Wage Cuts Will Not Cure a Depression, May Make It Worse.**—During a recession we usually hunt around for something to do which will stop the decline. Workers say prices should be reduced so that people can buy more and employers hire more. Employers are more apt to say that wages should be reduced so that prices can be reduced, more goods sold, and more workers hired. Most producers during recessions are unwilling to risk price cuts to test the elasticity of demand for their product.[2] It is doubtful if wage reductions would increase very much their willingness to cut prices. Fear of equal or greater price cuts by rivals remains a strong deterrent. Therefore, on this ground alone, economists would be warranted in opposing wage cuts as a general policy, although admitting the presence of exceptional cases.

There is also a roundabout effect of wage cuts to be considered. Wage-rate reductions may decrease the total of wage payments or may increase them, depending upon the elasticity of demand for labor, which in turn depends upon the elasticity of demand for the product

---

[1] Note that the assumption is one of a general decline in demand, not one of Ford falling behind in sales because competitors put out better cars.

[2] The producers referred to are, of course, those who can control their selling prices and increase output if market demand increases with a drop in price. The argument excludes farmers and other sellers in markets where there are very many rivals on the supply side.

whose price is now presumed to be cut.[3]  If we start with 1,000 workers earning $50 per week, the total payroll is $50,000.  A decline in demand and sales brings a 20 per cent layoff.  The total payroll drops to 800 times $50, or $40,000.  The question now is whether that $40,000 will be raised or lowered by a wage cut to $40 per week.  If there is no price cut (and if sales do not expand for any other reason), the number of employees will remain at 800 and the total payroll at the new rate will be $32,000.  This reduction of $8,000 in earnings will reduce spending by approximately that amount.  Sales will decline and the demand for workers will be less than before.  Laborers in general will have lost, not gained, by the wage cut.

Using the less likely assumption that price cuts do follow the wage cut, we note that sales probably would have to increase more than 25 per cent to raise the number of workers from 800 to a figure above 1,000.  A labor force of 1,100 would mean a total payroll of $44,000, up $4,000 from the previous total.  It is this $4,000 increase which is important, *if it occurs,* not the fact that $44,000 is still $6,000 below the original total payroll of $50,000.  But sales may not increase that much.  If they expand employment only up to 900 persons, the payroll of $36,000 would permit fewer purchases than the $40,000 received at the old wage of $50 for 800 employees.

The next question to be considered is the effect of wage cuts upon the volume of spending out of a given total wage income.  Consider, for instance, the two alternatives of $40,000 received by 800 workers at $50 each and $40,000 received by 1,000 workers at $40 each after wage rates have been cut.  It is probable that the latter group would spend more than the former.  The savings of the average family after a $10 weekly wage cut are likely to be small if not negative.  Approximately all the $40,000 would be spent.  But the 800 fortunate workers still getting $50 per week would continue to save, perhaps more than before, so that their aggregate spending might be only $36,000.  This would seem to imply that recovery would be promoted more by a wage cut than by wage rigidity.  The argument, however, neglects the probability that the wage cut would *not* restore employment to 1,000 workers.  The more probable result during a business recession would be only a very slight proximate increase, such as from 800 to 825 workers.  This would leave total payrolls at $33,000, much below the $36,000 spent by the 800 workers receiving $50 per

---

[3] This is a reasonable but not a necessary assumption.  There would be some cases where employers would be willing to hire more workers or to reduce their layoffs if wage rates were cut, even though sales volume were not expanded by price cuts or otherwise.

week and saving $5. The ultimate roundabout effect would be still worse.

There is still another possibility which might be significant in the short run when unemployment is not large. It is based upon the observation that when workers lose their jobs, they do not curtail their spending very much very soon. Ultimately they may have to reduce their level of living considerably, but at first they resist this change. They draw upon savings, borrow from friends and relatives, get loans on their life insurance, automobiles, or furniture, etc. Within a few weeks they may begin to draw unemployment insurance. After that runs out, they may get a relief dole, or charity aid. The 200 workers laid off in our illustration may spend as much as $40 per week during the first few weeks of unemployment. Total spending does not drop from $50,000 to $40,000, but only to $48,000. After several months the drop might be to $30 per week for the unemployed, or a total of $46,000. This is clearly larger than the amount that would be spent if the entire working force of 1,000 were employed at the lower weekly wage of $40. If total consumer spending is an important force in determining the level of business activity, it would seem better, at least at first, to keep wage rates rigid.

From several lines of reasoning we reach the conclusion that *as a general rule* wage cuts are more likely to accelerate a decline in total spending than to increase it. They should not be recommended as an appropriate cure for a business recession or depression. Wage cuts are not likely to increase very much the proximate demand for labor. Their roundabout effects on aggregate consumer spending would probably be deflationary. Investment to increase capacity or to modernize will not be stimulated during a recession by anything so simple as a few reductions in wage rates. However, certain exceptional cases can be found. Occasionally wage cuts keep a firm from shutting down entirely. There are also certain social advantages of private employment induced by wage cuts instead of relief or government work projects. But reducing the length of the workweek is a much quicker and surer way of securing this objective than the highly uncertain method of reducing wage rates.

**5. Wage Rates Promote Unemployment When Other Factors Become Relatively Cheaper Than Labor.**—Firms also dismiss workers when it becomes profitable to substitute other factors for labor. Changes of four types create that kind of situation. First, workers may raise their wage-rate demands. Second, interest rates or rents may fall. Third, the daily output of the average worker may decline. Fourth, the efficiency of other factors may rise, as when "labor-saving" devices are invented.

A fifth possibility may be mentioned briefly before passing to a more extensive study of the other four. It is a shift in consumer demand from one type of product to another. This will almost always bring some change in the kind of labor demanded, as when automobiles were purchased instead of carriages. The shift may also change the total quantity of labor demanded if the second article requires less labor per dollar value of finished product than the former. Beer versus milk is perhaps a good illustration.

**6. Unemployment May Be Caused by Wage Demands Being Too High.**—When workers raise their wage demands, employers may be unwilling or unable to pay the higher wage. As a result the workers and employers cannot agree on a mutually acceptable wage rate. Workers leave their jobs or refuse jobs offered to them. They may be counted among the unemployed. Eventually they may get jobs if employers agree to meet the wage demands or if the workers reduce those demands.

This analysis implies no blame upon either party. Each may have what it considers good and sufficient reasons for its refusal to accept the terms of the other. The workers may feel that their pay has not risen as fast as that of comparable workers. Perhaps wage rates have not kept pace with the rise in the cost of living. Or the employer is making huge profits and should share with his workers. On the other side the employer may feel he cannot pay higher wages without losing his profits or even going into the red. Perhaps he is now making large profits for the first time in many years. Or he may not see how he can shift part of the labor cost to his consumers through higher prices.

To pass judgment regarding partisan arguments of this type requires a criterion of economic justice, a philosophy of social welfare, or some ethical standard. If the economist wants to suggest what should be done in a given situation, he should first be clear in his own mind about his scale of values. He should recognize whence it came and what other people share it with him. When he speaks or writes his views, he should declare his objectives. This done, he can be as strong in his praise or condemnation as the facts warrant. Economic science requires only that economists be scientific in their approach to economic problems. It does not demand that they remain isolated in an ivory tower far from the issues of the day.

**7. Unemployment May Be Caused by Decreases in the Relative Prices of the Other Factors of Production.**—Another cause of unemployment may be found in the changing relative prices of the factors of production. Insofar as they are substitutes for one another in production, a fall in the price of one will tend to cause a decrease in the demand for others, and vice versa. Thus a fall in long-term interest rates may lead to some *substitution* of capital equipment for labor of certain types. The same tendency will prevail if there is a reduction in the market price of capital equipment, or a fall in rents and land values. Another illustration may be found when an employer fires one employee to hire another who has similar ability, but who is willing to work for less pay. In the days before workers became extensively organized, this sort of displacement was a common occurrence. One of the objections to immigration from Europe was the fact that the immigrants were willing to work at lower wages than those who had been here a generation or longer. The same is true today, but on a lesser scale, when migration occurs from farm to city or from the South to the North or West. The unemployment which results from causes of this type is probably not large in the aggregate at any one time, but it is a continuing irritant.

**8. A Decrease in Labor Efficiency Reduces the Demand for Labor Like an Increase in Pay.**—If the daily output per worker declines, the employer is hurt as badly as if he had to pay that much more in wages. He will strive to substitute other factors for the labor which has become more costly per unit of product. The long-run effect will be much the same. In the short run there may be some differences. There may be a gradual decline in efficiency over a period of good business which is not crucial for the employer until prices drop or sales fall off. It is then hard for management to make low productivity an issue. On the other hand, individual laborers may be fired if their output performance is not up to a set standard or not equal to the average for the group. And if the issue arises in a controversy over a labor contract with a union, the outcome may be voluntary quits or forced layoffs just as if the dispute were over wage demands. "Featherbedding" rules are well-known points of disagreement between employers and employees.

**9. Unemployment May Be Caused by Changes in Technology.**—Inventions may cause unemployment by reducing the amount of labor needed to produce a certain good. This occurs when a new process, machine, or product improves the physical efficiency of the labor employed with it so that an employer can produce more goods with the same amount of labor or the same quantity of goods with less labor. When he can sell profitably all that he can produce, the employer may not diminish his demand for labor. But when the demand curve for his product has appreciable inelasticity, the employer who introduces a labor-saving invention is very likely to discharge some of his workers. He can maximize his profit at less than capacity output, which usually means that he employs fewer workers than he hired before the change. Another possibility is that he will discharge skilled workers and hire unskilled workers instead, perhaps an equal number but less costly.

The loss of employment suffered by the technological victims of particular innovations is individually serious, but its effect on the economy as a whole is usually beneficial, not harmful. Offsetting increases in demand may occur in the market sense if the enterprising firm is led by competition to reduce its prices. If these products have a fairly elastic demand, they will be purchased in appreciably larger quantities and additional labor will be needed for the extra production (or not as many men need be laid off at the time of technological change). The decreased price of the first product may enable some people to purchase a larger quantity or variety of other goods. If the technological change requires machinery, people will be needed in its production. If larger profits are made by the innovating firm, its owners will have larger incomes which they may spend for consumption or may invest in creating new production facilities. To the extent that demand does increase in one or more of these ways, employment will rise. In the short run, occupational and geographical immobility may keep the displaced persons from shifting from areas of contracting employment to firms or regions where employment is expanding. In the long run labor-saving inventions do not increase the total volume of unemployment. At least they have not done so in the last 100 years.

The foregoing argument should not obscure certain important areas of unemployment which are so large as not to be dismissed lightly by reference to "the group as a whole." Technological change has been particularly rapid in agriculture, and displaced persons have found it difficult to move to cities or to find work once they got there. There are also numerous instances of areas where the major industry was forced to close down because of technological improvements which aided competitors elsewhere. The substitution of other fuels for coal, for instance, displaced many coal miners when their mines lost market outlets. Stranded skills are notorious. The general trend in mechanical improvements is to reduce the time required to train a worker for his task. Many with long apprenticeship now find their years of training no longer of any importance in the labor market. It is very difficult for such persons to make the mental adjustment necessary to shift downward in the economic and social scale. Therefore, they tend to remain unemployed longer than those who lose their jobs for other reasons than technological change. Finally, the rate of technological change at times may exceed the rate of reabsorption of displaced labor, as in depressions.

Sometimes changes in the demand for labor are the cause and not the effect of the introduction of labor-saving devices. In the first paragraph of this section the implication was that employers sought and introduced inventions because of their desire to increase profit. They may also be motivated to seek cost-reducing innovations by a desire to avoid loss. This latter situation may occur when workers take advantage of their organized strength or the scarcity of labor to force their employer to raise wages. As indicated above in Section 16 of Chapter 17, this may reduce profits so much as to prod the employer into more active cost competition than before. He will hunt energetically for ways to reduce his wage bill without diminishing his output. If these can be found and introduced, the workers of the firm may experience a setback which they did not contemplate at the time they demanded higher pay. However, for the working force of the economy as a whole the ultimate outcome will not be the same as that for the firm, since there are offsetting forces similar to those described above.

**10. Unemployment Caused by Appraisal Price Being or Becoming Too Low.**—The parallel but opposite situation to that of Section 6 occurs when employers reduce their wage bids or merely offer wage rates that potential new employees consider too low. The effects of wage cuts under various circumstances were treated in Sections 18 and 19 of Chapter 17. At this point it is merely necessary to repeat that wage cuts will not produce immediate unemployment if they are accepted by the workers. But if the laborers' asking wages are not reduced to match the wage cut, unemployment will result.

The wage bid of an employer tends to reflect his appraisal of the worth of the labor to him and will fall when that labor becomes less valuable. There are at least three major causes: (1) labor-saving changes in technology, (2) reductions in relative prices of other factors, and (3) decreases in the demand for the good made with the labor in question (or in the demand for the labor service where it is purchased by the ultimate consumer). Each of these causes has been treated in a separate section above. There is also a minor cause which may be described as changes in employer appraisals of labor's bargaining power. These result from observed variations in labor's organizational strength, the volume of unemployment, and the extent of governmental support.

**11. Cyclical Unemployment Is the Worst Type.**—The major problem in the theory of unemployment, numerically speaking, is why there are *many* people out of work at certain times and what can be done about it. The problems of temporary displacement by business failures, changes in desires, introduction of labor-saving processes and equipment, bargaining tiffs with employers, or slowness in learning about alternative job opportunities and deciding to accept them are all simple compared with the complexity of cyclical fluctuations in the volume of production and employment. Although extended answers cannot be given at this point, it is fitting to review the arguments found in the chapters on wages which indicate in what directions solutions of cyclical unemployment may be sought. These include (1) reducing laborers' asking prices, which may be too high, (2) reducing the cost of complementary factors such as interest rates on capital, (3) readjusting the relative prices of substitute goods, (4) increasing total demand for goods by expanding the volume of government spending, (5) furnishing consumers with subsidies so that those who want to spend more can do so, (6) subsidizing producers by guaranteeing them against losses of certain types, (7) improving producer and consumer confidence about the future in order to reduce liquidity preference, and (8) trying to prevent the use of any one or more of these devices from doing more harm than good through its direct and circular effects upon other causes of the volume of unemployment.

Section 4 analyzed the wage-cut proposal and reached an unfavorable conclusion. Since this chapter deals with business cycles only in connection with wage theory, the other seven proposals cannot now be treated at similar length. We should add only the comment that some people urge raising wages as a method of preventing a recession or starting an upturn. Organized labor is particularly pleased with this argument. But stable consumer buying or even buying increased by wage boosts is not enough to keep total demand stable or increasing. Therefore, it is inadequate to the task. Business demand for inventory accumulation, for modernization of equipment, and for expansion of capacity may still fluctuate, and usually does. Consumers also vary their own demands by borrowing more at one time than another, though their incomes remain constant. A buying boom for homes, automobiles, refrigerators, and other durable consumption goods is more stimulating to the economy than average or subnormal borrowing and buying in this field. The problem of business cycles is so complex that an analysis of their causes and cures would require at least a whole volume. Only certain negative arguments regarding wage-rate proposals can be mentioned here.

**12. Summary.**—One of the causes of unemployment may be found in wage rates. At some times wage rigidity is a contributing cause, as when the demand for a particular commodity falls. If the decline in demand is general, as in a business recession, wage rigidity probably does more good than harm. In most cases reduced wage rates would increase unemployment through their roundabout effect upon consumer purchasing power. To seek increased wages at such times probably would also cause unemployment. Strikes would be longer and less successful. Some firms would close entirely. Others would become more pessimistic about future profit prospects. Total business spending would decline.

Technological changes, demand shifts, and business failures are sources of unemployment at all stages of the cycle. Wage rigidities may be a contributing cause when these changes occur. But that is not sufficient reason for favoring wage cuts to avert this type of unemployment. It seems better to help workers find other jobs at prevailing wage rates and to care for their minimum needs by unemployment insurance and the like during the transition period.

Workers may voluntarily reduce their efficiency by setting limits upon daily output. They think to improve their health thereby, or to spread the work to make it last longer. But at the same time they may promote unemployment. The same is true if they demand higher pay. Gains may exceed losses, or vice versa. The economist can only say that workers should understand the risk before acting. If he is given some goal of social welfare as a judgment criterion, he might attempt an evaluation of particular proposals. But generalizations are difficult unless the whole problem is broken down into smaller groups of typical cases.

# Chapter 21

## RENT

**1. The Problem to Be Considered.**—The question of definition is much more important in the discussion of rent than it was for wages. Some prominent writers use the term *rent* in one way, some in another. The man-in-the-street is apt to have a still different idea. We shall see later that the terms *interest* and *profits* present similar semantic problems. Of the four terms in common use in distribution theory, only the term *wages* can be used widely without much fear of being misunderstood.

In this book on price economics, rent will be treated primarily as a price paid (and received) for the use of any durable good over a specified period of time. Adjectives will be used when other meanings are intended. Rent is a use-price, not an exchange price. In this respect it resembles the concepts of wages and interest which are used in this volume. The thing (factor source) which is rented, however, differs from the things which are hired or borrowed. For instance, the category of durable goods includes most tangible objects other than human beings and currency. Durable goods are often sold outright. Human beings are sold only under conditions of slavery. Currency is not bought and sold except in the foreign exchange markets.

Using this concept of rents as prices, we must ask much the same series of questions that we have asked about the other prices previously studied. Some special ones are also included in the following list of topics for the chapter:

1. How are specific rents determined? (Primarily an "institutional" approach.)
   (a) What forces determine the bid prices of demanders? (The concept of "income surplus.")
   (b) What forces determine the supply prices of suppliers?
2. Why do rents differ? (Primarily a "theoretical" approach.)
   (a) The average level of rents at one place or time as compared with another? (The Ricardian concepts of the relative intensity of use and the "product surplus.")

330

    (b) The rent of one durable good as compared with another? (The Ricardian concept of "differential surplus" based on differences in productivity.)

3. What are the effects of rents upon:
    (a) The supply of durable goods? (The concepts of reproducibility and durability.)
    (b) The prices of durable goods? (The concept of "capitalizing" rents.)

4. Do durable goods have "normal rents" comparable to "normal prices" of commodities?
    (a) In the long run? (No change in physical supply.)
    (b) In the short run? (No change in demand attitudes.)

5. How do royalties differ from ordinary rents?

**2. Alternative Definitions of "Rent."**—The definition of rent as a price paid for the services of a durable good is the concept most widely accepted. That is one of its merits. But economists have often used the word in other ways. Rent has been described, for instance, as the income derived from the use of any durable good, or from land alone, or from any natural resource. In a more general way it has been called the income from any factor fixed in supply, or from any which is scarce for natural or artificial reasons. Some writers emphasize the supply-side approach by identifying rents with surpluses over the costs of production of the thing rented (the factor source). Sometimes the surplus is an excess over the reservation price of the supplier. Chapter 22 will treat this problem of surpluses as a general one applying to all factor incomes. A few writers stress differences in the desirability or productivity of rented objects. The more desirable or more productive ones earn a rent. The least desirable and least productive ones do not.

When rent is defined as a price, it is sometimes called "contractual rent." If the owner of a durable good uses it himself instead of renting it to another, he is said to receive an "imputed rent" equal to the contractual rent he might have obtained. By a similar line of reasoning, the lessee (renter) is also said to receive an "imputed rent" equal to the contractual rent which he pays. But if the "rent" is thought of as something produced by the rented object, the rent imputed to that object may be greater or less than the contractual rent. Because of the confusion that arises from this alternative approach to "imputed rent," the term "income surplus" is offered as a substitute. The idea will be developed in Section 5 below.

The rental agreement between the owner and the user may be of various types. Most formally it is a written contract known as a lease which stipulates the rights and obligations of the two parties during a specified period of time. Ordinarily the lessee is expected to maintain the property in good condition so that at the end of the rental period it may be returned to the owner in substantially the same condition as received, normal wear and tear excepted. The contract may variously specify that certain upkeep expenses shall be borne by the lessor, for instance, or that depletion royalties should be paid by the lessee. Informal arrangements are also common as in the renting of dwellings where month-to-month payments without leases frequently continue indefinitely until terminated by one party or the other. Occasionally lessees sublet the property they have leased to some one else and thus become lessors even though not owners, as when a tenant housewife rents out rooms.

Sometimes the rental agreement is on a contingent basis, with the lessee agreeing to pay the lessor a fraction of the future gross product or gross income. Such agreements are common in farming (share-cropping) and in leases of retail stores. A special form of contingent rents known as royalties will be discussed in a later section. Royalties are usually on a percentage or per unit basis, as ten cents per ton of coal mined, or 15 per cent of the publisher's net on every book sold. The total royalty for any given *time* period is not known in advance. It depends upon the volume of output or sales. Sometimes there is a minimum amount per month or year with a royalty-type payment above that.

**3. The Peculiar Nature of Rentable Goods.**—The differences between rents and other factor prices stem chiefly from differences in the circumstances of supply. In the first place the units offered for rent are usually much less homogeneous than hours of labor, heterogeneous though the latter may be. Parcels of land differ from one another in size, shape, slope, improvement, location, etc. Buildings usually are rented with the land on which they stand. This introduces still greater heterogeneity. Rental units also differ widely in size, and there is no standard smaller unit into which they may be subdivided. It is therefore rarely possible for potential lessees to decide whether to rent more or to rent less of a given type of property. Usually they must choose between this aggregate or that, neither of which is quite what was wanted. Occasional exceptions may be found in the availability of office, storage, or factory space. Sometimes, but rarely, there are relatively homogeneous acres of farm land for lease on something other than an all-or-none basis.

In the second place, rentable goods differ from other goods in their greater durability. They may be used many times before wearing out or otherwise losing their usefulness. Single-use goods like food or fuel cannot be rented. Repeated-use goods like pianos or land may be either rented or purchased outright. Many durable goods also are purchasable only in large, expensive units so that those with limited capital are forced to rent them if they are to use them at all.

Thirdly, these expensive articles usually take a long time to produce. Some rented goods are not reproducible at all, such as land. Slowness to wear out and slowness to produce increase the fluctuations of rents, as a later section will point out. However, one must realize that the contrasts in durability and reproducibility mentioned here are intended to distinguish rented goods from nonrented goods, not from other factor sources. Laborers are also "durable" and require a long time to reproduce. Capital funds are "durable" in a different sense. They can be produced quickly by banks, although saving large amounts is usually a long process. A more complete comparison must await a later chapter.

The fourth peculiarity of rentable goods is related to their ownership rather than to the goods themselves. Many property owners do not possess more than one rental unit. If they do own more than one, the units are likely to be heterogeneous, like most houses or stores. This contributes to the bargaining which is so common in rental markets. Lessors cannot readily establish a fixed rental price for one or more units if they have only one of a kind to rent. Customary rents are less common than customary interest rates or wages.

**4. The Demand for Rentable Goods; Problems of Measuring Incremental Revenue.**—The lessee often wants the use of only one rentable unit. His problem is therefore not how many to rent, but how much to pay. He must also decide which of several different ones that may be available will give him the most for his money. This is true whether he is renting a home or leasing an office or a factory site. The ultimate consumer's choice will be determined by weighing the relative subjective merits of the different possibilities against the rents which owners demand for them. This is a utility or indifference problem resembling that arising in the purchase of consumer goods and needs no further treatment here. Our chief concern is with the businessman who must decide how much he can afford to pay for the services of a particular good and then must use his bargaining power to get the good for a smaller rent if possible. His calculations of maximum rent are often guesses rather than computations. He may decide that he is able to pay as much as his competitors are currently paying and therefore offers the going rent. Or he may find that he can get the property only by giving a long lease which requires such a distant look into the future that he cannot possibly make any precise calculation of revenue productivity.

Insofar as a producer does try to compute his probable gain from the lease of a rentable good, his task is that of estimating how much of the total revenue of his enterprise can be ascribed to the use of the rented factor of production. This may be done by the marginal factor revenue approach of the chapter on wages in the rare cases where the rented units are homogeneous. Usually the object to be rented is the only one of its kind used by the firm and therefore the incremental revenue to be attributed to it cannot be computed by applying the marginal revenue formula: $TFR_n - TFR_{n-1}$. For instance, a small merchant rents a store and thus becomes able to conduct business, or he does not and has no total revenue whatever.

Large firms may rent several pieces of real estate. Even though these differ from one another, a manager may be able to calculate how much would be added to his total income if one more building were leased and incorporated into the operations of the enterprise. Another circumstance which may permit the calculation of incremental gain occurs when a going firm of whatever size contemplates renting quarters different from those currently used. The manager may estimate how much the new property will add to (or subtract from) the total present revenue and then compare this amount with the difference in probable rent of the new and the old locations. He has no need to compute what the *total* worth of the rented property will be to his firm.

Nearly all of these decisions involve not only deciding whether the lessor's asking price can profitably be paid, but also which of two rental possibilities offers the best chance of gain. Here a second comparison is introduced: the excess of the estimated income increment from the use of property A over the stipulated rent of A as compared with the similar excess for B, C, etc. The property with the largest margin should obviously be chosen unless there is an opportunity to use bargaining to diminish the asking rent of one of the lessors. The excess in favor of property A when the owner gets the rent he asks may become smaller than that for property B if bargaining forces down the rent for B while the lessor of A remains adamant.

**5. Demand Appraisals by the Income Surplus Approach.**—If a given rentable good is indispensable to the operation of an enterprise and, when rented, no other like it will be needed, its worth to the firm may be calculated as a remainder or surplus by assuming that all other costs are known and fixed so that they can be subtracted from total revenue. With this approach an imputed normal profit must be included as a cost, thus reversing the usual view which makes rent a cost and profits the residual amount. Even though the estimates of future revenue, costs, and normal profits are difficult to make, there seems to be no other practicable way to calculate how much rent an enterprise can risk paying for a given piece of property under these circumstances. For instance, before they decide in favor of a certain site, certain chain stores make careful surveys of the number of families in the neighborhood or the number of persons who pass by a given location during a representative week. These surveys afford a basis for estimating gross revenues, while past experience tells the probable costs of business with the expected volume of sales.

A numerical illustration may help to clarify the argument about the use of the income surplus approach to rent *ex ante* (in prospect).

*Ex ante:* Assume that the manager's expectations are:

| | | |
|---|---:|---:|
| Total revenue .......................................... | | $10,000 |
| Total operating and overhead cost excluding rent ... | $7,500 | |
| Normal profit ................................... | 1,000 | |
| Total explicit and imputed costs ...................... | | 8,500 |
| Remainder or *income surplus* payable for prospective *rent* .. | | $ 1,500 |

If a business operation is viewed in *retrospect* instead of in prospect, total revenue and costs will be known. The rent that could have been paid for the property can easily be calculated if the firm makes normal profits. However, if profits exceed normal, then the economists will want to know why. Consider, for example, the following *ex post* illustration for the same firm whose hypothetical *ex ante* calculations led to a payment of $1,500 annual rent.

*Ex post:* At the end of the year the firm's books show:

| | | |
|---|---:|---:|
| Total revenue ......................................... | | $12,000 |
| Total operating and overhead cost excluding rent .. | $8,300 | |
| Normal profit (imputed) ........................ | 1,200 | |
| Total explicit and imputed costs ...................... | | 9,500 |
| Remainder or income surplus attributable to rented factor .. | | $ 2,500 |
| Rent actually paid ..................................... | | 1,500 |
| Excess, unaccounted for, which may be attributed either to the rented factor, to another factor, or just to luck .. | | $ 1,000 |

Was this $1,000 excess profit above normal due to the fact that the property was rented for the period at less than it was really worth? This question cannot be answered merely by a process of subtraction based on items in the profit and loss statement. The investigator must examine the circumstances of the case to discover other possible causes, such as (1) whether the property was obtained at a lower rent than competitors paid for similar property, or (2) there happened to be an unanticipated increase in demand for the products of the type of property under lease, or (3) the manager introduced a new cost-reducing process during the year, or (4) a bond issue was refunded at a lowered rate of interest, etc. Further comments on this problem of determining the components of profits in excess of normal must be deferred to the chapters on profits, but at this point it is necessary to insist that to impute any definite amount of rent income to either an owned or a leased factor one must answer questions such as these.

**6. Other Ways of Determining Demand Bids for Rentable Goods.**—Not all firms make estimates as detailed as the foregoing calculations of income surplus. Many small firms merely look to see if the lessor's asking rental is out of line with that paid by competitors for similar buildings and locations. If the rent is higher, they then guess whether it is worth the difference. If the rent is lower, the enterpriser hunts for a reason. In times of rising business volume and mounting profits, lessors may ask old tenants to pay more. The lessees then have to figure whether they can do better by moving elsewhere. Or they may bargain with the landlord to try to get him to take less than the rent he asks. The cost of moving is usually so great that lessors generally win the argument. They lose if the tenant is able to find a long lease elsewhere at a better rent, or if he is so weak in his field that the higher rent forces him out of business.

The nature of rental markets is such that a demand schedule has little significance in explaining how rents are determined. Under the assumption of supply heterogeneity, each rentable good must be considered separately. Therefore, demand must be for the rent of one good only. A series of potential demand bids by different firms for rental of this good might be ranged from high to low in cumulative fashion. The result would be a formal demand schedule. But a lessor rarely knows about all these potential bids. Therefore, he cannot choose the highest. There is no "intersection of demand and supply curves" in the usual sense. The lessor is likely to accept the first offer which equals or approximates his reservation rental price. Or he will engage any prospective tenant in a bargaining match.

**7. The Determination of Lessor's Asking Rentals.**—The owners of rentable property usually do not go to as much effort to determine its probable marginal productivity or income surplus as do potential lessees. Many of them have no thought of using their property themselves and therefore have no alternative save to ask the customary rent or to name a high figure and then yield as little as possible in subsequent bargaining. In reaching a decision about what rent to ask for leases of more than a year's duration, a careful lessor may survey economic trends which influence the probable demand for his property and its productiveness in business. These include movements of population, changes in transportation routes, trends of the business cycle, rise or fall of war demands, etc.

Sometimes the lessor is influenced by his ideas of a fair return on the total cost of the property to him. This may involve merely the application of a certain percentage, such as 1 per cent per month gross on the investment. Or it may include a more carefully calculated depreciation allowance for improvements plus enough to cover upkeep, insurance, taxes, and interest on cost. Occasionally a lessor is influenced to raise his asking rent by the fact that he has recently made improvements which were costly to him and were intended to make the property more attractive to potential lessees. The larger the investment in land, buildings, machinery, or other rentable goods the more carefully are rental calculations likely to be made. Millions of small owners do nothing more than imitate, guess, and higgle.

Renting resembles selling in another respect: the owner frequently incurs "selling expense" in trying to attract lessees. Since most rented property is immobile and cannot be brought to a central display place like a store, it is often quite necessary for lessors to use special contact methods like advertising in newspapers or listing with real estate brokers. The expense of advertising or commissions to brokers should be counted as a cost of doing business to be recovered, if possible, through gross rents. Another cost comparable to selling expense is that of product improvement through initial design or more often through remodeling, repairing, and redecorating.

One of the biggest "costs" to property owners is vacancy. That is why landlords will often make improvements or rental concessions to achieve the certainty of keeping a tenant because they fear having to make greater ones if a vacancy develops and they have to hunt a new lessee. In the rental business "time is of the essence" just as in the case of the worker hunting for a job. Every day lost without a rent-paying tenant deprives the owner of income with which to meet his unavoidable and continuing fixed costs. The higher the probable vacancy rate, the higher must be the asking price per unit for the periods of occupancy. The landlord often must choose between asking a high rent and risking a high vacancy rate or asking a low rent and having almost continuous occupancy. His problem is something like that of the merchant trying to decide whether to seek his maximum profit through a few sales at a high profit margin per unit or many sales at a small unit profit. Workers resisting wage cuts or negotiating for wage increases face a similar problem. Prevailing rental policies depend very much upon the general state of business as revealed by the average vacancy rate in the community. When it is low, lessors can afford to be "tough," but when it is high, a more conciliatory spirit is profitable. The labor float and vacancy rates are clearly analogous.

**8. Vacancies Compared with Unemployment.**—Vacancies of rental property resemble the unemployment of labor in that in each case a factor of production remains out of use because owner and potential user fail to agree on the terms of use. There are very few specific cases in which property could not be rented if the rent were low enough or a single worker employed if he were willing to work for next to nothing. But both people and property have maintenance expenses which they seek to cover and which tend to set a minimum below which wages and rents will not fall. Labor's minimum is probably more rigid than that for property, since eating cannot long be postponed. The minimum rent for property in the short run would have to cover taxes and any interest due on mortgage funds. Normal maintenance might be slighted, and insurance reduced or cancelled. The long-run expenses of depreciation and imputed interest may be treated as sunk costs and temporarily ignored. However, ideas of customary, fair, or normal returns usually put a brake upon reductions in both wages and rents long before the "logical" minimum is reached.

Individual instances of vacancy are caused also by the imperfection of the market, the failure of potential lessors and lessees to know about one another's bids and offers. But even as in the case of unemployment, the chief reason for extensive vacancies is the general decline in demand for factors of production which occurs during a business recession. In such times reducing rents is even less likely by itself to bring full utilization of rental property than reducing wages is to bring full employment.  Business property is empty because of the unprofitableness of business enterprise, and rent reductions would bring such a small cut in total cost as to do little to improve profit prospects.  Residence property is in less demand chiefly because workers are unemployed and have doubled up.  Rents would have to be reduced a long way to give very many unemployed workers the opportunity to have living quarters comparable to those they rented when employed.  In short, the demand for residences declines more rapidly than owner attitudes become readjusted downward, and much more rapidly than the physical supply wears out in use.

**9. Rents Differ with the Relative Intensity of Use: The Product Surplus above the Intensive Margin.**—We turn now from the question of how specific rents are determined to that of changes in the level of rents.  This is not a question of relative price levels at different phases of the business cycle.  It is related chiefly to changes in the intensity of use of land.  In many respects the question has the same answer as that regarding the differences in rents between regions. In one area or at one time the land is more intensively used than in another area or at another time.

The solution of this problem in classical rent theory used two principles.  The first was the theory of diminishing marginal physical returns with land fixed and labor as the independent variable.  The second was the competitive interchangeability of units of labor.  These two principles were combined in Sections 3 and 4 of Chapter 19.  The average real wage of workers was shown to equal approximately the marginal product of any one worker.  It decreases as the number of workers increases in a given region.  Competition prevents any worker from getting more than others like him so long as there is perfect mobility from job to job.[1]

Ricardo used these premises to argue that rent would emerge as soon as population increase forced production past the point of diminishing average returns.  See Figure 27 of Chapter 8, or Figure 65 below, which shows a simpler case in which diminishing returns occur immediately.  The landlord need not pay each of his two workers more than the marginal product of 7, but his total product is $9 + 7$.  Total product, 16, minus total wages, 14, yields a product surplus of 2.  Since the workers cannot claim this product, the landlord does.  It is his rent.

As the population rises further, rents also rise.  When three

---

[1] The inaccuracies in these assumptions are not so great as to invalidate their use in the present analysis.

workers must earn a living from this land, their marginal product will decline to 5, and total wages will be 3 × 5, or 15. Total product is 9 + 7 + 5, or 21. Rent is now 6. Similarly, with four workers, rent would be 12, and so on. This explains the rise in rents in regions with rising population. The declining marginal product is often said to represent the "intensive margin." (Cf. Fig. 66.) The argument also may be used to explain the difference in representative rents in regions which have different population densities, but which are otherwise similar. The rent of the fixed factor varies directly with the intensity of its use.

## FIGURE 65

### ESTIMATING RENT BY THE RICARDIAN PRODUCT SURPLUS APPROACH

#### (Diagrammatic Presentation)

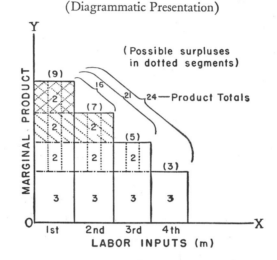

### TABULAR PRESENTATION

| Inputs of Labor $m$ | Total Product $TP$ | Average Product $AP$ | Marginal Product (Wage Rate) $MP$ | Wage Total $m(MP)$ | Product Surplus or Rent $R$ $(TP - mMP)$ or $m(AP - MP)$ |
|---|---|---|---|---|---|
| 1 | 9 | 9 | 9 | 9 | 0 |
| 2 | 16 | 8 | 7 | 14 | 2 |
| 3 | 21 | 7 | 5 | 15 | 6 |
| 4 | 24 | 6 | 3 | 12 | 12 |

The tabular presentation which accompanies Figure 65 shows that rents may be calculated in either of two ways by the Ricardian approach. The first formula is the one used in the numerical illustrations given above:

Rent$_I$ = Total Product minus $m$ times Marginal Product   or,
$R_I = TP - m(MP)$ (where $m$ = units of labor)

The second formula is based upon the fact that the average product exceeds the marginal product. It is sometimes more useful than the first.

Rent$_{II}$ = $m$ times (Average Product minus Marginal Product)   or,
$R_{II} = m(AP - MP)$ (where $m$ = units of labor)

The application of either formula will give the same result. For instance, when $m$ is 4,

Rent$_I = TP - m(MP) = 24 - 3(4) = 24 - 12 = 12$,   or
Rent$_{II} = 4 (6 - 3) = 4(3) = 12$

A few qualifications may now be added. The input dose of labor should really be labor-plus-capital. Output almost always requires that the worker use something more than his bare hands. But the result is unchanged. Rent increases while the return to the labor-plus-capital dose decreases. For the moment the question of how labor and capital split their return is irrelevant. Normal profits may also be introduced if desired. A second qualification is a little more difficult. If technology improves so that the total product curve rises, the marginal product will rise, but the rent or product surplus will not. In fact it is more likely to decline. The actual outcome depends upon the shift in the position of the point of diminishing average returns, as shown in Figure 64 of Chapter 19. Rent will also be affected by any change which may occur in the shape of the output curve beyond that point. Finally, the Ricardian approach to rent theory is based on physical product. It may be translated into monetary terms, if necessary, by giving each unit of product a uniform selling price. But this does not make it the same as the income surplus approach of Section 5. The latter is best used for explaining the demand estimates of individual firms. The former is best adapted to explain differences in typical rents between two different time periods or regions. Another application follows in the next section.

**10. Rents Differ with the Quality or Productivity of the Rented Good.**—The Ricardians also used this product surplus approach to explain the differences between the rents of various pieces of land.

Agricultural land obviously differs in its fertility and distance from the market. Urban land attracts more customers in certain desired locations than in others. But if labor and capital are mobile and their units generally interchangeable, then competition must make it impossible for one of these variable units to receive more than another in the same category. Hence they would distribute themselves over different pieces of land so that wherever employed their return would be the same. That is, the product yielded at the intensive margin would be the same on all land regardless of how productive the intramarginal input doses might be on the better lots. If there was any land so poor that the first input dose yielded no more than the additional product at the intensive margin on all other land, this poor land would produce no surplus. Such land was said to be at the "extensive margin" and was called "no rent" land. The following diagram reveals a hypothetical situation on three grades of land, A, B, and C, of which the last is "no rent" land. The intensive margins are equal on all three and the intensive and extensive margins coincide on Grade C land.

### FIGURE 66

#### Rents Equal to Differential Product Surpluses

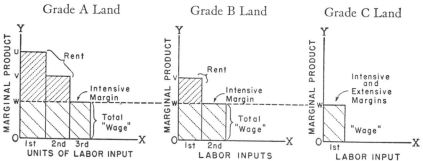

The Ricardian "differential surplus" theory of rent may now be summarized as follows: the rent of any given piece of land will tend to equal the total product of that land minus $m$ times the marginal product when $m$ is the number of units of the composite variable factor and when that factor is applied to such an extent that its marginal product is just equal to the cost of obtaining one unit of it on the competitive market. In symbols the formula is $R = TP - m(MP)$. This resembles the income surplus approach in that it explains the amount of rent as the surplus which a tenant ordinarily could afford to pay and which a land owner has it in his power to demand. Stated with appropriate qualifications and shorn of reference to the existence of "no rent" land and the alleged historical sequence of utilizing the better lands first, the Ricardian theory is a pretty good explanation of the absolute and relative amounts of rent. But it lacks the market realism of the income surplus explanation offered in the preceding sections. It is best seen as an *ex post* analysis based either on the average output of various grades of land over a considerable period or on the output of a "representative user" of average ability in any given production period.

**11. Differential Costs May Be Used Instead of Differential Product Surpluses.**—In an effort to bring the Ricardian approach into line with the current pattern of price and distribution theory, it has sometimes been presented in terms of increasing marginal money cost instead of diminishing marginal physical product. For instance, a smoothed curve of marginal money cost may be substituted for the successive product rectangles of the previous figure and the

FIGURE 67

RENTS EQUAL TO DIFFERENTIAL REVENUE SURPLUSES

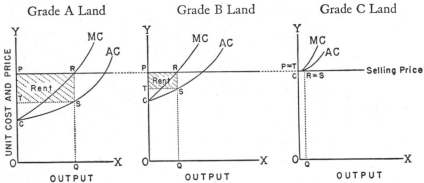

rent of Grade A and Grade B land may then be shown with or without a contrast with "no rent" Grade C land.

In using this approach one cannot apply a counterpart of the formula $R = TP - mMP$, but must turn to the first formula suggested above: $R = m(AP - MP)$. Revised to conform to the change from physical product to money cost, the rent formula now becomes $R = n(MC - AC)$. The marginal cost remains constant but the average cost rises as one moves from Grade A land to the inferior Grade B and the poorest Grade C, where it becomes equal to marginal cost. In the new formula $n$ replaces $m$ to indicate the change from inputs as the independent variable to outputs. These outputs are the result of input changes but must be used in any diagram which measures on $OY$ the cost per unit of output. The "differential" concept is found in the comparison between average cost and marginal cost when the latter is measured at either the "intensive margin" on any land or the "extensive-intensive margin" on Grade C land. For instance, the rent on Grade A land in Figure 67 is diagrammatically $OQ$ times $RS$, which is the difference between $RQ$ and $SQ$, or the rectangle $PRST$.

This approach using differential revenue surpluses seems more realistic than that using differential product surpluses. Revenues and costs are both measured in money units. It is easier to include in the composite variable such cost-raising factors as transportation to market, capital improvements, and normal profit. The value approach also is conceptually better adapted to the explanation of urban land rents.

The same sort of diagram can be used to demonstrate quite simply the income surplus approach of which it is a variant. It can be applied to any type of marketing situation and any type of rentable good. It requires no comparisons between "grades" of land, nor stipulations about identity between marginal costs and marginal revenue. Let $OP$ represent the selling price for the commodity produced by a firm using property A, and $OQ$ the output sold or expected to be sold. Then the total revenue becomes $OPRQ$. The total (nonrent) cost of producing the output sold to yield this revenue may be represented by the area under the curve $CR$, or $OCRQ$. The excess of total revenue over total cost is the income surplus area $CPR$ which is, of course, equal in area to $PRST$. A similar approach and diagrammatic technique may be used if the average revenue curve $PR$ slopes downward to the right.

**12. Normal Rents: Long Run, a Supply-Side Concept.**—Since rents are imputed or contractual prices paid for the temporary services of durable goods, it is fitting to inquire whether they resemble the exchange prices of commodities in tending toward a "normal" amount. Normal commodity price has been defined as that price which tended to keep the rate of supply constant in relation to a given demand and therefore to remain itself unchanged. The constant rate of supply was explained as being due to the fact that the normal price was equal to average total cost of production plus a normal profit and therefore encouraged neither entry nor exit, neither expansion nor contraction of production. This definition would hold in the moderately long run for expensive, durable goods just as well as for commodities which sell at a low price and are consumed in one using. Therefore, something like it should be applicable also to the rents or use-prices of those durable goods.

Thus one may speak logically of normal rents as existing in the long run for buildings and other man-made goods which can be reproduced as they wear out in use. Normal rents of this type would be those which were just sufficient to cover the time fraction of the total cost of reproducing it and making it available to the lessee. These generally would be the sum of (1) depreciation based on the fractional part of the useful life represented by the rental period, (2) upkeep expense, taxes, insurance, etc., borne by the lessor, and (3) normal profit to the lessor, which may be further subdivided into (a) interest, (b) wages of management, and (c) a possible compensation for risk of investment. Since it is *future* production that will determine whether there is to be a constant rate of supply of new buildings, the cost of reproduction should really be used in all of these interval cost estimates, not the prior cost of production of those buildings now being leased.

In actual practice, however, long-run normal rents are rarely calculated with any such precision. Usually they are figured as a gross percentage return on the investment which is approximately equal to what has been customary in the past or what can be earned currently on other types of new investment of similar expense, risk, and effort. Furthermore, most owners of rentable goods buy them secondhand from other investors; that is, they do not make them themselves nor buy them from the original producers. Therefore, a concept of short-run normal rent may possibly prove more useful in the analysis of most rental situations than that of normality in the moderately long run.[2]

First, however, the definition of normal price should be broadened to include the demand side as well as the supply side. A normal commodity price or a normal rent then becomes one which stimulates no change in demand or supply which would alter that price or rent.

**13. Normal Rents: Short Run, as Amounts and as Percentages.** —Short-run normal rents may be said to exist for any type of rented property when there is no trend upward or downward in the exchange price of that property in current buying and selling. The

___

[2] "Short run" here refers, as in Chapter 12, to the supply side and to goods already produced; in the "moderately long run" goods can be reproduced. On the demand side, the "short run" refers to fixed incomes, while the "long run" permits incomes to be changed by the prices paid.

number of persons actively seeking to buy is approximately equal to the number actively seeking to sell, and there is only the usual turn-over of property that occurs when a few owners desire cash and other persons want to invest funds they have accumulated. If the pre-vailing stable exchange price at any time happens to be equal to the reproduction cost of the rented property, short-run normal rent will equal long-run normal rent, but ordinarily the short-run normal rent will be less than or greater than this amount and will fluctuate much more rapidly.

The best way of generalizing particular instances of short-run normal rent is to express the amounts as percentage of the acquisition cost of the rented good, such as 12 per cent gross on the current ex-change prices of such goods. These exchange prices will then tend to remain stable when the going rents yield a percentage return which is generally acceptable for that class of rental property at that time. Any change in the rental demand for property will cause rents to depart from normal. The same effect will also occur if people's ideas change about the percentage return which current buyers of rental property ought to get.

**14. Rents Which Deviate from Short-Run Normal Cause Changes in the Demand for Rented Goods: Capitalization.**—Fluc-tuations in the purchase demand for rental property may be described as varying inversely with changes in the short-run normal percentage and directly with changes in expected rents. For instance, let us assume that investors currently accept 12 per cent as about right for gross investment returns on purchases of small apartment buildings in a given area and that a certain building returns $2,400 per year rent. If that rent may reasonably be expected to continue indefinitely into the future, the probable market value of the property may be esti-mated by the process of capitalizing the rent, i.e., by dividing $2,400 by 0.12 and getting $20,000. If the rent expectation should then drop to only $2,000, the capitalized income would decline to $16,667. But if the prevailing normal rent concept drops from 12 per cent to 10 per cent at the same time, the market value will not be $16,667, but $20,000, the same as before.

All such calculations are approximations only. The margin of error in predicting an exchange price from a known rent and normal percentage is much greater for rented property than in the case of bonds bearing a fixed interest rate. The market for realty is so im-perfect that urgent sellers often sell at prices which are "below the market" in that they represent abnormal yields. On the other hand buyers are frequently so ill-informed, impatient, or gullible that they pay relatively high prices which show subnormal yields on their investments.

It is important to note that land as well as buildings may have a short-run normal rent even though only the latter, and other reproducible goods, may have a long-run normal rent. When a normal rent is expressed as a percentage, it is the same fractional return at any given time for either short-run or long-run normal rents. In the former case the percentage is based on current acquisition cost, but in the latter on reproduction cost. For instance, during a depression a building whose reproduction cost is $10,000 may drop in market value to $5,000. Yet if people think that 15 per cent is a normal rate of return at that time, the property may remain stable in value when the rent is only $750 per year despite the fact that $750 is only 7½ per cent on reproduction cost. Similarly land, which is generally considered nonreproducible and therefore can have no normal *price* whatever, may at any time earn short-run normal rent on acquisition cost. The concept of short-run normal *rent* is really much broader than that of long-run normal rent. The former applies to all goods, both old and new, but the latter must be confined to new goods alone. To put it in another way, rents may be normal without the current exchange price of the rented good being normal.

**15. Other Causes of Changes in the Prices of Durable Goods.—** Fluctuations in the normal rent percentage are only one out of several important causes of change in the prices of durable goods. Others include changes in the relative desirability of rental property as compared with other forms of investment, and changes in the supply of rental property. For instance, rental property may become more attractive than other investments if rent incomes seem more likely to rise in the future (or to resist declines better) than dividend or interest income. Changes may occur to reduce the going rate of return on other investments, thus making real estate relatively more attractive than before. Speculative buyers, sellers, and producers may at times be numerous enough so that their actions influence the market price of durable goods. A good example is that of real estate in boom periods, such as that of coastal Florida in the 1920's.

On the supply side there may be changes in the rate at which old units are worn out or destroyed, as when fires, earthquakes, or wars accelerate the normal rate of deterioration. Important variations may also occur in the rate of production of new structures stimulated by changes in the rentals of existing property of the same type or by changes in the cost of producing such property.

In any case one must remember that some demand and supply variables in the realty market are independent of either rents or normal rent percentages. Their changes are not derived from variations in normal rent percentages by the capitalization process. Rather, they tend to change those percentages. If property values rise when rents remain constant, this change both indicates and determines a fall in the normal rent percentage. The same is true if rents fall while exchange prices remain unchanged.

**16. Fluctuations in Rents Tend to Be Wider Than Fluctuations in the Prices of Nonrented Commodities.**—When changes occur in schedule demand, rents tend to fluctuate more than other prices in both amplitude and duration. This is chiefly because rented objects characteristically have a longer time-elasticity of supply than objects purchased outright. In the first place rented goods are usually more expensive. Both businessmen and ultimate consumers usually buy the relatively cheap things they want, but rent the more costly ones like stores or homes. A second attribute of rented goods is also related to their expensiveness, the relatively long time required to reproduce them. Therefore, they have a long time-elasticity of supply expansion and their exchange prices or rents can rise farther and stay above long-run normal price longer than those of less expensive articles.

In the third place, the lessors of rentable goods more often follow monopolistic types of marketing policy than do sellers of goods. For instance, certain types of machinery like those used in shoe manufacture and record tabulating are withheld from sale by their producers and are obtainable for use only by lease, while at the same time patent controls prevent the entry of potential competitors. Other owners have a natural monopoly like those who own land containing valuable minerals or land which is located in particularly desirable spots. Entry of potential competitors is slowed by the difficulties of discovery or by the impossibility of finding another lot with the same location. Substitutes of an inferior type may be found or made, and they tend to check the upward rise of rents, but they cannot return rents to former levels since they are either imperfect substitutes or they cost more to produce. This is particularly obvious in the case of land when rising rents cause the use of less desirable land elsewhere, but the use of this land does not force the rent of better land back to zero. Monopoly-type rents cannot be forced downward without breaking the monopoly, i.e., without finding substitute durable goods which offer the user as much or more for his rent payments than those offered by the monopolist.

On the downside of rent fluctuations, the characteristically long time-elasticity of supply is due to the extreme durability of most rented objects. For reproducible goods such as buildings, a fall in rents below long-run normal rent will tend to stop construction, but it will not lead to a quick shrinkage in supply. Most buildings have a very long useful life, and this life often can be prolonged by repairs much more cheaply than new buildings can be erected. Hence, in bad times when rents have fallen below the level at which it is profitable to construct new buildings, there is a tendency to decrease rather than to increase the rate of obsolescence. Land in its spatial and location aspects never wears out in use, and its physical supply cannot diminish when contractual or imputed rents decline. Hence, its time-elasticity of supply on the downside is virtually infinite. Stated in another way, the long-run supply curve for land has zero elasticity downward.

**17. Substitution and Voluntary Vacancies Reduce the Amplitude of Rent Fluctuations.**—Certain qualifications to these broad generalizations must now be made. Usually it is particular types of land or improvements whose fluctuating rents are the subject of analysis rather than the rents of durable goods in general. In such cases supply-elasticity may be achieved by changing the use of certain land and buildings rather than by altering the total supply. For instance, during the war the congestion of certain cities increased the demand for residences while the demand for store leases declined. As a result many store buildings were converted into residences to swell the total when home-building programs proved inadequate. In many agricultural areas farmers have long made a practice of shifting from one crop to another as prices and revenue yields change. This is a method by which an owner-user maximizes his income surplus from alternate uses much as he might maximize his contractual rent by renting to a tenant who intended to plant corn and was therefore able to offer more rent than one who had recently planted wheat and intended to continue that crop. This possibility of substitution into or displacement out of varying employments of durable goods tends to limit the fluctuations in their rents. The more narrowly specialized the use of the good, the less substitution will be possible and the more its rent fluctuations may depart from the general level.

A second qualification of importance is found in the fact that owners of property may temporarily choose to let it lie vacant rather than to cut rents during a period of declining demand. The short-run supply curve for rental property is not perfectly inelastic downward, but slopes to the left as shown in Figure 68 because of the different reservation rent-prices of different owners. The physical supply does not shrink as rent bids fall, but rather the quantity offered for rent. In this respect rental property does not differ significantly from labor or from stocks of commodities in general. Vacancy rates are paral-

FIGURE 68

ELASTICITY OF SHORT-RUN SUPPLY
CURVE OF RENTABLE PROPERTY

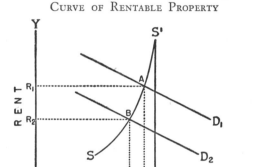

leled by unemployment and by accumulated inventories of unsold goods.

The degree of elasticity of the short-run supply curves of rentable property varies with the type of property and its ownership. It is probably greater for business property and multiple residence units than for single-family dwellings. Except when protected by long leases, the owners of apartment houses, office buildings, and the like may hesitate to reduce rents to get new tenants during depression periods for fear that the old tenants will be induced to demand similar reductions. Owners of this type usually do not depend upon any particular rentals for their essential income. For them to lose one tenant means that income will be reduced by only a small fraction and they may even have substantial nonrent sources of income to help out in bad times. Rents in this category are therefore likely to be more stable and vacancy rates may go higher than for individual residences. Owners of the latter usually do not own more than a few, and the loss of a single tenant may seriously diminish a relatively small income. There are also the difficulty and expense of keeping up the grounds around vacant residences, and a provision in many fire insurance policies makes them void after ten days of vacancy. Owners of small homes are more apt to be individualistic in their renting than are apartment or hotel owners and rarely belong to any organization which might urge them to refrain from cutting one another's throats by reducing rents. Under these circumstances a relatively inelastic short-run supply curve is to be expected. Neither group of property owners has anything to compare with the collective bargaining organizations of workers, since prospective tenants have in general no greater bargaining strength than lessors.

**18. Royalties Are a Special Form of Rents.**—To complete our study of rents it is necessary to consider "wasting assets" as well as land, buildings, and machinery. These include particularly various types of mineral deposits such as oil wells and coal mines where the one who uses the property extracts and sells some of the mineral wealth which makes the land desirable. A parallel situation occurs where land is leased for cutting its timber. There are numerous borderline cases including soil depletion by farm crops. The nature of the operations of the lessor is such that he is not expected to return the property in the same condition he received it. Hence he is made to pay for the damage done by including in his rent what is usually called a depletion allowance. The word *royalty* may be used for this concept, but it is more commonly used for the composite payment which includes both a use-price and a depletion allowance.

Royalties also differ from ordinary rents in that usually they are figured at so much per physical unit extracted or produced by the lessee instead of being stated as a certain amount per time unit of use. Thus an oil lease might be for one eighth of the oil recovered instead of for a given number of dollars per year. Royalties distantly resemble the depreciation allowances of building rents in that the lessor may be thought of as trying to get back through them enough to replace the leased good at the end of its useful life. Mineral deposits, however, are often of uncertain extent, and their current value need bear no close relation either to acquisition cost or to cost of replacement. Hence, a time depreciation method of figuring mineral royalties would be neither logical nor feasible.

The rent or use-price element of royalties paid for the right to exploit mineral deposits will vary with the desirability of using one particular area rather than another. This is usually an inverse function of the costs of extraction, processing, and transportation. Thus a relatively rich ore body near the surface will command a higher lease than a leaner one of similar extent or one located at lower depths. A mine near rail or water transportation will bring more than a less accessible one. Sometimes it is impossible to distinguish between rent and depletion elements in royalty payments, but both are always present.

The term royalty is also applied to payments made by licensees for the right to use privately owned patents. These royalties are also usually figured as a certain dollar or percentage amount per physical unit of use rather than per unit of time like ordinary rents. Patents have a fixed length of life and therefore may yield something like a depreciation or depletion element in their use, but these amounts would be quantitatively difficult if not impossible to calculate. Even if cost of production or acquisition is known, the cost of replacement is not. Replacement would have to be with something different, but of equal value. Current market value, however, is a function of the productivity of the patent in use, i.e., of something approximately equal to its current total royalty including both rent and "depreciation" elements. Physical replacement cost should relate to the depreciation element alone.

Royalties paid to authors by publishers are composite payments. Copyrights have a limited length of life like patents and mineral deposits, so that depreciation or depletion elements form a logical if indefinite amount of royalty payments. Copyrights also have different degrees of desirability or productivity in that certain publications catch the public fancy more than others. The amount of the author's total royalties rises or falls with the volume of sales, and this fluctuation reveals the rent element. Royalty percentages are usually about the same for all manuscripts of a given class, since relative worth to be revealed by future sales cannot often be determined in advance of publication. Patent royalties, on the other hand, are usually different for each patent. Sometimes they reflect an estimated cost savings to be achieved with each unit produced with their use.

### 19. Summary of Economic Principles in the Analysis of Rent as a Price.

    I. Specific rents are determined in most cases by the lessor whose offer price is accepted by the lessee, or by bargaining on the basis of this rent-price.

        A. Lessor supply prices are chiefly a function of custom modified by guesses as to future trends.

    B. Lessee demand prices for business uses are chiefly a function of estimated income surpluses. These involve estimates of future income and future costs other than rent.

II. The general level of rents at any given time or place is a function of the following. It is:
    A. Directly related to:
        1. The intensity of demand for the services of rentable goods (based on desire, income, and expected profit from use)
        2. The supply of other factors (labor, capital) combined with the fixed, rented factors (usually land, but also capital goods in short run). (The more of these other factors seeking employment, the higher the rents.)
        3. The cost of producing and renting reproducible goods. (Long-run normal rent includes depreciation, interest on investment, taxes, and operating costs.) (The higher the cost, the higher the rent.)
        4. The length of time required to reproduce rentable goods. (The longer it takes, the higher rents can be forced above long-run normal by rising demand or sudden destruction of part of the supply.)
    B. Inversely related to:
        1. The supply of the rentable goods in question. (The larger the supply, the lower the rent.)
        2. The length of time it takes for the rentable goods to wear out in use. (The longer it takes, the lower rents may fall below long-run normal.)
        3. The ease of substituting other factors when the rent of one type rises. (The easier it is for users to substitute, the less the rent can rise. Ease is a function of technology and the abundance of substitutable factors.)

III. Differences in rents at any given time are a function of:
    A. Differences in the quantities of the respective rented goods
    B. Differences in their physical productivities
    C. Differences in the demand for them, based on both physical and revenue productivities

IV. The short-run prices of rented goods are affected (through "capitalization"):
    A. Directly, by the rent expected
    B. Inversely, by the short-run normal rent percentage

V. Royalties differ from ordinary rents
    A. They include a charge for the depreciation of wasting assets
    B. They are calculated per unit of output not per unit of time

# Chapter 22

## SURPLUS ELEMENTS IN RENTS AND IN OTHER FACTOR INCOMES

**1. Statement of the Problem.**—In economic literature rent is often defined as a type of surplus and is sometimes called "economic rent." This book on price economics uses the word *rent* in the popular sense of a price paid for the services of land, buildings, machinery, or any other durable good. The student should understand both concepts. The task of the present chapter is threefold: first, to show how rent-prices may at times contain rent-surpluses; second, to show how rent-prices may at times contain three other types of surpluses; and third, to show how these four surpluses may also appear in other factor prices, here called factor incomes. Certain implications of this approach will also be considered.

The specific questions to be answered are the following:

1. What are the four types of surplus which may appear in factor incomes?
2. When may they appear in specific rents? in wages? in interest (as a price paid or income received)? in profits (as net income of a business unit)?
3. How may tax policies be influenced by concepts of surplus elements in factor incomes?
4. What are the relations between normal rent, normal interest, and normal profits?
5. Do rent-prices determine commodity prices, or vice versa?

**2. Four Types of Surpluses May Appear in Factor Incomes.**—Any factor price may at times exceed the cost of supplying the factor service. This excess over cost may be called a surplus on the grounds that the cost is all that actually needs to be paid to evoke the factor service. The surplus is "unnecessary." Or it may be called "undeserved," a "chance gain," the "reward for successful bargaining," etc. When received by the seller of the factor service, the surplus becomes part of his factor income.

The minimum factor supply price here called "cost" may be calculated in at least four different ways. Therefore, there are at least

354

four different types of surpluses. The size of these surplus elements in factor incomes depends upon both the minuend and the subtrahend in the formula:

$$\text{Factor price} - \text{Factor cost} = \text{Surplus}$$

The following table shows four possibilities under this formula:

*Four Possible Surpluses in Factor Incomes*

| Ways of Calculating "Factor Cost" | Suggested Descriptive Term for Each Type of Surplus |
|---|---|
| I. Short-run minimum supply price for the factor (owner's reservation price) | I. Lessor's surplus (or worker's or lender's surplus; resembles seller's surplus in commodity pricing) |
| II. Total *past* cost of providing the factor source and its service (usually equal to the pro rata share of the total cost of producing or buying the factor source plus the current cost of maintaining it and offering its services) | II. Residual surplus or accounting profit. (This view treats factor owning and offering as a form of business enterprise.) |
| III. Total *future* cost of reproducing the factor source plus the cost of maintaining and offering it | III. Economic surplus, more often called "economic rent" (like II, but better concept in explaining expansion and contraction of supply) |
| IV. The cost of getting a similar factor at the present time | IV. Opportunity-cost surplus |

These four surpluses have been defined in general terms to indicate that they do not apply alone to rent payments for the use of durable goods. They may be found also in wage payments, interest incomes, and profits. That is why we call even the third type "economic surplus" rather than "economic rent." It seems more logical to speak of "surplus" elements in rent incomes than to explain how there may be "rent" in "rents," "rent" in "wages," etc. The fourfold approach to surpluses is also more complete than that which defines "economic rent" as *the* surplus element in factor incomes. The next few sections of this chapter will discuss each of the four surpluses in turn, first in relation to rent-prices, and then briefly in relation to other factor incomes.

**3. The Lessor's Surplus (I) in Rent Incomes.**—Whenever a rent payment exceeds the minimum amount that a lessor would have been willing to take at that time for the good which he rented, that lessor receives a type of "seller's surplus." This explains his willingness to rent. That is, in order to be induced to rent, the potential lessor must be offered as much as or more than his minimum reservation rent-price.

The difficulty with the concept lies in the definition of this short-run minimum supply price. The economist would be likely to use the marginal cost idea. He would call this minimum rent the additional cost to the factor owner of supplying the service for that time period. But the thing that counts in the marketplace is the view of the factor owner. This is influenced strongly by custom, by memories of past cost, or by a sense of justice and personal ideas of a fair return. Therefore in most cases it is likely to be higher than the bare minimum conceivable to the economist.

If the highest specific rent offered by prospective lessees does not equal or exceed the factor owner's reservation rent, he will withhold his property from use, at least temporarily. If he employs the property himself, this does not constitute withholding from society unless he devotes it to a less productive use than would be made by a probable lessee (like using good farm land for pasture).

A positive lessor's surplus will emerge whenever a factor owner is successful in bargaining and obtains a higher rent than the minimum he was willing to take. It may also be found in those less frequent cases where the factor units offered by various lessors are relatively homogeneous and therefore capable of being assembled into a supply schedule. Supply interacts with demand to determine a uniform rent-price for all lessors which exceeds that which some of them were willing to accept because of their lower initial reservation figures. Least common of all in rental markets, though prevalent in many other types of seller's surpluses, is the situation in which a lessor rents more than one homogeneous unit at a given time. In this case, he may be considered to receive a subjective surplus on each of the intramarginal units.

Lessor surpluses should be contrasted with income surpluses, which are in a different category entirely. This may be shown by the following tabulation of the two methods of calculation:

| *Minuend* | — | *Subtrahend* | = | *Remainder* |
|---|---|---|---|---|
| 1. Specific rent income | — | Owner's reservation rent | = | Lessor's surplus |
| 2. Total business revenue | — | Total nonrent costs of doing business | = | Income surplus |

**4. Residual Surpluses (II) in Rent Incomes.**—The term *rent* is not often explicitly identified with the residual surplus or accounting profit concept defined in Section 2, but this viewpoint needs definition for future use in connection with proposed changes in tax policy. The residual surplus sometimes received by factor owners in excess of the cost of obtaining a factor source and supplying a factor service is not the same as the residual surplus of the business enterprise which rents and uses the factor. Both surpluses result from the accounting procedures of business units, but the former may be distinguished from the latter by saying that it is a factor-owner surplus and not a factor-user surplus.

A specific rent payment may yield a residual surplus to its recipient if it exceeds the pro rata cost to the owner of obtaining the land, building, or other rentable good plus the costs which the owner-lessor may have to bear in leasing it. Although the average lessor does not set up an accounting system to compute these costs and to derive a residual surplus or deficit, he could do so. He could think of himself as being in the factor-owner business and could figure his annual profit or loss from his purchase and rental operations. If his calculations revealed a profit, the terminology of this section would call that profit "a residual surplus in a rent income."

**5. Economic Surpluses (III) in Rent Incomes.**—The third of the factor income surpluses is often called "economic rent," and sometimes just plain "rent." For reasons previously explained, it is here called an "economic surplus." Like other surpluses, it may appear at times in either rent, wages, interest, or profits as defined herein. Economic surpluses differ from residual surpluses in being derived from reproduction cost instead of production cost.

This emphasis upon future cost instead of past cost makes the concept of economic surplus very useful in explaining the expansion and contraction of supply when rents deviate from long-run normal rent. When the rent of a reproducible good rises to exceed its pro rata cost of reproduction (and maintenance), its production will appear profitable. The supply of the rentable good will tend to expand through new production. The increase in supply will force specific rents down towards normal again. Whether rents will return exactly to their former level or not depends upon the future cost of production of the rented good. If this cost is higher than before, the new normal rent will be higher. If the reproduction cost is below the past production cost, the new normal rent will be lower.[1] In times of rising prices,

---

[1] There is a close parallel here with the concepts of increasing, decreasing, and constant cost for commodities as described in Section 7 of Chapter 13. The historical trend of costs and prices, however, should be given chief attention in dealing with the rents of long-lived durable goods. In the former discussion the emphasis was upon the effects of increased demand upon the economies of scale in production.

the desirability of comparing specific rents with reproduction cost rather than with past cost becomes obvious.

When specific rents fall, economic deficits may appear. These tend to stop current production of rentable goods, and the available supply gradually diminishes through wear and tear, fire, and other calamities. As soon as the place is reached where supply is shrinking more rapidly than the demand, rents will turn upward toward a new normal set by the then current cost of reproduction.

**6. Economic Surpluses in the Rent of Land and Other Nonreproducible Goods.**—If a good cannot be increased in supply as its rents mount, it is said to be nonreproducible. Land in its spatial aspect is the most common illustration. The reproduction cost of a nonreproducible good is zero. Therefore, one may argue that not part, but all of its specific rent at any given time is an economic surplus. That is why land rent has long been held to be the truest form of "rent." But one must be careful not to reason in a circle. Land rent is "true rent" only when *rent* means "economic rent" which is here called one form of surplus, the "economic surplus." And there remains the difficulty of defining "land" so as to eliminate all produced elements it may contain in any given situation which are capable of being reproduced. Defining *rent* as a rent-price paid for the use of *any* durable good seems a much simpler solution of the semantic problem.

Some goods, like buildings, cannot be reproduced quickly, but can be reproduced in the long run. During the time in which their supply is fixed, they resemble land. That is why Alfred Marshall and others who used the economic surplus concept of rent called building rent "quasi-rent." It resembles, but is not quite the same as their "true rent." Further comments on this term will be found in a later section dealing with "normal rents."

**7. Opportunity-Cost Surpluses (IV) May Arise in Rent Incomes from Long Leases.**—The concept of an opportunity-cost surplus is derived from the experience of those lessors who are successful in executing a long lease when rents are high and then having this contract remain in effect during a period when rents fall. When that happens, each specific rent payment brings the fortunate lessor a surplus over what he could obtain if he did not have a long lease and was forced to rent his property during the period of depressed rents.

The opportunity-cost terminology has been borrowed from the comparable buying-side situation where it is so well established that there seems no point in translating it into something like "opportunity revenue" merely for the sake of logical consistency. The opportunity-cost surplus which is a gain as seen by the lessor is of course a loss from the viewpoint of the lessee. Furthermore, opportunity-cost deficits probably occur as frequently or nearly as frequently in factor incomes as do opportunity-cost surpluses. Neither bears any necessary relationship to residual surpluses, but the probability is that opportunity-cost surpluses accompany accounting profits in factor ownership more often than they accompany accounting losses. Long-term leases are more willingly given by property owners during periods of expansion and prosperity than during a recession or depression.

The four classifications of surpluses are not mere terminological exercises, but are intended to help explain the differences in the behavior of various specific rents. They may be used also in the supply-side approach to the use-prices of other factors, as will be indicated shortly. Other terms might do just as well as these, provided they revealed equally well the significant differences in factor supply-elasticity and the manner in which these limit and determine use-price fluctuations.

## 8. Extending the Surplus Concepts to Wage Incomes.—As indicated above, surpluses of the four types which emerge clearly in the field of rent also occur at times in other factor incomes. Wages, for instance, may exceed the minimum amount which a worker would have accepted for a week's work if he had to take less or go without. Or the earlier hours of a day may be worked more willingly than the later hours. Therefore, part of some people's wages may be regarded as a worker's surplus. Residual surpluses, on the other hand, are not so logical in the wage field because of the fact that slavery no longer exists. An adult worker does not cost himself anything in most cases except upkeep; the past expenses of his rearing and training were borne by his parents or by the taxpayers of the community. Workers do not think of trying to make a profit on this investment. Nor does future cost of reproduction usually bear any close relationship to wages except as a worker believes it necessary to get enough to raise his family on the level to which they have been accustomed. For these and other reasons a normal wage concept is very difficult to define and therefore economic surpluses in the wage field must also be elusive.

Nevertheless, one may cogently argue that certain gifted or fortunate individuals receive salaries far above any conceivable past cost of rearing, training, and maintaining physical strength or mental energy.  These lucky persons may be said to receive residual surpluses in their salaries, surpluses which are akin to the high rents received by certain fortunate owners of plots of land which happen to be in great demand and limited supply.  These factor surpluses tend to remain undiminished for long periods of time because rare natural abilities, like rare mineral deposits or land locations, cannot be reproduced by man.

Acquired abilities also often have a long time-elasticity of supply upward because of the long time needed for the formal training and experience which makes great surgeons, musicians, executives, etc. Finally, opportunity-cost surpluses occur in the wage field whenever long-time contracts or the force of custom, bargaining power, or paternalism keep wages high in a given line or firm after declining demand has forced them down elsewhere.

**9. Surplus Elements in Interest Incomes.**—Lender's surpluses and opportunity-cost surpluses are common in the field of interest and are so obvious as to need no explanation.  The concept of residual surplus seems applicable to professional lending institutions, but not to individual lenders.  The former operate as business units in securing and lending funds.  They show profits or losses at the end of the year when receipts are balanced against expenditures. The small saver, however, experiences only the "real cost," if any, of foregoing spending or liquidity, and that cost is hard to express in monetary terms.  But if we shift to the concept of an economic surplus, we find that increases and decreases in the rate of interest alternately stimulate and depress a few people's willingness to lend. Therefore, there must be economic surpluses and deficits relative to some normal figure for these individuals, impossible though it is to define norms in numerical terms for lenders in general.

**10. Surplus Elements in Profits.**—The surplus concepts in the field of profits are best examined through the eyes of a person purchasing a share in a business unit.  There is no contract between the owner of potential equity capital and the firm in the making of which the former may say, "You must agree to give me at least this much or else I will not invest."  The business ownership relation is essentially a take-what-you-are-given proposition.  When a stockholder is dissatisfied with the dividends he is getting, there is nothing he can do to make the firm return his money unless he can get a majority of the other stockholders to agree to end the life of the business and liquidate its assets.  Even then the return of his investment intact is improbable, and when dividends are poor he usually cannot find some one who will buy his share for the price he paid. For these reasons, the concept of a business owner's surplus in the field of profits is either inapplicable or else the minimum supply price must be held equal to zero.

As regards the other surplus concepts, that of accounting profit in the business of business ownership is probably limited to investment trusts and holding companies. The concept of normal profit is widely accepted, even though difficult to define as noted in Section 9 of Chapter 10. Therefore one may speak of economic surpluses when profits are above normal and economic deficits when they are below. Finally, since profits are essentially residual incomes, they cannot be involved in long-term contracts, and opportunity-cost surpluses can hardly be said to exist, although a case might be made for putting participating dividends on preferred stock into this category.

**11. Some Tax Problems Involve Consideration of Factor Income Surpluses.**—If factor income surpluses are unnecessary payments to certain owners of the factors of production, people may well ask why they need to be paid. Or if it is difficult to keep factor owners from receiving these surpluses, why shouldn't the government aim at them in its tax program in order that the needs of the state be met as painlessly as possible? The answer must be that it should, provided that we can be sure about three things: (1) that reduction or elimination of the surpluses will not diminish the supply of vital factor services, (2) that we can measure the amount of these surpluses and devise taxes which will absorb them, and (3) that other criteria are not more important than painlessness in the collection of taxes. With these three qualifications in mind, let us briefly examine the taxability of the various surpluses that have been described above.

**12. The Taxation of Land and Improvements.**—For many years the followers of Henry George have contended that the total rent of pure land is an economic surplus and may be taxed away from the land owner without diminishing the supply of land. However it is difficult to estimate in advance just what the economic surplus will be in any future tax period. Both contractual and imputed rents fluctuate from year to year with changes in demand. Even the future average is uncertain. Hence the tax-collector hunting for economic surpluses may decide to be conservative and take only part of the probable land rent in order that private ownership of land shall not be made completely unprofitable. If the taxing agency should confuse lessor's surpluses with economic surpluses and tax too heavily the rent income from buildings, as well as from land, society might not suffer much in the short run. But in the long run the supply of buildings would diminish and rents would rise to cover the additional tax. The burden of the buildings tax would be shifted to lessees, and lessors would again get a normal return upon their investment.

In practice we find that although land and improvements are usually assessed separately for purposes of taxation, the same tax rate is imposed upon both. There is no attempt to make property taxation conform to the economic surplus viewpoint except as land may be relatively overvalued on the assessment rolls as compared with improvements. This failure to adopt a seemingly logical policy of imposing the property tax burden largely upon landowners is probably due first to a general feeling that it would be unjust to penalize one group of real property owners rather than another, and second to the political power of the land-owning groups who, of course, cultivate the foregoing concept of justice in their own defense.

**13. Taxes on Interest and Profits.**—There are two other forms of property income that may be taxed, that from loans and from business ownership. Interest income and dividend income are usually taxed on the same general basis as wage and salary income. But the corporation as a form of business unit is usually made to pay a special type of income tax which resembles real property taxes in the use of two implicit and rather vague assumptions, first that ability to produce income is sufficient ground for taxation, and second that the tax rate, ordinarily not very high, will not discourage either business ownership or the corporate form.

Frequently there is added to the corporation income tax a corporate excess profits tax which is clearly based upon the concept of economic surplus. Proponents argue in its favor that even high rates will not diminish either the number of new corporations or the efforts of corporate managers. Opponents claim that in any time except a war emergency excess profits taxation will be harmful to society, particularly when tax rates approach 100 per cent. They say that normal profits alone are not enough to induce most holders of liquid funds to take the risks of business ownership, but there must in addition be the chance to make and keep extra amounts. This is the same as saying that normal profits cannot be defined as a certain *average* percentage return on investment over a period of time or else that this average is well above the going rate of interest.

A decision between the pros and cons of this argument is rendered very difficult by the fact that it involves subjective imponderables. Owners of enterprise capital may even frighten themselves by shouting too loudly about the alleged menace of this form of taxation just as people raised their own fears about the size of the public debt during the New Deal deficit spending period. Further comments about the subjective and highly unstable determinants of the supply price of venture capital must be deferred until the chapter on profits.

**14. The Personal Income Tax Involves Surplus Problems.**—Another major source of tax revenue, the personal income tax, may also be construed as being aimed at an economic surplus, that portion of our incomes in excess of the amount needed to keep us functioning as workers. Like other normal supply prices, that for labor is uncertain and variable. The most generally accepted definition, that of the minimum cost of living, is annoyingly vague. It may apply to a single worker or to a worker's entire family. It is likely to change with fluctuations in the worker's bank balance, his trips to the movies, the pressures of union officials, and his wife's ability or willingness to economize. Even though hard to pin down, such a minimum is assumed to exist by legislators who propose that each taxpayer be allowed a minimum subsistence exemption for himself and an allowance for his dependents.

People with large incomes clearly have a larger surplus over minimum physical subsistence needs than do those with small incomes. Therefore it is logical to assume that they have a larger economic surplus even though their aspirations regarding living standards may also be higher. This is the justification of progression in income tax rates.

However one should note that the ability-to-pay argument really refers only to the higher *average* rate on higher incomes. It does not similarly justify the present American method of securing this higher average rate on large incomes. We levy a flat percentage as a basic tax on all incomes above a certain minimum and then secure progression by imposing a graduated surtax. This tends to discourage a few people from additional effort or entrepreneurial risk-taking which would be socially desirable. They see the last increment to income taxed at a high percentage, one much higher than the average for their incomes as a whole. If the tax laws were written so that only the lower average percentage were seen by the taxpayer, some of those who now are discouraged by the smallness of the net after taxes would put forth the marginal effort they now withhold. Society would gain, and the government would receive taxes from a larger surplus than would otherwise exist.

Another proposal of similar intent is that the tax on earned incomes combine a progressive normal tax with a regressive surtax. The taxpayer would be allowed to calculate his normal tax on the income received, say, five years before if it was lower than current income. The increase of present income over past income would be treated as a socially desirable increment. Surtax rates would be applied to it as they are at present to the portion of incomes above the minimum. But the rates would decline with successively higher brackets, instead of rising. A tax law of this type would tend to stimulate marginal effort and to increase the marginal surplus taxable by the government.[2]

Wartime experience has clearly shown that many people with relatively fixed incomes may be forced by the tax-collector to live on less than before without causing them to withhold their services or property from community use. Propaganda which causes people to accept increased taxes as a social necessity may be considered to diminish their minimum factor supply prices and to raise their economic surpluses.

**15. Summary of Rent and Surplus Concepts.**—The foregoing comments on various forms of factor surpluses and their implications were provoked by disagreement with the efforts of some writers to identify one or more of these surpluses with rent. The latter is best seen simply as a payment for the temporary services of a durable good. When such goods are used by the owner instead of being leased, they help to produce output or direct satisfaction. In this case they may be said to yield a rent type of income the amount of which may be imputed by comparison with the rents actually received for similar goods at the same time. Whether rented or used by the owner, the contribution of rentable goods in the production process may be estimated by the marginal productivity or income surplus methods, the latter being usually the most applicable. Specific rent incomes often contain one or more elements of surplus, but in this they do not differ greatly from other factor incomes. The surpluses arise for several reasons, of which probably the most frequent is inelasticity of supply (or long time-elasticity of supply) in the presence of rising demand, but each type and sometimes each case deserves separate analysis. Only thus can understanding be improved or public policy made more helpful.

---

[2] Cf. Kenneth E. Boulding, "The Concept of Economic Surplus," *American Economic Review,* Volume 35, December, 1945, p. 868.

**16. The Relation Between Normal Rent, Interest, and Profits.**
—It was suggested above that buying and renting durable goods often
can be considered a form of business enterprise like buying and selling commodities. The attractiveness of being a property owner-
lessor rises and falls with the general level of demand like any other
form of business ownership. The norm about which such fluctuations occur was described in terms of the gross rent income which
should be received if people are to find that type of business activity
desirable. If the normal gross rent is reduced to a net rent by subtracting depreciation and upkeep expense, the remainder may be considered the normal profit of owning-leasing. If desirable, one may
therefore say that normal (net) rent is equal to normal profit and
that it is not a distinct concept at all.[3]

From normal-profit rent one may also subtract wages of management and a risk premium, if either is present, and the final remainder
will be interest on the investment. At that point it may be argued that
if investment in durable goods does not yield as much interest through
gross rents as can be obtained from straight loans, people will tend
to move out of the former field into the latter and become pure creditors instead of realty owners. Or if property ownership comes to
yield more than lending, the number of people buying or building
will increase. In other words, the long-run normal (net) rent of
reproducible goods tends to equal the going rate of interest with due
allowance for differences in risk and management effort. This was
Alfred Marshall's view when he said that in the long run the "quasi-
rents" of buildings equal interest on reproduction cost, but that in the
short run they fluctuate like "true rent," which he described as a
"producer's surplus" of total revenue above the prime costs of producing goods with the use of a fixed factor.[4]

In time periods too short for supply adjustment through reproduction or contraction it is also possible to have short-run normal
rents equal to interest on *acquisition* cost. In fact, whenever
specific rents depart from this norm, the market price of the rented
goods tends to be bid upward or downward until the normal relationship is restored.

Another way of supporting the argument about the fundamental
identity between normal rent and interest is to describe buildings as

---

[3] But see the last paragraph of this section.

[4] Marshall's producer's surplus concept closely resembles the income surplus concept developed in Section 4 of Chapter 21. The latter, however, is broader and has
been presented not as "true rent," but as an estimating device for calculating factor
productivity. It may be used by a lessee, a lessor, or a third party either before or
after use of the factor. Cf. Alfred Marshall, *Principles of Economics,* 8th ed.,
London: Macmillan & Co., Ltd., 1930, pp. 412, 424, 657, 832, etc.

capital goods and interest as the return from the use of capital of all kinds. Thus, by the simple choice of certain definitions rather than others, the term *rent* is therefore confined to returns from the use of land. Some would go still further and say that all land has a "capital value" or is purchased with "capital funds" and therefore is a form of "capital" so that it, too, really earns interest, not something different called rent. However this terminological flight departs widely from the popular idea of rent as payment for the services of any durable good and cannot be justified since it contributes nothing to our understanding of the magnitude and fluctuations of rent incomes, which is our major objective.

From one viewpoint, it seems desirable to identify normal rent with normal profit rather than with the going rate of interest. This approach permits inclusion of the troublesome items of risk premium and wages of management, which are often much larger for lessors than for lenders. Furthermore, renting property involves prior buying or constructing plus upkeep expense. These make it resemble ordinary business enterprises much more closely than it resembles saving and lending.

Probably the best solution would be to abandon any effort to identify normal rent with either interest or profits. It is useful to point out similarities, but normal rent should be kept as a separate term. There are several good reasons for this. First, it is really a gross item, not net. Second, in all except land rents the depreciation element is usually a much greater part of total expense than in ordinary types of business enterprise. Third, the time frame of reference must not be obscured. Comparisons of rent with normal profit require an emphasis upon future reproduction cost and therefore must be limited to long-run normal rent and to reproducible goods. On the other hand, comparisons with the going rate of interest refer to acquisition costs, short-run normals, and to either reproducible or nonreproducible goods.

**17. In One Sense Commodity Prices Determine Rents.**—If a factor is reproducible and is destroyed by use, its use-price and exchange-price are influenced as much by the cost of producing the factor as by the demand for it. If, on the other hand, the supply of the factor is fixed, demand changes alone are responsible for *changes* in its price. Therefore if rent is given the narrow definition of payment for the use of a factor which is fixed in supply, then rents cannot fluctuate except as the demand for fixed supply factors fluctuates. This will occur when they become more or less profitable to use, i.e., when the price of the commodity being produced with their use rises or falls.

According to this line of reasoning it then becomes proper to argue that land rents, and building rents in the short run, are different from other factor costs in at least one respect. They do not fluctuate independently of the prices of commodities produced with their use, but are determined by those prices. The line of causation runs in one direction only, from commodity price to factor rent, and not vice versa. For other factors the causation runs in both directions: from commodity price by way of demand for the factor to factor rent, and from factor rent by way of cost of production of the commodity to commodity price.

For instance, the demand for wheat land and for harvesters rises and falls with the income which farmers can get from growing and selling wheat. If the supply of wheat land is fixed, its rent or exchange price rises or falls solely because of changes in the price of wheat. But the price of harvesting machines is influenced both by these demand changes and also by changes in the cost of producing the machines. In other words, the price of harvesters may vary because of forces external to the wheat market, but wheat land may not. In functional terms, the price of harvesters may be considered either an independent variable or a dependent variable as related to the price of wheat, i.e., either a cause or an effect, but the price of land is only a dependent variable. During a war or a prolonged strike the supply of harvesters might become temporarily inexpansible. The harvester price or rent then would tend to resemble land in that its upward fluctuations would depend solely upon increases in the price of wheat.

**18. In Another Sense Rents Determine Commodity Prices.—** The preceding arguments have considerable merit *if* the special definition of rent is accepted and all the premises are granted. But they do not add much to our knowledge of the reasons for rent-price magnitudes, fluctuations, and effects. Furthermore, the argument about rent thus defined being an effect of commodity prices and not a cause tends to introduce confusion in two major respects.

In the first place, the reasoning is valid only for *fluctuations* in rents. It does not apply to the relative magnitudes of different rents at the same time, nor to the absolute amount of a certain rent at any given time. In such problems *total supply* and *relative productivity,* even if unchanging, are just as important as the intensity of demand. For instance, rents for office building sites are not likely to rise as high in a city like Los Angeles, situated on a broad plain, as on the peninsula of San Francisco until the population of the former becomes many times greater than that of the latter.

In the second place, the sole dependence argument must specify that the rented fixed factor is highly specialized and not adapted to other uses. An illustration might be found in a waterfall that is useful only to furnish waterpower. In most cases, however, land has more than one profitable use. Much wheat land is really just "farm land" and may be used for growing corn or for pasture. Residence areas may be taken over for stores, and farms for factory sites. The same is true of buildings and most other man-made durable goods whose supply may be fixed in the short period. Whenever these alternative uses do exist, fluctuations in rents do not depend solely upon changes in the price of one commodity but upon several. They occur whenever variations in prospective income surpluses cause bidders for rival uses to raise or lower their maximum bids. In such cases changes in the rent of land available for producing a given commodity, X, become a cause of changes in the price of X.

Another illustration may be found in the case of a person wanting to open a men's haberdashery in the lobby of a fine hotel who may have to pay a very high rent in order to get space away from a florist or a beauty parlor. The haberdasher's total cost of production will be higher than that of competitors located outdoors a block or two away where rents are lower. Therefore he must ask more for his shirts and hats than they do if he is to survive. If he guesses right and if enough people patronize his store who are willing to pay these high prices, we have a case in which one of the determinants of commodity price is clearly space rent. However, it is not the only cause, for it operates on the supply side and the necessary demand conditions must also be present.

There is the further possibility that the haberdasher might have had the good fortune to secure his space on a long lease at a low rent before others realized how good the location was going to be. In this case the enterpriser is not forced by high rents to charge high prices in order to survive, but may choose to do so because he makes greater profits that way. He is in the position of a monopolist choosing the most profitable price at which to sell. His profit income includes a portion which may be attributed to unpaid rent, i.e., to what we have called an opportunity-cost surplus. This possibility should emphasize the fact that an explanation of either commodity prices or factor prices should always include consideration of *both* demand and supply forces regardless of how inconspicuous one of them may happen to be.

It should be apparent that land is not the only factor about which the foregoing propositions about lines of causation may be made. A change in the price of any factor will alter the cost of production of a firm using that factor and thus influence the supply price of its product. A common illustration may be found in the manner in which rising wages cause firms to ask more for the things they produce. On the other hand a rise in the price (or volume of sales) of a commodity will cause the demand for some factors to increase more than for others. The actual price history of a factor in such circumstances is a function of its technical substitutability and its time-elasticity of supply. Only in the latter respect do the peculiar characteristics of land set it apart from other factors, and even then the difference is often in degree rather than in kind.

**19. Summary of the Economic Principles and Concepts Regarding Surplus Elements in Factor Incomes.**—All factor incomes at times contain surpluses over the cost of inducing people to offer the factor services in the market. The amount of this surplus (or deficit) is a function of:

1. The size of the factor income (based upon the intensity of demand for the factor service relative to the supply of it)
2. The manner in which the factor service supply price is calculated. There are four possibilities:
   (a) Short-run minimum reservation price
   (b) Past cost of production [includes cost of creating the factor source (depreciation), maintaining it (interest and upkeep), and making it available (management)]
   (c) Future cost of reproduction (similarly computed)
   (d) Opportunity-cost of a current transaction of similar nature

These four subtrahends give rise to four types of surplus which may be called:

   (a) Lessor's surplus
   (b) Residual surplus (accounting profit in factor ownership)
   (c) Economic surplus
   (d) Opportunity-cost surplus

All of these surpluses differ from the concept of income surplus defined in the preceding chapter as appearing when a factor's contribution to the gross income of a business unit is computed by subtracting from that gross income the total of all nonrent costs. These surpluses are found in specific factor payments of all kinds, including wages, interest, and profits as well as rent.

In the long run, residual surpluses, the economic surpluses of re-producible goods, and opportunity-cost surpluses tend to disappear or average out. Net rents in the long run tend to equal interest on invest-ment in reproducible goods (when costs of production are deducted). Short-run departures from this norm were called "quasi-rents" by Marshall and were computed as the excess of specific rents over repro-duction cost, interest, and expenses, thus resembling most closely the economic surplus concept given here. Marshall's "true rent" is the specific rent of an object whose reproduction cost is zero and all of whose rent is therefore economic surplus. "Quasi-rents" arise be-cause of temporary fixity of supply when demand changes. "True rents" occur when there is permanent (upward) inflexibility of sup-ply.[5] Both of these concepts need redefinition and subdivision as at-tempted in this chapter with its four concepts of surplus. This pro-cedure seems more logical than to move in the opposite direction and consolidate them into a general term *rent*.

---

[5] This impossibility of increasing supply suggests a supply price of infinity, not zero, but Marshall chose to stress the origin of such rented objects as free gifts of nature.

# Chapter 23

## SPECIFIC INTEREST RATES: AN INSTITUTIONAL APPROACH

**1. Problems Connected with Interest.**—We must begin again with the problem of definition. This is particularly important because of the variety of meanings which the word *interest* may have. For this book on price economics, a price-type definition will be used. Unless otherwise indicated, interest here means the price paid (and received) for the temporary use of funds. The payer is called the borrower, and the receiver is called the lender. Other terms associated with borrowing and lending will be explained below.

The questions to be asked regarding this price resemble those which have been asked regarding other prices:

1. What are the *causes* of the *absolute* magnitudes of interest rates?
    (a) Who are the borrowers and what governs the demand bids they make?
    (b) Who are the lenders and what governs the supply prices they ask?

2. What is the nature of "credit" and where do lenders get it?

3. What are the *causes* of the *relative* magnitudes of interest rates?
    (a) For different types of loans—same place and time?
    (b) For the same type of loan:
        (1) At different times?
        (2) In different places?

4. What are the *effects* of changes in interest rates?
    (a) Upon the supply of funds?
    (b) Upon the demand for funds?

5. What are the relations between interest rates, roundabout production, and durable capital goods?
    (a) In a capitalistic society?
    (b) In a centrally planned society?

6. What are the strong and the weak points of the theories of pure interest?
    (a) The time preference theory?
    (b) The liquidity preference theory?
    (c) The cost of production theory?

7. What determines the long-run "normal" rate of interest?
   (a) How is it related to the general equilibrium of all prices and quantities?

There are two general approaches which one may take in answering these questions. The first is "institutional." It examines the actual market situations in which interest rates are determined, paid, and received. The borrowers and lenders are seen as actual businessmen, governments, banks, consumers, etc. Typical cases are described. From this information regarding what actually seems to happen in the country we live in, certain generalizations are reached. Major exceptions are noted. The approach is more inductive than deductive.

The second approach is usually called "theoretical." The term really means that deductive logic is employed more than inductive. Premises are stated in very general terms. The different segments of the funds market are not examined as much as the market as a whole. Attention centers on the entire economy or on all possible economies in the search for universal principles. Short-run phenomena are slighted in favor of long-run norms.

The institutional and theoretical approaches cannot be separated completely. Both propound theories, and both make use of observations of the world about us. But the primary emphasis of this chapter, after some preliminary definitions, will be institutional. It will consider the points raised under the first question in the above outline about the *causes* of actual interest rates. The next chapter will continue the same approach in giving answers to the questions about interest rate differences. Chapter 25 will analyze the last four problems dealing chiefly with interest rates as causes.

**2. The Borrower Seeks Improved Purchasing Power.**—What is it that a person wants when he borrows? Most borrowers would reply that they want "money." Economists would not disagree, but usually use the word *funds* instead, so that *money* may be used in a more precise sense. But what are these funds and why do borrowers want them? If a man borrows from a bank, he usually gets a bank deposit. He can draw checks against this deposit and pay his bills. If paper money or coins are more convenient than checks for certain purposes, he may secure these at the teller's window by giving the bank a check in exchange. When the same man borrows from friends, they may give him either checks or currency. If it is a corporation which is borrowing on its bonds, lenders will pay for the bonds with checks and these will be converted into a bank deposit.

In a few cases, businessmen borrow special drafts drawn by banks on other banks and then use these drafts to pay for goods, as in importing.

In all of these cases the borrower gets something which enables him to buy or to pay debts more easily than he could before he obtained the funds. Another way of describing it is to say that he borrows purchasing power. This phrase has some advantages, for it indicates that he gets the ability to purchase in the future. The borrowing and the buying do not always occur at the same time. Days, weeks, months, or even years may elapse between them. In some cases the borrower finds he does not have to buy, or changes his mind, and returns the funds without having spent them. But he had the power to purchase, if he had chosen to use his funds that way.

At the other extreme is that very common sort of borrowing where a buyer gets goods at once but defers payment. Here the borrowing and spending are simultaneous. The borrower never even sees the funds he borrows. He buys "on credit," "on open book account," etc. The lender and the seller of goods are one. A great deal of business as well as consumer buying is financed in this way. Sometimes the seller-lender himself has to borrow in order to be able to lend to his customers. He may borrow either from banks or from other seller-lenders from whom he buys. A large network of interdependent lending and borrowing of this type pervades our economy. It expands with the volume of business in good times and contracts during periods of recession and depression.

**3. Collateral as Well as Interest Often Must Be Pledged by Borrowers Seeking Loans.**—The promise to pay interest is often not enough to persuade a potential lender to part with his funds. The borrower also must offer collateral. Many different forms of property may be used such as land, buildings, automobiles, furniture, jewelry, stocks, and bonds. The lender usually requires that the collateral have a market value in excess of the loan. In large transactions the collateral is deposited with a trustee, such as the trust department of a bank. This trustee must turn over title to the lender if the borrower defaults. If the loan and interest are paid in full, the title deeds are returned to the borrower. Pawnbrokers, on the other hand, hold the collateral themselves, giving a receipt to the borrower.

The collateral aspect of loans is very important. Its use indicates the real nature of the borrowing-lending transaction. There is an exchange between borrower and lender. The borrower gives his note and collateral pledge to the lender in return for funds. The funds are more readily acceptable by most people than either the borrower's secured note or his collateral. That is why the borrower wants to make the exchange. The lender wants the interest. He also wants the return of his principal. If he has confidence in the borrower he may not demand specific collateral. He may be content merely to rely on his legal claim to the general assets and earning power of the borrower. When he does demand collateral, its excess value is merely his protection against a decline in the value of that collateral during the period of the loan. Further comment upon the lender's viewpoint will be found in the next section.

The foregoing concepts of the borrower's viewpoint in a loan transaction may now be summarized. He borrows funds, which may be called the factor source. (Funds are money, bank deposits, drafts, etc., whose full nature is yet to be explained.) The factor service is the way in which these funds may be used as purchasing power, actual or potential. Interest is the price paid for the temporary exchange of things of less wide acceptability for things of more wide acceptability.

**4. Lenders Demand Payment for the Service of Providing Funds Which They Create or Accumulate.**—Turning now to the lender's viewpoint, we find that he demands payment for providing funds which he has accumulated in the past or creates at the moment. Commercial banks supply deposit credit to borrowers. This credit is really only the promise of the bank to pay people who have a right to demand that payment. Because of the position which commercial banks occupy in our society, their promises to pay are considered better than the promises of borrowing firms or individuals. Borrowers exchange their own promises to pay for the bank's promises to pay. They pay interest for the privilege of getting credit (promises to pay) of greater acceptability than their own. Lenders demand pay for allowing borrowers to use their credit. There are two reasons which will be studied further in the next chapter but can only be mentioned here. The first is the cost of running the bank which supplies the credit. The other is recompense for bad debts. And of course profits should be included as a cost in a capitalistic society.

Some lenders provide borrowers with the funds which they have accumulated. These are held by them in the form of bank deposits which were obtained by depositing currency or checks received from others. When individuals are lenders, we speak of them as lending their "savings." The latter term will be analyzed further in the next chapter. When savings banks or loan companies are the lenders, we speak of them as lending their assets or their capital, not their savings. Nevertheless, the funds they lend represent the savings of the people who bought stock in the companies, or the reinvested profits of the companies themselves.

Governments may lend funds which they have borrowed, taxed, saved, or created. In "creating" funds they resemble commercial banks. The government orders paper currency to be printed or mints coins. Both represent government promises to pay. They are forms of credit which people are glad to borrow because of their general acceptability. Coins differ from paper currency chiefly in the fact that they cost more to make. Gold and silver cost more than paper and ink.

**5. There Are Various Meanings of Interest as a Price.**—Interest may be expressed as an amount or as a percentage of the funds loaned. The *amount* of interest paid per unit of time corresponds with wage payments and rents per unit of time. It is more common, however, to speak of the *rate* of interest. This is not merely a time rate, but a rate per dollar loaned per unit of time. It is the amount of interest for a given time period divided by the face value of the loan. Profits similarly may be expressed either as an amount or as a rate per dollar involved.

Several different types of interest rates should be distinguished. The *face rate* of interest (also called the *nominal rate* or *coupon rate*) is the percentage written on the face of the note. Or it is the amount of interest per time period divided by the principal. Thus a $1,000 bond may stipulate that the interest is to be computed at a face rate of 4 per cent or that the amount is to be $40 per year. Coupon bonds have $40 coupons attached, one to be removed each year. The *going rate* of interest for loans of a given type is the average face rate on new issues at the time they are issued. Or it is the average percentage obtained by dividing the interest amount paid on old issues of the same type by their current selling price, if time to maturity is ignored.[1] Since the securities of a given class are highly substitutable in the eyes of current lenders, these two percentages are usually equal. The going rate is also known as the *yield*. If most of the new ten-year government bonds which pay 3 per cent are being sold at par in a given day or week, the yield on old bonds will also be very close to 3 per cent. Thus, a 4 per cent bond would be selling for $133.33,

---

[1] When the time to maturity is considered, a more difficult computation gives what is known as "yield to maturity."

or thereabouts. In actual practice, the yield on old issues tends to determine the face rate on new issues, rather than vice versa, but they are clearly interdependent.[2]

Sometimes a *real rate* of interest is distinguished, like that of real wages. This is important in periods of rising or falling prices. It may be computed for a one-year note by the following rule. Compute the purchasing power of money at the end of the year as a percentage of what it was at the beginning of the year. Multiply the principal plus interest by this percentage and subtract the principal. Divide the remainder by the principal and the quotient will be the real rate of interest. Thus, if the purchasing power of money falls from 1.00 to 0.91 because prices rise 10 per cent in a given year, the real rate of interest in a 6 per cent loan is negative: $(0.91 \times 106) - 100 = -0.0354 = -3.54$ per cent. The lender has "made" 6 per cent on his investment, but he possesses less purchasing power at the end of the period than at the beginning. Nevertheless, he is better off than if he had left his funds idle during the period.

**6. Comparisons Between Interest on Loans and Rent on Capital Goods.**—Loans of funds differ from leases of capital goods in three respects. First, loans are stated in terms of money units which are perfectly divisible, but leases involve separate pieces of property like land or buildings. Second, the property owner in both cases expects to get his property back, but the lender does not insist upon the return of the precise dollars loaned, since all dollars are identical. Third, lenders frequently require the borrower to pledge collateral in excess of the value of the loan and often sue in cases of failure to pay interest or principal. Lessors require no collateral, but they may sue when tenants fail to pay rent, damage the property during occupancy, or refuse to vacate at the end of the lease.

**7. Funds Are One Form of "Capital."**—Funds are one form of "capital," a word with many meanings. In this book funds will refer to that form known as "capital purchasing power" or "liquid capital." They should be distinguished from "capital goods" or "capital equipment." The latter are tangible, durable goods used in making other goods or services. In the chapters on rent such goods were

---

[2] The illustration given here is only an approximation. It assumes that the $4 yield is capitalized at 3 per cent as though the annual payment extended indefinitely. More precisely, the current selling price of the 4 per cent bond of finite maturity would be the sum of two present worths: the present worth of the principal discounted at 3 per cent for the time to elapse before maturity, plus the present worth of each of the $4 interest payments discounted for its time distance. The latter may be expressed as the present value of a finite annuity.

said to be leased or rented. Occasionally they may be "borrowed" from friends, but when a payment is made for their use, it is called rent, not interest.

Accountants distinguish among several kinds of "capital." They speak of "working capital" to include not only cash on hand and bank deposits, but also government bonds inventories, and other "quick assets." The term "fixed capital" is used to refer to both land and capital goods owned by the firm. The total value of the securities issued by a corporation often is called the "capitalization" of the firm, or merely its "capital."

When loans are made, the promise to pay interest and repay principal is a credit instrument that may be called a "capital claim." The owner of this note or bond has a claim against the earnings of the firm and also against its "capital assets." The term capital claim may be applied also to leases and to shares of stock. All capital claims entitle the owner to income without working. Whether called rent, interest, or profits, they are all forms of property income. They should be contrasted with wages, which are claims against the income and assets of a firm for work performed.

**8. There Are Four Major Classes of Borrowers and Lenders.**— Because of the price approach with which this study of interest begins, the various market situations in which interest rates are determined by the forces of demand and supply must be classified and their differences explained. Business borrowing is usually the most important type, but in time of war it may be exceeded by the borrowing of governments. Quantitatively less important are the borrowings of consumers and banks. All of these four groups also appear on the lending side of the market, but the order of importance is different. Business firms are probably the major lenders, banks are second, private individuals next, and governments ordinarily are last.[3] Precise statistics on the distribution of demand and supply quantities are not available, but fortunately they are not essential to an understanding of the manner in which interest rates are determined and their fluctuations occur.

**9. Business Borrowing.**—Businessmen borrow chiefly because they think they see a profit opportunity which they cannot realize unless they possess additional goods to sell. They may get these goods by buying (borrowing) on open book account from producers or middlemen. Or, they may borrow funds from individuals or from

---

[3] N. H. Jacoby and R. J. Saulnier, *Business Finance and Banking*, New York: National Bureau of Economic Research, 1947, pp. 1–18.

specialized lenders such as commercial banks. With these funds, business borrowers can then "pay cash" for whatever they think they need, whether machinery, materials, land, or services. Funds also may be borrowed to pay taxes or to meet other pressing needs for cash to pay outstanding obligations. This latter motive for borrowing is defensive rather than offensive in the sense that it seeks to preserve the business as a going organization so that profits can be made in the future by other types of spending. Sometimes business firms borrow to refund existing loans at lower rates of interest, but this again may be included within the general objective of maximizing profit.[4]

Most firms do not borrow *all* of the funds used for buying goods, hiring factors of production, or paying tax obligations. They usually have some funds of their own, and a few firms have enough so that they never need to borrow at all. This is the result of managing operations so as to keep either a strong cash position or adequate investment in government bonds and other securities which can be liquidated when the need for funds develops. Small firms may also call upon the savings of owners which have not yet been put to business use but have been kept in the bank for other purposes. Either small or large firms may avoid borrowing by selling a part interest in the enterprise to people or institutions who are willing to accept the risks of ownership and do not confine their investments to loans. Corporations may sell stock instead of borrowing through bond issues. Individual proprietorships may get funds through conversion into partnerships by the sale of a part interest.

Current revenues pay for most current purchases. The need to raise additional funds may indicate that expansion is planned, that sales are falling more rapidly than purchases, that costs are rising while prices remain constant, that prices are falling while costs remain up, or that something else has happened to disturb the planned balance between income and outgo.

**10. Estimating the Worth of Funds to the Firm.**—Since business borrowing is usually a supplementary source of funds, the gains to be derived from borrowing and spending are incremental. Funds are divisible, and therefore it is appropriate to estimate these gains by the marginal factor revenue approach. The income surplus

---

[4] Some business managers go beyond the risk-taking of ordinary buying and selling of goods with equity or borrowed capital. They speculate with funds and sometimes borrow for that purpose. That is, they may borrow today to increase their cash balances for use on some future date when they expect borrowing to be more expensive or more difficult. This may be precautionary action, may be designed to make a speculative profit through purchasing more cheaply than usual, etc.

method may be used when firms make decisions not about how much to borrow, but whether to borrow this or that. Regardless of the use to which the funds are put, whether to buy machines, materials, labor, or to spend in some other way, it is obvious that a profit-minded manager will arrange the sequence of uses so that the most remunerative comes first. Any particular loan may be devoted entirely to one type of use, but even there the principle of diminishing marginal productivity is likely to apply. As a result an individual firm's demand for funds usually may be portrayed by the conventional type of demand curve sloping downward to the right. The more urgent the total need, the more inelastic will be the demand schedule or the more nearly perpendicular the demand curve.

The quantity borrowed by a firm at any given time will depend chiefly upon the magnitude of the particular project to be financed, the firm's own available funds, and the cost of borrowing. The individual borrower often has to accept an interest rate fixed by forces beyond his control, as will be explained below. His decision in such cases is limited to whether he should borrow and how much. If he has a mental picture of relative marginal factor revenues, he will tend to expand his borrowing so long as the marginal factor revenue exceeds the interest cost of borrowing one unit.[5] When these quantities are equal, he will have borrowed the amount which is most profitable for him to borrow. This general analysis of equilibrium at the point of marginal equality follows the familiar pattern of other explanations of quantities purchased and has logical validity under the assumptions. One should recognize, however, that there are many other variables which are often more important than the interest rate in determining when and how much a firm borrows.

In specific cases the particular needs of the moment may seem so pressing that the borrower does not make any calculations but merely says to himself, for instance, "I've got to get $10,000 and I'll get it even though the bank does charge me 6 per cent." Or a large corporation may be planning to build a new factory with an expected cost of $2,000,000 and realizes that the going rate for mortgage bonds of the type it can offer is 4 per cent. Its decision is whether to float the bond issue and build the factory, not how much to borrow. Optimism about future demand, general profit prospects, and the pressure of technological change are likely to be given more weight in the final decision of the board of directors than any argument that the inter-

---

[5] With a fixed interest rate, marginal factor cost is constant at an amount equal to that rate times the calculating unit. In business borrowing the calculating unit for such comparisons is often very large, $100, $1,000 or more.

est rate on the bond issue is now ¼ or ½ of 1 per cent higher or lower than it has been in the past.

**11. Banks May Supply Funds to Business Borrowers.**—There are three major markets for funds in which business borrowers and lenders meet and where the rates of interest and the quantities transferred are determined. The first is the commercial bank which is able to lend because people accept its promises to pay more readily than those of the ordinary firms.[6]

Commercial banks have varying policies in marketing their credit. Most small borrowers are asked to pay a fixed interest rate which is not subject to bargaining and does not change much from year to year. A higher rate is often quoted for unsecured loans than for those where collateral is offered.[7] There is little that resembles price competition in this field. The small businessman usually finds that it is easier to borrow from his own bank where he is known than from another bank. He chooses his own bank because it saves him time and paper work. Large borrowers are in a different category. They bargain with their bankers for the lowest possible rate of interest or the best repayment terms. Often there is much interest competition among banks for very large loans from good companies. This competition is particularly keen as between the banks in one city and those in another. New York banks, for instance, may outbid those of Los Angeles for loans to Southern California borrowers.

A comprehensive explanation of how interest rates are determined on bank loans to business firms must be deferred until other borrowing and lending situations have been described. However, it is clear that banks operate like business enterprises in the sale of their credit. They make many types of loans and determine their charges in many ways. In some cases the cost of the loan is dominant. In others, the major factor is the price (interest) charged by competitors, or the bargaining pressure of large borrowers. Custom also plays a part, particularly with small loans. The general level of rates will tend to rise as business demand for funds rises, and fall as demand falls. There is a significant degree of interdependence between the interest rates which prevail for various classes of loans. Bank loans

---

[6] Banks are fewer and better known than most business firms. They are supervised by state or federal authorities. They also make their credit available through a deposit and checking system which provides great flexibility and convenience. The ability to make checks payable to specific persons and in any amount makes bank credit in this form often preferable even to government credit in the form of paper currency.

[7] Sometimes interest rates differ because of the quality of the collateral (government bonds as opposed to commercial drafts).

to business firms form part of the credit structure, and their rates tend to rise and fall with the others.[8]

**12. Interest Rates on New Loans Are Influenced by the Going Rate on Old Loans as Determined on the Security Exchanges.—** A second market where the rate of interest is determined is the securities exchange where buyers' bids and sellers' offers are balanced. Except for the fact that buyers are lenders and sellers are borrowers, the securities exchange is much the same as the commodity exchange. There are speculators on both. The different maturity dates of securities influence their market prices somewhat like the different delivery dates for commodities. But for our present purposes, the major similarity is the fact that on both exchanges no single buyer or seller sets the market price. It is determined by the balancing of aggregate demands against aggregate supplies. Security prices rise and fall with changes in the quantities or the prices in particular collective demand and supply schedules.

The most important difference between commodity and security exchange pricing lies in the interdependence of security prices and security interest rates. The connection may be demonstrated in various ways, of which the following sequence is one simplified illustration:

First, let lenders (or speculators) become more eager to buy bonds.

Second, this will raise the price of bond issues already on the market, i.e., securities with fixed interest and fixed maturity dates.

Third, this will decrease the yield of these fixed interest securities. The new purchasers will get less return on their security investment than those who formerly purchased the securities for a lower price. [If a 4 per cent ($4) bond was selling for $100, it yielded 4 per cent. If now its price is bid up to $105, its current yield is only 3.81 per cent.]

Fourth, because of the interdependence of security prices, the diminished yield on the securities in demand will affect the yields or prices of other securities, including new issues.

Fifth, a new issue of very much the same type (same industry, similar maturity and probable risk) may now expect to find buyers willing to pay $105 for a 4 per cent bond, or $100 for a 3.81 per cent bond. (Because of custom and lender psychology, borrowing firms are more apt to use the former alternative in offering their new bonds than the latter. There may also be a

---

[8] See Sections 17, 18, and 21 below for further comments on the methods and basis of bank lending.

financial advantage in issuing bonds at interest rates which cause the bonds to sell above par. If, for instance, they sell at 101.5 and are called at 104, the calling firm loses less than if they were sold at 100, or at a discount.)

This simplified sequence shows the way in which the going rate of interest is determined for borrowers and lenders who get together in the securities market. The price of securities is influenced by changes in either the schedule demand for funds or the schedule supply of funds, or in both. The change in interest rates occurs simultaneously with the change in security prices as a joint result in the opposite direction.

In the structure of interest rates there is also interdependence. When 4 per cent bonds rise, more risky bonds paying 5 per cent also tend to rise. More conservative 3 per cent bonds do likewise. New issues are influenced in either their offering rate or their offering price by the going rate (the yield) on old issues of the same type. A more complete explanation of the absolute level of particular interest rates again must be postponed until more factual background has been presented.

### 13. Business Firms May Borrow from Individual Lenders.—
Business firms sometimes market their bonds directly to individual lenders by sales "over the counter." More often the bonds are sold to the investing public through investment bankers who either buy and resell or act as commission sellers.[9] In either case the bonds are sold ultimately to the same group of private and institutional lenders who might otherwise have purchased old issues through the organized bond market. The interest rate paid by the borrowers is likely to be much the same whether the marketing is direct or indirect. There is much fluidity of loanable funds, and it is usually easy for both borrowers and lenders to shift from one security market to another.

From the viewpoint of the large borrower, even the very small differences in interest rates or costs of borrowing by alternative methods may be decisive. The causes of such differences do not concern us here, only the fact that the differences are small. Our main problem is to explain interest rates as prices and the causes and effects of changes in those rates.

Business firms may also borrow directly from government lending agencies like the Reconstruction Finance Corporation, or indirectly

---

[9] Old securities which are not listed on the organized exchanges are also sold "over the counter" by security dealers. These dealers often aid investment bankers in marketing new issues, or operate in that role themselves.

by borrowing from banks which borrow from these agencies.[10]  Interest rates under such circumstances are usually lower than if such funds were borrowed from private lenders.  Political considerations are more important than economic considerations.

Occasionally large firms sell their bonds directly to insurance companies who have funds to invest.  Bargaining may enter into the determination of the precise price at which the issue is bought by the insurance company, but the yield will closely approximate the going rate prevailing for similar securities sold on the open market.

**14. The Proximate Supply of Funds Available to Government Borrowers.**—Governments borrow for a variety of reasons.  These include construction (public works), destruction (war), relief, relending, and tax anticipation.

The federal government sells most of its securities by public offering.  The Treasury Department announces how much it wishes to borrow at such and such terms and then waits for bids.  When enough bids are received, the books are closed.  If more than enough bids come in during the first day, as has often been the case, the lenders are given only a pro rata share of the total.  Bidders include banks, financial institutions, business firms, trusts, and private individuals.  Certain classes of securities appeal to one group of lenders more than to others.  For instance, very short-term, low-interest "certificates" are purchased almost entirely by the Federal Reserve banks, but some are sought by commercial banks and very large corporations.  Ten- or twenty-year bonds with higher interest rates usually attract life insurance companies, savings banks, and private individuals.  In short, the proximate supply of funds available to the federal government as borrower includes both (1) credit created for the occasion by commercial banks and (2) credit created by banks and governments at other times which has been accumulated as savings by individuals and business firms.

State and local governments also generally make a public announcement of the amount they want to borrow, but usually sell the whole block of securities for a lump sum to the highest bidder—a bank, other financial institution, or syndicate.  If purchased by the latter, the bonds are usually resold to the public in smaller amounts to fit the individual purse.[11]  Syndicate members prefer to make their

---

[10] The RFC gets its funds chiefly from the federal government. (See next section.)

[11] The above account is not intended to be all-inclusive. During the Civil War some federal issues were marketed to syndicates. Banks or other buyers of negotiable bonds may resell at any time.

profit by the margin between the buying and the selling price. Ultimate buyers prefer an interest reward, i.e., they are lenders, not enterprisers.

**15. Interest and Non-Interest Considerations in Government Borrowing.**—Federal borrowing may differ from state and local borrowing in the matter of interest rates. The federal government usually has some power to influence the rates in its favor, but minor governments do not. Both want to keep the interest cost of borrowing as low as possible. That is one reason why they use so many short-term (low-interest) issues. The national government has another method it can use. Through its influence on central bank policy, it may offset its own increased borrowing by causing the central bank to buy government bonds in the open market. Or the bank may depress interest rates in general by reducing the rediscount rate for commercial paper. Other methods, still more indirect, include reducing the legal reserve requirements of member banks, relaxing quality standards for central bank loans, etc. This topic will receive further discussion in the sections which summarize the forces determining interest rates.

Fiscal policy is often a more important consideration to the national government than the interest cost of borrowing. In wartime, for instance, rather than risk adverse economic and psychological reactions to heavier taxes, additional bond issues are sold, regardless of the size of the interest bill. Or the government may consider its major objective to be holding down prices. This requires absorbing purchasing power in the hands of consumers to prevent them from spending it in an inflationary manner. Securities may then be offered to individuals at high rates of interest to make them attractive, and expensive selling campaigns may be employed.

The amounts borrowed by state and local governments likewise depend more upon what the people want at the time than upon the prevailing interest rate. During depressions when interest rates are low, voters are very cautious. They are apt to disapprove bonds for new schools, court houses, and jails, unless, of course, these can be presented as projects which create employment. But in boom periods when interest rates are usually high, people vote much more willingly for all kinds of public works and the bond issues to finance them.

**16. The Proximate Supply of Funds Available to Consumer Borrowers.**—Consumers borrow to increase their present consumption of goods or services. In this country most of their borrowing is probably on open book accounts carried by the merchants

from whom they buy. Large purchases are often financed by signing contracts to pay on the installment plan. Merchants, in turn,
finance such deferred payment sales either out of their own capital
funds or out of funds borrowed from banks or private lenders. Consumers wishing to pay cash (or to quiet insistent creditors) borrow
directly from banks, finance companies, insurance companies, building and loan associations, pawnbrokers, etc.

When a consumer wishes to borrow funds for his own use in the
market, the place where he seeks a loan depends upon his knowledge
of opportunities, his connections, and his influence. Those with
checking or savings accounts are apt to think first of their bank as a
source of funds. Usually they do not bargain, but pay whatever
interest it demands. An alternative is to borrow on insurance policies for convenience, secrecy, or lower interest charges in that way.
Members of credit unions, which are co-operative banks, can usually
obtain better terms and lower interest rates from such organizations
than elsewhere. Poor people, or those already heavily in debt, generally resort to finance companies or pawnbrokers. Interest rates on
such loans are high both because of the high cost of making and collecting small loans and because of the urgency of the small borrower's
need. The state often has intervened with antiusury laws to try to
prevent lenders from taking undue advantage of persons in desperate
circumstances.

17. Non-Interest Determinants of the Amount of Consumer
Borrowing.—The quantity borrowed by consumers is not influenced
very much by the rate of interest they must pay. More important
determinants are the occurrence of personal emergency needs, changes
in income, and changes in the terms of payment. Although extremely
important for particular individuals, personal emergencies do not significantly affect fluctuations in the *total* amount borrowed by consumers at any given time. Therefore, they need not be examined in
detail in this study of the reasons for interest rates and their changes.

Income variations are very important in determining the amount
of consumer borrowing. When incomes fall, some people try to keep
up their levels of consumption by borrowing. Others reduce their
borrowing either voluntarily or because lenders will not continue to
extend credit. The net effect of a business decline and a rise in unemployment seems to be a reduction in total consumer loans outstanding. On the other hand, an upswing in employment and wage
rates tends to stimulate borrowing to buy automobiles, radios, refrigerators, homes, etc. The total volume of debt rises with the
boom and falls during the recession.

The amount borrowed by consumers seems to be influenced also by the terms on which the loan can be had. In the purchase of durable consumer goods the size of the down payment is important. If it is raised, installment buying declines; if it falls, buying on credit expands. This is clearly shown by the restrictive effect of action to raise down payments on consumer goods during the recent war. On the other hand, the lenient terms available under FHA loans offered a positive stimulus to home purchase.

The argument that consumer borrowing is not appreciably affected by changes in the level of interest rates must not be taken to mean that *individual* lenders may raise their rates with impunity. On the contrary, the large number of rival lenders gives the careful borrower the opportunity to shop around for the best rate and terms even though that only means hunting the pawnshop which will lend him the most on his watch. Banks compete with finance companies for small consumer loans. They also compete among themselves and with building and loan companies for mortgage loans. They may try to get borrower patronage by offering larger loans on a given piece of real estate than will their rivals. This is more common than the interest-cutting which would be analogous to the price-cutting of merchants. Although rivalry does occur among lenders with regard to interest rates, it is much more significant in determining *who* makes the loans than in determining the total amount borrowed.

**18. The Proximate Supply of Funds Available to Banker Borrowers.**—Commercial banks borrow as well as lend. The sources of funds open to them include other commercial banks, the central bank, or the national government through some special agency such as the Reconstruction Finance Corporation. Loans from one commercial bank to another are usually relatively small and are generally intended to meet temporary needs for funds. These loans can be concluded quickly and with a minimum of red tape. The interest rate is very low and does not constitute a serious deterrent to borrowing. In times of a monetary crisis, banks may refuse to lend or may impose onerous lending terms rather than try to discourage borrowing by raising the interest rate.

When commercial banks borrow from the central bank of the country, the loan may be obtained by signing a formal note for the funds desired. Less commonly, the central bank agrees to rediscount some of the commercial paper held by the borrowing bank. In either case, the rate of interest charged by the central bank is usually influenced by domestic or international fiscal policies. The profit considerations which govern ordinary banks in their lending are absent or unimportant in central bank decisions. National policies also influence the interest rates charged by the special government lending agencies set up to meet emergency situations such as wars or depressions, or to cater to particular groups such as the farmers.

The proximate supply of funds available to banks as borrowers is chiefly the credit of other banks. In a few cases funds may be borrowed from individual savers or business firms. Government lending agencies like the RFC and HOLC, for instance, may secure part of their funds by selling their own bonds on the open market. Savings banks, of course, receive deposits (borrow) before lending. But they are passive, not active, borrowers. Aside from general advertising, they do not approach potential lender-depositors and ask them for loans. Commercial banks may receive deposits of considerable magnitude from those wanting a place of safekeeping or the check-drawing privilege. Subsequently, some of these funds may be loaned, but they are received, not borrowed, funds. There is no specific solicitation and no interest is paid, except in rare instances.

**19. The Ultimate Supply of Funds Offered by Lenders.**— Lenders either create or accumulate the funds which they lend. The process of "creating" funds is one of extending to the borrower one's own promise to pay. Borrowers want these promises because they are more widely acceptable than their own. Credit of general acceptability is created chiefly by commercial banks and governments. The major lenders of our economy, business firms, usually accept their own credit immediately after creating it, as when they sell on open book account. Except when they allow drafts to be drawn upon them, they issue no credit instruments of general circulation. Business credit therefore is in a different category from bank notes, checks, and government currency.

Created credit may be either spent or saved. Those who borrow created credit usually spend it. People who think of themselves as savers accumulate credit instruments created by others. When they lend, they are really proximate and not ultimate sources of funds. Nevertheless, their ability to hoard saved funds instead of lending them does give them a significant place in the loan market. By increasing or decreasing the amount they are willing to lend, they influence interest rates.

The remainder of this chapter will develop the themes of the two preceding paragraphs.

**20. The Nature of Credit and How It Is "Created."**—Etymologically the word *credit* is derived from the Latin verb meaning "to trust." This is also the way in which it is popularly used. *Credit* in this sense is merely *the confidence which one person has in another that the latter will fulfill a promise to pay something in the future.* A store selling jewelry on the installment plan may advertise, "Your credit is good." The merchant is trying to convince people that he will accept their promises to pay in the future if they will sign purchase contracts. But he usually limits his sales to persons of good reputation who have jobs or property.

The merchant himself may find that when he wants to buy goods from a distant firm which he does not know very well, he may be told that his credit is not good. But at the same time, he is known to his banker, and the banker is well known throughout the country. Therefore, he offers to give his own note to the bank in exchange for notes of the bank and he pays for the privilege. If the exchange is merely a transfer of demand notes, as when the merchant writes his own check and gives it in exchange for a cashier's check, the payment is called a fee. But if the merchant gives a note, payable in the future, for bank notes or deposits payable now, the payment which balances the exchange is called interest. Inferior credit plus interest is given for superior credit.[12] In this sense credit is not created, it is merely exchanged.[13]

Another way of using the word *credit* is with reference to obligations to pay. Here it is the opposite of the word *debt.* A promise to pay money is known as a debt when viewed from the debtor's position, and as a credit from the creditor's position. Bank deposits are debts of the bank to depositors, but are often called bank credit. These deposits may arise from the borrowing-lending transaction. The borrower executes a note to the bank and receives in exchange a deposit credit. At the moment of exchange each is in debt to the other. Neither the debts nor the credits existed before. Therefore, in this sense of the word, bank lending may be said to "create" credit in the form of bank deposits.

To distinguish this second connotation of the term, it seems best to use adjectives. Bank lending creates *bank* credit. Business lend-

---

[12] This is the borrower's viewpoint. The lender requires that interest be paid for several reasons, not merely because he considers the loan risky. These additional causes on the supply side will be elaborated below.

[13] This type of credit may be "created" when a potential borrower, Jones, convinces a formerly reluctant lender, Smith, that a loan will be safe. Jones builds confidence in his ability and intent to pay in the future for what he gets today. Contrary to the usual interpretation, it is here the borrower, not the lender, who "creates" credit.

ing creates *business* or *commercial* credit. Some lending institutions (savings banks, etc.) transfer the credit of others, usually commercial bank credit or government credit (currency). The transfer involves accumulation in various ways and subsequent lending. Of course, every lending transaction requires the coöperation of a willing borrower and hence it takes *two* parties, not just one, to create a credit or a debt (in the second sense of an obligation to pay). It is only customary usage which permits us to forget the borrower and give all "credit" to the lender. (A third meaning of the term!)

The semantic confusion between "debts" and "credits" is a serious one. They are merely different ways of looking at the same transactions. One cannot be created without the other. (The "buying" versus the "selling" of goods furnishes a close analogy.) But the connotation of something "bad" is attached to "debts," while "credits" are "good." For instance, creating government debt by borrowing from the banks is widely thought to be bad. But when banks extend credit to the government they are thought to be performing a beneficial service.

**21. Credit Instruments and Their Uses.**—Credit instruments furnish evidence of an obligation to pay. They are used to transfer these obligations (credits in the second sense) from one person to another. The most common is the personal check drawn against a bank deposit. It is a draft, or order to pay to some one an amount which the bank owes the drawer. Such drafts against bank credit are widely acceptable because of the good credit (first sense) of the bank. Other forms of drafts may be drawn against banks without deposits having been previously created. In foreign trade, for instance, an importer may make an arrangement with his bank whereby, in return for the importer's promise to pay in the future, the bank allows the exporter to draw a draft against it. Commercial drafts are orders by a seller against a buyer commanding him to pay a debt arising from the purchase of goods. These credit instruments may be sold (transferred to others) if the buyer's credit (first sense) is good.[14]

Another very common form of credit instrument is the note, or direct promise to pay. It takes many forms in addition to the simple I.O.U. Most widely seen, though not often clearly recognized for what they signify, are various forms of national currency. "The United States of America will pay to the bearer on demand . . . dollars." Or, "The Federal Reserve Bank of San Francisco will pay

---

[14] The quality of the seller's credit is also involved when he indorses the draft.

to the bearer on demand . . . dollars." Formerly, we also saw similar promises of national banks, and still earlier, of state banks.

One important thing about these various types of credit instruments in the analysis of interest rates is that they have different degrees of acceptability. A man may trade his own I.O.U. which has limited acceptability for a bank deposit which permits him to draw checks of greater acceptability. One reason for the inferior status of the I.O.U. is its future date of payment. This is true whether the borrower is a private individual, a business firm, a bank, or even a government. In such cases interest may be thought of as comprising in part a payment which supplements a time credit instrument when it is given in exchange for demand instruments, i.e., funds. On other occasions, people trade bank deposits for checks or for note currency, or vice versa. Both are demand instruments, and therefore no interest payments are involved, but occasionally a fee may be charged. Domestic currency may also be exchanged for foreign currency, usually upon payment of a fee to cover bookkeeping and other expenses involved. There have been occasions when one type of currency became more desirable than another for which it ordinarily exchanged at par. Gold coins at times have sold at a premium over paper currency. Paper currency has also been preferred to bank deposits, as in the panic of 1907. But this premium is not the same as interest, since the transfer is not temporary. There is no time interval involved. If there were, the premium would be an interest payment exacted by the lender because there was a scarcity situation he could exploit.

An interesting anomaly that arises from this analysis occurs when the national government borrows from banks. According to most people's judgment, there is no institution with better credit than the government. Why, then, does the government exchange its credit for the (inferior) credit of banks? And pay interest for the privilege? The first answer might be that the government exchanges a time credit instrument (a bond) for a demand credit instrument (a deposit) against which checks may be drawn. But why does not the government issue its own sight drafts or promises to pay? Surely a government note is as widely acceptable as a bank note or check. An answer to this question might be that there is so much public disapproval of this method of using government credit that the more expensive and roundabout method must be used. In a free enterprise economy, people disapprove of government competition with private banks in the credit creation business. Some contend that governments lack sufficient self-restraint and that interest charges on a mounting public debt furnish a necessary restraining influence upon government spending. Others deny this argument. A third viewpoint is that governments borrow from banks as a subsidy to keep them alive for the benefit of the community or their stockholders.[15]

**22. Determinants of Interest Charges for Commercial Bank Credits, Most of Which Are "Created Credits."**—Commercial banks are business firms engaged in the selling of services. The major service which they offer is that of the right to use the credit of the bank for limited periods of time. The bank credit which they lend is chiefly credit which they "create." To a certain extent, however, commercial banks operate like savings banks. That is, they receive funds from stockholders and depositors part of which they may lend to others. These represent accumulated funds as distinct from the funds which the commercial banks themselves create. The interest charges which commercial banks exact from borrowers are payments for services rendered. Banks are organized to seek profit. They incur costs in the creation of the services which they sell to lenders. Therefore, many of the principles which govern the determination of commodity prices are useful here.

Like many other types of businesses, commercial banks also have various sidelines, some of which pay their way and some of which do not. Conspicuous among the latter is the provision of checking services for those who maintain deposits but do not borrow. In recent years fees often have been imposed upon small depositors to cover part or all of the cost of the services performed for them.

Commercial banks differ from other types of business in that they take payment for their product in a variety of ways. Some buyers promise to pay within a few days. Others ask the privilege of waiting several months or even many years. Some buyers offer good collateral; others offer only their general assets and earning power. This variety in the form of payments is equivalent to variety in the type of product sold. Reverting to conventional terminology, we may say that banks make many kinds of loans. Like many other enterprises, banks are therefore faced with the accounting and pricing problems associated with joint costs.

If banks follow customary business practices, their interest charges on loans should cover the direct cost of making those loans plus a share of the general overhead. These direct costs include those of investigation, entering the deposit credit, handling check debits, re-

---

[15] Cf. Anatol Murad, *The Credit System and Public Debt,* unpublished manuscript, Ch. 8.

ceiving or collecting payment, and a share of the bad debt losses associated with each type of loan. Expressed as a time percentage of the total loaned, these costs will differ. Chattel mortgage loans repaid on the installment plan usually are charged the highest interest rates because of their greater bookkeeping expense and default losses. Short-term loans to the government in amounts of hundreds of thousands of dollars at one time require less clerical effort per dollar loaned than a few thousand dollars borrowed by each of a score of merchants for the same length of time.

**23. Non-Cost Factors Influence Many Interest Rates of Commercial Banks.**—Bank interest rates, however, cannot be explained completely on a straight cost-of-production basis. The risk premium to be charged for bad debt losses is difficult to estimate, since it varies from borrower to borrower and it changes with the phases of the business cycle. There is also the problem of overhead. In good times, when banks are lending large amounts, the fixed charges per unit loaned should be low (and the risk premium, too), but interest rates are not often reduced as a consequence. In bad times these charges are high, but interest rates tend to fall. One reason is the fact that only the safest loans are made. Another is the decreased willingness of borrowers to pay high rates when the value productivity of the borrowed funds is low. And then there is the troublesome question of how much of the checking service expense should be borne by one class of borrowers as opposed to another or by borrowers in general as opposed to nonborrowing depositors. It should be clear, therefore, that bank interest rates like many other prices cannot be explained in terms of cost of production alone. Nor can cost of production be ignored, since banks must make a profit in order to continue in existence.

One of the other important factors on the supply side is the degree of interest competition. This comes from other commercial banks and sometimes from government agencies. But the most important competition in most lending fields is that offered by those who must save before they can lend. As explained in Section 18, this includes private individuals, industrial firms, insurance companies, and financial institutions such as building and loan companies, personal loan companies, savings banks, etc. All of these engage in direct or indirect lending competition with banks. In some fields of lending, competition is so keen that banks ignore overhead costs in setting the interest rates at which they offer funds. In others they are so free from interest rate competition that they may "charge what the traffic will bear." Monopolistic agreements, at least of the tacit type, have occurred in some cities. Outsiders furnish whatever lending competition exists.

Other determinants of bank interest charges include custom, government regulation or assistance, and bank management estimates of future trends in business. Custom has been strong, for instance, in the rural mortgage loan field, holding interest rates virtually fixed for decades at a time. Government regulation, aside from antiusury laws, has been confined chiefly to the types of permissible loans and to the total quantity that banks may lend. This has had an indirect effect on the interest rates charged by banks, as will be explained later.

**24. Limits to the Quantity Commercial Banks Can Lend.—** There are several apparent limits upon the amount commercial banks can lend, some effective and some ineffective. The first is based upon the fact that many people prefer currency to checks for certain purposes, such as small purchases, payrolls, bribes, gambling, hoards, etc. The quantity thus demanded tends to rise and fall with the volume of business. Therefore, as lending expands, banks must provide increased quantities of currency. This may be obtained from the central bank by selling government bonds or by borrowing. In modern times central banks rarely limit the amount of currency which they stand ready to provide as needed.[16] They only require that the demanding bank furnish good collateral and abide by certain rules in its lending.

The second limit also is more apparent than significant in modern banking practice. In the United States members of the Federal Reserve System must not lend more than a certain multiple of their reserves kept in the form of deposits in the Reserve Banks.[17] But these reserves may be increased by borrowing as needed. If that is not enough, the Board of Governors may cause the reserve ratio to be reduced, which is the same as increasing the multiple. Or the reserve banks may engage in active purchasing of government securities in

---

[16] Formerly, when currency was chiefly coin or coin certificates, the quantity available could not be increased rapidly. Banks had to plan to keep their loans within that certain multiple of their currency reserves which experience indicated was safe.

[17] Technically, reserves in the form of deposits in Federal Reserve banks must not be less than a certain percentage of the bank's own demand and time deposits. But the chief cause of deposit expansion by an individual bank is bank lending. Therefore, to speak of a loan : reserve ratio rather than a deposit : reserve ratio is to emphasize the most significant aspect of the problem. For the banking system as a whole this is even more true. An individual bank may receive primary deposits of both government currency and checks on other banks. Only the former remains as a nonloan source of deposits when all banks are grouped together.

the open market, thus raising member bank deposit reserves. However, if the government fiscal policy demands restriction, not expansion, the central banking mechanism may be put into reverse and thus limit the lending capacity of member banks.

A third limit is the cost of lending in relation to the interest income. If potential lenders compete actively for a given amount of borrowing business, they may force down interest yields on loans. This is done by interest competition on new loans and by bidding up the price of outstanding securities on the market. Eventually the yield may get so low that banks will prefer not to take the risks of further lending in some fields. Prospective bad debt losses plus operating expenses look larger than probable interest return. Over a period of years bank profits have not been so large as to indicate a wide margin for interest-cutting.

This leads to the fourth limit, the caution of bank managers. In addition to the danger of negative operating income, banks must also consider possible depreciation of outstanding loans at a time when depositors demand more cash than usual. Under the present system of federal deposit insurance in the United States, this risk is less than it used to be. But the fear of depressions and depositor panics still operates as something of a deterrent to indefinite loan expansion.

The fifth limit also is linked to the third. Although individual banks may compete in the open market and may purchase outstanding loans from some other lender, the total amount borrowed cannot be increased very much by banks in general. All that the banks can do is to make lending more attractive by offering lower interest charges or more lenient terms. If borrowers still fail to demand bank credit, there is not much that the banks can do. This is probably the major limit to bank loans and to lending in general. Under modern banking systems the legal lending ceiling is usually well above the aggregate demand for funds. For individual banks this may not be true, but it certainly holds for the banking system as a whole. Aside from the caution and the profit seeking of those who run our banks, there is no limit to their lending. The significance of this point relative to interest rates will be made clear in a later section.

**25. Individual and Business Savers of Funds May Lend, Hoard or Invest.**—Individuals obtain cash balances or liquid funds by receiving money income, by receiving gifts, or by selling some less liquid asset such as realty, merchandise, or securities. Most of the funds received from current income are usually spent for current consumption or for things needed in the ordinary course of business.

Some of the cash balances derived from periodic income receipts, however, may be considered to be larger than necessary for current needs. These are often called "savings." Persons with large incomes find it much easier to set aside such cash balances than those who have very little to spend for necessary food, clothing, and shelter. At this point, however, the most important consideration is not the origin of savings, but their disposition. They may be hoarded, loaned, or spent.

The decision which influences the disposition of the savings need have no connection with the decision which brought them into being. This is clearly true in the case of windfalls, like unexpected gifts or inheritances. On the other hand, savings out of current income may occur because of the desire for interest income. In that case both saving and lending spring from the same motive. Although saving with the intention of investing to get income is a very common motive, saving against future contingencies is also frequent, particularly among those with small incomes and among business firms. Contingency saving is apt to lead to hoarding in currency or in checking deposits, since liquidity is a major objective. However, persons with low incomes often consider savings banks or postal savings accounts as good as cash, and the interest is attractive. Such persons combine the contingency saving motive with that of earning interest. Business firms frequently invest part of their contingency reserves in short-term government bonds or commercial paper whenever they think the interest income is worth the slight reduction in liquidity which such lending involves. The final possibility is that of the arrival of the contingency itself. This causes the saved funds to be spent, whether taken from hoards or liquidated from loans. The secular upward trend of total savings seems to reveal, however, that contingencies do not occur with nearly the same frequency or magnitude as do savings. Regardless of the initial motive for saving, the ultimate purpose in most cases seems to be the accumulation of wealth for its own sake or for the income it will bring.

Much of the saving done by individuals is not directly loaned by them. It is used to purchase life insurance, where it accumulates as reserves and is loaned by the insurance companies. Or it may be put into savings banks or building and loan companies. Here, strictly speaking, the saver lends his savings to these firms and then they relend in larger amounts to various borrowers. Some saved funds are also used to contribute equity capital to various lending institutions and that which is not needed for fixed equipment and running expenses may be loaned out. All of these firms which stand between the individual saver and a loan market into which his funds eventually go may be called savings-transfer institutions. They accumulate funds and lend them under the profit-seeking motives of business firms. In this they differ from individual savers and play a different role in the loan markets.

Lending is only one of the ways of "investing" saved funds to earn income, but it is the one most directly related to the problem of interest rate determination.[18] Instead of buying bonds or notes (lending), a person or institution with surplus funds may buy shares of stock, leases, or rental property. They may also purchase things to hold for speculative gain rather than for interest, rent, or dividend income. The presence of these other alternatives reduces the amount of funds available for lending and therefore affects the interest rate.

The various forms of property income are interdependent. They should all be considered parts of a general structure of rates of return on investment of which interest income is a major element. The explanation of the level of these rates of return has already been given in part. A more complete analysis must wait until psychological and institutional forces influencing supply and demand have been further examined in the next chapter.

**26. Descriptive Summary of Loans and Interest Rates.**—The institutional approach of the foregoing pages has shown that there are many interest rates to be explained. There are different types of loan contracts, different markets for funds, and different ways in which interest rates are determined. The outline on page 397 summarizes the main features of the complex picture and furnishes a background for some concluding comments.

**27. Arbitrary Determinants of Interest Rates: Political Motives of Governments.**—In addition to the foregoing statement of the economic principles which determine interest rates, political principles should also be noted. In recent years national governments have come to dominate the activities of central banks in the major loan markets. There have been three chief motives. The first was to regulate the imports and exports of gold by controlling the rate of interest on short-term loans in relation to the rates in other countries. The second was to control the business cycle, particularly to combat depressions by "cheap money" which was supposed to induce bank and business borrowing. The third has been to hold down the cost of borrowing to meet anti-unemployment and anti-enemy expendi-

---

[18] The word *investing* is here used in the popular sense of purchasing some income-yielding property. Other meanings of the word will be considered later.

## MAJOR TYPES OF LOAN MARKETS WHERE INTEREST RATES ARE DETERMINED

| CREDIT INSTRUMENT | MARKET WHERE YIELD CHIEFLY DETERMINED VIA PRICE OR INTEREST RATE | PRINCIPAL BORROWERS | PRINCIPAL LENDERS |
|---|---|---|---|
| 1. Bonds (long term): <br>(a) Business <br>(b) Government | 1. Bond exchanges <br>Open market <br>Over-the-counter | 1. Large business firms <br>Governments | 1. Banks <br>Other financial institutions <br>Business firms <br>Individuals |
| 2. Drafts and acceptances: <br>(a) Commercial <br>(b) Bank | 2. Central bank (rediscount rate) <br>Bank (discount rate) <br>Open market | 2. Business firms | 2. Commercial banks <br>Large business firms |
| 3. Notes: <br>(a) Secured by mortgages: <br>(1) Realty | 3. <br>(a) <br>(1) Banks and other lending institutions | 3. <br>(a) <br>(1) Persons and firms | 3. <br>(a) <br>(1) Banks, building and loan companies, insurance companies, persons |
| (2) Chattel | (2) Finance companies and banks | (2) Persons | (2) Finance companies and banks |
| (b) Unsecured notes: <br>(1) Individual and business <br>(2) Government (short-term) | (b) <br>(1) Banks and other lending institutions <br>(2) Bond exchange and open market | (b) <br>(1) Persons and firms <br>(2) Governments | (b) <br>(1) Banks and finance companies <br>(2) Banks and large firms |
| 4. Open book accounts | 4. Business firms (interest rarely made an open charge) | 4. Business and persons as buyers of goods | 4. Business firms as sellers of goods |

tures which, for various reasons, were not financed by taxes. These three motives appear arbitrary because they follow no clear pattern of precedent. However, they help to explain the level of and the changes in interest rates and therefore must be included in interest theory.

The power of central banks to carry out government policies in this regard is exerted chiefly in three loan markets. Government bonds are bought and sold on the securities exchanges. Commercial paper is also bought and sold over the counter. In addition, the central bank sets the rate at which it will lend to member banks by rediscounting or otherwise. Through various substitution options of borrowers and lenders, central bank activity has significant effects upon many interest rates.

If, for instance, the government wants to keep interest rates from rising, it must keep the prices of bonds from falling. It orders the central bank to buy at a certain price all the government bonds offered at that price or lower. This tends to set the general level of rates for other securities, too. So long as the central bank stands willing to lend funds at a given rate (buy bonds at a given figure), other lenders cannot ask more. Interest rates on other types of loans tend to remain fixed at their normal differential from that for the government bonds which the central bank is buying. Therefore, as long as the central bank continues to lend at a fixed rate, there is a plateau in the general supply curve for funds.

The interest rate level set by the government in this way is largely arbitrary. It is based upon fiscal policies rather than economic costs. But ordinarily it cannot depart very much from the going rate which has been set by the joint action of all the demanders and suppliers of funds. The government cannot depress interest rates too far without hurting some of the other lenders. They have costs of production to meet and some of them are very influential in political circles.

In certain markets, however, the interest rate is fixed by the lender and does not change with every change in the yield on government bonds or commercial paper. Commercial banks, for instance, do not very often change the rates at which they offer to lend to various types of business borrowers. Even a major change in the interest rate of the central bank which may affect commercial bank costs of doing business has little if any effect upon their business loan rates. There is likely to be a plateau in the supply curves of commercial banks that resembles the one created by central banks when they offer to buy securities at a fixed price. Each is established as a matter of policy, the one in a quest for maximum profit in the long run and the other because of political decisions regarding national or group welfare.

The government may also influence the rate of interest in its role as a borrower. This is done by controlling the rates which it sets on new issues. If the government wants to depress interest rates, it may offer securities paying lower rates than those prevailing in the market and thus by the power of suggestion (including propaganda) induce lenders to take less. The subjective factor in lender decisions must not be minimized. Wartime bond-selling campaigns emphasize this point. On the other hand, if government officials believe that it would be good fiscal policy to raise the general level of interest rates, they may offer new issues at a higher rate than before. All of this activity on the borrowing side must, of course, be reinforced by the supply-side manipulations previously described.

28. Summary.—Interest is the price paid for the temporary use of funds. Borrowers usually want funds to increase their own purchasing power at that time. Funds, therefore, may consist of anything which is more acceptable to sellers or creditors than that which the borrower can offer before he borrows. In most cases, funds are in the form of promises to pay. They are credit instruments. The borrower exchanges his promise to pay for some one else's promise to pay which has greater acceptability. Inferior credit plus a promise to pay interest is exchanged temporarily for superior credit.

This superior credit may have been "created" or "saved." The creation of credit takes place chiefly in our commercial banking system. Business firms also create credit when they "extend" credit to their customers. Governments create credit when they issue currency. The credit instruments of banks and governments circulate as general purchasing power. When received as income, they may be spent as quickly as obtained. They also may be saved, i.e., they may be accumulated for future spending, for lending, or for the satisfaction of more hoarding. When savers lend, they are influenced chiefly by the subjective costs of opportunities foregone. When the creators of credit lend, the expected costs of doing business are the primary consideration.

The explanation of any particular rate requires an institutional study of the motives and practices of the borrowers and lenders involved. Business firms borrow to increase their profits through expanded purchase of goods and services, including durable capital goods. They lend to stimulate sales or to get interest from idle funds. Private individuals borrow to increase consumption, and lend to get income from savings. Governments borrow to fight wars, to combat depressions, to finance large construction programs, and to meet temporary deficits. They lend for various economic and political objectives.

The lending of accumulated funds is done by individuals, savings banks, loan companies, etc. Firms engaged in the lending business accumulate funds from stockholders, savers, and their own profits. Although it is not their chief function, commercial banks also lend funds accumulated in this way. In addition, they have a source of funds which other firms lack. They receive funds from people who want the convenience of a checking account. Large firms, for instance, may borrow by issuing bonds and then deposit the proceeds into their checking accounts to be used as needed. Some of these deposits remain unused by the depositors and can be loaned by the bank.

The lending of created funds is done chiefly by commercial banks. When they lend, however, there is no way to distinguish between the two sources of the funds loaned, whether received funds or created funds. Every loan begins by the bank creating a deposit against which checks may be drawn. A brief summary can only state that the amount of funds received from depositors is one of the several determinants of the total amount of loans that an individual commercial bank can make.

The interest rates charged by lending firms of either type depend upon a complex group of forces. These include the costs of making and collecting loans, the cost of interest paid to depositors (rare in commercial banks), the allocation of joint costs, the degree of lending competition, the force of custom, etc. Central banks and governments often arbitrarily fix certain interest rates. Or they may exert pressure indirectly as by the purchase or sale of securities on the open market.

No simple explanation of interest rates can portray all of the complex forces involved in any given loan market. The fundamental motives which govern borrowers and lenders must be understood. But one must know also the institutional setting in which these are given expression.

# Chapter 24

## DIFFERENCES AMONG INTEREST RATES

**1. The Problems of This Chapter.**—This chapter examines some specific questions regarding interest rates in modern capitalistic society. The institutional background which one must first understand has been outlined in the preceding chapter. The following explanation of interest rate differences furnishes something in the nature of a bridge to the more "theoretical" chapter which follows.

*Relative* magnitudes are the general theme. These are examined and explained under the following headings:

1. Why do different interest rates exist at any given time and place for loans of different types?
2. Why do interest rates on the same type of loan:
   (a) Differ from one time to another?
   (b) Differ from one place to another?

**2. Differences among Interest Rates at the Same Time: I. Risk.** —The reasons why some interest rates are usually higher than others may be found chiefly on the supply side. Demand differences also exist but are generally less important. High reservation prices in the supply schedules of high-interest markets often reflect differences in subjective or objective risk.

From a subjective viewpoint, risk refers to the lenders' fear of loss. Some of the principal may not be returned, interest may not be paid, or the lender may be put to expense to collect what should be regained without effort. This fear of loss is greater in some situations than in others. The experience of lenders in the past indicates that certain types of borrowers are less apt to default than others. Loans to large corporations with a long record of meeting their obligations generally are considered less risky than loans to small firms newly formed. Loans to the federal government are usually thought safer than those to small municipalities. Such is the general opinion of lenders.

Interest rate differences at any given time also result from the differences in expectations among lenders, even though the borrowers are of the same type. One banker may be more optimistic about the future than another who is also lending to local merchants. And noticeable differences may exist between cities. On the other hand, some lenders may lend at lower rates than others because the thought of possible loss does not worry them, as when government agencies make loans for semipolitical purposes.

From an objective viewpoint, risk is the known experience of loss in the past. It may be expressed as a percentage of the amount loaned. Large banks or banking systems have good records and can make such calculations. Others may read what published studies reveal. But the difference in riskiness between different classes of loans can never be given precise quantitative statement. The only definite *risk premium* that exists is the one revealed by the market itself. On the supply side of that market are many different lenders with varying opinions about the degrees of risk involved in different loans. Each separate lender may change his opinion frequently regarding future uncertainties and the risk class into which a given loan should be put. In short, despite the possibility of obtaining various objective measurements of loan risk, it is not definite like mortality risk, fire risk, etc. The subjective element is dominant.

One of the important causes of differences in risk is the length of the loan. We can predict what is likely to happen in the very near future with greater certainty than we can predict distant events. Therefore, the more remote the repayment date is, the greater the risk to the lender of not being able to collect. The second element of risk on long-term loans arises from the lender's own uncertainty regarding his own needs. He must recognize that unforeseen contingencies may develop before the maturity date of the loan. If these force him to sell his security, the price which he can get will be influenced by the going rate (yield) on such securities at the time of sale. If the going rate at that date exceeds the rate at time of purchase, the security will probably sell at less than its purchase price and the lender will lose.[1] For these two reasons, the risk of lending is generally thought to be proportionate to the length of the loan. The rate of increase in yield diminishes rapidly, however, as the duration of the loan increases. After eight or ten years' maturity is reached, additional time has little effect on interest rates.

### 3. Differences among Interest Rates at the Same Time: II. Cost.
—Some loans cost more per dollar to make and to collect than do others. It is therefore proper that they should yield a higher interest

---

[1] There are several exceptions which complicate the statement of the problem but do not change the fundamental principle. For instance, as a security approaches maturity, the influence of the going rate on its price diminishes.

rate. Prominent are installment loans on consumer durable goods. If losses on bad debts be counted as costs, then the risk differences described in the preceding section might be included here. Indeed, they often are.

Another cost difference that is sometimes important appears in loans by the national government to business, farmers, exporters, shipbuilders, foreign nations, etc. As indicated in Section 27 of Chapter 23, these loans are often made for policy reasons and therefore the interest rate charged is more or less arbitrary. However, in those cases where the government hopes to break even and cost is a factor, government lending costs may be less than those of institutional lenders. If the loaned funds are borrowed in both cases, the government can usually borrow more cheaply and therefore can lend for less. Certain elements of cost are also lacking or much reduced, such as rent or amortization of buildings, taxes, and normal profits.

**4. Differences among Interest Rates at the Same Time: III. Competition.**—In some fields there is much more interest rate competition than in others. The degree of monopolistic behavior by individual lenders or by groups is very important. The well-known story of Shylock illustrates the extreme case of monopolistic exploitation of a necessitous borrower. Bond purchases on the exchanges illustrate the other extreme of much competition among many lenders. A recent decision of the Interstate Commerce Commission to require open bidding by investment banker syndicates for railroad securities shows the significance of the problem. Discriminatory pricing by lenders of small amounts is not uncommon since secrecy usually prevails and relending does not occur.

There are also differences in the degree of monopsonistic behavior which should not be overlooked. When the federal government is the major borrower and therefore is the chief dependence of those who have funds to lend, it can depress interest rates in its favor. Because of the interdependence of interest rates previously described, this reduces other interest rates, too. Some are more markedly affected than others (state bonds vs. home mortgages) since they are better substitutes in the eyes of the class of lenders affected.

**5. Differences among Interest Rates at the Same Time: IV. Demand.**—The urgency of demand and the number of demanders also influence the rate of interest in some markets, although supply forces are usually dominant. An outstanding illustration occurred in the spring and summer of 1929 when call loans on stock collateral were in unusual demand because of the speculative boom. Interest rates on call loans are usually among the lowest of all because of their short duration and very low risk. But when the demand rose many-fold, call rates rose to 6, 10, 15 per cent and even more, thus proving the influence of demand. The supply of call funds from banks, large firms, and other lenders usually had been sufficient to balance aggregate demand at a very low interest rate in the neighborhood of 1 to 2 per cent. When schedule demand increased, additional supply had to come from other lenders less familiar with that loan market, or from less available funds of the usual lenders. Some lenders also probably felt that call loans were more risky than before.

The call loan illustration has been recounted in some detail because it illustrates the importance of the magnitude of demand whenever the supply of funds is not perfectly elastic. To put it in another way, so long as additional funds are forthcoming at constant marginal cost, demand seems unimportant. But when the marginal supply price rises, as it does in all cases beyond a certain magnitude, then demand quantities are very important. In diagrammatic terms, as the demand curve shifts to the right, it eventually encounters a rising portion of the supply curve and the joint result is a rise in the interest rate.

On the other hand there is the case of government borrowing in time of war whose magnitude and urgency cannot be disputed. Even though the amount borrowed each year increases many times over prewar quantities, the interest rate rarely rises much. In fact, the experience of the United States in the second world war shows that the banking system may be used to expand the supply of funds at progressively *lower* rates, not higher. This seems to show that in the government loan market, the supply curve is horizontal, or nearly so, for a very long range. However, if the government had to rely on loans from private individuals, the increased demand would quickly be reflected in rising interest rates. The collective supply curve of funds from this source rises fairly rapidly.

**6. The Interdependence of Interest Rates.**—There is much interdependence among the various interest rates. An individual may lend his funds in either one or several different markets. If he does not like the yield on one type of credit instrument, he may purchase or lend on another. He may also leave the loan market entirely and seek his investment return through profits or rent instead of interest. The range of options for bank lenders is not quite so wide. They are restricted by law to certain classes of loans. In some cases banks voluntarily limit their lending, such as loans on long-term realty mortgages. Business firms also may invest their surplus cash balances in several different fields.

On the borrowing side the possibility of substitution is not so great, although it definitely contributes to the interdependence of interest rates. Governments may borrow on either long-term bonds or short-term notes. Business firms have a similar option. They may also borrow from their suppliers on open book account or by requesting banks to discount drafts on their customers. Individuals have a more limited range of choice, although some kinds of loans may be obtained through more than one type of lending institution. In nearly every case, the possibility of shifting from one market to another, though present, is limited. For instance, when either governments or business firms want to borrow large amounts, they must usually sell long-term bond issues. Individuals without real property must rely on chattel mortgages or unsecured notes.

Because of the possibilities of substitution open to both lenders and borrowers, changes in the interest rates which prevail in one field influence those in others. The connection is close in some relationships, and remote in others. The yields on various types of government bonds tend to rise and fall at the same time, but the spread is not always constant. The general level of government bond yields also influences that for the best grade of utility and industrial bonds. These in turn affect medium-grade bonds and very high-grade preferred stocks. Low-grade bonds are speculative and tend to fluctuate more in keeping with speculative stocks. The different types of negotiable paper sell at rates which tend to move in unison.

Certain fields are relatively isolated, although not by any means completely independent of rates elsewhere. These include rural mortgages, and, to a lesser degree, urban mortgage loans on private dwellings. Pawnshop loans are largely in a field by themselves. In less extreme isolation are small loans made by banks or finance companies to private individuals.

Each loan market has its customary sources of demand and supply. These increase or decrease because of the changed desires of the parties involved. The cross-elasticity of interest rates which attracts or repels individuals at the margin does not remove the elements of difference among markets. The bond exchange still determines security prices and yields by the balancing of aggregate bids and offers. Building and loan companies continue to quote interest rates on mortgage loans in much the same manner that merchants quote commodity prices to customers. Banks either quote rates, as to merchants and home mortgage seekers, bargain, as with large business borrowers seeking medium-term loans, buy on the bond exchange, or buy on the open market. Pawnshops are notorious bargainers, although the chief issue is usually the size of the loan, not the interest rate.

**7. The Average Level of Interdependent Rates Will Be Explained Later.**—For these reasons a complete explanation of interest rates must examine each market, not just one. Independence in certain respects does not rule out general interdependence. The *average level* of interest rates, or the minimum rate in a series of rates, constitutes one question. It will be treated in the next chapter. But the question of why there are *individual differences* in interest rates and why these are greater at one time than another should be studied by itself, as we are doing in this chapter. In each specific situation, the forces which play the dominant role are different, or have different weights. No one generalization or theory will suffice to explain the absolute or relative level of all interest rates unless one falls back upon the too simplified abstraction "supply and demand."

Nevertheless, there are certain demand or supply forces which have appealed to various writers as being of major importance in borrowing and lending. These have become the center of different theories of interest. Because of their prominence in the literature of the subject and because they cast additional light upon the funds markets discussed in preceding sections, they will be analyzed in the next chapter.

Again it seems wise to interject a note of caution. Although loan markets are interdependent, they are not completely and perfectly interlocked. They extend like links in a slack chain, or even like a mesh net. The movement of any one influences first the movement of the adjacent ones. If stretched far enough the initial movement may thus reach more remote links, but their motion will not be as great as that which occurs in the first market. Some links will be so remote as not to move at all, or they may have independent motion of their own.

**8. Differences in Interest Rates at Different Times: Demand Side.**—The chief determinant of short-run fluctuations in interest rates lies on the demand side as it does with fluctuations in other prices. Changes in business profit expectations dominate cyclical variations in interest rates. Other fluctuations may be traced to changes in government demands for funds as the result of wars, depressions, or changes in fiscal policies. Long-run trends may be explained by reference to changes in our banking institutions, or savings habits, the stock of capital goods per capita, and the rate of technological change.

Another way of subdividing the problem is to study separately the different types of lending. This has already been done in the earlier institutional approach. At this point it is only necessary to recall the cyclical stability of some types of interest rates such as those on home mortgage loans and personal consumption loans. Other interest rates are quite unstable, like those of low-grade securities traded on the organized exchanges. Moderate fluctuations are shown by better-grade securities and by bank loans to large business firms. In this section attention will be devoted chiefly to interest rates on bonds, commercial paper, and term loans by banks.

Business demand for funds rises and falls with changes in the profit prospects of business. When the demand for industrial products rises, the profit return on the least productive funds employed exceeds the cost of borrowing such funds. Entrepreneurs are therefore stimulated to borrow and to use additional funds which will likewise yield a surplus over their interest cost. Equality of interest and incremental factor revenue will eventually be reached (at the margin) as borrowing expands. But in the meantime this increased demand for funds tends to raise the interest rate. The converse is true if profit prospects fall.

**9. Special Problems of Changes in the Demand for Funds.—** Several points in this simplified presentation deserve further elaboration. In the first place, the additional funds may be secured in other ways than by borrowing. These include the sale of stock and the reinvestment of earnings. But these possibilities are limited. Borrowing is the only option on some occasions. Or it seems the best method. Second, the borrowed funds may be used in many ways, for raw materials, for wages, to pay prior debts, or to improve or increase the stock of mechanical equipment. It is incorrect to associate borrowed funds exclusively with capital goods in the sense of buildings or machinery. The funds presumably are put to use in whatever way is best for the borrower, since he will seek to maximize the difference between his earnings from those funds and the interest cost of obtaining them. The term *marginal efficiency of capital* is most appropriately used with reference to increments of funds obtained in *any* way and put to *any* use. "Capital" here does not refer to buildings and machinery, but to what may be called, for want of a better phrase, "disbursed funds."

In the third place, the increased demand for funds is reflected in the securities markets by an increased supply of securities. This tends to depress the value of securities of the type being offered and to raise the yield to new purchasers. Stated in another way, lenders do not increase their demand for securities as rapidly as the supply increases. Therefore, the interest rate on each type thus affected tends to rise. Through chain substitution this rise is reflected in other markets not directly affected. However, it is probable that the good business conditions which increase the demand for funds in one market will raise it in several other markets also. One outstanding exception is federal borrowing, which tends to decline in good times. Tax receipts expand and the need diminishes for public works to create employment.

The increased demand for funds is also apparent in the calls upon the banks for short-term and medium-term loans. Here interest rates tend to rise chiefly because of diminished interest-rate competition among bank lenders. In bad times when borrowers are few, there is much interest-cutting to get loans. But when the business tide starts rolling in again, bankers stiffen their backs and become more reluctant to make concessions. That is when the rate starts rising on commercial paper and term loans.

Finally, it is well to remember the important part which government or central bank policy may play here. Through their control over open market operations, rediscount rates, legal reserve ratios, and other ways of influencing key interest rates they may offset to a significant degree the fluctuations in business demand for funds.

**10. Differences in Interest Rates at Different Times: Supply Side.**—The supply side of the picture is chiefly one of shifts from one type of investment of funds to another. In this it is to be contrasted with the demand side, where the shift is chiefly in the total demand for funds.[2] The total supply of newly saved funds seeking investment each year changes with the national income. But the major change in supply with regard to any one funds market comes from the actions of those old investors who are shifting out of one type of property ownership to seek greater income or safety in another.

Changes in the type of commercial bank lending are quite marked

---

[2] Reference is to business demand. Government demand may shift to offset somewhat the changes in aggregate business demand, as in depressions. Consumer demand does not change significantly except in the field of loans for installment buying of consumer durables, where interest rates are highly rigid. The process of disinvestment which creates the supply of funds in other markets is, of course, a demand for funds in the market where the securities are sold.

between phases of the business cycle. In boom times commercial banks lend chiefly to business firms at relatively high interest rates. In depressions, banks hesitate to make what few business loans are demanded and seek safety instead by purchasing government securities in spite of their low yields.

During the upswing of the business cycle private investors tend to shift from bonds to stock or to other forms of equity holding. Stocks appear more attractive than bonds because their dividends are rising and can expand beyond the fixed maximum interest on bonds. This brings greater opportunity for appreciation in the value of the shares. Business is good and stocks do not appear as unsafe relative to bonds as they did during the depression.

The sale of outstanding bonds that results from this demand shift to equities is partially offset by two compensating changes in demand. First, some people buy bonds with funds formerly held idle in safety deposit boxes or commercial accounts. As prosperity returns, bonds appear more safe than they seemed during the depression. People may also shift in similar fashion from savings deposits to bonds. The second offset is the increase in national income which gives habitual or potential bond buyers more funds with which to buy. However, this is not as important as it might seem, because bondholders themselves will get no additional interest income (except when defaulted bonds pay up). Only if they also have earned income or stock holdings will they benefit. And persons in either of these categories are apt to choose other ways of disposing of additional income.

There is a similar shift within the different classes of interest-earning securities. Banks, for instance, will be asked to make more short-term loans as business demand improves and therefore will feel able to invest larger amounts in less liquid long-term securities.

The result of these shifts of funds among various investment markets is to cause different security yields to fluctuate in different directions and with different amplitudes. High-grade bond yields tend to rise in boom times and to fall in depressions. The sum of new security offerings plus the liquidation of old issues by restless investors more than offsets the influx of funds from new savings, new bank buying, and favorable investment shifts. On the other hand, many people enter the stock market during booms as new, expanding, or transferring investors. Stock prices are forced very high and yields very low. Low-grade bonds tend to follow stock prices because they are somewhat speculative. Medium-grade bond yields come closer to the stock yield pattern than to that for very high-grade bonds. In periods of acute panic the desire for maximum liquidity sometimes becomes so great that even the best bonds fall in price and their yields rise.

**11. Differences in Interest Rates in Different Places: Demand Side.**—The third general problem of interest rate differences is that of variations from one place to another. The first two types of difference are eliminated by the stipulation that the comparison occurs at a given time and relative to loans of a particular type. At the outset the analyst must recognize the importance of institutional differences. Between two countries there may be great differences in the type of banking system, the distribution of income, the incentives to save and to invest, the attitudes of the people, and other variables. These all influence either the supply of funds, the demand for funds, the degree of competition on either side of the market, or the amount and direction of government intervention to influence interest rates. Since these influences cannot be systematized into any kind of formal theory, the analyst must be content to examine the differences which result from purely economic factors.

On the demand side, the determinants of business demand should receive first attention. Since cyclical fluctuations tend to follow parallel courses in different places, this factor in business demand may be excluded by the assumption that we are examining two places at the same time. Or one might take the long-run viewpoint and discuss averages over a period of years. This reduces the problem to the question: "Why is business demand for funds in some places larger relative to the supply than it is in others?" Or more simply, "What makes borrower demand large?"

The first answer is related to the profitableness of employing funds in business. That depends in part upon the number of business firms relative to the demand for their products or services. This in turn is a function of the economic maturity of the region. Newly settled or rapidly growing regions tend to increase in buying power more rapidly than firms are established. The average rate of profit is high. Entrepreneurs seek additional funds and are willing to pay well to get them. Another result of economic immaturity is the absence of many lines of business not yet developed. They offer good profit opportunities in addition to those which are already started and seek to expand.

A second reason why the demand for funds is large in some regions is related to technology. Those economies which make extensive use of capital goods need a much larger investment per unit of finished product than do those with more primitive technology. A large percentage of this capital equipment is purchased with borrowed funds, since it is easily mortgaged and used as collateral for loans. Industrialized countries also have a larger volume of production per capita. This requires more borrowing to finance firms while waiting for the time when they can sell their products.

The rate of change in technology is also important. When the state of the arts remains little changed for a long period of time, business firms gradually pay off their debts from their earnings. They have less need for borrowed funds. But if capital-using inventions follow one another rapidly and cause a rapid rate of obsolescence of equipment, the demand for loans will remain stronger. An offset to this tendency is found, however, in the way in which modern accounting methods establish depreciation reserves for capital equipment. The more equipment, the larger these reserves, and therefore the larger the amount of funds available within the firm to replace old machines with improved new ones. The need for borrowing in the loan markets therefore is an inverse function of the quantity of capital equipment accumulated and a direct function of its rate of obsolescence through technological change.

**12. Differences in Interest Rates in Different Places: Supply Side.**—On the supply side of funds markets there are two very important differences between regions: the banking systems and the rates of savings. As indicated earlier, the banking system is of paramount importance. A region that must rely upon savings and their transfer to get its capital funds is obviously much more handicapped than one which has a commercial banking system that can create funds by the mere exchange of credit. Regions also differ in the degree of development of their banking systems. Some of them have banks which provide only short-term credits, whereas other banking systems provide both intermediate and long-term credits. Whenever some of these facilities are lacking, it will be more difficult for borrowers to get funds and interest rates will be higher. Finally, the activity and goals of the central bank may differ greatly in two different places. For instance, it may or may not follow a low-interest policy designed to stimulate borrowing. It may make direct loans to business, or deny them. It may work intimately with a government program of industrialization or socialization, or it may not, etc.

If the banking systems are similar, there may be differences in the rates of saving which characterize the people and firms of two areas. Incomes in excess of bare subsistence are essential to saving. Hence, regions where there are very few people with large incomes will save less than other regions with the same number of people but a larger percentage in the upper brackets. Or with the same relative distribution of incomes, the region with the highest absolute levels of real income will save the most. On this latter point compare the United States and Britain. On the former, compare Britain with India. Both comparisons must be made, of course, on the basis of percentage of national income saved, not on dollar totals or equivalent.

The rate of saving is also a function of the feeling of security. If people are apprehensive regarding the unfortunate effects of illness, unemployment, old age, etc., upon their planes of living, they will save more than if they are happy-go-lucky like certain primitive tribes, or are protected by comprehensive social security systems as in the most advanced societies. If the typical citizen feels that his family, the state, or God will take care of him, he is likely to be less thrifty than if he believes he must or should take care of himself. Differences in the rate of saving are important because they influence the total amount that can be offered for loan at any given time.

There are also differences in regional culture patterns which influence interest rates in two other ways. First, there are differences in the amount loaned out of current savings or accumulated past savings. For instance, the tradition in favor of hoarding large amounts of currency or coin is stronger in some regions than in others. Second, institutional differences may influence the type of loan which most savers are willing to make. Certain loans are accepted in some places as being "sensible," while others are "too risky." Relative interest rates differ accordingly.

Other factors affect the rate of interest through the extent to which saved funds tend to be loaned. Individual savings may become more abundant than necessary to provide the liquid contingency reserve which is desired. Or, as with wealthy people, funds accumulate without effort and are loaned to get interest income for further accumulation. Also important is the presence of intermediate institutions which are highly developed in some areas. These are the savings banks, insurance companies, building and loan associations, and other firms which receive saved funds in various ways and transfer them to borrowers. These institutions mobilize savings and make interest rates lower than if borrowers had to go directly to savers, often a virtually impossible task.

**13. Some Cases of Interregional Interest Differences.**—By combining the supply and demand factors described in the two

preceding sections it is possible to explain various regional differences in interest rates.  For instance, the relatively low rates in
Britain as compared with the United States are the joint result of a
highly developed banking system, a high rate of saving, a somewhat
slow rate of technological obsolescence, and a high degree of economic
maturity.  A contrast between eastern and western or southern United
States reveals that in the Northeast there are more people with large
incomes per thousand inhabitants, and therefore more saving.  Banking institutions are more highly developed.  There are relatively
more business firms and lower rates of profit.  And so on.  A similar
comparison could be made between various frontier regions and the
areas from which their settlers came.

The interregional differences in interest rates which result from
demand and supply differences persist in spite of the mobility of
funds.  Credit can be transferred from one place to another by mail
or telegram with great ease and speed.  People wishing to lend their
own credit, or that of others which they have saved, want to get the
highest possible interest reward.  This incentive, combined with the
high mobility of funds, prevents interregional differences in interest
from being as great as interregional differences in wages.  But it
does not bring all interest rates to the same level.  Suppliers are influenced by subjective estimates of risk.  Loans to remote and less
well-known borrowers are considered more risky than loans to local
borrowers of equal repute.  Investigation of distant borrowers takes
more time and effort.  Collection is more difficult and expensive if
default occurs.  Interest rate differences measure the opinion of
marginal suppliers concerning differences in risk and trouble.

**14. Summary.**—An examination of the differences which exist
among interest rates reveals many of the basic forces in this price
field.  There is nothing automatic about interest, nothing mechanical which determines what interest rates must be.  Like other prices
they express the results of human actions based upon human impulses
and more or less rational human choice.  These motives and these
actions do not occur in a vacuum.  The demand for funds and the
supply of funds both spring from group life.  At any given time or
place they express the culture pattern of the group, with deviations
because of human differences.  Borrowing and lending occur also
against a background of social institutions such as banks, mortgage
companies, deficit financing, corporate securities, organized exchanges, laws, and customs.  These influence, limit, and guide but
do not completely determine the market activities of borrowers and

lenders. The most important of these relationships are summarized in the following outline:

I. Causes of interest rate differences at any given time and place:
   A. The terms of loan contracts are different as to time, collateral, repayment, etc.
   B. Lenders (suppliers of funds) are different.
      1. They have different ideas regarding the risks of lending.
      2. They have different (objective) costs of lending.
      3. Competition is more keen among some groups of lenders than among others.
   C. Borrowers (demanders of funds) are different.
      1. They have different use-opportunities and urgencies.
      2. They have different abilities to repay.
   D. Funds are not completely mobile on the supply side nor perfectly homogeneous as viewed from the demand side.

II. Yet the various loan markets are interdependent:
   A. Some lenders·do shift funds from one type of loan to another. (Some of them also shift back and forth from the lending to the proprietorship position, from bonds to stocks, etc.)
   B. Some borrowers can choose between one type of lender and another. (And sometimes they can obtain funds in other ways than by borrowing, e.g., equity capital, savings, etc.)

III. Causes of interest rate differences at different times:
   A. Changes in profit prospects (demand side).
   B. Variations in concepts of lending risk (supply side).
   C. Changes in government policies (demand or supply action).
   D. The interdependence of interest rates which may make one rate change when another changes.

IV. Causes of interest rate differences at different places, but at the same time:
   A. There are many different markets where borrowers and lenders meet.
   B. There is imperfect mobility of funds from one market to another.
   C. There are differences in the demand and supply situations in the markets where interest rates are determined.
      1. Countries, for instance, differ in banking systems, types of industry, amounts of capital goods accumulated, rates of saving, attitudes toward lending, government fiscal policies, etc.
      2. Regions within a given country often have similar though less extreme differences.

# Chapter 25

## SOME PROBLEMS OF INTEREST THEORY

**1. The Theoretical Approach.**—In this chapter interest problems are analyzed on a higher level of abstraction than in the two preceding ones. Those chapters contain much detail about specific borrowing and lending situations in modern "capitalistic" society. The present approach attempts to distill the essence of these institutions. It also uses models of hypothetical economics. This method limits the number of variables so much as to impress some observers as being unrealistic. But it need not be. It is really an application of the *ceteris paribus* method of analysis. The "realistic" variables which are excluded by omission are really just impounded while attention is centered upon the variations in others. Unrealism does not enter unless the partial picture is taken to be a complete one. Generalizations and partializations should not be confused with absolutes.

Some of the questions to be answered in this abstract, "theoretical" way are the following:

1. Why cannot interest rates fall to zero?
2. What are the strong and the weak points of certain theories which explain various things about interest rates?
   (a) The cost of production theory?
   (b) The waiting and time preference theories?
   (c) The liquidity preference theory?
3. What are the effects of interest rates and their changes upon:
   (a) The supply of funds from various sources?
   (b) The demand for funds from various sources?
   (c) The supply of durable capital goods and the length of the production process?
4. Is there a normal or equilibrium rate of interest:
   (a) In the short run?
   (b) In the long run?

**2. Minimum Interest Rates Must Pay for Marginal Risk and Trouble.**—Interest rates cannot fall to zero except in rare cases because the marginal lender feels the presence of risk, or trouble, or both. All loans involve time. Between the date of lending and that of repayment, many things may happen. The borrower may suffer unforeseen losses which affect his ability to repay. There is some danger of loss in nearly all cases, but by the requirement of ample collateral, the risk of financial loss from borrower default may be reduced virtually to zero. Another risk cannot be overcome so easily, if at all. It is the risk that the going rate of interest may rise during the life of a fixed interest loan. This depresses the market value of bonds and commercial paper. Hence there is always the risk of loss if the lender's financial needs force him to sell his securities before maturity.

The elimination of "trouble" is also difficult, if not impossible. At the beginning of each loan an agreement must be made regarding the terms. Funds must then be transferred. At the end of the time period they must be collected. These operations take time and effort. The owner of the funds may delegate this work to others and pay them for their services. Or he may perform this work himself. There is trouble of this type whether the loan is for a short or for a long time period. Risk also constitutes a sort of subjective "trouble." Even when experience proves that collateral has been ample, some uncertainty and hesitation may exist in the mind of the lender.

The marginal lender is influenced by his feeling of risk and trouble in lending even though some intramarginal lenders may not be. The supply of funds for lending comes from many different sources. Some lenders may be willing to lend for nothing, or even to pay for the privilege. To others the risk and trouble appear negligible. For instance, governments may make their credit available at zero interest rates, as in certain foreign loans. Lend-lease "loans" during the recent war perhaps were made with the expectation that they would not be repaid fully and therefore reveal negative interest rates. But these cases are exceptional. Most lenders would rather not lend if they cannot get interest or its equivalent. The demand for funds is so great and the various loan markets are so interdependent that most borrowers must solicit funds from these "risk and trouble" lenders. The acquisitive spirit of our society then drives more willing lenders to ask as much interest as the marginal, less willing lenders.

**3. The "Cost of Production" Theory of Interest.**—The foregoing argument may be called a "cost of production" theory of interest. Like the cost of production theory of commodity prices, it is useful but not complete. It is primarily a supply-side approach and ignores institutional forces, bargaining strength, and other possible determinants of interest rates. But it suggests two important truths.

First, the creation of funds involves a certain cost of production. This cost may be objective, or subjective, or both. It limits the supply of funds offered at any given interest rate (cf. Sections 7–12 on the interest-elasticity of supply of funds). This makes the total supply cumulative upwards, like other upward-sloping supply curves. The first part of this curve (assuming that a composite supply curve is possible) may be below the *OX* axis. But this is of only academic

### FIGURE 69

#### A Hypothetical Composite Supply Curve for Funds

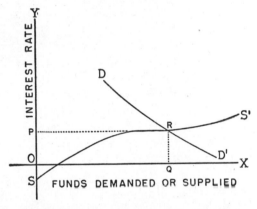

interest. The important thing is that the total demand for funds at zero interest far exceeds the supply offered at zero interest.[1] Therefore other funds are sought, funds that do have a positive cost of production. The cost of the last supply increment needed to balance demand may be called the marginal cost of funds. The interest rate cannot be less than this figure. The adjoining diagram portrays this hypothetical, composite supply curve for funds. Its shape to the left and right of *R* is highly conjectural, but *R* is surely above *OX*. That is the point of this section about the "cost of production" theory of interest.

Second, the height of each of the many distinct supply curves for funds is also a function of the cost of producing those funds. That is one major reason why interest rates differ on different types of loans made at the same time. Chapter 24 presented this argument

---

[1] There may be a few exceptions such as intergovernmental loans.

from an institutional approach. Installment loans cost more to make and collect than do others, some loans are better protected by collateral than others, etc. These may be called objective cost factors. Subjective costs will be discussed below in the sections on the waiting and liquidity preference theories of interest.

**4. Is There a Minimum Rate of "Pure Interest"?**—In their effort to make interest something quite distinct from other prices, some writers have tried to describe "pure interest." Some have called it payment for waiting; others emphasize the loss of liquidity. The foregoing argument suggests that perhaps "payment for trouble" or "cost of production" may be better approaches, but all are supply-side viewpoints and therefore incomplete. However, the "cost of production" approach has the advantage that it is applicable to more situations than the others. For instance, a loan payable on demand involves no involuntary waiting. If it is also secured by ample collateral, the risk element dwindles virtually to zero. These two provisions of collateral and permission to demand payment at any time reduce the usefulness of the liquidity preference theory in explaining "pure interest." But "trouble" always remains as a "cost of production."

Even so, it is difficult to find any *minimum* rate of "pure interest." Rather there are *different amounts* of "trouble" or different "costs of production." And different amounts of objective or subjective risk may be added.

Higher interest rates pay for more trouble or for more risk than do lower interest rates. For instance, a comparison may be made between the yield on long-term bonds of various types. The going rate of interest on "perfectly safe" government bonds is usually lower than that on industrial or utility bonds which are considered more risky. Another comparison may be made between long- and short-term securities issued by the same borrower. Government bonds of short maturity usually yield less than those of longer maturity. This seems to reflect lenders' ideas of differences in risk. Here the subjective feeling of risk is probably associated more closely with lenders' ideas of their own possible need to liquidate at a loss before maturity than with any belief that the government might possibly default. The influence of risk differences is found also in the presence of higher yields on trade acceptances than upon bank acceptances of equal maturity, on United States government bonds as compared with those issued by Peru, etc. Trouble differences have already been shown to reside chiefly in loan collections. There are also differences in the work which precedes lending as the lender tries to analyze the borrower's ability to pay.

**5. The Waiting and Time Preference Theories of "Pure Interest."**—Sometimes the supply side of the market in which interest rates are determined is interpreted in terms of the painfulness of waiting for future consumption. Those who supply funds are pictured as people who would not save and lend if they were not rewarded for the postponement of consumption which these acts make necessary. Saver-lenders are described as having positive time preference, at least at the margin of their saving and lending. That is, they prefer to consume now rather than to possess the prospect of consumption in the future when the loan is repaid. Under this analysis of human motivation, interest is said to be paid for the service of waiting, or of abstention. The height of the interest rate is supposed to measure the marginal degree of time preference. Interest rates could never fall to zero because people would rather consume than lend for nothing.

There is obviously a grain of truth in this approach, but it tries to explain too much. The time preference concept is helpful in explaining why some people save, but its chief usefulness lies in explaining why they save as much as they do. People save so long as they have positive time preference less than the interest reward from lending.[2] The limit to their saving is reached when the disutility of saving rises to equality with the utility of the interest which borrowers will pay. A better version of the argument would state that the initial satisfactions from saving are positive but smaller than the initial satisfactions from consumption. Both reveal a scale of diminishing marginal utility. If income is large enough, in most cases the marginal satisfactions from consumption will diminish to the place where they are less than the initial satisfactions from saving and some saving will occur. The equilibrium role of equality of satisfactions at the margin begins to apply to savings as one use of funds just as it does to categories of consumption which represent rival uses of total consumption.[3]

**6. Weaknesses of the Time Preference Theory of Interest Rates.**—Time preference is not a complete explanation of why people save. It assumes conscious choice, whereas many people save

---

[2] Zero and negative time preference will also induce saving. They may be considered extreme cases of the deviation of positive time preference below a positive interest rate.

[3] This is an application of the principle of maximizing total utility by equalizing satisfaction at the margin in each category of consumption.

because of habit, the compulsion of a contract, or impulse. Much saving by ultimate consumers in the modern world is done after they have deliberately or impulsively purchased something on the installment plan. There are also other bases of choice in addition to time-of-consumption comparisons. Those with very large incomes, for instance, may save merely because it requires less effort to do that than to find ways of spending their funds.

The theory that interest is payment for waiting also partly explains the fact that interest rates on long-term loans are higher than on short-term loans. As a matter of logic, however, this theory would merely require that the interest *amount* be greater for loans of longer duration, not the interest *rate*. There might be a way out by arguing that the irksomeness of prospective waiting increased progressively as the time of repayment was pushed further off, but that seems like stretching the time preference approach too much. After all, many people never expect to consume what they have saved. If they demand payment for abstention, the amount of that payment per year of abstaining should diminish, not increase with the number of years. The initial act is surely more painful, if painful at all, than the memory of that act as time goes by.

The time preference approach does not explain at all the differences in interest rates between different classes of loans of the same duration. Nor does it shed light on the differences in rates between places unless one were to argue that the culture patterns of time preference differed. The role of demand is also slighted, even though the valid argument is presented that borrowers are people with high positive time preference.

Another serious weakness lies in the fact that it does not explain divergences between the rate of saving and the rate of lending. Saving-lending is usually considered a simultaneous process although, by a twist in the traditional line of reasoning, time preference is sometimes described as preference for present liquidity rather than for present consumption. This approach tends to confuse the liquidity preference argument to be discussed in the next section with the risk and trouble of converting illiquid notes.

The major difficulty with the time preference approach is that it elevates a minor part of the picture into first place. The lending which takes place out of saved funds is secondary and inferior. The dominant forces in the loan market are those which govern the creators, not the savers of credit. Neither banks nor governments have time preference or subjective costs of waiting. Business firms also are motivated in their lending chiefly by objective costs,

The correct theory of the cause of *positive* interest rates in modern society must be sought in the trouble and risk approach. It has the added advantage of being clearly applicable to all types of situations in which funds are supplied, whether from private individuals who save, from institutional savers, or from those who lend their own credit, such as commercial banks.

**7. Liquidity Preference Theories of Supply and Demand for Funds.**—The liquidity preference approach to the supply side also has some truth in it. It is very useful in explaining *changes* in interest rates, but it does not help much in answering the question at hand regarding the existence or nature of "pure interest."

The liquidity preference approach separates the acts of saving and lending. Saving occurs for contingencies, for convenience, or for prospective interest reward, as explained in the preceding chapter. The saved funds are usually held in the form of government credit (paper currency) or bank credit (demand deposits), which are widely acceptable and therefore can be spent easily. When loaned, the savings are transformed into a note which is not so easily given in exchange for goods or in payment of debts. The saver, by the act of lending, sacrifices liquidity.

From this approach, interest becomes the payment which borrowers are willing to make to obtain liquidity and which lenders exact as the price of giving up liquidity. It is logical, therefore, that the more liquid the borrower's note, the less the lender will demand, and vice versa. The lowest rates are those paid on short-term notes which mature quickly and on notes issued by well-known borrowers of good reputation.

Examined more carefully, the liquidity of an asset may be measured in terms of the cost or loss involved in a prompt exchange of it for the most widely acceptable form of credit, namely, currency. In this case that means the difference between the amount loaned and the amount that can be realized by sale or discount of the note given by the borrower. If there has been no change in the prevailing interest rates, the cost of conversion will be merely that of the labor or trouble involved in making the exchange. A rise in interest rates, as explained earlier, will bring some additional loss of principal. When stated in these terms, the liquidity preference explanation of positive interest rates takes on many aspects of the trouble and risk theory expounded on pages 415–416.

**8. Weaknesses of the Liquidity Preference Explanation of Interest.**—The chief shortcoming of the liquidity preference approach is that it does not describe the role of commercial banks and other important lending institutions.   Commercial banks are in the business of lending funds.  *They usually want to become "illiquid"* because that is the way they make their profit.   In times of business uncertainty, it is true that banks may shift their investments so as to become *more* liquid, but to become completely so would mean that they had gone out of the lending business entirely.   There again, the trouble and risk theory explains the different interest rates which banks charge much better than the liquidity preference approach.[4]

Certain other lenders such as insurance companies, savings banks, and mortgage loan companies likewise operate under motives which do not fit the liquidity preference pattern.   For many of them there are no foreseeable contingencies which might make them want to liquidate their loans before maturity.   There is therefore no risk of loss through sale of securities whose value has depreciated because of increased interest rates.   The management need consider only the risk of borrower default and the costs of making and collecting. Some wealthy private individual lenders are in the same category. Liquidity preference does not exist for them.   They want their funds continually invested and earning something.   They are glad to get what they can, no matter how small it may be.   The same is also true of many lenders of moderate means.   Even speculators who want their assets liquid on certain occasions pending more advantageous investing opportunities do not require an interest reward to induce them to enter the market.   They seek to make their income chiefly by buying low and selling high, or by selling short and buying back at lower prices.   Their motivation is clearly different from that of potential lenders.

It is difficult to contend, therefore, that the reason for interest rates being greater than zero is the positive liquidity preference of those with funds to lend.   Trouble and risk offer a superior explanation and also are better adapted to explaining the differences in interest rates which exist at any given time.

The chief merit of the liquidity preference approach would seem to be in its separation of the motives of saving and lending.   Its major usefulness in dealing with current problems lies in the matter of *changes* in interest rates.   In economic dynamics, much of the emphasis shifts from the supply to the demand side.   Borrowers usually are persons who want funds to spend.   They want temporary

---

[4] This is not to deny that in the management of bank portfolios, the question of liquidity plays an important part. For instance, commercial loans eligible for rediscount at federal reserve banks are preferred to those which are ineligible, even though the trouble and the default risks are the same.

liquidity so that they can buy the particular objects of their desire. This is perhaps a form of liquidity preference. However described, its changes are a major cause of changes in interest rates.

**9. The Interest-Elasticity of Supply of Funds: General Aspects.**—The effects of interest rate changes upon the supply of funds are best studied by separating the sources. These include (1) commercial banks, (2) institutional savers, and (3) private savers, both individual and business. For each category there should be a further subdivision into short-run and long-run effects. Nor can the different classes of borrowers be overlooked in this supply-side problem. Very often what appears to be an increase or a decrease in the funds offered is merely a shift from one type of offering to another with no change in the total. Therefore, one constantly must remember that there are very many supply curves of funds and very many elasticity functions. The interdependence that exists among them merely makes the problem more complex.

**10. The Interest-Elasticity of Supply of Funds from Commercial Banks.**—Commercial banks lend in various ways as described in Chapter 23. When they lend at a fixed rate of interest, the elasticity of supply is infinite, at least for a certain range of lending. The banks supply whatever funds are demanded. Interest rates are set by the lending banks individually or in concert with others of the community or region. The question of supply-elasticity is not nearly so important as why banks change these asking rates of interest, and that has been answered above. (See Chapter 23, Sections 11 and 22.)

At times these infinitely elastic supply curves are deceptive. Banks put other restraints upon lending, either qualitative or quantitative. If there is a quantity limit, then the curve turns upward abruptly at that point and drops from infinite to zero elasticity. Where the restraint is qualitative, a two-dimensional supply curve would be utterly unrealistic.

Banks also lend by purchasing securities on the open market. This type of lending is hardly a function of the interest yield, and the total does not rise and fall appreciably because of changes in that yield. Therefore, the interest-elasticity for the total volume of this lending is virtually zero. Shifting occurs, however, between particular types of loans, as when one short-term rate becomes more attractive than another.

The same sort of observation may be made for bank lending to large borrowers where interest rate competition and bargaining frequently appear. There is little evidence that banks lend more at any given time because these rates have risen than they would have loaned if the rates had remained constant or fallen. It is true that the amount loaned has a positive correlation with the interest rate, but only because they are both a function of general business activity and optimism, not because interest rates are a determinant of bankers' decisions to expand or to contract the quantity of funds thus loaned.

Although what has been said about commercial bank lending thus far applies particularly to individual banks, it also holds for the system as a whole. Reductions in legal reserve ratios, increases in central bank gold reserves, relaxation of rediscount rules, and similar institutional developments have all accompanied the secular uptrend of the volume of bank lending.[5] Falling interest rates have certainly not diminished the total volume of funds offered by the banking systems of such countries as the United States and the United Kingdom.

**11. The Interest-Elasticity of Funds Supplied by Other Lending Institutions.**—The quantity of funds offered in various loan markets by savings institutions, life insurance companies, etc., is primarily a function of the quantity of savings. It is secondarily a function of the liquidity preference of the managers of the institutions. The question at issue is, therefore, "What effect, if any, does the rate of interest have upon either the volume of savings entering such institutions or the liquidity preference decisions of executives?" The savings question will be considered more thoroughly in a later section dealing with the savings of individuals. At this point the only comment that need be made is that some of the loanable funds of these lending institutions are derived from their reinvested profits, although most of such funds go into buildings and equipment. Insofar as higher interest rates mean larger earnings, there might be a long-run connection here, but it is of little significance at best.

The desire of managers of these institutions is to keep as fully loaned as possible with due regard to safety. Therefore they feel impelled to keep their liquid funds at a minimum and will lend approximately the same percentage of available funds whether the interest rate is high or low. A *change* in interest rates, however, as distinct from the *level* of those rates, may provoke abnormal entry into or exit from the loan market. When managers become apprehensive regarding safety, they may reduce their current rate of lending. A new feeling of optimism will produce an opposite result. As has been pointed out frequently, however, such changes in attitude

---

[5] The major determinant has been the rising level of general business activity.

are usually more the result of the general trend of business than specific changes in the interest rates that prevail. Furthermore, many of these institutions lend at rates of interest which they themselves determine as a matter of business policy. They do not take the initiative in making loans. They merely announce that they are willing to lend to those who want to borrow. Passive lenders of this type have infinite elasticity of supply in the usual sense. From another viewpoint they might be said to have zero elasticity of supply, since a general rise in interest rates does not cause them to offer more funds than before.

In the long run if interest rates decline, many institutional lenders will reduce the amount they pay the persons from whom they get their funds. This is particularly true of savings banks, insurance companies, and building and loan associations. If interest rates rise, the long-run effect may be reversed. Depositors and policy holders will be paid more in one way or another. If there is insufficient competition among such financial institutions, much of the gain from increased interest rates will become profits. In that category it may be reinvested by the firms or distributed as dividends. This brings us again to the question of the reactions of individual income receivers and holders of funds.

**12. The Interest-Elasticity of Funds Loaned by Private Savers.** —In discussing the problem of individual reaction to interest rate levels and changes, it is particularly important to keep the short-run and the long-run pictures separate. In the short run the important question is that of liquidity preference, which governs the percentage loaned out of savings. In the long run the amount of current savings is more significant. There may be also secular trends in habits of thrift akin to changes in the cultural pattern of liquidity preference.

Without repeating previous arguments too much, it may be stated that the level of interest rates has little to do with the rate of lending so long as interest is high enough to cover the expected risk of loss. If individuals believe that they can get their funds back at any time without loss, they are willing to lend at very low rates of interest. Savings banks experienced no decline in total deposits when their interest rates fell to 1 per cent as compared with 3 to 4 per cent twenty years earlier. A similar observation might be made about building and loan depositors, particularly since the federal government established its deposit insurance program. This guarantee, however, is not for immediate payment of the full amount loaned, and the memory of large depression losses in some instances still makes it necessary for such companies to pay higher rates than savings banks, whose record has been better.

So far as bonds are concerned, the level of interest rates has been brought much lower in recent years than was previously thought possible. Yet the rate of investing in these securities does not seem to have been adversely affected. One reason is the fact that the possible yield on alternative forms of investment has declined, too. People seem to prefer some interest to no interest. A very large percentage of saved funds is valued by their owners for potential income yield, not for use in foreseeable future contingencies. Therefore securities are purchased with an expectation of holding until maturity. This eliminates one of the major risks involved. Another major risk, seen by economists, that of a change in the general price level, is not usually considered a risk by investors and therefore does not influence their decisions.

Some lenders do at times become alarmed regarding the third big risk, that of a borrower default, but this is usually a result of major business declines or security market panics. People sell securities when they lose confidence. This raises interest rates. The adverse shift in estimates of risk constricts the rate of lending. This is the true causal sequence. It is the reverse of the usual elasticity approach. It is not a reaction of potential lenders to a drop in the rate of interest below their margins of liquidity preference. In formal terminology, the change in supply is a restriction in the schedule sense, not in the market sense.

**13. The Interest-Elasticity of the Amount of Current Saving.** —This topic must be divided into two parts. The first assumes that incomes are constant. The question becomes one of the influence of interest changes upon the percentage saved out of current income. This is the problem of incentives to saving in the sense of nonspending of money income. Does a rising interest rate, for instance, cause most people to want to save more out of their (unchanged) incomes? If so, then there is a positive interest-elasticity of saving. Then if lending rises as savings rise, there exists by this indirect route a positive interest-elasticity of lending. The supply curve of loanable funds available from individuals slopes upward to the right. The truth of this proposition will be appraised in the remainder of this section after a digression on the second division of the general topic.

Another part of the problem assumes that incomes may change. Do interest changes influence the level of money incomes? Authorities differ as to the correct answer. Some business cycle analysts,

for instance, contend that governments can stimulate business recovery from a depression by reducing interest rates. Others argue
that of itself that action is not enough. Conditions must be just
right for such manipulation to turn the tide. Or other action to
stimulate business borrowing must take place at the same time.[6] At
the opposite extreme stand those who say either that these other activities would do the trick without interest rate changes, or even that
the upturn would come more rapidly by itself if only the government
would do nothing at all. We cannot explore this controversy further
at this point.

There is much less dispute about the high positive correlation between the level of people's incomes and the amount they save. When
people get more pay, they have more income out of which to save.
Carefully collected statistics also show that the *percentage* saved
rises as incomes rise. For these two reasons, therefore, it is important to know whether interest rate changes influence those changes
in the business cycle which have such a strong bearing upon average
incomes.

Returning now to the first question regarding the possible direct
connection between interest rates and saving, we must examine four
motives for saving: (1) the expectation of interest reward, (2) the
expectation of producing other future income, (3) the anticipation
of contingencies, and (4) the reduction of effort.

**14. Saving Motivated by a Desire to Increase Income or
Wealth.**—Saving may be stimulated by the hope of financial gain
Most people like to get interest income if they can. But saving does
not seem to be stimulated very much by *increases* in interest rates,
nor discouraged by decreases. This is probably due to the fact that
other motives dominate saving and the hope of interest reward is a
very minor incentive. It is like eating because you are hungry, but
being thankful at the same time that the food is tasty.

At the extreme high and low ends of possible interest rate variations, the interest reward motive might be important. If the rate
jumped from 6 to 60 per cent per year, some would surely save who
otherwise would consume. Similarly, if the rate which saver-lenders
could get dropped from 4 per cent to $\frac{1}{4}$ of 1 per cent without any
change in the risk involved, some savers would undoubtedly choose
to spend instead. One must not, however, infer from these extreme
and hypothetical cases that the supply is similarly elastic for changes
between 6 and 7 or between 4 and 3 per cent. Within the customary

---

[6] These other activities may include deficit financing of armaments or public
works, devaluation of the currency, tariff changes, etc.

range, the small elasticity of individual supply curves of loanable funds that does exist is probably due more to liquidity motives than to the motive of interest gain through saving-lending.

One should note also that variations in the amount of funds saved out of current income do not change the total amount of funds in existence. Changes in total funds result from changes in total credit granted or created for production or consumption. Changes in saving merely influence the amount that individual savers (persons or firms) may lend. Another way of looking at it is to say that the velocity of circulation of funds is changed, not the total amount. It takes longer for funds to go through the received-saved-loaned-spent cycle than merely to be received as income and then spent.

Some people save to get a profit-type income by investing their savings in stock shares or directly in production goods. This desire for financial gain through the use of savings may also be seen in the activities of speculators and gamblers. The reward for the successful use of funds in these ways is usually called profit. But profit yields and interest yields generally rise and fall together. Therefore there is some positive correlation between interest rate changes and saving for profit-type income, even though the causal connection is weak.

Savings for business use do not enter the loan market. Their effect upon the rate of interest is indirect. Their presence diminishes the amount which businessmen need borrow. Reducing the demand for funds has the same restraining effect upon interest rates as increasing the supply. But our major attention here is upon interest rates as causes, not effects. If profit rates are raised by boom times, and interest rates too, then they stimulate saving which becomes available for use or lending, thus restraining the rise in interest and profit rates. The situation is somewhat analogous to that of commodity prices during a boom. Rising demand raises prices. These stimulate an expansion in supply. The increased supply does not usually offset all of the increase in demand, but only part of it. The price increase is slowed, not reversed, at least not at first.

**15. Saving to Meet Contingencies or to Reduce Effort.**—Most small savers think of themselves as saving "for a rainy day," for a vacation, for their old age, or for some similar contingency. This type of saving is little influenced by changes in the rate of interest. An infrequent exception may occur when an individual calculates very carefully how much he must save per year in order to accumulate a specified total on a certain date. Cases of this type have become in-

creasingly rare in this day of installment buying and salary loans.
Other contingency savers have no definite amount as a goal or do
not compute interest accumulations carefully.  For them saving becomes a habit of putting away a fixed amount each payday, or of
living as cheaply as possible and saving the rest.

For a few people with large incomes, saving may be easier than
spending.  When consumption patterns are fixed by habit and current income mounts, people sometimes save because it requires less
effort than deciding what to buy.  Lending is also more arduous than
mere accumulation.  Giving away surplus funds seems contrary to the
habits of a lifetime and may involve painful choice.  Sometimes such
a person hires an investment adviser and lets him do the work of discovering investment opportunities.  Many trust funds operate in
similar fashion.  Their budgeted outlay proves to be less than their
income.  The surplus is reinvested or held as a bank balance rather
than spent.

Business firms which accumulate large cash reserves usually have
a long-range plan of expansion or a loss prospect in mind.  But
occasionally stockholders get the idea that managerial habit is
stronger than judgment, stronger than the wails of people starved
for dividends.

In all these cases a rise in interest yields has no direct influence
upon the amount saved out of a given income level.  It may, however, raise that income or occur at the same time that there is a rise
in the general level of incomes.

**16. Collective Saving by Governments of Planned Economies.**
—The personal motive of saving for future income has its counterpart in the motives of leaders of socialist or fascist states.  When a
private individual saves, he diminishes his present consumption because of some greater pleasure.  This higher satisfaction may be the
thought of larger income, or wealth, or power, in the future.  When
government planners decide to forego present consumption for future
gain, they often have similar objectives in mind.

The economic planner must make two important estimates.  First,
he must make a technician's decision regarding the amount of future
output which will result from given present inputs diverted from
present consumption.  Second, he must make a social welfare decision
regarding the desirability of this output in relation to other possible
uses of the available inputs.  These alternative uses include production of other things in the future, production of things in the less
distant future, aesthetic enjoyments, etc.

A social welfare decision requires a scale of values. This is likely to be based upon some philosophy of welfare for the group, or even for the planner. In a democratic planned economy a vote may be taken in which the majority decides about each major project. Even in a capitalistic economy, voters are frequently called upon to approve or disapprove important public works like schools, bridges, dams, sewage systems, etc. The scale of values involved in such votes is not often clearly formulated. Affirmative votes may be cast by people who think they do not pay taxes, whose tax payments are expected to be less than the benefits, whose ideas are very hazy about the burden of higher prices, or who are swayed by emotional appeals and half-truths. In an authoritarian economy where saving-investment decisions are made by a few elected or self-appointed leaders, the scale of values is usually better understood. But it may change as conditions change, like the Communist "party line." Or top priority objectives may appear to outsiders to be evil and menacing, like the Nazi's belligerent slogan, "Guns, not butter."

Given a scale of values, good or bad, clear or vague, a choice can be made. The general principle that is applied can be stated formally as attempting to equalize the marginal utilities of expected goods which differ in time dimension as well as in cost, kind, quantity, and quality. The solution of such a problem in an exact way is impossible. The best that one can expect is a rough approximation.

**17. Use of Funds to Increase Consumption in Distant Future vs. in Near Future.**—With these cautions in mind a numerical illustration may be offered. If a planner today appraises 100 bushels of additional wheat at the end of one year at, say, $100 on a relative scale, and at the same time values an equal amount of extra wheat ten years from now at $80, he will choose the former. But the effort required to yield this year's 100-bushel increment may produce very much more wheat ten years hence if used to develop an irrigation project in the meantime. Then the planner should compare a possible 150-bushel return after waiting ten years compared to a 100-bushel return after waiting only one growing season. If the 150 distant dated bushels appear to be worth $110 in the planner's scale of values, he should choose them in preference to the 100 bushels worth only $100.[7]

This means diverting labor and materials from one form of employment to another. Granted the assumptions of the preceding

---

[7] The comparison should really be between two *streams* of inputs and outputs extending indefinitely into the future, but using only two dated amounts simplifies the presentation and does not distort the argument. Cf. Chapter 10, Section 5.

paragraph, this will be done in time choices only if there are *both* positive time preference and technical productivity. The diverted factors are "saved" in the sense that their product is not currently used. They are employed to make presently nonconsumable things which are expected to yield more consumable things in the long run than could be obtained by using the factors directly for the same time period. This is the so-called "roundabout method of production." It is described as being technically more efficient than "direct production," although the comparison in modern times is really between more and less roundaboutness, rather than between some and none.

There is the further possibility that present use may be sacrificed for some future use which is not commensurable with that given up. If the illustration is in terms of bushels of wheat, now and in the future, a comparison can be made which reveals a measurable gain (or loss). But if present skyscrapers are sacrificed to secure the building of a bridge which ultimately speeds the flow of automobiles across a bay, there is no common denominator. Soviet planners sacrificed food, clothing, and shelter during the First Five Year Plan to secure blast furnaces, copper mines, hydroelectric projects, and the like. Many of the latter are more easily connected with a self-sufficiency program or with armaments than with an increased per capita output and consumption of basic necessities, especially when trade opportunities are considered. It seems more logical to interpret such action as a choice of the more attractive of two alternative present satisfactions than as a manifestation of the "superior productivity of roundabout production." [8]

**18. The Interest-Elasticity of Demand for Funds in the Short Run When Rates Fall.**—The chief reason for examining the interest-elasticity of demand for funds in the short run is the power of the government to influence that rate. In modern banking systems a virtually unlimited amount of funds can be loaned without prior saving. The central bank of a nation cannot compel people to bor-

---

[8] It is conceivable, however, that future output might be less than at present, as with a natural resource subject to depletion. If this product seems highly desirable for the future, an economic planner might use current factors to create the means for insuring some future supply rather than none, or more rather than less, even though the "more" is less than could be obtained for an equivalent expenditure to secure current output. Such is the reasoning behind many conservation programs and certain aspects of "national defense" planning. When marginal increments of future oil, coal, steel, or other goods are preferred to present marginal increments of equal size, this must be called *negative* time preference. The common assumption of positive time preference should not blind us to the presence of these important exceptions.

row, but it can bid up the price of outstanding securities by purchasing them on the market.   This decreases the yield, as explained above, and brings lower interest rates for those who might want to borrow. Or the process may be reversed.   The effect of both a rise and a fall in interest rates should be considered.

When fiscal policies bring a fall in interest rates, what effect does that have upon the volume of borrowing?   The answer should be divided into several parts according to the potential borrowers involved and the time allowed.   A reduction in interest rates on government securities and on commercial paper will not cause a proportionate decline in interest charges on consumption loans.   Even if there is some reduction, consumer borrowing is not likely to be affected appreciably.   The volume of such loans is dependent almost entirely upon other things, such as the current income of consumers, repayment terms, etc., described in Chapter 23, Section 17.   This conclusion holds for both the short run and the long run.

Government borrowing is likewise only incidentally a function of interest rates.   Therefore, national government demand for funds will have very low interest-elasticity.   If the low-interest policy is born of a war situation when the government wants to borrow large amounts, it is true that the total interest bill will be less.   But one cannot argue with conviction that if interest charges had not been reduced the government would have borrowed less and taxed more. Surely it would not have spent less.   In antidepression borrowing and spending there is less unity of purpose.   Opponents do point with alarm at the interest cost of borrowing, but their main concern seems to be (or to have been) with the size of the public debt.   There are probably very few legislators whose votes swing one way or the other because of any change in the interest rate on government bonds. Arguments which hold for the short run are also probably true in the long run.   There seems to be no historical evidence that governments have become more profligate during secular downtrends in interest rates.

The crucial question remains, "What effect do reduced interest rates have upon business borrowing?" Here the fundamental criterion is their effect upon prospective profits.   In a dynamic society such as ours, profit expectations depend upon a host of cost and revenue considerations of which interest is only one.   The phase of the business cycle is very important.   When the future trend of sales points downward, businessmen are unlikely to increase their short-term borrowing even if interest rates should drop to zero.   At such times entrepreneurs prefer to pay off their prior loans and to reduce their indebtedness, not to increase it. Long-term borrowing will also decline in most cases, because a business recession is a time in which businessmen are usually gloomy about the distant future, too. This decline in schedule demand is not offset by the fall in interest rates which generally occurs during such periods. During the upswing, expectations of future earnings rise so rapidly that they offset any deterrent effect of rising interest rates. The record of net new issues of securities tends to follow the ups and downs of the interest rate, not the reverse. It is probable that, in the short run, factors other than the interest rate have greater potency in determining the amount borrowed by business.

On the other hand, a fall in the rate of interest may prove the crucial determinant of the level of business borrowing at times when there is no definite trend in sales. These are the trough and the summit phases of the cycle. Here there is no general consensus regarding the trend of other variables, and therefore changes in the interest rate may yield more than their usual influence.

**19. The Interest-Elasticity of Demand for Funds in the Short Run When Rates Rise.**—The probable effect of a *rise* in interest rates remains to be studied. Consumer and government demand is quite inelastic in the face of such change for much the same reasons as given above. Business demand will also be inelastic in periods of decided upward or downward trends in earnings. Nevertheless, business borrowing seems to be more easily discouraged than encouraged. Its demand is less inelastic when interest rates rise than when they fall. A very sharp increase may spread panic, but a sharp decrease does not seem to create confidence.

The elasticity of borrower demand, like that in other demand schedules, is a function of the rate of change of the independent variable. (Cf. Chapter 4, Sections 3 and 4.) A large and abrupt change in the interest rate will obviously have more effect on the quantity demanded than a smaller change or the same change achieved more gradually. This is important in two respects. Abrupt increases in interest yield occur more frequently than abrupt decreases. That is, large, panicky declines of the securities markets occur more frequently than equally large, optimistic rises. In the second place, central bank selling of securities becomes contagious more quickly than central bank buying.

This leads to the important observation that the market activity of central banks is not always sufficient to cause a decisive rise or fall in interest rates. The total volume of buying and selling of securities is so great that central bank participation is rarely more than a small fraction of the total. Usually it relies for its influence upon "tipping the scales" and setting a trend which will be copied by others until the desired effect is achieved. At other times the central bank may *force* certain commercial banks to offer securities for sale. This may occur when two conditions are present. First, commercial bank depositors buy the securities offered by the central bank. Second, these member banks do not possess excess reserves upon which they can draw. Therefore they must sell securities to be able to honor the buyers' checks tendered by the central bank. Furthermore, the central bank may raise reserve requirements at the same time, or quite independently. This may force member banks to sell securities to increase their reserves.

On the other hand, the speculative bearishness of private investors may start a downward trend that central bank activity is impotent to stop. Speculative booms are only slightly less difficult to control. Finally, one must remember that, regardless of how it starts, a marked trend in either direction will influence business chiefly through its effect upon forecasts of changes in sales, commodity prices, and other variables, *not* through the rate of interest.

**20. Interest Rates in the Long Run.**—If there is any such thing as a "long-run normal rate of interest," it will depend upon the position and the slope of the long-run demand and supply curves. The elasticity of demand will be a function of diminishing marginal productivity or utility. This includes, but is not limited to, the increase in the stock of producer's goods which is associated with lengthening the period of roundabout production. The elasticity of supply will be a function of motives for not saving, i.e., for not decreasing present consumption. These are usually grouped under the heading of positive time preference. One could also refer to the increasing marginal utility of funds resulting from increased subtractions from expendable balances.

The position, as distinguished from the slope, of the long-run demand curve for funds is chiefly a function of the level of business activity and of government deficit spending. Also important are the existing quantity of capital goods, their cost, and their physical productivity. The latter determinant is related to inventions and the state of the arts. Cultural factors which stimulate or restrict borrowing for enterprise or for consumption are very influential. Consumption, of course, includes government spending as well as individual.

The position of the long-run supply curve is dependent chiefly upon the number of financial institutions and their powers to create credit. Also of major importance are the level of income and its distribution among the people. Other forces include attitudes toward saving, laws which stimulate spending or saving, the incidence of taxation, the opportunities for installment buying, social security legislation, etc.

A stable equilibrium rate of interest in this long-run sense must do more than merely equate a long-run supply quantity of funds with a long-run demand quantity. It must also be neutral in its effect upon the positions of the two curves. That is, for the rate to remain stable it must not induce any shift in the demand or the supply curves in the cycle of events which follows the borrowing-lending which occurs at that rate.[9]

Complete equilibrium requires a balance among a whole host of variables. Labor and capital goods are sometimes substitutes for one another, and therefore the equilibrium interest rate must not disturb wage rates. Rent and profits are ways of getting property income which are substitutes for interest income from lending, and they, too, must be brought into the picture. The prices of commodities influence the revenue derived from using funds in business enterprise and must be considered by borrowers. When one looks far enough, he sees that to describe interest rate equilibrium in the hypothetical or long-run sense requires a survey of the entire economy and a statement of its many interrelationships. However, for most practical purposes of explanation, prediction, or control, partial equilibrium analysis or short-run determinants are enough.

**21. Summary.**—Interest theory is complicated by the large number of different sources of demand and supply, most of which are themselves interdependent. Different motives are involved and the dominance of certain motives changes from time to time. The short-run, day-to-day explanation of interest rates is very different from that for the long run. Analysis on any general plane must either shorten the list of independent variables or take refuge in a not very helpful statement that all prices, including interest rates, interact to determine a general equilibrium. Nevertheless, a review of the institutional material of Chapters 23–24 suggests certain dominant relationships which can be summarized profitably.

Pure interest, if it exists, is variously described as a function of

---

[9] Or the shifts must offset one another.

the following restraints upon supply, preferably the first, but having some connection with the others:

1. The minimum payment for the risk and trouble of the marginal lender on the shortest and safest of loans
2. The positive time preference of the marginal saver-lender
3. The liquidity preference of the marginal holder of funds

The interest-elasticity of *supply* of funds in the short run is chiefly a function of:

1. The way in which changes in interest rates influence expectations regarding future changes in:
    (a) The interest rates, especially relative to their effects upon possible speculative gains or losses in the security markets
    (b) The profit rates for investors in equities
    (c) The safety of principal against borrower defaults
2. The type of lender:
    (a) Institutional lenders: very little supply-elasticity, except that when loans are offered at a fixed rate, supply seems to have infinite elasticity at that rate
    (b) Individual lenders from funds saved out of current income: some elasticity, especially at very high and very low rates

The interest-elasticity of *demand* for funds in the short run is chiefly a function of:

1. The way in which changes in the interest rate influence expectations regarding future changes in:
    (a) The trend of security prices
    (b) The profit rates for business firms
2. The stage of the business cycle: very little elasticity of demand except at the top and the bottom, where no pronounced trends exist
3. The type of borrower: significant only in the case of business borrowing

In the long-run picture the level of interest rates becomes the major issue. Dynamic forces associated with changes in expectations can be eliminated. The positions of the demand and supply curves are as significant as their slopes. Major determinants of any "long-run normal" rate must include:

1. On the demand side:
    (a) The marginal productivity of additions to business resources, particularly durable capital goods. (This is a

function of (1) the total quantity of such goods in use and (2) the state of the arts.)

(b) The marginal utility of consumption spending by individuals and governments. (The decisions of the latter are best seen in a socialist economy.)

2. On the supply side:

(a) The financial institutions of the region and their policies

(b) The marginal propensity to consume, which is another way of describing the desire not to save out of current income

(c) The marginal liquidity preference for other than speculative purposes, particularly the desire to hold cash balances against contingencies

(d) The level and the distribution of individual incomes in relation to subsistence standards of living

# Chapter 26

## PROFITS: AN INSTITUTIONAL APPROACH

**1. Statement of the Problem.**—Like the first three distributive shares, profits may be analyzed from either an institutional or a theoretical approach. The institutional approach of the present chapter treats profits as an effect. It examines the causes of the relative and absolute magnitudes of profits and the causes of profit changes. The next chapter is concerned with theoretical problems. Most of them treat profits as a cause.

The specific questions to be answered in this chapter include the following:

1. What are the various meanings of the word *profits?*
    (a) Which of them is used in this chapter?
    (b) How do profits differ from wages, rent, or interest?
2. What problems are involved in determining:
    (a) Profit amounts?
        (1) Inventory valuation
        (2) Depreciation
    (b) Profit rates?
        (1) Computation of profit amounts
        (2) Choice of base
        (3) Valuation of base
3. What are the causes of differences in profit rates:
    (a) Among firms in the same industry?
    (b) For one firm from one time period to another?
    (c) Among industries?
    (d) Among regions?

**2. "Accounting Profits" Are the Chief Concern of This Chapter.**—There are several possible ways to define profits. The approach which fits best into the pattern of this volume is to begin with a definition which adheres as closely as possible to the connotation accepted by the typical "man in the street." From this viewpoint profits are the net income of business units figured by some type of accounting procedure which subtracts outgo from income.[1] The

---

[1] A more technical description of the accounting process will be given below as one which estimates the net increase in the value of the assets of a firm during a given period of time.

business unit is best known as a "firm." Its characteristic activity is buying and selling in the hope of taking in more than is paid out. From these elementary concepts we may develop others of importance.

In the first place, firms are owned by one or more individuals (or other firms). Sometimes the owner and the firm are so closely connected that there is nothing to be gained by trying to make a distinction between them. Such is the case of the small firm operated as a sole proprietorship. At other times the owner is clearly different from the firm, as in the case of the corporation. Partnerships lie in between. Generally speaking, it is wise to distinguish the owner from the firm he owns. *The firm "makes" profits; the owner merely receives profits from the firm.* He often gets or takes less than the total profits made. Sometimes he receives more than the firm made during the period. This disparity between profits made by the firm and profits received by the owners is most clearly seen in the case of large corporations. The total dividends to stockholders in a given year are usually smaller than profits, but are sometimes larger.

**3. Accounting "Profits" May Be Negative, i.e., May Be Losses.** —A second important group of observations about profits deals with their residual nature. Profits are not "paid" by one person to another. There is no contract agreed upon in advance to pay a certain amount, as in the case of nearly all wage, rent, and interest payments. Profits are uncertain until *after* a firm has done something. They are calculated by a process of subtraction. They are found by accountants to exist (or not to exist as the case may be). No one pays profits to a firm. They are a residual form of income and differ markedly in that respect from the contractual incomes popularly known as wages, rent, and interest. The significance of this contrast will be developed in many of the sections which follow.

A third distinct feature of profits which separates this form of return from the other distributive shares is the fact that profits are sometimes negative. Cases of negative wages, interest, and rent conceivably may be found by very careful search, but they are very, very rare. Negative accounting profits occur in a substantial minority of cases. Their occurrence is so common that they have been given a name of their own, i.e., *losses.* The financial statement of firms which deals with their income and expenditure record over a period of time is called the "profit and loss" statement.

The possibility of such loss is implicit in the nature of business activity. The simplest accounting approach implies in effect that expenditures are made out of income. The total spent is subtracted from the total income and a negative remainder may occur. In fact, however, buying usually precedes selling. Expenditures are made out of funds on hand and are subsequently recouped, if possible, by sales. Following the logic of the sequence of business activities, the subtraction might be reversed. Income might be subtracted from expenditures. Then the remainder, if positive, would indicate a loss. This inversion is useful in that it indicates how a firm may finance its losses. It shows how the dividing-up process known as distribution theory starts with something more than the total income of the period. The total to be distributed is that income plus the net worth of the firm. When the firm contracts to pay out more than the income it realizes during that period, it must draw upon its net worth. If the firm becomes obligated to pay more than its income plus its net worth, the firm is clearly bankrupt. It has undertaken to divide up more than it possesses.

In concluding those introductory remarks, it may be well to point out again the concept of profits which is chosen for the initial approach to the subject. Profits are defined as *accounting* profits. Whenever the term is used without a qualifying adjective, this is the meaning to be understood. In later sections we shall refer to "normal profits" in an effort to draw a parallel with the concept of "normal price." There will also be reference to "pure profits" in the discussion of deviations from "normal profits." It is very important not to confuse the concept of pure profits with that of accounting profits, and the adjectives should be used copiously. The former stresses a unique *type* of distributive income. The latter emphasizes a unique *way* of *receiving* income. Pure profits are supposed to be devoid of all wage, rent, or interest elements due to owners of business units. The concept of accounting profits avoids that issue by separating the firm from its owners and using a functional approach to explain what the firm and its accountants do to "make" profits. Various concepts of profits are useful and will be employed in the following analysis. No one concept should be singled out as "right" while all others are declared to be "wrong." All that is required of the economist is that he make his meaning clear and significant. He should define his terms so as to expedite that task.

**4. Problems Involved in Determining the Amount of Accounting Profits.**—Two problems of accounting theory are of special interest to economists. Both involve value estimates. The first is that of inventories. A firm usually enters an accounting period with some goods on hand and leaves that period with a different quantity.

Inventories of manufacturers may include raw materials, goods in process, and finished products. Some of these goods may be held for several months or longer. When they are held so long that prices change in the meantime, a valuation problem emerges. For instance, if raw materials are purchased at one price and are not used until after a later date on which the firm must calculate its profit or loss for the period, the accountant must decide whether to carry the inventory at original cost, at replacement cost, or at the price the goods would bring if sold. He is likely to be conservative and choose the lowest of the three figures. If he chooses one of the others, he will be able to show a larger profit for the period.

The second problem deals with estimates of depreciation. This is a valuation process at the outset, because a value must be placed upon the asset being depreciated. The usual procedure is to use the original cost of the good, but sometimes replacement or reproduction cost seems more appropriate. Depreciation, however, involves a more crucial decision than this one. It raises the question of how rapidly to depreciate an asset, and according to what formula. If a building has a probable lifetime of profitable use which is approximately 50 years, the annual depreciation may be calculated on a straight-line basis as 1/50th of the cost each year. More conservative practice would call for its depreciation more rapidly than this, as by 1/25th each year for an assumed life of 25 years. Or the depreciation could begin at a larger fraction and decline each year until the building was fully depreciated. There are a host of possible depreciation formulas. Some depart from the time approach and use a formula which considers the amount of use following one pattern of cost accounting. Others allow for special depreciation charges whenever there is evidence of unexpected obsolescence or sudden decline in demand for the product of the equipment.

**5. Valuation Problems Connected with the Rate of Profits.—** Valuation decisions enter into the determination of the *rate* of profits as well as their amount. The rate of profits is the percentage calculated by dividing the amount of profits by some other amount. This amount is usually the net worth of the enterprise, but it may be anything else that the calculator chooses. Sometimes it is the original purchase cost of the shares of stock held by an individual. Or it may be the amount he put into a sole proprietorship or partnership. A different approach uses as a divisor the amount which the individual could realize by *selling* his share of ownership in the firm. This may differ from the initial investment for a host of reasons including stock market gyrations, reinvestment of earnings, changes in technology, etc. From the viewpoint of the individual the numerator of the fraction should not be the total profits of the concern, but only that part which that individual receives, or to which he feels entitled.

The importance of estimates in calculations of the rate of profits can be further appreciated by considering the problem of valuation when net worth is used as the divisor. The net worth of a corporation, for instance, is the difference between total assets and total liabilities to persons other than the shareholders. Assets may be valued in various ways. The problem of inventory valuation has already been considered. More important quantitatively in most cases is the valuation of fixed assets. These may be carried in the balance sheet at original cost, reproduction cost, or present market value. If either of the latter alternatives is chosen, the personal bias of the valuator can be very important. Even original cost may be a larger or smaller amount, depending upon the carefulness with which the initial investment is made. This is revealed by public utility commission studies to determine "prudent investment" as compared with the "original cost" figures submitted by the firm.

Often there are also included among assets such intangible items as goodwill, trade-marks, value of patents originating within the firm, etc. The valuations required to make such entries often work backward from earnings by capitalization. This introduces circular reasoning when they are subsequently counted as part of the assets used to determine the current rate of profits on net worth.

Enough has been said to demonstrate the ambiguities and uncertainties involved in profit estimates, particularly when profits are expressed as a rate of return upon net worth. Additional items might be mentioned, but the point should have been well established by those already cited. If the owner does the estimating, he may get one figure; if an outsider performs the calculations, he may get another. The result may depend upon the skill or bias of the accountants used. Sometimes the purpose of the estimate is of major importance. When the rate of profit is being determined for tax purposes, efforts will be made to keep it low. When new capital funds are being sought, there is a temptation to exaggerate by one device or another. Public utility commissions have recognized this problem and at times have made a serious effort to secure the adoption of "uniform" accounting systems and methods. But they cannot standardize the accountants who apply the rules.

We are forced to the conclusion that there is no good answer to the question, "What is *the* rate of profits?" in any particular case. What one should do is to tell how the calculations were performed and what assumptions were used in the various valuation processes.  And when comparisons are made among the rates of profits of different firms or industries, one must examine accounting procedures to see whether they are similar.  If they are not, some highly erroneous conclusions may be reached.

**6. Profits May Include Work Income as Well as Property Income.**—The rate-of-profits concept wrongly implies that profits are always a form of property income.  When the profit amount expressed in dollars is divided by a chosen valuation expressed likewise in dollars, there is the clear implication that the profits are derived from the property thus valued.  This is often far from the case, as will be shown later in sections dealing with determinants of the amount of profits.  In small firms the residual income usually contains a large share properly attributable to the work efforts of the owner-manager.  In large firms, particularly of the corporate type of organization, *dividends to nonworking owners* become clearly a property type of income.  But these dividends must be distinguished from the *profits of the corporation* itself.  And one must not allow the prominence of large corporations to lead him to make generalizations about profits which exclude the host of cases involving partnerships, sole proprietorships, and small corporations.

Confusion will be avoided as suggested above, if profits are thought of as *a way of receiving income,* whether work income, property income, or both.  An individual in a capitalistic society has the option of seeking income in various ways.  If he has no property, he usually is forced to choose the contractual method and goes to work for some one else.  If the individual has property, his options broaden.  He may let some one else use that property for a contractual rent or interest payment as the case may be.  At the same time he may work for contractual wages.  If he chooses the alternative of seeking income residually, he has several further options.  He may purchase shares of stock or a silent interest in a partnership.  His return is then likely to be in the nature of interest residually received.  Or he may combine an "investment" of his time and effort with his investment of property.  That is, he may work in and manage or help to manage the business unit which seeks profit income.  The individual's return will then combine work and property returns.  The third possibility, residual work income without residual property income, is very rare, but it is conceivable.  A firm might have zero net worth appearing on its balance sheet and still show an accounting profit at the end of the year. According to strict logic, this income should not be associated with any property of the owners of the firm, but must be considered a result of the activities of the firm itself. These activities may be identified with the decisions of management, the efforts of labor, the passive receipt of chance gains, ownership supervision, or other things as the case may be. Various possibilities will be discussed below.

**7. Differences in Profit Rates Among Firms in the Same Industry.**—The nature and origin of accounting profits can be further illumined by examining differences among firms. For simplicity, it seems best to begin with firms in the same industry. Differences in size may be eliminated by using the concept of profit rates instead of profit amounts, remembering the problems associated with their calculation.

In the light of Sections 2, 3, and 4 above, the first observation must be that differences in accounting methods are of primary importance. Depreciation and valuation procedures may differ widely among firms in the same industry. This is particularly true for small business firms, although there are some notorious instances involving large corporations.

Among small firms there are also differences in the amount of labor contributed by the owner. If he hires a manager or mechanic to do the work he might do himself, profits will be less than if he does that work himself. For income tax purposes, any wages a sole proprietor (or partner) pays to himself cannot be counted as an expense to the firm. They are classified as profits presumably because the owner does not enter into a contract with himself for certain services. The nature of sole proprietorships is such that the owner must get residually whatever income he receives.

A similar observation might be made regarding those profit differences which stem from differences in the length of the owner's workweek. One complaint of white farmers in California against those of Japanese descent was that the latter worked too hard and too long! They made an unfairly large profit, saved too much, and thus got ahead too rapidly.

**8. Efficiency of Management as a Source of Profit Differences.**—Profit differences are often due to differences in the efficiency with which rival firms are managed. However, this topic must be approached with care. It is not efficiency in management *per se* which produces large profits, but *relatively greater* efficiency. If all the competing firms are equally well managed, their profits may be small because of competitive bidding up of purchase prices or cutting of selling prices.   In fact, it is hard to measure managerial efficiency except in terms of profits.   People have a tendency to reason backward from large profits to superior efficiency, although this inference may prove unwarranted when the acts of management are examined in detail.

A second caution might be given to the effect that attempts to infer relative efficiency from relative profits must start with the assumption either that the owners are the managers in each case or that the managers are paid alike.   Since firms being compared are usually of different sizes and are organized in different ways, this assumption is rarely in keeping with the facts.   The point is that hired managers of equal efficiency may be overpaid by one board of directors and underpaid by another, with obvious effects upon the residue called profits. If there are no hired managers, this discrepancy will not arise.

With these qualifications in mind, we may now approach the question regarding the nature of this attribute of a firm called "efficiency." It may be divided into three main parts: buying, selling, and operating.   A fourth might deal with planning and cover such things as the choice of time and place for an enterprise, for new investment, etc., akin to the production planning type of competition described in Chapter 11, Section 8.

**9. Efficiency Differences in Buying and in Selling.**—Successful management on the buying side includes bargaining and discovery.   Most materials are purchased by most firms at prices which are not subject to their control.   But there are exceptions.   Large buyers are often able to get price concessions not available to small buyers.   Sometimes the shrewdness of the purchasing agent makes the difference.   Success in discovery of willing sellers also contributes to profit opportunities, particularly when materials are scarce. In the factor markets, some firms get advantages by discovering rental opportunities and negotiating long-term leases at favorable terms. Or they may borrow at a time and place where lower interest rates are obtainable.

Probably the most important differences in buying efficiency, however, occur in the bargaining between management and labor.   Here the problem is to get a more favorable contract than your competitor and hold your workers to it.   Where there is industry-wide collective bargaining, no such differential is possible.   The problem then becomes one of striving for the most advantageous terms possible for the group as a whole.

When bargaining occurs between managers of business firms and those from whom they purchase, two effects are determined simultaneously. For instance, if organized workers succeed in getting a wage increase, management at the same time loses potential profit. Or if a lessor gets less of the gross income to be distributed, the lessee retains more. Changes in bargaining power are probably more important than changes in bargaining skill. But often superior skill is revealed in successful maneuvering for positions of power. The constant dickering between management and labor about who shall have the right to decide certain terms of employment is a case in point. By increasing its power in this field, labor is often able to increase its wage bill at management's expense. Each side may also plan how it can get outside support, as from other unions, from a trade association, or from the government. If the term *bargaining* is extended to include all these kinds of activity, efficiency of management becomes a wide phrase, indeed.

On the selling side there are also differences among the managers of firms which significantly influence the profits made. Bargaining is sometimes important, particularly when one firm sells to another rather than to the ultimate consumer. The chief difference, however, lies in the ability to promote sales inexpensively. Most firms have unused capacity most of the time and could increase their profit if they could raise their rate of sales. This requires selling efforts which succeed in attracting buyers without costing too much. It is the selling expense problem which was introduced above in Chapter 6, Section 1. Ingenuity in discovering effective sales appeals or astuteness in hiring advertising agencies or salesmen who can invent them are the conditions of success.

**10. Efficiency Differences in Production Cost or Output and in Planning.**—Profit differences also arise from differences in operating costs. This topic may be defined so as to eliminate those advantages which spring from fortunate purchases or bargaining successes. That management is most efficient which succeeds in devising ways of combining factors and materials so as to get more output per dollar's worth of inputs than do other managements. Success may come from inventing new machines, new processes, use of by-products, etc. It also requires either that competitors be kept ignorant of these inventions, or that the efficient management keep ahead by inventing something new while rivals are copying the old. Production efficiency is obviously an important source of profits in many cases. But it is only one source and should not be elevated into a complete theory of profits.

Finally there may be noted that group of efficiency attributes grouped under the head of planning. This includes superior foresight in knowing what to produce, when to produce it, and where. In order to expand at the right time, enterprises must make their plans far in advance. This requires good judgment of probable future actions by competitors, trend of the business cycle, legislation, consumer preferences, and the like.

This section should be concluded with the warning given at the outset: one must not infer high efficiency from high profits. Efficiency as defined here has covered many aspects of business, but there are other sources of profits, too. Some have been presented and others will be discussed shortly. And if *hired* management is paid in proportion to its efficiency, its contribution to profits will be nil. This point is so important that it will be analyzed further in the next section.

**11. Underpayment of Factors as a Source of Profits.**—Relative superiority in managerial efficiency will be a sure source of profits if the owners are the managers and take their pay residually. That is obvious. But if the managers are hired, another variable enters the picture, the pay given them for their services. This pay will be determined presumably by bargaining between the owners and the managers. If the owners can get a manager for less than he contributes through his efficiency to the income of the firm, there will be a profit residue from that manager's service. This is often the case for several reasons. A manager sometimes improves in skill at a given task more rapidly than his salary is raised. He is satisfied with the pay received, and his family likes the community. No one else has offered him enough more to warrant making a change. So he stays, and his employer profits.

Many such managers yearn for the day when they can have a business of their own and pocket the profits they feel they are making for their employers. Others work for such large-scale enterprises that such a hope seems futile. If not content with their pay, they merely seek to bargain for a higher salary. Then it is up to the owner, or whomever he hires to bargain for him (another form of manager!), to decide whether to pay the increase or to let the man go and hire a replacement who will probably need some training before becoming of equal worth.

The foregoing is not to imply that all managers are underpaid in this sense, but only that some of them surely are. Some also are overpaid, and the firm suffers losses accordingly. And again it must be said that neither profits nor losses are *prima facie* evidence of underpayment nor overpayment. There are so many possible causes that no one can be singled out by reasoning backward from the effect.

Other factors may be underpaid or overpaid, too. This was explained in the case of land during the discussion of various concepts of surplus (see Chapter 22, Section 6). Long-term loan contracts may give rise to opportunity-cost surpluses in relation to interest payments. And workers below the managerial level should not be ignored. They may also be underpaid, although probably not as often as they claim to be. When they are well organized, they bring constant pressure to bear to raise their pay to the level of their productivity. They often judge this productivity by the profits being made by the firm, although the profits might be ascribed by some one else to a different cause, such as the underpayment of a different factor. At times workers may demand a pay increase which is definitely beyond the capacity of the firm to pay and stay out of the red. These overpayment situations do not occur nearly so often as employers claim in their negotiations, but some cases are not to be denied.

None of this discussion is intended to imply any ethical judgment regarding underpayment or overpayment. The question of economic justice is far too complex for that. On the other hand, there are some occasions where one side or the other takes advantage of an unusually strong position to "drive a hard bargain." This may be sanctioned by the ethics of the competitive system, may be appraised as shortsighted, may be condemned as "exploitation," etc., depending upon the viewpoint of the person rendering judgment. No sweeping generalization seems possible. The presence of profits, even of large profits, in a particular case does not warrant the assumption that some factor hired by the firm was unjustly underpaid.

A final comment regarding underpayment takes us back to some points made in Section 6 of this chapter. In the corporate form of business enterprise an owner may be also a hired manager, or an employee may own some shares of stock. Differences in profit rates between corporations, particularly small ones, may arise from differences in the amount of salary paid for managerial labor contributed by the principal owner. It is also probable that there are differences in the degree of underpayment of owner-managers of various firms. One set of owner-managers may decide to overpay themselves, while another prefers underpayment so that profits will be larger. Sometimes the desire to reduce total tax burdens stimulates the payment of high executive salaries.

**12. Differences in Capital Structure Affect Equity Profits.**—Firms often differ in their capital structure, and this affects the rate of profits on the owner's equity. A firm whose owners supply all of the funds will be in a different profit position from one which borrows much of the funds invested. Consider, for instance, the following hypothetical cases:

|  FIRM A  |  |  FIRM B  |  |
| --- | --- | --- | --- |
| *Capital* |  | *Capital* |  |
| 10,000 shares common |  | 4% mortgage bonds .. | $ 400,000 |
| stock ............ | $1,000,000 | 6,000 shares common |  |
|  |  | stock ............ | 600,000 |
|  |  | Total | $1,000,000 |
|  |  |  |  |
| *Earnings in 1946* ..... | 100,000 | *Earnings in 1946* ...... | 100,000 |
| Earnings per share .. | $10 | Interest on bonds .... | 16,000 |
| Rate of profits per |  | Remainder ........ | $  84,000 |
| share ............ | 10% | Earnings per share .. | $14 |
|  |  | Rate of profits per |  |
|  |  | share ............ | 14% |

Firm B is said to have much greater "leverage" in good times. When net income before bond interest rises, the net per share of common stock will rise more rapidly than in Firm A. If earnings had been $200,000, a similar computation would show Firm A getting 20 per cent per share, and Firm B making 31 per cent for its shareholders. On a declining market the picture is not so rosy for Firm B. If earnings should drop to $16,000, all of this amount would have to go to the bondholders and stockholders would get nothing. But in Firm A, common stock profits would still show 1.6 per cent. The picture might be elaborated still further by showing other types of capitalization, such as those involving bonds and preferred stock. The fundamental argument would not change. Different capital structures often cause differences in profits when the latter is figured with reference to common stock. If the total capitalization of the firm is used as the divisor in calculating profit rates, then the explanation of interfirm differences must be found in the other causes cited above.

**13. Profits May Result from Lucky Events.**—Sometimes the profit or loss of a business firm results from occurrences which are clearly fortuitous. This appears most obviously in farming, where capricious storms may destroy the crops of one region while benefiting those of another. Locusts, boll weevils, beetles, and other pests may invade an area beyond the power of any farm manager to foresee or to control. Similarly, fire may destroy the plant of the major customer or supplier of a given factory. This may bring losses which no farsighted manager could avoid by insurance. It may also bring gains to rivals which are clearly windfalls. A war may bring losses to thousands of firms whose management could not prevent the war nor take action to avoid its harmful effects. On the other hand the same war may bring undreamed-of profits to other firms whose managers did not seek it. Scores of other lucky or unlucky events might be cited.

In addition to these clear-cut cases, there are many borderline situations. Here it is difficult to state whether the management deserves credit for the profits or blame for the losses. Certainly the management's own appraisal of its performance is suspect. A neutral judge would be best. However, no segregation of chance gains and losses is necessary in a residual theory of profits. The firm gets what is left regardless of the origin of that surplus. If the owners want to know whether the management of their firm is doing a good job under the circumstances, they can render their own decision or hire an efficiency expert to write a report. The appraisal will have its chief influence upon the amount of profits through its effect upon the salaries paid the managers. If the judgment is favorable, managers may be given or may bargain for more pay. Without any change in the operation of the firm, this will tend to reduce the profit residue. If luck is given the credit and not management, a salary increase is not likely to occur, and profits will be larger. A similar argument could be constructed on the other side of the picture for unlucky or inferior managers.

Luck is put toward the end of our list of the causes of profits in order that its importance should not be exaggerated. Yet it should not be overlooked. Every firm "takes a chance." That is the essence of putting oneself at the end of the line to take what is left. The remainder may be large or it may be small, depending upon the various determinants explained above. At the beginning of a venture period that return is uncertain. It cannot be predicted with precision. But fairly close estimates often can be made. These are based upon *probabilities* which must be distinguished from possibilities. A person is not said to be lucky or unlucky when the probable happens. But if the improbable occurs, which is always possible, we describe it as good luck or bad luck as the case may be. Therefore, the minor element of uncertainty in every probability must not be elevated into a theory which says that profits are essentially a chance return.[2]  The latter phrase should be restricted to its usual connotation of a highly uncertain event.  Luck may be present in every profit or loss situation, but it is not a complete explanation.  Usually it is one of the least important determinants of the size of the residual return which we call profits.

**14. Monopoly as a Cause of Profits.**—Monopoly profits, so called, may result from the actions of a firm's management in charging prices which are abnormally higher than the cost of supplying the goods sold.  This was explained in Chapter 8, Sections 12 and 13. The ability to charge high prices of this type for more than a very short period of time is described as a monopoly position in the market.  This favorable position is one which others cannot attain quickly, or without considerable expense.  It is obtained by the fortunate firm either by design or by chance.  For instance, management may seek it through collaboration to secure agreements which restrict competition and exclude potential entrants.  Or management may strive to obtain cost-reducing processes or equipment which are patented or kept secret as long as possible.  Sometimes chance discoveries or unforeseen changes in demand or supply bring a favorable position which is not easily duplicated by other firms.

It seems reasonable to conclude, therefore, that monopoly as a cause of profits is not as fundamental as the concepts given earlier to explain profits in general.  These include, particularly, the relative managerial efficiency factor, underpayment, and chance. When seen in the light of their causes, monopoly profits are not significantly different from other forms of profit, including those popularly called competitive. They become a distinct category only if defined very narrowly as those profits resulting from antisocial action to restrain some form of competition in an unethical or illegal way. And even these activities are managerial. All of which supports the approach of this chapter, which explains profits chiefly as a residual remuneration to a firm for the otherwise unpaid work performed by its employees and owners plus pay for the otherwise unpaid services of the property it owns and controls.

**15. Owner Profits Compared with Firm Profits.**—The business unit known as the firm makes profits in the first instance, but its rate of profits often differs from the rate of profits received by the owner. There are two main reasons for this difference. The first springs from

---

[2] One must remember that "profits" in this chapter means "accounting profits." On the concept of "pure profit" and its relation to chance gains, see the next chapter.

the interposition of the firm as an entity between the owner and the profit-making activities of the firm's employees. This is most readily seen in the corporate form of business enterprise. The directors of the corporation may distribute as dividends only part of the profits of the firm. The owner gets a second residue, as it were. First, the expenses of the firm are subtracted from gross revenue. Second, the firm sets aside that part of net revenue which it wants to keep for expansion or other reasons. Only the remainder is paid out as dividends. However, the owner's equity is increased because of retained profits. Some owners calculate their profits on the basis of reported net earnings per share instead of by the dividends they actually receive.

The second difference arises from the way in which each rate of profits is computed. For the firm the divisor is the net worth. For the individual owner the divisor usually is either the purchase cost of the shares he holds or their present market value. Either of these divisors will be different from the book value, which is based on net worth and sometimes they differ by several hundred per cent. Profit rates vary accordingly. This is important because owner profit rates have a greater effect than firm profit rates upon decisions to remain an owner, to become a new owner, or to expand ownership. This topic will be treated in the discussion of normal and abnormal profits below (Chapter 27, Sections 7–11).

**16. Changes in Profit Rate of a Firm from Year to Year.**—The profit rate of a firm may change from year to year for much the same reasons that have been advanced for the differences in profit rates among firms at any given time. Emphasis might be placed, however, on "lucky" changes in demand as the major variable in most cases. These include the cyclical ups and downs of business in general and of the particular industry of which the firm is a part. There also may be some counter-cyclical irregularities in demand affecting the individual firm, but not induced by the actions of its management. This last qualification is important if we are to segregate the chance developments from those stimulated by management. Among the latter would be changes in demand as affected by selling policies. It is obviously impossible to determine just where to draw the line in many cases such as that between sought and unsought increases in demand. But that difficulty does not destroy the advantage of recognizing that different causes of demand change do exist.

A second important variable from year to year is differences in cost of production. In recent times the negotiated rate of wages is and has become of major significance. The annual or other renewal of union labor contracts involves the setting of terms which may make the difference between large profit and small, or between profit and loss. Of a similar nature, but usually of smaller importance and less frequent occurrence, are negotiations for leases and for refunding loans. Management skills are important here. When labor wrests concessions from management, the taxonomist is confronted with the problem of deciding whether to ascribe the reduction in profits to overpayment of labor or overpayment of management. But again the classification is unimportant unless one is combating a monistic explanation of profit.

**17. The Role of Inventions in Causing Changes in the Rate of Profits.**—Costs of production also differ significantly with changes in the processes or equipment used. Technological improvements are a constant objective of management. Often their discovery, though consciously sought, should be ascribed to chance. Their introduction involves another complication. If the invention is patentable and is productive of an ascribable increment in profit through reduction in cost, its value may be determined by capitalization. If management pays this value amount for such an invention, there will be no gain unless in the particular firm the invention will yield more than the return estimated by the seller. Thus an invention may be appraised by its seller on the basis of an expected earnings rate of $10,000 per year for eighteen years. If the buyer-user can make it yield $11,000 per year, he will gain by purchasing it at the seller's figure.[3]

A different situation exists when the invention is developed by someone in the employ of the given firm, but is patented by that firm. Several new problems emerge. Should the invention be carried on the company's books at an estimated capitalized value, at a nominal $1, or at an estimated cost of development? The decision will influence the amount of net worth and therefore the rate of profits computed on that base. The invention itself will raise profits per share and therefore potential dividends. Stockholders usually are not concerned with the accounting decision regarding balance sheet entries, but there are some exceptions. The management may use increased net worth as grounds for an increase in the number of shares outstanding, thus diluting the return per share. Or an invention might be carried on the books at a high figure and depreciated over a

---

[3] Assuming, of course, that the seller does not use a lower discount rate than the buyer. Cf. Chapter 19, Section 6, and Chapter 21, Section 14.

seventeen-year period, thus reducing current dividend payments. Public utility shareholders may be glad to have net worth padded. It reduces the rate of profits without altering the absolute amount and may prove helpful in efforts to increase rates.

A few other causes of profit differences from year to year may be singled out for special mention. Accounting practice may change, particularly with reference to depreciation. Worker efficiency often is influenced by wage adjustments, union organization, the prevailing volume of unemployment, etc. Strikes hurt earnings, even if "won" by the management. Government action may grant or withhold subsidies, alter price control, revise tariffs, or change taxes. Key management officers may be changed through death, new hiring, promotions, and resignations. Volume of output may be curtailed at times by scarcity of essential raw materials.

**18. Differences in Average Profit Rate Among Industries.—** Further light may be shed upon the nature and source of profits by an examination of reasons for the differences that exist at any given time among the average profit rates of different industries. The list of determinants should include all of those previously explained for differences among firms in the same industry and differences from year to year for a given firm. For instance, changes in the intensity of schedule demand occur at different times for different industries. At the close of the second world war, the demand for construction materials rose and that for military airplanes declined. On the supply side, cycles of material costs also may differ in their peaks. This was particularly noticeable in the period of irregular decontrol of prices following the war. Labor gains at the expense of firms may come at different times in different industries. And of course, there are differences in accounting procedures in various industries.

The most important argument to be developed in Sections 18 and 19 is that the average rate of profits in an industry is a function of the productive capacity of that industry in relation to the demand for the goods it produces.[4] Total productive capacity is made up of two components, the number of firms and their several capacities. The determinants of each of these may be examined briefly. Ease of entry is an important determinant of the number of firms. The nature of the industry and its monopolistic practices suggest themselves as the major factors influencing ease of entry. Some firms, such as corner groceries, are easily established because they require little capital to

---

[4] The troublesome question of what constitutes an industry need not be discussed at this point. A commonsense criterion of high substitutability of firm products will be implied.

achieve a scale of operation which has relatively low unit costs. Others, such as automobile assembly plants, require large-scale production with huge capital investment. In some cases the lack of requisite skills limits entry, as in the manufacture of chemicals. In other cases potential entrants are held back by inability to secure the use of certain patents, materials, or sites. At times fear of retaliation by existing firms may be a deterrent. These and other points regarding the problem of entry were discussed in connection with the classification of forms of business activity in Chapter 11, Section 11.

**19. Industry Profit Differences Are Affected by Firm Expansion Programs.**—In addition to aids and obstacles to entry, current capacity is a function also of prior expansion of existing firms. Here the determinants are closely interrelated. Expansion will tend to occur when profit rates are high. Profits will be high when firms are operating at or near capacity. When operations approach capacity, firms begin to plan for expansion of that capacity. Expansion also is planned when it seems likely to permit production of larger volume at unit costs lower than would be possible by overtaxing present capacity. (Compare Chapter 13, Section 7.)

Occasionally capacity expansion is induced by technological change. New plants are erected using the new equipment or methods, but the old ones are not immediately scrapped. Sometimes this is also what happens when there is entry of new firms. The erection of new plants in new places to secure labor, material, or marketing economies is of the same pattern.

Some industries characteristically plan farther ahead than others. They expand capacity in order to be ready for an expected increase in demand, as in the case of electric utilities. Or they may anticipate declining supply from other sources, as in oil well development. Some try to get ahead of rivals by early development of choice but limited sites. In a few cases overcapacity with attendant low profits has been the result of vertical development of firms seeking to control sales outlets below them in the production-marketing process, such as gasoline service stations. Efforts to control raw materials are probably less frequent and do not often cause excess capacity. They are more apt to represent attempts to avoid paying high prices to cartels which themselves sprang from excess capacity situations.

Finally, there is the question of the availability of funds. When profits have been high in the past, funds for future expansion are relatively easy to obtain. If not present in the reserves of the firms themselves, they may be secured on good terms from the general public because of the attractive earnings record of the firm or industry.

In short, the profit differences among industries in a given year are a function of many variables. Chief among them are demand and investment fluctuations which differ in amplitude and in time of occurrence. The demand fluctuations relate to the year in question. The investment fluctuations relate chiefly to years prior to the year in question. A third important determinant is the extent of monopolistic activity which raises selling prices, resists increased buying prices, and restrains entry. It is often argued that profits are payment for taking risk, i.e., for assuming the chance of loss. This concept will be examined further in the next chapter, but at this point one must note that it does not serve as a good explanation of inter-industry differences in profit rates in any given year. For instance, there is a high mortality percentage for beginners both in retailing and farming. This indicates the high risk of entering such enterprises. But those industries usually have a very low rate of return relative to other industries. The argument of a correlation between risk and the rate of profits must be defended, if at all, on other grounds.

**20. Differences in the Average Profit Rate in Different Regions.** —A final approach to the institutional explanation of profits may be made by examining causes of differences in the average rate of profits of firms in a given year when the firms of two regions are compared. For instance, the average rate of profits of New England firms is probably less than that of those in California or Alaska. The reasons are complex and have their roots in the history, the culture pattern, and the natural resources of the two areas.

The explanation of differences in average profit rates between two regions should begin with an explanation of the differences in interest rates. The average rate of profits and the average rate of interest tend to be high or low together because they represent substitute uses of funds. (We ignore for the moment the possible wage element in managerial profits.) The explanation of interest rate differences was given in Chapter 24, Sections 11 and 12. Some specific determinants of profit rate differences should be given special mention.

If the producers of a certain good in two different regions sell that good in the same market with the same transportation costs, then those producers will have the greater profits who have the lower costs. The cost of producing a certain good may be lower in one region than another because the former has lower factor prices or greater factor efficiency.   Lower factor prices result from a relatively greater abundance of the cheap factors in one region than in another. The influence of cheap land and cheap labor has long been felt in international trade.   For some products, low cost results from abundant capital goods.

Abundance of the factors combined by business management would not of itself produce high profits.   Enterprise funds and ability must also be relatively more scarce in one region than in another. It is differences in the multiple ratios among the several factors in two regions which bring about differences in the profits made by producers of those goods which enter into international problems.   It is not merely greater abundance of one or all of them in one region as compared to another.

This argument is part of the theory of comparative costs in international trade and need not be given further elaboration here.   It holds most clearly for single products from two regions.   The low cost and high profit region may be either one of two types.   It may be one which has high profits in general as compared to another region.   Or it may be a region in which the given industry is new and in which the number of competing firms has not yet become large.

Differences in the average level of profits may also arise from differences in the general culture patterns of two areas.   One may be highly competitive and the other may have many obstacles of entry to protect existing firms.   Inventions may be frequent and technological change rapid in one area and slow in another.   Accounting practices may differ.   Tax structures are not often the same and occasionally may be quite different.   One may have more government ownership and control than the other.   Finally, the regions may differ in their stage of the business cycle.   One may be near the peak of its boom while another has not yet reached it or has gone beyond it.

**21. Summary.**—The concept of profits most commonly used in this chapter is that of the accounting profits of firms.   These are the net income which accountants compute by subtracting costs from gross income. They may be expressed as an amount or as a rate. Profits may also refer to the funds received by individual owners of a firm.   In either case they are a form of residual income which in most cases is derived from property, not from work.

The *magnitude* of the accounting profits of a *firm* is a function of:

1. The valuation processes used by accountants, especially regarding depreciation and inventories

2. The amount of uncompensated funds, labor, or durable goods contributed to the enterprise by the owner
3. The relative efficiency of the firm in comparison with competitors. This includes efficiency in production, buying, selling, and planning.
4. The amount paid to factors in relation to what they contribute to the efficiency of the firm. (Underpayments may be based upon the factor owner's bargaining weakness, ignorance, immobility, etc.)
5. The capital structure: the ratio of stock to bonds, etc.
6. Windfall gains not attributable to the actions of any factor
7. Monopoly position: usually a combination of management efficiency and luck

The *rate* of profits of an *equity owner* is a function of:

1. The amount of profits which the firm distributes to the owners
2. The purchase price of the owner's equity share; or its present market value
3. The difference between the purchase price and the sales price of shares the owner buys and sells ("speculative" gain or loss)

The profits of a firm *differ from year to year* because of changes in all the variables described above, but particularly because of changes in:

1. The demand for its products
2. Its costs of production: both factor unit costs and efficiency
3. Its accounting practices
4. Taxes

Differences in the average profit rates of *various industries* are a result of most of the above determinants for individual firms, but especially:

1. Different demand intensities for the products
2. Different aggregate capacities to meet the respective demands
   (a) The number of firms: past stimuli to and opportunities for entry
   (b) The size of firms: past stimuli to and opportunities for expansion

*Interregional differences* in average profit rates result from both general and particular relationships:

1. The current demand for and supply of funds for *all* productive uses, whether as loan capital or as equity capital

2. The relative costs of production of a certain good depending on factor costs and factor efficiencies, especially
  (a) The abundance of equity capital in that industry
  (b) The abundance of other factors in that region
3. Different culture patterns regarding business

# Chapter 27

## PROFITS: SOME THEORETICAL AND
## SOCIAL PROBLEMS

**1. Problems of Profit Theory.**—Up to this point we have been concerned chiefly with the institutional causes of profit, profit differences, and profit changes. In this chapter our attention shifts from profits as an effect to profits as a cause. Institutional explanations are supplemented by more general theories. The questions to be answered include the following:

1. What effect does the rate of profits have upon the supply of the factor which receives profit?
   (a) Upon the individual firm, its capacity and net worth
   (b) Upon the number and total capacity of firms in an industry
   (c) Upon individuals as equity owners
2. Why must the opportunity to earn profits exist in a free enterprise economy?
3. Why does the average rate of profits for industry as a whole tend to be positive?
4. Can a normal rate of profits be defined comparable to the concept of normal prices, normal wages, etc.?
5. What part does risk play in explaining the rate of profits in general or in particular cases?
6. What effect does the taxation of profits have upon the economy as a whole?

**2. The Profit-Elasticity of Supply.**—When profits are considered as a cause, the first problem to be considered is the way in which profits affect the supply of the factor which receives profit. This may be called the problem of the profit-elasticity of supply. It resembles the problems discussed in connection with the price-elasticity of supply of commodities, the wage-elasticity of the supply of labor, etc. In these other fields the effect of prices upon demand was also considered, but the nature of profits as a residual share makes the demand approach difficult and perhaps unimportant.

The profit-elasticity of supply of the profit-receiving factor cannot be analyzed until that factor is defined.  According to the argument of the preceding chapter, this factor seems best thought of as either (1) a firm or (2) an owner of an equity in a firm.  Both receive profits as a residual form of income.  The solution of the supply-elasticity problem requires a reasonable explanation of (1) the capacity and net worth of a given firm, (2) the number and total capacity of firms in a given industry, and (3) the entry of individuals into the equity ownership position and their exit from the equity ownership position.

**3. The Profit-Elasticity of Individual Firm Capacity.**—The profit-elasticity of supply relative to the individual firm must be examined in relation to the changes in the firm which are apt to be induced by changes in the rate of profits to net worth.  These include particularly (1) the capacity of the firm, (2) the percentage of net worth to total capitalization, (3) the output as a percentage of capacity, and (4) the cost of production.

**4. Firm Capacity Expansion When Profits Rise.**—The capacity of a firm tends to vary directly with the rate of profits.  The management is much more likely to plan expansion when earnings are good than when they are poor.  Funds for expansion are obtainable more readily when the firm's rate of profits has recently increased than when it has decreased.  Three reasons may be noted.  First, large profits permit large retention and reinvestment of earnings.  Second, they stimulate the allocation of previously accumulated cash reserves to an expansion type of investment.  Third, additional funds may be obtained more easily from outside the firm.  This is true whether the funds are sought from present owners, from potential new owners, or from lenders.  The correlation between changes in the rate of profits of firms and changes in capacity is probably positive, but not high.  It is highest when profits are increasing.

The minimum profit rate which a firm must earn if it is to attract *loan* capital for expansion cannot be defined in any general way.  Potential lenders demand ample security in terms of either the amount of profits or the collateral pledged.  The amount of profits, as distinguished from the rate on net worth, indicates the margin of protection afforded the lender.  The degree of safety is sometimes measured by expressing the total amount of profits as a multiple of the total amount of interest payable on the loan.  Another test is the ratio between the value of the collateral and the amount of the loan.  It is true that a high current rate of profits makes lenders less exacting in their safety margin demands or collateral requirements.  But there is no generally accepted minimum rate which they will demand as a condition for lending to a given company.

The same argument holds for equity capital. It is the peculiar nature of residual income that it may fluctuate widely and cannot be predicted with great certainty more than a short time in advance. Prospective earnings in future years may often be a greater inducement to equity investment than high earnings now. If this were not so, few firms would be able to get started or to grow from small beginnings. Many people buy stock chiefly for expected dividends and appreciation, factors which need bear no close relation to the present profit rate on net worth. In the light of these facts it is difficult to be sure how much correlation exists between a firm's rate of profits and its ability to attract new equity capital. Even though the evidence probably justifies a cautious affirmative answer, there is no definable minimum profit rate which must be exceeded at any given time before a firm can get equity capital. Certainly there is no normal rate below which existing equity capital will be withdrawn. Further comments on this point must be deferred until Section 10 where the discussion shifts from the rate of profits of the firm to the rate of profits of the stockholder.

**5. Firm Capacity Contraction When Profits Fall.**—When profits fall, but do not become negative, *capacity* to produce is not often diminished. *Output* may decline as firms shift to produce other things, as described above. Output also may be reduced by voluntary curtailment following the $MC = MR$ principle described in Chapters 8 and 10. But output is not diminished because of reduced capacity. The most that one can say is that falling profits generally restrain increases in capacity. Firm owners are reluctant to add to their investment in equipment. Lenders are not so willing to lend to the few brash owners who still want to expand. On the other hand, one should note that depreciation charges permit replacement of equipment. In periods of rapid technical progress, the replacement equipment may be more efficient or cheaper than the old. Under such circumstances, firms showing as little as zero profits *may* increase capacity. When a firm sells a part of its plant which it can no longer profitably operate, its capacity to produce is diminished. The proceeds from the sale, however, may be used to meet pressing obligations. This may help the firm to avoid still further contraction.

**6. The Profit-Elasticity of Other Determinants of the Profit of the Firm.**—In addition to the correlation between profits and capacity, a second supply-elasticity relationship should be noted. It is the manner in which the rate of profits on net worth is influenced by the percentage of net worth to total capitalization.   If a firm borrows a large part of the capital funds invested in fixed plant, the rate of profits on the remaining capital contributed by owners will fluctuate widely with changes in earnings.   The amount borrowed in this way is chiefly a function of the type of business and the arbitrary decisions of management.   In the case of railroads and public utilities, usually there is much real property against which mortgage bonds are relatively easy to sell.   In other cases, promoters, directors, or top management officials may decide to seek funds in the bond market or from banks rather than from potential investors in equity capital. Various motives may be present, such as the desire of present stockholders to retain full control.   The correlation between such decisions and the current rate of profit of the firm is probably so small as to be negligible.

A third correlation in this group is that between profits and output, capacity being held constant.   The output of a firm as a percentage of its capacity is influenced by the firm's rate of profit when the firm produces to stock rather than to order.   In such case a high profit rate often induces management to expand output in hopes of an increased rate of sales in the future.   This profit-elasticity of supply then operates in the usual manner to reduce the actual or potential future price of the product and tends to force the profit rate down again.   But there is no definable rate of profit which is generally considered "high."   This would require the presence of some normal rate to serve as a measuring stick, but this rate seems impossible to discover or to define.   A mere upturn in the rate of profits after a decline is likely to stimulate such expansion, regardless of the profit rate at which the trend is reversed.

The fourth possible source of a positive profit-elasticity of supply (mentioned in Section 3) is changes induced in the cost of production.   If a rising profit rate generally stimulates greater efforts to improve efficiency and to reduce costs, then a positive correlation exists.   If a falling rate more commonly provides such a stimulus, the correlation is negative.   If the efforts of management in this direction are continuous and persistent regardless of the profit rate, as is most generally the case, there is no correlation at all.   The first alternative seems less probable than the second or third.   If the correct generalization is in favor of a slight negative correlation, the supply effect offsets some of the slight positive correlations noted above.   Whichever conclusion is supported, there is no denying the argument that there is no "normal rate" of profit above which additional efforts are forthcoming and below which they are reduced. In an acquisitive society, the labor element of the ownership position tends constantly to press for more profits, regardless of the profit level currently attained.

**7. The Profit-Elasticity of Supply of Firms: The Problems of Entry and Exit.**—Our next questions relate to the possible connection between the rate of profits being made by the firms already in an industry and the probable entry of new firms or exit of existing firms. If a positive correlation exists, as seems likely, then a rise in the general profit rate will set in motion forces which subsequently will tend to reduce that rate.[1]

Entry into the position of business ownership is based upon choice and the ability to execute that choice. The amount of prospective profits influences the decision. The choice is not merely whether to enter or not, but what to enter, and what to do if one does not. The three major alternatives may be outlined as follows:

1. Whether to put one's factors to use or to keep them idle
2. Whether to put them to use in a contractual (interest or wage) position or in a residual (profit) position
3. In what industry and what firm to take the ownership position

The basic choice is that between keeping one's capital and labor idle or putting them to use in one way or another. When people enter the profit-seeking position, they demonstrate a preference for it over the other two alternatives. This preference is undoubtedly influenced by profit prospects. The higher the expected profit, the more capital and labor will be put to work in an ownership capacity. But there is no definable minimum rate which must be exceeded before this will occur. The trend of profits is more important than the amount, or rate. Nor can one be sure when entry occurs that the incoming factors come out of idleness rather than from other equity positions or from contractual employments. The labor element of the ownership position is also difficult to pin down. Probably more time is diverted from "idleness" to owner-management work when profits are falling than when they are rising. If this be true, labor inputs have an inverse relationship at the same time that capital inputs have a direct relationship to the rate of profits.

The second choice is that between seeking residual profits and lending at interest (or working for wages). It involves a compari-

---

[1] The subsidiary question of major importance is whether the correlation is positive for the entire range of profit rates from the highest down to zero or whether it becomes negative at some minimum rate before zero is reached. If there is some such minimum rate, how may it be defined? See Sections 12 and 13 below.

son chiefly between the loans that can be made and the business opportunities that appear open.  There is a definite tendency for investors to favor ownership when profits are relatively high and to
favor loans when profits are relatively low.  The potential entrant
who expects to contribute only capital differs from the one who expects to contribute management labor also.  The pure investor of
funds is likely to be influenced by calculations of relative interest and
profit returns more than is the potential owner-manager.  Those
who buy stock in new enterprises often are lured by tales of large
profits made by a few firms of that type in the past.  These profit
seekers rarely demand to see careful statistics proving that the current average profit rate in the industry exceeds the interest rate obtainable from bonds or realty mortgages.

**8. Choosing What Industry to Enter.**—For a potential entrant
the attractiveness of industry A as compared with other industries is
definitely a function of the rate of profit being made by the firms in
each.  The comparison may be in terms of averages, or of the number of firms in a given profit bracket (compare the bulk-line-cost
analysis of Chapter 10, Section 10).  The low average profit of an industry may be offset by the conspicuous success of a few firms.  This
is the lottery spirit bolstered by the chance to bet on one's own ability
as well as one's luck.  Another important basis of choice among industries is ease of entry, which will be explained shortly.

His ability to execute the decision to enter a particular industry
may often determine the choice of the potential entrant.  Ability to
enter is a function of (1) the amount of funds which the potential
entrant owns, can borrow, or can induce others to supply in the equity
position, (2) the skill and energy which the potential entrant can
bring to the organization of the enterprise, (3) legal obstacles to
entry, and (4) economic obstacles imposed by existing firms which
want to prevent entry of competitors.  The prospect of high profits
may make it easier to raise funds.  Economic obstacles to entry, and
sometimes legal obstacles, may be overcome by sufficient outlays,
but these raise the cost of production, which must be recouped
through sales.  Very high profits sometimes must be in prospect to
induce potential entrants to incur such expense.  In general, entry
will be more likely at high rates of profits than at low, although this
must not be taken to imply that other determinants can be ignored.

**9. The Profit Causes and Conditions of Exit.**—The chief type
of exit influenced by profits is that which occurs when a producer
shifts his facilities from the production of one commodity to the pro-

duction of another. This may be caused by falling profits in one line, or by rising profits in a substitutable alternative. An obvious illustration may be found in the case of farmers who shift from one crop to another when changes occur in the relative profitability of different crops as market prices rise and fall. Manufacturing equipment is sometimes so unspecialized that it, too, can be used for more than one type of product. During the second world war, many factories "converted" from peacetime products to munitions, and then after the war they "reconverted." The cost of such shifts obviously differs with the type of building and machinery involved.

In cases where the cost of conversion is so great that there would be no benefit from shifting facilities to another product, losses may not force exit but only recapitalization. Corporations with large interest charges on bonds or other loans often "go through the wringer." The creditors take over the business and oust the former stockholders. When the bondholders or banks become owners, their former fixed interest claims become contingent profit claims.[2] Costs are thus reduced and the firm continues in operation with its productive capacity unimpaired. It may even save so much on fixed charges as to be able to put aside or to borrow funds needed for new equipment.

To summarize, there is a much higher correlation between rising profits and entry than between falling profits and exit. Entry and exit occur in several ways. Basic factors such as land, labor, and capital funds may enter or leave a particular occupation. The alternatives to that occupation may be idleness or some other use. The same is true of specialized factors like buildings, equipment, administrative organization, etc. The more specialized the factors, the less the profit-elasticity of capacity governed by entry or exit. This is especially true for exit when profits fall. The profit-elasticity of output and capacity for existing firms was discussed in Sections 4 and 5.

**10. The Profit-Elasticity of Supply of Individual Equity Owners.**—The third major subdivision of the problem of the profit-elasticity of supply of the profit-receiving factor deals with particular individuals who may be induced to enter or to leave the equity ownership position. It follows logically after the question of the creation or the dissolution of producing units discussed in the preceding

---

[2] There are many variants. Entire replacement of stockholders need not occur. Owners of preferred stock may be given some common stock. Bondholders of various classes need not become stockholders, they may merely move down into positions of poorer priority in claims upon earnings, as by accepting income bonds in exchange for first mortgage bonds.

section. It is related also to the problem of expansion of firm capacity analyzed in relation to profits in Section 4.

The reactions of individuals to changes in profit rates depend primarily upon their expectations of yields on shares bought or sold. These yields depend proximately upon the price of the shares and the expected dividends. Ultimately they depend upon the amount of profits earned by the firm. In addition to yield expectations, individuals who buy or sell equities are influenced by expected appreciation or depreciation. Other subjective factors also may be important in certain cases, but do not give rise to significant generalizations.

The fundamental questions to be examined are two. First, is there a positive correlation between the current yield on equity shares and the entry or exit of people from the ownership position? This must be analyzed in terms both of firms in general and of particular firms. Second, is there some definable minimum profit rate below which there will be exit and above which there will be entry? If such a rate can be defined, it might be called the normal rate of profits to owners, since it would keep ownership constant.

When profits in the sense of stock yields rise, there is a definite inflow of funds into the equity ownership position. This is shown by the rise in the aggregate value of all shares traded on the stock markets. The profit-elasticity of supply of equity funds is so great that the average profit yield rises very little as dividends increase. At times the current yield actually declines because of large speculative bidding for securities, although not all of that bidding can be traced to realized increases in dividend yields. Much of it is based upon the *expectation* of a *further* rise in dividends. Other demand comes from the expectation of a rise in the prices of stock shares themselves. Motives are so mixed and vary so much from case to case that the generalization about the positive correlation between profit yields and entry must not be allowed to obscure the presence of other independent variables with which positive correlation also exists.

In addition to this purchase of outstanding stock shares at rising prices, individuals also enter the equity ownership position by buying new issues and by starting new companies. These new firms may be either of the proprietorship, the partnership, or the corporate form of organization. New security issues will attract new equity funds if their prospective yield is higher than the yield that could be obtained on similar shares in the recent past. Again other determinants are present, but they need not be elaborated. The amount of equity capital going into new companies at a time of rising profits will tend to exceed that going out. One reason is the optimism engendered by the profit trend. Another is the lower rate of bankruptcies during periods of general profit improvement.

**11. Other Alternatives Exist for Potential Takers of the Equity Position.**—The amount of funds which will enter the equity position under the stimulus of a rising profit level is limited by other opportunities for the use of funds. Most important among these alternatives is that of loan contracts. If many people try to sell their bonds, for instance, in order to buy stock, the interest yield on bonds may rise to the place where it appears so attractive to potential stockholders that they may prefer the contractual to the residual position. Individual preferences differ, but the aggregate response of all individuals is the focus of attention here. Other alternatives that may gain in relative attractiveness as one's equity investment increases include (1) increasing safety hoards of liquid funds, (2) reducing debt balances due others, and (3) consumption. These last three are mentioned to emphasize three other sources from which equity-seeking funds may be drawn: hoards, borrowings, and current saving out of income.

Despite the presence of these other opportunities for using funds, there seems to be no definable minimum profit rate for equity owners below which there will be exit and above which there will be entry. The most that one can say is that loans in general are a substitute for equities in general for investors in general. Substitution between loans and equities on the basis of relative yields does occur. The process tends to depress the current yields of the securities being bought and to raise the yields of those being sold. By a sort of arbitrage the range of interest rates tends to be kept fairly close to that of profit rates.

This brings up the question of the difference between current yields and what may be called investment yields. Current dividends constitute the numerator of the percentage fraction in each case, but the denominators are different. In the first, the divisor is the current price; in the second it is the past acquisition cost. Investment profit yields are often very large, particularly when stocks are held for a long time in growing companies. They may go as high as several thousand per cent per year on the original purchase price. Interest yields, similarly figured, do not go so high.[3] At the other extreme stand both bondholders and stockholders who have lost everything.

---

[3] There may be a few very rare cases where defaulted bonds have been bought at a few cents on the dollar and have later resumed interest payments, but even there a maximum interest rate holds down possible yields.

Lenders, however, do not get wiped out so frequently as equity owners, if only because lenders have a prior claim against assets when times are bad.

**12. The Concept of Normal Profits in Equilibrium Theory.—** In keeping with the pattern of price theory followed in this volume, normal profits may be defined as that rate of profits which tends to perpetuate itself unchanged. It stimulates no shift in supply or demand schedules. In profit theory the supply side is most amenable to analysis. Here we note that normal profits must be defined in three parts as suggested in the preceding sections of this chapter. The first deals with a given firm where the normal rate of return on net worth stimulates no change in capacity, output, or capitalization. The second concerns an entire industry, and normal profits provide no incentive to net entry or exit. The rate of profits involved in the industry approach may be either that of particular firms, the average for the industry, or that of equity owners in the firms. The third concerns enterprise in general relative to individuals in general. In this third case a normal rate of profits on equity ownership will stimulate no net entry nor exit in the aggregate.

The current profit rate should be seen as *only one* factor in the estimates of future profit-type gain which influence human action. The *opportunity* to make certain *expected* profits is what attracts or repels. These include accounting profit, dividends, and appreciation. There is much less certainty in predictions of this type of financial gain or income in the future than in the case of contractual incomes. In fact, the connection between current profit rates and future profit gains is so slight that one is tempted to omit it altogether. Nevertheless, expectations do spring in part from observations of recent conditions including the current rate of profits. Therefore, the remainder of the discussion will concentrate on that rate.

People with funds may use them in at least four other ways in addition to the quest for profits. For simplicity, funds are taken as representative of factors in general. The argument would not be changed if labor time and tangible property were included as things that people may use in profit-seeking in addition to funds. On the income side, there are lending opportunities. Non-income-producing uses include hoarding, spending for consumption, and paying debts. Normal profits exist when the pull toward the equity ownership position exerted by profit prospects for people in general just balances the pulls in these other four directions. This equilibrium position in the short run is best seen as a balancing of these five positive desires.

This approach seems preferable to a balance between profit prospects and an abstract negative force labeled "risk." Each possible use of funds has disadvantages, or risks. Each use represents the foregoing of an opportunity to put the funds to some other use with its own positive and negative aspects. When these opposing forces are enumerated as in the preceding paragraph, their differences and their influences become clear. They may be seen also as rivals among themselves, not only as rivals for the equity-position use of funds. For instance, the potential spender may choose to lend, to hoard, or to do something else with his funds.

We are here concerned with people in general as users of funds. They differ among themselves. For each particular use individuals will have different intensities of preference. For instance, a cumulative schedule for profit receivers would include many intramarginal people whose desire for profits was less intense than those at the margin. The aggregate demand and supply schedules for equity funds determine profit rates and profit prospects. Intramarginal people and intramarginal investments by any one individual receive a seller's surplus of the type described in Chapter 22, Section 3, and elsewhere.

**13. A Definition of Normal Profits for Short-Run Situations.** —A normal rate of profits may now be defined in summary as one which for its particular situation offsets the four forces which tend to pull funds away from investment in equity shares. Short-run profit equilibrium is thus defined in terms of at least five variables. These seem to be the only ones that need to be mentioned in a statement of the formal conditions of equilibrium unless the motives of firm managers be given further analysis. The long-run conditions of stability in a dynamic society, however, involve many more variables, such as all of the other things that influence profit expectations whether of the income or the appreciation type. One must not confuse the conditions of equilibrium in a hypothetical static state with the conditions needed for stability in our modern economy.

The price of equity shares should remain fairly constant in any situation in which normal profits exist. Their price stability under normal returns is probably less than that for bonds at times of normal interest or for tangible goods earning normal rent. The difference springs chiefly from the greater importance of expectations in the profit field. These enter even the definition of normal profits. Appreciation possibilities also are given more attention in the market for equity shares than for bonds, land, or buildings.

**14. Pure Profits as the Excess Above Business Profits (Opportunity-Costs).**—Some writers use the theory of opportunity-costs to derive a concept known as "business profits." This is described as the amount which an investor could obtain in the contractual markets for his funds, labor, and tangible property. He is then said to be unwilling to take ownership risks unless he receives at least as much in profits as the sum of these possible interest, wage, and rent returns.

The statistics of profits on net worth are then examined to derive so-called average profit rates to compare with average interest rates. When the former are found to be larger than the latter, the difference is said to represent "pure profits." This excess is claimed to prove that investors in general require additional recompense for taking their returns the risky, residual way instead of the safer, contractual way.

Our argument has been that current expectations are the most important thing to examine, not long-run averages. We want to explain the interdependence of interest and profit rates and the shift of people from one position to another. This involves the study of the various motives of potential equity owners, as explained in the preceding section on normal profits. It does not require any statistical average rates of profit on net worth. Attention focuses rather upon current yields on the cost of equity shares and the appreciation in income and market value which investors in general hope to realize. This avoids all the statistical difficulties which beset the analyst who tries to measure an arithmetical difference between some sort of average profit rate and an average of interest rates.

In cases where current profit yields exceed current interest yields, one may argue that investors attracted to this industry desire security against uncertain or diminished income more than they desire the possibility of increased income. This preference varies from industry to industry and from time to time. Where growth possibilities exist, profit yields tend to be less than interest yields. For mature industries or recession periods, the reverse is more often true.

**15. Profits as Payment for Taking Risk.**—"Pure profits" should not be made synonymous with payment for assuming risk. This identification is a major weakness of the theory which uses pure profits as a term to describe the excess of accounting profits above business profits. In the first place, risk begins the moment one takes the equity position. Risk does not remain absent until after a certain opportunity-cost level of profits has been reached.

In the second place, all those dependent upon a business enterprise for their income take some risk except, perhaps, those who receive payment in advance or at the moment of sale. The risk is in proportion to two things : (1) the legal sequence of claims against the firm's income or assets and (2) the length of time that elapses between the performance of service (including the delivery of goods) and the date of payment.

The equity holder is at the end of both the legal and temporal lists. Therefore, his position is particularly risky, but the difference is one of degree, not of kind. Interest contracts, for instance, are at higher rates for some types of loans than for others. These interest differences are usually ascribed in part to differences in risk as seen by lenders. An individual seeking income from his property balances his hopes against his fears in choosing which position to occupy. If his hopes prove the stronger, he chooses the tail-end position with its greater risk. If his fears win out, he chooses contractual income with its lesser risk. Or he may hedge by occupying both positions at the same time. For instance, he may sell his labor contractually and lend some of his funds. The rest of his funds may go into preferred or common stocks, the former being considered less risky than the latter because of precedence in the distribution of firm income. A particular individual's choice is a matter of temperament, experience, egotism, and opportunities. The generalization, however, must be that *one* restraining force which limits the flow of funds and labor into the residual position is its *relatively greater* risk.

A third difficulty with the theory which associates profits exclusively with the assumption of risk is that profits should then be proportionate to the risk assumed. The more risky the enterprise, the higher should be its average rate of profits to attract timid funds. An examination of profit statistics for a variety of industries, however, reveals no such correlation. Logic also denies the truth of any monistic explanation. In Chapter 26 a whole series of causes of profit differences were explained. In an earlier part of this chapter the profit-elasticity of the supply of equity funds has been examined. Taken together, these two approaches to the explanation of profits furnish a far better understanding of past and present profit rates than any argument about either the uniqueness or the primacy of risk in the determination of profit rates.

Only in the very difficult case of attempted comparison between the general level of profits for all enterprise over a long period of time and the general level of interest rates for all loans does the risk theory have possible merit. If it can be demonstrated that such an average level of profit rates to *owner*-investors is greater than the average level of interest rates to *lender*-investors, then some reason must be sought.   It might be found in a general margin of preference among investors for the greater certainty of contractual interest as compared with the greater opportunity for gain or loss from residual profit.   Statisticians are still examining the evidence and have reached no consensus regarding it.   In the meantime, there is little to be gained by *a priori* arguments about general investor aversion to risk.   There is much to be lost if it diverts attention from the specific causes of individual and average profits and the changes therein.

**16. The Motives of Equity Entry: Risks Deter and Profits Attract.**—Business enterprise resembles the so-called "games of skill and chance" in which the luck factor is very important but where skill is also useful.   Business enterprise, that is, consists of something more than a lottery gamble.   Potential enterprisers can bet not only upon their luck but also upon their ability.   People are induced to play games of chance and skill by the chance for rewards. It is difficult to state just how large the rewards must be, but the possibility of large winnings must be present.   If participants *never* obtained much more than they could get by using their time and funds in other ways, the game would not prove nearly so attractive.   But if there are a few big prizes known to have been won in the past, entrants will be attracted.   Like many commercial games of skill and chance, the average rate to the player may be less than zero.   The loss to the players represents the "take" to the owners of the game. In the field of business enterprise society gets the "take," if any.

Proponents of the risk theory of profits are often inclined to suggest that there is no "take."   They hold that, on the contrary, potential entrepreneurs have to be paid by society to play the enterprise game. These risk theorists argue from averages rather than from particular cases.   They contend that if individuals do not expect to earn from enterprise on the average more than they could get by lending or lending-working, they will sell their services contractually.   To bolster this argument they sometimes try to marshal figures to prove that on the average, in the long run, profits exceed interest.   There are many statistical pitfalls in such comparisons, such as the problem of allowing for the losses of those who vanish from the industrial scene entirely during the period being surveyed.   The *a priori* argument itself seems to misconstrue the motives of the players in the enterprise game.   Since statistical measurement is so difficult and when employed by different people yields such different results, there seems little likelihood that it can prove the arbiter in the controversy. People will still advance either the risk theory or the game-of-skill-and-chance theory according to their appraisals of human motivation.

The special rewards from this game are of two main types: (1) very large income and (2) appreciation. Since most people invest money with the objective of increasing their wealth and not their consumption, the second type is very important. Equity funds are attracted particularly by rising stock prices. Most of the funds thus attracted do not go into business expansion. They go into inflated values of old shares. This represents no gain to society. It often means genuine harm because a speculative boom in equity shares may hasten and magnify business collapse.

**17. Tax Policy in Relation to Profit Theories.**—Taxes on profit income probably discourage somewhat the quest for that income. In order to analyze this problem, however, we must ask what are the places in which taxes on profits are in addition to, or are greater than, the taxes on other forms of income. Notorious in this respect are corporation taxes and excess profits taxes. The funds frightened away from the equity position may go into (1) new loans, (2) bidding up the price of old loan securities, (3) hoards, and (4) spending. Since funds are accumulated primarily to get more funds, neither hoarding nor spending is likely to be increased by any particular *level* of profits taxation. One must not confuse the effect of upward changes in profits taxation with the effect of a general level of such taxes long sustained. It is obvious that only *changes* in tax rates would lead to a bidding up of the prices of old securities. Therefore we are left with only the first alternative in the above list.

Funds discouraged from taking the equity position may go into the loan position. This will have the effect of reducing the prevailing interest rate. In the long run this result seems unlikely to do any particular harm to the economy and if there is a downward secular trend, good may even result. In earlier chapters the argument was advanced that we do not today need to worry about too little saving but too much; therefore, declining interest rates are not a menace.

**18. General Social Objectives in Relation to Profits Taxation.**—The appropriate tax policy for our country can be decided only by examining a large group of factors. Among these are the various objectives which we may seek. Assuming that the question of the amount of total government spending may be ignored in the present discussion, the question then becomes *who* should bear *how much* of the tax burden in order that *we* shall get the things that *we* want.

When a person uses the first person plural in this sense, he often refers to the first person singular. Therefore, the following comments must be understood as one person's appraisal of what he thinks society does or should want.

There are three possible goals which to many people seem desirable. First, efficient use of available resources; second, increasing efficiency in their use, often called technical progress; and third, maximum individual freedom compatible with a large measure of success in achieving the first two objectives. Let us examine the possible effects of profits taxes upon enterprise in relation to these three criteria.

**19. Possible Effects of Profits Taxation upon Changes in the Business Cycle.**—An efficient use of available resources implies continuous and full use. This introduces the cyclical problem. According to the theories presented earlier in this volume, the end of the business upswing may be attributed to a lack of balance between the demand for goods and the supply of goods. This is sometimes explained as resulting from a decline in the rate of consumer spending or business spending. On other occasions, stress is laid upon a rise in the rate of production. When the flow of goods to market exceeds, for any appreciable length of time, the flow of purchasing power demanding goods, unsold goods will accumulate and profit prospects will darken. A given *level* of profits taxation seems unlikely to cause *changes* either in the rate of spending or in the rate of production. An *increase* in taxes upon profits is likely to diminish profit prospects. This in turn may decrease business spending more than it diminishes the flow of finished goods to the market because much business spending is preparatory to future production. On the other hand, a *reduction* in profits taxes may stimulate business spending. The actual effect of such changes upon the trend of the business cycle will depend, of course, upon the amplitude of the change, the time at which it occurs, its effect upon consumer spending, and a host of other factors. The point to be stressed here is that one must not confuse the effects of a *change* in profits taxes with the effects of a given *level* of such taxes.

Does the level of profits taxation have any effect at all upon cyclical fluctuations? Statistical studies by the TNEC experts and others seem to indicate that a major proportion of large incomes is derived from profits. Large incomes provide most of the savings. Therefore, heavy taxes on profits should reduce the rate of saving and increase at least somewhat the rate of spending. This should tend to prolong the upswing, particularly in comparison with its duration if equivalent tax revenue were to be derived from sales taxes.

The other side of the picture is the argument that profits taxation reduces the amount of investing which takes place out of currently saved funds. Reasons for doubting the significance of this contention have already been presented. If a high level of profits taxation induces spending rather than saving, that is to the good. If it stimulates hoarding saved funds, that would be bad. This possibility should be examined further.

There seems to be no major connection between profits taxes and the motives for hoarding. These include the desire for precautionary balances and the accumulation of funds for future large sum spending, lending, or giving. Hoarding for speculation might be reduced by the prospect of heavy taxes on speculative profits. But on the other side is the offsetting effect of a high level of profits taxation in stimulating people to lend rather than to buy equities. This will tend to reduce interest rates and may stimulate a slight increase in hoarding among those who are deterred from lending by the trouble and risk involved.

There is no apparent connection between profits taxation and operation of a business unit below capacity. The rate of output is determined by the relations between revenue and cost functions, in which profits do not appear.

**20. Possible Effects of Profits Taxation upon Economic Progress and Individual Freedom.**—Heavy taxation of profits might remove some of the incentives for industrial research aimed at methods of reducing costs. Much depends, however, upon the structure of profits taxation. If progressive rates are used or if flat rates do not go too high, business firms should still feel an incentive to increase profits before taxation. The prizes in the enterprise game are most effective if they can become large. A downward change in the possible maximum, such as might be caused by an increase in profits taxation, would probably discourage some types of research and betterment expenditures. The adverse effects, however, are likely to wear off and the business community would adjust itself to the lower maxima in such a way as to be stimulated to approximately the same type and amount of entrepreneurial expenditure or investment as before. To a certain extent high profits taxation may stimulate research expenditures as it has stimulated advertising and other outlays which are only indirectly connected with current revenue.

The third objective mentioned above was the preservation and expansion of the areas of individual freedom. This is more closely related to the structure of profits taxation than to its average level. If new firms are given special exemption from taxation or credits for early losses, they will be stimulated. Small firms should probably be given special treatment, although there must be some debate regarding where the line should be drawn between large and small firms. If society chooses to stimulate new firms and small firms, tax favoritism is one of the best devices. Tax revenues not obtained from such sources must, of course, come from someone else, presumably the larger and the more well-established firms. Another reason for stimulating small enterprises in this manner is the indirect stimulus which it may give both to technical progress and to price competition.

**21. Summary.**—The amplitude of possible fluctuations in the various rates of profit is restrained by the profit-elasticity of supply. Rising profits induce expansion of firm capacity, an increase in the number of firms, and a rise in the demand for equity shares. Each of these results tends to reduce the profits below that rate whose height stimulated the expansion. Falling profits do not produce a comparable contraction in the number of firms or in firm capacity, although they do diminish the demand for equity shares.

Normal profits are those which exert no influence to alter supply factors and therefore tend to remain unchanged. Expectations of future changes in the value of equity shares and in the rate of dividends are probably more important than the current yield in influencing the supply of equity funds. Equilibrium exists when the profit inducements balance four other incentives, chief among which are contractual income opportunities and the desire to avoid risk. If business profits are defined as being equal to opportunity-costs for the owners' factors, then pure profits or losses may be described. This approach tends to identify profits with payment for risk, an argument that has many weaknesses. Its grain of truth should be used with great care.

The average level of taxes on profits affects somewhat the volume of economic activity. Usually, it is not so important as the tax rate structure and the timing of changes in the tax rates.

# INDEX

Advertising, 118–122
Average factor revenue, 271

Balancing of aggregates, 80, 85
Banks,
central, 386–387, 398, 431–434
commercial,
costs and interest rates of, 391–392
as creators of credit, 387, 391
cyclical changes in lending by, 408–409
influence of, on interest rates, 423–424
as lenders to business, 380
limits to lending by, 393–394
savings, 387, 389
Bargaining,
and prices of commodities, 182–185
and rents, 336–337
and wages, 253, 268
Bargaining range, 183
Basing point system, 132–135
Borrowing,
business, 377–380, 382
consumer, 384–386
government, 383–384
non-interest determinants in, 384–385
for purchasing power, 372–373
Bulk-line cost, 152–154
Buyer's surplus, 184–185

Capacity,
of a firm, 106–107, 203–208, 455, 461–462
of an industry, 454–455
Capital (assets, claims, equipment, fixed, goods, liquid, working), 376–377
Capitalization, 346–347
Cobweb theorem, 226
Collateral, 373
Competition,
cost, 167
direct, 165–166
indirect, 167
marketing, 165
monopolistic, 111–112, 164–165, 196–197
predatory, 166
price, 165
product, 164, 177
production planning, 168
purchasing, 166
pure, 109–111, 162, 178, 180, 196–197, 247
unfair, 167

Competitive behavior, see *Competition*
Constant returns, 205
Consumer's surplus, 184–185
Cost,
acquisition, 365
decreasing, 205–209
monopoly conditions inevitable under, 208–209
increasing, 204
opportunity, 151, 358–359, 367–369, 471
reproduction, 355, 357–358, 365–366
selling, 118–123
Cost schedules of individual firms,
average fixed cost, 98
average total cost, 98
average variable cost, 98, 101–102
marginal cost, 99–102
total fixed cost, 96
total total cost, 97
total variable cost, 96
Credit,
created, 387–388, 391
instruments, 389–390
nature of, 388

Demand,
concepts, summary of, 15, 27
curves, 17, 24, 46, 48
arithmetic, 49
logarithmic, 49–50
statistical, 29–30, 233–237
derived, 245–246
elasticity of,
cross, 19–20, 66–67, 122, 125–128, 177, 245
income, 23–24, 69–71
logarithmic axes in estimates of, 49–50
price, 39–56, 71–73, 233, 245
joint, 245–246
law of, 28
market, 15
schedule, 15
causes of changes in, 17–24
diagrams of increase in, 24
schedules,
collective, 30–32
discontinuous, 36
instantaneous, 32
speculative, 36
statistical, 29–30, 233–237
successive, 32–34
time differences in, 33